Warriors and Fools
by Harry E. Rothmann
Colonel (US Army Retired)

Published by RCI Publications
All Rights Reserved. No part of this publication may be reproduced in any form or by any means, including scanning, photocopying, or otherwise without prior written permission of the copyright holder.
© 2018 Harry E. Rothmann

Table of Contents

Preface
Introduction
Chapter 1: The Best of Times; The Worst of Times
    Section 1.1 - The Story's Main Characters
    Section 1.2 - Post World War Two America
    Section 1.3 - The Cold War
Chapter 2: The Best and the Brightest
    Section 2.1 - JFK Administration
    Section 2.2 - Crucibles of Policy Making: Bay of Pigs, Laos, and the Cuban Missile Crisis
    Section 2.3 - JFK, Vietnam, and Counterinsurgency
Chapter 3: The Reluctant Commander-in- Chief
    Section 3.1 – LBJ Administration
    Section 3.2 - LBJ's Gradualism Approach for Vietnam
    Section 3.3 - LBJ Goes to War
    Section 3.4 - McNamara's War
    Section 3.5 – Personal Experiences, Observations, and Insights for Chapters 2 and 3
Chapter 4: America in Crisis
    Section 1 – Changes in America in the Sixties, the Great Society, and the Conduct of the Vietnam War
    Section 2 – The Civil Rights and Anti-War Movements and the Vietnam War
    Section 3 - The Media and Public Opinion and the Vietnam War
    Section 4 – The Congress and the Vietnam War
    Section 5 - Personal Experiences, Observations, and Conclusions
Chapter 5: Peace with Honor?
    Section 1 – Nixon Administration
    Section 2 - Nixon's Vietnam Strategy and The Policy of 'Vietnamization'
    Section 3 - The Search for Peace With Honor

Section 4 – Personal Experiences, Observations, and Insights for Chapter 5

Chapter 6: Know Your Enemy
    Section 1 – The Geopolitics of Vietnam
    Section 2 – Ho Chi Minh, Vo Nguyen Giap and The Road to Independence
    Section 3 - Victory at Any Cost: The First Indochina War
    Section 4 – Observations and Insights for Chapter 6

Chapter 7: 'The Enemy Gets a Vote'
    Section 1 - Le Duan, Le Duc Tho and the Road to Unification
    Section 2 – Victory at Any Cost: Confronting the United States' Military Power
    Section 3 - Personal Experiences, Observations, and Insights for Chapter 7

Chapter 8: The 'Unwinnable War'
    Section 1 – US Theater Military Strategies for Vietnam, 1954 to 1963
    Section 2 - Transition to an American War, 1964-1965
    Section 3 – Westmoreland's War, 1965-1966

Chapter 9: The Agony of Defeat
    Section 1 – Executing the Strategy of Attrition
    Section 2 - Taking the Offensive: Operations and Tactics, Summer 1966 to End 1967
    Section 3 - TET 1968

Chapter 10: A Better War?
    Section 1 – The Changing Nature of the War, Abrams' Theater Military Strategy and Vietnamization
    Section 2 – Buying Time, 1970 - 1972
    Section 3 - The Final Collapse

Chapter 11: The Failure of US Policies and Strategies for Vietnam, 1950-1975
    Section 1 - The Truman and Eisenhower Years: The Evolution of Vietnam as a Vital US Interest and the Quest for a Political-Military Solution for its Defense, 1950 to 1961
    Section 2 – The Kennedy Years: McNamara, The JCS, Harkins, and the US Counterinsurgency Strategy, 1961 - 1963

Section 3 – The LBJ – McNamara Years: Limited War, Graduated Response, and Westmoreland's Strategy of Attrition
Section 4 – The Nixon and Kissinger Years: Abrams, Vietnamization, and 'The Better War'
Section 5 - Conclusions
Chapter 12: The Heavy Shadow of Vietnam
Section 1 – Immediate Post-Vietnam Years, 1975 to 1988: America's Struggle to Find Meaning
Section 2 – Vietnam War Lessons Learned Applied: Panama, 1989
Section 3 - Vietnam War Lessons Learned and Applied: DESERT SHIELD and DESERT STORM, 1990-1991
Section 4 – Lessons Learned for the Future: Relationships Matter
Chapter 13: Have We Learned Anything?
Section 1 - The 21st Century American National Security Environment: From 'The End of History' to the 'Long War'
Section 2 – Observations, Insights, and Conclusions on Civil-Military Relations Pertinent for Today
Section 3 - Conclusion: Our Story's Main Characters… The Final Role They Played and What Happened to Them?
Epilogue
Source Notes
Bibliography

Preface

This book is about the Vietnam War. Its focus is on the American statesmen and soldiers who made some terrible, tragic mistakes and choices that led to the loss of that war; and over 58,000 American and unknown millions of Vietnamese lives.

As a young infantry officer, just a few years out of West Point, I led a platoon of thirty men and then a company of over one hundred soldiers in Vietnam. My unit lost several men killed and scores wounded. My West Point Class of 1967 lost twenty-nine killed in action - one of the highest tolls of the West Point classes that fought there.

When I returned from Vietnam, after two tours of duty training men to go to the battleground that I had left, the war ended for America. Then, while in graduate school preparing for a teaching assignment at West Point, Saigon fell to the Democratic Republic of Vietnam or Communist North Vietnam.

I wondered why this happened. After all, for over two decades Presidents had committed the US to a cause that was supposed to be right and just for both America and the Vietnamese. We also had spent much treasure in dead and wounded. I determined to find out the answers.

The story that unfolds in the pages ahead is what I discovered about the why and how we lost that war. It is also an account of my journey of over fifty years to uncover the reasons, motives, and lessons of this great tragedy.

Introduction

This book is a story, not a history.

I wanted to write this as a 'story' of a war that I fought in – an event that has played a large part in my life - because I knew that I could not be impartial. I wanted to compose a book that I could let out my feelings and passions. I could not do that and call it a history.

I have tried, however, to be as faithful to the history as I could. Therefore, I have included views that I do not agree with and accounts that I feel missed the point or tried to make one. I have also tried to be fair to those who had lived it – that is, to remember that the men who made recommendations, choices, and decisions for the Vietnam War were without foresight of what we now know.

I went into this project with a set notion of what went wrong and why. Some of that has survived in this story. Some of my preconceived notions have changed.

The essential points of this story are twofold. First, both US civilian and military leaders charged with making decisions and executing them during the Vietnam War failed America and its soldiers. Second, they also failed others, particularly the South Vietnamese, who depended on the US to keep its commitment to an independent South Vietnam free of communist subjugation.

Leader misjudgments and miscalculations were not the only reasons for this failure, as some have claimed. Rather, this narrative will show how they were more a result of personal faults and a lack of trust, honesty, and understanding among and between American civilian leaders and their military counterparts.

The enemy also had a great deal to do with it. Often overlooked in American histories of the conflict, North Vietnamese leaders persistently and decidedly pursued their goals. They also developed effective approaches to winning their war of unification. Their soldiers courageously and resolutely fought for its achievement. Yet, US leaders and advisors either ignored their enemy, or just did not understand them.

Thus, the purpose of this story is to understand and describe how and why the breakdown in US decision-making occurred, and why they did not consider their enemy properly. This account will also offer remedies for how to prevent similar circumstances in the future.

Background

When I entered West Point in July 1963, I had not even heard of Vietnam. In fact, the first I had become aware of Vietnam was sometime a year later. There was some talk of the war and our participation in it as advisors after graduation. I also remember reading an article or two in *Life Magazine* about the US military advisory operations.

In the summer of my sophomore year, the Academy assigned me to go on Army Orientation Training to the 25th Infantry Division in Hawaii. I got there in late June 1965. Some US combat units had already deployed to South Vietnam by then and had fought the Vietcong (the name usually used at that time for the Vietnamese Communists who were fighting the South Vietnamese Government).

A classmate and I ran into some infantry Lieutenants not much older than us at a small officers' club on Waikiki beach. They were on their way to Vietnam. They were eager to get there and experience combat; not knowing what it was all about yet. After several 'Singapore Slings,' we wondered how long the war would last and whether we would get there when we graduated in two years.

I trained with an infantry company in the 2d Battalion, 27th Infantry Regiment for the next month. Some of the soldiers in that battalion had just returned from Vietnam. They had volunteered to serve as door gunners for the US helicopters supporting the South Vietnamese Army. A few had shot their machine guns at elusive targets. No one that I know of had gotten wounded or hurt. Their stories of their experiences were usually about the strangeness of the country and its people, and how hot and wet it could be all at the same time.

The training in my company was intense. That was because the 25th Infantry Division – the parent unit of the battalion I was assigned to - knew that it would deploy to Vietnam sometime in the fall. It was the best experience a young cadet who wanted to join the infantry could get short of war.

After returning to West Point, I read sometime in the early winter a *New York Times* article about a unit in the 2d Battalion, 27th Infantry getting overrun in the 'Iron Triangle' (a Vietcong base area) outside of Saigon. It was the company I had trained with that summer. They had lost all their officers and most of their non-commissioned ones either killed or wounded. Suddenly, the war became very personal.

As graduation approached in the summer of 1967, we listened to press conferences and read articles about how well the war was going for us. We all became worried it would be over before we could get into it.

At the time the Army had a rule that recent graduates could not go directly to Vietnam. Instead, they would have an assignment with some Army unit not yet in Vietnam before going there. Upon graduation, I chose the infantry, got married, and left with my new wife to go to an airborne unit in Germany.

Optimism that the war would end proved folly. After a little more than a year I went to a battalion in the 101st Airborne Division in a place in Vietnam that I could not at first pronounce. By then already 19 of my classmates had been killed in action. I was fortunate. I returned home after my share of combat. In the year I was there, the war took another ten classmates.

Several years after my return I was a graduate student at the University of North Carolina. Studying history for a return to West Point as an instructor in the History Department, I had an opportunity to study the war – at least the materials that were then available. Several months after I began my studies, in April 1975 Saigon fell. That incident incited me to find out why we lost the war.

One day, I was reading some of the infamous *Pentagon Papers* – a top secret study that Robert McNamara had ordered while he was Secretary of Defense. One of the study's authors, a Daniel Ellsberg, had leaked it to the *New York Times*. I came across a memo that floored me.

An Assistant Secretary of Defense had written and sent it to McNamara on 24 March 1965. That date had been just sixteen days after the first American ground combat units landed in South Vietnam. The memo's title was 'Plan of Action for South Vietnam.' The first paragraph of that plan listed 'US aims' as: "70% to avoid a humiliating US defeat (to our reputation as guarantor); 20% to keep SVN (and then adjacent) territory from Chinese hands; 10% to permit the people of SVN to enjoy a better, freer way of life."

I was amazed, angry, and disgusted. So, this is what our government policy-makers had determined were the reasons for the employment of hundreds of thousands of American soldiers, marines, airmen, and sailors to Vietnam. Most hideously, I thought, these were the reasons that tens of thousands of them had already died there. I could not believe what I had just read.

I continued to read all four volumes of the Gavel Edition of the *Papers*. What I read further enraged me. I just could not believe the callous tone of the papers, and the lack of understanding of the nature of war as I had studied and experienced it.

I shared these findings in some of the papers I wrote for my graduate degree. Though I found my advisors and professors understanding of and sympathetic to my feelings, I was there to get a degree, not to draft any formal accusation or finding on the war. I harbored these feelings and kept them inside while I continued to read and study whatever I could get my hands on in the years that followed on how and why we got engaged in Vietnam.

In my last three years on active duty, I was a professor at the National War College. There I designed and taught a course of the 'History of the Vietnam War." As far as I had known none of the professional military war colleges then had yet taught such a course. I thought by then, 1995, it was worthy of study.

That opportunity gave me several terrific insights on the war. First, there had finally been some release of papers, mostly captured, of North Vietnamese documents that gave some understanding of their views and decisions on the course of the war. Several scholars wrote books offering their opinions on them. These presented interesting and valuable understandings of the consequences of US decisions on the war's conduct. Second, discussions with students at the time, mostly Lieutenant Colonels and Colonels, convinced me of the need and worthiness of further study of the war by senior officers – particularly of the decision-making issues and relationships between the senior military and civilian leaders involved in them.

The above journey of discovery led me to further study of the war, and eventually to the writing of this book and the telling of the story ahead.

What is Ahead?

What lies ahead are some of the thoughts and understandings I have gained through studying and teaching about the Vietnam War while in the Service, and my studies since my retirement. In my attempt to discover these insights, I have relied in part on the wisdom of an ancient Greek historian named Thucydides, whose work, *The Peloponnesian War*, I read at the Naval War College in the late seventies. While difficult to read, inside I found all kinds of historical 'analytical nuggets' on how nations, particularly democratic ones, wage war; the factors that one often considers in doing so; and the relationships between civilian leaders and soldiers in strategic formulation.

In Thucydides' examination of the decision-making, strategies and operations of the two primary antagonists of the Peloponnesian War – Athens and Sparta – he found five main factors that were important to understanding the outcomes of the war. They were: the personalities and abilities of the leaders; the geopolitical and historical settings of the two opponents and their allies; the major strategic decisions of the war and the underlying reasons for them.

Most importantly, Thucydides - like another theorist of war after him called Clausewitz – also stressed the difficulties in making these choices due to the many unknowns and uncertainties that people face in waging war. These war theorists further emphasized that war is a two-party affair between antagonists who have different views of war and how they go about waging it. To ignore the latter is to invite peril in one's decisions on how to conduct it.

I have organized my story around these main factors. Accordingly, the first chapter explains the situation and setting of the post-World War Two period, focusing on the US. It tries to place the overall climate of the later Vietnam crisis and issues in the context of American experiences and attitudes after the Second World War and during the first decade of the Cold War.

Chapters 2 and 3 examine the personalities and expertise of the American decision makers, and the major decisions and policies that they made during the Kennedy and Johnson Administrations. Here I targeted the relationships of the civilian and military people who were struggling with the Vietnam situation to address it as a war of national liberation and communist expansion, and how to counter it.

Chapter 4 describes the domestic environment that JFK and LBJ faced in making their major policy decisions toward Vietnam described in the two earlier chapters. The focus of this chapter is on the roles that the civil rights and antiwar movements, the Press, Public Opinion, and the Congress played in affecting how JFK and LBJ made their decisions on Vietnam.

Chapter 5 then returns to US policy-making over the war during the Nixon Administration. Here the story concentrates on Nixon's efforts to end the war favorably and 'honorably' for the US. The narrative attempts to show how his decisions and the factors affecting them led to the ultimate defeat of the original US policy aims, and the fall of the South Vietnamese government to Northern aggression.

Chapters 6 and 7 shift the view toward the North Vietnamese leaders of the Democratic Republic of Vietnam. These Chapters present their aims for the war, and how they conducted military and diplomatic actions toward the attainment of them. My purpose here was to show that the North Vietnamese had a substantial role in the American failure. I also wanted to show how US policy-makers misjudged or outright ignored their enemy's motives and actions to their peril.

Collectively, Chapters 8, 9, and 10 again change the viewpoint. This time the focus is on American military leaders and the strategies and operational concepts they employed to obtain their civilian leaders' political aims, as they knew and understood them. In these chapters I describe the numerous difficulties American leaders faced in waging a new kind of war in an unfamiliar environment, how they attempted to adapt to it, and the problems they tried to overcome.

In the first two of these chapters, I discuss General Westmoreland's Strategy of Attrition and compare it to what the North Vietnamese were trying to do. The narrative concentrates on the development of his theater military strategy and the critiques of it; both then and now. Chapter 9 also examines the TET offensive as a turning point in the war, both militarily and politically. Chapter 10 then discusses the change in the American command in Vietnam following the TET offensive. It assesses General Abrams' military strategic view and compares it to the one Westmoreland pursued. It also explains the US military's attempts to execute the Nixon policy of Vietnamization.

Chapter 11 summarizes and reviews the US policies toward Vietnam presented in Chapters 1, 2, 3, and 5 with the military strategies explained in Chapters 8, 9, and 10. It seeks to gain insights on the interfaces and integration of civilian policy making with military strategy formulation to determine the effectiveness of policy direction and military execution for the Vietnam War.

Chapter 12 examines the post-war reaction to Vietnam, the evolution of lessons learned, and how these lessons were applied to post-war events in the Carter, Reagan, and H.W. Bush Administrations. It concludes with a set of the Vietnam War's lessons learned that the author feels is most appropriate to explain why the US lost the war.

Chapter 13 is a logical follow-on to Chapter 12. It looks at what has occurred most recently in American national decision making during the "Global War on Terror" and the conflicts in the Clinton, George W. Bush, and Obama Administrations. It concludes the overall story by showing how the lessons of the Vietnam War still matter. The chapter proposes how the use of these lessons today can improve relations between American senior civilian and military leaders and enhance the formulation and execution of our national security strategy.

The principal view expressed here - and the overall theme of the story that follows - concentrates on a quote often misattributed to the Greek historian Thucydides. "A nation that makes a great distinction between its scholars and warriors will have its thinking done by cowards and its fighting done by fools." I believe that phrase, however misquoted or attributed, offers significant insights on the nature of the relationship of the US decision-makers, both civilian and military, that had a profound influence on the bad decisions made and their resultant failures in the Vietnam War.

As the reader will see ahead, the interrelationship between American civilian and military government leaders and advisors was extraordinarily divisive and dysfunctional. So much so that it resulted in flawed, timid policies and foolish strategies that led to defeat. Moreover, that troublesome interrelationship was a result of mistrusts, misunderstandings, and misperceptions on their roles, responsibilities, and what they thought would lead to a positive end to the war.

A significant conclusion is that these same poor relationships and their causes still exist in US national security institutions today. Moreover, they have resulted in the inability of the US to bring a favorable end to the current, endless 'Global War on Terror.' Therefore, the study of the lessons of the Vietnam War – notably what caused and resulted from the flawed relationships of American civilian and military leaders and their advisors – could result in a much-improved relationship, and more effective strategic formulation today.

Chapter 1: The Best of Times; The Worst of Times

On August 14, 1945, President Harry Truman announced the end of World War Two. From New York to San Francisco, people embraced and danced in the streets. There was much to rejoice and be proud of in America. The United States had unconditionally defeated the indomitable Nazis in Europe and a fanatic Japanese foe in the Pacific. The US now stood as the strongest military power on earth. It owned the most powerful weapon known to mankind. America also had been the arsenal of democracy. Now many thought its industrial might and wealth would lead to peace and prosperity in the aftermath of the war.

However, there were causes for concern and uncertainty on the horizon. As the war ended, our 'Grand Alliance' Soviet ally showed that it did not share the vision that America had for the post-war world. Domestically, there were people who had seen the potential of new horizons during their war service and sought better lives in America. While most were highly optimistic, some had concerns about a postwar recession, as there had been following the First World War. These changes, expectations, concerns, and uncertainties - and how they would come to influence the Vietnam War - are the subjects of this chapter.

Section 1.1 - The Story's Main Characters: Where They Were on V-J Day

As people throughout America and elsewhere rejoiced the end of the war, the prominent figures in the story that follows were in various locations in Europe, Asia, and the US. Some took part in the festivities or celebrated in their way. Others were too occupied with official or personal issues and could not take time out to rejoice. Regardless of their thoughts, feelings, or circumstances at the time, all wondered what was in store for them now that the war was over.

John Fitzgerald Kennedy was in London, England. He had just completed his latest assignment working as a news correspondent for the Hearst news corporation. The 28-year-old Kennedy was drafting a story on his observations of the Potsdam Conference, which he had just attended in Germany. The focus of that conference had been what to do about the defeated Axis powers and forming a new post-war world.

JFK was unable to celebrate Truman's victory announcement. He had entered the US Navy's dispensary in London for severe 'abdominal discomfort' and a recurrence of back spasms. Both ailments may have been a result of the injuries he attained when a Japanese destroyer in the Pacific had cut in half his patrol boat two years prior.

Treated and released after several weeks from the Navy's London dispensary, John Kennedy would go on to become a Senator from Massachusetts and later the 35th President of the United States. Ironically, some of the Potsdam Conference agreements, such as the division of Vietnam into occupation zones that would result in a permanent partition of that country, would have a decisive effect on his future presidency and this story.

In Washington, DC, **Lyndon Baines Johnson** was a serving representative from Texas in the US Congress. He was still mourning the death of his beloved Franklin Delano Roosevelt, who had played a role in his election to Congress before the war. LBJ had lost a bid for the Senate a few years ago and remained quite uncertain of his political future with Roosevelt gone. After hearing of the end of the war, he decided that with his uncertain political career, he did not have much cause for celebration.

As then Representative Johnson contemplated his situation, he was counting on his war service to have a positive effect on his political future. As a naval reserve officer visiting the Southwest Pacific on an inspection tour in 1942, he had been on board a US Navy aircraft in an air battle with some Japanese 'Zeros.' His later stories to his congressional colleagues of his heroics became increasingly vivid, even incredulous, as time passed. To show his wartime bravery, he proudly displayed on his lapel the Silver Star that General MacArthur had awarded him. He would make his war service a prominent part of his future campaigns. He was successful and eventually elected a Senator, a Vice President, and the 36th President of the US.

Paradoxically, when LBJ succeeded Kennedy after the latter's assassination, he did not want to become a wartime president. Nor, as we will see, would he have the where with all to become an effective one.

Richard Mulhouse Nixon was celebrating with the crowd in Times Square. He was still in the Navy, working on contract terminations. He and his wife, Pat, were expecting their first child. After their 'celebration' over the end of the war, they began to discuss their future.

A month after V-J Day, an old family friend and Republican Party leader sent him a letter. The family friend wanted to know if Nixon wanted to run for office. This letter settled his future in politics. He ran for Congress in 1946 and became a representative for California's 12th district. This episode began his career in politics, in which he later served as a US Senator, Vice President to Eisenhower, and 37th President of the United States.

Nixon's strong anti-communist rhetoric and actions would characterize his political career. He won an election in 1949 to the Senate, after smearing his opponent as soft on communism. As Vice President in 1959, he would debate Soviet Premier Khrushchev over the benefits of capitalism over communism. After losing in 1960 his first bid for the President to JFK, he would badger first Kennedy and then Johnson over their policies and actions toward Communist North Vietnam. After gaining the Presidency, as this narrative will show, he would eventually be the one who lost America's war against communism in Vietnam.

Robert Strange McNamara was in the Army Air Corps Regional Hospital in Dayton, Ohio. The hospital had admitted him and his wife for polio. McNamara, an officer in the Army Air Corps, had been serving overseas as a statistical control officer. His polio was mild. Doctors released him about two months later. However, his wife Marg, had a more severe attack. The future Secretary of Defense arranged for his wife's transfer to one of the top orthopedic clinics in the US in Baltimore. Doctors cured her polio. However, the medical bills were expensive.

McNamara had hoped to move back to Harvard in Cambridge, Massachusetts where he had gotten a degree in business before the war. The medical bills and his former boss in the Army Air Corps convinced him to join several of his wartime associates to form a team for industry to measure business cost effectiveness. Ford Motor Company hired them. In their work there, they became known as the 'Whiz Kids' for their abilities to create huge profits for the company. Eventually, McNamara became President of Ford. In that position, he made enough money to pay off his wife's medical bills, own a beautiful home in Michigan, and live comfortably.

Nearly fifteen years after the war ended, JFK would ask him to join his Administration. The new President wanted him to use the same techniques he had at Ford to reform the Department of Defense. McNamara would be a highly successful reformer of the Department's budget and programs. But, he would be a disastrous war advisor for the two Presidents he served. He would resign in 1968, having lost the confidence of LBJ.

In August 1945 Sergeant **Henry Alfred Kissinger** oversaw finding and rounding up ex-Nazis in Bensheim, Germany as part of the American occupation forces. He had fought in the Battle of the Bulge just last December. He was now, along with a small number of other GIs, the virtual ruler of this small town. Kissinger lived in a small villa untouched by the war. He usually got around town in his confiscated Mercedes. The Army had given him a sense of purpose for which he would ever be indebted.

Returning home to New York City at the age of twenty-four in 1947, he entered Harvard under the GI Bill to eventually study and later teach history and international relations there. In the 1950s, he gained a reputation as a brilliant professor of international politics and strategic affairs; having written several books on the matter that became bestsellers. Nelson Rockefeller – a prominent Republican politician – sought him as an advisor. After Rockefeller failed to get the nomination as a Presidential candidate in 1960, Kissinger went to work as a consultant for the Kennedy Administration.

In 1968 Nixon asked him to be his National Security Advisor. In that capacity, Kissinger was a faithful servant. He was a major actor in the President's desires to change relations with the Soviet Union and Communist China. Later he was also instrumental in obtaining a seriously flawed peace treaty with the Democratic Republic of Vietnam in 1973 to end the US military involvement in the war. For that work, he received the Noble Peace Prize. A few years later, North Vietnam defeated the South Vietnam Army and unified all of Vietnam.

When he heard of the end of the war, **Maxwell Davenport Taylor** was traveling through France visiting several former battlefields and conversing in fluent French with local villagers. In 1945 he was a Major General who had commanded one of the most renowned divisions of the war against the Nazis – the 101st Airborne Division. This is an outfit that had parachuted into Normandy in June 1944. Taylor had been one of the first to descend and land in Nazi-held Europe. Soon after he heard of the end of the war, the Army sent him orders to return to the US to take over as Superintendent of the United States Military Academy at West Point. Taylor would go on to be the Chief of Staff of the US Army during the Eisenhower Administration. Later he would serve first as a military advisor and then as Chairman of the Joint Chiefs of Staff for President Kennedy.

General Taylor would critically influence the conduct of military operations in Vietnam in several ways. First, his writings in the fifties on the use of military force would convince President Kennedy on the utility of the employment of US troops in limited wars, to include counterinsurgency operations in Vietnam in the early sixties. Second, he would influence the assignment of many of those whom he knew in the Army to serve in positions of command in the Vietnam War. Two of these 'Taylor Men,' Paul Harkins and William Westmoreland, became commanders of the US Military Command in Vietnam. Moreover, many of the subordinates he commanded in the 101st who were in their thirties during the war would become senior division commanders in their fifties in Vietnam.

Finally, as an Ambassador to South Vietnam for President Johnson, Taylor would make recommendations on the US policies and actions there from 1963 to 1968. These would eventually influence the decisions and outcomes of the war.

In August 1945 **William Childs Westmoreland** was a Colonel commanding an infantry regiment as part of the US occupation force in Germany when he heard of the Japanese surrender. He had commanded artillery units during the war; serving with distinction in North Africa, Sicily, and France. At the war's end in Europe, he had met the Russian soldiers invading Germany from the East. The ordinarily tacit Westmoreland reported to his superiors that "Vodka flowed like water; it was difficult to imbibe moderately and walk out under your own power. I succeeded. At the last party, we were served by female soldiers wearing boots and pistols. After the meal, they became our dancing partners and were very graceful dancers."

In a letter to this father a month after Truman's announcement, 'Westy,' as some colleagues would sometimes call him, lamented: "The deployment of troops [back to the United States] is progressing rapidly due to pressure from home." He worried that the effect of all of this would be an ineffective army which would result in "merely a group of more or less random troops." He indicated that he thought he did not want to be part of the resultant peacetime Army. He did not think he could endure such an ordinary life with soldiers who were difficult to motivate.

Nevertheless, he decided to remain in the Army. With Taylor's support, whom he had met in Sicily during the war, he steadily rose through the ranks. He commanded a prestigious airborne brigade in the Korean War. He then made general officer and followed in Taylor's footsteps as Superintendent of West Point and commander of the 101st Airborne Division. Taylor later recommended him as commander of US forces in Vietnam. Subsequently, Westmoreland worked with Taylor on responding to the crises of 1965 in South Vietnam that resulted in the employment of significant US ground combat forces there.

He continued to perform as LBJ's commander in the manner that had gotten him promoted throughout his career. He was a loyal supporter of his Commander-in-Chief regardless of the costs. He would not argue his views if he knew they were contrary to his superiors' opinions. The consequences for the American conduct of the Vietnam War would be catastrophic.

Creighton Williams Abrams was on the island of Leyte in the Philippines when he got word of the surrender. He was watching fireworks celebrating the news. 'Abe' - his Army given nickname - had just arrived with a group of fellow officers assigned to survey possible postwar base sites for future use by the American military in the Pacific.

He had come to the Philippines from Europe, where at the end of the war there, as a Colonel, he had commanded an armored task force in the 4th Armored Division. His outfit had led the way in the counterattack against the Nazis to relieve the American forces surrounded at Bastogne. Later, 'Abe' led the furthest thrust east of any American force to meet with the advancing Russians. He had been one of the most decorated soldiers of the war in Europe – winning the Distinguished Service Cross and two Silver Stars. General Patton, when asked about his combat skills, is purported to have said, "I'm supposed to be the best tank commander in the Army, but I have one peer — Abe Abrams. He's the world champion."

After the war and his return from the Philippines, Abrams served in a variety of assignments, leading to his command of a division, a corps, and other high ranking general officer positions in the Pentagon and elsewhere. He would serve as his West Point Classmate General Westmoreland's Deputy Commander in South Vietnam until taking over that position in May 1968. Then, as Commander MACV, he oversaw the implementation of Nixon's Vietnamization program and the withdrawal of US forces from Vietnam from 1969 to 1972.

His relationship deteriorated with Nixon, who would blame him for the poor South Vietnamese Army performance in its offensive in Laos in 1971, and its near failure to stop a major North Vietnamese offensive in 1972. It would be one of the greatest ironies of the Vietnam War that a man considered one of the greatest offensive tacticians and leaders in World War Two, would oversee the most humiliating withdrawal of US forces in history.

Over 8000 air miles west of Washington, DC, people in Vietnam could not listen to Truman's 14 August announcement of the end of the war. However, a few did hear Emperor Hirohito's announcement of Japan's surrender on 15 August. Two Vietnamese nationalists, **Ho Chi Minh** and **Vo Nguyen Giap**, were in a remote mountain area in northern Vietnam near the Chinese border when they heard the Emperor's announcement. Besides being nationalists, they were members of the Vietnamese Communist Party. They were also the political and military leaders of a growing political and guerrilla movement called the Viet-Minh. This organization had been fighting against the Japanese occupying their homeland. They had also resisted the French colonial forces to gain Vietnamese independence before the Japanese had taken control of French Indochina during the war.

Ho had been listening to events marking the end of the war on a small radio that an element of the United States Office of Strategic Services or OSS had provided. These Americans had parachuted into the Viet-Minh base area months ago to help train Giap's forces in their fight against the Japanese. The 54-year-old Ho, who had contracted tuberculosis in a Chinese prison a few years prior, had fallen ill recently from his overall weakened state. An American medic treated him, and perhaps had saved his life.

With the news of the Japanese surrender, a rejuvenated Ho called for a meeting of his communist colleagues. They were now gathering in the base area. He convinced them that now was the time to conduct their planned revolution and declare an independent Vietnam. Subsequent actions to achieve this would become known as the August Revolution. It would result in the founding of the Democratic Republic of Vietnam.

Giap would soon march his troops into Hanoi to affect this relatively bloodless revolution and set up a government there. Meanwhile, Ho drafted a declaration of independence. He showed it to the American OSS team leader for a critique. The opening phrase read, "All men are created equal. They are endowed by their creator with certain unalienable rights; among these are life, liberty, and the pursuit of happiness." Ho would carry this declaration with him into Hanoi. Before a crowd of hundreds of thousands of Vietnamese, after reading this passage, he announced the founding of a Vietnamese nation.

Despite Ho and Giap's attempts to peacefully establish an independent Vietnam state, they would have to fight to get one. First, they fought the French; then the Americans. Almost eight years after Ho's death in 1969, communist forces would finally establish a unified Vietnamese state through force of arms in 1975.

As Ho and Giap listened to the Japanese surrender on 15 August over an American OSS team radio, over 700 miles to the south another Communist Viet-Minh leader by the name of **Le Duan** had just gotten out of a French prison. He had spent almost the entire war there. Now free, his previous work in organizing resistance in the southern part of Vietnam against the French did not go unnoticed by the Viet-Minh leadership.

Several months later Ho's Vietnamese Communist Party appointed Le Duan as head of the Southern Territorial Committee. He located his headquarters in a small town in My Tho Province in the Mekong Delta southwest of Saigon. He would now oversee directing efforts in the south to set up a southern branch of a unified Democratic Republic of Vietnam. Soon it would become evident to Le Duan that the British occupation forces would be reestablishing French rule in that part of Vietnam. He would go into hiding and organize the Viet-Minh resistance during the coming war against the French.

Le Duan would be a key leader for Ho Chi Minh and Giap during the Viet-Minh's struggle for independence. After the victory against the French, he stayed in the South for a time to continue to organize and oversee communist political cells in preparation for unification. When that did not happen peacefully, he prepared and for a time led the southern communists in their struggle against the US-sponsored South Vietnamese government. As we will see in the narrative ahead, he would move to Hanoi to further lead and conduct the war against American forces, eventually gaining the unification of Vietnam.

Also in the southern part of Vietnam, word of the Japanese surrender and the end of the world war had reached another Vietnamese national by the name of **Ngo Dinh Diem**. Diem had been a member of the French puppet Vietnamese Government before the Japanese had taken over. After their occupation, he had refused to serve the Japanese for fear of being cast as a collaborator. At the time of the Emperor's announcement, Diem was hiding around the Saigon area. Now, hearing of the surrender, he tried to go north to prevent the current Vietnamese ruler from recognizing a communist-dominated government under Ho Chi Minh.

Diem was a staunch catholic and anti-communist. Before World War Two, he had served as a French administrator of a province, where he had suppressed a communist inspired uprising. Consequently, the Viet-Minh knew him well. On the way north after the end of the war, Viet-Minh communist elements captured and imprisoned him. A month later, Ho Chi Minh called for his release. The Vietnamese Communist leader then met with Diem and asked him to join the new government. Diem refused and left the country.

He would return after the Viet-Minh defeated the French in 1954. He would take over the newly formed Republic of South Vietnam set up to prevent the spread of communism. Diem's assassination in 1963, just days before JFK's, would be a significant factor in the future commitment of US ground combat forces in the war.

Section 1.2 - Post World War Two America

Of course, none of the above major players in the drama that follows had any specific notion that they would be involved in one of the most controversial wars of the twentieth century. They also could not have known precisely at the time the impact of their recent war experiences would have afterward. But for the Americans described above, they were confident that they could change the world in their image.

Indeed, for the United States and its people, the Second World War had further defined its image of itself and its future in the new world they faced. Their Revolutionary War had created an American state. Its bloody Civil War had shaped it as a nation. World War Two now fashioned the US as a global power. While the other victors and vanquished nations had suffered severe damage and destruction to their homeland, the US had not. America, prosperous and even delirious in victory, was now the premier power in the world.

Before the war, the notable *Times* publisher Henry Luce had predicted that the twentieth century would be the 'American Century.' It now appeared that his prediction had come true. Peter Jennings captured the state of mind in America after the war in his chronicle, *The Century*. He wrote, "Both capitalism and democracy had been redeemed and with the clearing of the dust of battle, the future of the nation most identified with both seemed, quite suddenly, limitless."

The great promoters of capitalism - the advertisers – took advantage of this mood that Jennings described. Homebuilder posters boasted, "After Total War, Comes Total Living." A toothpaste company advertisement proclaimed, "No child in the world has so bright a future."

Transition from War to Peace

As in its other wars, a triumphant America rushed to enjoy the victory and the 'best of times' that most expected to follow. The Armed Forces, which had grown to over 16 million during the war, by June 1946 had demobilized to 3 million personnel. In its rush to return to peace, Congress, in 1947, set the Army's authorized strength at 1 million. The returning veterans, of course, were anxious to get on with their lives. Most expected a different life than the one they had left - one more prosperous and promising than they had seen before the war. Their expectations were high.

Congress had already passed an act in preparation for the return of these veterans. A year before war's end, both the Congress and President Franklin Roosevelt - seeking to avoid the confusion and issues associated with the return of its warriors from World War I - worked on a post-war assistance program to help veterans transition from wartime. The result was the Servicemen's Readjustment Act of 1944, also called the G.I. Bill. Benefits from this bill included low- cost mortgages and business loans; payments for tuitions and expenses for education and vocational training; and unemployment insurance. By 1956, nearly half of World War Two veterans had benefited from the legislation.

In general, historians have proclaimed that the 1944 GI Bill had a revolutionary effect upon America. For example, James T. Patterson in his *Grand Expectations* describes its radical impact on small business growth, home building, consumer expenditure, and education. As for the latter, he writes, "it was the most significant development in the modern history of American education."

Other scholars agree; and further argue that the post-war booms, described below, could not have occurred if it were not for this extraordinary legislation.

The Post War Economic Boom

Despite all the expanded horizons and rosy outlooks, and the preparations for the return of over ten million veterans, there were those who had well-founded fears for the future and its uncertainties. In the words of a historian of the period Eric Goldman in his *The Crucial Decade*, "Would events follow the same pattern as during the last postwar? Was unprecedented boom to bring unprecedented bust? Was peace just a prelude to another war?"

There were also questions about whether the proactive governmental social and economic policies of Roosevelt's New Deal would continue; or would there be a backlash that would follow in the path of the conservative policies of the twenties? These fears and uncertainties loomed, despite the overall unprecedented progress and wealth that America experienced as the war ended. Some early spikes in inflation, shortages of certain foods, labor strikes, and dips in growth and employment fueled some doubts and fears.

However, the new President Harry Truman dealt with the initial post-war economic problems swiftly and effectively. Truman's Administration kept certain wartime price controls in place to help in controlling inflation. The President also dealt with several powerful labor union strikes as a threat to the national interest. He called upon the dissolving Army to temporarily keep some services going. In the end, any major threat to the economy was temporary and overcome.

One reason the Government avoided a major recession and accompanying inflation was the effects of the GI Bill. Because of its provisions mentioned above, the Bill created a well-educated workforce and offered financial opportunities for veterans to go into business or back to businesses they had left. It also helped finance home buying – the dream of so many returning veterans.

The Bill further gave a monthly stipend to Veterans who wanted to go to school. This grant entailed money for tuition and books. The total investment during the years of the program was a considerable amount for those days – 14.5 billion dollars. A total of 7.8 million veterans took advantage of this opportunity. Of that number, 2.2 million went to college; 3.5 went to technical schools; and the remaining participated in other authorized instructional programs.

By 1950, the number of college graduates had doubled that of the year before the war began. Indeed, as James Patterson explains, just before the war only a third of the 74.8 million Americans who were 25 or older had progressed beyond eighth grade. By 1950, a little over 57 percent of American teenagers had a high school education. Moreover, almost 48 percent enrolled in a college or university. By the Vietnam War, over 76 percent of teens had graduated from High School. 48 percent of them would enroll in college.

There was a corresponding growth in educational institutions to keep up with the demand. State Universities opened new colleges and distributed them throughout their respective States. There was an unprecedented growth in junior colleges and vocational schools, as well. All of this created a new expectation for the young children born during the late years of the war and in the years following. As the *Columbia History of Post-World War II America* notes, "Going to college became a much more widely shared goal in the 1950s and 1960s…. College became a mark of middle-class standing for the family and a route to future success for the child. "

As education expanded, GI Bill loans for home ownership decidedly influenced veteran demands for homes and prompted dramatic growth in the home building industry. The most notable was the Levittown. This was a suburban community of massed produced, pre-fabricated, low-cost homes.

The leading builders of these were William and Alfred Levitt. They had been small-scale home contractors in the thirties. During the war, they had worked for the Government to construct houses for defense factory workers. After the war, they turned to the mass production of domestic pre-assembled home sections that they could construct with plumbing and electricity in one day.

The most famous Levittown was near Hempstead, Long Island. It consisted of about 17,000 houses with over 80,000 white, middle-class residents (blacks could not live in Levittown communities). The Levitt brothers built others in Pennsylvania and New Jersey. Until the construction of these and other similar home building projects, which the GI Bill funded, the rich were the only ones who could have afforded a home in the suburbs. Now a veteran could buy a basic Levitt Cape Cod for $8,000.

Soon large communities grew outside of the cities. New single-family homes rose from a little over one-hundred thousand just before the war, to nearly one million by the end of 1946. By the end of the fifties, 33 percent of Americans lived in suburbia. By the beginning of the Vietnam War, 60 percent of Americans owned their homes, and as many people lived in the suburbs as lived in metropolitan areas. This shift in where and the way Americans lived would have substantial further economic, demographic, social, and cultural impacts on the population by the sixties and after.

Besides the GI Bill, the US war industry - undamaged by the war – would contribute significantly to the post-war economic growth. By the late forties, America accounted for half of the world's manufacturing production. This production included 57 percent of the steel; 43 percent of the electricity; 62 percent of the oil; and 80 percent of automobiles. At the end of the war, moreover, America dominated the international economy with an astonishing 75 percent of the world's Gold supplies. As Peter Jennings, the late ABC newscaster, noted, "The booming wartime economy had turned the Great Depression upside down…."

Indeed, the war had created capabilities and opportunities for the continued and new growth in peacetime of many industries. One was the automobile industry. While the US had been on the way to a motorized society in the 20s, the depression brought an abrupt halt to that. However, during the war America produced almost two and a half million vehicles, or about 60% of those used by the Grand Alliance of the US, Great Britain, and the Soviet Union. When the war ended, American industry, helped by Truman's postwar policies, transformed rapidly into a civilian market.

The automobile industry enabled many Americans to move away from the urban areas. American desires to set up households outside of the cities, in turn, prompted a growth in the use of the automobile. Masterful advertising helped. So did cheap energy costs due to increased oil productions for the war and low energy prices afterward. The big three auto-makers - General Motors, Ford, and Chrysler - produced more than two million autos between 1945 and 1946 alone. It leaped to over five million in 1949. This growth continued into the fifties. The number of automobiles annually quadrupled between the end of the forties up to 1955. By the Vietnam War, Americans owned more cars than the rest of the world put together.

During the fifties, President Dwight Eisenhower, who had commanded allied forces in Europe during the war, decided to sponsor an interstate highway system. Congress fully funded the project in the Highway Act of 1956, which turned out to be the largest public works expenditure in US history. The new freeway system, called the National System of Interstate and Defense Highways, was a monumental undertaking. Its proper completion was not until the early nineties. However, its influence on automobile production, ownership, and use in the decade after the war was profound.

The new automobiles and highways, likewise, had a profound impact on the movement of people and American goods across the country. Car ownership and the new local road building programs complemented the growth of the suburbs. The combination of cars, new roads, and the movement they created also brought about new phenomena called motels, fast food establishments, and shopping malls. These replaced the old main street focus of the city with dispersed locations throughout the suburbs. The familiar shopping mall gathering place of today, replaced the soda shops, drug stores, small family businesses, and downtown movie theaters of the prewar days.

Electronics was another area of industry growth. Scientists had used computers during the war; most notably in breaking German and Japanese codes, and in the development of the atomic bomb. The invention of the transistor in 1948 led to the further development of computers for initial use in science and research. Into the fifties, computers found their way into American business operations and telecommunications. By today's standards, these were crude and of limited capability (one narrator of the time noted that they had the computing power of an eighties pocket calculator).

Most notably, the development of the electronics of the cathode ray tube found its way into American households in the form of TVs. In the four years after the war, consumers were buying 250 thousand sets a month. By the end of the fifties, Americans had bought some forty-five million sets. Of course, these were still black and white ones. Not surprisingly, the television will come to significantly replace the traditional radio and touch every aspect of American life after that.

The growth and the use of the TV in the two decades after the war made many more aware of the happenings in America and the world. Soon the TV began to upstage the traditional movie theater. It also began to bring the news into the homes of families like no written or radio news media had ever done. By 1960, three-quarters of all American families owned at least one TV set. By then, families watched an average of five hours of television a day.

The TV also began to have a profound impact on how Americans perceived politics and their politicians. Likewise, TVs were starting to affect the election process. For example, per the *Columbia History*, in June 1948 television stations covered the Republican Convention held in Philadelphia. While the convention hall seated some fifteen thousand people, up to ten million people watched the event on TV.

One of the first regular users of the TV for political purposes was Harry Truman. During the 1948 election year, Truman used the TV eight times to communicate with the voters. Other politicians caught on. Congressmen Joseph McCarthy would use it to bring his hearings on communist infiltration of the government to the American people. Nixon used it to defend himself in refuting charges that he had accepted bribes or gifts for his favor as the Vice President. Kennedy would be most effective in his TV debate with Nixon in 1960 during which some seventy million Americans watched his performance.

The economic boom summarized above led to more prosperity domestically for Americans and tremendous international economic power for the US. American household wealth increased by 20% from the end of the war to 1960. Most startling by today's wealth statistics, this was evenly distributed between the top 10% and the rest of Americans. Correspondingly, American consumer spending increased dramatically.

The high employment rate, along with the growth in household income, led to a phenomenon that many called 'Consumerism.' Americans who could not buy consumer goods before the war because of the depression, or could not buy those items because of wartime rationing, were now spending their money on many items that had not been available or affordable.

Because of this dramatic postwar economic boom, American growth in Gross National Product – a measure of all goods and services produced – increased 56 percent from the end of the war until 1960. The US was now able to apply this economic power to rebuild and remake the world in the aftermath of the most devastating war in human history to assure the expansion of its economy abroad. American officials paved the way for continued US growth and use of its economic power on the international scene through such global mechanisms as the International Monetary Fund and the World Bank.

But not all was for selfish gains. As we will see the US will begin to offer large sums of economic aid to many countries that were suffering from the devastating destruction of the war. One such program, the Marshall Plan, will save Europe from the threat of communism and remake that continent.

The Baby Boom

Of course, what better way to celebrate the end of the war was there than having a baby? James Patterson stipulates that many were ready for marriage and children because they had consciously put that off during the Depression. Statistics support his claim. Marriage and fertility rates had dropped dramatically in the thirties. In the forties, marriage and fertility rates began to rise.

In 1946, per some figures, live births grew from about 220 thousand in January to almost 340 thousand by October. By the end of the year, there were 3.4 million babies born – more than 20% than had been in 1945. By 1950, the birthrate was 24 babies per 1,000 women of childbearing age. Family sizes rose accordingly; and continued to increase into the sixties.

It is not entirely clear whether homes rose due to birth and family increases or vice versa. Nevertheless, the growth in homes, and automobiles as well, were complementary to the Baby Boom. The economic boom certainly was a factor for sustaining family growth. The overall improvements in the economy - such as job growth, low unemployment rates, increases in per capita income, and growth in spending for consumer goods - offered the means and the confidence to grow and support families in ways that were unprecedented.

Another interrelationship between the rise in births and economic prosperity was the rise of a new 'juvenile market.' This development manifested itself in the increased production of toys, candies, children's clothes and, of course, diapers. The forties growth led to a corresponding advance in early teens in the late fifties. This increase, in turn, resulted in yet another impact on the economy, in particular on the entertainment industry. Music record companies saw a tremendous growth in sales. The radio industry survived the growing TV use with a demand to hear music on radios that were now an essential part of the family car. The movie industry saw a new market for teenage theme movies.

Social and Cultural Effects and Trends

The experience of war, the postwar economic improvements, the baby boom, and the growing confidence in and expectations for the future had significant social and cultural effects. Subsequently, they set trends that would affect America in the decades leading to and during the Vietnam War.

Young Americans began to marry earlier and have children sooner than at any time in the twentieth century. In 1946 a forty-three-year-old pediatrician by the name of Benjamin Spock published a book called *Baby and Child Care*. It caught on like wildfire. By the end of the fifties, per the *Columbia History*, this book was on the shelves of more homes in America than any book other than the Bible, and "it was far more likely to be read and followed."

Many families adopted Spock's views on child raising. He encouraged parents to treat children as adults and reason with them. He was firmly against strict disciplinary methods that had been the traditional way to raise children. He preached that children should not be treated as ones to "be seen and not heard." Instead, he favored verbalizing with them to explain what they did wrong. Some child psychologists claim that Spock's methods ruled the upbringing of the entire baby boomer generation.

Besides being subject to new child-rearing techniques, by the end of the fifties, the new teens of the post-World War Two era were subject to a bombardment of entertainment that portrayed themes of teen disillusionment, estrangement, and rebellion. One of the most significant examples was the work of film actor James Dean. His mid-fifties movies *Rebel Without a Cause*, *East of Eden*, and *Giant* made him a cultural icon for the growing youth movement. The young heroes he played continuously took stands against adults who portrayed authoritative figures against new ideas and change.

At the same time, Elvis Presley came along. His early fifties music, such as *Heartbreak Hotel* and *Love Me Tender*, along with his sexually provocative performance techniques introduced to young teens the musical era of 'Rock and Roll.' It also provoked somewhat of a backlash from the older generation, which thought that Presley's music and presentations encouraged sexual promiscuity and stood for a rebellion against their values.

While the booms and resultant prosperity of the post-war were remarkable and improved the lifestyles of most, there remained a group of Americans who did not fare well. That did not mean, however, that their expectations were any the less. As James Paterson writes, "African Americans, including many who were better off in the postwar era than ever before, grew more keenly aware of their relative deprivation." This was especially so amongst those who had served during the war.

Millions of Blacks had served in the Armed Forces and the Defense Industry. While the US military was segregated at the time, many Negro units distinguished themselves in combat. However, when they returned home, especially back to the South, they found that many things had not changed – the Jim Crow laws were intact and enforced. Despite their contributions to the war, Blacks, as well as other minorities, would continue to be disenfranchised from American politics and society.

The postwar era saw a mass exodus of Blacks from the South to the North. Some of this movement was to escape from the Jim Crow suppression and prosecution. Many sought and received meaningful employment and better lives. About a million Blacks made the move during the forties; followed by another 1.5 million in the fifties. As Patterson explains, this represented "one of the most monumental demographic shifts in American History."

Most of these migrants settled in urban areas. They created, like the many immigrants of the nineteenth century, enclaves within the cities where they could continue to live out their specific cultural rituals and events. These enclaves were also a result of many legal restrictions on where minorities could buy or rent a place to live, such as in the Levittowns. Northern Whites, moreover, exhibited the prejudices then still prevalent in American life in the 40s and 50s.

Black leaders, activists, writers, and athletes of the time began to make White America aware of the injustices that still existed. Martin Luther King, a recent graduate of Boston University's theology school, became engaged in several civil rights cases in Montgomery, Alabama – the most famous of which was the refusal of Rosa Parks to give up her seat on a bus to a white man. Because of his involvement, authorities arrested him. The incident resulted in a district court ruling that ended racial segregation on all Montgomery public buses. It also made King a major player in the growing civil rights movement that had started to blossom in the late fifties.

African American sports figures also began to have a significant role in furthering the cause of justice for their race. The most noted at the time was Jackie Robinson. He had been a commissioned officer during the war and had trained as an armor unit commander in Texas. However, his protest over segregation eventually led to court-martial proceedings. Though he was exonerated, the affair derailed his service in combat. After the war, he decided to play baseball in the all-Negro league.

The All-White Major League Brooklyn Dodgers learned of his abilities. He joined the team in 1947 as their starting shortstop – breaking the color barrier in professional sports. His prowess as a ballplayer and demeanor eventually drew praise and admiration from both the players and the fans by the early fifties. For many Americans, seeing Robinson excel in his sport and seeing how he overcame the adversity of prejudice produced a new awakening for the absurdity of discrimination and inequality due solely to the color of a person's skin.

One major event in the early post-war years that helped these young black men and women in their quest for equality was the integration of the US military. In July 1948 President Truman announced an executive order to integrate the US Armed Forces. The order said, "It is hereby declared to be the policy of the President that there shall be equality of treatment and opportunity for all persons in the armed services without regard to race, color, religion or national origin."

Truman had several reasons for this executive order. One was the need to keep black soldiers in the shrinking military. Another was that such an act Truman thought would enhance his standing in the Black Community and enhance his election that year. Nevertheless, his act was a monumental step in advancing civil rights not only in the military but the US. The US Army that fought in both Korea and Vietnam would be an integrated one.

Another landmark event of the post-war period for Black Americans was a Supreme Court of the United States ruling. In 1951, lawyers for thirteen parents in Topeka, Kansas filed a class action suit against the Board of Education of that city to reverse its policy of school segregation. At first, the

Court delayed its final hearing of the suit until early 1954. By that time a new Chief Justice, Earl Warren had taken over. He decided to end the Court's reluctance to take on segregation cases. He finally persuaded his colleagues not only to take on the class action, but to vote for it. On 17 May 1954, Warren announced the Courts' findings. He declared, "In the field of public education the doctrine of separate but equal had no place. Separate educational facilities are inherently unequal."

This act would have a critical impact not only in the Black Community, but much of White America. It helped spark the civil rights movement of the sixties. As James Paterson argues, "The Court, which enjoyed immense standing in the eyes of the people, had spoken, and in so doing had overturned nearly sixty years of legally sanctioned injustice. No longer, it seemed, could segregated public schools hide behind the law."

Paterson also noted, "Moreover, Americans had always placed tremendous faith in the capacity of schools to promote equal opportunity and social mobility. In 1954 they imagined optimistically that racial prejudice would decline if children of different colors were brought together in the classroom. For these reasons, Brown conveyed profound moral legitimacy to the struggle for racial justice, not only in the schools, but also in other walks of life."

Indeed, the war and its aftermath changed another minority's standing significantly - women. During the war, more than 6 million women worked in defense industries. Many performed jobs that society considered 'unwomanly' before the war – that is, industrial jobs. A wartime song called, 'Rosie the Riveter' came to symbolize them as a woman factory worker in the defense industry. Another 400,000 women served in the Armed Forces. Their duties ranged from clerks to testing planes to 'manning' anti-planes units. Their value during the war led to the recognition for their continued service in the Armed Forces in the Women's Armed Services Integration Act of 1948.

After the war, women either voluntarily left or were 'asked' to leave those jobs to make way for returning male veterans. Most did so without protest. The economic boom of the postwar era, however, soon led to the growth of massive new corporate bureaucracies that focused on the making and sale of consumer products. These, in turn, needed many secretaries and other office workers. Thus, many of these new companies began to rehire women to fulfill these jobs.

This demand for female labor soon skyrocketed. By the end of the fifties, nearly four in ten paid workers would be women. Much of this was also due to the need for women to find work. As their children began to get to college age, families had to find a way to pay the cost. The days of stay at home motherhood, as promoted in the immediate postwar years in advertisements and the media, began to change dramatically. Postwar Social Scientists and Historians postulated that women's wartime experiences and growing importance in the postwar workforce planted the seeds of later social legislation such as the Equal Rights Amendment, which many influential women pursued in the 40s and 50s; and later passed in the 60s.

Overall, the above summarized postwar booms and resultant social and cultural changes would have a profound effect on America in the sixties. The decades of expectation during the twenty years after the war would turn into an era of entitlement for many Americans. Young educated Americans, unlike their forebears, would come to question their traditions and institutions. This phenomenon would clash with the idea of John F. Kennedy of 'not asking what your country could do for you, but what you can do for your country.'

The postwar prosperity and growth – along with the resounding victories of World War Two - would have an equally profound effect on America's elite. In the sixties, it was not just JFK who felt that America could pay any price and bear any burden to further the American destiny of creating freedom and democracy in the world. It was also not just LBJ who thought that America was wealthy enough to both fight a war in Asia and build a great society at home at the same time.

The experiences and successes of the first two decades of the postwar produced and nourished these political ambitions and feelings among nearly all US leaders that America could accomplish anything it set out to do in the international arena. These beliefs and ambitions would not only have a decisive effect on the decisions leading to the Vietnam War, but on the domestic reactions and civil crisis that erupted during that war.

Personal Experiences and Observations of Post War America

I was born in 1944 during the war. My father and several relatives were away serving in the European Theater. I was too young to remember much until I got to be around four or five – 1949 or so. By that time, they were readjusting from the war, and beginning to take advantage of the changes that are described above. Beginning then and into the decade that followed, I was able to remember the stories of their experiences of the prewar, war and postwar world and America. They were remarkable.

Dad had served in the Railway Repair Engineers in the Army. He landed in Normandy, France in July 1944. Although he did not see any direct combat, he saw its aftermath. I do remember his stories of going through the French town of St. Lo and seeing many Nazi soldier bodies and destroyed vehicles from the fight there in late July. My Mom's brother, Uncle Andy, had served in the 82d Airborne Division. He took part in the operations in North Africa and Sicily. The Germans severely wounded him in the jump into Italy. After getting out of the field hospital, he served in a truck company until returning home.

I recall their contrasting stories of their overseas war service with what it was like before the war – especially life during the depression. That contrast was extraordinary. The accounts of the depression were gloomy and full of apprehension. Their stories of their overseas adventure and the victory over Nazism were so full of excitement and accomplishment. The contrast between the sorrow and gloom of the Great Depression and the exhilaration and success of the War and what was going on in America immediately after was amazing.

At family gatherings, the talk of the war usually was followed by discussions of the future. Both my father and my uncle were seeking more promising lives. Both had some financial help from the GI Bill to take some training or education for the future. My Uncle took advantage of Federal funding for small businesses and opened a car washing business. Both were elated about the ability to buy small homes in the suburbs of New York City.

I remember when my Dad bought a new 1949 Ford sedan. He washed and polished it every week. Soon after, we moved to a home in a small community in the suburbs. The town there consisted of around 2,000 people. Most lived in houses constructed right after the war. Our home was about 950 square feet with two bedrooms, one bath, a living room, small kitchen, and dining room. Mom and Dad were so proud to have their home, nestled in a quiet neighborhood with trees, shrubs, and dirt roads. It was a rural paradise; very different from the city surroundings in which they had grown up.

Dad worked hard. He took the train to New York City from the small station a couple of miles from our home. When he returned, Mom had dinner waiting. Afterward, we watched one of the few shows on our small black and white TV. It was all like the fifties TV show, Ozzie and Harriet.

On weekends, we piled into our sedan and drove somewhere. Usually, it was to visit family that still lived in the city. One week every summer we took a three or four-day auto trip to some destination of interest. We went to Washington, DC and toured our Nation's Capital. One summer we went to Lake George and enjoyed activities along the lake. Another summer we visited the battlefield of Gettysburg in Pennsylvania. That is where I got the notion of becoming someday a soldier. We lived close to the Military Academy at West Point, NY. We took several trips there, and I became interested in attending.

So, as I read and wrote about the accounts of the post-World War Two attitudes and expectations for the future related in this section, I could connect to them. My relatives' stories and discussions always seem to be confident for the future and full of pride of America. The war experience, moreover, had freed them from their limited, local view and understanding of the world. They had traveled aboard large ships and on airplanes to see the world - an experience that only the rich in America could have done before the war. At family gatherings, they talked about the people they met and the fact that they seemed just like us.

Now they could also see parts of America they could not have seen before owning an automobile and a TV. On television, they could hear and now see how other Americans lived from coast to coast. They could also see and listen to their political leaders, most of whom they admired and respected for their public service. They could also laugh and sing along with their growing families in their new homes, watching variety and comedy shows, and look to the future with hope rather than despair.

America seemed dramatically transformed to them from what they knew and felt before the war. There was a definite attitude that we were special, and the future was bright for us all.

Section 1.3 - The Cold War

While Americans viewed the end of the Second World War as a grand victory for a just cause and looked forward to a promising future, for many outside of the US, the war and its aftermath were the 'worst of times.' Indeed, the war's turmoil, death and destruction, and the post-war's pestilence and ruin bore the seeds of a 'Cold War' between the US and the Soviet Union that would dominate international relations for the next four and a half decades.

The Aftermath of War Abroad

World War Two had been the costliest one in modern history. In Professor Gerhard Weinberg's account of the war, total deaths reached 60 million souls; including about six million murdered Jews. Some other estimates go as high as 80 million. Using Weinberg's general estimates broken down by major belligerents the numbers are: Germany over 4 million; Japan over 2 million; Italy lost a little over 450,000; the United Kingdom had about 400,000; France around 550,000; the United States had 300,000; China between 10 and 20 million; and the Soviet Union more than 25 million deaths.

Deaths were but one measure of the war's effect on the world in general, and Europe in particular. Another was the displacement of peoples. During the war, there were millions of displaced refugees and deportees. Most of these had no home to return to. The redrawing of post-war boundaries displaced millions more. There was also the movement caused by the repatriation of prisoners of war. It seemed that the entire world was on the move. Disease, exposure, hunger, and just plain fear appeared to plague most of the globe along with this movement. This was except, of course, for Americans, who only had its returning veterans and internal migrations to worry about.

Moreover, the economic and infrastructure costs were enormous. The massive bombing campaigns and the large land battles had left entire industrial centers and cities obliterated; particularly in Europe and Japan. All belligerents, except for the US, had used up their financial resources. Colonial possessions, moreover, were now untenable for those nations that had held them before the war. In sum, as Weinberg wrote in *A World at Arms*, "the costs in human life and suffering, in destruction and economic dislocation, had been of absolutely unprecedented magnitude. "

Standing in the aftermath of this calamity stood two great powers – the United States and the Soviet Union. The former now found itself as a global power to which others looked for assistance, cooperation, and security in this post-war void and desolation. The latter sought compensation, reward and security for its sacrifice and losses, which far surpassed its American and British allies. Both powers had prospective goals for future security and stability. However, they had completely different ideas and views on the future of the world and how to achieve them.

Striving for a New World Order and Origins of the Cold War

During the world war the United States and the Soviet Union, along with the United Kingdom, had forged and kept together a Grand Alliance for one overriding reason – to defeat Germany. To obtain that goal, despite their differences in strategic approaches and national aims, this alliance had been one of the most cooperative in the history of warfare.

To coordinate strategic actions and perceived mutual interests, there had been a series of conferences between 1943 and 1945. During these meetings, the alliance leaders - Roosevelt, Churchill, and Stalin – and their military staffs met to plan and synchronize political-military goals and activities to defeat Germany. They also set up post-war international cooperative organizations for future peace.

There were three of these key conferences – one in Tehran, another at Yalta, and a third at Potsdam. The formulations and agreements at these were supposed to set the stage for how the war would end and what would the post-war would entail. There were significant agreements and resultant actions: such as the opening of the second front in France in 1944; the establishment of occupation zones in Germany; a Soviet offensive against Japan near the end of the war; and the creation of new international organizations for post-war cooperation, such as the United Nations.

However, as mentioned, these 'strange bedfellows' had differing expectations about security and interests in the postwar world. Roosevelt wanted to establish a lasting peace that accepted the principles of the Atlantic Charter, which expounded the freedom of nations to choose their destinies. Churchill wanted to keep certain areas of influence to maintain Britain's international stature in its waning empire and the new world order. Stalin wanted reparations, spheres of influence, and a secure zone for the Soviet Union that far surpassed what both Roosevelt and Churchill were willing to give or expected. It is this last factor that was the root of the geopolitical crises that led to the Cold War.

The most immediate events that led to the confrontation can be summarized. As the Soviet armies advanced into Eastern Europe, it became clear that Stalin was setting up communist regimes in these conquered territories that Moscow could control. For example, in Poland the Soviets rejected the installment of the Polish Government in exile and set up a puppet regime. Stalin further oversaw the founding of socialist (communist) satellite regimes and command economies in East Germany, Czechoslovakia, Hungary, Romania, Bulgaria, Albania, and Yugoslavia.

These states had Soviet-like secret police to silence any opposition. They also became members of a newly created Communist Information Bureau or COMINFORM. The latter was particularly alarming to the West because it sought to control all aspects of life in the satellite states and was reminiscent of the Communist International (COMINTERN) – a prewar organization of communist parties set to further the principles of communism around the globe.

As early as February-March of 1946 it had become evident to the US and UK that the Soviet Union would not take part in a peaceful, collaborative transition to a new world order. In early February Stalin stressed the incompatibility of communism and capitalism, and implied that unless the West made specific changes to his liking in the post-war arrangements, future war was 'inevitable.'

Later that month a respected American diplomat, George Kennan, sent a classified telegram from his post in Moscow elaborating his views on Soviet ambitions and intransigence to cooperation. He called for a hard stance against Soviet hegemony. He wrote that the Soviets were uncompromising, warlike, aggressive, neurotic, subversive, and 'intent upon destroying our traditional way of life.' His solution was for the US to lead the West in a long-term program of containing Soviet expansion using its considerable economic wealth.

Soon after, Winston Churchill, in a visit to a small American university in Missouri said, "From Stettin in the Baltic to Trieste in the Adriatic an iron curtain has descended across the Continent.

Behind that line lie all the capitals of the ancient states of Central and Eastern Europe. Warsaw, Berlin, Prague, Vienna, Budapest, Belgrade, Bucharest and Sofia, all these famous cities and the populations around them lie in what I must call the Soviet sphere, and all are subject in one form or another, not only to Soviet influence but to a very high and, in some cases, increasing measure of control from Moscow."

Stalin's words, Kennan's insights and warnings, and Churchill's ominous observations together placed a cloak over any optimism for future cooperation and agreement of the great powers over the new world order. Per John Gaddis – perhaps the most renown historian of the period - they gave precisely the justification for a reorientation of US policy.

Much of these happenings and words did not, at first, unsettle the US domestic scene and the American drive toward new cars, new homes, and new TVs. However, there was an awareness by the end of 1946 that something was up between the US and the Soviet Union. Early in 1947, in a now celebrated speech on the origins of the term, Bernard Baruch, a former economic advisor to President's Wilson and FDR, said, "Let us not be deceived: we are today in the midst of a cold war." A year later, the then well-known newspaper reporter Walter Lippmann gave the term wide currency in his book, *The Cold War*.

The US Policy of Containment

According to John Gaddis, it was not that the US or Great Britain had not expected Soviet hegemonic desires after the war. Before the war, both the US and Great Britain were staunch opponents of international communist expansionist and Soviet anti-capitalist ideology. Moreover, when the war began in Europe in 1939, the Soviets had cooperated with the Nazis in the invasion of Poland. Before the invasion, Stalin and Hitler had agreed to collaborate on a territorial division if the Soviets would agree to the invasion. Indeed, they did more than that. When Germany attacked in September 1939, the Soviets invaded and seized portions of eastern Poland, as they had agreed with the Nazis.

Of course, this all changed when Hitler invaded the Soviet Union in June 1941. Stalin was now amenable to 'an unholy alliance' with Britain and, following Pearl Harbor, America. Likewise, Britain and the US were eager to oblige. Churchill, who became the architect of the alliance against Hitler, said, "If Hitler invaded Hell, he would at least make favorable reference to the Devil."

During the war, to gain and keep the Soviet war effort sustainable against the Nazis and cooperation in his vision for a post-war world, FDR had adopted a policy of integration. Gaddis summarizes this approach in his seminal work on the Cold War, *Strategies of Containment*. He writes, "FDR sought to ensure a stable postwar order by offering Moscow a prominent place in it; by making it, so to speak, a member of the club. The assumption here—it is a critical one for understanding Roosevelt's policy—was that Soviet hostility stemmed from insecurity, but that the sources of that insecurity were external. They lay, the President thought, in the threats posed by Germany and Japan, in the West's longstanding aversion to Bolshevism, and in the refusal, accordingly, of much of the rest of the world to grant the Russians their legitimate position in international affairs." Gaddis further explains that to do so, Roosevelt sought to gain a sense of mutual trust between himself and Stalin.

Churchill, though willing to tip more than a few spirits with Stalin at their meetings, took a more bellicose view toward dealing with the possibility of Soviet aggressive behavior after the war. As

Gaddis describes, he advocated as early as 1943 the introduction of "Anglo-American forces into Eastern Europe and the Balkans, for the purpose, first, of defeating the Germans, but second, of barring the Red Army from the rest of Europe."

General George Marshall, the US Army Chief of Staff and principal military advisor to Roosevelt during the war, and General Dwight Eisenhower, Supreme Commander of Allied Forces in Europe, strongly opposed such a scheme. They objected primarily because it would divert their attention and resources from the planned invasion of France. Consequently, FDR eventually convinced Churchill to abandon his concept of a 'Mediterranean approach' for a cross-channel attack into France.

After Roosevelt's sudden death in April 1945, Harry Truman had become President. Truman had no sympathies or illusions about the Soviets. In fact, after the Nazi invasion of the Soviet Union, Truman - per a quote in the New York Times - said, "If we see that Germany is winning the war we ought to help Russia, and if Russia is winning, we ought to help Germany and in that way let them kill as many [of each other] as possible."

However, after FDR's passing, the US State Department was seeking a new way of influencing Stalin's behavior. Consequently, under advice from State, Truman initially tried to woo Stalin and convince him of the necessity of cooperation; namely by offering US loans and support for German reparations. This approach did not work.

Because of this failure to influence Stalin with financial incentives, and with the advice of those who seemed to know Soviet behavior best, the US changed course. This new path, again as Gaddis describes it, was one of "patience and firmness." That meant that the US would draw the line and make no more concessions to Soviet expansion. Avoiding any direct attempt to reverse Soviet control of Eastern Europe, the US would now follow this course of blocking Soviet adventurism and any new aggression.

This new policy is what Truman did in his proclamation in March 1947 on support for Greece in its struggle against communist insurgents that became known as the Truman Doctrine. Later, the US also was firm in resisting any role for the Soviets in the occupation of Japan, the continued occupation of North Korea, and influence in postwar issues in Turkey and Iran.

Soon after Truman's announcement of the Truman Doctrine in June 1947, the United States enacted the Marshall Plan. This was a pledge of economic recovery assistance for all European countries willing to take part, including the Soviet Union. The plan aimed to rebuild the democratic and economic systems of Europe and to counter perceived threats to Europe's balance of power - such as communist parties seizing control through revolutions or elections. The plan also stated that European prosperity was contingent upon German economic recovery.

In sum, the original instruments in the US arsenal called upon to implement this firm and patient response to the Soviets were three-fold. The first was a series of public pronouncements to ensure the commitment of the US to the security of a world free of subjugation (e.g., The Truman Doctrine). The second was a set of diplomatic actions and threats to thwart Soviet domination where feasible (e.g., Greece, Japan, and Korea). The third consisted of economic assistance to cure problems caused by the devastation of the war (Marshall Plan).

These instruments were exactly the ones that Kennan, who in early 1947 had returned from Moscow to the position of Deputy of Foreign Affairs at the National War College in DC, had in mind when he had written of ways to influence Soviet behavior in the long run. While at the College, Kennan lectured further on his views of containing Soviet power through patience and firmness. He emphasized that the Soviet critical weaknesses were in its command economy and ideology. Therefore, he argued, the US should take advantage of these shortcomings and use its economic power as it was doing through the Marshall Plan in promoting the ideals of democracy in those countries now in crisis.

Kennan further emphasized that the US needed to focus its attention on the use of these strengths on resisting Soviet aggression in the major geographic and industrial areas of the world. These included: The Atlantic community (Canada, British Isles and Western Europe and South America); the Middle East; and Japan and the Philippines). Significantly, these were the areas or regions that he thought were vital to US interests. He did not believe that America should get involved in the then growing areas of turmoil resulting from the ex-European colonies, such as was happening in Indochina.

Later, as Director of the State Department's Policy Planning Staff, Kennan wrote a series of policy letters further explaining his recommended approach toward the Soviets. Much of his thought, Kennan expressed to the public in a *Foreign Affairs* journal article he wrote, with a pen name of 'Mr. X' called 'The Sources of Soviet Conduct.' It is in this article that the term 'Containment' became of use in the public discourse.

The Red Scare: Berlin, the Soviet Bomb, China, and McCarthyism

A key feature to this new policy of containment was the rebuilding and recovery of the western portions of the German occupation areas. While the priority of Marshall Plan loans and grants went to the reconstruction of the Allies - Great Britain, France, and China - Germany was next in line. The US offered half a billion dollars toward the restoration of Western Europe. Along with those funds, the US and Great Britain, with a reluctant France following, supported the consolidation of the western German occupation zones. In early 1948, they announced the formation of the 'Federation of Germany.'

In reaction to the consolidation, Stalin ordered a blockade of Berlin, closing all land routes to the city, to include the American, British, and French administered West Berlin area. This action isolated the city from contact with the western occupation zones. The US, Britain, and France mustered their airlift forces and began a successful airlift of supplies to Berlin. While the Soviets were careful not to forcibly oppose the aerial resupply, the crisis created a tense atmosphere in Europe. Several Western leaders thought war could occur at any time.

Stalin finally lifted the blockade in May of the next year. However, several months later, the Soviets conducted their first test of an Atomic Bomb. The US discovered this successful test several weeks later. Suddenly, US confidence in its security with its sole possession of the bomb evaporated.

Meanwhile, the civil war between the Chinese Nationalists and Communists, which had begun before the war and renewed shortly after, had reached a climax. On 1 October 1949, Mao Zedong, the leader of the Chinese Communists, declared victory. The Nationalists fled to Taiwan off the coast of the mainland. Suddenly, it seemed, a quarter of the globe's population was under communist rule.

The Chinese Communist success incited much debate in the Congress. Many criticized the Truman administration for doing nothing to aid the Chinese Nationalists. The Republicans went on a fact-finding endeavor (really a blame game) to find out who 'lost China.'

For them it was a means to blame the Democrats so that the Republicans could take over control of the House. Some Democrats joined in on the criticism. A Congressman from Massachusetts, named John Kennedy, attacked the Administration's handling of China. He stated, "This is the tragic story of China, whose freedom we once fought to preserve. What our young men had saved, our diplomats and our Presidents have frittered away."

There was not much the Truman Administration could do at the time. The US had already been frustrated with the Nationalist Leader, Chiang Kai-shek, whose corrupt and inept handling of the war against the Japanese was legendary. The same poor leadership and incompetence had much to do with the communist success. As damaging, the US had given Chiang somewhere between two to three billion dollars in aid since the end of the war. No one knew where that had exactly gone.

The newspapers had a field day with this political infighting. Coupled with the news of the Soviet Atomic Bomb, the Press published a flurry of stories about the successes of communism in the world. Henry Luce, the editor of *Life* and *Time*, who had expounded on the American Century, severely attacked Truman and his State Department. He argued that the Administration just did not care, and that it was too focused on Europe.

By the end of the forties, the stories in the Press about a Cold War, the Berlin Crisis, the Chinese Communist takeover, and the Soviet possession of an Atom Bomb began to have a dramatic effect on the US domestic scene. Several historians of the period claim that all of this dampened the euphoria of the post-war mood and threatened to damage the positive mood in America permanently.

Taking advantage of these circumstances for his political advancement was a then little known Republican Senator from Wisconsin by the name of Joseph McCarthy. McCarthy had earned a degree in law, been a judge, and then served in the Marine Corps in the war. He became a Marine aviator and was a gunner-observer in the Pacific, which got him a nickname of 'Tail-Gunner Joe.' Later, during his time in Congress, he falsified documentation that got him the Distinguished Service Cross – the nation's second highest award for valor.

William Manchester, a popular historian who had served in the Marines during the war, claims that McCarthy's "only wartime injury, a broken leg, was incurred when he fell off a ladder during a party on a seaplane tender." After the war, to get elected in 1946 he made false accusations that his opponent was a coward who avoided service and had benefited from war profiteering.

Since his election, McCarthy had been an unremarkable member of the Congress. His claim to fame had been his fight against price controls. That issue had gotten him $20,000 from Pepsi Cola and a new nickname – 'The Pepsi Cola Kid.' In the flurry of the worries over communism, he pondered the upcoming election. As historian Eric Goldman argues, he decided to adopt an approach that would be sure to get him notoriety and reelected. He would attack Americans in Government and elsewhere as Communist 'Reds' who lost China and threatened the country.

In February 1950, McCarthy gave a speech to a women's club in Wheeling, West Virginia. Reports quoted him as saying that the government was full of communists and he had a list of them. The Senator claimed that the State Department was known to have anywhere between fifty to over a hundred known Communist Party members. He repeated these claims in speeches that followed. The newspapers jumped on the accusations and made the unknown Senator an overnight sensation.

With all this publicity, the Senate set up a subcommittee to investigate McCarthy's claims. The Democrats thought that this would present an opportunity to discredit the Republican Senator. During the subcommittee's hearing, no one could produce or discover any evidence of McCarthy's claims. However, the now famous anti-communist Senator came out of the hearings even better known.

McCarthy continued his crusade for years afterward. His outrageous claims of a communist conspiracy went far beyond the Government. They included actors, writers, and musicians. Finally, the Country and the Congress had had enough. In 1954, the Senate censured McCarthy. Three years later, at the age of 49, he died - from alcoholism.

Historians have labeled this time as the 'Red Scare,' and described the anti-communist crusade and the Senator's attacks as 'McCarthyism. The damage and the legacy of this period were profound. Competent, self-sacrificing individuals in Government resigned. This injured Asian State Department officials, who took the brunt of the 'Who lost China' inquiry; many of whom were on McCarthy's ever-growing communist lists.

The political fallout on the entire 'Who Lost China' issue would also come to affect Government politics well into the Vietnam War. Over the two decades, elected officials in America avoided at all costs being soft on communism. Especially important, was not to be someone who would give into communist aggression like those who 'lost China.'

Evolving US National Military Organizations and Plans in Support of Containment

As the US government sought ways of dealing first with the Soviets in Europe and then the Chinese Communists in Asia, there was little attempt in the beginning to bolster US military capabilities. In fact, following the rapid demobilization after the war, the Truman Administration and the Congress implemented a series of budgets in which Defense expenditures went from a wartime $83 billion in 1945 to $12.8 billion by fiscal year 1947. As John Gaddis notes, "The Truman Doctrine implied an open-ended commitment to resist Soviet expansionism at a time when the means to do so had almost entirely disappeared."

These reductions, however, did not prevent the American military from organizing and planning for future threats to US interests. Indeed, the Joint Chiefs of Staff, an organization that President Roosevelt and his right-hand man, General George Marshall, had created during the war was examining ways to posture the dwindling military forces to deal with the Soviet threat.

In the last year and a half of the war, the Joint Chiefs of Staff had begun looking at what and how the US military should do after the war. Most obvious to them was how to conduct the occupation of both Germany and Japan. However, as the Soviets became more intransigent and US policy began to confront them, it became apparent that the US military would have to do some planning on how to defend US forces and interests against this threat in both Europe and the Pacific where the Soviets had vast land and air forces.

Most clear to the military planners was the fact that America had become a world power with global interests. The post-war occupation of Germany and Japan, coupled with the economic aid that the

US was providing, demanded a US military presence there. To supplement and support that presence and the possibility of a war with the Soviets, the planners examined a series of other bases for postwar use, such as retaining specific air bases in Great Britain and naval bases in the Philippines.

Another issue was how to organize the US military for its new global responsibilities. The American military's experience in World War Two had demonstrated that the future of warfare was going to be joint and combined. That is, that all the different Services (then the Army and its Army Air Corps, the Navy, and its Marine Corps) and their various capabilities in the air, on the ground, and at sea would have to know how to operate and fight together to be successful in war. That is what ensured victory against the Nazis and Japanese Imperialists. So, any national military future organization would have to ensure a unified force.

Lessons from the war had also shown that the US Armed Forces would have to create a command structure that would ensure unity of effort on land, sea, and in the air. They would also need to develop a shared understanding of how the Services and their capabilities would work together. The American military leaders set out to work on both issues by developing a unified command plan and drafting an agreement of each Services roles and missions.

Both endeavors were difficult. This strain was chiefly because the US military was embarking upon a new era that demanded looking beyond its borders. First, there was the need to come to an understanding of what Services had the main oversight for what capabilities, and how to coordinate their use effectively worldwide over great distances. Second, there was the necessity of deciding on how to arrange for the command of these forces in various areas of the world with countless combinations of landmasses, seas and oceans, and airspaces.

The capabilities issue was complicated and controversial. There had been several relatively new capabilities used during the war that involved more than one Service. For example, there was the bomber and the fighter. The Army, Army Air Force, Navy, and Marine Corps had depended on these air capabilities for strategic bombardment of enemy production areas, battlefield attack of ground targets, and close air support for units in contact with the enemy.

Second, both the Navy and Marine Corps had used the carrier and its onboard array of airplanes for the attack of enemy naval forces, and support of amphibious and land operations. Third, the Army and the Marines had used the amphibious ship and landing craft for amphibious operations, as well as an array of armored vehicles and artillery for land operations.

The primary task after the war was not just how these would work together on the future battlefield, but to figure out what Service would have the major peacetime responsibility for the development and maintenance of these capabilities in a budget-constrained environment. This task would result in considerable arguments and disagreements that would have a major impact not only on how the US military would conduct the war in Vietnam, but on the American civilian and military leaders' and advisors' interrelationships.

The global command issue was the first addressed. President Truman approved, at the end of 1946, the final command arrangements for the US global post-war posture. It became known as the Unified Command Plan or UCP. That plan called for seven worldwide geographic regional commands, and one functional command – the latter being a new Strategic Air Command designed to develop and plan for US military nuclear capabilities.

The arrangements for command between Services were contentious. There were arguments over the suitability of one Service commander over another. These usually entailed the pros and cons of the use of naval or air or ground forces within a theater of operations. Sometimes it involved Service views on the kind of operations that may be suitable for the area.

For example, in Europe the Army argued that any war there would entail primarily ground operations on the continent. Thus, their Service should have command over all forces stationed there. The Navy and Air Force would counter that any war on the continent would depend of naval forces to transport reinforcements and supplies or would depend on air support and argue their case for the overall command.

Such issues would plague the attempts to gain a unified view and effective command in one or more of the geographical regions. These matters would also eventually lead to command problems in the war in Vietnam in the sixties, as well as arguments on how commanders would employ forces in that war.

The issue of Service roles and missions became so argumentative that the Services and Joint Staff were unable to come up with an agreed upon solution. As the official history of the Joint Chiefs of Staff explains, "The quarreling became so acrimonious and divisive that the Joint Chiefs in June 1946 felt it advisable to suspend their deliberations on roles and missions until Presidential or legislative action requires that consideration be revived."

Also looming large in the considerations of the American military was the future of the Atomic Bomb. When the war ended, as the JCS Official History and files in the National Archives explain, there were only a few fissionable cores and no assembled bombs that could be employed in the event of a Soviet attack against Western Europe. Indeed, even if the US military had them assembled and ready for employment, what to do about the bomb was still in question.

Early on after the war ended, President Truman did not at first see any future military use for the bomb. He wanted to examine ways to place the entire issue of atomic energy into civilian hands and control. Accordingly, the Administration supported legislation establishing the Atomic Energy Commission – a civic body that had authority over the Nation's nuclear program. There was also a move to place the atomic bomb under an international commission. In mid-1946 the US offered a plan before the UN to give up it an atomic monopoly in exchange for strict international controls and inspections of any country's nuclear programs. The Security Council rejected that plan due to the objections of the Soviets.

While the international issue of control was ongoing, the JCS and later the new Strategic Command considered the possibility of future employment of the bomb. They treated it as just another weapon, however potent it was. Of concern to military planners was how to deliver the munition given the vast distances that current bombers would have to travel to get to the chief industrial targets in the Soviet Union. This problem and its resolution would concern US military planning at first in the Truman Administration, but would later dominate that planning during the Eisenhower Administration when IKE decided to make the threat of the use of nuclear weapons the centerpiece of his national security policy.

Meanwhile, in July 1947 Congress passed a National Security Act. This Act mandated a major reorganization of the US foreign policy and military establishments in the executive branch of the government. In the months and years ahead there would be some follow-on legislation that would further clarify and change the Act's original provisions. The main provisions of the 1947 Act, however, created three new major institutions for the post-war era – the National Security Council or NSC, the Department of Defense or DOD, and the Central Intelligence Agency or the CIA.

The intent for the NSC was to provide the President an organization that could offer expert advice from various members of the executive branch on national security issues. The original act stipulated that this organization would consist of the President, Vice President, the Secretary of State, the head of a new Defense Department, and 'other members' as the President desired. Later, subsequent laws and Presidents stipulated that these other members would consist of a newly created chief military advisor, the head of the CIA, and an assistant for National Security Affairs who oversaw coordination of the council with a small staff of his own.

For the Defense Department, the national security laws further defined a chain of command for the military establishment. In so doing, the acts represented an overall compromise on the Service roles and missions issue. Congress created a dual operational command and administrative control organization. To command and coordinate military operations, the Act created a new cabinet position of Secretary of Defense. He further directed the geographic Commanders appointed in the UCP.

The Acts also formally set up a post-war Joint Chiefs of Staff composed of a Chairman, the Service Chiefs, and a small Joint Staff. The JCS, unlike its wartime organization, would become an advisory and planning organization for the Secretary of Defense. It was also to resolve roles and responsibilities between the Services. During the Eisenhower Administration, the law stipulated that it had no command authority over the geographic commanders. Only the President and Secretary of Defense could issue orders to them.

To oversee the post-war development and maintenance the Service capabilities, the laws provided for three Service military departments, each headed by a civilian Service Secretary answerable to the Secretary of Defense. These Departments had authority over their portions of the defense budget. Thus, this arrangement separated the resourcing of capabilities from the warfighters (that is the UCP commanders) and placed it in the hands of each Service. Each Service Chief, in turn, jealously created programs to protect their views of what each could offer to the warfighters rather than, necessarily, what they needed. As we will see, this separation of resource resolution and funding from the warfighter would plague field commanders in Vietnam and after.

Throughout the deliberations on the law, President Truman had tried to convince Congress of the need for a single military advisor directly reporting to and advising him on military matters. Such had been the case in the previous world war during which President Roosevelt had a senior military advisor to assist him in military matters.

Instead, the Act created the NSC as a collective body to advise the President on defense and foreign policy. As mentioned above, there was a Chairman of the JCS, but his role was intended to resolve Service issues and present combined JCS views on strategic matters, rather than to be the Commander-in-Chief's primary advisor. Thus, the Act did not give the President a close, trusted military advisor who was neutral from Service bickering and answerable directly to him. This situation would affect the nature of the advice that Presidents would receive for the Vietnam War.

As the US military addressed further plans for command and control, clarified Service roles and responsibilities for capabilities, and the implementation of the National Security Acts, American military planners continued to struggle with plans for operations against the post-war Soviet threat. Joint Staff Planners had been studying concepts on what to do about a possible Russian conflict as early as the end of 1945. These first studies embraced problems and issues that would plague planners throughout the Cold War.

The military analyses in late 1945 for these plans stated that the USSR had an estimated force of over 7.5 million under arms. They assessed that the Soviets were capable of overrunning all of Europe within six months of an opening conflict. The planners did not think that the Soviets wanted to wage a deliberate war, but that tensions between East and West may unwillingly lead to one. The problem then was that if some conflict was about to break out how to stop or limit it. As the discussions on the possibility of a war with the Soviets progressed, and the American military posture continued to deteriorate, it became apparent that the US would have to rely on the Atomic Bomb and bases located close enough to significant Soviet targets for strategic bombing operations.

As the result of this initial effort, American military planners derived their first global operational plan called 'PINCHER.' This plan envisioned an atomic offensive delivered by US bomber forces from critical bases in the UK and the Middle East. Per the JCS Official History, recognizing that such an offensive may not directly affect an attack in Europe, "it would buy time for the United States to mobilize forces, check the Soviet advance, and eventually mount counter-attacks."

This plan, however, was full of major uncertainties and disagreements. There were uncertainties about the availability of the bombs, whether the bases would be accessible, and, if they were, whether the bombers could effectively reach their targets to do the damage that would hamper any Soviet war effort. There were also disagreements between the Army Air Force, and later its successor the Department of the Air Force, and the Navy over whether land-based bombers or carrier-based aviation was best suited for the atomic offensive.

The Berlin Crisis, the 'fall of China,' and the Soviet tests of an atom bomb further exasperated these uncertainties and disagreements. Most importantly, the fate of US occupation forces in Europe was a major issue should a conflict break out. Consequently, the military planners drafted concepts of what to do with those forces in case of war. Realizing that the occupation forces could not halt a Russian assault, the planners' solution was to plan for their withdrawal from Germany through France, to either the Iberian Peninsula or North Africa. The key to making this plan work was France's cooperation in the planning and its recovery from the war's destruction.

Several factors made France critical to the withdrawal of US forces from Germany, should that become a necessity. First, to support any military resistance to a possible Russian attack, Western Forces would need the military supplies positioned in France during the war. Second, the withdrawal would have to take place over land and rail routes through France to potential areas in both Spain and southern France. Finally, French forces were necessary to help in the fight.

These factors made it of paramount military importance that the US repair and improve French infrastructure as quickly as possible and as a matter of priority. It was also important to support the reinstatement of a French government that would support US policies in Europe, to include the rebuilding eventually and rearming of a West Germany. As we will see, these dependencies would eventually tie US policies not only in Europe to French needs, but to their ambitions to restore their prewar colonial possessions, such as Indochina.

NATO: Containment in Europe

Throughout this intense period of trying to find and create a national strategy and corresponding plans in case of a conflict with the Soviets, defense budgets remained low and military capabilities mismatched to the needs of the policy of containment. The Truman Administration, while recognizing that there was a risk in underfunding defense, continued to pursue political, diplomatic, and economic solutions to the Soviet threat throughout the forties.

While the Marshall Plan aid was the main way the Administration pursued rebuilding western democracies to contain the Soviets, US Ambassadors were arguing that there was a psychological need as well as an economic one. As shown in State Department official papers in the *Foreign Relations of the United States*, several American diplomats were saying that there was a necessity for political assurance to the western European nations of US military support against the Soviet threat.

Meanwhile, US military commanders in Europe and Joint Staff planners from Washington were meeting with their European counterparts discussing contingency concepts should a conflict with the Soviets accidentally occur. They agreed that some organization was necessary to enable them to plan and train for that contingency constantly. They also concluded that a combined standing force would be required to at least deter such an attack.

By early 1948 to show their concern and entice the US to associate with it, the Western Europe states - namely Great Britain, France, and the Benelux countries - had decided to form a political-military alliance of their own called the Western European Union or WEU. Soon after, the Truman Administration decided to begin security discussions with the WEU.

Before that could happen, however, the Administration needed to prepare the way with the US Public and Congress. To enter a peacetime military alliance with European nations represented a revolutionary course of action for America. After all, the US had made it a matter of tradition of not getting involved in foreign 'entanglements.' While World War I had gone against that custom, there had been a backlash after the war in America. Some argued that a megalomaniac President, war profiteers, and European leaders had led us into that war under pretenses.

Hence, after the First World War, the US Senate had decided against joining the League of Nations – an organization that US President Wilson had argued for to prevent future conflicts. Indeed, even in the face of the threats of Germany and Japan, it took Pearl Harbor to get us into World War II. Now in the face of this tradition, and in the light of past popular policies of 'isolationism' or 'neutrality' in foreign affairs, the US was exploring an alliance in Europe to contain the Soviet Union.

As an indication of the Public and Congressional awareness of the Soviet threat and the impact of the Red Scare, it did not take too much of an effort to obtain US Senate approval to enter talks with the WEU and later sign a security treaty. The President led the effort in an address to the Joint Session of Congress in March 1948 called, "The Threat to the Freedom of Europe."

In this speech, Truman lauded the formation of the WEU, and emphasized that "the determination of the free countries of Europe to protect themselves will be matched by an equal determination on our part to help them to do so." He concluded by calling for universal military training legislation and reenactment of the Selective Service Act to show US resolve.

To further pave the way, State Department officials often met with the Senate Foreign Relations Committee. These meetings led to the adoption of a resolution authorizing the "progressive development of regional and other collective arrangements for individual and collective self-defense." Most press reports and public reactions were positive and supportive.

A year later, after many meetings on how to organize and plan for its defense, the United States signed the North Atlantic Treaty Organization (NATO). Signatories of the treaty agreed that an armed attack against any of them in Europe and North America would be an attack against them all. They also decided if an armed attack occurred, each of them would assist the attacked member "taking such action as it deemed necessary, including the use of armed force, to restore and maintain the security of the North Atlantic area." With the signing of the NATO agreement, and the commitment to defense of foreign states, the US had set a significant precedent for the future.

NSC 68: Containment as a Zero-Sum Confrontation

Up to this point, the US Containment Policy had been a statement, unofficially found in addresses and memos, on what the US should do in the face of the Soviet military and ideological threat to US global interests. While known to all in the government and made public, the Truman Administration had not, however, officially promulgated that policy into intergovernmental plans and actions. In short, there was no written, coordinated National Security Strategy for the US during this critical time in the Cold War.

Early in 1950 President Truman, seeing the need for a more coherent formulated strategy, directed the National Security Council to undertake a study to reevaluate US stated aims and plans for Containment and report on the results. Kennan's replacement in the State Department's Policy Planning Staff, Paul Nitze, set about to lead and write a comprehensive official policy and outline of its strategy in this report. The document, presented to the President several months later, became known as National Security Council Report 68, or NSC 68.

The foremost objective of the report, in Gaddis' words, "was to systemize containment, and to find the means to make it work." While endorsing Kennan's views on the Soviet Union and the need for firmness and patience against their aggressive behavior and ideology, it differed in how and where to confront and contain the Soviets. NSC 68 emphasized the need to bolster US military capabilities in this confrontation. It warned that without such an increase, now that the Soviets had the Bomb, US interests would be gravely threatened. Moreover, in a key phrase, the document warned, "a defeat of free institutions anywhere is a defeat everywhere." The report further explained that the US had to show the resolve to resist communist aggression wherever it occurred, because if it did not the Soviets would believe that America was weak and irresolute.

This zero-sum attitude, Gaddis argues, set the US toward a policy of needing to confront Soviet (and Chinese) Communism anywhere. Thus, NSC 68 represented a significant shift from a national strategy that emphasized political-economic means of containment in select areas such as Western Europe, to one that would use military means to thwart communist expansion everywhere in the world. "The implications were startling," Gaddis writes. "World order, and with it American security, had come to depend as much on perceptions of the balance of power as on what the balance actually was."

President Truman did not initially approve NSC 68. He refrained from the military buildup the document indicated was necessary. When presented to him and discussed in an NSC meeting on 7 April 1950, as David McCullough relates in his biography *Truman*, he said little and "put it away under lock and key." Perhaps it was too grandiose and costly (although the study did not give a cost figure, McCullough claims that costs discussed at the NSC meeting were from 40 to 50 billion US dollars). Besides, without an actual war, Truman may have thought it was just too unrealistic.

It would take an actual military conflict to resurrect the NSC assumptions that it was only with military force that they could contain communism. Moreover, to validate NSC 68's argument that military containment was necessary even outside Kennan's vital interest areas, there would have to be some future confrontation, crisis, or conflict outside of Europe that would warrant a major threat to US interests. Such a conflict was on the near horizon.

Korean War: Containment in the Pacific

Up until June 1950, NSC 68 and NATO were both paper tigers when it came to actual military capabilities to deter and thwart a Soviet attack against US interests. The former was a statement of what in the long term was militarily necessary to contain the Soviets without any commitments to the forces needed or the cost. The latter was little more than a political association to create a psychological effect and show resolve in Europe.
All of that changed when North Korean Forces, with the foreknowledge and approval of the Soviet Union and China, attacked South Korea on 25 June 1950.

At the end of World War Two, the Soviet Union and the US had agreed to occupy northern and southern portions of Korea, which the Japanese had used as a base for operations against China in the war. They had also agreed to turn over these areas to the respective Communist and Democratic Korean governments that now were to govern their portions, split at the 38th Parallel, of the peninsular.

Historians agree that the Korean War started because of miscalculations on both sides. Because the US had not taken any direct action in the Chinese Civil War, Stalin, and Mao Zedong, having signed a new treaty of cooperation, thought that military action to reunify the North and South under communist rule was possible. This assertion seemed even more promising when Truman's US Secretary of State, Dean Acheson, made a public statement in January 1950 that the US had defined interests in a strategic Asian Defense Perimeter that unintentionally excluded Korea.

Despite Acheson's statement, the US decided it had a vital interest in stopping the June 1950 communist aggression in Korea. The Truman Administration, backed by Congress, believed that not doing so would further encourage communist aggression elsewhere – particularly in Europe. This assertion was a key aspect and assumption of NSC 68.

Furthermore, American reaction to the aggression was swift. The US brought the matter before the UN. The Soviets were boycotting the Security Council at the time, and the Council quickly denounced the invasion. Truman ordered US forces in Japan under General Douglas MacArthur to go to Korea under a UN Command structure.

Initially, the US forces that employed - having been an occupation force from Japan and under-manned, ill-equipped, and untrained - did miserably. During the first months in the summer of

1950, UN forces fell back to a defensive perimeter around Pusan. Once reinforced and reorganized, however, MacArthur conducted a brilliant stroke with an amphibious landing behind enemy lines at Inchon. This attack outmaneuvered the North Koreans, cut their supply lines, and sent them in full retreat.

Then, overreaching initial objectives of restoring the border, the US decided to reunify the peninsula. This move prompted Chinese military intervention with Soviet help. The ultimate result was a web and flow of attacks and counterattacks until the war finally ended in an armistice in 1953.

This war turned out to be different than what MacArthur was willing to conduct. The General's famous phrase in World War Two was "there is no substitute for victory." That war's objective was to defeat the enemy unconditionally. The US had accomplished this aim with the employment of enormous land, sea, and air power, as well as with the use of the atom bomb against Japan.

However, Korea was now a limited war. With the risk that the conflict could embroil the US in a prolonged Asian war and a possible global nuclear war with the Soviets, Washington placed restrictions on field commanders on what targets they could attack and what force they could employ and where. It was also, in the words of another Second World War General Omar Bradley, who was now the Chairman of the Joint Chiefs of Staff, "the wrong war, at the wrong place, at the wrong time and with the wrong enemy." The JCS warned that the war could detract from what needed to be the priority theater for containing communist aggression – NATO Europe.

The *American Caesar*, as William Manchester called him in his biography of that name, was unwilling to bend to the controls that Washington imposed. Disregarding President Truman's intent and policies, General MacArthur set out to undermine the controls by eliciting his support in the Press and the Congress. He also directly contacted the Chinese and told them in effect to surrender or feel the full wrath of his power. These independent moves were completely counter to what President Truman wanted, and MacArthur knew it.

Truman had no choice. Despite that his popularity was low and the General's extraordinarily high, he relieved MacArthur of his command. The reaction at home was astonishing. Then Senator Richard Nixon at once called for the General's reinstatement. Others in Congress demanded Truman's impeachment. There were many public protests.

As Truman's biographer, David McCullough describes, "In New York two thousand longshoremen walked off their jobs in protest over the firing of MacArthur. A Baltimore women's group announced plans for a march on Washington in support of the general. Elsewhere enraged patriots flew flags at half-staff, or upside down. People signed petitions, fired off furious letters and telegrams to Washington. In Worcester, Massachusetts, and San Gabriel, California, Truman was burned in effigy. In Houston, a Protestant minister became so angry dictating a telegram to the White House that he died of a heart attack."

Truman waited out the reactions. He knew he was right and had no other recourse. Some supporters admirably told him that he had shown great courage in his decision. The President responded, "Courage didn't have anything to do with it. General MacArthur was insubordinate and I fired him. That's all there was to it."

Nevertheless, Truman's popularity continued to plummet. Many believe that this act had a decisive effect on his later failure to gain his party's nomination for President in 1952. This incident would be something for subsequent President aspirants to remember. Later, as LBJ was waging war in Vietnam, he would tell his general, "Don't Pull Another MacArthur."

To wage war in Korea, the US had mobilized significant forces and fielded them in a prolonged military struggle against the forces of Communist North Korea and Red China supported by the Soviet Union. Consequently, the austere budgets of the early postwar era went out the window. From 1950 to 1953, the US Defense budget jumped from around $12 billion to $43 billion. The strength of the US Armed Forces went from 1.4 million to 3.5 million. The Services central units – Army divisions, Navy ships, and Air Force Wings – doubled in size.

The Administration, furthermore, did not just send US forces to Korea. Recognizing that Europe remained the US top national interest and the Soviet Union as its number one threat there, Truman approved the deployment of additional forces to Germany as the Korean conflict dragged on. Therefore, by the end of the Korean War, the US had four Army divisions employed in West Germany, with another ten earmarked to reinforce them if needed. Truman approved sending more air forces as well. Thus, the US tripled the size of its bomber force in the UK.

The US also revitalized the war plans for the defense of Western Europe. For those plans, the US actively supported the rearmament and entry of West Germany into NATO to bolster the defense. To do that, Truman also began to support France in its efforts to reestablish its hold over Indochina. It was a price the US had to pay to obtain French support for the rearmament of its traditional enemy in Europe.

By the end of the Korean War in 1953, what had been a US policy to stem Communist Soviet hegemony in the world through a firm and patient but 'peaceful' means of Containment had become a military standoff between two major nuclear powers. It had also evolved into a policy of using military forces when needed to stop any communist aggression in the world. The Korean War thus validated and resourced the overall premise of the strategy outlined in NSC 68 of the necessity of a military confrontation with communism worldwide. This statement would be the bedrock of American policy and its national strategy leading up to and including the Vietnam War.

A New Look at Containment: Nuclear Weapons and Massive Retaliation

When the Korean War ended, Dwight Eisenhower had become President. With IKE in the White House, the Republicans now also controlled Congress. This was the first time in twenty-five years that the Republicans completely controlled the Government.

Journalists wrote that this marked the end of the Roosevelt-Democrat New Deal era. Eisenhower, sounding very much like another President some thirty years later, said that the Government's role should not attempt to direct the nation's economy. He further proclaimed that "he was trying to make it smaller rather than bigger and finding things it can stop doing instead of seeking new things for it to do." There were also hints in the Press that the new administration would take a new approach to Containment.

The Korean War brought two legacies to the new President and his administration. One was that the threat of the use of nuclear weapons might be a useful and significant deterrent to contain communist aggression. Another was that the buildup, use, and maintenance of conventional forces were extremely costly.

According to the JCS Official History, Eisenhower saw the use or threat of the US nuclear weapons during the Korean War as an option and had considered it. In fact, there were some who believed that the war had ended because IKE had sent a strong signal to the communists that if they did not agree to the cease-fire, he would employ nuclear weapons.

Moreover, the US military, unlike the late forties, had gone a long way toward curing its Atom Bomb weaknesses. First, after the revelation that the Soviets had the bomb and began to manufacture them, Truman had ordered both the testing of new Atom Bombs and development of the new Hydrogen Bomb. Second, the US had started to assemble significant numbers of weapons and placed them under control of the new Strategic Air Command (SAC).

Third, under its new commander General Curtis LeMay, who had led the bombing campaign against Japan in the Second World War, strategic bombers began intensive training programs for their delivery against planned targets. Finally, the JCS restudied its basing concepts, and SAC deployed some of its new strategic bombers to new or improved bases that could reach any target in the Soviet Union or China. Indeed, by the time Eisenhower took over as President, the US military had a significant nuclear capability, to include missile delivery systems, which gave the US a degree of superiority over the Soviet Union and Red China.

Moreover, IKE had become alarmed over the new alliance between growing defense industrial establishments, their expanding and costly government contracts, and the impact of defense spending on the economy. He now resolved to not only bring this phenomenon under control, but to shrink the defense budget so he could convince Congress to spend on domestic programs like the new international highway project he had in mind.

Consequently, during the Eisenhower administration, the US defense establishment began to shift its focus from reliance and maintenance of conventional forces to a 'New Look' (as the Press called the new defense strategy) of dependence on its Nuclear Forces to deter any further communist aggression. Central to this new strategy, Gaddis explains, "was the idea of regaining the initiative while lowering costs."

To justify and explain its new national security strategy, The IKE Administration criticized Truman's version of containment as having been too defensive and had surrendered the initiative to the communists. Thus, Truman had encouraged the Soviet Union, Red China, and their proxies to risk expansion of communism along the peripheries of our national interests to gain the upper-hand. Moreover, to hold the line against aggression everywhere with conventional forces was extremely costly. An attempt to do so would drive the country into an unsustainable deficit.

Instead, as Eisenhower's Secretary of State Dulles argued, the US should be able to employ our strengths and forces of our choosing, such as nuclear weapons, in a massive retaliation to communist threats worldwide. Eisenhower further clarified this massive retaliation policy as the ability to convince our adversaries that any conflict may escalate to one of nuclear war; thereby convincing them not to start one.

There were two major consequences of this 'New Look' that would have an impact on future defense policies and issues. First, the idea of the threat of massive retaliation as a deterrent policy would eventually lead to the political-military thought on 'Mutually Assured Destruction' or MAD. This was the dominant deterrence policy advocated in the last twenty years of the Cold War, which, in turn, led to the fear that any confrontation may bring about nuclear war between two nuclear powers.

The logic of MAD that the ability to guarantee the complete destruction of two adversaries with nuclear weapons will deter their use became a cottage industry among civilian military theorists arguing how to gain or maintain the advantage in a potential nuclear exchange. In turn, many military professionals abhorred, did not understand, or did not want to associate themselves with MAD. Instead, the military profession wanted to focus their study on the use of nuclear weapons as just another weapon for use on the battlefield, rather than as a doomsday device with no rational political-military operational aim.

A second major consequence of the 'New Look' Defense Policy was to create a schism among the military on the use and resourcing of nuclear and conventional military forces. This divisiveness was primarily a result of the cut in the defense budget and allocation of much of it to the Air Force. When Ike took over, he cut the defense budget from the $42 billion one that he inherited from Truman to $36 billion with a planned target of cutting another $12 billion.

With the new emphasis on massive retaliation, the Armed Forces' programs drastically changed. The Air Force, with the priority for the defense budget, further increased the size of its strategic forces, spending vast sums on new bombers like the B-52 and new intercontinental missiles. The other Services sought a piece of the nuclear weapons emphasis. The Navy concentrated on developing a new submarine-launched nuclear missile known as the Polaris. The Army reorganized its divisions to be able to fight on the nuclear battlefield and developed tactical nuclear weapons to support that new approach.

The conflict over the budgets now became even a more divisive bureaucratic war between the Service Chiefs of Staff. The battles over roles and mission also intensified. Thus, throughout the IKE Administration, the JCS had ceased to exist as a collaborative body to give coherent strategic advice to the President. To counter this intense bickering, Eisenhower sought to offset the power of the Service Chiefs. In 1958, he proposed, and the Congress passed another Defense Reorganization Act. It empowered the Chairman to the JCS as a voting member – he was not in the other Acts – and authorized him to select key members of the Joint Staff, which doubled in size.

While this act gave more power to the Chairman and enabled him to speak for the overall Chiefs directly to the President, it did not end the bickering. Nor did it prevent some of the Chiefs to go directly to the Congress to argue their views. In fact, the two most notable Army Chiefs of the time – Generals Matthew Ridgway and Maxwell Taylor – forcibly gave their arguments that the current defense policy was flawed. Taylor retired in protest and wrote a book called *The Uncertain Trumpet*. It called for a more flexible response strategy to deal with potential enemies who would not respond to nuclear threats.

Some notables in Congress thought the criticism of General Ridgeway and that of his successor Maxwell Taylor well founded. Senator John F. Kennedy was the most prominent. When he began running for President against Eisenhower's hand-picked replacement, Richard Nixon, Kennedy's defense policy was to develop more flexible forces that would allow for their use in limited wars, particularly the kind that seemed – insurrections and guerrilla conflicts in support of wars of national liberation.

The Eisenhower Administration, in fact, faced such a conflict in a remote place in Asia called Indochina that few Americans had heard of. There in 1954 a close ally and key member of NATO - France - was about to lose a war against a communist-dominated force called the Viet-Minh.

Indochina, France, and the US

To grasp US involvement in Vietnam one must more fully understand the importance of France to America during the Cold War, and why the US decided to support it in its war to regain control over its colonies in Indochina. This part of the narrative seeks to explain that importance and gain that understanding.

France had ruled Indochina - made up of Laos, Cambodia, and Vietnam - since the mid-19th Century. When the Second World War broke out, and Germany had defeated France in June 1940, the defeated French set up a government in Southern France that became known as the Vichy Government. That government continued to control Indochina.

To obtain the abundant resources of Southeast Asia for their war effort, the Japanese government in August pressured the Vichy to sign a treaty that granted Japanese forces movement into Indochina. The Vichy agreed. This arrangement was because the Nazis controlled the Vichy government, and Japan was an ally of Germany.

Subsequently, Japan moved its troops from China into Indochina, primarily focusing on Vietnam. It occupied the region until their surrender in August 1945. Afterwards, in line with the agreements in the Potsdam Conference, Great Britain and China took over the southern and northern areas, respectively, to manage and control the surrender of Japanese forces there. The real question that Great Britain, China, and the US, which had been a party to the surrender agreements, had was what next?

During the Japanese occupation, Vietnamese nationalists had fought a guerrilla war against both the Vichy French and Japanese forces. Now a group of those nationalists - calling themselves the Vietnam Independence League or Viet-Minh - sought independence from further French rule. Its leader was a communist by the name of Nguyen Ai Quoc, later known as Ho Chi Minh.

Though a communist, Ho was aware of US past declarations of support for the self-determination of people in European controlled colonies throughout the globe. As previously mentioned at the beginning of this chapter, he had also been in contact with American OSS teams in the area; assisting them in gaining information about the Japanese forces and downed Allied pilots in Indochina. After hearing of the surrender of Japan, Ho directed his military forces and his political teams to move on Hanoi and take control. They did. In September 1945, Ho, quoting from the US Declaration of Independence, declared the independence of the Democratic Republic of Vietnam and formed a provisional government.

Ho had good reason to be hopeful for US support for his new government. First, as a world traveler, he had gone to France near the end of the First World War. While there, he had become familiar with US President Wilson's call for self-determination at the Versailles Conference meeting in Paris to draft an end of war treaty. Ho drafted and presented a statement to that Conference pleading for the recognition of Vietnam as a sovereign state.

He also knew about the US and Great Britain's adoption of the Atlantic Charter at the beginning of the Second World War. This charter held to the Wilsonian principle of self-determination of oppressed peoples in the world as a war aim of those powers. Indeed, President Roosevelt, committed to the principles of the Charter, was against any restoration of European colonies during the war.

FDR had at one time in 1943 discussed the situation in Indochina, saying to his son that anything would be better for the native population than to live again under French colonial rule. His anti-colonialism was one reason that Roosevelt was not keen on giving France a say at any of the war councils and did not think they should have been part of the postwar settlements.

However, as the war progressed, a Free France government [a French Government in exile separate from the German established government at Vichy] began to make contributions to the fighting. FDR began to acquiesce to Free French requests for participation in the post-war deliberations. Also, the US-British Combined Chiefs of Staff – an organization formed to coordinate military plans - recommended French military involvement in defeating Japan. Roosevelt reluctantly approved this recommendation. Consequently, at the war's end, France had forces in the Pacific theater that they could send to regain their Indochina possessions.

Just a few months before the war ended, FDR died. While sick for some time, his death created a void initially in post-war planning. Truman filled that vacuum admirably. However, the new President was not anti-French, or anti-colonial, and was willing to do what was necessary to make the transition to peace as quickly as possible. Soon after Roosevelt's death, Truman concurred with a joint military staff and state department draft paper that set US policy as not opposing the restoration of Indochina to France. In return, the US obtained French military commitment toward the final defeat of Japan.

With the US now neutral to the fate of Indochina, the situation was in the hands of the British, Chinese, Viet-Minh, and the French. Ho Chi Minh took the initiative. He quickly engineered an election for a new government to replace the provisional one he had set up in September after the war ended. The national elections, held primarily in areas administered and controlled by the Viet-Minh, resulted in an overwhelming victory for them.

Promising the Chinese Nationalist General in charge of the occupation of the north that he would ensure that the new government would not be communist, he gained Chinese support. Soon afterward, Ho sent several letters to Truman pleading for recognition of the DRV and its newly elected government. They went unanswered. Meanwhile, he also began negotiations with the French to engineer some peaceful transition to an arrangement that would eventually guarantee Vietnamese independence.

At first, talks with the French seemed promising, with some French envoys indicating to Paris that Ho was a man they could trust. Ho believed that the French officials agreed to a temporary situation that would see Vietnam as a member of a French Union, with virtual independence sometime in the future. The French in Indochina meanwhile, wanting to get rid of the Chinese Nationalist Army in the north, negotiated a settlement with China to withdraw its Army in return for French concessions in China.

Ho Chi Minh's negotiations and compromises upset many in his Indochinese Communist Party. Having to placate those in the organization that were unhappy with this arrangement, he purportedly said, "The last time the Chinese came, they stayed a thousand years. The French are foreigners. They are weak. Colonialism is dying. The white man is finished in Asia. But if the Chinese stay now, they will never go. As for me, I prefer to sniff French shit for five years than to eat Chinese shit for the rest of my life."

But the new French Government in Paris, under the Free-French Force Commander Charles De Gaulle, was intent upon restoring full French rule. The British assisted. After arranging for transportation of French troops then deploying to the Pacific to Saigon, the British General in charge of the transition in the southern part of Vietnam turned southern Vietnam over to the French. Meanwhile, in the north, the negotiations with the Chinese and Viet Minh also allowed France to land some forces at Haiphong. These forces would aid in establishing French control as the Chinese troops left.

Clashes between Vietnamese people demonstrating against the re-entry of French forces in Vietnam occurred periodically after that first landing. Radical Viet-Minh leaders, who did not like Ho's policy of negotiating its freedom with France, sometimes organized, and instigated these. Sometimes arrogant French commanders prompted them. Amidst this anti-French climate, Ho continued to try to hold the militant faction of his Party in check while trying to negotiate a way to ensure a separate Vietnam entity. However, France was adamant for full control. Finally, a full-fledged battle broke out between Viet-Minh military forces and the French in Hanoi in December 1946. Negotiations ended. Ho and his Viet Minh leaders fled to the mountains to wage a guerrilla-type war.

At first, from 1946 to 1948, US policy toward the Indochina War was still neutral. Thus, it did not directly support the French war effort. However, the US – as mentioned previously - was adamant in supporting France in its recovery efforts in Europe. These two approaches were not compatible. The priority of US interests was to reestablish a functional, democratic French government in Europe supportive of the free world's struggle against communism. That interest sowed the seeds of US direct involvement in Vietnam.

When the Second World War ended, as mentioned at the beginning of this section, France faced a difficult ordeal ahead in the reconstruction of its infrastructure and restoration of its government. The physical destruction was enormous. The Allied Forces in preparation for the Normandy invasion and later the drive and fighting across France to defeat German forces caused much of this. The Allies had conducted massive interdiction efforts, sometimes aided by the French resistance, destroying factories and storage facilities; shattering the French railway system; and wrecking its bridges, canals, and harbors.

The German occupation contributed to this ruin. The Nazis had stripped France of its gold and had shipped to Germany anything worthwhile in its production capacity. The human destruction due to the occupation and liberation was equal to the physical. France lost over 550,000 lives due to the German invasion, the harsh occupation that followed, the resistance movement, and the Allied bombings. When the war ended in Europe, there were 6 million French that lacked housing and wandered the countryside.

Besides the physical destruction, there had been moral and psychological damages to France's reputation and self-confidence. The German defeat of the French Army in 1940 had been swift and humiliating. In the fierce fighting of the First World War, the French Army had proven itself as a noble institution amongst its population and internationally. Now with its defeat in 1940 in just four months, the Armed Forces reputation and honor seemed forever stained at home and abroad.

Traditionally the Army since France's Napoleonic era had stood for the soul of the French Nation. Despite the heroic and competent contributions of the Free French Army in the Allied cause and victory in the Second World War, the Army now had to regain the confidence of the Nation and prove itself again as an honorable representative of the French people.

The French provisional government, and those to follow, actively sought American assistance not only to reestablish an effective popular government, but also to restore the honor and capability of the Army. In so doing, they consciously, and as a matter of policy, used the threat of an internal communist takeover of its government [France had a strong Communist Party after the war]. The restored government also used the threat of communist military aggression in Europe and Indochina as bargaining chips to gain US help in its economic recovery and restoration of its postwar Army. The US would be a willing contributor.

As mentioned in the beginning of this section, France was an essential player in the establishment of NATO. Of importance was getting French agreement in the consolidation of the German western occupation zones, and the founding of the West German Federation. At first reluctant to acquiesce to this consolidation and formation, French leaders realized that this was another 'chip' they could play in getting further US assistance. The latter became more important to them than the traditional fear of a strong Germany again. So, they gave in and supported a new, even militarized West Germany as a means of making NATO a viable military as well as political alliance.

To facilitate all of this, the US agreed to provide substantial and direct economic assistance to France. The Marshall Plan also offered much economic aid. In fact, France was second only to Great Britain for overall financial outlays in the Plan. When the Marshall Plan ended, moreover, the US continued its economic and financial assistance. While most of this aid was to improve France's economy and infrastructure, there was another program that provided surplus military equipment for the French Armed Forces. All of this was the result of an aggressive diplomatic initiative of the French governments.

French leaders also asked for support for their struggle against the Viet-Minh in Indochina. For the French Government and their Army, regaining their prewar colonies was a matter of restoring France's power in the world and prestige in its Armed Forces. The US was at first careful not to oblige them. The only support from 1946 to 1948 that Truman was willing to give was to encourage France to set up an Indochinese Government with widespread support as an alternative to the communists. In fact, the US was insistent that its military and economic aid was for French recovery programs in Europe only, and agreements specified that they could not be used for overseas operations. Thus, while US dependency on French rehabilitation and restoration was significant, it was at first focused on and limited to Europe.

The Communist takeover of China in 1949 and the Korean War in 1950 changed that.

The Red Communist victory in China altered the Indochina situation in significant ways. For the Viet-Minh and its Democratic Republic of Vietnam (DRV), Communist Chinese support came soon after its victory over the Nationalists. It was significant. On 18 January 1950, the Chinese Communist Government, known as the People's Republic of China (PRC), formally recognized the

DRV. The Soviets followed two weeks later - and agreed to their requests for military aid. That soon came in the form of shipments of arms and ammunition to Viet-Minh forces.

The PRC also began employing significant military forces along the 500-mile-long border with Vietnam. Their purpose was two-fold. One, they helped in giving security for the safe havens within the PRC for Viet-Minh forces. Two, the Communist Chinese People's Liberation Army or PLA provided training for the Viet-Minh in its cross-border sanctuaries and advisors for its units. This training and advice focused on the lessons learned from its struggle in the Chinese Revolution and Mao's doctrine of revolutionary war.

Soon, as the Vietnamese scholar William Duiker explains, "the promise of weapons, advisers, and other war materiel provided the basis for a shift in [Viet-Minh] war strategy to the anticipated third stage of people's war—the general counteroffensive." In addition, the pretense that the Viet-Minh had distanced itself from the overall world communist movement and was a nationalist organization disappeared.

For France and the US, the PRC recognition of the DRV as the only legitimate government in Indochina, its military aid to the Viet Minh, and the presence of significant PLA forces on the border changed US support for the French war effort in Indochina. The Red Scare and McCarthy's constant attacks affected the Administration's deliberations as well.

In April 1950 President Truman approved National Security Council Memo 64. It declared that the US had to support the French war effort in Indochina to prevent its fall and the spread of communism to all Southeast Asia. Soon after, the US military set up a Military Advisory and Assistance Group (MAAG) in Vietnam headquartered in Saigon to oversee US military aid.

According to William Gibbons, in his series *The US Government and the Vietnam War*, NSC 64 was one of the first formally promulgated statements of US policy toward Vietnam that declared the region vital to US interests. It is the first justification of US involvement using what later became known as the Domino Theory – a statement that if Indochina fell to the communists than all Southeast Asia would fall. Interestingly, its focus was on the Red Chinese threat rather than that of the indigenous communist Viet-Minh. Consequently, in Gibbons words, this document had "profound and far-reaching" impacts on future US policy in Asia.

The Soviet and PRC sponsored North Korean invasion of South Korea in June 1950 solidified and accelerated US support to the French Indochina War and involvement in Southeast Asia. Southeast Asia now became a battle in the overall campaign against the global spread of communism, and an essential element of the US containment strategy, as delineated in NSC 68.

Furthermore, with the PLA intervention and participation in the Korean War, the possibility of its involvement in Indochina seemed not just possible but even probable. That probability advanced the cause of France in US aid in Indochina and European recovery as well. By 1954, total US military aid in the First Indochina War, as it later became known as, totaled more than a billion dollars.

Despite that assistance, in 1954 the communists won the war in Indochina. France, having to balance any commitment to Indochina with its restoration efforts and NATO responsibilities, could not provide enough forces to execute its ambitious military strategies to prosecute the war. There were also active political elements - to include its Communist Party - in France that opposed the war. Consequently, the French Parliament restricted service in Indochina by prohibiting the Government from sending there any Frenchmen conscripted into the Army. There were also strong political arguments that called for a negotiated settlement and supported the later French participation in the Geneva Convention to end the war.

Contributing to the call for a negotiated settlement and the eventual meetings in Geneva, were the failures of the US military assistance programs and the ineptness of the French military campaigns against the Viet-Minh. The US assistance program had been inefficient. Often the MAAG tried to dictate to the French where and how they could use it. The French resented that interference. American military officers blamed many of the French defeats or lack of ability to successfully conduct the war with disdain for the French Army. They continuously cited the fact that the Nazis had quickly defeated them without a major fight in 1940.

Moreover, French military leaders wasted their efforts in broad sweeps of areas that failed in cornering its elusive foe. Then in November 1953, General Navarre, the French Expeditionary Force (FEF) commander at the time, launched an assault into a valley around a place called Dien Bien Phu. In occupying that place, the French commander thought that he could control Viet-Minh movements in Laos and supplies coming from China. His forces there would also set up a series of strongpoint defenses and await a Viet-Minh attack. Navarre was confident those defenses would bleed the Viet-Minh much like Verdun had done to the Germans in the First World War.

The Viet-Minh, under their commander Vo Nguyen Giap, obliged. Using an extraordinary amount of manual labor, Giap skillfully employed his artillery on the high ground encircling the French redoubts. Much to the surprise of the French commander and his artillery advisor, they then proceeded to bombard the French positions. They also hindered and then prevented French forces from reinforcing and supplying the garrison. The French military leaders underestimated its foes determination and capabilities. Five months later the French surrendered.

For a time during that battle, the US contemplated direct military conventional involvement, and even nuclear weapons employment to save the French. President Eisenhower summoned some vital Congressional leaders to get their support. They, including one Senator by the name of Lyndon Johnson, voiced concerns over employing US troops or even airpower without Allied concurrence. Eisenhower queried the British and several other key NATO allies. They would not give their support to a venture that could detract from the defense of western Europe. IKE, also faced with his Army Chief of Staff Ridgway's candid estimate of the potentially prohibitive cost of a land war in Asia, decided against it.

The French defeat at Dien Bien Phu resulted in the recognition at the Geneva Conference of the DRV north of the 17th parallel and a separate, noncommunist South Vietnam south of it. The Conference called for elections on the future reunification of all of Vietnam. These elections would never occur.

According to Bernard Fall, the most noted historian of the First Indochina War, about 95,000 French troops (of all nationalities who served to include native Vietnamese), lost their lives on the battlefields or in prison camps. Viet-Minh casualties ranged from 300,000 to 500,000, including civilians. France lost its other colonial wars, and never gained back its prewar empire.

For many American officials, to include future Presidents, the war demonstrated that a monolithic communist movement continued to succeed in its planned conquest of the Free world – particularly in Asia. Moreover, this 'First Indochina War,' though not recognized at the time, was the cradle of much to follow in the American-Vietnamese relationship and experience there. The agreement to settle its division in an indeterminate election left much uncertainty about the future for the whole of Indochina and Vietnam. Both sides now had to wrestle with what to do.

For the North Vietnamese, while there was some division on how to attain it, the eventual unification of all of Vietnam was essential, even its 'manifest destiny.' Its leaders would struggle with the need for postwar consolidation, reconstituting and rebuilding an exhausted army, and seeking international support for both. This story will further elaborate upon this in Chapter 6.

For the US, in a rush to set up some base for halting the spread of communism, American policymakers hastily committed to building a democratic regime where there was no basis for such a system. Equally as foolish, the Eisenhower regime at Geneva hastily launched efforts for a security arrangement in Asia like NATO. The US labeled it the Southeast Asia Treaty Organization.

SEATO had no real backing from its supposed supporters in the region. The US never signed the treaty. It would turn out to be a 'paper tiger.' Furthermore, American military leaders sought to build a new South Vietnamese army that had no leadership base and had relied on the French for direction.

Neither the setting up of a new regional security regime or the development of a viable South Vietnamese Army had much chance of succeeding in the years to come. However, American confidence, bordering on arrogance, prevailed. Thus, shortly a new President pledged to "pay any price, bear any burden, meet any hardship, support any friend, oppose any foe, to assure the survival and success of liberty."

Chapters 2 and 3 that follow describe the Kennedy and Johnson Administrations' policies toward Vietnam, and their attempts to contain communist expansion in Southeast Asia through establishing South Vietnam as the bulwark of their defense against communist aggression there. Chapters 8 and 9 explain the American military strategies to attain the aims of these policies.

Personal Experiences and Observations of the Cold War

Personal Experiences

As I grew up in the suburbs of New York City, I do not remember ever hearing the term 'Cold War.' Recalling that time, it does not surprise me. Our family was typical of the middle class of the late forties and fifties. We continued to focus on our community events such as our church and school activities and participating in sports on nearby playing fields.

Yet, I do have some vivid memories as a child in the 50s about the Atomic Bomb. As early as third grade in elementary school we practiced drills on how to protect yourself from the effects of an atomic attack from Soviet and Red Chinese bombs and missiles. After a while, it became just something you did, like fire drills, and you never really thought too much about it.

We sometimes viewed films of actual nuclear tests that were taking place. Watching these, it just did not seem possible that anyone would want to launch an atom bomb attack. That possibility was something of the imagination of Hollywood. Filmmakers obliged the public curiosity of what would happen in movies such as *On the Beach*. Producers also portrayed the idiocy of such an event in *Fail Safe* and *Dr. Strangelove*.

I do remember discussions or conversations at some family gatherings about the 'Reds' or 'Commies.' I recall these sometimes to be about a few Americans being in the Communist Party and about the Korean War. Two of my most prominent memories were when President Truman relieved General MacArthur and the announcement of the Korean War armistice. The Korean War armistice news, as I recollect, was on one of the three TV news shows that had started to occupy fifteen minutes of our nighttime viewing.

My mother was furious about the MacArthur dismissal; as many in the family thought highly of him because of the publicity he received in World War Two and during the Inchon operation. In fact, a poll taken during these times that asked to name the greatest figure in world history had him ranked fifth - after FDR, Lincoln, Jesus Christ, and Washington.

When I attended junior high and high school, I remember films on TV about World War Two and Korea. These usually portrayed the good guys (American soldiers and leaders) overcoming the powerful 'Japs" or the evil, supermen Nazis. Some of these movies, now on TV after having shown in the movie theaters, depicted outnumbered American soldiers overcoming Red Chinese fanatical human wave attacks in Korea. These movies often portrayed Asian soldiers and leaders as not caring about their lives but committed to a totalitarian communism way of life.

The US Army produced a show entitled *The Big Picture*. It often showed combat footage of operations in the Second World War and Korea. However, it did, from time to time talk about the Army being overseas to protect American friends. I think I remember some footage about the Berlin Airlift. Also, Hollywood produced many films about World War Two and the Korean War. I do not remember much, if any, film or news or discussions of the French in Indochina.

After I had graduated from High School in June 1962, I went to a small college in Maine while I waited for a chance to get into West Point. There in October, we heard about the Cuban Missile Crisis. As a Freshman, I was trying to acclimate and just started to play my first season of college football. So, quite honestly, this great crisis in which the US and the Soviet Union were on the precipice of a nuclear war, passed without much concern or focus on my part.

It was when I entered the United States Military Academy that I began to hear more about the Cold War and the Army's role in it. I entered West Point in the summer of 1963. Of course, now I was a soldier in the 'Cold War.' We did not study much the origins or what even the Cold War was. At first, we did not even know much about what was happening in Vietnam. But while there we did have instruction on Army tactics and doctrine, which focused on a future conflict with the Soviet Armed Forces in Europe.

After I graduated from West Point in 1967, Class members who chose the Infantry, like myself, attended the Infantry Officer's Basic School at Fort Benning, Georgia. There, despite the ongoing war in Vietnam in which much of the Army was then engaged, we continued our studies of Army tactics and doctrine for a war in Europe against the Soviets.

For those of us who were curious about what was happening in Vietnam – and most of us were - we began to study on our own the events there. That was primarily through first-hand accounts related in a publication called *Infantry Magazine*. I also read Bernard Fall's histories of the French

Indochina wars, namely his *Street Without Joy* and *Hell in a Very Small Place*. The Infantry School then did not officially teach its new officers about the Vietnam War.

My first assignment was to the First Battalion, 509th Airborne Infantry at Mainz, Germany. Our focus and training there was on a possible Soviet invasion of Western Germany. My duties included instructing soldiers and training teams on the employment of tactical nuclear weapons on the battlefield and their effects. On occasion, we moved our unit to our General Defensive Position on the West-East German border near Fulda, Germany. There we practiced our 'wartime' defensive operations.

It was evident, and strange, that while the Vietnam War was on everyone's mind - and that members of our class were already serving and dying there - the official Army was almost ignoring it. It was bizarre that our doctrine and training disregarded the war. My mind and body became very much focused on Vietnam in April 1969 when I deployed and served there as an infantry leader in the 101st Airborne Division.

Several years after I returned from Vietnam, the Army sent me to Graduate School to prepare for an assignment as an Associate Professor of History at West Point. I attended the University of North Carolina from 1974 to 1976. While there the Vietnam War ended. North Vietnam, or the Democratic Republic of Vietnam as it was officially named, invaded the South in 1975 and in April captured Saigon, renaming it Ho Chi Minh City. I had woken up to the news in the papers. I was devastated.

During my studies to get a degree, I now decided to find out why we had gotten involved there. I wanted to know what the overall objectives and strategy were and how the North Vietnamese Communist had won. I had not thought about or questioned any of this before I went to Vietnam, or certainly when I was there. I had been an infantry soldier, a grunt, fighting along with other grunts to stay alive. Now I needed to know why we lost the war. I needed answers for all the death, destruction, and sacrifice.

I was fortunate to have several history professors who would guide and teach me how to proceed to obtain - not definitive answers - but some understanding of what had happened. First and foremost, there was my Academic Advisor, Dr. Samuel Williamson, who had been a student at Harvard under Henry Kissinger. He had researched and written a book on how Great Britain had gotten involved in World War I. He oversaw my overall graduate education and gave guidance and advice on all my studies. But he also gave me some crucial counsel on how to approach the questions I had about Vietnam, and whom to seek out for further direction and help.

With his guidance, I took courses, sought recommendations, and followed up on the instructions on my way forward from three other notable University Professors. Dr. Gerhard Weinberg, a distinguished and internationally renowned historian of the Second World War, guided me on how to pursue my quest through a logical and thorough historical inquiry of available materials. Dr. Samuel Wells, a noted US diplomatic historian, suggested ways to approach the US Government's primary sources to discover political issues and motives. Dr. William Leutze, who studied under the brilliant strategist and military historian Liddell-Hart, gave me some ideas on how to approach civil-military relations and military strategic analysis. Armed with all this wisdom and historical know how I set out on my quest.

My journey started with a study to gain an understanding of the times that the major decision makers lived. All my academic counselors hammered into me that I could only understand what happened and why people gave recommendations and made the choices they did if I could relate to the times they had lived in. I had to know and recognize the lessons they had learned from life; appreciate the pressures and influences in which they worked and served; and grasp the reasons for their actions.

All of this led me to a study of the events recounted in this Chapter, as well as some of the Chapters to follow. This corporate, educational guidance resulted in a study of much of the US involvement in the Cold War, especially in the formation of NATO in Europe. It also led to a discovery of how the US got involved in Southeast Asia and the war in Vietnam. It further resulted in many hours of study of US Government papers and documents in the National Archives.

Observations and Conclusions

My intent is designing and writing this chapter was to present two main conclusions that the reader needs to keep in mind as you go through the rest of this book. The first is that most of the people whom you will read about had lived through the Great Depression, the Second World War, and the early years of Containment. For many, these times were watershed experiences in their lives and influenced them dramatically as they struggled with the ends, ways, and means to deal with the issue of Vietnam.

In general, they acquired several major lessons from the Great Depression and the War that would affect them. The depression affected some more than others. A few, such as LBJ, saw that poverty almost ruined America. Thus, to ensure America's greatness Johnson wanted to focus on economic and social reform before all else. Others, who had escaped the worst of these years through educational opportunities – like most of the 'Best and Brightest' in the two chapters that follow - depended on their learning experience to solve any problem; no matter how intractable it may seem. Thus, men like McNamara and his 'Whiz Kids, McGeorge Bundy, and many other of the 'Best and Brightest' depended on educational theories or processes to solve the national security issues they faced.

Moreover, from the depression, most had learned that when confronted with a difficult problem or situation take some action. Any action is better than none. Inaction can only lead to further despair and destitution. You can only affect change by doing something; waiting for events to solve the problem is only to have more of the same or worse.

From the war, the American decision makers and their advisors gained an unquestioning belief in the power and a sense of destiny in the United States of America in the world. All of them, to a degree, thought that there was nothing that the US could not do. All that had to be done was to muster the natural strength of the nation and its people, and act upon its power and ideals.

Most of all, they also drew a major lesson from the causes of World War Two. Universally, American officials believed that Great Britain's policy of appeasement of Hitler's demands for a reunited Germany had led to war. In oversimplified terms, appeasement encouraged aggression. Therefore, in the future, if a nation wanted to deter a conflict it had to be firm and resolute in confronting the threats to its security.

A corollary to this argument was that one should not wait until that aggression starts. The confrontation must be early and at a place where the containment or defeat of that aggression was possible and did not threaten the vital interest of the nation.

The second significant finding is that, despite the experiences and lessons described above, US policymakers had faced a situation in the Post World War Two that none of them were fully prepared for. America was now a Global Great Power. It was the leader of the Free World. It also confronted another Great Power that seemed intent on destroying its way of life. Thus, war could occur at any moment. Furthermore, with the advent of Nuclear weapons, that conflict could lead to the destruction of humanity.

Most important is that this environment was entirely different from their typical view that they and most Americans had on the relationship between war and peace. That view was, per a scholar of US foreign policy named John Spanier, "that war was an interruption of the normal state of harmony among nations." As the Cold War was showing, nations could no longer view war as something abnormal; it was part of everyday thinking in international politics and peacetime defense planning.

Moreover, the issues that American national security leaders and advisors had to consider in this new era of global politics – some identified above – were profound. How could US Administrations develop and maintain international institutions and diplomatic relations on such a global scale when the US had rejected participation in them before? How could any Administration build a consensus for and obtain action on political, economic, and military actions when America had held a traditional isolationist view of the world and a pacifist outlook on war?

Furthermore, how could the Government sustain support for military action if needed? How could the US military posture itself in the world to act upon its now global interests? Where and how should the US bring its use of military force, whether conventional or nuclear or both, to bear on a perceived threat? What if that threat is not an obvious danger to a vital interest, then where and when might that threat become one against a vital interest?

Then there was the question of civil-military relations. Up to the Second World War the US military was a fairly sequestered institution. Its interface with the government had been minimal in peacetime. In fact, ingrained in American culture and politics was not only the traditional anti-militarism, non-interference in politics, and civil control, but a distaste and even anxiety over standing armies and general staffs.

Now in this new era of permanent 'Cold War' the need for an American standing armed force and the promulgation by the National Security Acts of a peacetime permanent general staff raised new questions on US civil-military relations. Indeed, a Harvard professor by the name of Samuel Huntington in 1957 published a book called *The Soldier and the State* examining this new relationship. In this book and a later one called *The Common Defense*, he expounded on the need for a new theoretical framework to examine new issues in the relationships between civil and military authorities, and their roles in defense affairs.

As explained in some of the anthologies in Don Snider's and Suzanne Nielsen's *American Civil-Military Relations: The Soldier and the State in a New Era,* the US would now have to confront such issues as: how would an enlarged professional military perform its new major role in national life indefinitely rather than episodically; what is the proper degree of professional military involvement in policy and strategy; how would the military ensure it provides quality advice to its civilian leaders; and what is the appropriate way for the military to voice its views, especially if they vary with their civilian leaders?

All of the above were the great questions that future governments would now have to face. Up to the late fifties the Truman and Eisenhower Administrations had faced them well. Some argued that both Presidents had handled tough civil-military issues firmly and successfully - especially a revolt of several Navy Admirals over roles and missions; and, of course, MacArthur's insubordination in Korea. Some would argue that they also handled the international demands creatively and decisively, thus leaving a baseline of ways to deal with future threats.

In fact, as Henry Kissinger noted in the first volume of his memoirs, "It is to the last credit of that generation of Americans that they assumed these responsibilities with energy, imagination, and skill. By helping Europe rebuild, encouraging European unity, shaping institutions of economic cooperation, and extending the protection of our alliances, they saved the possibilities of freedom. This burst of creativity is one of the glorious moments of American history."

The leaders and advisors in the Administrations that followed – those who had to confront the strategic questions surrounding whether to commit US military forces to combat a communist enemy threat in a faraway place - had to deal with these same issues under much continued uncertainty and confusion. Therefore, as we examine ahead the question of US policy toward Vietnam in the sixties, one must be aware of the contradictions, uncertainties, and new relationships that US policymakers and military leaders labored under.

On the one hand, they had an unshakeable confidence in America's now global destiny of leader of the free world, and its power to act as one and solve all issues. On the other hand, most political and military leaders had neither the long-term preparation for or experience in solving the issues at hand on such a global scale for an unknown future or duration. We will see, in the Chapters ahead, how they struggled to reconcile their beliefs and their confidence in America's power with situations that they had no experience in or preparation for. The reader, therefore, must put themselves in their shoes and, as best as one can, imagine the times and circumstances that they lived in, and what they knew then and not now.

This is all easier said, then done.

Chapter 2: The Best and the Brightest

In January 1961, as John F. Kennedy took office after his stirring inaugural address that month, the mood in Washington bordered on euphoric. As David Halberstam noted in his book, *The Best and the Brightest*: "It was a glittering time. [The new Kennedy administration] literally swept into office, ready, moving, generating their style, their confidence — they were going to get America moving again. There was a sense that these were brilliant men, men of force who acted rather than waited.... The word went out quickly around the Eastern seacoast, at the universities and in the political clubs, that the best men were going to Washington."

Despite this enthusiasm and confidence, there was much on the international agenda to challenge these scholars and warriors. Their remarkable intellects and skills would be tested as they had never been before. This chapter describes who these best and brightest were, what influenced them, and the nature of their relationships with one another. It also describes the key policy decisions they made or were a part of and their effect on the Vietnam War during the Kennedy Administration.

Section 2.1 - JFK Administration

During his campaign and in his inaugural address, President Kennedy elaborated that his approach to the Presidency would differ from his predecessor in two significant ways. The first was that his government would represent 'a new generation of Americans' – one that would renew America's sense of purpose in the world and reenergize its commitment to its ideals of service to the country. JFK intended that theme to portray an administration that was - like himself - young, energetic, confident, and willing to adopt new ways to govern. Per his confidant and speechwriter, Arthur Schlesinger, Kennedy wanted this theme to reflect a political movement that stood for a new era of forward progress rather than the 'stagnation' that the earlier administration seemed to epitomize to the new President, his advisors, and to the public in general.

JFK referred to this movement as "The New Frontier." He introduced this phrase in his nomination speech at the Democratic Convention in 1960. There, Kennedy had proclaimed, "We stand today on the edge of a New Frontier--the frontier of the 1960's, the frontier of unknown opportunities and perils, the frontier of unfilled hopes and unfilled threats. Beyond that frontier are uncharted areas of science and space, unsolved problems of peace and war, unconquered problems of ignorance and prejudice, unanswered questions of poverty and surplus." His inaugural address call for paying any price and bearing any burden for the advance of freedom represented what he thought every American would be willing to do to attain his new frontier goals.

The second way that his approach would be different was that the US needed a new method of dealing with the looming communist threat in the world. Unlike the Eisenhower policy, it did not rely on the threat of use of nuclear weapons for security and containment. Kennedy would call for a national security policy and capability that would enable the US to respond to threats and shape our interests with a more flexible mix of military, economic and diplomatic means to 'to assure the survival and success of liberty.' Underlying the need for this more flexible strategy and force structure was the belief that the new battlefields of the Cold War would involve third-world confrontations as well as the need to protect Europe.

To implement his vision for progress in this new frontier, Kennedy sought the most brilliant men for his government. JFK also thought that to deal with the world's security issues and obtain the best advice from these men to solve them, he had to change the apparatus for making national security policy.

While the National Security Act of 1947 had created a formal structure, namely creating a National Security Council and an assistant, it was subject to how the President desired to use it. For example, President Truman, who would rather deal directly with individuals or a select group of advisors on these matters, did not use it much. In fact, of the 55 meetings of the Council, he attended only 10.

President Eisenhower, on the other hand, had used the Council more formally and frequently. Indeed, he wanted to have most security matters thoroughly staffed, presented in papers, and officially documented. Accordingly, the Council formed several subordinate organizations to do the staff work and submit the results to the President and the principal members of the Council. By the late fifties, however, some believed the Council had become too formalized and structured; and its processes too rigid and slow.

Kennedy rejected the need for an overly used formal process; especially one so rigid and confining to him as the one that Eisenhower had set up. As Larry Freedman explains in his book, *Kennedy's Wars*, JFK preferred a more academic, collegial approach than the more military one like the one of IKE.

Freedman explains the new President's rationale for such a process. "This model offered influence on merit, while the military model required a clear line of command. Kennedy saw hierarchy as an obstacle, a means of filtering out the unorthodox and the awkward while giving undue prominence to the bureaucratic interests of the key agencies. Kennedy wanted a system that extended the range of his options and did not box him in when the moment came to choose. He disliked organizational charts, elaborate committee structures, and large formal gatherings, preferring small, intense groups."

The closest that JFK came to some more formal organization was an executive committee of the Council called an 'EXCOM.' He used that when confronted with a clear and critical national security issue that needed immediate attention. The personnel on that committee did not necessarily consist of the statutory members that the law had put in place. Rather, it included those whom the President felt should deliberate such matters, and, more importantly, the people he had confidence in and trusted.

Accordingly, the people JFK chose for his administration and formed the center for his national security policy apparatus both reflected and suited his approach of a 'new era of forward movement,' and his desire for qualified, smart advisors whom he could trust. He also wanted advisors who were comfortable with discussing issues in an environment that was open to discussion and debate. In short, he wanted and favored smart, educated people over experienced ones.

JFK as President and Commander-in-Chief

John F. Kennedy, as most Americans are aware because of his tragic assassination, was born in a large New England Irish family of wealth. His father, Joe, Sr., had made his millions in the banking industry and other business ventures. In the late thirties, Joseph Kennedy would serve under FDR as his ambassador to Great Britain. His money and influence played an essential part in JFK's political rise.

John Kennedy's mother, Rose Fitzgerald, was from a prominent Boston political background; resulting in his maternal Grandfather giving significant electoral support for JFK's elections as a Representative and later Senator from Massachusetts. Therefore, many in his Party, as well as the Republican, believed that Kennedy's meteoric rise to the Presidency at the age of forty-three was due mostly to the political and monetary support of his family.

The tragedies of the Kennedy Family are well known. JFK's older brother died in World War Two on a bombing mission in Europe. A Brother-in-Law also perished in the war. A plane crash resulted in the death of one of his sisters. Another sibling languished in a mental institution. Some Kennedy biographers argue that JFK's experience with death, as well as his suffering from a series of chronic ailments and war experience, accounted for his needs for early fame. Some historians argue that it was this profound sense of impending tragedy in JFK that motivated his, now famous, womanizing both before and during his marriage.

Despite his Father's wealth and support, John Kennedy was a man and leader of his own making. Throughout his illnesses as a youth and injuries as a Congressman, he became an avid reader of history. JFK was particularly fond of the writings of the Founding Fathers. He also read treatises on military policy and strategy. Coupled with his education in international affairs at Harvard, and his later writings and publication of *Why England Slept* and *Profiles in Courage*, he had become an educated and thoughtful scholar in his own right.

Arthur Schlesinger noted that he was intensely inquisitive and curious in his search for self-knowledge. Indeed, at one point after he married Jacqueline Bouvier, he asked Jackie to translate from French books about Indochina, and then read the translations. His extensive travels, and his opportunities to meet accomplished diplomats, political leaders, and military commanders gave him an astonishing amount of first-hand know-how on the art of politics and international affairs before he had become President.

He was a war hero as well. Not accepted by the Army to serve after Pearl Harbor because of his chronic back ailments, he joined the Navy and, with the help of his father's influence, went to the Southwest Pacific. There he was the commander of a Torpedo Boat – PT109 – and in 1942 survived a clash with the Japanese in which he saved many of his crew. His wartime experiences, chronicled for his political benefit in a book in 1961, had given him a distaste for war. It also contributed to his aversion toward high-ranking military brass; whom he characterized as inflexible and unable to think on their own. This attitude would influence his relationship with his military advisors. Unlike other politicians of his time, he did not embellish or make up stories of his service. When asked how he became a hero, he responded, "It was involuntary. They sank my boat."

JFK had given much thought to his transition to the Presidency. After the election, he met with several advisors at his family home at Cape Cod on how to execute the changeover. One such advisor was Professor Richard Neustadt of Columbia University, who had written an insightful account of the Presidency and government called, *Presidential Power*. Neustadt's observations impressed Kennedy that the President's real power consisted of the ability to persuade others. It also depended, Neustadt argued, upon the President's ability to focus on and deal with energetic, talented, and motivated people in government more than bureaucratic processes.

These ideas fit well with JFK's philosophy of the Chief Executive as someone who would be the "vital center of action in our whole scheme of government." Moreover, Neustadt's arguments that FDR was one of the most effective Presidents because of his less formal and more open approach to policy making was a primary reason for the new President's desire to have a collegial based national security process. Kennedy knew this meant not only finding the right men for the right jobs, but these new advisors had to be men who relied more on intelligence and their instincts based on intellect, rather than on experience and bureaucratic procedural prowess.

In the two months before his inauguration, Kennedy set out to find the right men that fit the above criteria. There were over a thousand positions to fill in 1960 (more today). JFK focused on those that he considered being the most important. He decentralized the choices of others to those principals he focused upon.

There were five principals, whom JFK chose personally. They would play critical roles in the policy making for the Vietnam War. These were: Secretary of State, Dean Rusk; Secretary of Defense, Robert McNamara; Assistant for National Security Affairs, McGeorge Bundy; Deputy

Assistant for National Security Affairs, Walt Rostow; and his Military Assistant and later Chairman of the Joint Chiefs of Staff, General Maxwell Taylor.

There were two individuals that the President did not directly choose for his administration, but who would serve important positions in State and Defense during the Vietnam debates. These were Assistant Secretary of State George Ball and Assistant Secretary of Defense John McNaughton. Finally, there were another two who, while the President did not directly appoint, would also be crucial to the decision-making process. These were: Ambassador to the Republic of South Vietnam – Frederick Nolting; and Commander, Military Assistance Command Vietnam (MACV) – General Paul Harkins.

JFK's Scholars and Warriors

Usually, the Secretary of State, who is fourth in the Constitutional line of succession, is one of the most important positions that the President can appoint to his Cabinet. In the Truman and Eisenhower administrations, the people who held this position had already made a mark on history. These had been such notables as George C. Marshall, Dean Acheson, and John Foster Dulles. Kennedy had decided, however, that he wanted to act as his own Secretary of State. Therefore, during the transition, he sought someone who could be a good team player and would be amenable to his dominance in foreign policy formulation.

Kennedy chose Dean Rusk. Rusk had the credentials for State. He had served in the State Department as the Assistant Secretary of State for Far Eastern Affairs. Most importantly to JFK, he had the academic qualifications, as well. He had been a Rhodes Scholar (one of the six such scholars that would serve in the Administration). Most of all, Rusk was known as a competent manager, but not one who was comfortable in taking the initiative in policy-making.

Dean Rusk had served in the military in World War II. He had been General Joseph Stillwell's Chief of Staff in the China-Burma Theater. He also was an ardent anti-communist; believing that the US had to contain communism wherever it was by military force. Rusk often justified these views with the use of a historical analogy that the mistakes of appeasement led to the outbreak of the war in Europe. These attitudes would consistently influence his view of US policy toward Vietnam. While Rusk was not a prominent figure during Kennedy's time as President, he would become much more influential for JFK's next in line – Lyndon Johnson.

For the Defense Department, JFK thought he needed a reformist – someone who could shake up the Department and revolutionize its management. This task was necessary and urgent because Defense had grown into a vast bureaucracy, which now entailed 20,000 employees in the Pentagon. Kennedy also wanted a Secretary who was confident and able enough to control the military establishment and execute the changes he foresaw in defense policy.

For this job, Kennedy picked Robert McNamara. JFK did not personally know him. However, members of his transition team did. All of them recommended him. He was then several years into his term as President of Ford Motor Company where, as mentioned in Chapter 1, he had earned a reputation for his work ethic and results-driven management style. That style focused on the intensive use of statistical measurements on performance to make decisions. McNamara had learned and taught this method at the University of California and as a professor at the Harvard Business School. His academic credentials fit in well with what Kennedy wanted.

In an interview with JFK, McNamara had impressed him with his statement that he would take the position, even though he felt uneducated for the job if he could choose his people. Remarking that there were no schools for Presidents and Defense Secretaries, Kennedy agreed to McNamara's precondition. Soon after his swearing in, the new Secretary brought in a group of people he had worked with at Ford or knew at the Rand Corporation to overhaul the Department. These men were highly educated (two were Rhodes Scholars, and the majority had graduated from Ivy League schools).

Under McNamara's close supervision, they set up new organizations to scrutinize and analyze all aspects of the budget and force management through a new process called the Planning, Programming, and Budgeting System or PPBS. The Defense Department still uses the system. The group became known as the 'Whiz Kids;' the same moniker some of them had when they were at Ford with McNamara. Many in the military also used other less flattering labels when referring to them. We will see why in the story ahead.

McNamara would use his management methods in assessments and recommendations on how to respond to strategic military situations, as well as in his reform activities. Specifically, in addressing the situation in Vietnam, he would institute a rigid method of measuring progress in the military operations. We will see ahead that McNamara's methodology, coupled with his lack of understanding of military operations, will have a major - even catastrophic - impact on the choices and decisions for the Vietnam War.

For the Special Assistant for National Security Affairs, JFK appointed McGeorge Bundy – a Bostonian whom Kennedy knew, liked, and admired. Though Bundy had voted for Republicans from time to time, he was an extraordinary intellectual whom everyone admired. He had graduated from Yale, served in the war as an intelligence officer, and had been a Dean at Harvard. He was also a student of foreign policy, and as a member of the Council on Foreign Relations (a Washington 'Think Tank') assisted in a study of how to implement the Marshall Plan. Though Bundy could be witty and entertaining at social events, at work he was often condescending and arrogant. Above all, he thought there was an answer for everything, and he could find it.

In several ways, Bundy was the ideal man for the job. He and Kennedy were on the same intellectual wavelength. JFK also thought that Bundy was the only person who could change and administer the national security process that the new President sought to create – a consortium of intellectuals. Bundy could handle these kinds of men. After all, this new special assistant had just been the Dean of Harvard University, where he had already demonstrated that he could oversee hard to manage intellectuals from the most prestigious university in America.

Under Bundy, the National Security Process would change dramatically and according to the way the new President wanted. As both Andrew Preston in *The War Council* and Daalder and Destler in their *In the Shadow of the Oval Office* argue, "Kennedy and Bundy would end up revolutionizing White House foreign policy making" because they focused all policy-making in the offices of the White House. Before, in the Truman and Eisenhower Administrations, the office had functioned as mostly a glorified clerk and coordinator of the growing national security bureaucracy. Now everything to do with foreign and national security went directly through Bundy. Key agencies - such as the CIA, the State's policy-making group, and Ambassadors abroad – fed him information unfiltered by their hierarchical bureaucracies. He, in turn, would decide what the crucial issues were, and what the main courses of action were to address them.

Bundy recruited for his personal staff a subset of the 'best and brightest' – young intellectuals who were known for 'out of the box' thinking. He would give them access, through him of course, to the President. This method offered Kennedy, Bundy thought, with various views on subjects unvarnished by years of bureaucratic experience on mundane matters. Bundy's primary intention was to use his people to bypass the Government's tedious and, as he thought, often dull thinking recommendations.

The new Assistant for National Security Affairs was confident enough to handle the pressure and responsibility that went with the job. As we will see he would not hesitate to execute his powers and apply his considerable talents to the fundamental issues confronting the Presidents he served. However, despite his undeniable intellect, he brought to the position of National Security Advisor a set of assumptions toward problem-solving that would affect his judgments of Vietnam.

For example, as mentioned, he thought all problems had a solution. All that one had to do was to apply the mind to analyze its premises and calculate the odds of a plausible resolution. He also believed that most people reacted to situations in the same way. The key when dealing with foreign adversaries, therefore, was to measure what their choices were and affect the one they must reasonably accept. In part, Bundy based his thoughts on this interaction of options on 'game theory' – a model of conflict and cooperation between rational decision makers developed in the late forties and fifties. It was a model he had studied and applied extensively in the academic world.

Herein, is Bundy's tragic flaw. He succumbed to his credence in rational choices. He believed everyone could be persuaded, as a rational actor, to give in to some stimulus or demand and accept an outcome adverse to his or her original desire. Thus, when confronted with the irrationality of war and conflict, he just did not understand Clausewitz's characterization of war in which, "all information and assumptions are open to doubt, and with chance at work everywhere, the commander continually finds that things are not as he expected." This tragic flaw will have a major impact on both JFK's and later LBJ's policymaking for Vietnam.

To complete his White House 'National Security Team' Kennedy selected Walt Rostow as Bundy's deputy. He complemented Bundy in several ways. First, he possessed as strong an intellect. Rostow had graduated from Yale, where he had received a doctorate in economic history. He also was a Rhodes Scholar. Second, Rostow had been a close advisor during the campaign and had offered valuable inputs to JFK's platform and speeches. His most significant contribution to the platform was the need to focus on aid to Third World countries to counter communist support for wars of national liberation.

Rostow had also coined the phrase "New Frontier" that JFK had used to denote his policy for a new forward movement in international relations in the world. Thirdly, he had also served as an advisor and speechwriter for Eisenhower, and had experience in government, whereas Bundy had none. Finally, he had extensive travel experience abroad and written a book that gave an intellectual counter to the ideas of communism. Indeed, of all JFK's advisors, Rostow was the most ardent opponent of communism.

Kennedy had decided before he took office not to make any changes to the Joint Chiefs of Staff, who were, as outlined in the first chapter, charged to advise on military matters. This decision, as we will see, would be a mistake. Eisenhower had 'groomed' the current members not to question his policy of massive retaliation. They had also been involved in the planning for the military use of the nuclear weapons should deterrence fail. In so doing, these military men had adopted the use of nuclear weapons as just another way of employing force in crises.

JFK would become dissatisfied and dismayed with the Joint Chiefs advice in several crises early on in his Administration. He could never understand their tendency to rely on the use of nuclear weapons in addressing military employment issues. For this reason and several others mentioned below, Kennedy would remain prejudiced against the Chiefs for the rest of his term. His disdain and distrust of his senior military advisors would rub off on his successor as well.

Because of his frustration with the JCS, President Kennedy called back to active duty and appointed General Maxwell Taylor as a 'Military Representative to the President.' There were other reasons for this appointment as well. The first is that like Truman JFK wanted to resurrect the wartime role of FDR's military advisor. Despite the National Security Act's establishment of a Chairman of the Joint Chiefs as one who could fill that role, Kennedy did not want to risk the situation where the Chairman would merely present the group think advice of the Joint Chiefs. He wanted an unfiltered view on military affairs; not one that the Service Chiefs primarily tainted with their parochial views.

A second reason was that JFK liked men who could think. He sought a military man with brains, not just one with an excellent combat record. Max Taylor met these prerequisites. He had a reputation as a soldier-scholar. His service in both World War Two as the commander of the 101st Airborne Division and later in the Korean War were exemplary. General Matthew Ridgeway, who had replaced MacArthur in Korea and whom Kennedy had admired, was Taylor's mentor. Thereby, Taylor replaced Ridgeway as Army Chief of Staff under Eisenhower. However, during his tour, Taylor disagreed with the 'New Look' Strategy and retired. The retired General wrote a book on his views on defense strategy called the *Uncertain Trumpet*.

Kennedy had read Taylor's book. It argued for a more balanced military force with the capability to respond to smaller conflicts that did not call for the threat of massive retaliation or require the use of nuclear weapons. This policy was precisely what the President was looking for in a new national security strategy. In fact, as he was building his new team, JFK told those whom he interviewed to read the book, for it was what he wanted to establish as the centerpiece of his Administration.

Taylor, moreover, fit more like the general that JFK had in mind - one that was intelligent, rational, cultured, and articulate. David Halberstam summed it all up well: "The general seemed almost invented for the Kennedy years; he was cool, correct, handsome and athletic. As an airborne general, he was more modern in outlook than other generals; he spoke several languages and had written a book. Moreover, he was imposing, always in control."

The new military advisor to the President was so like the Kennedys that he became a close family friend – especially to JFK's brother Robert, who often had him over to his Washington house to have dinner. As Matthew Moten writes in his *American Presidents and Their Generals*, "Handsome, cerebral, urbane, and skillful with a tennis racket, he fit right in at Hyannis Port. Robert Kennedy named a son after him. Fawning admirers suggested that Taylor was the General that Harvard might have produced."

Taylor's appointment would cause much consternation, confusion, and eventually, distrust amongst the Joint Chiefs. It appeared to them that Kennedy was circumventing their advisory role. It also strained the relationships between the JCS and McNamara. This tension was because McNamara turned more to Taylor than the Chiefs for military advice.

Aware of this tension, by the end of 1962, the President appointed Taylor as Chairman of the Joint Chiefs. However, the lack of trust, stressed loyalties, and even disingenuous behavior between Taylor, McNamara and the Chiefs would continue. It would have a dramatic effect on policymaking toward Vietnam not only during Kennedy's presidency but much of LBJ's.

Two other Washington, DC officials served both Kennedy and his successor bear mention in this group of best and brightest. These are John McNaughton and George Ball. These two would come to represent the two opposite poles of advice on Vietnam; the former a staunch supporter of military intervention and the latter not.

McNaughton had been a Harvard Professor of strategic studies. He joined the Defense Department because – like Bundy - of his ability to think through any problem and arrive at a solution using game theory. He became McNamara's closest advisor. As Assistant Secretary of Defense for International Security Affairs, he drafted many of the memos and thinking papers that McNamara used when advising his Presidents. Many of these papers are part of what became known as the *Pentagon Papers*. They reveal McNaughton's role in the decision-making process of the times and the nature of his recommendations.

As Halberstam wrote, "In the Pentagon Papers he seemed to symbolize the inhumane and insensitive quality of that era, undoubting, unreflective, putting the quantifying of deaths and killing and destruction into neat, cold, antiseptic statistics, devoid of blood and heart…as if human beings never entered the calculations." McNaughton also held a dislike for the military and made it obvious. Uniformed officers who worked for him thought he was cold, aloof, brusque, and contemptible.

Ball, who joined the State Department at the onset of JFK's Presidency as Under Secretary of State, had been a member of Adlai Stevenson's law firm. He had served on Stevenson's staff during his run for the Presidency against Eisenhower in the fifties. He had also worked as a director of the Strategic Bombing Survey, which analyzed the effectiveness of strategic bombing in the war.

During his tenure at State – based in part on the results of the strategic bombing survey he had taken part in - Ball would write papers questioning the viability of bombing North Vietnam to convince the North Vietnamese to cease operations in South Vietnam. In so doing, he would regularly be at odds with his direct boss, Dean Rusk.

George Ball garnered a reputation as a 'devil's advocate' on military intervention to both JFK and LBJ. Later, as we will see in the next chapter, LBJ took advantage of his role as such to show that he was considering all points of view in his policymaking. Unfortunately, though Ball may have been genuine in his assessments, LBJ never seemed to take his advice in hand and act on it.

To complete this set of characters in the JFK Administration, there is the Ambassador to the Republic of South Vietnam, Frederick Nolting, and the Commander of MACV General Paul Harkins. These two men would give the first-hand accounts and assessments to Kennedy and his principal advisors on how the President's policies and its resulting programs were working in Vietnam.

'Fritz' Nolting had joined the diplomatic corps after the war. Previously, he had graduated from the University of Virginia, where he earned a doctorate in history. He also later attended Harvard. Having served a brief tour in the Navy during the war, Nolting joined the State Department in 1946.

By the Eisenhower Administration, he moved up the bureaucratic ladder as a member of the foreign service to become a special assistant to the then-Secretary of State John Foster Dulles. Afterward, he went to NATO as a member of the US delegation. He later became the Permanent Representative to NATO – the highest State Department official there.

When JFK became President, the State Department was looking for a replacement for their Ambassador in South Vietnam, who had a poor relationship with the head of the government, Ngo Dinh Diem. The Department nominated, and JFK approved, Nolting. The new Ambassador had no experience in Asian affairs. However, the Europeanists in the State Department dominated the entire organization. They knew Fritz from his days in NATO as an honest, hardworking, loyal official who would follow orders, do his job, and get along with the South Vietnamese. He would also do his best to make the best out of an unfortunate situation.

Ambassador Nolting would fulfill his prescribed role well. He would work hard at ensuring a favorable relationship with Diem. In so doing, there were times when he was overly optimistic about Diem's abilities and American progress. Some US reporters, such as David Halberstam and Neil Sheehan, believed Nolting 'cooked the books' and reported on only those matters that looked favorable to Diem and demonstrated progress. In support of these two journalist's views, there is evidence to show that his reports were more optimistic than some of JFK's advisors making fact-finding trips to South Vietnam. These mixed reports would affect JFK's policymaking – particularly his support for Diem.

The Ambassador, however, had a great relationship with JFK's main military man in South Vietnam. That man was General Paul D. Harkins, Commander of MACV. Harkins was a West Point graduate of the Class of 1929. During the war, he had been General George Patton's Deputy Chief of Staff for Operations of the Third Army. Patton's aggressive can-do attitude rubbed off on this man who would plan and coordinate the operations of his Army, particularly its drive across France. The cloning was so compelling that Harkins acquired the nickname, 'Ramrod.'

After the war, Harkins served as Commandant of Cadets at West Point. Then he went to Washington, where he was a staff officer working for the Army's then Chief of Operations, General Maxwell Taylor at the Pentagon. Taylor took Harkins with him to Korea. There Taylor commanded the Eighth Army and Harkins served as his Chief of Staff. During the Korean War Harkins commanded an Army Infantry Division.

Following Korea, Harkins held several positions primarily overseeing and coordinating military assistance in some forty-two different countries. Just before coming to South Vietnam, he had been in Hawaii, coordinating aid and support to the Pacific region for the Army. The General's experiences in foreign assistance and the region seemed to make him a qualified commander. The real reason he got the job was that he was a 'Taylor Man.'

Harkins took charge of MACV – the successor to the Military Assistance Advisory Group set up during the French Indochina War – on 13 February 1962. Militarily, the new command came under the Commander in Chief, Pacific Command – a joint command headed by a Navy Admiral based on the Unified Command procedures set up under the National Security Act and the Unified Command Plan.

MACV then consisted of some 5,000 American military personnel. Some of these were advising South Vietnamese military forces; others were providing direct combat support such as flying helicopters supporting ground operations and manning small boats patrolling coastal waters. Some had been wounded. By this time twenty-five US personnel had died in their service in South Vietnam.

General Harkins tasks were complex and challenging. First, he had to support the nation-building activities that the Ambassador's Country Team planned, coordinated, and executed. Second, he oversaw the support and logistics operations that sought to arm, equip, and train the South Vietnamese Army. Finally, and most challenging, the Command supervised the advice and training of the Army of South Vietnam or ARVN.

As mentioned, the Ambassador and MACV Commander got along very well. There was a reason for that. Both supported one another in their attitudes toward these challenges. There was no alternative to success. Not surprisingly, both were optimistic about the progress during their tenures. Both were ardent about the prospects of success when faced with situations that showed otherwise.

Sometimes Nolting's and Harkins' desire to emphasize progress conflicted with some of the military advisors who saw it otherwise. Some in the Press caught on to these disagreements and accused Harkins and the Ambassador of overzealous, even duplicitous reporting of progress. These reporting discrepancies would become problematic for JFK. Over the several years of his presidency, he would receive decidedly different reports of improvement from several sources. These different assessments caused the President much consternation and confusion. They would also affect his decision-making adversely on his program of counterinsurgency.

To summarize this description of JFK's key advisors, there were two distinguishing features that the President wanted in and from them. First, they had to be educated to the point of being considered brilliant. As Kennedy often told his closest confidants, "you can't beat brains." He much preferred smart advisors rather than seasoned ones.

The new President also made it known that he sought not thoroughly prepared papers or briefings, which he was suspicious of and thought trivial, but wanted open debate and innovative ideas that challenged the status quo. In today's overused rhetoric, he sought 'out of the box' thinking.

As we will see ahead, while brains and innovative thinking are two traits that one would want in making decisions, they are no substitute for the hard work of studying, learning, and experience that people who spend their lives in getting to know their profession offer. This is especially so in the areas of foreign and military service. Kennedy would not live long enough to learn this fact of government service. His policies would suffer. His successors would fail.

Section 2.2 - Crucibles of Policy Making: Bay of Pigs, Laos, and the Cuban Missile Crisis

It was not long after John F. Kennedy took office that he had to deal with his first two crises. One involved an invasion by Cuban exiles of Cuba around an area called the 'Bay of Pigs.' Another involved what to do about a conflict in Laos that threatened the security of Southeast Asia and the policies and nation-building programs for South Vietnam.

Bay of Pigs

The CIA during IKE's Administration had drafted a concept and plan for confronting the communist-leaning regime of Castro Cuba. IKE had informed Kennedy of that plan during the transition period. Its primary goal was to overthrow Castro. The latter had led a revolution resulting in the ouster in 1959 of a right-wing dictator who had close ties with the US. Castro seized control of some US industry assets, such as several oil refineries, and set in motion links with the Soviet Union. The CIA recruited, equipped, and trained fleeing Cuban exiles in secrecy to return to overthrow the Cuban Communists eventually. They formed them into a paramilitary brigade located in Guatemala in Central America.

Soon after JFK took office, the CIA briefed the new President on the status of their invasion plans. They pressured Kennedy for a decision, arguing that the longer they waited, the more likely someone would discover the covert operation. Uneasy with the entire concept, JFK convened several meetings with some of his 'Ministry of Talent' – a term coined by one of his White House counsels, Ted Sorenson, for the advisor team Kennedy had mustered. McGeorge Bundy and Robert McNamara, believing that the Castro regime had not yet consolidated its power, recommended he approve the plan. Rusk had misgivings but did not vigorously object.

JFK further turned to the Joint Chiefs of Staff for a recommendation on the military aspects of the CIA's plans. He had become concerned about the assumptions and objectives of the invasion, which, in his view, seemed overly ambitious. Kennedy also wanted to ensure that the US did not give direct military support to the Cuban paramilitary force, lest this become an internationally explosive issue with the US as a foreign aggressor.

Per the JCS official history, the JCS had not been included in the planning or even known of the plans until Kennedy had taken over. JCS planners, responding to the President's request for an assessment, told their Chiefs that they felt the chances of success were 'very doubtful.' However, the JCS in their hastily offered final assessment gave a more upbeat version saying that it had a "fair chance of ultimate success."

In early April, JFK gave his reluctant approval. The invasion took place on April 17, 1961. Leaks and Soviet Agents alerted the Cubans of the attack. They were waiting. Without US military direct support, the invading force was no match for Castro's forces. The Cubans quickly defeated the invaders in three days.

Afterward, the President directed his new military representative, General Taylor, to investigate what went wrong. Taylor's report, presented to Kennedy in June, blamed the Chiefs for not considering closely enough the risks involved. This criticism, most historians judge, was unfair. The General did not inform the President that the CIA had not brought the Chiefs in early enough for their assessment to be thorough. Further, JFK's new military advisor did not inform the President that the JCS had not been in on all the details of the plan.

JFK accepted the blame for the failures that became public. The Bay of Pigs incident, however, tainted the President's views on his current senior military advisors. It reinforced his preconceived notions that the military Chiefs could not think beyond their narrow Service parochial views. To his close advisors, as one of Kennedy's biographers wrote, "he confided that he had assumed, the military and intelligence people have some secret skill not available to ordinary mortals." The experience taught him "never to rely on the experts." He told one of his press advisors, "The first advice I'm going to give my successor is to watch the generals and to avoid feeling that just because they were military men their opinions on military matters were worth a damn."

The international situation did not give the President much time to dwell on the perceived failures at the Bay of Pigs. Another crisis simultaneously needed his attention and a decision on how to respond. This one was in Indochina. It involved the conflict in Laos, which sat astride of Vietnam. It concerned the ongoing struggle between the US-backed Royal Laotian Government and the Communist Pathet Lao forces supported by the Soviets, Red China, and North Vietnam.

Like the Bay of Pigs, this crisis was not one of Kennedy's making. He inherited it from IKE's support to the Laos Royal Government. Eisenhower had spoken of the importance of Laos not only to the rest of Indochina but also to all Southeast Asia. He argued that the fall of Laos to communism would result in the demise of the rest of Southeast Asia and its dominance by Red China like the falling of dominoes.

During the transition, JFK had listed the situation in Laos as one of his top priorities to discuss with IKE and his outgoing team. Kennedy wrote, "I was anxious to get some commitment from the outgoing administration as to how they would deal with Laos, which they were handing to us. I thought particularly it would be helpful to have some idea as to how prepared they were for military intervention." He soon found out, however, that the Eisenhower Administration plans for Laos were full of erroneous or risky assumptions and concepts on how to deal militarily with the situations there.

Since taking office, the Press had been asking Kennedy about his views on the deteriorating situation in Laos. There it appeared that the Communist Pathet Lao might win its conflict with the national government the Geneva Convention had set up. He responded, "Laos is far away from America, but the world is small... The security of all Southeast Asia will be at risk if Laos loses its neutral independence. Its safety runs with the safety of us." A month later, after a report from the US Ambassador there that the communists would gain control unless the US took some action, the President called a rare meeting of the entire National Security Council

As the JCS official history records, at that meeting the JCS urged US military intervention in Laos. They argued that South Vietnam and the rest of Southeast Asia would be strategically untenable should the communists control Laos. This judgment was primarily because the North Vietnamese were building and using an infiltration route to the South that supported the insurgency there.

Walt Rostow, who was present at the meeting, supported the Chiefs position. He further reasoned that to win the insurgency in the South the US needed to isolate it from any Northern support. He argued that North Vietnam was directing the conflict and was the base for communist action in South Vietnam.

Kennedy turned his attention to the military plans for Laos. The JCS and the Pacific Command had been working on these since the first term of the Eisenhower Administration. They were combined plans; drafted as part of the SEATO Alliance military strategy to defend parts of the Southeast Asia region. Ike's intent in the development of these plans was to ensure allied participation, as well as support for any unilateral US action. However, because the American military planners had developed them under the Eisenhower policy of massive retaliation, they included the employment of strategic bombings against the Chinese mainland and the use of nuclear weapons.

As Lawrence Freedman describes in his *Kennedy Wars*, the current Chairman, General Lyman Lemnitzer, gave a lengthy briefing on the JCS plans several times in the first seven months of 1961. These briefings unsettled the President. On several occasions JFK asked questions about what military force would be necessary; would they be sufficient; how long it would take to marshal them; where they would come from, and how would the military support them logistically. The answers showed that the planners had not considered significant logistic factors or had assumed they could be carried out without taking into account important matters - such as whether ports or airfields were operable or could support the forces needed.

In one such briefing, JFK asked General Lemnitzer what they would do if the Chinese intervened. The CJCS, knowing that the plans had considered that situation and called for the use of tactical nuclear weapons, responded, "if we are given the right to use nuclear weapons, we can guarantee victory."

Robert Dallek in his biography *An Unfinished Life* writes that JFK thought the statement absurd. Kennedy felt that the JCS had not considered the ramifications of such an action. The President quickly rejected it. JFK then tried to obtain some agreement on what would deter the communists from outright seizing control of the Laotian government. He did not get any convincing military options. As discussions continued, Bundy noted, "Questions from the President showed that the detailed aspects of this military plan had not been developed … The President made clear his own deep concern with the need for realism and accuracy in military planning."

In all fairness to the JCS and their planners, as its official history explains, they were aware of some of the problems with the plans for Laos (to include those the regional commander developed). Indeed, in the JCS version of the meeting, Lemnitzer admitted such, saying that operations would be, "handicapped by logistical limitations." However, trying to show a positive attitude, he stated that many of these they could remedy and that the commander in the field was working on them. It just would take some time.

Moreover, as William Gibbons explains in his *US Government and the Vietnam War*, neither the President or the Secretary of Defense had yet issued any political guidance for use in these plans. Thus, again, they were based on previous Administration political guidance and goals. The Kennedy stated policy of Flexible Response and its intent to use an appropriate level force to avoid nuclear war had not yet been promulgated. Neither Kennedy or McNamara was willing to acknowledge this lack of political guidance and its effect on sound military planning.

Despite his dismissal of the JCS recommendation to employ major US combat forces in Laos, the President did authorize, as William Conrad Gibbons' account notes, the dispatch of three aircraft carriers with 1400 Marines toward Laos. He also authorized increased reconnaissance flights and the continued effort to refine the plans and resolve some of the logistical issues.

Eventually, the Administration through diplomatic actions generated a temporary arrangement in the fall of 1961 for a ceasefire and the formation of a provisional unity government. These actions seemed to settle the immediate crisis. Kennedy felt relieved that such a diplomatic arrangement bypassed the use of military force problem.

Laos would continue to plague Kennedy throughout his term. The conflict between the loyalist forces and the communists, to include North Vietnam regulars, waged back and forth. Meanwhile, JFK continued to meet with the JCS to get updates on their planning. He remained dissatisfied and felt that the military recommendations were too risky or did not show enough original thought to offer any practical solution.

Some historians, such as Mark Moyar and Andrew Birtle, fault Kennedy for not taking military action in Laos early enough to prevent its use as a lifeline of support to the war in the South. They argue that by not taking such action he "hammered a large nail into South Vietnam's coffin."

In fairness to Kennedy, the evidence shows that any effective action may not have been possible militarily. The military plans for intervention in Laos in the early sixties were not realistic. The fact is that the use of the main ground forces in Laos was just not feasible mainly due to the lack of support bases and extended logistic lines vulnerable to attack. Some of the planning explored alternatives, such as the insertion of the forces through Thailand. The movement of these further into Laos, however, would have been highly problematic.

Despite the arguments of the JCS and Rostow, it was not entirely clear at the time what the North was doing in building a route through Laos and sending material and some military units to South Vietnam. Most of the intelligence community assessments then judged that the war in the south was not dependent on the few items and cadres that moved over this Lao infiltration route.

They also argued, as did some in the military, that the insurgency was more dependent upon and was being successful in recruiting and supplying the VC forces from the South Vietnam populace and the ARVN. One National Intelligence Estimate, for example, in October 1961 reported that "80 to 90 percent of the estimated 17,000 Viet Cong had been recruited locally and there was little evidence that they relied on external supplies." In short then, the North Vietnamese activities in Laos, during this time, did not seem to present a threat sufficient enough to warrant a significant American military intervention there.

Furthermore, as we will see in the chapters ahead, though the North had decided to step up its infiltration in support of military actions to defeat the ARVN, its Ho Chi Minh Trail in 1961 was not yet mature enough to support major movements of supplies and forces. A Rand study available to Kennedy's advisors noted that the trail was "no more than paths running through the mountains, unsuitable for large shipments."

This episode, like the Bay of Pigs intervention, is vital to the story that follows in that it furthered Kennedy's dissatisfaction with the advice of the Joint Chiefs. It may have also been "a nail in the coffin" of accepting any of their advice on Vietnam. In fact, to Ted Sorenson, his primary speechwriter who had written his famous inaugural address, Kennedy quipped several weeks after the crisis abated, "Thank goodness the Bay of Pigs happened when it did. Otherwise, we could be in Laos right now – and that could be a hundred times worse."

In sum, per historian H. R. McMaster in his work *Dereliction of Duty* on the Vietnam War, "During the Laotian crisis, the president was again dissatisfied with the advice of the Joint Chiefs, whose thinking he regarded as outmoded and unimaginative… He believed that strategic options in military affairs should give him more flexibility than a stark choice between inaction and large-scale commitment."

During the first year of his Presidency then the relationship between the Commander-in-Chief and his principal military advisors had been disastrous. JFK thought that their advice was far from realistic and did not consider the situation beyond just military factors. To his credit, the President told the Chiefs just that. In a meeting arranged by General Taylor, Kennedy encouraged them to think more about the political ramifications of their advice. Unfortunately, most of them thought that this was outside of their purview as military men.

From the JCS perspective, they had made recommendations based on the current military planning carried out during the Eisenhower administration. They had not had enough time or opportunity with the President to understand his thinking on military matters or his approach to national security problems. Their immediate boss, Robert McNamara, moreover, focused more on program and budget issues and reforms, rather than strategic military policy.

Throughout the rest of his first year, JFK continued his attempt to alter the nation's approach to threaten the use of nuclear weapons as a means of dealing with national security crises. For him, the January 1961 announcement of Nikita Khrushchev's support for wars of national liberation was a clarion call to develop the means to counter insurgencies backed by the communists.

As the Laotian issue continued to come to his attention, JFK and his advisors continued to grope for a solution. Eventually, they would settle for a less than satisfactory diplomatic one of neutrality. The President saw no alternative given what he knew in 1961 and early 1962. In so doing, he continued to ignore what was happening in Laos, and may even have wished that it just go away. He turned his attention to where his belief in countering insurgency may work.

As we will see later in this chapter, while JFK had ample information to discourage any significant military action in Laos in 1961 and into 1962, by early 1963 the situation was changing. Communist military action in South Vietnam would increase and gain some significant victories. Furthermore, that activity and success was a direct consequence of the North's increased infiltration over a significantly improved Ho Chi Minh Trail through Laos. But Kennedy, perhaps a result of the distaste he had for early military plans and his military advisors, did not notice these changes.

Thus, as we will further see, the problem is that the President and most of his advisors ignored the fact that the conflict in the south was a regional problem that required action not just in South Vietnam, but throughout the Southeast Asia region. In short, JFK's mistrust and distaste for the military tainted his view on Laos so much that he overlooked the changing strategic calculus in the region.

Though Southeast Asia was a major issue early on in his Administration, throughout the rest of 1961 and into 1962, there continued to be significant problems and challenges in other security affairs elsewhere. The Soviets continued their threats over Berlin. They also continued nuclear testing, which JFK was trying to get a treaty to ban. Furthermore, the Chinese threatened military action over Taiwan. Finally, there was the Cuban interference in the Western Hemisphere and continued ties to and aid from the Soviets.

The Cuban Missile Crisis: The Birth of Graduated Response

Following the Bay of Pigs crisis, the Soviets had set up a military presence in Cuba. The US maintained surveillance of the Soviet force to ensure that it would not be a threat to the US. The Soviets argued that their presence was nothing more than an assurance to the Cubans and deterrence to US attack. Nevertheless, McNamara tasked the JCS to come up with plans for an all-out assault on Cuba if it produced a significant threat to the US homeland. It was over Cuba and their support from the Soviet Union that JFK's Administration would meet its greatest challenge in the fall of 1962.

Early on the 15th of October, Bundy went to the President's quarters in the White House and informed him that US intelligence aircraft had detected conclusive evidence of Soviet offensive missiles in Cuba. JFK called for a meeting of his EXCOM. It met just before noon in the cabinet room. Bundy, Rusk, Ball, McNamara, the President's brother Robert, Vice President Johnson and seven others were in attendance. The only military man present was General Taylor, who was now the Chairman of the Joint Chiefs.

The focus of this meeting was to figure out courses of action to remove the missiles. According to Robert Dallek, the President concentrated the initial discussions on four possible military actions: "an air strike against the missile installations; a more general air attack against a wide array of targets; a blockade; and an invasion." Though the entire JCS was not present, General Taylor represented them and tried to submit their views on the crisis.

Throughout the next couple of days, the EXCOM met and discussed the courses of action. During this time, the military conducted more reconnaissance flights. They further verified the presence of the missiles and types, found the exact sites and numbers, and eventually could assess when the nuclear warheads could be ready to launch.

Meanwhile, McNamara and Taylor continued to represent the JCS views in EXCOM meetings. At first, they presented that view that highly favored air strikes to take out the missiles and an invasion to ensure that all of them were inoperable. As McMaster recounts, "The JCS resented being excluded from the EXCOM meetings. Every evening during the crisis, Taylor found the Chiefs anxiously awaiting his return from the White House. They grilled him to ensure that he had accurately represented their recommendation to bomb the missile sites and follow the air strike quickly with a ground invasion of Cuba."

By the 17th McNamara, without consulting the Chiefs, changed his view. He strongly suggested a blockade of Cuba accompanied by a mobilization and assembly of forces for an invasion. He also recommended the dispatch of messages to the Soviet Premier indicating some approach for a peaceful solution.

The Defense Secretary argued that such a course would give the Soviets some time to respond to diplomatic initiatives, while still presenting the threat of force should those initiatives fail. This approach, he explained, would allow the President to gradually increase the threat of the use of force; rather than just conducting military strikes from the outset that might trigger a war. After a strong endorsement from JFK's brother Bobby, the EXCOM, with the Chiefs absent, agreed with this course. The President approved it.

Under pressure from the Chiefs, and after the decision on the blockade option approved, General Taylor arranged for a meeting with the Chiefs with the President - ostensibly to obtain their views. The meeting's purpose was to get the Chiefs' acquiescence to the naval blockade, now called a 'quarantine' to seem less warmongering.

Early on the 19th, the President met with the JCS for forty-five minutes in the White House. The historians who edited the tapes on this meeting noted that JFK was already in a sour mood toward listening to the Chiefs. Just weeks earlier, in an incident over the use of troops to offer security in the riots in reaction to the admittance of a black student in Mississippi, Kennedy had asked for answers on the availability and timeliness of sending active duty forces there. The JCS was hesitant to do so and did not give answers to JFK's satisfaction. Soon afterward, the President remarked to an aide, "They always give you their bullshit about their instant reaction and their split-timing, but it never works out. No wonder it is so hard to win a war."

Nevertheless, the President was cordial when the Chiefs arrived. He opened the session explaining his concerns over a quick, massive strike against Cuba, which he knew the Chiefs favored. General Taylor, duplicitous and seemingly supporting the Chiefs, reinforced the validity of the President's concerns, but then argued that without a robust military response US credibility would suffer.

General LeMay, the Air Force Chief, led the Chiefs' argument. He emphatically said that there was no other viable solution to a strong military strike to take out all the missiles and supporting sites. The General argued that the blockade would be seen as a weakness on the part of the US, and eventually an appeasement like Munich. The other Chiefs agreed.

Then, captured on JFK's Presidential tapes, LeMay said, "You're in a pretty bad fix at the present time." JFK asked the General to repeat what he just said. After repeating it, Kennedy responded, "Well you're in there with me!"

The tense meeting broke up with the President restating his decision for the quarantine. Afterward, per Robert Dallek, JFK turned to several in his group and said, "Can you imagine LeMay saying a thing like that? These brass hats have one great advantage in their favor. If we listen to them and do what they want us to do, none of us will be alive later to tell them that they were wrong."

After the meeting, the Chiefs continued to discuss their views on the crisis and Kennedy's reaction to their recommendations. The White House taping system recorded their conversation. As the tapes reveal, they not only remained adamantly opposed to the blockade option, but to the entire idea of gradual response.

General Shoup, the Marine Corps Commandant who had won the medal of honor at Tarawa in World War Two, seemed to be the most adamant in his opposition, but the others disagreed with the blockade as well. In reaction to the idea of gradual responses in the use of military force, Shoup said, "if somebody could keep them from doing the god damn thing piecemeal. That's the problem…. Either do this son of bitch and do it right, and quit friggin around."

The meeting on the 19th was remarkable. It showed how great the 'divide' was in the military-civil relationships between the President and his military advisors. It also showed how damaged the mechanism for military consultation had become in the Kennedy Administration. This damage was not entirely the Chiefs fault or their attitudes toward their civilian leaders. Kennedy and his civilian advisors had failed to communicate what their political goals were for solving the crisis to the JCS. They had never confided in them that they wanted a diplomatic solution to avoid a major military confrontation with the Soviets. Consequently, the Chiefs and their planners were entirely out of sync in what they had recommended to the President.

Future deliberations on security matters, especially what to do about the situation in Vietnam, would reflect this lack of communication, distrust, and lack of confidence between the President and his military advisors. Such would also be the case when Johnson took over after Kennedy's assassination. Therefore, as H. R. McMaster observes, "The divergent civilian and military views on American objectives during the Cuban missile crisis foreshadowed what would become a major obstacle to the development of a strategy for the Vietnam War."

As for the crisis itself, eventually, after several exchanges with the Soviets, the ultimate peaceful solution became a 'trade.' The Soviets would remove the weapons; the US would issue a statement renouncing any intent to invade Cuba. Secretly the US also agreed to withdraw their offensive missiles from Turkey.

Section 2.3 - JFK, Vietnam, and Counterinsurgency

Concurrent with many of the crucibles described above, the President and his advisors continued to address the question of policy and action over the aggression and insurrection in South Vietnam. While they understood, as early as 1961, that North Vietnam supported the conflict in South Vietnam, they chose to direct most of their attention on the way to counter the insurgency in the South.

Even though Kennedy had mostly inherited the national security issue of Vietnam from earlier Presidents, he had already established himself as a proponent who supported drawing the defense line in Southeast Asia in general, and supporting South Vietnam against the spread of communism in particular.

For example, in 1951 after his visit there he declared that the US should support the establishment of a free Vietnamese government to "check the southern drive of communism" and "protect vital US interests in the area." Accordingly, in 1954 and 1955 he also strongly supported the choice of Ngo Dinh Diem as the Premier of South Vietnam. Moreover, as a keynote speaker at a symposium on Vietnam in 1956 JFK declared that Vietnam "represents the cornerstone of the Free World in Southeast Asia, the keystone to the arch, the finger in the dike." He further stated that "Vietnam represents a test of American responsibility and determination in Asia."

From the onset of his Presidency, Kennedy reaffirmed not only his previous support for Vietnam but pledged US support for all those in the Third World involved in the struggle for finding their way in the aftermath of colonial rule. Thus, in his inaugural speech he declared, "To those new states whom we welcome to the ranks of the free, we pledge our word that one form of colonial control shall not have passed away merely to be replaced by a far more iron tyranny." He further said that the US would assist those trying to "help themselves for whatever period is required, not because the Communists may be doing it, not because we seek their votes, but because it is right."

In short, John F. Kennedy was not just a presidential inheritor of others' commitments. He had committed himself before and at the beginning of his presidency to supporting Vietnam in its quest to create a state free from communism. As William Gibbons writes, JFK's "statement of intent, together with [his] own beliefs about the importance of defending Southeast Asia, and making American power credible throughout the world, had a direct, and, as it turned out, critical bearing on the Kennedy administration's decision to reaffirm and to expand the US commitment" to Vietnam.

Development of Counterinsurgency Strategy: Vietnam as a Test Bed

Furthermore, as mentioned previously, Kennedy saw the situation in South Vietnam as a 'test bed' for an original approach to counter Soviet and Chinese Communist support for wars of national liberation. The Kennedy Administration labeled this approach as a counterinsurgency strategy. It was, by late 1961, a key part of the President's new overall 'Flexible Response' security policy.

JFK was confident that his new policy and approach could, in the words of his inaugural speech, "assure the survival and the success of liberty" in Southeast Asia. He was confident that his 'ministry of talent' was up to the task, and that he could mobilize a 'new generation of Americans' to 'pay the price' and 'bear the burden.'

A key influence on Kennedy for his counterinsurgency strategy early on in his Presidency was a military man by the name of Edward Lansdale. Lansdale had been an Army intelligence officer for the OSS in the Philippines during World War Two. He transferred to the Air Force after the war and returned to the Philippines to help Ramon Magsaysay, its defense minister, in the war against the Communist Huks. Magsaysay - who eventually became President of the fledgling new republic - with Lansdale's help and friendship, successfully suppressed the rebellion. Thus, began Lansdale's reputation as a counterinsurgent expert.

In the early fifties, Lansdale had become a member of the US Military Assistance and Advisory Group in French Indochina. He stayed there after the French left and became an advisor to Diem, whom he helped gain power early in the establishment of the South Vietnam regime. By this time, Lansdale's reputation as a counter-guerrilla and Asian expert was approaching legendary status. It is purported that he was the model for Graham Greene's immensely popular novel on the events in Southeast Asia, *The Quiet American*, published in 1952, as well as the leading character in *The Ugly American* later in 1958. In the late fifties, Lansdale arrived at the Pentagon to serve in the defense department as a special operations expert.

Soon after JFK took office, Lansdale had written an assessment of the situation in South Vietnam based on a recent visit there. Walt Rostow brought it to Kennedy's attention. The thrust of that evaluation was that the insurgency could be defeated if the US gave its wholehearted support to President Diem and furnished him the political-military aid that he needed. His specific recommendations were to give over 28 million dollars to expand the South Vietnamese Army and another 12 million to improve its local guard forces. Lansdale also recommended an expansion of the advisory effort, and that they "be allowed to work in combat areas."

Lansdale's assessment and recommendations convinced the President that the US had to take immediate action to save Vietnam from a communist takeover. Subsequently, Lansdale became a key assistant to Secretary McNamara and an influential member of JFK's interagency group on counterinsurgency. JFK would also send him along with his principal advisors to Vietnam to make further assessments on the implementation of his policies and programs.

At this time, with Vietnam seen as a minor conflict that was primarily an internal affair of the South Vietnamese government, the JCS did not take on an overall national military strategy to offer overall direction for counterinsurgency operations in that country or the region. For the most part, they were intent at this point to just see South Vietnam as a booster to the Service budgets. The Army and Marine Corps were especially keen to reinvigorate their forces after years of neglect under the policies of the Eisenhower years.

McNamara oversaw, through his trusted Deputy of the time Roswell Gilpatric, the conduct of the interagency study of the concept of counterinsurgency and the means for its execution. Because Vietnam was the test case, the interagency group would also make recommendations on how to employ forces to counter the insurgency there. The study would use, as its start point, a Pacific Command plan, called 'Basic Counterinsurgency Plan for Viet Nam.'

Soon after the Bay of Pigs affair, the interagency group presented its recommended actions, entitled "Program of Action to Prevent Communist Domination of South Vietnam." Approved by the President a month later and incorporated into a National Security Action Memorandum called NSAM 52, it formed the initial basis for JFK's policy in South Vietnam. The entire program became known simply as the Counterinsurgency Plan or CIP. Its focus was on producing the capabilities to counter communist support for wars of national liberation as it was unfolding in South Vietnam.

The NSAM affirmed US policy aim to "prevent communist domination of South Vietnam and create in that country a viable and increasingly democratic society; and to initiate, on an accelerated basis, a series of mutually supporting actions to achieve this objective." Kennedy followed up this memorandum with another, days later. Labeled NSAM 111, it called for increased economic and military aid to the South.

Because of these two policy papers, follow-on actions included the dispatch of 400 Special Forces troops to South Vietnam and authorization of covert sabotage and harassment missions against the Democratic Republic of Vietnam or North Vietnam. This marked the first significant buildup of America's military effort to counter communist aggression in South Vietnam.

Several of the deliberations in the development of these two policy documents had discussed more than just the growth of capabilities to counter insurgencies. For example, people like Lansdale and Rostow had brought up the importance of Laos to the defense not only of Vietnam but to the overall region. Though not significant at the time, the two warned of the apparent intent of North Vietnam to use Laos as a springboard and link to its support of the southern insurgency. Lansdale emphasized Diem's concern that there was no possibility of his forces to counter any significant infiltration of North Vietnam regular forces through Laos to the south.

In addition, Lansdale pushed the group to study "mutually supporting actions of a military, political, economic, psychological and covert character" designed to achieve the study's stated objective. He emphasized that much of what worked in the counterinsurgency arena, such as the moral character of its political leaders and achieving moral support for the government could not be easily measured, but were important to try to institute nevertheless.

However, key members of the group ignored these strategic issues and non-military programs. Primarily this was a result of McNamara's insistence on focusing on the development of forces necessary to counter not only insurgencies but to avoid the reliance on nuclear and other strategic forces that could lead to rapid escalation to nuclear war. Indeed, as Max Boot argues in his book on Lansdale, *The Road Not Taken*, it appears that McNamara was uneasy with the unconventional thinker and made a conscious effort to minimize his presence and influence both in the counterinsurgency policy development and in getting face time before JFK.

Moreover, the President had continually emphasized the need to get things moving. As Gibbons explains, "Kennedy's major concern seems to have been to make the US role more effective, to get moving. He wanted to do more not less, including undertaking, among other things, espionage and sabotage by guerrilla infiltration into the North Vietnam." Thus, progress in developing the means to conduct counterguerrilla operations far outweighed thinking about strategies for their use.

New counterinsurgency capabilities did follow quickly. With McNamara's emphasis on programs and forces that could be produced and measured under his supervision, most of this progress was in the form of military capabilities instead of the other economic, political, and social initiatives that the original task force study group recommended.

For example, soon after Kennedy had directed the development of these capabilities in mid-1961, the Army increased and further developed several Special Forces units and a Special Warfare Center at Fort Bragg, NC for the training of these forces. The other Services, knowing that the budget would have a high priority for such organizations, began to look at how they could adjust as well.

The Taylor-Rostow Visit and Report

In early fall of 1961, President Diem, whom Vice President Johnson had called the Winston Churchill of Asia when visiting South Vietnam in Spring 1961, sent a formal request for further aid. He asked the President to add 100,000 men to his armed forces to counter the growing Viet Cong threat. In response to this request and later discussions of it at an NSC meeting, JFK dispatched General Maxwell Taylor, then still his military representative, and Walt Rostow, his Deputy Assistant for National Security Affairs, to assess the situation in South Vietnam and the validity of Diem's request.

Rostow was an early proponent of increasing military support to the South Vietnamese beyond just advisors. Months before he and Taylor left for South Vietnam, he had proposed that the US organize and lead an international force for deployment along the demilitarized zone between the North and the South. While the JCS dismissed the proposal, it showed the Deputy Assistant for National Security Affairs' militant view on solving the communist threat to South Vietnam.

Rostow also continued to argue that to counter the insurgency in South Vietnam the US could only be successful if it could isolate the conflict there from the support it was receiving from the North. Thus, as previously discussed, he had supported the JCS in their views to use military force in Laos to prevent the North from building a lifeline to the South. Publicly, per Lawrence Freedman, Rostow argued that the origins of the fighting in the South "lay outside the country in which it occurred. For this reason, it was not simply a symptom of dissatisfaction with a particular government. With an external sanctuary, it was very easy for a small band of men to impose a terrible burden on any government in a society making its way toward modernization."

In a series of papers to Kennedy before the President had decided on sending him on his fact-finding trip, the Deputy National Security Advisor contended that the Administration should go to the United Nations and make its case that the conflict in the South was primarily the result of Northern aggression, not an internal insurrection. If the UN sanctioned this view, then the US should take the war to the North.

Rostow argued further for an intensive air and naval campaign against the North "to impose about the same level of damage and inconvenience that the Viet Cong are imposing in the south." In this way, Rostow reasoned the North would have to give up its support, or if they chose to continue, the US could legitimately deploy combat forces to attack its forces in Laos and seal off its principal support routes.

Rostow had support for his views at that time from General Maxwell Taylor. According to John Taylor – Maxwell Taylor's biographer and son - the General had run into Kennedy in the White House right after Diem's request for aid had hit his desk. JFK asked him what he thought. Taylor said he would get with Rostow and some others to discuss the matter.

In his following discussions with the Deputy National Security Advisor and some others, Taylor found that he agreed with Rostow's argument that support for the insurgency from the North was key to defeating the conflict in the South. He further agreed with Rostow that the conflict in South Vietnam was a regional issue that the US had to address in an overall national strategy for the

Southeast Asia region.

Moreover, Taylor thought that the insertion of an American ground force, either in the South or Thailand, would serve as some deterrence of any further outright North Vietnamese aggression, and even convince them to decrease their support to the VC. He also believed that a punishing bombing campaign against the North would do much to convince them to cease their aggression in the South.

Because of his meetings and before he knew of Kennedy's desire to send him to Vietnam, the General drafted and sent JFK a memo with a set of options for Vietnam. As described in John Taylor's *An American Soldier* they were: first, disengage from Vietnam; second, attack the regional source of the conflict by attacking Hanoi; and third, build up the South Vietnamese 'to the greatest extent possible' while preparing to 'intervene with US military force.'

In a later discussion with the President, Taylor found out that JFK had no intention of getting out of Vietnam. On the other hand, the General also sensed that Kennedy was uneasy with the thought of employing large numbers of American ground forces.

Though Kennedy had personally chosen them, Rostow's militant calls for action and Taylor's support for them did not resonate with the President. In his guidance on counterinsurgency and in his NSAMs, JFK felt that the US should avoid a major military commitment. There appear to be at least four reasons for Kennedy's resolve to avoid the use of major combat forces.

First, he continued to lack confidence in his senior military advisors. Second, he remained unsure whether the insertion or use of military forces was a practical option anywhere in the region. In that belief, the lack of realistic planning for the use of force in Laos influenced him. Third, he had been in contact with General Douglas MacArthur, who adamantly recommended against the use of significant US combat forces "on the mainland of Asia." Fourth, he was also intent on showing that the utilization of the counterinsurgency capabilities he had called for could offer a solution to the communist strategy of supporting wars of national liberation. Thus, he wanted to avoid the use of conventional force as long as possible.

Given his proclivity to not use major US combat forces, JFK was now intent that the real problem was to shore up the South Vietnamese government and its forces. Whereas Kennedy had publicly spoken of the importance of offering military aid to South Vietnam to stop communist aggression in Asia, in private, he cautioned all his advisors to concentrate primarily on economic and political support. While the President's instructions for a visit directed that the team examine the political and military feasibility of military intervention, he privately instructed both Rostow and Taylor in their visit to focus on providing assistance and avoiding any discussion of the use of US combat troops.

The Taylor-Rostow visit was over several weeks in October 1961. On the way to South Vietnam the group stopped in Hawaii to obtain the views of the US Pacific Command, primarily on their ideas in their original Counterinsurgency Plan for Vietnam. When in South Vietnam, Taylor and Rostow met with President Diem and one of his top generals, General Duong Van Minh, who would later become the leader of a coup that resulted in Diem's assassination.

While Taylor spent much of his time with Diem, trying to convince the President of the utility of accepting some US combat troops as a deterrent to further Northern infiltration, Rostow met with several Vietnamese, to include a captured VC, to find out for himself the roots of the conflict. They returned to Washington the first week of November.

The Taylor-Rostow mission produced a fifty-five-page report of assessments and recommendations to the President. The report emphasized the critical situation found in South Vietnam in the fall of 1961. Taylor and Rostow noted the dire military circumstances that the South Vietnamese government faced. This was primarily due to a conscious North Vietnamese decision to support the insurgency in the South through infiltration of more supplies and PAVN 'cadres' from the North via the Ho Chi Minh Trail. Indeed, just before Taylor and Rostow had arrived, the Viet Cong (VC) had seized a provincial capital just eighty kilometers from Saigon. General Taylor noted that both President Diem and the South Vietnamese military command had become unnerved by these latest VC successes. Their morale and confidence, he emphasized, were extremely low.

Importantly, General Taylor further emphasized in his report that the Administration had to consider that there was a critical linkage between the war of liberation in South Vietnam and the North's support for it. Therefore, he stated that the US might have to punish the North for its support and aggression eventually. In a separate cable, dispatched before the formal report, both Taylor and Rostow had written that "NVN is extremely vulnerable to conventional bombing, a weakness which should be exploited diplomatically in convincing Hanoi to lay off SVN."

Rostow's comments in the report, as Lawrence Freedman explains, further focused on the strategic implications of the North's support for the war. He argued that North Vietnam purposely followed a public relations campaign to present a ruse that the war in the South was purely an internal one. What distinguished the conflict in the South from other wars of national liberation in Malaysia and the Philippines, Rostow emphasized, was the infiltration that supported the communist forces there. He elaborated that though that infiltration now was not yet decisive, it could be if the North decided to send regular troops into the conflict. These observations and assessments would prove to be prophetic.

The Taylor-Rostow report recommended a substantial increase in US military aid. This assistance, they suggested, should focus on the creation and training of South Vietnamese self-defense forces. The South Vietnamese government could then employ these at the village level to protect the population from VC guerrilla forces. This new self-defense force could then allow an expanded Army of South Vietnam (ARVN) regular forces to concentrate on defeating the VC main military units.

In addition, Taylor recommended an emergency increase in US military advisors to plan and actively take part in combat operations. To oversee this increased American aid and growing military involvement, the General further recommended the formation of a command to supervise and plan US military strategy for South Vietnam.

The most controversial feature of Taylor's report was his recommendation for the deployment of a US military task force of some 7-8,000 men to South Vietnam. This proposal was ostensibly to assist in a significant flood in the Mekong Delta region that devastated much of the rice production there.

As Taylor explained in his report, however, such a force could also serve as a strategic reserve that the US could employ in the country if needed. Moreover, as some of the evidence shows, both Taylor and Rostow thought that this force could also later serve as an advance unit that with reinforcement could employ into Laos and cut the Ho Chi Minh Trail.

The General further emphasized that US combat forces could be a leverage to get the North to either desist its support or to impose such an objective by the strength of American arms. Taylor argued that the presence alone of such a force would offer the South Vietnamese a welcome boost in confidence and show US resolve to prevent the fall of South Vietnam.

When the report hit the desk of JFK, simultaneously the President and his advisors received updates from the intelligence community that supported much of Taylor's and Rostow's findings. In fact, US intelligence was at the end of 1961 and into 1962 beginning to detect the growth of the VC in the South and the role that the North was having in the war. Though they stayed ignorant of the degree of intent of the North Vietnamese to win militarily and who was directing the war, it had accurately reported that the VC forces had dramatically increased over the last year from some 4,000 at the beginning of 1960 to about 17,000 by late 1961.

US intelligence was also beginning to see evidence and assess that the Democratic Republic of Vietnam (aka North Vietnam) gave direction of the forces in the South – known as the People's Liberation Armed Force or PLAF – through a command structure called the National Liberation Front (NLF). Thus, evolving US intelligence assessments began supporting the calamitous appraisal of the Taylor-Rostow report and its recommendations.

For the next several weeks the report sparked much discussion and debate in the Kennedy Administration. Interestingly, though the entire counterinsurgency effort had taken off with the adoption of the Pacific Command's initial version, now JFK officials no longer consulted the Command. Moreover, they had also left out the Joint Chiefs of Staff in the face-to-face discussions on the entire effort. The President did not ask to see them to obtain their views. This lack of consultation was indicative of JFK's lack of trust in their judgment.

However, the Defense Secretary agreed with the Chiefs' assessment, who had seen the Taylor-Rostow report and the current supporting intelligence estimates, that the situation in Vietnam was critical. McNamara also believed that any commitment of US troops should be more decisive than Taylor had recommended. So, he asked the JCS for a plan on how to counter the communist insurrection with an increase in direct military action to turn the tide.

As a result, the JCS proposed, and McNamara approved, a concept for South Vietnam that they labeled a "Win Plan." It involved the deployment of six divisions to South Vietnam to assist in battling the main force VC, and the bombing of the North. McNamara, however, never sent this plan to the President. He did send a memo, however, outlining more militant recommendations in general.

Later in his memoirs *In Retrospect*, McNamara states that as soon as he sent the memo, he started to worry that "we had been too hasty in our advice to the President. For the next couple of days, I dug deeper into the Vietnam problem. The more I probed, the more the complexity of the situation and the uncertainties of our ability to deal with it by military means became apparent. I realized that seconding the Taylor-Rostow memo had been a bad idea."

The evidence contradicts these later statements. Despite the claims in his memoirs, as William Gibbons' detailed analysis and reevaluation of the records in *The US Government and the Vietnam War* show, McNamara strongly supported the Taylor-Rostow report. He especially liked Taylor's idea on using combat forces to show US willingness to confront communist expansion in Southeast Asia. The Secretary thought that this was one more action that the US could take to ratchet up the pressure on the North to cease its support for the insurgency. That notion fit well into his overall gradual escalation philosophy toward crises that he supported since the Cuban Missile Crisis.

The fact is that in late 1961 McNamara was one of the more hawkish advisors on the use of force in South Vietnam. He would remain so for the rest of Kennedy's Administration. He would still be one when Johnson took over. Only after the employment of US armed forces failed to convince the North to stop its aggression would he become dismayed and doubtful.

Indeed, it was the shattering of his confidence by the failure of his policy of gradualism in the employment of US forces in Vietnam that eventually convinced him that Vietnam was not worth the effort. By that time, he would suffer what amounted to a nervous breakdown. He would willingly leave his post at the height of the conflict that he was most responsible for as a primary advisor on South Vietnam for two Presidents.

In the fall of 1961, besides McNamara and the JCS, most of the President's other advisors also recommended some degree of US military intervention in Vietnam. McGeorge Bundy and Dean Rusk were champions of naval and air operations against the North as well as supporting some ground intervention in the South. Moreover, both General Taylor and Walt Rostow continued to support the intervention they had proposed in their report. The only naysayer was George Ball who, to the frustration of his boss Rusk, argued that US military intervention would be a huge mistake.

By most accounts, the President, in these meetings did not waver in his desire not to involve major US combat forces in Vietnam or Asia for that matter. According to Arthur Schlesinger in his memoir, *A Thousand Days*, JFK said to him about the report, "They want a force of American troops. They say it's necessary to restore confidence and maintain morale. However, it will be just like Berlin. The troops will march in; the bands will play; the crowds will cheer, and in four days everyone will have forgotten. Then we will be told we have to send in more troops. It's like taking a drink. The effect wears off, and you have to take another. The war in Vietnam could be won only so long as it was their war. If it were ever converted into a white man's war, we would lose as the French had lost a decade earlier."

Thus, Kennedy rejected not only the Taylor-Rostow report but the JCS recommendations that, taken together and compared to the unfolding new intelligence, could have formed the basis of a regionally focused US national military strategy. Such a strategy may have been exactly what was needed in providing direction to the military commanders responsible for efforts in South Vietnam and the Southeast Asia region to counter North Vietnam's bid to win the war in the south and unify Vietnam under a communist regime.

But JFK was not inclined to accept any significant military action in Indochina or Vietnam. This inclination was especially because of his lack of confidence in his military advisors and commanders. In addition, Bundy, the national security assistant who should have brought these recommendations together, and McNamara, who was his civilian advisor most responsible for military recommendations, were also not inclined to make military recommendations that their boss was likely to not be in favor.

Kennedy approved, however, many of the other report's recommendations. The resulting decision, dated November 22, 1961 - called National Security Action Memorandum 111 and entitled "First Phase of Viet-Nam Program" - increased US military support and assistance dramatically in the South. This included the deployment of eventually up to 15,000 advisors. It also enlarged helicopter support, air and naval reconnaissance, and intelligence operations. Most importantly, it committed the US to a substantial military solution to the conflict. It also left open the possibility of US conventional combat operations against the North.

While some historians applaud Kennedy for facing up to his advisors, seeing the wisdom of staying away from a significant military commitment to the defense of South Vietnam, and avoiding the quagmire that followed, the evidence suggests otherwise. Up to this point, JFK's decision over the Taylor-Rostow report had other influences. First, of course, he was leery of committing large combat forces because he did not trust that the US military was competent enough to turn such an action into a success. Second, he continued to believe that his idea of defeating the insurgency with a counterinsurgency approach was a better way. It would also be cheaper and prove his testbed theories. Third, and what characterizes his actions as President thus far, he just was not sure about what to do. Thus, he decided to take the least risky course – continue along the lines he was going with a little more.

Regardless of his motives, the results of JFK's decisions on the Taylor-Rostow report would have major consequences for US policies ahead. One, he did not recognize and take action that the war in South Vietnam was a regional conflict whose chief instigator was North Vietnam. With no significant action against them, the North was free to continue and increase its military pressure on the South.

Yet, he authorized the use of force in terms of more advisors whom he knew would become involved in the fighting because they were there. He increased the American role in fighting with helicopters and other aviation assets with Americans piloting them, shooting from them, and advisors on the ground directing them. In short, without saying so, and most likely not recognizing it, John F. Kennedy had committed the US to a land conflict in Asia.

Kennedy's 'Advise and Train' War

The Taylor-Rostow Report and its subsequent actions resulted in real growth in forces and programs in Vietnam. As the JCS history summarizes, by October 1962, the ARVN totaled some 200,000 men, a 30,000 increase from the previous year. South Vietnamese civil guard and home defense units increased to 154,000. This latter increase resulted in almost a thousand self-defense units at the village level.

American military strength also increased significantly. At the time of the Taylor and Rostow visit in late 1961, there were a modest number of US military in Vietnam (948). By the end of 1962 there were 11,300 US servicemen serving in various capacities with about 2500 in the South Vietnamese Armed Forces as advisors. That number would continue to grow in 1963. By JFK's death, there were more than 16,000 US servicemen in South Vietnam, more than are currently deployed in the wars in Iraq and Afghanistan.

By mid-1962, moreover, American advisors and other supporting forces, such as helicopter gunships, were involved in direct combat in Vietnam. Reports of wounded and killed Americans began to become more common. *Life Magazine* began showing pictures of American officers accompanying South Vietnamese units on combat operations. Pictures of dead Vietnamese and wounded Americans began to populate newspapers and TV programs.

In news conferences and interviews, President Kennedy continually avoided admitting that the US was involved in direct combat. When asked if the US was in combat in Vietnam, he either said 'no' or explained that we were advising and training South Vietnamese and if shot at would shoot back.

Throughout 1962 and 1963 the situation in South Vietnam ebbed and flowed. Among the successes was the standup of the headquarters US Military Assistance Command Vietnam, commanded by

General Paul Harkins. The employment of new helicopter operations proved invaluable to the movement of ARVN forces throughout the vast areas of South Vietnam. US Special Forces set up base camps along the western borders to train and lead mountain tribes on surveillance and interdiction operations against North Vietnamese soldiers moving into the South.

On a follow-up visit to Vietnam in September 1962, General Taylor, now Chairman of the Joint Chiefs of Staff, reported, "much progress has been accomplished... The most notable perhaps is the snowballing of the strategic hamlet program which has resulted in some 5,000 hamlets being fortified or in process of fortification." Both General Harkins and Ambassador Nolting reinforced this good news. They reported to Washington that "the military progress has been little short of sensational."

Secretary McNamara, with confidence that his new defense policies and programs had brought the military brass under control, also made several fact-finding trips to Vietnam in 1962 and 63. Impressed with General Harkins and Ambassador Nolting's use of statistics and reports of improvements, the Secretary often supported reports on the progress in South Vietnam. His assessments to the President and statements to the Press were full of optimism. He used such phrases as the actions the South Vietnamese have undertaken "are beginning to be effective…. Our military assistance to Vietnam is paying off…. The sign posts are encouraging…. A tremendous amount of progress is being made."

When reporter Neil Sheehan asked McNamara to speak the truth about progress in Vietnam, the Secretary looked him in the eye and said, "every quantitative measure we have shows we are winning this war." McNamara had become a prisoner of his reliance on quantitative measurement that had worked so well for him in the business world and defense reform.

Amidst this optimism, wishful thinking, and can-do spirit, President Kennedy considered withdrawing some of the advisors and other forces he had committed under his NSAM 111. According to McGeorge Bundy, JFK was looking for any reports that could justify a pullback from the militarization that he had approved. So, he ordered McNamara to draw up plans for the reduction of US forces, beginning with some 1000 advisors by 1965 to lower the public profile of military operations. Moreover, the President also ordered strict control over Government officials traveling to Vietnam.

Several historians, Vietnam War pundits, and film-makers have made much out of this episode in which JFK directed plans for withdrawal. Their basic theme is that it showed that if he had lived, JFK would have withdrawn all US forces from Vietnam, avoided the war that LBJ later waged, and prevented the disaster it turned out to be.

Along with some other scholars such as Larry Berman and Mark Moyar, John Prados takes apart this theory in his *The Hidden History of the Vietnam War*. Prados examination of the evidence and his primary analysis leads him to conclude that the withdrawal was a Kennedy ploy to get the South Vietnamese to do more and increase their burden of their defense. To further dispel the JFK 'would have gotten out of Vietnam" theory, Prados shows that at the same time as the President had ordered this withdrawal he was ordering increases in the use of US covert forces in Laos. As he concludes, "It is difficult to reconcile this Laos policy with the assertion that Kennedy intended total withdrawal from Vietnam."

Despite the improvement of programs, growth in forces, and wishful thinking, there were ample signs that the American aid and South Vietnam civil and military operations were not going as well as hoped and reported. A significant sign was a military operation near a village called Ap Bac in January 1963. There an ARVN force of some 2,000 attacked a PLAF unit of around 400 entrenched troops. Although the South Vietnamese, relying on its US advisors, used American mechanized armored vehicles and American flown helicopters and air support, it suffered almost 200 casualties. The VC soldiers escaped the ARVN's poorly attempted encirclement.

A senior US advisor, Lieutenant Colonel John Vann, witnessing the fight assessed that the South Vietnamese soldiers had fought well. However, he was incensed about the lack of leadership and even the cowardice shown by their higher ARVN commanders. He also was impressed with the ability of the VC to confront successfully a combined South Vietnamese and American support force about three times its size. He wrote up a detailed after-action report on the episode.

General Harkins and others were incensed with its assessment and suppressed it. The Press, however, noticed the battle and its results. The news media published what they saw as a more accurate portrayal of the ARVN progress – what Vann had told them. Their stories were the prevalent accounts of the battle and the overall lack of progress of the South Vietnamese in their fight against communism.

Recently, historian Mark Moyar has questioned the story of what happened at Ap Bac. He claims in his book, *Triumph Forsaken*, that what happened at Ap Bac was primarily based on several falsehoods about the battle that Vann made to cover up his errors in judgment. Thus, because of Halberstam's and Sheehan's reliance on Vann and the popularity of their accounts of the battle, the ARVN poor performance had been grossly exaggerated.

More important than the impact of the American reporters' accounts, was the North Vietnamese assessment of the battle. When their Southern Communist leaders' accounts for the fight reached Hanoi, there was much elation. The leaders in the Politburo were now convinced that the combined forces of the PAVN and PLAF could stand up to the ARVN and its American advisors. They became further emboldened. As we will see in Chapter 7, their assessment of the battle will further incite them to infiltrate regular Peoples' Army of North Vietnam units to the fight in the South.

Meanwhile, Kennedy was upset with the negativity of the news reporting coming out of South Vietnam. At one point, he contacted some publishers and heads of newspapers to encourage them to relook their editorials. In the case of the *New York Times* reporter David Halberstam, he even encouraged the *Times* managers to recall him from Vietnam.

Whether it was these reports or his sensing about Vietnam, the President, by mid-1963, began to have severe doubts about official progress reports. There were also vast differences of views in his Administration of progress. These disparities were divided along organizational and civil-military lines. Defense officials tended to say that the US aid and war efforts were working. If there was something to be done that could further improve circumstances, more US assistance was needed.

Two Assassinations Create a Turning Point Toward War

Officials in the State Department, on the other hand, said that the lack of political improvements was undermining the overall war effort. They had doubts as to whether Diem could ever be an effective leader. Some were saying that the only way that South Vietnam could improve was to remove Diem.

Kennedy came to believe that some changes in the US country team in Vietnam were necessary.

This need was because he thought the Ambassador and Harkins had become too close to Diem and the main problem – a lack of adequate reform in the South Vietnamese Government and military. His immediate action was to send Henry Cabot Lodge to take over from Nolting with instructions to reevaluate Diem's effectiveness and the potential for political reform. He also told McNamara to begin looking for a replacement for Harkins.

There is no greater example of the frustration that Kennedy felt and had to deal with during most of 1963 than a report on a visit to South Vietnam in September of that year. The Defense Department representative, Marine General Victor Krulak, reported to JFK in a National Security Council meeting that military operations were overall going well. He said that Diem was a staunch anti-Communist who was effectively trying to defeat the insurgency. He argued that the problems that Diem was having were attributive to the need for more aid.

Meanwhile, in the same meeting, the State Department official, Joseph Mendenhall, said that the struggle was not going well because Diem was an obstacle to effective reform and ultimate success. He further noted that most of the populace and many in the South Vietnamese military detested Diem. The President's rhetorical question to these conflicting reports was, "You did visit the same country, didn't you?

Administration divisions on what to do about Vietnam manifested themselves in a debate as to whether to support a South Vietnamese military coup to remove Diem and his brother. The two had in 1963 cracked down on a Buddhist movement against the Government. On television Americans watched Monks set fire to themselves to protest a Government that the US was supporting. David Halberstam wrote a series of articles that denounced Diem for his hand in attacking the Monks who had gathered at a monastery. American public opinion, dormant at the time, began to believe that the US was supporting a regime unable to offer the legitimacy that the Kennedy Administration said was necessary to defeat the communist insurgency.

Moreover, there was evidence that Diem's brother, Ngo Dinh Nhu, who had lead the movement against the Buddhists, was making secret overtures to the North Vietnamese on arranging some compromise political solution to the insurgency and their support for it. This information (which was true), coupled with Nhu's constant anti-American rhetoric and the maligned views of Nhu's wife whom the South Vietnamese elites despised, further incited American officials in South Vietnam to argue for a change in government.

The new Ambassador Lodge soon began to argue forcefully for Diem's removal. He had become convinced that the war could not be won, short of an American military intervention, if Diem and his family remained in power. Some State Department Asian experts agreed. They argued that the South Vietnamese military had to remove Diem because he would not voluntarily step down. McNamara and Taylor argued for his remaining in power. They saw no workable alternative in the South Vietnamese military who could reform and govern.

Kennedy, per biographer Robert Dallek, was frustrated and distraught over the divisiveness and lack of clear answers to the Vietnam problem in general and Diem in particular. The President gave mixed signals as to what to do about Diem. Sometimes he indicated that the US must stick it out with Diem because he was the only one who could hold any government together. At other times, JFK thought if there was an alternative it would be better to try someone else who could be useful in achieving the reform that was so necessary to a South Vietnamese led successful conclusion to the war.

As a result, the President indicated to his advisors that he would support a coup if there were a replacement General they could trust to be effective. Like the Bay of Pigs, however, JFK wanted to be discreet about US support. He did not want it to appear that the US directly influenced a military coup of a foreign national government.

By November things had gotten out of control. State Department officials, including Ambassador Lodge, had been sending strong signals to the South Vietnamese military command that the US supported a military coup to overthrow Diem. The State official in Washington that was most adamant in engineering Diem's removal was a man named Roger Hilsman.

Hilsman in many ways epitomizes the kind of best and brightest that one would think could have given the right kind of expert advice on the situation in Vietnam at the time. As noted by Andrew Preston in *The War Council*, Hilsman was the one expert who should have "completely understood the subtleties of both guerrilla warfare (and thus, its remedy, counterinsurgency) and what President Kennedy wanted."

A 1943 West Point graduate, Hilsman had joined the infamous 'Merrill's Marauders' in World War Two. This unit was the forerunner of the elite ranger-type organizations of today. It had conducted behind the lines operations against the Japanese in Burma. Hilsman had been severely wounded there. After a lengthy recovery, he decided to join the Office of Strategic Services or OSS – the forerunner of the CIA. As a detachment leader, he again conducted operations behind enemy lines in Burma. However, in that instance, he led a series of guerrilla attacks employing 'hit and run' techniques much like the local VC guerrillas were now conducting in South Vietnam.

After the war, Hilsman earned a doctors' degree in International Affairs at Yale. He then went on to lecture as a fellow at Princeton, Johns Hopkins, and Columbia. He joined the Kennedy election committee in 1960 and provided JFK with some foreign policy speech drafts. One of Rusk's Undersecretaries hired him to join the department. Because of his knowledge and experiences in guerrilla operations, he became an influential expert on the Interagency Group on Counterinsurgency. There he was instrumental in devising guidance for the development of capabilities for counter-guerrilla warfare.

Hilsman became friends with one of Bundy's staff members - James Forrestal. The two had met in several of the interagency meetings on Vietnam and became close. Forrestal and Hilsman had also become close friends with Bundy. The former, whose father was the first Secretary of Defense, was an academician – having graduated from Princeton for his undergraduate degree and then attended Harvard Law School. Bundy saw him as an intellectual equal. In many ways, he became the National Security Advisor's alter ego. Unlike Bundy, he was outgoing with everyone and easy to make friends. He had even made the acquaintance of JFK's journalist nemesis – David Halberstam.

Bundy and Forrestal eventually introduced Hilsman to the President. They emphasized his military background and his experiences in guerrilla warfare. Kennedy was ecstatic. He not only had an experienced military man who was unconventional in his thinking, but he had another highly-educated man with brains. As Andrew Preston further explains, by 1963 Kennedy "thought of the Bundy-Forrestal-Hilsman triumvirate as his 'inner club' on Vietnam.

Despite Forrestal's association with Halberstam, Kennedy grew fond of him. One reason was that this NSC staff member was as avid a sailor as the President. JFK also loved his quick wit. In one early conversation, Forrestal lamented to the President that he knew little about the Far East. To which Kennedy typically responded, "That's just what we want. Somebody without preconceptions and prejudices."

By the fall of 1963, 'The Triumvirate' had decided that something had to be done about the Diem regime if US policy was to succeed in Vietnam. In previous cables to Ambassador Lodge, mostly drafted by Hilsman, they encouraged the removal of Diem's relatives from power. They thought these relatives had been too influential in Diem's actions, and the primary cause of the instability and dislike of the regime.

The critical part of one cable, sent in August, was that if Diem did not remove these people than the US should encourage the ARVN generals to remove Diem. The South Vietnam President, adamant now that the US was meddling in his affairs and did not understand Vietnam, refused to remove his relatives who were his principal advisors.

As Mark Moyer details in his *Triumph Forsaken*, the process for coordinating and the sending of these directions to the Saigon embassy was seriously flawed. The August cable did not get the proper venting among key officials. Rather, Forrestal and Hilsman, following their beliefs that Diem must go, ramrodded the staffing through critical members of the Government. In so doing, they bypassed McNamara and Taylor and convinced Rusk that JFK had approved of the message. It seems that Moyer's explanation is reasonably accurate, but not entirely.

The memoirs of McNamara and Ball indicate that the two sponsors of the cable did pressure others to approve by saying Lodge needed a prompt answer. But, in fact, George Ball, as acting Secretary of State, did coordinate the message with McNamara with both Rusk's and the President's approval. Taylor was not available, so Ball contacted his deputy, who approved for the General.

Regardless of the hasty staffing, in yet another exchange of messages over the next several weeks, the movement to remove Diem gained momentum. Finally, in October, Bundy sent a cable stating that "Once a coup under responsible leadership has begun…it is in the best interest of the US Government that it should succeed." That message settled the issue.

On 1 November, the coup was underway. Diem telephoned Lodge and asked, "what is the attitude [on the actions of his generals] of the US?" Lodge duplicitously told him that he was not aware of what was going on so could not say. By that evening, Diem and his brother Nhu were dead – killed while being transported to the Saigon airport by two soldiers under the orders of the Coup leader, General Duong Van Minh - the general Taylor had met in his fact-finding visit in October 1961.

On November 2d, news of the coup and assassination of Diem and his brother reached Washington. Kennedy was visibly shaken in front of his 'Triumvirate" advisors. Forrestal offered his resignation. JFK responded, "You're not worth firing. You owe me something, so you stick around."

In a private dictation for his memoirs in the Oval Office, now part of the Presidential Recordings, he lamented the entire affair. In a somber tone, JFK implied that it might have been a mistake. To a friend who tried to console Kennedy by saying that Diem and Nhu had been tyrants, Kennedy snapped back, "No. They were in a difficult position. They did the best they could for their country."

Historians have viewed the Diem assassination as a turning point in the US involvement in Vietnam. Gordon Goldstein, in his work on McGeorge Bundy aptly called *Lessons in Disaster*, noted that the affair demonstrated the weakness of JFK's mode of national security policy-making process. The President, Goldstein argues, "allowed the bureaucracy to elude his firm command."

In this case, the "you can't beat brains" trust that he had in his best and brightest failed him. As Goldstein further explains, the 'Triumvirate" just did not understand the Vietnam situation and the consequences of the removal of a man who saw himself, perhaps rightly so, as a modern Mandarin who could create a new South Vietnam consistent with its heritage, and not one as America desired.

This characteristic of not understanding Vietnam among most American senior advisors would not end with the Kennedy Presidency. Though some knowledgeable American government experts did study and understand Vietnamese history and culture, as we will see ahead, they would be virtually ignored. This ignorance, lack of understanding, and neglect of not only the Southern Vietnamese but the Northern leaders would eventually be a significant cause of America's failure there.

The observations of some scholars on the Diem assassination are worthy of note here. Journalist Kai Bird - in his biography of the Bundy brothers' involvement in Vietnam policy, *The Color of Truth* – observed, "Diem was gone and with him a regime that had been closely allied to Washington for nine long years. After his death in a coup intimately promoted by an American president, it would be much harder for Washington to avoid responsibility for a war that would not end. As Bill Bundy [McGeorge's brother] put it later, 'In an intangible way, Americans in both public and policy circles were bound henceforth to feel more responsible for what happened in Vietnam."

History professor Mark Moyar's assessment is harsher; and among some historians controversial. "While South Vietnam's President was ousted and killed by certain of his countrymen, ultimate responsibility for his fate belonged to Henry Cabot Lodge, to the President who appointed and refused to fire Lodge, and to the individuals who were giving Lodge information and advice on the political situation – a few State Department officials in Saigon and Washington and a handful of resident journalists.

As Moyar further observes, "Lodge had overridden a much larger and better informed group of Americans who had opposed a coup, including most of Kennedy's top advisers, the top CIA and military officials in Vietnam, and veteran American journalists, and he had disregarded orders against encouraging a coup from President Kennedy, who himself was torn by serious doubts about removing Diem. With Diem gone, America lost its best last hope of succeeding in Vietnam."

On 22^d November Lee Harvey Oswald assassinated the President in Dallas, Texas. John F. Kennedy would not live to see the results of Diem's coup and death – turmoil and instability in South Vietnam's politics and a near North Vietnam victory over the South in 1965. All of which would lead to a significant US military intervention of combat troops in the war. A result JFK had sought to avoid.

The Transition: I Will Not be the First President to Lose a War

The assassination of JFK marked the seventh transition of a Vice President to President while in office in US history. Some political scientists argue that these smooth transitions of power are a testament to our democracy and its constitution. Robert Caro, Lyndon Johnson's most recent biographer, argues that this transition was the most efficient one in history because of Johnson's masterful handling of it. In so doing, as Doris Kearns Goodwin writes in her *Lyndon Johnson and the American Dream*, "Johnson was able to act as both apprentice and caretaker – faithful agent of Kennedy's intentions and the healing leader of a stunned and baffled nation." It was LBJ's finest hour.

What made this transition so masterful was Johnson's adroit recognition of the situation he found himself after JFK's death. As LBJ later told Goodwin, "I became President. But for millions of Americans I was still illegitimate, a naked man with no presidential covering, a pretender to the throne, an illegal usurper. And then there was Texas, my home, the home of both the murder and the murder of the murderer. And then there were the bigots and the dividers and the Eastern intellectuals, who were waiting to knock me down before I could even begin to stand up. The whole thing was almost unbearable."

Most importantly, as LBJ also told her, "I needed that White House staff. Without them I would have lost my link to John Kennedy, and without that I would have had absolutely no chance of gaining the support of the media or the Easterners or the intellectuals. And without that support I would have had absolutely no chance of governing the country."

Thus, acutely aware of his circumstances, LBJ set out to ensure a smooth and efficient transition in several ways. He carefully controlled his demeanor during the assassination crisis and its aftermath. He was extraordinarily diffident as he assumed office and dolefully took part in the nation's mourning and burial of JFK. He purposefully stayed in the background for Kennedy's national funeral and public grieving.

Johnson further grasped that the American people, and many in the world, had come to admire and respect John Kennedy and his image as the President of the United States. He recognized JFK's death had come as a shock to most Americans. He also realized that the American public did not know him. If anything, he had often been ridiculed; called names by many in Kennedy's Administration and the Washington Press.

The new President gave the Government and the people a sense of continuity to JFK's governance. In doing so, he gave assurance that his Government would continue to function and move in the direction set by the murdered President. To do this, he quickly went about to convince most of JFK's senior advisors and cabinet members to remain in his administration. Successful, he announced this continuity to the public.

LBJ also showed after the formal grievance was over that he was Presidential. At a joint session of Congress in December and then in his State of the Union speech in January 1964, while staying respectful to the memory of Kennedy and reiterating his goal to carry on his legislative agenda, he proved that he was Presidential and in charge. There was no doubt in the audience and the Press coverage afterward that he was in command now. He was the President.

There was one overriding and pressing need that Johnson had to confront and address at once – become the head of a great nation and the leader of the Free World. It required his talents and ability to promote solutions to difficult problems and persuade others to act on them. These attributes, he thought, he had acquired through decades of campaigning for and serving as a Congressman, Senator, and Vice President. Now, he had an election to prepare for and win. He needed to be a real President – one elected by the American people in November of 1964 – just ten months away. This opportunity is what he had prepared for his entire life.

While Vietnam was becoming a major foreign policy issue in 1964, it was not yet at the forefront of domestic American politics. Civil rights, poverty, immigration, medical care for the elderly were. Hence, these issues would become the centerpiece of Johnson's platform for the 1964 election and remain so afterward. What soon became 'The Great Society Program' would be Johnson's love. Obtaining Congressional action to obtain its goals was LBJ's forte. He was a master politician who could convince, cajole, and pressure Congress to get his way in domestic affairs. Everything else would have to be secondary.

So, as the situation in Vietnam continued to deteriorate in 1964, LBJ gambled that he could put that issue on hold. He told his national security team to manage the Vietnam situation with more direct assistance and aid, and more clandestine actions hidden from the public eye until after the 1964 election. He did remind them, however, that he would not be the first President to lose a war. He would not be someone known as losing another 'China.' Winning would just have to wait a few months.

Chapter 3: The Reluctant Commander-in-Chief

LBJ won the 1964 election by a landslide. He received the highest popular vote in history over his opponent Barry Goldwater. The margin in the electoral college was 486 to 52. These were figures that only Franklin Roosevelt had approached. Like FDR, during his presidency Johnson would pursue two major agendas - one domestic and the other international. Just as the Second World War interrupted FDR's 'New Deal,' so would the Vietnam War disrupt LBJ's 'Great Society.'

Unlike Roosevelt, who was one of the most effective Commanders-in-Chief in US history, Johnson did not embrace his wartime role. Of all the US wartime Chiefs, LBJ would be the most reluctant. This is because he found himself caught up in the dilemma of choosing between his treasured domestic program and a war that he did not want. As he later told his biographer Doris Kearns Goodwin, "If I left the woman I really loved — the Great Society — to get involved with that bitch of a war on the other side of the world, then I would lose everything at home. ...But if I left that war and let the Communists take over South Vietnam, then I would be seen as a coward...."

LBJ's solution was to wage a limited war in Vietnam, while seeking to carry out his Great Society reforms at home. Later, Johnson found out he could not do both. In 1968, he abandoned victory in Vietnam. True to his words to Goodwin, he thereby became the most cowardly Commander-in-Chief in American history.

Section 3.1 – LBJ Administration

This chapter describes LBJ's handling of the Vietnam War from 1965 to 1968. While he inherited earlier Presidents' policies toward Vietnam, he would commit large US combat forces to wage a major war there; something his predecessors sought to avoid. Yet, LBJ tried to limit the US involvement as JFK had done previously.

Initially, he would also mimic Kennedy's concept of gradualism – the employment of just enough force to convince the communists to give up its aggressive policies. He chose gradualism because his principal advisors recommended it. He also felt that this method of increasing the use of force incrementally allowed him to control the war; so he could continue to devote resources and efforts to his Great Society programs.

This section describes LBJ's background and influences that characterized his role as Commander-in-Chief. It also explains the relationship that the newly elected President forged with the advisors in his Administration. It further portrays how they convinced Johnson to wage a limited war in Vietnam using the doctrine of gradual escalation. In so doing, as the narrative that follows explains, that approach failed to convince the North Vietnamese to stop its aggression in 1965. This left the reluctant commander little choice but to commit US combat ground forces to battle to save a faltering South Vietnam from near defeat.

LBJ as President and Commander-in-Chief

Lyndon Baines Johnson was as different as one could be from the 'Best and Brightest' that he asked to stay in his government. He had been born and raised in Texas, and was out of tune with the eastern social establishment that many of the Kennedy men stood for. He had grown up in the dirt-poor hill country around Austin, Texas. His family had been poor.

LBJ had been the only one in the family to go to college – Southwest Texas State Teachers' College, not an Ivy League school. Throughout his schooling, he was not known for his intelligence. He was known for his aversion to demanding situations and backing down when confronted with his behavior. He was also known for his ability to spin a yarn, often exaggerating his stories to make himself seem more important.

Unlike many of JFK's appointees Lyndon Johnson had not made it in academia or traveled extensively abroad. All he had ever wanted to do was be a politician. He had done that well; at least by the standards of Texas politics. As a recent biographer Robert Caro explains, he bribed, bought, flattered, threatened, cajoled, and bullied his way to being a representative in Congress in 1937.

As a junior member of Congress, he relied on his mentor, Sam Rayburn the Speaker of the House, whom he had befriended early in his career. He supported the New Deal when it was making sense, that is, brought money to Texas. In so doing, he became known to and a favorite of President Roosevelt. Later he abandoned New Deal policies when Texans turned against them. He was the consummate politician – a pragmatist who went with the voters' mood to get reelected.

During World War Two, still a Congressman, he was a member of the Naval Reserve. FDR appointed him to inspect facilities and report on the situation in the Southwest Pacific. As mentioned at the beginning of Chapter 1, there he managed to go with a bomber force on a combat mission ostensibly to get first-hand knowledge of their capabilities and needs.

LBJ's main motive, however, was to be able to brag that he had experienced combat so that it would enhance his postwar political career. While on the mission, Japanese planes attacked the squadron he had accompanied. There is some confusion in the official records of what happened to Johnson's plane. However, after the mission, General MacArthur awarded him the Silver Star.

The award had the intended effect. Upon Johnson's return to Washington, DC, he persuasively argued for more resources for MacArthur's theater of operations. After the war, LBJ wore the Silver Star pin on his lapel. His stories of how he shot down Japanese Zeroes to earn the medal became publicly famous and laughed at privately. He sometimes compared himself to Kennedy as a war hero – and reminded people that JFK had not earned the Silver Star.

After the war, Johnson was elected to the Senate. It had been his second attempt. He had learned from his earlier failure in 1941. As Robert Caro relates, he stole the 1948 election through illegal campaign contributions, by paying for votes and rigging tens of thousands of ballots. In the Senate, he later became the Majority Leader known for his suspicious growth in personal wealth, his style of getting in your face to convince you to vote the way he wanted, and his propensity for extramarital 'excursions' in a Senate office room he labeled as his 'nooky room.' Above all, he had become a master politician and effective Congressional leader.

After he had successfully engineered the transition following JFK's death, LBJ established his style of leadership as President. Like Kennedy, he did not like to do business through formal processes. Unlike Kennedy, he did not feel comfortable in large group debates on issues with differences of opinion that he would have to settle. Instead, he preferred small discussions or meetings with people he could control, convince of his views, and trust there would be no dissension. Above all, he wanted loyalty rather than honesty and bold ideas. He made sure that those who were not loyal or did not seem to be, were no longer working for him.

He had observed as Vice President some of the difficulties JFK had with his military generals. LBJ was determined to avoid that. He was intent on controlling the military by appointing people who had a reputation for obeying orders and being loyal – not a reputation for military strategy and operations, intelligence, honesty, or constructive criticism. He would avoid meeting with the Joint Chiefs of Staff as a group. However, he mastered his meetings with the Chairman or any of the other Chiefs individually, whom he knew he could control.

He was ill-suited to be a Commander-in-Chief for two primary reasons. First, he was even more distrustful of the military than Kennedy. As he said to one of his close Congressional associates, "And the generals. Oh, they'd love the war, too. It's hard to be a military hero without a war. Heroes need battles and bombs and bullets in order to be heroic. That's why I am suspicious of the military. They're always so narrow in their appraisal of everything. They see everything in military terms."

Second, as Professor Goodwin relates, LBJ's life was politics. He had volunteered to serve in the war so that he could use that service to gain votes rather than to obtain any knowledge of military affairs. Unlike Kennedy, "who had a voracious appetite for relevant reading material," Johnson did not read much. When he did, he abhorred military history.

However, he knew a lot about bargaining and getting votes. He believed everyone had a price. He knew how to cajole and convince politicians on how to vote. As Goodwin observes, "the experience of a long political career had confirmed him in the belief that there were no differences that could not be settled by upping the ante. That conviction was part of his character, and had shaped his mode of conduct throughout a long and successful political career."

After several years as a wartime President, Johnson would learn the hard way that his experience in the American domestic political arena did not prepare him to be for Commander-in-Chief in wartime. He knew nothing about the conduct of war. He had no desire to learn about it. He sought only to have the war wishfully go away. He thought he could do that by offering Ho Chi Minh what any American politician would crave for – a way to show his people that he got something for them to improve their way of life. Ho, and other influential North Vietnamese Communists, would have none of it.

LBJ's Scholars and Warriors

For various reasons, most of the prominent Kennedy officials stayed on with LBJ, as he had hoped. Bobby Kennedy - with whom LBJ had always feuded - left after only a couple of months of showing some semblance of support. Arthur Schlesinger and Ted Sorensen, still grieving for their lost leader, left early as well.

McGeorge Bundy, Walt Rostow, Dean Rusk, and Robert McNamara stayed in office. With the latter two, Johnson grew a personal and close relationship. Dean Rusk, whom Kennedy had relegated to a manager of his Department rather than policy participant, became a close advisor on Vietnam. This was mainly because the Secretary of State was a loyal servant and supported Johnson in whatever LBJ chose to do. Rusk continued to be a staunch Cold Warrior intent on the containment of communism in Asia, and fervently supported committing US combat military forces to stave defeat in Vietnam.

Robert McNamara, who among all of JFK's brightest was closest to the Kennedy family, became a loyal servant as well. Johnson genuinely admired his Secretary of Defense. Both shared an immense work ethic; often working almost twenty-hour days. LBJ also enjoyed McNamara's intense desire to control the military establishment. He could count on him to keep the JCS in line with his policies. Four years later, however, the principal architect of US military intervention in Vietnam seemed to doubt his and the President's actions toward Vietnam. McNamara appeared to strain from his consumption with work. LBJ would have to replace him at a critical time.

Johnson also admired the work ethic and intelligence of his Assistant for National Security Affairs. Bundy appeared to have the national security apparatus under control. This gave the President the time and opportunity to concentrate on his domestic agenda. Moreover, when LBJ became overwhelmed and frustrated with the situation in Vietnam, mainly because it conflicted with his Great Society programs, Bundy seemed to have all the answers for the Vietnam quandary. Because his recommendations seemed to avoid tough decisions, Johnson initially agreed with his National Security Advisor's solutions.

However, Bundy later began to wander out on his own to challenge and debate the growing anti-war movement. LBJ felt these debates were counterproductive. He worried that they would result in too much press coverage, threatening his control of the message on Vietnam. More important to LBJ, Bundy decided to take on the critics against his advice. The President thought this action brought unneeded scrutiny to his war policies. Johnson finally concluded that his National Security Assistant crossed the line of loyalty that he demanded.

As for Bundy, he found it difficult adjusting to Johnson. In their classic study of the NSC process, Daalder and Destler explain, "The Johnson style was ebullience, overstatement, passion, wearing his emotions on his sleeve, a sharp contrast to Kennedy's style and a poor fit with Bundy's. Bundy realized, of course, that it was he who would have to adjust, and he made considerable efforts to do so. But it was never easy. The discomfort could only fuel resentment on both sides, and ultimately a lessening of mutual confidence and respect." Eventually, Johnson would remove the frustrated Bundy.

In his place, LBJ would bring back Walt Rostow. JFK had moved Rostow to the State Department to get him out of the discussions about Vietnam because of his militant views. Now he returned to the White House to continue his support for military solutions to the Vietnam problem.

The President appointed three other people who would perform essential roles in his future Vietnam policy. They were Generals William Westmoreland and Earle Wheeler, and Clark Clifford. The President assigned General Westmoreland, whom Taylor had positioned as a Deputy to General Harkins in preparation for the latter's removal, as Commander, MACV in April 1964. General Earle Wheeler, who had been the Army Chief of Staff for most of Kennedy's administration, was now the new Chairman of the Joint Chiefs. Clark Clifford, a seasoned Washington DC insider, would take over for McNamara when he left in February 1968.

General William Westmoreland had graduated from West Point in 1936. As outlined in Chapter 1, he had fought in World War Two. During this time, he commanded several artillery units in campaigns in North Africa, Sicily, Normandy, and Germany. In Sicily, he had performed well in support of the 82d Airborne Division and its Artillery Commander; then Brigadier General Maxwell Taylor. After the war, Westmoreland held several positions in US Army airborne organizations to include the command of a brigade in the Korean War.

After Korea, he served in various positions that would ensure his ultimate promotion to General Officer – to include General Taylor's principal chief in the Pentagon. He later served as a commander of the 101st Airborne Division and Superintendent of the United States Military Academy. At the military academy, 'Westy' had introduced 'counterinsurgency' to the curricula. Whether that had been to prepare cadets for future service, or merely to show he was on board with the new administration is open to conjecture.

Westmoreland had a reputation for being a serious man with little humor. His looks, with a square jaw and straight posture, impressed those whom he met. Many thought that his demeanor and appearance destined him for General Officer. According to some who knew him, however, he was more of a good manager than a warrior; and more loyal soldier than a bold leader. He had attended Harvard Business school, which led some to claim, "Westy was a corporation executive in uniform."

Westmoreland got ahead because of those he knew and had served well. Like Harkins, he was a Taylor man. After LBJ had selected him to command and direct operations in Vietnam, he told the General that he was counting on him and said, "I hope you don't pull a MacArthur on me." Westmoreland did not respond. Johnson needed none. Both men knew that 'Westy' would never do so. He was the right man to execute LBJ's policy in Vietnam. He would never seriously or outwardly challenge his superiors.

General Earle 'Bus' Wheeler, was a 1932 West Point graduate. As the Army Chief of Staff during the Kennedy Administration, he had garnered a reputation for supporting positive thinking about policies toward Vietnam. In fact, McNamara had dispatched him to Vietnam to investigate the battle of Ap Bac, which, as mentioned in the last chapter, the Press had reported as a disaster for the US aid and training program for the South Vietnamese forces. Wheeler reported to McNamara that it had been a military victory, unlike what the Press was reporting.

Wheeler had a reputation as an excellent staff officer. Unlike most officers of his year group, he had not seen any combat. After the war, he had several assignments in the Pentagon in a senior staff position in both the Army and Joint Staffs before he became the Army Chief. These assignments reinforced his reputation as a superlative staff soldier who knew the 'politics' of the Pentagon.

Johnson selected Wheeler as the new Chairman of the Joint Chiefs because LBJ knew he would be a loyal team player. McNamara, moreover, liked him. Wheeler had been a math instructor at West Point and had an affinity for numbers. Unlike most military men, he had worked well as the Army Chief with the 'Whiz Kids' that the Secretary had set up to reform the Pentagon. As recorded in Mark Perry's history of the Joint Chiefs called *Four Stars*, Wheeler was "living proof that his get along, go along the road to high command attitude bred mediocrity."

This 'get along mentality' was especially true of his relationship with the President. Wheeler, in an oral testimony in the Johnson library, said that he and LBJ formed a close relationship. The President had told him that he considered him as one of the ten closest friends in DC. 'Bus' would do his best to be an admirer and loyal supporter of his friend, the President. He would also do his best to help the President and ameliorate any differences in the Joint Chiefs of Staff. However, the General would not do his best to give the most effective and convincing military advice.

Clark Clifford was also one of LBJ's closest friends in DC. He had been friends and an advisor to earlier Democratic presidents as well. A fellow Missourian, Harry Truman asked him to be his Naval Aide during the latter stages of the war. A lawyer, he stayed on as Truman's legal counsel after the war. He also helped Truman get reelected.

Afterward, Clifford ran a law firm in Washington. During that time, he became a private counsel and advisor to Kennedy. He served LBJ in the same capacity for a while. As an advisor, from time to time, he went with other officials on trips to Vietnam. Although he had counseled LBJ against sending US combat forces to Vietnam, he was an articulate supporter of the President's policies in the Press. His reputation as a hawk on Vietnam would later lead to his eventual choice as a replacement for McNamara. As Secretary of Defense, Clifford would convince Johnson to change course in Vietnam that would eventually lead to defeat.

To recap LBJ's new national security team, in taking over the Presidency in the most difficult of circumstances, Johnson had succeeded in building a team he felt confident about. He had succeeded in keeping on most of the high-level members of JFK's Administration. Thus, he could show continuity between his and Kennedy's governance.

Most importantly, he was also able to appoint people that fit his view of an effective government – one that showed unanimity in policy and purpose. LBJ was also able to appoint military officers that he felt would support him and be loyal. He wanted his generals to first, not let the Vietnam War dominate his bid for reelection; and second, not oppose his decisions on how to prosecute a limited war that would enable his domestic agenda.

Section 3.2 - LBJ's Gradualism Approach for Vietnam

In consonance with his theme of 'continuity' with the Kennedy Administration, LBJ, four days after becoming President, reaffirmed his commitment to the support of South Vietnam in National Security Action Memorandum (NSAM) – 273. This document declared that "it remains the central object of the United States in South Vietnam to assist the people and government of that country to win their contest against the externally directed and supported communist conspiracy. The test of all US decisions and actions in this area should be the effectiveness of their contribution to this purpose."

The memo gave support to the new post-Diem regime and increased economic and military aid. It also tasked the National Security establishment to develop plans for covert actions against North Vietnamese lines of supply in Laos, as well as other operations. The latter prompted the development of an operations plan labeled OPLAN 34.

Johnson was looking for a solution that would meet his desires to focus on his domestic agenda and not lose South Vietnam. He dispatched McNamara on yet another series of fact-finding missions to Vietnam. He also sought the advice of Maxwell Taylor before he retired as Chairman on the situation. Both argued for a series of increasing covert operations against North Vietnam as a means of sending a signal to their leaders that the US would not abandon South Vietnam. Meanwhile, they recommended planning for gradual overt military pressure on the North through aerial 'retaliatory strikes' should the President later decide to up the pressure.

At a National Security Council meeting in March 1964, LBJ formalized this approach in the publication of NSAM 288. That memorandum specified that the US sought an independent, non-communist South Vietnam to thwart further expansion of communism in Asia. Thereby, the President confirmed his support of the Domino Theory set by both Eisenhower and Kennedy, and affirmed the vital interest of Vietnam to US national security.

Johnson also approved of McNamara's approach of gradually more aggressive covert military actions, such as the bombing of selective targets in North Vietnam, and the possibility of introducing US ground forces in the south to bring pressure on the North Vietnamese to cease their aggressive support for the war. The commanders of the Pacific Command and MACV, Admiral Sharp and General Westmoreland, respectively, included this policy and its concepts into a revised OPLAN 34A.

While this approach appealed to Johnson, it was fraught with miscalculations and invalid assumptions. The JCS decided in April to assess the gradual pressure concept through a series of war games in the Pentagon called Sigma I-64 and Sigma II-64. The conclusion of these assessments – captured in the JCS official history and detailed in Gibbons' Vietnam War study - was that the North Vietnamese would respond to the pressure of US bombing strikes and other actions by increasing, not decreasing, its efforts in the South. That increased commitment, moreover, may compel the US to commit significant combat forces to the defense of the south. Further, the Sigma II games "predicted that the escalation of American military involvement would erode public support for the war in the United States."

While these games were prophetic, according to H.R. McMaster and other historians, neither Johnson, Taylor or McNamara thought much of this wargaming activity at the time. Moreover, as we will see, LBJ, McNamara and other civilian policymakers will continue in the years ahead to ignore similar military assessments to their peril.

Meanwhile, the CIA produced an estimate in early June that questioned the 'Domino Theory.' Like some of the intelligence estimates of the time, it brought a sense of realism to the underlying assumptions of policy-making in these years. The estimate, called a National Intelligence Estimate or NIE, stated that it was highly doubtful that the fall of Vietnam would affect any other nation in Southeast Asia. Of course, one could argue the premises of the CIA's argument. However, the document, which Bundy should have seen and further staffed, was ignored.

During the six months after Johnson took over as President, it was becoming clear that there were three people whom LBJ trusted and relied upon – McNamara, Rusk, and Bundy. Equally as clear, the new President, while giving an aura of respect, ignored the collective advice of the Joint Chiefs. While LBJ liked␣Wheeler, he did not yet include him in the President's 'Tuesday Luncheons,' which became Johnson's preferred policy making venue, and were made up of only civilians. Instead, he relied on McNamara for military guidance and keeping the JCS in line and on board.

For his part, McNamara felt entirely comfortable in his role and the President's dependence on him for military analysis. The Secretary of Defense learned from his experience, especially during the Cuban Missile Crisis, that the Chiefs were too narrow-minded. Moreover, he had learned the effectiveness of a gradual approach to the employment of military force. In his view, such an approach allowed for political, diplomatic maneuvering and signal sending during a crisis to affect an opponent's will.

LBJ also grew close to Dean Rusk. Rusk's simple views of a monolithic communist adversary intent on ruling the world, and that America was the only power that could defend against them, corresponded to Johnson's. Moreover, Rusk gave confidence to a new President who had no experience in international affairs. Despite his strong views on the need to confront aggression with force, the newly empowered head of the State Department was unwilling to go against the President when he would seek a negotiated approach to the war.

Though less close to Bundy, mainly because of his advisor's educational background and intellect, LBJ relied on him to keep the national security affairs of his Administration on track. Bundy's extraordinary abilities to absorb information and analyze the myriad of issues, and then present them confidently with straightforward solutions, allowed the President to focus on his first love – his domestic agenda.

While McNamara, Rusk, and Bundy had served in World War Two, none of them had served in the field or been in combat. They had experienced war through the eyes of a desk officer. They had no direct experience in developing military strategies or the employment of forces on the battlefield. They had no or, in the case of Rusk, limited education on military affairs. At the beginning of August 1964, with its uniformed military advisors either ignored or sidelined, the Johnson Administration was about to make its first major decisions on what to do about the vastly deteriorating situation in Vietnam.

The Seeds of an American War in Vietnam

On August 2, 1964, North Vietnamese torpedo boats attacked the US destroyer Maddox in the Tonkin Gulf off the coast of North Vietnam. The destroyer was conducting electronic intelligence gathering operations. The USS Maddox returned fire and asked for air support from a nearby US Carrier. The planes from the carrier attacked and damaged three of the boats.

Two days later the Maddox and another destroyer, the USS C. Turner Joy, reported more attacks. These attacks were much less certain than the earlier ones. They were at night, and there was much doubt by the ships' Captains whether the suspected torpedoes and enemy boats were real or perhaps sonar or radar misreading's. Nevertheless, the US Pacific Command reported both attacks to Washington.

Based on this second attack, the President, upon the recommendation of Secretary McNamara, ordered air strikes in retaliation against North Vietnamese Torpedo bases. In addition, Johnson decided to seek a Congressional resolution for further military action in case of further North Vietnamese attacks against US forces. Going on television, LBJ announced his request for a resolution to express "the unity and determination of the United States in supporting freedom and protecting peace in southeast Asia." The American public, many of whom did not even know where Indochina or Vietnam was, rallied around the President.

The Congress approved the resolution on 10 August. It stated, "That the Congress approves and supports the determination of the President, as Commander in Chief, to take all necessary measures to repel any armed attack against the forces of the United States and to prevent further aggression." Section 2 of this resolution further said, "The United States regards as vital to its national interest and to world peace the maintenance of international peace and security in southeast Asia," and would take "all necessary steps, including the use of armed force," to assist South Vietnam in defense of its freedom.

The House passed it unanimously. The Senate passed it by a vote of 88-2. Senator Wayne Morse of Oregon, one of the dissenters said, "I believe this resolution to be a historic mistake."

To this day, the Gulf of Tonkin incident and its following resolution are matters of debate. Administration officials defended their actions then and well after. McNamara, in his memoirs *In Retrospect*, claimed that there were conflicting and ambiguous reports over the attack of the USS Turner Joy. The deciding factor for him was when Admiral Sharp, the US Commander in the Pacific, said that there was no doubt in his mind the attack occurred. Thus, the Secretary of Defense 'passed the buck' of responsibility to the military.

Well after the incident and the end of the war, Government investigations, as well as Democratic Republic of Vietnam reports, showed that there were no second attacks. Indeed, for those Americans who believed that the events that followed the incident and resolution were a conspiracy to start a US war in Vietnam, the affair was the first of several Government schemes to falsify and keep actions secret from the American people.

What can be discerned is that the President and his advisors, namely McGeorge Bundy, who had the lead, had decided before the crisis that they may need a Congressional resolution to support expected US military actions against North Vietnam. Therefore, the intent to gain Congressional approval for increased military activity preceded the Tonkin Gulf incidents. This was what LBJ, an astute politician, would want to justify further significant US military actions whatever they may be.

In addition, covert military activities ordered and carried out under OPLAN 34A had already prompted North Vietnamese military actions in and around the Tonkin Gulf area. Though the actions by the two US destroyers were not directly part of the OPLAN 34A operations, the North Vietnamese attacks were not unprovoked as claimed by the Johnson Administration. To the North Vietnamese, the actions of the two destroyers were just a continuation of OPLAN 34A actions against its homeland. Thus, in this sense, the Administration had falsely claimed unprovoked attacks against US forces to gain Congressional and Public support.

Regardless of the debate over motive, duplicitousness, or outright deceit of the Johnson Administration over the affair, the effect of the Gulf of Tonkin incident was monumental to the subsequent road to increased US military involvement in Vietnam. The near-unanimous Congressional resolution, while not a declaration of war, gave Lyndon Johnson the political cover that he felt he would need to make decisions regarding the use of US combat forces and actions in South Vietnam. This was especially so since the American public during the Gulf of Tonkin crisis overwhelmingly approved of his 'retaliatory strikes' against 'unprovoked' enemy attacks on US military activities.

In November 1964, LBJ won the election. As mentioned, it had been decisive. It did not matter that he may have gained votes by invoking an image of a peace candidate who would not "send American boys nine or 10,000 miles away from home to do what Asian boys ought to be doing for themselves." Rather, LBJ was now an elected President in his own right. He soon turned to his trusted advisors and indicated that he was now ready to deal with Vietnam.

While Johnson had put Vietnam on the back burner for most of 1964, his principal advisors, notably McGeorge Bundy and McNamara, had been working on what to do with the Vietnam dilemma. Four main factors created this great dilemma as they saw it after the Tonkin Gulf Affair. First, the US had committed itself to the defense of South Vietnam and ensuring its fate as a non-communist state. Official executive branch national security documents, such as NSAMs 273 and 288, had declared South Vietnam in the vital interest of the US. The Congressional Gulf of Tonkin resolution had further stated the area was vital to world peace. Moreover, publicly and privately, officials had also invoked commitment to the SEATO agreements to defend not only Vietnam but also all Southeast Asia. In short, the US had placed its reputation as a guarantor of freedom on the line for all the world to judge if it failed in Southeast Asia.

The second factor that created this dilemma was that the Republic of Vietnam was increasingly showing that it was unable to both govern itself and resist communist aggression. Its government was a 'revolving door' of different heads of state who could not gain widespread support or establish any semblance of stability. Its military was unable to defeat VC military units and resist the communist takeover of large chunks of territory and population. In short, it was losing the war, and losing badly.

The third factor adding to this predicament was that the US had been unable to dissuade the North Vietnamese from supporting the aggression in the South. The Northern Communists had shown that they were committed to unification despite the possibility that it could face the terrible consequences of war with the US – the world's guarantor of resistance to communism.

A fourth factor was that the American Commander-in-Chief was a reluctant warrior. While committing the nation to the defense of South Vietnam and adamant that he would not lose 'another China,' LBJ was loath to commit the full fury of US military force to defend a declared vital interest.

He was worried that such a commitment would incite Chinese military intervention as it had done in Korea. He was troubled that such a commitment would embroil the US in a broader war that could overtake his goal to create a Great Society.

This dilemma would plague US policymakers throughout the Johnson years. It would become the dominant policy issue that both the civilian and military members of LBJ's 'team' had to struggle with. As *The Pentagon Papers* noted back in the sixties, "The basic problem in US policy was to generate programs and other means adequate to secure the objectives being pursued. The central dilemma lay in the fact that while US policy objectives were stated in the very most comprehensive terms, the means employed were both consciously limited and purposely indirect." The *Papers* appropriately referred to this quandary as the use of 'limited measures for limitless aims,' and the result that was 'limited escalation' led to 'open-ended intervention.'

The evidence since *The Pentagon Papers*, however, shows that the 'problem' was not only that the stated political aims demanded more than the means the President was willing to commit, but that the civilian and military leaders and advisors could not agree upon or follow the same objectives or means. This major issue was both a symptom of the appalling civil-military relations of the times and the cause of an inability to derive an effective national strategy to solve the dilemma described.

LBJ's civilian advisors were aware of and attempted to propose ways to eventually use military force to solve this issue in late 1964, right after the election and before the significant decisions to commit substantial ground forces to the war in 1965. As several historians have explained, Bundy, McNamara and their like-minded assistants and others in the State Department created during this time objectives and proposed ways to address the situation in Vietnam. Their options and goals would differ significantly from what the military advisors and staffs in Washington thought was necessary to defend South Vietnam and prevent a communist takeover, the stated objectives of NSAMs 273 and 288.

Through several ad hoc committees the civilian advisors - ignorant of military strategic theory and planning, and feeling it unnecessary to consult the JCS - drafted what became in the words of Carl Clausewitz a "policy demanding things that go against the nature of war." The resulting vague options and supporting actions called for efforts to gradually put the "squeeze" on the North Vietnamese to persuade them to give up its support for aggression in the south and pursuit of unification. The primary aims of this way forward were to "(A) protect US reputation as a counter-subversion guarantor; (B) avoid domino effect especially in Southeast Asia; (C) keep South Vietnamese territory from Red hands, and (D) emerge from crisis without considerable taint from methods."

The historical evidence on this work further shows that Bundy and McNamara, and their assistants working on this policy and planning, thought that "it would be preferable to fail in Vietnam after trying some level of military action than to withdraw without first committing the US military to direct action against North Vietnam." Moreover, as explained by McNamara's assistant John McNaughton, the loss of South Vietnam after the direct intervention of US forces "would leave behind a better odor" than an immediate withdrawal and would portray the US as "a good doctor willing to keep promises, be tough, take risks, get bloodied, and hurt the enemy badly." Yet, there was no detailed concept of operations for the use of this force, or any detail on what kind or what level of force would be necessary.

As mentioned, this policy-making and plan development took place without any participation or direct inputs from the chief military advisors. The JCS did provide some of the facts or data for the civilians' use. However, strategic advice was neither asked for or offered. There were two major reasons for this lack of civilian-military interaction.

The first primary reason was that there was a different view of the purpose of any military action against the North. The civilians, as explained above, thought the principal object was to protect the US reputation with gradual military pressure to 'persuade' the North to give up its aggression. The Military Chiefs thought, per the standing NSAM political objectives, that the US had to employ adequate military power to 'force' the North to give up. These were opposing views on the purpose and use of force.

A second main reason for the Chiefs not providing their views was that they were divided by parochial interests on how to wage any major military campaign against the North or in the South. The Chief of the Air Force and Navy recommended substantial bombing operations against military North Vietnam significant targets. The Marine Corps Commandant wanted to send marine forces to South Vietnam, to set up enclaves along the coast, and take part in securing the populated areas against communist attacks. The Army Chief wanted to send Army forces to the South that could not only secure the population but attack the VC main forces.

The above discontinuity in views, which LBJ contributed to with his vague guidance, would continue throughout the war. They would be a cause of disagreement and dissatisfaction between civilian and military officials in the government throughout Johnson's tenure. This discontent would further paralyze effective national strategic formulation and advice for the President and the field commanders until 1968, when the President would seek an entirely different approach to the conflict.

The 'Fork in the Road'

As the Johnson Administration officials struggled with the above-described dilemma and confused or vague objectives, the situation in Vietnam at the beginning of 1965 had become critical. Some 23,000 US military personnel there, an increase from 16,000 when LBJ had taken over from JFK, had come under more brazen and targeted attacks.

In the first week of February VC saboteurs attacked a hotel that billeted US soldiers in Saigon killing two Americans, and wounding over 107 other Westerners and Vietnamese. The VC also struck a US air base at Pleiku that killed 8 Americans and damaged scores of planes. They further attacked another US billet in Qui Nhon and killed 23 Americans. The ARVN seemed helpless to combat the VC in the countryside. One CIA analyst estimated the VC now controlled about 50% of the rural populated areas in the South.

These VC attacks and the North's increased infiltration of its forces gave impetus to a new direction for the Johnson Administration. In a memo that McNamara would later label the "Fork in the Road" memo, McGeorge Bundy, who had just returned from South Vietnam where he had witnessed the aftermath of the Pleiku attack, and Robert McNamara argued for a change of course.

The most immediate change they recommended was to increase US air attacks from just retaliation strikes to a concerted air campaign against the North. Bundy, McNamara, and later Rusk argued forcefully for the efficacy of bombing as the means to punish North Vietnam for these attacks and bring their leaders to the negotiating table. They also believed that the bombing could affect North Vietnamese infiltration of troops and supplies to the South.

For Bundy, this approach fit well with his belief in game theory. The airstrikes, carefully controlled and calibrated, would send a series of signals of the intent of the US to punish the North for its aggression in the south. The North Vietnamese, as rational actors would recognize this intent, and determine that it could not succeed against the US. The underlying assumption was that the North would find that it could not sustain the damages that the US could inflict. Therefore, it would eventually, in line with game modeling, give up its pursuit of supporting the war against the Southern Vietnamese Government.

LBJ approved the increased bombing. According to his biographers, the main reason for this approval was because it would not interfere with his domestic agenda. He also sought to show his restraint publicly, so that it appeared that he did not want a widened conflict. Along with that demonstration, he could continue to argue overtly that he was seeking peace and not war. The President, moreover, could closely orchestrate these air operations to ensure that the targets did not incite further direct involvement of the Soviet Union and China. The spectra of Chinese intervention, as had happened in Korea, continuously haunted Johnson when considering actions against the North.

Lyndon Johnson also knew, as he admits in his memoirs, that he had to take some military action to prevent a loss of South Vietnam to the communists. As he explained, "I knew that if we let Communist aggression succeed in taking over South Vietnam, there would follow in this country an endless national debate—a mean and destructive debate—that would shatter my Presidency, kill my administration, and damage our democracy. I knew that Harry Truman and Dean Acheson had lost their effectiveness from the day that Communists took over in China. I believed that the loss of China had played a large role in the rise of Joe McCarthy. Moreover, I knew that all these problems, taken together, were 'chickenshit' compared with what might happen if we lost Vietnam."

The CIA, the JCS and the American military field commanders who had to execute the air operations were mixed in their views of the aims of the strikes and their potential effects. CIA assessments doubted the effectiveness of bombing against a non-industrial nation whose military capabilities depended on both Chinese and Soviet support. They also disagreed that the North Vietnamese Leaders would pay any attention to the 'signals' being sent; primarily because they had everything to lose and nothing to gain from any negotiated settlement. The CIA understood that the North was winning the war - estimating, correctly, that there were now (March 1965) 37,000 regular NVA forces and 100,000 irregular VC forces in the South.

The Joint Chiefs continued to be divided along service parochial views. The new Air Force Chief, General John McDonnell, who had replaced LeMay, supported an air campaign. However, he argued that the strikes needed to be more massive and the targets more expansive. The Chief of Naval Operations, Admiral David McDonald, supported the Air Force view, indicating that US carriers could support such a campaign from positions off the coast of North Vietnam.

The two Army officers, Army Chief, General Harold Johnson, and the Chairman, General 'Bus' Wheeler, along with Marine Corps Commandant General Greene, had doubts about the ability of bombing alone to decisively affect the conflict. In fact, Wheeler and Johnson began to further exam options for the employment of significant US Army combat forces in Vietnam. They both thought this was the only answer to the significant successes of the North Vietnamese and VC onslaught that was coming close to defeating the South Vietnamese. However, neither were willing to challenge their civil leaders who were intent on relying on the less controversial bombing option.

In the field, Maxwell Taylor, now ambassador to Vietnam, thought that the bombing was a great alternative to employing ground combat forces. He also believed that it would significantly improve the morale of the South Vietnamese leaders and forces. General Westmoreland, who had taken over from General Harkins, was neutral to the bombing; thinking that it was worth a try. However, now, more than ever, he believed the only solution to the war was a US force ground intervention. Admiral US Sharp, the US Commander of Pacific Command, argued for a two-month air operation focused on the logistical lines through Laos.

Bundy, McNamara, and Rusk muzzled or minimized most of the disagreement on the 'air war' to the President. Wheeler, for his part, worked behind the scenes to plan for an eventual expansion of the use of military force; but chose to present a consensus of the JCS in supporting the gradual pressure approach. Meanwhile, the President dismissed those, like George Ball from the State Department, who could get opposing views to him, as playing the 'devil's advocate.'

The extended bombing campaign, dubbed 'ROLLING THUNDER,' which would go on for three more years, got off to a rocky start. Terrible weather at first hampered it. However, the real hampering, especially from the Air Force perspective, was the Administration's unprecedented control. LBJ would come to boast that there was not a target that could be struck without his approval. He even chose some of the targets personally. His choices were not based on military worth, but what he thought would send the proper signals to the DRV leadership and affect their will to wage war, while preventing any threat to the Soviets and the Chinese.

As the bombing continued, as McMaster relates in his critique of civil-military relations in Vietnam *Dereliction of Duty*, there was growing confusion and lack of transparency over what the overall US objectives of this US graduated pressure policy were. As mentioned above, the confusion continued between the civilians, who were considering different political aims for the gradualism policy than the official ones, and the military, who were considering the military objectives on the use of force to support the NSAM political goals.

McGeorge Bundy, at the White House, and John McNaughton, at the Pentagon, set out to bring 'clarity' to the political aims. The ones they now proposed were like those proposed earlier in the post-1964 election aftermath. These aims thus continued to differ significantly with those presented in official documents, such as previous NSAMs. They also continued to be widely dissimilar from what the Administration had publicized in press releases, interviews, and speeches. Most importantly, these objectives - never officially approved or provided to the military - were the ones that the senior civilian leaders and advisors – to include Robert McNamara – sought to achieve throughout 1965 to 1968.

For Bundy and McNaughton, both students of 'game theory' and 'conflict management,' any US military action in Vietnam, no matter what the result, would continue to show resolve and thus be sufficient to stem the tide of communism in Southeast Asia. So, in their minds the US political objective of the graduated response approach needed to be 'show the US resolve to contain the spread of communism in Southeast Asia.'

Therefore, the conflict in Vietnam could no longer be up to the South Vietnamese. The stakes were now too high to leave it to them. As Bundy explained in the notes he kept for a memoir he never completed, "The international prestige of the United States, and a substantial part of our influence, are directly at risk in Vietnam." Thus, he pressed those who worked for him and to his close associates like McNamara to devise US actions that would 'preserve the deterrent value of the US to its Allies and others in the Southeast Asia area.'

John McNaughton, in a memo called "Action for South Vietnam" sent to McNamara in March, exactly defined what the objectives were, as he and Bundy saw them, and assigned a percentage for each. They were: "70% - To avoid a humiliating US defeat (to our reputation as guarantor); 20% - To keep SVN (and then adjacent) territory from Chinese hands; 10% - To permit the people of SVN to enjoy a better, freer way of life; ALSO – To emerge from crisis without unacceptable taint from methods used; NOT – To 'help a friend,' although it would be hard to stay if asked out."

McNamara saw these papers and agreed with them. But, as far as the evidence shows, he never transmitted or discussed them with the military. The JCS and Commanders in the field, i.e., Sharp and Westmoreland, continued to believe that the primary political objective was an independent non-communist Vietnam. As we will see later, even if they did know, deriving clear military objectives would have been problematic at best.

Having ignored the earlier results of war games that showed bombing would not achieve what the Administration wanted, there were now some civilian naysayers, besides CIA analysts, who cautioned Johnson on his gradual bombing policy. Vice President Hubert Humphrey, who had read the CIA assessments questioning the viability of bombing Hanoi into submission, sent a memo to the President in February warning against the US being unable to convince the North to stop its aggression.

The Vice President argued that now was the time for the US to get out of Vietnam. Humphrey said now was the time because the President had gained a considerable political advantage in the elections. Therefore, he could use his peace image, and the public's lack of knowledge of Vietnam, to extract America from an unwinnable war. LBJ ignored his advice. The President, moreover, now excluded his Vice President from future discussions of Vietnam.

Meanwhile, George Ball, who had supported the bombing concept earlier in 1964, now feared that the current direction of using military force risked the commitment of US ground combat units. Therefore, he advocated getting out of Vietnam as well. Johnson liked Ball. As mentioned, he had established him as his official 'devil's advocate.' Ball's presence at meetings gave some semblance that LBJ was seeking all sides of the issue of Vietnam. Thus, though he thought Ball's advice defeatist, the President continued to want his presence at his meetings on Vietnam.

To counter Ball, and any others who may advocate a withdrawal, the President continually brought up that such a withdrawal from the US commitment would be contrary to earlier Administrations. He would tell his advisors of his telephone conversations with President Eisenhower in which the ex-five-star general would tell him that he could not lose Vietnam. LBJ would also remind them that abandonment would be akin to the British appeasement at Munich before World War Two.

Throughout all of this, LBJ remained ambivalent, unaware, or in disregard of whatever his Administration's unfolding political and military objectives were in the worsening situation in Vietnam. In a brief telephone conversation with McNamara, he did make a feeble attempt to give his input. He told his Defense Secretary that he wanted better plans for Vietnam in which he wanted "to whip the hell out of them," and "wants to kill them." McNamara, his voice reflecting a reaction that was cordial but surprised, agreed and said he would get right on it. Johnson's attempt to give direction was hardly helpful. He would repeat this 'guidance' later, as American servicemen were about to die in the hundreds on the battlefield he would send them.

There appear to be two reasons for LBJ's lack of attention to the importance of setting concise, useful political aims toward Vietnam in the first year after his election. One was that he just did not understand their importance. He did not understand the critical relationship between the political aim and how they should drive the military objectives supporting them.

The historical evidence further shows that he just wished all of this away, so that he could get on with his Great Society. There is also evidence that Johnson wanted to keep any semblance of a change in policy in Vietnam out of the public view. Both Bundy and McNamara tried to convince him that the US was headed in a far different direction with the use of airpower against the North. They recommended that the President should inform the public of this fact. LBJ chose not to inform the Congress, or the Press, or the Public. His motive, of course, was that it would detract from his Great Society program.

Up to this point in the Vietnam problem, that is late February and into the first week of March 1965, LBJ had placed his hope in just a little more of this or that would convince the North to desist its actions in supporting the war in the South. In early 1964, he had given permission for covert actions, increased the number of American advisors to South Vietnam, and given South Vietnam's revolving governments more aid to hopefully stop the instability.

Then in late 1964 he had given permission for airstrikes in retaliation for Northern actions in the Gulf of Tonkin, and for VC attacks in the South. Following these 'tit for tat' raids, now LBJ had given his authorization to 'unleash' an American bombing operation to show resolve, meaning 'you Communist North Vietnamese guys should realize who you are against.' None of it was working. The Vietnam conflict was still a dilemma that ROLLING THUNDER had not solved. The hopes for an easy victory using limited air strikes to persuade the enemy to give up had not worked.

The President and his top civilian advisors could not understand why the North Vietnamese continued to not respond as a rational actor would. Did they not realize that they were dealing with the United States of America? Did they not understand that the US had defeated two great world powers nearly simultaneously in the Second World War? Did they not know America had rebuilt the postwar world and contained the spread of Soviet Communism in Europe?

As explained in Mark Clodfelter's study of the bombing campaign in his *Limits of Air Power*, "It seemed inconceivable [to Johnson and his advisors] that the lightly armed and poorly equipped Communist forces could maintain their momentum against, first, increasing amounts of American assistance to the Vietnamese Army, and subsequently, American bombing,"

LBJ and his advisors did not know or even suspect that the Democratic Republic of Vietnam Politburo had decided to go to war to defeat the South before any more American military force could be brought to bear. As we will see in Chapter 7 ahead, the communist leaders were intent on taking advantage of American reluctance to employ force, while they intended to impose a military solution on the South Vietnamese by defeating its Army, toppling its government, all before the Americans could react.

But how could the American leaders know this intent? They did not even know who was in charge or know what the North Vietnamese strategy was. Now, in March 1965, all the US had was an unbridled belief that it could convince someone they did not know, or even care to know, that just showing its muscle was enough, in Johnson's words, to "whip the hell out of them…kill more VC…and win" in South Vietnam.

Section 3.3 - LBJ Goes to War

Many of ROLLING THUNDER's air bases were in South Vietnam. As the situation there grew worse, these bases were at growing risk to attack. General Westmoreland asked for US troops to protect them. Without much controversy, though he had voiced to one Senator that committing the marines was a substantial step toward war, the President approved two battalions of Marines for the most important bases operating out of the northern provinces of South Vietnam. On 8 March 1965 Marines out of Okinawa landed at Da Nang, South Vietnam. Their mission was to protect the airbase complex there.

Soon after the Marines arrival, LBJ, McNamara, Bundy, and Rusk met at Camp David to discuss what to do next. Previously, LBJ had been on the phone with President Eisenhower and several of his close associates in the Senate. Once again, he had gotten conflicting advice from them. IKE was supportive of military action and encouraged Johnson to support his military commanders should he choose to commit significant ground forces. His Senate colleagues continued to advise restraint and offer sympathy to the President's predicament.

For sure, Johnson was disturbed that the easier way of bombing had yet no effect on the North's actions. However, he was equally disturbed about making a decision to commit ground combat troops to the South. In the end, he indicated that he would not abandon the South. He told those present at Camp David that to do so would to be the equivalent of what the British did at Munich in 1938. With no further discussion, it seemed to all present that withdrawing could not be an option.

General Harold Johnson Visit to Vietnam, March 1965

Just before the marine landing at Da Nang, the President had dispatched Army Chief General Harold Johnson on a fact-finding tour in Saigon. Before leaving, LBJ met with the General. Pressing his finger against his chest, he said, "Now get things bubbling." He also told him to return with recommendations that would not draw public attention to any escalation of the war. The Army General departed Washington with directions from McNamara that included an assumption that there would be "no limitation on funds, equipment or personnel."

In a week-long visit, General Johnson met with Taylor and Westmoreland and got an ear full of bad news. The MACV commander thought that only the use of US military ground force could now save the South from defeat. He also felt it would take significant numbers. Taylor, on the other hand, was reluctant about the ground forces. He still believed that the North would give in to sustained bombing. However, he also knew from what LBJ had told him in late 1964, that the President did not think that bombing by itself would work, and was willing to commit US combat forces to turn the table on the North. Thus, in these discussions the Ambassador did not forcibly object to the introduction of Army forces on the ground.

The Army Chief, himself a survivor or the infamous Bataan Death march, did not pull any punches when he returned to Washington. On 14 March, less than a week after the Marines had first landed in Da Nang, General Johnson provided his report to McNamara, the JCS, and the President. The Army Chief's report said that the US would lose the war in Vietnam if it did not commit ground forces there.

The General estimated that it would take up to 500,000 troops and five years to complete the mission. He further listed three categories of actions with over twenty specific measures of recommendations. Among these, as described in the Joint Chiefs of Staff official history, was the "emplacement of a US or SEATO anti- infiltration cordon of at least four divisions below the Demilitarized Zone and across the Laotian panhandle" to stop infiltration. No one, as McNamara recalled in his memoirs, had been thinking in terms of the numbers of personnel that General Johnson had mentioned in his recommendations, much less actions in other areas of Indochina.

Meanwhile, the Joint Staff continued its estimates of what forces would be necessary. So did General Westmoreland. Unlike the JCS, the Pacific Command or the Defense Department, the MACV commander was trying to reconcile his thoughts on the size of the US force needed to stem the tide against the communist forces with the genuine logistics problem of supporting them in a very austere environment. Thus, he began to outline to his superiors in Hawaii and Washington what he thought would be needed in reinforcements and his general concept for their use. This outline, called 'Estimate of the Situation' also went to McNamara, who ignored it.

On 15 March the President called a rare meeting of the JCS in the White House. He wanted to discuss General Johnson's report and recommendations. Exhibiting his often-used tactic of talking tough, LBJ told them that he would take any action necessary to 'kill more VC' to win the war. As related in the JCS official history, he also told the Chiefs that he would hold them accountable to improve the situation in Vietnam, and wanted them to come back and recommend ways to do that.

As reported in some sources, the Marine Corps Commandant General Wallace Greene immediately recommended that the President approve sending additional Marines to set up beachheads or enclaves along the coast from Da Nang all the way to the Mekong Delta. LBJ seemed pleased to receive such a recommendation but was adamant that sending large combat units at this stage may invoke Chinese intervention. He ended the gathering by approving 'in principle' General Johnson's recommendations, but would hold off on the deployment of large ground forces for the time being.

April Fool's Day: Offensive Operations Authorized to 'Kill More VC'

Two weeks later President Johnson, in a meeting on 'April Fool's Day,' met again with the JCS and other advisors about Vietnam, to include Bundy, McNamara, and Rusk. General Wheeler reemphasized messages from both Ambassador Taylor and General Westmoreland that the VC, supported now by contingents of regular North Vietnamese units, were winning the war. He told the President that the JCS were recommending the deployment of three US Army divisions to prevent South Vietnam from 'losing the war.' The Chairman also wanted a reserve call-up to both support this deployment and replenish the strategic reserve in the US.

McNamara and Rusk, according to the Department of Defense official history, recommended "deferring any decision on the JCS proposals", but said that the deployment of some additional forces, especially support units, could prepare the way for any future need to reinforce the South Vietnamese forces in their fight. The President agreed and decided upon the deployment of some added Marine battalions with a support force for a total of 20,000 men.

This decision, issued on 6 April, was codified in NSAM 328 entitled "Decisions With Respect to Vietnam." The most important action in this memo was its paragraph 7. It stated, "The President approved a change of mission for all Marine Battalions deployed to Vietnam to permit their more active use under conditions to be established and approved by the Secretary of Defense in consultation with the Secretary of State." While LBJ emphasized to his senior advisors that his approvals in the memo should be "understood" as "wholly consistent with existing policy," the memo categorically changed the missions of US combat forces deploying to Vietnam from purely defensive to "permit their more active use."

Despite the President's caveat on his decision, it de facto gave the go-ahead to General Westmoreland to use US combat forces offensively – something the General had been clamoring for over the last several weeks. Whether President Johnson wanted to admit it or not, the US involvement in Vietnam had taken a decisive turn toward an American War.

One primary reason that LBJ agreed to change the mission is that McNamara argued that the use of US ground forces in Vietnam would send a further signal to the North that the US was serious. In conjunction with the bombing campaign, the Secretary reasoned, the presence of US troops on the ground fighting alongside South Vietnam forces would show greater resolve. Certainly then, he felt, the North would come to reason and cease its aggression. What no one in the Administration discussed in any detail was what would be the likelihood of the Communist North Vietnamese leaders' abdication, or what was the general strategic concept for the use of these US ground forces.

Almost a week after the April 1st Fool's Day meeting the President gave a nationally televised address on TV on Vietnam at Johns Hopkins University. He reiterated the US commitment to guarantee the independence of South Vietnam and freedom from aggression. He also vowed to continue to seek a negotiated settlement should the North Vietnamese show that they were ready to discuss one. However, he reemphasized that the goal to keep South Vietnam, and all Southeast Asia, from being communist had been and still is in the vital interest of the US.

Much of the Johns Hopkins speech reflected Johnson's uncertainty on what to do in Vietnam at this time. Over much of his tenure in office up to this moment, he was reluctant to execute his responsibilities as Commander-in-Chief forcefully and effectively. Some of this, as already explained, was his lack of knowledge and dislike for foreign and military affairs. These were alien to him. However, much of it was due to an innate fear of failure and need to attract sympathy for his situation as a reluctant wartime President.

This fear and need for sympathy for his plight are apparent in many of his continued telephone discussions with fellow politicians recorded and preserved in the Presidential Tapes. In looking at the transcripts and listening to the tapes of telephone calls with his former Congressional colleagues like Fulbright, Russell, Mansfield, Dirksen, and McCormick, Johnson's attempts to get them to show empathy for the Vietnam dilemma is startling.

They also are indicative of his reluctant performance as a Commander-in-Chief of the US Armed Forces about to go to war. He blames his advisors from time to time as presenting inadequate and often poorly thought out solutions. He is unmerciful in his description of his military advisors who, he says, are trying to get him deeper into a war without regard to the consequences.

Furthermore, though LBJ often gives the impression in these conversations that he had in-depth discussions with his military advisors about what to do in Vietnam, up to this point in the Spring of 1965, despite Westmoreland's messages outlining a way ahead for use of more ground combat forces, there had been no systematic discussion in Washington of any national military strategy for the unfolding changes in South Vietnam. There had been some talk and debate about keeping American troops in enclaves along the coast to protect major population areas and bases, with limited spoiling attacks against VC bases in South Vietnam. Most of that, however, was discussion amongst staff officers, or limited, fleeting discussions in small meetings of senior advisors, or some articles in the press.

With the change in mission at the April Fools' Day meeting, both Westmoreland and Wheeler continued working to obtain more US ground combat units to Vietnam to stem the tide of VC victories. Pressing the need for more troops was the recent intelligence that the VC, and its now supporting North Vietnamese Army regular forces, were planning to finish the South Vietnamese military off before the US got more combat forces into the South. Confronted with this revealing intelligence, in Washington Wheeler and the JCS took the initiative to convince the President to give Westmoreland the troops he needed to stem the tide.

On 8 April, they once again met with Johnson at the White House to give their views on the numbers of troops that MACV needed to keep the VC at bay and prevent the South Vietnamese government from falling. They also wanted to clarify his earlier statement that to win we must 'kill more Viet Cong.' LBJ, according to McMaster's account, wanted to make clear to the Chiefs that he expected results from them in Vietnam, despite the restrictions he has imposed on the air strikes and limitations on calling up the reserves.

The President opened the meeting, which McNamara also attended, asking for an assessment of the ROLLING THUNDER operations. Wheeler and the Air Force Chief General McConnell both gave dismal assessments of the bombing operations and recommended the lifting of current restrictions. This set the President off on a tirade of blaming the military for the poor results and saying, "I want you to tell me how to win." LBJ then went on and said, "You're graduates of the Military Academy and you should be able to give me an answer." He then told them to come back with the answers on how to kill more Viet Cong." Johnson finally reiterated his previous pledges "to spend the money and, if necessary move the JCS to Saigon to improve the situation."

For most of that meeting, McNamara stayed silent. As Secretary of Defense, he had not fulfilled his responsibility to press for better guidance than 'kill more VC." As the one senior civilian advisor responsible to the President to ensure a thorough discussion of the strategic implications of going to war in Vietnam, he had failed to do so and would continue to fail. As for the LBJ's actions up to this point, General Wallace Greene - in the extensive notes he kept of his meetings with the President - noted that Johnson "did not seem to grasp the military details of what can and cannot be done in Vietnam." As we will see, this was a vast understatement of this Commander-in-Chief's inability to understand the use of force and his responsibility to give clear guidance ot his senior military advisors and commanders.

After this meeting, LBJ met further with his closed group at one of his Tuesday luncheons. Present were Bundy, Rusk, McNamara, and a few other close associates, such as his confidant Clark Clifford. At that meeting, Johnson agreed to the deployment of an Army brigade already forward stationed in the Pacific to boost US signals to the North Vietnamese.

The next day on 15 April McNamara dispatched a directive approved by the President that called for several 'experimental steps' that "must be added to the South to achieve victory." One of these 'steps' included the "introduction of a brigade-size force into the Bien Hoa-Vung Tau areas, both to act as a security force for our installations and also to participate in counter-insurgency combat operations." Another step called for the "introduction of a battalion or multi-battalion forces into 2 or 3 additional locations along the coast…to experiment further with US forces in a counter-insurgency role."

Thus, despite the recent intelligence that the North was intent on defeating the South before US combat forces could 'stem the tide,' the President and his principal civilian advisors continued to cling to their hope and belief in a gradual approach to convince the communist Politburo leaders to give up and negotiate an end to the war.

After these early April discussions and decisions, McNamara held a conference in Honolulu on 20 April to discuss the future of the war. There McNamara discussed with Westmoreland, Taylor, Wheeler, and Sharp US troop deployments. The Secretary of Defense convinced Taylor, who had resisted sending US forces in large numbers and had protested the 15 April directive, to accept the need for an increase in US ground forces to reverse the situation in country by mid-1965. The levels then agreed to amounted to an increase to 82,000 from what was then present. They also agreed that another 41,000 at some later date would deploy if the President approved.

The group further discussed goals for the war which the US would now dominate. Without setting a time limit, they agreed that the object was to deny the North Vietnamese and VC a victory – a vague one but one that was at least consistent with those already officially proclaimed. When he returned to Washington, McNamara told the President that in one or two years, with the troop levels discussed, the US could "demonstrate VC failure in the South."

Not aware of what their defense secretary was telling the President about objectives, Westmoreland and Sharp returned to their commands to devise a theater military strategy for the possible employment of US combat ground forces to defend South Vietnam from Communist aggression and deny the VC a victory.

May 1965 would be a month of firsts for the future of US military involvement in Vietnam. The first Army brigade size (3000 soldiers) combat unit deployed to Vietnam – the 173rd Airborne Brigade out of Okinawa. Westy would employ it shortly in combat against VC and PAVN main force base areas northwest of Saigon.

Meanwhile, President Johnson ordered the first orchestrated halt in the bombing of North Vietnam in the hopes of getting the DRV leadership to the negotiating table. This was the first of several such halts seeking a negotiated peace over the next three years. The North Vietnamese refused – the first of many refusals to come to the peace table and abandon their aggression. They also took advantage of the bombing halt to further build up their forces in the South to defeat the Southern armed forces and topple its government before the US could prevent that from happening.

The 7 June 1965 Westmoreland "Bombshell" Message

Despite all the signals that McNamara had told the President that the North would take into consideration, on 11 May the VC, with NVA units participating, launched an all-out offensive in the South to split South Vietnam in half and eventually defeat the ARVN. After a series of major battles from the end of May through the first couple of days in June, the ARVN lost heavily and conceded large chunks of territory. This set back was even though at the beginning of June there were more than fifty thousand US troops in South Vietnam with another thirty thousand on the way. From Saigon, both Westmoreland and Taylor warned that "further VC victories might lead to a complete collapse of the ARVN."

On 7 June, seeking to get formal approval of the troops he needed to stem the tide of the communist offensive, Westmoreland sent, as McNamara calls it in his memoirs, a 'bombshell' memo. Sending his message to the JCS and McNamara after he had coordinated with Ambassador Taylor and Admiral Sharp, the MACV commander once again painted a dim picture of the situation in South Vietnam. He said that he saw "no course of action open to us except to reinforce our efforts in SVN with additional US or Third Country forces as rapidly as is practical during the critical weeks ahead." He then asked for 41,000 more troops as soon as possible, followed by another 52,000 later. This would bring the total US force level to 175,000 troops by the end of the year. This message became known as the '44 battalion request' in Washington circles.

In his memoirs, McNamara states, "Of the thousands of cables I received during my seven years in the Defense Department, this one disturbed me the most." There were two apparent reasons for this statement. First, the Secretary must have finally realized the magnitude of the US force commitment that a military commander on the ground said he needed to persecute the war in Vietnam. Therefore, he was caught off guard by it. This surprise was because he had been complicit in LBJ's middle of the road course of trying to keep the US commitment to the war minimal; and as if it was not even a war to the Congress and the Public.

Second, because the memo demanded a detailed look at how these forces were going to be employed, he found himself deficient in that there had been no Defense Department military strategy for the pursuit of a ground war in Vietnam. As he admits in his memoir, "I should have been more forceful in developing a military strategy and long-term plan for the force structure required to carry [the war] out." What he does not mention in his memoir is that he had not done so because he had continued to believe and advocate in the spurious and defunct approach of gradualism, despite evidence that the North was not paying any attention to it.

For the next six weeks, LBJ, McNamara and his 'Whiz kids,' and others in the Johnson Administration puzzled over what to do with this request. Interestingly, McNamara claims that he had to deal with Westmoreland's "shifting plans and requirements' with no clear explanation of how the forces were to be used. In Westmoreland's memoirs, the General claims that he had sent several papers outlining his concept of operations to Washington for deliberation in the NSC and other meetings with the President and the Secretary. Furthermore, he had assumed "absent any word to the contrary that they had been approved."

The historical record, principally *The Pentagon Papers*, shows that Westmoreland had indeed sent several detailed analyses, concepts, and rationale for the forces he was asking for. They were clear and complete about his troop requirements and their use. He also warned that his requirements might have to shift if the enemy plans change. The General had further cautioned that it might take several years to defeat the communist forces. Chapters 8 and 9 will discuss in detail Westmoreland's troop requirements and his military strategy.

Regardless of who was in the dark or confused, the request caught the attention of the President. LBJ now was asking all kinds of questions about what were these forces supposed to do; how long would it take for them to be successful; what would be the cost in terms of dollars and casualties; what would the Congressional and Public reactions be if he authorized these additional forces for deployment? At the same time that the President was making these queries, an article in the *New York Times* based on a cursory statement of a Public Affairs official reported that the US was "now involved in a land war in Asia." This report further sparked the President's concern and urgency, as well as his wrath that the war genie was out of the bottle.

The Pentagon Papers state that Westmoreland's 44 battalion request and the search for answers to questions from an upset President "stirred up a veritable hornet's nest in Washington." Over the next several weeks, administration officials – especially Bundy, McNamara, and Rusk - conducted many meetings to discuss the MACV commander's urgent request. Meanwhile, LBJ set out to minimize the damage of the *New York Times* June article and other news about a pending increase in US deployments, and rumors of a significant change in Administration policy. As usual, he decided to conduct a series of telephone discussions with key people in the Congress.

LBJ started on 8 June with Senator Mike Mansfield, who was then the Senate Majority Leader. He was known as an expert on Southeast Asia in general and Vietnam specifically. He had often traveled there over the years and had become disturbed about the militarization of US actions there. The Senator had just recently written a series of memos to the President explaining his opposition to further military involvement.

In his first call, recorded in the Miller Center's tapes and transcribed in Michael Beschloss' *Reaching For Glory*, LBJ typically set out to make Mansfield feel sorry for the pressures and lack of definitive answers he was getting from his policy advisors on Vietnam. At one point, he told the Senator that they had discussed getting out of Vietnam and said that he was thinking this over. He adds that none of his key advisors knew he was considering withdrawal. Saying that he was under tremendous pressure to give in to his advisors to commit major combat troops, he asks for Mansfield's advice.

As Mansfield gives alternatives to sending more troops, Johnson deftly countered the Senator's options. For example, Mansfield suggests pressuring the South Vietnamese to provide more of their soldiers to combat the North's buildup. The President dismisses this suggestion by saying that would not work because of the significant desertion rates in the ARVN. In the end, LBJ tells the majority leader that he may have to send in more troops as Westmoreland, Taylor and all his leading advisors have recommended. He further informs him that he needs his help and others in Congress to tell him what he may need from them to do so.

_{To several other less senior members of Congress, LBJ ranted about the military advice he was then getting. To Indiana Senator Vance Hartke he said, "If you'd see what some of the Joint Chiefs are recommending here to me, you'd drop the phone and go see your grandchild." To another he claimed, "Now, none of us want to do what the Joint Chiefs of Staff say you ought to do to win—and that's 'go in and bomb the hell out of them. And I'm refusing to do that." To Senator Richard Russell, he lamented that the Joint Chiefs were "awfully irresponsible… "They just scare you. They're ready to put a million men in there real quick and all that."}

In looking at this conversation and others, it is evident that Johnson is distraught over the aspect of committing the combat troops that his military advisors were recommending. However, also apparent is that his intent in making these calls was to gain sympathy for his dilemma more than getting answers from his former colleagues. He further intended to offer the semblance of consultation with Congress on his decision to send the troops and to obtain their support without having to go to the overall Congress and risk a debate over the war. It worked for his 1965 summer decision to go to war in South Vietnam. LBJ would continue to do this throughout his Presidency.

For several days after Westmoreland's request, there were constant meetings. The President again indicated in telephone calls with senior members of the Congress and in conversations with his senior civilian counsellors that all his military advisors had "no plan for victory militarily." After dozens of these calls, he ultimately turned to the man he trusted most to resolve this situation – Robert McNamara.

McNamara could not give the President what he wanted – a sure way to victory. He was personally unable to do that given his complete lack of understanding of military affairs and strategy. Besides, he still had faith in gradualism and continued to search for ways to convince the North to desist its aggression. He went to the President with a plan to introduce just enough military force to prevent the South from defeat for the next few months. He convinced the Johnson to formally approve only a part of Westmoreland's request.

In a meeting with the President on 9 June, attended by only his senior civilian advisors and including his close friend Senator Richard Russell, McNamara made his recommendation official. He proposed approval of only a little more than half of the force that Westmoreland recommended in his 7 June request. The Defense Secretary said that this force "would cover us until the end of the year." LBJ asked what the object of this limited force deployment was. McNamara and Rusk responded to produce a "stalemate in the South." However, they also said that it may yet convince the North to negotiate. LBJ approved McNamara's recommendation.

McNamara then turned his attention to selling this decision to the Chiefs and his military commanders. He solicited General Taylor's help, who agreed with McNamara on the limited reinforcement. The Ambassador, however, failed to convince Westmoreland and Sharp that this was a temporary decision based on the President's need to pave the way with Congress toward a greater commitment of force in Vietnam. The two Commanders responsible for carrying out the political objectives as expounded in the formal policy documents countered that any delay in the full reinforcement level could severely inhibit stabilizing the situation and saving South Vietnam.

McNamara was less up front with the military Chiefs. He did not inform them of what had occurred until just before a NSC meeting on 11 June. Even then the Secretary duplicitously hinted that the President was in favor of deploying Westmorland's full request and wanted to win militarily with whatever it takes, to include a possible increased bombing campaign. Then he informed the Chiefs that the Commander-in-Chief was unsure of what to do because he was unhappy that there was no definitive plan for victory from his military advisors.

At the 11 June NSC meeting with the President, however, the Chiefs were not present. General Wheeler represented them. As described in McMaster's *Dereliction of Duty*, the Defense Secretary started that meeting by saying that the Chiefs did not fully support Westmoreland's request. He used the knowledge that the Marines were unhappy with the levels of forces in the request and that the Air Force and Navy had recommended an increase in air operations over Vietnam (but had not objected to the request). General Wheeler challenged his boss's depiction of the JCS position, and - not knowing the President had already decided on the matter - argued for the approval of full deployment package.

Of course, the President supported McNamara's position that he not approve the full force reinforcement package. He ended the meeting saying, "We must delay and deter the North Vietnamese and Viet Cong as much as we can, as simply as we can, without going all out. When we grant General Westmoreland's request, it means that we get in deeper and it is harder to get out." It was apparent to all but Wheeler that the President, as the consummate politician that he had become, wanted to keep his options open. Most of all, what all did not surmise, was that the reluctant Commander-in-Chief wanted to avoid a war that could possibly derail his domestic programs.

Several weeks later US Army units in the States, among them the newest organization explicitly designed for combat in Vietnam – the 1st Cavalry Division (Airmobile) – would be alerted for deployment. Even before this organization and others could get to Vietnam, however, main force VC regiments were overrunning ARVN units in the Central Highlands on the way to splitting South Vietnam in half. Even before that – the same day as the 11 June NSC meeting - the South Vietnamese government gave way once again. Two South Vietnamese military men, Air Vice Marshal Ky, took over as Premier, while General Thieu took over as temporary President.

LBJ Wants a Guarantee for Victory

Even before he became aware of the latest adverse developments in Vietnam, LBJ, was not entirely happy with or confident in this half measure. Should the limited force and delay tactic choice fail, he needed some course to follow to prevent the fall of another Asian country to communism. Thus, during the rest of June and into July, LBJ's constant question was if he decides to fully commit to an American war to save South Vietnam 'could the US win.'

McNamara, still wedded to the gradualism approach, needed to pass the buck on this inquiry. He tried at first to get Westmoreland to give the President the assurances he was seeking. However, the MACV commander did not take the bait. He continued to answer that due to the many unknowns, especially the reaction of the North, he could not offer such a guarantee. In fact, he cautioned everyone that any success would take time. McNamara then tasked General Wheeler to come up with a strategic concept paper for whether they could 'win' the war 'if the US did everything it could to win.' Wheeler accepted this challenge and directed his assistant, Lieutenant General Andrew Goodpaster, in early July to come up with an answer.

As it turned out, Goodpaster was the perfect officer to oversee such a study. He was a rare General officer who had a reputation as a soldier-scholar with experience in political-military affairs. He had come to the position as the assistant to the Chairman of the JCS via General Maxwell Taylor, who had appointed him as his Special Assistant in 1962.

A 1939 West Point graduate, 'Andy' Goodpaster had been second in his class in academic and leadership ranking. Commissioned in the engineers, he saw extensive combat in Italy in the war. There he was wounded twice and awarded the Silver Star and Distinguished Service Cross for gallantry in action. By war's end, he had risen to the rank of Lieutenant Colonel.

After the war, he spent some time as a strategic planner for General Marshall, worked on the joint group that produced the first war plan for a potential conflict in Europe with the Soviets, and then went off to Princeton University to earn his doctorate in international relations. In 1954 President Eisenhower appointed him as his staff secretary and defense liaison officer, where he participated in IKE's national security council meetings, among other personal duties.

His rapid rise to General officer, which he attained in 1957 at the age of 42, gained him a reputation as one of the military services' most respected officers, who was also self-effacing and a team player. By July 1965, he had already participated in the Sigma war games, had worked with McGeorge Bundy as a representative of the Chairman – making several trips to Vietnam at the beginning of 1965, and served as a special liaison to Eisenhower for President Johnson.

Thus, Goodpaster was well acquainted with what was going on in Vietnam, aware of the current civilian thinking on gradual response, and knew of LBJ's desires to limit the war for fear of a Chinese intervention. However, he was not sold on this thinking or the current assumptions for limiting any potential commitment of US forces to halt the current North Vietnamese campaign. Indeed, in a meeting with McNamara on sending signals to the North to convince them to negotiate - according to one of his biographers, C. Richard Nelson - Goodpaster, cautioned McNamara, "Sir, the one thing you cannot do is program the enemy. We can program ourselves, but you have to understand that the enemy will make his own decision."

As Goodpaster was forming his study group, on 2 July, McNamara's assistant John McNaughton, having heard of Wheeler's task, decided to provide some further guidance to the General. It is interesting to examine this guidance because McNaughton was obviously trying to influence the parameters and results of the study. His memo to Goodpaster suggested that the General set as the overall US political aim to "show to the VC that they cannot win." He also suggested some of the assumptions for the study. An important one was that the "questions of calling up reserves and extending tours of duty are outside the scope of this study."

These objectives and bounding assumptions were intended to limit the scope and what was needed and how long it would take to win in Vietnam. However, they also could severely inhibit the studies' strategic concept of what was needed to execute a winning strategy. Most of all, they were in line with what McNaughton and other McNamara assistants had in mind to support their views on how to win a limited war as they had previously outlined in their memos to McNamara.

Oral testimonies after the war, described in Gibbon's Vietnam studies, show that Goodpaster did not consider McNaughton's limiting goals and guidelines. He set as the political aim what had been stated officially and written in the National Security documents: defending South Vietnam from aggression and maintaining a stable and independent non-communist government. He also would assume that the reserves would be available. Importantly, the General further assumed that the US military would be able to directly attack enemy lines of communication through Laos, and defeat any of the enemy's main forces sent to counter such a move.

As the Goodpaster study group went about its work, LBJ began efforts to build a consensus for fulfilling all of Westmoreland's request should it be necessary. From time to time he had members of Congress, some of whom he had had telephone conversations with, to the White House. There he had McNamara or Bundy brief them on the situation in Vietnam, to include updates on the bombing. All of this was to continue to show that he was consulting with Congress, albeit select individuals. He would also inform them that he had met with his team of experts outside of the Administration, called the 'Wise Men,' and obtained their views.

One such meeting in July of the 'Wise Men' specifically addressed the Westmoreland request. These men were 16 prominent Americans who had advised LBJ on foreign affairs during his 1964 election campaign. It consisted of experienced civilian and military policymakers such as former Secretary of State, Dean Acheson, ex-CIA chief, Allen Dulles, and previous Chairman of the Joint Chiefs, General Omar Bradley. They met in Washington from 8 to 9 July and attended a series of panel discussions on the issues of sending the forces.

There is no formal record of those meetings. However, Dean Acheson sent a note to President Truman on LBJ's actions and statements in a meeting at the White House on the evening of 8 July.

Acheson's observations in this letter are stark. They reveal the way LBJ was handling the crisis of deciding to go to war in the summer of 1965. They are overall enlightening of how LBJ executed his role as Commander-in-Chief at the time.

As related in Gibbons *Part III, The US Government and the Vietnam War*, Acheson wrote, "We were all disturbed by the long complaint about how mean everything and everybody was to him – Fate, the Press, the Congress, the Intellectuals and so on. For a long time he fought the problem of Vietnam (every course of action was wrong; he had no support from anyone at home or abroad: it interfered with all his programs, etc.,etc.)....I got to thinking about you and General Marshall and how we never wasted time 'fighting the problem' or endlessly reconsidering decisions, or feeling sorry for ourselves....I blew my top and told him he was wholly right on Vietnam, that he had no choice except to press on, that explanations were not as important as successful action."

Meanwhile, as both the Wise men met and as the Goodpaster group continued its work, LBJ reversed himself on the Westmoreland full reinforcement request. On 8 July he approved the deployment of the entire force package. McNamara assured him that the forces, totaling more than two-hundred thousand, would be in Vietnam by November 1. Both the Defense Secretary and the President would later renege on this promise.

While the President was trying to get sympathy for his predicament and support in Congress for his ordering American soldiers into harms' way, General Goodpaster and his ad hoc study group were completing their study on how to win in Vietnam. On 14 July, the General, after discussing it with Wheeler, sent the results to McNamara's office. The Chairman also sent copies to the other Chiefs with a note that he would discuss the results in a meeting in Vietnam with McNamara, Sharp, and Westmoreland. He told them that he would further discuss the report's conclusions upon his return. Wheeler and McNamara left for Saigon the next day.

The 128-page report outlined a military strategy for the defeat of the communist aggression in South Vietnam. It included military actions throughout the Indochina area to achieve its stated military objectives. According to excerpts of the report in the *Foreign Relations of the US*, these were: to "destroy the war-supporting power of North Vietnam"; "press the fight against VC/DRV main force units in SVN to destroy them;" and "cause them to stop the war, or to render them ineffective if they seek to pursue it."

Importantly, the main thrust of the strategy was not to rely on sending signals to the North to stop. To the contrary, the study's central concept was to employ US military forces to impose conditions on the North to force it to cease its aggression. To do so, Goodpaster set force levels that could defeat the North Vietnamese main force units and the VC in the south, while destroying the war supporting efforts of the North – to include effective interdiction of the Ho Chi Minh Trail.

Although he presumed that the Administration would not allow an invasion of North Vietnam, he did not rule out ground operations against the trail in Laos. He also envisioned an unrestricted air attack against the North and the mining of its major ports. The only exceptions were that there would be no use of nuclear weapons and no mass bombing of the North's population. The study also assumed that there would be no armed intervention by the Chinese and the Soviets. It concluded, "within the bounds of reasonable assumptions… there appears no reason we cannot win if such is our will – and that will be manifested in strategy and tactical operations."

Just before Goodpaster completed his study, McNamara, puzzled by the President's turn around on the Westmoreland force request but determined to find out how this force was to be employed, called for a meeting in Saigon with his military commanders on their views of their use. General Wheeler would accompany him, along with his most trusted advisor, John McNaughton.

General Goodpaster went with McNamara and Wheeler on their mid-July trip to Saigon. While there, the Chairman and his assistant discussed the study's results with McNamara and Westmoreland. As McNamara recalls in his memoirs, he was uneasy with the study's findings. The Defense Secretary did not like the assumptions about the restrictions and authorizations. Especially worrisome to him were the expectations that there would be a call-up of the reserves, no restrictions on the bombing of the North, and ground attacks beyond the borders of South Vietnam. He asked the General to alter these. Goodpaster replied that without those he would not report that they could win. The Secretary allowed them to stay.

Westmoreland and his superior Admiral Sharp were comfortable with the study. They believed it closely reflected their views about how to conduct the war. The study also, according to Westmoreland's recollection and official Army histories, detailed the phases and forces needed to carry out proper military objectives to achieve the established political aims of the Administration.

McNamara later reflected in his memoirs that he "clearly erred by not forcing – then or later, in Saigon or Washington - a knock-down, drag-out debate over the loose assumptions, unasked questions, and thin analyses underlying our military strategy in Vietnam." In truth, as most of the historical record shows, McNamara fully supported even the assumption on mobilization and the need to attack the lines of communication at the time. As for those 'loose analyses,' neither he or his assistants, really studied or analyzed the strategic concepts of the Goodpaster study's or Westmoreland's military strategy sent to Washington. In their stead, they continued to rely on the same statistical analyses that had made them fortunes in the business world.

As explained in Gibbons' Vietnam Study, and in an oral interview that Goodpaster did years later, McNamara never passed the study on to the President. Nor did he use it as part of wider discussions. While the study made it to Bundy's desk, he labeled it as background for later discussions on Vietnam. It ended up in the dusty bins of the Johnson Presidential Library.

The Goodpaster study is the nearest document that explains what the US military in Washington – at least those who worked on the study - was thinking of a national military strategy for victory in Vietnam. It stated that to be successful, the US had to impose its will upon the enemy to force it to give up its aggression in Vietnam. Its military strategy rejected the use of force as signals to convince the enemy that it could not win. It also recognized that the military strategy that was necessary for achieving victory had to be regionally and not just locally oriented – that US force had to be applied and coordinated throughout the Indochina and Southeast Asia region, not just in South Vietnam.

Most remarkably, in retrospect, is that the critical concept for the strategy was to isolate the battlefield in the South from its support from the North. To do this, the key operational maneuver was to strike against the Ho Chi Minh Trail in Laos with enough ground forces to prevent the North from using it as its lifeline to the South.

The Road to War Meetings in July 1965

After McNamara's return from Saigon in July, LBJ indicated that he would formally approve committing major combat forces to save South Vietnam. However, informed by his Defense Secretary on the size of future troop deployments and the possible length of the conflict, the President worried over the magnitude of these and future deployments, and the Congressional and public reactions to them. He was aware, as well, that the JCS was worried over replenishing the strategic reserve, which would have to support Vietnam deployments. He was also mindful that McNamara and the JCS would be asking for his permission to execute specific mobilization laws.

There were several reasons that LBJ would indicate in the next several weeks that he would not permit the numbers of reinforcements in the year ahead that he had approved, and the mobilization measures that his chief advisors recommended. First, was the need not to alarm Congress on the full potential of the costs. This was especially because he had an unprecedented number of domestic programs already in the legislative process that he needed to get through and approved over the next year. Second, as mentioned in his memoirs, he was worried about Chinese and Soviet reactions to putting the US on a war footing. Finally, it just went against his natural political instincts to give the military everything they wanted. He did not trust the military who had not provided, to his satisfaction or as far as he knew, a way ahead that would guarantee victory.

In his memoirs, *Vantage Point*, LBJ gives further insight and justification into his reasoning. He states, "I believed that we should do what was necessary to resist aggression, but we should not be provoked into a major war…. We would not make threatening noises to the Chinese or the Russians by calling up the reserves in large numbers. At the same time, we would press hard on the diplomatic front to try to find some path to a peaceful solution."

However, the President's thinking did not account for the thinking or motivation of his enemies. Though there were ample intelligence estimates on enemy intentions and capabilities, none of his senior civilian advisors brought them to his attention, much less have a discussion on them. Besides, the President, Bundy, and McNamara all thought that they would respond to US actions, as they would.

LBJ's limitations, and similar ones that followed, would have a significant impact on the conduct of the war. Without specific mobilization authorizations units deploying to Vietnam could not allow individuals with less than a certain amount of time to go in their service to deploy with the unit. This deprived specific units, such as the Army's only airmobile division, of key leaders and other soldiers who had been training in preparation for combat in Vietnam. It would also affect the overall authorized strength of the units deploying as well as the equipment and armaments they would need.

In addition, the Army depended on specific support units in the reserve forces in its structure for logistical and sustainment operations. Being deprived of these, had a considerable influence on the ability of Westmoreland to build up and support combat units in Vietnam. Finally, the impact on the Army worldwide was critical. To make up for forces and individuals not mobilized, the Army would have to draw from units stationed in other overseas areas, such as Europe. That would have a significant effect on the readiness of those units to perform their missions. Chapters 8 and 9 will further discuss the military impacts of the President's decision not to call up the reserves on the conduct of the war and its operations, as well as other restrictions.

From 21 to 28 July LBJ and his civilian advisors would focus on three main tasks. First, they needed to struggle with exactly how to fund the deployments that the President had approved.

Second, they needed to convince the military that they would not be able to do everything they wanted to do – like increase bombing operations, execute a blockade against North Vietnam, and execute mobilization measures. And finally, they needed to hide the potential full costs of the war and any domestic impacts on the Congress and Public.

To accomplish all of the above, LBJ had to bring on board his 'team' of military advisors and commanders, get their acquiescence on his 'limited war' restrictions, and show to the Public and Congress that his Administration was in unanimous agreement on how to fight in Vietnam and win. Thus, though he had already in principle approved the Westmoreland June requests, the President needed to hold counsel enough to convince himself and his advisors in Washington that he had done everything possible to justify his overall war decisions.

The centerpiece of the meetings, consultations, and discussions from 21 to 27 July - culminating in a public announcement to send significant combat troops to defend South Vietnam - were three options that McNamara had developed and sent out for discussion after his mid-July visit to Saigon. These options, as depicted in the Defense Department official history of the Vietnam War were: "(1) a humiliating withdrawal; (2) holding on at current levels; or (3) escalating US military pressure." Curiously, these options had been the same ones that McNamara and Bundy, and their assistants, had been discussing since mid-1984.

George Ball, recalling his participation in these deliberations, said of these options, "Working groups of seasoned bureaucrats deliberately control the outcome of a study assignment by recommending three choices, exploiting what we referred to as 'the Goldilocks Principle.' By including with their favored choice one too soft and one too hard, they assume that the powers deciding the issue will almost invariably opt for the one just right." In this case, it was option (3) that was 'just right.' It was the one that both McNamara and Bundy had thought the best one to follow given the dilemma they had discussed and described already in this chapter.

Moreover, in the author's experience in the Pentagon and with similar deliberations on important national security issues, the wording of the options is also important to controlling the choice. In this instance, option one included 'humiliating,' and option two had 'holding on.' The first word connotated defeat, while the second phrase indicated more of the same leading to nowhere. However, 'escalating' indicated continued calculated control over the situation.

According to the Defense Department history and the State Department's *Foreign Relations of the United States*, LBJ's officials gathered several times a day over the next six days for deliberations. The first meetings with the President were on 21 and 22 July. Each would consist of several sessions of two to three hours and be in the cabinet room in the White House. The July 21 meeting consisted of three sessions. The first was a preparation gathering in the morning. The next two involved the President from 11:30 until 1:00 PM, and then from 2:30 until 5:30. At the two with the President, discussions focused on the McNamara options and gaining LBJ's inputs on them as well an attempt on the President's part to reach a consensus on a recommendation.

The 21 July meetings focused on a series of questions that LBJ asked about the viability of the RVN government and could we be successful in a war in which they are so unpopular and unstable. The President also inquired about the level of troops and what were they supposed to do; could they fight successfully in the terrain of Southeast Asia; when would he be forced to decide on mobilization; and can we win given the forces recommended?

General Wheeler told the President that the forces were prepared and could engage the VC successfully especially given their mobility using helicopters. He also countered some of the civilian and President's concerns about finding such an elusive enemy. He emphasized that Westmoreland would be going after the enemy's main forces, and by continuing to conduct offensive operations this would force them to fight.

All except Under Secretary of State George Ball felt that McNamara's option three (to escalate military pressure by sending the forces that Westmoreland asked for and by continuing the bombing of the North) was the best option to pursue. No one, however, was willing to ensure success if the President decided for that option. LBJ ended the meeting asking that George Ball suggest an alternative to McNamara's three that may warrant further consideration.

In the afternoon session of 21 July, the focus was on an alternative that Secretary Ball offered. The alternative he proposed, according to the notes in the *FRUS* of the meeting, was to fight for one more year and if not successful "to let the GVN decide it doesn't want us" and get out of Vietnam. That incited a flurry of backlash from the others.

The theme they all followed was that such a course would be disastrous in that it would give the wrong signal to our allies, encourage communist support to other wars of national liberation, and would not be as costly as Ball estimated in dollars and casualties. Wheeler added that getting out after only one year of fighting was unreasonable because there was no way that we could show any success or evaluate our combat effectiveness in that limited period.

The President made no decision. The meetings continued. There would be another at the White House the next day, several further gatherings at Camp David from the 24th to the 27th, and the last one on the 28th at which LBJ chose to follow McNamara's option three. In so doing, he formally approved the 44 battalion force deployments with some modifications, primarily in timing. Moreover, ten of those battalions would come from other countries, like from Korea and Australia.

Most importantly, Johnson decided not to call up the reserves. He also told McNamara to minimize the necessary budget request for Congress' approval. As an alternative, the Secretary would delay further budget requests until the following year and raise draft calls. He also decided against the JCS and Admiral Sharp recommendations for increased bombing against an expanded target list, and a blockade of North Vietnamese ports. He further emphasized that his advisors would treat his decision, not as a change of policy but just an increase in 'requirements to meet that policy."

The dismay of the Chiefs over the lack of mobilization is succinctly described in the JCS History. "The Joint Chiefs were dismayed by this development, which they knew
would slow down the deployment of the requested forces, cause long-term deterioration
of readiness in their Services, and degrade the United States' ability to respond to other
contingencies. Nevertheless, individually and collectively, the Joint Chiefs of Staff supported their Commander in Chief; they defended his policy in administration councils
and meetings with Congressional leaders."

The official history continues and states that "At the 27 July NSC meeting General Wheeler remained silent when the President asked for objections to his plan. General Johnson, who would see the Army nearly wrecked by the attempt to wage war without mobilization, eventually considered resigning in protest. In the end, he joined the other Chiefs in acquiescence—a decision he later characterized as the worst, the most immoral of his career. "

In sum, the Joint Chiefs were more than just the 'six silent men' whom H.R. McMaster describes in his work on their advice on Vietnam. They were men who acquiesced to a decision that they knew was wrong, was not in the best interest of the country, and placed American troops that were about to go into harms' way in grave danger.

The Curious Dissent of George Ball

Throughout the above meetings and other less formal ones, there were two leading dissenters – Clarke Clifford - at the time an informal advisor to LBJ – and Under Secretary of State George Ball. Clifford, in public forum from time to time, had agreed on actions to counter the communist aggression in Vietnam, making him seem like a hawk to many. In private, however, he had his reservations. On 25 July, at Camp David for example, he told the President "I don't' believe we can win in South Vietnam. If we send in 100,00 more, the North will meet us. If the North runs out of men, the Chinese will send in volunteers. Russia and China don't intend for us to win the war. If we don't win, it is a catastrophe. If we lose 50,000 plus it will ruin us. Five years, billions of dollars, 50,000 men, it is not for us."

But it is George Ball's dissent that has captured the eye of most historians. That is because the historical evidence shows that he appears to have been the most consistent and ardent resister to US direct military action in Vietnam. The fundamental questions are what was the nature of his dissent; what influenced his disagreement; and why did no one concur with him?

So, what was the nature of his dissent and what influenced it? As mentioned in Chapter 2, Ball, whom Kennedy had appointed as an Under Secretary in the State Department, had already objected to the insertion of US forces during the Kennedy Administration. He had done so in reaction to the Taylor-Rostow's recommendations to move combat forces into either Thailand or South Vietnam. But since Kennedy had resisted the deployment of large numbers of ground combat forces, the Under-Secretary's objections were then irrelevant, and, thus, unremarkable.

However, in the fall of 1964, as Johnson's primary advisors became more favorable to taking military action against the North and in the South, Ball decided to voice his views and doubts on the use of military force to his boss Dean Rusk, as well as to Bundy and McNamara. As recalled in Larry Berman's *Planning A Tragedy: The Americanization of the War in Vietnam*, he first did so in a memo entitled, "How Valid are the Assumptions Underlying our Vietnam Policies?"

In that paper of sixty-seven pages, Ball - as Kay Bird in *The Color of Truth* mentions -sensed "the US drift toward intervention" and questioned, "the current notion that we can take offensive action while controlling the risks." He argued that he did not think that gradual bombing or other US military actions would convince the North to desist its efforts against the South. Ball further warned of the risks of a protracted conflict with a motivated adversary, writing that "once on the tiger's back we cannot be sure of picking the place to dismount."

In subsequent discussions with the memo's addressees, according to Ball in his memoirs, "my colleagues were dead set against the views I presented and uninterested in the in the point-by-point discussion I had hoped to provoke. He further relates that McNamara treated his ideas "like a poisonous snake" and "treasonous." In McNamara's version of the meeting the Defense Secretary says that he had agreed with much of Ball's views on what needed to be done, but that his argument was "tantamount to advocating unconditional withdrawal," and that was "clearly unacceptable." The memo went nowhere at the time.

Having been encouraged by the President to play the devil's advocate, Ball took up the gauntlet again in the discussions on Vietnam from February 1965, when he objected to ROLLING THUNDER, up to the decision to intervene with combat troops in late July 1965. Many of these Devil's Advocate's ideas and arguments were in today's jargon 'out of the box.' There are three examples that best illustrate his thinking and the nature of his dissent.

First, in a May 13, 1965 memo to McNamara, Bundy, and the latter's brother William entitled "A Plan for a Political Resolution in South Vietnam," Ball proposed halting the war in the south and inviting the Viet Cong supporters to take part in the national life of South Vietnam. He thought that if the VC did not do so, then that action would provide at least justification for further US combat deployments and provide some moral support to the President that he had done everything possible to avoid war.

Second, in another memo on June 18 entitled, "Keeping the Power of Decision," Ball told LBJ that he thought "the momentum of events was taking over," thus preventing the President "from finding a way to keep control of policy." He further argued that "the best formula for maintaining freedom of action" was "to limit our commitments in time and magnitude." As Ball further explained that meant not taking any action that would commit the US to a course it could not reverse, i.e., approving increased bombing of the North and committing significant combat forces in the South. Instead, as he argued in other meetings, he called for the temporary employment of forces already there in coastal enclaves until the situation allowed for further clarification on what to do.

Finally, on June 28 he wrote a paper entitled "Cutting Our Losses in South Vietnam." Here he argued that the US should force the current South Vietnamese military leaders to "put together a government of national union under civilian leadership" or the US would reconsider its commitment and withdraw its forces. Like some of his previous arguments, this would justify a withdrawal should the South Vietnamese not comply.

In the above-described papers, Ball argued and justified his points using three major themes. The first was that the US, like the French, had made a terrible mistake in trying to find a military solution to a political problem. The second was that what was at stake for the US in Vietnam was not preserving its credibility by defending against communist aggression, but showing the world that it had the wisdom to pull out because it recognized that Vietnam was not worth the cost or in the US vital interest.

Finally, the third was that the US could justify its withdrawal by showing that it had done its best, but the South Vietnamese leaders were not worthy of support because they neither represented their people or could reasonably govern. In short, the overall nature of Ball's dissent was that Vietnam was an unwinnable war, was not in the vital interests of the US, and was not worth the cost to defend.

So why did Ball feel it necessary to object as consistently as he did? What formed his views and made them so different from his colleagues? Historians and his memoirs reveal several influences. The first was that Lyndon Johnson encouraged George Ball to do so. Historians attribute that encouragement to LBJ's need to show that he had considered all angles of a problem in reaching a consensus for a decision. Thus, the President chose Ball to be a devil's advocate to play a role that would, in turn, show that he considered disparate, even controversial views.

Was this true? Johnson seems to support that view in his memoirs indicating that Ball decided to play that role at his request. Ball admits in his recollection that LBJ wanted him to voice opposition to the prevailing views because he knew that Ball would be loyal regardless of his disagreement and not express his dissent publicly. Moreover, to many in the Administration, Ball was expected to be the voice of the counterarguments against the consensus on Vietnam from late 1964 to his resignation in 1966. Thus, Ball felt that he had an obligation or at least the opportunity to be a dissenter in an otherwise atmosphere of general consensual agreement.

However, this role-playing is not the main story of his dissent. It appears that Ball's arguments were genuine and based on his knowledge of the French experience in Indochina. Ball had in the postwar period spent much of his time as an attorney for the European Recovery team – a group that was working to implement the Marshall Plan. In that position, he spent much of his time working with French leaders in effecting their implementation of the recovery. In that work, the future US government dissident had observed, up close, what the French had practiced and experienced in Indochina in the late forties and early fifties.

Ball mentions several times in his memoirs that his involvement with the French had a significant impact on his views about Vietnam. For example, he states that "I had listened to innumerable French military and civilian experts discuss their nation's plans, fears, and doubts and shared vicariously in my French friends' agony over Dien Bien Phu."

Moreover, Professor Yuen Foong Khong masterfully demonstrates in his *Analogies of War* Ball's use of the French experience in his arguments. As he points out, the Under Secretary used analogies of the French experience, to various degrees, in all the papers and memos mentioned above. Khong observes that Ball's use of the French experience was quite masterful and, in retrospect, prophetic in that he predicted both the motivation and intransigence of the North Vietnamese in their struggle and the US public lack of support for a far-off conflict that seemed to have little interest.

Khong further elaborates, "Ball's prescience is stunning in retrospect, yet his reasoning fell on deaf ears." So Why? The Oxford professor explains, "No other high-level policymaker had intimate knowledge about, or took seriously, the French experience in Vietnam." Ball confirms this. In his memoirs, *The Past Has Another Pattern*, he writes "I knew substantially more than most of my colleagues about France's unhappy experience in Indochina." Moreover, "I knew Indochina's recent history better than most."

However, it had to be more than just a lack of knowledge of the French experience. The men whom Ball confronted were not stupid. There must have been some reason other than they did not know much about the French experience in Vietnam. They could have researched it themselves. There were ample accounts that they could have consulted.

Professor Khong again offers some insights. He states, "few senior policymakers in the Johnson Administration saw the position of the United States in 1965 analogous that of France in 1954," because "it was too much at variance with the national self-perception of most of the policymakers." Moreover, "the policy makers were uninterested in learning from losers." Ball confirms this observation. He laments, "It was useless for me to point out the meaning of the French experience; they thought that experience without relevance."

Ball offers another reason as well. He observed that many of the 'best and brightest' fell into the mindset of those who too often become enamored with the aura of power in Washington. He writes, "Men with minds trained to be critical within the four walls of their own disciplines – to accept no proposition without adequate proof – shed their critical habits and abjured the critical question why. Once they caught hold of the levers of power in Washington, they all too frequently subordinated objectivity to the exhilaration of working those levers and watching things happen."

Whatever the real reasons that Ball's arguments 'fell on deaf ears,' the 'curious dissent of George Ball' demonstrates that American policy-making over going to war in Vietnam was characterized by the inability to question the critical assumptions that the US leaders chose to believe. This, in part, resulted in their choice to fight a limited war in Vietnam without regard to historical precedence or experiences.

Moreover, the inability to question assumptions and beliefs was not the sole providence of the civilians. As we have seen, and will continue to see, military advisors and leaders had their blind spots and incapacities to question the courses they chose to follow in the prosecution of the war launched by their civilian leaders. They too will not take into consideration their enemy's past experiences and underestimate their abilities to challenge US military power in ways they had not experienced before.

The Decision for War or Something Like War

As recounted in George Herring's *LBJ and Vietnam*, on 28 July President Johnson made a televised address to the nation on Vietnam. He announced his decision to send an added 50,000 troops there, far less than he knew he had approved in Westmoreland's June request. The President also mentioned that most likely there would be others to follow, but gave no clue as to what that may entail.

In fact, by the end of 1965 LBJ would approve the deployment of some 185,000 troops to Vietnam. This would rise to nearly 500,000 by the beginning of 1968. In trying to show how difficult his decision was, he said, "I do not find it easy to send the flower of our youth, our finest young men, into battle." The President then invoked the lessons of Munich and Korea, not the French Indochina War or Dien Bien Phu, in justifying his decision.

Herring further notes that "his message was received by the media in much the spirit it was delivered, seriously, but without any sense of urgency or impending crisis. The *New York Times* gave it a modest, five-column headline." Time magazine speculated about US casualties and how long it might take to win against the communists. But its main cover story, like that of the Reluctant Commander-in-Chief, was to note "the remarkable historic week of legislative accomplishment in US history" with the passing of the Civil-Rights act – the first of many legislative actions for LBJ's Great Society.

As Herring so eloquently describes the moment, "July 28, 1965, might, therefore, be called the day the United States went to war without knowing it, and it's now clear that this was no accident. Johnson's 28 July press conference culminated six weeks of deliberation and an intensive week of meetings resulting in a decision for an open-ended military commitment in Vietnam. The press conference was also part of a carefully orchestrated strategy for waging limited war. The Johnson administration set out to fight this different kind of war, in cold blood. In Secretary of State Dean Rusk's words; that is, without mobilization and without arousing popular emotion."

Support for LBJ's decision in the Congress was widespread. According to Gibbons in his *The US Government and the Vietnam War*, while there were some naysayers such as Mike Mansfield, most agreed to support the President and fund whatever he needed for the time being. Most of that support, however, Gibbons argues was because members felt they had to support the troops.

Another reason was that polls were showing public support for LBJ's decision and the war. Gallop polls in August, for example, showed that 57% of the people approved of the way the Johnson Administration was "handling the situation in Vietnam, while only 25% disapproved. When asked whether "the US made a mistake sending troops to fight in Vietnam" a resounding 61% said it was not a mistake.

Meanwhile, in the remaining months in 1965 and into the beginning of 1966, the President, McNamara, and other civilian advisors, would focus on the rising costs of the war in budgets and programs, while reporting on the progress of the war in the South and the bombing in the North. The JCS and its military staffs would primarily focus on the risks to the US worldwide military force status and service force structures; the ability of the services to meet Westmoreland's force goals; and recommending increased efforts in ROLLING THUNDER.

General Westmoreland would be left to devise a military strategy for the war as he saw fit and within the limits of his area of responsibility and Presidential restrictions. Some would claim in Washington that he was the commander in the field, and thus it was fit and proper that he devise his way to fight the war. Westmoreland would seem at ease with being left alone at first to do so. However, this schism between the development of a theater military strategy for Vietnam, and the development of a national strategy to both direct and support it would come to haunt the execution of the war. This is a significant topic for further detailed discussion in Chapters 8 and 9.

From 1965 to 1968, Westmoreland continued to devise and then execute a theater of war strategy to employ these troops against a determined North Vietnamese and VC adversary. The General describes in his memoirs this military strategy as one of attrition – meaning, in his words, one that he had to choose because it was "dictated by political decisions." It envisioned, again in his words, "seeking, fighting, and destroying the enemy." Many, then and through the years, have criticized the effectiveness of his approach and questioned the General's reasoning for choosing it. Chapters 8 and 9 will further examine that strategy and the operations supporting it.

However, for most of the public and the later Congressional critics, the war that the Johnson Administration pursued became known as 'McNamara's War." That is because the Congress, the Public, and Press most associated it with the face of this Secretary of Defense. The images of Robert Strange McNamara remain today as a symbol of the war and his principal part in it. Those images show him in his finest scholarly appearance, wearing his wire-rim spectacles, confidently briefing with all sorts of maps and statistics, and convincingly arguing progress in the pursuit of victory.

Unfortunately, that pursuit would turn out to be a shameful anathema. The President and his Secretary would not provide all the forces or in a timely fashion that their military commander said he needed. Moreover, the civilian war managers in Washington would continually try to gradually convince their enemies to give up the fight while not providing the where with all to do so. Despite these efforts, they would not understand why the North would not bend to their demands.

The advisors' reluctant Commander-in-Chief agreed that the North Vietnam Communists must realize that they faced the strongest nation on earth, and would eventually do their bidding. So, in addition to committing the "flower of our youth, our finest young men, into battle," he would offer vast sums of money to rebuild and remake Vietnam in America's image. How, in this master politician's mind, could they not concede. As we will see, the communists had other ideas and motives that US policymakers just did not understand or choose to appreciate.

General Westmoreland's image became known to the Congress and Public as well. For the Johnson administration, he was a perfect public relations man. Primarily, they knew that he would be loyal and supportive of their policies. They could count on him to be positive, even uplifting on the military progress. After all, he was a Maxwell Taylor protégé.

Moreover, he looked like a military man who knew what he was doing. As David Halberstam wrote, "he looked like a general, the jaw jutted out, the features were forceful and handsome, there was no extra poundage…. Even Generals around him looked like Generals." Pictures on the covers of *Time* and *Life* Magazines confirm that portrait. Initially, in 1965 and 1966, public opinion polls supported the favorable view of the General who would undoubtedly bring victory in Vietnam. Moreover, why not? Westmoreland was supremely confident he would deliver.

Section 3.4 - McNamara's War

A month after his June request deployments began to arrive, Westmoreland would be ordering US units out to execute his search and destroy operational design and fight the enemy. In August Marines based along the coast engaged main force VC organizations in an operation that would demonstrate the difficulties of fighting in the numerous populated small hamlets that characterized South Vietnam's coastal areas. Enemy units there mostly chose to flee from the Marines at first.

However elsewhere, mostly in the Central Highlands region, the communist main forces, namely the North Vietnamese regulars, would be more than willing to fight when they thought they had the advantage. In November 1965, there would be a series of large engagements in a place called the Ia Drang Valley. American casualties would be in the hundreds; communist force casualties would be in the thousands. As these numbers began to pour into the halls of the Pentagon, McNamara's Whiz Kids would begin to measure and analyze them, form them into kill ratios, and report on the degree that the US was winning the war.

Westmoreland saw the Ia Drang Campaign as proof that his concept of operations would eventually kill enough enemy to deny the communists in the North their goals in South Vietnam. On the other side, Vietnamese Communist military leaders thought they had met the Americans on their terms, performed well, and could ultimately succeed with what they learned about the American way of war.

The MACV commander, though confident after his lopsided victories in November, was cautious in his first progress reports on the war. He did not want Washington to think that his initial successes meant a short war. The battles in late 1965 had prevented the North's main offensives from toppling the ARVN. Westmoreland could rightly report that he had stemmed the tide of the communist attacks to defeat the ARVN and overthrow the South Vietnamese government.

Yet, he knew that the North continued to reinforce in large numbers their forces in the South. His staff revised the estimate he had given McNamara in July for the forces he would need in 1966 to gain the initiative and launch his Phase II offensive. Westmoreland would change his reinforcement requests accordingly. McNamara, not aware that war had its own logic and could not be measured to success, became dismayed that Westmoreland's numbers still fluctuated from and did not fit into the mode of the Defense Secretary's certainty in mathematics and systems analysis.

Strategy Debates Without a Strategy

Meanwhile, debates in Washington soon surfaced on the efficacy and effectiveness of the bombing operations in the North, and reactions of the North Vietnamese to the US deployments in the South. Another JCS war game and accompanying intelligence estimate assessed that the North would increase its efforts in the South rather than cease, and would not seek any negotiations regardless of the US commitment of force. Though McNamara was aware of these results and was concerned, he continued to believe in the validity of controlled escalation to bring the North to the negotiating table.

Before the fall 1965 battles, and as the initial increments of the June requested reinforcements were reaching Vietnam, the Joint Staff had conducted another review and study of a future military strategy for the war. The JCS sent the study results to the Secretary of Defense in late August. The Chairman and the JCS were seeking McNamara's approval of the study's military strategy, and his endorsement to send it on to the President. It was a bold concept that not only was meant to fill the void of a national military strategy, but was intended to lift the main restrictions so that the US military could force, rather than convince, the North to desist its aggression.

The JCS recommendations were strikingly like those in the Goodpaster Study completed in July. As described in Gibbons' work, it recommended the lifting of many of the current restrictions of ROLLING THUNDER, attacking the Ho Chi Minh Trail with air and land forces to deny the North infiltration of its forces, and continuing the use of US forces to find, fix and destroy enemy main forces in the South. In addition, the JCS strategy recommended the deployment of other US land forces into Thailand to deter China from intervening in the war with its land forces.

Clearly the JCS recommendations were out of tune with both McNamara's and Johnson's thoughts on how to wage a limited war in Southeast Asia. The Secretary treated it accordingly. He first sent it to his right-hand man, John McNaughton, for dissection and destruction of its rationale, lack of systems analysis, and dismissal of political considerations. He did that.

McNamara then sent the JCS strategy on to McGeorge Bundy's office, where, like the Goodpaster study, it was put in a file for future consideration. The President never saw it. Later, General Wheeler would lament that not getting this recommendation approved was one of the worst mistakes he made as Chairman.

Despite this lack of consideration and approval, the JCS continued to bombard the Secretary with recommendations for increased bombing and lifting of restrictions. Admiral Sharp, the commander of Pacific Command who had overall oversight of ROLLING THUNDER, chimed in as well. Besides the increase in bombing targets, the Admiral recommended, and the JCS concurred with, the mining of the key North Vietnamese port of Haiphong.

For McNamara, the recommendation for the mining of a port that the Soviets were using to supply the Communist North's war effort represented a significant escalation of the war, and severely risked the chances of a Soviet military intervention. Moreover, yet another intelligence estimate indicated that the bombing was not hurting North Vietnam; contrary it was hardening their position on any negotiations, increasing rather than decreasing infiltration, and rallying their people to the cause. These two occurrences further shook the Secretary's hopes for a favorable end to the war and his concerns over its costs.

Consequently, from October to November 1965, as American soldiers were dying on the battlefields of South Vietnam, Secretary McNamara decided to conduct an internal office review on the war of attrition in the South and the bombing of the North. He intended to measure the progress of Westmoreland's strategy, determine the effectiveness of the bombing campaign, and recommend whether the President should approve the anticipated considerable number of deployments for 1966 as well.

As he recalls in his memoirs, the Defense Secretary says that Westmoreland's inability to guarantee victory despite the increases of forces he was requesting "was troubling" to him. He states that "I sensed things were slipping out of control" especially because the "chiefs urged expanding US air attacks against North Vietnam." To assist in his review, particularly bombing operations against the North, he recommended to the President the formation of a special study group to assess the air war effectiveness and the risks of expanding it.

That special study group, which consisted of entirely civilians inclined to support McNamara's views, came back, and warned against an expansion of ROLLING THUNDER and mining of Haiphong, which they argued risked bringing both China and the Soviet Union into the war. Not surprisingly, reflecting the views of McNamara and Johnson already well known to them, the group also recommended a substantial bombing pause that would enable serious negotiations and a possible political rather than military end to the war.

Upon reflection on the study group's recommendations, McNamara reported the result of this review to LBJ in a "Draft Memorandum From Secretary of Defense McNamara to President Johnson dated 3 November 1965." Its subject was "Courses of Action in Vietnam." It is a remarkable document given the fact that just three months ago the President had embarked upon a US war in Vietnam that McNamara had encouraged. Furthermore, the paper did not make any clearer the US purpose for the war, nor did it offer any succinct future course that could have been of any strategic military use for the President or Westmoreland.

The document begins by defining what the study group thought the political goals were for Vietnam. Despite McNamara's claims in his memoirs that they reiterated the objectives published in the NSAMs, the paper outlines a set of desired outcomes explained in "nine fundamental elements" that had nothing to do with the original official political objectives for US policy in Vietnam.

Instead, they reflected what McNamara thought that he could measure or what he desired for the unfolding conflict. These were: "DRV reduces infiltration to a trickle" …" Communists remain quiescent in Laos and Thailand" …"DRV withdraws PAVN forces and other North Vietnamese infiltrators from South Vietnam." Moreover, there was no military analysis of the feasibility or the achievability of these general outcomes that McNamara set as future US desires.

The body of the document then lists and describes a series of what the memo labeled "military variables," "Illustrative scenarios;" and "Considerations." The variables and scenarios were a combination of actions for bombing, reinforcement levels, and diplomatic initiatives. McNamara portrayed these combined actions as gradual signals to the North that he hoped would solicit a favorable reaction from the communist leaders for a diplomatic solution.

The memo concluded with a recommendation for its "Hard-Line Pause, then evolving Rolling Thunder, and then Phase II." As described in the memo that meant an extended bombing pause to allow time for the North Vietnamese to consider US proposals for negotiation, followed by the continuance of the bombing of the North - which would not be intensified as the JCS was recommending but remain limited - followed by the execution of the Phase II reinforcements. Even this option, the memo explained did not ensure the achievement of the favorable outcomes. It stated, "the odds are even that, despite our efforts, we will be faced in early 1967 with stagnation at a higher level and with a need to decide whether to deploy Phase III forces, probably in Laos as well as in South Vietnam."

This memo is extraordinary for several reasons other than it further confused US aims for South Vietnam. The first is that McNamara, despite the decision to use significant military force in Vietnam, continued to rely on his belief in a calculated, gradual management of signals to convince the North to stop its aggression. This is despite the evidence in all the assessments over the last months that the DRV was increasing its efforts in the face of the bombings and commitment of major US forces to combat.

Second, regardless of past communist actions to refuse to negotiate, McNamara was once again recommending a pause to implore them to do so. What made it such an outrageous recommendation is that US forces were now involved in combat and dying, and such a pause was sure to give the North a military advantage. The third reason is that McNamara had not only ignored the earlier JCS recommendation of a military strategy in his memo, but he had not included any consultation with the military in the drafting of his courses of action in this document.

After several meetings with the President in November and in early December, the President agreed to a bombing pause and to further address the Phase II deployments in Honolulu at the beginning of the next year. The pause, without prior knowledge of the military commanders in the field, went into effect over the Christmas holidays and into January, ending at the end of that month. It included some revised 14 US negotiating points.

Not surprising, the North Vietnamese denounced the pause and the peace points as tricks. They not only continued their attacks against the ARVN and US forces but, taking advantage of the bombing pause, once again increased their infiltration of troops and supplies dramatically.

Though the pause had given the North an ideal opportunity to reinforce its units in the south, Westmoreland continued to execute his attrition strategy in a vacuum of any real overarching military guidance from Washington. Over the course of the next year, in pursuit of his 'big unit war' as later critics would call it, several large engagements with the North Vietnamese and VC main units resulted in huge enemy losses.

The kill ratios, which McNamara had set as the key variable to measure whether the enemy was losing more forces than he could provide to the conflict, seemed to indicate some success in the ground war in the south. The Secretary's staff of Whiz Kids were now demanding and analyzing kill ratios on a regular basis to determine the cost-effectiveness of the war and to recommend future force deployments.

Throughout 1966, Westmoreland continued to report that his big battles prevented the enemy from executing their strategy of dividing the country and overwhelming the South Vietnamese forces. At the end of that year, the MACV commander was ready to execute his offensive phase of his theater strategy. Though he would not get all the forces he continued to ask for, the General would continue to report successes in more big battles based on field 'body counts.' McNamara's staff would take his body count reports and continue to measure kill ratios.

Doubts, Protests, and Persistence

Despite reports of progress, there was growing dissent and opposition in the US over the war, especially as US casualties rose. Some just did not understand why we were fighting a major war in such a faraway place that no one had ever heard of before. The rhetoric of their Government that this was somehow vital to our national interests just did not make sense to them. Others grew cynical of the constant reference to battle deaths or 'body counts' that seemed to dominate the US Government's measure of progress. Others just did not feel that the US was doing everything it could to win.

Yet others protested because, despite Johnson's attempt to wage war without it affecting Americans, the draft potentially changed their lives. The selective service law was unfair. Its deferments allowed too many educated and well-off men to escape service. The draft seemed to select many from lower-middle-class citizens and minorities. This exasperated many men, and their families, who were just starting their young lives. Many asked themselves why should I give up the opportunities that the times provided for education and economic advancement?

Johnson's actions caused much of this exasperation and dissent. The President, wanting to downplay the war and not wanting to incite emotions for it, avoided convincing Americans that the war in Vietnam as one that was in the dire interest of the US. LBJ himself had said that he would not send American boys to do what Asian boys should be doing. Now he was doing just that. Moreover, his July 1965 announcement indicated that the employment of US combat forces would be limited. The President, after all, wanted to negotiate, not wage war. This all confused many Americans, and encouraged the communists.

The news media coverage of the war was becoming even more critical and dubious about the rationale and achievability of the stated goals as the war progressed. This was primarily so as Americans began to shed blood for a South Vietnamese Government and its Army that seemed corrupt and incompetent. The media now also brought the fighting and dying into the living rooms of many families through the TV, which had become a mainstay of American life. It was not comfortable for mothers and fathers to see US soldiers killed and wounded.

Some protests were peaceful and well organized. Some were radical and violent. They began to affect the Administration. One protest at the Pentagon resulted in a person taking his own life outside of the offices of the Secretary of Defense. McNamara was visibly shaken. Although Johnson tried to publicly dismiss the growing numbers of protests, they affected him as well. He continually watched the TV coverage – particularly that of Walter Cronkite, the most famous newscaster of the day (Chapter 4 presents in more detail the domestic reactions to the war summarized above and their effect upon the government).

As the battles raged in South Vietnam and on TV sets in America, both Johnson and McNamara were beginning to have frustrations and further doubts about its progress. LBJ was always on his telephone to his former Senate colleagues telling them his misgivings about how the military was conducting the war.

The President's chief theme during these discussions was his effort to keep it limited to avoid escalation and intervention by the Chinese and Soviets. He was also concerned about the need for the South Vietnamese to do more of the fighting, and the necessity to improve pacification efforts. He continued to voice his discontent with the American military. He blamed the failure of his efforts to convince the North Vietnamese to negotiate an end to the conflict on the US generals. LBJ expressed his frustrations to some of his closest Senate friends and told them that the military brass wanted to keep the war going for their advancement.

By the beginning of 1967, with the Chairman of the Joint Chiefs and the Army Chief giving warning signs of the effects of the Vietnam deployments on the force and the budget beginning the strain, McNamara continued to delay and then hold back some of Westmoreland's requested reinforcements. Unknown at first to the American military commanders in the field, the Secretary was now telling the President that he should level-off force levels in Vietnam, accept a stalemate, and seek a negotiated peace as he continued to think that the North would undoubtedly give in eventually.

During the first half of 1967, moreover, Westmoreland was beginning to have his doubts about his attrition strategy (Chapters 8 and 9 give details of the campaigns and battles, and their successes and failures). His intelligence was showing that the massive casualties his search and destroy operations were causing were not preventing the North from replacing its losses. In fact, one estimate proposed that the enemy forces had increased in the first few months of 1967, over the same period the previous year.

Consequently, in the spring of 1967, the MACV commander decided to test the waters for a change. He had his staff draw up plans for a bold, large-scale US offensive to cut the Ho Chi Minh Trail in Laos. Without forcibly arguing for this plan, he sent his 1968 force requirements with an 'Optimum Force' package to execute this bold stroke to the JCS and Secretary of Defense. As we will see in some detail in Chapter 9, LBJ denied the optimum force, primarily because McNamara opposed it; but also because the President still did not want to put the country on a 'war-footing.'

As McNamara touted his peace plan, and after the Secretary had recommended and LBJ disapproved the optimum force reinforcement package to sever the Ho Chi Minh Trail, the North Vietnamese were meeting to plan and execute its largest offensive of the war. Its objective was to defeat the South's armed forces, topple its government with the assistance of South Vietnamese insurgents and dissidents, and force America to see that its efforts in Vietnam had failed. The centerpiece of this plan would be to send reinforcements and supplies over the Ho chi Minh Trail to ensure victory.

In the latter part of 1967, Johnson brought his primary field commander back to the States to address the American public on the war's progress. Despite his misgivings at the beginning of the year, General Westmoreland reported that US forces had set back the enemy's efforts to control the countryside, giving the South Vietnamese Army and its government the necessary security to reestablish political control in the hamlets and cities. He further said before the National Press Club of the war, "the end comes into view."

The General did not report, however, that the enemy engagements usually happened because the PAVN or VC chose to so, not because the large sweeps had trapped them. He also did not report that the enemy had the initiative. This was because they had sanctuaries in Laos and Cambodia to which they could withdraw, refit, and then return to the South. Finally, he did not report that the political viability of the South Vietnamese government was still in question in the eyes of the Southern populace.

When Westmoreland was not doing his pep talks, McNamara was. While sometimes publicly cautious about progress, he always had some quantifiable measure of improvement that he could report. The Secretary, along with the President, often reminded every one of their attempts to bring the North to the peace table through their policy of inflicting damage of the North through their air campaign coupled with voluntary bombing halts.

This combination of McNamara's and Westmoreland's progress reports, despite rumblings from the Service Chiefs about gradualism in Congressional hearings, gave some feeling of confidence to the Congress and Public on the war effort at the end of 1967.

Then TET happened.

The TET Offensive: Victory or Defeat?

On 31 January 1968, the NVA and the VC, during a traditional Vietnamese holiday truce called TET, launched major attacks against over 100 cities throughout South Vietnam. Involving more than 85,000 enemy troops, this offensive, planned well beforehand, was the largest of the war thus far. The goal of the attacks was to inflict significant battlefield defeats on the ARVN, spark a national uprising of the South Vietnamese people, and end the war on Communist North Vietnam terms.

After a little over a month of fierce fighting, the US and ARVN units won a significant military victory. US Marines destroyed the NVA forces that had seized the citadel in the ancient capital of Hue. US Army forces destroyed the NVA forces that tried to reinforce them and elsewhere. US and ARVN forces defeated VC forces that had attacked Saigon and had briefly penetrated the American Embassy.

After this first offensive, there were several waves of attacks that followed. One was in early summer; and another two months later. Evidently, the North Vietnamese thought these attacks could severely weaken the ARVN and would keep the pressure on the Americans as the November elections approached. These attacks, while defeats for the North, wreaked havoc on South Vietnam during the year; and, of course, caught the attention of America.

Across Vietnam, the fighting during the main TET offensive from January through March had cost over 4000 Americans and other Allies' soldiers, nearly 5000 ARVN troops, about 15,000 civilians and over 20,000 NVA and VC forces. The VC guerrilla forces and political infrastructure suffered a crippling blow. The uprising did not occur. With their American advisors and support, the ARVN had fought well. Though the VC had attacked their headquarters palace, the South Vietnamese government lay intact and functioning.

According to his memoirs, the TET offensive did not surprise General Westmoreland. He had intelligence in late 1967 that some big communist move was going to happen in early 1968. He also had some assessments that it could occur during the TET holiday. However, though Westmoreland minimizes them, there were two big surprises.

The first was that he had thought the enemy would start any significant attack against the American base at Khe Sanh. This was a position the US marines established in the fall of 1967 to interdict any PAVN force moving into the South from Laos. Consequently, his and the Administration's focus had been on the defense of that base. In fact, when the NVA/VC attacks began against the cities, he thought they were a diversion. He still expected the enemy main attack to be against Khe Sanh.

The second surprise was the extent and coordination of the attacks against the population areas. Though Westmoreland had moved some American units to those areas on indications of possible enemy attacks against them, many US combat units had still been postured to thwart attacks against major US bases, such as Khe Sanh, and near the border areas.

The TET offensive's primary impact was on the American psyche. Given the Administration's statements in the latter part of 1967 of success against the NVA and VC forces in the South, Americans were confused. The President and his generals had told them the US was winning. How could the VC have launched such an attack if they were near defeat? Walter Cronkite perhaps voiced what most had felt when he said, "What the hell's going on here? I thought we were winning this war."

For some Americans, this enemy attack came as proof that the Government had duped their citizens. The continual reports of progress were all lies. The most recent statements of General Westmoreland, who had visited the States several times in 1967, were either gross distortions of the truth or deceptions to hide the failures of the costs of American lives. TET further fueled the peace movement and the protests. Congress, moreover, now began to confront the Johnson Administration on its conduct of the war.

President Johnson and Secretary McNamara were incredulous. Immediately they sensed that this offensive was going to have a decisive impact on their policy toward the war. Already exhausted from long hours of work and shaken by the protests that had included vehement personal attacks, they pondered what to do.

McNamara was particularly affected. He was on his way out before TET. Johnson had lost faith in him. The Secretary had begun to voice increasing dismay over their policy on Vietnam. He had ordered a massive in-depth study of its strategy [later referred to as *The Pentagon Papers*] to evaluate the stalemate he had observed during 1967. He had also written LBJ a defeatist memo questioning the wisdom of continued pursuit of the war. Now, McNamara had to confront the greatest crisis of the war. He would not be up to the task. Neither would the President.

At first, Westmoreland was confident about the success of military operations against the VC and the PAVN. He initially indicated to LBJ that he could handle the situation with what he had except for a few more support units. The Ambassador, now Daniel Ellsworth, was confident that the situation, while serious, could be managed. They both at first sought to ease the anxieties of Washington. In short, they conveyed that the US and ARVN military had been successful in defeating the offensive. The RVN, moreover, had survived and was still in charge.

Then, on 7 February, the CJCS, General Wheeler, decided to step in and take advantage of what he perceived as the right moment to change course in the war. The historical evidence shows that he saw the TET offensive as an opportunity. He believed that the crisis could force the mobilization that the JCS had recommended to the President on several occasions. This would relieve the drastic worldwide shortages caused by the war and ease the risk should another conflict occur in Europe, the Middle East, or Korea.

The Chairman also thought that the Administration could be convinced now that a change in strategy was necessary. That change would be predicated on the premise that the North could not be persuaded to come to the bargaining table unless it was forced to understand that its war effort could not succeed. The way to accomplish this was to cut the Ho Chi Minh trail and threaten an invasion of the North in the aftermath of its failed general offensive.

Wheeler started what was to become a flurry of messages back and forth with Westmoreland on what to do about reinforcements and follow-on actions to the enemy offensive. On 7 February, he sent a message to MACV about providing the 82d Airborne Division and some Marines to counterattack the PAVN forces in the northern provinces of South Vietnam. At the end of the cable, he emphasized, "if you need more troops, ask for them."

The next day there were other exchanges. Wheeler revealed his thinking about changing the approach to the theater military strategy and said, "the critical phase of the war is upon us." Westmoreland, thinking about the CJCS encouragements on more forces and potential changes to the restrictions he had been operating under, requested additional forces beyond some marines and a brigade of the 82d Airborne Division. Referring to the future use of these forces as a contingency, he emphasized: "particularly if operations in Laos are authorized."

On 9 February, Wheeler attended a meeting with LBJ, McNamara, and Clifford. The latter was to take over the Secretary of Defense position on the 1st of March. The subject of the meeting was the immediate deployment of the 82d brigade and the marines. LBJ and his advisors expected that this would be a cautionary reinforcement to deal with any other NVA/VC surprises. This was prudent, they thought, but only temporary until the situation stabilized.

At this meeting, Wheeler surprised and perplexed all by painting a bleak picture of what was going on in Vietnam. He warned that there might be a second wave of attacks like the one that just occurred. That afternoon after the meeting, Westmoreland sent yet another message to the Secretary of Defense that showed a need for further reinforcements. He said that he would welcome any troops available, and justifies this saying, these are needed to "turn the tide to the point where the enemy might see the light." Neither Wheeler or Westmoreland was clear, however, on how they could turn the tide.

LBJ, McNamara, Clifford, and Rusk were now more confused about the situation in Vietnam and what their military was telling them about it. To sort it out, the President called for another meeting on the 11th. At that meeting, LBJ showed his dismay at the picture that Westmoreland was portraying about the current state of affairs in Vietnam and whether he was asking for added forces. Rusk indicated his frustration with a remark about poorly drafted messages coming out of MACV that are at fault. He hinted that the CJCS needed to sort it all out. McNamara and Wheeler agreed to get a firmer grasp of the situation.

Afterwards, an apparently frustrated General Wheeler sent yet another cable to Westmoreland. Telling him of the meeting he just left, he wrote that the conferees had concluded: "you could use additional US troop units, but you are not expressing a firm demand for them; in sum, you do not fear defeat if you are not reinforced."

Westmoreland now got the message. Writing in his memoirs that with this 'encouragement,' he wrote a 'formal' request the next day that he "desperately needed reinforcements." The General further emphasized that "time was of the essence" to ensure that the enemy could be defeated in the northern part of South Vietnam. He added that he also wanted "to capitalize on enemy losses by seizing the initiative in other areas." He is unclear in the message on what 'seizing the initiative' meant or how he planned to 'capitalize on his losses.'

The Debate over Reinforcements and A Change of Course

Trying to understand what his military commanders and advisors needed, McNamara became particularly dismayed and what to do about it. He tried to support some reinforcement for Westmoreland. He also saw the need for some mobilization to fill the voids that existed in other overseas areas that the JCS wanted. However, he had lost favor with LBJ. He had lost faith in his belief that there was a solution for the war, and Johnson knew it. The most he could do right now was to get the immediate reinforcements from the 82d and a Marine regiment on the way, which LBJ agreed to. He then told Wheeler that the President was also considering some mobilization.

Because of the confusion over the assessments of the situation and requests for reinforcements, the President, at the end of February, sent Wheeler to Vietnam. The Chairman was to confer with Westmoreland and "get a comprehensive view of where we stand today."

Wheeler met with Westmoreland in Vietnam from the 23rd to the 26th of February. Understanding the need to make a comprehensive request for reinforcements and explaining their rationale for them, the two sat down and composed a message to Washington. On the way back from Vietnam, Wheeler dispatched this request as a memo to the President. Its subject was "Military Situation and Requirements in South Vietnam" and dated 27 February 1968. It called for an increase in troop levels of some 206,000 troops. It does not explain how these forces would change the situation decisively.

Several other events on the 27th of February would shape future discussions and resultant decisions on this significant troop request. The first was a meeting at the State Department between McNamara, Clifford, Rostow, and Rusk to discuss the Wheeler memo that they had just received. It was an extraordinary meeting.

McNamara led off summarizing what this request meant. The outgoing Secretary explained that it would need a significant reserve call up and increased draft. These would require a total increase in military strength of 400,000 at the cost of at least $15 billion in the defense budget. He then led a debate of alternatives for discussion with the President the next day. McNamara expressed that he was confused over the request, that it did not present a strategy for the use of the forces it asked for, nor offer any sign on what it was designed to change from past operations.

In contrast to McNamara's pessimism, Rostow was enthusiastic. He strongly favored the reinforcement request, arguing that it came at a critical juncture of the war and could enable a change in strategy to take the war to the North Vietnamese. He referred to captured enemy documents that showed their assessment of failure in the offensive and inability to launch further attacks. Rostow then alluded to the opportunities that he had long advocated to win the war. He argued that now the US would have the forces to launch an offensive against the Ho Chi Minh trail to isolate the conflict in the South.

This was just too much for McNamara. One of the President's close domestic advisors, Joseph Califano, who was also present, described the Secretary's demeanor and ensuing arguments. He became visibly upset and "called the request madness." With just two days left in his tenure, he broke down. "What then?" he said to Rostow. "The bombing campaign has been worth nothing…. We've dropped more bombs than all of Europe in all of World War II and it hasn't done a thing." Alluding to the PAVN and the VC, he shouted, "Let's not delude ourselves into thinking they cannot maintain pressure [on the ARVN]." He turned to Clifford and emotionally appealed to "end this thing…. It is out of control." According to Clifford and Rostow, the Secretary of Defense then 'disintegrated' into 'suppressed sobs.'

That evening, after a two-week tour of Vietnam sparked by the TET offensive, Walter Cronkite went on national TV to give his assessment of what had happened in Vietnam. He concluded that the US was "mired in stalemate," and said, "the only rational way out would be to negotiate—not as victims, but as an honorable people who lived up to their pledge to victory and democracy and did the best they could." According to some sources, President Johnson after watching the report proclaimed, "if I have lost Cronkite, I have lost middle America."

The next morning, General Wheeler met with the President and his primary national security advisors at the White House to discuss his memo. As the notes of that meeting in the *Foreign Relations of the United States* series describe, the Chairman led off explaining what he discussed and assessed in his meeting with Westmoreland in Vietnam. His words were not encouraging. He stated that "The TET attack was very powerful and nationwide.... The margin of victory was very thin in a number of battles.... The enemy is still hanging around.... What the future intensity of the conflict will be is an unknown.... We do know that more TET-type attacks are planned."

He then tried to balance these statements by showing a captured enemy document that indicated the PAVN/VC objectives had failed; and that they had suffered heavy casualties. However, he reiterated that the "margin between defeat and victory in many areas was surprisingly narrow." Then Wheeler argued for the increase in the force levels in the request. He concluded his argument by saying that if Westmoreland does not get these forces "we should be prepared to give up the two northern provinces of South Vietnam...that would give the North Vietnamese a strong position for negotiating" and, he believed, "cause the collapse of the ARVN." There was a pause of silence in the room.

Clifford had advised the President not to make any commitments at this meeting. LBJ did not. In the end, Johnson asked the soon to be Secretary of Defense to head a task force to study the request and report back on 4 March. Then all left for the White House ceremony honoring McNamara's service at which the President awarded him the Medal of Freedom – the nation's highest civilian award. At the end of that service, holding back tears, McNamara acknowledged the President's thanks for the work he did over the last eight years. He went off the head the World Bank.

The next day Wheeler cabled Westmoreland and said, "My report on the situation in South Vietnam and your force requirements touched off an intense discussion of where we stand and where we are going in the war." The official history of the JCS says of this cable, "The Chairman's words were a masterpiece of understatement. Wheeler's report was a staggering blow to a politically beleaguered administration already shaken by the TET assault."

Instead of clarifying the situation in Vietnam and the military rationale for the troop increase, the memo and Wheeler's meeting further confused LBJ and his civilian advisors – most notably Clark Clifford. The new Secretary did not understand what the new levels of forces would attempt to accomplish. More importantly, in his astute political sense, he knew that the mood of the country and the Congress had been shaken in the few weeks after the TET offensive. Clifford instinctively thought and believed that even if he and the President did understand what the need was, no power of persuasion could get support for a decision to raise the forces.

The subsequent task force meetings did not change what the new Defense Secretary instinctively had come to understand already. The Joint Staff briefings did not clarify anything for him. According to Clifford, he could not understand, or the military explain, what the outcome would be if they agreed to deploy the troops. There was no assessment of the effect on Hanoi.

In interview years later, he recalled: "We met hour after hour.... I asked how long would it take to turn the war around? No one knew.... Do you think 206 thousand would be enough, if not how much more may be needed? No one knew.... Do you find any diminution in the enemy's will to fight? They said, we don't…." Of these answers, Clifford concluded, "After all of this interrogation at the end of four to five days my thinking had undergone a substantial revolution." The one-time public supporter of the war and advisor to three Presidents was convinced that the US had to disengage from Vietnam.

The lack of answers to Clifford's queries is difficult to understand – why had not the Joint Staff made a better case for the use of the reinforcements? They had been reviewing and studying not only their plans for the use of more forces in Vietnam but those of General Westmoreland. These plans (the one residing in the Joint Staff was dubbed 'MULE SHOE') called for an amphibious attack along the southern coast of North Vietnam just north of the DMZ, and, as mentioned, the MACV commander's contingency was for cutting the Ho Chi Minh Trail in Laos.

The answer may be that the staff did not have the authorization to raise the concepts of either their plan or the Pacific Command's. One reason for that, according to the JCS History, may have been that the Army Chief of Staff, General Harold Johnson, had objected to the further development of these plans and advocating their use. The Army Chief felt that none of them had any hope of execution given the President's stated aims and restrictions, and that the JCS was overstepping their bounds in pursuing such a concept.

Like Westmoreland, General Harold Johnson was the dutiful soldier who was unwilling to argue or voice dissent with his civilian overseers once they had made a decision. As Lewis Sorley noted in his biography of him, Johnson told others, that if a military man's advice was rejected, then he should just be a good soldier and do what he was told. Given Johnson's unwillingness to agree to support any change in strategy that would include an offensive into Laos or against the North's homeland, Wheeler did not push the matter with Clifford or others.

As for General Wheeler, he had most likely rejected the idea of presenting a new strategic concept to his civilian advisors for more bureaucratic reasons. As he had told Westmoreland in Saigon during their recent meeting, he thought it would just confuse Clifford and his people. The best approach, Wheeler believed, was to concentrate on the numbers and how they would lessen the risk of failure in South Vietnam, serve to reconstitute the strategic reserve, and provide a reserve to the MACV commander for future operations.

In his memoirs, Westmoreland says that he could not fault Wheeler's approach, for "better to exploit their [civilian defense advisors'] belief in crisis to get the troops, then argue new strategy later. One thing at a time." When queried after the war about the entire affair, Westmoreland further indicated that his entire support for the 206K reinforcement was mostly Wheeler's idea, and his support was more to obtain forces for further contingencies than an immediate use in a counterblow. This attitude may have been the reasons why he also did not push for the change of strategy with Clifford or the President. There may have been others that the then MACV commander did not divulge. Chapters 9 and 11 will further discuss this issue in detail.

The lack of a coherent strategic reason for the troops was the deciding factor for the new Defense Chief. Clifford left his meetings with the military not just confused but with no understanding of why the reinforcement request was necessary. Consequently, at his 4 March meeting with the President, Clifford recommended, with Wheeler present, only a limited reinforcement of the troops. He argued that the never-ending dispatch of troops seemed like a bottomless pit. If the President agreed to this troop request, moreover, it would not be long before there was "another 200,000 or 300,000 with no end in sight."

The new Defense Secretary further related to the President that there was a definite need to relook at all the premises and assumptions about US policy and military strategy in Vietnam. His most forceful argument, which resonated with LBJ, was that he did not think the Administration had the political support to do anything further until there was an in-depth look at how to change Vietnam policies. According to the oral histories of several at this meeting, "Clifford's blunt appraisal shook the President to his very core."

In reaction to this report and a further recommendation from Clifford, the President decided to convene the 'Wise Men' group to review and make a further recommendation on changes to policy and military strategy. These Wise Men were now made up of such notables like Dean Acheson, former Ambassador Henry Cabot Lodge, former National Security Advisor McGeorge Bundy, and military notables Generals Omar Bradley, Maxwell Taylor, and Matthew Ridgeway. One more individual that the President had curiously added was George Ball – the 'devil's advocate' who had left the government in 1966.

As previously noted, many of these men had met before and had blessed LBJ's approach to the war. It was not to be that way this time. The atmosphere was different. Just before they met, a *New York Times* article leaked the 206K request for troops. It included a story of the debate it had caused within the Administration. The public reaction was entirely negative, as well as, of course, that of Congress.

In the atmosphere of post-TET, the group had become tired and cynical of the military briefs. At one point, one of the Wise Group members tore apart a briefer's estimates of enemy casualties and other measures of careful assessments of near victories that needed to be exploited with additional reinforcements. Once again, Wheeler remained unconvincing, even contradictory with his updates on progress since the beginning of TET that seemed to outdate the end of February request.

Before the Wise Men's recommendation was complete, perhaps because he knew that Clifford was against the full reinforcement, LBJ sent Wheeler to meet once again with Westmoreland and get his agreement with the much smaller reinforcement that had been already agreed to. Wheeler met with the MACV commander in the Philippines on 24 March. He told him that the full 206K force was "out of the question. Westmoreland did not object.

Wheeler then returned to DC with General Abrams, whom LBJ had already designated as Westmoreland's replacement. In a meeting with the President on 26 March, the CJCS told LBJ that Westy had acquiesced to the smaller reinforcement. General Abrams concurred that the increase was not necessary. He went even further and told the President that their post-TET strategy was sound and would be able to defeat the remaining enemy attacks. Johnson was happy.

He had covered his bases. He wanted to ensure that he could not be seen as someone who denied the warfighting commander what he asked to win the war. Now frantic calls for more reinforcements had ceased. Military men were telling him that all was ok. The crisis had passed. Johnson now contemplated, without his key advisors, what he would do next.

On the 27th of March, Dean Acheson presented the group's recommendation. In sum, he said that "we can no longer do the job we set out to do in the time we have left, and we must begin steps to disengage." The Wise Men also recommended a reduction in the bombing of North Vietnam. Some argued for re-engaging the North along with bombing halts to obtain negotiations to end the conflict.

By the time of the Wise Men's report, LBJ had already decided upon a course of action. He planned a TV announcement of a new initiative for peace through the cessation of the bombing of the North. The principal objects of this pause were to regain public support for the Administration's policy of opposing aggression against the South, and place the onus of stopping the killing on the North. What he revealed to some, was that he would also inform the American people of his decision not to seek a nomination for another term as President.

On 31 March President Johnson addressed the nation on public television. He proclaimed his willingness to "move immediately toward peace through negotiation." He said to take steps toward that he would "de-escalate the conflict" by ordering no attacks against the North, except around the demilitarized zone. The President then said the US was "ready to send its representatives to any forum, at any time, to discuss means of bringing this ugly war to an end."

To address the public knowledge of the 206K increase request and the possible draft increases and reserve call-ups associated with such an increase, he assured the public that only 13,500 more troops would be sent over the next few months to Vietnam. Then he finished by saying, "I shall not seek, and I will not accept, the nomination of my party for another term as your President."

Most retrospective analyses of his speech marked it as the beginning of a steady process of American disengagement from Vietnam. Though, of course, not known at the time, it began America's ignoble retreat from a noble effort to defend people from unwanted subjugation by a communist-inspired government. That initial effort went astray and led to an ignominious result in the loss of life and the loss of freedom of millions of souls.

As for LBJ and McNamara, George Herring summarized it best: "McNamara's tearful departure from the Pentagon at the height of the Tet Offensive in early 1968, as much as Lyndon B. Johnson's March 31, 1968 speech, marked the inglorious end of an era once bright with promise."

Section 3.5 – Personal Experiences, Observations, and Insights for Chapters 2 and 3

This section summarizes and presents insights on the narrative in Chapters 2 and 3. It also presents some pertinent personal experiences and observations of the events described in those two chapters.

Personal Experiences

When Kennedy and his 'best and brightest' came into office in January 1961, I was still in high school. As mentioned previously, I entered West Point in the third year of JFK's first term – July 1963. A little over four months later, Lee Harvey Oswald assassinated him in Dallas, Texas.

Kennedy had spoken at the Class of 1963 graduation a month before my entry. As I later read his remarks, I found that they were remarkably prescient of what was to happen in the world I would soon join as a soldier. He said that even though we were not at war like the US experienced in World War Two or Korea, the use of the military in the future would still be a challenge to keep the world at peace. He said that we would face severe tests to our profession of arms ahead with the threats to our interests less direct, but as important as those in the past.

JFK, reflecting the defense policy of his administration, further cited the need to understand limited wars of national liberation. He emphasized that the communists had proclaimed support for such wars. This meant that the US might have to assist countries subjected to communist subjugation of legitimate governments that wanted to be democratic. He also mentioned that there were considerable uncertainties ahead, and the need for the Army to be able to respond to any contingencies in the nation's struggle to contain communism and protect democratic ideals.

Of course, Kennedy was speaking about his policy of supporting the Government in South Vietnam, a place that many West Pointers at the time knew nothing about. Frankly, we did not even know then where Vietnam was. Neither did we see much on the horizon, other than serving in Europe to guard against a Soviet conventional threat there. Just six years later, I would end up in Vietnam fighting an unconventional war against a highly competent enemy.

My experience was a microcosm of my entire West Point Class. That would also be the fate of the other 587 cadets in my class when we graduated in 1967. 29 would never make it back. It had always seemed ironic to me that many in our class marched in the inauguration parade of the President who decided to go to war over Vietnam – Lyndon Baines Johnson.

Before I went to Vietnam, I saw the effects of President Johnson's decision not to mobilize or call up the reserves to meet the Armed Forces' worldwide security commitments. The Army brigade (a unit of about 2000 soldiers) I was assigned to in Europe was woefully understrength. Most disturbing was the lack of senior (Captain and above) officers and the rapid rotation of noncommissioned officers between Europe and Vietnam. Many of our tracked armored vehicles, which were an anathema to most of us because we were also a parachute infantry outfit, did not work either. There were not enough repair parts due to the priorities going to Vietnam.

As a Lieutenant, I held a position usually held by a Captain. The officer I worked for was a Lieutenant as well, a few months senior, who held a Major's position. If the Soviets had decided to launch an offensive against NATO, most of the American units that would have been called upon, both in Europe and stateside, would have been led by junior, inexperienced officers. The shortage of senior officers was entirely due to the needs in Southeast Asia and the personnel policies gauged toward short twelve-month rotations in the Vietnam War.

The noncommissioned officer situation was also in disarray. The sergeants I served with in 1967 and 1968 already had at least one tour in Vietnam. Everyone had been wounded at least once. Many were alcoholics and divorced husbands and fathers. Most of them were only in the unit for a few months. Their rotation between Vietnam and elsewhere was even shorter than that of the officers. Thus, if there had been a war in Europe American units would have had serious problems with small unit leadership.

This dire situation described above was a warning to things to come in the Army in the last two years in Vietnam and in the decade following the end of the war there. The Vietnam War decimated the commissioned and noncommissioned officer corps. It killed off a generation of leaders. Some of those had served in and survived the two previous wars only to die in some godforsaken jungle mountain-top or rice paddy. The Army after Vietnam almost disintegrated because of that war.

I was one of the lucky ones. I survived the war and its aftermath. I stayed on to lead and train soldiers in the new volunteer force. It was a challenging experience. In the early seventies, the experiment almost failed. However, the Army made it. Through the efforts and struggles of the survivors of Vietnam rose a new Army. It took the better part of a decade to recover and build this Army. The successes of the late and early nineties in Panama and the Persian Gulf were due to these efforts and struggles.

Along the way, I had the opportunity to study and teach about the Vietnam War. As previously mentioned in Chapter 1, in Graduate School I researched and wrote about the years leading to our military involvement there. I was incensed about the lack of understanding of military affairs that I found amongst the obviously educated and brilliant best and brightest advisors to the Presidents.

I was also enraged by the lack of courage amongst the senior military officers who also advised the Presidents to confront a flawed strategic policy - what H.R. McMaster labeled as a 'dereliction of duty.' I was exasperated by the foolishness of the field commanders who directed the use of military force under conditions that were impossible to surmount. Yet, they continued to do so and waste lives along the way. The full reckoning of that story and the findings are yet to be told in the later chapters.

What I had learned I tried to teach first to young students at West Point, and then to senior officers at the prestigious National War College at Fort McNair in Washington, DC. I was cautious and not very introspective when teaching cadets. There I talked mostly about what it was like as an untried junior officer in combat. However, at the National War College I dwelled on the meaning of the war; how we got involved, and some of the difficulties in strategic formulation at the national and theater levels. That meant getting into the how's and whys of policymaking.

In constructing the course at the National War College and in preparation for its seminars, I improved upon my research that I did in graduate school. This was in 1996, and there were then already a plethora books consisting of memoirs, reminiscences, monographs, and official documents about the war and its causes and implications. These fell into several categories.

First, there were those that argued that the US participation in the war had been a mistake. It had not been in our national interest. We had gotten involved in a series of blunders caused by mistaken assumptions about the threat to our interests. This argument contends that the US had foolhardily tried to protect an illegitimate or incompetent South Vietnam government. Many authors in this category further asserted that our involvement was either immoral or result of our arrogance or both. Some also claimed that US decision-makers had gotten involved in a 'quagmire' of seemingly irreversible commitments that had to be honored or the world would have lost faith in the US.

The second category of works on the war, which came out generally after the first category, argued that the US military could have won the war had it not been for the restrictions placed upon them by the politicians. This argument primarily focused on President Johnson's decisions to not mobilize for the conflict, the prohibition of attacks against the NVA sanctuaries and supply routes in Laos and Cambodia, and the restrictions on the bombing of the North. The authors of these works seem to place the onus of failure in Vietnam on the back of the civilian decision makers. One of their central premises was that the US military could have won the war if 'they did not have to fight with one hand tied behind their back.'

The final category of materials on the war in the mid-nineties consisted of documents that provided me and my students some insights into the war through original policy papers, analyses, transcripts, and personal notes and accounts. From the US side, these were primarily the *Pentagon Papers* and documents in the State Department's *Foreign Relations of the United States* series. These provided actual intelligence estimates, minutes of meetings and policy papers of the US government. Some monographs also provided excerpts and descriptions of captured North Vietnamese and Viet Cong documents. Although these materials were invaluable to recount some of the decision making at the time, by themselves, they did not entirely account for the influences of or reasons for that decision making.

Despite some shortcomings, all this enabled lively debate of the Vietnam War. The discussions focused on the US government administrations' decision-making processes, and the resultant military courses of action and strategies. These conversations were amongst a group that consisted of senior-level military officers at the Lieutenant Colonel and Colonel ranks who would go on to senior positions in the military and the government.

I was further aided in these discussions by my experiences as part of the national security apparatus like that of the JFK and LBJ era. In the early eighties, I had served on the Army Staff in the Pentagon. In 1990, I returned there to serve on the Joint Staff. These tours exposed me to the immense bureaucracy of the Department of Defense.

In my first tour, the Services dominated military discussions on strategies and force structure. Like those during the Vietnam War, interservice rivalries over the budget were intense; often overpowering any useful, unified examination of joint warfighting capabilities and approaches to military doctrine and strategies. The duplication of roles and capabilities led to a bloated defense budget. Coordination and planning were cumbersome and time-consuming. The civilians in the Office of the Secretary of Defense were frustrated with military bureaucratic maneuvering over priorities in the budget.

In my second tour on the Joint Staff in the early nineties the Goldwater-Nichols Act, which was promulgated to move the Services more to joint organizations and operations, had taken hold. The Chairman of the Joint Chiefs of Staff, then General Colin Powell, had significantly increased power as the primary military advisor to the President. The Joint Staff was now organized and empowered to serve primarily the Chairman. All of this meant more meaningful strategic advice during the first Gulf War and sound recommendations on post-Cold War force structure.

My experience in these tours demonstrated the tremendously slow and inept movement of the Pentagon bureaucracy in military affairs. The second tour also showed that to overcome this bureaucracy you need an influential military primary advisor to the President who knows the politics associated with the Executive and Legislative branches of Government. General Powell had been such a person as the newly empowered Chairman of the Joint Chiefs of Staff. In that position, he could both plan and execute a new military strategy for the post-Cold War and the first Gulf War, and reconstruct a new force structure that made sense for a new world after the fall of the Soviet Union.

Much of this experience, study, and dialogue gave me knowledge and insights for this book. My tours in the Pentagon gave me an acquaintance with the same bureaucracy of the Defense Department that affected the JFK and LBJ administrations in the sixties. But, my studies of the Vietnam War then were limited to the materials at the time and our knowledge of what had occurred.

Since then, I have had the opportunity to study the war further and gain more insights. The recent material, described in detail at the end of the book, consists of the same categories already described, but enhanced by the wide release of US government sources and the Democratic Republic of Vietnam materials. Moreover, there has been a treasure trove of thousands of tapes of conversations in the Kennedy, Johnson, and Nixon Administration's meetings, telephone conversations, and private dialogues that have offered insights on individual and group emotions, thoughts, and motives on decision making that are invaluable to this story.

Observations and Insights

What I have found throughout my search for insights on how the US got involved in Vietnam is that the general thinking and beliefs of their times significantly influenced US policymakers. This observation should be obvious. However, too often some historians and most amateur critics ignore the influence of the times that people live in when they judge their actions. Such has particularly been the case in assessing US policymakers during the Vietnam War era.

As described in this and the earlier chapters, the experiences of World War Two, the onset of the Cold War, and the domestic reactions to both were powerful forces that predisposed some of the decision makings of both the Kennedy and Johnson Administrations.

Accordingly, the victories in the Second World War showed that the US could overcome the most difficult circumstances. In James Patterson's words, "Americans, having fought to win the war, expected to dominate the world order to come. Although worried about a return of economic depression, they had reason to hope that wartime prosperity would continue. The enemies had been defeated; the soldiers and sailors would soon return; families would reunite; the future promised a great deal more than the past. In this optimistic mood, millions of Americans plunged hopefully into the new postwar world."

Moreover, faced after the war with unsettling times – that is the emergence of the Soviet Union as a threat and the unraveling of prewar colonies - the US had prevailed in Europe, the Middle East, and in North East Asia. Indeed, it is not too much of an exaggeration to say that American leadership in an uncertain era had triumphed.

As David Rothkopf states in his history of the US national security apparatus in the postwar world, "The sweep and scope of that transformation was stunning. Within a decade of the Pearl Harbor attack, the United States had led the Allies to victory in the Second World War; signed the United Nations Charter with nearly unanimous approval from the Senate; implemented the Marshall Plan; fulfilled the promise of the Truman Doctrine with substantial peacetime aid to Greece, Turkey, Western Europe, and Japan; and committed itself to the North Atlantic Alliance, the Military Defense Assistance Program, the creation of the International Monetary Fund, the World Bank, the International Labor Organizations

He continues, "In addition, to manage what it saw as its permanent role in executing those programs, it transformed its national security apparatus, modernizing its military, and creating the Department of Defense, the modern Joint Chiefs of Staff, the U.S. Air Force, and two potentially powerful new agencies to focus exclusively on ensuring successful management of our world affairs: The Central Intelligence Agency and the National Security Council. It was one of the few occasions when what came out of a transformation was as stunning as the transformation itself."

The key people in both JFK's and LBJ's administrations - and as we will see later others as well - were very susceptible to the atmosphere of the post-Second World War decade of success. The idea of a powerful America that emerged from that war dominated much of their thinking about Southeast Asia. Thus, the 'Best and Brightest' thought that the US could successfully affect an intractable situation in South Vietnam. Policymakers in both administrations could rightly believe that if America could thwart Soviet expansion in Europe and communist exploitation of North East Asia, then what prevented the US from succeeding in Southeast Asia? Why could it not do in Vietnam what it had done in Europe and North-East Asia?

JFK's call to pay any price, bear any burden and endure any hardship epitomized that confidence. The scholars and soldiers of both administrations were representative of America's confidence and ability to succeed in difficult situations. In retrospect, this may appear as overconfidence, even as arrogance. For the times in which these men lived, it just reflects the optimism and assurance in American influence and capabilities at the time.

Despite this confidence in the ability of America to shape the world, there was the challenge of Soviet Communism that the US still had to confront. The Truman and Eisenhower Administrations were successful in meeting this challenge. However, while dealing with the international threat of communism, domestic overreactions to it would surface. These would become a detriment to sound policymaking. Both the Red Scare period, characterized by McCarthyism, and the emergence of the communist takeover of China would come to haunt US global policy. The Communist Soviet and China obtainment of nuclear capabilities exasperated and fueled the fear.

These reactions had a significant bearing on decisions in both the Kennedy and Johnson Administrations, and, as we will see, even the later Nixon government. For example, all Presidents, to various degrees, often referred to domestic political concerns of being soft on communism and not being the President to lose Vietnam during their policy deliberations.

Moreover, some previous setbacks were of almost equal influence. The 'loss of China' and the later Korean War Chinese aggression and stalemate turned America's attention from Europe to Asia and focused attention to Indochina and Vietnam. As George Herring points out in his seminal work on the Vietnam War, *America's Longest War*, these events turned the area of Southeast Asia and Vietnam into an international issue, rather than a local anti-colonial conflict between the Viet-Minh and the French.

Meanwhile, the Soviet and Communist Chinese possession of atomic weaponry would also be a decisive influence on policymaking in Vietnam. Now, without sole possession of these powerful devices, US actions, particularly considering the Chinese intervention in Korea, would have to consider that any conflict in Vietnam could escalate into a global nuclear war.

These influences go a long way to explaining the JFK and LBJ assumptions and actions over Vietnam described in the two previous chapters. For example, both adopted the Eisenhower argument of the Domino Theory. Two foreign policy precedents seemingly made that theory legitimate at the time. The first was the US policy of containment. Less than fifteen years old by the time JFK took office, the policy had shown that it had been successful in thwarting Soviet expansionism in Europe. Moreover, the policy had also afforded needed continuity in US foreign affairs. Therefore, it was understandable to American leaders at the time of our first involvement in Vietnam that containment of communism in Asia, which was the object of the theory, was both proper and necessary.

The second precedent was the lesson of appeasement. As mentioned, many foreign policy analysts and practitioners after the Second World War thought the great lesson of that war was that appeasement of aggression leads to more aggression. Hence, if the US was to allow the fall of Vietnam, the Chinese Communists would naturally want to conquer the rest of Southeast Asia. History had proclaimed so. This lesson not only underwrote the Domino Theory but also turned Vietnam into a perceived vital interest worthy of the commitment of US military power to protect from communism.

Besides these influences of US Vietnam policy during the Kennedy and Johnson years, there was another factor that came to bear considerably in their decision-making. This was the organizational and bureaucratic revolution occurring in the National Security apparatus of the US government in the post-World War Two world.

During the war, the US realized that it would have an entirely different position in the world than ever before. To the credit of the FDR Administration, both its civilian and military leaders recognized this and sought to prepare for America's global power responsibilities. With the wartime experience and lesson of the interdependence of land, naval and air power, they also realized that the application of military force had changed dramatically. Recognizing that the Soviets would be an adversary in that world as well, the American military initiated plans to organize and institute a post-war establishment that could fulfill the US role as a global power.

The overall result was the National Security Act of 1947 and the Unified Command Plan. These decrees and others plus the events of the late forties and fifties, by 1960 had set up a vast, cumbersome government bureaucracy. Indeed, JFK primarily appointed Robert McNamara to his cabinet not to deal with the Vietnam situation but to reform and manage the Defense Department – the largest and most unwieldy of the Government post-war entities.

There were primarily four major organizations that made up this bureaucracy for executive policy making - the National Security Council, the Intelligence Agencies, the Defense, and the State Departments. To be efficient and effective in national security matters, these organizations depended upon the expertise, loyalty, trust, and cooperation of the civilians and military personnel who comprised them. This was woefully lacking or ignored, in both JFK's and LBJ's administrations. That flaw severely hampered sound decisions on the policies and strategies for Vietnam.

Much of this lack of full venting with the experts was a direct result of how both Kennedy and Johnson used their national security apparatus. As explained, both Presidents were uncomfortable in using the formal structure. They thought the formal structure, as used during the Eisenhower years, was too cumbersome and restrictive to debate and receive good counsel. Kennedy preferred large groups made up of trusted agents and their principals from his selected agencies and Departments. Johnson favored smaller groups and weekly luncheons with his principal secretaries and selected advisors. Both methods allowed the Presidents to choose, and omit, those advisors that they wanted or did not want as part of their decision-making process.

The consequence of this restriction and control was that often the two Presidents did not obtain detailed, thorough interagency vetting of courses of action. Moreover, because the Presidents usually chose those they were comfortable with in making their decisions, and sometimes chose, especially in the case of LBJ, those that they could rely on to recommend and pursue a course that the President wanted, other adverse or contrary positions were often avoided, whether they were valid or not. Much of the time, for better or worse, this led to the avoidance of, or a vacuum, in military advice.

For example, leading civilian policymakers ignored or did not consider Joint Staff and CIA analyses of the effectiveness of strategic bombing and its impact on North Vietnam. Moreover, plans for offensives against the North Vietnamese lines of communication, namely the Ho Chi Minh Trail, never received a thorough discussion and consideration. The best example of this was when McGeorge Bundy and McNamara ignored the Goodpaster study in 1965, which LBJ had personally directed.

This control and limitation further allowed the Presidents to govern the debate and the message that they wanted to ensure public support for their decisions. For JFK that message on Vietnam was that it was not a war for the US. The US role was to help the South Vietnamese set up a workable government that could succeed against the communist insurgents. For LBJ the message was that a US limited war could succeed without putting the nation on a war footing. That would ensure his Great Society programs could take priority and be implemented. Both these messages, we now know, were false. They were also, at best, influenced by wishful thinking; or, at worst, an intent to deceive the American people.

Another result of this lack of formal advice and careful study of policy options was that national security policy became subject to the individual beliefs, experiences, and attitudes of the Presidents and their closest chosen advisors without genuine and thoughtful consideration of opposing points of view. Of course, this is often the case. However, in this instance, it became more so, and led to profoundly unfavorable outcomes.

Exasperating the above inadequate and closed processes for decisions on the use of force, the civilian policymakers' experiences and knowledge of military strategies and operations were limited or woefully lacking. While the principal advisors - such as Bundy, Rostow, McNamara, Clifford, and Rusk - all had military experience in the Second World War, they had been staff officers. All except for Rusk, who had been a Chief of Staff to General Joseph Stillwell in China, had been far from the fighting.

Thus, these men had no idea of what war was about, or what it took to plan and execute military operations. Not surprisingly, they relied not on their wartime experience but on their personal professional background in national security issues. That was in the realm of academics and, in some cases, the business world. They were all highly educated and intellectual – no doubt. But, none – again except for Rusk - had attended or received any military education or subjected to meaningful military experience.

Likewise, the military advisors' experience and knowledge on political matters were limited or nonexistent. Most had little understanding and acquaintance of the interplay between policy, strategy, and operations. Nor did they recognize the innuendos, subtleties of the international environment and diplomacy. The supreme example of this lack of understanding was when General Curtis LeMay during the Cuban Missile Crisis said to JFK that the President was in 'quite a fix.' Kennedy had to remind the Chief of Staff of the Air Force that he was in that 'fix' as well.

Moreover, many senior military officers were not only unfamiliar, but abhorrent to the nature of diplomacy and international affairs when it came to interfere or shape the nature of military force. Compromise and innuendo were contrary to the military logic of there is no substitute for victory – a phrase MacArthur made famous in the US Armed Forces after the war. Moreover, the military ethos demanded a positive attitude. Again, a favorite refrain was the 'improbable we do immediately; the impossible takes a little longer.' No wonder senior military officers such as General Harkens in Vietnam emphasized the positives – leading to overzealous reporting on progress.

Compounding the lack of political shrewdness and inexperience, many military officers did not have a grasp of nuclear weapons and their dramatic effect on the future of military strategy and national security affairs. Generally, military officers then looked at nuclear armaments as just another weapon employed on the battlefield or as a part of a strategic bombing operation.

This condition was partly because the military had divorced itself from the study and theory of the use of atomic weaponry. Another influence was that the IKE Administration's emphasis on massive retaliation had encouraged the view that nuclear weapons were just another means to employ during military operations in support of national policy.

Therefore, when the JFK and LBJ Administrations asked for military solutions during crises the senior military officers often included options for the use of nuclear weapons as just another means to employ force on the battlefield. In this context, it is understandable that the civilian decision makers and advisors lost faith with some of the military advice that included apparently flippant counsel on the use of nuclear weapons that could result in a global nuclear annihilation

In addition, the post-war military was, like their civilian counterparts, new at planning and executing operations in a protracted situation somewhere between peace and war on a global scale. The situation they faced was unprecedented. There had been no earlier experience to rely upon. Moreover, though a system for military education and thinking was in place with military colleges for the development of future senior officers, these institutions, at the time, were more focused on education for military subjects than the consideration of political-military issues.

With no experience in political-military issues and no educational opportunities to consider such, not surprisingly senior military officers tended to rely on what they were familiar with in their past. That was primarily their Service experience. That experience was not conducive to the thinking that was now needed for a new joint, unified military force. The resultant in-fighting over Service roles and missions for budget priorities was a symptom of this uncertainty. That inter-service rivalry, in turn, further inflamed the civilian members of government, who saw that as another sign that Service parochialism was the primary motivation for much of the military advice.

Despite the above organizational and bureaucratic reasons for the nature of the policy-making in both the Kennedy and Johnson Administrations, the Commander-in-Chiefs remained both responsible and influential for the decisions leading to US involvement in a major war in Southeast Asia and Vietnam. The Presidents not only set the stage for policymaking but, in the case of JFK and LBJ, influenced it decisively. In short, they not only made the decisions; they also guided their advisors toward those decisions. In the case of JFK, it was to stay away from a substantial US combat commitment to South Vietnam. In LBJ's case, it was to keep the war limited, and thus not interfere with his domestic program.

Kennedy and Johnson, moreover, had striking similarities in the way they managed national security affairs. Already mentioned was the desire to use its apparatus less formally than the law intended. Another similar aspect of their management was the intentional undermining of the influence of the military because they did not trust their military advisors. That lack of trust, moreover, had its roots in both men's past experiences and how they viewed military culture.

Both had seen military incompetence during their service in the war, and that had an influence. Moreover, for Kennedy, his experience during the Bay of Pigs and Cuban Missile Crises further led him to virtually ignore all but his most trusted picked military man – General Maxwell Taylor. JFK just did not think that the military understood the complexity of the new international arena. He also thought that they were wedded to old ideas on the use of force. Consequently, he came to believe that if he followed their advice, like what happened during the crises in August 1914, the country could end up in a world war it did not want.

If JFK chose to ignore the military, LBJ set out to control it. He chose his Chairman of the Joint Chiefs of Staff, General Wheeler, based on the General's reputation for being a team man, a manager whom he could trust to be loyal to the President. He relied on General Westmoreland to not pull another MacArthur in Vietnam. He met with all the Chiefs on occasion to put them through the 'Johnson treatment,' and get them to understand his predicament as a political leader who needed their support to get Congress to fund the military. As a reluctant Commander-in-Chief he asked for ways to kill more VC or how to guarantee victory in Vietnam. Yet, as President all he really wanted was for his commanders to wage war on the cheap, and not do anything that would lead to a wider, more costly war that would interfere with his domestic program.

In Chapters 8 through 11, we will take a closer look at the US military commanders and advisors and how they interfaced with their civilian superiors during the war. The perspective in these chapters will focus on how the military commanders and their staffs, particularly at the theater level – that is, in South Vietnam and its contingent areas – tried to develop and execute a military strategy that would meet the objectives and desires, as they saw them, of their political leaders.

We will also further examine the Nixon era decision making in Chapter 5, and some other influences that governed that Administration's decisions over the conduct of the war in Vietnam. But before doing that, the next chapter will take a closer look at the tremendous domestic factors that influenced not only the policymakers in Washington in making their decisions, but would impact on American military commanders in Southeast Asia and how they employed forces to meet the President's political aims.

Chapter 4: America in Crisis

In his history of *The Peloponnesian War*, Thucydides complained that in a democracy domestic matters often adversely affect decisions to go to war. He lamented that often these internal affairs interfered with the leaders' ability to develop and execute sound military strategies and operations. This chapter explores the 'interference' of domestic affairs in the waging of the Vietnam War up to Nixon's election in 1968.

The US domestic scene during this period was in tremendous turmoil. While the war escalated, America was in crisis at home. That turbulence was a result of many factors. However, the leading cause of this crisis had its roots in the tremendous post-war booms, and resultant political, social, and cultural changes they began in America already explained in Chapter 1. As the Vietnam War continued with no end in sight and casualties increasing, the war further inflamed certain sectors of the US populace, which the post-war changes had most affected. The result was a vitriol reaction not only to the war, but to long-standing US institutions, politics, and social norms that touched most Americans and their lives.

The first part of this chapter describes the connection between the post-war booms and the resultant social and cultural changes that prompted the reactions to the war in the sixties. In so doing, it also examines the Great Society program impacts and the interaction between those programs and the war. This first part intends to provide an overall understanding and nature of the crisis in America and show the interrelationship to both the Great Society programs and the war.

The rest of the chapter then describes specific domestic actions and factors that may have affected and been affected by the policy-making and the war itself. This includes a synopsis and view of the civil rights and anti-war movements; the media's part in covering the war; the role of public opinion; and the role and accountability of Congress in waging war. The chapter concludes with a description of the author's experiences with domestic affairs during the sixties, and some observations and conclusions on their impact on the war.

Section 4.1 – Changes in America in the Sixties, the Great Society, and the Conduct of the Vietnam War

This section assesses the impact of the Post War Booms and how they affected social and cultural change in American in the sixties. The section also focuses on the interrelationship of the war and LBJ's Great Society programs, and their probable impact on domestic affairs and LBJ.

Exactly how and the degree that domestic affairs affected policy making for the Vietnam War is debatable. Some scholars argue that one or a combination of internal factors had a decisive impact. One strain of that is that domestic factors constrained or inhibited US policymakers from choosing courses of action that may have avoided defeat in Vietnam. Another is that one or several factors brought an end to an unlawful and immoral war. Other scholars say that they had some impact, but did not measurably alter the policies or their effects. Still other experts argue that Government leaders should and could have managed these influences on the war more successfully. And if they had, their options could have been less restrictive and would have led to a better outcome.

America in the Sixties

By the early sixties, the booms and changes that Chapter 1 describes began to have a significant effect on US economy, politics, and culture. The economy was still growing. According to John Andrew in his work *Lyndon Johnson and the Great Society*, workers' pay rose in the first five years of the decade by some 21 percent. Meanwhile, the consumer price index only increased 1.3 percent annually. This absence of inflation and the growth in incomes resulted in about a 25 percent overall increase in wealth in America during this timeframe. As in the previous decade, the increase in wealth was nearly equal between the top ten percent rich and the rest of America.

Meanwhile, the leading edge of the baby boomer generation had now reached eighteen years old. Thus, there was a glut of young people about to seek entry into the job market or higher education. As a result, there was twice the number of people about to enter the job market than in the earlier decade. Some economists now predicted a labor crisis. They forecasted that there might not be the kind and number of jobs available for these potential young workers. Meanwhile, for those not going into the job market, trade schools, community colleges, and state universities were trying to adjust to the new influx of students.

Despite some misgivings about overburdening of the job market, the widespread consensus of the times was that the growth in the economy and wealth would continue indefinitely. The 'baby boomers' setting out to go to college or trade school or out to get a job had lofty expectations. They thought that the affluence that the postwar booms had created in the late forties and fifties would continue unabated into the sixties.

For most of the sixties, according to James Paterson, the prosperity not only continued but increased. He notes that "the 1960s were the longest period of uninterrupted economic growth in United States history. Per capita income (in constant 1958 dollars) rose from $2,157 in 1960 to $3,050 in 1970, an unprecedented decadal increase of 41 percent. Prices stayed stable until the late 1960s. Although unemployment among 16- to 19-year-olds rose alarmingly, overall unemployment stayed low, falling to 3.5 percent in 1969. Poverty, as measured by the government, declined rapidly, from an estimated 22 percent of the population in 1960 to 12 percent in 1969."

The 'baby boomers' that were coming of age during this period began criticizing the prevailing ideas, values, and social attitudes of the what they called 'the stagnant fifties.' Encouraged by their parents, who naturally expected more for their children than they had had, the baby boomer generation had a new idealism centered on the belief that their futures were bound to be unlimited and of their choosing. Politicians took up on this theme. Thus, Kennedy's inaugural address appealed to the era of "a new generation" and "a new frontier" for the future.

As James Paterson further notes, "Millions of young people, especially those with the resources to pursue higher education, were swept up in the hopes for change that civil rights activists and others had done much to unleash and that Kennedy and Johnson had appealed to promote liberal programs. As Bob Dylan had prophesied in his song 'The Times They Are a-Changin,' many young people thought they had the potential to transform American life. Rarely before had two such interrelated and dominant trends—demographic and ideological—occurred at the same time. Reinforcing each other, they underlay much of the turmoil that distinguished the 1960s from the 1950s."

Along with this overall hope for change and opportunity, America's population continued to be on the move. The drift from urban areas to suburbs continued into the sixties. Major businesses and corporations had followed the movement to the suburbs; robbing the inner cities of the tax revenues they provided. By 1963, the effects of this movement were becoming quite noticeable. City housing, infrastructure, and schools crumbled. Job opportunities dropped. The jobs available were not in the higher wage categories.

The great black migration from the South to the North regions in the early postwar years had also continued into these same affected urban areas. An influx of minority immigrants joined them there. In New York City, for example, between the end of World War Two and 1965, more than a million Blacks and several hundred thousand Latinos had moved there. Thus, Blacks and other minorities – mostly Hispanic – were not experiencing the growth in income and wealth as the rest of America. Nor were they beneficiaries of the improvements in housing, education, and public services.

Further affecting the Black community, in general, was that the Supreme Court ruling in 'Brown versus the Board of Education' in the fifties had not made much progress. Segregation was still prevalent in both the North and the South. In the South, only 1.2 percent of black children were attending school with white children. In the North, Blacks were not allowed the same housing opportunities as Whites in the growing suburban areas. Moreover, as Blacks moved from the South into Northern urban neighborhoods, White people, who had not yet gone to the outlying areas, either now moved to them, or moved into new affluent urban adjacent areas, leaving the inner cities mainly minority inhabited. Consequently, de facto segregation in the North flourished.

Compounding continued segregation in the South was the fact that more than half of all Southern Blacks remained disfranchised. In hundreds of counties, less than 25 percent of the Black population registered to vote. While in some instances Blacks made up the majority in a voting district, only one to two percent were registered voters. Much of this was due to voting laws and restrictions that White officeholders passed to inhibit Black voting rights. All this further enabled the Jim Crow acts to continue to exclude Blacks from their rights, and segregation continued unabated.

Thus, within the overall hope of prosperity and promise that most of America was experiencing, there was a part of the populace, mainly minorities and lower income whites, not experiencing the benefits that such affluence seemed to ensure. Moreover, there was another portion, namely the growing numbers of those with the opportunity to obtain a higher education, that was becoming increasingly aware that their good fortunes and futures were not available to all of America as they should have been.

The unfolding war in Vietnam would affect both groups. The disenfranchised minorities and lower income would see the war as a distraction to their hopes for more equality and wealth in the future. The educated youth would see it as an interference in their hopes for a better and more prosperous life that their parents had told them they were entitled to and deserved.

The Great Society and its Domestic Effects

Amidst all the above ongoing changes, Lyndon Johnson became President. In many ways, he was an ideal person to use Government powers to improve the status of every American. LBJ had grown up in a family and a region in Texas in which he had lived amongst and observed the typical effects of poverty upon people. As a young Congressman, he had worked to enable and install several FDR's New Deal programs in his district. His experiences and relationship with the Congress as a Senator and then-Majority Leader had prepared him for dealing with those who would have to pass the laws and obtain the funds for legislation to affect change for the underprivileged and disenfranchised.

Johnson believed as President in 1964 that he had the opportunity and means to implement his domestic vision. He was not ashamed to use JFK's death and the public sentiment that followed to cloak his program as a continuance of Kennedy's legacy when he meant it for his own. Johnson also believed that the landslide victory over Goldwater provided him with the necessary public mandate. Moreover, the public mood seemed to be for change. Lastly, his economic advisors had told him that he would have the revenues to execute it. They projected a $35 billion increase in federal monies over the next five years.

As James Paterson explains, "After the election Johnson drove ahead with all of his legendary energy, for he was certain that his mandate would not last on Capitol Hill. 'You've got to give it all you can, that first year,' he told an aide. 'Doesn't matter what kind of a majority you come in with. You've got just one year when they treat you right, and before they start worrying about themselves."

The historian further notes, "And Congress did his bidding, enacting the most significant domestic legislation since FDR's first term and accelerating the rights-consciousness of the people. The GOP Congressional Committee grumbled that it was the 'Three-B Congress—bullied, badgered, and brainwashed.' The journalist James Reston marveled that LBJ was getting everything through the Congress but the abolition of the Republican party, and he hasn't tried that yet."

The Great Society programs that LBJ sent to Congress were broad in scope and ambitious. They targeted all the American political, economic, and societal problems of the past and the present. While its first and arguably most famous acts – the Civil Rights and Voting Rights – focused on the most critical actions for the segregated and disenfranchised, the myriad of other programs addressed almost every domestic sector – from education to health and welfare.

There would be some 200 significant pieces of legislation sent to Congress to do so. One of his aides noted, LBJ adopted programs "the way a child eats rich chocolate-chip cookies." In trying to raise the statue of his domestic agenda in the face of the growing concern for the Vietnam War he declared that his programs consisted of a "War on Poverty."

LBJ's rhetoric sought American voter support for his domestic agenda. At a commencement address at the University of Michigan in May 1964, he explained that we wanted "abundance and liberty for all." He promised, "We are going to assemble the best thought and the broadest knowledge from all over the world to find" the solutions." A month later to an audience in Detroit he assured all, "that America possesses the resources, properly marshaled, and directed by social purpose, to rid our civilization of the ills that have plagued mankind from the beginning of time." Meanwhile, as described in the previous chapter, he sought to minimize actions in Vietnam and tried to convince the Congress and the Public that it would not interfere with his domestic agenda.

There would be several problems that hampered the execution and results of the Great Society programs. The first was that the President and his economic advisors underestimated the extent of the difficulties they thought the legislation could solve and its costs. As John Andrew explains, "Eliminating poverty [was] expensive, far more expensive than anyone imagined in 1964. While the Great Society released about six million Americans from the bonds of poverty between 1964 and 1969, it did so with ever-escalating bureaucratic and financial costs. Forty-five federal social programs spent $9.9 billion in 1961; eight years later 435 programs spent $25.6 billion. Yet the $1.5 billion authorized for the War on Poverty in 1966 represented only 1.5 percent of the total federal budget. The OEO [The Office of Economic Opportunity's] annual expenditures between 1965 and 1968 averaged just $50 to $65 per year for each American in poverty, and much of that went to administrative costs."

The second problem was that government administration of the programs was fraught with fraud, ineptitude, inefficiencies, mistakes, and lack of overall supervision. As an example, 1964 funds authorized for the construction of 200,000 new public housing units to solve the rundown of city dwellings only resulted in some 23,000 constructed. Instead of investing in the restoration of city centers by creating new or refurbished business areas and improving adjacent housing, administrators chose to bulldoze large areas of ghetto housing. In their place, they reconstructed new facilities, such as colleges and local government administration offices, that were irrelevant to improving the inner-city problems.

The result was that most of the impoverished minorities and lower income whites remained in the rundown housing areas. In addition, absent any workable new business support, stores and companies kept moving to the suburbs. This movement further created an inordinate number of unemployed minorities or poor whites unable to either make the transfer to the suburbs or improve their living in the cities.

The third problem was that most of the Great Society programs addressed race-related, especially African American, problems. There was a considerable number of poor White Americans who were by-passed or received little improvement. This inadvertently created a backlash from White and local Communities on Federal efforts to improve racial problems. The result was further unintended segregation in suburban areas. Black protests and violent riots in cities like Los Angeles, Detroit and hundreds of others added to this backlash. By the late sixties, earlier majority support for the Great Society began to wither away.

A fourth problem hindering the execution and results was LBJ's overzealous rhetoric on his domestic program. The President promised that the Great Society could improve all the past and evolving problems in America. James Paterson argues that "As LBJ jetted about the country to publicize and to sign the landmark acts of his administration, he (and others) offered soaring descriptions of what he had done. The OEO could end poverty in ten years. Aid to education would provide the only valid passport from poverty. Medicare would advance the healing miracle of modern medicine."

When the programs were unable to solve the most intractable issues swiftly, hopes for solving the problems of race relations and poverty in America began to fade. As with the Vietnam War, the American public in short order grew restless and lost faith when their leaders did not solve things rapidly.

The Vietnam War, the Great Society, and Domestic Unrest

By far, the most extensive problem that the Great Society would confront was the competing Vietnam War costs. Indeed, the entire cost of LBJ's domestic programs eventually paled in comparison to the spending on the war. For example, by 1967 almost 75 percent of the budget was on the war or war-related costs. Funds authorized for health, education, and welfare represented only 12.2 percent.

LBJ and McNamara tried to hide the increasing costs of the war. In the early years 1965 to the end of 1966, they attempted to shift funds in the defense budget between programs to minimize the rising costs of the war to Congress and their potential impact on inflation. LBJ thought that this tactic would allow Congress to fund his domestic programs without concern for the costs of inflation. Johnson continued to do this as long as possible despite warnings from his economic advisors.

As the first combat ground troops were arriving in South Vietnam and by the time of the significant engagements in the Ia Drang Valley in the fall of 1965, prices started to rise. By late 1966, it became apparent even to Johnson that the US economy was beginning to see an increase in prices while wages remained stagnant. The economy was starting to feel the effects of inflation.

LBJ and McNamara continued to manipulate the budgets and its programs to manage and hide the costs of the war and its impact on domestic programs. Despite Johnson's constant pledges to give his military commanders in the field all that they needed to win the war, he and McNamara withheld critical resources. The President would not seek a call-up of the reserves. The Defense Secretary, assisted by his 'Whiz Kids' who worked the numbers, would not support the full reinforcements that his military commander said he needed throughout 1966 to 1968.

To make up the losses in the war and to minimize its impact on US global military balance, LBJ and McNamara ingeniously came up with alternative solutions. They relied on increases in the draft. For example, for 1965 and 1966 draft calls rose by some 120,000 and 150,000 personnel respectively. This manipulation of the draft, however, could only replace some of the losses. Moreover, they could not provide the manpower resources that Westmoreland needed in the time-frame he needed them.

Increasing draft calls soon backfired. As notices increased, and the war seemed to have no end in sight, they became an incentive for some to protest the war. Sudden notices interfered with the baby boomer generation's desires to seek higher education or a better life. They upset their dreams for the future. As the Government's rhetoric and waging of the war began to make little sense to many, dissents on the draft and the war grew. By 1967, burning draft cards was a principal method of protesting.

Furthering discord was the fact that draft exemptions and deferments favored those who were in higher education, married with children, and had key professional callings. Also, approval for medical exemptions was lax; and, if one had the money, could be bought. Moreover, one could also escape service in Vietnam by joining the reserves. With LBJ's decision to not call up or mobilize them, service there became a safe-haven from the war. The effect was to polarize America further and incite dissent over the war.

As mentioned, President Johnson made most of his crucial decisions on the war with the idea of minimizing the war's effects on his Great Society. For example, his decision in July 1965 to not call up the reserves was to avoid any debate or confrontation with the Congress. His primary incentive was to buy time to obtain the votes for his initial programs of the Great Society. As adeptly outlined by Larry Berman in *Planning a Tragedy*, "[LBJ's] own priority was to get agreement, at the lowest level of intensity he could, on a course that would meet the present need in Vietnam and not derail his legislative calendar."

As previously described as well, LBJ's attempt to manage the war included the manipulation of Congressional leaders. He primarily relied on techniques that he had learned in his years in the Senate. Thus, to those – especially the Republicans – who favored taking military action to save South Vietnam, he committed enough combat ground forces, he hoped, to thwart the communist offensive in the South. To keep the support of his Democratic colleagues for his Great Society, LBJ needed to minimize the view that the war would take precedence over domestic affairs – that he could wage limited war in Vietnam while continuing his war on poverty at home. Thus, he did not want to mobilize the reserves because this would signal that the country was on a wartime footing. So, as Berman argues, what he chose to do was a mid-course solution that afforded him a way out of this conundrum.

At first, by the end of 1965 and into 1966, it appeared that LBJ's decisions had paid off. As Berman further explains, "in the short run Johnson succeeded—only to prove the bankruptcy of his leadership. Six months following the July 28 decision Johnson went to Congress and declared, 'I believe we can continue the Great Society while we fight in Vietnam.' Johnson wrote in The Vantage Point, in that sentence, to which the Congress responded with heartening applause, the turmoil of months was resolved, and the Great Society moved through mid-passage into its final years of creative activity and accomplishment."

However, by the fall of 1967, as the costs of the war grew significantly from 1965 and as Johnson's campaign to sell the war to the American public was in full swing, LBJ asked Congress for a 6 percent surcharge tax increase. As he had feared in 1965, the 'beautiful woman' dream of his domestic programs suffered a significant reduction of funds in late 1967. Then came the TET offensive in January 1968. It became clear to the President that his Great Society had suffered a fatal blow, while his attempts to win in Vietnam appeared shattered.

LBJ suffered immensely from these two blows to his legacy. In the first two months of 1968, it became evident that the pressures had shaken him. He may have been on the verge of a nervous breakdown. His good friend and colleague in the Senate Richard Russell hesitated to visit him at the

White House in the early months of 1968. As the Senator related later, he could not stand to see LBJ sob uncontrollably.

Indeed, Johnson was having severe trouble sleeping. When he did, he had terrible nightmares. As he related to Doris Kearns Goodwin years afterward, "Every night when I fell asleep I would see myself tied to the ground in the middle of a long, open space. In the distance, I could hear the voices of thousands of people. They were all shouting at me and running toward me: 'Coward! Traitor! Weakling!' They kept coming closer. They began throwing stones. At exactly that moment I would generally wake up ... terribly shaken."

The twin pillars of Johnson's Administration – the Great Society and the Vietnam War – would both become failures. This outcome was not entirely clear in 1968 as LBJ announced that he would not run for another term. However, what was evident then was that both the war and the Great Society – along with the dramatic effects that the postwar booms brought about in culture and society - had the effect of breaking not only a President but also severely polarizing America.

This polarization had already found its outlet and expression in the Civil Rights movement. These, in turn, had already begun to protest the conduct of the war in Vietnam as early as 1966 and would continue to do so. As the war continued, and as the Great Society programs began to fail, other movements' protests, particularly against the war, would intensify. These, in turn, would have an impact on the media and public opinion on the legitimacy and handling of the war.

Section 4.2 – The Civil Rights and Anti-War Movements and the Vietnam War

This section describes the effect that both the Sixties Civil Rights and Anti-War movements may have had on the courses of action and decisions made in JFK and LBJ's administrations. It also sets the stage for the impact of these movements on the Nixon Presidency described in Chapter 5 to follow. It includes an explanation of how the civil-rights anti-war movements related to and affected one another and the nature of their relationship with war policies and actions.

The Growth of the Civil Rights Movement in the Sixties

The momentous events and actions of the Civil Rights movement during the Vietnam War had its roots in the postwar actions described in Chapter 1. For example, as mentioned above the landmark decision of the Supreme Court in 1954 on desegregation did not result in much change. The expectations of those in the movement in the fifties, like Dr. Martin Luther King, were not met by any stretch of the imagination. This was not only true about desegregation, but relatedly the distribution of wealth, voting rights, housing improvement, access to education, and job satisfaction.

The hotspots of civil rights discord for the Black community in the early sixties were primarily in the deep South and the Northern urban areas that were now taking shape as Black ghettos. In the South, segregation and discrimination were still the mainstays of southern politics, culture, society, and education. In the North, Blacks experienced problems of inadequate housing, poor schools, and reduced opportunities for jobs in the inner cities. Increasing use of drugs and lawlessness became a symptom of the plight of minorities there, especially in large city communities such as Watts in Los Angeles, California.

Despite years of sit-ins, other non-violent protests, and forced federal support for entry of Blacks into southern universities, there was yet no large-scale American public support for change. Up to this time, Black churches and their communities, with some support from student and religious activists, were primarily responsible for most of the advances in civil rights. An event in 1963 - the march on Washington and Dr. King's "I have a Dream" speech - would begin to make other Americans aware of the movement and begin to propel the civil rights crusade forward.

However, as moving as the event and King's rhetoric were, it was not the march or the Reverend's words that prompted the dramatic changes in the early sixties. It was when film and television brought images of the brutal beatings of marchers in Birmingham, Alabama, and other key places that public support in the North began to take hold. It also served as the impetus for the Civil Rights Act passed in 1964 and the Voting Rights Act in 1965. Throughout 1965 and 1966, large groups of Americans, both White and Black, demonstrated for civil and voting rights. Dr. King shifted much of his focus from the South to the troubled cities in the North.

Eventually, there would be measurable and real gains from these two acts and broader public support, especially in attacking the voting problems in the South. However, as mentioned in the previous section, the growing Black riots in the cities created significant backlashes. The growth of the Black power movement and the militant groups like the Black Panthers reinforced this reaction. In some cases, a few whites began to believe that communist agents had infiltrated and manipulated these movements and their leaders to protest and end the war in Vietnam. On the other hand, minority leaders, like Martin Luther King, began to protest the war because they felt that its burdens fell inordinately on minorities.

Ultimately the civil-rights movement – like the Great Society – helped in creating rather than solving the unfolding discord in American society. For like the President's well-meaning domestic programs it caused much division and resulted in polarizing America. The reactions to the assassinations of Martin Luther King and Robert Kennedy within months of each other in 1968 were more likely symptoms rather than causes of that discord and division.

On the other hand, the civil rights movement, like some of the legislation of the President's Great Society program, left a permanent positive mark on American society in the years after the war. It further energized important social groups to assert their rights in other areas. For example, the women's and gay rights movements started in earnest from the atmosphere of the Black community civil rights protest. As the Columbia History of Post-World War II in America notes, "The rebellious mood of the 1960s, and particularly the example of the civil rights movement, changed the political climate" in the US. One such impact with that change in political climate was the attitude toward and support for the war.

The Nature of the Civil-Rights Movement and the War

Like the Great Society programs, the Civil-Rights movement, and the changed political climate it produced had a reciprocal relationship with the Vietnam War. The war policies and events incited more radicalization of the movement. Meanwhile, the movement and claims of some of its leaders and supporters made statements about the conflict that added to the anti-war rhetoric. The question is how much it affected decision making on the American conduct of the war.

One of the significant effects that the Civil Right Movement had on the war and its decision-making, some scholars argue, was that it directly affected the public's dismay over government institutions and their ability to foster change. As historian Christian Appy explains, "Thousands of future antiwar activists participated in or were deeply inspired by, the boycotts, sit-ins, freedom rides, and community organizing that comprised the mass movement to end racial discrimination in the United States. The experience and example of challenging legal, political, economic, and cultural institutions that sustained racial inequality and division provided valuable political training for many who would later oppose America's actions in Vietnam."

Thus, Appy convincingly argues that "the civil rights movement provided a way of questioning power that was directly transferable to the antiwar movement. For years civil rights activists had measured official claims of justice against the grim racial realities of American life. As the war dragged on, more and more Americans would ask similar questions of official statements about Vietnam."

Another effect that the movement would have on the war was on the Congress. As the *Columbia History of Postwar America* explains, "obtaining support for a change in the civil rights meant dislodging the old Southern congressional hold over legislation for it. As support for civil rights grew in both the North and the South, the elections brought younger more liberal-minded members to the Congress. These began to both ignore the old norms for procedures in that legislative body and fight to produce new ones. Indeed, some of these more inexperienced and liberal members were key to the ultimate passage of crucial legislation affecting civil rights. It was among these newer, liberal-minded members that began not only to question the war but vote against Administration measures to wage it."

In their fight to change Congressional ways, and later to challenge Presidential actions in Vietnam, these young, liberal-minded congressmen began to use the media to further their views. They also sought support from like-minded members in the Executive Branch. This latter action created more leaks from some in the government to both the media and Congress. Consequently, increasingly administration officials shunned informing some members in Congress on policies and actions on the war for fear they would leak it to the press. In turn, the Congress began to feel that the President and his principal cabinet members were not willing to include and inform them of war actions and policies.

This all, despite LBJ's attempts with Senior Congressional leaders to continue to gain sympathy and support for his Vietnam policy, began to create an atmosphere of distrust between the executive and legislative branches of government. It later would lead to catastrophe in the Nixon Administration that would directly affect the conduct and end of the war in the early seventies.

Besides creating a new generational group in Congress, the civil rights enthusiasts began to ally themselves with the peace movement. Members, especially its most vocal advocates, began to follow the lead of King and other senior leaders and make claims about the unfairness to and unequal burdens of the war on the Black community. For example, one typical statement was that a disproportionate number of Blacks were being killed in the war and consequently black soldiers were being used as cannon fodder by their white officers.' The movement's leader Dr. King declared that Vietnam was "a white man's war, a black man's fight."

It is difficult to assess how much the argument that it was a Black man's fight had on the Black community or the public in general. These claims were so frequent that they became part of the myth of the injustice and immorality of the war for America. The facts are that about 12.5% of those killed were black. This number was about one percent higher than the overall ratio of the black population in America.

Often rhetoric of a respected leader trumps truth. Indeed, after the assassination of Dr. King, some Blacks in the Armed Forces reacted against their superiors, some deserted. Despite the press coverage of this, the actual incidents were not as prominent as the media indicated at the time or as the historians claim later.

Later in the Nixon years, there was a more pronounced increase in racial violence and discord in the US Armed Forces. This rise perhaps was the most significant impact on the waging of the war. However, then the US had already decided to withdraw from Vietnam. Chapter 10 will further examine the issue of criminality and the deterioration of the US Armed Forces in Vietnam.

As for the movements' direct effect on decision making for the war, its impact was, at best, minimal during the Kennedy Administration. JFK's policies on Vietnam were not affected because most of the Public, and those involved in the movement, did not see the US involvement there as a threat to domestic politics or programs. Indeed, most then did not even know where Vietnam was.

There is evidence, however, that the civil-rights movement and its protests eventually added to the pressures on LBJ. As Doris Kearns Goodwin relates, LBJ wondered why the Black community did not realize that he was their friend. After he had left public life, he told her: "How is it possible that all these people could be so ungrateful to me after I had given them so much? Take the Negroes. I fought for them from the first day I came into office. I spilled my guts out in getting the Civil Rights Act of 1964 through Congress. I put everything I had into that speech before the joint session in 1965.

LBJ continued, "I tried to make it possible for every child of every color to grow up in a nice house, to eat a solid breakfast, to attend a decent school, and to get a good and lasting job. I asked so little in return. Just a little thanks. Just a little appreciation. That's all. But look at what I got instead. Riots in 175 cities. Looting. Burning. Shooting. It ruined everything." Thus, though its effect on LBJ's decision making is difficult to correlate directly, one can reasonably surmise that it certainly added to the frustration and stress that Johnson experienced.

There was one group of decision-makers involved in the war, however, that the civil rights movement had a major, even crucial, impact upon US involvement in Vietnam from its onset. The growing discord and anti-war sentiment of the civil rights movement certainly caught the attention of the North Vietnamese, particularly after 1965. Much of the new evidence on North Vietnam decision making during the war shows that it was, in fact, instrumental in their strategy to defeat American arms.

As we will see in the Chapters ahead, the civil rights movement, along with the overall domestic reactions to the war, gave sustenance to the North Vietnamese leaders to prevail in their goals to unify Vietnam using force. They knew that they could not militarily defeat American combat forces. They did think that they could win if the American public and Congress would stop its support for the war. They would be right.

The Anti-War Movement

Anti-war sentiment during the Vietnam War was not new to American politics. While the Vietnam anti-war protests exceeded in scale other US anti-war movements, America had a long tradition of peace activism and anti-militarism. For example, several prominent citizens, to include future president Abraham Lincoln, protested the Mexican War in 1846. In the early 20th Century, in reaction to the Spanish-American War and later the First World War, there was a proliferation of peace organizations, such as the Carnegie Endowment for International Peace, the National Peace Federation, and the American Union Against Militarism.

In reaction to the disillusionment after the First World War, moreover, Congress passed a series of laws designed to keep America out of a future war. These 'neutrality acts' inhibited US support of Great Britain when the Second World War broke out. Even after Pearl Harbor and America's entry, there were pacifist organizations that encouraged draftees to become conscientious objectors.

The rise of communism, the Cold War, and the Red Scare of the late 40s and the 50s had curbed much of these anti-war sentiments. By the end of the fifties and early sixties, however, they began to emerge as a significant force in America. The first organized groups of the movement focused then on the limitation of and control of nuclear weapons. Two such groups became major players in the Vietnam War. One was the National Committee for a Sane Nuclear Policy (SANE). The other was the Students for a Democratic Society or SDS.

The baby boomers of the post-world war era made up many of these groups' members. These were also mostly college-educated young people who had benefited from the educational growth after the

World War. Two of the most notable members and leaders were Dr. Benjamin Spock in SANE and Tom Hayden in the SDS.

The SDS, in early 1965, organized the first national demonstration against the Vietnam War in the nation's capital. In November of that year, both the SDS and SANE organized an anti-war march on Washington that encompassed some 30,000 people. It was during that march that Norman Morrison, a civilian Quaker upset over the killings he saw in the media, set fire to himself in protest to the war in front of Robert McNamara as the Secretary watched from his Pentagon office. The movement grew significantly in both numbers and activism, to include violence, as President Nixon took office in 1969.

The movement had its greatest effect on universities and colleges throughout the country. The SDS and other organizations prepared 'sit-ins' and occupations of campus buildings. This demonstration affected their Reserve Officer Training Center (ROTC) programs. Some schools shut them down. Others experienced a decrease in membership. Overall, student enrollment in ROTC dropped from almost 200,000 in 1966 to a little over 72,000 by 1973.

ROTC sources of commission were essential to keep a quality officer corps, particularly in the Army. To make up for these reductions, and the casualties of junior officers in Vietnam, the Army increased its outputs from its Officer Candidate Schools or OCS. These schools produced many of its junior officers in eight weeks – significantly less time than ROTC and military academy commissioned officers.

While many officer candidate graduates proved themselves capable and brave in the war, many others accounted for a decline in the professionalism of the junior leader force. One such product of the OCS program was Lieutenant William Calley, who led the infantry platoon in the infamous My Lai Massacre.

Despite the attempts of the Johnson and later Nixon Administrations to label the movement as solely a radical student protest of the war, the movement was quite diverse. It eventually included many sectors of American society. For example, groups demonstrating for women's rights, some led by ladies who had fought in World War Two and had become dissatisfied with conditions for women in post-war America, joined in on the anti-war demonstrations. In addition, as mentioned, non-violent Civil Rights organizations, led by Martin Luther King, united with the movement.

Besides being broad, the movement grew to encompass tens of thousands of protesters. George Herring provides a sense of the size and nature of some of the more prominent protests. For example, he notes that "The most dramatic act of protest came on October 21, 1967, with the March on the Pentagon, the culmination of Stop the Draft Week. A diverse group estimated at 100,000 including colorfully arrayed hippies and intellectuals such as Mailer, gathered at the Lincoln Memorial for songs of protest by performers such as Peter, Paul, and Mary and Phil Ochs and speeches proclaiming the beginning of active resistance."

As Herring continues to explain, "As many as 35,000 protesters subsequently crossed the Potomac and advanced on the Pentagon. Some carried NLF flags, others smoked marijuana, and a few put flowers in the barrels of the rifles of soldiers guarding the building. Soldiers were challenged to leave their posts. The demonstration ended that evening in violence when federal marshals moved in with clubs and tear gas and arrested nearly 700 demonstrators."

A small portion of the overall movement, Herring notes, was extremely radical. Those in these groups incited, created, and took part in violent demonstrations and criminal behavior. The prime example of this was the 'Weathermen Group.' This group was a splinter organization of the SDS. Taking their name from a Bob Dylan song, they advocated revolutionary positions characterized by Black Power and opposition to the Vietnam War. The group conducted a campaign of bombings through the mid-1970s – to include one of the Capital Building. It also took part in actions such as a riot in Chicago timed to coincide with the trial of the Chicago Seven, a group of protest leaders led by Tom Haden. In 1970, the group issued a "Declaration of a State of War" against the United States government, under the name "Weather Underground Organization."

This radicalization of the anti-war or peace movement had an adverse impact on the overall movement itself. Like the riots in the name of civil rights, it lead to more division of the already polarized public. It also led to extreme governmental intelligence and law enforcement involvement in private citizen affairs and lives. For example, LBJ, believing the peace movement was turning the public against the war effort and even controlled by communist elements, instructed the CIA and the FBI to conduct surveillance and collect information on movement leaders and most notorious actors.

Formalized into a program called Operation CHAOS the CIA began to listen in to private conversations of American citizens suspected of collusion with communist agents. Meanwhile, the FBI collected and compiled dossiers on such people as Martin Luther King, Jr, and Malcolm X and organizations such as the Black Panthers. All in all government intelligence and law enforcement agencies created some 7,000 files during the operation without finding any substantial evidence of collusion with communist bloc or Vietnamese leaders.

This does not mean that there was no relationship between the antiwar movement and Communist North Vietnam. As we will see, particularly in Chapter 7, there were significant contacts and exchanges between North Vietnam propagandists and antiwar leaders. Again, however, the impact on the war would mainly be on the North Vietnam leaders hopes for and actions in their prosecution of the war.

The Impact of the Anti-War Movement on the Government and the War

While the antiwar movement included an amalgamation of civil rights, peace advocates, draft dodgers, antigovernment and other protest groups, according to two scholars - Simon Hall and David Steigerwald - most leaders and members of the movement focused on legitimate concerns about the war. One of the primary ones was that they believed the Government had acted unconstitutionally in its waging of the war. They also argued that much of the decision making on the war was hidden from both the people and its representatives in Congress.

They further reasoned that it was their right as citizens to demand more transparency from their government on what was happening in the conflict. Many also thought that the war was a mistake. They contended that the US should not have engaged in a revolutionary or civil war so far from our shores and outside of US national interest.

Much of this criticism and argument was logical, and some had validity. Some of it was also a result of misperceptions and mistruths. For example, many scholars and journalists painted the war as a purely revolutionary war in which a distraught Southern Vietnamese faction led the fight against an unjust autocratic government. This group mostly ignored the support and direction the

North was giving to the conflict. They also misrepresented the fact that the PAVN was the main enemy force fighting the American and ARVN forces. They further fell victim to the mistruth that the DRV leaders were more nationalists than communists who just wanted to reunite Vietnam.

Of course, the DRV promoted and took advantage of this misinformation. They further encouraged through a vast propaganda program the ruse that the revolutionaries of the South, the indigenous Viet Cong, were the main arm that was fighting for their rights against a corrupt Southern government. The Republic of South Vietnam, the DRV propaganda argued, would not be able to exist without American support because it did not represent the Vietnamese people.

As we will see in Chapter 7, the North Vietnamese even hosted conferences that invited many of the American protest leaders and groups to give them this propaganda to fuel the anti-war and peace movements in the US. In turn, some American antiwar leaders made broadcasts or videos for the Communist North Vietnamese to use in their propaganda campaigns against the US.

One of the more intriguing arguments on the overall movement comes from retired Colonel Harry Summers in his book *On Strategy*. Like other analysts, Summers reiterates that Americans have had a tradition of anti-militarism, which naturally sparks protests of wars and foreign adventures. The Vietnam War protests were no exception to this tradition.

However, in the case of the Vietnam War, Summers argues that the protests were a direct result of the fact that the Government failed to be open with the people on what their policies were and why they were pursuing them. Summers faults the Presidents, mostly LBJ, for lack of transparency and candidness in explaining the war to the American people. He believes that the Johnson Administration, rather than ignoring the protests or dismissing them as out of the mainstream, should have had a program to discuss the issues that aggravated them.

In short, US policy-makers should have had an active agenda to build a consensus for their policies that went beyond just controlling their message and giving some speeches. He writes, "Instead of building this moral consensus and taking action to smooth the natural friction that exists between the American people and their Army, Vietnam war policies tended to aggravate it."

One policy, Summers notes particularly 'aggravated' the friction. This was the decision not to call up the reserves and put the country on a war footing. As he explains, this decision sent a negative message to the public on the worthiness of the war. That is, the signal he was sending to the American population was that if the President did not think that the conflict was worth mobilizing the populace to fight it, then it must not have been worth the sacrifice.

This retired Army Colonel and Vietnam veteran further speculates that this lack of consensus building for the war eventually led to a schism between those who supported the movement and the Army that fought the war. The Army, he argues, eventually became a symbol of everything that was wrong with the war. If one felt that the war was immoral, then the Army became a bastion of immorality.

This may explain, Summer surmises, why soldiers were spat upon and called baby killers during the war's later years. The massacre at My Lai village in 1968 and the Army's incompetent handling of it rightfully added to this image. The media's portrayal of the Army's reliance on firepower that resulted in unnecessary civilian killing in the war and its use of such phrases as 'search and destroy' operations furthered the impression of the US Army's immoral approach to the war.

Of all the evidence on the impact of the anti-war movement on the war and its conduct, the one clear, most evident impact was on one person in particular – Lyndon Baines Johnson. Like those of the civil-rights movement, the anti-war protests severely affected LBJ personally. His statements and later memoirs, as well as those who knew him at the time, support a significant impact these movements had upon the President. It may have so affected him that he could no longer make sound decisions. He certainly, by his acts in 1968, was unable to carry on his duties as Commander-in-Chief.

Take his statements to his post Presidency biographer. As with the lack of Black appreciation already mentioned, he lamented to Professor Goodwin, "Then take the students. I wanted to help them, too. I fought on their behalf for scholarships and loans and grants. I fought for better teachers and better schools. And look what I got back. Young people by the thousands leaving their universities, marching in the streets, chanting that horrible song about how many kids I had killed that day."

Doris Kearns Goodwin's conclusion about the effects of both the civil rights and anti-war movements on LBJ seems to be on the mark. She states, "So strong was Johnson's need for affection, and so vital his need for public gratitude, that he experienced this rejection of his "good works" as an absolute rejection of himself. Denied the appreciation which not only empowered but sustained his self, the love which validated his identity, the anatomy which gave Lyndon Johnson's ego its shape was dissolved. His energy and capacity to direct that energy outward abandoned him. Every presidential responsibility (speeches, conducting meetings, greeting visitors) took inordinate effort."

In more stark terms, by 1968, Johnson had lost any courage he had to deal with the tough decisions. This loss of nerve was the most critical factor in his decision to abandon his policies to continue to wage war against the North. As the evidence shows, the protests of the civil rights and its related anti-war movements added to the pressures and stress on the President, as well as some of his key advisors – most notably Robert McNamara.

How much that related directly to the entire decision making for the war is impossible to measure or assess. However, it had to matter. It certainly did matter during the first three months of 1968 when LBJ had to confront the TET crisis and lost his nerve. Thereby, the 'Reluctant Commander-in-Chief' retreated from the war he had chosen to wage and abandoned the nearly 500,000 American soldiers then on the field of battle.

War, and in this case reactions and protests to it, puts immense pressure on both military and civilian leaders. Carl Von Clausewitz in his treatise *On War* recounts the nature of that pressure and what it takes to overcome it. He explains: "The personalities of statesmen and soldiers are such important factors that in war above all it is vital not to underrate them…. Since all information and assumptions are open to doubt, and with chance at work everywhere, the commander continually finds that things are not as he expected…."

The theorist then argues that "If the mind is to emerge unscathed from this relentless struggle with the unforeseen, two qualities are indispensable: first, an intellect that, even in the darkest hour, retains some glimmerings of the inner light which leads to truth; and, second, the courage to follow this faint light wherever it may lead." That courage, he further explains, is expressed, in both battle and in making decisions on war, in determination – the determination to accept responsibility and "overcome doubt and the perils of hesitation."

In that sense, as Clausewitz explains, commanders must learn how to develop this determination, which "in a single instance is an expression of courage; if it becomes characteristic, a mental habit…. But here we are referring not to physical courage but to the courage to accept responsibility, and maintain the ability to keep one's head at times of exceptional stress and violent emotion."

On this point, Clausewitz concludes that determination can best be acquired through the study of and an education on war and its nature. For him, this is the central point of his work – that it is through the continued study of war that one can best develop an understanding and determination for its conduct.

LBJ had neither an understanding of, or determination for, the conduct of the Vietnam War. Nor did his primary civilian advisor - Robert McNamara. Thus, both were susceptible to and eventually overcome not only by the war's innumerable surprises and doubts but also by the significant protests they witnessed and experienced.

Section 4.3 - The Media and Public Opinion and the Vietnam War

As stated at the beginning of this chapter, both Presidents Kennedy and Johnson tried to control the message to the Public and Congress of their intent and purpose of their war policies. They, of course, tried to use the media as a principal means to convey those messages. On the other hand, civil-rights and anti-war movement leaders also used the Press to get their views to the Public. Media leaders had to sort out these opposed messages and views, based on the statements of leaders of all sides, as well as what they could report on in the events of the war and at home they observed.

Not only was this a complex undertaking, but it involved questions of who influences whom, and how much and what kind of influence did it have on the waging of the war. With the advance and changes in news gathering and reporting changing dramatically - especially with the growth of television and the lack of censorship during the war- the impact of the media is one of the most difficult questions to undertake. This section attempts to examine the issue of how much the Media and Public Opinion influenced the decisions on the Vietnam War and its outcome.

Early Media Reactions to Vietnam Intervention

At the beginning of the sixties, when members of the Press began to cover the US support for South Vietnam and its assistance programs, generally the media was supportive of the American government's goal to prevent a communist subjugation of South Vietnam. They bought into the political assumption of the Domino Theory. Their early coverage portrayed US involvement as purely advisory and a noble cause. Pictures in the major news magazines and their stories displayed and narrated the efforts of American soldiers to help the ARVN to defeat a communist insurrection insistent on overthrowing a regime struggling to set up a democratic government.

However, American reporters also ran into problems with the South Vietnamese Government in their coverage of the US support and the conduct of the war. That interference led to some news people's bitterness. Resentment resulted in questioning the commitment of the RVN leaders to democracy. That led to criticism, even distaste of the South Vietnamese regime.

President Diem thought the Press had no role in his country. He banned press coverage of the war from the field. The Kennedy Administration faced a dilemma. It recognized that banning the Press did not fit with trying to develop a democratic South Vietnamese Government. On the other hand, some US officials understood that the Diem regime faced a situation where it felt that it had to control news reports about its progress in suppressing the insurrection. Moreover, the role of the press in the US was different from most Asian experiences. In Korea, for example, the government strictly controlled the Press.

The State Department, with the Ambassador's approval, decided to issue a policy statement to the media in South Vietnam explaining this dilemma, and setting up what it thought were reasonable rules for news coverage. It published a directive, called Cable 1006, that stressed the need for sensitivity. The cable emphasized that the conflict was a South Vietnamese affair, and the latter did not have any tradition or inclination for freedom of the press. The directive further encouraged positive reporting to reassure South Vietnamese efforts. The US Information Agency organization, which was a part of the State Department, issued this document to US government officials in South Vietnam to give guidance to the press, not to prohibit their reporting.

The directive did not work as intended. US officials in South Vietnam began to make a concerted effort to paint overly optimistic pictures of success in the training and advisory efforts. American news people saw it as an attempt, which it was, to control the Press news and views. Meanwhile, Diem's intransigence and hostility toward American news media increased. Some noted media people reacted negatively. They began to rebel against the attempts to propagandize the story out of Vietnam and attack the person they saw as responsible for the failure to democratize South Vietnam – Ngo Dinh Diem.

Homer Bigart of the *New York Times* was one such newsman. Returning from Vietnam in the summer of 1962, Bigart wrote, "The issue remains in doubt because the Vietnamese president seems incapable of winning the loyalty of his people. Should the situation disintegrate further, Washington may face the alternative of ditching Ngo Dinh Diem for a military junta or sending combat troops to bolster the regime."

Replacing Bigart for the *Times* was David Halberstam. He, like most of the other members of the small press corps at the time, did not question the need for the US to confront communism in South Vietnam. In fact, soon after arriving, Halberstam reported on several successes and attributed them to the enhanced US military aid to the South Vietnamese.

Shortly after, however, he and several other reporters began to report on the ineptness of the South Vietnamese Government to gain widespread support. They also criticized its military for its inability to engage and defeat the growing VC threat; and the need to find a replacement for Diem.

Becoming increasingly frustrated with the optimism of administration officials, Halberstam and Associated Press reporter Neil Sheehan turned to US advisors in the field for their sources. While under pressure to report good news, these officers were experiencing increased frustration with the South Vietnamese Army leadership. This led to some advisors giving candid reports on military deficiencies and defeats to anyone who would listen. Frustrated reporters welcomed their views, primarily because it was newsworthy and made for great copy.

One of the most famous examples of the Press use of the advisor was an assessment of the Battle of Ap Bac in January 1963. Both Halberstam and Sheehan reported the battle as a significant defeat of the South Vietnamese Army. Their reports quoted American officers, such as the ARVN division advisor named Lieutenant Colonel John Vann, that the performance of the ARVN was miserable, and that the VC fought more effectively. Both Ambassador Nutting and General Harkins were incensed over the news report and the fact that an advisor was its source. They tried to place a more positive spin on the battle. Meanwhile, they counseled Vann for his interview with Halberstam and Sheehan.

Hence, according to these journalists, American efforts to find a way to solve the dilemma of fixing a South Vietnamese Government and its Army were doomed to fail. This failure, moreover, was primarily because of the incompetent and duplicitous leadership and mismanagement of US efforts in the entire Vietnam War. As the title of Sheehan's history simply explains it, the war was nothing more than a *Bright and Shining Lie*. This view remains today the crux of the orthodox view of the Vietnam War.

As mentioned in Chapter 2, more recently, however, there is more information about the event and more people who are arriving at conclusions different from that of Halberstam and Sheehan. Professors Mark Moyar and Andrew Birtle are two historians who take a different view. Moyar, a Harvard and Cambridge educated historian, in his *Triumph Forsaken* argues that the ARVN "did not perform well at Ap Bac, but neither did they display gross ineptitude or cowardice. Most of their troubles could be traced to the terrain, to the prowess of crack Viet Cong troops, or to Clausewitzian friction –the inevitable mishaps that make easy tasks difficult in war."

Again, as briefly explained in Chapter 2, Moyar further claims that "Colonel John Paul Vann committed the most grievous error of the battle by landing the reserve company too close to the western edge of the Viet Cong's defensive positions, which he mistakenly believed to be free of enemy forces." The Harvard Professor also argues that "Vann succeeded in misleading the American press corps, and hence the world, about the events at Ap Bac by exaggerating the faults of the South Vietnamese and hiding his own. The mischaracterization of Ap Bac as the epitome of the Diem government's incompetence would not take root so quickly, since contrary evidence abounded at the time. The rise of that misinterpretation, like that of many other denigrations of the Diem regime, would have to await the overthrow of the Diem government."

Professor Birtle supports Moyar's view that the ARVN performance at Ap Bac was not as bad as portrayed. He also agrees that Halberstam's and Sheehan's reports and others overexaggerated the South Vietnamese Army's faults. On the other hand, Birtle supports the newsmen's views that the Diem's interference with and control of the ARVN command structure severely hampered overall ARVN competence and performance at the time. Birtle further believes that the Diem interference would have a lasting effect on South Vietnamese Army performance throughout the war. However, like Moyar, Birtle emphasizes that the two newsmen's description of the battle exaggerate the ARVN mistakes, and does not account enough for the fact that the VC were better armed and prepared.

The US Army's official history, *The Military and the Media, 1962-1968*, states that much of the controversy over Ap Bac and further critical reporting was due to the way the Diem regime treated the US media. The history also comments on the Ambassador and US commander for the way they handled the press – providing their spin on that battle as well as other actions that were starkly different from what the history argues happened. Thus, the early 1963 battle is a turning point in the development of animosity and differences of view between the senior US military and other government officials and the Press.

The Army Media history continues, "Ap Bac and the controversy surrounding it marked a divide in the history of U.S. relations with the news media in South Vietnam. Before, the battle newsmen criticized Diem, badgered American officials, and argued for more US control of the war, but were still agreeable. After it, correspondents became convinced that they were being lied to and withdrew, embittered, into their community. Although Ambassador Nolting and General Harkins professed to be accessible to the press at any time, most senior American civilian and military officials in South Vietnam limited their contacts with newsmen to formal occasions such as news conferences and briefings, where they turned an ever more optimistic face toward their critics."

Because of the stories about Ap Bac and other events in South Vietnam in early 1963, US newspapers and television stations began to question the Kennedy Administration's policies more earnestly. They stepped up their editorials about the ineffectiveness and the corruptness of the South Vietnamese Government. They ran stories on Diem's unjustified attacks against those in

South Vietnam that openly opposed his actions, such as his arrests of protesting Buddhist Monks and attacks against their pagodas. Several journalists further assessed that Diem's Government could never be a democratic one.

Moreover, based on field reports on the use of US armed helicopters and fixed-wing air support of ARVN operations, the Press began publishing commentaries that raised the issue of how much was the US military effort solely advisory and how much was devoted to a war that the US was directly trying to influence.

One of the most famous American newspapermen of the time was Walter Lippmann. In the early sixties, he was writing for the *Washington Post*. Lippmann questioned the capability of the Diem Regime or any other South Vietnamese government's ability to defeat the insurgency. He further argued that only US direct military intervention could do that. However, he warned that any significant and direct US military intervention would be risky because of the strong possibility of another war with China.

The three national television stations at the time – ABC, NBC, and CBS – also reported on the news coming out of Vietnam. However, in the early sixties, the networks had not yet fully established themselves there. Coverage and reporting were primarily based on the newspaper and wire agency reports. In fact, most news broadcasts were only fifteen minutes long then.

By the end of 1963, it became apparent to reporters that the brief successes of the year before in Vietnam had eroded. By then, the TV broadcasting news had expanded to thirty minutes. Coverage of Vietnam became more extensive. These TV reports were becoming quite astonishing. One report, aired on all three major stations, showed a Monk set himself aflame in protest to the Diem Regime's policy toward Buddhists. The American public beheld a human engulfed in flames and slowly slumping over to his agonizing death. This sensationalism was just a precursor to the violence and horror that would engulf the TV news on Vietnam during the height of the US involvement.

JFK Administration officials granted interviews to explain its policies and deliver its message on the war. McNamara would extol his figures showing success in US aid programs. He was a master at using these measures of effectiveness to show progress and dispel contrary views. Newspapers and magazines published pictures of him pointing at these charts and maps as if it was a presentation to a board of directors of a large corporation reporting on its profits.

Two months before his death and Diem's assassination, President Kennedy granted an interview to Walter Cronkite, the CBS news anchorman. He reiterated his theme that the war was a South Vietnamese affair and could only be won by them. He optimistically said that the South Vietnamese government could gain the support of the people, "with changes of policy and perhaps personnel." After the Diem coup, some newspapers reiterated JFK's reference to changes in personnel as a reason to believe that the US had engineered the coup and killing. Of course, the Government denied involvement.

Despite these reports, film coverage, and interviews, Vietnam was not yet on the public's 'radar' in the early sixties. Moreover, most stories, whether on TV or in the newspapers or magazines, were not focusing on the US involvement there. The worthier news stories were still of what was happening in Europe, and the situation in Cuba.

In addition, as mentioned, most stories did not challenge the reason for US involvement. They questioned matters such as tactics and politics in Vietnam, which the US public did not have much interest in. US deaths and other losses had not been significant. All of that would soon change, with the upcoming commitment to combat of American soldiers, marines, airmen, and sailors.

The Americanization of the War and the Media

The 1964 Gulf of Tonkin crisis and later bombing reprisals began to garner more press and public attention. These incidents raised the stakes for our continued involvement in Indochina. Though they were mostly naval and air, now the US had outwardly committed its forces to battle.

Not knowing the full circumstances that led to or occurred in the Gulf of Tonkin, the media supported Johnson's actions. Marguerite Higgins, a famous newspaper editorialist who had covered the Korean War, wrote in *Newsday* that at last, the US had decided to strike at communist sanctuaries. Walter Lippmann praised Johnson for the effective use of naval and air power which, he argued, could offer the means of punishing the communists for their aggression without getting involved in a ground war in Asia.

There were some, however, who had misgivings. James Reston, a protégé of Lippmann's, wrote prophetically in the *Times* that Congress's resolution" demonstrates just how much the powers of the presidency have grown and how those of Congress have declined in foreign affairs." He reminded those who read his editorials, now that the US has committed its military in the area it has "proclaimed that the maintenance of peace and security in all of Southeast Asia is vital to its national interest and to world peace." The implication was that this commitment might even grow.

President Johnson was pleased with this support. With the media mainly behind him, he could now interject in his campaign that while he was not a warmonger like his opponent Senator Goldwater, he had stood firm against communist aggression. Johnson reinforced the notion that he had used only limited force, and said at a news conference, "We are not about to send American boys 9 or 10 thousand miles away from home to do what Asian boys ought to be doing for themselves." However, if the war turned bad in the South, LBJ felt he had the overall support of the news media to make decisions for further US military action if need be.

However, with an election coming up, Johnson still felt that he needed to portray himself as a peace candidate rather than someone, like Goldwater, who could get the US involved in a war in Asia, or even more catastrophic, involved in yet another war with China – a nuclear power. Accordingly, his campaign put together the now famous TV political ad showing a little girl picking the petals from a flower and counting down to the last one, when a nuclear explosion occurs at the end. Thus, LBJ seemed successful, especially with his victory in November 1964, to have portrayed himself as one who would not decide to go to war flippantly.

When the decision for war came in July of 1965, the mainstream media continued to support Johnson. As with the retaliatory bombing for the attacks in the Tonkin Gulf, the media response reflected public support for the deployment of American troops to Vietnam. For example, Joe Alsop wrote that US combat involvement was critical to our past President's commitment to the preservation of the South and containment of communism in Asia.

Joe Alsop was one of the most prominent journalists of his time. Though not renown as Lippmann, he had been a Washington mainstay reporter who had written for the *Saturday Evening Post* and the

New York Herald. He had also been a Kennedy favorite and hawk when it came to Vietnam. Alsop had served in the Pacific as a naval officer, where he had been captured and then released by the Japanese. He had also won the Pulitzer for his reporting during the Korean War. Thus, he was a respected and considered competent war reporter. Now he was an independently syndicated columnist. In the aftermath of LBJ's commitment of troops, Alsop would continue to be supportive and became a favorite of US military commanders in Vietnam because of his backing.

Other notable news editors, however, took different views of LBJ's escalation. Walter Lippmann, though overall supportive, warned of a widening war. Based on what had happened in Korea, he counseled that the Chinese, whom he saw as the primary culprit in the aggression, may eventually intervene. Several in Congress and the news media adopted this "Korean War assumption" as the most critical consideration in the US intervention. As previously discussed, President Johnson agreed with this cautionary warning.

Now that he had committed combat troops to the conflict, LBJ wanted to 'control' the story of the escalation. He especially wanted to continue portraying his policy toward the Vietnam War as one of restraint. He wanted the blame for US military actions to be squarely on the Communist North Vietnamese and their Soviet and Chinese sponsors. This approach, Johnson believed, would convince Congress that the US was not on a 'war footing,' and was only going to commit enough resources to contain communist advances. In turn, LBJ expected the Congress to protect his domestic agenda. Accordingly, the Administration gave MACV guidance that the mission of US forces in the initial build-up was purely defensive to protect key installations.

Under White House direction, General Westmoreland and his public affairs officers in country in early 1965 were cautious in their press releases and briefings on their mission. They sought to conceal the fact that the Administration had given MACV permission to conduct offensive operations to support the ARVN and prevent further deterioration of the situation. By June 1965, US forces in country, however, were conducting offensive operations, and American correspondents were reporting on these so-called, 'Counterinsurgency Combat Operations.'

It did not take long for the correspondents to reveal the obvious. One reporter from the *New York Times*, Arthur Krock, wrote an article entitled, *By Any Other Name, It's Still War*. He wrote that despite what the US wanted to call it, US combat operations in Vietnam had heralded a 'fundamental change' to the conflict there.

When LBJ went on TV in later July 1965 to announce the deployment of major combat ground forces, several reporters at the July press conference did ask him if the deployments he announced were a shift in policy. LBJ testily shot back, "no it does not." That was the end of any further questioning; but the beginning of a long road of inept, or deceitful, or duplicitous attempts to control the message and misinform or deceive the Press, the Public, and the Congress on what was going on in Vietnam.

Despite the Administration's attempts to downplay the commitment and depict US operations as solely supporting South Vietnamese war efforts, by August 1965 the major news stories that came from South Vietnam were about US combat operations. Correspondents, which had increased four-fold from the Advisory years to several hundred with about sixty in the field, reported on the 'big war' search and destroy operations.

Media stories soon included such unknown and strange place names as the Ia Drang Valley, the Iron Triangle, and War Zone C. As one historian noted, overall "the press coverage gave the impression that the United States, through the massive military power it was bringing to bear on a small Southeast Asian nation, had the initiative in the contest."

News coverage at home similarly focused on the US combat operations and the decisions for continued gradual escalation of US deployments and bombing. CBS News did a series of reports on the war, primarily inviting Johnson Administration officials to explain their policies. To the personal chagrin of President Johnson, Morey Shafer did a CBS story that aired in August 1965 about a Marine unit that torched a Vietnamese village at Cam Ne.

The story brought out the extreme complexity of the war for American soldiers and marines who had to fight a ruthless enemy who used the local populace to its advantage against US forces. Later, Morey Safer also did a story that Walter Cronkite introduced and co-narrated on the Ia Drang Valley campaign in November 1965. It was a startling account with pictures of the aftermath of the battle that included dead US soldiers. Soon this will come all too familiar to American families watching the news on TV.

While filming operations in Vietnam was limited to technologies available then, newscasts on all three networks often included dramatic film footages of operations and fierce battles. As in the Ia Drang battles, they included dead and wounded American soldiers and marines; something the FDR Administration had in their war tried to minimize. They also included stories of the increasing number of captured air force and naval aviators over North Vietnam.

On many occasions, the combat film clips and pictures exceeded in graphic depiction the death and destruction photos of the famous American Civil War photographers Matthew Brady and James Gardner. Like the Civil War pictures, the film clips, many of which were in color, would have a profound effect on the public.

Meanwhile, from the end of 1965 through 1967, the media also covered the anti-war movement. Scenes of protesters marching in the streets of Washington, DC, coupled with University sit-ins and some violent protests in other cities, often were shown along with reports of the battles and engagements on the ground and in the air in Vietnam. The contrast, especially with graphic film of dead American soldiers, gave emotional boosts to the antiwar messages.

As the battles in Vietnam grew more intense, the casualty lists increased. By the beginning of 1967, the number of killed in action were over 300 per week. By the end of the year, the news media was full of reports on the siege of the US base at Khe Sanh – making all sorts of comparisons to the French siege at Dien Bien Phu almost 20 years previous.

News film clips of Khe Sanh had a particular effect. Over and over there were pictures and movies of Marines taking cover during North Vietnamese artillery attacks. A compelling picture was one of the few Air Force airlift planes that enemy artillery had struck on the base's landing pad. Journalists used it as a constant backdrop for their reports from the base. Even today when viewed, one gets the impression that the North Vietnamese were about to overrun the US defenses.

In contrast, news coverage of Johnson, McNamara and Westmoreland 1967 interviews and press conferences stayed full of favorable progress reports on military operations against the NVA and VC. As mentioned in Chapter 3, Westmoreland told the National Press that "the end was in view."

No wonder by the end of 1967, what the public saw in the media and what their government leaders were telling them confused Americans.

The TET Offensive and the Media

Then North Vietnam launched the TET offensive. The first reports out of Vietnam were confusing and contradictory – as are most initial statements on chaotic events in the war. Many of these, mostly those coming from the Saigon press corps, reflected the overall shock of the offensive on Americans in general.

There were several compelling news stories especially on American TV, in retrospect arguably the most powerful of the war, that came only days into the attacks. They would stun the American public. The first emanated from the news wires and reports on the assault on the US Embassy. The second came from pictures and film of the killing of a VC prisoner on the streets of Saigon.

Each of the four major newspapers in Vietnam – *Los Angeles Times, Christian Science Monitor, New York Times,* and *Washington Post* - had journalists in Saigon who reported the attacks on the Embassy and Saigon on the 31st of January. They indicated that many of the attackers were either 'wiped out' or had suffered 'massive casualties.' The *Washington Post* accurately reported that the enemy had briefly penetrated the Embassy grounds but not held it.

The next day the *New York Times* and *LA Times* stories indicated that VC sappers had held the Embassy building for some time. This report was not accurate. However, soon attention focused on the fact that the enemy had attacked and held the symbol of US prestige and power in Vietnam. The effect was startling to most Americans.

On 1 February, Westmoreland arrived at the Embassy. A CBS TV news team quickly interviewed him. They asked him for an assessment of the overall enemy offensive. He declared that the attack was deceitful and had taken advantage of a highly regarded traditional holiday for all Vietnamese. Then the MACV commander said that this attack against the cities was but a ruse on the part of the VC. The real target - Khe Sanh -was yet to be attacked. Westmoreland's remarks visibly confused and disturbed the news team.

Soon after this interview, *New York Times* and *LA Times'* editorials added fuel to the fire by misrepresenting that the Embassy had been seized and held for some time. They wrote that the bold VC attack had embarrassed the US and that the VC had sought and gained a significant political victory. The *LA Times* editorial included a cartoon of LBJ calling our Embassy with a caption that read, "What the hell's Ho Chi Minh doing answering our Saigon Embassy phone?"

The *Washington Post* evidently did not want to be outdone by this sensationalized reporting. It followed with its characterization of the situation. On 2 February, it showed a cartoon of General Westmoreland under a desk in his Saigon headquarters saying, "we now have the initiative" and "the enemy offensive has been foiled…" He then says, "Everything's Okay…They never reached the mimeograph machine."

Time magazine added to the misrepresentation of the attack on the Embassy with a news article in its February 9th edition. The article was cleverly entitled, "The Battle of Bunker's Bunker." The first 'Bunker' referred to the then Ambassador to South Vietnam, Ellsworth Bunker, who was not at the Embassy at the time.

The storyline was sensational. It portrayed the defenses of the Embassy as 'impregnable,' which was hardly the case. It then described the VC attack as 'overwhelming' and that the VC had 'rampaged' through the Embassy for six and a half hours before troops from the 101st Airborne Division finally retook it. The article had several photographs of the dead US Embassy guards and ended with an editorial paragraph of how this attack, along with the overall enemy offensive, was 'humiliating' for the US.

Both *Life* and *Newsweek* magazines followed with their stories on the TET offensive. Like the *Time* article, they implied that the Embassy attack was a 'victory of sorts.' The *Life* article was entitled, "New Frenzy in the War, Vietcong Terrorize the Cities: Suicide Raid On The Embassy." It showed a picture of a VC soldier captured during the raid, which was not the case since all had been killed. The image had two US military policemen escorting the VC soldier, whose face was battered and bleeding. The picture, per some critics of the coverage of TET, evoked feelings of pity and sympathy for the captured soldier. The overall article implied, like the *Times* story, that the attack was a humiliating psychological blow to the US.

Newsweek featured the Embassy attack as its cover story for its February 12th issue. The title was, "Hanoi Attacks and Scores a Major Psychological Blow." The article included a summary of the overall NVA/VC offensive. But it was clear that the Embassy attack was a symbol to the editors of the overall negative effect on American war efforts.

The article further proclaimed, "On Capitol Hill, hawks and doves alike lamented the 'humiliation' inflicted on the Allied cause and complained that they had been misled about the Communists' capability. And on the home front, bewildered Americans sitting before their TV sets watched the stunning spectacle of U.S. troops storming their embassy in Saigon to oust guerrilla invaders."

Of all the reports, pictures and film bombarding Americans during TET, there was one that was particularly shocking and memorable. On 1 February, the South Vietnam Chief of Police, General Nguyen Loan, confronted a captured VC officer on the streets of Saigon. He summarily executed him with a shot to the head. Nearby, the Associated Press photographer Eddie Adams took a picture. The next morning the picture was in all the major US newspapers. That evening it was on the network news programs.

Two camera teams from NBC and ABC had also filmed the execution. The ABC cameraman did not get a clear and complete shot. The NBC crew did. It was put on a Friday night 6:30 PM NBC news program. The film clip showed an outwardly nonchalant Loan cold-bloodedly raising his pistol to the VC soldier's head and firing. The man's face quickly became contorted. As he fell to the ground a stream of blood burst from his temple, the film clip briefly followed the VC to the street. Blood continued to pour from his temple, forming a pool on the street. A week later NBC showed the film clip once again. This time some previously omitted footage was included.

Reactions poured into the newspapers and networks. Overwhelmingly they reflected the horror of the event. Comments saw this act as a cowardly South Vietnamese officer murdering in cold blood an innocent Vietnamese civilian or, at the least, killing a POW with no reason. The news stories and commentaries did nothing or said nothing to correct this impression.

The public view was that this murder was but a microcosm of what had happened in Vietnam. The South Vietnamese were incapable of ruling themselves. The US had backed the wrong side. The

VC were rightly fighting for an independent nation free of outside interference. Some viewers expressed that they wanted to become part of the anti-war movement.

Then and in retrospect, many argue that the episode of General Loan killing of the VC soldier underscored and poignantly ingrained the overall negative news coverage of the TET offensive in the minds of most Americans. This school of thought argues that TET was a defeat of many dimensions. It was a defeat of President Johnson's policy of escalation in a war of attrition to convince the North to cease its aggression against the South. It was a defeat of the idea that a workable democratic South Vietnamese government could win the support of its people. It was a defeat of the idea that the South Vietnamese military could defend its country.

Historians and other scholars, as well as participants who saw otherwise, have tried to set the record straight. One of those who wanted to correct the record was Eddie Adams, who had won a Pulitzer Prize for his photo. When Nguyen Loan passed away decades later in California after trying to make it as a Liquor Store owner but failed due to his notoriety, Adams wrote a letter to the LA Times.

He told about how the picture he had taken was really of two deaths. The most obvious one was the VC officer whom Loan had killed that day. The other was the person who had pulled the trigger. He then explained how the General had lost his family to the VC, and how the VC he had killed had been leading assassination squads roaming Saigon looking to kill South Vietnamese officials and their families.

Adams then related how Loan had escaped only to meet animosity at the hands of some in the US who had known of his role in the picture. He lamented that his picture had led to the slow death of a Vietnamese patriot who was on the wrong side of history. Adams later told about how when he had gone back to visit Ho Chi Minh City in the 80s, the Democratic Republic of Vietnam hailed him as a hero for his photo's contribution to the DRV's war effort.

Another one who set out to make the record straight was the *Washington Post* Saigon Bureau Chief during TET – Peter Braestrup. Braestrup, who had served in the Marine Corps in Korea where he was wounded, wrote a study on the overall media coverage during TET called *The Big Story*. In it, he found a startling number of factual errors in the reporting. He attributes them, in part, to the confusion and complexity of the events surrounding the offensive and the reaction to them.

Braestrup, however, also faults the media for its one-sided reporting of the offensive. He argues that much of the media reporting gave the impression that the NVA/VC attacks had been successful; while overall, they failed. He shows that the American news media gave the general impression that the offensive had demonstrated that US policies had failed in South Vietnam. He shows where the media harshly criticized the South Vietnamese Government and Military, while both handled the attacks rather well. Indeed, while the American news reports denigrated the South Vietnamese Army and gave the impression that US forces were doing most of the fighting, the exact opposite occurred.

Braestrup's conclusion is both bold and, to those who were in the Press at the time, extreme. He writes, "The generalized effect of the news media's contemporary output in February – March 1968 was a distortion of reality – through sins of omission and commission – on a scale that helped shape Tet's political repercussions in Washington and the Administrations' response."

He further explores in his work, "Why the distortion?" Braestrup argues, "I find simple ideological explanations of media flaws gravely insufficient, particularly as applied to the Tet coverage. In my view, the distortions at Tet resulted from the impact of a rare combination of circumstances on the various habits, incentives, economic constraints, and managerial and manpower limitations peculiar to each of the major US news organizations." He then goes into detail what all those circumstances were: such as the inexperience of some reporters; the haste and difficulties in getting stories to their medium; the competition and desire to outdo each other, and various others.

Supporting Braestrup's argument is Richard Hammond in the US Army's *The Military and the Media, 1968-1973*. He shows that overall the media shifted dramatically in its views of the war just after TET. For example, he noted that the news reports for the war outnumbered those against by 5 to 1 before TET. By mid-1968 there were at par. Afterward, news reports would be overwhelmingly against the war.

Throughout all this reporting and editorializing, the Johnson Administration stayed, for the most part, silent. LBJ acted besieged in the White House. At a moment when the President should have strongly assured the American people that the NVA and VC had failed, and the US and South Vietnam had won decisively, the President was quiet. He should have corrected the impression that the news media was presenting. Johnson should have shown that he was as resolute and determined as those American and South Vietnamese forces were on the battlefield. Yet he did not do so.

On this silence and lack of leadership, Peter Braestrup makes a most interesting observation that supports the above assertion. He notes, "One possible underlying explanation of the unusual media malfunction during the Tet period needs more emphasis. This involves the public performance of President Johnson." He explains, "during a foreign policy crisis; the Chief Executive plays a special role with respect to the practical needs of the press and television. American news managers (like other Americans) look to him to define the new situation, at least initially, and to provide a coherent response to it."

About TET, he goes on, "Lyndon Johnson, willy-nilly, helped create conditions that led to an unusual failure in US crisis journalism…Possibly owing to the deep contradictions of his own 'guns and butter' war policy, Johnson did not give the news media (or the public) a coherent scenario [for what was going on in the TET offensive]. In that sense, the President's political crisis in Washington after Tet was a self-inflicted wound."

Thus, to conclude this portion, LBJ's lack of leadership shaped both the nature of and the reactions of many in Washington – including his advisors - to the TET offensive. In military terminology, 'he simply quit his post' as the nation's Commander-in-Chief. Thus, on 31 March, after being bombarded by news in the papers, magazines and on television, Johnson went on TV to announce that he would not seek another term and that he would seek a negotiated settlement to the war.

The President of the United States surrendered to the negativity of the Press coverage of TET. The North Vietnamese, who had targeted American public opinion in its offensive, had struck a decisive blow against the Commander-in-Chief of the Armed Forces of the United States of America. From now on the US would not only be mostly on the defensive in the war but on its way to defeat.

Public Opinion

Perhaps the most interesting question of the media coverage of the war, in general, and its portrayal of TET specifically, is how did this affect American public opinion? Although the degree and nature are in dispute, most scholars argue that the media – the press (written and wired) and television – had a significant impact on the American public during the war. Its influence was more significant than on any other US war to date. There were several reasons for this.

The first is that the coverage of the war lacked government censorship. In both the First and Second World Wars, reports from the field had to go through government offices whose sole purpose was to both alter the tone of the reports and strike out passages that they thought would reveal operational details harmful to the war effort. Officials also censored or edited film strips before released for public consumption. As mentioned previously, often this censorship focused on the showing of dead US servicemen, which leaders knew, if the public saw, would incite public dismay or even engender discontent over support for the war. This censorship was not the case for the Vietnam War. While US officials tried to convince the media of progress in the war, they did not prohibit or edit stories and film clips sent to their editors.

A second reason for the major impact was the advent of the use of the television in news reporting. As described in Chapter 1, after World War Two, there was a television boom in the US. By 1968, there were 78 million television sets in American homes. With a total population of some 202 million that was an astounding figure. Many of these were color. Most Americans now got their news from television. As mentioned, news on the Vietnam War included graphic film clips and soundtracks of the horrors of combat. While there was some graphic film from World War Two and Korea, the American public could only see them if they went to the theater. Now they viewed them in the sanctuaries of their living rooms. How could that not affect US public attitudes about the Vietnam War or any war for that matter?

Some historians and commentators on Vietnam claim that the media had a decisive impact on the American public's view of and support for the war. They argue that it was the primary factor for America's withdrawal and eventual defeat. Many US military men believed, and still do, that the media was the blame for their defeat because of its decisive impact on public opinion. However, was that the case? How did the public view the war as it started, as it progressed before TET and then after? Was public opinion - fueled by the Press' adverse reports - the main reason for our failure in South Vietnam?

Shortly after the Vietnam War ended for America, there were extensive studies done on wartime public opinion polls. They set out to figure out what these polls showed of public opinion on Vietnam. There were several polls of note that they examined. The most prominent were the Harris and the Gallop Polls. One of the more comprehensive and interesting studies is William Lunch and Peter Sperlich's paper published in *The Western Political Quarterly* entitled, "American Public Opinion and the War in Vietnam."

That study divided the nature of public opinion on the Vietnam War into four phases. They labeled the first phase, 'From Innocence to Rally-Round-the-Flag.' During this phase, which corresponded to the years just before the commitment of US troops, circa mid-1964 to mid-1965, they found that the polls first showed no to a brief interest in Vietnam. Many people did not even know about the advisory effort there. Those who seemed interested had heard of Vietnam and our advisory efforts through the news media but had no opinion on its effectiveness. Thus, it appears that JFK's concern for public support of his policies received little notice, at least from the polls.

The second phase the study called, "A Permissive Majority." In this phase, which stretches from mid-1965 to mid-1966, the Lunch and Sperlich analysis shows that the public was now aware of the war and supportive of LBJ's rationale for the US commitment there. However, due mostly to some warnings of an open-ended commitment and mounting casualties, there was a sentiment amongst a few that we may have made a mistake.

From mid-1966 to nearly the end of 1967, the public opinion polls favored, 'A Preference for Escalation." This phrase characterizes a predilection amongst Americans to want to escalate the war. Lunch and Sperlich's examination of the poll data and other materials conclude that the reason for this preference is the public's disenchantment with the lack of results in the war and their frustration with its prolongation without any resolution in sight.

The Study labels its last phase, 'Disillusionment and Withdrawal.' This segment corresponds to the Post TET period. It marks the height of discontent with the war effort and a call for withdrawal from Vietnam. This is the first time in the polls that they see a clear call for withdrawal from Vietnam that continues to increase, not surprisingly, as Nixon becomes President and the US starts a voluntary withdrawal from Vietnam.

This 'lumping' or 'characterization' of the public opinion polls is not the entire story of public support for or against the war according to this study. Looking at the actual questions and answers of the specific polling queries over time shows much more. It can enlighten us further on the role of public opinion on the war.

There were three central questions that the polls used consistently throughout the Vietnam War. These questions were: do you think the war was a mistake; do you think the US should withdraw from Vietnam; and do you think the US should escalate the war? The quantities of yes's or no's and when these answers were provided, give insight into the extent of public support for or against the war and when.

It also offers some measure of the impact of the media coverage during TET. Of note, the study proves that the polling answers during the TET period - from January through the last offensive in August 1968 - show that the media may not have been as decisive on the public as some have thought or argued.

While support for the war by the end of 1967 was declining, at TET about 42% of those polled still did not believe the war was a mistake. At that time, only 10% believed we should withdraw, while 53% thought the US should escalate its military involvement (to include more bombing of North). Six months after the start of TET, the withdraw figure only increased to 15%. Yet, 40% of Americans still thought that the US should escalate. The support for the war had declined, but there was still substantial support to do something that might lead to success.

Thus, as this study reveals, there was much consensus, despite the media negativity, in America to do something more militarily about the war. Much of the public's discontent was on how the war was being waged and that there had been no clear victory in sight. More importantly, had there been any effort by the Administration to shore up the support that the January figures show existed, certainly, the backing for escalation may have been at least maintained.

In short, what the polls remarkably show – in the study noted - is that most of the public confusion and lack of support over the war up to TET was on how US leaders were waging war with no end in sight. Moreover, during TET, there was no significant defeatist landslide in the face of TET attacks amongst the American public. Most importantly and startling, is that the figures show there was a considerable number of Americans whom LBJ may have been able to persuade in early 1968 to support further decisive military operations against the communist to end the war favorably to the US.

Impacts on Decision-Making during TET

These figures and analyses show that the ones who were most affected by the negative media and the shock of TET were in the Government, not the public. As testimonies demonstrate, LBJ succumbed to that malaise and lost faith in any bold military action that may have yet been possible. He refused to accept operational and intelligence reports and assessments about the failure of the NVA/VC to obtain their aims and the defeats that the US and ARVN forces inflicted. Instead, he surrendered to the sensational negative media frenzy.

Meanwhile his civilian advisors - in particular, the outgoing and incoming Secretaries of Defense - also ignored the field reports and yielded to the defeatist attitude of the media. All of this occurred while the polls indicated that some support for military action was not out of the possible.

Moreover, while his military commanders and chief military advisor were more optimistic, they did not explicitly and forcefully convey that positive attitude to the President or the Secretary of Defense. In fact, his primary military advisor – The Chairman of the Joint Chiefs – may have even added to the negativism with his reports and assessments that, as the evidence shows, were geared toward putting pressure on the President to make decisions that he had staunchly avoided. In short, LBJ's war advisors, both civilian and military, failed him at a critical time.

William Hammond - one of the most noted scholars of public opinion, the media, and the war – made an observation that is most astute on the relationship and opportunities between the Administration and the public during this period. He stated, "If Americans were unwilling to repudiate the war, they nonetheless appeared increasingly dissatisfied with their President. Willing to back any decision he made, they saw little forward motion on his part…. If the gloomy reporting of the press had little effect on American public opinion, it nonetheless reinforced doubts already circulating within the Johnson Administration."

Thus, it appears that President Johnson - and his top civilian advisors - took counsel of their fears at a vital time in the conduct of the war. As Peter Braestrup noticed above, when he should have taken charge of the 'story' of what was happening, LBJ chose to do little. Much of this was due to their sensitivity to the media reports, which did not offer an accurate portrayal of the situation on the ground in Vietnam during TET and afterward. As we will see in more detail in Chapters 9 and 10, LBJ's senior military advisor and commander also had a decisive role in this.

In sum, at least at this critical juncture of the war, it appears that neither the media nor the anti-war movement had a decisive impact on public opinion. From 1965 through 1967 the Public's discontent seems to have focused on the way the President was conducting a war that seemed unending. Moreover, as the evidence demonstrates, during TET the Public did not panic as much as the media and the Administration. Therefore, the argument that TET was a turning point in the war because public opinion went sour and prevented any action to preclude a US defeat is just not correct. More accurately - it seems to this author at least - the President was incapacitated, in part, because his advisors did not convincingly provide an assessment and viable course of action that could rouse the President to remedy what appeared to him through the Press to be a defeat.

TET may have been a 'turning point,' but it was due more to a failure in senior civil and military leader and advisor competency and performance more than public opinion. While the media had a profound role in this, LBJ and his civilian advisors succumbed to the unbalanced accounts of what had happened during TET. That in turn, gave them a preconceived negative notion of the situation during that offensive and its aftermath. Due to their lack of resolve at the time, the President and his senior civilian advisors were unable to overcome this notion. As a result, the one person most responsible for the war – the US Commander-in-Chief - succumbed and surrendered to the enemy's offensive, which had militarily failed.

Section 4.4 – The Congress and the Vietnam War

One of the important and pertinent debates surrounding the Vietnam War was the role and responsibility of the US Congress. The arguments are two-fold. First, Congress failed to exercise its constitutional powers of declaring war. In so doing, it allowed, through the Gulf of Tonkin Resolution, President Johnson to commit the US to an immoral and illegal war that had no vital interest. A corollary of this argument is that, by reneging on its Constitutional right to declare war, the Congress allowed the President to pursue war without committing the nation to victory.

The second claim is that when Congress finally decided to act, it contributed to the loss of the war. It did this by using its constitutional powers to authorize government spending. For example, it used legislative vehicles such as foreign aid or defense funding bills to restrict military activities in areas of Indochina – such as operations into Cambodia and Laos. Thus, the argument is that these restrictions hampered the use of US military forces in critical areas that could have made a difference in the successful conduct of the war.

A corollary to this claim is that after the departure of US Forces, Congress further cut military aid to the South Vietnamese to the degree that the ARVN could no longer wage a successful defense against a major Northern invasion. The central premise of this argument is that South Vietnam could have won, had Congress given the military aid funds to enable the Armed Forces of the Republic of South Vietnam to resist North Vietnamese aggression.

While there is some truth in these arguments and validity in the debates over them, the role of Congress was more complicated and less decisive to the conduct and the outcome of the war than other factors. In the final analysis and opinion of this work, Congress followed what it believed to be the proper exercise of its constitutional powers in war, and its part as representative of the people. What influenced that exercise and role, however, is more important to the story.

Thus, to determine what influenced the Congress' role and impact may have been, it is best to examine the motives of why and how these powers were, or were not, exercised. The evidence shows that, while they debated Constitutional Powers, the role was less a story of Constitutional law, and more an account of the personal views and interactions of legislators and executive branch leaders and public servants.

These views and interactions, moreover, involved personal beliefs, political opinions and ambitions, and interpretations of constitutional powers. Furthermore, these interactions sometimes involved reactions to the domestic upheavals, such as the anti-war demonstrations. Other times, media reporting prompted Congressional members to act. On several occasions, especially after Nixon took over, they were reactions to the abuse of power in Presidential behavior and actions.

The rest of this section, therefore, examines these interactions and motives to conclude the role of Congress from 1950 to 1968 on policies on and actions in Vietnam, with a focus on the Kennedy and Johnson Administrations. The next Chapter will examine the interactions during the Nixon era.

Congress and Vietnam, 1950- 1960

As noted in Chapter 1, with the 'Loss of China' in late 1949, President Truman sent military aid to the French in their war against the Communist-dominated Vietminh in Indochina. He also set up a military assistance group to oversee that aid – the precursor of MACV. The Congress strongly supported this first direct involvement, which grew dramatically after the Korean War broke out in June 1950. As Gibbons points out in *The US Government and the Vietnam War*, the fears of communist expansion in Asia and the necessity to contain it significantly influenced this support.

According to Fredrik Logevall – a noted scholar of the First Indochina War and the origins of the US Vietnam War – an "apocalyptic anti-communism [mood] was the order of the day in Congress in 1950. Members of Congress, Republicans, and Democrats, had already begun a ferocious assault on the Truman Administration on its failures to oppose communism. Indeed, the Republican majority, which would only hold a majority twice over the next forty-eight years, held the Truman Administration liable for both the China debacle and the Soviet bomb development."

"Now all of Asia was ripe for communist plucking, argued a young congressman named Richard Nixon. He noted that now the deck was stacked on the communist side of the table. Another Congressman by the name of Joseph McCarthy claimed Truman's Secretary of State, Dean Acheson, knew and supported communist agents in Washington. Nixon chimed in by referring to the Secretary as the "Red Dean of the College of Cowardly Containment."

While the American public had not taken note of Vietnam, members of Congress took trips there to draw their conclusions on the viability of American support to the French to contain communism there. One such person was a young Senator from Massachusetts by the name of John F. Kennedy.

JFK had already supported the Truman critics of being too defensive toward communism. He had also joined some Republicans, namely Joe McCarthy, in blaming the Democrats for the loss of China. So, when Truman began the aid program, the Senator, along with his brother Robert and sister Patricia, went to Vietnam in October 1951 to see for himself what was going on there.

The thirty-four-year-old Senator landed at Tan Son Nhut Airport near Saigon. Their French escorts soon drove them to the Majestic Hotel in Saigon. Their first day there they received the regular French visitors briefing, which was very upbeat and optimistic about the war (just like the future President's officials would offer ten years later).

However, the next day Kennedy went off on his own. He visited an AP reporter's flat in the 'Chinese district' of the bustling city. There he got a sobering view of the war. Soon after, JFK visited the US Counsel. He asked tough questions based on his previous day's sojourn. The future President left with the impression that the war could only be won if the Vietnamese decided it would result in their eventual freedom from French colonial rule and a better way of life.

After Kennedy had returned to the US, he remained a staunch supporter of resisting communist rule in Southeast Asia. However, he had reservations about the way the French were waging war in Indochina. He questioned whether it could be won without a major effort to establish a free Vietnamese government that had the loyalty of its people.

Many in Congress shared this view. There were some who had reservations, as well. These members thought that the US should be wary of taking over the war from the French and getting too involved in another Korean like war. Others felt that the US should be leery of seeming too sympathetic to the French. It might look like America supported imperialism in a new world in which many ex-colonies were pawns in the Cold War struggle. However, enthusiasm supporting American help to France was strong. This support became more so as knowledge of the significant Communist Chinese military support to the Viet-Minh became known to the legislators.

As the war dragged on, Congress grew more pessimistic about whether the French could prevail. Many believed that the US was backing a losing cause; mainly because the French military seemed so incompetent – as they had been in losing to Hitler in 1940.

Early in 1954 – as related in Chapter 1 - President Eisenhower, who had ended the Korean conflict, contemplated committing American combat forces to the conflict to save the French at Dien Bien Phu. While rejecting the use of ground troops, IKE decided to consult Congress to see if they would support a military intervention with a joint resolution authorizing the use of air and naval power in Indochina.

As briefly mentioned in Chapter 1, Eisenhower and several vital advisors met select Congressional members at the State Department on 3 April 1954 to ask for such a resolution. Among the members was the Senate's minority leader – Lyndon Johnson. The Administration arguments during the meeting would become all too familiar in the future.

Secretary of State Dulles contended that the resolution would give the President with a commitment of the American people to face communist aggression. The Chairman of the Joint Chiefs Admiral Radford briefed the French situation. He assessed that the Viet-Minh were sure to defeat the French if US arms were not able to support them. Dulles chimed in and said without that intervention, "it was only a question of time until all of Southeast Asia falls along with Indonesia."

After these remarks, Senator Johnson asked the fundamental questions. He also made some of the more pertinent comments. The Senator wished to know whether the US had allied support and involvement. He reminded his colleagues that one of the problems in Korea was that the US had given ninety percent of the forces and bore ninety percent of the costs. He also asked about how long the commitment would take. The answer to the first question was negative. The best that Admiral Radford could say about the duration was that he expected it to be 'limited.'

Not convinced, Johnson and others questioned whether this assurance could eventually lead to a ground force commitment. The Chairman said that the French and its Vietnamese loyalists would continue to do the ground fighting. That did not satisfy anyone. The meeting ended with the Congressional members giving a 'sine qua none' for its commitment. The US needed allied support. Without such, they would not support a resolution.

IKE never got an Ally to support military intervention. The US did not commit significant combat forces (it did deploy some air forces to help in the supply of engaged French troops). Dien Bien Phu fell to the Vietminh.

Before that decisive battle ended, the IKE administration had committed itself to a British-proposed meeting at Geneva, Switzerland. The purpose would be to discuss the situation in Korea and Indochina. The conference met in May, a day after the French had capitulated at Dien Bien Phu. The major attendees were the US, Britain, France, China, and the Soviet Union.

This gathering would be the first time that US diplomats were meeting with communists over an issue that the latter had the upper hand and had much to gain. Dulles and his team were very much aware of the Congressional criticism about how China was lost. Now there was talk about another defeat to communism in Southeast Asia. Thus, appearances were crucial. Dulles announced that the only way he would be seen with the Red Chinese chief representative, Zhou En-Lai, would be if his car ran into Zhou's automobile.

After several days at the conference, Dulles left and turned over US participation to a deputy. Meanwhile, the US delegation informed attendees that the US was contemplating military intervention in Indochina. This information was a ruse, given Congressional reluctance to offer support. However, it did make some delegates take notice – mainly the Chinese, who had been surprised about the US intervention in Korea in 1950.

After a month of talks, it became apparent that conference attendees were going to agree to a temporary partition of Vietnam. They also agreed to a national election to follow. The intent was for this election to settle a unified Vietnam government structure. China pressured Ho Chi Minh to accept this division. They argued that if they pushed for a unified communist government, it would prompt direct US military involvement. The US threat of intervention had an effect.

As George Herring explains, Dulles approached congressional leaders at the end of June, before the Geneva accords were to be signed and presented a novel approach to lessen the adverse effects of Geneva. Dulles argued that the Geneva agreements would be something no one would want or could support. To 'salvage something" the US must establish an international, regional security apparatus in Asia much like NATO. That way the US would 'draw a line' that the communists could not cross without facing military conflict. That organization would call for the US to give its support, along with other countries, to defending Southeast Asia against any further communist aggression.

The Congressional leaders at this meeting supported the idea. They also agreed to support a US commitment to set up a non-communist government in the southern part of Vietnam. It seemed to Congressional members that the Korea solution might work in Indochina.

Armed with this Congressional support, Dulles worked feverishly to set up such a mechanism. Eventually, the countries of Great Britain, France, Australia, New Zealand, the Philippines, Pakistan, and Thailand became part of the Alliance (the Geneva Accords prohibited the independent states of Indochina from joining). Thus was born the Southeast Asia Collective Defense Treaty or SEATO.

The US Senate ratified it by a vote of 82 to 1. There was little debate. Mainly founded to appease Congress - less the Eisenhower Administration seem too weak on communism and having loss 'Indochina - future Administrations would use the treaty as justification for its commitment to South Vietnam. It is ironic, therefore, that Congress may have been both a key player at the beginning of US involvement in South Vietnam in 1954 and its defeat a little over twenty years later.

As for the Geneva accords, the US never signed them. The IKE Administration felt that to do so would gain the wrath of the US Congress. Indeed, one Republican Senator later referred to the accords as "the greatest victory the communists have won in twenty years."

Though the agreements set up a temporary partition of Vietnam at the 17th Parallel and called for a national vote to unify the country, the election never occurred. The new head of the South

Vietnamese Government, Ngo Dinh Diem, with US encouragement, decided that such a vote would undoubtedly go to the communists.

The US had now put their trust in SEATO, and their support to a new South Vietnam led by Diem. The latter was a 'darling' of the US Congress and the Media. He was also a hero to several political action groups influencing Congress – namely the American Friends of Vietnam whose main supporter was Senator John F. Kennedy.

Dulles, at a news conference after the signing of the accords, discussed the future of Southeast Asia. He noted that the "important thing was not to mourn the past but to seize the future opportunity to prevent the loss in Northern Vietnam from leading to the extension of communism throughout Southeast Asia and the Southwest Pacific." This 'future opportunity' would soon become an albatross for the Kennedy, Johnson, and Nixon Administrations.

To sum up Congress' role in these early years, in the atmosphere of the 'Red Scare,' the 'loss of China,' the Korean War, and the defeat of France in Indochina the US Congress was more than acceptable to stemming communism in Southeast Asia. Accordingly, members fully supported the Eisenhower Administration's creation of a security mechanism like NATO, called SEATO.

That organization intended to create a multi-national organization to support the future defense of the Southeast Asia region threatened by communism. For the most part, the IKE Administration championed the formation and support for SEATO to placate Congress that it had not abandoned Southeast Asia, as Truman did China.

For some members, such as future Presidents Kennedy and Nixon, they eagerly supported SEATO and had taken an active role in supporting the IKE led the establishment of a friendly non-communist government in South Vietnam to serve as a proxy for the containment of the communist expansionist tendencies of China and North Vietnam. They would have to not only live with that support later but become tied to its survival.

Kennedy, Vietnam, and the Congress

Several years after forming SEATO and the Republic of South Vietnam, Senator Kennedy met with the American Friends of Vietnam to give his opinion about Southeast Asia and South Vietnam's role in it. Reflecting the attitude of the Congress, as previously quoted, he said, "the fundamental tenets of this nation's foreign policy. …depend in considerable measure upon a strong and free Vietnamese nation. Vietnam represents the cornerstone of the Free World in Southeast Asia, the keystone in the arch, the finger in the dike."

From 1955 to 1960, according to George Herring, America made an investment that supported this political commitment. Congress gave over $1.5 billion in economic and mostly military aid to the South. With it, the American presence in South Vietnam grew. The US mission in Saigon would become the largest in the world. The Military Assistance Group exceeded the Geneva accord authorizations by twice as much, numbering almost 700 men. In Congressional hearings, Senators touted South Vietnam as a model of nation-building and 'helping others to help themselves.'

When JFK became President, as briefly explained in Chapter 2, he was true to his views of the fifties. He believed that the only way to ensure success in Vietnam was to have the Vietnamese build their nation and wage its struggle for survival. At first, He thus tried to aid the South

Vietnamese, but not take over entirely the task from them. He placed his hope, as most American politicians did in the late fifties and early sixties, in the hands of Diem. In Congress, the South Vietnamese leader found staunch support.

Despite the relative success that immediately followed after the establishment of the Diem regime in the fifties, by the beginning of 1961 it was becoming clear that Diem was not up to the task, at least as the Americans defined it. No matter how much money the US spent on nation-building programs - building a nation depends on a 'nation' to build it.

Most notably, that effort now faced an enemy determined to defeat a government that they portrayed, quite successfully, as a Western puppet regime. By the end of 1961, the South was losing badly on the battlefield. All of that was certainly evident to President Kennedy. However, how did the Congress, at that time, view the situation in the South?

There were two critical issues that Kennedy faced with the Congress during his Presidency that would provide him with a sensing of his support from Congress over Vietnam. The first was a Congressional reaction to and support for his initial foreign policy crucibles over Cuba. These involved the Bay of Pigs and the Cuban missile crises. The second involved his actions over both Laos and his policies toward Diem and South Vietnam.

With the failure at the Bay of Pigs, the Republicans, led by both former President Eisenhower and JFK's Presidential rival Nixon, criticized him for not being more supportive of the Cuban nationals. Senator Barry Goldwater, who would become LBJ's opponent in 1964, also claimed that the country should feel shame at the lack of support for the invasion. Republicans used the tainted word of 'appeasement' and analogy to Munich to describe what they saw as a lack of courage and vision to deal with the Cuban Communist threat.

During the Cuban missile crisis, Kennedy also had to endure some dissatisfaction within his party. This discontent would be particularly relevant to him because his party held the majority in both the House and Senate. In a meeting afterward with Congressional leaders Richard Russell and William Fulbright, they told the President that they thought he had been too cautious. They felt that he should have either taken out the missile sites with a massive air attack or invaded Cuba and gotten rid of Castro. The Joint Chiefs views were well known to them, as relayed by Kennedy's nemesis General Curtis LeMay. The implications were clear. Some, even in his party, thought JFK was not up to the task of being a President who could halt communism.

With his first test in Southeast Asia in the Laos crisis, the Republicans again criticized JFK for being too cautious. They felt he was giving in to communist actions. They used that analogy again that invoked weakness and lack of resolve – Munich. They had wanted some military intervention. Again, members of Congress used the Munich analogy and described Kennedy as an appeaser.

As two historians – Robert Dallek and Andrew Johns – of the Kennedy Administration explain, this early Congressional scrutiny and criticism affected President Kennedy's Vietnam policies. As Johns notes, "he feared being portrayed as an appeaser— a charge that had crippled his father's political career after comments about Germany during the elder Kennedy's tenure as ambassador to Britain— and realized that Republicans like Representative Melvin Laird (R-WI) would assail him for failing 'to act with sufficient vigor to frustrate the achievement of Communist objectives'."

Johns further explains that "JFK said that he thought a communist takeover of Vietnam would "produce a debate in the country more acute than the loss of China." The President told a friend, "We don't have a prayer of staying in Vietnam. Those people hate us. They are going to throw our asses out of there at almost any point. But I can't give up a piece of territory like that to the Communists and then get the American people to reelect me."

Regardless of how these pressures may have motivated JFK, we know that he dealt with these Congressional concerns in two ways. First, he tried to soothe GOP criticism by meeting with their leaders. Thus, he had frequent visits with ex-President Eisenhower. He also met with Richard Nixon, who was considered its Right-Wing leader. At the least, these meetings kept up the façade of Bipartisan cooperation. They also had an effect in ameliorating Republican opposition to his Vietnam policy. They may have, certainly in the case of his meetings with IKE, have had an impact on his continued support to the South Vietnamese.

The second way JFK dealt with these domestic political pressures was to try to downplay the American direct military efforts in South Vietnam. As noted already several times, it was important to him that he emphasize the successes in the South Vietnamese nation building and fighting efforts against the VC. Thus, as we have seen, he wanted to control the message coming out in the media on US military activities in South Vietnam. Consequently, he was upset with those reports that seemed to show Diem and the ARVN as incompetent.

Kennedy also encouraged a positive picture before the Congress of progress in Vietnam. In the President's mind, this was more to provide him with freedom of choice in how to execute his policies without Congressional interference, but with their continued support for military assistance. In trying to do so, he began what would eventually become in the public mind and associated with the war, a deliberate policy of Government deceit.

In sum of this period of Congressional reaction to Vietnam, there are two notable trends. First, Congress continued to see South Vietnam as the bulwark of US policy of containment in Asia. Therefore, it continued to fully support the President's efforts to make South Vietnam fulfill that role. Second, there were members of the Congress, both Republican and Democratic, who thought that Kennedy might be too reticent and not willing to use military force to contain communism there. These two trends undoubtedly put pressure on JFK to stay the course with defending Vietnam against communist expansion. These trends, moreover, do not support the argument that Kennedy would have withdrawn its support of South Vietnam should have lived.

Congress, LBJ, and The Tonkin Gulf Resolution

As Johnson took office, Congressional attitude toward US actions in Vietnam fell mostly along Party lines. The Republicans tended to support more forceful actions based on their continued belief in thwarting communist expansion in Asia. They criticized actions when they appeared to be too accommodating to communist expansion or too defensive. Their criticism also continued to use the analogy of Munich or appeasement. They further alluded to the lessons of the loss of China. In 1964, there was only a tiny minority who questioned the viability to succeed in Vietnam.

The Democrats also criticized the actions based on appeasement and the Munich analogy. They too supported containment of communism in Southeast Asia. However, when they condemned actions in Vietnam or Southeast Asia, it was regarding whether the South Vietnamese were doing enough in their own defense, and whether our allies could contribute in the US effort to contain communism there.

Overall, LBJ was aware that he could not only count on the Congress for support of his policies for Vietnam but also, more importantly, his intended domestic programs. This backing was because the Democratic Party dominated the 88th Congress. In the Senate - the body that LBJ had directed for so many years as its Majority Leader - the Democrats outnumbered Republicans 67 to 33. In the House, it was much closer, 234 to 201. For the most part, the House and Senate leaders were Democrats with whom he had served for most of his political life. Many were either personal friends or who owed their positions to Johnson.

Despite this early support from Congress, Johnson knew he would eventually need further backing if the conflict in Vietnam widened. A few months after taking office, he told Dean Rusk, "If we stay in South Vietnam much longer or have to take firmer action, we've got to go to Congress," Accordingly, he tasked McGeorge Bundy to draft a Congressional Resolution supporting the war for use when the time came.

Meanwhile, he reached out to Congress's key leaders to figure out where they stood on the situation in Vietnam. In the sixties, Congressional key leaders - namely the House and Senate majority and minority leaders, and the chairmen of the most influential committees such as foreign affairs, armed services, ways and means, and appropriations – held the power of persuasion over other party members and worked out the key compromises between parties. Thus, they were the pivotal players in Congress to get appropriations and legislation accomplished.

As previously noted, LBJ's conversations with them are full of words to extract sympathy, which he evidently equated to support, for his anguish over having to take further military action to defend South Vietnam. This is the 'Johnson technique' he had used in Congress as the Majority Leader in the Senate to great effectiveness.

There were several major members of the Senate that LBJ would be in contact with to either gauge the mood of Congress or to convince them to do his bidding. One of the first that he turned to was his mentor and friend Richard Russell. Russell was the senior member of the Senate and the Chairman of the powerful Senate Armed Services Committee.

While the senior Senator was cautious about US involvement in Indochina from the beginning, he felt that American policy there was the primary purview of the President. Also, Russell was devotedly patriotic and loved the military. He could, moreover, keep a secret, unlike most politicians in Washington. Johnson knew he could confide in him without it showing up in the media. LBJ further knew that he could count on Russell's sense of patriotism for his support.

The senior Senator from Georgia wanted to help his friend as much as he could – at least initially. He was a bachelor and lived alone. The Johnsons had had him over often for dinner in their homes in Washington both before and after LBJ was President. The Johnson children called him 'Uncle Dick.' LBJ on occasion would tell him he was like a father. The aging Senator had certainly been a mentor to Johnson. Along with the now deceased former House Speaker and fellow Texan Sam Rayburn, the two had taken LBJ on board when he first arrived in the Congress and showed him the ropes around Washington's political and social circles.

Russell was also the leader of the strong Southern click in both the Senate and the House. That group had opposed several civil rights bills in earlier administrations. Johnson, of course, knew that. Now he would primarily use his old friend to eventually overcome Southern obstructionist actions in his civil rights bill and other Great Society programs.

As for Vietnam, LBJ leaned on Russell to back the necessary appropriations support for the bombing operations and the American troop buildup there. This Russell did; despite the Senators early warnings (as recorded in a telephone conversation soon after LBJ had become President) that "it was the damned worse mess I ever saw...." Johnson most needed him, however, to obtain sympathy for his dismay when he ran into opposition or criticism. Thus, the President often called Russell when things were tough.

To a lesser extent, Johnson also asked for the views of the Senate resident expert in Asian Affairs, Senator Mike Mansfield. Mansfield had replaced LBJ as the Senate Majority Leader in 1961. As a sailor and then Marine before the Second World War, he had served in the Pacific area. Afterward, he studied and taught Asian history in his home state of Montana. When he entered the Senate, Mansfield became interested in foreign affairs and turned his attention to the situation in Vietnam in the late fifties. He made many trips there and had become an early supporter of Diem.

In 1962, after one of these visits, the new Majority Leader had become convinced that Diem would never be able to gain the support of his people. He reported the same to Kennedy. After that, he became a behind the scenes naysayer and honest broker about the increased involvement in Vietnam not only for the President but in the Congress in general. LBJ had respected him for his loyalty and honesty.

Johnson also knew that despite Mansfield's negative views on the situation in Vietnam, like Russell, the Senator would never challenge the Presidency or voice his dissent publicly. A major reason for that loyalty was that the Senate in the fifties and sixties was made up of a click of lifetime politicians whose main motivation was to keep their private lives secret and their public lives protected. Thus, the principal ethic was not to cross one another if you can compromise and share political gain to ensure reelection.

The Senator that the President first turned to for Vietnam policy support in the Congress was the 'intellectual leader' of the Senate, J. William Fulbright. Fulbright was a Rhodes Scholar. When LBJ was Majority Leader, he referred to the Senator as his 'Secretary of State.' Now Fulbright was the Chairman of the powerful Senate Foreign Relations Committee.

He was the perfect person to carry forth LBJ's draft resolution over the Tonkin Gulf incident. So, in August 1964, as he was getting into full swing for the fall election, Johnson called on his 'Secretary of State' in the Senate to manage the resolution through that body.

Despite his reservations, Fulbright deftly did so. At a joint meeting of the Armed Services and Foreign Relations Committees, he explained that the resolution was meant to give the President the authority needed to retaliate and bring air and naval military power to convince the North to desist in its aggression. That is how McNamara and Rusk had explained it to him. Fulbright may even have believed the reasoning at the time.

When several legislators asked whether the resolution would authorize a later commitment of ground forces, Fulbright indicated that it could. He then provided a warning: "If a situation later developed in which we thought the approval should be withdrawn, it could be withdrawn by concurrent resolution. That is the reason for the third section." The third section included a statement that the Congress could later terminate the authority. What Fulbright and others did not consider is that it would be tough to change that third section after American forces were committed to combat.

At the beginning of his Presidency, LBJ was extraordinarily pleased with Fulbright's support. However, soon after the passage of the Tonkin Gulf resolution, Fulbright began to feel that the President had tricked him. Against his staff's advice, he began making speeches in the Senate questioning the entire rationale for the commitment of US combat forces in a war in Indochina. When Johnson got feedback on Fulbright's statements, he started to leave him out of his periodic telephone calls and meetings; as well as calling him names not worthy of repeating here.

Congress and the Decision for War in 1965

As the situation in Vietnam grew worse after his election to the Presidency in November 1964, LBJ kept touch with senior members of Congress. As previously explained, he did this mostly through his many telephone talks, but also from time to time, inviting them to the White House either for private talks or briefings from his key advisors.

Though the Tonkin Gulf resolution gave him the go-ahead for future military actions of an unspecified number of forces and with no time limit, Johnson felt the need to continue these talks and briefings. This necessity was to prepare senior Congressional leaders for the possibility of a US military ground force intervention. He recognized, of course, that Congress had the power of the purse to conduct any intervention as well as to fund his beloved Great Society programs, which was then being prepared for submission.

These consultations continued up to the day that he announced his decision to deploy significant combat forces on 28 July and afterward. As mentioned in Chapter 3, according to William Gibbons' study *The US Government and the Vietnam War*, Congress supported the President's decision to send US forces to Vietnam. There were, however, several prominent members, such as Senator Mike Mansfield, who had expressed to LBJ grave misgivings on the use of significant forces there. There were also some members who were "apprehensive" about the deployment of such a large contingent of forces. Gibbons estimates that these amounted to a dozen senators and three dozen representatives.

To address this apprehension, as described in the previous chapter, LBJ's July announcement assured the public, and mostly the Congress, his desire to limit the war and seek a negotiated peace. Moreover, Johnson not only continued his telephone campaign but sent McNamara and Rusk to the Congress to testify and justify the funds that were needed to support the commitment of the Phase I reinforcements to Westmoreland.

While there, the Defense Secretary ensured, and deceived, Congressional members that further deployments would not need any major funding increases beyond the maintenance of the forces already there and some others to follow. In short, the true nature of the forces that Westmoreland had requested in June 1965, and had further estimated for 1966, was not revealed to the Congress in the first six months of the war.

To keep support from Congress, especially the Republicans, LBJ continued to consult and make known his telephone calls to Eisenhower, whom he called his chief military advisor. The President also dispatched General Andrew Goodpaster, who had been an assistant to Eisenhower during his presidency, to his home in Gettysburg to keep him updated on the situation in Vietnam personally. As a result, IKE came through. On several occasions, the former President publicly announced support for what Johnson was doing in Vietnam and for the American troops employed there.

According to William Gibbons, two significant factors were working for the President in getting this support from the Congress. First, he was Commander-in-Chief in a wartime situation. Second, significant American forces were now in harms' way. Thus, Mansfield, his most ardent personal adversary on the commitment of significant forces to Vietnam, was not willing to challenge him publicly because the Senator, and most in Congress, thought it was their duty to support the President in wartime.

Moreover, even his most public adversary on the war, Senator Wayne Morse, who had voted against the Tonkin Gulf resolution and had publicly voiced his opposition to the deployments, voted for the funds to support the forces. As he justified his vote, Morse said, "As long as [US Forces] are there, they must have every possible bit of protection that can be given to them."

Congressional Doubts and Differences Grow: The Fulbright and Stennis Hearings on the War

As the war progressed, Fulbright became the unofficial leader of a small movement in the Senate questioning policies toward the war. Wayne Morse was a young Senator at 64 and a member of that group. Another in the movement was Frank Church, a new member of the Senate. In his thirties, he stood for the newer breed of Senators willing to challenge its antiquated procedures. He also was not an admirer of Johnson during the President's days as Majority Leader.

Early in 1966 Fulbright started television hearings on the war. These hearings focused on the reasons for the war and whether it was in our national interest. Fulbright invited and queried key officials such as McNamara and Rusk, and distinguished statesmen such as George Kennan at these hearings. The hearings became unique events for national network TV shows and the mainstream written media.

By some accounts, these hearings also fueled the antiwar sentiment and demonstrations. As a result, LBJ soon turned nasty toward Fulbright. He put him under FBI surveillance for leaks of any classified materials he may have had access to. Privately, he called him a 'son of a bitch' and 'traitor.'

To offset the views of Mansfield and counter the public hearings of Fulbright, LBJ turned to Everett Dirksen. He was the Senate Republican Minority Leader. Both Dirksen and Johnson had been in the House together just before the Second World War. They had, despite their different political parties, become close friends.

By the early sixties, Dirksen had become a celebrity. He had an incredible speaking voice. He had won a Grammy for a documentary he had narrated called "Gallant Men" – a tribute to the American soldier. The celebrity Senator frequented the television circuit; showing up occasionally on variety shows and the new late-night talk show, "The Johnny Carson Show."

Johnson called upon him often to get his Great Society programs through the Senate, and to influence overall Republican caucus meetings in the Congress. In true LBJ fashion, the President consistently and lavishly complimented him. He often used the phrase "you're worthy of the Land of Lincoln," referring to Dirksen's home state of Illinois. When Johnson used his friend 'Eve' to rally Republicans to the cause of civil rights, it put political pressure on his southern Democratic senators and his anti-civil rights friend Richard Russell.

Dirksen was not the only Republican that LBJ courted. For example, from time to time he even talked to Richard Nixon, ostensibly to get his views, but also to remind him that he had President Eisenhower on his side as his chief military advisor.

Indeed, Johnson needed Republican support because early in the conflict they supported escalating the war, and he needed to try to control that pressure. For example, when the President committed American combat forces in 1965, Republicans rallied around the 'troops.' Sometimes they mocked those few Democrats, who early in 1965 and 1966, were critical of the President's policies, even though the US was now at war. LBJ, the master politician, while trying to manage Republican calls for more force, also used this right-wing support to offset some of the criticisms and doubts on the war of his liberal colleagues.

Though supportive of the war to stem communism in Indochina, the Republicans frequently criticized Johnson not only for his limited war policy but his lack of candor with the public. For example, the House Minority Leader Gerald Ford was a vocal critic of Johnson's gradualist approach. He even appeared with Senator Dirksen in TV press conferences challenging Dirksen's defense of the President and calling for "a more muscular approach" to defeating the communist insurgency and the North's support. To his colleagues, Ford showed that he thought the President was not keeping the Congress or the public informed. He believed that LBJ was trying to conceal aspects of his policies toward Vietnam. As the war progressed he said to his colleagues, "There's not just a credibility gap – it's become a credibility canyon."

Another critic of LBJ's war policies was Senator John Stennis from Mississippi. Stennis was a member of Fulbright's the Senate Foreign Relations Committee. Like Fulbright, he saw the need for hearings on the war to enlighten both the Congress and the Public. Unlike Fulbright, whose hearings were challenging the reasons for the war, Stennis had become concerned more about whether the President had listened to his military advisors and had employed the Armed Forces effectively. So, in August 1967, he began his hearings. Unlike the Fulbright hearings, these were closed to the public.

A main reason Stennis wanted the hearings closed was to offer the opportunity for the military to give their honest and unrestrained opinions on the conduct of the war. He was particularly interested in challenging the imposed Johnson Administration approach to the ROLLING THUNDER bombing campaign. According to Joseph Fry in his book *Debating Vietnam*, the Committee did all it could to motivate and to ensure the military realized that they had the constitutional duty to give their views to the Committee despite what they had been ordered to do.

In so doing, the members of the Committee also tried to put them at ease, and even coach them ahead of time on what the questions would be. Notwithstanding the fact that these hearings were closed, Committee members would ensure that sanitized, unclassified summaries would be offered to the media. In short, Stennis' motivation was clear. He wanted to bring pressure to bear on the gradualism policy of the President, and attack Secretary of Defense McNamara's advocacy for that policy.

On the first day of the Stennis hearings, the Pacific Commander, Admiral Sharp, and members of the JCS - to include General Wheeler, Admiral Moorer, and the Air Force Chief, General McDonald - testified. Their testimonies and the Committee inquiries focused on the effectiveness of the air campaign against the North. The next day the Committee scheduled Secretary of Defense McNamara to testify on the overall efficacy and rationale of the Administration's war policies. The day following the Defense Secretary's attendance, the Army Chief General Johnson and the Marine Corps Commandant General Greene were called upon to give the ground perspective on the contributions of the bombing in the North to the ground war in the South. They mainly were interested in their assessment of the effectiveness of the interdiction of the Ho Chi Minh trail.

The military testimonies were outwardly respectful toward their civilian superiors but candid. Their views were that the Administration's gradual application of air power and the restrictions on targets significantly hampered the effectiveness of the bombing and interdiction campaigns. Of note, they pointed out were the restrictions on the main lines of communication from China over which much of the war-making logistics flowed. Also, they argued that the inability to mine and attack the vital port facilities in Haiphong had a significant impact on the ability to critically affect the flow of supplies to the North's war effort. They further said that any cessation of the bombing effort - as the Johnson Administration was once again discussing to bring North Vietnam to the negotiating table - would allow the enemy to increase its flow of troops to the South and severely affect the US war effort there.

Finally, upon being asked how the restrictions and the policy of gradualism had affected the overall war effort to date, they said that it had prolonged the war and increased American casualties. In sum, these senior military officers, while being careful to point out that some operations had been effective, overall discredited the Administration's conduct of the war at a time in which Johnson and McNamara were telling the American people that the US was winning.

McNamara's testimony to the Committee in that summer of 1967 was especially dramatic. It was forceful and opinionated. In the views of some Senators present, he was arrogant and unwilling to concede to any other opinion rather than his own. The Secretary, in his opening statement, claimed that ROLLING THUNDER had achieved US aims of reducing the flow of men and supplies to the South and increasing the cost of waging war to the North. Under questioning, McNamara, citing his usual grasp of statistics, refuted any implication that unnecessary restrictions and a coordinated bombing campaign on the North had hampered or could have adversely affected the war effort.

The Defense Secretary further contested the military's claims that increased and unrestricted bombing would lead to a faster or decisive conclusion to the war. Citing lessons from the strategic bombing in World War Two he avowed that such arguments were "completely illusory and futile." He emphasized, with some credibility, that the North was not an industrial nation and therefore was not as vulnerable to strategic bombing as more developed countries would be. Finally, the Secretary took liberty in citing the JCS's many past statements supporting, or according to some, misrepresenting the conduct of the war.

What the Secretary did not address was that the military Chiefs recognized that at this juncture of the war the industrial base of North Vietnam was not what was critical to the strategic bombing campaign. What they wanted to do was to lift the restrictions on air interdiction of the supply lines out of China that were close to that nation's borders, and mine the key ports through which Soviet military aid was sent to the North.

While McNamara's ability to cite from memory an extraordinary number of statistics and weave them into impeccably logical arguments impressed many, he did not convince or sway most on the Committee. Several attacked the Secretary's ability to be open to differences in opinion and his inability to listen to military advice. In response to a question of whether he or the President had confidence in the Joint Chiefs and their recommendations, McNamara argued that there was no rule or law that he or the President had to follow their advice or "judgment in every instance."

However, McNamara took this opportunity, contrary to his knowledge that there was much friction between himself and the Joint Chiefs, that he did not think there was any "gulf between the military leaders and the civilian leaders in the executive branch." These responses, in Professor Fry's words, "typified McNamara's day before the Senate Committee—articulate, highly informed, often brilliant, unyielding on either fact or interpretation but also evasive, intermittently disingenuous, and willing to distort the military's positions for his own ends."

McNamara would later say in his memoirs that this day was amongst the most difficult to bear during his tenure as Secretary of Defense. However, even in retrospect, he remained adamant that he was right and everyone else wrong. In his memoirs, he says, "The case against expanding the air war was clear. All you had to do was look at the numbers."

McNamara's testimony in August 1967 brought to light the serious difference of views between himself and the President's military advisors. However, it went beyond just a difference in views. Per the JCS history, the Stennis hearings and discussions in its aftermath accurately portrayed the severe lack of trust between the American military leaders and the President and his advisors by the fall of 1967. The history states, "the chiefs were dismayed, and in the aftermath of the hearings, relations between the JCS and the Secretary of Defense sank to a new low. Leaks to the press of growing dissension within the Pentagon inevitably followed."

The Fulbright and Stennis hearings opened for the first time in public the disagreements and doubts about the policies for and the conduct of the Vietnam War. Their effect upon the public was minimal at this point. Most importantly, however, they started the Congress down the road to questioning seriously the Executive Branch's wisdom, or lack thereof, in the conduct of the war. From here on the Legislative Branch would try to narrow the perceived 'Credibility Gap' that a growing number believed was driving public dissatisfaction with the war and with the Government in general.

The impact of these Congressional hearings and criticisms on the actual war policies, at this stage and time, were also minimal. LBJ did decide, because of the testimonies on the bombing, to enlarge the target set and remove some restrictions on the ROLLING THUNDER campaign. These did not include, however, the restrictions on attacks against the Chinese major supply lines near the DRV-China border, or the mining of Haiphong harbor.

According to some sources the Stennis hearings had a profound impact on the President's confidence in his Secretary of Defense. Some claim that it prompted LBJ to move McNamara out of office and to the World Bank. However, the Secretary would leave the Government shortly after the beginning of the next year. Whether this was due to the hearings or to McNamara's continued advocation of a 'stabilization' policy for the war in Vietnam and a no conditional call for further negotiations is not clear. Johnson does not reveal anything in his memoirs on this issue.

LBJ also decided to involve Wheeler on a more regular basis in his policy-making gatherings, specifically his Tuesday luncheons. Until mid-1967, the Chairman had not always participated. General Wheeler would not partake much, however, in these meetings. He died shortly afterward from a heart attack.

Because this was the first time that the Senate began to take part in examining the conduct of the war, in the longer view, these hearings became the forerunner of more forceful Congressional action to follow. For example, between 1970 and 1973 there would be six major appropriation bills that would prohibit certain military actions in the Southeast Asia theater of operations. There were also six amendments in bills that did not restrict funding but did restrict certain military operations or actions. They would prevent the Nixon Administration from supporting principal activities and actions that they saw as crucial to their policies toward Vietnam.

As we will see in the next Chapter, Congressional involvement and action in the Nixon years will have a major impact on Presidential policymaking for the war. It would both affect the conduct of actual operations in time and scope, and give further sustenance to North Vietnamese leaders in their decisions on the war.

Section 4.5 - Personal Experiences, Observations, and Conclusions

Personal Experiences

My experiences in the topics in this Chapter began in the Memorial Day parade in New York City in 1966. I had just entered my senior year at West Point. It was a tradition for the military academy to take part in that parade. It was supposed to be an event honoring the sacrifice of American servicemen and women in defending our freedoms.

My West Point company of 100 cadets marched along Fifth Avenue to shouts - not cheers - along the way. It was my first exposure to the anti-war protest. I noticed that there could not have been more than fifty protestors. There was about double that number of media people with cameras filming and taping the demonstration. That evening, over a TV news program, I saw the footage and heard the narration. The presentation made it seem that thousands were protesting. It was my first observation that the news was trying to make something out of nothing – news for the news people so the media could sell something.

In 1968, an assassin killed President Kennedy's brother, Robert. I was in Europe then, serving my first tour as a new second lieutenant in the infantry. We had a small black and white TV. The only station was the Armed Forces Network, which relayed news stories and film clips from the States. I saw pictures of the RFK assassination. They were coupled with extracts from the now famous Zapruder film of JFK's shooting. The TV reporter's comments were that America was in turmoil, even falling apart. He further claimed that the Vietnam War was the main reason for that.

Soon after, I also saw protest marchers for civil rights and against the war. This time there were thousands, even tens of thousands, of protesters. This dissent was followed by yet another assassination – of Martin Luther King, who had made a famous speech in Washington that I had not heard of until after his death. From outside of the States, it all seemed so strange and unreal. What was real to me was the death, up to that time, of 15 of my classmates – killed in action in the now raging war in South Vietnam. By the beginning of 1969, over 36,000 US soldiers had been killed there.

As mentioned in Chapter 1, I deployed to Vietnam in April 1969. I returned in March of 1970. 14 more of my classmates were killed in action that year, along with another 11,780 American soldiers. While there I had heard of men landing on the moon and returning to earth. While I was checking our defensive positions one night on some unknown hill, I listened to a soldier over the command radio say, "If they cannot get us out of Vietnam, how in the hell are they going to get those men back from the moon?"

Upon my return to the US in San Francisco, a long hair unruly looking young man spat at my feet and called me names. What had happened to America I asked myself? More painfully, my son, who was now a year and a half-year-old, did not recognize me. He would remain distant for another year after my return. I felt like I had gone to and lived on another planet.

I missed much of the sixties in America. Most of what had happened I observed in a sequestered environment like West Point, or from afar in my military service in Europe and Asia. My wife had been closer to it. She related that she had a tough time getting a place to stay while I was in Vietnam. No one in her hometown in New Jersey would rent a place for her to stay since she was a soldier's wife whose husband was away at war. That was until her mother asked a friend of a friend to help.

My wife related to me how, along with my Mom and Dad, the nightly news stories with their graphic film clips had frightened her. Six months into my year in Vietnam, a classmate whose wife and mine had been very close in Germany and after, had been killed in action in the same division I was serving. My wife went to be with her and console her through the long ordeal of the return of his body and his burial at Arlington Cemetery. This of course had frightened her more; but she still had to put up with the television news, which seemed to her to be against the war.

My exposure to the media and protests when I returned disgusted me. I recall one incident in particular. One night I watched a CBS TV documentary on the conduct of the war. It infuriated me. In the show, a CBS reporter was interviewing soldiers in the field. As they moved through the typical heavy jungle brush in temperatures nearing a hundred degrees with rucksacks that looked like they weighed about sixty pounds, the reporter poked his microphone in the face of one struggling, sweating soldier and asked, 'How do you feel about the War soldier?'

The soldier replied, in true grunt fashion given the circumstances, 'it fricking sucks,' or something like that. Then the reporter gleefully continued, 'What do you think about what you are doing – are we winning the war?' The soldier responds, 'No fricking way are we going to win, this is BS, and I want to go home.' The reporter then turns toward the camera and makes his commentary, "You now have seen and heard firsthand how the American soldier feels about this war; how hopeless he knows it is, and how all he wants to do is to get home and end it all."

It was this kind of reporting of the Vietnam War that made many of us in the military not like and distrust the press. I had had my experience with reporters in Vietnam. On one operation in the fall of 1969, we had air assaulted into an area that higher intelligence had indicated was a prisoner of war camp. A reporter from some national newspaper, whose name I cannot remember, went with us for what he had hoped to be, I was sure, a sensational news story. At the end of the day, after we had found nothing, the reporter, who was supposed to spend some extended time with us to write about the infantry in Vietnam, returned via helicopter to one of the large base camps to the rear.

Sadly, as far as my experience went, I did not know of or heard of any reporters like Ernie Pyle or Robert Capa caliber in the Vietnam War. Later I found out that there were some who understood the plight of the infantryman and were intent on giving their stories. These journalists, such as Catherine Leroy, Larry Burrows, and Joe Galloway, were not trying to make stories based on political issues. Since the end of the war, I have also had the opportunity to meet other reporters of the military like Richard Halloran formerly from the New York Times who were also fair and honest in their reporting of military affairs.

But media coverage of the war, as I remember it while in Vietnam and afterward into the seventies, seemed biased against the war and the military. Of course, this was well into the fighting – 1968 to 1975. The effect on my wife and others in my family of that coverage was devastating. Not only did it trouble them to see the bloodshed and feel for my safety, but the antimilitary and pro antiwar bias that they experienced affected their entire attitude about the worthiness of it all.

From time to time in my service, I also had contacts with members of the Congress. When I was at Fort Lewis, Washington I was an aide to the Commanding General there. While in that position, the

General allowed me to sit in on several of his meetings with visiting dignitaries. On several occasions, I met Senators John Stennis and 'Scoop' Jackson. In sitting in on the General's discussions with them, I found how much they supported the military.

Senator Stennis, on one occasion in 1974, talked about his role during the Vietnam War, which was still going on. He told the General that he felt that the war was going to be lost because the South Vietnamese Army would not be able to stand up to a major Northern offensive that he was certain would soon come. He lamented that when the US military was still engaged, it was not able to bring the full weight of its power to bear to win the war. By that time, the Senator looked particularly feeble. Several months before this meeting two teenagers had shot and mugged him outside his Washington home. Stennis, who had never served in the military, would die in 1993 right after the victory of the first Gulf War.

When I was later stationed at the Pentagon on the Army Staff, I had some more direct experiences with members of Congress. From time to time, as a staff officer in the Army War Plans Division the Army leadership sent me with others to brief both Senators and Representatives on what the wartime missions were for Army forces. This entailed going from the Pentagon to the 'Hill' and briefing the Congressman and his staff in their offices in one of the buildings adjacent to the Capital. Since I was a junior field grade officer at the time, a General Officer would accompany me; just to make sure that the Congressman did not feel that the Army thought he was not important.

I was startled how little the Congressmen knew about the military. Most of their staff members were equally as ignorant. They were focused more on what the Army was going to acquire for its organizations than the training and readiness of the force. Their interest, therefore, was on how much of the defense budget they could tap into to support a defense program for their district or State. Otherwise, they seemed to care less about anything the military was about. In short, what this experience taught me was that for most members of Congress politics is usually all local.

Later, I served as a Senior Planner to the Chairman of the Joint Chiefs of Staff. I had frequent contact with the then Chairman, General Colin Powell. Here I got yet another view of the Congress. General Powell knew and was constantly in touch with the Chairs of the Senate and House Armed Services Committees. From time to time the General would share with his senior staff, of which I was a member, his views on Congress in general, and the two Congressmen. They were insightful. From these, I learned the following.

As a military man dealing with Congress, you need to know who has had military experience or service. Absent the experience or service, a Congressman or woman would only be able to relate to the Armed Forces in what acquisition program or military base gives jobs or revenues to their district or State. The old cliché that 'all politics is local' is true to most members. This I hand already experienced. Now my earlier observations seemed confirmed.

Because this is their primary, or for some, only interest, you must make an opportunity to educate them in subtle ways on what the military is all about. By subtle he explained, you cannot make them feel 'like a dummy' or talk down to them. However, you should inform them of what the military missions and needs are, regardless of the direct economic benefits to their constituents. This would always be an uphill battle and the most challenging task in briefing a member of Congress who fits into this category of no experience with the US Armed Forces.

For those with military experience or service, you must relate the issue that you are bringing to their attention to their experience or prior service. If you can make that link, it will be easy to get the member to understand what the needs or solutions are for that issue. However, there are some who, because of their position in Congress and their background in military affairs, think they know the answer even if they do not have all the facts and considerations. In that case, ensure that you do not insult them, but use the tact that this issue is different from their experience and service and show how.

In any case, senior military personnel must understand that members of Congress can be critical to solving military problems in this country. They can and will challenge the Executive Branch and the Department of Defense in such ways as to make it most difficult to obtain support for military strategies and policies. General Powell would always remind us that this was a direct result of the Vietnam War. Before the Vietnam experience, most members of the Congress accepted that foreign affairs and national security were the Executive Branch's primary function and Congress needed to let the President take the lead.

Observations and Conclusions

What can we summarize, observe, and conclude about US domestic affairs and their impact on the conduct of the Vietnam War discussed in this chapter? Did events at home significantly affect policies and actions in Vietnam? If so, how much did the civil-rights and anti-war movements, the media, public opinion, and the Congress influence JFK and LBJ policy making for Vietnam? Moreover, how much did the war affect these movements, reactions to it, and the American crisis of the sixties?

First some general observations on how the Presidents and their senior advisors on Vietnam reacted to the American crisis in the sixties, and the groups and activities that incited it or reacted to it. As for JFK, America's domestic scene had not reached a level of major concern. Kennedy was involved in the civil rights' issues during his administration and had sent troops to enforce law and order in several instances. However, his civil-rights legislation got nowhere, primarily due to the obstruction of the Senate southern click that blocked his program.

As we saw in Chapter 2, the President was concerned about the media's portrayal of his policy of counterinsurgency, and his message that America could not solve South Vietnam's problems using military action alone. He also did not want the media or the Congress to know about the growing role the US military was taking in the insurgency there. Though JFK did not want his military assistance program to be too militant, he was concerned that if he was not successful, and Vietnam fell to the communists, he would face a backlash equal to the 'Who Lost China' affair of the fifties.

It was not until after Kennedy's assassination that the country began to show signs of major concern and some discord over the course America was taking for them. Ironically the mood reflected in JFK's 1961 call for 'ask not what the country can do for you, but what you can do for your country' by 1965 was changing. More accurately, Kennedy's inaugural words were now flipping toward 'what can my country not only do for me, but what can I do not to have it interfere with me.' The 'me' represented the majority White, Male citizens – and a growing number of baby boomers who were reaching early adulthood – all of whom wanted to ensure the prosperity and hope that they now thought they were entitled to.

For the minority - those Black, Hispanic immigrants, and urban and rural poor Whites who were left out of the prosperity of the post-World War Two era – they were anxious and hopeful that LBJ's great society programs and war on poverty would cure their plight as Johnson told them they would. They were also fearful that a growing war in far-off Southeast Asia might steer the President's promises off course.

As explained in the first part of this chapter, it was not until the mid-sixties that the major social, political, and cultural effects of the post-war changes now caught up with America at home. By then, American outlooks had broadened dramatically. Educational opportunities furthered these outlooks and sparked a new generation to question the social attitudes and values of the fifties, and begin to further question its government and other institutions in the sixties. LBJ's contributions through his Great Society, especially the Civil Rights and War on Poverty legislation, also pushed American minority reactions and desires for further change in the status quo at home, and further affected their views of and hopes for the future.

Moreover, the emerging youth of the country – the baby boomers - had grown up under the threat of nuclear war. They had practiced ducking under school desks in case of a nuclear attack. There had also been all this rhetoric of 'massive nuclear retaliation.' It was not logical to many for one nation to threaten another's annihilation to 'deter' war. Thus, was born the student movements against the specter of nuclear war. It naturally came to question the government's waging of a conflict for the sake of deterrence of further war, or the waging of a war in Vietnam thousands of miles away to stop communism before it reached the shores of America.

The corresponding undertaking for civil rights and other group liberties, such as women rights, now was becoming intermingled - even intertwined – with a growing anti-war movement fueled in part by uncertainty and confusion over the future. These movements, in turn, questioned the rights of the 'yellow man' and why was America trying to decide the future of an Asian people engaged in a war for their own future. The diversity of the anti-war movement, as discussed in this Chapter, showed that it engaged many segments of American society. Thus, the questioning of the Vietnam War in such a cross section of America was very much related to the overall search for America's future at home and abroad.

For the most part, these movements were reactions to and even symptoms of profound social and cultural changes in the US. But, they were also further fueled by the waging of a war that few understood, many were confused over, and others abhorred. The conflict further exasperated movement participants, especially the more militant ones, to protest what they saw as an illegal and immoral war waged for no good reason. As the war escalated, and draft calls increased, the protests became larger and more militant from frustration and anger.

So how did LBJ and his Administration deal with this crisis as they waged war in Vietnam? The last chapter recounts that LBJ and his civilian advisors were very much, by the beginning of 1967, aware that the American domestic scene was in turmoil, and much of it was related to the war. They were also concerned about how it may further affect its conduct; especially because it now appeared that the war would be longer than expected. Thus, the President finally decided to launch a public affairs campaign to affect public, and in turn, Congressional attitudes.

Indeed, recall that Johnson's advisors, both civilian and military, had argued in 1965 that instead of trying to minimize the costs and necessity of war he should have considered a program of keeping the public informed of the need to conduct military operations and the reasons for them. Instead,

LBJ decided to minimize the importance, potential costs, and nature of the war. He did so because - as mentioned several, perhaps now dozens of times – he wanted to downplay his commitment to the use of force and not seem to put the nation on a war footing primarily for fear of failing to get his domestic programs through Congress.

Now faced with a prolonged war, LBJ saw that he had to convince the public and Congress that it was worth the cost. However, there were two factors about this campaign that detracted from the effectiveness of its effort from the beginning. First, by 1967 it may have been too late to build any kind of majority consensus that the US was on the right course to winning and just needed more time for that victory. Second, and related to the first, LBJ's reputation for telling the truth and thus convincing the populace and Congress of its continued path to victory were already severely damaged. Thus, attempting now to build a consensus for the war seemed like more of the same deception of past years. This attitude, of course, accelerated after TET.

The media, and some of the public and in Congress by this time, had already seen through Johnson's attempt to minimize his administration's commitment to a major war in Vietnam. Indeed, it began for some with Johnson's denials in 1965 that the deployment of major US ground units meant 'no change in policy' just did not pass the 'makes sense' test. By then, it had become clear that there had been a failure to build a workable South Vietnamese Government and Army that could counter the NVA/VC aggression in the south by itself. Thus, LBJ's refusal from the onset to show that it was going to take substantial American combat forces on the ground to reverse the situation had already created a 'credibility gap' between the Administration and the media, the public, and the Congress.

Moreover, as he committed America's sons to combat in 1965, which he had said to Americans he would not do in 1964, Johnson told American mothers and fathers that he did not want war and sought a negotiated peace. While Americans were dying on far away battlefields in 1966, the President said he did not want to bomb or damage the enemy too much. Now, while the war reached millions of Americans via television in their living rooms and they saw American boys killed and maimed, LBJ said that with a little more fighting and dying the war would result in victory.

These words in 1967 reached and reverberated in the ears of many Americans who had fought or supported a war with unconditional terms to force the defeat of powerful military opponents. Their children, who were now eligible for the draft and could go over to Vietnam and die, heard them as well. Why would there not be a 'credibility gap?' Why would people listening to his Administration's words and seeing what was happening on TV believe LBJ, and agree to more of the same with no end in sight other than more American casualties? Thus, despite his campaign to show that the US was winning it would just take a little more time, the protests continued.

So how did the two major protest activities then or after, affect the war's conduct? In general, scholars on the civil and anti-war movements argue that they were not a major factor in shaping the war or ending it. Yet, as one reads about them and particularly sees these movement protests on film, that rather trite conclusion does not entirely make sense. For many Americans who lived through this period to include me, the movements - certainly the more virulent and violent faction - divided the American polity and made civil discourse difficult. The movement also divided families. This often led to family disarray. That grew as the war went on into the late sixties and early seventies – and even lasted after US forces no longer played a key role.

By late 1967, however, these movements, despite the turmoil they exhibited, had not yet brought any major changes to the US conduct of the war. They did influence two people in the Administration, the Secretary of Defense, and the President. We will examine that influence more closely below.

In addition, during the Nixon years, as we will see in the next chapter, they would begin to affect the attitudes of the Congress on support for further military actions. But, the movements, as we will see, did not alter Presidential policy to bring the war to some sort of 'honorable' end. So, despite the divisions, they caused in America, by themselves these movements did not cause any major changes to the course of the Vietnam War.

So, what of the media's role in the war? Undoubtedly, the domestic movements and their protests provided ample storylines for them, as well of course, the war itself. While there were certainly honorable, well-intentioned reporters, the stories of the activism at home often focused on those people and events that would sensationalize or make for a good story. They were particularly effective on TV - especially when paired with reports from the battlefield that seem to support the protest messages.

The media was also a factor in affecting the disharmony portrayed in the protest movements and reactions to them. It had a duty, of course, to report the events, opinions, and causes of the domestic disturbances. And some of the occurrences associated with the turmoil made for important as well as sensational news – such as the 1968 assassinations of King and Kennedy, and the Chicago riots and brutality at the Democratic Convention. But, in examining the media's coverage of these events and the movements in general from 1965 to the end of TET in 1968, there were more than a few instances of hyperbole and editorial license overdramatizing the size or extent of the movements, protests, and events, and how they surmised they impacted on the war. Some overeager journalists even made correlations between the domestic disturbances and their effect on the morale of the American forces fighting the war.

To be fair, much of the coverage of the war in 1965 and 1966 was honest and straightforward, though tainted by some frustration and skepticism. For example, Walter Cronkite and Morey Shaffer of CBS did a show on the operations in the Ia Drang Valley in 1965 that was accurate, well informed, and presented without bias. However, as the news coverage, especially the graphic film reports on national TV stations, continued to bring the war home to Americans, the media began to convey its doubts about the war to the public. Coverage increasingly focused on not just showing and reporting on events and people, but included editorial comment on what the reporter or the news editors thought was happening.

As for its editorial opinions of the war, by 1967 the media seems to have turned sour because of having lost confidence in the viability of a corrupt South Vietnam Government, an inept Army of South Vietnam, and an ineffectual strategic US approach of attrition in winning it.

However, some reporters lost track of the fact that reports and criticisms of battles and campaigns are not easily discernible as successes or gains because wars are messy affairs. Often the fighting does not reveal or relate to any logical course, utility or consequences beyond the death and destruction they display. This applies particularly when the journalists are ignorant of military affairs and eager to get a story that their editors want quickly to compete in the growing news media struggles to gain audiences and profit.

Moreover, it is the nature of the media to focus on the dramatic and the perceived more newsworthy events and activities. What is not visible or difficult to report objectively goes unseen or unreported. In some of this, the military itself is to blame. While more than 50% of senior officers in Vietnam – as reported in Kinnard's *The War Managers* - thought the media was not reporting the war correctly, much of this was a result of military briefings that were often staged and valuable information that was not always forthcoming. Senior commanders grew too suspicious of the press. Instead, they should have been better at ensuring that the media understood what was happening, or more importantly, what was going wrong and right.

Without a familiarity with the subject and knowledge of the big picture - or when some reporters jumped to conclusions because of their narrow points of view - too often the media assumed a 'truth' about the entire war, not just the news event related. Thus, when a news film or picture shot showed a soldier with a zippo lighter setting fire to a thatched roof village home, the commentary added that this is what was going on all over Vietnam as part of the 'Search and Destroy' concept of operations. Other pictures, such as the killing of a VC officer during TET, were not reported with the entire facts. These reports were the precursor to today's media aggressive news reporting of 'breaking' and 'exclusive' news stories. The bias in news reporting during TET and after became the rule rather than the exception.

Competition among news agencies, TV stations, and broadcasters, and even among news people in Vietnam contributed as well. Though not as prevalent as today, owners and editors of the news media during the Vietnam War competed to give more prompt and sensationalized coverage. In a rush to provide the then 'breaking news,' as in the case of the attack on the American embassy during TET, the familiar aphorism, "In war, the first casualty is truth" can be attributed to much of the American media's reports.

While it is difficult to assess the degree that media reporting affected opinions toward the war and its conduct, some interesting conclusions can be made. First, having lived through the times, I can say that the reporting reached about everyone I knew – former teachers and coaches, and classmates, family members, neighbors, and closest friends. In the early to mid-sixties – both before and at the first stages of the ground commitment and combat – most that I knew, who did not understand anything about the military, were simply curious as to what was happening after they had seen or read news reports on Vietnam.

By the latter part of the sixties, some I knew had become disgusted with the war. Now the message was, 'we should just get out.' The same numbers of disgusted said, 'we should just win.' When I returned from the war in 1970 most were sour on Vietnam. Implanted in all their minds, it seemed to me, were ideas on Vietnam that they had acquired from the media; not from speeches or sound bites from Government sources, and certainly not from most returning veterans, who were shunned or did not want to talk about it anyway.

But, it seems unfair, and giving more than its fair due, to say that the media alone brought an end to the war. It is immoral and dangerous to claim that the press purposefully undermined the US military and was to blame for the Vietnam failure. American military leaders made enough mistakes on their own to contribute to their losing the war. Moreover, as we will see in the Chapters ahead, the enemy had something to do with the loss as well.

Nevertheless, the media did have an impact. As the narrative in Sections 2 and 3 demonstrate, the effect of the media on the war was most prominent and pervasive during TET. The evidence is quite clear that the negative and misleading reporting at that time had a significant effect on President Johnson and his civilian advisors. Along with the pressures of the domestic protests, the media accounts convinced LBJ and his Secretary of Defense that the war could not be won, not just at acceptable costs but any costs in 1968. These accounts added to the demoralization of the President to the extent that he could no longer listen to any other account that TET was a military victory. More to follow on that below.

How about public opinion? As mentioned, the Polls, despite the growing media negativism, showed that public opinion seemed to mostly favor escalation, not a limitation of US military actions during much of the war. The indication is that Americans were dismayed that the Government was unable to apply its vast military power to bring the war to a favorable conclusion. There was also some bewilderment over the government's lack of ability to defeat the communists in Vietnam. This then turned to a feeling that the government, namely LBJ, was not forthright in what was going on in the war. By 1967, this impacted the President, who finally decided that he had to garner positive support for an anticipated prolonged war through a public affairs campaign.

When TET happened, the public was obviously as surprised and shocked as the President and his advisors and commanders. Johnson's previous 'victory is near campaign' added to this shock. The media reporting further reinforced the public's reaction. But, there was still support for a brief period after the first TET attacks for escalation, not retreat or clamor for peace. Therefore, the argument that TET adversely affected public opinion, which in turn caused the failure in Vietnam, is not valid. Rather, public opinion seemed to await the President's reaction to TET, and what he thought should happen next. As we have seen, Johnson failed to rally public support for further significant military action. Hence, after his I will not run speech, public support for the war turned entirely negative.

Later, Nixon would announce his policy of Vietnamization and the unilateral withdrawal of US troops. It was then that public opinion polls began to show continuously a lack of support for the war, and most people indicating that the Vietnam War was a mistake. Hence, one can conclude that rather than decisively influencing Presidential policy on the war, public opinion followed the President's lead and decisions on Vietnam.

How about the overall role and effect of Congress in the outcome of the war? As for the criticism of Congress not addressing a declaration of war, there are many reasonable explanations for having not done so. First, by 1965 the Cold War was going into its third decade. Thus, for twenty years the country had been in constant confrontation and, at times, actual military conflict with communism. The United States was in a continuous 'crisis-situation' that may have demanded the use of force quickly. Thus, the US was now experiencing a new international situation it had never been in before.

That situation was that the use of force or going to war was no longer just a break from peace, but was an everyday possibility. In that sense, waiting for a declaration of war before employing military force, especially if that employment were intended as limited in scope and time or to deter an enemy from some action, did not make sense. The President had to have the authorization - as Commander-in-Chief of the armed forces and in his main responsibility to act for the common defense - to enter into conflicts or war without a formal declaration from Congress.

Second, the US was now faced with the constant fear in the age of nuclear weapons of a nuclear holocaust. In those circumstances, a declaration of war might prompt or incite an uncontrolled escalation toward nuclear war. Yet, as both Kennedy and Johnson argued, that did not negate the need to use of limited force under circumstances not requiring the use of nuclear weapons. However, if a nation with nuclear weapons were to declare war, then it may indicate it was preparing to use all its military power, to include nuclear weapons, to achieve its aims. Given these conditions, it made sense to the President and many in Congress to stay under the so-called 'threshold of nuclear war' by not asking or proceeding for a formal declaration of war.

A third explanation for not declaring war is that members of Congress now believed it was in the Constitutional powers of the President, particularly with the precedence of the Berlin and Cuban Missile Crisis, to employ military forces to meet military threats to our interests. The Gulf of Tonkin crisis seemed to fit that mold. To say that the Congress reneged on its responsibility to declare war just does not make sense at the time.

Besides, the Resolution's Section 3 stated, "This resolution shall expire when the President shall determine that the peace and security of the area are reasonably assured by international conditions created by the action of the United Nations or otherwise, except that it may be terminated earlier by concurrent resolution of the Congress." Thus, Congress held the authority to end the President's powers under the resolution at any time after its promulgation. This is hardly an indication that the US Congress forsook its Constitutional responsibilities as some critics' claim.

In January 1971, Congress did repeal the Resolution. It also acted to restrict further the President's power to wage war by limiting funds for the conflict. All those actions, though later Nixon would blame these Congressional acts for losing the war, were legitimate activities demonstrating Congress's role under the Constitution to exercise its intended part in waging war.

It was in the third year of LBJ's first term as an elected President that Congress began to reassert itself in the Vietnam conflict. It started in 1966 through hearings on certain issues that indirectly challenged the President's war power activity in Vietnam. However, as we will see in the next Chapter, it was not until the Nixon Presidency - with a stated policy of withdrawing from Vietnam without a clear military victory - that the Congress forcefully exerted its powers and began to limit actions in the war primarily through its Constitutional power of the purse.

As for the overall role of Congress in the war, up until TET it was as much responsible for the US involvement in Indochina and South Vietnam as the office of the Presidency. This is a constant theme throughout William Gibbons' excellent work on government actions in the history of US involvement in Southeast Asia. Though there were a few naysayers, the most notable being Senator Mansfield, the Congress as a whole - Republican and Democrat – supported from 1950 through 1968 the Presidents' increasing militant actions to defend South Vietnam from aggression.

The reasons for that support were threefold. First, there was a consensus in both the House and the Senate for containment of communism in Asia, and to defeat it in South Vietnam. Second, most in Congress saw the commitment of forces in Vietnam within the powers of the President; especially under the Tonkin Resolution. Third, once American soldiers, marines, airmen, and sailors were committed to battle, even those who thought Vietnam was a mistake, voted to support the funding of the war because Americans were in harm's way.

Overall then, in looking at each of these factors or domestic actors or activities – the civil rights and antiwar movements, the media reporting of the war, and public opinion and Congressional reactions to it, and comparing them to JFK's and LBJ's wartime decisions up until 1968, they had no major impact on the conduct of the war.

Yes, both Administrations were concerned for Congressional support, but it was primarily to ensure no major dissent would derail their policies toward Vietnam. Even the Fulbright and Stennis hearings, while a nuisance and infuriating to LBJ, in of themselves caused no major changes to the conduct of the war. Yes, these factors and their key players had a role in the domestic unrest and turmoil, but they did not alter the conduct of operations in Vietnam significantly.

But what does become evident from this examination of these domestic factors and the crisis in America in the sixties, is that by 1968, together these activities had a major effect on one individual – Lyndon Baines Johnson. Furthermore, together these factors not only brought his Presidency down, but launched the US on a road to defeat in Vietnam. This then is the main impact of domestic affairs in the sixties on the Vietnam War.

There is much evidence to support this assertion. First, reading accounts of LBJ's and his family's reactions to the protests, one gets a sense that the events of the time deeply affected them personally. For example, Lady Bird Johnson wrote in her diary how the protests and riots made her depressed. At one point, after the assassinations of Robert Kennedy and Martin Luther King, she wrote, "What is happening to us? What is the country coming to? Are we a sick society?" Moreover, the Johnson's oldest daughter, Lynda, whose husband had deployed as a Marine to Vietnam in 1968, recounted that from the White House you could often hear the protesters shouting, "baby killer" and "how many kids did you kill today." Her younger sister, Luci said that the shouted words, "Hey, hey LBJ, how many kids did you kill today," was often her "wake up call" at the White House.

All of this affected their husband and father. At family dinners and meetings in the White House they discussed these observations and their reactions to them. Johnson's own remarks show that he was very much affected. LBJ, speaking after the 1968 assassinations, said of the climate of the 60s in America, "those awful events give us ample warning that in an atmosphere of extremism, of disrespect for law, of contempt for the rights of others, violence may bring down the very best among us."

Indeed, that 'bringing down the very best among us' may very well be adjudged not only of his Presidency but himself personally. As Doris Kearns Goodwin relates, the President admitted that he felt betrayed by these student protests, as well as the dissents of the civil-rights leaders. Many of LBJ's personal assistants, such as his spokesman Jack Valenti and his domestic advisor Joseph Califano, testified that he was "bewildered by the demonstrations." Bewilderment then turned to anger. Anger then turned to anguish.

Moreover, amidst all the dissent, protest, and violence in late 1967 and into 1968, Lyndon Johnson's most respected civilian advisor abandoned him. In the fall of 1967, McNamara had once again recommended what his eventual replacement Clark Clifford and others called a "pull-back strategy" that they argued would mean defeat for the US. His Secretary of Defense – a man he most admired and respected and had counted on to pull him through the war he did not want - had lost all hope for victory in a war LBJ had promised he would never lose. It must have devastated him.

His senior military advisors and his commanders in the field failed him as well. While LBJ was at fault in demanding only views from them that fit into his ill-advised limited war policies that would not work, these military men had responsibilities to their civilian leaders to tell them what would work and not work in war. They did not; at least not in terms that he could understand or in ways that were convincing.

Mark Updegrove, a director of the LBJ Presidential Library, further captured Johnson's mood by 1968 in his book, *Indomitable Will*. The author, using interviews with LBJ confidants, notes, "increasingly the president appeared wrought physically and emotionally, his weathered face, deeply creviced with worry, aged beyond its fifty-nine years. Leaving the White House became difficult for Johnson in those latter days. Protesters were everywhere, and Johnson kept his distance, fearing that exposing himself to the torrent of dissent would be to diminish the presidency itself."

Images of Lyndon Johnson in late 1967 and 1968 are telltale signs of his demoralization and despair. White House pictures, taken to show a President hard at work for the people, show LBJ hunched over a meeting table with his head to his lap; or at his desk in the Oval Office without a jacket, his tie undone, and his hand touching his brow as if trying to make his worries go away. Indeed, the pressure of the protests added to the burden of his decisions on the war and inability to end it.

All this pressure, dismay, and even disillusionment and defeat appeared to reach a climax during TET. The President was a beaten, downtrodden man when he decided to not run for another term. It is reasonable to think that the movement could have had a significant impact on the primary decision maker for the Vietnam War – the 36th President of the United States.

Thus, this story argues that the domestic unrest - and how it was portrayed, perceived, and felt - in America during LBJ's terms in office had a critical effect upon him. His decision in 1968 to reject any military victory was a result, in large part, of the pressure of the dissent upon him and his loss of courage. As the Commander-in-Chief, he abandoned his duty to the American military to seek an alternative strategy to end the war positively. As President of the American people he failed to show determination in the face of adversity, and courage to convince them that it was the US responsibility to take further action to ensure the freedom of millions of Vietnamese.

In sum, all the examined evidence supports the supposition that Johnson lost his nerve in the few months following the first stages of the TET offensive. While his military and civilian commanders and advisors contributed, his character faltered. He lost faith in his abilities to lead, and the support that he so desperately needed from the domestic scene to make a decisive, if difficult decision to change the course of the war to win it. As Peter Braestrup notes, it was then that LBJ should have taken charge, acted like a Commander-in-Chief of the military and President of the people, and grabbed hold of the situation to turn the message of defeat to an opportunity to exploit and win the war. Johnson did not. In doing nothing, above all others, he lost the war.

To conclude this chapter, we have seen that domestic circumstances do exert a critical influence on a nation's ability to wage war. To ignore domestic attitudes and support invites disaster for the conduct of the war, particularly in a democracy.

The domestic crisis in America in the sixties was particularly tumultuous. The discord and attendant violence were a result of a perfect storm of unsurpassed hopes for the future, inept handling of a long and contentious war, and real inequities resulting from uneven distribution of unequaled post World War Two growth in wealth and opportunity.

While the American domestic crisis added pressures on President Johnson and affected him personally, he did not effectively address them and provide the leadership that was necessary to see

America through the most difficult challenges of the war. There is evidence that strong Presidential leadership could have rallied support for decisive military action after TET if the military commanders and advisors had provided him with a convincing incentive to do so.

Also, as briefly mentioned above, the North Vietnamese leaders paid close attention to the American domestic scene and their apparent and potential effects on US decision makers. As already noted, the Politburo made American will a major element and calculus in its strategy for waging war in the South. We will see in Chapter 7 and elsewhere ahead, how important a role they placed on American politics in their strategy and make a judgment there, and the greater, even critical, importance they placed on the civil-rights and anti-war movements, the media, and public opinion and the Congress reactions to it as a measure of US will.

We will also see in the next chapter that President Nixon continued initially to ignore the importance of engendering domestic and congressional support for military actions. This will incite the Congress to act. It will pass legislation decisively restricting US operations. These restrictions, and anticipation of them, as we will see did have a more decisive impact on the conduct of the war in the Nixon years.

Chapter 5: Peace with Honor?

This chapter continues the explanation of the US government's policies toward Vietnam and their effects on the war waged there. It covers the years from the election of Richard Nixon in 1968 to the fall of Saigon in 1975. The focus is on President Nixon's policy of ending the war, which he labeled 'Peace with Honor,' and his Administration's main approach to gain that peace through 'Vietnamization' of the conflict. It also continues the explanation of the role that domestic factors had on Nixon's attempts to end the war favorably for the United States.

Nixon thought that he could terminate the war in his first two years as President. Though he portrayed his 'plan' to end the war as something different from his predecessor, he pursued the same goals – to end the war by convincing the North Vietnam that it could not win. He employed military force, however, in ways and in places that Johnson thought too risky to limit the conflict.

Nixon also pursued diplomacy more effectively. His negotiations with China and the Soviet Union enabled him to bring international pressure against the North to negotiate an end of the war for the United States. In question, is whether that negotiation and its results were, in fact, a 'Peace with Honor.'

Section 5.1 – Nixon Administration

After LBJ's announcement in March that he would not run for another term but would seek a negotiated settlement of the war, an old nemesis of the Democratic party, Richard Nixon, decided to run again for the Presidency. Nixon's campaign charted a careful course in addressing the future conduct of the war. On the one hand, he had always been a staunch anti-communist. Indeed, much of his past political success had been due to his fervor over not just containing communism but defeating it. As Vice President to Eisenhower, he was at the forefront in defending IKE's massive retaliation policy toward communist aggression, and his Domino Theory regarding the containment of Chinese Communism in Southeast Asia.

On the other hand, Nixon was a master politician adept at reading the public's temperament on the key issues. The central one he now confronted was domestic support for the Vietnam War. He recognized, in 1968, that the sentiment was to end the war, even if it meant concessions to the communists. Effectively reading the 'tea leaves,' he knew that he needed some policy that would give hope in doing so without it being a 'defeat' for the US. Nixon also wanted to have a platform that would distance himself from LBJ's successor, Hubert Humphrey. He chose to shackle the Democratic nominee to Johnson's failure in Vietnam, and the significant debt resulting from LBJ's domestic agenda and war policies.

In Nixon's words, "I wanted the war to end, but in a manner that would save the South Vietnamese people from military defeat and subjection to the domination of the North Vietnamese Communist regime." As he further explained in his memoirs, "I believed that we could use our armed strength more effectively to convince the North Vietnamese that a military victory was not possible. We also needed to step up our programs for training and equipping the South Vietnamese so that they could develop the capability of defending themselves. Most important, I believed that we were not making adequate use of our vast diplomatic resources and powers. The heart of the problem lay more in Peking and Moscow than in Hanoi."

During his campaign for the Presidency, the mainstream media, seldom Nixon supporters, asked for details on his views on ending the war. The Republican nominee refrained from offering any. The media derisively called this policy Nixon's 'secret plan.' One reporter for the *Washington Post* observed that Nixon was trying to portray himself "just dovish enough to make Humphrey look like the hard-liner and Nixon the sensible peacemaker." The fact is that he did not have a preconceived plan, only some ideas that would take on more substance later.

During the campaign, Nixon portrayed himself as a capable and experienced leader who had assisted Eisenhower admirably and competently for eight years in government service. IKE supported this claim. As part of the platform, Nixon further sought to show that he could end the war that Democratic leaders had started and conducted. Thus, most of his campaign speeches had the phrase, 'New leadership will end the war and win the peace in the Pacific.'

However, one action during the campaign kept secret until years afterward, would indicate how Nixon would eventually run and ruin his Presidency. Detailed in Ken Hughes' book *Chasing Shadows*, the future president found out in September 1968 that there had been a breakthrough in LBJ's diplomatic actions directed toward North Vietnam. The North Vietnamese had agreed to talk in Paris if Johnson would continue to stop the bombing. At the end of October, the day that LBJ announced the suspension of bombing and the imminent start of the talks, Nixon ordered his campaign manager to see if he could derail the talks for fear that they may give his opponent, Hubert Humphrey, a boost at the upcoming November polls.

Through a contact named Anna Chennault, a Chinese-born widow of an American war hero who had led air operations in support of the nationalist Chinese in the world war, Nixon arranged for the sending of a secret cable to the South Vietnamese Government. That message said that if they held off in any negotiations until he got into office Nixon would get them "a better deal." Consequently, the South Vietnamese leader announced he would not attend any meeting with the North. The negotiations never took place. Whether this act got him elected is impossible to say. However, Nixon did win by a very narrow margin. To LBJ's credit, he refused to acknowledge Nixon's treason, though he knew about it through the FBI.

As we will see in this chapter and later, the North Vietnamese approach for these talks was to stall until there was some breakthrough on the battlefield. So, the negotiations were bound to fail. Regardless, this was an illegal act and, as Hughes argues, led to the formation of a secret White House group called "The Plumbers" to cover up this 'treasonous act." It would be Nixon's later use of this group that would lead to Watergate Affair and his resignation.

As we will also see, Nixon's policies toward Vietnam and his conduct of the war were consistent with some of his campaign proclamations. He and his National Security Advisor, Henry Kissinger, sought to bring the North Vietnamese to a negotiated settlement through a combination of military actions against both North Vietnam and its lifelines in Cambodia and Laos; and diplomatic measures that brought pressure on the Democratic Republic of Vietnam leaders from its supporters – Red China and the Soviet Union.

Later, well after the war, evidence would surface that his "plans" – more accurately 'ideas' about how to obtain peace with honor - would entail Machiavellian designs which historians would variously label, 'The Madman Theory,' 'Decent Interval,' and 'Permanent War.' This Chapter will discuss these later in some detail.

Nixon as President and Commander-in-Chief

Nixon took the reins of Government confidently, forcibly, and decisively. He had decided - as Robert Dallek relates in *Nixon and Kissinger: Partners in Power* - that he was now, as his hero Teddy Roosevelt had written, the 'man in the arena.'

Notwithstanding the malaise that hounded the end of the Johnson Administration, and the pessimistic mood of the media and the public at the beginning of 1969, Nixon was almost giddy during his inauguration and for a few weeks after. One observer wrote of his demeanor at the time, "The expression on his face was unforgettable. This was the time! He had arrived, he was in full command; someone said he felt he saw rays coming from his eyes." Richard Mulhouse Nixon had resurrected himself from his JFK defeat in 1960, and a trouncing he had experience in the running for governor of California afterward. He boldly pronounced to the despised Washington news media that "he was back."

Nixon's personality, background, and experience would govern his philosophy and methods of his Administration. Like LBJ - brought up in a rural, low-income family - he saw himself as a 'self-made' man. As one of his biographers Stephen Ambrose points out, Richard Nixon came to believe in himself as in control of his destiny through perseverance, hard work, and practical application of his earned education and intellectual skills. Along the way, he had gained distrust for people who had not earned their way, and who had gained fame and fortune through others. He had also learned to trust only a few carefully chosen people. These would become members of his inner circle of faithful and loyal agents.

Nixon had also learned to be insistent and persistent. As a young man going to school, he loved to debate. As a member of formal debate teams in college, he mastered the techniques of argument. In fact, his mastery of them led to rare accolades from his father; whom some say had ignored him at best and physically abused him at worst.

His father's abuse, as Evan Thomas claims in *Being Nixon*, may have also accounted later for his deep inner instinct for self-protection and introversion. Thomas also argues that as a youngster Nixon avoided his father, and that may have resulted in Nixon's reflections of his father when he admitted later, "Perhaps my own aversion to personal confrontations dates to these early recollections."

As a young congressman from California after the war his persistence in action and his distrust of intellectuals paid off for him. In 1948, he served on the House Un-American Activities Committee. This organization was investigating reports of communist infiltration of government and the affairs of the American Communist party. One such report came from a State Department official who had been a member of the American Communist Party by the name of Whittaker Chambers. He named a close associate of then Secretary of State Dean Acheson as a communist spy. The man's name was Alger Hiss.

Hiss denied the allegations. He further filed a defamation suit against Chambers and insisted on testifying before the Un-American Activities Committee to clear his name. The loyal State Department official had the full support of Dean Acheson. His testimony and demeanor convinced many that he was not a spy. Nixon thought differently. Through much of his effort, the FBI found evidence that Hiss may have conducted espionage. Later a court found Hiss guilty.

The Alger Hiss affair led to two primary results. One is that it elevated Nixon's name in the Republican Party. That would help him get elected to the Senate in 1950. In his memoirs, Nixon claims that this incident was the first to raise him up to the national scene and establish his political future. Another result of the incident was that a Congressman by the name of McCarthy would use the publicity of the trial and conviction as a platform for his election.

Besides persistent, by most accounts, Nixon was also brilliant. He was a top student in the state of California when he graduated from high school. Consequently, there were opportunities to attend some of the top schools in the east – namely Harvard and Yale. However, family circumstances demanded that he remain near home, so he accepted a scholarship at Whittier College. While there, through mostly self-study, he came to grasp fundamental concepts and events in his most favored subjects - history, foreign affairs, and politics. He could easily retain myriads of information and complex concepts. He had an innate ability to remember facts and challenging issues.

However, Nixon was not a leader. He did not know how to effectively communicate with people whom he did not know. He was painfully shy, and only able to break down communication barriers with those he knew and learned to trust. Nixon also detested confrontation.

During his administration, he would delegate differences of opinion for a solution to his closest advisors – primarily his Chief of Staff and National Security Advisor. He avoided meetings in which his subordinates would argue their views. His meetings were information briefs or consultations. He made decisions either afterward or made them ahead of the meeting; using the later gatherings to appease his subordinates so they could air their differences.

There were times that Nixon could also be belligerent and cantankerous. This behavior usually happened when he drank alcohol. His Chief of Staff, H. R. Haldeman claims that, as President, he drank moderately during dinner occasions; and only when there were no pressing issues.

However, some biographers argue that it was much more frequent. They contend that he had an alcohol problem that gradually became worse as his Presidency underwent increased scrutiny and the pressure on him intensified. As we will see ahead, apparently because he had imbibed too many spirits, on several critical occasions when he had to confront a crisis in the Vietnam War his demeanor did change, and judgment clouded.

As he set-up his Presidency in 1969, Nixon, like JFK, wanted to control his foreign policy and be his own Secretary of State. Unlike JFK and LBJ, he wanted to use a more formalized National Security System. However, he insisted that this system, with a council of a small number of picked advisors, be under his direct control. Thus, he established a miniature version of the National Security Council in the White House.

In Nixon's view, this Council would be the principal advisory body to the President. It would give that advice based on careful study and assessments from several interagency groups. The White House would closely supervise them. These groups, through the Council, would then offer the President alternatives of action to solve issues and recommend solutions and initiatives.

The Council and its subgroups would answer to only Nixon and his trusted agent – the person he would personally select as Assistant for National Security Affairs. In the words of David Rothkopf in his history of the NSC, *Running the World*, this set up "concentrated unprecedented power in the hands of the national security advisor and his team at the NSC, and ensured that the White House would drive national security policy."

The main reason the new President thought that this was necessary was his distaste, like JFK, for bureaucracies. Per Robert Dallek, Nixon believed "that the primary enemy of a wise, more successful diplomacy was a turgid, self-serving bureaucracy. His study of past and contemporary history convinced him that for a successful foreign policy…a statesman needed to free himself from the accepted wisdoms of cautious bureaucrats frightened by innovative thinking."

Nixon also believed that government bureaucracies in Washington were the primary sources of leaks to the Press. Like JFK and LBJ, he knew that these leaks could derail his attempts to control his message to the public. They would also fuel media attempts to personally attack him, which he felt the press was determined to do. Finally, they could damage his approach to foreign and security affairs, which he intended to run secretly without oversight from the Congress or knowledge of other parts of his Administration, such as the State Department.

Nixon's feelings toward leaks bordered on hysteria, according to his biographers and those close to him who later wrote memoirs. During his administration, the President would become obsessive about catching anyone leaking stories to the Press. He later put out memos to his departments warning against talking to the press and proclaiming that the "Press is the enemy." As criticism increased during the President's tenure, according to a close counsel William Safire, Nixon's obsession with leaks and the Press became 'the cause of his downfall.'

Nixon's attitude toward bureaucracies also molded his attitude toward the military in general, and the Joint Chiefs and its staff. Some close to him throughout his political life have testified that he believed military men had 'mediocre minds.' He thought they were, by nature, not very innovative and ignorant of domestic and international political factors. Accordingly, Nixon would set up his own small military advisory cell within the NSC, seek to bypass deliberations of the full JCS, and establish direct communications with the Chairman of the JCS and commanders in the field. In so doing he would often and willfully bypass his Secretary of Defense.

The new President's service in World War Two influenced his views of the military. Recognizing that any future he had in politics needed war service, he volunteered to join the Navy soon after Pearl Harbor. After two months at naval officer 'indoctrination' school in Rhode Island, where he "learned to stand straight and keep my shoes shined," the Navy assigned him to a staff job at a Naval Air Station in Iowa. Fearing that he would sit out the war 'landlocked in Iowa,' he applied for sea duty. Consequently, Nixon deployed to the Southwest Pacific.

In later staff positions - first at New Caledonia and then Bougainville - the closest Nixon got to combat was to see wounded soldiers evacuated to hospitals and some Japanese long-range shelling. His job was to assist in plans for transportation and supply operations for the dispersed bases throughout the Southwest Pacific. As he recalled in his memoirs, he spent much of his time playing poker and cooking hamburgers. Nixon admitted that these diversions from his duties were a cure for the 'oppressive monotony' of military service.

With his extensive winnings from poker, he finally redeployed from the Pacific in January 1945 to a position overseeing Navy contracts on the east coast. There he stayed until the war ended. He had experienced the military bureaucracy at its worst and would not forget it.

As Vice President in the Eisenhower administration, Nixon also felt that many leaks came from officers in the Pentagon seeking to enhance their views. That belief may have originated from what he had observed of the Service bickering during IKE's presidency. He witnessed some senior military officers disagreeing behind the scenes with the Administration's massive retaliation policy. He vowed to prevent such leaks during his Presidency vigorously.

Thus, during his administration, Nixon came to rely on his small, selected, and close-knit group of trusted military officers working for his National Security Assistant in the White House for many sensitive military options. He also seldom asked for or met with the corporate body of the Joint Chiefs for military advice.

As the Joint Chiefs' official history states, Nixon, "had no qualms about second-guessing or even belittling the chiefs' advice. Indeed, he was fond of citing H.G. Wells' observation that military people had mediocre minds because intelligent people would never contemplate a military career." Instead, he dealt with the Chiefs by calling or meeting directly with the Chairman. Often the meetings included his National Security Advisor, who would mediate and offer a course of action that the two had previously agreed upon.

Nixon's Scholars and Warriors

Given Nixon's approach to governing, he picked the perfect person to join him as his Special Assistant for National Security Affairs – Henry Kissinger. He had known Kissinger for years as a foreign policy advisor to a Republican rival, Nelson Rockefeller. Before he took office, Nixon's transition team had been in touch with Kissinger, who was then a consultant to the Johnson administration's negotiations with the North Vietnamese. Indeed, Kissinger was passing essential information to the Nixon team about the meetings that were occurring between negotiators. This action was to keep the President-elect informed of the proceedings. However, Nixon would use this information, as mentioned above, to scuttle the Johnson Administration negotiations before the election.

Because Kissinger had been instrumental in informing him of the progress of the talks, Nixon felt that he owed him in part for his election. In early December, after a brief meeting between the two, the President-elect named Kissinger as his primary national security policy man to work with him in the White House.

Henry A. Kissinger, along with his Jewish-German family, had in 1938 migrated to New York to escape Nazi prosecution. Embracing his new country and culture, he chose to keep his German identity and accent throughout his early years in America. His biographers surmise that this may have been an effort to overcome the tortured discrimination he had suffered in Germany. He devoted his energies to his studies, excelled in school, and went to New York's City College until the war broke out.

The Army drafted him. They sent him off to training and afterward assigned him to the 84th Infantry Division. There he served as an 'education officer' instructing other soldiers on the German language and history. Deploying to Europe in 1944, he served as a translator and then as a counter-intelligence specialist in the European Theater. The German offensive in late 1944 surprised his unit, and he fought at the Battle of the Bulge for a brief time as an infantryman. After the victory in Europe, as mentioned in Chapter 1, he helped in finding and arresting Nazi officials.

While proud of his wartime service, Kissinger's military experience left him a lingering distaste for what he called the military traditionalism. He felt that such ingrained conventionalism led to the inability to grasp complex problems. It also, in his view, promoted too much loyalty that hampered healthy differences of opinion. For example, later in his memoirs, Kissinger chastised the military hierarchy for not opposing some of the gradualism invoked by the Johnson Administration.

While he writes about the military in laudatory terms in his memoirs, in the Nixon tape recordings Kissinger's general aversion toward the military is evident. He derides, often in inflammatory language, their bickering. He also often refers disparagingly to the Joint Chiefs of Staff and the MACV commander, General Creighton Abrams. Interestingly, Kissinger never seems to take the lead on these remarks. He only does so when Nixon makes the same kind of comments criticizing the military and their thinking or advice.

After coming home after the war, Kissinger had taken advantage of the G.I. Bill of Rights and attended Harvard University. There he found his life's interest and calling – government and foreign affairs. Working twelve to sixteen hours a day at his studies, he ranked at the top of his class. His mentor, William Elliot, was one of the most influential professors at Harvard. He used Henry as a teaching assistant, and later ensured his entry into the University's graduate programs.

Kissinger excelled in international politics and graduated summa cum laude in 1950. He then went on to achieve his masters and doctorate degrees.

Kissinger stayed at Harvard as the executive director of a University summer international seminar under Elliot's supervision and tutelage. The latter asked several international and national government officials to attend Henry's seminar. These included foreign presidents, premiers, and cabinet members. Notable Americans who attended were Eleanor Roosevelt, columnist James Reston, General James Gavin, and Arthur Schlesinger. All of this built a reputation for Kissinger and would forward his desires and ambitions to serve in Government in a prominent post.

Dr. Kissinger also wrote several major books and published articles in prominent international affairs journals. His notable books included *A World Restored, Nuclear Weapons and Foreign Policy,* and *The Necessity of Choice.* The latter two explained his views toward nuclear weapons and foreign policy in the debates surrounding massive retaliation and flexible response policies in the later fifties and early sixties. *A World Restored* presented his arguments and views from his doctoral thesis. It outlines his support for international power politics and advocates a balance of power approach to world affairs. These, to one degree or another, supported Nixon's views on foreign policy.

By Nixon's account of his meetings with Kissinger, he had wanted to interview him because he thought that they shared the same opinion that a foreign policy needed to be "strong and credible." This shared outlook most likely resulted from Nixon's reading of some of Kissinger's works mentioned above. Nixon further states that in their first meeting he "had a strong intuition about Henry Kissinger, and I decided on the spot that he should be my National Security Advisor." They also discussed the need for a strong, but closely controlled national security apparatus. Kissinger, to Nixon's delight, recommended that he "structure a national security apparatus within the White House that, in addition to coordinating foreign and defense policy, could also develop policy options for me to consider before making decisions."

Thus began what would become one of the strongest personal foreign policy teams the US government would ever know. In his memoirs, Nixon explains, "The combination was unlikely— the grocer's son from Whittier and the refugee from Hitler's Germany, the politician and the academic. But our differences helped make the partnership work." Historian Robert Dallek argues that this arrangement "made [Kissinger] a kind of co-president," and made them a "brethren of a kind." Between the two of them, they would rule US international affairs unlike any other foreign policy oligarchy in American history.

Although there was mutual respect and even admiration, their relationship could also be strange and at times tumultuous. Nixon always wanted the upper hand. In private, he would sometimes ridicule Kissinger; even, as some sources claim, call him his 'little Jew boy.' Kissinger, on the other hand, felt that Nixon did not understand and could not deal with the interpersonal necessities of managing and affecting foreign affairs and the personal skills of statecraft. Nevertheless, when one listens to their recorded conversations, Kissinger always seems not only respectful, but subservient to the man who put him in a key position of power in US national security affairs.

On occasion, both would seek allies in their self-made inner bureaucracies to gain favor or support for differences of opinion. Kissinger likened this to competition for barons in the hidden feudal world in the government they created. In the end, however, it was always Kissinger who sought to improve any differences. He was a master at flattery and would quickly use it to gain and keep favor with his President. Kissinger cared about what his legacy would be as the prime minister of Nixon's 'Imperial Presidency.'

Since Nixon wanted to be his own Secretary of State and directly control foreign policy from the White House, like JFK, he did not want a powerful Secretary of State in his cabinet. So, he chose William Rogers. Rogers had served honorably in the Navy during the war. He saw combat in the Pacific; especially at Okinawa where Japanese Kamikazes attacked the ship he was on. After the war, he became a noted New York attorney while Nixon practiced law there. Later, during the McCarthy years, he helped Nixon in the Alger Hiss case. Rogers had also been IKE's Attorney General. He and Nixon thus became close friends in the fifties.

By admission, Nixon chose Rogers for his lack of background in foreign affairs. He told Kissinger that he "considered Rogers unfamiliarity with the subject an asset because it guaranteed that policy direction would remain in the White House." However, Nixon did feel that Rogers would make a good negotiator because of his loyalty to him and his tough-mindedness. Rogers lack of expertise in foreign affairs would lead him to listen to those in the State Department that would become disenchanted with the Nixon-Kissinger approach. It would cause some difficulties in Nixon's first term.

For Secretary of Defense, Nixon did not want someone like McNamara or Clifford. They had been too influential and as well-known as their Presidents. Nixon picked Melvin Laird. He selected Laird because of his sixteen-year experience in Congress. That involvement, Nixon felt, would make him a perfect Cabinet front man in dealings and negotiations with the Congress.

Nixon also needed someone who could focus on the defense budget. He knew that Laird had been an experienced member of the House Appropriations Committee. That made him an expert on defense budgets. Laird thus seemed perfect for the job as Defense Secretary. Busy with defense budgets and the Congress, Nixon counted on his defense chief being busy enough with managing budget issues that Laird would not have time for other security and defense matters the President expected to run from the White House without him.

Yet, Laird was not someone to be ignored or left out of a job that he thought was important to the nation. In fact, early in his life, he had wanted to join the military. According to his authorized biographer, Dale Atta, that desire resulted from his meeting at the age of 10 a young Navy Commander walking down a street in his hometown in 1932. The Commander's name was John McCain, Sr. He was the father of Admiral John McCain, Jr., who would command the Navy in the Pacific and hold overall command of US forces in Vietnam when Laird became Secretary of Defense. McCain Jr.'s son John McCain III would become a prisoner of war and later run for President of the US against Barrack Obama.

The onset of World War Two had given Laird his opportunity for military service. Up to that point, Mel Laird lived an inauspicious life. He graduated from a small college in Minnesota just after the war started. Then he enlisted in the Navy. As an Ensign, on-board the destroyer *Maddox* (the same destroyer involved in the later Tonkin Gulf crisis in 1964) he was wounded when a kamikaze bomber hit his ship on operations in the South China Sea (close to Vietnam). His wounds were not severe. When he returned from the war, he entered politics; first serving in State Government and then in the Congress.

As Secretary of Defense, Laird would not sit on the sidelines, as Nixon desired. As we will see, he was very influential in the design and execution of Nixon's Vietnamization policy. He also had a great relationship with the MACV Commander in Vietnam during the Nixon Administration - General Abrams. Laird would defend him on occasion when both Nixon and Kissinger chastised their commander in Vietnam when unhappy with events there. However, Laird also deviated at times from Nixon and Kissinger on policy for the conduct of the war. This diversion would lead to some confusion for both Abrams and the Joint Chiefs on the overall direction of the war as US troops withdrew from Vietnam.

As for his military advisors and commanders, Nixon decided, at first, to keep on General 'Bus' Wheeler as Chairman of the Joint Chiefs. He held onto Wheeler for two reasons. One, the new President felt he needed some continuity with the Johnson Administration on the war. More importantly, he had observed that Wheeler had been an extremely loyal servant to Johnson and had successfully managed the other Service Chiefs to keep their support for the President's war policies. He was also further known to detest the usual leaks that came from the Pentagon. However, Wheeler had a heart attack in 1968. Though he continued the arduous duty of Chairman for a year, it was clear that Nixon would have to make another appointee soon.

When Wheeler retired in mid-1970, Nixon chose Admiral Thomas Moorer, who was then Chief of Naval Operations. For much of 1970, Moorer had been acting Chairman. Nixon and Kissinger liked his loyalty. They became convinced that he would be just what they wanted as a successor to Wheeler. In the words of the authors of the JCS official history, Moorer "shunned the role of 'team player' and viewed himself primarily as an agent and spokesman for the administration. According to one official account, Moorer's influence as Chairman was so thoroughly pervasive that he was now the only JCS member who really counted.'"

That turned out to be precisely the kind of Chairman that Nixon and Kissinger needed for their secret schemes for security policy-making. As the Presidential tapes reveal, Nixon and Kissinger would use the loyal Admiral to keep valuable information away from those they did not trust, or those who they just did not want to know what they were up to. This included key people involved in the war, such as their Secretary of Defense, the military Service Chiefs, and the Commander of MACV.

In their design for the functioning of their national security apparatus, Nixon and Kissinger wanted some military expertise working directly for them in the White House that they could control and trust. They found just the right person for that role in Colonel Alexander Haig.

Haig was a 1947 West Point graduate. He already had an extraordinarily diverse military career when he met Kissinger for an interview as his military assistant in New York early in 1969. After graduation from the Academy, Haig had served on the staff of General McArthur in Japan. When the Korean War broke out, he served with distinction there as an aide to an Army Corps commander. Later, he led an infantry command in combat. He was daring and brave, winning two Silver Stars for gallantry.

After the Korean War, Haig had served in various command and staff positions. One was a tour in the Pentagon as a special assistant and executive officer to an Assistant Secretary of the Army and the Deputy Secretary of Defense. In the latter position, he caught the eye of Robert McNamara. He had also earned an MBA from Columbia and a Masters in International Relations from Georgetown. Moreover, he had graduated from the Army War College. Then in 1966, he deployed to Vietnam.

There he commanded an infantry battalion in combat and earned the Distinguished Service Cross – the nation's second-highest award for valor.

Following his interview with Haig, Kissinger at once selected him as his assistant. His job at first was to aid and coordinate the two dozen foreign policy experts hired to fill the unique groups he wanted in the NSC. Soon he became a close confidant to Kissinger. One reason he became close was that he survived the excessive demands and working hours in the small office in the White House better than any other in the NSC Council staff. Another reason is that Haig was smart and had both field and Pentagon experience. The latter enabled him to informally contact other officers serving in the Department of Defense and gather intelligence for Kissinger.

Haig would become a favorite of the President. He would come to serve both Nixon and Kissinger as a personal assistant whom they would consult with on military matters before and after receiving such from the Chairman. Haig would also serve as an emissary abroad to assess the military situation in Vietnam for the President and National Security Advisor privately and independently. In short, Nixon and Kissinger selected Haig to offer them the political-military advice they did not think they would get from the JCS or the commanders in the field.

With all his intellect and practical understanding of politics and bravery in combat, Haig was also extraordinarily ambitious and arrogant. He got much of that from Douglas MacArthur, who was his military mentor. He would take the opportunity, as most arrogant people do, to undermine and ridicule those who were his superiors and those for whom he worked.

Though he was always loyal and in admiration of Nixon, Haig often talked about Kissinger behind his boss' back. As Kissinger's biographer Walter Isaacson describes, "When talking to military leaders, Haig tended to blame Kissinger rather than Nixon for any softness in American policy on Vietnam and arms control." For example, he confided to Bruce Palmer, the Army's vice chief of staff, "that there were times when he wondered whether Kissinger had the inner toughness and tenacity to stay the course." It was his role, Haig liked to say, "to stiffen Kissinger's backbone." Haig's criticisms, moreover, often involved anti-Semitic slurs.

As we will see ahead, as military aide to Kissinger and a junior to the commander in Vietnam, he would not hesitate to not only criticize his military senior, but also seek to offer himself as an alternative to his command.

Finally, Nixon inherited a new commander in Vietnam – General Creighton Abrams. Abrams had taken over from Westmoreland in April 1968 when the later took over as Chief of Staff of the Army. Westmoreland and Abrams were West Point classmates – Class of 1936. General Abrams had also served in World War Two. Unlike Westy, who had been in the artillery and had mostly seen combat from afar, Abe had been in the armor and saw combat as a tank battalion commander always leading from the front in his tank. He had been famous for leading the counterattack of Patton's Army in the Battle of the Bulge.

In the post-World War Two military, Abrams had served in Korea as a staff officer. Afterward, the Army promoted him and gave him all the prime duty assignments from battalion to brigade to division and finally to corps command. He also had attended the Army's War College and had assignments in the Pentagon on the Army Staff. His last position as Westmoreland's deputy, which he had held for a year, gave him the experience and insight he needed to continue the conduct of the war.

As we will see in the chapters ahead, General Abrams demeanor and manner of command were different from his predecessor's. He was abrupt and straightforward. He disliked the pomp and ceremony of office. He had also been, as Westmoreland's deputy, in charge of overseeing and reporting on the progress of ARVN performance in the war. That seemed to give Nixon the perfect man for managing his withdrawal of US forces and the turnover of the war to the South Vietnamese.

Initial reports from the field seemed to confirm Nixon's choice. Abrams informed him that the TET counter-offensives had turned the tide in the military equation in late 1968. By the beginning of 1969, there seemed to be the military success that the President could capitalize upon at the negotiating table. So it made sense to keep the General on and rely on him in the war that they inherited.

We will see ahead, however, that both Nixon's and Kissinger's trust in Abrams would not last long. When the conduct of the war stayed favorable, as it seemed it would be in 1969 and into early 1970, everything was ok. When operations did not go their way, then their inherent distrust of the military would come to play, and they would begin to belittle and attack Abrams. They called him a 'drunk,' and talked of his removal.

All of this would influence the unraveling of the military efforts to end the war favorably between 1970 and 1973. This chapter will describe how this was to happen primarily from the Washington point of view. Chapter 10 will provide more detail primarily from the Saigon point of view.

Section 5.2 - Nixon's Vietnam Strategy and The Policy of 'Vietnamization'

As Nixon and Kissinger were selecting personnel and setting up their organization for conducting national security affairs, there was an urgency to assess the current situation in Vietnam and derive a policy and strategy to affect 'peace with honor.' Now that the elections were over, the media and the public mood grew for a hastened end to the war. Nixon said he had a plan to do so. While the President could expect some grace period to arrange for and execute his 'plan,' he recognized that Americans were impatient to see some movement toward resolving the conflict.

There had been no substantive progress in the negotiations with the North Vietnamese, which had begun in Paris in 1968. Since then there had been mostly arguments over procedural questions; such as the shape of the negotiating table. Meanwhile, intelligence sources were showing that the North Vietnamese were preparing for some military operation in the South at the beginning of 1969.

As they turned their attention to the primary task of negotiating a treaty to end the war, Nixon and Kissinger agreed that the US could not negotiate a peace that would undermine US credibility. As Kissinger explained, "For a great power to abandon a small ally to tyranny simply to obtain a respite from its domestic travail seemed to Nixon—and still seems—profoundly immoral and destructive of efforts to build a new and ultimately more peaceful pattern of international relations. The American people wanted to end the war, but every poll, and indeed Nixon's election (not to mention the 13 percent vote for pro-war George Wallace), made it equally clear that they saw their country's aims as honorable and did not relish America's humiliation."

As mentioned, Nixon thought that a way to get the North Vietnamese to negotiate a peace that the US could agree to was to put pressure on the leaders through their Allies – the Soviets and the Chinese. He and Kissinger agreed that they needed to tie Soviet desires for meaningful talks on strategic disarmaments to putting pressure on North Vietnam to meet some of the US demands. This linkage was especially crucial to the US proposal at Paris to put into effect a cease-fire and then proceed with the mutual withdrawal of forces before any reasonable peace agreement could be reached.

Nixon also said that he wanted to approach the Chinese to lessen tensions with them. He wanted to convince them that it was not in their interest to continue to support the war in Southeast Asia. Kissinger was less enthusiastic about the probability of a Chinese rapprochement.

Another component of Nixon's strategy was to put military pressure on the North. The new President, while emphasizing his peace-seeking attempts, also realized that Northern leaders would only agree to some meaningful agreement if they thought they could not win on the battlefield. Both Nixon and Kissinger agreed that diplomatic pressures alone would not result in a peace that they could live with. The trick was how to use US military power in a domestic environment that was against further conflict and American casualties.

NSSM-1: A Review of the Current Situation and Finding a Way Ahead

The President and his National Security Advisor turned their attention to obtaining some understanding for a way ahead and developing a coordinated and workable policy and plan for

Vietnam. On 21 January, Dr. Kissinger issued National Security Study Memorandum One or NSSM-1. The memorandum tasked the Secretaries of State and Defense, the Director of Central Intelligence, the JCS, and the Ambassador and Commander in Vietnam to review six broad categories of questions on Vietnam. These inquiries ranged from matters of past, current, and future negotiation environments to assessments on current and future military operations.

According to Kissinger, the forty-four-page responses fell into two main divisions. There was the group that he called the 'optimistic school.' That faction was made up primarily of the military – the JCS, General Abrams the MACV commander, and Admiral McCain, who then was Abrams superior as Commander of the Pacific Command. They thought that the North Vietnamese had decided to negotiate because they had suffered a severe military blow during the 1968 TET offensive. They also believed that the renewed pacification effort undertaken as a priority under Abrams had made real gains in the last six months and continued to progress favorably.

Finally, this group emphasized that there were improvements in the capability of the South Vietnamese Army that could affect positive military operations ahead. The South's army performance during TET showed that, with added improvements, the ARVN could handle any further NVA and PLAF military action in South Vietnam. In question, however, was the North's continued capability to infiltrate its forces to the South in support of future communist offensives like that of TET. Thus, most in this group argued that any withdrawals of US forces would need a "vigorous interdiction campaign against land and sea supply routes."

Civilian officials made up the second group. That included primarily personnel in the State and Defense Department and the CIA. They thought that MACV had inflated the pacification gains. They also did not believe that the South Vietnamese Government, though much more stable than in earlier years, had made the reforms necessary to obtain widespread support. They argued that the only way to settle the war was by a compromise settlement.

There was one issue, however, that all were unanimous on. As Ken Hughes explains in his *Fatal Politics,* there was a question about whether the South Vietnamese Armed Forces could "survive on its own without American soldiers." All groups and agencies - military and civilian, defense and state – answered: "not for the foreseeable future."

Thus, there were two central issues that Nixon had to face in executing his publicly announced action to withdraw US military forces from South Vietnam. One was how to gain the time to build the Vietnamese Armed Forces to defend themselves from a North Vietnamese major offensive so that the US could withdraw its combat forces. The second was what US military capability would be necessary to support the ARVN after American combat forces were withdrawn.

Overall, the responses to NSSM-1 gave no clear-cut way ahead. Nixon and Kissinger discussed future courses of action given these diverse views over the next month and a half. Complicating the search for a policy was the fact that the North Vietnamese launched a major offensive at the end of February. It resulted in a series attacks that were causing over 250 American casualties a week. Their discussions now included how to respond to these attacks.

Abrams and Laird March 1969 Meeting: Discussions on Turning the War over to the South Vietnamese Armed Forces

At first, the JCS primary response was to begin a new bombing campaign of the North. Nixon and Kissinger thought that doing such would undermine their current favorable support to end the war from the American public. The urgency for a military response was somewhat ameliorated by reports from General Abrams, which indicated that this offensive was nothing like the 1968 TET attack. Abrams also indicated that US and ARVN forces could quickly bring the assault to a favorable conclusion. However, in his continued search for a plan to bring military pressure to bear on negotiations, Nixon decided to dispatch Laird to Vietnam to get an update on the situation and some recommendations from the field commander on future operations.

Secretary Laird and General Wheeler went to South Vietnam for five days at the beginning of March to discuss matters with General Abrams and Ambassador Bunker. The MACV commander gave a favorable report on the ability to defeat the North's current offensive. They also convinced Laird of the viability of improving the ARVN and the South Vietnamese regional and local security forces. That effort, they indicated, would allow some withdrawal of US forces during 1969. It would also offer the President an opportunity to show that the US was beginning to end its overall massive combat mission in South Vietnam.

The Secretary further discussed this possibility with the South Vietnam President Thieu, who said he would support some US troop withdrawals. Laird reported this good news to the President. However, he caveated this news with a report that none of the US or ARVN leaders saw an end to the war in the 'foreseeable' future.

According to the JCS official history, while in Saigon in March 1969, the Secretary of Defense also conveyed to the US command in Vietnam a clear, but grim picture of public opinion for the war. "Mr. Laird told the US military commanders that the American people expected the new administration to bring the war to a satisfactory conclusion, and to most Americans, that meant eventual disengagement of US troops from combat. He informed his audience that it was their task to find the means to shift the combat burden 'promptly, and methodically,' to the South Vietnamese."

There was a difference of opinion, however, between the Secretary and the MACV commander on the nature of the withdrawal and the need for residual US forces. As we will see in more detail in Chapter 10, the MACV commander had already been working on his plans for 'Vietnamization' before Nixon had taken office. This effort had been ongoing since the Johnson Administration had directed it in the late summer of 1968.

Briefly explained, Abrams had been planning for the withdrawal of US forces in an orderly, strategically sound way. As deputy commander under Westmoreland, one of his duties had been to track ARVN performance. He saw just that during TET and knew their strengths and weaknesses. The relatively new MACV commander, therefore, argued that the withdrawal had to correlate to both the ARVN improvements to make up for any US drawdown, and to North Vietnam's actions in the war. Regarding the latter, Abrams argued if enemy infiltration from the North persisted or increased and their offensive actions continued to threaten South Vietnamese cities, then the US should not unilaterally withdraw its forces. Moreover, total withdrawal of US forces needed to match the complete withdrawal of NVA troops in the South.

General Abrams further explained to the Secretary that his program to build the ARVN forces to cope with the fighting depended on the continued use of American advisors and some combat forces. He explained that the ARVN and Southern regional defense forces could now cope with the enemy forces in the South. However, they needed the US advisors and some American combat forces to ensure that the South would be able to resist any significant offensive from the North. Besides, Abrams further argued, like Korea, a continued US combat force presence could enable future stability in the region once the diplomats negotiated a peace treaty.

The JCS official history notes that Secretary Laird was not willing to acquiesce that the withdrawals be tied either to the total withdrawal of North Vietnamese forces or to a residual force presence to deter or defend against North Vietnamese invasion. In fact, when he sent his report to the President, though he included MACV's arguments on both, Laird argued for the reduction of forces to enhance US security interests worldwide, to sustain US public support for further actions, and to stimulate self-reliance on the part of the South Vietnamese.

This argument showed that Laird, as both Nixon and Kissinger would come to agree to, recognized that overall the American public would settle for nothing less than total withdrawal of US forces from the South regardless of the military situation there. This became the underlying assumption for the Nixon Administration's policy of Vietnamization. It would undermine any effective US military strategy to end the war.

National Security Decision Memorandum (NSDM) 9 and Nixon's Grand Strategy to End the War

On 28 March, the President convened a rare formal meeting of the NSC. In this session, the Principals discussed progress in the war: especially improvements to South Vietnamese forces; NVA/VC military operations and posture; future US troop withdrawals; and current negotiations and a future negotiating strategy. The focus was on US policy toward the removal of forces. The President moved the discussion toward the risks and nature of US force withdrawals. He indicated that he wanted to make some announcement soon on his efforts to change the nature of the war and to 'de-Americanize it.'

General Goodpaster, now Deputy Commander to General Abrams, represented MACV and gave an upbeat presentation on the improvements to the South Vietnamese forces. Afterward, those present discussed three issues. The first was how much improvement was necessary to begin US troop withdrawals. The second was when and how to tie them not only to ARVN improvements but enemy actions. A third was whether there should be any residual US forces left behind as part of any final treaty.

The meeting did not solve all these issues. However, Secretary Laird suggested that instead of calling the withdrawals 'de-Americanization,' they refer to this policy as 'Vietnamization.' The President liked that phrase. He directed that from now on it be the word to use when referring to improvements to the South Vietnam military, which would further enable the withdrawal of US forces and the turning of the war over to the South Vietnamese. Nixon also said that as the US withdrew its forces, it should attempt to tie its force levels to North Vietnam actions. The President added that the US should not expect any of its combat forces to be left behind in South Vietnam.

On 1 April 1969, the President signed and issued a National Security Decision Memorandum, called NSDM 9. It conveyed to the Administration the decisions of the 28 March meeting. The focus of the decision was the establishment of the US policy of Vietnamization and a directive to prepare detailed plans for the withdrawal of US forces. In the memo, Nixon emphasized that US withdrawal actions would be tied to the North's military activities in the South, and to their willingness to remove its forces from South Vietnam, Laos, and Cambodia. These conditions showed that the President, at this juncture, heeded most of MACV's concerns about the withdrawal process. The document did not, however, discuss the issue of any US residual forces in the South.

Meanwhile, Nixon prepared to announce this policy as his plan to wind down American involvement in the war and seek a negotiated settlement. He wanted to appease the growing Congressional and public anxiety for some announcement of the plan that he had hinted he had before the elections. So, on 14 May he went before the American public and explained this 'new' policy.

During his talk, Nixon summarized the attempts of his Administration to kick-start the Paris negotiations. He pointed out the obstructionism of the North Vietnamese. He promised he would reveal shortly his detailed plan for the withdrawal of US forces, which he emphasized would match the North Vietnamese military action against South Vietnam. Nixon further stressed that it would be his Administration's priority to turn the war over to the South and that the US would do what was necessary to ensure they had the capabilities to win against the communist forces.

However, the President also added that the South Vietnamese should be free to decide their future. This was a subtle, but important, change from the previous Administration's announced aims of ensuring South Vietnam would be a free, noncommunist government. Nixon now was signaling that the road would be open at the negotiating table on the future of the government structure of South Vietnam as the Vietnamese would determine for themselves.

The decision on Vietnamization, with its inherent assumption of a total withdrawal of US combat forces, represented the beginning of a 'slippery slope' towards ending the war. Turning the war effort over to the South Vietnamese as a way of extricating America from the conflict was full of uncertainties and risks. Some scholars have argued that Nixon and Kissinger recognized from the start that this policy would not work. In their view, the President intended from the beginning to leave Vietnam without regard to the viability of the South Vietnamese Government. This argument – often referred to by scholars as the 'decent interval '- assumes that Nixon and Kissinger were merely buying time to extricate America from Southeast Asia at the cost of thousands more American and Vietnamese lives.

George Herring, on the other hand, argues in his *America's Longest War* that the policy initially tried to carry out what previous Administrations had also tried. In his words, "their policy suffered from the same flaws as those of their predecessors. Although disguising it in the rhetoric of peace with honor, the Nixon administration persisted in the quixotic search for an independent, non-Communist Vietnam." Thus, for Herring, Nixon's 14 May statement was merely meant to placate the American public, rather than to announce a new negotiating strategy.

Vietnamization, Herring argues, was nothing more than a way that others had already tried, that is, end the war militarily. The difference was now the US would rely on South Vietnamese forces rather than American forces fighting a war of attrition. Moreover, Herring emphasizes, that policy was subject to the same foibles of earlier attempts to carry out that goal – it depended on the South Vietnamese Government's willingness to govern and successfully wage war against both external and internal threats. It also depended upon the North's willingness to accept a compromise peace.

Yet, the current evidence, mainly recorded conversations and published meeting minutes, shows that while both Nixon and Kissinger wanted to continue to use military force to convince the North to seek a negotiated settlement, they more carefully integrated that force with other efforts to reach an end to the conflict favorable to the US. Moreover, while they recognized the inherent flaws of their policy of Vietnamization from the start, they thought, at first, that it had a decent chance of succeeding. Finally, while they understood that their strategy depended upon both the South's willingness to govern and wage war and the North's willingness to negotiate, they felt that they had a grand strategy that could positively affect both.

Thus, contrary to persisting in a quixotic search for a solution using military means or seeking just some time for an excuse to get out, throughout most of Nixon's first term, the President and his National Security Advisor thought their overall policy had a decent chance for success for three primary reasons.

First, both General Abrams and Ambassador Bunker reported during that period vast improvements both politically and militarily in South Vietnam. South Vietnamese actions seem to collaborate these claims in 1969 and 1970. As historian Guenter Lewy points out in his book, *America in Vietnam*, by 1970 the South Vietnamese carried out almost three times as many operations as they had done in 1966-67. They were now taking the preponderance of the casualties.

President Thieu had also stabilized the South Vietnamese government. While he authoritatively ruled, there was a semblance of political and land reform that had never occurred before. At the hamlet level, moreover, most of the population was under South Vietnamese control. This was attributive to two factors. First, the populace in these hamlets felt more secure by the presence of South Vietnamese local and regional forces. Second, was the fact that the NVA/VC were too weak to control the hamlets permanently.

The second reason for confidence in success is that Nixon believed that he could bring pressure to bear on North Vietnam through his diplomatic linkage policy with both the Soviets and Chinese. That policy would tie US cooperation, arms control, and trade in return for their pressures on the North to negotiate reasonably. This pursuit of linkage, slow at first, began to demonstrate some headway by the beginning of 1971. As US diplomacy began to show progress the President argued the North would start to feel, at the very least, isolated. At best, the North's allies would eventually bring the necessary pressure on them to compromise at the negotiating table.

A third reason to believe in success is that both the President and his National Security Advisor felt that the North must have a 'breaking point.' Therefore, in conjunction with their diplomatic actions and efforts to turn the war over to the South, Nixon intended to increase American military pressure against the North and their lines of communication in Cambodia and Laos. This military action would not only serve to gain time for Vietnamization to work, but also put further pressure on the North to negotiate an end to the war.

Previous Presidents had not earnestly tried these aggressive military actions - mainly because of the fear of Chinese intervention. Now the effects of the Chinese domestic turmoil associated with Mao's 'Cultural Revolution' were well known to the Americans. The threat of Chinese intervention seemed less real and fearful. Thus, both Nixon and Kissinger thought it was less risky to use more offensive military action outside of South Vietnam to gain an advantage that would complement their diplomatic actions.

Accordingly, the threat and use of greater military action were significant parts of Nixon's approach to convincing the North that he would stop at nothing to end the war on terms favorable to the US.

Moreover, Nixon was willing for Kissinger, in his dealings with all the communist diplomats, to use his reputation as a staunch anti-communist and therefore would stop at nothing to prevent a communist takeover of the South. He also sanctioned his chief negotiator to portray him as one who was unpredictable and impulsive.

Indeed, as Nixon's Chief of Staff, H. R. Haldeman wrote in his memoirs, the President wanted his opponents to "believe any threat of force Nixon makes because it's Nixon. We'll just slip the word to them that, for God's sake, you know Nixon's obsessed about Communism. . . and he has his hand on the nuclear button." This technique of making his enemies uncertain of Nixon's actions, and producing a fear that his behavior could be erratic and irrational, evolved into what some have called Nixon's 'Madman theory.'

The Madman theory, several recent historians argue, was central to Nixon's dealings with North Vietnam and its allies. This approach also differed significantly from LBJ's gradualist policy. For example, though Nixon used bomb pauses from time to time, he usually followed these pauses with some increased military action. Thus, he carefully linked the use of military force to diplomatic actions.

Moreover, as historians Burr and Kimball in *Nixon's Nuclear Specter* reveal, Nixon told Kissinger and his small military planning group to plan for the use of tactical nuclear weapons. He wanted this option to convince the North to cease its aggression and negotiate in earnest. Also, according to Burr and Kimball, in October 1969 Nixon ordered a global secret nuclear alert to send a warning to the Soviets and the Chinese that he would be willing to use nuclear force should they continue to support North Vietnam aggression.

Thus, historians that claim that Nixon and Kissinger from the onset were intent upon arranging some deal to give an excuse for the US to get out of Vietnam does not stand up to the evidence. To the contrary, while recognizing the risks and problems, they both believed there was a fair chance for their approach to work.

Furthermore, Herring's claim that Nixon's approach was merely the same as his predecessors seems to be an overstatement. Though Nixon did rely on the use of military power to convince the North to cease its aggression against the South, his strategy differed significantly from LBJ in that he more closely tied aggressive military and diplomatic actions and aims to get the North to negotiate. Moreover, while LBJ wanted to limit the war and was not willing to employ the military to force the North to end the war by attacking their sanctuaries, Nixon was willing to risk military ground operations outside of South Vietnam.

In sum, the use of military force would be an important feature of Nixon's foreign policy and his approach to settling the war in Vietnam. But it would be more integrated and linked with other actions than ever before. Both Nixon and Kissinger saw Vietnamization, continued military action, and diplomatic pressure on the Soviet Union and China as key elements in getting North Vietnam to negotiate an end to the war in a way that would allow a US military withdrawal and obtain a peace favorable to US interests.

As we will see ahead, this approach will change as the President realizes that he miscalculated, as his predecessors had done, the capability and will of their opponents. As US and South Vietnamese military actions faltered, and as time for Vietnamization dwindled, both Nixon and Kissinger gave up on their grandiose 1969 plans. It was then that both would seek a decent interval that would allow them to withdraw from Vietnam and 'save face' with the American public. That seemed to work for a while in 1973 and early 1974; then in 1975 everything crumbled under Nixon's paranoia with his enemies, destroying his Presidency and leaving South Vietnam vulnerable to North Vietnam aggression.

Cambodia 'Secret Bombings.'

As the Administration continued to formulate its policies and plans for Vietnamization and its overall program to settle the war, the North continued to launch attacks to disrupt the pacification programs that Abrams was now placing a priority on. Nixon was incensed. When he and Kissinger asked Wheeler how to retaliate, all they got again was to renew bombing of the North.

Meanwhile, General Abrams was reporting on the importance of Cambodia to the North Vietnamese offensive. He also reported that US intelligence had found the main headquarters for NVA/VC operations in the South – called the Central Committee of the Communist party in South Vietnam (COSVN) - in Cambodia.

There had been some disagreement in US intelligence on just how vital the Cambodian bases were. That dissension surrounded the amount of supplies that flowed through Cambodia to support the NVA in the South. The CIA argued that the movement of supplies was not significant. Their analysis showed that the supplies flowing over the Ho Chi Minh trail through Laos were more than enough to supply all forces in South Vietnam.

MACV was arguing that it was significant because the Chinese were using the Cambodian port of Sihanoukville to funnel substantial amounts of supplies to the bases along the Cambodian-South Vietnam border. These, in turn, supported North Vietnamese operations in the southernmost areas of South Vietnam, to include the critical environs of Saigon. Without those supplies, the Command suggested that North Vietnamese operations would suffer a severe setback and could not continue on a large scale.

Nixon had early in his Presidency asked for a study of communist activity in Cambodia. He had suspected that the North was using it as a primary base for operations. Now he instinctively believed that an attack against Cambodia could seriously affect the North Vietnamese offensive against the South. Abrams agreed. Wheeler concurred. Kissinger thought it would be worth a try.

Consequently, Nixon ordered on March 15th massive B-52 air attacks. He also ordered that the strikes be secret. The pilots themselves did not know the targets they were dropping their bombs on were even in Cambodia. Nixon and Kissinger did not want to stir US public opinion on this expansion of the war against the NVA.

As it turned out, initially there was not much publicity on the bombing. This was because neither the Cambodians nor the North Vietnamese protested. The Cambodian regime had been trying to remain neutral in the war. They had acquiesced to North Vietnamese bases if they did not threaten the regime. At the same time, they were trying to obtain US aid against an indigent communist insurgency. The North Vietnamese did not protest because they did not want to acknowledge their presence in Cambodia. In fact, as Abrams and the President had surmised, the Cambodia bases and lines of communication had become as important to their attacks against the South as their Laotian supply line.

Soon after the B52 raids began, the news media noticed the secret air attacks. In May, the *New York Times* ran a front-page story on them. Nixon and Kissinger were outraged. The President sought to find who in the Administration leaked information on the attacks. He ordered Haldeman to see who had done it. The FBI established, on Nixon's orders, wiretaps on suspected members who may have talked to reporters. This action included several members of Kissinger's small personal staff.

Nixon also began to think that the culprits may have been Democratic government employees in both the Defense and State Departments. Thus, the President began to contemplate the use of his 'Plumbers' team of entrusted agents, under his Chief of Staff, to investigate Democratic sympathizers who may be trying to undermine his Presidency. He gave Haldeman a 'warning order' but did not yet pursue any action.

Despite the news reports, the public reaction to the bombings was not significant. Nixon, therefore, ordered the Cambodia B-52 raids to continue well into the year. The code name for the overall operation was 'Menu,' with several iterations called, Breakfast, Lunch, etc. MACV soon reported to Washington that they were "one of the most telling operations in the entire war." Although post-strike reconnaissance could not tell whether the COSVN headquarters had been destroyed or even significantly damaged, there had been many large explosions showing damage to ammunition supply areas near the suspected headquarters location.

The positive psychological effects on Saigon were noticeable. Now the new President was authorizing attacks that could significantly affect the North Vietnamese war efforts. There were even some in Washington and Saigon who now believed that they could win the war. At Abrams staff briefings and discussions with Commanders, recorded and transcribed in Lewis Sorley's *Vietnam Chronicles, The Abrams Tapes, 1968 – 1972*, all present were full of confidence that they could gain the necessary time to execute Vietnamization successfully.

Abrams Change of Mission

The Cambodian bombings supported what General Abrams called his 'one war' strategy. That entailed simultaneous pursuit of combat operations, pacification, and South Vietnamese Armed Forces (RVNAF) improvements. According to the JCS official history, the strategy envisioned a "mission of defeating the VC/NVA forces and assisting the Republic of Vietnam to extend control throughout South Vietnam.

To combat the enemy, the plan called for sustained, joint ground, air, and naval operations against VC/NVA forces, base areas, and lines of communication. For extension of RVN control, the plan envisioned securing towns, cities, and military bases, using measures to prevent infiltration, 'clear and hold' military operations, and increased support of pacification." Chapter 10 will discuss this military strategy and its operations and effects in more detail.

Secretary Laird felt a certain uneasiness when briefed on this strategy during his March visit. His biographer claims that he did not believe that it agreed with his views on Vietnamization or the President's announcements on how to end the war. In Laird's dealings with Congress, moreover, he knew that the Administration could not sustain continued military actions to solve the conundrum of Vietnam. The Defense Secretary also instinctively recognized that the American public would soon turn on the Administration should it continue to rely on military force to 'win the war.'

At first, Laird's views were an apparent contradiction to those of the President. Nixon was much more bellicose toward future military actions than the Defense Secretary. As mentioned above, the President envisioned in 1969 the use of US military force as a key element in his strategy to force the North to give up their firm position on a negotiated peace. The Cambodian bombings had been but the beginning of these military actions.

In fact, Nixon and his National Security Advisor would start secret planning within a small group of people in the NSC headed by Colonel Al Haig to quickly end the war using military means if North Vietnam did not change its negotiating position. That plan - called 'DUCK HOOK' and developed in the summer of 1969 - envisioned the mining of North Vietnamese ports and harbors, the sustained B52 bombing of military and economic targets, and even an offensive across the DMZ into North Vietnam.

According to Jeffrey Kimball in his work, *No Peace, No Honor*, Haig later shared this plan with Admiral Moorer and a small group of the Joint Staff for further details. The President would keep its actions, however, from the Secretary of Defense until the later part of the year. At that time, Nixon discussed its execution with Rogers and Laird after the failure of the North to respond to his overtures in the negotiations in Paris.

When it was completed, Nixon decided not to order the execution of the plan. In part, this was due to objections of his two top cabinet officers. The President also became concerned at the end of his first year about the resurgence of the antiwar movement demonstrations, and Congressional reactions to the Administration's bombing of Cambodia. Thus, he felt that such a bold military offensive as that envisioned in DUCK HOOK would have to await some sort of strong military action by the North that would threaten South Vietnam's survival. Besides, he was confident enough at this point that his Vietnamization, diplomatic actions, bombing in Cambodia, and Abrams' military activities in South Vietnam would all eventually work.

Toward the latter part of the first year of the Nixon Presidency, reactions to the war in America showed that Laird was closer to the realities of continued military efforts in Vietnam considering the national mood. Despite the knowledge of the 1969 North Vietnamese offensive and acquiescence to the Cambodia bombings, the Media, Public and Congress began to show increasing concern over the loss of lives of American soldiers.

For example, earlier in May, casualties in the Battle of Hamburger Hill in northern South Vietnam near the Laotian border prompted a firestorm of protests in the news, on the streets, and in the halls of Congress. Led by Senator Ted Kennedy, several Congressmen, and ex-officials of the Johnson Administration began to question publicly the need for US offensive combat operations to continue. They argued that they did not make sense because they entailed so many losses and were not congruent with the President's Vietnamization policy.

Life magazine, the week after the battle, had published the pictures of over two-hundred soldiers who had died in Vietnam in one week. While the dead were from military actions throughout South Vietnam, the public mistook the pictures to be of soldiers killed on Hamburger Hill. This misperception added to the public outcry in support of Kennedy and the other Senators.

On 24 May Senator J. William Fulbright, the Chairman of the Senate Foreign Relations Committee, asked Laird for the Department's orders to Commanders in South Vietnam. The Senator wanted to see whether they were consistent with the President's 14 May rhetoric on winding down US military operations and letting the South Vietnamese pick up most of the fighting.

The Secretary, in turn, asked General Wheeler to provide an answer to the Senator's inquiry. This episode, coupled with continued Congressional concerns about US combat operations and resultant casualties, would spark a major Defense Department review of operational guidance to Commanders in South Vietnam.

The response that Wheeler gave Laird restated the standing mission statement in the Chairman's Joint Strategic Capabilities Plan or JSCP (pronounced JAYSCAP in military jargon). As the JCS Official History states, the mission was "to defeat the externally directed and supported Communist subversion and aggression" and to attain "a stable and independent noncommunist government" there. This was consistent with the officially published political aims provided to the military during the Johnson years.

In addition, the JSCP assigned the following subordinate undertakings: " (1) make as difficult and costly as possible the continued support of the Viet Cong by North Vietnam, and cause North Vietnam to cease its direction of the Viet Cong insurgency; (2) defeat the Viet Cong and North Vietnamese Armed Forces in South Vietnam and force withdrawal of the North Vietnamese Armed Forces; (3) extend Government of Vietnam dominion, direction, and control over all of South Vietnam; (4) deter [Chinese People's Republic] intervention and defeat such intervention if it occurred." These are the tasks that Westmoreland and now Abrams were to carry out and those that they further assigned in their guidance to their subordinate commanders.

Secretary Laird sent an abbreviated response to Fulbright. It said that US operations in Vietnam were consistent with Administration's policy goals. They were following the prudent judgment of the President's military commanders and advisors to conduct operations that would decrease the enemy's ability to inflict damage on US and Vietnam forces and protect South Vietnam. However, Laird felt concern that the essence of the JSCP language was not in consonance with what the Administration's new policy of Vietnamization needed of the military. It undoubtedly did not, he surmised, reflect the wording of the President's 14 May announcement. Therefore, in early July he ordered the JCS to review its military strategy guidance for Vietnam.

Inconsistency between political guidance and military operations had already been a problem in the war. As we have seen in Chapter 3, US political leaders did not transmit clearly or entirely to the commanders in the field what they wanted to accomplish to end the war in terms that could force or impose their will on the enemy.

Now, these inconsistencies were not only between political leaders in Washington and military commanders in the field, but between major civilian leaders in the Administration. By mid-1969, Laird, at least, was pursuing a political aim of allowing the South to decide its fate (whatever that meant), based on what he thought the President wanted because of a speech he had made to pacify domestic unrest on the conduct of the war. To him, the speech and other Nixon remarks meant eventual, but complete withdrawal of US forces no matter what the North was doing, or what the South was accomplishing.

General Abrams, on the other hand, operating off previously established political objectives, thought that he needed to keep the pressure on the communist forces in the South by engaging them and destroying them or making them ineffective. While doing all of that he was trying to create a South Vietnamese force that could withstand further operations against the main enemy forces in the south; further gain control of the cities, hamlets, and villages in the countryside; and defend an invasion or offensive from North Vietnamese regular forces sent into the South. All of this, he knew, could only occur with the help of American advisors and airpower for the long term.

General Wheeler, still the Chairman, had already raised the issue of potential mission changes with General Abrams. Both were concerned that their civilian leaders thought the US military should assume a defensive posture to reduce casualties. Wheeler assured Abrams that he could deal with the 'semantics' and produce new words for the mission statement that would appease Laird and the other civilian leaders, while still allowing for operations to maintain pressure on the enemy.

The Chairman took up the mantle to make the changes that both the civilian leaders and General Abrams and his commanders could live with. In several sessions with Secretary Laird, the Chairman and the other Joint Chiefs argued that General Abrams must continue to conduct mobile, offensive operations or else the enemy would gain the initiative and cause more unacceptable casualties. What they could do is discontinue the use of phrases such as 'search and destroy,' which had lost favor in the field.

Secretary Laird continued to indicate that he thought the current mission statement was not congruent with Vietnamization. At the end of July, the Defense chief presented his mission statement which he said, "more adequately met current and anticipate conditions in Vietnam." The JCS still attempted to dissuade the Secretary from this change, but Laird insisted upon it. Once again, as he had done in 1968, General Wheeler failed in his task to ensure that the civilian leaders in Washington understood the nature of military operations that were necessary to meet official, stated Presidential aims for the war. Most grievously, Abrams would now be faced with a situation, like Westmoreland had in 1967 and 1968, in which his civilian leaders did not understand the approach necessary to achieve a favorable military situation in South Vietnam.

Thus, the JCS guidance by the summer of 1969 changed. The new mission now read: "CINCPAC and COMUSMACV should assist the Republic of Vietnam Armed Forces to take over an increasing share of combat operations. The tactical goal of the combat operations is to defeat the subversion and aggression which is intended to deny self-determination to the RVN people."

The guidance further stipulated that "The overall mission encompasses the following undertakings: (a) Provide maximum assistance in developing, training, and equipping the RVNAF as rapidly as possible; (b) Continue military support for accelerated pacification, civic action and security programs; (c) Conduct military operations designed to accelerate improvement in the RVNAF and to continue to provide security for US forces; (d) Conduct military operations to reduce the flow of materiel and manpower support for enemy forces in SVN [South Vietnam]; (e) Maintain plans for a comprehensive air and naval campaign in Vietnam."

As its official history explains, the JCS took the new mission statement as a definite change in the operational tempo of US forces. Indeed, soon after the Chairman issued the modified mission to MACV, there was a corresponding reduction in the military budget that affected the operational capabilities in the war in the South. Consequently, there was a decline in Abrams' B-52 and tactical air sorties that began to take effect at once. What Wheeler thought would be an exercise in semantics would increasingly have grave implications for field commanders in the way they could conduct operations in South Vietnam.

While Laird saw this mission change as a necessary and crucial step in implementing the Vietnamization policy, neither Nixon nor Kissinger paid much attention to it when the Secretary informed them of the modification. In fact, as Kissinger recalls, Nixon thought of canceling the new mission statement but decided it did not matter because they were going to do whatever was necessary. As LBJ and McNamara had done in managing the war during their tenure, Nixon and Kissinger were now following in their footsteps – ignoring the military strategy in the field that may have led to a better situation in South Vietnam than eventually would occur.

Meanwhile, true to their mode of operating, both the President and his National Security Advisory continued to look for military ways in their view that would affect the negotiations and retaliate for North Vietnam's offensive operations in the South. For the military commanders in Vietnam, however, the new mission statement would limit large-scale operations against enemy base areas and place US forces on the defensive throughout South Vietnam. We will further see in Chapter 10 the effects on operations and how they handicapped seriously, even decisively, General Abrams in his pursuit of achieving the military objective of creating a capable South Vietnamese Armed Forces that could defend its country, while US forces withdrew from Vietnam.

Nixon Administration Negotiation Initiatives

As his Defense Secretary and commanders were struggling with a new mission statement, Nixon's attention was on formulating and initiating action to enhance negotiations. As previously outlined, these had stalled in Paris since they had begun in the Johnson Administration. It was apparent to the new President that the North Vietnamese were only stalling so that they could somehow gain the upper military hand again in the South.

Per Kissinger in the first volume of his memoirs *White House Years*, to jump-start the negotiations the National Security Advisor suggested in June 1969 a meeting between the President and a Frenchman by the name of Jean Sainteny. Sainteny was a longtime friend of Kissinger's. More importantly, he knew Ho Chi Minh. During the turbulent period after the Second World War when Ho was seeking some arrangement with France that would result in independence and unification of Vietnam, Sainteny was the French delegate that Ho worked with to obtain an agreement. Though the agreement eventually fell through, it was not due to Sainteny. He had faithfully worked with Ho to somehow arrange for an understanding that would have avoided war. Since the Indochina War, the two had stayed in touch.

The purpose of the meeting was to get Sainteny to carry a personal message from Nixon to Ho suggesting a new initiative to open meaningful dialogue to settle the war. Kissinger also wanted the Frenchman to arrange a secret meeting between himself and a top Northern diplomat in Paris to begin meaningful discussions.

Nixon agreed to meet with him. The Frenchman traveled to DC from his home in France and met the President in the Oval Office on July 15, 1969. He agreed to carry a letter to Hanoi and present it to someone close to Ho for delivery. Meanwhile, after he left, Sainteny arranged for the meeting that Kissinger had suggested in Paris.

Eventually, Ho received Nixon's letter. The US President started with regrets that the war had caused much damage and death to both sides. He also repeated his comments on May 14 that the US goals were "to assure the right of the South Vietnamese people to determine their fate free of outside coercion." However, as Ken Hughes in his *Fatal Politics* relates, the real purpose of the letter was to make Ho understand that Nixon was ready to use force if necessary to end the war.

In fact, Hughes argues that the words that Nixon told Sainteny to convey to Ho were an ultimatum. These were, "if no valid solution has been reached, he will regretfully find himself obliged to have recourse to measures of great consequence and force.... Regardless of public opinion or opposition, Mr. Nixon is determined to bring this war to an early conclusion. He totally rejects continued talking and fighting. If this diplomatic approach fails, he will resort to any means necessary." These words were congruent with Nixon's belief in the use of his madman theory.

Ho's response was typically full of lofty words of Vietnam's long struggle to free itself from Western colonialism. Without acknowledging Nixon's call for peace, it indicated that - as Larry Berman in his *No Peace, No Honor* explains - that no threats could ever lead to peace. Thus, it appears that Nixon's use of his madman theory with the North failed. Of course, as we will see in Chapter 7, Ho by this time was sick and had little to do with the direction of the war. The real Northerner in charge could not be intimated and had already decided to continue to seek a military solution though he knew the costs would be high.

Despite the lack of progress in direct communication with Ho, Sainteny's travels and contacts led to a secret meeting between Kissinger and high-ranking Northern diplomats. These in turn eventually resulted in the meeting between himself and a man who would become Kissinger's capable adversary in the negotiations – Le Duc Tho.

This first meeting proved to be nothing more than a social call. However, in Larry Berman's words, "Although little was accomplished, this first meeting opened the door for the secret parallel negotiating meetings that would soon begin between Kissinger and Le Duc Tho. The story of Paris would henceforth be a dual tale of the official talks (the plenary sessions), with South Vietnam present, and the real talks (private meetings) between the United States and the North Vietnamese."

The Cambodia Incursion

In early 1970, with little movement on the diplomatic side, Nixon began contemplating offensive ground operations against the Cambodian sanctuaries. In fact, during the first months in 1970, the North's infiltration of forces into those bases had increased, as well as supplies coming through Sihanoukville. By some estimates, there were almost 300,000 North Vietnamese troops there, which showed the importance of Cambodia to the war effort in the South. In March Admiral McCain - overall Commander of US Pacific Region and Abrams' commander - proposed to the JCS covert operations against the bases. General Abrams, meanwhile, began making plans to launch limited ground attacks against them.

The North Vietnamese buildup in Cambodia threatened the entire process of Vietnamization. Withdrawal of US forces, first announced publicly by Nixon in June 1969, by the beginning of 1970 was in full swing. During 1969, US military strength in Vietnam had dropped a little over 60,000 troops. Nixon had also linked these withdrawals to reductions in the draft call. Recognizing the role of the unfair draft rules, he wanted to ameliorate its impact on the antiwar movement. He had also made ending the draft part of his campaign platform. In a few years, the President would act on that promise.

Despite the draft reductions and the beginning of troop withdrawals, the antiwar movement continued and even grew in reaction to the Cambodian bombings and military losses in Vietnam. Both Nixon and Kissinger began to realize that, despite their desires of tying US troop withdrawals to North Vietnamese military aggression against the South, it may not be possible to link the extraction of forces to enemy actions. In addition to the protests bringing pressure to extract US troops from combat, once the announced withdrawals began and the troops started coming home, the public clamor for more and faster return of American military personnel created pressure on both Nixon and the Congress.

Yet, there remained public support for pursuing an 'honorable' withdrawal – whatever that meant. As mentioned, in November of 1969 Nixon had gone on national TV to explain his approach to ending the war and bringing the troops home. He had also described the obstinacy of the North Vietnamese to the negotiations. He emphasized that "North Vietnam cannot humiliate the United States. Only Americans can do that." The presentation, afterwards referred to as the 'silent majority' speech because of his appeal to the 'great silent majority' of Americans supporting the President, was a public opinion success story. It even received much publicity and favorable comments in the media.

The overwhelming positive feedback and the poll information that Nixon received gave him, in his mind, a popular mandate to continue the road he was on to obtain peace without capitulation. By the beginning of 1970, Nixon felt he had some relief from the anti-war protests and anti-Nixon media to pursue his vision of getting out of Vietnam with the use of force as well as Vietnamization.

By the end of March of 1970, the situation in Cambodia had turned critical to the Administration's Vietnam policy. Nixon would now face a situation that would require his use of the clear mandate he had gained from his 'silent majority' speech.

That 'situation' was that the Cambodian National Assembly had announced the removal of the Chief of State, Prince Sihanouk, who had been visiting in France. The Cambodian Prince had walked a fragile line between allowing the North Vietnamese to use the eastern part of his country as a base to persecute the war in the South. He had also been silent about the secret bombing campaign that the US had launched and tolerated the 'violations' of his border area by the South Vietnamese Army limited forays against NVA forces that had made significant attacks in the South.

Finding out about the removal while in France, Sihanouk decided to fight back. He solicited the help of the North and the use of their and the indigenous communist resistance forces in Cambodia. A civil war ensued.

The pro-western National Assembly members initiating Sihanouk's removal now sought Western aid against the Cambodian Communists. The considerable number of North Vietnamese Army forces along its eastern border prompted this help. Concurrently, North Vietnam declared the new Cambodian government as a pro-American ultra-rightist group and claimed that the US had engineered the coup. Soon after this proclamation, North Vietnam forces from their Cambodia bases began an offensive to secure its lines of communication from the port of Sihanoukville to their positions along the South Vietnam border.

President Nixon asked for plans from the JCS and his commanders to aid the pro-western Nationalist forces. Meanwhile, Kissinger convened one of his small NSC groups to discuss and come up with a course of action to assist the new Premier of Cambodia, Lon Nol, who had requested US aid to deal with the communists.

In later NSC meetings, Nixon and his advisors debated several courses of action. These varied significantly, but they considered two of them seriously. One was an attack against two major base areas in Cambodia with a combination of South Vietnamese and US forces. The other was to attack one of the largest bases, called the 'Parrot's Beak,' which most threatened the Saigon area. The latter attack would be with only South Vietnamese forces. Nixon decided upon the first of the two alternatives.

The South Vietnamese forces began the combined attack on 28 April in the 'Parrot's Beak' area. US troops joined in on 1 May with its offensive against an adjacent base area called the 'Fishhook.' On 30 April Nixon went on national TV and announced the attacks.

Most sources claim that this decision put Nixon "through an emotional ringer." Haldeman noted that he seemed drained and distraught. Kissinger and Nixon's military aide pointed out that Nixon started drinking heavily. Following a cruise along the Potomac on which he consumed two to three alcoholic beverages, he decided to retire to Camp David to watch his favorite Hollywood film 'Patton.' The picture, along with the alcohol, seemed to soothe his spirits.

MACV and the JCS later reported that the overall Cambodian invasion achieved the US goal of disrupting the North Vietnamese timetable for offensive operations in the South. Although it did not capture or destroy the COSVN headquarters, it did significantly disrupt the flow of supplies and soldiers into the bases for follow-on operations. Units captured or destroyed tens of thousands of weapons, hundreds of thousands of pounds of supplies, and a myriad of important documents.

However, Nixon's time and distance limitations of thirty days and thirty miles for the operation of US forces affected the overall effectiveness of the incursion. That did not allow for a more sustained operation that could have engaged decisively enemy forces and captured or destroyed more supplies and base areas. Abrams, in a meeting with his commanders, lamented that if he could only have pursued the NVA as he had done the Nazis in World War Two, he could have genuinely achieved a decisive victory in this indecisive war.

When the operation ended, Abrams reported that overall the ARVN forces had performed admirably. Along with their performance during TET, there was much optimism in the road ahead with further improvements. The MACV commander noted, however, one critical deficiency. The South Vietnamese Armed Forces still depended heavily on US support for planning, for executing air and artillery support, and for logistical sustainment. These were deficiencies that would be very difficult for the US to overcome in the time ahead.

The air and ground operations against Cambodia from 1969 to 1970 had both positive and adverse effects for the Nixon Administration. On the one hand, the invasion had sparked the anti-war movement in the US. Protests continued to grow in the summer of 1970; especially after some National Guard troops fired upon and killed some students during a demonstration at Kent State University. Also, despite the overall public approval of Nixon's decision, Senator George McGovern introduced a bill requiring the US withdrawal from Vietnam by the end of the year. Though it had some support, it did not pass the Senate.

Months later, the Congress overrode a Presidential veto and passed The Cooper-Church Act. It prevented US forces from participation in further land offensives outside of South Vietnam. That meant that only South Vietnamese Armed forces could conduct these out of country operations. It further meant that they would have no direct support of accompanying American advisors and land units. Congress finally had a significant impact on the President's ability to conduct operations in the war.

On the positive side, the Cambodia operations had set back North Vietnamese offensive operations in the South. Captured documents showed that many of their units had to cease operations due to lack of supplies and ammunition. The intended effect to provide for more time for Vietnamization had worked. However, how much time was still an issue. The 'race to Vietnamization' remained the key to any perceived honorable settlement, but how much time was available to achieve it still an unknown.

Most importantly in the overall scheme of using military force to end the war, the Congressional restrictions on operations now would affect the ability to gain time through cross-border actions. As both Nixon and Kissinger had already surmised, it was just a matter of time that further restrictions, especially those cutting funds for the war, would have a major, if not critical effect, on their use of US forces to enable Vietnamization.

Therefore, the President and his National Security Advisor needed to derive some further ways to circumvent these restrictions while increasing their efforts to gain a negotiated agreement that would be favorable to the outcome of the war. Whatever the latter was, at this time at least, they both had not yet decided. It would depend on the diplomatic efforts with the Chinese and Soviets, their ability to get concessions from the North, and progress in Vietnamization.

Laos Operations – Lam Son 719

Despite the attempts to reach some agreement on how to end the war, the talks with the North Vietnamese remained deadlocked into 1971. Even though US and South Vietnamese operations along the Cambodian border had hampered communist threats against Saigon, they had not decisively affected the North's overall infiltration operations.

In fact, at the beginning of 1971, the North increased the infiltration of both troops and supplies over the Ho Chi Minh Trail. US intelligence estimated that the North was now infiltrating six thousand combat troops a month through Laos. It soon became apparent that the North was preparing for a spring offensive aimed at the two northern South Vietnamese provinces.

In late 1970 Admiral McCain and his subordinate General Abrams had begun discussions and planning for next years' operations. The Admiral was keen for an operation in Laos. He recognized, as the JCS official history relates, that with the damage done to its Cambodian bases and denial of the use of the port there, Laos had become particularly critical to the North Vietnamese war effort. Consequently, he told Abrams to start planning for an attack into southern Laos.

General Abrams, working with the South Vietnamese high command and staff, began work on such a plan. The scheme called for a multi-division ARVN attack toward the vital area of Tchepone, Laos to destroy stockpiles and facilities there. They would then operate against NVA base areas to disrupt their preparations for a dry season offensive. American forces would support the attack by re-establishing a base at Khe Sanh from which the ARVN could launch the assault.

US forces would further support the ARVN in its drive into Laos with helicopters for lift and aerial fire support, air force fighter-bombers and B-52s, and long-range artillery. Abrams recognized that such an operation would be risky and had some initial reservations. However, as the South Vietnamese grew more enthusiastic toward such an offensive, he thought the ARVN had a reasonable chance to accomplish it successfully.

Meanwhile, from late in 1970 through the beginning of 1971, Dr. Kissinger had several meetings with his small planning group of the NSC to discuss the North's buildup and preparations for an offensive in 1971 or 1972. Participants in these meetings, documented in the *Foreign Relations of the United States* papers, discussed the several US and South Vietnamese options to deal with the buildup and possible enemy offensive. These possibilities ranged from attacks again into Cambodia, to an offensive into Laos to cut the Ho Chi Minh trail there, to ground force raids into the DMZ.

In early December 1970, Haig - now a Brigadier General and the man who had led the NSC planning - visited Saigon to discuss these alternatives and any others that MACV thought practical. He reported back to Kissinger that both Abrams and the South Vietnamese military and civilian leadership thought that a multi-division drive from northern South Vietnam into the southern part of Laos could be a decisive blow against the NVA. Haig wrote that "all here are extremely enthusiastic about this operation."

Just before Christmas, Kissinger, prompted by the President for some preemptive offensive action in 1971, called a meeting with Admiral Moorer, now the CJCS, to discuss plans for actions during the upcoming year. The Admiral had been in communication with both McCain and Abrams. Consequently, Moorer briefed the same plan that Abrams had developed a month earlier.

Pleased with what both the Commanders in the field had planned and what the JCS had endorsed, Kissinger took the Laotian offensive concept to a meeting with Nixon and Laird. Laird liked it, arguing the operation would be a great test of Vietnamization. Nixon approved both the Cambodian and Laotian options for further planning.

Both the military and the civilian advisors continued to refine these two options. In January, the MACV staff briefed a refined Abrams' plan to the JCS. The Joint Chiefs again endorsed it. About the same time, Kissinger's NSC planning group further discussed both the Cambodia and Laos options. This group had reservations about the risks associated with the Laos operation.

Kissinger went back to both the JCS and the field commanders on the risks versus benefits. Abrams gave the Laotian operation his 'unqualified support.' McCain called it 'an exceptional opportunity to inflict maximum damage against enemy personnel, materiel, and psychological pressure." Kissinger then sought Nixon's approval of what became known as Lam Son 719 – named by the South Vietnamese after a Vietnamese hero who had defeated the Chinese in the fifteenth century.

On 27 January Nixon approved. The first phase of the operation, the American establishment of a support base around Khe San, went ahead soon after. The 'decisive moment' about the progress of Vietnamization was underway. The US military leadership, both in Washington and Saigon, thought that this operation "would be the real turning point of the war." They were right. But it would not be the decisive moment they had in mind.

The ARVN attack into Laos started on 8 February. Already aware that this region had become critical to their war effort, the North Vietnamese had by the end of 1970 begun to reinforce the area. Moreover, by February they had learned of the plans for Lam Son 719. They began massing some 63,000 soldiers in the suspected area of the South Vietnamese offensive. These included units with tanks, heavy artillery, and air defense capabilities. Aware that the ARVN would be using Route 9 for their primary ground thrust, the PAVN had prepared defensive positions to resist such an advance.

Aided by the American B-52 bombing preparation ahead of their advance, the ARVN armored column moved into Laos with light resistance. The helicopter assaults that occurred along that route to secure its flanks, however, ran into intense fires from the start. The ARVN ground advance toward Tchepone met increasingly stiff resistance. Air assaults in support of that advance also faced stiff opposition. South Vietnamese armor and mechanized units confronted North Vietnamese armored organizations; US helicopters met heavy antiaircraft fires.

The war had taken a distinctly different turn from its original insurgency. Now the conflict was mostly conventional. As described in the JCS official history, "What the allies had envisioned as a search-and-destroy operation like those in Cambodia turned into an intense combined arms conventional battle for which the ARVN was poorly prepared."

Despite the enemy's heavily conventional response, Abrams' reports were confident throughout the first weeks of the operation. Within days of the attack, the General said he was "very pleased with the progress." As it became apparent that the North Vietnamese were prepared for the assault and began to mass forces against it, both Abrams and McCain indicated they welcomed the response because the massed forces would present easy targets to continued air attacks. To the Media, this was all too reminiscent of Westmoreland's claims during TET that the communist forces had exposed themselves to destruction.

Both Nixon and Kissinger wanted to believe their military assessments. This was despite the news reports coming out of Vietnam and intelligence reports of North Vietnamese effective resistance. Kissinger heard that General Westmoreland, now the Army Chief of Staff, had made plans of his own when he was the commander of MACV for such an assault. He asked for his assessment.

The Joint Staff had briefed Westmoreland on the plans for Lam Son weeks before the attack. Then he had said nothing. Now he told Kissinger and Moorer that the entire plan had been too risky. The Chairman, irate at the Army Chief for his reversal of opinion and apparent disloyalty to the field commander, supported Abrams and assured Kissinger of the soundness of the operation.

Meanwhile, General Haig questioned the apparent lack of aggressiveness of the ARVN commanders. Later, Haig, dispatched to Vietnam to evaluate the situation, further gave a scathing critique of Abrams' performance to Kissinger. These conflicting opinions unnerved the National Security Advisor. He began to criticize both Abrams and Moorer to Nixon.

In his memoirs, Kissinger blames the military for lack of innovative thinking and a reliance on "superior resources rather than the bold stroke." The Presidential tapes show that the National Security Advisor directed his more vehement criticism toward the military's lack of aggressiveness due to lack of courage. His language of the military's performance was full of expletives and derisiveness. He often referred to US military leaders and advisors as 'bastards' and 'fools.' In a March 23 meeting, Nixon agreed with his National Security Advisor. At one point, for the first time, they talked of relieving General Abrams.

The American media and peace movement, as expected, was highly critical and active against yet another Nixon attempt to spread the conflict in Southeast Asia instead of putting an end to it. Nixon went on national TV to assure the public of the merits of the operation. He praised the actions of the South Vietnamese Armed Forces and repeated Abrams positive assessments.

The media continued to bombard the American people with negative reports, as it had done during TET. One such story reported an incident where the North Vietnamese were about to overrun an ARVN outpost. In this situation American helicopters helped in the evacuation of the ARVN unit there. Pictures and film depicted South Vietnamese soldiers holding on to the helicopter skids as the aircraft moved away from the outpost. Like other similar spectacular pictures or film strips of the war, it came to represent in the public eye the truth of the war in Vietnam, that is, the South Vietnamese military was cowardly and inept.

Ultimately, the South Vietnamese armed forces seized the sizeable communist base at Tchepone – its primary objective. They also started to clear other known base areas in southern Laos. However, South Vietnamese President Thieu, a month into the assault, began to lose his nerve over the reports of fierce North Vietnamese resistance and heavy ARVN casualties. He ordered a change of plans. He directed a withdrawal from Laos much sooner than either Nixon and Kissinger had expected.

The American President and his principal advisors wanted South Vietnamese forces to stay in Laos long enough – into the second week of April - to demonstrate an actual severing of the Ho Chi Minh Trail. They did not want the operation to look like just a raid against Northern base camps. However, without their American advisors, the ARVN commanders had difficulty in coordinating artillery and aerial strikes. More importantly, Thieu and his senior commanders had lost the stomach for the fight. By March 25, ARVN forces were back in South Vietnam.

Both sides claimed a victory. Both sides had made gains that could warrant such a claim. The South Vietnamese and their American supporters had destroyed large caches of enemy supplies. They also inflicted significant casualties on North Vietnamese units. Their operation precluded any North Vietnamese major offensive in 1971.

The North Vietnamese had inflicted substantial casualties on the ARVN. They had overrun several of their fire support bases, despite the significant American aviation and fire support. They succeeded in proving to themselves that they could take on the ARVN and defeat it in a large-scale conventional battle. In sum, Lam Son 719 gave the South a year without a significant enemy offensive and some breathing room for continued preparations. It also resulted in emboldening the North for another offensive after it recouped its losses.

Section 5.3 - The Search for Peace with Honor

Nixon publicly proclaimed that the Laos operation was a resounding success. He announced that it had shown the effectiveness of Vietnamization. The President also asserted that now the South Vietnamese could take on the North by itself, allowing for the complete withdrawal of US combat forces.

The reality was much different. Nixon and Kissinger now knew that Vietnamization had not really worked. They began to realize that their entire scheme for an end to the war through military pressure on the North would not work. In their overall grand strategic design, they now had to turn to diplomacy as their key to achieving peace with honor.

Post Lam Son 719 Assessments

In the beginning of 1972, Nixon announced yet another withdrawal of US forces. Three months into the year there would be only 69,000 American military troops in South Vietnam. These were mostly support and advisory personnel. By April 1972 then, there were no more capable US ground combat units available to aid the South Vietnamese Armed Forces.

Privately, as demonstrated in the Presidential tapes, Nixon indicated that he did not think the South Vietnamese would ever be able to defend themselves against the North without US support. In his memoirs, he claims that the overall Laos operation was a 'psychological defeat' caused by the negative media coverage. Kissinger was more realistic. He argued that the operation far exceeded the capabilities of the ARVN. He also said that he then had grave doubts that the ARVN could ever stand up to the North.

Thus, after Lam Son 719 it seems that both Nixon and Kissinger were looking for some way out regardless of what happened to South Vietnam. The conversations between them, captured in the Nixon Presidential Tapes after Lam Son, show the depth of their dilemma and their need to create some apparent 'victory with honor' so that they could rid themselves of the Vietnam conundrum.

They accepted three major notions that affected that future. One was that they now knew that there needed to be a complete withdrawal of American forces. There would not be any residual force there as in Korea. They also knew that eventually, with the power of the purse, Congress would play a vital role in inhibiting the President in his ability to use force. Finally, they realized that they would have to accept the idea that the North Vietnamese would not agree to a complete withdrawal of their forces from the South.

Another significant result of Lam Son 719 was to demonstrate that the ARVN could only stand up to the North with significant American firepower. It further showed that, without American advisors on the ground, South Vietnamese leaders could not conduct effective sustained combat operations. While their soldiers showed courage and stamina, their leader's ability to react to the changing circumstances of battle was poor. They could not coordinate the activities of units between and amongst themselves without American advisors. They also were no able to call for, apply, and adjust fire support from the air or ground effectively.

In short, Nixon's continued pronunciations on the overall success of Vietnamization were false. It had not succeeded. Furthermore, after the Laos operation, ARVN's future success against the PAVN remained hostage to the American ability to man, equip and train its forces before the complete withdrawal of US forces. However, there was no longer enough US public support to provide that time. Now, 71 percent of the American people thought the war was a mistake. Meanwhile, Congress was looking for more legislation to prevent Nixon from further military adventures that would prolong US involvement in the Southeast Asia region.

The Laos operation also had some resounding effects on the confidence between the American civilian and military leaders. As mentioned above, during Lam Son 719, Nixon and Kissinger had become distraught with the advice and performance of General Abrams, some of his subordinate commanders, and the JCS. Despite claims to the contrary in their memoirs, they both were furious with their field Commander. Nixon, on several occasions, the Presidential tapes show, claimed that Abrams had been drinking too heavily and threatened to relieve him.

Most astonishing, as Alexander Haig relates in his memoirs, the President told him, now a one-star general, to take over command from Abrams, a four-star commander. What is equally astonishing is that Haig thought about doing so. Fortunately, Secretary Laird intervened and convinced Nixon to calm down and consider the consequences of such a move.

Nixon also derided Admiral Moorer, whom the President claimed had not presented the risks of the operations beforehand. The CJCS, the consummate staff officer, told the President that he had to rely on the commander in the field for such an assessment and was only doing so. Nixon turned to Kissinger and said that Moorer was only a sailor who wanted to look after the Navy and did not have the qualifications to be his military advisor. The only reason that they still needed him, Nixon admitted, was that he was willing to keep matters away from other key members of the government – namely Defense Secretary Laird. Moorer was also willing to send orders from the President to the field commanders bypassing the other Chiefs, and, on occasion not informing Abrams.

Nixon and Kissinger also discussed the need to get Haig, the only military man they trusted and who had ample ambition to do so, over to the Pentagon to oversee the JCS. In short, after this operation, it became apparent that both Nixon and Kissinger would no longer rely on any US military advice from Saigon or Hawaii or, for that matter, from the JCS in Washington on Vietnam.

The Nixon tapes during late 1971 and throughout 1972 show how both the President and his National Security Advisor mistrusted and even loathed their military commanders and advisors. Nixon and Kissinger often used expletives – supposedly learned during their military service – when referring to the military in general or addressing them over some issue. They called certain officers 'sons of bitches' and 'bastards.' Many of these tapes illustrate that both saw themselves as more knowledgeable and capable of applying military strategy and operations. Sometimes they tried to impress one another with their knowledge of military history. Other times they talked about how to use military forces at the tactical level.

Most startling, Nixon often in 1971 and after gave orders on how to move ships and employ airpower. He reminded his senior military advisor that he was Commander-in-Chief. As such, he ran the war. The result was that, as the US military force in Southeast Asia redeployed, any semblance of a US military strategy to end the war disappeared. Nixon and Kissinger, with Haig often transmitting orders or offering feedback from meetings in Saigon, would consult and connive among themselves on how to end it. They disregarded and bypassed their senior military advisors and commanders in the field.

US Diplomacy and 'The Decent Interval'

Up to mid-1971, the President had taken unprecedented military action against North Vietnam's lines of communication and bases outside of South Vietnam. This action was despite the growing domestic disillusionment with the war and gathering opposition in Congress. He had lived up to the persona that he had wanted to portray at home and to the communists abroad. He had been effective in explaining his actions to most of the American public. Despite the radicals in the peace movement or the adversarial press, Nixon continued to be tough and forceful toward communist expansionism in Southeast Asia.

Nixon continued to want his international antagonists to believe he was irrational or unpredictable when it came to the use of power. Despite the occasional distraught over the pressures and continuous resentment toward the Press and anyone who opposed him, he believed he was doing the difficult but right thing as the man in the arena, like his hero Teddy Roosevelt would have done.

However, he and Kissinger were becoming increasingly frustrated with the lack of movement in the secret talks with the North. They also had not much success in their attempts to use the Soviet and China 'cards' to influence those negotiations. Some of this was due to Nixon's offensives in Cambodia and Laos. Some of this, we will see in Chapter 7, is due to the diplomatic efforts of North Vietnam with their allies.

Just after the Lam Son 719 operation, there finally came some breakthroughs with both China and the Soviet Union. In May, the Soviet Union indicated that they were ready to go ahead with improved relations with the US. The carrot that Nixon had offered was an agreement over the Strategic Arms Limitation Talks or SALT. He had also shown that there would be a 'linkage' between any concessions or agreements and 'progress in other areas'- meaning pressure on the North to break the impasse in the negotiations in Paris. On 20 May both the US and Soviets issued statements that they intended to reach an agreement on the SALT, as well as have a summit between their leaders in Moscow in the Spring of 1972.

The renewed SALT discussions, which had formally begun in the fall of 1969, addressed much more than just the limitations on nuclear weapons. They included issues on Berlin, Cuba, and US-Soviet trade. The talks now linked these issues to Soviet pledges to prompt the North Vietnamese to make some meaningful progress on peace in Vietnam. The American negotiators emphasized that the US had already made significant concessions on mutual withdrawal issues and the inclusion of the National Liberation Front in the peace process. The central message was that now was the time for the Soviets to pressure the DRV to become reasonable at the negotiating table.

Because of meaningful talks between American and Soviet diplomats throughout most of 1971, Nixon and the Soviet Premier Brezhnev signed an agreement at a summit in Moscow in May 1972 on the above SALT issues. This agreement formed the basis of the President's new détente policy toward the Soviets. Despite some rough roads ahead, such as the future mining of the Haiphong harbor and a crisis over the interdiction of Soviet supplies to North Vietnam, Nixon obtained an agreement for Soviet pressure on the North in the Paris negotiations.

The US-Soviet SALT talks in mid-1971 also had an impact on US-Chinese relations. The Chinese were leery of the possibility of a new Soviet-American agreement. They felt that the US was taking advantage of the China-Soviet rivalry, which was true. However, they too wanted to lessen the tensions with the West and gain some quid pro quos.

Soon after the SALT talks started, Nixon finally received a response from the Chinese Premier, Chou En-Lai, to a message he had sent in late 1970 suggesting a high-level visit to Peking. This reply showed a willingness to receive a special envoy from the US to discuss fundamental issues between the two countries. The two most pressing for China were its acceptance as the one China nation representative (over Taiwan) at the United Nations and US-China trade relations.

Nixon responded quickly and favorably. The result was a secret meeting first of Kissinger in July, followed in February of the next year by Nixon's visit with Chou and Mao. Nixon announced these exciting diplomatic initiatives during the summer of 1971. They would all be crucial to getting the negotiations with North Vietnam moving in 1972. They would also give a boost to Nixon's reelection in the fall of that year.

Revelations in the Nixon Tapes, secret papers from the Nixon library files, and some State Department papers on the behind the scenes diplomacy and discussions with the Chinese and Soviets are essential to an understanding of what Kissinger and Nixon negotiated with them. These also help in understanding their subsequent discussions with the North Vietnamese, what concessions resulted and why, and how the war ended.

The evidence further reveals some interesting aspects of whether these negotiations and their results reflected Nixon's intent to terminate the war knowing that they may have led to the downfall of the South Vietnamese in what historians have labeled a 'decent interval.' They also disclose how the 1972 US national elections and American troop withdrawals influenced these negotiations and the Paris Peace Treaty in January 1973.

The issue of troop withdrawals was at the center of Kissinger's secret negotiations with the North Vietnamese in Paris and even before. Now they would become center stage, along with the release of US prisoners of war and some concessions so the US could get out of Vietnam.

LBJ's initiatives in late 1968 had established both sides initial views on withdrawals. The US and North Vietnamese had entirely different stands from the onset of talks. The US wanted a cease-fire followed by a mutual withdrawal of all foreign forces. The North called for a total unilateral withdrawal of US forces and the removal of Thieu Government before it would even agree to significant talks on how to end the war.

When Nixon became President, he continued to support the mutual withdrawal argument. Thus, throughout the secret talks between the North's representatives and Kissinger in Paris, both sides continued their hard lines on withdrawal, and the talks could not break through the deadlock on them.

While publicly Nixon continued to support that view, in 1971 he and Kissinger discussed alternatives. There may have been several reasons for this. The need to break the impasse over the withdrawal issue was the primary factor. However, related was the fact that the Administration was now fully committed to the pullout of US forces. As mentioned, as the troop pullout continued in earnest into 1971, Nixon and Kissinger now thought it inevitable that the US public and Congress would argue for its continuance despite what the North did. If that was the case, then holding a hard line on mutual withdrawal did not make sense.

What mattered, however, was the timing of the withdrawal. Kissinger, as Ken Hughes tells it and supported by the tapes and Haldeman diaries, argued that they should consider total withdrawal relative to the 1972 elections. He argued that if a total withdrawal happened before the elections, and the North attacked and defeated the South, then the Congress and the Public would hold Nixon responsible and label him as the first American President to lose a war. So, he recommended to Nixon some interval between the signing of an agreement that called for a US withdrawal and the actual movement of forces out of Vietnam.

Nixon accepted his advisor's argument and reasoning. Discussions turned toward the timing of a full withdrawal, the signing of a treaty, and the potential impact on the South Vietnamese. Kissinger argued that they would need about eighteen months between a unilateral total withdrawal and an inevitable defeat of the South to avoid being blamed for the South's fall.

This eighteen-month period is what some historians refer to as 'a decent interval.' Meanwhile, however, the discussions also show that Nixon felt uneasy about a communist victory over the South. He noted that the complete removal of ground forces in Vietnam still gave him the option to use airpower out of Thailand or other locations to punish Northern aggression and even prevent the South from total defeat.

Nixon then authorized Kissinger to try to break the deadlock in Paris by changing their stance on withdrawals. Accordingly, the National Security Advisor in one of his meetings in Paris in late May 1971 told the North's representatives that the US would drop its insistence on mutual withdrawals. He told him that once they returned all American POWs and agreed to a ceasefire, the US would withdraw all its forces within seven months without demanding a corresponding one from the North. Kissinger also said that the North would have to stop all infiltration once the withdrawal began.

North Vietnam rejected this offer. George Herring states that it was because they did not want to give up their primary bargaining chip- the US POWs. Le Duc Tho, the principal negotiator, countered that they would agree if the US dropped its support for Thieu before any settlement. Kissinger refused. He returned to Washington telling Nixon that he thought that though the North Vietnamese had refused to accept their offer, there was, for the first time, some serious negotiation and perhaps a breakthrough.

Nixon and Kissinger now turned their attention to talks with the Chinese. Their contacts with the Chinese thus far had gained a summer audience between Kissinger and Premier Zhou Enlai. Kissinger was due to fly to China in July 1971 for a first meeting. On June 30, Nixon offered his advisor some guidance. Most of it was for Kissinger to remind the Chinese Premier how tough the President had been on communism in the past, and how he was now using military force as he sought fit "without regards to political considerations" to end the war. Nixon said to tell them that he would further escalate the war if necessary.

Kissinger left several days later. His primary purpose with the Chinese was to play the 'decent interval' card to get their support and pressure on North Vietnam to yield in the negotiations to their reasonable recent proposals. His visit began with a meeting with Zhou in a stately Victorian house on a lake outside of Beijing at 4:30 PM on July 9th.

Ken Hughes account, based on recently released transcripts of the meetings, relates the results. With his briefing notes for his meetings having a notation, "We want a decent interval, Kissinger quickly began dropping hints that a Communist victory [in Vietnam] would not be unacceptable." He then outlined what their proposals for negotiations were and expressed, "somewhat vaguely" that the US hoped that once a ceasefire was in effect that hostilities would not "start again." Most astounding, Kissinger "implied that American intervention would be unlikely, but he didn't rule it out."

As Kissinger explains in his memoirs, their conversation ran several hours into the evening. The National Security Advisor was much impressed with the Premier, who was "one of the two or three most impressive men I have ever met." Zhou then invited Kissinger to dinner. In a lighter conversation during the meal, the American diplomat wrote that he felt that the Communist Chinese leader understood him "without any need for translation."

Afterward, they continued their exchange of views on the war. The National Security Advisor did not address these discussions in his memoirs. Knowing that the Chinese were taping all the conversations, several Americans took notes. These notes are the transcripts in the State papers mentioned earlier.

As Hughes further relates in his book on these negotiations, Kissinger was now most blunt and clear on US intent should an agreement with the North occur. "If the agreement breaks down, then it is possible that the people in Vietnam will fight it out," he acknowledged. "If [the South Vietnamese Government] is overthrown after we withdraw, we will not intervene." Kissinger further offered a timeframe or "period of time" between the ceasefire and the outbreak of further hostilities of "18 months or some period." Though it is not yet clear how the Chinese may or may not have used this information in 1971, the Nixon-Kissinger decent interval policy was now cast and tied to further relations with the Chinese.

After Kissinger returned to the US and informed Nixon of his meetings, on July 15[th,] the President publicly read an announcement of a Chinese invitation to come to China the next year. He said, "I want to put our policy in the clearest possible context. Our action in seeking a new relationship with the People's Republic of China will not be at the expense of our old friends."

Meanwhile, the President and his National Security Advisor continued their talk about how to follow up to the meeting with the Chinese and begin working on how to get their 'decent interval' across to the Soviets. They went to work to suggest a summit between Nixon and Soviet Communist Party Leader General Secretary Brezhnev sometime early next year.

The beginning of 1972 would shine brightly for Nixon's diplomacy and his intent to obtain Soviet-Chinese support and pressure for a reasonable negotiation based on a 'decent interval.' The Soviets had agreed to a summit in late month of May. In February, Nixon went to China. There he had conversations with Mao Zedong.

Nixon warned him about the Soviet build-up of forces along the border. Then he subtlety talked about an end to the war in Vietnam and the need to ensure that all of Indochina does not become a sphere of North Vietnam. This then led to Nixon's remarks about the need for the US to leave Vietnam in a way that would not need its return militarily – a hint of the decent interval solution.

When Nixon returned home, the Press and the Public were all in support of his breakthrough with the Chinese. The President, of course, was mum over the entire sell out of South Vietnam as the means to get China's and later the Soviet Union's support in these breakthrough diplomatic actions.

The Easter Offensive

Though not precisely told of what happened in Kissinger's meetings in China and the behind the scenes preparations for the Soviet summit, the North Vietnamese were very much aware of the discussions between the US and the Chinese and Soviets. They were worried. They had already felt concerned about the rivalry and tension between their two allies, which had developed over the late fifties and had become highly public in the late sixties. The North had had to walk a fine line between pleasing the two since they both had a significant role in their aid in the war of unification.

Now they saw the US trying to influence their allies and bring pressure upon them to make concessions in Paris. As George Herring noted in his book *America's Longest War*, "Chinese and Soviet willingness to talk with the United States evoked from North Vietnamese leaders still bitter memories from Geneva 1954 and angry charges of betrayal." They did not want to have once again to yield to their allies and give up their goal of unification.

Realizing that a decision on the battlefield could preempt any 'deals' between their allies and the US, and encouraged by their victory in Lam Son 719, the DRV launched on 30 March 1972 its most massive offensive of the war. This assault became known in the US as the Spring or Easter Offensive. The communist goal was to defeat militarily the South Vietnamese so that any peace negotiation to end the war unfavorably to them would become impossible. They also thought that even a partial victory would give them further negotiating leverage; especially in a US Presidential election year.

The offensive did not surprise the Nixon Administration. General Abrams had alerted Washington months in advance of the buildup. Nevertheless, like TET 68, they were startled at the size and initial momentum of the attacks. The NVA launched four major assaults. One was across the DMZ and directed toward Hue city. A secondary attack from the A Shau Valley supported it. The second came out of Laos. It focused on the central highland cities of Kontum and Pleiku. The third came from Cambodia. It headed in the direction of Saigon via An Loc. A fourth also came out of the Parrott's Beak area of Cambodia and went into the Delta region of South Vietnam's southernmost provinces.

Overall, the total invasion force numbered over 200,000 regular NVA soldiers in thirteen divisions. The entire offensive was a large-scale conventional attack with armor, heavy artillery, and mechanized infantry. There was no pretense of a Southern guerrilla uprising supporting it.

Initially, the assaults were successful. In one week, the four NVA divisions attacking across the DMV threatened to take Quang Tri City just north of Hue. The attack out of southern Laos met tough resistance but was making good headway toward Kontum. The Cambodian advance quickly took the border town of Loc Ninh. It was approaching An Loc, which was just sixty miles from Saigon. Unlike Lam Son 719, General Abrams was not positive in his reports. After several weeks, he assessed that the ARVN might not be able to defend its principal cities and the "whole thing may be lost."

When the offensive began, Nixon had just returned from his trip to China several weeks before. He was now preparing for his journey to Moscow seven weeks away. The President was not deterred by the possibility of a cancellation of that summit given the circumstances. He and Kissinger knew that a North Vietnamese victory would nullify his diplomatic initiatives and his decent interval solution to the war.

In several meetings with his advisors, Nixon was adamant that "there will be no consideration of restraints." He quickly ordered the massing of air and naval power to defeat the offensive. As a priority, these attacks would target North Vietnam's war-making facilities. He also wanted the supply lines out of China interdicted. Later he would also order the mining of Haiphong Harbor.

Nixon did not worry about the domestic reaction. He knew that the survival of the South and his political future were at stake. The President had also seen several polls that showed the public would support massive bombing and other military measures against the North primarily to stop them from seizing South Vietnam and make the return of POWs more problematic than it already was.

He was also not waiting for the advice of his military commanders. He was the Commander-in-Chief and was now exercising that authority by directly controlling operational decisions. He announced to all that unlike Johnson in 1968, he had the "will" and would take "whatever steps are necessary" to end the war.

Admiral Moorer and the JCS felt elated that the handcuffs were now off. They poured themselves into the massing of US air and naval power in Southeast Asia and bringing that military power to bear on North Vietnam and its forces.

However, the personal directions of the President soon contradicted Abrams schemes to thwart the ground attacks in South Vietnam. Nixon wanted the main effort to target the Northern attack across the DMV. He also wanted to attack North Vietnam's ability to sustain the effort from its homeland, and the supply lines and facilities of its leading supporters. Abrams needed to mass airpower against the threats to Pleiku and Saigon.

Abrams threatened to resign. Nixon wanted to fire him. Cooler heads prevailed. Secretary Laird smoothed the ruffles for Abrams. He pleaded with Nixon to rethink his desire to fire his Commander in Vietnam at such a crucial time.

On May 8, as the battles raged in the South and their overall outcomes still in question, Nixon announced to the American people his steps of a sustained bombing campaign of North Vietnam and the mining of Haiphong Harbor. Initially, there was a tremendous outcry from the antiwar leaders, along with a wave of protests in major US cities. The Congress also reacted negatively with calls to end funding for the war. The overall public support, as usual for a crisis of this proportion and for a President willing to step up to it, was supportive. Nixon's approval rating shot up.

With the apparent support of many Americans and with no significant Congressional move to inhibit military action, Nixon's aggressive attitude skyrocketed. As LBJ had done over Khe Sanh, he began to daily track all military actions. He took an interest in the aggressive air campaign now underway against the North. He was not satisfied with that effort – often attacking the courage and determination of the military commanders in charge.

It is at this time that he issued an extraordinary order. As Tim Weiner recounts in his biography of Nixon, *One Man Against the World*, he told Kissinger, "I have decided to take the command of all strikes in North Vietnam in the Hanoi–Haiphong area out from under any Air Force jurisdiction whatever.... I want you to convey my utter disgust to Moorer which he in turn can pass on to the Chiefs... It is time for these people either to shape up or get out." Soon after, "the president boarded Air Force One, bound for Moscow, where he would drink toasts and sign treaties with the men who were arming his enemies."

Meanwhile, both China and the Soviet Union were careful and cautious in their opposition to the US military moves. The Soviets did not cancel the Moscow summit. In fact, with the full brunt of airpower now attacking the North, Nixon went to Moscow. While Brezhnev and his foreign minister Gromyko urged restraint on the bombing, they were sympathetic to Nixon's and Kissinger's explanation of what they hoped to achieve with his decent interval scheme. Months later, both the Soviets and Chinese urged Hanoi to compromise with the US in the negotiations.

By late May as the Soviet Summit was ending, ARVN forces, with massive tactical air support and US advisors' help, halted the NVA assaults. Major operations ended in June. The sustained bombing operations, both against the North (called LINEBACKER) and against the lines of communication supporting the operations into South Vietnam, were highly effective. They significantly contributed to the halt of the North's offensive. They were mainly so because the North was fighting a conventional war with corresponding dependence on fuel and ammunition. That required transportation on roads and storage at depots, which were much more susceptible to aerial interdiction than the primitive means supporting unconventional forces and methods used before.

Although the primary offensive ended, fighting continued unabated in the South. The South tried to win back some lost territory. The North continued to develop more base areas next to the borders and build up supplies and reinforcements for the war that was to continue regardless of the outcome of the Paris negotiations. The US bombing campaign went on until October. Unfortunately, according to the JCS, Nixon called off the high-intensity bombing effort that Moorer insisted could have brought the North to its knees without a negotiated settlement.

George Herring's assessment of these events is worth noting. "In the final analysis, the ferocious campaigns of the summer of 1972 merely raised the stalemate to a new level of violence. Both sides endured huge losses—the North Vietnamese suffered an estimated 100,000 casualties, and the South Vietnamese lost as many as 30,000 killed, 78,000 wounded, and 14,000 missing in action—but neither emerged appreciably stronger.... North Vietnam had exposed ARVN's continued vulnerability, gained a sizable slice of territory along the Laotian and Cambodian borders that would be important in its final offensive, and retained sizable troops in the South. The NLF scored some major gains in the Mekong Delta. But Hanoi had again badly miscalculated the U.S. response."

There were two critical outcomes – both favorable to Nixon. First, in July the North returned to the negotiating table. They had refused to meet after their last meeting in May as the Northern offensive was ongoing. They had waited to see if results on the battlefield would give them the leverage they needed to end the war on their terms. Urged on by their allies, the DRV participants now indicated that they were willing to move forward earnestly toward a compromise settlement. So much, that in October Kissinger announced, prematurely as it turned out, "peace is at hand."

Then in November, Nixon won a resounding victory over the Democratic peace candidate, George McGovern, to gain a second term as President. His reelection gave him the boost and confidence he needed to continue with his actions. Nixon now felt confident about his use of military force to bring the North to their senses. He also thought that if the North seriously violated any agreement that they reached on ending the war and that threatened the South's existence, he could continue to use air power to punish them. This is what some historians have labeled Nixon's 'Permanent War' approach to solving the Vietnam conundrum and obtaining his 'Peace with Honor.'

Paris Peace Negotiations, The Treaty, and the End for the United States

The inconclusive Easter Offensive, coupled with the Soviet and Chinese encouragements to compromise on their peace agenda, brought the North Vietnamese back in July 1972 to the negotiating table in Paris and secret talks between their envoys and Dr. Kissinger. Up to this point, after four years of negotiation, there had been 174 formal and eighteen secret meetings. The diplomats had settled nothing of substance.

Now, the LINEBACKER bombings and the interdiction of its primary port and routes of supply had severely hurt the Democratic Republic of Vietnam. Their forces in the South were hurt and needed to regroup. Their Allies had indicated that they should begin to listen to US terms for a settlement and respond accordingly. The Communist Politburo was ready to negotiate seriously. However, it still had an agenda that would give them the upper hand in that negotiation.

Three key issues were confronting the consultations in mid-summer 1972. The first was who would take part in the negotiations and the transition to a final settlement. The second involved the nature of the military ceasefire and the presence of Northern forces in South Vietnam and its neighbors. The third was the disposition of all prisoners of war and detainees.

As mentioned, Nixon and Kissinger had already backed off its position for a mutual withdrawal of forces. They had agreed, primarily influenced by the negotiations and results with the Soviets and Chinese explained above, to allow a considerable number of NVA forces to remain in South Vietnam. Now the DRV wanted not only to confirm this position but also wanted to have the additional forces and territories from its recent offensive included. Kissinger agreed to this. It would seal the fate of South Vietnam.

The DRV had, up to this point, refused to negotiate any peace agreement if President Thieu was in power. They also had wanted a coalition government formed before a final settlement. They, furthermore, wanted to approve the makeup of that coalition, which could not include any members of the current Saigon 'clique,' but would include representatives from the Southern Communists.

The North Vietnamese now said that it would drop its demands for Thieu's removal and a coalition government. In the latter's stead, it wanted an independent organization to oversee the transition to a final settlement. This latter organization, called the National Council of Reconciliation or NCR, would consist of the Saigon regime, a group of neutralists, and a new organization called the Provisional Revolutionary Government (PRG), which was the old NLF. The PRG was supposedly representative of the southern insurgents but controlled by the North.

Finally, the DRV now agreed to return all US POWs forty-five days after a cease-fire. They also dropped their demand for the release of all the communist cadre personnel in South Vietnamese jails, over ten thousand overall, before final settlement negotiations. For the North, as we will see in the chapters ahead, dropping the release of the communist prisoners would fit into their post-war intent to seize control of the government structure in the south, without resistance from the original southern communist leadership, many of whom were among those in captivity in southern jails.

After all his time and effort to reach an agreement, Kissinger felt elated when the North Vietnamese chief negotiator, Le Duc Tho, provided him with a written document explaining the new positions. Kissinger agreed to these new points and indicated to Tho that they would be acceptable for a peace treaty between the US and the DRV. He then went to Saigon to brief President Thieu. After Saigon, he returned to Washington to discuss with President Nixon.

Kissinger underestimated the reaction of the South Vietnamese President and his advisors. As chronicled in Dr. Larry Berman's *No Peace, No Honor*, when the National Security Advisor explained the new provisions to Thieu and his advisors they vehemently objected. They brought to his attention several significant differences between the English version and the Vietnamese. Most of all Thieu said that acceptance of NVA forces in South Vietnam would mean the defeat of his Government and eventually lead to a North Vietnamese victory.

Nixon was sympathetic to Thieu's situation and his concerns over the draft accord. In several messages, the President assured the South Vietnam leader that should the North violate the agreement and conduct military operations, he would retaliate against them just as he had recently done during their Easter Offensive. He then instructed a reluctant and now demoralized Kissinger to return to Paris and present Thieu's concerns to the North Vietnamese.

In the meantime, as mentioned, Nixon had won a resounding victory as President. He beat McGovern in the popular vote by 60.7 percent to 37.5 percent. Nixon was sure that this would provide him with the power to end the Vietnam War. Dr. Berman argues that it provided him with the confidence to continue his punishment of the North Vietnamese if they did not abide by the peace accords – the so-called 'Permanent War' interpretation. Ken Hughes and others argue that Nixon was content with his 'decent interval' approach.

Kissinger returned to Paris at the end of November. He presented the South Vietnamese issues. The North Vietnam negotiators were unyielding in their opposition to any changes. In fact, now Le Duc Tho revived their call to remove Thieu before agreeing to any accord. Kissinger returned to Washington in early December and met with a furious Nixon, who felt that his chief negotiator had erred grievously in not getting an agreement between the North and South.

The President now contemplated a renewal of the bombing of the North. He asked Laird for sensing support from Congress. The Secretary said there would be none. This reflected the Gallop polls. The American public wanted nothing more than to end the conflict. 60 percent thought sending US troops to Vietnam had been a mistake. Moreover, at the end of November, 47 percent thought the South would never be able to resist a communist takeover after a withdrawal.

Nevertheless, over the Christmas holiday, Nixon ordered the renewal of the bombing of the North. This campaign was the most devastating of the war. LINEBACKER II dropped about 20,000 tons of bombs. B-52s bombed Hanoi and Haiphong continuously. The North ran out of surface to air missiles. While they protested the bombings much more than in LINEBACKER I, the Soviets and Chinese still pressured the North to return to the peace talks. Despite the overall American domestic adverse reaction to the bombings, the peace talks resumed.

Notwithstanding Saigon's continued view that the settlement was a 'surrender,' Nixon instructed Kissinger to agree to "almost any settlement" that he could get to end the war. Meanwhile, he reiterated to Thieu his secret pledge to use force if the North Vietnamese violated it. The North's negotiators knew that an agreement that left their soldiers in the South would only be a temporary truce, despite how the US leaders peddled it to their public. They also surmised that Nixon would not have the political power to renew the use of force such as what the President unleashed over Christmas. Thus, in their view, agreeing to this settlement was not a surrender. To the contrary, they now thought it would lead to victory.

On 23 January 1973, Nixon announced on national TV that he had reached an agreement with the North. It was the 'Peace with Honor,' he had promised. The Administration never gave the agreement to the Senate for approval. It would not become a ratified 'treaty.' Thus, the agreement was not a 'law of the land.' Congress had no obligation to assure its future.

Watergate and the End for South Vietnam

The 1973 Paris "Agreement Ending the War and Restoring Peace in Vietnam" was only a peace settlement on paper. Weeks after the signing, the North and South were battling over areas for their control. The US media asked Kissinger about the fighting that was still taking place. He said, "they have been fighting for over twenty-five years" and that the "necessary pressure could be brought to bear to maintain the peace." That 'necessary pressure' from Nixon's pledge to Thieu to use force was never 'brought to bear.'

By the end of 1973, all known US prisoners of war had returned. US combat forces had withdrawn from South Vietnam. For a while, Nixon and Kissinger reveled in their success. Kissinger received the Nobel Peace Prize for his role in the treaty. His counterpart, Le Duc Tho, refused his prize rightfully saying that peace had not yet occurred.

That summer, Congress further asserted itself in attempts to ensure that the President would be unable to use US military forces in South Vietnam. In June, the Congress passed the Case-Church Amendment. It prohibited further US military actions in Indochina unless the President obtained Congressional approval in advance. Previously defeated a year earlier, this time it had received the necessary votes in both chambers to override a Presidential veto.

Ken Hughes argues that Nixon deliberately did not try to mobilize Republicans to vote against the bill. It is an interesting claim, but difficult to prove. Toward the end of the year, North Vietnam stepped up its military activities in the South in preparation for another major offensive. Nixon could do nothing. President Thieu decreed that the Paris Peace Accord was no longer in effect.

Despite his success in getting the US out of the war, Nixon's obsession to rid himself of his perceived antagonists, both political and media, continued. The release of *The Pentagon Papers* to the public in 1971 had incensed Nixon. He had 'The Plumbers' group of ex-CIA and FBI aides break in and search the office of Daniel Ellsberg, the Government official who had given them to the *New York Times*, to discredit him.

It is this group that later broke into the Democratic National Committee office at the Watergate complex in downtown DC. The so-called Watergate Affair, which dragged on for more than a year, led to Nixon's resignation on the 9th August 1974. Soon after, Congress drastically cut aid to South Vietnam.

A couple of months later, the North Vietnamese Politburo planned a major offensive to capture large areas in the South's central highland region. Then on 10 March 1975, they launched an attack against Ban Me Thuot in the Central Highlands. This was 'to test the waters' for an all-out assault later. They wanted to see what the US response would be.

ARVN forces, down to several artillery rounds a day, without air support and suffering from desertions, soon collapsed. Gone was the fierce resistance that they had been able to put up in the 1972 Easter Offensive with American support. The NVA, again with tanks and heavy artillery in a conventional attack, soon began to have other successes.

What started as a limited attack grew into the general offensive the North Vietnamese had sought several times before. This final offensive overwhelmed a demoralized ARVN. Weeks after the NVA main attack, the South Vietnamese Government resigned and fled the country. President Thieu declared that the US had betrayed the country. He said, "It is so easy to be an enemy of the United States, but so difficult to be a friend." He then quickly left for Taiwan.

By the end of April, the NVA had encircled Saigon. South Vietnamese civilians, particularly government officials and others who had supported the US, panicked. The US Ambassador had delayed the US evacuation to try to avoid such a panic. Now, with a hundred thousand NVA soldiers surrounding the city and about to attack, he finally gave the evacuation order.

Thousands of Vietnamese tried to get out on American evacuation helicopters. There was not enough time or helicopters to evacuate all who deserved to be. Numerous loyal to the US were left behind and incarcerated in 're-education camps.' Many of those died or just disappeared.

As it had become clear that the NVA offensive could decisively defeat the South, now President Gerald Ford, who had become Nixon's second term Vice-President, tried to get Congress to pass emergency funding to shore up the situation. He failed. Ford on the 23rd of April declared an end to the war for the US. Of course, it had already ended. We were just picking up the pieces. In a version of the speech handed to him by aides, he crossed out the words 'honorable' end to the conflict.

On April 30th, after the Americans had completed their hasty evacuation from the US Embassy roof, NVA units overwhelmed the last fragments of resistance in Saigon. A solitary tank broke through the gates of the South Vietnamese Independence Palace and raised the Viet Cong flag. The victors renamed Saigon, Ho Chi Minh City. The war was over.

Section 5.4 – Personal Experiences, Observations, and Insights for Chapter 5

This section provides some personal experiences of the author's service in Vietnam during the first year of Nixon's presidency, and some observations and insights on the events and commentary in this chapter.

Personal Experiences

When Nixon took the oath of President on 20 January 1969, I was in Germany assigned to the 1st Battalion, 509th Infantry (Airborne). A month previously I had written a letter to my assignment officer in Washington, DC asking when I would get orders for Vietnam. Right after Nixon's inaugural, I received a response. The letter ordered me to report to duty there on 15 April.

When I got to Vietnam in April, there was 543,400 US military personnel there - the peak of our military strength in country. There was no talk or hint at peace with honor or any withdrawal of forces. From my reception and training area at Bien Hoa, I flew via Chinook Helicopter to my assignment – 3rd Battalion, 506th Infantry (Air Assault), 101st Airborne Division. The unit - about 550 men of average age 22 of whom 67% were white and about the same number volunteers - was located at a base called LZ Betty some hundred miles northeast of Saigon.

Three days later I was flying on a troop Huey helicopter and dropped in an area where I would join 30 other American soldiers as their Platoon Leader. "Welcome to the Nam, LT," my new platoon sergeant greeted me with a look that I never forgot – 'another new lieutenant who will get us all killed!' About a third of this infantry platoon soldiers had already been wounded at least once.

I was finally accepted as their leader after I had demonstrated that I would not get them killed – only the NVA and VC in the area would do that. I acclimated as well. I joined the 'Grunt Brotherhood' after I had seen the prerequisite number of dead bodies, had killed an enemy soldier, and showed that I would not order them to do anything I would not first do.

The day that Nixon announced the first increment of 25 thousand American soldiers to withdraw from Vietnam (June 8th) the NVA in our area of operations attacked my unit's night position. We all survived. There were four wounded. We recovered a half dozen enemy bodies and gleefully reported six enemy Killed in Actions or KIAs. Chalk up a win in Vietnam. Another body count closer to going home.

I served six weeks as a platoon leader before my battalion commander assigned me as a company commander, where I served another six months in charge of over 100 grunts. Then someone picked me to join the division headquarters group near Phu Bai, up in the northernmost province of South Vietnam. It was there that I got a real sense of what might be happening in the war in 1969. By then the strength of US soldiers in Vietnam had dropped to about 500,000.

My position at the headquarters brought me in contact with several senior officers serving in Vietnam at the time. I got to meet General Abrams, the MACV commander; Lieutenant General Melvin Zais, who was the US Corps commander; and Major General Wright, who was the Division

Commander in that area. On several occasions, I listened to them discuss the situation in Vietnam – particularly the withdrawal of US forces under Nixon's Vietnamization policy.

As I recall these conversations, those Generals had major concerns about the withdrawal plan and its impact on further combat operations. The one issue that was been particularly relevant to the 101st generals was the continued use of base areas in Laos and NVA infiltration routes into the northern provinces of South Vietnam. All of them worried that as the withdrawals continued, the ability of US forces to interdict NVA infiltration through the A Shau Valley and the potential threat to Hue would become at high risk. This was almost three years before the North's major offensive in 1972 that would use these approaches to Hue to seize major cities in the 101st Airborne's area of operations. The 101st would not be there to make any difference.

I heard these Generals discussing the long-term withdrawal plan that Abrams' staff had drafted. That plan had several options for the withdrawal schedule. The options went from the removal of a small number of units to a modest one to a 'worst case' option. The latter was a course that the commanders feared the most.

When Nixon made another announcement of a second withdrawal of 60 thousand troops in December 1969, it was clear that the Administration was intent on the more accelerated schedule. All the Generals thought that this choice was not only imprudent, but that it would lead to defeat in Vietnam.

They also discussed the impact that the withdrawal would have on the first line soldiers – the 'grunt' infantrymen. These officers had fought in World War Two. It was evident listening to them that they were dismayed over the President's intent to withdraw combat troops from Vietnam regardless of the situation.

I recall General Zais, who had parachuted into Italy and France in World War Two, saying that the soldiers would certainly know that America's leaders were not willing to win in Vietnam. He emphasized that this would undoubtedly affect their morale and willingness to fight for a 'lost cause.'

Personally, I knew from my experience that infantry 'grunts' did not care about the 'cause'. All they wanted was to survive and get home regardless of any President's or General's desire to win. I was one of the fortunate grunts. I survived and returned to the 'world' in mid-March 1970. It was a month earlier than expected because of the withdrawal demands of the President.

The Army assigned me to Fort Benning, Georgia upon my return. There I trained Army Ranger volunteers who would be filling the important Long-Range Reconnaissance units in Vietnam. The Generals would be relying on these units more than ever now. They would be the soldiers who would patrol the infiltration routes and potential assembly areas for NVA units threatening South Vietnam's population centers during the US pullout.

I left this assignment after a year and went to the Infantry Officers Advanced Course at Benning. There I studied how Army organizations at the battalion (about 600 soldiers) and brigade (multiple battalions) levels would fight the next war – on the plains of Europe and against the Soviet Army. It was if the Army was already hoping that it could erase the Vietnam experience and get on with preparing for a war that it would be 'comfortable' fighting!

As that school ended in July 1971, regardless of what we had studied, many of us expected to return to Vietnam. Due to the Administration's withdrawal program, most of us did not return. I went on to Fort Lewis, Washington to command one of the new volunteer Army units there.

Observations and Insights

Historians have and will continue to argue about which one of the US presidents was most responsible for our commitment to the defense of South Vietnam and its failure. As Chapter 1 depicted, Truman certainly initiated this undertaking. He then increased its military component after the Communist takeover of China and the Korean War.

Eisenhower continued the aid that Truman had begun. However, he also declared that if the Asian communists took over South Vietnam, then the rest of Southeast Asia would follow. IKE's 'Domino Theory' thus extended the importance of South Vietnam and in so doing make it a vital interest of the national security of the US.

As we saw in Chapter 2, JFK inherited this commitment and reinforced the importance of South Vietnam to US security policy. He did so by saying that it had, in the early sixties, become a testing ground for the containment of a new and emerging communist means to expand – support for wars of national liberation. Kennedy sought to find a way to counter this new communist way of expansion by introducing counterinsurgency doctrine and forces. In so doing, he raised the ante of US commitment to Indochina by introducing the first combat troops to the conflict there.

LBJ was the reluctant recipient of his predecessors' policies and commitments. As we saw in Chapter 3, he further inherited the results of JFK's failed counterinsurgent approach. He also inherited the architects of not only Kennedy's doctrine, but their belief and faith in limited war through the gradual application of military force. Initially, ignorant and unable to grasp international and strategic concepts, he bought into their gradualism approach because it would not interfere with his main domestic programs. He chose war on the cheap.

Johnson's military advisors were unable or unwilling to convince or cajole him on an alternative course. His field commander, neither by nature bold or willing to disagree, failed to provide his President with a viable alternative to just "killing more VC" as LBJ had told his military to do in 1965. His senior military advisor, schooled in numbers and staff processes, attempted first to scare him and then persuade him to throw more military force into the situation without any reasoning for doing so. By 1967, the war was a stalemate. In 1968, his opponent achieved a political triumph. LBJ - distraught over the opposition to the war, haunted by stories of failure, gloom, and defeat, and unsure of himself - folded and resigned.

Enter Richard Nixon on this stage. So where does he fit in this saga? How was he like his predecessors? How was he not?

While Nixon appeared devoted to an eventual negotiated and honorable course to end the war, he was not the reluctant warrior that LBJ had been. Speaking of ending the war and implying it would be through a masterful, statesman-like approach, he was intent at first to pursue a military solution to impose his will upon his enemy. He had to. He had already shared in the US commitment to contain communism there. Indeed, he had led the way.

In fact, Jeffrey Kimball in his book, *Nixon's Vietnam War*, shows how Nixon had played a crucial and a continued role in the American commitment to stem communism in Vietnam. He says that throughout the fifties and early sixties, "Nixon advocated policies that drew the United States more deeply into the quagmire of Vietnam." Indeed, of all the five Presidents who had a role in the US commitment to South Vietnam, Nixon had been and continued to be the most adamant to end it on favorable terms to the US. He wanted to be the one President who would not hesitate to impose his will upon the enemy and be able to do so.

Therefore, it should not be surprising that Nixon at first tried to win the war militarily. Most of the evidence shows that he intended from the beginning of his Presidency to do that through a combination of diplomatic and military moves. This consisted of détente with the Soviets, and recognition of and cooperation with China. That would bring pressure to bear on North Vietnam to negotiate a meaningful peace. He saw himself as a practitioner of the balance of power, realpolitik international affairs. Therefore, he knew that diplomacy would not just work against a military opponent without the corresponding pressure of the use of force.

Militarily, Nixon wanted to launch massive attacks against the supply routes and bases of North Vietnam. That, coupled with a more intense bombing of the North later, would bring military pressures to offer further leverage in the negotiations. Nixon's military actions also would gain time for the Vietnamization of the war – that is, turn the fighting over to an improved South Vietnamese Armed Forces that could resist and even prevent communist domination of the South.

Overall, this strategy made eminent good sense. However, it was dependent on time to improve the South's military forces. Most importantly, it would also depend on support from a war-weary American public and Congress to give that time.

Nixon's Vietnamization policy was also a way of convincing the public and Congress to give the time for it to work. Nixon calculated that turning the fighting over to a capable South Vietnamese military and reducing American casualties would be an acceptable solution to the American public and Congress. Proof of a successful Vietnamization policy, moreover, was the actual withdrawal of American ground forces. Thus, in this overall strategic scheme of winning the war, American public support depended on the pullout of American troops from Vietnam.

While this appeared to be a workable strategic policy, there were four critical factors that this policy was dependent upon. One was the ability of the South Vietnamese Armed Forces to take over the mantle of combat from US forces effectively. A second was the viability of military actions to disrupt the North's support of the war in the South. The third was the will of the North Vietnamese to negotiate a peace that would enable a divided Vietnam. The fourth was the ability to gain support from the Congress and the public. The Nixon Administration was unable to achieve the first and second. Thus, it could not successfully affect the third and fourth.

As a result, Nixon came to recognize that the best that he could do was to show the semblance of success. Hence, the withdrawal of US forces was on a schedule that was not dependent on the success of Vietnamization. Indeed, post-TET 68 operations like Lam Son 719 and The Easter Offensive, demonstrated, despite the political rhetoric otherwise, that Vietnamese forces were unable to fight without US support.

US military actions against the routes of infiltration eventually became constrained by Congress and hence limited in both time and scope. Consequently, the US could not affect Northern infiltration into the South. It even grew. US policymakers restricted their attacks against the North to air and naval activities and limited them until 1972. Hence the North did not seriously negotiate until it became apparent that it would gain the advantage that would guarantee an eventual takeover of the South. The American Congress and the public just ran out of patience.

Nixon's 'Peace with Honor" turned out to be neither peaceful nor honorable. The evidence - mainly the Presidential tapes as well as recent documentation in the Foreign Relations series - indicates that both Nixon and Kissinger recognized that they could not win the war nor the peace on favorable terms. They acknowledged that the price they had to pay to obtain a signed settlement would lead to the demise of the South Vietnamese independent state.

Thus, those who argue that all that Nixon and Kissinger wanted was a 'decent interval' of the appearance of a viable peace before the treaty broke down are right, at least after his attempt to force the North to the negotiating table and obtain a favorable agreement failed. What honor exists in such a sell-out to those Vietnamese that had died to protect their families and perhaps someday create a life free from subjugation?

The Nixon-Kissinger method for making national security policy exhibited similarities and differences from the previous administrations. It suffered from the same weaknesses. More openly distrustful of government bureaucracies, the Nixon-Kissinger process was also a closed one. While Nixon and Kissinger announced the use of a more formal national security apparatus, they formed a small organization located in the White House. It excluded relevant Cabinet members and the JCS advisors. Also, Nixon and Kissinger were not open to debate, even from members of their inner circle in the White House.

The Nixon Tapes show that in conversations between Nixon and Kissinger or Nixon, Kissinger, and other White House inner circle officials such as Haig, the President often dominated them. Many of the transcripts of the tapes show how most officials often ingratiated themselves to the President. The atmosphere portrayed in these tapes was one in which the advisors – particularly Kissinger, Moorer, and Haig – told the President what he wanted to hear and seldom disagreed with him.

Nixon's and Kissinger's relationship with their military advisors and commanders suffered from the same misunderstandings and lack of trust as did Kennedy's and Johnson's. While their memoirs were full of praise for the military, the taped conversations and remarks were much less flattering, very critical, and full of disdain for their military commanders and advisors.

They thought that Moorer was only good enough to understand what the Navy did. However, found him useful to send their orders, often by-passing the military chain of command. As a CJCS, he was also an unquestioning servant. They lost trust in Abrams, especially after Lam Son 719. As mentioned, Nixon wanted to relieve him, but Laird said it would further enrage those who opposed Nixon's conduct of the war.

Both Nixon and Kissinger over-relied on their only trusted military man. They relied on Haig, who was a junior officer when he took over his position, to provide them with views and critiques that he was hardly able to do. Yes, he was an experienced and brave soldier in the field. But his experience and know-how of national security matters and high command were limited.

The fact that Haig freely gave his criticisms of the field commander – General Abrams – and was listened to without question was extraordinary. That Nixon wanted Haig to take over Abrams command is equally astonishing. The fact that, per his memoirs, Haig thought he could perform better than Abrams is even more amazing. Clearly, Nixon and Kissinger did not understand the military's culture, which contributed to their disregard for it. Moreover, Haig's actions show his ambitions surpassed his sense of duty to his profession and the nation.

Finally, Nixon, like his predecessors, continually misread his opponents. He underestimated their will and determination for a military solution to the war. Thus, despite his willingness to conduct operations in those areas that had afforded the North sanctuary, these operations were too limited in scope or lacked the requisite combat power to make a difference in imposing conditions that would force the North to negotiate.

Indeed, one primary constant throughout each Administration's policy and actions toward the conflict in South Vietnam and Indochina was that they did not know their enemy. They thought that US actions would decide the course of the war. They ignored the fact that in armed conflict the enemy has a vote.

Thus, to understand the US failure in South Vietnam, we must turn our attention to the enemy. Who were the main leaders making the decisions to employ military might to achieve their aims to unify Vietnam? How did they wage their war for reunification? What were their means to do so? What were their vulnerabilities? What were their strengths? What would have forced them to end the war in a way that could have been favorable to the US? Knowing your enemy is the subject of the next two chapters. How the North Vietnam Communists used their strengths to overcome their adversaries is the main topic that they address. In doing so these chapters will provide insights on how North Vietnam won and the US lost the war.

Chapter 6: Know Your Enemy

Two great theorists of war, Thucydides and Clausewitz, remind us in their writings that war is a conflict of human wills and emotions between two or more parties seeking to impose their views upon one another using force. Thus, to be successful in war, in terms of another theorist, Sun Tzu, you must 'know your enemy as yourself.'

Yet the history of the US involvement in Vietnam is full of criticisms and examples of how much senior American decision makers either did not know about their enemy or how much they misunderstood or misjudged them. The next two chapters explain who the key North Vietnamese leaders were and how they sought to conduct their war of independence and unification. The purpose is to gain an appreciation of how these communist leaders took into consideration their opponents capabilities, strengths, and weaknesses, and devised a strategy to defeat them.

This chapter begins with a description of the geography, history, and culture of Vietnam, which American decision makers largely disregarded. It then describes two of the best known of the Northern Vietnamese leaders – Ho Chi Minh and Vo Nguyen Giap. It explains their experiences, motives, and decisions in their struggle for independence and ultimate unification of Vietnam. The narrative further elucidates their policies and strategies to reach those goals before their major confrontation with the US. The chapter concludes with some observations on how the US leadership in their pursuit of the policies and strategies explained in the earlier chapters ignored at their peril the experiences of these two leaders in their struggle against France.

Section 6.1 – The Geopolitics of Vietnam

Geopolitics is the study of the effects of geography (human and physical) on international politics and relations. Most scholars of international relations, to include those who focus on conflict as a form of those relations, view geopolitics as relevant to their study as a doctor's knowledge of anatomy to surgery.

Most major American policymakers knew nothing of the geopolitics of Southeast Asia, much less Vietnam. Robert McNamara admits in his *In Retrospect*, that he "did not understand or appreciate Vietnam's history, language, culture or values." He further states that neither did "President Kennedy, Secretary of State Dean Rusk, National Security Advisor McGeorge Bundy, military advisor Maxwell Taylor, and many others. When it came to Vietnam, we found ourselves setting policy for a region that was terra incognita."

This section, therefore, begins with an explanation of the geopolitical backdrop of Vietnam and its possible influence on the behavior and decisions of its leaders. It is my firm belief that this can lead to a better understanding of what happened during the war and furnish further insights into why and how the US lost the war and North Vietnam won it.

Vietnam Geography

Vietnam is part of the Southeast Asia region. Geographers describe this region as consisting of the countries that are south of China, east of India, west of New Guinea and north of Australia. They also further divide the region into 'mainland' and 'maritime' portions. The former entails modern-day Cambodia, Laos, Vietnam, Myanmar (formerly known as Burma), Thailand, and West Malaysia. The latter contains East Malaysia, Singapore, Indonesia, and the Philippines.

The region encompasses almost two million square miles. It is a very diverse area; made up of all kinds of flora, terrain, climates, and peoples. The Javanese are the largest ethnic group, mostly concentrated in Java and Indonesia. In Myanmar, the Burmese account for more than two-thirds of the ethnic stock in this country, while ethnic Thais and Vietnamese account for about four-fifths of the respective populations of those countries. The most substantial religious group in the region is Islam; other religions consist of Buddhism, Hinduism, Confucianism, Catholicism, and a group of localized religious affiliations.

This region is important from a global perspective because of its principal sea lines of communication that run between Europe, the Middle East, East Asia seaports and the Northeast Asian region of Japan and Korea. Those lanes traverse the northern portions of the Indian Ocean through the Malaccan Straights into the South China, Java, and Philippine Seas. Southeast Asia also has key resources for commerce and industry; including rice, forestry products, fisheries, rubber, tin, tungsten, iron ore, oil, and gas.

Vietnam occupies a strategically unique position in this region. On the eastern side of the Indochina peninsula, it runs from the Chinese border south to the Gulf of Thailand. As a coastal country, it sits astride the eastern part of the mainland sub-region and affords access to the maritime portion. The extensive coastline that runs about three thousand miles also provides harbors along the seafaring route in the South China Sea toward the eastern coast of China.

This unique position appealed to western colonial powers in the nineteenth century seeking maritime access to the east and Chinese resources, consumers via South Asia and the Middle East, and other areas of the West Pacific region. For these reasons the French would later call Vietnam their "balcony to the Pacific." Today that position remains important. Vietnam geopolitically offers land and coastal areas that can serve as important bases in disputes over ownership of valuable resources in the adjoining oceans and seas.

Traditionally the Vietnamese have viewed their country as distinctly divided into three portions – North, Center, and South. The northern part (known as Tonkin to the French) consists of the highlands of the north and the Red River Delta. The main population center is Hanoi. There is a major harbor at Haiphong. The center (also known as Annam) consists of the central highlands and a narrow and long coastal area. The ancient capital of Hue and the major harbor city of Da Nang is located here. The southern area (called Cochinchina) consists primarily of a lowland area that includes the principal city of Saigon (now Ho Chi Minh City) and in its southern extremity the Mekong River Delta.

William Duiker, one of the most renowned scholars on Vietnam, says that it is common among the Vietnamese people to see their country as analogous to a long shoulder pole that carries two rice baskets. This seems like a perfect analogy because the Red River and Mekong River Deltas in the northern and southern extremities of the country are the richest rice-producing regions, while the 'pole' that connects these two areas is narrow and its proximity to the sea makes fishing and maritime trade a vital part of the overall economy of the area.

Whereas water and rice paddies inundate much of the 'basket' rice areas, another striking feature of the geography of Vietnam is the mountainous regions. In the north, there is a range of mountains that is the source of the water for the Red River. These mountains can serve as a barrier to the northern border with China. With the many streams, caves, and dense vegetation it can also function as a refuge for any group or armed force that seeks protection or to avoid detection.

Along the western side of the 'long pole,' there is a range of mountains that primarily define the border between Laos and Vietnam. This range runs southeast looking like a protracted spike and ending with its continuation into the central region of Vietnam. While the mountains can serve as a natural barrier, they also have numerous valleys and streams that flow from the north and west to the south and east. These natural geographic avenues allow for concealed movement between the North and West to the South and East of Vietnam.

The most dominant feature of this 'pole' is the Central Highlands. The vegetation there varies. At the foothills of the highlands and extending to the lowland areas, there can be a mixture of bamboo, ferns, palms, and tall elephant grasses. Along the peaks of its surrounding mountains, one can find a triple canopy of large trees, smaller trees, tall shrubs, and climbing vines typical of tropical rain forests. In some areas, there are also large plateaus with tropical grasslands. Peoples, or Armies, moving through the mountainous areas from the west reach these highlands, can then move quickly to the eastern coast and control, or block any movements from the south to the north.

Finally, in the southern part of Vietnam, there is also a mountain massif southwest of Nha Trang and northeast of Saigon (or today known as Ho Chi Minh City). Much like the other mountainous tropical forest areas, it is ideal for concealing small settlements and potential military base areas.

From these peoples or armies can easily access any populated or rice growing regions near and in the Mekong Delta as well as to the east and the coast.

Vietnam History and Culture

The above-described geography naturally led to the settlement and location of the indigenous population in the fertile delta regions for sustenance, and eventually along the coastlines for travel and trade. Indeed, the historical record places the core of the modern Vietnamese people as settling in the Red River Delta area. From there, from time to time and under pressure from their Chinese cousins to the north, some of these people drifted southward along the coastal flatlands and adjacent seas.

As part of the Indochina peninsula, Vietnam became a crossroad for the movement of peoples and invasions of outside powers from both the west, northwest, and north. These movements and invasions sought both the rice producing area of the delta regions and access to the seas and oceans to the south and east. Indeed, the French called the area 'Indochine' meaning between India and China mostly because of these movements and invasions.

In the northern part, Vietnam's early record was a history of Chinese invasions and rule. For about a thousand years, starting with the Chinese Han Dynasty in the second century BC, Tonkin Vietnam was subject to these incursions and subjugations. These invasions left an indelible imprint of Chinese ways on Vietnam culture. China's Confucianism and Mandarin rule were the two most recognizable marks on that culture. However, the Tonkin Vietnamese eventually won their independence and gained a sense of nationality by the ninth century AD.

After that, a succession of strongman dynasties ruled a series of Vietnam northern political entities. These powers eventually were united under the rule of first the Ly and then the Nguyen Dynasties. This unified northern part of Vietnam was known as Dai Viet or Great Viet. It was under this rule that Dai Viet leaders eyed expansion toward central and south Vietnam, bringing their version of the Chinese imprint.

In the south, peoples from India seem to have eventually formed a kingdom in that part of Vietnam. The origins of these groups are subject to conjecture, but historical records and artifacts support that they were of Indian origin with ties to Hindu religious roots. They formed, in the first century AD, the Kingdom of Funan. It centered on the Mekong River basin but stretched from the Malay Peninsula to the eastern coast of modern Vietnam to Sumatra.

Another migration of peoples out of modern-day Burma and Cambodia supplanted this polity in 800 AD. This was primarily a Buddhist-oriented society and named after the language of a group of people who called themselves the Khmers. The capital of this kingdom was at Angkor whose ruins is a tourist attraction in present-day Cambodia. This kingdom lasted until about 1460.

The central region of Vietnam evolved eventually into a kingdom of its own in the ninth century called Champa. It was made up of some peoples who had migrated from the Red River Delta; others from the west out of modern-day Thailand and Laos; and some peoples from Polynesia. These mixed migrations along with a small indigenous population led to a stratified society. The populace spoke several languages. They practiced a mix of Hindu and Buddhist religions. They eventually worked a seafaring economy using its coastal dominated features to trade with China and southwest Pacific settlements. Champa, from time to time, was at war with both the

Khmer and Dai Viet Kingdoms. Dai Viet eventually conquered and entirely absorbed Champa at the beginning of the 19th Century.

After the conquest of Champa, the Dai Viet dynasties further expanded to the south. They fought a series of wars that eventually brought a semblance of unity to what we know as modern Vietnam. In fact, the traditional date for the founding of a unified Vietnam is 1802. That is when a member of the Nguyen dynasty declared himself Emperor at the City of Hue. That dynasty would last until the abdication of Bao Dai, a French puppet ruler, in 1954.

After this unification, several landlords ruled the conquered areas. These lords represented family dynasties, such as the Nguyen and Trinh families, who continued to fight among themselves but were successful in holding on to their conquests. Ironically, the Nguyens even hired French mercenaries at times to aid in their holding of power against rebellious rivals.

Despite all this movement, conflict and conquest, the Vietnamese rulers assimilated most of the disparate ethnic and religious peoples within the conquered lands. There were two dominant features of this assimilation. One was its focus on the local village or hamlet whose loyalties were to some landlord or Mandarin. The other was the adherence to a Vietnamese brand of religious beliefs. Both features were primarily inherited from the Chinese. However, there was a Vietnamese flavor to them that blended into a political and social structure that held the Emperor, the local Mandarins, and village elders together.

As Francis Fitzgerald explains in her popular book, *Fire in the Lake*, Vietnamese religious, social, and political beliefs were a combination of Confucianism, Buddhism, Taoism and even some animism connected to a strong bond to the land and the family. This all became "the authority for, and the confirmation of, an entire way of life – an agriculture, a social structure, and a political system."

As a result, Fitzgerald says, "For the traditional villager, who spent his life immobile, bound to the rice land of his ancestors, the world was a very small place. It was, in fact, the village or xa, a word that in its original Chinese roots signified 'the place where people come together to worship the spirits.' In this definition of society, the character 'earth' took precedence, for, as the source of life, the earth was the basis for the social contract between the members of the family and the members of the village."

The West's intervention in Vietnam would upset most, but not all, of this structure by the mid-nineteenth century. That intrusion started with the arrival of French missionaries spreading Christianity through a small Portuguese settlement called Faifo, near the modern city of Da Nang. Later, under the pretext of protection for the noble cause of civilizing the primitive peoples of Asia, France launched a naval expedition. In 1848, as a result, the French captured the Vietnamese city of Tourane, the pre-colonial name for Da Nang. They followed this attack with several other expeditions that eventually conquered all of Vietnam and the surrounding countries of Cambodia and Laos. That conquest ultimately led to the formation of the French Indochina Union by 1887.

French motives, administration, and the rule of its Vietnam colony would have significant implications for the Vietnamese and the future of their country. Unlike most of the British colonial policies - which sought to build a colonial society and governance based on the indigenous populations' history, culture, and values – French colonial policy in Vietnam tried to exploit the country in every way to extract economic benefits for France at the expense of the indigenous populace.

As Fredrick Logevall, in his Pulitzer Prize-winning *Embers of War* writes, "From early on, the lure of profit was the engine that drove French colonial policy. Commercial interests and government officials sought economic gain by exploiting the area's natural resources and opening up new markets for the manufactured goods of metropolitan France." As a result, as Mark Bradley notes in his acclaimed, *Vietnam at War*, "For much of the first half of the twentieth century, French colonialism posed both a political and an existential crisis for many Vietnamese as they experienced the collapse of the pre-colonial imperial order and the searing material, intellectual, and spiritual dislocations of French rule."

In short, French colonial government in Vietnam served France at the expense of the Vietnamese. French rulers did not entice or motivate the Vietnamese to develop self-rule institutions or economic systems. Quite the contrary, as Logevall argues, "The first elected political entities in Indochina, which took the form of municipal councils in the larger cities and assemblies at the provincial level, lacked meaningful decision-making power and were composed mostly of Europeans or wealthy local elites prepared to work within the colonial system. Unlike in India, where the emergence of the Indian Congress Party allowed nationalists to pursue their quest for independence partly through constitutional means, Ho Chi Minh and his colleagues were forced down revolutionary roads."

Furthermore, France implemented their colonial policies differently in each area of Indochina and each region of Vietnam. For example, in Vietnam's delta areas where most of the population lived but which did not offer much to France regarding natural resources, the French colonial government did not try to build any schools of note or develop any sustained economic structure. Nor did these regions attract any French national settlement.

On the other hand, Cochin China, especially around the Saigon area where there was fertile soil and less Chinese cultural influence, French immigrant nationals predominantly settled. There was also a similar development of schools, social establishments such as hotels and restaurants, and economic producing entities such as rubber plantations. Consequently, Saigon became the colony's capital and commercial center. Saigon became known to French nationals as the 'Pearl of the Far East' and 'Paris of the Orient.'

Thus, this area of southern Vietnam became more westernized. The French educational, economic, and political institutions there sought to make civilized Frenchmen out of the Vietnamese; both those who lived in the area and those who traveled there from other regions to obtain a different life than that in the villages. Prompted by French approved and financially favored Vietnamese Mandarins, some of the village populations moved to the coastal cities.

An affluent Vietnamese bourgeoisie arose in and around Saigon and some of the other mostly southern cities. They came to admire French culture, language, and institutions. Despite their attempts to become French, the French émigrés scorned them. They soon also became disillusioned with the inability of the French colonial government to impart any form of genuine self-rule.

Many of these Vietnamese became a source of agitation and later would bestow substance on Vietnamese revolutionary ideas and independence movements. They gained encouragement from the Russo-Japanese War of the early 1900s, in which an Asian people defeated a Western power.

Many of these also fought for France in World War One. When the war was over, they returned home expecting some reward for their sacrifice.

Regardless of some French attempts to westernize the upper strata of Vietnamese society, the French Colonial Government continued to exploit Vietnam, like its other Indochinese colonies, rather than develop them for eventual self-rule. As Logevall further explains in his *Origins of the Vietnam War*, "This situation [the French colonial policies] deeply affected the development of the Vietnamese nationalist movement, which emerged among educated Vietnamese in the first quarter of the twentieth century." The inability of the French colonial rulers to produce any real reform "gave impetus to more revolutionary approaches" and "in provincial and district capitals scattered throughout Vietnam, anti-colonial elements began to form clandestine political organizations dedicated to the eviction of the French and the restoration of national independence."

Vietnamese Nationalism and Sectionalism: A Historical View

In the aftermath of the American experience in Vietnam, it became a standard argument amongst many historians and other scholars that US policymakers ignored the nationalist spirit prevalent from their history – mainly developed in their long history of fighting Chinese aggression. The collective wisdom among them was that the North Vietnamese were merely following the course of Vietnamese history in their war of unification against the South and their American supporters. The premise of this argument was that there was a large group of South Vietnamese that yearned for unification with the North because the North and its leaders most represented historically Vietnamese national fervor. In fact, that longing and attraction, along with dissatisfaction with their government, was the primary cause of the insurgency in the South.

A more thorough and accurate view of Vietnam history reveals that the development of nationalist fervor in Vietnam was not that simple. As Mark Moyar has recently argued, "driving out foreign invaders was not the main chord of Vietnam's national song; infighting was the primary chord, and aggression against the southern neighbors of Champa and Cambodia rivaled the struggle against foreign invasion for second place." The fact is that the southern portion of Vietnam historically was much different from its northern. The French subjugation, moreover, further enhanced these differences. In the South, French rule and imprint, for better or worse, was more pronounced.

This is a significant point that Bruce Lockhart and William Duiker make in their *Historical Dictionary of Vietnam*. As they conclude, "The result [of the historical infighting between various ruling families in the North and the South] was a [southern] society that was more ethnically and culturally diverse than its northern counterpart and had undergone a very different historical and political experience, a fact that would have implications for future attempts to reunify the country under a single government."

Thus, some lose sight that Vietnamese nationalism was not just a phenomenon of the northern part of Vietnam. As Mark Atwood Lawrence reminds us in his *The Vietnam War*, "The first crucial step [in Vietnamese nationalism] came in the early twentieth century, when a new generation of nationalists began to look abroad for inspiration. The most influential was Phan Boi Chau, a scholar from central Vietnam who embraced Western rationalism and science as the keys to creating a robust, modern Vietnam." He "agitated tirelessly for the overthrow of French colonialism and the establishment of a constitution monarchy." Lawrence further explains that many Vietnamese in the central and southern parts of Vietnam took the ideas of such men as Chau and others to form nationalist groups in that area. The movement, however, could not overcome their differences to form a unified group to further Vietnamese nationalism and unification.

Furthermore, in their wars for independence and unification, there were distinct differences of opinions between 'Southern' and 'Northern' Vietnamese on how to achieve the ultimate aims of both freedom from colonial rule and a unified nation. These differences were prevalent not just within those Vietnamese who chose to call themselves communists, but also those who affiliated themselves with organizations outside of communist domination. Unfortunately, not only did American leaders not capitalize on these differences, they were not aware of them enough to do so.

Thus, to conclude this section, the division of Vietnam was not just of foreign making and the result of the 1954 Geneva Accords, as many scholars argue. Geopolitically the northern and southern parts of Vietnam had distinct differences. The variances were significant enough to warrant the possibility of and to argue for a division of the North and South into two distinct nation-states. Moreover, the Northern portion of Vietnam did not have a monopoly on the origin or growth of Vietnamese nationalism. Significant feelings existed in the central and southern portions as well.

Thus, from a historical view, it was not inevitable that Vietnamese unification under Northern Vietnam rule would be, or should have been, the outcome of the Indochina wars. What did happen, of course, was that in the northern part of Vietnam there was born one of the "most influential Vietnamese leaders of all" – one who became known as Ho Chi Minh. This man "showed a remarkable ideological flexibility and tactical genius that enabled him to succeed where earlier nationalists had failed." The fact that he and his key subordinates were communists also played an essential part in their ability to institute control over the Vietnamese people in the north – for they chose ways to force the populace, as well as to convince them, to accept their rule.

Section 6.2 – Ho Chi Minh, Vo Nguyen Giap and The Road to Independence

The leaders who organized and directed the Vietnamese wars of independence against the French and unification against the Americans were a product of and influenced by the above geopolitical factors. Where they grew up, what they knew of their history, what they witnessed of their colonial rule and their choices on how to respond to all of this defined their roles and motives in the story ahead.

As mentioned in Chapter 1, after World War Two had ended, Ho Chi Minh, the primary leader of the Vietnamese resistance movement against the Japanese, declared a new democratic Vietnam. Seeking an accommodation with the French who were trying to reassert their rule over their long-held Indochina colonies, Ho tried to convince French colonial leaders to grant an independent Vietnam as part of the French Union. Talks and negotiations to do so broke down. War soon seemed inevitable. In a final attempt to convince them of the futility of armed conflict, Ho Chi Minh turned to the French Colonial leaders and said, "you can kill ten of my men for every one I kill of yours, but even at those odds you will lose, and I will win."

Similarly, later in the war against the Americans, the communist military leader General Giap warned, "we will fight for ten, fifteen, twenty, fifty years, regardless of cost, until final victory." Despite both proclamations, neither the French nor the Americans heeded this commitment of North Vietnam's primary leaders to winning at any cost solution. Indeed, the defeat of both France and the US, in part, resulted from a gross underestimation of the will and commitment of their Vietnamese opponent to 'victory at any cost.'

This section and the next reconstruct and explain who some of the North Vietnam's key leaders were and what they did to win their war for the independence of Vietnam from 1946 through 1954. This section begins with a summary of the lives of two of the its most prominent figures – Ho Chi Minh and Vo Nguyen Giap. It tells of their involvement in the organization of political groups protesting and trying to gain favor for the independence of Vietnam. It then explains how their attempts to reach a peaceful solution failed, leading to a war against the French to gain independence in the northern area of Vietnam.

This story is essential to the American experience in Vietnam; for what North Vietnamese leaders decided in the war against the Americans can be traced to their experiences in their war against the French.

Ho Chi Minh

In his biography of Ho Chi Minh, William Duiker writes that the Democratic Republic of Vietnam's victory in 1975 was the "legacy of the vision, will and the leadership of one man: Ho Chi Minh...." He further argues that, given his importance to this conflict and the international political impact that surrounded it, Ho "unquestionably was one of the most influential political figures of the twentieth century." Duiker explains, however, that despite this prominence in history, Ho was a man of mystery who lived his entire life mostly as an enigmatic figure.

This diminutive looking, and humble acting Asian was a multifaceted human being. Those who knew him described him as both devious and trustworthy, simple in appearance but complex in his views; and a selfless patriot who also was a dedicated communist. One of Ho's ministers described him as a man of "paradoxes – a nationalist, humanist, Marxist-Leninist, Machiavellian, Confucianist." Despite all this complexity and mystery, one cannot view and explain the Vietnam War without trying to understand his role in and the measure of his influence upon it.

Ho was born Nguyen Sinh Cung in 1890 in a village in central Vietnam. The central part of Vietnam by then had become a significant crossroad between those in the north - who were still primarily of Chinese culture and religion - and those in the south - where there were those who saw themselves as more enlightened and willing to learn Western ways. Moreover, the growing movement for independence, or at least more rights from French rule, was affecting the central region as the new revolutionaries passed between the north and south. Indeed, the French colonial masters at the time knew the area of Ho's village as the heart of the anti-French resistance in central Vietnam.

Cung's father, Nguyen Sinh Sac, was a Confucian scholar who taught in several local schools in the Province. Recalling these years, Ho recounts that his father and other relatives told him stories of former Vietnamese heroic figures in their struggles against the Chinese. Later his father - to gain a higher position for himself as a teacher - moved his family to the ancient Vietnamese capital of Hue. This city was then the seat of the French ruled Vietnamese Government. There the young child pursued further studies to become a teacher like his father. He would also gain further insights into the inequities of French colonial rule there.

While in Hue Father Sac enrolled Cung in a local Vietnamese school that taught the Confucian classics in Chinese. The boy did well. It was becoming clear that Cung had a keen intellect and a curious mind. However, in 1901 Cung's mother became ill and died. As recorded in some of Ho's autobiographies, the young boy ran around the neighborhood crying from house to house over his mother's death. Afterward, Father Sac decided to take the imperial examinations to receive a higher degree. He earned a doctorate. It was a great honor. The now prestigious Confucian scholar returned with his family to his native village where Cung had been born.

Cung was happy to return. In Hue, he had met French provincial officials who treated the native Vietnamese population with contempt. The future "Ho' had also seen the cruelty of the French overseers to Vietnamese workers. Now, he was back where he belonged – in a small village void of French colonialists and direct influence.

His father opened a local school that Cung attended. Sac also arranged for some tutors for the young lad who concentrated on teaching him the French language and classics. They also continued to teach him Vietnamese history and the conquests of lands to the south to build a united Vietnamese nation. From one of his autobiographical sketches, Ho recalled several of his radical nationalist tutors telling him, "if you want to defeat the French, you must understand them." When Cung reached eleven years, per Vietnamese traditions, he assumed another name - Nguyen Tat Thanh, or 'he who will succeed.'

With his degree and his reputation as a man of profound knowledge, Ho's father could no longer resist French requests to join the colonial government. In 1906, he returned to Hue as an administrator at the Imperial Academy. That position required attendance, from time to time, at the Imperial Court as well. He, his son Thanh, and another son moved into a small house near the eastern gate to the Imperial grounds. Sac then enrolled his two sons in a school that was part of a new Franco-Vietnamese educational system located just outside of Hue's citadel walls.

The next year, Thanh passed the entrance examinations for the National Academy. The academy was the highest-level Franco-Vietnamese school in Hue and arguably the most prestigious in Indochina. There he gained a reputation as a serious student who questioned his instructors often. He studied geography, history, literature, and science. His favorite subject appeared to be the French philosophers of the 18th Century who formed the intellectual basis of the American and French Revolutions.

Because of this study, Thanh also became interested in politics. Some of his instructors, who had displayed some anti-French views in their classes, also talked about the recent victory of Japan against Russia in 1905. They emphasized that this was the first instance in modern times that an Asian nation had dealt such a blow to a Western one. It was also a school that other key Vietnamese of the wars ahead would attend – like Vo Nguyen Giap and Ngo Dinh Diem.

During Thanh's early time in Hue, in the northern part of Vietnam around Hanoi, Vietnamese protests began to grow against the unfair French colonial policies. Led by Vietnamese progressive scholars, the protests sometimes became violent. They also spread southward. In early May 1908, these protests reached the gates of the Imperial City. Thanh witnessed this dissent and decided that someone needed to serve as an interpreter for the Vietnamese who were demonstrating and the French officials who had gathered to control it.

As related in Duiker's biography, on 9 May a French official ordered French militia troops to disperse the crowd. At the front was Thanh, who was trying to convey some of the protest leaders' grievances to the French. Someone struck him, sending him stumbling to the ground. After he recovered, one of the French officials, to bring a peaceful resolution to the situation, invited Thanh to sit down with him in his office to serve as an interpreter with leaders of the protest group.

Despite this attempt at a peaceful resolution, the protest continued. French regular troops arrived, fired into the crowd, dispersing the protestors. The next day some French officials remembered Thanh as one of the instigators of the protest. Authorities dismissed him from the school. Court officials also reprimanded his father for the behavior of his son.

Fleeing Hue, the future Ho Chi Minh would become a fugitive from constant French attempts to monitor his activities. From time to time, he would change names. At one time, Ho became a teacher at a small school in the city of Phan Thiet in southern Cochinchina. There he stayed at various homes and villages of friends of his father. He seldom saw his father, who also was under French surveillance. After three years in Phan Thiet, Thanh went further south to Saigon. There he hired on as a cook aboard a steamship bound for the French city of Marseille. He was determined, as his tutor had told him, to 'understand the French.'

According to Duiker, it appears for the next two years that Thanh spent most of his time at sea, visiting various ports of call. These included places in Europe, Asia, North America, Africa, and South America. His voyages took him back to Saigon at times, where he tried to contact his father but failed. He may have even visited America, spending some time in New York City, and briefly staying in Boston where he may have worked as a pastry chef. As a best guess, Duiker claims that Thanh briefly settled in London in late 1913. There he worked several temporary jobs and studied

English. It appears that Ho stayed in Great Britain until 1917. Then, at the age of twenty-seven, he moved to Paris. It was the height of the First World War.

By 1917 the Vietnamese population in Paris had grown (by the end of 1918 there would be as many as 50,000 Vietnamese in France). That was a result of conscription of Vietnamese whom the French colonial government had sent as replacements for workers serving in the armed forces. Some also served on the front lines and fought gallantly. Many of these soldiers, after the war, would return to Vietnam expecting a reward for their service. They would be ignored or impressed into service for further French military purposes.

Paris at that time was a hotbed of dissent. A revolution had begun in Russia. French soldiers had rebelled against their commanders who had continued to order needless bloody assaults on the western front of the war. Paris had now become a place where many socialists, inspired by the ideas of the Russian revolution, were organizing political groups to protest the Government's domestic and war policies. They had frequent meetings during which they discussed the socialist ideas of Hegel and Marx, and how they wanted to form a socialist party. It is at one of these meetings that Thanh showed up to take part in the French Socialist movement.

He was not a very impressive figure. Pictures of the times portray him as frail and dressed in shoddy clothing. The stress of his worldwide travels, and his meager subsistence and current living arrangements in Paris, made him look sickly and older than he was. However, as some observers later wrote, Thanh had deep penetrating brown eyes that held some mystique, showed devotion to his ideas, and seemed to "penetrate the soul of the observer."

When he initially spoke at these meetings, he was timid and nervous. Some remembered that he stuttered severely. The emotions he expressed, however, moved many to applaud his remarks. After several meetings, he was called upon for his views in discussions. Socialists wanted to hear his views on French colonial questions.

When not working or attending meetings, Thanh read vociferously. His encounters with French socialists sparked an interest in Karl Marx and Vladimir Lenin. In Duiker's view, it was natural for him to attract to the ideas of these two men for two reasons. One, their writings appealed to his natural attraction to and teachings in Confucianism, since both authors emphasized community over individualism. Second, both expounded upon the evils of capitalism; especially its exploitation of others under colonial rule. It appears then that it is during this time in Paris that the future Ho Chi Minh found the intellectual underpinnings of his future politics.

When the First World War ended, Thanh read Woodrow Wilson's fourteen principles, which the American President had expounded for use in the development of the peace treaty at Versailles. The most appealing of these to Thanh was the call for self-determination of all peoples in the post-war years ahead. Consequently, he drafted a petition that asked the leaders at Versailles to apply this principle of self-determination to French colonial possessions in Southeast Asia. He signed the petition Nguyen Ai Quoc, meaning 'Nguyen the Patriot.' He would use this new name until he finally adopted Ho Chi Minh.

Quoc personally delivered the petition to the French President and other dignitaries at the Palace of Versailles. He also arranged for a Socialist newspaper to publish it. Furthermore, he elicited the aid of some of his Socialist friends to have the petition printed and delivered to individuals on the streets of Paris. Although he received a polite response from the American delegation at Versailles that they would deliver it to President Wilson, nothing ever came of the petition.

For the next four years, 'Nguyen the Patriot' continued his political involvement in Socialist Party affairs. He also joined the French Communist Party when it broke off from the more moderate Socialists in the early twenties. For three years, Quoc wrote for various journals expressing his anti-colonial views. During these years, French authorities closely tracked and watched his activities.

Then in 1923, the Russian Communists invited him to a meeting of the COMINTERN – an organization of international communist parties directed from Moscow to implement communist doctrine worldwide. While in Russia he met such notables as Joseph Stalin and Leon Trotsky and became an agent of the COMINTERN. The future Ho Chi Minh was now not just a member of the Communist Party, but a notable one.

At the end of 1924, as an agent of the COMINTERN, Quoc traveled to China to support the unfolding socialist revolution there. When he arrived, he joined the Chinese Communist Party's efforts along with Sun Yet-Sen's more moderate movement to overthrow the Manchu Dynasty's warlords and unite China. He also contacted several Vietnamese exiles who had been active in the protests against the French but had sought refuge in China to escape imprisonment. While there, he watched the increasing unrest and protests in Indochina over French post world war rule. He wrote to protest leaders still in Vietnam to stay in contact.

Led by the Vietnamese intellectuals and returning Vietnamese laborers and soldiers from France, the French colonial government could no longer quickly control or subdue the growing protests. It was now clear to Quoc that Vietnam was prime for a revolution of its own. Working with those exiles in China and in contact with the radicals in Vietnam, in February of 1925 Quoc formed a secret organization called the Indochinese Nationalist Party. The Party's stated object was the independence of all of Indochina from French rule.

In a couple of months, Quoc would also focus on Vietnam's independence. To achieve a youthful attraction to a new organization specifically geared toward that, he formed the Vietnamese Revolutionary Youth League. Many future Vietnamese Communist leaders, such as a future leader of the Party named Le Duan, began their association with Ho as a member of this league.

Meanwhile, the socialist revolution in China in these years saw much ebb and flow. While China was finally united, the Nationalist Party, under Chiang Kai-shek, fought with its communist counterpart and gained the upper hand in 1927. Chiang then instituted a vicious crack-down on left-wing radicals, to include members of the Vietnamese Revolutionary Youth League. Quoc had to flee China to escape imprisonment. He initially fled to the Soviet Union where he spent the next few years. Occasionally he would travel back to China to meet with his growing Vietnamese recruits for independence.

By 1930 the future Ho decided to settle in Hong Kong, where he had access to the sea and, under British protection, could avoid French capture. While there, he founded the Vietnamese Communist Party, later renaming it to the Indochinese Communist Party under pressure from Moscow to broaden the communist hold over Southeast Asia. He had finally decided to not only seek independence for Vietnam but wanted it also to be communist. After a year, however, the British under French pressure arrested and imprisoned him for two years for his revolutionary activities.

In 1933, upon his release from jail in Hong Kong, Quoc again fled from French attempts to arrest him. He again ended up in the Soviet Union, stayed there until 1938. From there he again went to China. There he served again as an agent of the COMINTERN to report on the progress of the revolution against the Nationalist Chinese and the war against Japan. Over the next three years, Quoc stayed there as an observer.

During this time, he kept in touch with leaders of the ICP infrastructure and checked its activities in Vietnam. He also provided ICP leaders written materials on the benefits of communism for their use. Sometime in late 1940, after the Second World War had broken out in Europe, Quoc met a young Vietnamese man who had just joined the Party and had already gained a reputation as a potential leader. His name was Vo Nguyen Giap. The two liked one another and quickly grew to admire the dedication they shared for Vietnamese independence.

While Ho and Giap were in China, Germany defeated France. As noted in Chapter 1, the Japanese decided to take advantage of the French defeat. They arranged with the new French 'Vichy' government to deploy forces to Vietnam. This gave the Japanese the ability to secure bases for its fight against the Chinese forces in southern China and seize the resources in Indochina and maritime areas of the South China Sea. Recognizing the potential opportunity for his vision of an eventual independent Vietnam, Quoc decided that now was the time to return to Vietnam to actively take part and direct the independent movement there.

He dispatched an advance party, which included Giap, to go to Southern China and pick out a base across the border in northern Vietnam. In January 1941, Quoc joined Giap and others in the advanced party at their established base at the village of Pac Bo. They settled on a cave complex near the village to set up their headquarters. It is here that Quoc would change his name and adopt the new pseudonym of Ho Chi Minh ("He who enlightens"). He also would find the League for the Independence of Vietnam (known as the Viet-Minh).

From his newly found secure base and with this organization, Ho and his colleagues waged war against the Japanese and French for independence. Vo Nguyen Giap would be his right-hand man. Ho appointed him to recruit, organize, and lead the Viet-Minh military forces in the fight for independence ahead.

Vo Nguyen Giap

Giap had been born in August 1911 in central Vietnam in a small village called An Xa. His father held a position in the colonial administration and taught elementary school there. He, like Ho's father, was a Confucian scholar. His mother told him stories of her father, who was a rebel commander in an uprising against the French in 1885.

Like Ho Chi Minh, Giap studied at the National School in Hue, winning high grades especially in history and geography, and learning French. It was there that he also began reading and studying military history. He would continue to explore military history throughout his life – especially the campaigns of Napoleon and, a favorite of his, T.E. Lawrence's *Pillars of Wisdom* about the British organization and implementation of irregular forces in World War I.

When he was in Hue, Giap joined in several demonstrations against the French. He organized a group that protested the suppression of political views at his school. For that, the school administration expelled him and sent him back to his home village. While home he published an editorial for a French-language newspaper in Saigon about how his school suppressed views critical of French rule.

Giap then returned to Hue where he became active in several secret organizations that worked for Vietnamese independence. One of these was a group called 'Tan Viet.' After reading communist literature, he formed a cell within that group that eventually splintered away and became part of the Vietnamese Communist Party. He may have also joined Ho Chi Minh's Revolutionary Youth League.

As a biographer Cecil Currey relates by the early thirties Giap had become known as one of the brightest stars of the fledgling Vietnamese Communist Party in central Vietnam. He was active in organizing small Party cells in the villages and cities that spread communist views. Giap also began to lead protests and attacks against colonial authorities.

Moving to Saigon, he became part of the Central Committee of the Vietnamese Communists operating in Vietnam. While there, French authorities captured and sent him to jail. Upon release, he married, settled down and raised a family. He also resumed his formal schooling, attending the University of Hanoi. Later he taught history at this University and became known for his lectures on Napoleon's campaigns.

In the late thirties, French authorities became more tolerant of Vietnamese political movements, to include that of the Vietnamese Communist Party. This toleration was partly due to the rise of French Socialism and Communism in France, and the coming to power of a French Socialist government.

Thus, Giap could continue his activities openly for the Party. He wrote articles in a French-language newspaper that was popular in Vietnamese cities on communist ideas that were pertinent to the country. By 1939, per some sources, there were over 2,000 members of the Vietnamese Communist Party in Vietnam and almost 40,000 followers.

In late 1939, French authorities reasserted a crackdown on subversive activities in Indochina – especially those of the communists. This action resulted from the pact between the Soviet Union and Nazi Germany. Politicians in office now saw the French Communist Party as an agent of the Soviets and after France's declaration of war against Germany an instrument of passing secrets to the Nazis. Although the French police arrested about a thousand members of the ICP, Giap eluded arrest, and once again went into hiding along with other prominent Vietnamese Communists and Nationalists.

The Beginning of the Struggle for Independence

From various hiding places, Giap read about the war in Europe. When Germany defeated France in May 1940, both Giap and Ho Chi Minh thought that the defeat would present an opportunity for independence. That opportunity grew when the new defeated French government gave directions to its Indochina colonial government officials to grant bases to the Japanese in Vietnam.

Soon Japanese troops were landing in North Vietnam and setting up air bases for attacks against the Chinese in support of their ground campaign there. Most French soldiers in the area withdrew to the southern part of Vietnam. Japan, by this time, saw all of Indochina as vital to their war effort regarding oil and other natural resources. It could also serve as an interim base area for future operations against Burma and India in the years to come.

While the Japanese occupation was underway, Ho and other ICP committee members thought it would be good to have Giap cross into China and join the communist forces there to learn about the practice of military strategy and tactics. Ho had already served some time with the Chinese armies and had gained some valuable insights on military operations. Giap packed a few items and, saying goodbye to his wife and small child, took off on foot for southern China.

While in China, Giap studied the works of Mao Tse Tung. He read his writings on the experiences in China fighting the Japanese and, most importantly, Mao's 1937 treatise called *Guerrilla Warfare*. He also heard of his wife's capture and imprisonment in Vietnam. The French later executed her. Giap felt devastated; but kept up on his studies and observations of the war in China, waiting to return and avenge the death of his wife.

He returned in 1941. His first significant act, mentioned above, was to build the base at Pac Bo. While at Pac Bo, Giap and Ho talked about and planned for the eventual formation of a Vietnamese National Army. They further discussed the possibility of a general uprising of the Vietnamese people against the remnants of the French colonial regime. Both surmised the eventual defeat of Japan. They agreed that it would offer the best opportunity for an uprising and eventual independence.

While at Pac Bo, Ho organized and conducted the Eighth Plenum of the ICP on May 10, 1941. It was the first meeting of the key Vietnamese Communist leaders and party members since the early thirties. In this session, which Ho chaired, the members agreed to formally establish the Viet-Minh Front. They then drafted a resolution that set goals for that organization. At the top was to struggle for national liberation of Vietnam from the French colonial regime and the Japanese occupation forces.

This goal was a departure from an earlier one that called for the independence of all of Indochina. As Duiker relates, Ho pushed for this goal to focus the revolution that was to follow on Vietnam first; then follow it with the rest of Indochina. To prepare for the latter, the leaders instructed the regional committees to set up cells in both Laos and Cambodia. The committee then agreed to adopt Mao's doctrine for guerrilla warfare as its primary design for winning independence.

The final act of the Plenum was to choose a new Party leader, called the General Secretary. Ho pushed for a long time friend named Truong Chinh. He believed that Chinh was a perfect choice. Chinh was a prime believer in the need for the Vietnamese to prepare themselves politically before any move toward a military solution. Therefore, he would be a leader who could keep the more militant factions of the movement in check.

With Ho's staunch support, the Committee chose Chinh. However, as William Duiker states, Ho remained the "spiritual head of the Viet-Minh." After the meeting, the members dispersed to various locales to prepare for the revolution. There had not been any agreement yet on the date it would begin. Ho and Giap stayed for the time being at Pac Bo.

Ho decided that the area around Pac Bo, which was then a French provisional province called Cao Bang, would be the ideal main base for the revolution. Ho and Giap discussed how to expand the movement from the base southward in stages. Ho cautioned Giap that any military operations needed to be well planned, and, more importantly, only launched after careful preparation to gain the support of the majority of the people.

Leaving Pac Bo in early June, both Ho and Giap made frequent visits to other secure base sites throughout the Cao Bang area for the next eighteen months, preparing for the revolution. It was during this period that Giap also began to launch small attacks against Japanese and any remaining French posts in the northern part of Vietnam. These forays prepared his growing military forces for future offensives.

In August 1942 Ho decided to return to China to gain Chinese support for the future Vietnamese Revolution. Soon after, the Nationalist Chinese captured and jailed him. Party members attempted to gain his release. They failed. Then, several months after knowledge of his arrest, reports came that Ho had died in captivity. All were in despair, especially Giap. They felt that at a critical time they had lost the movement's critical spiritual leader.

Ho languished in jail for over a year. Then Chou En Lai, at the time a little-known lieutenant of Mao's, managed to get him released. Chou argued that Ho, though he was a communist, was also an inspirational leader to all Chinese in their fight against Japan. After his release, Ho stayed in China to continue his fight to gain support for the Vietnamese Communists. Then in August 1944, he returned to Vietnam.

Ho found that under Giap's considerable efforts the Viet-Minh had made substantial gains in the Tonkin region – all the way to the Red River Delta. Elsewhere in Vietnam, the Viet-Minh had also created political cells and organized small guerrilla forces to support them. The great famine that had spread throughout Vietnam from 1943 to the beginning of 1945 played a role. While the Japanese and French troops in Vietnam hoarded much of the grain and kept it away from the general population during this famine, the Viet-Minh seized large grain stocks and gave it to the starving general population. Thus, the Viet-Minh forces were gaining a reputation for being a Liberation Army for Vietnam. These forces continued to grow in numbers and size. Giap now had organized many into special platoons (of 20 to 30 men) that would eventually form the nucleus of his regular army.

These paramilitary forces gained the attention of the American Office of Strategic Services or OSS – the forerunner of the CIA and American Special Forces. Having heard of the Viet-Minh and its leader from some nationalist Chinese, the OSS set out to contact their leaders. They needed someone who could report on Japanese activities and rescue downed pilots conducting missions in support of operations in China.

Indeed, when Ho was in China after his release from jail, he had already sought out American officials to gain support for his organization. Ho had known of President Roosevelt's commitment to end colonialism as part of the original Atlantic Charter published in 1941. Reminiscent of Wilson's fourteen points, the Viet-Minh leader thought he could gain FDR's approval of his Viet-Minh Front as the government to rule post-World War Vietnam.

In March 1944, Ho met with an OSS official by the name of Captain Charles Fenn, who headed the OSS office in Southern China. They mutually agreed to cooperate in intelligence gathering of Japanese forces in Vietnam, sabotaging their facilities, and rescuing downed pilots. Ho also met with the American aviation advisor to Chiang Kai-shek and commander of the US Army Air Force in China, Claire Chennault. Chennault supplied a signed photograph of the two posed together. To show his American support, Ho would show his comrades the picture when he returned to Vietnam.

After he returned, the OSS sent a team of personnel to give radio support and medical aid. From time to time, the OSS airdropped supplies to Ho and his Patriots at the Pac Bo headquarters. Afterward, they sent another team under a Colonel Allison Thomas to evaluate Ho and his forces.

Thomas reported back that the Viet-Minh had the broad support of the Vietnamese people against the Japanese occupation and the harsh French colonial rule. On one occasion an OSS team medic treated Ho for malaria and dysentery. As the mutual support continued into 1945, Americans also furnished some weapons and training to the Viet-Minh.

On March 9, 1945, with their defeat becoming increasingly evident, the Japanese seized all of Vietnam from the French. They also imprisoned French regular soldiers who did not flee into China. The Japanese then incorporated some of the Vietnamese who served under the French into their units. Japanese officials further created a puppet government headed by the Emperor Bao Dai, the last in the line of Nguyen family rulers still alive. Japanese authorities then abandoned the northern part of Vietnam.

As William Duiker noted, "by abolishing the colonial administration and replacing it with a puppet imperial government headed by Emperor Bao Dai but firmly under their domination, the Japanese had inadvertently opened up the entire region north of the delta to a revolutionary takeover."

Ho and Giap quickly took advantage of the situation. They decided to move their command post further south to improve their ability to control Viet-Minh forces for an uprising. They moved there in late May, as reports came in about the surrender of Germany in Europe. The American OSS members went with them.

The place of the new command post was Tan Trao. From there Ho and Giap ordered their cadres to begin seizing vast land holdings of landlords for redistribution to village leaders chosen under Viet-Minh supervision. Ho also sent messages to OSS leaders in southern China offering them the use of one thousand Viet-Minh guerrillas against the Japanese in Vietnam.

The Americans responded favorably. They asked for the location of airfields to airdrop more OSS personnel to coordinate operations. Some soon parachuted into Tan Trao. Ho and Giap received them as their 'American friends.' Ho asked them if they knew the words of their 'Declaration of Independence.' Embarrassed, they said they could not remember them. Ho then cited the first line for them to jog their memory. These OSS members soon turned their attention to further train and better equip the Viet-Minh forces for operations against the Japanese.

Over the next couple of months, Ho got wind of Allied plans to send troops to occupy Vietnam in case of the inevitable Japanese defeat. The Chinese were to occupy the northern part and accept the surrender of Japanese forces there. British forces would take the surrender in the south.

As recounted at the beginning of Chapter 1, Ho quickly called for a Party conference at Tan Trao. It met in mid-August. There the Party leaders heard of the Hiroshima bombing and the Japanese surrender over OSS radios. Recognizing that the time was right, Ho urged the Party to launch the general uprising to seize power. He argued that the Viet-Minh must be in a position of power to convince the Allies to support its authority over an independent Vietnam.

The August Revolution

On 16 August Viet-Minh led popular uprisings broke out throughout North Vietnam. Previously, a famine had swept the region. Once again, the Viet-Minh attacked colonial landlords and the Japanese occupation forces to gain rice stocks that they had been depriving the people. In so doing, the Viet-Minh then distributed the rice to the starving people. What would become known as the 'August Revolution,' spread further south throughout Vietnam.

The Revolution in the northern region was swift and successful. As Logevall describes, "Viet-Minh forces took control in towns and villages in various parts of Annam and Tonkin. Resistance was usually minimal, as local authorities simply handed over power to the insurgents and as Japanese forces, now part of a defeated empire, stayed neutral."

On August 19, Giap's People's Army consisting of some one thousand troops seized control of all relevant public buildings in Hanoi and raised their new bright red flag with a yellow star in the middle. On August 25 in Hue, with many Vietnamese demanding he renounce his throne, the Japanese puppet Emperor Bao Dai announced he would support a new Viet-Minh government headed by Ho Chi Minh.

In the South, the revolution developed more slowly. This was because the French and later Japanese had been somewhat successful in discovering and rooting out the Viet-Minh infrastructure in the early forties. Nevertheless, the Party had put in place clandestine cells primarily in the industrial establishments around Saigon numbering by 1945 some 3000 workers.

Back in the North, on 25 August, Ho Chi Minh entered Hanoi. It was the first time in fifty-five years that he had been there. He at once went about forming a new Vietnamese Government. Though it would be several weeks before Chinese troops would arrive to affect the occupation and surrender, American OSS members came to Hanoi around the same time to coordinate the turnover and surrender. One of these was a Captain Archimedes Patti, whom Ho had met when he was in southern China.

Accompanying Patti was a French official by the name of Jean Sainteny (the same man whom Nixon and Kissinger would use to send a message to Ho in 1969). The Frenchman was a representative of the Free French Force Commander, General Charles DeGaulle. De Gaulle was also the President of a Provisional French Government in liberated France. Officially Sainteny was to account for the French citizens and soldiers in Vietnam. His secret orders, however, were to arrange for the retention of Vietnam as part of a restored French Empire.

Ho tried to use the presence of Captain Patti and other OSS members as an American endorsement of the government he was forming. Patti would not take the bite. He had queried his superiors on US policy on the events unfolding in Vietnam. The State Department had informed all that the US would not encourage nor oppose the return of French power to Vietnam and Indochina. Thus, Patti told Ho that the US was neutral at this time about what was happening in Vietnam.

Meanwhile, Ho went forward with the formation of a new provisional government. He purposefully included in that government more than just members of his Communist Party and the Viet-Minh movement. He wanted to show broad base support and representation of all in Vietnam. Then on 2 September, Ho, and his newly appointed ministers – with Giap as his new Minister of Interior –

drove into the center square of Hanoi. It was the same day that Japan signed its surrender on the deck of the Battleship Missouri in Tokyo Bay.

Hundreds of thousands of Vietnamese had gathered to see the birth of their newly independent nation. Ho took the podium and declared the formation of a new independent Vietnam. In a short speech, he included words from the American Declaration of Independence and mentioned the French Declaration of the Rights of Man and the ideals of the French Revolution.

Ho then listed a litany of crimes committed by the French colonial regime over the Vietnam people. He concluded, "Viet Nam has the right to enjoy freedom and independence and in fact has become a free and independent country. The entire Vietnamese people are determined to mobilize all their physical and mental strength, to sacrifice their lives and property to safeguard their freedom and independence."

As his words ended, a squadron of US P-38 fighter-bombers passed overhead. No one had agreed to or had planned the flyby. Nevertheless, such a show of force was sure to impress all present that Ho had the support of the United States of America.

In the South news of the declaration and the formation of a Vietnamese government also sparked much excitement. A young Vietnamese pharmacist by the name of Truong Nhu Tang - who would later become a vital member of the South's war against the French and Americans – expressed later in a memoir his feelings over the events of August and September. "All around me…the air was charged with excitement and anticipation…. Caught in a tide of emotional patriotism and excited by danger and the idea of independence, all of Saigon's young people seemed to be joining [the Revolution]."

However, the attendant violence against the French that accompanied this excitement soon dulled Troung's enthusiasm. It would take a later meeting with Ho Chi Minh himself to reignite his desire to fight for independence.

Back in the North, there was much to do in the weeks and months that followed. Several weeks after the declaration ceremony, the provisional government issued a decree announcing the elections for a constituent assembly to draft a new constitution. All citizens over the age of 18 could vote. Other decrees on taxation, abolishment of the Mandarin and French colonial administrations, and freedom of worship followed.

Ho was deliberately cautious and did not announce any other reforms that the ICP platform entailed. He did not want the government to seem too socialist or, most importantly, communist to the West. His focus was to ensure that the government would appear moderate and capable of replacing the French imperialistic administration.

While to the outside world, this conservative and all-inclusive look of the leadership of a new provisional government may have had some effect, there were some Vietnamese who knew what a communist leadership dominated government meant for the future of their country. For example, members of a nationalist party by the name of Dai Viet or 'Greater Vietnam', which had struggled with the Communist Party of Vietnam over the future of Vietnam for some time, were not only leery of the way things were going in September, but outright distrustful of Ho and his selected members who were overseeing the formation of a new government.

One such member of the Dai Viet was Bui Diem. A northerner by birth, Diem had joined the Dai Viet in 1944 as it became clear that the end for the Japanese may mean independence for Vietnam. He was from the upper crust of Vietnamese society. His father had been a Mandarin scholar. Diem had attended the best of schools, and excelled in them. One of his teachers at a prestigious high school in Hanoi had been Giap, whom he had admired for his love of history and his dynamic lectures – especially the ones on Napoleon. Now he was taking part of some of the events in Hanoi wondering what it all meant for his future.

Bui Diem sat in several of the meetings that Ho held in his attempts to mobilize all segments of northern Vietnamese society and politics to support his provisional government and the tasks that lie before it. His observations, written in his memoir, *In the Jaws of History*, are interesting for someone who wants an understanding of how Ho and the communists gained power in 1945 from the viewpoint of a noncommunist Vietnamese.

At one such meeting, Diem met Ho. As he recalls, "I was standing just a few feet from Ho, watching him carefully. Here he was, the Chief of State, and the man didn't have a pretentious bone in him…But I thought to myself that this was a truly capable man, relaxed and unflappable – a consummate politician. It was an impressive performance." Thus, Diem, like most Vietnamese of the time, took to Ho, who shrewdly portrayed himself as a humble man, but one who could easily get others to follow him.

Another observation from Diem is essential to how the educated Vietnamese looked at America at the time. The Dai Viet member said that regardless of their political view at the time, all who participated in politics in Vietnam as the war ended looked up to the Americans. Like Ho, they expected that the US would support their bid for independence from the French. Diem also recalls that Ho took care at the time to create a belief that the US was supporting him as the rightful future leader of Vietnamese freedom.

On 9 September, the National Chinese occupation force reached Hanoi. Unsure about what the Chinese would do or what their aims were, Ho decided to ensure its leader that his government would cooperate with the occupation and surrender of the Japanese forces. He also hoped that his American contacts would be able to convince the Chinese to support his government.

Ho was unaware that the new Truman Administration was becoming eager to ensure that the French in Europe would cooperate in building a post-war Europe. In fact, the State Department had already recommended to the new President after FDR's death that the US not support an independent Vietnam, but acquiesce to French rule. Ho's continued efforts to gain American support would turn out to be futile. He even wrote a letter appealing to Truman to support his new government. The US President did not respond.

Fortunately for Ho, the Chinese commander wanted nothing to do with the occupation. Ho's supply of opium for his personal use convinced the Chinese General that the Viet-Minh could assist in expediting the task of surrender and evacuation of the Japanese forces. This would ensure that the Chinese stay in Vietnam would not be extended. The General seemed happy that he could return home soon; with an abundant amount of the drug for future use. Ho's drug diplomacy with the Chinese seemed to at least create the conditions that the Chinese would not stay as long as they had in the past.

About the same time the Chinese were occupying northern Vietnam; the British forces moved into the South. The Viet-Minh southern leaders were eager to show they could govern and hasten the surrender. The British Commander had other ideas. His higher authority had instructed him to install law and order 'until the restoration of French colonial authority.' The British were in no mood to conduct a lengthy occupation that could result in violence and unnecessary costs to its government. Besides, a former colonial power itself, the British were sympathetic to the desire of the French to regain their Indochina colonies.

Eager to end its involvement in the occupation, the British completed their handover to the French quickly and without regard to the Vietnamese. The Viet-Minh southern political leader had called for a general strike to put pressure on the British to recognize the Viet-Minh as a government that could rule and control the population. However, the strike turned violent.

This violence prompted the British commander to quickly release and rearm the French prisoners in Saigon and turn them over to the Free French Commander. Clashes followed between Viet-Minh forces and the French. The French commander ordered his troops to take control over key installations and bring law and order to Saigon and its surrounding regions. Some 20,000 French residents there helped the French soldiers.

As sporadic violence continued for several weeks, the senior US representative in Saigon, an OSS officer by the name of Lieutenant Colonel Peter Dewey, went to the British and tried to get them to stop the reinstatement of French rule. He did not know of the official US position. The British Commander gave him a hostile reception; blaming the OSS for inciting the violence that had occurred. He ordered Dewey to leave the country.

After reporting to his headquarters that "Cochin China is burning" and recommending that all Americans "ought to clear out of Southeast Asia,' Dewey left for the airport. The OSS officer was fluent in French. He had lived with his father, a foreign-service officer in France for a while. On the way to the airport in a jeep, Dewey came upon a roadblock. The American called out in French to the soldiers manning it to identify himself. A Viet-Minh detachment, believing him to be French, shot and killed him. He was the first of over 58,000 Americans to die in Vietnam.

Meanwhile, the Provisional French government had gained the approval of Allied Commanders in the Pacific and China-Burma-India Theaters to send more forces to Vietnam. The British provided US lend-lease transport ships for the movement. In early October, French soldiers began to arrive in Saigon. General Henri Leclerc – a hero of the Free French Army during the war and a close friend to DeGaulle – commanded them.

Upon landing, the British Commander, eager to give up his responsibilities, turned over occupation authority to Leclerc in all areas in Vietnam south of the 16th parallel. These French reinforcements, wearing American uniforms and carrying US weapons, outnumbered and outgunned the Viet-Minh around Saigon. Under the leadership of a man by the name of Le Duan, the Viet-Minh major paramilitary forces dispersed to the Mekong Delta to regroup and await instructions.

Along with Leclerc and the troops came the newly named French high commissioner for Indochina. George d'Argenlieu had been a naval officer in both World Wars. Between the wars, however, he had resigned his commission and become a priest. Now he wanted, without hesitation, to reassert French authority and restore the Indochina colonies to France. As Logevall states in his *Embers of*

War, "His policy decisions in the year that followed would set the conditions and the course of the outbreak of a full-scale war."

It was now becoming apparent to Ho Chi Minh he had to act to ensure some sort of government for Vietnam would survive all this turmoil. His most prominent problems were to ensure the withdrawal of the Chinese, and, with the fait accompli of their return in the South, negotiate with the French to ensure the survival of the Democratic Republic of Vietnam. In so doing the Vietnamese leader showed that he was a pragmatist, willing to give up some of his communist cloaks to ensure his greatest vision – an independent Vietnam.

In the latter part of 1945, Ho sought to broaden further his government's support. He first dissolved the Indochina Communist Party. This action eased any problems he may have had with the Nationalist Chinese whose conflict with the Communist Chinese had picked up after the surrender of Japan. It also sought to ensure the Americans who were still in Vietnam that he was more a nationalist than a communist. Ho proclaimed publicly and privately to the Americans that "his country was his party." After that, he included some Vietnamese nationalists who had not here before participated. However, the new Prime Minister of the DRV also ensured that none of these non-communists had any following or desire to challenge his authority.

Ho then began negotiations with the French. In December, he sat down with Jean Sainteny and started to talk about a treaty that would be beneficial to both sides. Together in 1946, they began to hammer out a deal. Sainteny's primary goal, which both d'Argenlieu and Leclerc desired, was to get Ho's assent to the return of French troops in the north; ostensibly to protect the twenty thousand French citizens who lived there. To get Ho to do this, Sainteny would also get the Chinese to agree to a withdrawal sometime in early 1946. Ho's end game was to get French agreement to an eventual unified and independent Vietnam.

In February, they reached a deal. Ho would agree to the return of French troops in the North. In exchange for that, the French, as Sainteny informed the DRV leaders, would agree to recognition for an eventual entirely independent and 'free state' of Vietnam. In the meantime, Vietnam would become a member of the French Union – a federation of semi-independent ex-colonies.

Before the French, Chinese and newly elected Vietnamese National Assembly in Hanoi fully accepted the deal, twenty-five thousand French troops on 6 March arrived at Haiphong harbor. Chinese batteries greeted them. Quickly, however, the Chinese, Vietnamese and French came to an agreement that ended this brief conflict. The Chinese agreed to withdraw within a year. The French agreed to recognize the Vietnam free state in its Union with a future popular referendum on the issue of full independence and unification. The Vietnamese decided to let French troops relieve Chinese occupation forces and remain in Vietnam for five years.

Not all Viet-Minh leaders were pleased. Ho was not entirely pleased either. However, he felt this is the best deal they could get at the time. The Viet-Minh military forces were hardly ready to take on the French troops, some of which had fought against the Japanese in the Pacific and the Nazis in Europe and were well armed by the Americans. However, as previously quoted in Chapter 1, Ho turned to his comrades and countrymen and purportedly said, "I prefer to sniff French shit for five years than eat Chinese shit for the rest of my life." Most agreed that this was the best they could do at that time.

Section 6.3 - Victory at Any Cost: The First Indochina War

For much of the remaining year in 1946, Ho tried to seal the deal with the French. He spent much of his time in Paris trying to get a formal treaty. Before he had left Vietnam, however, he and Giap had met and agreed to enlarge and improve the armed forces of the DRV, in case diplomacy failed.

Giap spent most of the year increasing his forces from about 5,000 at the time of the August Revolution to some 25,000 by mid-1946. These forces were not well armed – some carried old flintlock muskets. However, they were devoted to their newly founded country. Nevertheless, Giap continued to train them hard. Also, Giap had organized and could count on the support of another 80,000 guerrilla forces in the local districts and villages throughout Vietnam.

As it turned out, from the Vietnamese Communist view, these preparations were fortunate. By June, French Commissioner d'Argenlieu, on his own accord and without informing Paris, declared that the southern region of Vietnam was an autonomous 'Republic of Cochin China' under French rule. After word of this reached France; most French politicians applauded d'Argenlieu's actions. A recently formed Government, favorable to restoring its colonies in Indochina, sanctioned the move.

Hearing about this action, Ho desperately attempted to salvage the situation. In Paris, he and a close friend Pham Van Dong sought American pressure to get the French to abide by the March accords. The low-level State Department Officials to whom Ho and Pham talked indicated that the US would not support him - saying that communism is not compatible with freedom. The American Ambassador in Paris, Jefferson Caffery, denied his request.

An American journalist in Paris interviewed Ho over the French decision to not grant full independence. The Journalist implied that the Vietnamese would have no course but to submit because of the significant French military presence in Vietnam. Ho replied, "It will be a war between an elephant and a tiger. If the tiger ever stands still the elephant will crush him with his mighty tusks. However, the tiger does not stand still. He lurks in the jungle by day and emerges only at night. He will leap upon the back of the elephant, tearing huge chunks from his hide, and then he will leap back into the dark jungle. Moreover, slowly the elephant will bleed to death. That will be the war of Indochina."

Another Vietnamese who was then in Paris was Truong Nhu Tang – the young Southern Vietnamese man who had witnessed the excitement and violence in Saigon in August and September of 1945. Tang was now with some other Vietnamese youths undergoing a higher education in Paris. As was his habit, Ho met with his countrymen and women while he was in that city negotiating with the French on Vietnam's future. One-day Ho met Truong at the home that the Vietnamese President was staying during his negotiations.

As Truong recalls in his *A Viet Cong Memoir*, when he first met Ho "he gave off an air of fragility, almost sickliness. However, these impressions only contributed to the dignity that enveloped him as though it were something tangible…Ho exuded a combination of inner strength and personal generosity that struck me with something like a physical blow. He looked directly at me, and at the others, with a magnetic expression of intensity and warmth. Almost reflexively I found myself thinking of my grandfather." In fact, Ho told him and the others as their conversations continued for several hours, to call him 'Uncle Ho' instead of President.

The above passage reflects both how Ho wanted his countrymen to see him, and how many of his fellow Vietnamese viewed the man throughout the rest of his life and struggles. The effects of his life as a revolutionary – the long, arduous travels, often on foot; his years at sea; the loneliness and punishments in many jails; and his travails as the spiritual leader of a nationalist movement – all gave him a worn and fragile outward appearance. Physically the grueling travel and troubling times in terrible jail conditions would eventually kill him.

Yet, his inner confidence, tranquility, and devotion – as those Vietnamese, even the nationalist Bui Diem, and some others who saw him and came to admire him observed – made him an older, wiser family member to be listened to and revered. This fits in well with the Mandarin and Confucian way of life of quiet obedience in the face of hardship in the struggle for a better life. Even though Ho had a lead role in a vicious struggle over many decades that resulted in millions of Vietnamese deaths - and that his or his comrades' policies led to much suffering, inequities, and hardships - that is the way most Vietnamese viewed this revolutionary. It will serve his cause well in the struggle for unification.

Most American senior policymakers, however, never understood how Ho's background and revolutionary experience motivated him for his trying quest for both independence and unification. Neither did they understand how this diminutive, sickly-looking Asian man could motivate other Vietnamese to join his cause and fight for his vision. For most of these Western cultured, highly educated, and wealthy men, Ho was someone who was wedded to communism and taking the direction of his supporters in the Soviet Union and Communist China.

Despite his statesman qualities and diplomatic abilities, and the admiration of many Frenchmen that he met, Ho's efforts in France failed. He was unable to get the assurances that he sought. He returned to Vietnam. Landing in Saigon in October 1946, he obtained an audience with d'Argenlieu. The latter tried to get Ho to agree to withdraw Viet-Minh armed forces from the South. Ho saw that the Commissioner was not about to compromise on what he had announced earlier about French control over the south.

Not recognizing de facto French control of the South, Ho then sailed North. When he got to Hanoi, he found the situation tense between the French and his government. He also found that his colleagues were in no way in a mood to further compromise with the French. Some were highly critical of Ho and his willingness to deal with them. Nevertheless, the peoples' reception demonstrated that they remained dedicated to him.

At the end of October, in response to attempts by the Viet-Minh to smuggle more modern arms into the country, a French warship bombarded the Vietnamese area in Haiphong. Soon after, French airstrikes supported them. Over two days the French attacks killed more than a thousand civilians. They were under orders from d'Argenlieu. When Ho found out that the French High Commissioner had given the orders to the troops to use force, he gave up any hope of reconciliation.

By December conflicts continued with the French troops who were trying to take control over DRV facilities in Hanoi. Ho officially declared war against the French on 19 December. The fight for independence was underway.

At once, Giap launched an offensive against French facilities in Hanoi. What became known as the Battle for Hanoi did not turn out well for the Viet-Minh. They were no match for the regular French forces they faced. After two months, they fled to the base areas that Giap had set up over the last several years.

In the South, the Viet-Minh stepped up their fight against the French. But here too, the Viet-Minh had to retreat to and operate out of secluded, hidden bases in the mountains and the Mekong Delta regions. By February, the French reported losing almost 2,000 men killed or wounded throughout Vietnam. The Viet-Minh losses are unknown.

Meanwhile, in the US, the Truman Administration had concluded that the war was a result of a collusion between the Communist Vietnamese Government under Ho Chi Minh and the Soviets and Red Chinese under Stalin and Mao. The Americans believed that the latter two were furnishing advice and instructions to the Viet-Minh. The primary evidence for this conclusion, at first, was French provided intelligence. Nevertheless, currently the official US line was that it was neutral in the conflict.

By late February 1947 the French Expeditionary Force, now commanded by Leclerc's replacement General John Etienne Valluy and numbering upwards of 100,000 men throughout Indochina, had taken control of Hanoi, Haiphong, Hue, and most of the Red River Delta. Ho and Giap – along with most of the Viet-Minh government - had planted themselves primarily in the northern Viet Bac base area. Small guerilla units, along with political cadres, remained embedded in many of the villages throughout the Tonkin region.

Giap began to prepare for a long war, to include more conventional battles eventually. Accordingly, he began to organize some of the Viet-Minh forces into larger units. They hid in the highly-vegetated mountains and valleys of the secure base areas near the Chinese border awaiting orders. Meanwhile, Ho emphasized and oversaw the organization of small communist political cells. These were infiltrated or covertly initiated both in the densely populated urban areas and the cluster of villages in the surrounding rural regions. They would be protected by locally recruited militias whose members continued to be shop owners or farmers when not taking armed action.

In the South, particularly around Saigon, French forces continued to have the upper hand. Some clashes occurred from time to time with the Viet-Minh forces. These also were primarily found in their various mountainous and jungle hideouts. Some guerrilla forces operated in and near villages and hamlets. Their leading role, like those in the North, was to protect and act as a militant arm to the Viet-Minh political cadres there. These worked to convince the population that the August Revolution had enacted an independent Vietnam, which the French were trying to nullify.

Now throughout Vietnam and in other parts of Indochina, acting as farmers during the day, the local guerrilla forces conducted operations against any vulnerable French forces at night. Sometimes, a few main force Viet-Minh organizations from their hidden base camps further away from the populated areas supported these guerrillas. However, unlike their brethren in the North, these main force units did not yet have the supplies and equipment to conduct sustained combat operations against the French.

In both the North and the South, as Bernard Fall wrote in his *Street Without Joy*, the French 'control' of Vietnam, in general, was primarily in and around the urban areas. Along the roads in between, they controlled about "two hundred yards on either side." There simply was not enough manpower to do otherwise.

The French Expeditionary Forces numbered more colonial troops and Foreign Legionnaires than Frenchmen. The Government could not afford politically and economically to put national French Army forces in the field. Nevertheless, General Valluy, who was a decorated veteran of the two world wars, felt confident that he could readily destroy the Viet-Minh military forces.

Viet-Minh Strategy – A People's War

In their base at Tan Trao, Ho and Giap continued to plan for their 'People's War.' They agreed that their core strategy would follow Mao's doctrine. Both had learned its basic principles and had observed its successful implementation while in China. Both had also indoctrinated their subordinates on Mao's political-military approach to revolutionary warfare over the last several years. These subordinates, in turn, drilled it into the minds of their political cadres and military commanders.

As William Duiker explains, the Viet-Minh revolutionary strategy for its war against France in the late forties evolved from Ho's early pronouncements at the beginning of World War II when the Viet-Minh front first formed. At a plenum meeting outside of Saigon in 1939 and later in several papers, Ho argued that their struggle would begin with the building of a mass base among the people. The intent was to obtain their support to recruit at first some small units, which would then gradually form a military force to wage an armed struggle against both the Japanese and French military units in Indochina. Indeed, during 1941 some Viet-Minh elements, numbering between thirty to a hundred, had conducted a few small unit operations against the French, followed by increasing size elements – to two hundred - against the Japanese in 1945.

As Douglas Pike describes in his book, *People's Army of Vietnam*, Ho's and Giap's version of Mao's People's War had a distinctly different approach from the Chinese leader's. First, they made several adaptations based on their above experiences in the early forties. Second, its political actions differed somewhat from those specified in Mao's approach because their political circumstances were unlike those of the Chinese revolution. Therefore, their overall method, adapted for the specific conditions in Indochina and Vietnam, called for a more closely integrated political and military struggle, which they labeled the 'Dau Tranh' Strategy.

That strategy's dominant political component would consist of three main elements: the Dan Van, Binh Van, and Dich Van. Dan Van described the actions to accomplish in dealing with the Vietnamese people to gain their support. These consisted of activities to motivate and unite the populace to its cause. It included instructions on how to act particularly around the mostly peasant population to gain their favor.

The Binh Van element consisted of actions directed toward the enemy's military. These included acts to subvert the enemy's military effectiveness, such as propaganda to undermine their support for their government and encourage lower morale and defection.

Finally, the Dich Van element of the political strategy consisted of specific activities directed toward the Vietnamese people who had given their support to the enemy government and its military. It included acts and propaganda to sow discontent and create disfavor toward the enemy state.

In conjunction with the above political program, the military component of their overall strategy more closely followed Mao's strategic doctrine for a three-stage war of independence. In the first stage, aggressive political activities would dominate actions to gain the support of the people for the revolutionary forces. That would entail the setting up of political-military cells in or in proximity to the population's cities, hamlets, and villages. These cells would educate the people on revolutionary principles, in this case, communist and nationalist ideas and values, and serve as the local governing political arm of the revolution. They would also use coercion to convince key people to support the movement and to recruit people for local guerrilla units.

Actions at this stage would include the assassination of existing government officials – particularly those who were competent and successful in their office. The locally organized guerrilla forces would carry these out under the direction of the cell leaders. Meanwhile, the revolutionary main forces would organize and prepare for an eventual move to the second phase. Military operations in this stage would be mainly defensive – protecting bases, husbanding forces, and conducting spoiling attacks against the most vulnerable enemy locales and forces. As much as possible the revolutionary forces would avoid open and large-scale engagements.

In the second stage - launched when first stage preparations were complete, and some military parity reached with the enemy – revolutionary main forces would appear from their base areas and aided by both the local guerrilla forces and population, launch surprise attacks against critical enemy installations and units. The object of this phase was to spread the revolution and show the people that the existing regime was both illegitimate and unworthy of ruling.

In the third stage, referred to as 'the general offensive,' revolutionary forces would launch an all-out attack to defeat the enemy's military, overthrow its political institutions, and take over. During this stage, the goal was for the general population, aided by both the political and military revolutionary forces, to revolt against the enemy regime and further assist the revolutionary main military units in their endeavor. This stage, per Mao's doctrine, would only begin when the revolutionary forces had gained superiority in the military balance and support from the people.

As rigid as Mao's military strategy seemed, both Ho and Giap anticipated that in executing it in the circumstances they would face, the movement into and between phases might have to experience an ebb and flow. That is, in a move from one phase to another the revolutionary forces may suffer or experience a defeat or setback that would require a regrouping and another launch at some later time. Time was a critical factor in this doctrine. Those implementing it should expect decades or more to obtain victory.

It is important to emphasize here that while both Ho and Giap believed in the efficacy of Mao's overall strategy, they expected that they needed to adjust it as necessary to the Vietnamese situation and their overall successes or defeats on the battlefield in the long term. As their war against the French experienced a series of both successes and setbacks, that situation further reinforced for them the need to be flexible in moving between Mao's designated stages and their integrated use of regular main and guerrilla forces.

At this stage of their struggle, in executing their above described political-military strategy, Ho continually argued for the accommodation of the non-communist elements of the Viet-Minh. Thus, in most of his and his communist subordinate dealings with them, they kept their ideas on communist social and economic philosophies subdued. The crux of their propaganda, therefore, focused on nationalist themes rather than communist political doctrine. This also enabled them to argue in the international arena that the Viet-Minh and the DRV were primarily nationalist rather than communist based organizations.

Meanwhile, Giap recognized that their military arm was not yet strong enough at this stage to directly challenge the French forces. Moreover, their recruitment base included several non-Vietnamese areas and mostly limited to the rural areas of northern Vietnam and even more restricted areas in the South. Thus, both Ho and Giap comprehended that their struggle might be more prolonged and not precisely follow the Chinese experience.

In sum, Ho and Giap were not concerned so much about moving from guerrilla to more conventional operations based solely on the balance of forces in the region of operations. Instead, they felt that if they could challenge the French in larger scale operations in one area of Indochina they would; while still conducting guerrilla operations in another. Moreover, as we will see, if they failed in their major unit engagements they were willing to then revert to small-scale guerrilla-type operations if need be to gain time to launch larger-scale operations when circumstances permitted. Furthermore, unlike the Chinese and Mao's doctrine, they more closely integrated guerrilla actions with their larger scale, main force, operations.

Later we will see that this flexibility would pay off in their struggle against the French. It would then become a hallmark of North Vietnamese military operations in their war against the Americans. As we will also see, US civilian and military leaders would never understand this flexibility. It would haunt them in their estimations of their enemy's intent and capabilities to conduct operations against them.

Viet-Minh Military Forces - The Founding of the People's Army of Vietnam (PAVN)

Ho and Giap recognized that the key to this doctrine would be how to organize the forces, both political and military, to execute it. In this area, Giap brought Ho up to date on the status of the Viet-Minh military. His military forces had come far from its earlier days of its formation.

As Douglas Pike relates, the Viet-Minh military arm had its beginning in the latter part of 1944. That is, as previously mentioned, when Giap began to form his first official military organizations. These were three small teams each made up of ten to twelve men and women. Collectively Giap referred to these teams as the 'Armed Propaganda Platoons.' While armed and used for military operations, they also at first primarily trained and acted for political purposes. Their armaments consisted of a variety of pistols, old rifles – and even ancient flintlock muskets.

As this force grew, it would become increasingly a military organization, commanded by trained officers, and accompanied by political commissars like other communist military organizations. Much of its armament before the Chinese support consisted of arms captured from the Colonial French and Japanese occupation forces. Some of it was, before the war's end, also made up of American-supplied World War Two rifles.

Over the last several years, notably when Ho was a prisoner in China during 1946, Giap had made significant headway in training his forces. He had also judiciously employed them primarily in small unit actions against vulnerable units of the French Expeditionary Force. It was now variously called the Vietnam Liberation Army or, what its leaders finally decided upon, the People's Army of Vietnam or PAVN. While the strength of this Army varies with many sources, it now consisted of some 50,000 main force troops, with 30,000 primarily in the North.

Giap had begun at the end of 1946 to organize his main forces into larger units – mostly companies and battalions of one hundred to three hundred soldiers each. By the end of 1947, he further formed some battalions into divisions of around 9,000 soldiers. Though he dispersed most of these divisional units, Giap felt he could assemble them if necessary with some preparation time to engage in battle where and when he chose.

Although not armed entirely as well as the French, their weapons were improving. This improvement was mostly a result of obtaining arms from China. Weapons continued to include captured French arms from some depots and defeated units, as well. In sum, the PAVN were becoming a well-trained Army, and, with its political commissars continually teaching communist doctrine, thoroughly indoctrinated to the cause.

Giap informed Ho that he thought, though he and others were never certain, that the Viet-Minh also had guerrilla forces numbering somewhere between 80-100,000 men and women. These were scattered throughout the country. They had a vital role to play. As mentioned, they would protect the political cells, harass the enemy, and give necessary intelligence to the main forces. With the paucity of regular forces in the South, the Viet-Minh leaders there came to rely on recruiting mostly guerrilla forces, both at the local and regional levels.

Viet-Minh Early Tactics Prove Effective – OPERATION LEA

The French commander, General Valluy, was also doing his organizing and planning. Having gained control of Hanoi and most of the Red River Delta, where the majority of the population in the North lived, he decided to strike out against the Viet-Minh base areas along the Chinese border. After seven months of preparation, on October 7, 1947, he launched OPERATION LEA.

LEA was a large-scale attack. It consisted of about 15,000 soldiers organized into three main thrusts directed toward the Viet Bac base area. Valluy aimed to surprise and surround the Viet-Minh leadership, capture, or kill Ho and Giap, and annihilate the main forces of the Viet-Minh. The French General thought he would crush Viet-Minh resistance in one blow and end the war.

Problems plagued the operation from the start. First, the Viet-Minh became aware of the plans through their embedded agents amongst the population and in some French headquarters units. This intelligence enabled Giap to move and concentrate his forces to counter the primary French attacks. Second, Valluy could not muster enough forces to support all three of his attacks. He had to keep forces tied up securing roads and key installations. Thus, none of his maneuvers had enough combat power to achieve their goals.

Despite these problems, one of the leading thrusts – a French airborne assault near the Viet-Minh headquarters – killed several of Giap's subordinate leaders. It also nearly captured Ho, who narrowly escaped. The other two attacks, one an armored attack along the main roads leading into the area from the west, and the other a river bound assault using some small boats and landing craft, confronted stiff resistance. It was the result of ample warnings of the timing and direction of the attacks.

The fighting mainly consisted of a series of ambushes and night attacks that the Viet-Minh initiated and that surprised French units. Throughout, the Viet-Minh chose hit and run attacks using unmapped trails and small roads that local scouts knew well. After the first attacks caused casualties and halted the French advance, the Viet-Minh units would then disperse and move away, avoiding further battle.

The fighting continued for a month. The French claimed a significant victory. They estimated that they inflicted significant casualties – about 9,500 according to some sources. They had also forced the Viet-Minh to give up their headquarters and seized some logistic stockpiles.

In the following weeks, the French withdrew back to the Delta region. They left behind a series of forts along the China-Vietnam border with small garrisons to patrol and harass the enemy in the vast areas of mostly jungle mountainous terrain. Valluy reported to Paris that Lea was a success in causing considerable damage to the Viet-Minh and bringing stability back to Indochina. His offensive did not, however, drastically affect the morale or capability of the Viet-Minh to fight on.

OPERATION LEA, in the view of Bernard Fall's two books in *Street Without Joy* and *Hell in a Very Small Place*, was the first example of a flawed French strategy to launch large unit operations to create, what the French Generals were to label, a 'set-piece battle' to bring the Viet-Minh to defeat. The French search for the decisive battle to end the war would continue for the next seven years.

Following LEA both sides seemed satisfied with the status quo for the time being. Neither launched any major offensives. The Viet-Minh reoccupied the Viet Bac area. Giap was content to reestablish his logistics, continue to grow and train his forces, and harass the French forts on the China frontier. While he was overall pleased with his troop's performance, he remained determined to wait for an opportune moment to launch a major offensive of his choosing. The French continued to hold on to the major cities, control the major roads, and patrol the frontier from their forts near the Chinese border.

The only significant move was a political one. The French created the semblance of a legitimate "independent Vietnam within the French Union." Their motives were two-fold. First, they wanted to discredit the Viet-Minh's claim that it was fighting for Vietnamese independence. Second, they wanted to show the Americans, who were becoming their main supporter of military arms and equipment, that it was trying to create an independent, noncommunist state eventually.

In setting up this new 'Vietnamese' political entity, the French government reached out to Bao Dai, the last Emperor of the Nguyen Dynasty who had fled to France when the conflict broke out. They convinced him to return as the nominal head of the new government. This new government soon had its inaugural ceremony in Hanoi. Fewer than fifty Vietnamese attended. Everyone saw this for what it was. What became known as the 'Bao Dai solution' was nothing more than a puppet government that had little power and no independence. It was a sham. Ho proclaimed it so, and Bao Dai, a traitor. The Emperor soon sailed back to Europe to enjoy the resorts, casinos, and parties given in his honor.

By late 1948 and early 1949, the situation changed drastically for Ho and Giap. In the fall of 1948, Mao was on the verge of winning the civil war against the Chinese Nationalists. Giap increased the harassment of the French forts along the border in anticipation of the Red Chinese victory. In the South, Viet-Minh forces boosted their attacks against French convoys and posts, as well.

By the end of the year, while the French Expeditionary Force (FEF) numbers had not changed since the Lea attacks, Giap had increased his military to some 250,000. He had also completed the further organization and training of these forces. The Viet-Minh Armed forces now consisted of three distinct, but complementary components.

There was its regular army, now commonly referred to as the PAVN. These units were his best trained armed forces designed to engage the French regulars. Then there were the regional units sometimes referred to as district forces. These were well armed and trained, but not as well as the regulars. They were to assist both the regular forces when engaged and the local forces as needed. The last contingent was the local guerrilla-militia forces. By year's end, these elements were throughout Vietnam. Now, about half of the Vietnamese population lived in Viet-Minh controlled territory.

Internationalization of the Conflict - Red Chinese Civil War Victory and Korean War

At the end of 1949, Mao won his civil war and declared the establishment of the Communist People's Republic of China (PRC). In January the next year, he recognized Ho Chi Minh's DRV as the legitimate Vietnamese Government. Several weeks after, the Soviet Union followed suit.

That same month Ho arrived in Beijing to meet with PRC officials about support for the DRV. He quickly obtained assurances for significant economic and military aid. Mao told him "Whatever China had and Vietnam needs, we will provide." Ho then went on to Moscow where he met with both Stalin and Mao. Stalin gave his support, though he appeared more subdued and less excited about the Vietnamese war against the French than Mao did.

A month later, the PRC set up an advisory group to train and assist the Viet-Minh. Over the next six months, Red Chinese advisors, veterans who had fought in their Civil War, would be in Viet-Minh units down to battalion size. Arms and supplies flowed into North Vietnam. According to Mark Moyar, "during the first nine months of 1950, the Chinese shipped 14,000 rifles, 1,700 machine guns and recoilless rifles, 60 artillery pieces, 300 bazookas, and a variety of other military equipment." By the end of 1950, the regular Viet-Minh Army's firepower was equal to the French Expeditionary Forces.

From the US perspective, this Soviet and Communist Chinese recognition and aid was evidence of a communist move to take over Southeast Asia. The French fueled this perception by continuously reminding the Truman Administration that they were the sole protector against communist aggression there. When North Korea attacked the South in June of 1950 that sealed the French argument. To the US, the invasion was proof of the intent of the communists to threaten all of Asia and its southeastern rim.

Truman committed, under pressure from the Congress, support for the French in Indochina. He further recognized the Bao Dai government as a free nation in the French Union. By mid-1950, the war in Indochina in general, and the fighting in Vietnam specifically, had become an international affair and part of the Cold War global confrontation.

With the Red Chinese aid, Giap felt that the time to launch an offensive was opportune. He targeted the dispersed French forts situated along what the French called Route Colonial 4 or RC4 on the China-Vietnam border. Ho approved his scheme. The object was to clear the border of French units. This action would then allow for more freedom of movement between northern Vietnam and southern China.

During the summer Giap prepared his forces for the offensive. They meticulously scouted the French forts. Viet-Minh leaders with their Chinese advisors built replicas and rehearsed their attacks on each position. Confident that he had the proper balance of forces, Giap planned for a major offensive in September 1950.

French leaders got wind of this attack. However, they underestimated Viet-Minh capabilities. They did not think they were as numerous, well trained, and well-armed as Giap's forces now were. Moreover, French commanders, as would happen again at Dien Bien Phu four years later, did not think that the Viet-Minh had or could employ heavy weapons to support their attacks.

On 16 September 1950, Giap began his offensive against the French fort at Dong Khe. After two days of fierce fighting, the post fell. A succession of battles for the other forts followed. In a month of exhaustive fighting, the French withdrew from their border redoubts. Overall the FEF suffered 6,000 casualties of the 10,000 garrisoning the forts. They also lost a host of weapons, munitions, and vehicles; much of which the Viet-Minh captured. Of the 30,000 Viet-Minh troops in the fight, 9,000 may have been killed. Despite the fall of the forts, this was a significant loss for Giap's forces.

Bernard Fall would later state that "the French suffered their greatest colonial defeat since Montcalm had died at Quebec" in 1759. Logevall wrote of this defeat, "the French had been driven out of northern Tonkin, from the sea to the Red River. The border to China was completely open, from Lao Cai to coastal Mong Cai. The French fell back on a 375-mile northern perimeter, with Hanoi at its core. Panic swept the French communities in Hanoi and elsewhere in the delta, and there was open talk of abandoning Tonkin entirely."

The De Lattre Line

By January 1951, the French had abandoned all northern Vietnam north of the Red River. At home, the public and politicians were calling for a complete withdrawal from all of Indochina. The French Government, seeking to remedy the dour situation they now faced, sent the most distinguished General they had to take over as both the new High Commissioner for Indochina and commander of the FEF – Marshal Jean de Lattre de Tassigny.

King 'Jean,' as many of his countrymen often called him, was a highly-decorated soldier during World War One. He had been wounded three times at Sedan – one of the bloodiest battles of that war. During the Battle of France in May 1940, he was one of the few French commanders who had beaten the invading Nazi forces in combat. After the fall of France, the General went to fight for the free French forces. He reached the rank of full general, and, under Eisenhower's command, led the First French Army in the liberation of his country in 1944.

Arriving in December 1950, the French 'MacArthur,' as some Americans called him, quickly gained the confidence of his troops. He ordered the execution of a new theater strategy. Taking the advice of his son who was an infantry lieutenant serving in the FEF, de Lattre decided to concentrate his forces to protect the population and start a pacification program to bring peace and stability. He chose the Tonkin region as his central operational area. Within it, he set up a defensive enclave to secure and protect the densely populated and rice producing region of the Red River Delta and its principal city, Hanoi.

What became known as the 'De Lattre Line' – the outer perimeter of the enclave – consisted of a chain of mutually supporting fortified positions. The FEF commander planned to quickly move forces to reinforce and counterattack any of these posts as needed. To do so, he also organized his more elite units into mobile groups commanded by his most trusted Colonels, whom he dubbed his 'Marshals' – a term reminiscent of Napoleons' trusted subordinates.

Knowing that the French government remained unwilling to send significant other forces to bolster the FEF, de Lattre further began to organize friendly indigenous Vietnamese forces into units in support of the FEF. Their mission, primarily, would be to protect the native Vietnamese population under French control and execute the pacification program.

Hearing of the arrival of Marshal de Lattre, Giap sought to move quickly. He wanted to attack the French around the Delta region before the French General could fully set up his defenses. Giap, now "brimming with confidence following his victories in northern Tonkin" wanted to move into the last stage of Mao's Revolutionary War doctrine – the general offensive.

This sparked a debate in Viet-Minh councils. Some questioned whether the timing and the balance of forces were right to go on the general offensive. Giap, now having much political capital because of the border success, convinced reluctant Viet-Minh members that any delay would only reduce the chances of victory. Ho agreed and gave the final go ahead.

In mid-January 1951, Giap attacked. The Viet-Minh struck at three separate locations. The first was at a critical road junction northwest of Hanoi. A communist victory there would open the way to an attack against Hanoi itself. That attack was at the head or furthest point of the de Lattre Line. The other two attacks were at the base of the line – one at the northern and the other at the southern. In military terms, the two thrusts at the base represented a classic attempt at a double envelopment. If the maneuver succeeded, it could lead to the disintegration and later annihilation of the entire FEF manning the defensive line.

These Viet-Minh attacks were not simultaneous. They lacked overall coordination. The Viet-Minh high command had trouble controlling large bodies of forces in big battles. These mistakes allowed de Lattre to move his mobile groups from one battle to another over the course of the campaign. The FEF also received help from newly arrived American airplanes, weapons, and ammunition. The air strikes in support of the French defenses were particularly effective – especially the use of a new napalm munition first employed in Korea.

French leadership was equally effective. De Lattre was present at most of the battles. He encouraged his commanders and uplifted the morale of his soldiers. As a result, after four months of fierce fighting, Giap withdrew. The revitalized FEF had put up an unexpected successful mobile defense. On the other hand, the Viet-Minh forces had not been ready for the general offensive that Giap had insisted upon.

Some recriminations followed. Giap admitted his errors. Ho Chi Minh calmed most of the dissent. He told the Viet-Minh senior leaders that they must learn from their mistakes. The general offensive failed because all had been overconfident. He vowed that that should never occur again.

The victory elated the French, both in Indochina and in France. De Lattre was a hero and a savior. Unfortunately, his son died in the fighting. That would eventually break the FEF commander's spirit. The General also found out he had cancer. Trying to overcome these afflictions, he continued to work hard at bolstering the defenses around the Red River Delta area. He also worked at trying to set up a legitimate government and build a Vietnamese Army. However, the Vietnamese leader the French counted on, Bao Dai, did not have the stomach for it – he much preferred spending his time gambling and playing tennis on the French Riviera.

While Giap retreated and prepared for the future, de Lattre worked feverishly to gain material support from both the Americans and his politicians. He visited the US; where he received a hero's welcome. In a speech to the US Congress, he argued that the war in Indochina and Korea were interdependent, and part of the communist goal of spreading their dogma and hold over Asia. The Truman Administration and the public voiced their support and pledged more aid. A young Republican Senator named John F. Kennedy decided to take a trip to Vietnam to see for himself what was going on because of de Lattre's words to the Congress.

Afterward, de Lattre went to France before returning to Indochina. The French General plead for more forces from his government. They ignored him. The postwar French governments were too unstable and divided to reach an agreement. The Public wanted nothing to do with the war in far-off Indochina.

Indochina Misunderstood

By the end of the year, de Lattre relinquished his command for health reasons. In January 1952, he died in Paris. From time to time on his deathbed, he called out for his son. In the end, he muttered, "I have never completely understood Indochina…." This statement would later be a frequent lament of American leaders facing similar circumstances there.

De Lattre's successors would not heed his revelations about Vietnam. They continued to seek an easy one battle or campaign to end the conflict. His first replacement, General Raoul Salan, was, in the minds of the French general staff, an Indochina expert. He had served there for much of his professional career and had married a Laotian woman. He followed in the footsteps of pre-de Lattre commanders.

Soon after taking over, Salan ordered yet another large force offensive. Called OPERATION LORRAINE once again the object was to end the war by destroying the main forces of the Viet-Minh. Launched in the Fall of 1952, it was the most massive French offensive of the war. It consisted of over thirty thousand men of the FEF with thousands of American provided planes, tanks, and artillery.

Giap chose not to engage decisively. Instead, he employed his regional forces to harass the supply lines of the road bound French Expeditionary Force. Meanwhile, he used his regular forces to conduct raids and ambushes against targets presenting an opportunity for a Viet-Minh victory. One such opportunity was the ambush of two French mobile groups in the highlands outside of the Red River Delta near the Laotian border. The groups lost heavily. Overall the operation cost some 1,200 FEF casualties and resulted in yet another hasty retreat to the lowlands of the delta region.

LORRAINE was not without some Viet-Minh mishaps, however. At one-point Giap again became overconfident and counterattacked a remote French outpost at a place called Na San. The French fought back fiercely. They decisively defeated Giap's onslaught. This Viet-Minh set back further fueled the French belief that they could eventually lure the communists into a set piece battle that would end the war in their favor.

At the beginning of 1953 Giap, with Ho's approval, decided to launch an assault on the now dispersed French military units. He directed this one not at the main French forces in the Delta region, but against small FEF garrisons spread out in Laos. Giap felt that an offensive there would further attract support from the mountain tribes in that area that had not yet lent support to the Viet-Minh movement. He also reasoned that the French could be drawn to the Laotian area and defeated in a series of fights of his choosing. Giap thought that with a series of successes, the French public would then bring pressure on its government to end the war.

As Giap planned for this new campaign, Ho assessed the political climate. He recognized that the Vietnamese War for independence had become an international affair. Both the Americans and Chinese Communists had become heavily involved in supporting the opposing sides. The US by 1953 supplied most of the money, weapons, equipment, and supplies for the French. Its Military Assistance and Advisor Group or MAAG had begun taking a more active part in getting the French to be more aggressive. Meanwhile, the Chinese had also played a pivotal role. They not only gave sanctuaries to the Viet-Minh forces in the North but, through its own Military Assistance Group, continued to provide significant material aid and military advisors.

Ho now assessed that the overall situation favored the Viet-Minh. De Lattre had left. His replacement was not as talented. The French public had decidedly turned against the war. Meanwhile, the Americans under Eisenhower were pursuing a negotiated settlement over Korea. The US and China had arranged for a ceasefire in June 1953. This arrangement released the Chinese from a costly war in Korea to focus on their support for the Viet-Minh. What the Viet-Minh needed and hoped for was a significant victory that would influence the French and the international community to negotiate an end to their war favorably.

Ho would get his wish. In May 1953, a new French commander, General Henri Navarre, had taken command of the FEF. Immediately he faced two significant challenges. Giap's Laos offensive had produced several significant victories over French defensive outposts there. The French high command had done nothing to prevent these positions from falling. Navarre was now under intense pressure from his government and the Americans to take the offensive. In fact, the US government had made it evident that they would tie any continued aid to more aggressive French action.

Moreover, the French government, observing that the US was willing to seek a negotiated settlement to their own 'dirty war' in Korea, now sought such a settlement in Indochina. They reasoned that a decisive battle against the Viet-Minh would be just the right catalyst for such an end to their 'dirty war.' They urged Navarre to take the offensive.

According to Frederick Logevall, Navarre accommodated both the Americans and his politicians and declared, "We will take the offensive... We shall give back to our troops the mobility and aggressiveness they have sometimes lacked." He further proclaimed that "victory was certain." His plan - some historians argue it was more an American plan - was to put in place an air-ground base along the Laotian border to goad Giap into attacking a strong, entrenched French force. That force could then act as a strong point, resisting the first onslaught, and holding its position. That would then enable superior firepower to defeat the Viet-Minh engaged there in battle.

This approach was precisely what had happened earlier at the battle at Na San. All that was needed now was to repeat that victory on a larger scale. Such a victory would as the French high command explained and hoped, "break the organized body of Communist aggression" and give the French the victory it needed to settle the war favorably.

Dien Bien Phu and the Geneva Conference

In November 1953, the French launched OPERATION CASTOR. They began with an airborne drop of 2200 paratroopers to occupy a place called Dien Bien Phu along the northwestern Vietnam and Laotian border. The FEF employed there almost 15,000 troops to establish a series of strongpoints protecting two airfields in a mile-wide valley between two major mountain ridges.

The French commander at Dien Bien Phu, relying on the advice of his artillery commander and his disdain for the Viet-Minh, was confident that the communist forces would not be able to employ artillery or air defense units that could seriously threaten these strongpoints, or interdict aerial resupply and reinforcement of his base. He also calculated that his adversary would not be able to sustain large regular forces against his positions in such a remote area. These calculations would prove foolhardy and wrong.

Though surprised by the quickness of the French move, Giap decided to quickly mass forces to confront it. His first action was to send reconnaissance elements to scout the activity at Dien Bien Phu. This force included elements to intercept French radio reports. These activities soon informed Giap of the intended employment of a large force there.

The Viet-Minh General, with Ho's and the Vietnamese Communist Party approval, quickly concentrated most of his northern regular force divisions in the vicinity. By extraordinary efforts, he was not only able to concentrate his infantry there but the artillery, air defense, and sustainment that the French never thought he could do. That effort required a support force of porters using some 20,000 bicycles. Eventually, this extraordinary feat enabled Giap to bring a force of almost 49,000 men to bear on the French base.

As this concentration was taking place, Ho said to Giap, "You are the general commanding the troops on the outer frontier.... I give you complete authority to make all decisions. If victory is certain, then you are to attack. If victory is not certain, then you must resolutely refrain from attacking."

Giap, however, did not have complete freedom of command. Because of the Viet-Minh dependence upon Communist Chinese assistance, he had to listen and consider his Chinese advisors. They were pressing him to adopt their Korean War tactics of massive frontal assaults to overrun French resistance, which they labeled 'swift attack, swift victory.'

From the end of the year to the third week of January 1954, Giap and his Chinese advisors discussed and argued about their plan of attack. The Vietnamese commander advocated a more prudent and methodical approach, which he called 'steady attack, steady advance.' The phrase was a euphemism for his concept of keeping the pressure on the base through artillery bombardments coupled with the digging of trenches closer and closer to the French outposts each of which would then be overrun in detail. At first, however, the Chinese concept won over the Vietnamese. Thus, Giap ordered an all-out assault on 24 January - Chinese Korean War style.

Giap countermanded the order, however, before it began. The ultimate reason is not apparent. Logevall lists several. The most compelling is that Giap felt that the French position was stronger than the Chinese realized. A massive all-out assault would risk everything at one time. He chose to be more methodical because he recalled his hastiness in his past approaches that had led to failure.

Giap later claimed that Ho's guidance had convinced him to wait and ensure his attack had a very high chance of success. He waited until all his artillery was in place, and his infantry could approach from covered positions. Then on 13 March, he launched his first major assault. His artillery was in place, ready, and supplied. His infantry had dug trenches to surround the strong points, enabling them to attack from close in. He had prepared the battlefield well.

By then international political and diplomatic events on Indochina had dramatically changed. At the beginning of January, the 'big four' superpowers of the day - the US, Great Britain, France, and the Soviet Union - had met in Berlin to discuss international issues, to include a formal ending of the conflict in Korea. At the end of their meeting, they agreed to convene an expanded conference in Geneva, Switzerland to further discuss Korea, but to also include talks on how to end the war in Indochina. At Geneva, the big four would include the Peoples' Republic of China, because of its involvement in both conflicts. Present also were the Viet-Minh and Bao Dai governments for the Indochina issue. The conference was to begin in late April.

A week before the Geneva Convention, Giap launched his final attack on Dien Bien Phu. Preceded by a massive artillery bombardment, three Viet-Minh regular divisions attacked the five French redoubt strongholds. One fell that day. Another two the next. Soon another Viet-Minh division joined in the assault and overran the fourth stronghold. The one remaining outpost, containing the French command group, finally fell on May 7th.

It was a historic victory for Giap and his bloodied and exhausted troops. As Fredrik Lodevall writes in his *Embers of War*, "For the first time in the annals of colonial warfare, Asian troops had defeated a European army in fixed battle." Dien Bien Phu had been a dramatic and devastating victory as well as historic. Of some 15,000 men who had served there under the French flag, less than half ever made it home. The Viet-Minh suffered over 10,000 deaths, and at least 15,000 wounded.

The Viet-Minh victory astonished the diplomats who had gathered at Geneva. They recognized at once that Dien Bien Phu had been one of the decisive victories in the history of warfare. Now they focused on Indochina rather than Korea or any other agenda items they had agreed to discuss.

Giap had timed his final offensive perfectly with the expected conference in Geneva. When the conference met, despite heavy losses and some setbacks, the Viet-Minh successes made it clear that the French at Dien Bien Phu were on the verge of collapse. As the conference met, it appeared to Ho Chi Minh that victory was now within his grasp.

However, the Soviets and Red China were worried that the US might intervene militarily in Indochina to save the French. Its recent intervention in Korea had caught them by surprise. They did not want to make that mistake again. American rhetoric remained bellicose both before, during, and after the fall of Dien Bien Phu. Reinforcing this fear, IKE and his representatives at Geneva hinted the use of force to resolve the overall Indochina question, especially in Laos.

The Viet-Minh benefactors were now intent upon some political rather than military solution. China wanted their presence at Geneva and its actions to "solidify her membership in the great-power club." In meetings before the Convention, Soviet and Chinese diplomats conveyed their feelings and advice to Ho and his party. It soon became obvious to Ho that his 'victory' would not be the complete one he had hoped for.

Therefore, the Viet-Minh delegation, led by Ho's close associate Pham Van Dong, had instructions from the Politburo to seek a compromise solution based on earlier discussions with their allies. What that exact compromise was, however, differed between them and their primary supporters – the Chinese Communist delegation headed by Zhou Enlai.

Ho and the Vietnamese Communists wanted to have both Laos and Cambodia recognized as independent. However, they also wanted the communist elements there, namely the Pathet Lao and Khmer parties, to head the Governments. These would then be tied to the DRV. The PRC, however, did not want to see a powerful Vietnam dominate the rest of Indochina. Zhou Enlai warned that communist regimes throughout Indochina might incite the US to act militarily there. He, therefore, argued for the creation of neutral regimes free of any outside party bases or forces.

During a recess in the proceedings at Geneva in early July, the Vietnamese Workers Party held its sixth Central Committee Plenum. The purpose was to discuss their final negotiating position for the conference. Several present had heard of the compromises discussed in Geneva. They did not want to settle for anything other than total victory over the French and immediate unification of the country.

Ho led the way in the discussions on the need for a peaceful, compromise solution. He voiced that his primary concern was that the US would intervene militarily and that would mean a continuation of a costly war – now with the World's greatest power. Ho further emphasized that the losses at Dien Bien Phu had left most of the Viet-Minh army bloodied and exhausted. He then argued that a political division of Vietnam could only be temporary. He convinced all that the southern portion would voluntarily vote for unification. With these convincing arguments, everyone agreed to support Ho's position.

When the convention reconvened, the participants reached an agreement. The principals signed and announced a treaty. There were six main provisions. The first was the temporary division of Vietnam at the 17th parallel. Second, there would be a demilitarized zone on each side of that demarcation line. Third, French and Viet-Minh forces would move to the south and north, respectively, of that line. Fourth, there would be a free movement of populations between the zones for 300 days. Fifth, parties would set up two administrative governing organizations in Vietnam. The Viet-Minh would lead the northern one. The French established Bao Dai government would lead the one in the south. Finally, there would be an International Control Commission to oversee the execution of the accords and ensure elections for the unification of the northern and southern zones in two years.

France and the Democratic Republic of Vietnam, along with the Soviets, PRC, and UK, signed the treaty and its accords. The US and a newly designated political organization in the South – the Republic of South Vietnam – did not. Ironically, the DRV signed to prevent the US from a military intervention in Indochina. Though the US distanced itself from the settlement, it increased its military aid to the newly created southern regime. The Eisenhower Administration hoped to create a stable government suitable for unifying a southern Vietnam like what the South Koreans had done after the Korean armistice.

As mentioned in Chapter 1, the US also set out to establish an international organization that would serve as a security mechanism to preserve that area from future communist attack. As previously explained, the Southeast Asia Treaty Organization, however, would become a 'paper tiger' – one that did not have an adequate military force or the political commitment to enforce any military containment in the area.

The transfer of authority from the French to the DRV in the North would take months to execute. So would the relocation of Viet-Minh political and military units in the South. In October, the victorious Vietnam People's Army once again marched into Hanoi. Among them were officials of the DRV to include their victorious military commander – Vo Nguyen Giap. They were setting foot in their capital for the first time in nearly eight years. Ho Chi Minh was not part of the parade. He would slip into the city quietly several days later.

The first thing Ho did was to seek out medical treatment for exhaustion and what would eventually kill him – heart disease from years of smoking and health neglect. He refused to settle in the French Governor-General's Palace, as the new DRV administration wanted. Instead, he chose a small gardener's house on the palace grounds.

He knew that the long struggle of the past was not yet over. He now needed to create a functioning government that could consolidate its gains in the North; while awaiting the resolution of the Geneva accords in the South.

Section 6.4 – Observations and Insights for Chapter 6

What can one observe and surmise about Vietnam geopolitics, its two main leaders in its quest for independence and unification, and US knowledge and understanding of both Vietnam and its leaders?

First, it is instructive to view Vietnam's geopolitics considering the evolution of the US containment policy during the Cold War. Indeed, that view provides an interesting supposition on why Vietnam became so important, even vital, to US policymakers from the Truman to the Johnson Administrations.

Several scholars argue that American policy toward Indochina in general and Vietnam was misguided. For example, George Herring states in his *America's Longest War*, "that the containment policy was misapplied in Vietnam seems beyond question." Cold War historian John Gaddis and others agree. At the heart of this argument is that neither Vietnam or Southeast Asia were of vital interest to the US. There was no overriding economic, social, or political factors that would have made it so.

There is evidence that supports Herring's and Gaddis' arguments. As discussed in Chapter 1, the initial US policy of containment, at least as George Kennan originally conceived it in 1946-7, sought to deter the Soviet aggressive behavior and contain it through a balance of power politics aimed at the protection of specific priority regions. In that scheme, Kennan and his State Department colleagues did not include Southeast Asia. Indeed, even one of the principal architects of implementing containment, Secretary of State Dean Acheson, in a speech in early 1950, did not include Southeast Asia in his perimeter defense of Asian countries against communist expansion.

However, in this author's view, it seems quite logical that the American leaders at the time deduced that Vietnam, considering the Chinese Communist threat perceived in Asia at the time, to be vital to US national security policy of containment. For example, when the US adopted NSC 68 in April 1950, several months after Acheson's Asian speech, the policy of containment began to take on a geopolitically extended and more zero-sum game approach. The underlying assumption of US national security policy became that any communist gain would result in a 'loss' to the US containment policy.

Thus, between the establishment in 1947 of the containment policy, as Kennan had described it and as Herring and Gaddis explained its original intent, and NSC 68's version of the policy of 1950, the purpose and extent of containment had changed dramatically. Why? One reason is that the NSC 68 version was after the communists had gained control in China and had recognized the Democratic Republic of Vietnam under Ho's leadership. It was also put into effect after the Korean War broke out. Thus, the situation had changed significantly, especially in Asia, between 1947 and 1950.

Another reason, related to the first, is that the drafters of NSC 68 adopted a more wide-ranging global geopolitical posture for containment than Kennan and his colleagues. To understand this more extensive view, one needs to read the rationale within the NSC 68 document carefully. When one does, you can see that the document reflects the arguments of two geopolitical theorists' – Sir Halford Mackinder and Nicholas Spykman – and their views on the world geographic influence on

US strategic policy. Indeed, the logic for NSC 68 follows the geopolitical ideas and premises of these two theorists.

For example, these theorists' premises, in very general terms, argue that the world divided into two major strategic geopolitical zones or areas. The predominant zone, the 'Heartland' – encompassing the central Eurasia landmass – offers any nation or nations in control of that area a critical geographic central position from which those powers could eventually control the globe. The two powers in the 1950s that could potentially control that position were the Soviet Union and Communist China.

On the other hand, the littoral regions of the heartland referred to as the 'Rimland,' offers a counter or defense to the projection of power by those in control of the Heartland. The premise here is that the nation or nations that control the Rimland can contain the outward movement of those in the Heartland, and thereby prevent their eventual control of the globe.

After the Second World War, the nation that could control the Rimland was the United States. It chose to do so by setting up bases along its exterior lines, and arranging for alliances, such as NATO and later SEATO, to further contain land operations that threatened to expand outward of the Heartland. The operative premise here in Spykman's words is: "Who controls the Rimland rules Eurasia; Who rules Eurasia rules the world."

This control of the Rimland area is exactly what the US military planners in the post-World War Two years attempted to incorporate in the US national military strategy for the policy of containment explained in Chapter 1. Indeed, that geopolitical reasoning had led to the establishment of a global posture outlined in the Unified Command Plan and subsequent stationing of US military forces in Europe, Japan, the Philippines and elsewhere around the globe.

From that perspective, Vietnam's critical geographic position on the eastern border of the Rimland is critical to the containment of the communist powers seeking control of the overall Eurasian landmass that includes central and western Europe and all South and Southeast Asia. This is the geopolitical logic of NSC 68. It is also the view implied in Eisenhower's original argument for the Domino effect in Southeast Asia adopted by both Kennedy and Johnson Administrations.

In the mid-fifties and early sixties, these views seem both logical and valid. Control of that part of the Rimland, i.e., Vietnam, which could further allow a hostile power's access to the entire maritime portions of Southeast Asia, could be essential. In fact, without directly quoting either the Mackinder or Spykman theories, the CIA gave an estimate of the loss of Vietnam and Southeast Asia to the communists in geopolitical terms like their theories and its premises explained above. The estimate posited that both were critical geographical locations that, if under communist control, would vitally threaten US global interests.

Thus, it seems that not only was it logical to view Vietnam as vital to US interests by the Kennedy, Johnson, and Nixon Administrations, but, particularly from a geopolitical perspective, very much worthy of the commitment of American Arms to resist its control by communist states.

However, while American policymakers judged Vietnam as vital to US security, it is undeniable that many American decision-makers ignored Vietnam history and culture at their peril. They misunderstood or disregarded the experiences and strategic policies of Ho and Giap, the two leaders most responsible for the Viet-Minh victory over the French. In so doing, they underestimated the intentions and capabilities of the North Vietnamese, overestimated the abilities of the South Vietnamese, and ignored the entire French experiences in Vietnam and Indochina. In this sense, George Herring's argument that the US ignored local forces to their peril in their policies toward Southeast Asia seems valid.

US senior policymakers should have noticed that the long history of conflict in and conquest over Vietnam demonstrated an unquestionable resolve to fight a prolonged war against any intruder threatening national unification and survival. They should have also recognized that internal conflicts within the bounds of the Vietnam area of Indochina indicate that not all of Vietnam was destined to be unified by those who fought the Chinese. Moreover, the lengthy nature of the conflict in Vietnam culture should have alerted the US policymakers that getting them to settle easily and quickly based on limited and graduated military pressure was neither practical nor probable.

Instead, American leaders and their senior advisors either disregarded past pronouncements of both Ho and Giap for total victory at any cost; or, like Westmoreland in his memoirs, dismissed them as merely some distinct Asian trait for disregard of the value of human life. Furthermore, American leaders overlooked or disregarded lessons they should have learned from the DRV's war with the French – a war that America was, by 1950, heavily involved in.

Yet, the primary assumption of American policy toward North Vietnam during the Kennedy, Johnson and Nixon administrations was that the US could convince the DRV leaders to desist in their desire to unify the South and North. Presidents and most of their principal advisors just ignored or dismissed the extended period of resistance to French colonial rule, and the successes of the Viet-Minh over the French to eventually gain independence.

Moreover, if decision makers had been knowledgeable of the failures of French colonialism and the reasons for Vietnamese resistance, they might have recognized that the South Vietnamese government reflected more of the policies of their former French masters than a genuinely nationalist movement. Also, American decision-makers seemed to dismiss the Vietnamese victory over their former western colonial masters a result more of French ineptness rather than Viet-Minh prowess.

That is not to say that all in the Kennedy, Johnson, and Nixon Administrations were ignorant of this history. One can find many US documents, such as the national intelligence estimates, that pay tribute to the will of the North Vietnamese movement and its resilience to resist force to desist its war on the South. There were also State Department and Defense Department papers that produced insights on Vietnamese history and culture. One of the most famous, of course, is the McNamara directed *Pentagon Papers*. Then, let us not forget George Ball, who argued vehemently and cogently to avoid the French experience with their Vietnamese opponents to no avail.

However, like several Joint Staff studies showing the weaknesses of pursuing a War of Attrition, the top policymakers, for several reasons, just ignored the counterarguments and warnings on Vietnam. One might judge from this that 'The Best and Brightest' thought they knew better than the bureaucratic experts. Their reliance on their intellectual powers led them to believe that they were right, and their ideas would prevail over historical evidence that suggested otherwise.

Above all, American senior policymakers did not know very much about the nature of the North Vietnamese key leaders in their war for independence or their experiences or those of their principal subordinates and compatriots. As we have noted in the earlier chapters, American leaders and advisors primarily viewed Ho and Giap as being devoted communists who, with Communist Soviet and Chinese sponsorship, were intent on establishing a communist state by force over all of Vietnam. They virtually disregarded their dedication, learned military skills, determination, and nationalist fervor to unify Vietnam eventually.

Ironically, as we will see in the next chapter, the two North Vietnamese leaders that the American decision makers and policy advisors sometimes paid attention to, Ho and Giap, were not the primary decision-makers during the American war. As the Vietnamese-born historian Lie-Hang Nguyen recently wrote in a *New York Times* article "Who Called the Shots in Hanoi" wrote, "Even by 1967, America's military, intelligence and civilian leaders had no real idea who was calling the shots in Hanoi." How can one base a strategy on convincing your enemy to stop his aggression when you do not even know who that opponent is? The next chapter will explore who was calling the shots.

Moreover, one must wonder why US decision makers so blatantly mistook or ignored their North Vietnamese opponents? There may have been three primary reasons for this that are instructive. At first, when American decision makers got involved in Vietnam, Presidents Truman and Eisenhower ignored first the Viet-Minh and then the Democratic Republic of Vietnam's leaders. For the most part, they believed the Vietnamese were mere 'lackeys' of the Stalin and Mao regimes. Thus, their focus was on how to counteract Moscow and Beijing assumed directions to the Vietnamese Communists, rather than focus on what the Vietnam Communists were trying to carry out for themselves.

Later, Presidents JFK, LBJ, and Nixon further misunderstood and did not grasp Hanoi's determination to pursue the war. As mentioned, much of that misunderstanding resulted from an ignorance of the North Vietnamese long struggle and sacrifice for independence. They also were arrogant toward the French experience; believing that the French did not prevail because of their inherent weaknesses and ineptness.

On the other hand, America had been successful in the Second World War. It had saved the French from Nazi rule. It had defeated the most powerful Asian power of the time. It would just be a matter of taking over the war from another inept colonial regime and applying American military power properly through calculated actions before victory at minimal cost could be achieved.

Moreover, the American civilian and military leaders and policymakers looked at their ideas and concepts for waging war in Vietnam from their personal experiences, perspectives, and beliefs about what the US could do to convince the DRV leadership to cease its aggressive policies and negotiate. In so doing, they mirror-imaged their beliefs on how the Northern leadership should respond to their action despite who they were.

The prime example of this was an offer that LBJ made to Ho in 1966 in exchange for a meeting to negotiate an end to the conflict. Doris Kearns Goodwin in her *Lyndon Johnson and the American Dream* claims "Johnson had grounded his actions all his life on the conviction that every man had his price. That must also be true of Ho Chi Minh…. Johnson persisted in the belief that if he ever met with Ho, he would reach the private man beneath the public image. If Ho Chi Minh were a reasonable man, then he, too, would recognize superior resources, just as Richard Russell had done when he had finally acknowledged the strength of the forces against him on civil rights. The war, Johnson said, would be "like a filibuster—enormous resistance at first, then a steady whittling away, then Ho hurrying to get it over with."

As Goodwin further relates, Johnson said that he "had a plan and a generous promise—a billion-dollar project for the social and economic betterment of both Vietnams, and the rest of Southeast Asia. Ever since his first trip to Saigon in 1961, Johnson had been intrigued by the idea of developing the Mekong River to give food, water, and power on a scale so immense as to dwarf even the TVA. Now this noble concept could also serve the cause of peace." That plan and offer were sent to Ho. However, the North Vietnam leader never accepted it. Johnson could never understand why. He just did not accept the fact that Ho did not see the benefits of his offer. After all, he and any right-minded American could see the wisdom behind accepting it.

This incident is a prime example of how and why LBJ, and his similar minded advisors, did not know their enemy. Like his predecessor and successor, President Johnson did not study or understand the years and the effort that North Vietnamese leaders had spent to reach their dream of a unified Vietnam. They did not know how each of these men, and men like them, had endured in French prisons and had lived in mountain caves to achieve a dream they cherished from the time they were young men living under the domination of French colonialism.

After all, in war, as Sun Tzu argues, "Know your enemy as you know yourself and you can fight a hundred battles without disaster." The corollary is if you do not know your enemy a hundred battles fought and won can still bring disaster – as it did for America.

The next chapter further demonstrates how American decision makers misjudged, misunderstood, or ignored the North Vietnamese leaders in their commitment of significant forces to convince the DRV to cease its aggression against the South in its consistent goal of reunifying Vietnam. This time the Americans would face adversaries who were not as well-known publicly to them as Ho and Giap. These men would be as committed to a military struggle against the US as Ho or Giap had been against the French.

Chapter 7: 'The Enemy Gets a Vote'

This chapter resumes the discussion of the North Vietnamese leaders and what they did to gain independence for and unification of Vietnam. It continues the dominant theme of the previous chapter – that US leaders misunderstood, misjudged, or ignored who these North Vietnamese leaders were, what motivated them in their pursuit for the unification of Vietnam, and how they set out to achieve that quest. As a result, American decision makers, both civilian and military, chose misguided and ineffective policies and strategies in the Vietnam War in part due to their disregard for their opponents and miscalculation of their actions. In short, they forgot that 'the enemy gets a vote.'

This part of the story covers two far less known Democratic Republic of Vietnam decision makers – Le Duan and his right-hand man, Le Duc Tho. Thanks to the ground-breaking research of several historians, we now know much more about the crucial role these two men played in the development and execution of DRV policies and strategies against the United States from 1954 to 1973. We can also gain further insights on how much their policies, strategies, and actions affected the conduct and outcome of the Vietnam War.

Section 7.1 - Le Duan, Le Duc Tho and the Road to Unification

As Ho Chi Minh and the Vietnam Workers Party Politburo took over in Hanoi in late 1954, they formulated a domestic and international policy to consolidate their control in the North, and plan for the future unification with the South. The DRV leadership formally named this as the 'North First' policy.

At first, they continued to be cautious in their approach to their goal of adopting communist economic and social agendas. For example, they were initially conservative in institutionalizing land reform and government ownership of industry. They did not want to scare away the current land, factory, and business owners.

The new DRV regime needed these managers to assist initially in the rebuilding of the country in the aftermath of a war that devastated much of North Vietnam. While seeking to control the news and public media, they assured their personnel, many of whom had helped in their revolutionary cause, that they would not suppress their reporting. The Party argued that the new government would only temporarily inhibit commentary to assure the public of a positive future and prevent unrest.

Ho, moreover, wanted to ensure the Western international community that his regime would be moderate in its approach to socialism. He thought that domestic actions should show to the West that the DRV could be an independent international actor and not a proxy of either the Soviets or Chinese. That way, Ho thought that he could minimize American intervention in the South and reconcile with the French. These actions would facilitate the latter's withdrawal from all of Vietnam and inhibit American resistance to unification.

Giap supported this policy. He recognized that his Army could not withstand another conflict with the West. The head of the Peoples Army of Vietnam needed to give his forces a rest. He also wanted to embark upon a significant reorganization and modernization of the PAVN. Meanwhile, the other leaders, especially the Party Secretary Truong Chinh, needed time to plan for the massive land reform program and socialist transformation that the regime wanted to institute.

Though many in the DRV, in the words of William Duiker, shared a "genuine apprehension that the accords would not be honored," the official pronouncement coming out of the Politburo was to honor its provisions. According to Pierre Asselin in *Hanoi's Road to the Vietnam War*, "Wary—and weary—of war, these men pinned their hopes on the Geneva accords and political struggle in the South to peacefully bring about national reunification under communist rule."

Despite some misgivings over the results of the Geneva Conference, the post-war DRV government and its ruling Communist Party now held both Ho Chi Minh and Nguyen Van Giap in high esteem. The North Vietnamese public saw them as the two men most responsible for the victory over their former colonial masters.

Ho and Giap were also well known in American intelligence circles. National Intelligence Estimates or NIEs throughout the mid to late fifties name both men as the principal leaders of the DRV. For example, NIE 63.1-55 dated July 1956 stated that "Ho Chi Minh, President of the DRV, is probably the ultimate authority within the regime. No other Vietnamese currently possesses his great popular appeal among the Vietnamese as the symbol of nationalism." The same document then named "Giap, as the capable Commander-in-Chief of the Vietnam People's Army."

While the US Intelligence Community accurately assessed that these two leaders would be trying to consolidate their forces and building a communist regime in the North, their documents further judged that their ultimate aims were to reunify Vietnam under their control. Thus, in the early sixties as JFK came into office, American intelligence fed the Kennedy Administration reports of Ho and Giap's role in supporting the insurgency in the South.

Interestingly, however, US intelligence assessments in the fifties and early sixties usually did not refer to the motives or directions of Ho and Giap or detail the capabilities of the DRV and its PAVN. They mostly referred to the Communist Bloc intentions or the Chinese Communists capabilities. For example, an NIE labeled as 10-62, dated 21 February 1962 and entitled "Communist Objectives, Capabilities, and Intentions in Southeast Asia" focused on the long-range objectives of the "Communist bloc" countries of the Soviet Union and Communist China and the capabilities of Red China, "with the largest land army in the world," which had "the capability to overrun Southeast Asia and defeat the combined indigenous armed forces of the area."

There were now two other men, moreover, not widely known to the Northern Vietnamese public or US policymakers, joining the Politburo in the mid-1950s – Le Duan and Le Duc Tho. These two had gained a reputation amongst the Communist Vietnamese Workers Party for their thankless leadership of the Viet-Minh forces and the Party in the struggle in the South. American leaders, though aware through intelligence and State assessments of DRV members of the Politburo, did not include them much in their policy or decision-making calculations.

As the war in the South continued and after US combat involvement, US policymakers continued to see Ho and Giap as the principal leaders who directed the war efforts. However, as we will see ahead, both Le Duan and Le Duc Tho would come to dominate North Vietnamese policies and strategies in the struggle with the US. For the most part, these two North Vietnamese Politburo leaders would remain relatively unknown to American decision makers.

Le Duan

As we have seen, the DRV had primarily waged its war of independence against the French in the northern area of Vietnam. It was there that the Viet-Minh had fought its largest and most significant battles. In the South, on the other hand, the French had mostly dominated and been successful. For most of the war, the leaders of the rebellion there had to confront strong FEF forces supported by significant loyal southern Vietnamese.

They did so without most of the regular Viet-Minh forces, which Giap had concentrated in the North. Moreover, the revolutionary troops in the South were without the significant Chinese support that its northern forces enjoyed. Thus, they lacked the more modern weaponry that the northern-based troops had. During most of the war, the political leader for the DRV who met these challenges was Le Duan.

Born in 1907 as Le Van Nhuan in a small village in Quan Tri Province of central Vietnam, Le Duan was the second of five children raised in a poor family. After marrying a local girl, he moved north to Hanoi to work in the Indochinese Railway office.

He soon became caught up in the anti-colonial movement there. Like so many in the movement, he had to change his name to avoid French police detection and arrest. He then joined the Ho Chi Minh founded Vietnam Revolutionary Youth Movement. In 1929, he joined Ho in what became the Indochinese Communist Party.

Le Duan quickly rose through the ranks of the Party. According to William Duiker, this was because he was a capable organizer and a hard worker. Lacking the intellectual and educational background of the likes of Ho and Giap, he showed self-confidence and zealous dedication to the cause. By most accounts, he was also arrogant toward and stubborn in considering those who opposed his ideas.

French agents caught up with him in 1931 in Hai Phong and arrested him. Upon his release five years later, Le Duan rejoined his comrades in central Vietnam close to where he was born. Because of his hard work, he became a member of the ICP's Central Committee. On the eve of World War Two, the Party sent him south to Saigon to incite rebellion.

The French again arrested him there in 1940. This time they sent him away to one of the most notorious French colonial prisons on an island off the coast of southern Vietnam. He stayed there until freed in 1945. According to historians of this period, this experience further welded him into "a stern, dogmatic, and stoic revolutionary."

Upon his release, Le Duan once again traveled to Hanoi where he joined the newly proclaimed DRV under Ho. There he became a member of the Vietnam Workers Party's (VWP) Central Committee. Because of his knowledge of the South, Ho sent him back when war with the French broke out to coordinate political activities.

His untiring work in the South under challenging conditions earned him a seat in absentia on the VWP's Politburo in 1950. At war's end, he stayed in the South. There, in the words of Pierre Asselin in his work *Hanoi's Road to the Vietnam War*, "he was fully determined to achieve prompt reunification of Vietnam, whatever the cost."

Le Duan remained clandestinely in the Mekong Delta region along with some 10,000 Viet-Minh political personnel and troops. He oversaw efforts to influence the Geneva accords' elections for reunification.

According to Asselin, this stay behind force was "a hedge against failure of the unification of Vietnam." Meanwhile, Le Duan's deputy, a man named Le Duc Tho, left via ship for Hanoi. Le Duc Tho was one of about 87,000 Viet-Minh troops and 43,000 other revolutionaries and their families to move north under the Geneva Agreements.

Le Duc Tho

Le Duc Tho and Le Duan by this time had welded a close and professional relationship. They shared similar backgrounds and personalities. Both had spent considerable time in French prisons. Both had gone south to oversee the political aspects of the war with the French there. Both had moved up to the Vietnam Workers Party Central Committee because of their hard work and dedication to the cause. Both were "devious in manner and dour in their public image."

Unlike Le Duan, Le Duc Tho was born in the North – in a small village in the Red River Delta. He was also, unlike Le Duan, from a scholarly gentry family more like Ho Chi Minh's. Because of his experience in organizing the party and helping in the formation of the DRV government, Le Duc Tho had a reputation as a ruthless politician with a talent for weeding out incompetent bureaucrats. The Politburo had dispatched him to the South to help Le Duan in keeping the various other political factions outside of the party in line with the DRV goals.

Le Duan, four years older, had quickly recognized the value of Le Duc Tho to his efforts to oversee the challenging and chaotic efforts in the South. In turn, Le Duc Tho realized that Le Duan was in charge and was equally as ruthless in ridding any opposition to his way of doing things. Both effectively cooperated in overseeing the operations against the French, as well as getting rid of those rivals who challenged their leadership. When Le Duc Tho left to go North, Le Duan knew he would have a friend and supporter in the Party councils in Hanoi.

Neither of these two Communist Politburo members was confident that the DRV's policy to support the Geneva convention would work. Le Duan believed that they would have to revert to the use of military force to obtain unification. However, during 1955, he followed the Party policy and sought to control those militants in the South that wanted to use force against the American-supported Southern government.

Making control more difficult was the campaign of the South's new leader, Ngo Dinh Diem, to rid the communists in South Vietnam. While he was an ally of the US - and his role in the American experience, as already surveyed, was important - his relationship and actions directly and profoundly affected the Northern leadership. Thus, the next several paragraphs describe how he affected Northern reactions to the events in the South during his rule and their decisions toward their ultimate aggression there.

Diem and the 'Struggle' in the South

The government now forming in the South, initially called the State of Vietnam, was a replica of the one that the French had created during the First Indochina War. Its nominal head was Bao Dai; whom, as mentioned in the last chapter, the French had installed as the leader of a puppet government in their attempts at 'Vietnamization' in the late forties. That was the same Bao Dai who had taken refuge in the French Rivera during the August Revolution and spent most of the First Indochina War overseas.

The Geneva Convention Accords on Indochina reinstalled this last of the Vietnam Emperors as a figurehead for the Southern government. Knowing that the US would approve, Bao Dai appointed an experienced, former colonial government administrator and Southern-born Vietnamese Catholic as his new Premier – Ngo Dinh Diem.

Diem had grown up in a devout Catholic family north of Hue in the early 1900s. He followed in his father's footsteps and obtained a formal French education in the same school in Hue as Ho Chi Minh and Giap. Later he studied law in Hanoi. He then became a civil servant in the French colonial government in the 1920s.

Diem rose rapidly. He became a district, then provincial chief overseeing 300 villages near his hometown. While in that position he began to aid in the rounding up and arrest of Viet-Minh communists. The French rewarded him with the Governorship of Binh Thuan Province. There he suppressed communist lead revolts in collaboration with French forces. As a result, the French wanted him to play a more significant role in their colonial bureaucracy.

However, Diem called for more autonomy for the Vietnamese. When the French ignored his demands, he resigned. His later denouncements of French rule led to a threat of arrest and exile. Diem withdrew from his political activities. He chose to live in relative recluse in Hue with his family.

While there, he considered becoming a priest. During the Japanese occupation in World War Two, he briefly contemplated joining the Japanese organized Vietnamese government but thought doing so may label him as a collaborationist. Consequently, he wisely did not join Bao Dai's Japanese collaboration government.

At the outbreak of the French–Viet-Minh war, Diem sought refuge in America. Despite his anti-communist and anti-colonial views and before his trip to the US, both the French and the Viet-Minh had asked him to join their organizations. He had turned them down. He wanted nothing to do with the French puppet government. He equally despised the communists, who had earlier killed one of his brothers and had briefly held him prisoner.

During his visit to the US, Diem gained a reputation as a Vietnamese Nationalist who would make a formidable opponent to the communists. He gained favor with influential US statesmen such as Senators John F. Kennedy and John Mansfield. These and several other American anti-communists, to include Senator McCarthy, began to see him as the solution for a democratic South Vietnam. Eventually, Eisenhower and his Secretary of State Dulles embraced him as the one who could stem the communist expansion in Asia.

As depicted previously, Diem eventually turned out to be a failure in the eyes of many - especially American newsmen such as David Halberstam and Neil Sheehan who led the criticism on him. Some of his American military and political advisors thought the US had backed the wrong man. So much so that, as explained previously, the Kennedy Administration engineered his removal - during which opponents killed him and his brother Nhu.

This criticism and early orthodox historical accounts of Diem seem to have ignored his triumphs. From 1954 to 1958, he had quickly and successfully installed his rule in South Vietnam. This had been no small feat.

There had been many obstacles to overcome in 1954. First, Diem had to control the Army. The post-Geneva South Vietnamese Army was a remnant of the Vietnamese National Army formed under the French Expeditionary Force in the First Indochina War. Though the total number of the Vietnamese forces created during the war for the French cause is uncertain, most accounts show that the figures had been approximately 150,000 men. At war's end, the number dwindled drastically. Desertions were rampant, and some went over to the Viet-Minh. By the end of 1954, there were approximately 100,000 personnel still available to the newly forming South Vietnamese Army.

The immediate problem for Diem was its leadership. The French had trained its senior leaders, and that training had been haphazard. The major problem was that the General Staff stilled owed its loyalty to the departing French, who were encouraging them to fend for themselves. Meanwhile, several regional commanders were aligning themselves with the local religious and criminal sects and gangs. As a result, there was little sense of a Vietnamese National Army. There was no sense of loyalty or obedience to the new South Vietnamese government forming under the premiership of Diem. The Prime Minister set out quickly to change this.

The newly positioned American advisors supported Diem in this endeavor. In fact, the Americans now were replacing the departing French as the primary benefactor of the unfolding southern political structure. Diem's most close and personal advisor was now a CIA officer by the name of Colonel Edward Lansdale – the same officer who would become an advisor to JFK on counterinsurgency later.

As mentioned in Chapter 2, Lansdale had gained a reputation as a counterinsurgent and foreign government- building expert in the Philippines; where he had advised the Philippine leader on how to suppress a rebel uprising. He had been successful in this endeavor. Thus, American military commanders assigned him to support the US aid program for southern Vietnam. He quickly gave encouragement and support to Diem; backed by large quantities of American dollars.

According to Max Boot in *Road Not Taken* Lansdale took a liking to the strange looking 'roly-poly' oriental man, who he found "unexpectedly humorous but also courageous, and deeply in love with his country." Far from the caricatures of American journalists Halberstam and Sheehan, the CIA officer also found Diem dedicated and hard-working, but one who "Tended to want to do most of the work himself, instead of delegating to a member of his personal staff or someone."

One of the most important actions that Lansdale undertook was in heading off an Army coup against Diem. He had arranged to send its leaders to an all paid vacation to Manila; where they were lavishly wined, dined, and furnished women. He then paid off other senior officers to not interfere with his attempts to form a palace guard of hundreds of troops, themselves paid by American dollars to protect Diem.

Feeling secure under Lansdale's battalion of bodyguards, Diem quickly appointed a loyal cabinet member to oversee the General Staff. He then ruthlessly replaced the key senior commanders and gained sole authority over the appointment of officers who would serve in the Army.

This force was now an Army reorganizing under the advice of the US Military Advisory Group that had expanded after the Geneva Convention. Heading this command was one of Eisenhower's most trusted World War Two leaders – General Lawton Collins. While Collins was not a supporter of Diem and came to recommend his removal, the IKE Administration had cast its full support to the building of the South Vietnamese Army whose loyalty would be to Premier Diem.

To ensure so, the US funded the construction of the Army, to include its salaries, through Diem. By the end of 1954, the Premier held the purse strings and thus the control of an Army that the American military was now equipping and training.

Securing his hold over the Army, Diem turned to his other potent enemies. These were two of the largest religious sects in the South called the 'Cao Dai' (pronounced 'kow dye') and the 'Hoa Hao' ('hwah how'). He also sought to eliminate the large crime syndicate centered in the Saigon area called the 'Binh Xuyen' ('bin swyen'). The significance of these groups was in their powerful armed forces, and the control their leaders exercised over areas of the Mekong Delta and Saigon.

That power emanated from the French colonial leaders who had allowed and even helped pay these groups for their allegiance in the struggle against the anti-colonial forces in Vietnam. The French had also integrated some of the armed members of the sects into the Vietnamese National Army during their war against the Viet-Minh.

In early 1955 these groups, some with communist agents in them, had united in their opposition to Diem. This antagonism was primarily due to four Diem actions. The first was the new Premier moves to end subsidies that the French had offered to the religious sects. Second, he had separated their forces from the Army. A third act was the revocation of the licenses and practices the French had given to the syndicate for continued criminal activities in Saigon. Finally, Diem had also denied appointing any individuals of these groups to his government. All of this eventually led to armed conflict.

A fierce battle ensued in Saigon in April 1955. After several days of intensive fighting, the Vietnamese National Army units in the area stayed loyal to Diem and competent enough to defeat the rebel armed forces both in Saigon and eventually in their base areas in the Mekong Delta. Lansdale also helped. He bribed many of the group leaders to flee the country.

With his victory in "The Battle of Saigon," Diem solidified his hold over the new South Vietnamese government. Several influential members of the American Congress, such as Senators Mansfield and Kennedy, highly lauded his triumph. The IKE Administration thought it now had the leader they needed to support and strengthen an anti-communist regime in Southeast Asia.

After establishing control over the developing South Vietnamese Government, Diem turned his attention to the remnants of the Viet-Minh in the South. According to Mark Moyar in his *Triumph Forsaken*, the Premier planned and executed a ruthless 'Denounce the Communists' campaign. "The campaign, unfolding progressively across 1955, saw Diem's security forces and officials fan out into the rural districts and set up permanent control over great numbers of villages while hunting down Communists and preaching Diem's propaganda."

William Turley further argues in his *Second Indochina War* that this campaign was highly successful. It reduced the communist membership in the South from between 50 – 60,000 in 1954 to about 15,000 in 1956. The PAVN official history confirms the effectiveness of Diem's actions. That history also admits that the communist movement in the south was near collapse.

Having subdued the immediate communist threat, Diem then turned to the Geneva proposed Vietnam reunification elections due in 1956. Since the State of Vietnam was not a signatory to that treaty, Diem reasoned that he was not violating any international laws by not agreeing to hold the elections. Besides, he argued to the Americans, any election in 1956 would sure to be a communist victory because the Northern Communists would control and manipulate the results.

Rejecting several DRV attempts to compromise over unification elections, Diem accepted a call from the State of South Vietnam's quasi-democratic committee set up during the Battle of Saigon to form a new democratic government. He called for a referendum to decide whether to keep a monarchy-based government with Bao Dai, or a republic with himself as President.

On October 23, 1955, the referendum occurred. Diem won 98.2 percent of the vote. In Saigon, he captured some 605,000 votes; more ballots than those who had registered to vote. Thus was born the Republic of Vietnam with Diem as its President.

Diem had succeeded in gaining control of the newly formed Republic of South Vietnam mostly because of his prodigious work ethic, and his undaunted devotion to an anti-communist cause. Like the Vietnamese Mandarins before him, he kept power to himself and seldom relegated it. Moreover, he only chose and appointed those he could trust to carry out his will. That usually meant he would rely mostly on his family members. In the military, he would continue to control the appointments of and orders to the high command and senior officers all the way down to battalion level.

Many historians, in retrospect, have pointed to Diem as one who was incapable of governing the South. Thus, they argue, the failure of America in Vietnam was due, in large part, to the backing of the wrong horse. Bui Diem, the Vietnamese Nationalist who had admired Ho in Hanoi in 1945, agrees with this view. He argues that had the US been more interested in creating a genuinely diverse South Vietnam, they may have found an alternative to Diem from someone from the Vietnamese nationalist organizations. As it was, Bui Diem argues, the US was more interested in stability and an anti-communist government than a democratic one.

There is evidence, however, that shows or argues a different story; depending on when one assesses the actions of Diem's rule. More recently, especially as Mark Moyar tells it, some point out that Diem was highly successful in bringing a factious society in political turmoil into a political entity that, without outside interference, could have survived. In fact, in the late fifties one could rightfully argue, America had what it wanted – a South Vietnamese leader and government that could defeat a communist insurrection in Vietnam.

The Road to Another War: Hanoi's Reaction to the Diem Regime and Resolution 15

Diem's ruthless actions against the communists in the South presented a dilemma to Ho's and the Party's policy of peaceful unification. Those supporting the 'North First Strategy' thought that the Party had to rebuild infrastructure, reorganize, and revitalize the Army, and institute land reform before anything else to ensure the future of a viable Democratic Republic of Vietnam. Once completed, then they could go ahead with a forceful reunification, which was slowly becoming clear as the more likely case. The programs to fulfill these actions were either faltering or needed time to carry out. Any move to counteract and protect the Southern Communist infrastructure, now referred to as the Viet Cong by the Diem Government, was problematic.

There were three primary reasons that supporting the VC in the South with any militant action was difficult in 1956-8. The first was the dire situation in the North. The land reform program, which the Party was executing with much inefficiency and violence, was failing. The people's reaction to it had grown violent. The Party had to call upon the People's Army to suppress several peasant revolts. The leading man who oversaw the reform program, General Secretary Truong Chinh, had to resign. There was a further 'shake up' in the Politburo. Ho eventually had to offer a public apology for the government's failures. In sum, the entire 'North First Strategy' was uncertain.

Second, The DRV's main international benefactors - the Soviet Union and Communist China - were not supportive at this time for any military action to reunify Vietnam. The Russians, under its new Premier Nikita Khrushchev, were advocating 'peaceful coexistence' with the West. The use of force in the South would run counter to that policy.

The Chinese, moreover, were recovering from its war with the Americans in Korea. They did not want to incite any military confrontation over Vietnam. They were also struggling with their own internal economic and social problems, which would result in Mao's pursuit of his 'Great Leap

Forward' reforms. Consequently, both the Soviets and the Red Chinese indicated that they would not support any use of armed force in the South that may result in direct American military intervention.

The third primary reason that a military solution for unification at this time was infeasible is that there just was not a military capability to accomplish it. According to the PAVN's official history, *Victory in Vietnam*, there were only about 2,000 ex Viet-Minh soldiers in the South. Most of these had dispersed into base areas that they had used in the war against the French. Others had joined the Sects to try to recruit their thugs against Diem's anti-communist movement. These forces, mostly organized as propaganda teams and security units from 10 to 20 men and women, were hardly capable of overthrowing the Diem regime or enhancing any strong military action against it.

Moreover, the entire regular PAVN in the North had been reorganizing and retraining. While its numbers had grown to over 330,000 during the war against the French, it now numbered some 170,000. It was unable to launch any conventional attack against the South. Moreover, the North did not yet have the means to infiltrate to the South, as it would later in the sixties. The Ho Chi Minh Trail did not exist. Besides, the Peoples' Army had to aid in the control of a growing public unrest against land reform.

In the South, Le Duan's need for action was much less uncertain. He had to act soon to impede or at least survive the continued success of Diem's counter communist campaign. As Lien-Hang Nguyen mentions in her *Hanoi's War*, he was growing increasingly concerned in 1956 with the situation. He began to waiver and cautiously change the Party's official policy toward militant actions.

As Nguyen describes, "Traveling around the western Mekong Delta, the southern countryside, and even the cities, Le Duan undermined Hanoi's orders by mobilizing irregular and regular troops to prepare for an eventual war. At the same time, he reined in more 'hotheaded' southern comrades lest they destroy the resistance with their call to arms or, just as disconcerting, lest they—and not he—reap any rewards if the masses responded."

Le Duan also changed his Territorial Committee's location from the waters of the Mekong Delta to Saigon. Though it exposed him and the Committee to Diem's crackdown, the move allowed him to tap into spies or political agents who would inform him of the South's military actions and plans.

One such spy worked for the chief American advisor to Diem, Colonel Edward Lansdale. His name was Pham Xuan An. An sent much of the South's plans for building its Army, its military operations, and its Strategic Hamlet construction plans to Le Duan and Northern leaders. This intelligence also allowed the Southern Communist leader to move about in Saigon and its environs, avoiding detection and escaping arrest.

Le Duan benefited from information by another agent – Truong Nhu Tang. Tang was the same young southern Vietnamese who had met Ho Chi Minh in Paris soon after the August Revolution. Inspired by that meeting, Tang had returned to Saigon and joined other southern dissidents in what would later become known as the National Liberation Front. He had also become a successful businessman and as such enjoyed contacts with many senior officials in the Diem regime. He not only gave some useful information about the Diem regime to Le Duan, but further solicited young men to join the movement.

Le Duan further acted to convince the Northern leaders to abandon their current policy in the South. While in Saigon, he wrote one of the more influential documents of the coming struggle, 'The Path of Revolution in the South.' This was a bleak assessment of the situation there. As Pierre Asselin summarizes the main theme of this document, he called "for abandoning the party's current line and at once resuming armed struggle in the South, with comprehensive northern backing."

Le Duan's manifesto, as some called it, fell on sympathetic ears in the Workers Party's Central Committee when it arrived in early 1957. One reason it was well received was that his former comrade, Le Duc Tho, who now held a powerful position in that committee, fully supported his previous commander's views. Another reason, according to Lien-Hang Nguyen, was that others in the Politburo thought it had become time to renew the armed struggle.

One such new member was Nguyen Chi Thanh – an Army Political General who had grown to favor for his successful efforts at suppressing some dissent amongst Army officers disillusioned with the Party's crackdown on the people. Thanh would eventually become an opponent to Giap in the conduct of military actions in the South and become head of the North's political-military organization in South Vietnam that oversaw the war there.

Despite the overall support for and consideration of Le Duan's views, the resultant Party's new directive to the Southern leaders remained cautious and reserved. While it endorsed more aggressive measures to protect the movement in the South - such as authorizing the kidnapping or assassination of South Vietnamese officials - it still emphasized that the policy of the Party was not to overthrow the Diem regime using violence.

The Southern revolutionaries would continue to build support for an anti-Diem government. They would do so primarily by gaining the backing of the Southern people through propaganda and social program advocacy. Meanwhile, the Communist Vietnamese Workers Party leaders in the North would continue to try to get Diem to agree to negotiate a peaceful resolution of the unification issue.

For a while in 1957, according to historian William Turley and others, the communist political struggle in the South seemed to make some gains. The 'Viet Cong' cadre propaganda campaign had some positive effects amongst the Southern population for their cause. However, most VC gains were a result of the internal Southern push back to many of Diem's reforms, particularly his attempts to uproot peasants into newly concentrated areas called 'Agrovilles.' These were actions to move the peasants from their hamlets to government-controlled villages to convince them of the benefits of Diem's reforms.

Bolstered by an increasing American influx of military aid, Diem's policies and forces prevailed. The situation by 1959, as portrayed in most communist documents, remained bleak. These documents referred to these times as the 'darkest days' of the struggle. While they could continue to hold some of their base areas, the political cadre dwindled, and control over the population dropped. As Mark Lawrence summarizes in his work *The Vietnam War* on this period, "The party lost 90 percent of its cadres and members in the South from 1955 to 1958," and "saw much of its following disintegrate."

Therefore, by the end of 1958 it had become clear to the Politburo, which had experienced increased pressure from its militant 'pro-South faction,' that armed struggle against the South was going to be necessary to achieve reunification.

The Party's leaders met in January 1959 to specifically deal with the Southern policy and situation – a meeting called the 15th Plenum of the Central Committee. Le Duan, who had returned to Hanoi in late 1957 and appointed by Ho as the acting secretary of the party, would play a significant part in the results. Mark Lawrence rightly marked this gathering as "the key turning point' in the North's policy and future actions toward the South.

Preparation for this meeting had been in progress for over a year. Recognizing that the situation in the South had become critical, Ho saw the need for increased military action other than the one authorized in the cautious 1957 directive. He began preparing for a full-blown Central Committee meeting before the scheduled Fifteenth session of the Party Congress.

Ho first engaged his old comrade Giap to draft a resolution to focus on the failing struggle in the South. But for some undiscovered reason, he turned the document over to Le Duan months before the Plenary. Speculation is that Ho needed to have the imprint of a southerner to appease the growing militant faction of the Party. For whatever reason, when the Plenum in January reviewed Le Duan's draft resolution for action, called Resolution 15, they found a definitive call for a complete change in policy to reunify Vietnam through force.

The Plenum's review led to debates on how to continue. Not all thought that the use of military force should be the primary means at this time for unification. The 'Northern First' group, which Giap headed, wanted a more cautious approach that still emphasized political means with some increase in a 'guerrilla' military campaign. The 'Southern First' group, led by Le Duan and supported by Le Duc Tho and Thanh, argued that the only way to save the South was a massive influx of Northern troops to reinforce Southern Communist forces. The debate continued for months on the proper course.

Ho, whose role was increasingly shifting to that of senior diplomat and advisor to the Le Duan power clique, tried to mediate the debate. He warned against a military conflict that could involve substantial American military intervention. He also cautioned that international support from the Chinese and Soviets would be contingent upon avoiding all-out conflict with the US.

However, Le Duan, who had been slowly but resolutely gaining power in the Central Committee, forcefully argued that without military support and action the revolution in the South would fail. He further emphasized that significant military action could not only offer the necessary protection and salvation for cause in the South but turn the tide in its favor. To bolster his view, he argued that Diem's policies were creating increasing dissatisfaction amongst critical factions there, and that this is the moment to take advantage of that dissent.

Le Duan – now viewed as the 'expert on the South' - by May 1959 won the debate. While the Politburo did not specify the actual amount and degree of force, its resolution stated: "The fundamental path of development for the revolution in South Vietnam is that of violent struggle. Based on the concrete conditions and existing requirements of revolution, then, the road of violent struggle is: to use the strength of the masses, with political strength as the main factor, in combination with military strength to a greater or lesser degree depending on the situation, in order to overthrow the ruling power of the imperialist and feudalist forces and build the revolutionary power of the people."

This document, Resolution 15, was one of the most important of the entire war to come. It was a declaration of war not just against the Diem regime, but the Americans who were supporting it.

Whatever the original intention of the document, it resulted in preparations for a war and a commitment of Politburo leaders and Northern based forces that were sure to further involve a military struggle with a western power for unification. This time, however, the struggle would be against the most powerful nation in the world.

Building the Ho Chi Minh Trail, the National Liberation Front (NLF) and the People's Liberation Army Forces (NLAF)

Following the issuance of the resolution, the North's General Military Party Committee members, led by General Thanh and encouraged by Le Duan, set out to prepare for the war to come. They undertook three significant actions before the end of 1959. The first was to accelerate the buildup and modernization of the PAVN to support the Southern forces in the conflict ahead.

The second was to form several 'cadre units' of southern 'regroupees' who had come north under the Geneva accords. These forces were to be specially prepared and trained to return to the South and help in the military struggle there. The intent was to disguise them as Southern revolutionary forces. Thereby, the North could argue that the southern struggle was an insurgency against a corrupt Diem regime.

The third action was the establishment of a transportation route to send the returning southern PAVN cadres and supplies to the South. To execute the later, the Politburo, according to the PAVN official history, "directed that a special communications group be formed to set up routes to send cadre, weapons and other needed supplies to South Vietnam."

The PAVN official history includes much detail on the building of both a land route - named the Ho Chi Minh Trail - and a sea route to South Vietnam. It emphasizes that "this was a tremendous job of strategic importance that would play a direct role in the liberation of South Vietnam and the liberation of our nation." Indeed, by the middle of the year, the organization set up to build and furnish support troops for the land route, named Military Transportation Group 559, would begin the transport of 542 PAVN 'regroupee' troops to "perform their revolutionary duties" in the South.

By the end of 1959, some 3,000 other members joined them. They wore no PAVN uniforms. Because of their southern origins, they also remained indiscernible in looks and language to many in the South who supported Diem or who were neutral. Many were returning to battlefields they were all too familiar with during the war against the French. Now that combat experience, their northern training and indoctrination, and their familiarity with the area would begin to turn the tide in the South. They would serve as the advance element for hundreds of thousands more PAVN soldiers to follow.

Most importantly, they allowed the North to continue to deny that they were supporting the Southern insurrection directly with its forces. This ruse was effective until about 1965 when American intelligence would confirm PAVN regular forces in regimental strength in South Vietnam. Even afterward, the ruse continued to work because many Americans would continue to believe that Southern Revolutionaries were the ones primarily fighting the war.

By the beginning of 1961 - as a new President in the US was taking office and calling for the American people to "pay any price, bear any burden, meet any hardship, support any friend, oppose any foe, to assure the survival and the success of liberty" – the Southern revolutionaries were striking back. In one year, they assassinated about 1700 South Vietnamese officials and employees, and kidnapped almost 2000 others. Small guerrilla forces had successfully conducted ambushes and raids against ARVN or regional force outposts.

Southern Communists, now universally known as the Viet Cong or VC, further organized several 'popular uprisings' in mostly remote, minority-dominated mountain tribal regions. According to the PAVN official history - which is suspect in its positive claims - VC forces had by 1961 regained control of thousands of hamlets in the Central Highlands and the Mekong Delta region. They had recruited again around 7,000 guerrilla forces and had reconstituted an equal number of provincial and district main forces.

To further rally sympathy and support for the Viet Cong and present a semblance of Southern leadership of the revitalized war effort, the Politburo also moved to form a new organization in the South. It would become the National Liberation Front or NLF. Patterned after the Viet-Minh Front during the war against the French, the NLF served to reach out to non-communists who would rebel against Diem's rule. One of the first members of this organization was Truong Nhu Tang - the businessman in Saigon who was an agent reporting on Southern government actions. He would become a secret member of its Central Committee in 1962.

Gathering in a heavily forested area near the Cambodia border in December 1960, several members of the Territorial Committee, some representing the North and others representing various factions of the Southern rebels, agreed to its structure. Its purpose was to oversee important revolutionary tasks. The most critical one was the establishment of a political structure at every level of South Vietnamese social and political strata. After several days, they further appointed leaders and organized groups to carry out the tasks of forming district and province shadow governments and political committees.

They also fashioned an overall military organization encompassing all the armed elements fighting against Diem in the South. They called it the Peoples' Liberation Army Forces or PLAF. As explained in the official PAVN history, the Northern Politburo made it clear at the time that the PLAF was to be "a part of the People's Army of Vietnam, having been organized, developed, educated, and led by the Party."

The NLF leaders organized it along the same lines as the Viet-Minh in the First Indochina War – local and guerrilla forces; district and province main force units; and regular units of the supporting PAVN organizations that infiltrated from the North. By 1961, the PLAF numbered about fifteen thousand main force troops, with, according to William Duiker, about five thousand of those infiltrators from the North.

Along with these two organizations, the Northern Communist Workers Party Politburo decided to reestablish the Central Office for South Vietnam or COSVN. This command organization, which would receive much notoriety during the war, had existed during the First Indochina War to oversee operations in the South. Le Duan had been its political officer. Now the North reinstated it as an operational command to direct and coordinate political-military operations. According to Tang, this organization would become more of a group of individuals than a place – meaning it did not have a permanent headquarters and could often move to avoid detection.

To further coordinate operations, the North also began setting up various subordinate command and administrative areas that were geographically oriented. For example, the PAVN High Command designated the coastal region with its populated and some rich rice-producing areas from Danang to

Nha Trang and about 75 kilometers inland as the B1 Front. They organized the southernmost area of South Vietnam, encompassing the Saigon and Delta regions and much of the plateau area north to the city of Dalat into the B2 Front. Within that Front, there were four Military Regions, numbered one through four. The B3 and B4 Fronts encompassed the mountainous highland Cambodia border area to 100 kilometers inland, and the Laos border region in the north to the coast, respectively.

The North further set out to directly control COSVN and its subordinate geographic commands. It did so through the Politburo appointed political and military officers in the most essential and authoritative positions. Moreover, Le Duan would ensure that he had complete control through personal appointments. To guarantee this Le Duan appointed an old friend, Nguyen Van Linh, as the first leader of COSVN. Le Duan would continue to personally choose later COSVN leaders to control the war in the South. Indeed, the most celebrated myth of the entire war and the most significant achievement of the North was that Southern leaders directed the war in South Vietnam.

Meanwhile, in Hanoi Le Duan courted a member of the PAVN General Staff - General Nguyen Chi Thanh - to win him over to his views. Thanh had been born in Thua Thien Province which was the northernmost area in South Vietnam. At an early age, he had taken part in demonstrations and strikes there and had joined the Communist Party at the age of twenty-three. In one year, he became the Secretary of the party committee in the province.

This, young, ambitious, and quickly advancing Communist Party member had gained a reputation even before the French war began. Ho and particularly Le Duan observed that he had "a commanding presence, an infectious enthusiasm, and organizational talent." Thanh also, like most of the higher leadership of the Communist Vietnamese Workers Party had served several years in a French prison during World War Two. As the war was ending, Thanh got out of prison. Soon after, Ho invited him to the party conference at Tan Trao in 1945, where Party leaders elected him to the Central Committee. The Committee later put him in charge of the resistance movement against the French in central Vietnam.

After the war with the French, Ho had promoted him to General of the Army, a rank equal to that of Giap. In the reform of the PAVN, the two began to clash over how the new army would fight, particularly in any future expected clash with the Americans. Giap still favored an emphasis on guerrilla operations, while Thanh emphasized the need to build a main force focus to confront the Americans.

Thus, General Thanh, by 1961, had already become a nemesis to Giap on how to conduct military operations. He would fit in well with Le Duan's ideas on the conduct of the war. The increasingly outspoken Le Duan began to argue for the use of more large force operations to enable the North's army to confront both the ARVN and American better armed and more mobile armed forces.

With the passage and later implementation of the above actions and organizations of Resolution 15, what exactly was the intended DRV military strategy for the war? Many of the sources are vague. Historian speculation is widespread. The PAVN history is unclear. The most convincing theory comes from William Duiker in an article he wrote in *The Vietnam War: Vietnamese and American Perspectives* called "Waging Revolutionary War: The Evolution of Hanoi's Strategy in the South, 1959-1965."

Duiker argues that no specific, detailed written strategy came out of the Politburo after the Fifteenth Plenum on how to execute its resolution. However, there are recent pieces of information from

Northern sources - particularly some papers and writings of Le Duan and postwar interviews and articles of some of the PAVN and VC military leaders - on some details of the what and how they intended to pursue the war against Diem and his American supporters. Duiker further emphasizes that the overall strategic concept revealed in these documents show that the Northern plans and operational concepts for the war evolved from 1959 to 1963, and represented a compromise between those who sought more military emphasis than political.

As Duiker reconstructs it, the main thrust of the strategy followed what the Northerners had pursued during their war with the French - that is, a modification of Mao's Revolutionary Theory previously described. The overall goal was to conduct operations that would lead to a condition in which the 'balance of forces,' both political and military, would enable a general uprising of the people of the South against the Diem regime. In Mao's terminology, this was his Phase III of his Peoples' War military doctrine.

A favorable 'balance of forces' for the North Vietnamese Communists would be contingent on two broad capabilities. The first was when the NLF would be able to have the military advantage over the South Vietnamese armed forces. The second would be when would most the people of the South supported their cause and were dissatisfied enough with the Diem regime to conduct a general uprising.

The key to the first was the ability to sustain and support the military operations in the South. Crucial to the latter would be the communist political shadow infrastructure to both spark rebellion and administer the main villages, districts, and provinces during and after the general uprising.

As previously mentioned, but worthy of repetition, Northern civilian and military leaders had learned from their experience with the French that the execution of this strategy would have to be flexible. That is, the balance of forces and timing of when to seek a general uprising would fluctuate back and forth depending on the successes of both the political and military operations.

Critical to the North Vietnamese leaders in general, and Le Duan in particular was the amount of effort and resources placed on the political versus the military aspects of this strategy. The Politburo was concerned about the ability of the Americans to respond to their military actions. The timing of US elections, reactions of the Americans to the war, and the mix of small guerrilla and sizeable main force actions on the battlefield were the main factors that the North Vietnamese debated during the war, both in its early stages and later.

The Emergence of Le Duan as War Leader

With the execution of this strategy in the early sixties, Duiker, as well as others such as Lien-Hang Nguyen, found that Le Duan was intent upon furthering his control over the war. He thus ruthlessly strengthened his power in the North. With his key people in place, namely Le Duc Tho on the political side and Nguyen Chi Thanh on the military, he went on to neutralize Ho, marginalize Giap, and negate the influence of other Politburo members.

Throughout the war with the Americans, though the Northern Communist strategy would change in several ways, it would be Le Duan who would have the ultimate say on its main concepts, timing, and execution. However, he would have to wrestle control from both Ho and Giap. This would not be an easy undertaking. The story of his efforts and actions to do so was one of the best-kept secrets of the war.

As Lien-Hang Nguyen masterfully explains, Le Duan began neutralizing Ho by presenting him as the elder statesman who could best further the war effort for unification by building international support – especially from his contacts with the Soviet Union and China. This role suited Ho well; primarily because of his failing health and ability to manage the myriad of issues surrounding the waging of war in the South.

To deal with Giap, Le Duan used Thanh as a counterweight to the Minister of Defense. He also appointed other key military officers to the influential Party's Military Committee. The latter had much more power in decisions involving the Army than the Ministry of Defense, headed by Giap. Increasingly, Giap became an administrative manager of military affairs and a figurehead in the decisions about the war.

For other Politburo members, Le Duan, as Lien-Hang further clarifies, constructed "a complex structure that involved multiple committees nominally performing the same tasks. This arrangement allowed the first secretary to undercut his opponents by getting them mired in powerless committees while he stood at the center of the key decision-making bodies in Hanoi."

Le Duan completed the establishment of his control over most aspects of North Vietnamese policy, both domestic and international, with the use of powerful security forces that had been set up earlier to deal with the internal unrest over the original reform programs. As summarized in *Hanoi's War*, "In effect, Le Duan laid the foundation for the sturdiest power structure the Party had ever seen, and whose vestiges continued to loom over Hanoi decades after the war ended."

The irony of these revelations from recently released and available North Vietnamese sources, is that as American decision makers became more focused and committed to the defense of South Vietnam, they continued to think that Ho Chi Minh and Giap were the DRV leaders driving the North's decisions. Le Duan was a shadowy, behind the scenes figure to most major American policymakers until the end of US involvement.

In a recent article in the *New York Times*, Lien-Hang writes, "to some extent, this is what the North wanted." That is because Le Duan suspected that the Americans would focus on the ailing Ho and believe they could reach a compromise solution with him as they had done in Geneva in 1954. That would, in Le Duan's thinking, serve to encourage the US leaders to continue to limit the war, while allowing the DRV to control the tempo and build up its forces for its unlimited war. This, in turn, gave the North Vietnamese both the tactical initiative in the South, as well as the overall strategic initiative in the war.

Ap Bac and Resolution 9: Defeating the US 'Special War'

By the end of 1960, measures to execute the policy and its resultant strategy of Resolution 15 were well underway. Soon it became clear that the NLF and its PLAF military arm were making slow but steady headway against Diem's anti-communist campaign and his military.

However, in early 1962, a year after Kennedy had come into power, approved a Counterinsurgency Plan, increased US advisors, and enhanced the US combat actions in the country, the NLF experienced some setbacks. As the PAVN official history admits, Diem's strategic hamlet program, in particular, had caused some alarming loss of control of the countryside.

However, as Le Duan reminded his comrades from time to time, Diem would never be able to connect with the rural populace as the NLF political cadres were doing. The VC shadow governments and agents became master propagandists. They used Vietnamese history to their advantage, preaching to the ordinary peasants that all of Vietnam was destined to be unified.

They also used the successes of the First Indochina War to argue that the North was the instrument to ensure victory against the corrupt Southern government and the US, which the North portrayed as but another foreign power intent on colonizing Vietnam through its puppet Southern regime. At the end of 1962, with almost 11,000 US soldiers in South Vietnam – albeit mostly advisors - it was clear that the NLF was winning the political battle for "the hearts and minds" of the southern populace.

The PLAF's military efforts soon flourished as well. Increasingly in late 1962, 'VC' units were being successful in their attacks against the South Vietnamese military and their US advisors. Much of that was the result of a combination of recruitment in the South and the reinforcement from the North. According to US government estimates, found in the *Pentagon Papers*, the PLAF grew from 17,000 in late 1961 to 25,000 in 1963 in its main forces. Its irregular forces also grew from 3,000 in 1960 to nearly 70,000 by mid-1963. This estimate of forces approximates the figures in the PAVN official history.

It was not, however, just a matter of numbers. The main force VC were well trained and motivated. There is no other battle in the entire war that proved to both sides that the VC could stand toe to toe with an American equipped, armed, trained and helicopter supported ARVN than Ap Bac in January 1963. We have already seen how the battle had an impact on how many Americans viewed the competency of the ARVN versus the VC from this encounter. As mentioned, though contested by the American military command when the American news accounts depicted it as a defeat, Ap Bac became a symbol of ARVN incompetence.

The battle did not just hit a nerve amongst Americans. As mentioned briefly in Chapter 2, the DRV Politburo noticed the event as well. According to Lien-Hang Nguyen, the battlefield success at Ap Bac "pointed toward an imminent victory for Le Duan" in his policy to take up military action in the South. Because of the fight there, "Party leaders now possessed a clear example of the fallibility of American-style counterinsurgency."

The PAVN official history reinforces this view and further recounts that the battle showed the PLAF, with Northern support, was "capable of defeating sweep operations by the United States and its puppets…." The success of the fight soon spurned a new slogan for the PLAF - "Emulate Ap Bac, Kill Pirates, Attack."

During the Spring and Summer of 1963, PLAF attacks – following the creed to 'Emulate Ap Bac' - seem to be successful wherever they occurred. Like their war against the French, the assaults were all carefully planned and launched after the leaders thought there was a high chance of success. These 'Emulate Ap Bac battlefield victories', coupled with the assassinations of both Diem and Kennedy in November, caused an uproar in the Communist Party Central Committee by the end of the year.

Many Northerners now believed that a significant obstacle to their revolution had been eliminated – Diem. Their military success also gave them confidence that they could end it before the US further intervened militarily. Ironically, they thought that the Americans, whom they suspected had a hand in the Diem Coup, had changed the situation in the South favorably for them. It now became clear that some assessment of the meaning of it all was necessary. The Politburo called for meeting to do so.

Le Duan was keenly aware that the events of 1963 called for some reassessment of the Resolution 15 strategy. These circumstances presented Le Duan, in the words of Lien-Hang Nguyen, with "a fork in the road at the end of 1963 similar to the one Kennedy's successor, Lyndon B. Johnson, faced a year later."

Historians differ on exactly how the Diem assassination prompted this reevaluation. Lien-Hang Nguyen supports the idea that with Diem gone, the North's Politburo members thought the time was ripe to take advantage of the vacuum and certain turmoil to follow in the South's government and military and go for an all-out military victory.

Ang Cheng Guan in *The Vietnam War from the Other Side* supports this view. Pierre Asselin claims that the Northern leaders worried that the Americans may now commit large contingents of combat forces to the war, and that some Politburo members thought a more aggressive strategy was needed to preempt the anticipated US move. David Elliott in his *The Vietnamese War*, on the other hand, suggests that some thought the time may now be right to negotiate with Diem's successors and create a coalition government without recourse to further conflict and loss.

Whatever the motives, throughout the rest of November 1963 and after, the Communist Vietnamese Workers' Party leaders mulled over their options. One possibility was to continue applying the same pressure on the ARVN and Diem's successors using limited North Vietnamese reinforcements and increased growth of the forces in the South to seek a negotiated settlement before further American intervention.

Another choice was to significantly accelerate the infiltration and military efforts of both the North's regular and South's revolutionary forces to achieve total military victory before the Americans could significantly intervene directly with combat military forces. Before the Plenum met, Le Duan had settled on a course. He chose the latter.

While the intent of Resolution 15 had been to defeat the Southern political and military in a protracted struggle leading to the overthrow of the Diem regime, Le Duan, the most militant in the Politburo, now wanted to seek a quick military solution. The aim, as his contemporary writings show, was to defeat what he called the American 'Special War' of aiding the South to prevent unification under the North. To do this, the Northern Politburo leader wanted to quickly destroy the South's military forces and topple the weak South Vietnam government. The result would be that the US would have nothing left to support, and thus have to withdraw from its Vietnam venture.

Sometime in late November or early December 1963, the Central Committee of the Vietnamese Workers' Party convened its Ninth Plenum in Hanoi. Though there are no official released papers on the Plenum, some recent scholars have been able to gather some ideas of what those present discussed using interviews and related documents.

Plenum discussions lasted several weeks. There were a wide variety of topics: from the growing divisions of views of the Soviets and Chinese support; to whether the Americans would commit combat troops to South Vietnam; to whether the Party should seek negotiations with the South's new government. According to historians Pierre Asselin, William Duiker, Lien-Hang Nguyen and Ang Cheng Guan, these discussions were "contentious."

Giap made a presentation on the status of the progress of the PAVN in its modernization and growth. He tried to make a point that any assessment to take increased military measures needed to take into consideration that the Army was not yet fully prepared to take on a major conflict – especially one with the Americans. His comments sparked an argument over the risks of US military direct intervention. The differences between the North First and Southern factions threatened to divide the meeting seriously.

The contention may have been too much for Ho Chi Minh. Some sources report that he walked out of the debates. He then told a member of the Soviet embassy that he had decided that he had enough and that he no longer held sway over the more bellicose members of the Party. He may have even said that he was exhausted and going to retire from politics. Other sources say that Le Duan and his allies used Ho's two greatest disappointments, the failure to get concessions from the French in 1946 and the inability to get reunification at Geneva in 1954, to discredit him at the meetings. Whatever the actions, Le Duan neutralized both Ho and Giap, the two greatest Vietnamese revolutionaries, in the debate.

Le Duan then dominated the proceedings and held sway over the discussions. He forcefully presented his views on the escalation of military force. He attacked those who were advocating a more cautious, more of the same approach to the North's policy and strategy in the South. Le Duan then allegedly told the Plenum, "Revolution is not on the defensive, and the strategy of revolution should not be a defensive one." In Vietnam, as elsewhere in the colonial and semi-colonial world, he argued that the "strategy of revolution" must be "an offensive strategy to smash one by one the war policies of imperialism headed by the United States until its war plans are completely smashed." He then concluded that the time had come to "take the offensive against imperialist war policy and defeat it." His words carried the debate in the Plenum.

The resultant Resolution 9 was more forceful and detailed than the earlier resolution. The Plenum labeled it "Strive to Struggle, Rush Forward to Win New Victories in the South." Unlike Resolution 15, "it spelled out in explicit terms the guidelines for implementing the new strategy." The document called for operations leading to a "general offensive and uprising for the 'annihilation' and complete 'disintegration' of the ARVN forces." It further emphasized that the North's war effort and operations throughout Indochina were critical to success.

Remarkably - at least when one considers that most Americans then and some even now think that North Vietnam's approach to war was revolutionary and guerrilla operations oriented – the Resolution was replete with emphasis on large-scale offensive operations using main forces to destroy the enemy's forces. In doing so, it further emphasized the use of 'annihilation attacks' and to destroy the sources of the enemy's strength and the war effort. In short, the resolution's words in describing its military strategy and the war it was intended to wage were more in tune with Clausewitz's than Sun Tzu's or Mao's treatises on warfare.

To ensure the resolutions' intended outcomes, the North would now send major combat forces south, as well as to Laos to secure the major lifeline to the fight in South Vietnam. While political action stayed relevant to the cause, the Resolution made it clear that the armed struggle was now the decisive means to reach a 'direct and decisive' victory over the South and prevent America from intervening militarily.

Le Duan's central assumption, noticeable throughout Resolution 9, was that decisive PAVN/PLAF victories over the ARVN would convince the US that trying to save the corrupt and inept South regime would be futile, and, therefore, it could not intervene militarily with any sizeable military effort.

Meanwhile, the North Vietnamese war leader - aided by his trusted comrade, Le Duc Tho – purged Party moderates from any key positions they held in the government and party hierarchies. As quoted by Asselin, Le Duc Tho reasoned that these moderates had to go to develop "unequivocal and definite" support for the new direction. Le Duan's major supporter in the Politburo also said, "We are determined not to tolerate the practice of expressing views in an unorganized manner on the party's lines, policies, resolutions, and instructions."

Section 7.2 – Victory at Any Cost: Confronting the United States' Military Power

Right after the Ninth Plenum, the Party's Executive Committee put the DRV on a full wartime footing. Accordingly, they authorized the PAVN to go to 500,000 regular forces by the end of 1965. Soon after the DRV leaders began to mobilize for war, they enacted universal conscription.

For the first time, the North also began infiltrating entire PAVN units to the southern battlefield. To handle the increased traffic of personnel and supplies, the Army General Staff reinforced units responsible for the land routes into South Vietnam to further develop them. These reinforcements began a significant expansion of the existing, primitive route south to an elaborate network of trails, supply depots, base camps and training areas that became the Ho Chi Minh Trail.

Preparations for War: Mobilization, Training, Self Defense, Command and Control Enhancements

Many narratives of the Vietnam War note that while the nature of the war was a limited one for the US, it was an unlimited or all-out one for the North. Studies and books on the DRV's efforts to support and wage its war against the South and its American supporters demonstrate that the North totally mobilized its resources to go to war.

According to a US defense department contractor study in the seventies, in 1964 the DRV total population was approximately 18 million people. Of this, the North could produce about 100,000 eligible males fit for service each year. Also, to continue its food production and other areas of its meager economy, and to support other facets of its wartime needs, the DRV called upon a pool of nearly seven million women.

Many of these women performed manual labor in support of the PAVN. Some served in certain direct support combat specialties as well. To further support the war effort, the Chinese provided almost 40,000 laborers who worked on the North's transportation system to aid in the flow of armaments and other supplies from China.

The DRV Universal Military System law called for conscription for eligible males at the beginning of each year. Once called up and assembled in their districts, buses or trains or watercraft or a combination of them transported the recruits to their respective military bases for initial training. Basic training lasted between eight to twelve weeks depending on their military specialties – infantry soldiers were eight; mortarmen, radiomen, and engineers twelve. The initial entry training oriented on necessary soldierly skills. Unit training at divisional training centers followed.

The training in the North was mostly conventional. It did not focus on specific training for their area of destination in the South. The lack of focus on specific training for the South, according to several authors on the subject, "was because experienced combat troops were seldom rotated back north and there was little effort to collect and pass on lessons learned at the troop level. Infantry training was limited only to squad-level movement formations, attack maneuvers, defensive tactics, camouflage measures, defense against air attack (returning fire with small arms), digging fighting positions and individual movement techniques."

There was more intense training for specialists in the Army. Take that of Nguyen Van Troung, who was drafted in early 1965 and assigned to a reconnaissance unit. In an interview after US units captured him, he told the interrogator that after he had a period of basic training, as described above, he underwent intense added training consisting of special weapons firing, map reading, land navigation, camouflage techniques, and many others. He said this took up to an extra year before he went south because intelligence units were the most elite in the Army.

The DRV Armed Forces units not going south - primarily air defense, security, and logistics units - prepared to defend critical targets against US naval and air strikes and any subversive activities. North Vietnam was now the great base for directing and supporting the war for unification.

Besides the support of the nature mentioned above, the DRV further called upon their Chinese cousins to aid in that defense. In addition to the civilian labor mentioned, the PRC would eventually station some 170,000 engineering, support, and air defense military personnel in the DRV during the war.

Meanwhile, despite some disfavor the Soviets had at first with the DRV's new aggressive policy, they too would provide material, supplies, and advisors in the North. Though they at times argued for Hanoi to negotiate an end to the conflict, the Soviets provided over a thousand personnel, primarily to aid in or operate its surface to air missile systems that made the Hanoi area so deadly for American pilots. According to records released after the Cold War ended, Moscow would by 1967 overcome the PRC in the provision of overall supplies and material to the DRV.

In addition to its moves to mobilize its military resources and bolster its homeland defenses, the Politburo also beefed up COSVN headquarters in the South as it dramatically increased infiltration of PAVN forces there. Under Le Duan's appointment, in the late summer of 1964, General Tranh went south to take command of this important headquarters. His assignment would ensure the Northern direction of the new strategy. As historian Lien-Hang Nguyen noted his assignment also "marked the beginning of the end of southern autonomy in the field of military matters."

Lieutenant General Tran Van Tra, the PAVN Deputy Chief of Staff who was a southerner by birth, went with Thanh. He became Tranh's deputy and commander of the important Front in the Saigon area. His primary duty was to assist the COSVN political and military chief in expanding his forces and setting up a new command structure for the war. Tra directly commanded the PLAF troops, while the former was overall responsible to the Politburo (i.e., Le Duan) for political-military matters.

Le Duan sent Van Tra to play an important role. There had been some tension between southern communists and their northern brethren in who was running the war there. Van Tra was to placate the southerners. He would also ensure the execution of the North's strategic concepts.

Build Up and Operations: 1964 to Summer 1965

The war footing in the North, the changes in the COSVN headquarters, and increased infiltration measures soon paid high dividends for operations in the South. The PAVN history boasts that "the quantity of supplies shipped to the battlefields in 1964 was four times greater than that transported in 1963. During 1964, almost 9,000 cadre and soldiers marched down our commo-liaison route to fight in the South. Included in this were a number of full strength battalions and regiments."

As William Duiker further notes, over the twelve months of 1964 "Hanoi's gamble proved to be, on most counts, a success. …The PLAF imposed severe losses on the armed forces of the Saigon regime, while the political situation in South Vietnam continued to deteriorate." Toward the end of the year "US intelligence estimates were predicting a Communist victory within six months in the absence of a major US response."

Then came the Tonkin Gulf incident in August 1964. As mentioned in Chapter 3, soon after the US launched retaliatory strikes against the North. These strikes evolved into sustained bombings. As these were occurring, the US landed its first element of US Marines in South Vietnam during March 1965.

According to communist sources and those historians who analyzed them, the Gulf of Tonkin affair, the US subsequent bombings, and the later deployment of combat forces into the South in early 1965 accelerated Hanoi's implementation of its Resolution 9. As Pierre Asselin writes, "The revolution was now in a race against the clock; it had to redouble its efforts to annihilate ARVN forces and complete that tasks before Washington could get its forces into Vietnam in sufficient numbers to fight effectively."

In fact, as the evidence from the communist side shows, the US actions to show its resolve and convince the DRV to give up its aggression in the South had the exact opposite effect – in the words of some observers "it aroused them to still greater efforts." One of the 'greater efforts,' as the PAVN official history explains, resulted from an October 1964 directive from the Central Military Party Committee, endorsed by Le Duan, "to launch a campaign during the 1964-1965 winter-spring period aimed at destroying a significant number of puppet regular army units and expanding our liberated zones. Eastern Cochin China, the central part of Central Vietnam, and the Central Highlands would be the main battlefronts for this campaign."

Thus, as the retaliatory air strikes in the aftermath of the Tonkin Gulf incident were underway and the LBJ Administration was planning to launch ROLLING THUNDER, both meant to convince the North to desist its aggression, the communists were about to launch an all-out campaign to eliminate South Vietnam.

The ensuing Binh Gia campaign, according to the history, ended in January 1965 in a victory. "In more than one month of combat, our soldiers had fought five regiment level and two battalion-level battles, wiping out two entire battalions of enemy regulars (including one battalion of the enemy's strategic reserve forces) and one armored troop and inflicting severe casualties on three other battalions." The history continues, "Many strategic hamlets along Route 2 and Route 15 in Dat Do, Long Thanh, and Nhon Trach districts had been destroyed. Hoai Duc district was liberated. The Hat Dich base area in Ba Ria province and the southern part of Binh Thuan province was consolidated and expanded, thereby protecting the sea transportation route from North Vietnam to eastern Cochin China and extreme southern Central Vietnam."

Meanwhile, as the first US marines were landing in Da Nang and later reinforced with others and an American airborne brigade, Le Duan, aided by Ho Chi Minh and the North's chief diplomat Pham Van Dong, opened a campaign to ensure Chinese and Soviet support for the impending conflict with US forces in the south. That support, Le Duan felt, was not just in the military assistance arena. He wanted either assurances or threats from China to come to their support with their forces. The threat of China's military intervention, as it had done in Korea, was a significant part of Le Duan's strategy to keep the US from committing its ground forces outside of South Vietnam's borders.

Therefore, Le Duan traveled to China in April and Ho followed in May to solicit support for defense against a possible US full-scale intervention in the South. Mao agreed to provide "whatever support was needed by the Vietnamese." While such support would be substantial, it was limited. For example, there was some requested assistance, such as Chinese combat pilots to fly against US air strikes, that the Chinese were not willing to provide. As sources after the war would also reveal, the Chinese were willing to threaten intervention, but it was something they would not do.

Meanwhile, Le Duan and Ho continued to reject US diplomatic attempts to negotiate. A significant reason for so doing was their belief that eventually the US people would not support a major conflict spanning years in Vietnam. Another reason is that they both felt that conditions were not right for any negotiations. They both felt that they needed a significant military victory before any negotiations could begin in which they intended to show the US how futile it was to continue its military support for the South. Now in the Spring of 1965 another communist offensive in South Vietnam appeared on the verge of victory.

Thus, both Ho and Le Duan still believed that the Southern armies and its government might fall before the US military power could make any difference. Negotiating an end to the conflict, as LBJ and McNamara wanted in their show of resolve, was the farthest thing on their minds.

In late spring and early summer 1965, the limited US combat forces then in country were now fighting main PLAF and some PAVN units and inflicting heavy casualties. Nevertheless, Le Duan sent messages south encouraging his commanders to not shy from engaging US forces. Ho was no less sanguine. A week before LBJ would announce his commitment of US combat forces and declare that he wanted to end the war quickly, Ho declared that regardless of "whether the war would go on for another five, ten, 20 years or even longer the people must fight to achieve total victory."

If the US Wants a Protracted War; We Will Give it to Them

By the end of the summer of 1965, it became apparent that Le Duan had miscalculated in his assessment that the US would not commit major forces to the South's defense. His strategy to defeat the ARVN before the US could react decisively had failed.

One would think that there may have been in Hanoi some rumblings about this miscalculation. There very well may have been some. However, Le Duan and Le Duc Tho and their security services continued to keep any dissent under wrap. Security henchmen cracked down and arrested those they suspected of 'revisionist anti-party' thinking. Le Duan stuck to his decision for a military solution.

He did not ignore, however, this primary American intervention. He realized that any quick end to the Saigon regime now may not be possible. However, he did not think that the US would have the will for a protracted war. Le Duan voiced this often to his comrades - supporters and secret naysayers alike. He said that "if the US wants a protracted war, we will give it to them."

In discussions over a possible protracted war with the US, Le Duan often argued that the Americans would not have the support of their people, and that "we will ultimately win." He reminded all of what had happened in the French War. There were already some indications of dissatisfaction for and protests of American involvement in Vietnam. The growing US public dissent, moreover, made his argument plausible that the Americans would eventually lose because of dissension on the home front.

Letters between Le Duan and General Thanh indicate that their operational approach to execute their Resolution 9 strategy entailed matching the US build-up and confronting American units in large-scale battles. The primary units to do this were the PAVN regular (and some main PLAF) battalions, regiments and even divisions during 1965 and 1966. The primary theater where they thought they would have the advantage was in the Central Highlands.

The North Vietnam war leaders surmised that in the highland area their main force units would be able to hide in the thickly covered base camp areas. There, the base camps were mostly in the same locations that they had used during the French War. There, they would have the great advantage of knowing the terrain. There, they would also be able to withdraw to the safety of Cambodia or southern Laos in the event they needed to do so.

Meanwhile, most of the PLAF main force province, district, and local units could take on the ARVN. Le Duan and his Generals knew that they could not outright defeat the Americans. However, they continued to think they could defeat the ARVN. They further reasoned, if the PLAF (reinforced at times) defeated the Southern Army, then the general uprising could occur. They also further reasoned that if the Americans faced these conditions, they would have to sue for peace on the North's terms.

The key throughout, Le Duan believed, was to keep the political pressure on the Americans. To do that the North needed victories over the ARVN and to bloody the American Army. With American losses, he thought, American will for the war would crumble. The opportunities would then arise for a settlement in their favor. His most repeated phrase was 'fight to negotiate.' His mantra was 'diplomacy without military superiority should be avoided at all costs.'

It is interesting to contemplate, at this juncture, how the North Vietnamese military leaders who would carry the battle to the Americans thought they could fight successfully against the growing US combat forces in the South. Though statements in the official history of the PAVN are full of bombastic rhetoric and claims of inevitable victory, there were some thoughtful analyses from senior PAVN military leaders outlining how they believed they could confront successfully a far technologically superior US force and win.

Two such PAVN leaders were General Nguyen Chi Thanh – the Politburo general in overall charge of COSVN and operations in the South - and General Van Tien Dung, who was then Chief of the PAVN General Staff in Hanoi. They both made statements or wrote articles during the 1965-1967 timeframe explaining their thoughts on fighting the Americans. These statements, and in the case of General Dung some lectures he gave to fellow officers, are strikingly similar in the benefits or advantages both believed the PAVN and its southern army the PLAF enjoyed over the Americans. They are also in line with Le Duan's thinking at the time. There were four advantages that they noted.

The first advantage they mentioned was the familiarity of the terrain and the preparations of the theater of operations in the South for their main force units. In this case, both Dung and Thanh believed and stated that the Americans would be unprepared for the terrain and weather that they would be fighting in. Their forces, on the other hand, they reasoned would be not only acclimated to the weather but familiar with the terrain – especially those units that had already infiltrated into the

South and were training in their border base areas. Follow on PAVN elements, moreover, would also become familiar with the areas they would fight in as they prepared for combat in their base camps before employing against American and ARVN units.

In fact, as mentioned, the PAVN and PLAF base areas that supported them had already been carefully prepared and stocked. This groundwork had been one of the tasks for the stay behind cadre after the Geneva convention. Regroupee units that had returned in the early sixties had gone to these areas; where some had fought the French in the fifties. Moreover, population areas near these bases had local guerrilla forces and political cadres in position. These forces and individuals were well prepared to do advanced reconnaissance and surveillance of deploying US troops for them before they would engage the Americans.

Indeed, the second primary advantage that the North's two generals thought they had over the Americans was preparation for and actual conduct of intelligence operations. As the preparations and set up of the base areas went ahead, there was a move to recruit and place personnel to recon and report on ARVN and US force movements in the vicinity. Communist leaders and their subordinates further recruited agents and positioned them at or near American unit locations. Finally, they were also prepositioned in and around key population centers, and in the major posts of the ARVN forces and US headquarters.

The use of southern Vietnamese to provide this essential information and intelligence varied in sophistication, importance, and usefulness throughout the war. At the very local level, members of local guerrilla elements or individual communist sympathizers gathered information about ARVN and US base defenses and movements. This information ranged from the surveillance of the bases and routes to actual gathering of intelligence from personnel that worked in the US and ARVN base areas and installations as cooks, barbers, and maids. Most of this intelligence was tactical in nature.

On the other end of the spectrum, COSVN and other more regional headquarters recruited Vietnamese to work in and live around ARVN and US headquarters. Some claim that there may have been as many as 14,000 spies and informants that the DRV and COSVN put in place and relied upon for operational and strategic intelligence throughout the war. Claims are that one may have worked as a civilian aide to Westmoreland. Another – called Vu Ngoc Nha - was a close associate of the last GVN President. Still, another named Pham Chuyen was a double agent for the CIA. One of the most famous and already mentioned of these - Pham Xuan An – is worth a look at to show the importance and impact of their activities to the North Vietnamese war effort.

Larry Berman, a professor of Political Science at the University of California, has written a book on him called *Perfect Spy: The Incredible Double Life of Pham Xuan An*. In it, Berman traces An's life from his roots in South Vietnam as a child growing up in Saigon under French rule, to his service in the Viet-Minh against the Japanese and French, to his recruitment, training, and operations as a spy for COSVN and the DRV. It is a remarkable story.

An was unique among spies for the North Vietnamese, particularly against the US. He trained in the US as a journalist. Afterward, he was a reporter first as a *Reuters* and then as a *Times* correspondent in Saigon. In that role, he made the acquaintance and gained the trust of senior CIA officials – early on as mentioned Colonel Edward Lansdale during the Diem Regime – and then made it as a colleague with noted US reporters David Halberstam, Stanley Karnow, and Neil Sheehan. In fact, Max Boot claims that An actually got his first training in espionage and intelligence from Lansdale, who also was the one that made arrangements for the spy's education in the States.

His contacts, expertise, and experience not only influenced American attitudes about the war, but also directly provided to the COSVN and the Politburo crucial information and intelligence on the plans, movements, and intentions of both ARVN and American military leaders and their forces.

Specifically, he gave information on ARVN movements and tactics before the famous Battle of Ap Bac. For example, one document that he provided was on helicopter capabilities and techniques. After sent to the PAVN general staff, they were further distributed to the field. PAVN and VC units trained to counter these tactics and develop ways to shoot down helicopters. The unit at Ap Bac had done so.

An had also meticulously scouted the US and South Vietnamese potential targets in Saigon. This intelligence not only played a role in the selection of the targets for sabotage but aided in the actual communist attacks against Saigon in TET 1968. In sum, his intelligence was so crucial to the Northern civilian and military leaders during the war that afterward the high command appointed him a General in the PAVN and awarded him several high decorations.

The third major feature – and perhaps most critical - that Generals Dung and Thanh thought provided them an advantage in their campaigns against the US combat forces was the central line of supply they had to their main strategic base in the North. They - as well as their civilian Politburo members in the North and their subordinate front and military district leaders in the South - recognized that without this lifeline and its base areas along the borders the war in the South would be virtually unwinnable for them.

The Ho Chi Minh Trail, along with other reinforcement routes to the South such as the Sihanouk Trail in Cambodia and the sea-lane routes along the eastern Vietnamese coast, provided not only critical supplies and forces from the North, but deployed them in the numbers and quickly enough to match the American build up. Thus, the PAVN official history repeatedly describes how critical the Ho Chi Minh Trail was to the overall war effort in the South.

As an example, though there were some 50,000 North Vietnamese that went to the South in the ten years from 1955 to 1964, that figure doubled in in 1965 as Thanh and Van Tra launched their campaigns against the Americans. The next year that figure would double again. Thus, as the North's Politburo and PAVN high command decided upon specific offensives, they made improvements to the Trail accordingly. In turn, throughout the war, the Trail could transport and provide the troops and supplies as needed to launch these offensives.

As mentioned, the forces sent up to 1964 were primarily regroupees, small military units for training indigenous recruits, political cadres for indoctrination, and a few combat forces. The forces in 1965, however, were mostly all PAVN combat regiments and their divisional support units. By the end of 1966, according to the official history, there were a total of 230,000 PAVN soldiers available in the South to the COSVN military leaders for their campaigns.

These reinforcements not only allowed Thanh and Van Tra to match the American deployments, but enabled them to replace the soldiers, equipment, and armament they needed to continue to engage the US and ARVN forces without fear of decisive attrition to their troops. There is little doubt, therefore, that the Trail was, in Clausewitz's terms, the 'Center of Gravity' or "the source of power that provides moral or physical strength, freedom of action, or will to act" for the North's strategy to win the war.

The final significant advantage that Generals Dung and Thanh figured they had over the Americans was that US combat forces would be spread thin and would not be able to carry out what they had to do to defeat the North's operations in the South. Thanh in 1965 told Le Duan that he thought that "the forces of the United States had committed were insufficient for the multiple objectives assigned to them. The enemy himself deplores that these mobile forces often have to carry out occupation and pacification duties while Vietcong regiments are entirely mobile units."

Dung further stated a year later, "[the US enemy] was vainly trying to muster a bigger mobile force but his troops remain scattered around his bases and posts. If he withdraws from his posts and watch towers to have more mobile forces he will not be able to control the population and the areas under his control will shrink." As we will see in Chapters 8 and 9 ahead, North Vietnamese leaders had indeed identified the fundamental dilemma that Westmoreland would face in the execution of his military strategy in the war.

With their confidence in the above advantages, Thanh and Van Tra developed their campaign plans for their operations in the South against the ARVN and American forces. As described in the PAVN official history and Wilkins' *Grab Their Belts*, they wanted to use their main PAVN and PLAF forces operating out of their prepared base areas in the central region and around the Saigon area to engage and bloody American units to prevent them from preventing the collapse of the ARVN. Meanwhile, their main force units operating out of their bases next to the populated areas along the central coast and around Saigon and aided by the local and guerrilla forces there would engage and destroy the ARVN forces.

The overall intent was to so destroy and demoralize the ARVN that they would be unable to prevent the fall of the South Vietnamese government. This goal would ultimately be accomplished by the seizure of the main cities in the central region and perhaps Saigon itself. Meanwhile, PAVN forces in and adjacent to the Demilitarized Zone would engage US forces located there to prevent their movement elsewhere. They would also maneuver units out of Laos toward the cities of Danang and Hue. Thanh set specific goals to "strive to annihilate between 30,000 and 40,000 US troops and 200,000 puppet and satellite (allied) troops" a year during 1965 and 1966.

The PAVN and PLAF Operational Campaigns, 1965 to Mid-1967

The PAVN units that gathered in their base areas astride the borders of South Vietnam and those that further moved to bases near the populated areas in 1965 were ready for a fight. To protect their bases, the forces already there had constructed elaborate tunnel complexes and bunker systems. The NVA located and hid these bases mostly in mountainous regions, obscuring them from aerial view by dense and triple canopy trees and undergrowth. For the defense of bases close to villages and hamlets, PAVN and PLAF forces depended on local VC forces and guerrillas for early warning of approaching enemy forces and to provide guides for movement away from American units approaching their bases. Moreover, units moved these local bases and camps often to avoid detection.

Prepositioned NVA cadres and leaders and the nearby PLAF units provided security and combat specific training to any infiltrating PAVN regulars as they arrived in their base camps. They instructed them on how to move quickly and silently toward the enemy using the carefully prepared trail network in the area. They further taught them how to assemble quietly with the use of local guides, use the night to get close to the enemy positions, and conduct mass frontal assaults to overwhelm the enemy before their commanders can bring their massive firepower to bear.

In attacking American units, the PAVN often targeted American support and firebases. If these were large, then they would usually attack using the indirect fires of their mortars or in some cases artillery and rockets. If small then they would first infiltrate small units, called sappers, to attack command posts and create gaps in the defenses. Quick, overwhelming infantry assaults would follow. As a matter of habit, units carefully planned and thoroughly scouted their attacks and ambushes, often with the support of local spies or sympathetic southern Vietnamese.

A favorite tactic in the assaults against large bases, or those that the enemy felt important, was to feign an attack and then prepare a large ambush for any relief force sent to reinforce the base. This had been a common type of operation against the ARVN forces, which were primarily road bound. As the American combat units arrived in South Vietnam, the PAVN/PLAF commanders were unsure if this tactic would work. However, they were willing to try it.

One operation at the end of 1965, conducted in a way similar to the above descriptions, gave the North confidence that their tactics and their PAVN (and some PLAF) regular forces could indeed match the Americans. It served as a testing place not only of the tactics but also for the operational strategy outlined above. Ironically, it would be the campaign that would give the US Commander in South Vietnam at the time confidence that his operational concept, search and destroy, could win, as well. It was the Ia Drang campaign in November 1965.

According to captured documents, and North Vietnamese and VC interviews and discussions, the PAVN command in the Highlands designed the campaign to lure ARVN forces toward an ambush area and destroy them. They further expected that American troops would respond. The PAVN forces would then attack the American units in areas in which their use of helicopter tactics would be vulnerable to NVA crew-served weapons.

As described in Warren Wilkins' *Grab Their Belts To Fight Against Them* the campaign started with an attack against a US Special Forces Camp at Plei Me in October 1965. The first phase consisted of the newly infiltrated 33rd NVA Regiment (about 2000 soldiers) encircling the camp. Another NVA Regiment, the 320th, set up an ambush along a route that an ARVN relief force would take. A third Regiment, along with a VC Main Force Battalion, would be in reserve to react to any American helicopter operation.

The PAVN units initially conducted the operations successfully. However, American massive air attacks and a sudden movement of an entire US airmobile division caused concern to the PAVN commander. He ordered the withdrawal of the forces to the highland base areas near the Cambodian border.

Unexpectedly, the US Airmobile Division commander air assaulted a battalion of American infantry right near the regimental reserve base. A three-day fight ensued with heavy casualties on both sides. The NVA took severe losses to air and artillery strikes. Undeterred, in the next several days NVA forces stalked other American infantry sent to the area. In a fierce battle between a regiment of both NVA and VC main forces and the US infantry, a significant part of the American unit took heavy casualties. The rest of the American force withdrew.

For the first part of the campaign and the battle that took place at a place called Landing Zone X-Ray, the US took credit for winning the battle. As we will see in the next chapter, General William Westmoreland claimed that the PAVN/PLAF significant casualties showed the validity of his search and destroy concept and the efficacy of the use of helicopters in Vietnam.

For the second part of the campaign and the battle that took place near a place called Landing Zone Albany, the NVA took credit for winning. General Thanh claimed a great victory over the Americans. He professed that the big unit confrontation with the Americans was working.

The PAVN official history, of course, claims today the same as General Thanh did then. It argues, "The Plei Me victory demonstrated that our main force troops had high combat morale and a high resolve to defeat the Americans. It also demonstrated the clever and innovative campaign and tactical combat techniques of our main force army. This victory proved our army was capable of annihilating U.S. battalions operating in large formations and that we could disrupt the helicopter-assault tactics and defeat the most elite, most modernly equipped units of the American army even under the most difficult and savage conditions."

As the first round of fighting ended in 1965, PAVN and US commanders extracted what they wanted out of the battles to show that their operational concepts were correct and working. Each side drew heavy casualties borne by soldiers who mostly knew nothing of the strategies. It seems now in retrospect that these first battles were so appropriate to the entire war that would follow.

The fighting and bloodshed continued throughout 1966 and into the first six months of 1967. Most of it, as described in the NVA/VC tactics above, was now familiar to the PAVN, PLAF, and ARVN, US forces alike. The PAVN official history is full of descriptions of victories and significant losses for the ARVN and Americans. It relates how, "by mid-1966, after six months of fierce and arduous fighting, our soldiers and civilians in South Vietnam had defeated the first strategic counteroffensive conducted by 200,000 American and satellite troops and almost 500,000 puppet troops." The communist forces, the history claims, 'eliminated' some "70,000 enemy troops (including 30,000 Americans)."

Despite these inflated claims, the history admits that there were some setbacks and lessons to be learned from the fighting. It emphasizes that the American tactics were significantly different than PAVN and PLAF leaders had experienced during the war against the French. US firepower, both from artillery and the air, caused heavy casualties. They often prevented successful massive ground attacks during the day and often disrupted assembling of forces at night.

Also disconcerting, the history shows, was the American use of helicopters in the movement of US troops. US combat units were not constrained to roads. Thus, customary planned ambushes that worked so well against French and ARVN units were not as effective against US forces. Moreover, the sudden and continual movement of American units not only kept their forces always on the move, but often placed US soldiers into positions that their units could not always escape from. This, in turn, was an added strain on PAVN and PLAF mobile forces. These official history comments, often confirmed by captured enemy documents and prisoners, are quite honest in their assessments.

The PAVN history is particularly valuable in describing its mobilization efforts in the North, the infiltration along the Ho Chi Minh Trail to the South, and its use of base areas along the borders of South Vietnam. It states that these were all significant factors in their ability to continue the fight despite heavy casualties. As a result, "By the end of 1966 the total strength of our armed forces was 690,000 soldiers. The number of troops training in North Vietnam was 460,000, and the number of troops fighting on the battlefields of South Vietnam was 230,000. The number of replacement troops sent south in 1966 was six times greater than the number sent in 1965. Our combat battalions in South Vietnam increased from 103 battalions… in 1965 to 136 battalions… in 1966."

By mid-1967, it had become noticeable to Le Duan and other Northern leaders that their strategy of destroying the ARVN and bloodying the Americans had not worked. Though they had been able to replace them, their forces in the South had taken significant losses.
Giving them hope, however, was the growing antiwar movement in the US.

As mentioned, part of their strategy in the war against the Americans was to gauge their operations to influence domestic support for the war, as they had done against the French. Thus, especially throughout 1966 and into early 1967, as casualties grew, they continuously watched the unrest in America, even trying to incite it by making contacts with some prominent American antiwar leaders and members of Congress. While Le Duan and the Politburo had taken heart over Congressional hearings, especially the Fulbright one, they were dismayed that there was a sizable number of Americans who supported the war and even wanted it escalated, especially in the American Republican party.

Moreover, as the war progressed, and casualties grew it would not just be the American leaders who would be questioned over the costs of the war and the efficacies of the strategies. Despite their security services, Le Duan and his militant supporters in the Politburo, especially Le Duc Tho, would come under scrutiny from time to time – particularly over any overtures for negotiations with the Americans.

This growing dissatisfaction was most prominent during the Johnson bombing halts. While it cannot be called a 'peace party,' with the growing costs of the war, there was a 'negotiations' faction in the Party. However, that faction was never strong enough or allowed to get so, to make any difference to Le Duan's determination to fight the Americans.

There was also one individual, however, who stayed a thorn in the side of Le Duan and his supporters. That was General Giap. Though coy and cautious, Giap took the opportunity to voice in late 1966 some subtle criticism of Le Duan's big unit war and its casualties. With his experience in journalism, the Defense Minister took advantage of his war hero image to criticize General Thanh's neglect of the guerrilla war aspects of the war in the South.

Giap voiced concern over the 'suicidal nature' of some of the attacks. He criticized the PAVN for launching them without thorough preparation, which would have minimized such casualties. Giap's reproaches were careful not to attack the Le Duan- General Thanh approach. He suggested subtleties in the degree in the use of guerrilla and main force attacks. For a while, Giap's old French Indochina War comrade, Ho Chi Minh, supported him in these criticisms.

Giap's public 'suggestions' continued into 1967. They then suddenly stopped. In the late Spring of that year, Giap met with the PAVN leadership to discuss the apparent stalemate that had developed. Le Duan may have prompted this meeting to examine how to overcome the impasse in the South. He also wanted to create conditions for a decisive victory in the upcoming US Presidential elections in 1968. In June, the Politburo recalled General Thanh from the South to take part in these discussions.

The TET Offensive

These meetings and later ones in the Politburo would result in the infamous Communist TET Offensive in January 1968. From the Communist North Vietnam perspective, what did they hope to gain? How did they think they could achieve victory? Most of all how did the results affect the Vietnamese Communists' future conduct of the war?

Historians Lien-Hang Nguyen and An Cheng Guan offer some views and insights from their research on North Vietnamese documents on the decision for the offensive. Historian William Turley, some post-war revelations from PAVN General Tran Van Tra, and the PAVN official history also give some assessments of its results.

The above sources agree on the rationale for that offensive. As Lien-Hang explains, there were four plausible reasons for the 1968 TET offensive. Some of them related. The first was that, despite their ability to withstand the damage and losses, the North Vietnamese had to take some decisive action to address the US bombing campaign.

That campaign had been unprecedented in scope and size since the end of World War Two. Since the beginning of ROLLING THUNDER in late March 1965, the US had been bombing northern targets on almost a daily basis. The sorties (numbers of aircraft missions flown per day) had progressively grown from 25,000 in 1965 to 79,000 in 1966. They would total 108,000 for 1967.

Targets had progressively become more inclusive and damaging. By 1967 the American bombers were attacking industrial, commercial, and even city centers. There was a sense of frustration and damage enough (particularly with the ability to produce food and basic necessities of life) to cause North Vietnamese dismay at not being able to stop the incessant strikes. Faced with the prospects of a prolonged war, some Politburo members were concerned about the North's continued ability to survive the continued bombing.

Second, the Politburo felt that they could not expect their chief supporters, the PRC and the Soviets, to deliver the level and kind of support indefinitely. The DRV had already been playing a balancing act between these ever-growing rivalries in the communist world. While the Chinese reveled in the bloodletting the war was causing to the US military and the disruption in American society; the Soviets wanted, in the long run, to pursue détente with the West.

How much longer could these two be convinced it was in their best interest to provide support? What would happen if one or both supporters suddenly thought it in their best interest to try to end the war? Would such a negotiated peace result in a Geneva-like compromise? Would that lead to the continued division of Vietnam? The Politburo pondered these unknowns with no assurances for positive outcomes.

A third reason, which historians have most recently speculated upon, was that there might have been the real possibility of a power struggle on the horizon for the Vietnamese Communist militants, and those who opposed them in the Politburo. Ho's failing health had gotten worse. What would happen when he died? While Giap and other less militant Party members had been suppressed, they may make a challenge should Ho pass away soon – especially if the war remained in a deadlock and casualties high from the battles and bombing.

A fourth possible influence on a change of course in the South was that Le Duan realized that the war in the South had reached an impasse. He had hoped that he still could have kept the Americans at bay while destroying the South's armed forces and toppling its regime. That did not happen. Meanwhile, his confrontation with the Americans had not been able to inflict enough casualties to convince the American public to call for an end to US support for the South Vietnamese 'puppet' regime. Though he held the home front at bay, he just did not think he could go on with the same strategy. He needed some dramatic military action that would, if not turn the tide militarily, do so politically.

So, by mid-1967 it became apparent to the militants in the Politburo that the stalemate needed to be broken. It seemed that the timing was right. Peace protests had gotten more vocal and rampant in the US. It had become reminiscent of the protests in France during the First Indochina War around the time of the Dien Bien Phu campaign. A US presidential election was coming up in 1968. Might some dramatic action sway both?

According to Lien-Hang Nguyen, the debates in the summer of 1967 broke down along the same lines of the old North First and Southern Liberation group arguments about transitioning to a more considerable military effort in the South in the late fifties. The former reiterated its cautionary, protracted war approach; while the latter argued that the time was right for a decisive offensive that would lead to a general uprising. Again, as in the earlier debates, Le Duan dominated the discussions.

The June Politburo discussions further pitted Le Duan and General Thanh against Giap and a few of his followers. The latter agreed that some decisive move was necessary to break the stalemate in 1968. They disagreed that the attack should be an all-out offensive focused on the cities with the hope that a spontaneous uprising would occur.

Giap offered that there should be a more carefully prepared and prolonged campaign. He argued for a combination of sizeable main force unit attacks with guerrilla unit harassment attacks on the outskirts that would lure American forces away from the cities. This distraction would eventually make the ARVN forces weakened, and the cities vulnerable to an all-out offensive.

General Thanh offered his ideas based on planning he and his COSVN military commanders had already accomplished. According to Vietnamese scholars Ang Cheng Guan and Lien-Hang Nguyen, Thanh had convened a meeting in May 1967 at his COSVN headquarters to review and discuss their operations in the South. Agreeing that the Americans continued to reinforce their forces and that, although they had stood up to them in many battles, they needed to change the tempo of their fighting.

Thanh, ever the believer that they could hold off the Americans and defeat the ARVN with his main forces, came up with a concept where there would be an all-out coordinated offensive against the major southern cities. That massive offensive, Thanh believed, would incite a popular uprising and topple the South's hold over them for good. With the sure turmoil to follow, the COSVN commander thought he could then destroy the ARVN forces defending the populated areas, and throw the American forces in disarray. The DRV commander in chief in the South had relayed this proposal to Hanoi in June. Le Duan was pleased with and agreed with Thanh's strategic concept because it was bold, if not imaginative.

It seems that the main difference between Le Duan and his supporter General Thanh and Giap was in the type of force, timing, intensity, and location of the overall decisive attack in 1968. The natural compromise or conclusion was to combine the best aspects of each's ideas and concepts.

At the beginning of July Thanh suddenly died of a heart attack. Some say a B52 strike killed him. There is even some speculation that some disgruntled PAVN staff officers may have assassinated him. Whatever the cause, it appears that General Thanh had been the original author of the concept plan for an all-out general offensive. Thus, with him gone, the principal author of the general offensive concept would not be available to defend it further.

More importantly, Le Duan appeared to have lost his leading supporter for the all-out offensive he wanted. He had also lost his main military counterweight to Giap. According to Lien-Hang Nguyen's account, Le Duan set out to find a replacement of some stature amongst the military brass to continue to counter Giap.

He found that in a General Van Tien Dung. Dung was the PAVN Chief of Staff and viewed as second in command behind Giap. According to Douglas Pike, Dung's primary duties were to oversee the defense of the DRV, especially air defense measures. He had been Giap's Chief of Staff at Dien Bien Phu. An ambitious general, he had a reputation for attention to detail in military planning. Many thought that Dien Bien Phu would not have been successful without his planning.

Dung was also a member of the Central Military Committee and an alternate in the Politburo. He was an outright ambitious man, who continually sought more power in both the Army and in the Workers Party hierarchy. All of that made him prime pickings for Le Duan.

Sometime in July after Thanh's death, Le Duan met with Dung privately and promoted him to full general and gave him the prominent seat in the Military Committee, which the Politburo had tasked to reconcile the concepts of Thanh and Giap. He then turned to his newly found military comrade and told him to continue to draft plans for the 1968 offensive in the way the Party Secretary wanted, and Thanh had proposed.

At a two-day high-level Politburo meeting, late in July – just three weeks after Thanh's death - Le Duan and General Dung presented the results of this planning. It incorporated some suggestions from Giap regarding attacks against American forces – mostly to lure them away from the lowlands and urban areas. However, to the astonishment of many there, it called for a PLAF led offensive throughout South Vietnam against hundreds of cities that were primarily seats of government for the RVN. It also included the killing of many RVN high-level officials and their replacement with National Liberation Front (NLF) governments in anticipation of a popular uprising against the South Vietnamese government.

The Le Duan- Dung plan had three central assumptions. One was that the major American combat units would be unable to affect the main attacks. A second was that the ARVN could be quickly defeated. The third was that the Southern populace would welcome the NLF.

The most vocal and leading voice against the plan turned out to be Ho Chi Minh. The aged and frail leader questioned the plans optimistic assumptions and its prediction for a quick and decisive victory. He asked what if the assumptions turned out to be wrong? He then thought that there should be more preparation time for any offensive and that plans should include the use of small units and guerrillas to wear down the enemy beforehand. He also recommended that plans take into consideration that the initial attacks may not be successful. In short, Ho thought the entire plan too risky.

Le Duan must have felt confident and powerful enough to dismiss Ho's concerns. After the high-level meeting, he gave permission to General Dung for further planning based upon an all-out attack against the urban centers. He then appointed a replacement for Thanh – an old comrade from his time in the South in the war against the French and a man whom he had spent some prison time together, General Pham Hung. Hung went south with outlines of the plans to ensure PAVN and PLAF military commanders would execute the plan as Le Duan envisioned.

Meanwhile, Giap, who was silent during the July Politburo meeting, left for Eastern Europe. In protest over the resultant plans for TET, he would not return until after the PAVN had launched the offensive. Ho also left the country. He traveled to China, where he stayed to recuperate from the illness that eventually would kill him.

With his two primary opponents out of the country, Le Duan once again turned to his security apparatus to remove any others who may have opposition to his TET plans. He had loyal members of Giap's staff arrested and jailed. He also ordered the detention of several of Ho's comrades who had sympathized with his views against Le Duan. There would be no further dissent.

In December, the Workers' Party members met once again to discuss the final plan. Ho had returned and vainly tried to convince his comrades of the risks of the all-out large-scale attack. He was unsuccessful. He had lost control of the Politburo.

PAVN and PLAF forces had already launched attacks in the latter part of 1967 before the final orders for the overall offensive. Per Giap's ideas, they were to lure US troops away from the urban areas. These attacks were primarily in the border regions in ARVN Corps II and III. These worked to a degree. However, they also cost high casualties among the PAVN regulars and PLAF main forces.

Then in the last week of January just before the primary attacks, the PAVN launched an offensive against the US Marine Corps base at Khe Sanh. This action would become the most famous of the diversions; if it was one. From the evidence, thus far from communist sources, it is not clear why Khe Sanh became such an attraction for the PAVN. After the war, Giap claimed that the attack was to draw Westmoreland forces away from the critical targets not only in the I Corps region, such as Quan Tri City and Hue, but from all over Vietnam.

However, some documents show that this may not have been all that Giap and others made it out to be. An Cheng Guan explains why. First, it appears that the PAVN High Command may have ordered the Khe Sanh operation launched at the same time as the general offensive. This would indicate that the PAVN high command may have planned it for more than a diversion, but a support attack for Hue.

The PAVN commander responsible for the attacks there had to hurry his assault. The result was that PAVN forces were confused, support units did not move as directed, and the main infantry arrived in piecemeal. Thus, there is some speculation that the move to Khe Sanh was a last-minute afterthought.

Second, a reason for the movement to Khe Sanh may have been because Westmoreland had sent reinforcements there to bolster the original Marine Corps presence. That reinforcement prompted the PAVN command to send forces there to protect the movement of forces toward their assembly and attack positions for the TET main offensive. Thus, Westmoreland's move may have diverted PAVN reinforcements for any expected successes against Quan Tri and Hue.

Whatever the reasons for Khe Sanh, the battle there, as well as the other diversion attacks, were costly for the PAVN and PLAF main forces. Moreover, though the attacks diverted some US combat forces, at the last moment, Westmoreland had gained enough intelligence to redeploy some forces back to the Saigon area and toward Hue and Quan Tri. They would play a significant role in TET's outcome.

However, whatever the North's intent, as we will see in Chapter 9 the battle around Khe Shan did attract attention at MACV. Not only was Westmoreland under much pressure from the President over Khe Sanh, but after the offensive began, he continued to think that the North's main offensive would be there.

In December 1967, the Politburo passed a resolution officially sanctioning the offensive. The Central Committee voted on and approved it at its Plenary Session in early January. On 18 January 1968, Le Duan issued a letter to the COSVN providing the general thinking about the offensive, its objectives and desired outcomes.

The principal objective was to defeat the enemy forces around Saigon to topple its government. Other main attacks would be directed at Hue and Da Nang to destroy the ARVN forces there, capture critical facilities, seize important local government sites, and, with the help of the people, set up liberation governments. The most desired outcome, the letter pronounced, would be to "deal the enemy thundering blows to change the face of the war, further shake the aggressive will of US imperialism, compel it to change its strategy and de-escalate the war."

As for the attacks of the main offensive, they were overall well-coordinated and overall caught the ARVN off balance as well as some American units. However, due to the last-minute distribution of orders and preparations the attacks were not as coordinated or as effective as planned. Some units, mistaking the date and times, launched their assaults a couple of days early, preventing a complete surprise.

The offensive, as already related in Chapter 3 and will be in more detail in Chapter 9, was a shock to the US and ARVN forces in the scope and intensity. However, the reliance on the PLAF and the revealing of the VC infrastructure would cost the North's war effort dearly overall. The risky operational assumptions proved false. There were no general uprisings. The ARVN performed well and did not, as expected, disintegrate. While the diversions may have lured some away, many US forces reacted quickly and counterattacked successfully in support of ARVN and local South Vietnamese forces.

It is interesting to read the PAVN's official history of the TET offensive. It claims that the diversions were highly successful. The offensive, it states, was launched as planned. The history further claims that the "population of Hue rose up in insurrection"; and that, in general, "the people of the villages and hamlets rose up and eliminated tyrants and traitors."

In truth, while there were some successes in Hue and other cities, several weeks after the offensive most of the PLAF and PAVN forces in Hue and elsewhere that attacked perished with only a small number escaping. The South Vietnamese populace in most of the cities fled the communists during their attack and returned to their homes when the ARVN obtained control again. In the countryside, the PLAF held onto villages and hamlets for several months, but eventually, Allied forces drove them out as well.

In fact, as already mentioned, the initial offensive was a disaster for the PLA. In particular, the local and the main military forces, and the political cadres, severely lost personnel. The genuinely southern VC would never recover.

While he is highly laudatory of his soldiers' performance during the offensive, General Tran Van Tra, who headed the attacks against the Saigon area, made some admissions that seem credible about the overall offensive. His main critique was that he thought that the Politburo and PAVN high command gave their final directions much too late.

Tra further believed that there were too much time and resources devoted to the phase to lure American forces away from the cities. Consequently, there just was not enough time to do the typically thorough planning and other preparations that he oversaw in other main attacks. He also thought that they had overestimated their strength and underestimated the enemy's. In short, they overreached their capabilities in launching such a country-wide attack against an ARVN foe who had more fighting ability than they gave them credit for.

The PAVN history, in less direct terms, supports these comments. It does admit that "we had somewhat underestimated the capabilities and reactions of the enemy and set our goals too high." Moreover, it states, "our preparations of supplies, spiritual preparations, and preparation of tactics were insufficient." Finally, "our arrangements for carrying out and coordinating combat operations by our forces for coordination between battlefields and between military attacks and mass uprisings were disjointed."

The PAVN history also reflects upon the impacts the offensive had on domestic affairs in the US. It says that the "American people believed the TET offensive had caused the failure of the US effort to achieve its objectives in Vietnam." It adds, "the US President Johnson rejected General Westmoreland's recommendation that an additional 200,000 soldiers be sent to Vietnam," and "announces he would not run for a second term as President."

Because of these events, the history claims, "The TET General Offensive and Uprising conducted by our soldiers and civilians secured a great strategic victory." The overall conclusion of the history's rendition of TET is that Le Duan achieved his primary goal. The attack crippled the political will of the US in a critical election year.

For the Vietnamese Communists, LBJ's announcement not to run for another term was an unexpected positive result of TET. It caught Le Duan and all the Politburo members by surprise. Indeed, it was welcome news amidst all the bad news on the military front.

When Johnson called for Hanoi to honestly reciprocate his call for a negotiated settlement in March 1968, Le Duan decided to dispatch a delegation to Paris to begin talks. To ensure that he would have strict control over these discussions, he sent Le Duc Tho to be the special advisor to his diplomatic team. He gave his trusted comrade instructions that there would be no real negotiations, - 'just talks about talks,' until there was a military victory in the South.

Meanwhile, Le Duan gave orders to launch the second phase of attacks beginning 4 May. This phase caused some significant fighting and damage in Saigon. However, it resulted, yet again, in high casualties for the PLAF. These actions gained nothing.

Le Duan stubbornly refused to give up on his desire to win a military victory to defeat the ARVN and topple the RVN government. So, when this second phase failed, he ordered yet another series of attacks that lasted from mid-August to the end of September. Similar results followed. DRV representatives in Paris continued to have 'talks about the talks.'

As 1968 ended, it became apparent to Le Duan that whoever was going to be the new US President, the political atmosphere in America was such that the US would have to do something to draw down its military commitment in South Vietnam. Though the general offensive had failed in 1968, there had been no combined American-South Vietnamese Counteroffensive. As Van Tra later noted, though the communist forces "had to retreat," they did so "to their strategic positions in the outlying areas" where they maintained their "staging areas for later attacks."

Thus, as Le Duan realized, many of the PAVN and PLAF main forces in the border sanctuaries were intact and unharmed. He knew that his troops also continued to have the capability to infiltrate further and reinforce the decimated forces in the South. Most importantly the General Secretary would have the capacity for some military solution in 1969 or later to defeat the RVN. Therefore, the North Vietnamese leader continued to instruct his diplomats in Paris not to negotiate until fighting in the South renewed.

In 1969, the fighting continued in the South. Replenishing some of its forces, North Vietnam launched several offensives early on with the hope of some military gains that it could use at the Paris talks. This continued combat was to no avail. The balance of forces had significantly changed for the US and RVN.

The PLAF could no longer sustain any significant attack against the cities. PAVN forces now were replacing VC main and local force personnel losses. Neither the PLAF or PAVN forces could assemble enough combat power to regain even a semblance of any serious offensive. There were a half a million American forces still in South Vietnam.

1969 began a period for the PLAF and PAVN that most communist sources describe as 'difficult.' Even the PAVN official history characterized the period 1969 to 1970 as one in which "to maintain and employ our main force units became a critical issue for all battlefields…and many were forced to withdraw to our base areas."

As Lien-Hang Nguyen notes, "With reports reaching Hanoi of the deteriorating military picture in South Vietnam, the Party leadership had no choice but to advance the diplomatic struggle in Paris in order to provide much-needed support for the weakened military and political struggles in South Vietnam." In other words, the 'diplomatic struggle' became a means to gain time to build future capabilities for another military offensive. LBJ furthered the 'means to gain time to build future capabilities' by ordering a halt to the bombing of the North. Accordingly, infiltration operations went on unhindered.

Throughout the negotiations that would follow Le Duan and Le Duc Tho dominated the diplomatic agenda. Ho Chi Minh died in September 1969. He never really affected the North Vietnamese positions in the negotiations or in the fighting in the South. Giap's influence was minimal. After it had become evident to the Politburo that any more conventional offensives in the South were neither practical nor desirable at this time, Giap's call for a more protracted struggle using guerrilla tactics gained favor – at least for the time being.

Though there were a few significant battles between US and PAVN main units- such as the one at Hamburger Hill - most of the fighting in 1969 entailed small unit engagements. When there a few large-scale PAVN/PLAF attacks, they involved attempts to weaken the RVN's resurgent pacification program. These efforts to turn back pacification, by the PAVN history's admission, failed.

In sum, Le Duan had to bid his time for any other future significant military move until he could rebuild his forces. He still had not given up his quest for a military solution. He still could build and train new forces in the North. Most importantly, he still had his lifeline to the South – the always improving Ho Chi Minh Trail.

North Vietnam and the US Anti-War Movement

Because the US reaction to the North's TET offensive was an essential part of the results of TET, it is proper here to take a moment and look at the DRV role in and use of the anti-war sentiment in the US. It is one of the most controversial issues of the war. The topic is also a fundamental aspect of understanding the attitudes of and the decisions of Northern leaders - from Ho Chi Minh to Le Duan - toward the war and how much US public opinion and the antiwar movement gave not only sustenance to their cause but direction.

First, the evidence is undeniable that US domestic opinion and support were very much a part of the DRV's overall policy and strategy in its war against the Americans. It was a crucial part of Resolution 9 – the key Central Committee policy document declaring the Vietnam Workers Party policy in its impending conflict with the US in 1963.

That document stated, "We must make every effort to motivate various peace organizations, labor unions, youths, women, lawyers, [and] other professional organizations of various peoples in the world" to "take stronger actions in asking the U.S. imperialists to end their aggressive war, withdraw their troops, military personnel, and weapons from South Vietnam, and let the South Vietnamese people settle their own problems."

The resolution further declared that one of its primary tasks was to win "the sympathy and support of the people of the nationalist and imperialist countries and gaining the sympathy of antiwar groups in the United States and taking full advantage of the dissensions among the imperialists."

This point should not be so startling. As mentioned and known to the North's leaders, French public opinion had been a fundamental part of the Communist Vietnamese war against France. Ho Chi Minh and other Vietnamese Workers Party members paid close attention to it then; why would not they do so now?

Second, most of the evidence on the DRV's conduct of the war shows that American domestic affairs - particularly dissent against the war, Congressional reaction to it, and the politics surrounding election years - remained a constant concern of the North's leaders. These were frequent topics discussed in the Politburo.

Bui Tin, a former North Vietnamese Colonel and editor of the People's Daily, in his memoirs, said that the antiwar movement "was essential to our strategy. Support of the war from our rear was completely secure while the American rear was vulnerable. Every day our leadership would listen to world news over the radio at 9 a.m. to follow the growth of the American antiwar movement."

Indeed, as we have seen, North Vietnamese leaders and advisors took into consideration US public reactions to the war in every significant decision they considered. This included their decisions to send regroupees in the late fifties to South Vietnam; the stepped-up military campaign to defeat the ARVN in 1963-4; to engage US forces in combat in 1965; and the TET 1968 general offensive. This focus on American reactions to the war, we will see in the pages ahead, will continue in every subsequent major decision to include the final offensive resulting in the fall of South Vietnam in 1975.

Though North Vietnam agents did not directly control and direct the US peace and anti-war movements, the Vietnamese Workers Party members did take a role in instigating and promoting US dissent. For example, communist officials granted and facilitated US visitor support to North Vietnam. These visits were ostensibly to gain access to American POWs for humanitarian reasons. However, they often consisted of the North's active manipulation and use of antiwar activists who wanted to gain favor and information to further their cause on the international scene or at home. In so doing, communist officials gave ample photo opportunities and propaganda for their use.

In several instances, American activists willingly gave radio interviews and made broadcasts that were in turn aired over communist airwaves to US troops in South Vietnam and elsewhere. Most of these were well-known leaders of the more vocal or militant groups, such as Michael Haden.

The most infamous of these was Hayden's wife at the time, Jane Fonda - a well-known Hollywood actress. Not only did she make radio broadcasts attacking American government policies on the war and expounding on the suffering of the Vietnamese people, but she made film interviews of American POWs to show how well their captives were treating them. By far, her most notorious act was posing around North Vietnamese soldiers and manning an antiaircraft gun appearing to want to shoot down US aircraft. For these acts, she became known to US servicemen then and always as 'Hanoi Jane.'

The American activist interface and propaganda making went beyond the confines of North Vietnam. Much of this is described in Frank Rafalko's work *MH/Chaos: The CIA's Campaign Against the Radical New Left*. For example, American antiwar and government activists arranged meetings between North Vietnamese officials and VC leaders at several international conferences. There they discussed "how to conduct their psychological warfare campaign against the United States."

At one such conference, Tom Hayden advocated ways to "sabotage the American war effort." At yet another, Black Panther leaders discussed with some officials how to incite draft evasion and unrest in the American military. These conferences and meetings varied in frequency and locations, from Eastern Europe to Sweden to Cuba. In most instances, the activists did not pay for the costs of transportation or stay; rather communist organizations operating in favor with the North did.

At these meetings and conferences, the North's propagandists went beyond the how to influence the anti-war sentiment in the US. They provided 'evidence' that they said documented American servicemen atrocities in the south, as well as giving many photos of women and children killed in airstrikes in the North as well as against southern villages. Some American antiwar activists returned to the States armed with these and provided some of the visuals and testimonies to the American Press and Congress. Some of this, in turn, made it into the Congressional record by American veterans against the war - an organization funded by Jane Fonda.

Finally, the North's Politburo used the antiwar movement and dissent in the US to shore up its domestic front. As an example, the story of the American Quaker Norman Morrison's self-immolation on the grounds of the Pentagon was turned into a song that the North Vietnamese leaders required children to sing in their schools and at other public gatherings. Moreover, the DRV government turned his image into a stamp. Meanwhile, Northern communist newspapers regularly carried stories of Congressional hearings on the war as well as the numerous demonstrations in the US against the war.

In sum, Le Duan and his Politburo cohorts consistently tracked US domestic opposition to the war. They consistently took that opposition into account in their combined political and military activities and actions, domestically and internationally. They also took an active part to influence American antiwar activist leaders by inviting them to the North to view the damage, and through the use of international conferences on war atrocities. At home, the Vietnamese Workers Party applied its propaganda using it to shore up the population, while internationally the Northern Communists used it to attack the legitimacy and legality of US actions.

Defending the Cambodia Sanctuaries

In his first year, as mentioned in Chapter 5, Nixon thought that he had some respite from the domestic unrest and antiwar sentiment that marked LBJ's last year of his Presidency. In fact, the domestic reactions to the Vietnam War experienced some relief in 1969 from the frenzied unrest of the prior year. Americans, it appears, were willing to give Nixon a chance on his peace with honor pledge and Vietnamization policies.

To recall from Chapter 5, soon after the Nixon – Kissinger team came into office, the new Administration continued to pursue a military solution to Vietnam. In 1970 Nixon decided to bomb and then conduct a ground offensive against the North Vietnamese sanctuaries in Cambodia. The reason was to gain time for his Vietnamization effort. However, as we have seen, Nixon also believed that if he could effectively attack North Vietnam and its sanctuaries, he could convince Hanoi to give up support for the war in the South and reach a compromise solution at the Paris talks.

Le Duan would not oblige Nixon. Despite adverse reports from the battlefield and pessimism from some comrades in the Politburo, he was still intent on achieving a military solution. In fact, in Nixon's personal message to Ho in 1969 proclaiming his desire for peace but warning of further US military action, it was Le Duan who wrote the response telling Nixon that the North would never yield to US demands.

Moreover, when Le Duan got word of the activities in Cambodia removing its leader who had allowed the North to build and use bases there, and the later US bombings and ground attacks there, he decided to outwardly support the Communist Khmer Rouge and conduct military operations to secure their bases of supply in Cambodia.

The Cambodia sanctuaries were a critical part of the war for the North. By 1970, the North Vietnamese support system for the campaign in the South had become extensive and intricate and extended far into Cambodia along the South Vietnamese border. The Ho Chi Minh Trail now consisted of an elaborate mix of trails, roads (some now paved), base areas, depots, and defenses. At its height, it would consist of 12,500 miles of trails and roads and 3,000 miles of pipeline in an overall complex of six main north-south routes and twenty-one east-west crossways running from North Vietnam to Cambodia.

As the PAVN history describes, approximately 50,000 engineer troops and another 12,000 other security troops now maintained and secured it. Approximately two million PAVN troops moved over the trail in its lifetime. At its peak, the system could transport twenty thousand tons of supplies per month. In the annals of military history, it was a monumental undertaking. As the PAVN history attests, the North could not have won the war without this supply and reinforcement complex.

The North Vietnamese called the part of the extended supply line that went through Cambodia the Sihanouk Trail. It not only ran from the southern part of Laos down toward Saigon but reached from the port of Sihanoukville in the southwestern portion of Cambodia to the inner eastern border with South Vietnam.

Much of the ship-borne supplies that moved along the NVA sea lines of supply from Haiphong to the Delta and Saigon regions ran through that port. Along the Cambodian – South Vietnamese border the NVA forces continued to have many base areas it used to attack ARVN and American troops in the Delta and around the Tay Ninh – An Loc – Saigon area. The COSVN headquarters was also located in the border region. That command center was mostly mobile, never large, and often displaced to avoid detection.

So extensive and useful was this complex that the system, by 1970, equipped and supplied most of the NVA and VC main force units in the southern regions of South Vietnam. The extended trail had been crucial to the simultaneous attacks during TET in the ARVN III and IV Corps regions.

After the TET offensives, the communist forces in the South had spent much of its supplies and equipment. PLAF forces within South Vietnam had a difficult time even feeding themselves. Ammunition sustainment was so critical that most engagements had to be curtailed due to ammo shortages. By 1970 the communists were replenishing their forces in the South mostly using the Sihanouk Trail.

As briefly related, political events during late 1969 and early 1970 in Cambodia now threatened North Vietnamese use of the Cambodian resupply lines and their base areas. As detailed in Chapter 5, the Cambodian Prime Minister, Lon Nol, and some in the cabinet had decided to challenge the reigning Monarch, Prince Sihanouk. While the latter was away visiting France, Lon Nol sought to reverse Sihanouk's arrangements with the North by renouncing the presence of North Vietnamese forces and demanding their removal from Cambodia. Clashes between Cambodian and North Vietnamese troops and the burning of the DRV Embassy in the capital, Phnom Penh, followed. Soon afterward, Lon Nol seized power.

Following the Coup, the Nixon administration tried to arm and support Lon Nol. A civil war broke out between the Lon Nol faction and the Khmer Rouge Communists who were supporting the North

Vietnamese. Consequently, the North Vietnamese Politburo decided to outwardly use its forces in Cambodia to aid the Khmer Rouge and secure their lines of communication.

NVA forces, in cooperation with the Khmer Communists, were initially successful against a weak Cambodian national army. Operations increasingly drove westward; to protect the lines of supply to the NVA bases. These attacks threatened the capital, Phnom Penh, and the Lon Nol Government. Partly in response to this threat, Nixon ordered US forces to invade Cambodia along with the ARVN.

Despite the tight operational security of the American command, communist spies and informants alerted NVA forces to the invasion a few days before it occurred. Most of the force, to include the PLAF and COSVN headquarters, moved deeper into Cambodia to avoid battle and capture.

Though the US and ARVN forces did capture some supplies and material, the COSVN had moved much of their support and sustainment deeper into Cambodia. These moves, along with the restrictions that Nixon placed on the depth of the offensive, averted a disaster to the North Vietnamese stocks and forces in Cambodia.

After the American and later ARVN forces withdrew, the North continued its support to the Communist Khmer Rouge under a ruthless leader called Pol Pot. Much of Cambodia would continue to fall to the communists; later resulting in the infamous 'killing fields of Cambodia.' Ironically, the Cambodian Communists would later turn on their NVA allies. After the Vietnam War, a unified Communist Vietnam under Le Duan would fight a war against Cambodia and occupy it for some time.

Protecting the Laotian Life Line

With the Cambodian lifeline and its bases disrupted, the PAVN high command now depended on its Laotian lines of communication, well extended into South Vietnam, to take up the slack. Aware that these supply lines were critical to the war effort, its defenses were increased following the US/ARVN attacks into Cambodia.

In January 1971 Hanoi received warnings of a South Vietnamese attack directed toward Tchepone in Laos. Some sources indicate that NVA spies in ARVN headquarters units may have given forewarning. For sure, later US News reports of American movements toward the border to support the attack confirmed their earlier intelligence. Unlike the Cambodian invasion, however, the NVA would stand and fight.

Just before the offensive began, the North Vietnamese Politburo sent the PAVN chief of the general staff, General Van Tien Dung, to the vicinity of Tchepone to address the commanders of the troops concentrated there. On 31 January, he said to them: "The coming engagement will be a strategically decisive battle. We will fight not only to retain control of the strategic transportation corridor, but also to annihilate a number of units of the enemy's strategic reserve forces to... deal a significant defeat to a portion of their 'Vietnamization' plot, to advance our resistance effort to liberate South Vietnam and defend North Vietnam, to gloriously fulfill our international duty, and to hone our main force troops in the fires of combat. Our Army must certainly win this battle."

As described in Chapter 5, on 8 February 1971 a three-division ARVN force of some 17,000 troops crossed the border and attacked west along an east-west road called Route 9. As the North

Vietnamese had been told, their principal aim was an NVA base area near the Laotian town of Tchepone.

The 23,000 PAVN forces in Laos charged with the defense of the Ho Chi Minh Trail were prepared. Moreover, PAVN units in North Vietnam near Laos, which had begun to modernize into a combined arms force with tanks, artillery, and air defense weapons, were ready to reinforce and counterattack. These capabilities would be more than a match for the best that the ARVN employed in Lam Son 719 in a real test of Vietnamization.

Adding to the North's advantage was the fact that the US Congress had prohibited American commanders from committing its ground forces and advisors with the South Vietnamese in their offensive. The North Vietnamese leadership knew of this restriction and was waiting to take advantage of it.

Le Duan and the Politburo were aware of the criticality of the defense of the lines of communication that ran through Laos toward South Vietnam. For Le Duan, his future designs for another general offensive were utterly dependent upon the road network, logistical depots, supply stocks, and prepared assembly areas there.

Hence, the First Secretary ordered the commander of the PAVN modernized Corps, previously designated as the principal counterattack force for the ARVN invaders, to annihilate them. Such a victory to Le Duan would also boost his "fight and talk" strategy at the Paris Talks. It would further preserve the support of his Soviet and Chinese benefactors. At home, it would provide good news to a home front dismayed and troubled by years of bombing. In short, much was riding on an NVA victory.

According to James Willbanks' account of the operation in *A Raid Too Far*, "By the end of the campaign, the North Vietnamese were to throw elements of five main-force divisions, two separate regiments, eight artillery regiments, three engineer regiments, three tank battalions, six anti-aircraft regiments, and eight sapper battalions plus associated logistical and transportation units into the battle." This 60,000-soldier force had outnumbered the ARVN by more than three to one. The result was the significant bloodletting and the retreat of the ARVN forces in what the Western Press reported and showed on TV as a frantic rout.

While both sides claimed victory, Willbanks' overall assessment seems balanced: "The truth was that three of the finest South Vietnamese divisions—the 1st Infantry, Airborne, and Marine Divisions—had been bested by the North Vietnamese and were heavily battered in the bitter fighting in Laos." Moreover, the campaign had demonstrated that "the South Vietnamese had grown far too dependent on US advisers and American support. Many of the things that the ARVN commanders had routinely relied upon their US advisers to accomplish were not done or were done poorly."

Most significantly, "the leadership in Hanoi came to the conclusion that the outcome of the campaign in Laos "signaled a new step forward in the development of Vietnam's campaign arts." That meant that the army had "moved into a new era" in which it was now capable of conducting large-scale, conventional, combined arms operations. Thus, "In the eyes of Lao Dong Party First Secretary Le Duan and his supporters among the senior political and military leadership in Hanoi, the performance of the ARVN during Lam Son 719 was proof that the South Vietnamese were incapable of standing up to the NVA, even with US air support."

In sum, Le Duan and many in the Politburo were emboldened that they had defeated the Vietnamization program and could proceed soon with another general offensive to finally win the war. According to William Turley, soon after the campaign, "the Political Bureau resolved to make 1972 the year of decisive victory."

The Nguyen Hue (or Easter) Offensive: The Beginning of the End

The American domestic reactions to both the Cambodian and Laotian war incursions gave further encouragement to Northern leaders. They were very much aware of the US Congress' trend toward more active involvement in restricting Presidential war-making abilities. They concluded that Nixon's hands would be tied, and he would not be able to use significant US combat forces to affect an eventual North Vietnamese military victory. Besides, there were few US ground combat forces available in South Vietnam to save the ARVN.

Moreover, as Lien-Hang Nguyen argues in her history, the Northern Politburo was now very much aware of Nixon's diplomacy toward both the Soviets and Chinese. She writes, "Events on the world stage hastened Hanoi's ambitious military planning in 1972. Nixon's superpower diplomacy now threatened relations with Beijing and Moscow, whose assistance was vital to continuing the war."

Thus, Le Duan and Le Duc Tho argued that the time was right to end the war. That could now be accomplished by rolling back the South Vietnamese pacification gains, reasserting control over the rural areas and some large cities and defeating the ARVN. These military gains, these two powerful Politburo members argued, would force the US to come to terms favorable to the North at the Paris talks.

Plans progressed quickly toward a 1972 Spring Offensive. The PAVN High Command would call that operation the 'Nguyen Hue' offensive – named after the Vietnamese emperor who had defeated the Chinese in 1789. Unlike TET, these plans focused on conventional force operations. The offensive would rely primarily on PAVN units attacking across several fronts. These forces now had significant numbers of tanks, motor vehicles and heavy artillery, which the Soviet Union primarily provided.

While the PAVN had trained hard on this new equipment and was confident in its capabilities, it also made the offensive heavily dependent on a logistical tail, which, in turn, was dependent on road movement and susceptible to air attack. Moreover, PAVN high-level commanders had never maneuvered such a large conventional force before over large areas. These differences would all have an impact on the offensive.

The plan, which a reinstated and reluctant General Giap oversaw, called for four major attacks. In the Northern part of South Vietnam, six PAVN divisions would attack across the DMZ and from Laos toward the northern cities of Quang Tri and Hue. The goal here was to seize significant territory that North Vietnamese Communists could bargain with at any subsequent peace conference should any of the other attacks fail. In the central part, one PAVN and one PLAF division (the latter mostly made up of North Vietnamese soldiers) would attack toward Kontum to draw ARVN forces away from the coast. Then one PLAF division would attack the lowland cities.

In the South, three PLAF divisions –also mainly made up of PAVN soldiers – would attack toward An Loc. From there several NVA units would reinforce them and then continued toward Saigon. Out of southern Cambodia, two divisions would attack into the Mekong Delta area of the ARVN IV

Corps. These PAVN divisions would then turn toward Saigon to support the final assault against the South's capital.

The offensive began with the assault across the DMZ on 30 March 1972. Initially, all four attacks were successful. The northern thrust quickly took Quang Tri on 1 May. In the process, NVA forces destroyed an entire ARVN division and routed three others. In the Central Region, they quickly surrounded ARVN bases in the Dak To area and forced the ARVN from a critical position defending Kontum. The attack toward An Loc in the south resulted in the overrunning of its airfield and the seizure of the northern outskirts of the city by 1 May.

Le Duan, the rest of the Politburo, and the PAVN leadership, however, miscalculated the American response. Ignoring domestic opinion and Congressional opposition, Nixon's massive use of US airpower soon had a devastating effect. Strikes against NVA armored columns moving along roads and their supporting logistics sites and organizations halted their attacks. PAVN commanders lost control of their forces. Attempts to renew assaults were uncoordinated and piecemeal. Meanwhile, ARVN forces, still helped by their American advisors, counterattacked successfully. PAVN and PLAF unit losses were heavy.

Meanwhile, as described in Chapter 5, Nixon unleashed an all-out B52 bombing offensive against logistics facilities and transportation routes in the DRV that were supporting the attacks in the northern part of South Vietnam. This bombing operation, named LINEBACKER, dropped over a hundred thousand tons of bombs in one month alone. Le Duan and the Politburo had their first taste of what a strategic bombing operation could be like when unleashed with few restrictions.

By June, both sides had ceased major operations. Both had suffered huge losses. The North Vietnamese lost over 100,000 personnel. PAVN units had lost most of their tanks and heavy artillery. While they had expanded their control of land areas in the South, they could no longer sustain significant operations. The South's casualties exceeded 105,000. The ARVN was exhausted. It had almost broken apart. However, a few brave and competent leaders and soldiers held on at critical times. Of course, American support had made the difference.

With the failure of the Nguyen Hue Offensive, General Giap lost his PAVN command. He took the blame for its failure; although he had warned that it might not succeed. His health had a role as well. After relinquishing command, he would not be heard from for several months until North Vietnam withstood the worst of another brutal B52 assault in December 1972.

The Paris Peace Agreement, Ho Chi Minh Offensive, and Final Victory

While the ability to have launched this Spring Offensive was much due to the DRV Soviet and Chinese allies' material support, those same allies were now pressuring Le Duan to reach a negotiated peace. In the summer of 1972, as Lien Hang T. Nguyen explains, "Beijing and Moscow, urged on by Nixon, pulled out all the stops to pressure Hanoi to accept American terms... With the failure of his 1972 Spring–Summer Offensive to achieve a decisive victory, the first secretary, who long abhorred relying on diplomacy during the war, focused the Party's resources on the talking portion of his policy [because] fighting had failed to achieve the Party's goals."

As outlined previously, the talks, both official and secret, had been going on for almost four years now. Most of these had been meaningless or deadlocked in coming to any peace agreement. Recently, Kissinger had agreed to decouple any agreement from the American demand for a mutual withdrawal of forces from South Vietnam. Now the US conceded, unknown to this point to the RVN leaders, that North Vietnam forces could stay in the South before any permanent political solution to the war.

This change was a fatal concession for the South and a decided advantage for the North. After the Spring Offensive, there were over 140,000 PAVN soldiers still in the South in control of large areas that were still being contended. They would play a decisive role in the victory campaign ahead.

In early July 1972, the Politburo recalled Le Duc Tho to Hanoi to discuss how to go ahead with a new diplomatic initiative given the failure of the 1972 Offensive, and the Soviet-Chinese pressures for a negotiated peace. Le Duan and the Politburo instructed him on several modifications to their principles for the negotiations. There were two that would be essential to getting a settlement from Nixon and Kissinger.

The first was that they would now agree to releasing US prisoners of war without linking that release to other conditions. The second was that they would also agree to allow the current Government of South Vietnam under Thieu's Presidency be a part of the reconciliation administration. Armed with these and several other concessions, Le Duc Tho returned to Paris for yet another round of secret meetings with Kissinger.

On 1 August, the DRV diplomat offered these new proposals to Kissinger. The US National Security Advisor realized the importance of these changes, and the two continued to work on other contentious issues. In later meetings, they hammered out the wording of a new agreement to end the fighting. As detailed in Chapter 5, by the end of the month, Kissinger, under Nixon's direction, went to Saigon to finally coordinate with Thieu and his government on what was discussed in these secret negotiations. Kissinger and Le Duc Tho agreed to meet again in mid-September.

When Kissinger returned to the negotiations, he presented the South Vietnamese changes that Thieu had demanded and Nixon had agreed to. Le Duc Tho rejected them out of hand. Further negotiations fell apart. While both the North and the US tried to revitalize negotiations in November and December, these also did not break the deadlock over changes that the South wanted to be implemented. Frustrated, Nixon launched LINEBACKER II.

For two weeks American aircraft, primarily B52s, dropped over thirty-six thousand tons of bombs on North Vietnamese transportation facilities and routes, factories and warehouses, and ports. Though the DRV had mostly evacuated large population centers, these took hits as well; to include Hanoi's largest hospital. The US bombing of these targets caused over two thousand deaths and brought international condemnation.

The bombings caused significant even catastrophic damage. Supply routes out of China, as well as those going to the South, were reduced to a fifth of what they were before the bombings began. With the North's complement of the surface to air missiles nearly depleted into the second week, air strikes could be made without fear of losses. Le Duan and the Politburo, under pressure by the Chinese and the intensity of the bombing, let Washington know that they were ready to come back to the negotiating table after the start of the New Year.

All parties finally signed an agreement at the end of January. Summing up what this treaty represented for the Vietnamese Lien-Hang T. Nguyen states, "After more than four years of acrimonious negotiations and bitter fighting, the Paris agreement and cease-fire signed in late

January 1973 managed to end the American phase of the war but gave little respite to the Vietnamese."

The cease-fire went into effect the day the Parties signed the treaty – 27 January 1973. At once, the North, as well as the South, violated the treaty's provisions. Thieu had no intention of honoring it. Before the treaty had been signed he had ordered his troops to seize as much territory as they could. He later also refused to negotiate any national reconciliation seriously. Thus, only weeks after signing the treaty, any semblance of negotiation broke down. Recognizing that the agreement that he had worked so hard at finally getting signed was a fraud, Le Duc Tho refused to accept the Nobel Prize that Henry Kissinger had embraced.

As Lien-Hang T. Nguyen explains, "A new stage of fighting—the war of the flags—ensued as Hanoi and Saigon scrambled to stake out territory and ground while the Americans, Chinese, and Soviets watched. Although Le Duan may not have definitively won the war for peace, he managed to prevent Nixon and Thieu from gaining victory with a negotiated settlement that could have resulted in the permanent division of Vietnam. True victory, however, would have to wait."

According to Lien-Hang T. Nguyen's analysis of North Vietnamese documents and interviews, at first Le Duan and the Politburo had sought to honor the agreement. They hoped that it would give the necessary cease-fire that would allow a recovery from the military and economic devastation that both the 1972 Offensive and the American bombing had caused.

However, reminiscent of what had occurred after the Geneva Convention of the fifties, Southern Communist commanders would not abide by the official Northern policy. According to General Van Tra, Southern leaders once again felt sold out. In reaction to the ARVN successes, COSVN military commanders ordered their forces to take as much territory as they could.

Late in 1973, the Politburo recognized that the treaty was not going to give them the respite they wanted. They fervently continued to rebuild their military, once again revitalize and expand the Ho Chi Minh trail system, and reinvigorate its infiltration of PAVN forces to the South. During 1974, the North moved somewhere between 100,000 to 120,000 troops to South Vietnam and adjacent base areas. By the end of that year, the total PLAF and PAVN forces there were about 230,000.

The ARVN during the same period grew to a total of about one million men under arms. However, the numbers were deceiving. American aid was dwindling drastically. In 1974 alone Congress cut aid by half. The US withdrawal had also caused severe economic problems in the South. With few Americans present and fewer American facilities to keep running, unemployment skyrocketed. With the economic downturn, corruption - especially amongst the military brass - was growing.

The mobilization strain on South Vietnam families to support their livelihood on the land was dramatic. As Mark Bradley notes, "With most ARVN recruits drawn from peasant families, the rapid build-up of the army and length of required service posed severe problems for household agricultural production. As one Mekong Delta farmer recalled, 'We lived through French imperialism, the war against the fascists, a liberation war with the French, and never had we known such problems. In the days before the ARVN draft, if families needed labor they could always hire from local families with more sons. The draft took all our sons and made farming almost impossible."

Because of the hardship to their families, ARVN soldiers by 1975 were deserting dramatically. The personnel figures on paper no way matched what was present for duty. Morale was also dropping; almost as fast as the Army's stocks of ammunition and fuel. Moreover, the success of President Thieu's policy of regaining control of the countryside had spread the ARVN thin.

It appeared to the Communist Politburo and PAVN High Command that the beginning of 1975 was about right for another major attack. Unlike the 1972 offensive, however, they decided to be cautious. Instead of a simultaneous all-out assault from the beginning, they planned for an initial attack into the Central Highlands to test ARVN defenses and to discover what the American reaction would be.

They chose that area because the ARVN was spread thin there. An attack there also had an excellent chance to gain the north-south and coastal road network between Pleiku to Dalat and Danang to Cam Ranh Bay. Seizure of this area and communication network would place the North's forces in an excellent position for a final general offensive the next year.

In March, the PAVN command, headed by Giap's successor, General Dung, launched the limited offensive in the Central Highlands. Its first objective now aimed at Ban Me Thuot (pronounced 'ban me to it') because it was the least defended of the major cities in the Highlands. By 9 March the NVA had encircled the city. 48 hours later PAVN forces seized it.

Over the next couple of days, the PAVN command was surprised at the ease in which their forces defeated the ARVN. They then quickly routed an ARVN counteroffensive to relieve Ban Me Thuot. For various reasons, the ARVN troops in the Central Region conducted a disorderly withdrawal southward.

This success further surprised the PAVN High Command. They quickly recovered. Given that there was no military response from the US, Le Duan ordered an offensive by forces in the ARVN I Corps area as well as those in the central region forces. Soon these forces were also successful. A PAVN army soon took Quang Tri City, which they had briefly held in the 1972 offensive but had lost. Next, they took Hue, the citadel which they had briefly held in 1968. Danang to the south fell next.

Overall the ARVN forces were disintegrating; many fled by sea to get south. Most just faded into the growing refugees who were fleeing the cities. The communists eventually claimed that the population had finally conducted a general uprising in support of their attacks. The truth was more that the South Vietnamese were fleeing to get away from the fighting. If they contributed anything to the communist cause, it was that the disorder and pandemonium disrupted any attempt of the ARVN to resist. The retreat continued south.

On 1 April – ten years after LBJ's April Fool's Day meeting in which he had ordered US Marines on the offensive in the South - the Politburo met to discuss the reaction of the US government. Seeing that the Americans were not willing to intervene, it ordered a general offensive. Le Duan sent his trusted friend and colleague Le Duc Tho south to COSVN headquarters. He was to relay orders for the general offensive as he did in 1968 and to conduct last-minute discussions for the final push – now dubbed the Ho Chi Minh Campaign. As he did so at the headquarters, PAVN forces had already reached the suburbs of Saigon.

On 26 April, some fifteen PAVN divisions began their final assaults on Saigon. Two days later, ARVN General Duong Van Minh, the same who had ordered and taken over after the Diem assassination, assumed the head of the RVN government. He indicated that he was ready to surrender and negotiate an end to the fighting. Ignoring this appeal, on 29 April PAVN forces continued their attack on the center of Saigon.

On 30 April, the war ended when a Soviet-made T-54 tank, manned by PAVN regulars, broke through the gates of the Republic of Vietnam's Independence Palace – the seat of its national government. Vietnam was finally reunited.

Right to the end, the North continued its ruse that the PLAF and VC had won its insurgent war. The forces that took the Palace flew the VC, not the PAVN flag. Its soldiers dressed in PLAF, rather than PAVN uniforms. In fact, the NLF political organization, while still consisting of some loyal, dedicated Southerners like Troung Nhu Tong, was no longer the master of its fate. Le Duan and Le Duc Tho would rule a united Vietnam as a totalitarian communist state.

Section 7.3 - Personal Experiences, Observations, and Insights for Chapter 7

This section first offers some personal experiences in conducting research of the Vietnam War, especially the early gathering and use of materials on the North Vietnam leaders' actions. It then gives some general observations and insights on the author's view of North Vietnam's strategy and execution of the war, and how the Americans reacted to it.

Personal Experiences

In the 'twilight years' of my service in the Army, I ended up at the National War College at Fort McNair in Washington, DC. As mentioned in Chapter 2, there I taught courses in military strategy and operations to officers from all the US Armed Services and civilians from Government Agencies. These were senior officers and career civil servants, some of whom their organizations thought would eventually occupy the top positions in the military and government.

I saw this as an opportunity to engage these students in my thoughts and experiences of almost thirty years of service. It turned out to be that and more. I gained insights from the teaching process on what they thought and experienced as well. I also saw this as a great occasion to continue my quest to find out why we had lost the Vietnam War. I had the time.

I also had the opportunity to discover new materials about the war that I had not yet noticed or had not yet been available. Lastly, I could share revelations and questions about the war with a captive audience of experienced military and civilian leaders who might be able to assist me in understanding what happened.

I found that the best way to do this was to develop a course entitled "A History of the Vietnam War." The College Administration supported the development and teaching of this course mainly because, at the time, the Vietnam War had not been taught formally at any of the Senior Service Colleges. They thought it was about time it was.

In the development of the materials and the lesson plans for this course, I discovered, even then, that a few scholars were pursuing research on who the North Vietnamese leaders were, how they engaged the US in this war, and what they did to defeat them. Up to that point, most of the unfolding history of the war had focused on the American side. Indeed, much of it still does.

In so doing I discovered a seminal work from the North Vietnamese Communist view by William Duiker – then a relatively unknown scholar who had been a State Department, foreign service officer in South Vietnam. The book was *The Communist Road to Power in Vietnam*. After reading it, I decided to make it one of the centerpiece materials for the course. Based on mostly then publicized North Vietnam documents and captured materials, Duiker masterfully wove these into a fascinating history of the war from the North's perspective.

That work provided the basis of my attempt to capture and use information on who the enemy was and what strategy he pursued against America in Vietnam. It became one of the most important sources for the course. It was the central source in sparking discussions on and criticisms of the US decision-making during the war and understanding the war's outcome.

In sum, Duiker's work gave us insights on 'knowing the enemy' so we could figure out what had happened, and how the war was a result of the fact that 'the enemy has a vote' and that vote contributed significantly to the US defeat.

In this Chapter, like the last, I have used several works like Duiker's groundbreaking book to obtain a view of 'the enemy.' I feel they have served the same role that the *Communist Road to Power in Vietnam* did in my war college course in this story – providing pivotal sources for understanding why we lost in Vietnam.

Observations and Insights

What can we discern from the story in this chapter and the previous one about who the main North Vietnamese leaders were; what they tried to accomplish and how; why they made the decisions they did; and how did those decisions affect the war's outcome?

Moreover, contrasting what we know about how US decision makers waged their war in Vietnam, with what we now know about the DRV leaders, what can we discover about what senior American decision makers knew about their enemy? For example, how much did they understand them and their actions? Alternatively, how much did they misunderstand or ignore them?

The most glaring and profound observation is that the person responsible for the North's conduct of the war against the US is not whom our leaders thought it was. We now know, due to the release of and research on select sources from Vietnam's archives and interviews with Vietnamese who took part in the war on the northern side, that it was not Ho Chi Minh making the decisions in Hanoi on the American war, but Le Duan.

We now know that Vo Nguyen Giap was not the mastermind strategist against the US. Le Duan was. Moreover, Le Duc Tho, a faithful and loyal comrade whom the Party leader trusted, most competently supported him. Generals Nguyen Chi Thanh and Van Tien Dung, whom the communist leader appointed to key positions because they were of a like-mind, executed his strategic ideas.

If one examines the personal memoirs and tape transcripts of the central American leaders they hardly mention Le Duan or his principal assistants. LBJ cites Ho Chi Minh twenty-seven times in his memoirs. There is no mention of Le Duan. There is no mention of him in any of the publicized transcripts of his Presidential Tapes as well.

McNamara cites Ho six times, Giap once, and never mentions Le Duan in his *In Retrospect*. Westmoreland does not cite him at all. He does mention Giap seven times, and Thanh twice; but portrays most of the actions, particularly Khe Sanh, as Giap driven. Nixon does not reference the North Vietnam leader in his memoirs but does mention Ho seventeen times (he frequently mentions Le Duc Tho, but only because of his notoriety as the Chief DRV negotiator at the Paris talks). Nixon does refer to Le Duan in his later work, *No More Vietnams*, but only as "Ho's right-hand man" during the war.

Furthermore, the Nixon tape transcripts that I have had access to mention Le Duan several times, but only as the General Secretary – not as a significant decision maker of the war. Kissinger mentions Le Duc Tho many times, because of his relationship with him in the peace talks, but there is no mention of Le Duan. The National Security Advisor names Giap several times as an important determiner of the North's strategy. In sum, as Lien-Hang T. Nguyen states, Le Duan was an unknown figure during the war for the Americans, even 'an obscure figure' who resided 'on the historical margins' of the Vietnam War – until now.

Interestingly, this does not mean that US experts on Southeast Asian Affairs or the North's military efforts did not know of Le Duan or some of his military subordinates. American State and intelligence experts discussed him and some of his principals more regularly as the war continued. On several occasions, these 'bureaucrats' indicated that Le Duan was the man in charge, and 'calling the shots.'

One can also find mention of him in *The Pentagon Papers'* analyses, and in State, CIA and other Defense Department Papers discovered in the archives or other published sources. However, once again, the US main policymakers who considered themselves the 'best and the brightest' ignored the 'experts,' whom they viewed as entrenched bureaucrats unable to think innovatively. In short, those in the US government, civilian and military alike, who were most responsible for the war simply did not know their enemy.

The theme of this and the last chapter is that it is of vital importance, as Sun Tzu says, to "know your enemy as yourself" to understand one's enemy's military strategies and plans for waging war. As for the Vietnam War, Lien-Hang Nguyen notes, "the key to unlocking these puzzles [what, why and how did North Vietnam prevail] lies with one individual who has managed to escape scrutiny: Le Duan" ... - the architect, main strategist, and commander-in-chief of the communist Vietnam's war effort...."

What do the 'unlocked' puzzles in the two previous chapters reveal? Foremost is that Le Duan wanted complete control of the Communist Vietnamese Workers Party, its policies, and its conduct of operations in the South. Lacking the personal appeal and statesmanship of Ho, and the military knowledge of Giap, Le Duan had an iron will to pursue the conduct of the war as he thought it should be conducted. He chose his political and military supporters and appointed them to key positions to keep this iron hand.

Furthermore, Le Duan had a determined view on what meant success in his conduct of the war – offensive operations to bring about the defeat of the ARVN on the battlefield, the collapse of the RVN, and withdrawal of support from America. He did not believe that the North could defeat the US military directly. However, he did think that he could confront American forces, and inflict enough casualties to cause the American public to lose support for the war.

While military victory was his prime goal, in not achieving this object at first, Le Duan then turned to diplomacy. However, significantly, the North Vietnam war leader did not believe that diplomacy alone could achieve his aims until he had success on the battlefield. Conversely, Le Duan used negotiations to gain an advantage in the war. In the Paris Treaty, he achieved that end. Thus, the North Vietnam war leader was determined to use military force and diplomacy as complementary actions to achieve his ultimate aim – the unconditional unification of Vietnam on his terms.

What does 'know your enemy' and 'the enemy has a vote' reveal about how America approached the war? First, it shows the futility and foolhardiness of the pursuit of a strategy that sought to convince the North through military signals, or gradual escalation, or a combination of those with economic incentives that it should withdraw its support of the insurgency in the South. Le Duan, and his supporters, would have none of that.

Furthermore, the US strategic policy of gradualism and its waging of a limited war, in fact, encouraged the North for a quicker military resolution of the goal of unification through military means before any greater US military ground involvement was possible. Ironically, US signals through a combination of limited bombing with announced bombing halts benefited the North's pursuit of its aims, rather than convincing them to give them up voluntarily.

A second revelation is that those who claim that the US lost the Vietnam War because it chose to depend on the so-called big unit war, and in so doing ignored the pacification effort and neglected the guerrilla nature of the conflict, should reexamine the evidence. The North determined the nature of the conflict in the South – all the evidence supports that – and it did not see its guerrilla forces as the principal means to achieve their aims.

The most recent North Vietnamese evidence shows that guerrilla actions, as Le Duan and his select commanders on the ground such as Nguyen Chi Thanh saw it, was a secondary supporting effort to the Main Force general offensive. Indeed, as early as 1965 when US ground forces were deploying, Le Duan and the PAVN high command wanted to confront them with their regular PAVN forces to show that they could deal with the American military effort in a limited war, defeat the ARVN forces, and topple the Republic of Vietnam. In so doing, they would produce a situation in Vietnam in which the US would have to give up its efforts in South Vietnam and perhaps all of Indochina.

In this light, as we will see in the chapters ahead, Westmoreland's so-called large unit war was necessary to thwart the North's main force effort. To focus mostly or solely on guerrilla warfare and pacification would have diverted resources needed to confront the North's regular and main PLAF units from 1965 through 1967 at the peril of protecting the population. In fact, the North skillfully used the ruse of conducting a guerrilla war to divert attention from its concept of relying on its PAVN to achieve success. Chapters 8, 9 and 10 ahead will further discuss this, and its effect on US military operations.

On the other hand, those who argue that the US should have focused solely on defeating the PAVN regulars and the North's support base neglect the importance of the local and guerrilla forces to the overall North Vietnam war effort up to the conventional invasions of 1972 and 1975. These forces provided an invaluable, what the US military calls, 'force multiplier.'

From their experiences in the French War, the PAVN high command knew that they could gain the advantage over the Americans and the ARVN using intelligence, sabotage, assassination, political propaganda, and small unit actions that the local guerrilla force organizations and their political cells provided. It gave them a distinct advantage on knowing the terrain and the local situation. These forces were an integral part of the North Vietnamese 'way of war.'

That 'way' differed, moreover, from Mao's People's War doctrine. The PAVN and PLAF leaders did not follow a scheme of military operations that gradually progressed from a phase that focused on small unit operations to a final phase in which the Main forces would conduct operations that would overwhelm their enemy. Rather, forces at every level were dependent upon one another at different times based on the overall balance of forces and the situation on the ground. We will see in the chapters ahead how US military commanders, for the most part, did not understand this complementary nature of the North's use of its forces.

Thus, to have focused on only one aspect of the North's scheme of operations in the South, as necessary as it was to protect the people and gain their support, would put at risk the very thing that you wanted to preserve – the support of the people. The real strategic issue for the American military and their civilian leaders was how to defeat the main forces so that they would not be able to support the communist effort at subjugating or winning over the South Vietnamese populace.

In addition, there was also the need to counter local communist efforts to gain the support of the people through political propaganda and coercion. Westmoreland and Abrams recognized this and attempted to address it. But, Westmoreland never had enough forces to do so, and take on the enemy main units. Abrams, though more successful, never had the time to improve the ARVN to enable it to stave off the North's main forces as the US withdrew its. As we will see in the next three chapters, this is the dilemma that had to be confronted. The question is: was there a way to do that, and if so, why was it not pursued as an alternative to the chosen course? The chapters ahead will try to answer this inquiry.

What the chapters ahead will also demonstrate is that Westmoreland and his superiors had no idea of what value the North could put on its blood and treasure when it came to the cause of unification of Vietnam and the survival of its regime. Besides, the NVA and PLAF had the advantage of its sanctuaries in Cambodia and Laos to which they could withdraw to obtain reinforcements and recover for subsequent operations. Moreover, the US never seriously threatened these, as well as the critical lifeline of the Ho Chi Minh trail, during the war.

The US never seriously threatened these key components of the North's military strategy primarily because, as explained in Chapter 2, LBJ sought to limit the war. The President wanted to avoid Chinese intervention, as they had done in the Korean War. The conditions that he and some of his chief civilian advisors assumed would incite such a Chinese move were three-fold. First, a major land invasion of the North. Second, an attack against North Vietnam forces into Laos. Third, an all-out bombing campaign against the North, especially if it threatened to harm Chinese forces or supplies moving into North Vietnam from roads out of China or through ports such as Haiphong. Later, Nixon would authorize attacks against all of these, but either place restrictions on time and duration, such as in Cambodia in 1970, or the Congress and his South Vietnam ally would place them on him, such as in Laos.

Indeed, the North's military strategy for the war, as executed, was not only masterful but one of the main reasons it won. In addition to having the tactical initiative as already described, the North's strategy gave them not only significant advantages in its operations in the South but the strategic initiative as well.

Though there is yet no single document describing the North's military strategy in these specific terms, one can deduce from what their leaders said, and how they pursued the war, that the main components for this strategy were four-fold. The first is that they established the North as the great base for their war of unification of the South. From this base, they provided the leadership, forces, supplies, and material that were critical to winning the war. Second, they built, maintained, protected, and used the Ho Chi Minh Trail and other subsidiary routes to move the above critical war essentials to prepared bases astride the South's borders. Third, they took advantage of the South's terrain and weather, as well as the US political climate, to choose the when and where to launch its operational offensives to its advantage in the South. Finally, they pursued a masterful propaganda campaign and deception operations to both protect its vital strategic assets and affect the US domestic support for the war.

This work has already described in some detail the advantages and roles that the first three components had and played. More needs to be said, however, about the last component to understand the North's overall strategy and why it was so masterful. In particular, what role and what advantages did the North's propaganda and deceptions give to the North? How did it fit into their overall strategy described above? To address this issue, we need to explain further what the North's central deceptions were, what relation they had with its propaganda campaign, and what advantages they produced.

The DRV's main ruse was that the war in the South was an insurrection of the Southern Vietnamese populace against an illegitimate, corrupt regime. The North, moreover, as the representative state of Vietnamese nationalism had the moral right to help in that revolution. Its military aid, furthermore, aimed at giving the revolutionaries the means to do so. Therefore, North Vietnam was not a foreign aggressor, but a legitimate part of the struggle to gain the Vietnamese unity that the actions of the Geneva Convention, the ruler of the Southern puppet government, and the United States had wrongly and illegitimately prevented.

The North's propaganda campaign targeted both the international arena and the American public on that message. The DRV sought not only to justify its support for the conflict in the South but cast the US as the aggressor and violator of international law. In short, the US was not fighting, in international terms, a 'just war.' North Vietnam was.

What advantages then did the North expect to gain? It appears from North Vietnamese documents, such as Resolution 9, and Politburo discussions, that the North intended its propaganda and deception operations to not only affect US popular support adversely but also to play a role in limiting the use of American power against its strategic base and its vital lines of communication.

In every instance it could, North Vietnam argued that the American bombing was not only a violation of international law but immoral as well. The North also denied a significant military presence in Laos and Cambodia and argued that their presence there was to aid other communist movements in seeking their independence, as they had successfully done from the French.

Though it is arguable how much North Vietnam's propaganda campaign and deception operations protected its home base and its use of lines of communication, there is evidence that it succeeded in hampering US bombing operations, and was a factor in US restrictions against attacking their bases in Laos and elsewhere. In fact, until 1971, there was much hesitation to attack the lines of communication in Laos and Cambodia decisively; especially with any significant ground operation. Moreover, in many instances, US civilian control and limitation of bombing in the North always considered the effects of damage on the civilians and economic targets, and its corresponding effect upon the international arena.

Here it is important to note that the above description of a masterful North Vietnamese strategy certainly does not mean that any US conduct of the war was doomed to failure. As this Chapter shows, the North made significant mistakes and miscalculations. These resulted in major setbacks; some could have been fatal to their unification war aim if the US had taken advantage of these errors.

The costliest mistake was the 1968 TET offensive. Despite the labeling of TET as a strategic success, by all Northern accounts and sources, it was nearly a cataclysmic military failure. The entire VC/Southern Communist infrastructure was almost destroyed. That seriously affected subsequent military operations in several ways.

First, the support that the PAVN and PLAF main forces had received locally after 1968 was never the same. The intelligence apparatus was never as capable. Communist local recruitment declined dramatically and to the point that they could no longer sustain local or regional forces without PAVN replacements. Political cadres, which had been so essential to the VC ability to control the rural areas, were nearly wiped out. Those that had survived had revealed themselves or had to seek refuge in areas away from the villages.

Second, prepositioned supply and material sites that stored and distributed ammunition and arms coming off the Ho Chi Minh Trail were destroyed or severely damaged. Major base areas, particularly those near the populated lowlands, were devastated. This damage and devastation dramatically curtailed military operations, particularly from 1969 to 1971. It is no wonder that most Northern sources refer to those years as their 'Darkest Time' in the war.

Another costly mistake was Le Duan's 1972 Easter Offensive. While it resulted in some regained and even additional gains of territory and hamlets, like TET it also decimated its military. In this case, it was its regular PAVN and NVA filled PLAF main forces. Fortunately for the communists, the RVN was unable to capitalize on this – the Nixon Administration was losing its support for the war. Moreover, time was running out for its Vietnamization program, which, after the Easter offensive, soon lost its direct American military support – mainly the 'glue' that kept it together – American advisors and air support.

However, US decision-makers were unwilling or unable to capitalize quickly on these mistakes. This lack of timely counteraction was mostly because senior leaders and advisors, civilian and military, never accurately analyzed the North's strategic approach as explained above. Thus, they were unable to assess the situation accurately or argue convincingly for a counteroffensive at a time that it may have decisively turned the tide against the North.

Again, American decision-makers did not focus on their enemy. Thus, they did not take advantage of the mistakes that the DRV, PAVN and PLAF made. They were not accounted for in their calculus of decision making. Instead, it was their values, attitudes, and intellect that mattered and little else. As Jeffrey Record states in his take on the failure to win in Vietnam, "The key to US defeat was a profound underestimation of enemy tenacity and fighting power - an underestimation born of a happy ignorance of Vietnamese history." As this chapter shows, it was not just an ignorance of history that was the key. It was also a failure to 'know your enemy' and to realize that your 'enemy has a vote.'

The three chapters that follow will focus on how the US military commanders sought to achieve their civilian leaders' direction and goals for the war. In that description, the reader should keep in mind that in every instance in which there was a decision or direction for the employment of US forces to counter the North's strategy and operations, American commanders failed to account fully or appropriately for their enemy.

Chapter 8: The 'Unwinnable War'

During a visit to Hanoi in 1975, an American military officer said to a member of the North Vietnamese negotiation team, "You know you never defeated us on the battlefield." Calmly, the North Vietnamese delegate replied, "That may be so, but it is also irrelevant." Indeed, it was irrelevant by the measure of the original political aims of both sides. By those objectives, in which the US pledged to defend South Vietnam from communist aggression and Communist North Vietnam sought to unify all of Vietnam, what was relevant is that the Democratic Republic of Vietnam had won the Vietnam War.

The next three chapters examine the various US military strategies and operations to defeat the North's pursuit of conquest of the South. The purpose of this examination is twofold. The first is to compare these military aspects of the overall US approach to the war to see if they were compatible with what their Commanders-in-Chief wanted to achieve. The second is to determine whether the Presidents and their advisors gave the direction and means for their commanders to achieve what they wanted.

This chapter reviews the early American military strategies designed to thwart the communist insurgency in the South and the North's support for it. It then focuses on the 'Strategy of Attrition" that General Westmoreland formulated to defeat the North's aggression. It additionally explores the operational effectiveness of that strategy from 1965 to 1967.

Many scholars blame Westmoreland's strategy for the US failure in Vietnam. They argue that his attrition approach, based on killing more enemy forces than the communists could replace and thus convincing them to give up their aggression, was faulty. It focused on the wrong military objective of destroying the communist military forces rather than protecting the population and did nothing but prolong the war. Moreover, by prolonging the war, ultimately the US public lost support for it. The Vietnam War was then, as these critics see it, an 'unwinnable war.'

Section 8.1 – US Theater Military Strategies for Vietnam, 1954 to 1963

Before examining the military strategies for the Vietnam War, we should look at what is a military strategy? How does it relate to what civilian leaders set as policy and who is responsible for its execution? In this case, of course, we will look at how the US military did it during the Vietnam War era.

The term 'strategy' is an often-used term that can mean anything from an idea to a vision to a plan to solve some problem or initiate some action. For this story, a military strategy is the combination of specific military objectives, along with the forces and a set of concepts or ways for their use, to achieve some political purpose against a threat to national interests. Senior military commanders in the Vietnam War, as the national security laws during the forties and fifties stipulated, would derive their military strategy from the President's policy on how to provide for the nation's common defense.

In Chapters 2, 3, and 5, we looked at the Vietnam policies of the Kennedy, Johnson, and Nixon Administrations. At the highest level of the US Government, per the US Constitution, the President has a responsibility as the Executive Head of State and Commander-in-Chief of the Armed Forces for US international relations and national defense. In that capacity and to fulfill his responsibilities, the President sets the policy of our nation toward others, and for the defense of threats to our nation. These policies usually include a stated purpose or aim that the US needs to achieve.

Presidents set policies in several ways. The most familiar way is to make statements, formal or informal, oral or written, on our international affairs and interests, and how the US will protect them. In modern times, US Presidents usually promulgate these statements through some form of documentation. In the case of the timeframe covered in this story, formal documentation took the form of National Security Policy Memoranda – several of which we have already scrutinized in the fore-mentioned chapters.

In the years after the Second World War through the Vietnam War, most policy statements, or memoranda, as discussed in earlier chapters, set the overall US policy as the 'Containment' of communism. Containment's implied purpose or aim was to stop the spread of communism beyond the borders of the Soviet Union, and later Communist China, and its post-war occupied territories. For instance, as we have seen, NSC Memo 68, signed by President Truman in 1950, formally instituted 'Containment' as our national security policy for the Cold War period. In general, it served as an overall official statement of the national security policy for Presidents Kennedy through Nixon.

In each Administration, moreover, there have also been several policy memoranda that were specific to that Presidency. For instance, Kennedy issued National Security Action Memoranda (NSAM) 52 and 111. The former reaffirmed Ike's commitment to prevent communist domination of South Vietnam. The latter inaugurated JFK's pursuit of counterinsurgency operations in support of the Diem regime to prevent it from becoming a communist state.

As we have seen, President Johnson further supported JFK's policies toward South Vietnam in NSAMs 273, 288 and 328. NSAM 273 continued US interests in keeping South Vietnam free from communism and authorized the use of covert operations against the North. In NSAMs 288 and 328, LBJ declared the US political aim for South Vietnam as ensuring that it would be an independent, non-communist state, and committed US combat troops to Vietnam in a limited war against the North. Relevant to the military in the Vietnam War was that these documents instituted the overall aim to defend South Vietnam from a communist takeover.

As we have also seen in Chapters 2, 3 and 5, US policymakers also instituted national security goals in other documents. Sometimes, these contradicted or confused the official NSC promulgated NSAMs. Sometimes, the President may not have officially approved these documents or their declared aims. Nonetheless, they served on occasion as an understanding between the Defense Secretary and his senior assistants of what was needed to accomplish in Washington for a national security mission overseas.

For example, as explained in Chapter 3, McNamara's Whiz Kids further defined aims for the unfolding war in Vietnam in 1965 separate from official documents. Instead of denying South Vietnam to communism, several of these stated that US aims were to avoid a humiliating defeat and to maintain US prestige. These latter objectives were much different from the ones promulgated in the NSAMs. In part, this led to a lack of clarity of what to do in South Vietnam for the military. This chapter and the next two will show how that affected military strategy and operations.

US Command Responsibilities for Military Strategies and Operations During the Vietnam War

As Chapter 1 described, the post-war National Security Defense Acts in the forties and fifties created the Joint Chiefs of Staff and its Joint Staff as the government body that took the Executive Branch's policy and developed national military strategies and plans to execute that policy. During the Vietnam War, the Chairman of the Joint Chiefs of Staff or CJCS, in the name of the Secretary of Defense and President, gave guidance for the development of military plans and strategies through a document they variously called the Joint Strategic Operational Planning Document or the Joint Strategic Capabilities Plan. We discussed one such document in Chapter 5.

Also mentioned in Chapter 1, the Acts set up the Chairman's position to coordinate national military affairs. In so doing, the CJCS represented the collective views of the other Service Chiefs, who had equal status in strategic matters with the Chairman when advising their civilian superiors. If any of the Chiefs disagreed with the others or the Chairman, that Chief had the right by law to present his dissenting views to the Secretary of Defense and the President.

The Security Acts also stipulated that the Secretary of Defense, in coordination with the Joint Chiefs, would set up a set of US Commanders to execute those strategies or plans. They would do so within an assigned geographic area of responsibility or AOR. These areas corresponded to geographic regions or areas encompassing more than one country and adjacent oceans and seas. Within these AORs, the US Commanders - usually senior four-star generals or admirals - established theaters of operations for their subordinates. Within these theaters, or specific other geographic areas within the overall commander's area of responsibility, the subordinates executed a version of the plan for their AOR.

However, again as mentioned in Chapter 1, it is important to note that the Security Acts also set up a dual chain of command. While the geographic commanders had operational command over army, navy, marine corps, and air force units performing tasks in their AORs, the Service Chiefs had administrative command of the geographic commander's subordinate Service leaders working for him. That meant that too often the Service Chiefs in Washington could influence the Service leaders in the AOR on matters like Service regulations on doctrine, organization, training and equipping of their forces. We will see ahead how this dual organization also complicated matters for the Vietnam War.

For the Vietnam War, the Commander of the Pacific Region oversaw the execution of the operations in his AOR – a vast area encompassing all the Pacific Ocean – to include the oceans, seas, and islands within - and land masses adjacent to those oceans and seas. As noted, subordinate to him were commanders responsible for land and supporting air and naval operations in South Vietnam. However, there were also subordinate commanders for naval and air operations in other countries and areas outside but next to South Vietnam.

General Westmoreland, from 1964 to 1968, oversaw overall operations in South Vietnam as Commander of the US Military Assistance Command Vietnam or MACV – a subordinate command of the Pacific Commander. However, naval operations conducted in the adjacent South China Sea that may have affected what Westmoreland was doing in South Vietnam came under another commander. The latter was directly responsible to the Commander of the Pacific, not to Westmoreland. Likewise, air operations conducted in North Vietnam, or those against the Ho Chi Minh Trail in Laos and Cambodia, fell under yet another commander. He was also subordinate to the Commander, Pacific not the MACV commander.

For the Vietnam War, these command arrangements and responsibilities were complicated and often convoluted. For example, one commander oversaw the strategic bombing of the North. Another was responsible for the interdiction campaign for PAVN forces moving to the South. While the MACV commander handled the conduct of the war in South Vietnam waged against the PAVN (aka NVA) and the PLAF (aka VC), these other operations were critical to that conduct. He was to coordinate that strategy with other Commanders that had responsibilities for operations supporting MACV. However, he could not direct these other commanders what to do with that support. These burdensome command relationships led to problems with the overall conduct of the war against North Vietnam. This and the following chapters will note the most severe examples.

Further complicating military operations in the Indochina region and South Vietnam was the State Department's arrangements in the foreign countries there. For example, by law, the President's senior diplomat in each country and his Embassy staff did not answer to the military commander in that country or the region of the Ambassador's foreign country. Instead, the Ambassador officially outranked these military commanders. Further, no US military commander could conduct military operations without the American Ambassador's approval. Such was the case for South Vietnam as well.

Given the above circumstances and arrangements, it was the responsibility of the military commander in charge of forces and operations in South Vietnam, i.e., the MACV commander, to develop a military strategy for his area – also known in military parlance as a theater of operations. His higher headquarters, in this case, the US Pacific Command, and national higher staff organizations, such as the Chairman of the Joint Chiefs and his staff, had the responsibility to offer guidance and send orders from the President and the Secretary of Defense to the theater commander on his conduct of the war. The MACV Commander, moreover, technically was subordinate to the Ambassador there, and could not conduct operations out of country to adjacent areas without approval of that country's US Ambassador.

Finally, as stipulated in the military doctrine and directives of the day, geographic military commanders and their staffs usually drew up a strategic plan or military strategy that provided the military objectives to achieve, the means to achieve them, and the concept of operations to execute their political objectives as provided by the President and Secretary of Defense. Thus, General Westmoreland was the one who was responsible for carrying out this. However, as surveyed above, the dual command arrangements and multiple other civilian and military people who had overlapping responsibilities, as we will see, often produced contradictions and confusion.

One needs to understand here that there were some civilian and military leaders who were not happy with the above arrangements and wished to change them during the war. For example, both Secretary McNamara in Washington and General Westmoreland in Saigon, knew they were not only burdensome, but, as we will see, often interfered with or questioned ways to execute the war in South Vietnam and operations against North Vietnam.

However, the reader should recall from Chapter 1 that setting up the US national command structure after the Second World War necessitated a compromise solution between and among the various Service organizations, each having their interests in preserving and preparing their personnel, equipment, and training for armed conflict in various areas of the world. These military organizations all had, in turn, support from various factions of the US Congress. Moreover, as a result of the conflict and competition over resources, these bureaucracies were compromises arranged in the first two decades following the war to enable the Department of Defense, however inefficient, to manage its budget and operations.

Early Theater Military Strategies for the Defense of South Vietnam

Also recall from Chapter 1 that President Truman decided to support the French war in Indochina shortly after the Korean War began. To do that, he ordered the establishment a small Military Assistance Advisory Group or MAAG to manage American aid to the French military. After the French had left Indochina a few years following the Geneva Conference, the IKE Administration expanded that Group. To prevent the further spread of communism into South Vietnam, the MAAG's mission was to "organize, train and advise" the armed of forces of the Republic of Vietnam (RVN) with the objective of creating a force that could defend a new South Vietnam government from aggression.

The Commander, US Pacific tasked that MAAG, as one of its subordinate commands, to further develop a draft plan for the combined defense of South Vietnam against an invasion from the North. The Pacific commander did this under guidance from his civilian superiors in Washington, who had decided to develop a military defense plan for South Vietnam under the auspices of the Southeast Asia Treaty Organization or SEATO. This early planning, which included the cooperation of several SEATO country's militaries, became the first instance of a US theater military strategy for South Vietnam.

Significantly, that military strategy was primarily conventional in scope. Though the US military in both South Vietnam and its parent Pacific Command headquarters realized at times that there was an indigenous communist movement supported by the North seeking to overthrow the Diem regime, the planners felt then that the primary threat was a conventional one from the PAVN forces in North Vietnam. Thus, according to research into these early plans by Alexander Cochran published in the military journal *Parameters*, this early planning called for reinforcement of the newly organized and inexperienced ARVN by US forces stationed in the Pacific Command area to defend South Vietnam from an attack from North Vietnam.

The initial concept for this strategic planning called for the creation of coastal enclaves for US deploying forces, which would serve to both protect principal ports and airfields for continued reinforcement, and defense of the populated coastal areas and their cities. It also envisioned the further employment of these US Army ground divisions to blocking positions alongside ARVN forces on probable avenues of invasion by the PAVN forces. Eerily, in retrospect, those avenues happened to be the same that PAVN forces would use in their offensives in 1972 and 1975.

An essential aspect of this planning was that the MAAG and its advisors initially based the organization and training of the ARVN primarily on this strategic concept of a conventional defense against an invasion from the North. By 1959 then, according to the US Army official history of this period, the ARVN "consisted of seven infantry divisions patterned on those of the US Army in World War II."

However, though patterned after US divisions of the Second World War, these ARVN main maneuver units were 'light divisions' or organizations that possessed little heavy equipment and were not designed to counter enemy units that had a lot of firepower and armored organizations. Moreover, the MAAG leaders felt that, because these ARVN units were 'light infantry,' they could be used against any serious insurgency.

The above outline of the early development of a theater military strategy for South Vietnam and the resultant formation of the ARVN is essential to the story ahead. This is because some contemporaries and future critics cite this initial strategy and organization of the South Vietnamese Army as being misplaced and faulty. They argue, particularly in hindsight, that the focus should have been on the potential insurgency in the South, and that the ARVN was ill-designed from the onset to deal with it.

However, as a close reading of the evidence shows, the ARVN divisions, though designed to thwart a Korean type conventional invasion from the North, were more than capable as light units to b against any light guerrilla force in case of a pure insurgency effort. The reason that they would not be able to fight successfully against the Northern directed aggression later is much more complicated than the American initial 'conventional' design of its forces. This issue will be further addressed in this chapter and the two following it.

Evolution of the Counterinsurgency Plan (CIP) Strategy

When the PLAF (VC) military insurgency began to challenge the ARVN in 1960 seriously, it became evident to both the MAAG and Pacific Command that the thrust of the overall organization of South Vietnam's armed forces and its planning to maintain a viable South Vietnam government needed to change. This change resulted in a Pacific Command and MAAG document called "The Counterinsurgency Plan or CIP."

As one of the volumes of the US Army's official Vietnam War history, called *MACV: The Joint Command in the Years of Escalation,* explains, the CIP presented a comprehensive approach to addressing the growing VC insurgency. It altered the original MAAG military strategy for South Vietnam described above, as well as calling for augmentation to the overall force structure of the

South's armed forces. That plan prescribed a three-phase offensive strategy to defeat the PLAF insurgency, and the formation of local security forces to protect the mainly rural populated areas.

On paper, the CIP offensive concept envisioned, first, the use of ARVN forces to engage main force PLAF units to destroy them or to clear them from designated priority areas – the latter being primarily populated regions. Once the ARVN regular units cleared the area of enemy main forces, other ARVN forces and newly formed territorial forces would continue to keep clear and hold these protected zones. Finally, once security was fully set up, RVN political cadres with local security elements would indoctrinate the population on government policies and programs, such as land reform and economic development.

After President Kennedy came into office, the Commander of the Pacific Command sent the CIP to Washington for consideration. This was in response to JFK's new push on counterinsurgency. From the perspective of the US Pacific Command and its MAAG, South Vietnam was becoming the new practical "testing ground for the Kennedy Administration's counterinsurgency doctrines and programs." The CIP thus was intended as an input to those programs.

The new Administration was less interested in the operational concepts in the plan than its call for the reorganization, growth, and retraining of the South Vietnamese armed forces. Of interest, was its call to improve South Vietnam's regional and local territorial forces to protect the population. These were the type of military actions that the Interagency Counterinsurgency Study Group under the guidance of Defense Secretary McNamara, as mentioned in Chapter 2, were interested in.

After considering this plan, JFK approved NSAM 52 in May 1961 and gave the go-ahead on the CIP's recommendations for resources to increase Diem's forces by 20,000 men. Soon after, the President would further approve a total increase of more than 100,000 personnel to Diem's armed forces. Kennedy also approved the dispatch of 400 US Special Forces troops to help in its training and the conduct of counterinsurgency operations.

After this surge of US aid and in response to the Taylor-Rostow visit in the fall of 1961, McNamara approved of the deployment of some other newly created US counterinsurgency forces. These forces were a result of the US military services' reaction to the Administration's budget increases for counterinsurgency programs.

The MACV history notes that "Before the end of 1961, an Air Force counterinsurgency tactical air unit was establishing itself in South Vietnam, as were two Army helicopter companies. Navy minesweepers meanwhile, took up coastal patrol stations just below the 17th Parallel. Army and Air Force specialists began building and manning communications and tactical air control systems. Still, other Americans arrived to improve and expand South Vietnamese government military intelligence." Finally, McNamara also sent a new directive to the US MAAG to increase its intelligence collection capabilities and "to deploy battalion and province advisers to help the Vietnamese plan and conduct combat and pacification operations."

One of the most promising activities of the CIP that was also included in the NSAM 52 initiatives was the effort to create the Civilian Irregular Defense Group (CIDG) program. The CIA had begun this effort in late 1960. Its goal was to use US Army Special Forces Teams to organize and train Vietnamese mountain tribesmen, called Montagnards, for the defense of their villages. The program also sought to use these tribesmen along with American green berets for offensive anti-guerrilla operations and border surveillance.

This program had caught the eye of McNamara as a cost-effective method of affecting the conflict. He argued for and obtained control over it. With Defense Department now in charge of the program was now growing to a total of thirty-nine Special Forces detachments to organ, equip and train a projected 100,000 irregulars. The MAAG organized these SF teams and the Montagnards into small units and placed them in a series of outposts, or camps, mainly along the border regions of South Vietnam to monitor infiltration and conduct counterinsurgency operations against nearby communist base camps.

Soon it became clear that these new forces and added responsibilities demanded a corresponding change to MAAG. After much infighting between the State and Defense Departments, and Service debates on the roles and missions of their forces in Vietnam, McNamara ordered the creation of the Military Assistance Command or MACV. Its newly stated mission was "to direct U.S. military activities and advise the Saigon government on internal security and the organization, deployment, and operations of the armed forces."

The real result of all this change was the creation of a US military headquarters capable of commanding American forces in an ever-growing conflict without relying solely on the South Vietnam military. Thus, without admitting it to the American public, during 1962 JFK and McNamara had committed the American military to an armed conflict without the outright employment of major US combat units.

The Secretary of Defense activated MACV on 8 February 1962. Five days later its first commander, General Paul Harkins, landed at Saigon's Tan Son Nhut Air Base to take command. That command now consisted of almost 5,000 American military personnel. Many of these, particularly those who were helicopter crews and advisors in the field, were now involved in a shooting war with the Viet Cong.

With US military assistance dollars growing, the plan now was to increase the South Vietnamese Armed Forces to a strength of 458,000. Of that force, a little more than half would consist of Regular Forces, while the rest would perform the mission to protect the population and conduct what became known as pacification operations.

These latter activities were to win the support of the people through the building of infrastructures, such as schools and hospitals, and to provide some loyal South Vietnamese officials to gain the support of the people for the government. Some of this growth also went to the further enhancement of mobile forces – ranger, airborne and marine units – that the South Vietnamese high command could move throughout South Vietnam as necessary.

One of Harkins' first tasks was to gain Diem's acceptance of the CIP operational concept and to improve the South Vietnamese Military Chain of Command to execute it. Thus, he went to Diem and suggested that he and his military advisors develop a "nationwide offensive campaign…to destroy the VC and restore control of the country to the duly constituted government." While the South Vietnam leader outwardly gave his support, he was less than enthusiastic about offensive operations and more in tune with the use of his military to ensure support for himself and his loyal appointees.

Diem had already sought the advice of a British expert on counterinsurgency by the name of Robert Thompson. Thompson was a member of the British Advisory Mission in Saigon. He and the other members had gained experience in a successful counterinsurgency campaign in British Malaysia.

This campaign was primarily against a predominantly Chinese minority that had sought the overthrow of that commonwealth nation. One of Thompson's concepts for success in that war was called the 'strategic hamlet' program. It found favor with Diem because it fit into his ideas of solidifying his hold on the people in the vast rural areas of the South.

This program called for the gathering of the indigenous population from various, dispersed villages, and bringing them together into a 'strategic hamlet.' Theoretically, and in Malaysia, the host government could separate and then protect the people from the insurgents and offer government-led economic and social reforms. Diem was enthusiastic about this concept because it was very similar to the 'Agroville' Program he had tried to implement in the first years of his administration.

The difficulty with this program in Vietnam was that the strategic hamlets had worked for the British because they had been able to separate the indigenous people, who were Malaysian, from the guerrillas, who were Chinese. No such delineation existed in Vietnam, where both the people in South Vietnam and the guerrillas were Vietnamese.

General Harkins was successful in getting Diem to implement the overall counterinsurgency plan that MACV had envisioned. He succeeded because he incorporated the strategic hamlet program into it, and the Kennedy Administration thought it a great idea.

However, the hamlet concept soon took on a life of its own. Both the US and RVN leaders became so enthralled with their construction that they began to lose track of the importance of the security operations. Before long, as the numbers of hamlets became the critical measure of success against the insurgency, the effectiveness of the actions to provide the clear and hold operations that should have accompanied their construction faded into the background. Instead, Diem and the Americans just continued to build more hamlets without regard to whether they really provided the security as well as the government benefits they were supposed to offer.

The entire CIP as a military strategy would become a sham. This was not only because of the poor execution of the strategic hamlet program, but because the entire strategy was focused on measuring statistics that would show progress in combating the insurgency. The factors that were easy to measure - such as number of hamlets, increases in local security forces, and the growth of the ARVN - became center stage instead of how well security programs were protecting the populace or whether government programs were providing any support to the people in their daily lives.

The MACV commander also got an agreement from Diem to reorganize and revitalize the ARVN high command – another action called for under NSAM 52. Thus, the ARVN high command, referred to as the Joint General Command, was to direct and oversee all operations for the 'General Offensive Campaign Plan,' supervise its execution through several regional Corps headquarters, and implement its concepts through the regional ARVN divisions and territorial forces.

However, like the Strategic Hamlet program soon this campaign plan demonstrated more emphasis on measuring success than creating it. Harkins and Diem began reporting on the number of ARVN operations and the number of days of their duration rather than how much they were able to contribute to the security of the countryside or prevent enemy disruption to the pacification efforts.

For example, even before the final approval of this nationwide campaign plan, ARVN forces had begun major offensive operations against the VC in sixteen of the RVN's forty provinces. Thus, in March 1962 the ARVN had launched 'OPERATION SUNRISE' as the 'proof of principle' for the strategic hamlet program as well as the offensive campaign plan. It began with a sweep of the ARVN 5th Division across the Binh Dong Province.

The ARVN commander intended to engage and destroy the main VC forces in the Province. The VC did not oblige. They refused to take part in any significant battles, and only fought small unit actions when they could gain the advantage. Nevertheless, the operation went ahead to employ ARVN forces in the countryside, often in places that they knew there was no VC present. That did not seem to matter. The South Vietnam high command and the US MACV commander were pleased that the ARVN was in the field operating for whatever number of days they reported.

The ARVN and some government officials further oversaw and participated in the building strategic hamlets, which consisted of several small peasant dwellings surrounded by barbed wire. The operations and hamlets were touted as successes. This optimism seemed to ignore that "many sullen peasants forcibly herded from their homes into the new settlements" were angry and despondent about being uprooted from their ancestral lands.

Soon after, General Harkins briefed the favorable results of this operation to Secretary McNamara and others from the US Defense and State Departments. McNamara was particularly impressed with the statistics that were being kept on the number of secure strategic hamlets, the growing areas under ARVN control, and the number of operational days ARVN units launched.

Secretary McNamara used these as measures of progress for counterinsurgency as a whole. He was also impressed with the progress in the increase of the South Vietnamese Armed Forces, to include the Territorial Force improvements. The Secretary was further delighted when General Harkins reported a significant upsurge in readiness of the ARVN forces. In most cases, these improvements and readiness measurements were in growth in numbers rather than any measure of valid military progress such as denial of VC units to key areas, or protection of government officials or programs from VC interruption.

In fact, numbers now drove McNamara's assessment of progress. By the end of 1962, for example, every quantifying element that the Defense Secretary tracked was showing that the US and South Vietnam were winning the insurgency. From an initial force of 150,000 now the regular South Vietnam Army numbered 219,000. This would further grow to 225,000 in the first months of 1963. In addition, US aid for self-defense forces, a hallmark of US recent assistance for defense at the local level, grew to more than 170,000. Indeed, by April 1963, out of a goal of 11,000 strategic hamlets already the Diem government had established 6,000. The estimate was now that the GVN controlled over 60% of the population, out of a goal of 90%.

Soon in Washington, the only American measures of progress in the counterinsurgency strategy became 'numbers of strategic hamlets' and 'areas under RVN control.' Harkins began feeding McNamara what the Secretary wanted to see – an increase in both. It mattered not whether these numbers provided real security and pacification to the South Vietnamese countryside. It mattered not that South Vietnamese officials were reporting that a strategic hamlet complete and secure only because someone had circled a number of villages with barbed wire.

In fact, there is some debate on how well the strategic hamlet program worked and for how long. Most sources indicate that they initially had some effect in pacifying the countryside. Indeed, some North Vietnamese documents claim that they set back for a while their campaign to control the rural areas of the South. However, as the North began to infiltrate more PAVN forces and arms and counter the ARVN forces, strategic hamlet local forces could not defend against an increasingly improved VC supported by their NVA cousins.

Nevertheless, initial favorable reports seemed to show considerable progress throughout 1961 and into late 1962. The JFK Administration was becoming confident that they had turned the corner in South Vietnam. As mentioned in Chapter 2, they began to make plans for the withdrawal of some one-thousand American advisors. The real story of how much progress was, and still is, contentious.

There were improvements. US military strength and corresponding operations using armed helicopters grew. By early 1963, US personnel had increased from about 900 to almost 15,000 from the time Kennedy had taken over. There was a corresponding improvement in the advisory effort, which jumped from around 540 at the time of JFK's inauguration to 2600 by mid-June 1963. As mentioned, the ARVN also grew; as did the territorial forces. Strategic hamlets did increase, and a number proved useful in separating the population from the guerrillas. ARVN operations were increasing every month.

While these improvements were primarily measures in numbers, proof of the overall effectiveness in the insurgency, some historians have noted, is that several post-war North Vietnamese documents have recounted South Vietnamese successes in curtailing VC control of the countryside, growth in VC sympathizers, and reductions in VC strength. One historian, Mark Moyer, has gone as far as to say that these efforts, under Diem's direction, were so successful that the ultimate overthrow and loss of Diem was a *Triumph Forsaken*.

No doubt, under General Harkins tenue, MACV, from its perspective, had accomplished much in what Harkins' superiors in Washington had told him to do. The General had focused his efforts on the actions that JFK's NSAMS 52 and 111 had called for. Though there were problems, mainly in some instances where the ARVN had not done well against the VC in battle, the MACV commander had mostly accomplished the measures of effectiveness that his direct boss, the Secretary of Defense, had set for progress in South Vietnam.

The Linchpin of US Theater Strategy in South Vietnam: ARVN Effectiveness

As mentioned in Chapter 2, despite all the favorable reports and the optimistic statistics that McNamara kept track of for Vietnam, there were rumblings from the field. A major one was that some American advisors were reporting about the lack of aggressiveness and incompetence of ARVN senior commanders. As the MACV history explains, advisor field assessments reported that too often ARVN operations "produced no enemy contact; and when government troops did encounter the Viet Cong, they often faced stubborn, effective resistance by units better trained and armed than in the ARVN."

Moreover, despite the new high command reorganization and training, it was troublesome that Diem still had total and direct control over his senior commanders. He often bypassed his military chain of command calling directly to Division commanders using an unsecured phone from his palace. Too often these calls countermanded orders that the ARVN high command had issued. Command effectiveness was never a McNamara measure for the war. It was arguably the most crucial aspect of ARVN performance.

As explained in earlier chapters, the American Press in South Vietnam reported these inadequacies and incompetencies more often and in more detail than MACV headquarters. On occasion, American military personnel, dispatched by the President to report back on progress, verified these negative reports. Some of these assessments were completely counter to those JFK was getting from his Commander and Ambassador in Saigon. Problems in solving ARVN weaknesses would not only plague the Kennedy Administration. ARVN competency was a significant issue throughout the war.

Indeed, some historians have claimed that ARVN incompetency was a significant cause of the American defeat. Journalists turned historians Stanley Karnow, David Halberstam and Neil Sheehan in their popular selling books *Vietnam: A History*; *The Best and the Brightest;* and *A Bright Shining Lie* portray the South Vietnamese Army as a forever ill-matched force against the PAVN and PLA. Sheehan sums up their views on the ARVN during the war. He argues that "the Saigon armed forces commanded by thieving incompetents were doomed." His hero, John Paul Vann "would deceive himself" that they were improving even after the 68 TET offensive.

Other historians have kept this criticism alive as part of the main reason the US failed in Vietnam. Some agree that the leading cause was the corrupt Government oversight and over-politicized military command. Others claim that the American military command's lack of attention to ARVN leader growth and low priority to providing modern armaments and other equipment influenced their defeat. Still others took the result of their defeat in 1975 as ultimate proof of the ARVN's poor performance during the war.

More recently, some scholars depict a more positive and balanced view. Though Mark Moyar, in his *Triumph Forsaken*, portrays an ARVN plagued by command problems at the highest echelon, he also shows that it was an Army that continued to improve, despite being outgunned by the PAVN/PLAF. The South Vietnamese soldiers just could not put up with the better trained and equipped PAVN forces for most of the war.

Andrew Wiest in *Vietnam's Forgotten Army* and James Willbanks in *A Raid Too Far* present a fair and balanced view of a South Vietnamese Army, especially after TET 68. They argue that the ARVN fought bravely and well in TET and other operations through the Easter Offensive of 1972. It had many competent and courageous mid-grade officers (primarily battalion commanders) and junior leaders, with a few senior leaders as well.

However, they both argue, the South Vietnamese Army was never able to overcome two critical flaws. One was that its senior commanders were politicized; that is, they owed its promotion and continued service to the political head of the government. Thus, its loyalty was to the head of state and not to the nation. Second, it was entirely dependent on US support – especially American advisors and firepower.

Because ARVN competence and capabilities were central to the American military strategies pursued in South Vietnam, it is worthwhile to examine the issue further here. So how competent was the ARVN? What were the factors that influenced its strengths and weaknesses? How culpable was the US leadership in its failures? Would it ever have been able to stand on its own against the very capable PAVN? To try to answer these questions, the following paragraphs examine in more detail the origins of the ARVN; its values and social makeup; its leadership; its training and organization; and its use as part of the American directed strategy from 1965 – 1972.

Most of the evidence shows that the ARVN's origins had a considerable impact on its performance, especially in the early years from 1955 to 1965, but even after that. As mentioned in Chapter 1, this army evolved from the Vietnamese National Army (VNA) that served in the French Expeditionary Force (FEF) in the First Indochina War. Thus, formerly French-led and trained officers, and noncommissioned officers (NCOs) made up the core of the ARVN from its very beginning.

As a result, the ARVN core leadership and training were sorely lacking from its beginning. It reflected the French attitude toward its colonial indigenous peoples in that French leaders refused to develop or place any responsibility on its Vietnamese small unit leaders. Thus, the French military officers never promoted any South Vietnamese beyond the rank of junior officer. French commanders, moreover, often ignored the VNA noncommissioned officers.

As Andrew Wiest argues in his intriguing study of the ARVN, the French experience systemically plagued the ARVN. French tutelage ignored leadership training and growth. It disregarded the importance of loyalty to the ordinary soldier and caring for them as a fundamental tenet of military leadership. That had a lasting effect on ARVN senior leaders who remained focused continuously not on improving themselves as soldiers and leaders, but on surviving constant political upheavals.

Moreover, their French experience implanted an inherent hesitancy toward western advice and help. In the interim between the end of the First Indochina War and the departure of the French, key VNA leaders had mixed emotions and loyalties toward new Western efforts to form a new army. For one thing, the French officers had often shunned and looked down to their colonial underlings. The resultant feelings engendered into the Vietnamese from this early experience transferred to the American Advisors. Many resented being cajoled by yet another Westerner who came to a Vietnam he did not understand. They became frustrated when told that it had to conform to yet another mode of warfighting that they thought was European in style.

As the VNA transitioned to a new ARVN, moreover, the equipment and material it received severely hampered its combat capability. As the French left, they took most of the best equipment and armament. The new South Vietnamese Army thus inherited mostly unserviceable or older, less capable equipment and armament. Even as the US military aid program kicked in, most of the material given to replace the old French equipment consisted of Korean War vintage. In fact, it was not until 1968 that the Americans began supplying new modern armaments, such as the M16 rifle, in the quantities needed.

The impact, especially in the early sixties, was that the PAVN would have modern armaments offered by the Chinese and Soviets, such as the AK47 rifle, which later some American soldiers thought even superior to theirs. The ARVN would still have to rely on its World War Two and Korean War weapons such as the M1 carbine. This had a significant impact on the confidence of the ordinary South Vietnamese soldier. It was also a factor that gave much confidence to their PAVN and PLAF counterparts. Consequently, as American advisors reported, many ARVN units avoided contact with the enemy because they felt outgunned.

Another common early trait associated with the ARVN was that there was no real attachment to the nation that they were fighting for. In a groundbreaking social study of the makeup and behavior of the ARVN, Robert Brigham, in his *ARVN: Life and Death in the South Vietnamese Army*, takes on this criticism. He explains that many in the officer corps came from the upper strata of the Vietnamese society. As such, they were brought up in French colonial schools. Many also had served in the FEF during the First Indochina War. Thus, many in the South Vietnamese populace associated the ARVN officer corps with the earlier French colonial rule, rather than the new nation that their Government was trying to create.

Brigham also explains that the average ARVN soldier and its junior leaders possessed primarily a local family focus more than a national one. For example, sources about South Vietnam and its Army state that much of the desertion rate was because soldiers, many draftees, were still the principal 'bread-winners' for their families. Thus, when Government forced them to leave their family units to serve in the military away from their geographic area, they had little choice but to leave their unit and go home to assist in tending the rice paddies and livestock. Moreover, government pay for their service was meager. Therefore, they could not offset their absence with any substantial funds for their families to subsist on.

A high-level American veteran of the war and one-time senior advisor to the ARVN, General Bruce Palmer, supports this view of the ARVN soldier. As he explains in his book, *25 Year War*, the "ARVN was a territorially based and supported army. The families of ARVN soldiers lived near their home stations and were partially sustained by local ARVN resources - housing, for example. Historically ARVN regiments and divisions had not performed well when deployed any great distance from their families. In the Vietnamese culture, particularly in the South, family ties were stronger than loyalty to ARVN or the government, and if the families needed help when so separated, the soldiers simply deserted."

In fact, ARVN families were the primary motivating factor for the individual South Vietnamese soldier in the war. As Brigham writes, "Over time the ARVN created a subnational culture that focused the war's meaning on family survival. Servicemen arrived at a shared understanding that the war was no longer about 'the national question' but about something more elemental. Drawing on cultural and historical traditions, the ARVN redefined the meaning of the war. What held it together in the face of enormous difficulties was a growing belief among soldiers that military service was a way to increase the odds that their families would survive intact.... Still, most soldiers accepted (and continue to accept) an unfavorable reputation as a small price to pay for accomplishing their main objective: saving their families."

This is the main reason, Brigham contends, that the ARVN did so poorly when forced to support US units away from their assigned areas of responsibility. It was also a contributing factor to the ARVN performance in the 1975 NVA invasion. In responding to that PAVN offensive, the ARVN command moved the units away from their traditional area of service, which coincided with where their families lived. Thus, the regular ARVN units did not fight well and dissolved, in part because their soldiers worried about their families' fate.

Brigham and most historians further add that the ARVN soldier's senior leaders also had little association with the new nation. From its onset, most of the Army's senior-level commanders, division level and above, fought primarily to establish and keep Diem and his autocratic style of government in power. After Diem, the Army leaders remained embroiled in political issues surrounding their existence, rather than the building of an efficient armed forces. In short, Army officers had every reason to be more loyal to the RVN political leaders than to the army and the nation that they were supposed to defend.

Brigham and others also point out that senior officers who survived and were loyal to the ruling regime were powerful political entities who ruled their areas like feudal warlords. The most powerful were the four Corps Commanders who ruled each of the four military regions of South Vietnam. General Bruce Palmer, as mentioned one who served as an ARVN Corps advisor, supports this view. He relates in his book on the war: "The ARVN corps commanders, three-star ARVN generals, were also military region governors responsible for civil administration. Exercising both political and military control, they enjoyed great authority and prestige. They reported directly to Saigon—the president at the palace on political matters, and the Joint General Staff (JGS) for military affairs."

Andrew Wiest in his *Vietnam's Forgotten Army*, further explains that these ARVN senior leaders "were all too often interested first in obtaining and then in retaining personal power. With political loyalty serving as the ultimate arbiter of worth within the upper echelons of the ARVN command structure, there was little impetus for far-reaching military and societal reform." With political infighting and survival their primary task, there was also little impetus or time for sound military tactical decision-making and certainly no reason for risk of life.

Besides, political power, favor and corrupt behavior went hand in hand. Senior commanders, in the words of historian Jeffrey Clarke, "routinely supplemented low government salaries with a wide variety of extralegal practices, such as the sale of draft deferments, land titles and other licenses; the levy of protection fees for various commercial activities; and the general diversion of government monies and materiel into private hands." General Palmer experienced this corruption first hand. "In one instance our advisory group discovered that the commanding general of 5th ARVN Division, using ARVN trucks and ARVN soldiers, was running a black-market rubber business in cahoots with the French rubber plantation managers in his area."

Throughout the brief history of the ARVN, corruption was thus endemic to its high command structure. The more junior officers - many of whom fought valiantly and led courageously and effectively – were, in the words of Andrew Wiest, left to "struggle for the soul of the ARVN and the South Vietnamese State." Indeed, the main reason that the ARVN improved from 1965 to 1972 was because of the competency and combat experience of its mid-level officers. For Wiest, the key question was "would the junior leadership have time to transform the ARVN?" Of course, in retrospect, we know it would not have the time or the opportunity because of the precipitous American withdrawal and faulty Paris treaty.

There were also factors that influenced ARVN performance associated with the American organization and training of, advisory efforts for, and how the US command would employ the ARVN in support of its military strategy for the war. As mentioned earlier, when the US military aid program began to focus on the new ARVN organization, the MAAG wanted that organization to be able to defend South Vietnam primarily from a conventional invasion from the North. Consequently, the fundamental ARVN divisional structure was the traditional infantry outfit, primarily geared toward defensive operations against a conventional type invasion from North Vietnam.

Per the US Army Vietnam Study on *The Development and Training of the South Vietnamese Army*, to both save money and simplify training, the American design for the ARVN infantry division was void of several key capabilities that US infantry units of similar design and purpose had. These were primarily heavy artillery, logistics, intelligence, and aviation unit equipment and skills. The development of these skills and capabilities seemed beyond the ability of the ARVN, and certainly beyond the monies that would be necessary.

In addition, those who were responsible for the ARVN's early design also thought that American Army units, which were supposed to supplement the ARVN in the event of a PAVN invasion, would make up for the South Vietnam Army deficiencies. Later, as American aide and units poured into South Vietnam, and as the ARVN force structure grew, it became dependent on the US combat and combat support units, and their American advisors, to make up for the deficiencies in their original design in fighting the more capable PAVN units as well.

This reliance continued throughout the war. Consequently, when US forces were no longer available, the ARVN had a challenging time in creating them through not only getting the right equipment and munitions, but also the training, which was the most time-consuming activity of all. Although the US Vietnamization program attempted to make up for these deficiencies in the early seventies, it would take more time than was available to institute the manning, equipping, and training of the absent US capabilities.

Moreover, as mentioned in Chapter 5, and as we will see in Chapter 10 in more detail, General Abrams, the MACV commander in 1972, recognized this weakness. He therefore sought an American military 'residual force' presence in Vietnam to give some capability in these areas for the ARVN. However, as we will see, the Nixon Administration would have none of it. The ARVN collapse in 1975 can be attributed, in part, to these deficiencies.

While training and assistance were significant parts of the MAAG and then MACV mission, its field advisory task was, arguably, its most important. When it began in the 1950s, advisors were few. Moreover, their primary purpose was to direct the flow of equipment and armament to the newly formed ARVN units. Later, some advisors went to ARVN JCS, Corps and Division headquarters units. By the early sixties, JFK's emphasis on counterinsurgency pushed the advisor mission down to battalion (units with several hundreds of soldiers) level and, in some instances, to the company (smaller organizations within the battalion of about one hundred soldiers).

The numbers of field advisors increased accordingly. They went from about one thousand in the late fifties; to over three thousand by the end of Kennedy's first year as President; to more than eight thousand at the end of 1965. The major field team in the ARVN battalions consisted of five members, with a US Major or Captain at its head. At first, these advisors were officers with considerable field, and in some cases, combat experience. Later, as the requirements increased, junior field grade officers made up many of the teams; some with little field experience.

Accounts of the US advisory effectiveness, to include some first-hand South Vietnamese memoirs, list several severe flaws in the American efforts. Primarily, advisors lacked language skills and knowledge of Vietnamese culture. Though the US set up pre-deployment training for them, it was limited in time and scope. With the effectiveness of the advisory role dependent on the nature of the personal relationship between the American advisor and Vietnamese commander, the lack of understanding of language and culture invariably led to a weakness in communication and comprehension in decision making.

US policy toward advisor assignment further contributed to ineffectiveness. MACV, with the Army's approval, assigned American advisors for a one-year tour. However, in many incidents, field advisors' tour of duty in ARVN combat units were for only six months. Personnel policies called for the transfer of the advisor at the end of that half-year to an ARVN staff position. This action was primarily due to account for the difficulty and danger of serving in ARVN units. The impact was that even if the American advisor and ARVN commander could construct a productive relationship, the advisor would be gone after a brief time. Consequently, some ARVN leaders had up to a dozen different advisors in their command time.

Furthermore, as the American unit presence in South Vietnam grew, most American officers sought assignment to US units. US military personnel policies favored the promotion of officers who had combat tours with American units ahead of those who had a tour with ARVN units. Thus, in many incidents, US military personnel sought and could arrange for their transfer from an advisor assignment to a more 'prestigious' American unit after they arrived in country. This would not only give an opportunity to experience combat with an American unit, but promotions favored those serving in combat positions in US organizations.

That notion was, in part, the result of the mission relationship between the US and ARVN forces that General Westmoreland first set up. In his operational scheme, as we will see in more detail ahead, the ARVN were to defend the highly-populated areas and have the primary responsibility for security and pacification operations. Meanwhile, the US forces took part in offensive operations to seek and destroy the enemy main forces. American military officers saw the latter as a much more desirable and prestigious mission to be part of.

Westmoreland's division of tasks between the ARVN and the US forces, some argue, also had a profound and long-term effect on the ARVN. Between 1965 and 1968, the ARVN was mainly a static defensive force tied to specific areas. As the war changed after TET, and the need for the ARVN to take on a more offensive role with the withdrawal of US forces, it found itself untrained and unfamiliar with such offensive operations. This would later affect its capability to counter the North's offensives in 1972 and 1975, and the ARVN's effectiveness in its operations in Cambodia and Laos in 1970 and 1971.

Yet of all the discussion and reasons for the ARVN performance in the war, perhaps the predominant factor causing the overall lack of effectiveness - according to Moyar and documented in US Army histories - can be attributed to one major event. That was the assassination of President Diem in November of 1963.

We have already seen that the US played a significant role in Diem's removal. While President Kennedy was surprised at its brutal ending and seemed to regret the coup, his Administration, particularly the State Department and Ambassador Lodge, encouraged and gave their tacit approval for the coup. Afterward, the South Vietnamese government was in complete turmoil. Indeed, the predictions of some US supporters of Diem - namely Generals Harkins and Taylor, as well as McNamara – came to fruition.

During the next two years, South Vietnam had nine different governments. The successive military officers and some civilians who tried to rule were mostly incompetent and unable to offer any legitimacy and stability. In their quest to keep power, they continually removed senior leaders appointed by Diem and each succeeding head of government. As an example, the 1st ARVN Division changed commanders four times in a single year; while one of its regiments had three different regimental and four battalion commanders.

The results were devastating. According to Mark Moyar, "As the struggle for military and political control became more chaotic, the leadership of the ARVN fragmented into smaller and smaller groups of loyalty ... In the wake of political instability, ARVN morale plummeted, and a military that had been holding its own against the Viet Cong both stagnated and lost the initiative as offensive operations and pacification efforts in several areas simply ground to a halt." Andrew Wiest agrees with this assessment. As he notes after Diem's removal, "The political and military chaos struck the ARVN like a typhoon and served to destroy much of the fitful gains made by the South Vietnamese military in recent years."

As Moyar continues, "these changes would help propel Hanoi toward a strategy of seeking a decisive victory through the destruction of South Vietnam's armed forces, which in turn would eventually force the Americans to decide either to introduce US ground troops or to abandon South Vietnam." For the ARVN, the tremendous upheaval caused by the many changes in command at every level from Corps to battalion following Diem's assassination would have a lasting effect that it could never recover from in the years after.

To sum and conclude this analysis of ARVN capability and its role in the loss of the war, many factors influenced its ability to fight the main PLAF/VC forces and the PAVN regular forces that Hanoi relied upon to eventually win the war. As explained, some of these were peculiar to its origins, such as a lack of capable weaponry and other material. This continued as the American combat units withdrew and it was unable to make up for its provision of the key capabilities in aviation, heavy artillery, logistics, and intelligence.

Throughout the history of the ARVN, its leadership remained wanting as well. Some of that was a result of the French lack of professional leadership development. Much of that was also because of its continual involvement in politics. The South Vietnamese high command was unable to solve this issue. There was never any serious reform.

American efforts, as we will see ahead, would never be able to convince the South Vietnamese leaders to affect senior leader improvement that made a difference. Westmoreland's attempts, explained in what follows, never seemed to have been forceful enough. Besides, he would rely on Ambassador Taylor to cajole the various leaders. Taylor would become too frustrated to make a difference.

Later Westy's successor, General Abrams, would have a better relationship with the two RVN leaders who would become relatively stable in office – President Thieu and Premier Ky. However, as we will see in Chapter 10, reform still never took hold. Most importantly, Thieu continued to insist on appointing and controlling the ARVN senior leadership, which remained highly politicized and corrupt. Just as important, perhaps, was that the US withdrawal gained a momentum of its own and, along with the decision not to maintain a permanent military presence in Vietnam after the peace accords, the US military was never able to assist or accelerate improvements.

As their combat experience and confidence grew, there were undoubtedly courageous and capable divisional and junior leaders, who fought bravely and competently. The ARVN's performance during TET 68, the Easter Offensive, and its invasion of Laos was as good, in some respects, as any of the US combat units during the war. Moreover, from time to time, Thieu would take Abrams' advice on firing incompetent senior officers, mainly when the choice was defeat or holding on until the NVA had to give in.

However, as explained later, time would run out for US efforts to build a combat effective ARVN that could defend its territory from the more capable North Vietnam regulars. With the right kind of military support over the long run, the US may have eventually been successful in pressuring for reform and building the capabilities needed. Over time, perhaps, the competent and loyal junior South Vietnamese officers could have supplanted the bureaucratic, corrupt, and incompetent senior ARVN commanders. However, we will never know whether the ARVN could have gained the capabilities to withstand the North's aggression.

What the evidence does show conclusively is that in the end, the ARVN failure was also an American failure. The US was never able to offer the wherewithal the ARVN needed to defeat a relentless and more capable foe – the PAVN. Only the American military could fight and win over that main force the North depended upon for its victory.

In the end, the US abandoned that Army of its making. The pages and chapters ahead tell a more detailed, if not satisfying, story of its end. That narration, moreover, will further chronicle the bravery and failures of a South Vietnamese Army that America created, fought alongside, and then left stranded.

Section 8.2 - Transition to an American War, 1964-1965

Despite the progress that General Harkins had confidence in and that he could show, as explained in Chapter 7, the North Vietnamese stepped up its support for the war dramatically in 1963 and into early 1964. Ironically, the progress in ARVN operations and growth in the strategic hamlet program late 1962, coupled with the VC military successes in early 1963 and the Diem assassination later that year, all incited Le Duan to order an all-out North Vietnam offensive in early 1964. A new US Commander-in-Chief now thought Harkins needed to go. He wanted someone, he told McNamara, that could turn things around and "whip the hell out of the VC."

As the overall situation in South Vietnam deteriorated in 1964, it is not surprising the new American commander, General William Westmoreland, sought ways to affect the situation. MACV, and its higher headquarters US Pacific Command, began to take an increasingly more direct involvement in the war. They began to launch operations that were either done by US forces or by US-directed irregular South Vietnamese units. Some of these were planned and conducted as covert operations against North Vietnam.

OPLAN 34A

MACV created a new staff section to oversee the covert operations. Activated in January 1964, the command initially labeled the unit the Special Operations Group or SOG. Later SOG changed its name to the Studies and Observations Group to avoid any scrutiny for its covert mission. It took over the CIA's covert operations against the North, which had been ongoing since Colonel Lansdale had executed propaganda and sabotage activities in the fifties.

Most of these activities fell under OPLAN 34A mentioned in Chapter 3. The OPLAN, which began as an extension of the original CIP, soon took on a life of its own separate from the operations waged in South Vietnam. It consisted of "over 2,000 activities, in three ascending categories of scale and severity, to include reconnaissance, psychological warfare, and sabotage operations as well as small-scale military attacks." At first, these were to consist of only South Vietnamese, with some support of 'volunteers' from Nationalist China. American units supplied their equipment, and in some cases, their transportation.

MACV's SOG also stepped up and tried to make the agent operations in the North more effective. Up to 1964, these operations had been a complete failure. According to one source - Robert Gillespie's *Black Ops Vietnam* - the communists captured or killed these CIA teams. SOG's operations in 1964 were no more successful. Of the 22 teams they trained in secret, they employed half of them by the end of the year. The North captured all of them – consisting of seventy-five agents. We now know that much of their demise was due to Northern spies well placed in Saigon who alerted the North's leaders on the times and the whereabouts of the CIA teams when they were inserted.

After the assassinations of Kennedy and Diem, the US military took an even more direct role in OPLAN 34A. Most of this consisted of secret US air attacks on the Ho Chi Minh trail in Laos and, to a minor extent, in Cambodia. In some instances, CIDG units, advised by and often led by American Special Forces personnel, conducted border raids. MACV SOG also increased its aerial operations, flown by National Chinese crews, dropping propaganda materials over the North.

Meanwhile, US naval patrols supported South Vietnamese raids against North Vietnamese coastal facilities – one of which led to the Tonkin Gulf incident in August 1964.

These early supporting and direct US military actions were symptomatic of a growing belief that only direct and significant US military involvement would ensure success in Vietnam. They were part of McNamara's gradual escalation campaign designed to convince the North that the US was going to commit more combat forces should it continue to support the insurgency in the South.

Despite these increased covert and overt operations, the situation in the South continued to unravel. As we have seen, the North had decided to increase its infiltration of PAVN forces to seek an end to the conflict through military means. As argued by Mark Moyar, President Johnson's speeches and actions in 1964 – indicating he was for peace and that he sought no wider war – may have encouraged the North to win the war before the US could intervene. Ironically, the limited military response of the LBJ Administration to the Tonkin Gulf incident enhanced Le Duan's belief that he could defeat the ARVN before the US could deploy significant forces if it had the will to do so.

In late 1964 and early 1965, while the increased PAVN and PLAF main forces began attacking ARVN unit formations, the local VC forces stepped up small group actions against vulnerable ARVN and US bases and other facilities. One of the more effective VC attacks was against the airbase at Pleiku. It had resulted in some significant loss of life and aircraft.

As mentioned in Chapter 3, the Johnson Administration had already been wrestling with what to do with the increased NVA/PLAF activities. Some Advisors, the most prevalent being McGeorge Bundy, Robert McNamara, and Maxwell Taylor, had called for, and the Administration had begun planning for, air attacks against the North. Once again, the purpose of these attacks was primarily to show resolve and convince the DRV leaders to cease their support for the war in the South.

Ironically, Bundy was in country during the Pleiku attack. Westmoreland observed that he seemed to have taken it personally. The National Security Advisor now strongly urged the President to make retaliatory air strikes for the attacks against US bases in South Vietnam.

The President gave the go ahead. On 7 February, the Commander, US Pacific ordered 49 aircraft from naval carriers in the South China Sea to attack North Vietnamese barracks at Dong Hoi in southern North Vietnam. The next day, South Vietnamese aircraft, accompanied by the US fighters, attacked similar targets. Operation 'FLAMING DART,' a very limited 'tit for tat' operation to deter Northern operations in the South, was underway.

US Theater Strategy: Airpower and the Enclave Concept

FLAMING DART did not last long. Soon after it began, the President gave the green light for the sustained, but limited air campaign against the North called ROLLING THUNDER. As explained previously, LBJ and his advisors had conceived ROLLING THUNDER in November 1964 just before the national elections. As recommended in McNamara's and Bundy's 'Fork in the Road' memorandum, this operation called for a carefully controlled but sustained strategic bombing of North Vietnam.

As the US Air Force history of the Vietnam War describes, "The strikes had a threefold purpose: to raise the morale of the South Vietnamese, impose a penalty on Hanoi for its support of aggression in the South, and reduce the infiltration of men and supplies into the South. The air campaign also was based on the hope that the gradual destruction of North Vietnam's military bases and constant harassment and attacks on its LOCs would bring its leaders to the negotiating table."

The campaign was extraordinarily complex. It involved planes from both inside South Vietnam, consisting of both US and South Vietnamese Air Force aircraft, and from Navy Carriers in the South China Sea. Admiral Sharp – the Commander of the Pacific when it started – had overall operational direction. Westmoreland was a supporting commander responsible for the security and provision of the planes launched from South Vietnam. Making all of this more complicated was that Sharp had to coordinate with the various Ambassadors of the regional countries from which the military planes employed to seek their approval of the use of airfields there.

The most complicating factor was that Washington, specifically the President, personally controlled the air operations. In the words of the Air Force history, "The President retained such firm control of the air campaign against the North that no important target or new target areas could be hit without his approval." As mentioned in Chapter 3, the primary reason for this close control was to avoid any mishaps against Chinese and Soviet forces or citizens that were supporting North Vietnam or any inadvertent strikes or violations of Chinese airspace. Another was the President's desire not to seem like the US wanted to hinder or destroy the North's economy or harm its civilians.

Unlike the aerial campaigns of the Second World War, the restrictions on targets and geographic areas were extraordinary. Again, as explained in the official history, "The initial air strikes were limited primarily to enemy radar and bridges between the 17th and 19th parallels. Later, the airmen could hit a number of other military targets below the 20th parallel." These parallel restrictions defined the geographic areas for targets, with the areas above and below prohibited primarily because of the above described LBJ concerns.

The history further describes the targets involved. "The first target hit above the 20th parallel, the Quang Soui barracks, was attacked on 22 May 1965 by Air Force F-105s and the first above Hanoi in late June. After mid-1965, the airmen were authorized to attack important bridges and segments of the northwest and northeast rail lines between Hanoi and the Chinese border. For an extended period, Washington exempted from attack sanctuary areas around Hanoi and Haiphong, a buffer zone near China, surface-to-air missile (SAM) sites, and MIG bases located within the Hanoi-Haiphong areas."

Because of these restrictions, the history explains, "war materiel from the Soviet Union, China, and other Communist countries flowed in easily through Haiphong and other North Vietnamese ports and over rail lines from Kunming and Nanning, China - all of which helped Hanoi to make up for its losses and which facilitated a rapid air defense buildup."

"These limitations also frustrated American pilots, who had to repeatedly use ingress routes to their targets. This made them particularly vulnerable to Northern surface to air missile and conventional anti-aircraft attacks. With Soviet and Chinese aid, the North Vietnam air defense system became one of the most effective and sophisticated in military history. As a result, the US military lost over 900 planes, and 745 crewmen shot down during the war."

Because the Administration launched ROLLING THUNDER primarily to send signals of US resolve to convince DRV leaders to cease its support of the war in the South, the President ordered a series of bombing 'pauses' to allow the North Vietnamese leaders to respond. The first was in mid-

May 1965. The President also directed one that began Christmas Eve 1965, which continued until the end of January 1966. North Vietnam did not respond to either of these or others following.

Rather, as mentioned, the North skillfully used these halts to repair facilities and lines of communication. Infiltration also increased during the bombing respites. From time to time LBJ gradually increased the number of targets and intensified the bombing. By the time the bombing ended in 1968, the US had estimated that these air attacks destroyed over 60% of the North Vietnamese power plants, 50% of its bridges, and 40% of its railroad shops.

This calculated bombing campaign, however, never convinced the North to give up its struggle in the South. It was not until President Johnson in 1968 finally called an end to ROLLING THUNDER, and announced he would not run for another term, that the North finally decided to come to the negotiating table. However, as explained in Chapter 7, that decision was not a result of the bombing. It was because of the need for some relief to recoup its losses from the TET offensive.

While the chief instrument of convincing the DRV to stop its aggression was the strategic bombing of the North, airpower in support of the ground forces in the South was also necessary to engage the increasing VC attacks. Heretofore, the Kennedy and Johnson Administrations had restricted the small US Air Force tactical support presence there to supporting Vietnamese Air Force operations.

Now, shortly after the FLAMING DART operations had begun, Westmoreland asked for authorization to reinforce and use US aircraft in the South without Vietnamese crew members. He argued, along with Ambassador Taylor, that such use would not only be necessary to support ARVN forces, but also give confidence to the South's government. In early March 1965, Washington gave that approval.

With the growth of US Air Force power in the South, the security of its bases was becoming increasingly important. The ability of the South's forces to protect these bases, and other US installations, however, was growing suspect. Of importance was the massive US airbase and installation at Da Nang. Much of the airpower stationed there was, in the early Spring of 1965, supporting ROLLING THUNDER as well as close air support for the fighting in the South. Compounding this insecurity was the ever-increasing success of the PAVN/PLF offensive directly threatening Da Nang.

Recall from Chapter 3 that during late 1964 and early 1965 both Ambassador Taylor and General Westmoreland had sent cables to the Johnson Administration warning of the increasing failure of the RVN to combat the Communist offensive and the need for security of US air bases. Both had hoped that their push on the RVN leaders for an expansion of the ARVN would enable greater capabilities to thwart the PAVN/VC.

A few months into 1965, it became clear to them that this expansion was not going to work. As noted in the US Army history of MACV, "In Westmoreland's assessment, the South Vietnamese Army, which handled protecting the American bases, could do so only by diverting already thinly spread units from pacification and territorial security missions at the risk of serious loss of government control over sizeable areas and their populations."

Accordingly, the Commander of MACV initially asked for the deployment of either a Marine or Army Brigade to South Vietnam to protect these important, but vulnerable bases. He also requested air defense units in the unlikely but within the capability of a Northern air attack in retaliation for the ROLLING THUNDER bombings.

In response, President Johnson approved the dispatch of an air defense unit right after the VC attacks against Pleiku in February 1965. In the weeks following, as that unit deployed, the Johnson Administration briefly debated the dispatch of a Marine Expeditionary Brigade to guard the facilities at Da Nang. On 26 February LBJ approved the deployment. Ambassador Taylor paved the way with the current RVN government. On 8 March Marines from the 9th Marine Expeditionary Brigade stationed in Okinawa came ashore near Da Nang with South Vietnamese flower girls there to greet them.

The MACV history states that "During their first month on shore, the Marines operated under highly restrictive instructions from General Westmoreland. Issued on 8 March, the instructions specified that the 9th MEB would not engage in combat operations against enemy forces except for its own protection or the protection of installations, facilities, or other units it is charged with defending or assisting in defending. The marines were not to perform any counterinsurgency functions. Under the operational control of MACV, the brigade was to work with the ARVN corps on the basis of coordination and cooperation in the mutual self-interest of both commands."

While Westmoreland denounced afterward claims that he had any scheme to get his foot in the door for greater American ground involvement in South Vietnam, he and others in the Johnson Administration understood that the commitment of the Marines changed the game. Despite this awareness, Westmoreland was under strict orders to downplay their deployment and emphasize that they were only there for security purposes.

Yet, as noted in the official MACV history, "the landing at Da Nang on 8 March was to acquire in retrospect precisely the significance which Westmoreland claimed it did not have. Even as the Marines settled into their bunkers and ran their first patrols, General Westmoreland and his superiors, on the basis of a growing volume of disturbing information about the military situation in South Vietnam, were beginning to consider seriously the most drastic intensification yet of the U.S. commitment: the direct engagement of large American ground forces in the battle against the Viet Cong."

The *Pentagon Papers* - as well as other primary sources like the *Foreign Relations of the United States* and official histories such as the *US Army History, MACV: The Early Days* - carefully detail the circumstances that those in Saigon played in leading to that commitment. They also demonstrate that the role General Westmoreland played in the decision toward war was substantial – even critical.

Contrary to some claims of Westmoreland's role and his motives, these sources also show that there was nothing underhanded, or as some have since claimed conspiratorial, to start an American War in South Vietnam on the part of General Westmoreland or the American military. Instead, the MACV Commander professionally offered his views and opinions - in detail and stated in official cables - on how to achieve militarily the then issued US objective to enable a "stable and independent noncommunist government in the Republic of South Vietnam (RVN)."

Ironically, Ambassador Taylor also played a pivotal role. It is ironic because, despite his previous argument during JFK's Administration for US troop commitment to South Vietnam, in late 1964 and into early 1965 he had urged restraint. The General did so because he believed that any significant US ground commitment would discourage rather than encourage South Vietnamese performance and reform. Besides, he still held out hope that the South Vietnamese would still be able to rally and get its Army to fight to a standstill the aggressive VC forces. He also believed that ROLLING THUNDER might work, thus negating the need for US combat force commitment.

Taylor's confidence in the bombing, however, had not found favor with the President. In his memoirs, *Swords and Plowshares*, the General now turned Ambassador relates how at one point when he was in Washington talking with LBJ on what to do with the deteriorating situation in the South told him that the key was to lift the restrictions on the bombing. When the President asked whether that may encourage the Chinese to get more involved, the Ambassador said he did not think the Chinese would dare enter even if some US bombs hit their territory. The President snapped back, "Didn't MacArthur say the same just before the Chinese poured into Korea?" The President then, a bit testy toward the Ambassador, sent him back to Vietnam saying, "we will rely on you to bring some political stability before we take any military action."

After he returned to Vietnam, the Ambassador faced yet another turnover of the South Vietnamese government. He now believed that 'bringing some political stability' was not possible, especially with the mounting pressures on the South with the deteriorating military situation. There appeared to be no one in South Vietnam who could stabilize the situation. By March of 1965, he began to reluctantly support Westmoreland's call for the insertion of US forces inland to 'stem the tide.'

In this reevaluation on the use of US ground forces in South Vietnam, Taylor, at first, favored their employment in enclaves near major population centers and in proximity to US bases. That way the Ambassador thought they could serve as a demonstration to the North that the US was seriously committed to stopping northern aggression.

He also felt that such a demonstration now could further bolster South Vietnamese resolve. Finally, US forces postured in such a way would then be able to act as a reserve for any reinforcements or be withdrawn should the US decide that the South could no longer fight. In sum, it provided the Administration flexibility in its deployment of US combat forces. Though he was not aware of it, Ambassador Taylor's thinking in Saigon was precisely what George Ball was arguing at the same time in Washington.

The Ambassador's thinking on the use of US troops, however, would not be the ignition that would jump-start the move toward US combat ground force commitment in South Vietnam from Saigon. That would come from Westmoreland. General Taylor would, though a reluctant player, provide some spark for his protégé for the latter's actions in that direction.

By mid-March, General Westmoreland had become aware that the timing was now right to push his views for a stronger US military ground intervention. In conversations with his mentor General Taylor, he knew that the Ambassador would not now actively resist him. Besides, he learned from Taylor that the President had also become convinced that the air campaign would not work.

Taylor, in fact, related to the MACV commander conversations he had had with the President on the latter's dismay over the ineffectiveness of the bombing. He told Westy that LBJ said, "I have never felt that this war will be won from the air, and it seems to me that what is much more needed and would be more effective is a larger and stronger use of rangers and special forces and marines or other appropriate military strength on the ground and on the scene. I am ready to look with great favor on that kind of increased American effort, directed at the guerrillas and aimed to stiffen the aggressiveness of Vietnamese military units up and down the line. Any recommendation that you or

General Westmoreland make in this sense will have immediate attention from me...."

Thus, the real ignition for US ground intervention came from the President and not from his Generals. Westmoreland's initiative for the further use of combat troops, in fact, only came because he knew that LBJ would favor such action. After all, Westy was not the kind of military commander who took the initiative upon himself. He never wanted to do anything unless he knew that his superiors would be in favor it beforehand.

Adding to the support that Westmoreland now seemed to have on more ground forces was, early in March, LBJ's dispatch of the Army Chief of Staff, General Harold K. Johnson, to Saigon. As mentioned in Chapter 3 and related in the MACV official history, "After a breakfast meeting on the day of General Johnson's departure for Saigon, the Army chief of staff later recalled, the president 'bored his finger into my chest and . . . said get things bubbling' in Vietnam."

In conversations with General Johnson during that visit, Westy judged that their views on the need to deploy US ground forces to stop the Northern offensive were very similar. As he relates in his memoirs, "If the President was determined to succeed in Vietnam, as General Johnson communicated to me, I saw no solution, while awaiting results from the bombing and expanded ARVN forces, other than to put our own finger in the dike." He later learned that both the President and Secretary McNamara had discussed General Johnson's trip report and it "reflected much of my thinking."

That report, as related in Chapter 3, shocked the President. As McNamara remembers, "The President and I met with General Johnson and the other chiefs at the White House on 15 March to review his report. General Johnson estimated it could take 500,000 US troops five years to win the war. His estimate shocked not just the president and me but the other chiefs as well. None of us had been thinking in anything approaching such terms."

Thus, with the timing right, Westmoreland finally sent on 26 March to the JCS a detailed "Estimate of the Situation" for the use of US ground troops. In the words of the analysts of the *Pentagon Papers*, "The Commander's Estimate of the Situation prepared by General Westmoreland and his staff during the early weeks of March and completed on the 26th was a classic Leavenworth style analysis, detailed and thorough in its consideration of possible U.S. courses of action. Copies of the Estimate, which in bulk amounted to a full half inch of foolscap paper, were delivered to Washington by Brigadier General De Puy, Westmoreland's J'-3, who was traveling with Ambassador Taylor to the NSC meetings of 1-2 April."

The 'Estimate' outlined a limited theater military strategy that assumed the strategic bombing campaign would eventually convince the North to cease its support of the war in the South. However, as an interim measure, the US, and other 'Free World Countries,' would need to deploy to South Vietnam to support the Government of Vietnam in 'surviving' so that "it may defeat the VC insurgency inside SVN." Evidently, the ever-cautious Westmoreland did not want to step outside the current policy and thus presented his estimate for the use of US ground troops assuming the bombing would work, even though he was aware of the President's dismay on the bombing's effectiveness.

The 'Estimate' presented several courses of action for the employment of US forces. All were variations of one basic course. That was for the US 7th Fleet to "quarantine the coast against infiltration of men and arms and continue US logistical support as required." The US would then commit up to two divisions to "secure vital US installations and defeat VC efforts to control the Kontum, Pleiku, Binh Dinh region, or to secure critical enclaves in coastal regions, or to do a combination of both." Finally, in conjunction with the concepts of operation for those two US divisions, the theater strategic concept called for "a cordon across SVN and the Laotian panhandle manned up to three US divisions coupled with ARVN, Thai, and Laos forces."

The 'Estimate' went on to further detail what the necessary US force size was and the timing of its deployment to South Vietnam. It recommended for each course a buildup of US forces "to 17 battalions by early June at latest." Westmoreland warned that if the bombing did not work by the end of the year, more forces might be necessary.

It is not clear from the *Pentagon Papers*, or other sources, who saw or what exactly was discussed about this estimate. Westmoreland assumed the NSC discussed it at its 1 April meeting. As mentioned in Chapter 3, that April fools' day meeting did result in several decisions affecting changes to the US posture and strength in South Vietnam. The President approved two more marine battalions for base security and 20,000 more support troops. The deployment of a larger force, as Westmoreland was advocating, was relegated to further planning. However, there is no mention of Westmoreland's 26 March estimate as influencing any of these decisions.

Most important as far as Westmoreland was concerned was that the President had changed the mission for US forces in South Vietnam from one of purely defensive to the more offensively minded mission of taking part in counterinsurgency operations. However, still of concern for the MACV commander, LBJ made it clear that any US troops, either deploying now or in the future, would be operating out of secure 'enclaves' and not conducting offensive operations inland.

As explained in the *Pentagon Papers* this enclave strategy, as understood by those in Washington, "proposed that US troops occupy coastal areas, accept full responsibility for their security, and be prepared to go to the rescue of the RVNAF as far as 50 miles outside of them. Initially, the US was to experiment with four Marine battalions in two coastal enclaves to see if the concept and the rules for operating with the RVNAF (which were to be worked out with the GVN) were feasible."

The military proponents of the enclave concept, who were mainly the Marine Corps Commandant and some retired Army officers, argued rightly that the logistical situation in the South at the time necessitated the employment of US forces in these coastal bastions. In fact, and as Westmoreland admitted in his 26 March estimate, it would take some time to build up the necessary supplies to sustain any considerable force and further employ them away from the coastal areas. It was also highly problematic and risky to move supplies from the coastal ports and airfields to support operations inland.

The political proponents, who included Taylor and George Ball from the State Department, argued that the use of US forces to fight the main forces and attack their base areas would relegate the ARVN to a secondary mission. In so doing, they contended that the ARVN would grow too defensive oriented and not able to conduct operations against the primary threat to security and stability throughout the South. Besides, as both the military and political proponents further reasoned, the bulk of the population lived in coastal areas. It was therefore there that the main effort was necessary to ensure the security of the population and the success of pacification that were so critical to success against the insurgency.

Westmoreland Takes the Initiative for the Way Ahead

At this point, in early April 1965, though satisfied that he had proposed his views for US ground actions in South Vietnam, Westmoreland was not entirely happy with the recent decisions from Washington. He was especially concerned about the enclave strategic concept that seemed to have gained favor. As he recalls in his memoirs, "I disagreed with the enclave strategy. As my staff study put it at the time, it stood for an inglorious, static use of US forces in overpopulated areas with little chance of direct or immediate outcome on the events."

He further explained, "it would position American troops in what would be in effect a series of unconnected beachheads, their back to the sea, essentially in a defensive posture. That would leave the decision of when and where to strike to the enemy, invite defeat of each in turn, [and] virtually foreordain combat in densely populated locales." In the months ahead, he would work to change the strategic approach to a more offensive one of his liking.

He would get his first opportunity at a conference at the end of April in Honolulu. After the April Fool's Day NSC decisions and later discussions in Washington about future deployment options of US forces, McNamara called for a conference in Hawaii to discuss further actions. The main participants were McNamara and several of his deputies from the Department of Defense; Admiral Sharp, the US Commander, Pacific; General Wheeler, the Chairman, JCS; and Ambassador Taylor and General Westmoreland. The conference began on 20 April in Honolulu.

The most crucial development discussed at the conference was the recent US intelligence on the buildup of PAVN regular forces in the South. Specifically, a defector from the 101st PAVN regiment (around 2000 soldiers) in late March had revealed that his regiment was operating in the central region province of Kontum as one of three regiments in the 325th PAVN division. Subsequent ground operations verified this story. Thus, US intelligence officials, to include MACV's and the CIA, confirmed Westmoreland's suspicions that Hanoi's regular forces had joined the VC in strength in the South and intended to defeat ARVN forces.

As he relates in his memoirs, the MACV commander now thought that the Communist High Command had decided to launch into Mao's third phase of his people's war doctrine. This was the most alarming signal for him. He was now assured that either the US deploy significant combat forces quickly and in strength to counteract this move, or South Vietnam would fall. Moreover, Westy judged that the combined PAVN/PLAF offensive's main attack was in the central region and designed to split South Vietnam in half. This intelligence, in the words of Mark Moyar, "inspired America's military leaders to advocate additional ground deployments...."

According to the documentation in the *Pentagon Papers*, those attending the conference reached a consensus that "the DRV was unlikely to in the next six months and probably would only give up because of VC 'pain' in the South rather than bomb damage in the North." Thus, the "best strategy would be to break the DRV/VC will by effectively denying them victory [in the South] and bringing about negotiations through the enemy's impotence." However, what the *Papers* do not reveal is what exactly did the major conference leaders think would cause the 'enemy's impotence.'

They did discuss and agree upon the concept of creating four brigade-sized enclaves to accept US forces and launch future operations. While Westmoreland was against any enclave strategy for the war, he did not challenge the deployment of forces to coastal enclaves at this point. One reason is that he saw this as a temporary solution for the deployment of forces into the theater. In fact, moreover, the first stage of his strategic concept called for the deployments into secure coastal reception areas – in fact enclaves – so it did not matter at this point. What did matter is that it looked like his request for troops was moving in the right direction and going to get Washington's approval.

At the end of the meetings, all agreed to the deployment of two US Army brigades, three more Marine battalions, and another 18,000 support troops. This reinforcement would increase the total of US forces from 33,000 to 82,000. Moreover, some 'Allied' forces, specifically the South Koreans and Australians, agreed to deploy several battalions in the overall effort to "deny a VC victory." McNamara put on hold further consideration on future deployments of the new US Army airmobile division, an added Korean division, and more Marine battalions pending discussion with the President.

When McNamara returned to Washington, he met with LBJ to discuss the results of the conference. Though during the Hawaii meetings, the JCS members and Admiral Sharp had pushed for a dramatic increase in ROLLING THUNDER, McNamara never brought that to the President. The Secretary did get Johnson's approval for all the force deployments. However, he agreed to deploy these reinforcements slowly to avoid any public or Congressional scrutiny.

The April Honolulu conference was a crucial turning point in the march to war scenario unfolding in early 1965. As the MACV history states, "the 20 April decisions committed the United States to large-scale ground combat in Vietnam. Under them, indeed, Westmoreland obtained as many battalions as he had requested in his March commander's estimate, though not [at this time] the [airmobile] division for the Central Highlands." As the *Pentagon Papers'* analysts commenting on the decisions in Honolulu observed, missing from the conference discussions and decisions was any formal adoption or statement on a specific US military strategy for those forces.

After the conference, Taylor and Westmoreland returned to South Vietnam to gain approval from the RVN government for these American troops. Paramount in the MACV commander's mind was the command and control organization between the ARVN and US forces that was needed. He and Taylor desired a combined command much like what the US had in the Korean War. That sort of arrangement, with the ARVN and American forces under the direction of a combined organization with Westmoreland in overall command – would ensure unity of effort for military operations against the PAVN/PLAF.

By this time the RVN government had evolved into an arrangement between the Premier, now a civilian named Phan Huy Quat, and a military group referred to as the 'Young Turks.' The latter was a collection of powerful military Generals who were tired of the merry go round of governments, and who wanted to bring some government stability to fight the war. Amongst the most powerful of the 'Young Turks' were General Nguyen Van Thieu and Air Marshal Nguyen Cao Ky. Thieu and Ky recognized the dire circumstances that the ARVN faced with the PAVN buildup and the current offensive. As a result, they favored and called for the US troop deployments. The Quat government, under this pressure, agreed.

Thieu and Ky, and consequently the current RVN government, were dead set against a combined command. One factor was that they were unsure just how much power they would lose in such an arrangement. The Americans had not indicated whom they favored for the most critical posts in that command. More important to the Vietnamese generals, was that with American leadership, no matter how many ARVN generals were in the chain of command, the ARVN would once again seem to be an Army prostituting itself to western command. It would undoubtedly have the semblance of - if not the actual - loss of Vietnamese sovereignty.

Westmoreland, in his memoirs, recalls that "several factors other than Vietnamese sensitivity mitigated against a combined command... Most important of all, we were in Vietnam to help the Vietnamese, not to do the job for them, and to enable them to increase and improve their armed forces to the point when they could do the job alone. If we did it for them, how were they to learn? Junior and senior commanders alike learn to assume responsibility only from experience." Besides, he argues, he had the leverage to influence ARVN operations and already had a mechanism to do so – the advisory organization.

The MACV history portrays a different picture. It says that Westmoreland favored a combined allied command that would have placed the ARVN under his operational control (Westmoreland could direct ARVN commanders what to do). It further states, "He believed that, beyond any military benefits, such a command would enhance the Saigon government's stability by bringing politically active South Vietnamese generals under American supervision and restraint." Nevertheless, the history states Westmoreland and Taylor had decided that such an arrangement was "no longer politically feasible or desirable."

Westmoreland believed that he could achieve that through personal relationships and the power of the US aid carrot. It is difficult to assess whether any such formal agreement would have increased Westmoreland's influence over the various South Vietnamese leaders to reform its command structure. However, much was at stake. In complex military situations, especially when the enemy is united in his will to win and the other side is unsure and hesitant of what to do, a unified command is much more effective in obtaining decisive action.

It can never be determined whether such a command would have altered any of the results of the war. However, such an arrangement is what, in part, enabled an efficient combined use of South Korean and US forces in the Korean War. Moreover, the setting up of such a command may have fostered a permanent command that could have survived the later withdrawal of major US forces and may have favored the leaving of a US residual force.

Section 8.3 – Westmoreland's War, 1965-1966

Having reneged on the unified command and control concept but having gotten enough forces to begin operations to counter the enemy offensive, Westmoreland now turned his attention to the enclave versus offensive strategy debate. He was unhappy with the Honolulu conference endorsement of the enclave concept. He recognized, however, that he had no formal proclamation out of Washington, or from his superior commander in Honolulu, detailing a military strategy for his Theater.

With more US forces now approved for deployment to South Vietnam, the circumstances now seemed right to take the initiative and further push for his theater strategic views. Therefore, to gain formal recognition of his strategic concept, on 8 May, he sent a "Concept of Operations by US/Allied Ground Combat Forces in support of the Republic of Vietnam Armed Forces (RVNAF)" to the Commander, Pacific Command, the Chairman, JCS and the Secretary of Defense.

Concepts for Defeating the North's Aggression

According to Westmoreland in his memoirs, and as detailed in the *Pentagon Papers*, that strategic concept consisted of three main stages of operations that sought to "take the war to the enemy." In Stage I, US forces would focus on the security of their base areas. These areas would be centered on ports and airfields that they would deploy to and assemble in. For the most part, these base areas and support facilities corresponded to the same areas considered in the enclave concept. In Stage II, US and Allied Forces would conduct "deep patrolling and offensive operations" in coordination with the [Republic of Vietnam Armed Forces]. These would be in planned and coordinated "Tactical Areas of Responsibilities" (TAORs) assigned to each force unit.

Stage III was, in the wording of the concept paper, the "Search and Destroy" stage. It consisted of four phases. In the first phase, forces would continue to improve their base areas, which he continued to call coastal enclaves. In the second phase, those forces would conduct actions in support of ARVN operations. As Westy explained, "units were to engage in offensive operations and deep patrolling in cooperation with the ARVN." For the third phase, US forces would then secure inland bases and areas for further operations against the PAVN/PLAF forces and their bases. The implied task for this phase was that the US and other Allied Forces would strike at the enemy's main forces and bases while ARVN forces secured the coastal population areas.

This 8 May message was the first mentioning of the phrase 'Search and Destroy.' Moreover, at this point, there were no timelines associated with the overall stages or phases. While there was no definitive schedule, the concept envisioned the stages progressing one after another with some overlap. The most important aspects of this concept were that it was offensive and envisioned the future conduct of operations away from the coastal base areas or enclaves.

The MACV history observations are useful on where this theater strategy stood at the beginning of May 1965. "Westmoreland's 8 May concept of operations laid out how individual units were to go about entering the fight, but it hardly constituted a plan of conduct for the war. Instead, it treated the introduction of ground combat units as simply an extension of American advice and assistance to the South Vietnamese armed forces. The troops would function, Westmoreland said, in a logical extension and expansion of [the] role already performed by a wide range of US units and forces throughout RVN."

The history continues with an assessment of the anticipated follow-on operations of Westmoreland's strategic concept. It explains that "this formula, adequate for the limited forces thus far committed, would wear thin as American numbers and firepower overwhelmed those of the army they were supporting. Until the beginning of June, it seemed as if the Johnson administration would have time to work out these problems during a continued gradual introduction of American forces. Time, however, was about to run out."

Whatever its intent or however it served at this time as a strategy for US forces, it is not entirely clear who saw, commented on, recognized the importance of, or approved Westmoreland's concept in Washington. The General said in his memoirs, "I assumed in the absence of any word to the contrary that Washington... approved." Again, there is currently no definitive evidence that there was any proper staffing or discussion of Westmoreland's 8 May message among the President or his senior civilian advisors.

Soon after its dispatch, several significant developments may have distracted Washington's decision makers from any formal or detailed consideration of Westmoreland's future concept of operations or any immediate follow-up query by MACV. The first, and most likely interruption, was a crisis over the Dominican Republic.

There a coup and civil conflict had occurred that, in LBJ's mind, might result in the establishment of another Communist Cuba in the Caribbean. In reaction, LBJ had decided to intervene with American troops. Marines started to land there on 16 May to establish order. Apparently, the President and his advisors during the entire month of May paid a lot of their attention to this crisis.

Meanwhile, as mentioned in Chapter 3, the Press and Congress were bombarding the Johnson Administration with questions about the future of US military operations in South Vietnam. Inciting Congressional concerns was the fact that the Administration had just sent a supplemental budget request to fund the forces called for in the Honolulu Conference. LBJ and his cabinet, besides dealing with the Dominican crisis, thus had their hands full attempting to downplay the new deployments and defending its request, all of which many in the Press and Congress rightly thought represented a notable change in the American role in the war.

Furthermore, McNamara may have just ignored Westmoreland's summary of his strategic approach and his concept of operations. As we have already seen in Chapter 3, in July and later in November of 1965, the Secretary would ignore strategies proposed by General Goodpaster and then Wheeler. He just did not pay attention to these military strategies for Vietnam; they did not matter to him as much as his focus on numbers of troops and their costs.

A week after Westmoreland sent his 8 May message to Washington, in the words of Mark Moyar, the communist forces launched an offensive which "exceeded all previous Communist offensives in strength and ambition. The North Vietnamese leadership sought to kill South Vietnamese regulars at such a pace that the South Vietnamese Army's total combat losses for the year would reach a level of between 30,000 and 40,000, which they predicted would be high enough to allow Communist forces to capture Saigon and the other cities before the Americans could stop them". As discussed in the previous chapter, Le Duan had launched the main phase of his general offensive to defeat the South before the US military could do anything about it.

As summarized in the MACV history, "Between mid-May and mid-June, Viet Cong troops in at least regimental strength fought three sustained battles with government regulars—at Song Be and Dong Xoai north of Saigon in III Corps and Ba Gia in southern I Corps. In each, the enemy attacked district towns, or small ARVN units to draw out relief forces and then slaughtered the reinforcements piecemeal as they arrived."

The history further explains, "In the engagement at Dong Xoai, the worst government defeat of the three, several Viet Cong battalions stormed a South Vietnamese Special Forces camp and district town, then stayed in the vicinity for five days to maul a succession of South Vietnamese reinforcement battalions, including one from the elite airborne. Over 400 government soldiers died before the enemy broke contact and withdrew, and the toll of missing men and lost equipment was high."

The MACV document concludes that "In all these fights, the Viet Cong showed continued improvement in tactical proficiency and weaponry, as well as determination to destroy government forces in prolonged combat, even at the cost of heavy casualties to themselves. South Vietnamese commanders, by contrast, became ever more defensive minded. In some regions, notably II Corps, they became hesitant to reinforce posts under attack or simply gave up exposed positions, including half a dozen district headquarters."

Indeed, it was in the South Vietnamese II Corps area that most of the infiltrated PAVN main forces were concentrating. That Corps area encompassed most of the central highland region of South Vietnam. As Mark Moyar relates, "The Highlands offered the Communists critical advantages, both as bases and as operational areas. Hanoi could supply the highlands relatively easily, via the Ho Chi Minh Trail, because of their proximity to Laos and North Vietnam."

Moreover, the monsoon season in this region started in mid-May and would last until September. This afforded the communist main forces in the area considerable relief from any accurate airpower strikes. It also would inhibit US Army airmobile operations and the use of supporting helicopter gunships.

As we had discussed in the previous chapter, the PAVN and PLAF generals had made their estimates on how to confront the American forces. They were not only ready but now eager to engage them. Their main PAVN forces were to inflict significant casualties to affect the will of the American people's support for the US 'Limited War.' At the same time, the PLAF main troops, supported by their local units and guerrillas were to confront and defeat the ARVN forces to topple its government.

General Westmoreland had skillfully expected the developments that were unfolding as June approached. He had been working on a plan that would stem the tide if he could only get the forces that he deemed necessary to do that, and approval of their employment as he saw fit – that is in offensive operations that would seek out and destroy the enemy main elements near their base camp areas. Now, with the enemy offensive in full swing, he had to act to get approval for further reinforcements, and obtain at least tacit approval on how to use them.

The "Bombshell": Westmoreland's 44 Battalion Request

Both Taylor and Westmoreland were now seriously alarmed over the ever-growing communist successes against ARVN forces. On 5 June, the Ambassador sent a message to Washington giving a general assessment of the current political-military situation. He outlined the continued political infighting amongst the South Vietnamese politicians and military, the deterioration of the ARVN, and the offensive operations of the communists. He assessed that the communists seemed to be 'winning the war.' He emphasized, "the cumulative psychological impact could lead to a collapse in ARVN's will to continue to fight."

Meanwhile, General Wheeler, also concerned over the deteriorating situation, cabled Westmoreland. He asked about his views on some of the added deployments discussed at the Honolulu Conference, but not yet approved for deployment. Concerned about the PAVN build up, the notable PLAF victories, and the ARVN deterioration in both capability and morale, Westmoreland responded on 7 June through Admiral Sharp.

As described in the *Pentagon Papers*, the message pointed to the increasing use of enemy large unit operations. Westmoreland emphasized that "In pressing their campaign, the Viet Cong are capable of mounting regimental-size operations in all four ARVN Corps areas, and at least battalion-sized attacks in virtually all provinces." Moreover, the "DRV will commit whatever forces it deems necessary to tip the balance and that the GVN cannot stand up successfully to this kind of pressure without reinforcement."

To counter this increase in PAVN regular forces he concluded, "In order to cope with the situation outlined above, I see no course of action open to us except to reinforce our efforts in SVN with additional US or Third Country forces as rapidly as is practical during the critical weeks ahead. Additionally, studies must continue, and plans developed to deploy even greater forces, if and when required, to attain our objectives or counter enemy initiatives..."

He continued, "Although they have not yet engaged the enemy in strength, I am convinced that U.S. troops with their energy, mobility, and firepower can successfully take the fight to the VC. The basic purpose of the additional deployments recommended below is to give us a substantial and hard-hitting offensive capability on the ground to convince the VC that they cannot win...."

In all, Westmoreland's message asked for some additional forty-four battalions be deployed to South Vietnam. Hence, policy-makers in Washington referred to this cable as the '44 battalion request'. This was more troops than the MACV commander had requested in Honolulu, but it reflected his previous caveats that 'US reinforcements may have to be greater as the enemy commits more forces to battle, and as the situation continues to deteriorate.' In short, it was not an unreasonable request for troops given the unfolding situation and the consistent warnings that had proceeded it.

As described in Chapter 3, this is the message that Secretary McNamara called a 'bombshell' in his memoirs. As he also noted, "of the thousands of cables I received during my seven years in the Defense Department, this one disturbed me the most." That was because there was now no doubt that the LBJ Administration must commit itself to taking over the ground war in South Vietnam or lose Vietnam. Moreover, President Johnson, despite all his despair over the 'bitch of a war in Vietnam,' was not willing to lose the war in the summer of 1965.

As further related in Chapter 3, Westmoreland eventually got the commitment he was looking for. However, what is most disturbing about the approval is that McNamara claimed in his memoirs that Westmoreland did not describe how these forces were to be used, or what strategy the MACV commander would use to pursue the ground war. Apparently, either he had not seen any of the

MACV commander's estimates outlining his proposed use of these forces or had not paid much attention to them. The LBJ Administration thus went to war not knowing how it was going to wage it.

Afterward, the President did ask whether the force he approved was enough to win. McNamara queried the Chairman, JCS whether the new 44 battalion reinforcement would be "enough to convince the VC/DRV that they could not win." As related in Chapter 3, the result was the Goodpaster study that the Washington leaders subsequently dismissed or ignored.

The JCS further met and debated the impact of this request on the overall US global force posture rather than how the forces were going to be used or whether they were enough. The Chiefs also discussed the need for a reserve call-up to fulfill the numbers that the theater commander said he needed.

The later discussions in Washington on Westmoreland's request, already discussed in detail in Chapter 3, were many and contradictory. Recall that Defense Department advisors, to include McNamara, were saying that the war had become a matter of 'prestige' and that all the US had to do was show resolve. If that failed, they surmised, the Administration could withdraw and declare, like a good doctor, it had done its best, but the disease was incurable.

Meanwhile, the JCS continued to focus on a bombing campaign that they wanted intensified. If unleashed, the Air Force and Navy were predicting that the North could be brought to the negotiating table. However, McNamara and LBJ would not approve an all-out bombing campaign. They wanted to control it. At the same time, the President had indicated and would continue to advocate, that he wanted to kill more VC to end the war.

Amidst all this confusion, contradiction, and vague guidance, the only clear statement of political aims for Westmoreland's use remained the NSAMs that had outlined US intent to defend South Victnam from the communists. Those objectives are the ones that the MACV commander focused on in his theater strategic concept. Had Westmoreland been present or privy to the Washington deliberations, he would probably have been confused as to the real intent of the Administration toward South Vietnam's survival.

Because of the Washington meetings, there was a flurry of messages back and forth between Generals Wheeler and Westmoreland. Most of them intended to explain the MACV commander's reinforcement needs in more detail. In some frustration over these cables and their apparent underlying call for a quick and straightforward solution to the military situation in Vietnam, Westmoreland emphasized, "We are in for the long pull. The struggle has become a war of attrition. Short of [a] decision to introduce nuclear weapons against sources and channels of enemy power, I see no likelihood of achieving a quick, favorable end to the war."

To his credit, Westmoreland sought to emphasize his assessment that US military operations would take considerable time to have an effect. Thus, he further declared to Wheeler, "We are deluding ourselves if we feel some novel arrangement is going to get quick results. We must think in terms of an extended conflict; be prepared to support a greatly increased effort; give the commander on the scene the troops that he requires and the authority to deploy these troops in accordance with his best judgment. We need more troops, and we need them quickly."

Senior civilian leaders in Washington, not knowledgeable of military affairs and strategies and confronted with a situation demanding action, did what they do best - they called for a meeting.

Thus, Secretary McNamara called for a meeting in Saigon to discuss the added deployments and their use. The Secretary also wanted to discuss what forces may be needed during the next year to "prove to the VC/DRV that they cannot win in South Vietnam." What the Secretary meant by win, at this time, was not clearly explained to Westmoreland. It is doubtful that McNamara, or any of his Whiz Kids, could explain what win meant in useful military terms anyway.

US Theater of War Strategy: Attrition

General Westmoreland assumed win meant to defeat the main NVA/VC forces that threatened to defeat the ARVN, provide the necessary security to ensure a stable and functioning RVN Government, and reestablish RVN hold over the countryside. These were military objectives he had developed to guide his action. They matched the political ones in the current government NSAM on Vietnam. The MACV commander had referred to them as the political goals for his concept of operations in his 8 May and 7 June messages to Washington. These are the same two messages that McNamara and his Whiz Kids seem to have ignored.

McNamara arrived in Saigon on 16 July with General Wheeler and Ambassador Taylor's replacement, Henry Cabot Lodge – the same Ambassador who had engineered the removal of Diem. One of the first meetings in their five-day visit was with the newest members of the Government, Generals and Chief of State Thieu and Premier Ky.

These two military men had arranged for the abdication of the earlier civilian government. They met dressed in their military uniforms and accompanied by their military aides. President Thieu presented his views on the situation and agreed with the need for Westmoreland's troop reinforcements. They also discussed their plans for their new government.

Afterward, Westmoreland's operations deputy, General DePuy, presented a briefing to McNamara on MACV's concept for the '44 battalion request.' The concept he presented was somewhat different from the one in Westmoreland's earlier estimates. As the MACV history explains, "DePuy laid out MACV's force requirements in two phases, each of which denoted a stage in the progress of the military campaign as well as a reinforcement increment. In Phase I, the 44-battalion reinforcement would enable the allies to stem the tide that until then had been running against them. This meant holding the Viet Cong offensive during the rest of the year and preventing a South Vietnamese political or military collapse."

The history continues, "In Phase II, which should begin early in 1966, the second contingent of American reinforcements would give the allies the strength to turn the tide by attacking enemy main forces and base areas while simultaneously resuming the pacification of economically and politically important regions. This phase would require an estimated 24 additional American maneuver and 17 combat support battalions with helicopter and logistic units and 9 Air Force squadrons. "

Westmoreland elaborates on his thinking on these phases in his memoirs, *A Soldier Reports*. He explains that in his July meeting with McNamara, "I told him that I thought twenty-four more battalions [in 1966] in addition to the forty-four under consideration, plus more combat support and logistical troops, would put us in a position to begin the 'win phase' of our strategy. That meant about 175,000 American troops at the start, followed by about 100,000. Yet I warned that VC and North Vietnamese actions well might alter the figures..."

He further explains, "I based my reckoning on a concept of operations to be executed in three general phases...." These were: "Commit those American and Allied forces necessary to 'halt the losing trend' by the end of 1965 [Phase One]. 'During the first half of 1966', take the offensive with the American and Allied forces in 'high priority areas' to destroy enemy forces and reinstitute pacification programs [Phase Two]. If the enemy persisted, he might be defeated, and his forces and base areas destroyed during a period of a year and a half following Phase II."

The MACV commander added that the Secretary endorsed the forces and concepts. They also discussed the necessity of a temporary call-up of the National Guard and Reserves. Westmoreland strangely considered that 'premature' in that without a Congressional authorization for mobilization, such a call-up would only be temporary.

For some reason, he did not recognize how critical a call-up of reserves meant for his deploying forces. Evidently, no one of the Joint Chiefs – even Army Chief Harold Johnson - cared to remind him of that criticality. A few days into the meeting all this discussion seemed overtaken by events. The President gave his approval in principle of the 'forty-four battalion' reinforcement but did not authorize any call-up or mobilization.

This would be the first of many instances that Westmoreland, Wheeler, the Service Chiefs, McNamara, the President, and other advisors discussed the need for some call-up of the reserves or a more significant mobilization to support troop levels and the conduct of the war in Vietnam. This chapter and the next will focus on Westmoreland's views and part in that debate.

From the onset, the MACV commander played a curiously ambiguous role. Now - in mid-July 1965 just as the major deployment of US forces was to begin - he did not see the need for it. He says in his memoirs that he thought this issue was under the purview of those in Washington. His view at this time, he further states, was that there was no need to place the nation on a war footing. What he did not seem to realize was that even this early in the reinforcement flow not calling up the reserves would have an immediate adverse impact on his capabilities to achieve his concept of operations.

Despite his shortsightedness on the reserves issue - because of the President's approval of the 44 Battalions and McNamara's apparent agreement with his general concept for those forces - Westmoreland now thought he had the authority to maneuver forces as he saw fit. He also believed that this all meant an end to the enclave concept that some had advocated. As he emphasizes in his memoirs, "The restrictive enclave strategy with which I had disagreed from the first was finally rejected... I was convinced my plan was sound."

The Commander of the war in South Vietnam still experienced, however, what he saw as interference or reluctance in his authorities to execute his offensive concept. There were two specific instances he describes in his memoirs. One was with Admiral Sharp, his commander in Hawaii. As American reinforcements began to arrive in the late summer and early fall of 1965, Sharp tried to influence Westmoreland to use caution in their employment inland away from the coastal assembly areas. Sharp's concern was the ability to logistically support forces moved inland at some distances away from their support bases. The Admiral was also concerned, as Westmoreland recounts in *A Soldier Reports* and as Sharp confirms in his *Strategy for Defeat*, that forces employed inland could be subject to enemy ambushes such as that occurred to the French in their war, or, even worse, to some situation reminiscent of Bien Dien Phu.

The second instant surrounded the employment of Marine units in the Northern I Corps region. As Westmoreland relates, both the Commandant of Marines, General Wallace Greene, and the

Commander of the III Marine Amphibious Force in I Corps, General Lewis Walt, still favored their versions of the enclave strategy. The MACV commander thought the Marines were too wedded to think "in terms of beachheads."

Both Greene and Walt wanted to use Marine forces more defensively to protect the populous coastal regions, with occasional counter strikes against main NVA/VC forces that could threaten the pacification efforts along the populous coastal villages, hamlets, and cities. It appears from his memoirs, that General Walt's reasons were operationally motivated. At this time, he did not feel that stemming the tide could be accomplished with going after, rather than defending, the Vietnamese Armed Forces and its populace. On the other hand, from his comments in his *Papers*, General Greene seemed more concerned that his Marines obtain a mission more in tune with what he saw as the Marine Corps roles and missions debate in Washington.

Westmoreland, in explaining his rejection of these cautions and opposing arguments, states, "Although a commander must observe caution, he wins no battles by sitting back waiting for the enemy to come to him." He further argues that his strategy and its concept of operations considered the Pacific Commander and Marine Corps concerns. As he explains, in his first phase he already envisioned that most forces would be employed "to protect developing logistical bases, although some might have to be committed from time to time as 'fire brigades' whenever the enemy's big units posed a threat...." The implication is that he did not intend to employ forces until they could be supported, and that he realized his initial employments would have to fight closer to the coastal areas to prevent an ARVN defeat.

Later, Westmoreland, to his benefit, would continue to send cables to General Walt supporting his desires to protect the populated coastal regions, but reminding him that his principal object was the destruction of the enemy's main forces that threaten the population and any security that can be provided. Walt would respond that he understood that objective, but that he needed to be sure that he could find the enemy's main forces before committing his marine units to searching and destroying them.

Westmoreland further explained to the III Amphibious Corps commander, as well as all his principal subordinate commanders and Admiral Sharp, that he envisioned most US forces would engage the enemy's main forces while the ARVN protects the population based on his assessment of US and ARVN capabilities. As he explains in his memoirs, the MACV commander thought that "American mobility, firepower, and flexible logistical support more than balance the equation" of the enemy force knowledge of the terrain and closeness to their own supply lines if attacked inland. Thus, the risks the Sharp was concerned with would be alleviated in this first phase."

The General then explains that his offensive concept did not ignore the protection of the coastal population centers nor the pacification that the Marines were concerned about. Indeed, in his strategy, this was the focus of the ARVN forces who - "by language, culture, and local knowledge" - were better suited for that mission. Moreover, Westmoreland clarifies that throughout his phases, he expected that wherever American forces operated, they would be involved in protecting the people and pacification operations.

Clearly, Westmoreland's concept, as he elaborates more fully in his chapter entitled "Evolution of Strategy," reflects his belief that the key to winning the war in the South was by focusing on offensive operations. Indeed, the critical phase of his military strategy was Phase II. He emphasizes that it would be during this phase that, "we were to gain the initiative, penetrate and whenever possible eliminate the enemy's base camps and sanctuaries."

The MACV commander further reasoned that "so long as the Communists were free to emerge from those hideouts to terrorize the people, recruit and impress conscripts, glean food, levy taxes, and attack government troops and installations, then to retire with impunity back into their sanctuaries, there was little hope of defeating the insurgency. Invading the sanctuaries also might bring the elusive enemy to battle, affording an opportunity to destroy his main forces." This critical second phase would also naturally lead, if necessary, to a third and final phase when "sustained ground combat and mop up" would occur to destroy them or "at least push them across the frontiers where we could try to contain them."

In explaining the rationale for his strategy, Westmoreland argues that he had to engage the enemy big units because you ignored them at your peril. "They had to be pounded with artillery and bombs and eventually brought to battle on the ground if they were not forever to remain a threat." He contends that this 'war of attrition' was dictated by political decisions and that there was no other alternative given the restrictions against a ground invasion of North Vietnam and "attacking the enemy inside Laos and Cambodia, which, was beyond my means for months, even years." Later, as we will see, he will revisit the idea of attacking the enemy in Laos.

In sum, in General Westmoreland's view, it appears that the urgency of executing this offensive strategy was keyed to the enemy situation at the time and his own capabilities. As he was deriving his ideas in early 1965, it was clear to him that "the enemy clearly was moving into the third phase of revolutionary warfare, committing regiments and subsequently divisions to seize and retain territory and to destroy the government's troops and eliminate all vestiges of government control." Thus, from the field commander's view, there would be no need for a strategy at all if something was not done quickly to 'stem the tide.'

Theater Strategy Phase I: Stemming the Tide - US Operations and Tactics from 1965 to 1966

Following the conferences in Honolulu and Saigon and LBJ's July decision for more reinforcements, Westmoreland further refined his operational concepts for each phase of his theater war strategy. In his strategic phase one, which he alternately called his 'halt the losing trend' or 'stemming the tide' phase, he wanted to set up secure base areas from which he could begin offensive operations against the enemy's main force units.

These initial base areas were essential for follow-on operations. They would be secure sites to receive forces and their necessary equipment and supplies. After putting these in place, Westmoreland and his planners envisioned that American forces would then be able to build up the necessary logistics to support and sustain themselves for further operations beyond these original coastal sites. Finally, the early bases would also offer training areas in which American troops could acclimate and prepare for later offensive operations.

Upon completing these essential tasks, Westmoreland intended moving US forces inland to build tactical bases further into South Vietnam and engaging the enemy main force units in spoiling attacks. These preliminary attacks would keep the main enemy units from further damaging the ARVN units and begin to restore the protection of the densely populated cities and coastal areas. Throughout 1965 and later, Westmoreland issued 'letters of instruction' and directives to his subordinates to communicate his intent and operational ideas.

As mentioned, the first forces to deploy and set up bases were the Marines in the northern ARVN I Corps. Of course, the Marines had already deployed a battalion-size force to Da Nang in March 1965. The Presidential decisions in April and June expanded this force to include, by the summer, a reinforced brigade, and its parent Division headquarters – the 3rd Marine Division from Okinawa, Japan. The 3rd Marine Division had fought at Iwo Jima, and some of its current leaders were veterans of that battle. Many of its marines, especially non-commissioned officers, were also Korean War veterans.

Meanwhile, Westmoreland also sent incoming logistical units to areas for follow-on forces. For example, in June, he sent Army engineer units from Saigon to the Cam Ranh Bay area to begin the building of an extensive port and airfield complex there. He also sent construction units to the Qui Non coastal area. Both bases were intended for follow-on reinforcements to the ARVN II Corps area for later operations against the NVA main force build up in that region.

As the Army's official history *Stemming the Tide* explains, Westmoreland was taking significant risks in the first employment of his forces in South Vietnam. First, he had decided to deploy an equal number of combat and logistics forces at the same time. Typically, US Army combat forces deploying overseas are preceded by their support forces, which set up the facilities and stockpile supplies for the combat unit subsequent employment into combat. Second, and related to the first, he was employing combat forces into battle before their usual supplies were in place. This decision puts those units at risk if they got engaged in sustained battles. For example, the some of the first Army units went into battle with only a day's supply of ammunition.

Westmoreland's deployment and use of the Marines in the I Corps area was less of a risk, especially considering his logistics problem. First, the Marines had their own logistical support over the shore from Navy ships in the South China Sea. Thus, they did not need a mature, land-based logistical facility. The ships that off-loaded them, moreover, had supplies that could support them for over thirty days in combat operations. The Marines also had their own tactical air support. Thus, for his phase one approach, he could depend upon the Marines providing the necessary means to secure a 'beachhead' for follow-on operations and to conduct limited offensive operations inland.

Furthermore, the Marine Corps organization gave him a headquarters to receive follow-on forces and to command and control other units in the ARVN I Corps area of operations. This was because a Marine Corps division had some augmentation to serve as a higher headquarters for other Marine divisions. Moreover, the Third Marine Division commander, General Lewis Walt – a highly decorated World War Two and Korean War veteran – was more than capable of commanding larger forces.

The Marine Corps capability explained above is precisely what Westmoreland needed for the northern South Vietnam area. This is because it was a region that North Vietnam threatened continuously by attacks across the DMZ separating the North from the South. It was also the region of South Vietnam closest to the Ho Chi Minh Trail complex. Westmoreland, of course, realized that he would need more than a division to defend against conventional attacks across the DMZ and subdue the insurgency in the region. As we will later see this area would become a magnet for forces, both friendly and enemy, almost as much as the critical Saigon area.

The first employment of the Marines around and out of the initial base area at Da Nang offered a microcosmic experience of what many US forces would later have in the war. First, according to the *Marine Corps History of the Vietnam War*, while the Marine forces had little difficulty in establishing themselves in their secure area, they soon had difficulty adjusting to working with the ARVN forces stationed there.

The ARVN Corps commander - a General by the name of Nguyen Chanh Thi - was a politically ambitious and powerful officer. He resisted American encroachment upon his rule of his Corps area. Known as 'Warlord of the North' General Thi would have to approve any movement of Marine forces in the region. Unfortunately, the War Lord would continuously resist or delay American attempts to expand their defensive perimeter or come to the aid of ARVN forces.

Also, by Westmoreland's concept of command and control between ARVN and American forces, the senior US commander - in this case, the Commander of the US Marines around Da Nang - was also an advisor who would cooperate on operations with the ARVN. Thus, General Walt became an advisor as well as commander. His relationship with the haughty Thi did not lend to effective ARVN and American force cooperation. Such would be the case for other senior US officers from time to time throughout the war.

Because the Marines were the first combat ground forces to employ to Vietnam, their first experiences showed the complications of operations they and other American forces would face throughout the war. For example, early patrol operations demonstrated the difficulty of finding and fixing the enemy in an area of dense civilian populations in which the VC tried to hide. Commanders had to put in place, and Marines had to follow, strict rules of engagement to try to avoid innocent civilian casualties.

Pacification operations further showed the difficulty in dealing with South Vietnamese officials who did not want to cooperate, either out of fear or indifference or both. Equally as frustrating were the difficulties of using fire support in enemy engagements when protection of the civilians in the area was necessary. All of this was compounded by the fact that most American units had little time, in the beginning, to train in such conditions they now faced.

An operational example of all of this was an incident involving the Marine forces early in this phase of the war - made famous on American TV - and described in *the US Marines in Vietnam: Volume II, The Landing and the Buildup, 1965*. By the end of July 1965, the Marines had built up to a full division in and around the Da Nang area. Periodically, the VC launched mortar rounds and rockets into their positions surrounding the airfield there. When they had General Thi's authorization, frustrated Marines patrolled outside of their locations trying to find and destroy VC positions that had attacked them.

Many of these patrolling operations included pacification actions, which General Walt had initiated as part of his counterinsurgency operations. The commander of a battalion of Marines launched such an operation at the end of July against a series of small villages near the Cau Do River southwest of Da Nang. One such village was called Cam Ne. American intelligence had shown it was a well-known VC stronghold. In fact, from this village VC elements had fired upon earlier Marine patrols in the area.

On 3 August, accompanied by CBS news correspondent Morley Safer, a company of Marines moved to Cam Ne to clear it of VC forces. In the initial movement toward the village, the Marines took fire, wounding one Marine. As they continued forward, the VC withdrew. However, the Marines encountered booby traps. According to the Marine Corps history, "The entire Cam Ne complex favored the enemy hit-and-run methods. The innocent-looking collection of crude structures harbored punji sticks, spider holes, interconnecting tunnels between houses, and an uncooperative civilian population. The Marines would search one hut, only to have a VC sniper turn up behind them, shoot, and disappear. "

As the arduous task to clear the VC continued, troops from one of the platoons began to burn the huts from which they had received fire. As the Marines engaged the other VC, many of the enemy deliberately took refuge among the unarmed civilians, continuing to fire on the Marines. As the official history notes, "Cam Ne forcibly brought to the attention of the American command both the political and military dilemmas inherent in the Vietnam War where the enemy could and did use the civilian population as a shield. Among the casualties at Cam Ne were a dead 10-year-old Vietnamese boy and four wounded villagers, who were caught in the crossfire between the Viet Cong and the
Marines."

The History goes on to explain, "The nastiness of the village war was dramatized for millions of Americans on their television screens. A CBS television crew had gone with the Marine company into Cam Ne, and American viewers saw a Marine casually set a hut on fire with his cigarette lighter while an old woman pleaded for the preservation of her home. The CBS film version of the action showed the Marines meeting little or no resistance, and indeed, Morley Safer, the CBS reporter narrating the film, bluntly said that 'If there were Viet Cong in the hamlets they were long gone.'" Such was the precursor of a situation that would repeat itself many times for both Marine and Army forces throughout the war.

As the buildup and Phase I operations continued in the northern region of South Vietnam, US forces began to arrive and conduct training exercises and patrols in other areas. In the ARVN III Corps region, which encompassed Saigon and its built up populated environs, the 173rd Airborne Brigade, also form Okinawa, had begun arriving in early May.

The first elements of this airborne brigade landed at Bien Hoa Air Base some twenty kilometers northeast of Saigon. The entire organization minus one battalion, numbering almost 2000 soldiers, completed its move by mid-May. Westmoreland assigned it to protect the airbase and to serve as the quick reaction force he had envisioned to reinforce the ARVN divisions in the area or to reinforce arriving US forces if necessary.

The III Corps area was the top priority for American deploying forces in these preliminary stages. It stayed so for the duration of the war. The region would have some of the largest and most contested battles. A significant reason is that the territory around the South Vietnamese capital had the largest NVA/PLAF base areas in the South.

For example, just north of the city was a place called the Iron Triangle – it had been a famous base area of the Vietminh during the First Indochina War. It encompassed a series of hamlets and villages notoriously known as sympathetic to the communist cause. It also had the famous 'tunnels of Chu Chi'- a complex of underground passageways some hundreds of miles that ran all the way to the Cambodian border in some areas.

Further northwest and east of the triangle, were the equally as famous War Zones C and D. These areas had also been traditional Viet-Minh bases in their fight against the French. Now they were the main bases for two PLAF main force divisions, numbering a little over ten thousand main force VC soldiers.

War Zone C was astride of the Cambodian border and contained, from time to time, the COSVN headquarters and the North Vietnamese B2 Front headquarters. The enemy units there in 1965 were to defeat the three ARVN divisions protecting the capital, force the surrender or the flight of the RVN government, and ultimately seize Saigon before US units could have an effect.

Now an American brigade was in the vicinity to help the ARVN prevent that from happening. Of course, one brigade numbering about two-thousand soldiers would not be enough. Westmoreland, in his 44-battalion reinforcement concept, also hoped to deploy there an entire US division - the 1st Infantry 'Big Red One' - from the states by the latter part of 1965. After that, the MACV commander planned to deploy several American separate infantry brigades to spoil any significant communist offensives further.

As he had mentioned in several of his messages in early 1965, General Westmoreland continued to be concerned about the NVA main force build up in the highland region as well. This corresponded to the ARVN II Corps area. MACV thought that the increase in PAVN forces in regimental and division strength there was intended to strike from their bases along the Cambodian or Laotian borders eastwards along highway 15 toward the coast. That would cut South Vietnam in half and prevent the road bound ARVN from moving forces between the southern and northern provinces.

By mid-June, as Washington was debating Westmoreland's 7 June 'bombshell' message, the 1st Brigade of the 101st Airborne Division was ready to deploy into the theater. The MACV commander directed its leader, Colonel James Timothy, a decorated World War Two veteran, to deploy to the Cam Ranh Bay port and airfield complex, which was still under construction.

At first, the brigade, like other US forces coming into theater, would protect its bases and gradually patrol outward while preparing its soldiers for follow-on operations. The brigade closed at Cam Ranh at the end of July. Its deployment followed the pattern of other US forces already in country - most of its personnel and light equipment deployed via aircraft, while its heavy equipment went by sealift.

By the end of July, as LBJ was announcing the deployment of more combat forces to Vietnam to the American public, Westmoreland now had American forces in each of the three regions profoundly threatened by the summer PAVN/PLAF offensive underway. He had almost an entire Marine Division in I Corps, operating out of Da Nang. He had the 173rd Airborne Brigade in III Corps, operating out of Bien Hoa. Moreover, the 1st Brigade of the 101st Airborne Division was setting up a base near Cam Ranh Bay.

These forces were light and mobile; but well-armed, equipped, and trained. Many of its leaders - officers at the Division, Brigade, and Battalion level, and senior noncommissioned officers of the Company and even Platoon level - were combat veterans of either World War Two or Korea or both. The organizations' soldiers and marines were ready to engage the enemy.

For the first four months of their deployment to South Vietnam, American forces met light contact. Much of that was with local VC elements. Concentrating on destroying the ARVN, the PAVN/PLAF main forces either avoided or were not yet able to make significant contact with the Americans. By August this began to change.

As explained in Chapter 7, the Communist High Command knew it needed its main forces to challenge the Americans. They understood that they were up against a modern, well-trained opponent who had vast capabilities in mobility and firepower that neither the French nor ARVN had. They had to find out how to cope with those capabilities. They reasoned that this was mainly necessary if there were to be a prolonged war with the US. As mentioned, General Thanh, the commander of communist forces in the South, ordered his forces to seek battle to figure out how to confront the Americans and to 'bloody' them.

The continued expansion of the American base areas and the patrolling from them offered the circumstances for confrontation. In the Da Nang area, the Marines had expanded the most. By August they had also established 'enclaves' or beachheads near Chu Lai to the south of Da Nang and Phu Bai to the north.

Marines were now patrolling some six hundred square miles of territory around these and the Da Nang base. At Chu Lai, in mid-August, a VC deserter indicated that the 1st PLAF Regiment had occupied a series of hamlets 15 kilometers to the south near a place called the Van Tuong Peninsula. The 7th Marine Regiment planned a two-battalion assault to surround the VC and destroy it.

The resulting action, dubbed OPERATION STARLITE, consisted of an overland, amphibious, and helicopter assault to surround and destroy the suspected VC force. It resulted in the first major battle of the American and communist main forces.

According to the Marine Corps history, the air, sea, and land assault caught the VC by surprise. The maneuver trapped at least a battalion of the 1st PLAF regiment. As their history of the war recounts, "The Marines had killed 614 VC, by body count, taken 9 prisoners, held 42 suspects, and collected 109 assorted weapons, at the cost of 45 Marines dead and 203 wounded."

The official Marine Corps history also states that the Marine commanders learned key lessons from this fight. They realized that they had to use a variety of methods to corner the VC; such as moving by multiple means from several directions to try to encircle the enemy before he could escape. They also grasped that the use of firepower – artillery, helicopter gunships, naval gunfire, and close air support – was fundamental in defeating the enemy with minimal friendly casualties.

The most famous of the early battles between American and main NVA forces occurred in the Ia Drang Valley in the central highlands in November 1965. It involved the Army's first, and then only, Airmobile organization – the 1st Cavalry Division.

The US Army had specifically organized and trained this division to conduct operations against an enemy and in an environment much like Vietnam. Its new aviation organizations - made up primarily of the UH-1 'Huey' troop lift helicopters and gunships - could maneuver and insert forces over long distances, into widely dispersed locations, and in terrain that would be difficult to move forces by land routes. Aviation units had trained with their combat infantry and artillery organizations in such operations at Fort Benning, Georgia before their deployment.

As related in Chapter 6, the senior communist military leaders thought the Central Highlands would be an ideal first 'killing ground' for its main forces to engage the Americans. They felt that the terrain and weather would favor their PAVN regular forces, which had been infiltrating the region using the Ho Chi Minh trail to bases astride the South Vietnamese border areas.

Indeed, according to Warren Wilkins' book, *Grab Their Belts to Fight Them: The Viet Cong's Big-Unit War Against the US, 1965-1966*, the commander of the three NVA regiments that had just arrived in the South had made their base in the Chu Pong mountains astride the Cambodian border. They were eager to fight the Americans. They devised in September 1965 a plan to lure them into a fight.

That commander, General Chu Huy Man – a respected veteran of the French war - drew up his plans to engage them. He described them as follows: "First, we attack Plei Me, then the ARVN reinforcements come into our ambush…. Then, I was confident, the Americans will use their helicopters to land in our rear…. It was our intention to draw the Americans out of [the American base] An Khe. We did not have any plans to liberate the land; only to destroy troops."

In a later interview for the popular Vietnam War book about the campaign, *We Were Soldiers Once and Young*, General Man said, "We wanted to urge the tiger out of the mountain…We would attack the ARVN – but we would be ready to fight the Americans." One of his regimental commanders, in an interview after the war added, "we were ready, had prepared for you and expected you to come."

The 1st Cavalry Division had deployed to Vietnam shortly after OPERATION STARLITE. Its main port of entry had been at Qui Nhon, where Westmoreland's logistics units were working frantically to improve the port, airfield, and facilities. As soon as possible, Westmoreland wanted to send the division deep into the Highland region all the way to Pleiku to engage the NVA forces staging there.

As previously mentioned, his superior, Admiral Sharp had disagreed. He felt that such a move was too risky. They had compromised and settled for An Khe – a small highland town midway between the coast and Pleiku.

The Cavalry set up at An Khe one of those forward 'tactical bases' that Westmoreland had discussed in his concept of operations from which American combat units would attack the PAVN/PLAF main forces. Its construction was somewhat of a military marvel. An engineer unit - as the Army official history *Stemming the Tide* notes - completed in several weeks the base structures of "bridges, roads, helipads, guard towers, ammunition storage areas, administration buildings, a hospital and a 20,000-man cantonment for the division's personnel."

The deployment of the 1st Cavalry had been a much different experience from that of the Marines and the 173rd. The latter organizations came from forward-deployed bases in the Pacific region. They were fully manned and trained, and relatively unaffected by the President's decision not to call up the reserves and declare a national emergency. For an Army division stationed in the US, however, specific regulations inhibited the overseas deployment of all the personnel in the Division.

Explicitly, they prohibited the deployment of personnel if they had just returned from another overseas tour or were close to their end of enlistment. Moreover, unlike forward deployed forces, stateside divisions needed specific logistics units and personnel from outside of the division for it to be combat ready when deployed. Many of those shortages and augmentations came from the reserve forces. Without a Presidential declaration of emergency and reserve call-up, those shortages and needs had to be fulfilled from other active duty forces and units in the states.

Such had happened to the 1st Cavalry before it deployed from Fort Benning, Georgia. Soldiers, even many leaders, that had trained with the unit as it developed its airmobile skills and prepared for combat could not be deployed without a declaration of emergency. Several support units and personnel slots from the reserves, with whom they had trained in the States, could not deploy without a call-up. So, before it could deploy the division needed an infusion of some 6,000 new soldiers who had not trained with the others.

The shortages were not just a matter of numbers. Some critical specialties, such as helicopter pilots and mechanics, could not be filled because they would have to have been called up from the reserves, or would have needed some additional pilot training, or would have needed to extend their enlistments.

Complicating these personnel issues was the fact that because the unit was a relatively new organization, it was short new items and repair parts. To fill them in time for the unit's deployment, the industry would have to be put on a war footing. LBJ, however, was unwilling to do so, less the Congress and the News media become more aroused than they already were over the decision to send more American soldiers to Vietnam.

The Army Chief of Staff, General Harold Johnson, in commenting on this situation at the time said: "this is a special type division, unique to the Army, which has demonstrated the potential of bold and imaginative tactical concepts. It would be unfortunate if this division were employed in combat prematurely."

Unfortunate was undoubtedly a kind word. It was then, and is now, a euphemism for irresponsibility. According to some sources, General Johnson had contemplated resignation over the situation. He did not. Such a move on his part may have had an impact and saved lives early in the commitment of American soldiers to battle. At the very least, his resignation may have sent a signal to all that without a reserve call-up Army forces would be deploying to war without the full resources they would need to be in harm's way.

Consequently, as this 'special type division' was deploying, it struggled to train its new people further and regain the unit cohesion it had before its deployment. It also had to adjust its tactical methods, particularly because of the aviation personnel and equipment shortages. Now that it had fewer helicopters, infantry company organizations - numbering about 160 men - could not lift its soldiers into combat in one move. Now it would take several 'lifts' to move a unit's combat power into battle. Such a situation put the first soldiers on the ground at grave risk in the event of any enemy immediate attacks.

In late October, as it completed its move to Vietnam and its base preparations, it looked very much like elements of the 1st Cavalry would be in harm's way. PAVN General Man had moved two of his PAVN regiments toward the Plei Mei special forces camp and laid siege to it.

The 1st Cavalry Division commander, Major General Harry Kinnard, who was a World War Two combat veteran of General Taylor's 101st Airborne Division, asked for permission to deploy forward to the Pleiku area to be able to support the American Special Forces at Plei Me. Upon receiving permission, he ordered his 1st Brigade and divisional artillery, aviation, and air cavalry units forward to tactical bases near Pleiku.

Soon after arriving on 22 October, the artillery organizations were giving support to the besieged special forces camp. That artillery, plus a massive airpower pounding of General Man's soldiers, forced the PAVN units to withdraw to their bases along the Cambodian border.

General Kinnard seized the initiative. He sent his air cavalry battalion, a unit made up of a combination of scout helicopters called OH-1s, Huey that served as both aerial gunships and infantry troop carriers, and specially trained aviation and infantry personnel, to pursue the PAVN forces. This move marked the beginning of the most extensive US offensive of 1965 against the enemy main forces. The campaign in the Ia Drang Valley would last from late October until the end of November.

At first, the air cavalry had difficulty in finding enemy units because of the terrain. However, in the first week of November, they spotted some NVA soldiers – it was a unit of the 33rd PAVN regiment that was guarding a medical station treating wounded from its actions at Plei Me. The cavalry commander inserted an infantry force that engaged the NVA. After a fierce firefight, the NVA withdrew, leaving behind some key documents that showed regimental plans and base areas.

Kinnard now had what he needed to conduct a reconnaissance in force to find the major PAVN units. The General ordered his 2d Brigade to insert forces in several locations. All units made contact. He then decided to insert a battalion of airmobile infantry from another brigade into a location called Landing Zone (LZ) – X-Ray in the Ia Drang Valley. That unit, the 1st Battalion, 7th Cavalry, commanded by Korean War Veteran Lieutenant Colonel Hal Moore, would be landing amongst the 33rd's sister regiment, the 66th.

On 14 November LTC Moore had begun the insertion of his battalion. Due to the number of helicopters available, the loads they could carry in the high altitudes of the Highlands, and the size of the LZ, Moore would have to insert his unit in several lifts. Each lift, numbering about 16 helicopters, would be able to insert a half infantry company size on each turn, or about 70-80 troopers at a time. Initially, the battalion landed three lifts without any significant contact.

Soon after landing, however, the American infantry captured an enemy soldier. He told them that a large NVA force was in the area and wanted to kill Americans. One infantry platoon patrolling out from the LZ perimeter ran after a trail watcher. That enemy soldier led them into an ambush. About the same time, a large NVA force, at first surprised by the air assault, attacked the battalion gathering at the LZ. Moore now had about one-half of his unit on the ground. He knew he was outnumbered and had a major battle on his hands.

Indeed, the situation for the air cavalry battalion was grave. As described in *Stemming the Tide*, "Unknown to Colonel Moore, the 7th and 9th Battalions, 66th PAVN Regiment, and a composite battalion of the 33d PAVN Regiment had massed near the Chu Pong and were on a ridge above X-Ray. Although some of these units had been bloodied in the fighting around Plei Me, they still constituted a substantial force - up to sixteen hundred troops - and were well positioned to attack. In addition, the 32d PAVN Regiment, the H15 Local Force Battalion, and the 66th Regiment's 8th Battalion stood nearby."

For the next three days, Moore's outfit fought a courageous battle, as did the PAVN. In the first twenty-four hours, the aviation unit supporting them continued to reinforce the LZ until all the battalion's soldiers were on the ground. It was touch and go at times. Outnumbered, Colonel Moore had to continually shift his arriving forces – brought in by brave helicopter pilots and their crews. Those pilots and crews provided the lifeline for the soldiers on the ground. Vulnerable to NVA ground fire, they continually brought in ammunition and water, taking wounded on their way out.

Critical to the fight was the amount of American firepower that could keep the massive NVA forces at bay. This included division artillery firing from forward fire support bases and its aviation gunships – called aerial rocket artillery. It also included Air Force close air support planes, and newly created gunships – converted C130 cargo aircraft carrying all sorts of firepower. Further, General Westmoreland authorized for the first time the launching of B52 bombers in support of tactical operations. They flew ninety-six sorties overall, dropping their bombs on the Chu Pong Massif, where the NVA had built their base camps. Moore's Brigade Commander ordered other infantry forces into the battle. Because the LZ was under fire, most of these came overland. Due to high casualties, General Man ordered a halt to the assaults on the 16th. As described in the Army official history, "Colonel Moore surveyed the field of battle. It was, he later wrote, 'a sobering sight': enemy dead 'sprawled by ones and twos and heaps across a torn and gouged land' that was littered with body fragments, torn and bloody uniforms, and shattered weapons. Those North Vietnamese who had survived were moving away from the battle area, heading north and west along the base of the Chu Pong Massif...."

As the history concludes, "The clash between American and North Vietnamese forces at X-RAY represented the largest single action of the war so far. By body count, the Americans had killed 634 of the enemy and by estimate another 1,215. American casualties were 79 killed, with 121 wounded. The toll on the enemy was clearly substantial."

The battle at X-Ray drew the immediate attention of General Westmoreland. Afterward, the MACV commander went to where the battalion was to rest, equip and review lessons learned. To reporters there, the MACV commander claimed that the battle was an "unprecedented victory" for the Americans. General Kinnard was more adamant. In his report on the campaign, he asserted that the overall Ia Drang campaign had prevented the Communists from cutting South Vietnam in half because his forces had "depleted the enemy's ability to continue combat in the region."

In its aftermath, as the Army official history states, "the main conclusion seemed clear: American forces had killed hundreds of enemy and had won a victory in their first major fight against North Vietnamese regulars." Thus, it seemed in late 1965 - and the key word is 'seemed'- that with the American military's capability to maneuver via the helicopter and airmobile tactics, and bring massive firepower to bear on the enemy, it was entirely possible to deny the enemy from achieving his major objectives in the South. To Westmoreland at the time it appeared entirely possible to inflict more casualties on the North's military than Hanoi could replace.

This optimism over the battle at X-Ray ignored some stark realities. The enemy was extraordinarily persistent despite high casualties. Many of the PAVN soldiers and their units that fought at X-Ray escaped across the border to Cambodia where they could refit to fight another time and place in the South. PAVN and some PLAF units, which fought in the Plei Me campaign and at X-Ray - despite their losses - were able to regroup.

Once back to their parent units near their main base area, PAVN units further positioned themselves to ambush American forces that had moved after the battle from X-Ray to another landing zone. At that location, called LZ Albany, an American infantry battalion "had experienced a terrible bloodletting." It lost 151 killed, 121 wounded, and 5 missing, representing almost 70% of the overall battalion field strength. Yet, the American high command ignored that engagement. It chose to use X-Ray to illustrate the effectiveness of search and destroy tactics, and the attrition strategy.

General Westmoreland, as 1965 ended, felt he had good reason to be confident and optimistic. *Stemming the Tide* summarizes his views of the situation. "Although deeply concerned about improving his command's tactics, General Westmoreland never doubted that his forces would prevail and that his concept of how to fight the war was sound. For him, the evidence was compelling. Earlier in 1965, before the arrival of the combat units, both he and Ambassador Taylor had informed officials in Washington that South Vietnam would never survive another year without drastic steps to avert collapse."

However, as the official history continues, "In the ensuing months, he oversaw the introduction of the first U.S. brigades and divisions into Vietnam and watched those units stabilize the situation by their very presence. The battles of November and December followed, producing lopsided kill ratios in favor of the United States, and putting an abrupt end to all thought of collapse. By January 1966 he believed Phase I of his three-part campaign plan was complete and that Phase II could begin a relentless effort that would subvert the enemy's ambitions and, once and for all, secure the future of South Vietnam."

Yet, as related in Chapter 2, what Westmoreland did not know at the end of 1965 was that in Washington, DC Secretary McNamara was already having second thoughts about his support for the deployment of large US combat units to Vietnam. The MACV commander would soon find out that the reinforcements he sought for the offensive phase of his campaign would not be forthcoming at the beginning of 1966. Thus, his enemy, especially the PAVN and PLAF main units, would get an opportunity to continue its campaign to bloody American forces and continue its attempts to defeat the ARVN units guarding the populated areas.

Chapter 9: The Agony of Defeat

This chapter continues the examination of Westmoreland's Strategy of Attrition. It focuses on his 1966-67 campaigns and how he tried to execute that military strategy and achieve its objectives. As in Chapter 8, we will scrutinize how the American military attempted to achieve the policies and its objectives for the war set by their Commander-in-Chief and his national security advisors.

The narrative that follows explains the issues that confronted Westmoreland and his attempts to successfully execute a strategy that he thought would win the war. Those issues were the constraints that the Administration's limited war policy placed on the conflict; the changing nature of the reinforcements that LBJ and McNamara were willing to send; and the role that the MACV commander played in dealing with these limitations and changes.

The chapter also describes his attempts on two occasions to pursue an alternative to attrition in which he sought to sever the Ho Chi Minh trail in Laos. The narrative concludes with an account of the communist TET 1968 offensive, and the military results.

Section 9.1 – Executing the Strategy of Attrition

At the very beginning of 1966, General Westmoreland had begun to feel comfortable with the viability of his theater strategy and its campaign plan. As summarized at the end of the previous chapter, he had been successful in denying the enemy's goals of defeating the ARVN and overthrowing the Saigon government.

He had done that by getting enough US combat force into the theater to conduct spoiling attacks to disrupt Hanoi's planned offensives with their PAVN and PLAF units. American forces had engaged these main forces and inflicted heavy casualties. Remarkably, the MACV commander and his forces achieved this while simultaneously creating the critical support and logistics structure necessary to bring US combat power to bear on the communists. By the end of January 1966, Westmoreland had twenty-two Army and thirteen Marine battalions in country. The General was contemplating what he now needed to move into the offensive Phase II of his concept of operations.

Command Arrangements and Plans for Follow-on Operations

With the President's previous commitment for further reinforcements of some four to five additional US divisions and support troops, Westmoreland had also begun to devise a command structure to control the incoming forces and to continue his offensive in the most critical ARVN Corps areas. Thus, in early 1966, he set up a US Corps level headquarters in each of the northern three ARVN corps areas to oversee their operations.

In the northern I Corps region, he formalized the III Marine Amphibious Force or MAF, with General Walt as the commander, as one of his subordinate corps. General Walt would control all US forces there – not just his Marines - and continue to serve as the senior advisor to the ARVN I Corps commander.

In the ARVN II Corps area covering mostly the highlands region, he created Task Force Alpha, which he renamed I Field Force Vietnam, commanded at the beginning of 1966 by US Army General Stanley Larsen. Its headquarters would be located at the growing military support complex at Nha Trang. General Larsen would also advise the ARVN Corps commander in that area and be ready to employ new US forces to carry out MACV's designs for 1966.

Finally, in the ARVN III Corps area, which encompassed Saigon and its surrounding environs, he set up II Field Force Vietnam. The newly promoted 1st Infantry Division commander, General Jonathan Seaman, led this force. Seaman, like the other Corps level commanders, would also be the advisor to the areas' ARVN commander. The II Field Force would receive the preponderance of US military power to protect Saigon and continue to attack the main PAVN/PLAF forces in their base areas close to the South Vietnamese capital and along the Cambodian border.

General Westmoreland relied heavily on these Corps commanders to ensure cooperation and coordination of ARVN and US operations. As previously mentioned, he had issued periodic directives to these subordinate elements to manage the overall theater strategy and operations. The MACV commander usually followed the issuance of these with visits to his major commands to discuss his concepts and obtain situation reports. He would continue to do so. In December 1965, in coordination with the South Vietnamese High Command, he issued a Combined Campaign Plan for 1966 to his newly created commands.

As *Stemming the Tide* explains, "the allies declared their 'basic objective' for the year to be clearing, securing, and developing the densely populated regions around Saigon, in the Mekong Delta, and in selected portions of the I and II Corps coastal plain. Coincident with this effort, they would defend significant outlying government and population centers and conduct search and destroy operations against major VC/PAVN forces."

As the history further states, "In pursuit of these objectives, South Vietnam's army would concentrate on defending, clearing, and securing the designated strategic areas. American and third-country forces [some Australian and Korean forces had begun to arrive in theater], besides securing their bases and helping to protect rice-producing areas, were to conduct operations outside of the secure areas against VC forces and bases. Implicit in these words was the *de facto* division of labor between the South Vietnamese and Americans that had been in effect since the summer."

Despite the successes of 1965 and his intended offensive operations for the beginning of 1966, Westmoreland knew that he still could not move into his second, all-out offensive phase of operations until he was sure to get the necessary reinforcements. That was the phase in which he wanted to conduct a sustained offensive against the enemy base areas, bring much of the enemy main forces to battle, destroy most of them, and force the rest across the borders. He just did not have the combat units that he needed at this point to even begin his offensive much less turn his attention to security for pacification afterward.

Related to the need for more combat units, the MACV commander still required an enlarged support structure and force that could sustain large-scale operations. As the Army official history emphasizes, "The task before him was daunting. He had to keep the enemy at bay while laying the foundations for the effort to come." What he so sorely needed "for the effort to come" were his requested US combat troops and their necessary support forces as fast as he could get them.

The Honolulu Conference: January-February 1966

In January, LBJ and McNamara called for another meeting in Honolulu to discuss the war's progress and way ahead. This one would include the current South Vietnamese Government, President Thieu, and Premier Ky. These leaders had steadied the merry-go-round of RVN rulers. Now there was some US optimism that the South would have a stable government. Though it stayed corrupt, it was becoming efficient. McNamara would also have his 'Whiz Kids' there to discuss future reinforcements and their plans for deployment. They also came with a prerequisite set of measures to gauge progress in the war.

Westmoreland had his operations deputy, General DePuy, prepare a briefing on his strategy and the necessary schedule of deployments for the year to support his concept of operations. This presentation would be an important briefing. The MACV commander wanted to not only give a status of ongoing operations, but he wanted to explain what he needed for future operations and why.

Westy was concerned over the continued buildup of PAVN forces during 1965. He expected that to continue. His intelligence at MACV had estimated the strength of both the PAVN and PLAF forces at the end of the year at 99,600 in combat units, 16,900 in combat support units, and 103,600 in guerrilla forces.

The US Army official history clarifies his primary concerns over those enemy figures, the infiltration, and the current US reinforcement plans. It states that "In Westmoreland's opinion, the

United States had no alternative but to commit more forces just to counter the immediate threat and, more importantly, agree to much larger troop deployments in the future to ensure the success of Phase II operations."

Therefore, as the MACV history further explains, in their preparations for the upcoming conference, "General Westmoreland and his superior, Admiral Sharp, developed their comprehensive reinforcement plan, combining the approved buildup of forty-four battalions in 1965 with the added troops under consideration for 1966. Under the scenario, Sharp and Westmoreland envisioned, more than 440,000 U.S. and third-country troops - including one hundred two maneuver battalions, seventy-nine of them American - would be present in Vietnam by the end of 1966." Westmoreland and Sharp had sent this updated plan to the JCS before the conference. General Wheeler, in turn, sent it on to the Secretary of Defense.

Before the Honolulu Conference, the Joint Chiefs deliberated on the MACV commander's increased reinforcement needs. Seeing it, The Army Chief of Staff, General Harold Johnson, took another fact-finding mission in December to discuss it with Army commanders. Thus, the General agreed with the need for more forces as quickly as possible. He asserted in a Memo to the JCS, "the U.S. would be well advised to make a sizeable increase in the shortest time possible in additional forces ... in order to create a favorable power balance suddenly and achieve a maximum destruction of the increased enemy presence."

General Wheeler and the JCS agreed but were becoming concerned with the impact on US force requirements worldwide. There was also considerable concern from General Johnson on whether the Army could meet all the deployment requirements without a call-up of the reserves.

Although throughout 1965 LBJ and McNamara had specified that they would fully support Westmoreland in what he needed to prosecute the war successfully, as revealed in Chapter 3, they were now privately having misgivings. The President, in conversations with his old Senate colleagues, was indicating his continued lack of confidence in the military and his confusion over the war and how to continue. He again voiced his concerns over how the Soviets and Chinese would react to the growing commitment of US ground and other forces to Southeast Asia. Most of all, he remained troubled about the potential cost of the war and what putting the nation on a wartime footing would do to his Great Society programs.

As an example, in a recorded telephone conversation with Senator Mansfield, LBJ said that he wanted just to give the military enough to prevent defeat, but not too much to raise the ire of the Soviets, Chinese, or the US Congress. He said: "But I'm doing my best to hold this thing in balance just as long as I can. I can't run out; I'm not going to run in; I can't just let them sit there and let them be murdered."

Johnson continued, "So I've got to put enough there to hold them and protect them. And I don't believe if we don't heat it up ourself [sic], if we don't dramatize it, we don't play it up and say we're appropriating billions and we're sending millions and all that kind of stuff and men - I don't think that you could get the Russians worked up or the Chinese worked up about it. And that's what we're hoping ".

These words were hardly the strong ones that LBJ was announcing to the public, his administration, and his military leaders to 'kill more VC' to win. They certainly did not reflect his pledge to Westmoreland that he would give 'whatever the commander needs to win.'

McNamara, in his memoirs, also emphasizes his continued doubts at that time. The Secretary states that when he saw Westmoreland's November 1965 request to increase deployments, "it came as a shattering blow." After a last-minute trip to Vietnam to confer with Sharp and Westmoreland on future deployments and progress, McNamara claims that he became disillusioned with the war. In a meeting with the President in December, he recalled telling him that "our military action approach is an unacceptable way to a successful conclusion."

As further explained in Chapter 3, the Secretary then recommended that they seek a negotiated diplomatic approach with the North Vietnamese. LBJ, accepting this advice, ordered a bombing pause over the Christmas holidays, which extended into the conference. The pause came as a surprise to the commander charged with overseeing the overall bombing campaign – Admiral Sharp. General Westmoreland, who had virtually no input to the air operations in the North, did not voice any concern. Meanwhile, the North Vietnamese dismissed the gesture as a ploy and trick. More importantly, it gave them some respite to further increase their infiltration of forces to the South.

Thus, the two top American civilian leaders in the war were going to Honolulu to assess the situation already full of hesitation and doubt only months after they had decided to send American forces into combat. They had serious misgivings about finding a way to apply military force to achieve a favorable outcome that met the US established aims. Yet, they had ignored most of the inputs of their military commander in the field and their advisors in Washington on what was needed to, in their views, achieve the political object to defend South Vietnam from aggression.

Neither Sharp nor Westmoreland knew of these hesitancies or reservations. Nor did the American people, who by a 2 to 1 margin in the polls in early 1966 favored either 'an all-out victory' or 'to get out.' Nor had the nearly 2,000 American military that had been killed in action in 1965.

The conference opened in Honolulu on 17 January and would run through 9 February. It consisted of two major parts. In the first, over 450 staff officers and civilians would deliberate several 'cases' for further deployments. A set of different force levels and provided the basis of these assumptions – the most important one being the degree of mobilization that would support each case.

The second part of the conference would be a political summit meeting between the Americans and the South Vietnamese. This latter summit was a way of showing solidarity for the South Vietnamese cause, and, in turn, a demonstration of Republic of South Vietnam's gratitude for US actions and a commitment of the RVN to American plans. For this political phase, the US (Secretary McNamara) drew up a set of pacification and government reform measures to improve upon for the RVN, the ARVN, and MACV.

It was the first part of the conference that was important to the way ahead for Westmoreland and his military strategy. Although MACV had emphasized the need for security and pacification in its directives and plans, Westmoreland saw his most critical task for 1966 the defeat of the enemy's main forces. Without that, he believed, there was no way that any pacification program would succeed. Hence, in his view, the deliberations and decisions on the details of the air and ground deployments and campaign plans for the coming year were the most important and vital to the war effort. McNamara and his team drove the discussions on three deployment 'cases' that they had derived for the conference. As described in *MACV: The Years of Escalation*, "Case I called for a reserve mobilization and extension of enlistments. Cases II and III did not…. The first two cases would offer [the full request of] all 102 maneuver battalions, but in Case II the deployment of 9 would not begin until early 1967."

The MACV account further states that "Case III required outright deletion of 18 American battalions, including a complete division, 2 brigades, and some smaller combat elements." The reason for the smaller force levels in Case III was to reduce the cost on an already strained Federal Budget. Of course, what was also attractive to the civilian leaders, especially McNamara and LBJ, is that Case II and III did not require any mobilization authorization from the Congress.

Though the Joint Staff presented the above force cases at the conference, McNamara's staff had given the total numbers. These figures included the potential costs, effects on the Service budgets, and the impact on the domestic economy. Weighing heavily on the cases was the probability of congressional and domestic support. Of note, emphasized by McNamara, was the impact of a call-up of reserves or a declaration of emergency would have on public opinion, the economy, and the probability that the President would approve them.

During the deliberations, General DePuy presented the MACV campaign plan, and how each of the 'cases' supported it. He emphasized Case I was the best in supporting the plan and Westmoreland's desire to begin his Phase II major offensive early in 1966. He also indicated, however, that Case II was 'acceptable,' but added risk to MACV's achievement of military objectives because it did not give the support forces needed or the combat forces soon enough.

On the other hand, Case III, DePuy argued, would not offer the forces necessary to take the offensive that MACV envisioned for 1966. It also would not provide the forces needed to secure some areas in the high priority areas identified in the campaign plan. Admiral Sharp and the JCS concurred with this appraisal. Wheeler and the JCS, however, wanted to delay some of the deployments into 1967 to minimize the impacts on the US military posture in other areas.

Near the end of the conference - after the plenary session involving the President was over and the dignitaries had left - McNamara, Wheeler, Sharp, and Westmoreland came to an agreement on what the Secretary and his staff called a modified Case I schedule. The modifications, however, made it look more like Case II.

As the conference was about to end, McNamara told Westmoreland that he would not get all that he wanted when he wanted them. However, the Secretary assured the General that he would go to the President and request deployments that did not include any mobilization or declaration of emergency. What he did not tell Westmoreland was that the President had already told his Defense Secretary he would not approve of any forces requiring mobilization. They both acknowledged that there would be some logistics shortages and a delay in some reinforcements into 1967. In short, the General was not getting all that he needed to support his campaign plan.

At the end of the conference, all, to include the South Vietnamese present, adopted a set of goals and performance measures to guide actions into 1966. As explained in the MACV history, "The objectives included defending key military and civilian centers and food-producing areas, opening roads and railroads, clearing and securing the four national priority pacification zones, and bringing 60 percent of South Vietnam's people within secure territory by the end of 1966."

The history further states that "Along with these security-related goals, the leaders promised to intensify their offensive against Viet Cong and North Vietnamese units, bases, and lines of communication within South Vietnam and infiltration routes in Laos and North Vietnam, with the objective of destroying 40–50 percent of the enemy's base areas during the coming year and inflicting casualties on their forces at a rate as high as their capability to put men into the field."

In retrospect, this conference would turn out to be the most important one for Westmoreland's theater strategy and his goal to defeat the North's aggression in the South. As *Stemming of the Tide* asserts, "the new schedule contained a serious strategic flaw. By extending the troop deployments well into 1967, the sudden powerful surge in forces that General [Westmoreland and] Johnson had sought would never become a reality. Thus, Westmoreland during most of 1966 would not have in hand the troops - both maneuver battalions and support units - that he needed to implement the second, or offensive phase of his campaign, forcing him to spend some months buying time while the buildup proceeded. More importantly, the stretch-out also meant that the enemy would be able to nullify the US buildup by expanding his own forces at the same or even faster pace than the Americans."

Nevertheless, Westmoreland remained an optimist. He continued to show his 'can do' spirit. He thought he had enough eventually to do the job. The MACV commander was not overly concerned at this point about the lack of mobilization and was overall pleased with the results of the conference. He had not gotten everything he wanted. No commander ever does, he thought. The goals and measures, he believed, were consistent with his own.

In his memoirs, General Westmoreland does not mention much about the conference results regarding reinforcements. He does recall three occurrences. The first was that LBJ "seemed intense, perturbed, uncertain how to proceed with the Vietnam problem, [and] torn by the magnitude of it." The second was the President's remarks to him, "I hope you won't pull a MacArthur on me."

Of course, as he admits in his memoirs, Westmoreland had never held any thoughts about disagreeing with his President or the Secretary of Defense. He was not that kind of military officer. He had never questioned his superiors. His loyalty was one of the characteristics always marked high on his career efficiency assessments. Moreover, LBJ had chosen him for the command based on the General's reputation as a loyal officer.

The third incident he recollects in his memoirs of this conference was his concluding remarks. He recalls saying, "There comes a time in every battle – in every war - when both sides become discouraged by the seemingly endless requirement for more effort, more resources, and more faith. At this point, the side which presses on with renewed vigor is the one to win." These turned out to be prophetic words.

These recollections are also remarkably strange given his lack of concern with the conference results. Why if he did not object to the reduced force levels and arrivals would he make or even recall these remarks? Why would he have made them if he was overall pleased with the results of the conference? Unfortunately, he does not address these questions in his memoirs, or in oral histories in the Presidential libraries.

Here is yet another instance where the overall American commander did not forcibly press for the means that he needed to give at least a reasonable chance for his concept of operations to work. Westmoreland once again gave into the perceived 'truths' that Washington forced upon him – no reserve call-up and a delay in the deployment schedule that he thought would provide the forces he needed to defeat the enemy.

Most critically, he gave the Secretary of Defense and his advisors the impression that he could still carry out his mission, it would just take a little longer. All of this would haunt him during the next year and after when he would argue for forces well beyond what he had said he could win the war in 1966.

The Build Up and Buying Time

In the way forward, both the President and his Defense Secretary would continue to lose 'faith' and any remaining 'vigor' for Westmoreland's war strategy. Both would continue with no further guidance on how to wage a war that the American public was not only becoming more focused on but disillusioned with – some now calling for getting out, some calling for escalation. Hereafter, Washington leaders, and the Press and the Public, would be focused on numbers – deployments, casualties, and polls – more than anything else.

Many of those numbers were critical to the execution of the theater of war strategy in Vietnam. Deployment numbers stood for the means that they would need to execute Westmoreland's concept of operations and to achieve his military objectives. At the end of 1965, there were some 150,000 American soldiers and Marines in South Vietnam. By the end of 1966, this number was to increase more than two-fold.

However, sheer numbers can be deceiving. Of the 150,000, for example, only about a third were in maneuver units – those that were the most capable of conducting the search and destroy part of the strategy. While MACV kept watch over the ratio of maneuver versus other types of forces - such as supporting artillery, engineer, and aviation and servicing transportation, maintenance, construction and medical – there would still be a problem with getting enough maneuver combat forces into the field to 'find, fix, and destroy' the enemy.

After the conference, Westmoreland returned to Saigon and looked toward taking the war to the enemy. He could not yet do that in earnest until he had at least the next quarters' reinforcements. In that time, one infantry division – the 1st Marine - and elements of a second – the US Army's 25th Infantry – would close in country. Deployment plans also called for another infantry division, the 4th, to arrive in June. Along with them, the remaining forces of the 1st Infantry Division, another battalion for the 173rd Airborne Brigade, some more Korean forces, and the sorely needed support forces necessary for an offensive completed their movement to Vietnam. Thus, it would not be until June 1966 that he would be able to launch the Phase II all-out offensive he had originally envisioned.

Not having the full complement of forces that he would need to execute his strategy as planned, the MACV commander would have to prioritize. As the MACV history explains, "he assigned the highest operational priority to the populated areas in III Corps around Saigon and then to those of the coastal lowlands in I and II Corps. In other regions, such as the Central Highlands, he planned to respond to enemy initiatives when they occurred, but otherwise maintain no more of a US presence than necessary."

Moreover, "With the III Corps area being the most critical, the MACV commander set about installing a set of major bases surrounding the Saigon area that could support the ARVN forces there and periodically conduct attacks against the key PLAF/PAVN bases in War Zones C and D, and the Iron Triangle."

Of course, the enemy was not waiting for the Americans to bring in more reinforcements. They continued to fight the ARVN in and around the populated areas; and attack American units when they seemed vulnerable or when they threatened vital base areas. As described in Chapter 7, they continued to move significant PAVN regular forces and supplies down the Ho Chi Minh Trail in large numbers.

Meanwhile, the advantages that Le Duan and General Thanh had counted on in their battles with the Americans were undoubtedly making a difference. Though losses were high, the North could replace them. Though the American military was attacking them, they could escape when need be across the borders to regroup. Though the American leaders were continuing their limited war, the peace atmosphere in the US was growing. Though they had not defeated the ARVN and toppled their government, time was on their side.

Westmoreland, to buy time until he could get the required forces for his offensive, continued his spoiling attacks as he could. In the III Corps area at the end of February the 1st Infantry Division, less its forces due in June, conducted operations astride War Zone C. The purpose was to keep critical routes open in areas that the ARVN were trying to clear local VC forces and start their pacification programs. In March, Big Red One units, along with those of the 173rd, continued their operations into War Zone D. The object was to find and destroy the enemy's B2 Front headquarters and supply depots.

The Army official history summarizes these operations against War Zone D. "In all, the two units had killed 353 Viet Cong soldiers and estimated an additional 218 killed. American losses came to 11 killed and 228 wounded. The two brigades had found and destroyed some three hundred seventy tons of rice, had interdicted the enemy's lines of communication, and had disrupted one of the major Viet Cong sanctuaries in III Corps."

In the first few months of 1966, Westmoreland also ordered the 1st Brigade of the 101st Airborne Division, which had built a base camp at Phan Rang, to protect the lowland areas in II Corps that were rich rice-producing regions. One area, from which the communist forces of the central region in 1965 had requisitioned most of their sustenance, was the rice fertile Tuy Hoa Valley in Phu Yen Province. Somewhere near there was also the suspected central base area for the 95th Regiment of the 5th PAVN Division. As a result, the 101st Brigade commander launched a brigade-size operation into the valley; setting up a brigade forward base near the provincial capital of Tuy Hoa.

The operation would last for almost six months. It became an operation that was typical of most infantry actions during the war. The American paratroopers conducted a series of patrolling operations near the lowlands from several fire support bases put in place there to provide artillery fire for the infantry. Several of these patrols intercepted NVA soldiers who had come from their base areas in the adjacent mountains to gather rice from villages. Other patrols caught local VC and guerrilla units who were supporting the PAVN forces in ambushes.

The longer the US infantry was in the area operating near the villages, the more frequent became the contacts. Some of these were a matter of brief firefights lasting from several minutes to a few hours that came to typify combat operations in South Vietnam throughout the war. Several were intense battles involving several US battalions [and Korean forces also operating in this II Corps area] for a couple of days.

The larger engagements in the lowlands usually occurred when the NVA and VC main forces had gathered in strength and decided to engage the Americans. PAVN/PLAF sustained large unit combats were only possible while these forces were near their base areas, both in the vicinity of the lowlands and the more distant ones near the borders. The notion that these forces obtained their capabilities to fight from the populace, often reported in the Press then and now in some books on the war, was, and still is, a myth. For by mid-1966 the Ho Chi Minh Trail was providing most of the supplies and munitions for the communists to fight the Americans and South Vietnamese in any prolonged battles.

As the lowland operations continued for several months, US units, sometimes in concert with the South Vietnamese, began to show some progress regarding security for the population and effectiveness of pacification programs. As described in the US Army Official History of Vietnam, "America's stock among the people rose, buoyed both by its military successes and the civic action programs of the 1st Brigade, 101st Airborne Division. The paratroopers distributed food and clothing to villagers, aided in the government's effort to rebuild houses damaged during operations, and protected Army engineers assigned to repair roads and bridges. Army psychological warfare specialists helped South Vietnamese officials restore government authority, while medical personnel established the first dispensary in Tuy Hoa in many years, treating approximately one thousand patients per month."

Operations in the lowlands also produced some excellent intelligence from captured NVA soldiers and documents. These led to some 101st Airborne battalion size search and destroy operations into the surrounding mountainous terrain containing NVA bases. They lasted from April through July in the assigned 1st Brigade area of operation. They typified much of the tactics American forces would use throughout the war.

As an example, before infantry forces began the operation, especially if it was away from the densely populated village and hamlet areas, commanders would order the establishment of a new fire support base or FSB to give adequate firepower both for the air assault into selected landing zones and later operations. These FSBs would consist of one or two artillery batteries (usually of five 105mm howitzers each), the battalion headquarters element to command and control the operation, and some infantry for protection. The LZs, in general, could only support a platoon or two (5 – 10 helicopters) insertion at any one time – sometimes less.

Therefore, like the LZ-X-Ray operation, forces would be vulnerable at first. Thus, also like X-Ray, the units wanted to get as much force as possible into the LZ or multiple LZs as quickly as possible. Moreover, like the LZ-X-Ray operation, coordinated air and artillery strikes would prepare the landing zones, in case the enemy was at or near that zone.

Once inserted, American forces, because of some of the densely vegetated jungle and mountainous terrain where the communist lowland base areas were situated, could not move in battalion-size units. Multiple companies would move together, usually very slowly, seeking to keep within a proper distance to support one another. Often infantry companies had to move in platoon size formations; often going ahead in a single file, i.e., with one soldier behind another.

The most critical soldiers in these formations were the two or three that walked 'point' – those first in the line of march. They would be the ones to indicate if there was enemy sighted or signs of imminent contact such as footprints, booby traps or abandoned enemy equipment. Many times, these movements ended with no contact. Sometimes they erupted into fierce, but brief battles. Sometimes the first contacts lasted for several days if the NVA decided that they could damage the American units or if, by chance, the US elements had trapped them.

While the results of the Screaming Eagles brigade's operations in the lowlands of Phu Yen Province were encouraging, Westmoreland still had his focus on the NVA/PLAF main forces wherever he could find them. He continued to believe that, if left alone, these regular units could easily undo any attempt to bring security and pacification to the South Vietnamese populated areas. No matter how promising the results were in the populated lowland areas were, the enemy could continue to feed forces into battle there and disrupt the security and pacification gains from their main bases. So, as the 101st was engaging in the protection of the rice harvest, he sent units of the 1st Cavalry Division into Binh Dinh Province, just to the north.

Intelligence activities had shown in that area the presence of the 3rd PAVN Division, which had three regiments in country. One regiment had been fighting in the South since 1962. In fact, large segments of the Binh Dinh Province had been a redoubt for the communists for almost thirty years. The ARVN 22d Division in this Province had fought several difficult battles with NVA regulars who had easily bloodied them. During the first months of 1966, the division was on the verge of disintegration.

The Airmobile Division operation, initially called 'MASHER' but renamed because of the Administration's concern over such 'provocative names,' employed two of its three brigades, almost all its helicopters, and much of its combat support elements. Such a large size operation, almost a division in strength, foretold what many of the large-unit sweeps of Westmoreland's offensive phase would look like later in the year and into the next.

The Cavalry Division's commander, still Major General Kinnard who had overseen the IA Drang campaign, devised a two-phase operation. In the first phase, he would insert one brigade task force south of the predetermined primary area of operations into a flatland called the Bong Son Plain. Kinnard intended this move as a diversion for the enemy forces, and to form a reserve for further operations once his main element had found and engaged the enemy.

In the second phase, the 1st Cavalry commander planned to insert another brigade task force into the mountain area to the east of the An Lao Valley and west of the Bong Son plain. From there this task force would conduct operations out of two firebases to find and engage the enemy. A US Marine task force would seal the An Lao Valley from the north to prevent any NVA from escaping.

Kinnard further planned for an ARVN airborne brigade to move along the main highway along the Bong Son plain to prevent any escape of enemy forces via the highway. Thus, MASHER, renamed WHITE WING, would be the first of other similar large-scale operations that used a hammer and anvil tactic to seal off escape routes (the anvil) and attack with forces against trapped enemy main forces (the hammer).

This operation lasted from the latter part of January to the middle of March 1966. Like most hammer and anvil operations, the enemy knew the terrain well enough not to get cornered. When it appeared that PAVN large units might get trapped, they dispersed, received help from the locals, and avoided battle. When they had the advantage, mainly when something went wrong like weather interference of air movements and air support, PAVN units would attack isolated American companies, and inflict severe casualties on the American infantry who endured most of the fighting.

General Kinnard's operation, on the other hand, showed the advantages that the airmobile concept and capabilities offered American forces. When he failed to trap or engage the enemy, he shifted units about the area of operations using his helicopter assets. Eventually, he managed to engage some PAVN forces. Often, he would first employ massive air and artillery strikes to damage them before engaging with his infantry.

On other occasions, American infantry showed up using their airmobile assets in areas the enemy did not suspect them to be. Using evolving techniques such as night ambushes and aggressive patrolling out of night defensive positions, US units - mainly small elements of platoon (about 30 men) and company (120 soldiers) - surprised the NVA and inflicted heavy casualties. In almost every case these units employed artillery, gunships, and close air support to overcome the enemy's numbers and knowledge of the area.

However, the communist forces continued to adapt to these tactics. NVA and PLAF units, when engaged with American forces, tried to stay as close as they could to avoid US supporting artillery and airpower. They also employed mines and ambushes along suspected landing zones to catch American infantry at their most vulnerable times when landing.

To counter American search and destroy techniques, the PAVN/PLAF began to create areas astride their major base areas designed to engage approaching infantry into kill zones. They carefully concealed their positions using heavily camouflaged bunkers, and small foxholes dug into the ground, which US infantrymen dubbed 'spider holes.'

The Communist forces also began to employ heavily constructed bunkers in their base camps, connecting them with numerous underground tunnels. Of course, they had learned much during the French war; but their techniques had to be improved or changed to adapt to the American more powerful fires and maneuverability.

At the end of MASHER/WHITE WING, the US military claimed a victory once again. As the official history states, "In forty-one days of campaigning the 1st Cavalry Division had killed more than 1,300 main force regulars, captured over 600 more, and received almost 500 defectors. Also, Kinnard's men had seized or destroyed over two hundred individual and fifty-two crew-served weapons, large quantities of ammunition, many useful documents, and communications gear."

"Finally, the division had uncovered ninety-one tons of rice and fourteen tons of salt that were distributed to the South Vietnamese refugees. Overall, MASHER/WHITE WING had dissolved any doubts that remained about the ability of the division to conduct sustained operations and to take the war to the enemy. But the price of progress was high: 228 Americans had died, and 834 had been wounded. And Binh Dinh, which was still dotted with fortified villages and mountain hideouts, was not yet secure."

Besides inflicting damage on the PAVN/PLAF main forces, these types of lowland operations around the hamlets and villages brought further security and pacification program benefits to the people. As the official history recounts, "American sweeps on the coastal plain had prompted Viet Cong to surrender in record numbers and prevented main forces from massing near population centers. Under the division's protective umbrella, the government was also able to extend its presence into several previously contested areas, at least temporarily. Village self-defense groups were formed, the Popular Forces achieved nearly full strength by June, at least on paper; and the police increased their network of informers by 50 percent in the villages, producing new intelligence."

The history also states that "the provincial economy also perked up, thanks in part to the presence of allied garrisons and their success in keeping portions of Highway 1 open for commerce during the day. Most notably WHITE WING enabled the government to secure over 80 percent of Binh Dinh's winter rice harvest, adding to the Communists' supply troubles. The one negative aspect in what was an otherwise encouraging if still fragile political picture was Binh Dinh's swelling refugee population-approximately 120,000 people, more than any other province in South Vietnam."

Despite these favorable outcomes, what the US Army's official history does not say is that the Bong Son Plain, An Lao Valley, and its surrounding mountains would never be entirely secure from NVA main forces. Subsequent similar operations to WHITE WING would create some of the same results. However, American units never had enough forces to sustain the security and pacification programs while conducting operations to keep the communist main forces at bay.

Nor did the regular ARVN forces in the area. Most of the time, South Vietnam territorial forces took over the security mission. As too often the case, however, they usually withdrew from the populated areas and built small 'forts' to protect themselves from any enemy main forces that remained in the mountainous, vegetated base areas adjacent to the lowland villages. As a result, the main force NVA and some PLAF remained in their local Binh Dinh base areas until the North's final victory in 1975.

Alternatives to Search and Destroy: The Marine Corps Combined Action Program

As the Army's spoiling attacks and denial operations took place against NVA/PLAF main force suspected base camps and war zones in the ARVN II and III Corps areas, the Marines focused on somewhat of a different enemy and area of operations in Northern I Corps. North Vietnam had not yet sent large PAVN forces into northern South Vietnam to engage the Marines there. The enemy in the first months of 1966 were primarily VC main and local force units located in hard to detect base camps near the coastal region villages. Some were also well entrenched at the hamlet level, like those that the Marines battled in operation STARLIGHT.

These VC forces, at first, avoided battle against the Marines as much as possible. They usually concentrated on engaging nearby ARVN forces and protecting their hamlet infrastructure. Moreover, unlike the Highlands region, this northern region of the country was relatively flat and open. Its mountainous area was to the Western extreme along the Laotian border and somewhat isolated. Its most prominent terrain feature was its extended coastal area with sand flatlands and rice patties. That area consisted of some 570 villages with approximately 2.4 million inhabitants or 80% of the total I Corps' population.

When a second Marine division arrived early in 1966, General Walt devised what he called in his memoir a 'balanced strategy' for his area of operations. The Commander of III MAF sent his own directive to his subordinates outlining this operational approach. It took into consideration the kind of enemy he faced at the time, the nature of the population and terrain in his area, the capabilities of the ARVN, and General Westmorland's priorities in the MACV Commanders' campaign plan. This 'balanced strategy' took on the characteristics of the 'enclave strategy' that Westmoreland thought he had eradicated a year previously.

As described in Walt's memoirs and the Marine Corps' official history for Vietnam, the Marine General's method consisted of a three-prong campaign plan. It would follow the guidance of MACV and seek out and destroy enemy main force units, "when there is good intelligence" that can be acted upon. However, the focus of his operations would be on protecting the local population and instituting pacification actions to gain their trust and loyalty to the local RVN officials.

As this protection and pacification took root, the Marines would expand out, clear and control additional areas like a spreading 'ink blot.' As the Marine official history describes General Walt's operational directive, it "consisted of a counter-guerrilla campaign within the TAORs [Tactical Areas of Operations], search and destroy operations against enemy main force troops outside the TAORs, and a pacification campaign within the hamlets to eradicate the VC 'infrastructure….'"

The operational technique of the 'Ink Blot' was not new. The French had tried a similar method in the early fifties. Under the Pacific Command and MACV's original Counterinsurgency Plan for the ARVN in the late fifties and early sixties, this technique was also used. In both cases, they had failed.

The failure was usually a result of just not having enough forces to execute it. Often the elements used for 'protection and pacification' had to face determined Viet-Minh or VC main units which struck back and threatened the destruction of the security units and their pacification efforts. In most cases, this more substantial threat demanded the use of larger units employed to thwart the enemy attacks. The demand to overcome VC significant threats to the security operations then detracted from the sustainment of the security operations. General Walt would soon experience the same dilemma.

The Marines also derived a unique tactic to bring security and pacification within these TAORs. It became known as the "Combined Action Platoon" or CAP Program. This program began in late 1965 as a 'grassroots' attempt to deal with local security for the villages and hamlets around the Phu Bai 'enclave.' The concept called for a Marine infantry squad of approximately ten to twelve men teamed with a local Vietnamese territorial Popular Force unit.

The latter were like local American national guard forces; but not as well organized, equipped, experienced, or trained. The Marine leadership that initiated the concept saw the CAP as a way to improve these Popular Force units so they could eventually combat VC forces on their own. Thus, operating together initially for some time, the Marines saw this as a way to offer long-term security for villages or hamlets.

General Walt embraced the concept to support his goal of providing long-term security for pacification in his entire area of operations. The Marine Command would develop over a hundred of these CAPs concentrated in their enclave areas at Phu Bai, Da Nang, and Chu Chi. Marine Corps leaders in Washington, such as Generals Greene and Krulak, always willing to sell Marine force capabilities, touted them as an alternative operational approach to search and destroy.

Francis J. West, a Marine who served in Vietnam with some of the CAPs, wrote a fascinating book entitled, *The Village*, which documents the success and the agony of the CAP experience. Some historians, citing this book and others about the CAPs, argue that they could have been a useful tactic that may have won the war only if the concept had been adopted theater wide.

General Westmoreland applauded the idea in his memoirs, and states that he "disseminated the information on the platoons and their success to other commands." However, he added, adopting it throughout his Corps areas "would have been fragmenting resources and exposing them to defeat in detail."

In fact, enemy actions would eventually inhibit General Walt and his successors from fully implementing the CAP concept and their overall pacification programs throughout the vastly populated areas in the I Corps region. By mid-1966, the North Vietnamese decided to threaten the area by infiltrating PAVN units across the DMZ and from Laos via the Ho Chi Minh Trail system.

As Douglas Pike in his book *People's Army of Vietnam* describes this move, the reinforcements followed the usual pattern of at first sending fillers for the VC casualties. Then, PAVN regular units infiltrated in large numbers. Most of these NVA units settled in the A Shau Valley and other western portions of I Corps, where there could readily conceal themselves. From base camps set up there, these regular NVA units could regularly and seriously threaten the populated areas on the coast.

Recognizing this threat, Walt would have to employ most of the arriving 1st Marine Division in reaction to the enemy movement. That response would ultimately result in much of that Division's combat power engaging PAVN forces along the DMZ, in the A Shau Valley, and a place called Khe Sanh near the Laotian border. This diversion was the main reason for the Marine commanders' inability to fully implement CAP.

The Combined Action Program was highly successful where and when the Marines could implement the tactic. However, the fact is that there were not enough American and South Vietnamese forces to apply it throughout the South's populated areas. Moreover, the CAP concept was highly vulnerable to any concentration of PAVN/PLAF main forces. Where and when these main force elements thought the CAPs had been a threat, they could mass and attack them. If these small units could not call on reinforcements, those enemy attacks were bound to be successful.

General Walt admitted such in his memoir. There he states, "Until early 1966 my men had been widely dispersed, exercising the greatest amount of security over the greatest number of people…. Now [most of 1966 and after] we were in a situation similar to that in Korea in 1950 – an army coming down from the north to seize and hold ground. This was a turning point [for us] in the conflict."

Alternatives to Search and Destroy: The Program for the Pacification and Long-Term Development of South Vietnam or PROVN

The Combined Action Program was not the only concept that some argue should have been adopted as an alternative to Westmoreland's search and destroy approach. Historian Lewis Sorley has proposed that an Army concept called the Program for the Pacification and Long-Term Development of South Vietnam could have been more effective. Indeed, Sorley argues in several of his works – namely *A Better War* and *Honorable Warrior* – that the program's approach may have won the war.

As Sorley explains, General Harold K. Johnson, the US Army Chief of Staff, as early as April of 1965, sensed that engaging the enemy main forces while giving protection for the people would be the primary problem for the US military in the entire war. Therefore, after he had returned from Vietnam in the Spring of 1965, he formed a small team to study "new sources of action to be taken in South Vietnam by the United States and its allies, which will, in conjunction with current actions, lead in due time to successful accomplishment of US aims and objectives." The team presented their results in March 1966. It became known as the PROVN study.

The study's primary conclusion was "the Vietnamese people are, and must remain, the true and paramount objective of all US-Government of Vietnam efforts." It emphasized that 'victory' could only be achieved through bringing the population to "support willingly the Government of South Vietnam." It further warned that the deployment of US forces may detract from this truism and that the battle against enemy forces was secondary to the political struggle. The PROVN conclusions thus seemed to imply that the conduct of pacification operations was the priority action above all others.

Yet, as explained by historian Andrew Birtle in his treatment of the PROVN study in *The Journal of Military History*, the report did not dismiss the need for military operations against the enemy's main forces to provide the security necessary for pacification. Nor was it intended, as Sorley proclaimed, as a repudiation of Westmoreland's military strategy, whose execution was only in its preliminary stages as the study was underway.

Indeed, the report gave some relevant recommendations that General Westmoreland tried to adopt. In particular - as the MACV commander had already requested from both Ambassadors Lodge and Taylor - the PROVN study recommended that the pacification effort be under his control. Both Ambassadors had denied this request. The report also recommended the integration of other economic, political, and diplomatic efforts that Westmoreland supported and felt he could coordinate with military actions if he had more of a say in pacification.

In short, one of the leading recommendations of the study was that there be a more concerted and coordinated effort to meld the military operations of both the ARVN and the main American units with the security efforts of the South Vietnamese territorial forces and the pacification programs of the South Vietnamese Government. A close examination of Westmoreland's directives and orders show that that is precisely what he wanted as well.

However, there had been two obstacles in 1966 to doing so. First, the American ambassadors had resisted that such an effort be under MACV control. Second, enemy main forces had effectively disrupted any South Vietnamese government, and ARVN attempts to improve local security and the effective establishment of pacification in the populated areas.

The PROVN study further emphasized several factors that would become critical to the future waging of the war. Many of these are ones that Westmoreland was trying to get approval for but had failed. One was the study's argument that the Administration needed to recognize that the war would be a long one. Accordingly, the report recommended that the Administration prepare the American public for a protracted war.

Also, the study's conclusion emphasized that the Command needed more forces than had then (late 1965 to early 1966) been authorized. As we have seen the Administration had already decided to both send fewer forces than Westmoreland had asked for and delay the others. Moreover, though Westmoreland had not yet asked for this action, the study called for the isolation of the battlefield and the necessity to prevent, through ground action against the Ho Chi Minh Trail, the continued infiltration of the PAVN forces into the South.

A careful reading of the PROVN report and General Walt's operational concept show that the approaches in each were dependent on the level of forces or means to achieve what Westmoreland ultimately wanted to accomplish – pacification of the countryside and establishment of the South Vietnam Government's control. Both the PROVN and General Walt concepts, moreover, realized that the result could not be successful unless 'free-world' forces could defeat the enemy main forces. Therefore, both recognized that the central issue in achieving success in South Vietnam was the competition for resources in defeating the main forces and giving security and pacification programs to the population.

Indeed, defeating the enemy's main forces and providing security and pacification to the populated area was the principal strategic dilemma and problem that both the civilian leaders in Washington and General Westmoreland needed to solve. The solution, as far as Westmoreland was concerned in 1966, was for the President and his Secretary of Defense to give him the forces necessary to do so.

Contrary to some historians' views then, Westmoreland recognized that the population security, pacification, and the defeat of the main forces were interrelated. However, the General just did not have enough US combat power to do them all at the same time. Contemporary sources show that he did not ignore pacification. Instead, he made a conscious choice to prioritize and allocate US combat forces to defeat the main forces. He relied on the ARVN and regional security forces to execute local security and pacification operations with US support when available.

As the MACV commander received more troops in 1966, he would continue to be confident that he could solve one part of his problem – defeat the PAVN/PLAF main forces by attacking their base camps. Then, he thought, he could turn his attention to the pacification effort. What he did not expect at first was that he would not be able to defeat his main force enemy. By the beginning of 1967, a few months into his Phase II offensive, he would begin to understand that he had miscalculated. This is the story that unfolds in Section 2.

Section 9.2 - Taking the Offensive: Operations and Tactics, Summer 1966 to End 1967

By the late summer of 1966, Westmoreland thought he had enough combat forces to undertake his Phase II offensive. In the words of the US Army Vietnam War history, *Taking the Offensive*, "for the first time since the spring of 1965, when the American phase of the Vietnam War began in earnest, Westmoreland felt he had enough troops to strike at the enemy, pin him down, and inflict heavy casualties."

There were now 350,000 American soldiers in country. Along with other Free World Forces, mostly South Korean troops, this amounted to 102 battalions available for the offensive – compared to some 45 in the previous twelve months. The ARVN, whose main units had been static and recovering from their near 1965 defeat, also increased its strength somewhat. It now had 163 maneuver battalions. Most of these would be only capable of defensive operations in the populated areas. Some - mainly the ranger, airborne, and marine units - could operate with their advisors in support of US offensive operations. The MACV commander, furthermore, expected in the second half of 1966 and the first month of 1967, an additional nine US battalions.

Evaluating the friendly force situation, Westmoreland assessed that his spoiling attacks had been successful. They had kept the PAVN/PLAF main forces from defeating the ARVN and given them some reprieve to recover. The US attacks had also prevented most of the enemy main forces from penetrating the major population areas permanently. Another plus was that kill ratios (enemy killed in action versus Allied) in the first months of 1966 had increased over those in 1965.

Also encouraging were the statistics on enemy activities in the lowlands, which were dropping. Along with those, a new Hamlet Evaluation System, or HES, reported that pacification efforts had increased. These figures, kept by MACV staff and sent to McNamara's Whiz Kids, were an important measure of effectiveness to Washington. McNamara's staff would track them to produce reports on how well the attrition strategy and the Honolulu goals were progressing.

On the downside, US operations had not had a significant impact on the ability of the North to infiltrate forces to the South. They also had not denied the enemy from its principal base areas along the borders, and in South Vietnam, such as War Zone D. Moreover, US casualties were increasing. Over the same six-month period of the kill ratio figures, US killed in action doubled over the earlier 1965 ones.

Meanwhile, ARVN KIAs declined. The American Press, more than McNamara's staff, took note of these latter statistics. Newspaper and Magazine stories reported them with their accounts of the battles. They also accompanied American TV network coverage, which now was daily reporting the war with dramatic battle film to the public. The US Congress was also taking note of the disparity of casualties between US and ARVN forces as a measure of how well the RVN government and its armed forces were fighting their own battles.

The Key Enablers: Intelligence and Logistics

In planning for his late 1966 offensive, Westmoreland struggled with estimating the enemy strength and the location of its principal bases and units. His MACV intelligence apparatus, as the US Army official histories recount, was not yet mature enough to give enough confidence in its assessments. Therefore, the General had to rely on CIA figures. Even after the MACV intelligence organization grew in its effectiveness, there would continue to be a reliance on the two offices; mainly because Washington continued to favor the CIA estimates. This would eventually lead to differences of opinion on general enemy capabilities, and specific infiltration figures.

Both estimates were usually close to the strength of the enemy main forces, which they assessed in 1966 as around 114,000, including approximately 46,300 PAVN. Their estimates of guerrillas (local VC forces and cadre), however, were significantly different. The MACV estimated 112,000. The CIA proposed around 600,000.

These figures would plague the accounting system that McNamara was relying on to assess the war's progress. The difficulty of assessing the guerrilla figures, of course, was enormous. Even the North's estimate of 320,000, their official history admits was uncertain. This problem was because it was impossible to know how many guerrillas supported the communist war effort. It did not substantially upset the North's strategists, but, because it was crucial to the body count ratio that McNamara set up, it was essential to the Whiz Kids.

Intelligence on base areas, furthermore, was of paramount importance to Westmoreland. He had based his strategy on being able to threaten them to get the enemy main forces to engage in combat. This intelligence was a result of several factors. MACV, with ARVN input, knew of the locations of traditional bases from the First Indochina War, which captured documents often verified. For those along the borders, MACV and CIA relied mostly on radio intercepts and captured documents.

Intelligence on enemy bases turned out to be much more reliable than that on the total PAVN/PLAF main forces, guerrillas, and cadre. The most significant problem for US operations against the bases would not be the intelligence on their general location. The main problem was after finding them, getting the enemy forces to stand and fight.

Another critical enabler for Westmoreland's planned offensive was logistics. As previously mentioned, the General had made a conscious decision in the Spring of 1965 to deploy both combat and logistics units at the same time. However, the critical situation of a near collapse of the ARVN forced a MACV decision to get as many US combat forces in country as quickly as possible. Thus, in the course of executing the deployments, the deployment of combat and support units had become imbalanced in favor of combat units.

At the end of 1965, Westmoreland tried to alleviate the risk his forces had been operating under with this imbalance. He decided to get more support forces in the deployment flow. The result was that by the summer of 1966 he was getting the logistics units in country as fast as they could deploy from the States and US bases in the Pacific.

The logistics challenge, however, continued to be immense. South Vietnam did not have the ports, airfields, roads, railroads, pipelines, or other infrastructure to support the buildup of American forces envisioned for Westmoreland's offensive. While the US had begun in late 1965 to deploy the needed forces and materials to construct the required infrastructure and reception and onward movement capabilities to support and sustain the buildup of US combat forces, there was still a critical lack of facilities and shortages in supplies.

By Spring 1966, however, the imbalance had become rectified, and MACV had accelerated its program to build the necessary support infrastructure. The resultant effort and outcome were extraordinary. The most critical logistical need was for ports and airfields, with the former a priority. Most of the US combat divisions equipment came into country through those ports. Initially, the only capable port was at Saigon. It had the deep-water peers required for offloading cargo from large oceangoing ships carrying most of the needed equipment and bulk supplies for American combat units.

However, even the Saigon port had significant limitations in off-loading capacity, storage areas, facilities, and transportation capability. To support the build-up, US military logistics units and contractors began to correct these limitations. They had also started improving other ports at Cam Ranh Bay and Da Nang. To accommodate the required offensive force, however, Westmoreland needed more.

A new Army logistics command, and its subordinate units distributed to key locations, rapidly expanded the required ports, facilities, and onward movement capabilities for US forces. By late summer of 1966, there were now deep-water ports and airfields available at an expanded Saigon Port and Vung Tau, and nearby airfields. Logistics units built other similar capable ports and airfields at Cam Ranh Bay, Nha Trang, and Qui Nhon. By the end of 1967, there would be ten; plus, three other shallower ports.

Many of these were made more effective through the use of artificial structures, called DaLong Piers. These allowed the handling of more cargo ships and faster unloading, and ship to shore vessels, which support units used at shallower ports. There was also a tremendous construction effort to create cargo holding areas and depots for receipt and distribution of materials. As the need for more supplies and equipment increased because of the offensive - especially for aviation fuels and ammunition - facilities further increased to keep pace.

US Engineer and other logistic units also expanded the base camps of the major combat and combat support commands. For the combat units, these camps usually were home to US divisions and separate brigades. In turn, as divisional units arrived, their major subordinate elements, usually brigades, built their own forward base camps. As these units launched their offensive operations, they further set up fire support bases that gave artillery support to their infantry. At the height of Westmoreland' upcoming offensive, there would be some twenty-seven major base camps and cantonment areas. There would also be fifty-three major forward base camps and hundreds of fire support bases, some temporary and some permanent, throughout South Vietnam.

Campaign Planning for Phase II Offensive: Setting up Command Priorities

Westmoreland's updated campaign for the 1966 offensive designated several 'mission-oriented areas' for the employment of all forces. The most critical were his 'National Priority Areas and 'Areas of Priority for Military Offensive Operations.' These "two priority categories comprised about half of South Vietnam and included about 77 percent of its population, 85 percent of its food production, and 75 percent of its roads."

The MACV headquarters also estimated that these areas contained "77 percent of the enemy's conventional units and 43 percent of his bases". General Westmoreland assigned primarily the National Priority Areas, which corresponded to the major population centers, to the ARVN. He assigned operations in the Areas of Priority for Offensive Operations, which entailed mostly the known enemy base areas in the unpopulated regions, to the US and other Allied forces.

Within these ranked areas, the MACV commander further prioritized force dispositions and operations in the ARVN regions for his Corps headquarters – the III Marine Amphibious Force, II Field Force, and I Field Force. His first priority was still the ARVN III Corps (his I Field Force) region, which encompassed the environs of Saigon and the largest communist base camps. Saigon was close to those camps and the Cambodia border, where more camps and the infamous COSVN headquarters lurked. His intelligence had also informed him of the buildup of communist forces in Cambodia, which the Cambodian leader, Prince Sihanouk, had allowed.

His second priority was now the I Corps region, where the III MAF conducted its operations. There, as 1966 progressed, Westmoreland was increasingly worried about the buildup of PAVN forces at the DMZ and along the western border near the Ho Chi Minh Trail. He thought that an enemy attack there might quickly overrun the northern provinces. Such a move would give an opportunity for the Northern Communists to set up an alternative government there. He reasoned that such a government would offer a way for the North Vietnamese to negotiate an interim solution to end the fighting, obtain the withdrawal of US forces, and then reunify Vietnam eventually under communist rule.

Westmoreland also thought that the presence of the very capable PAVN divisions in II Corps, his third priority region, could do something similar. From their border base areas, they could launch operations to seize key areas along the major west to east Route 15, sever the RVN, and set up a provincial communist government. That outcome, MACV thought, could easily be accomplished because the ARVN forces in the Highland Region were the least capable and most corrupt in the South Vietnamese Armed Forces.

Finally, the last of his priorities, at least for now, was the rice rich IV Corps region. It had been the birth of the insurgency in the south. It still was mostly communist controlled. Left alone, enemy forces there, mainly PLAF, could assist any drive on Saigon. Though Westmoreland had not been able to allocate any US forces there, by 1967 he thought he would be able to do so.

With this in mind, MACV began exploring the possibility of creating a unique Army-Navy Task Force that would be able to operate in the predominant marshy rice bogs along the Mekong Delta that dominated the region. This initiative came to fruition in 1967, when elements of the US 9th Infantry Division teamed with the Navy to form the Riverine Force.

The First of the 'Big Unit' Operations - OPERATION ATTLEBORO

Completing his plans and issuing them to his subordinates, Westmoreland pondered when to begin his primary offensive. He decided to wait until the early fall - after the monsoon season was over in his III Corps priority region, thus providing the best weather for his aviation capabilities. The MACV commander also thought that this timing would give his newly arrived units a period to adjust and acclimate to Vietnam. Meanwhile, he felt comfortable that his ring of bases around the Saigon area would protect the RVN capital from any enemy threat.

The enemy in III Corps did not wait for Westmoreland to have the favorable weather he sought. General Thanh, the COSVN commander that Le Duan had sent South to do his bidding, directed the 9th PLAF Division to attack out of its War Zone C base the American forces in Tay Ninh Province.

Its objective was to inflict heavy casualties on the newly arrived US 196th Infantry Brigade, disrupt the ARVN pacification effort in the province, seize control of areas not yet 'liberated,' and counter any plans for attacks against his base areas. On 14 September, the 9th struck a battalion of the 196th just outside of the city of Tay Ninh, the Province capital.

Over the next two months, this first contact turned into the first American Corps size offensive of the war – OPERATION ATTLEBORO. The US II Field Force commander, General Seaman, would eventually employ not just the 196th Brigade in a series of battles, but elements of the US 25th Infantry and the 1st Infantry Division, as well. The 9th PLAF Division would employ all its three regiments and involve many of the local VC forces in the Province. For two months, there were dozens of small, but fierce engagements involving US and PLAF platoons and companies that lasted less than an hour.

There were also several larger engagements involving battalions, with thousands of soldiers involved on both sides, which lasted several days. American units unexpectedly ran into carefully prepared entrenched enemy positions. Just as surprisingly, PLAF units ran into US ambushes. US commanders maneuvered to entrap the VC units. The latter managed, with knowledge of the area, to escape. After the operation, American commanders learned to employ new tactics and techniques to counter a competent enemy. PLAF commanders continued to learn how to engage the superior mobility and firepower of its enemy.

On both sides, there were many instances of bravery. Over 20,000 American soldiers took part in this first major 'Big Unit' war, as some would refer to this kind of operation. US units captured or destroyed vast quantities of supplies and scores of base camps. They killed over a thousand PLAF soldiers; with a loss of 155 killed in action, and 494 wounded. McNamara's Whiz Kids loved the kill ratios.

American senior leaders involved reported that the operation virtually destroyed the 9th Division. Captured enemy documents later revealed that the PLAF division, though it had taken heavy casualties, had escaped destruction, and survived the American attack. It did so by fleeing to Cambodia, where it would refit to rejoin the fight in War Zone C and the III Corps region many times after.

For Westmoreland, OPERATION ATTLEBORO showed that the elusive communist forces in the South would fight to protect its base areas. Thus, his focus on attacking them with major US forces could lead to their destruction at best, or at least to the heavy casualties he sought in his attrition strategy. Like the Ia Drang campaign in the fall of 1965, the first operation of his 1966 offensive confirmed for him his strategic approach.

The Battles for the Enemy Base Areas in III Corps – OPERATIONS CEDAR FALLS and JUNCTION CITY

Confident that these operations could succeed, Westmoreland in early January 1967 decided to attack the Iron Triangle base area less than 10 miles southeast from War Zone C and about 35 miles from Saigon. Before this time, he had only conducted small, brigade-size operations there. Now, it would be a Corps multiple-division operation using thousands of soldiers commanded by the II Field Force Commander. The name of this operation was CEDAR FALLS.

General Seaman's plan for the operation was the classic military one already used in the war – the 'Hammer and Anvil' tactic. He would employ two brigades, one from the 25th Infantry Division and the 196th Separate Infantry Brigade, to the southwest side of the Triangle along the Saigon River. Along the northern and eastern sides of the triangular base area, he placed brigades from the 1st Infantry Division, reinforced by the 173rd Airborne Brigade, the 11th Armored Cavalry Regiment, and some ARVN forces. These units would be the 'Hammer.' They would conduct an attack on the base area, seeking to destroy it and the enemy soldiers in it. The forces allocated to the 'Anvil' southwest side of the base were designated to stop any enemy from escaping.

The operation began on 5 January with some battalions of the 25th Division and the 173rd Airborne using helicopters to air assault to their positions in the 'Hammer and Anvil' scheme. This was to deceive the enemy as to the actual scheme of maneuver and the intent to employ such a massive force against its base area. Four days later, battalion units from the 1st Division air assaulted into the triangle area along landing zones on the northern and eastern side of the triangle. Additional units followed to form the entire 'Hammer and Anvil' encirclement.

For the next two weeks, American infantry and armored vehicles, accompanied by engineer plows that were to destroy bunkers and collapse tunnels, swept the base area. No large battles, like those of ATTLEBORO, occurred. However, there were a series of small firefights that were frightening enough to the infantry soldiers or 'grunts' as they called themselves. These fights were fierce enough to cause 750 enemy KIA and the capture of 280 more. Friendly casualties included 72 American soldiers killed and 337 wounded. There were also 3 ARVN soldiers killed and eight wounded.

Like many of these large-scale operations, CEDAR FALLS caused the uprooting of the South Vietnamese civilians within and along the triangle area. This dislodgement resulted in the movement of almost 3,000 civilians by the ARVN and Americans to new areas just outside and within Saigon. Meanwhile, their villages were destroyed, livestock lost, and rice harvest ruined so it could not be of use to the VC. The Press, of course, captured all the devastation to the South Vietnamese civilians and their homes, and showed it all on the TV sets in America.

Taking the Offensive sums up much of the positive results of the operation. "When CEDAR FALLS ended on 26 January, the combined American and South Vietnamese force had found and destroyed all the main headquarters installations in *Military Region* 4, including over 1,100 bunkers, 400 tunnels, and 500 other structures. They had captured over 600 weapons along with large quantities of ammunition, mines, and booby traps and had seized over 3,700 tons of rice...."

The history further states that "The intelligence windfall from CEDAR FALLS was even greater than expected. Of 491,553 pages of enemy documents captured, 52,797 (11 percent) were either summarized or fully translated by the Combined Document Exploitation Center in Saigon. Those documents containing perishable intelligence-information, which required immediate action if it was to have value, received the highest priority."

General DePuy, now the American commander of the 1st Infantry Division in the operation, declared the Iron Triangle destroyed and denied to the VC. This was hardly the situation. Despite the employment of several US divisions, the main PLAF units operating there had escaped. While the VC would not use the Iron Triangle for some time, they would return. It would be a significant area for the launch of the 1968 TET offensive. It would later become an important stepping stone to the attack on Saigon in 1975.

In early 1967, soon after CEDAR FALLS, Westmoreland approved of another Corps size operation. This one would attack War Zone C. While earlier assaults there were 'spoiling' ones intended to disrupt enemy offensives, this one was to permanently deny its use to the communist command and destroy the VC and NVA forces there. This operation, called JUNCTION CITY, was the largest operation of the war involving American forces.

Like CEDAR FALLS, the plan entailed another 'Hammer and Anvil' tactic intended to encircle the PLAF forces and its main headquarters. On the first day, three brigades [almost 6,000 soldiers] would air assault into positions north of the base area and between the Cambodia-South Vietnam border. This force would be the 'Anvil.' Two other brigades would move overland and establish a north to south arch on the west and another on the east to further seal the area. Finally, another two-brigade size force would form the 'Hammer' and sweep War Zone C from the south to the north toward the Cambodia border.

This maneuver involved almost all the I Field Force combat units, some 35,000 American soldiers. Nearly 200 artillery guns would provide fire support, along with more than 4,000 Air Force sorties [number of aircraft support missions]. It also employed almost 250 helicopters, "making JUNCTION CITY the largest air assault in the history of US Army aviation." Finally, thirteen Air Force C-130 transports dropped paratroopers from the 173rd Airborne Brigade as part of the eastern sealing force in the first and the last US combat parachute assault in the war.

Preceded by a massive B52 strike and Air Force fighter and Army gunship preparations of the landing zones, the entire Anvil force was in place on the first day, the 22d of February. They prepared defensive positions, ambushes, and sent out patrols. At first, they met light resistance. The next day the other forces were in place, and the 'Hammer' brigades launched their attack north into the base area. For the next week, allied units – including ARVN marines – swept the entire war zone. Despite some fierce fighting, most of the PLAF/NVA forces and the COSVN headquarters escaped.

Nevertheless, the Communist Front commander decided to counter, at places of his choosing, the US troops. This included attacking mostly American small unit night defensive positions, remote fire support bases, and ambushing vulnerable and surprised US infantry patrols. Several significant attacks included battalion size assaults, at night, against well-defended American companies.

One attack against a firebase encountered an American infantry battalion and nearly overran the base. With massive US employment of fire support, the attack resulted in 647 VC dead. In the assault, PLAF soldiers nearly killed a future Chairman of the Joint Chiefs of Staff, Lieutenant Colonel John Vessey.

Another major attack involved an American battalion at a firebase commanded by LTC Alexander Haig, who would later be Henry Kissinger's primary military advisor. It too resulted in massive VC ground assaults, with significant casualties. However, even though an entire PLAF Division was involved in these attacks and took heavy losses, US forces were never able to trap or destroy it.

The US Army official histories and studies, namely *Taking the Offensive* and *Cedar Falls - Junction City: Turning Point*, characterize JUNCTION CITY as a highly successful offensive with very positive results. American units, especially engineers with plows, did severe damage to the bunkers, tunnels, and training areas of the PLAF. They uncovered and destroyed hundreds of tons of food and munitions, thousands of weapons, and one-half million pages of documents. They also killed 2,728 VC soldiers.

However, as the history admits, once again the operation "had not proved to be the victory that Westmoreland had wanted." Major VC units and the COSVN headquarters escaped. American commanders - though this was the largest force put together for an operation during the war - knew that they just did not have enough forces to destroy the enemy base areas, occupy them permanently, and thus deny them to the enemy.

More importantly, they knew that, despite the casualties that occurred, the enemy had the initiative. He chose when and where to attack. For a strategy that depended on finding and engaging an enemy to attrite his forces, this was problematic, to say the least.

In fact, though he was positive about his ability to conduct offensive operations against the enemy's main base areas, Westmoreland recognized that the enemy still had the initiative. He was becoming increasingly aware that despite enemy losses of about 72,000 in the last six months of 1966, infiltration from the North continued. MACV staff officers began to feel that enemy forces could continue to send troops south to increase its troops there indefinitely unless some dramatic campaign brought the bulk of the PAVN reinforcements to battle and its lifeline of the Ho Chi Minh Trail severed.

OPERATION PERSHING and the Battles Along the II CORPS Borders

In the II Corps area, Westmoreland's forces were spread thin. Despite the arrival of the 4th Infantry Division by the summer of 1966, he could not sustain simultaneous offensives against the PAVN border base areas and those located in the mountainous regions near the coastal population centers. He had, by October 1966, two Korean Divisions, which he positioned along the coast with division bases at Qui Non and Nha Trang. The American Field Force Commander decided to use them to conduct operations in those populated areas and to protect the vital logistics bases there.

In addition, Westmoreland had the brigade of the 101st, positioned in October at Tuy Hoa. He saw that unit as a MACV reserve that he could use wherever needed. There were also two major US divisions available for offensive operations - the 1st Cavalry, with its base at An Khe, and the 4th Infantry at Pleiku.

From October 1966 to April 1967, the 4th Infantry took on the PAVN forces in the II Corps border areas. Several operations focused on PAVN Base Area 702 astride the Cambodia border. There American forces periodically engaged four NVA regiments from October 1966 to April 1967. The battles here were different from any other American unit operating against the PAVN or PLAF forces that were not along the Cambodian or Laotian border.

These border battles were some of the most intense and bloody of the war. This was because the PAVN forces along the frontier were well rested and armed. They could conduct sustained operations against ARVN and US forces. This capability was due to their proximity to their primary base camps there, and the resultant ability to have more food and ammunition stocks to draw upon.

They were also able to escape across the borders to Cambodia or Laos when necessary. This ability was a great morale booster for the North Vietnam soldiers. The above factors made the PAVN in the border areas much more aggressive and able to inflict severe losses on American forces when it favored them. Thus, nine of eleven engagements (involving battalion size forces) fought there occurred within three miles of the border.

The US 4th Division's border battles would last until the end of 1967. Like other places in South Vietnam, along these boundaries with Laos and Cambodia, there were Special Forces Camps positioned to monitor PAVN infiltration into the South. These had many things in common regarding the combined forces manning them and their layout. However, there was one characteristic that they had most in common - they were 'magnets' for PAVN and PLAF assaults.

Such was the case for a Special Forces camp at Dak To in Kontum Province. In 1966, the NVA had attacked that camp and nearly overrun it; but elements of the brigade of the 101st Airborne sent to rescue it prevented this. Now by mid-1967, the 4th Infantry had set up its forward headquarters there to command and control operations in the western extremities of the Province.

The North Vietnamese Front Commander, General Thao, had orders to attack the Camp and draw US forces into the mountains surrounding it. The PAVN command intended this operation to divert American troops from the lowlands for a country-wide offensive at the beginning of the next year. To accomplish this task, PAVN regulars had been moving along the Ho Chi Minh Trail and reinforcing other NVA forces just inside the Cambodian-Laotian borders.

Four PAVN regiments were in the hills surrounding Dak To. They were well entrenched and looked-for opportunities to lure US forces into prearranged ambushes and longer fights. Acting on the intelligence of this build up, the 4th Division, now reinforced with the 173rd Airborne Brigade, which had become the theater reserve after Westmoreland sent the 101st brigade north to reinforce the Marines, moved to find the PAVN and spoil any attack against Dak To and other ARVN positions in the Kontum area.

According to US Army's official history *Staying the Course*, after some small skirmishes through October 1967, a battalion of the 4th engaged the PAVN 32d Regiment, dug in on top of one of the many hills surrounding Dak To on 3 November. For the next month, battles raged along the mountain ridges and hilltops on which the NVA had set up their redoubts. Casualties were high on both sides. As usual, American firepower - artillery and air strikes - was intense and, on several occasions, saved outnumbered American infantry units from being overrun. PAVN losses were estimated at over 1600, while Americans suffered 289 killed in action and South Vietnamese paratroopers 73. Publicly, both sides claimed a victory.

While the above American forces battled inland and near the borders of the II Corps area, the 1st Cavalry Division at the end of 1966 still focused on the fertile and populous Bong Son Plain area in Binh Dinh Province. At the beginning of 1967, the then 1st Cavalry commander, Major General Norton, decided that he would employ portions of his division to "finish off NVA forces" in the northern part of the Province. He launched Operation PERSHING to do so. For the first time in over a year, all the brigades of his division fought a running battle with the PAVN and PLAF forces in the Province.

The campaign would last into the fall. During that time, elements of the division engaged all three PAVN regiments in the area. Many of these engagements were small skirmishes. Some were significant battles involving multiple battalions. The American air assault capabilities allowed divisional units to shift quickly about the battlefields.

At the end of the operation, the three PAVN regiments lost two-thirds of its total strength of 11,000 soldiers. They had to withdraw deep into the highlands. The Hamlet Evaluation System reported that within the Province 68% of the hamlets were now under RVN control. That was an increase from 22% from the end of 1966. However, the campaign also uprooted some 140,000 Vietnamese civilians from their homes. By the end of 1967, the refugee problem throughout South Vietnam had become a significant issue.

Also by the end of 1967, American forces had learned a great deal about their enemies. The PAVN and PLAF main force units were dedicated forces, well trained, and acclimated to the weather and terrain better than their American opponents. Along the borders, in their well-built and entrenched base camps, these forces were well armed and employed aggressive tactics to lure the Americans into ambushes and fire zones. If large US combat formations could penetrate and even destroy these formidable base camps, NVA and VC main forces could withdraw across the international border and regroup and refit to return, often at full strength.

Near the coastal areas, enemy forces operating from their long established and hidden base areas in difficult tripled canopy jungle and mountainous terrain could threaten populated areas almost at will if they had adequate support from their local forces. However, they often could not engage in a sustained battle for several days with US forces. This was because they were far from the supply lines along the Ho Chi Minh Trail complex and the depots in their major base camps. Nevertheless, the VC local security forces and their political cadres still could threaten and, in many instances, hold sway over numerous hamlets and villages if not the cities.

US combat units learned and adapted to this varied enemy and the environment by altering their tactics and techniques. Contrary to many accounts, American forces did not operate as if they were in a conventional war environment such as Europe. They did not blindly act per doctrine developed for a conventional war. The American Army developed new tactics, techniques, and procedures that they used throughout the war.

For example, as described in Erik Villard's *Staying the Course*, American forces employed new tactics such as 'pile on' operations, 'checkerboard' and 'cloverleaf' reconnaissance in force missions, and night defensive positions – such as the DePuy bunker. US units developed their ambush techniques and employed them along the routes that enemy units habitually used to travel between their jungle and mountain hideouts and their targeted hamlets and villages. Moreover, American use of new air assault procedures countered enemy actions to attack US units landing in vulnerable landing zones.

American unit use of its available firepower was a prerequisite for survival. Too often US infantry organizations found themselves outnumbered because they were fighting on their enemy's terrain and country. Indirect firepower, artillery, and air support, was the equalizer. Unfortunately, when fighting in populated areas, too often this dependence resulted in unintended civilian casualties.

To both maintain their proficiency in all the above and to further train new replacements, US divisions and separate brigades created in-country training facilities to train new soldiers in these adaptations, as well as give refresher training opportunities to units not engaged in an active operation. Often this training was among the best that any US soldier or marine would ever receive in their service. Often this experience also overcame some deficiencies in combat effectiveness due to rotational policies, though not all. Most often, this training was much different from the traditional doctrine of the US Army for a fight against the Soviets on the plains of Europe. The argument of some scholars that the US Army somehow clung to its conventional ways during the war is just false.

The 'Big Unit' War in the North

In the ARVN I Corps northern region, Westmoreland was aware that the Marines could not counter the PAVN build up along the DMZ and to the west and conduct operations along the breadth of the populated coastal regions. By the end of 1966 and into the beginning of 1967, General Walt had to increasingly concentrate on the PAVN threat in the northern and western reaches of I Corps.

The III Marine Amphibious Force commander had to withdraw the 3rd Marine Division from its operations along the densely populated coastal region and employ it in the DMZ area to counter infiltration and attacks against the northern Quang Tri Province. Soon a line of Marine Corps outposts ran from the eastern main north-south highway, Route 1 at Dong Ha, along the east to west highway, Route 9, toward the Laotian border where the Marines had a battalion outpost at Khe Sanh. The PAVN forces in that area, who had established themselves in the DMZ generally along the Ben Hai River, regularly attacked the US Marines primarily with rockets and artillery, and, from time to time, with some infantry as well.

North Vietnam, moreover, periodically infiltrated large PAVN forces across the DMZ to attack key installations in Quang Tri. To thwart some of this, the Marines conducted patrols to detect these movements and counter them with quick reaction forces nearby. In the last months of 1966, several of these patrols had detected PAVN main forces moving into the South. Elements of the 3rd Marine Division had fought several battles that seemed much more conventional than what was then attributed to the war.

Back in Washington, McNamara took notice of the situation along the DMZ. He commissioned a study on how developing technologies could help. In September 1966, he gave the results to both the JCS and Admiral Sharp, Westmoreland's superior. Neither thought the concept was worth the effort. Despite resistance on the feasibility of the study, the Secretary ordered that the study's concept of an electronic barrier system be employed.

McNamara felt that it could be a substitute for more deployments that he knew Westmoreland would be asking for. The concept also fit well in the Secretary's effort, as explained in Chapter 3, to change the war into one that he could level off forces and wait for the North to give up and seek a negotiated settlement.

In January 1967, LBJ approved of the concept, and the Administration budgeted $1.5 billion for its construction. Erection would begin in the summer of 1967. The 3rd Marine Division had to devote resources toward construction that took away already short infantry assets for their combat patrols from their outposts. Despite the Secretary's support, MACV never completed the so-called McNamara Line. Despite the expenditures, the project never created, in the terms of the McNamara Whiz Kids, 'cost effective' results.

As the Marines were trying to complete the construction of this 'barrier,' the infiltration continued and even increased. So did the many encounters between Marines and the PAVN infiltrators. Meanwhile, the NVA also increased their attacks against the Marines at Khe Sanh. Their VC counterparts increased their operations in the southern part of I Corps. This proved too much for the overcommitted Marines to handle effectively. Westmoreland formed an Army Task Force made up of several separate Army brigades, to include his then theater reserve, the brigade from the 101st, and sent it to the I Corps area to aid the Marines.

While the resultant Army Task Force Oregon helped to thwart enemy attacks along the coast, the Marines had to reinforce, toward the end of 1967, the beleaguered forces at Khe Sanh. They also continued to fight a series of engagements along their outpost line south of the DMZ for the rest of the year.

One post, that at Con Thien, fought off an attack by an NVA regiment dressed in Marine uniforms. That outpost turned out to be one of the worst experiences for American infantrymen in the war. In several months, PAVN heavy artillery and rocket units attacked the Marines there with over 3,000 rocket and artillery rounds.

Soon, the PAVN activities in the I Corps region began to change Westmoreland's campaign plan priorities to that area. That shift from 1966 to the end of 1967 was the result of two decisions. Both decisions involved Khe Sanh. One was the enemy's choice to build up around Khe Sanh. This action, as Chapter 7 describes, was perhaps to lure American forces away from the populated areas in preparation for a general uprising offensive planned for the beginning of 1968.

The other was General Westmoreland's idea in March of 1967 to start building a base for an eventual strike against the Ho Chi Minh Trail in Laos. He thought that Khe Sanh could be an ideal base, primarily due to its proximity to the Laotian border and access to routes from South Vietnam for support for such an attack. We will further see that this contingency never became a reality.

The Debate Over the Transition to Phase III in 1968 and the Search for an Alternative Strategy

As operations had continued into 1967, Westmoreland was beginning to have mixed feelings about the success of his attrition strategy. On the plus side, he felt that his offensive had again foiled the enemy's designs to defeat the ARVN and had gained more control of the South Vietnamese population. Moreover, the battles of 1966 and into 1967 had produced massive enemy casualties, confirmed by captured documents and prisoner interrogations.

Over two dozen of these operations had caused over 500 enemy KIA in each – amounting to an estimated 81,000. His argument back in March 1965 that US forces could bring firepower and mobility to bear on the enemy throughout the South seemed validated by his ability to move forces between regions and confront threats to the coastal population centers while attacking the border bases. Thus, he continued to believe that his large unit operations, while not able to destroy the enemy's main forces, could engage significant enough numbers to over time convince the North that it could not win militarily.

Looking at these successes into 1967, Westmoreland proclaimed in his memoirs, "I envisioned 1968 to be the year of the third phase, in which we would continue to help strengthen the Vietnamese Armed Forces - turning over more of the war effort to increasingly capable and better-armed forces." However, he remained unsure of the South Vietnamese ability to significantly contribute to his offensive strategy. He also continued to recognize that he did not have enough combat power to defeat the enemy's main forces and support the security and pacification that was critically necessary to ensure a free and independent South Vietnam.

At the same time, the General was beginning to doubt that his strategy to keep the fight in South Vietnam would be decisive. An essential parameter for him was the fact that despite the casualties that his forces could inflict, the North's infiltration had been able to replace them. In a message to the JCS in January 1967, he had reported that despite their heavy losses the PAVN might have replaced its forces in 1966 by some 12,000 per month. Thus, his staff estimated a strength increase during that year of 42,000. Later, he followed up this statistic with another estimate that was cause for concern. During the first few months of 1967, enemy attacks had increased two-fold during the same period in 1966.

Another critical parameter for Westmoreland as he assessed his strategy in early 1967 was US public support for the war. He had warned from the beginning that achieving his goal to defend South Vietnam and convincing the North it could not win would take time. At the Honolulu Conference, he had warned that the enemy was continuing his aggression because he was counting on the US public to give up its support. His sensing was that the antiwar movement in the States was taking on steam as the war continued.

Therefore, the MACV commander thought it prudent to begin to devise an alternative to his strategy of attrition. That strategy envisioned attacking the Ho Chi Minh complex in Laos. He had originally considered doing so back in his March 1965 concept but had backed off when his civilian superiors indicated that they wanted to avoid any situation that may cause Chinese intervention.

According to Colonel (Retired) Casey Brower in his paper, "Strategic Assessment in Vietnam: The Westmoreland Alternative Strategy of 1967-1968," Westmoreland now thought it viable because it could deny the North's capability to infiltrate forces and continue to threaten pacification efforts in the South. He also would have by the end of the year, with a few more support units, the logistical capability to sustain such an assault.

MACV had already been at work on contingency plans for the trail. Some of these were raids; others were limited attacks in size and duration but more substantial than the raids. There also was a plan for a Corps size (multiple divisions consisting of tens of thousands of troops) offensive. Now Westmoreland tasked his staff to 'dust these off' and put more substance to them, but to do so in the "utmost secrecy."

Staff officers labeled the resultant plan for the attack into Laos, OPERATION EL PASO. Its concept of operations called for a Corps sized force of several US divisions with the necessary support forces, to attack out of northern South Vietnam along the west-east Highway 9 into Laos. Khe Sanh, which Westmoreland had already built up, was to be the jump-off point and the main sustainment base for the attack.

The objective of the operations was to seize major North Vietnamese depots, destroy base areas, and block the major infiltration route into the South. The plan intended to permanently interdict the trail in Laos so that the North would be denied its use to reinforce its forces in South Vietnam. In Brower's explanation, the end state was to isolate the battlefield (the South) and in turn then destroy the PAVN and PLAF main forces in South Vietnam. Thus, the strategy's primary purpose was to impose on North Vietnam the need for a settlement. All that was needed were the forces to execute it.

In March, while his 1967 operations described above were ongoing, Westmoreland sent his troop requirements for 1968. His staff drafted several force options. They based these various troop levels on assumptions of availability of forces, mobilization decisions, and contingency plans. For each possibility, Westmoreland gave a concept of how the added forces would be employed.

He labeled the options as the 'optimum force' and the 'minimum essential force.' The optimum called for a reinforcement of 4 and 2/3 divisions and support units or some 201,250 soldiers, representing an increase in his current ceiling of 470,366 to 671,616. The minimum represented an increase of 2 and 1/3 divisions and would add another 80,576 troops.

The 'optimum force' option fulfilled the necessary combat power and support units Westmoreland felt he needed for the Laotian offensive. His message forwarding the options emphasized that it would expedite the achievement of success; thus offering the Administration a way of ending the war more quickly and providing a way of avoiding the growing dissent in America over the conflict. This was no small incentive for the President, with an election year coming up in 1968.

On the other hand, there were significant drawbacks and risks involved. Westmoreland was not sure that LBJ would chance such an increase in forces given public opinion polls showing some resistance to the war – mainly because in just another year there would be an election coming up. The increased costs of the war, he surmised, would also come into question. Finally, he would have to defend the issue on how long could the North hold out with the trail interdicted, and how long would he be able to sustain forces in Laos?

The *Pentagon Papers* states that the debate in Washington over these options' forces and numbers was extensive and intense. It lasted until the fall of 1967. The results were not favorable to the campaign planned for 1968 – nor certainly for any contingency to sever the Ho Chi Minh Trail. McNamara's civilian defense analysts ignored the employment concepts for the force levels. Troop numbers, kill ratios, costs, and political decisions on what it would necessitate providing the forces dominated the debate.

At first, the JCS led the argument for the optimum force levels proposed by Westmoreland. McNamara and his Whiz Kid analysts led the fight against it. The JCS argued that the higher force provisions would allow the MACV commander "to reduce and obstruct the enemy capability to import the material support to sustain the war effort." The defense analysts were against the significant increase and called for more efficiency in the kill ratios.

The Defense analysts' principal argument was that MACV had not accurately tracked infiltration rates versus attrition of enemy forces in the South. They hoped that with a more accurate assessment, the Administration would see that the war could be won over time with just the minimum option number of troops. They also argued for the more efficient use of the ARVN to offset any American added forces.

Again, the basis of the Defense analysts' argument was what the numbers showed. The method for the conclusion was systems analysis. The number one concern was cost-effectiveness; not what the theater commander needed to win the war. McNamara dominated this view.

As mentioned, the Defense Secretary had grown disillusioned with the war. The Secretary now sought to keep the force levels in South Vietnam at around the 500,000 mark. He also thought once again as he had done the previous year that the Administration should seek a negotiated settlement.

Amidst the debate, Westmoreland returned to the US to undertake a review of the situation in South Vietnam, and, at the behest of the President, to gather support for the war effort. On 27 April 1967, he met with the President at the White House. The most prominent people present were Secretary McNamara, Secretary of State Rusk, Walt Rostow the National Security Advisor, and General Wheeler, the Chairman of the JCS. The primary subject was MACV's troop request for 1968.

This meeting shows how LBJ and his principal advisors viewed the war in Spring 1967. It also is an example of how well Johnson's military commander and principal advisor could convey their case for a new approach on how to win the war. Finally, it may have been, in retrospect, the best opportunity to change the military course in Vietnam and compel, rather than convince, the North to cease its support for the conflict in South Vietnam.

As documents in the *Foreign Relations of the United States*, the *Pentagon Papers*, *The US Government and the Vietnam War*, and Westmoreland's and McNamara's memoirs describe, the discussion was detailed, but curiously subdued on the part of the MACV commander. Westmoreland began by briefing the President on his strategy for the war, the current situation and his rationale for the additional forces requested. LBJ asked pointed questions on several issues. Wheeler chimed in on several of Westmoreland's answers. In the end, McNamara provided his pessimistic thoughts on the war to date and the request for reinforcements.

On his strategy, Westmoreland summarized what he had already told the President. He said, "we are fighting a war of attrition in Southeast Asia." He further explained that this approach was like a "meat-grinder" in which we had to "kill large numbers of the enemy" to get a result that would convince him to give up. The General then reported he thought that "last month we reached the crossover point. In areas excluding the two northern provinces, attrition will be greater than additions to the force."

The MACV commander then provided a short assessment of his current troop levels by saying, "with the troops now in country, we are not going to lose, but progress will be slowed down. This is not an encouraging outlook, but it's is a realistic one." His troop request, he explained, would accelerate the enemy losses, and would expedite the war's end from five years to three years. Indeed, he further emphasized, if given his optimum force, he could further cut the period to even two years.

LBJ seemed most concerned about the infiltration abilities of the North. He asked, "When we add divisions can't the enemy add divisions? If so, where does it all end?" Surprisingly, Westmoreland did not have a definitive answer. He avoided one, by explaining that he thought with the additional forces he could attrite the enemy at a cost that the North eventually could not replenish. He implied, however, that North Vietnamese infiltration could be severely damaged by a military operation into Laos that "would take the pressure off the South."

Curiously, Westmoreland did not divulge or explain or argue forcibly or cogently for his US force contingency plan. His tack, and that of Wheeler's, was to tie the increased US force commitment to reducing the time to win the war.

The President further asked, "What if we do not add the 2-1/3 divisions?" General Wheeler responded, "The momentum will die; in some areas the enemy will recapture the initiative. We won't lose the war, but it will be a longer one." LBJ retorted, "we should make certain we are getting value received from the South Vietnamese troops." He also asked about forming an "international division" with more Korean, Thai, and Australian troops. There was no response recorded.

According to Westmoreland, the meeting adjourned with no decision. He sensed, however, that McNamara was not supportive. In his memoirs, the General wrote, "As the discussion neared a close, Secretary McNamara wrung from me an estimate of how long 'it would take to wind down our involvement' under each of my two plans. Assuming that the air war against North Vietnam and in the Laotian panhandle would continue, I said finally: 'With the optimum force, about three years: with the minimum force, at least five.'"

Unknown to Westmoreland at the time was that the Defense Secretary in listening to the arguments for more troops thought, as revealed in his memoirs, "that all of this demonstrated that our policy was failing: bombing and ground operations were not working, and our diplomatic initiatives, such as they were, were proving clumsy and ineffective. These harsh facts led me to conclude…that it was time to change our objectives in Vietnam and the means by which we sought to achieve them."

As the totality of the current evidence shows, for McNamara that change meant keeping the costs of the war down and placing more emphasis on peace initiatives and the use of bombing pauses as incentives for starting negotiations. He had completely lost faith in the war, which led to a gradual, apparent and slow deterioration in his ability to further function as a war advisor.

The MACV commander, reflecting in his memoirs years later, had sensed from his 27 April meeting that the President was also reticent about progress in the war. Again, curiously, his recollections of this meeting do not offer any further clues on why he did not provide a more detailed and convincing argument for his alternative strategy.

He had a perfect opportunity to do so given the President's concern over infiltration. Thus, the General may have been able to convince LBJ that with the additional forces and interdiction of the Trail in Laos he could have compelled the North to give up by denying him the ability to reinforce the South. Perhaps it was because he sensed that both the Secretary and the President would not have approved. Westy was not one to push his superiors when he sensed they would not agree with him.

The notes in both the *Pentagon Papers* and in the *Foreign Relations* documents do not reveal any discussion on an alternative strategy - only on numbers of reinforcements and the enemy's ability to match them. Westmoreland does mention the possibility of attacking the Laos lines of communication but states that ARVN forces would conduct it and implies that it would be more a raid than an offensive to change the war.

The General went on to give a speech at West Point and then appeared before a joint session of Congress to give an upbeat progress report. To Congress he reported, "Given the nature of the enemy, it seems to me that the strategy that we are following at this time is the proper one, and that is producing results. While he is obviously far from quitting, there are signs that his morale and his military structure are beginning to deteriorate. The rate of decline will be in proportion to the pressure directed against him."

As he had done at the Honolulu Conference at the beginning of 1966, he prophetically mentioned, "As I have said before, in evaluating the enemy strategy it is evident to me that he believes our Achilles' heel is our resolve. Your continued strong support is vital to the success of our mission…." While he received vigorous applause for his remarks and he offered an impressive military salute in response, it would not be long before the North Vietnamese would attack that Achilles' heel.

Getting reinforcements to quicken the war's end or, at the least, stealing public support, was now almost entirely hostage to the Administration's domestic concerns. Adding significant numbers of troops was now becoming a problem of not just getting an agreement to do so. Any more above the current levels would require the President to order the execution of a national emergency and call-up of the reserves that were necessary for the Services to provide them. Moreover, as Doris Kearns relates, "the President was now terribly worried about the inflation and economic ramifications of his decision to fight a war and acquire a Great Society at the same time without raising taxes. He needed to cap the amount of forces deploying to Vietnam. "

Moreover, as mentioned several times, McNamara was convinced that the war was becoming a stalemate and that any course to increase US forces would not be cost-effective. He continued to work on a program for leveling off the final numbers of forces in Vietnam. Moreover, the JCS was inadvertently supporting the Defense Secretary's approach by estimating that to fill Westmoreland's optimum reinforcement requirements would dangerously weaken US-NATO forces, and require the call-up of some 600,000 reservists.

Toward the end of the year, absent any convincing military argument and logic, the President approved a modified 'minimum option' for MACV's 1968 campaign. McNamara and his Whiz Kids had convinced LBJ that more troops would not produce higher kill ratio results. The critical factor for the President in getting the needed reinforcements, however, were not kill ratios or military concepts of operation. He again was concerned about further putting the nation, in his words, "on a war footing."

Thus, the JCS informed the Westmoreland that his full reinforcement package and the approved force levels might not be possible. Westmoreland apparently abandoned any hope for his alternative strategy and ordered his staff to study "a possible leveling off point for our forces which might take place after the first of the year."

When McNamara paid a visit in October 1967 to discuss the problem of force levels for 1968, the General informed the Secretary that he could live with a "level-off force" and agreed that such a force should not require any reserve call-up. Westy further gave a 'best estimate' of between 480,000 and 500,000 men. When McNamara returned to Washington, he told the President that he had the field commander's full concurrence in limiting force levels.

General Westmoreland, once again, bent to the will of his superiors without explaining possible adverse outcomes. There also is no indication in any of the evidence that he tried to rebut the Defense Secretary on force issues by making a compelling argument for the Optimum Case for his Operation FULL CRY during the rest of 1967. The only conclusion that one can draw is that the MACV commander remained confident he could still defeat the enemy with a little more than he had by keep doing more of the same. He either did not believe strongly enough in the need to conduct a bold operation in Laos, or he did not want to argue for what he thought he could not obtain. It could have been a combination of both reasons.

Whatever the reasons, Westmoreland obeyed LBJ's request not to pull a MacArthur. Neither did he tell any in Congress that he had misgivings over the current course. He certainly did not contemplate resignation as a show of any conviction in his alternative strategy. He would not have the fortitude or the sense of duty to strongly argue for an attack against the Ho Chi Minh Trail – a move that perhaps would have rivaled MacArthur's brilliant maneuver at Inchon during the Korean War.

The Issue of Combat Power in South Vietnam

With all the number crunching done between Saigon, Hawaii, and Washington, there were two numbers that Westmoreland had direct control of that could influence his ability to execute his attrition strategy and search and destroy operational concept. They were the number and strength of combat forces in the field that could find, fix, and destroy the enemy.

The General, during his tenure as MACV commander, made two significant decisions affecting those numbers. One was the number of base camps and other facilities that American units constructed and the nature of that construction and their security requirements. Another was the rotational policy of soldiers in Vietnam.

As Westmoreland describes in his memoirs, the establishment of base camps throughout South Vietnam was a vital part of his ability to conduct search and destroy operations. As he explains, "Under my plan of operations, every American division and separate brigade was to build a base camp, in effect a home station, which was essential for such rear echelon functions of the division as record keeping and maintaining reserve supplies. When moving far from the base camp, a unit would leave behind a small security and house-keeping cadre. In the field, the unit would erect fire-support bases to serve as protected artillery positions and as combat bases for patrols and for sweeps to find the enemy and his supply caches. Smaller fire-support bases might house artillery along with a small security force."

The US Army's Vietnam Studies volume *Logistics Support* further describes and explains the need and reason for this base camp structure. It emphasizes, "South Vietnam was an austere theater demanding a huge effort to create support bases and troop cantonment areas to sustain combat for an unknown duration. Setting up these bases and areas was critical to combat operations. They would provide the indefinite combat support factors for their sustainment – such as food, clothing, fuel, ammunition, water, material parts, and a host of other factors. Also impacting was the 12,000-mile supply line from the US, and the need to move forward combat sustainment supplies from ports of entry over hundreds of miles forward to combat organizations."

Proudly – and rightly so - this study further states, "the construction done in 1965-68 in South Vietnam enabled the United States to deploy and operate a modern 500,000-man military force in an underdeveloped area. The ground combat force of 165,000 men was able to combat an enemy force effectively from an adequate facility base which permitted US and allied forces to concentrate and operate when and where they wished." To emphasize the magnitude of this effort, the study shows a table of 28 major bases - of division, separate brigade, and supporting logistics units - that could offer housing at any one time for over 210,000 soldiers.

While Westmoreland claims that he "had to maintain a constant vigil to ensure that these camps remained relatively austere," such austerity was not the case – certainly not for the 28 major bases listed in the Army logistics study. These had all the amenities of any stateside base – to include well-constructed wooden barracks, mess halls, movie theaters, food stores, libraries, enlisted and officer clubs. Many of them grew to the size of small American towns and even cities – expanding over hundreds of acres of the South Vietnamese countryside.

Perhaps there is no better compelling source on this extravagance – and its cost to generate combat power in the field - then General Bruce Palmer's memoir of the war, *The 25 Year War*. He writes, "The most pernicious policy encountered was the base camp idea. The manpower it soaked up was appalling, not to mention the waste of material resources and the handicap of having to defend and take care of these albatrosses. We found one separate infantry brigade, operating by itself a long distance from the headquarters to which it reported, that habitually kept almost one-third of its strength, fighting, and support, in an elaborate base camp that could have carried out support missions for a much larger force. It made little sense. Base camps occupied large areas which generated correspondingly large security requirements and almost immobilized the parent unit."

Except for anecdotal information like that above, there appears to be no one document or source that offers in detail all the combat manpower required at any one time to secure these bases and how much it drained, along with other losses, combat power in the field. Some sources provide general estimates of maneuver strength – that is the number of soldiers in the field who were conducting tactical operations. For example, Robert Thompson in his 1969 book *No Exit From Vietnam* claimed, without justifying his numbers, that "in 1968 it was estimated that, out of a total strength of 500,000 American Troops, only 100,000 were operational and only 80,000 could be deployed in sustained operations." More recently, Eric Villard in the Army's official history *Staying the Course* states that in December 1967 "only about 74,000 were in combat maneuver battalions." These numbers are startling figures.

In the Defense Department, where McNamara's Whiz Kids resided, there was also an attempt to assess overall Allied combat field strength to arrive at effective kill ratios. Thomas Thayer, one of those analysts, in his book *War Without Fronts* gives a mountain of numbers on combat ratios regarding maneuver battalions and other figures.

In the end, with the caveats of "rough estimates" and "figures not precise," Thayer claims that "an analysis of force allocations in January 1968 suggests that only 40 percent of the allied maneuver forces were available for offensive operations during that month…. The data may be rough, but the findings seem roughly right, and they are in accord with Sir Robert Thompson's observation." Actually 40% of the 165,000-ground maneuver force, the number in the Army's *Logistics Support* study, is 115,000 and thus is still off by 15,000, which is almost a US division strength.

Whatever the precise figure that either the US Army *Logistics Support* study or the Thompson or Villard or Thayer books claim, none of these give details on how exactly they arrived at these figures, and certainly do not estimate how much such duties as security at these many bases affected their conclusions.

Given the total number of these bases and combining them with the author's combat experiences and involvements in providing this security, one can derive a reasonable estimate. The combat unit forward bases - those subject to either guerrilla harassments, or actual PAVN/PLAF attacks - always had some contingent of infantry support. Westmoreland seems to imply that this protection was a 'small security force.'

However, by most accounts and the author's experiences, the Division size bases sometimes had up to an infantry battalion for protection. For a Brigade camp, as General Palmer claims in one instance, it was also an entire battalion. However, most accounts and in my experience, it was usually an infantry company. Fire support bases varied, but in many instances had an infantry company as well.

Many of the logistics bases tried to use their own forces. However, if there was a significant threat or a VC sapper attack had occurred, infantry units would be called upon to provide a response and subsequent security for a period afterward. Of course, these infantry units did not always just secure the base. They often conducted patrols from them. In populated areas, they also conducted pacification operations. So what does all of this mean toward estimating what the actual US forces were that were available to conduct search and destroy operations?

Assuming a tooth to tail ratio of about 50-50 by the end of 1967, of about 500,000 in country, generally, there were about 250,000 combat troops available for search and destroy missions. This is a somewhat higher figure from the *Logistics Support* study, which may have only included maneuver units in US Army definitions, which did not include specific units that could have conducted tactical operations in the field.

At any one time, however, at least half of that - or approximately 125,000 troops – most likely performed security missions for bases. That left 125,000 for maneuver forces – those that would conduct the search and destroy operations. This number is reasonably close to the one that Thompson and Thayer estimated. However, as will be shown below, this figure still does not offer a reasonable estimation of actual combat strength or the numbers of soldiers available to engage the enemy directly.

For example, other activities and factors had an impact on maneuver unit field strength in the fighting or what was referred to as 'foxhole strength' in Vietnam. For example, another drain on manpower strength and available effective combat power in the Vietnam War for American units was the rotational policies. There were two of them that affected performance and the amount of combat power MACV could field in the theater at any one time. The first was to limit the time that personnel were in country to one year.

In his memoirs, Westmoreland explains his support of this policy. "The harsh conditions provided one of the strongest arguments for a one-year tour of duty, a policy that was in effect when I arrived, and I saw no reason to change it." He further states, "In keeping with my belief that it was going to be a long war, the one-year tour gave a man a goal. That was good for morale. It was also advisable from the standpoint of health, and it spread the burden of a long war over a broader spectrum of both Army regulars and American draftees."

Those rationales were reasonable from a personnel viewpoint, but the impact on unit cohesion, and, most importantly, unit combat effectiveness was extraordinary – particularly for organizations that deployed to Vietnam as units in the first two years. For example, as explained in the MACV history, when the one-year mark came to the 196th Separate Infantry Brigade in 1967, it lost two-thirds of its total officers – to include its commander and all three battalion leaders – that rotated home to the States. In addition, the brigade also lost 2,166 enlisted men or 58% of its total enlisted strength.

The impact on combat operations was not just from these losses. Their replacements mostly came all at once to the brigade; demanding a retraining and acclimation period. The result was that most of the brigade was not available for combat operations for several weeks. Another example was the 4th Infantry Division. From August to October 1967, it lost 10,000 officers and men, or three-fourths of its total authorized strength.

While this rotational impact was a one-time occurrence for units deploying to Vietnam, the one-year rotation policy continued to affect the combat effectiveness of organizations as units received replacements. Sometimes there were days and months that the units would have many soldiers depart on leave. In some instances, they lost all their key personnel - and large chunks of infantrymen.

To alleviate the impact, Commanders tried to manage rotations. At the Field Force level, for instance, in anticipation of significant turnover in one unit, Commanders would send fillers from another unit to one that would experience a significant turnover. However, then, to a smaller extent, both organizations would have a personnel turnover problem. The impact on field strength was significant.

A second rotation policy further exasperated the situation. That policy put in place a rule that critical leaders – mostly battalion, company, and platoon commanders – would only spend six months in their duty position. Again, as Westmoreland explains, "Although there were advantages in a commander holding the same job for a full year, such as cumulative experience and knowledge of his troops, the broader experience was also worthwhile, and a man with command experience could make important contributions to staff work…There were, in any case, good enough officers to take the place of those who moved on from command to staff."

However, 'good enough' does not count as much as combat experience. Besides, as the war continued the field strength of infantry officers at company and below became critical from combat losses. Thus, replacements from hasty production facilities, such as Officer Candidate Schools, did not always produce 'good enough' officers. This resulted in severe leadership problems, like the massacre at My Lai.

Furthermore, the six-month rotation policy often came at odds with operational plans, which sometimes had to change due to the administrative loss of experienced leaders at crucial moments. Moreover, the policy had a tremendous poor morale impact on the infantry 'grunt' soldier, who sometimes saw as many as three to five platoon leaders and company commanders in his unit due to the six-month rotation rule and casualties to these small unit leaders.

Security for bases and rotations alone do not yet offer an answer to total foxhole strength estimate for Westmoreland's search and destroy operations. There were further drains, such as leaves of absence, illnesses, and, of course, casualties. The US Army's official history gives an estimate of the toll of these on field strength in infantry units. As *Taking the Offensive* notes, "Between casualties, illnesses, troop rotations, and rear area duties, rifle companies sometimes took the field with less than half of their men present for duty."

The authorized strength of a US Army infantry company at the time was about 175 soldiers. With the average losses through combat wounds, sickness and injury, and rotations usually an infantry company in the field on combat operations had 80 to 90 soldiers. Marine Corps companies were a bit larger. Allied ones were in between. Assuming that at this time there were approximately 85 Allied maneuver battalions available to MACV with four infantry companies per, that would result in approximately 30,600 foxhole strength combat soldiers available for search and destroy operations at any one time. These calculations seem extraordinarily low. They are more than half of the Thompson, Villard, and Thayer assessments.

Whatever the exact numbers several conclusions can be drawn about US maneuver strength and Westmoreland's strategy of attrition to destroy the enemy's main forces. The actual combat strength in the field was very low. That strength, in turn, had an adverse impact on the war in several ways. First, it limited the number of troops on the ground to find, fix and destroy the enemy. Thus, it may have contributed as much to the inability to engage enemy forces as the NVA/VC prowess to avoid combat when they wanted.

Second, it put tremendous pressure on the individual infantry grunt, who bore the brunt of the fighting and surviving in the challenging environment of South Vietnam. The ultimate cost to the infantry soldier was that of the total casualties of the war, according to US government statistics, the grunt made up 80% of those killed in action. Moreover, the constant strain of search and destroy operations in a demanding environment on a small number of soldiers and marines, especially the enlisted infantryman, affected their abilities to be psychologically and physically alert and capable to fight, which, in turn, resulted in exhaustion and the need to pull units out of the field to refit and recover. This further affected maneuver strength in the war.

Third, from strictly a military operational view, the low foxhole infantry strength available to find, fix, and 'finish' the enemy favored a maneuver to concentrate, rather than disperse your maneuver units to gain maximum combat power. In Westmoreland's scheme in which he allocated his combat maneuver units across all regions, and his concept of building a series of outposts in numerous areas of operations, these units were spread way too thin to accomplish his strategy of attrition.

Though he may not have been aware of the overall effects of personnel policies, security requirements, and operational losses had on effective combat strength, Westmoreland was aware of the dwindling reinforcements from a strained pool of available Army and Marine units on his operational plans. The prime impact, as he saw it at the end of 1967, was to prolong the war. The General thought, as his memoirs and statements at the time indicate, that North Vietnam would eventually give up the fight.

He was not the only one in Saigon to feel that way. Ambassadors Bunker and Komer were optimistic as well. The former had taken over duties from Lodge in the Spring of 1967 with enthusiasm. The latter was the new Ambassador for CORDS, or Civil Operation and Revolutionary Development Support. He was now a Deputy to Westmoreland, which the MACV commander welcomed to oversee and coordinate pacification activities with the search and destroy operations.

Komer would bring a renewed emphasis to pacification, oversee the regional and local force improvements, and would help Westmoreland with handling the GVN rulers. His office, now a regular staff element within MACV, oversaw training and coordination of US pacification efforts in South Vietnam. The CORDS organization improved the revolutionary development efforts. It also dramatically enhanced the overall effectiveness of province and district defense forces through its assigned US advisors.

Finally, the Ambassador personally took an interest in the Phoenix Program, which came under his control. Though controversial because some of its actions, such as CIA 'hit team' assassinations, entailed getting rid of the VC infrastructure, Phoenix would later reap dividends in reducing the VC political cells at the local level.

Komer felt confident that these areas would continue to improve in 1968. He had already offered Washington much needed optimism in progress in the pacification of the countryside at the end of 1967. Indeed, the US Embassy was enthusiastic about the coming year. On invitations to its New Year's Party in Saigon, the Embassy had printed, "Come see the light at the end of the tunnel."

Section 9.3 - TET 1968

Despite this optimism, intelligence reports caused Westmoreland to have concerns for the northern I Corps area. In the fall of 1967, the enemy had reinforced its forces around Khe Sanh. MACV intelligence was estimating at the end of the year that there were upwards of two PAVN divisions now around the Marine Corps base. General Robert Cushman, the Marine commander who had taken over from General Walt in April 1967, responded by sending in two more battalions to reinforce the unit that had been manning the defenses.

At the end of 1967 and into 1968, the NVA launched daily artillery and rocket attacks at the Marines. Skirmishes around it became frequent occurrences. Soon the US Press began to make analogies between Khe Sanh and the battle and defeat of the French at Dien Bien Phu. President Johnson, concerned with the North Vietnam apparent preparations to attack the Marines, sought assurances from the JCS and Westmoreland that Khe Sanh would not be, in his words, another 'DIN BIN FOO.'

By mid-January, Khe Sanh had become a magnet for US forces. There were now 6,000 Marines dug in there at both the primary base and at several outposts in the surrounding hills. More importantly, the base and the NVA siege had become a magnet for attention for the MACV commander and his Commander-in-Chief as well. Consequently, believing the NVA attack on the base would be a prelude to a significant communist offensive in the north, by the end of January about 50% of Westmoreland's combat forces, to include newly arrived brigades from the 101st Airborne Division and a portion of the 1st Cavalry Division, were now deployed to or deploying in the I Corps region.

Moreover, these US troop employments in reaction to stepped up NVA activity along the border regions were not restricted to I Corps. As mentioned in the previous section, in the ARVN II Corps highland region major US combat forces were fighting near the Laotian and Cambodia borders, especially around Dak To. By the end of 1967, US combat units were also conducting operations near the Cambodia border in the now familiar War Zone C and Iron Triangle. Thus, at the beginning of 1968, US combat forces were mostly employed away from the population centers, per Westmoreland's directives.

Review of PAVN and PLAF Plans and Preparations

As explained in Chapter 7, the North's Politburo, led by Le Duan, had decided by mid-1967 to conduct a general offensive campaign commencing with the beginning of the 1968 TET new year on 31 January. Le Duan, along with a hand-picked officer on the PAVN general staff – General Van Tien Dung - had worked out the general outline of the campaign in Hanoi in the last several weeks of July. General Pham Hung, Le Duan's hand-picked man who had replaced the former COSVN leader, General Nguyen Thanh, had been in the South working out the details and preparing his forces for the offensive.

Those preparations had been extensive throughout the fall of 1967. Forces continued to infiltrate in large numbers. Because recruitment in the South had not been high enough to replace VC losses, PAVN troops now began to fill those positions – a trend that would continue throughout the war. Per the PAVN official history, the North also moved over 61,000 tons of supplies for the offensive.

That was two times the tonnage of the previous year. Select PLAF/VC units, in the last months of 1967, were guiding and moving these reinforcements and supplies further into the South to be near the three most important focal points of the offensive – Saigon, Da Nang, and Hue.

Meanwhile, the November 1967 attacks in Kontum Province and the battle of Dak To, as well as other NVA attacks out of their base camps near Cambodia, were important parts of the plan. Along with the reinforcement of forces near Khe Sanh and their attacks against the Marines there, these operations, as already mentioned, sought to divert American troops from the cities and lowlands.

Should the country-wide offensive be successful in the beginning stages, these PAVN forces could also reinforce efforts in both the ARVN I and II Corps regions. Moreover, PLAF forces had moved from their base areas in the Iron Triangle and War Zone C toward Saigon to get in between the American bases screening the city. Once inside this screen, these VC main forces were to conduct operations within the RVN capital against vital government installations.

As described in Turley's *Second Indochina War* and based on North Vietnamese documents, in the first weeks of January 1968 "some 84,000 Communist troops moved toward their targets in five municipalities, thirty-six province capitals, and sixty-four district seats. In prearranged and scouted assembly areas, they would marry up with the weapons and ammunition pre-stocked there. The bulk of the assault forces were indigenous Southern irregulars, and the preparations for the offensive required at least the passive collusion of many urban residents whom the US and its allies supposed were its victims."

According to Mark Bowen in his recent book, *HUE 1968*, among those gathering for the assault were special 'sapper' teams that would attack specific American and South Vietnamese targets in the cities. Also assembling were political cadres. These would lead the way in setting up new communist governments in the urban areas. The new political entities would serve as an alternative to the current regime should the offensive be successful. Aiding them were special units formed to capture or kill key RVN officials.

US Intelligence and Warnings

With all this activity, American and South Vietnam intelligence sources knew that some general offensive was going to happen - either before, during or after the TET holiday. The MACV history of this period claims that "American and South Vietnamese intelligence organizations during the fall and winter [1967] steadily accumulated evidence, primarily from captured documents and prisoner interrogations, of the scale, objectives, and timing of the attack."

Some of this intelligence was quite specific. For example, as early as October 1967, ARVN units had captured specific orders outlining the upcoming communist campaign to include its aims and concepts of operations. James Willbanks, in his *The TET Offensive*, states that a month later a US unit operating in the ARVN II Corps area captured a notebook entitled, "Ho Chi Minh's Order for Implementation of General Counteroffensive and General Uprising during 1967 Winter and 1968 Spring and Summer." MACV translated and disseminated the details in this directive to its major commands. The same month US units captured another document that seemed to substantiate the Ho Chi Minh order.

The problem with all this intelligence is typical in war. Intelligence analysts and commanders need to sort out and determine whether there are 'collaborating' materials that they can believe. Some of the information was contradictory. Some of it was not believable at the time. The difficulty was trying to see what and how much of the intelligence made sense regarding enemy capabilities, patterns of operations, and possible intent. In some cases, such as a double spy's information in the Hue area indicating an attack there, US intelligence analysts may not have considered the sources reliable.

As explained in the MACV official history, the MACV intelligence organization and the CIA Saigon station issued a series of studies on what they thought the plethora of materials indicated. These remarkably "predicted a nationwide enemy offensive, including major attacks on the cities. The CIA study, finished in November, accurately forecast the successive phases of the coming campaign. Its drafters suggested that the border battles were part of the first phase and that a second phase, possibly including the city attacks, would begin in January."

Of course, knowing the enemy's military leaders and their thinking helps a great deal as one attempts to deduce what this intelligence meant. Most analysts and commanders looked at this material from the viewpoint of the writings of Ho Chi Minh and Giap, rather than a Le Duan. Thus, some, like Westmoreland and his Intelligence Chief did not think that Ho or Giap would expose their forces in an all-out assault against the cities.

The MACV commander thought any offensive would still be directed at seizing large areas that would allow the communists to set up an alternative government in South Vietnam and then seek some negotiated solution. For Westmoreland that meant the main attack in I Corps. Reinforcing his belief, was US intelligence that General Giap oversaw the forces around Khe Sanh. As we now know and recounted in Chapter 7, Giap was actually in Eastern Europe at the time and stayed there well into 1968.

Westmoreland, in his memoirs, describes in general terms the intelligence that he had and his thoughts on what it meant. The movement of major PAVN forces in the region and their posturing for an attack at Khe Sanh, along with the reports that it was General Giap personally directing these forces, reinforced his thinking about the main attack in I Corps. Any other attacks, he believed, would be diversionary to that. Thus, he dismissed the intelligence that showed there would be a massive attack against the cities. He did not believe that the enemy could do so; nor did he believe that General Giap would be so foolish as to expose his units to American counterattacks in such vulnerable areas.

As the MACV history sums up the pre-attack thinking on this intelligence, "An all-out nationwide offensive seemed clearly beyond the capabilities of the North Vietnamese and Viet Cong and seemed inconsistent with their presumed strategy of protracted attritional warfare. An attempt to capture the cities, where the enemy hitherto had confined his efforts to terrorism, espionage, and political agitation, appeared especially improbable."

The history continues, "The Communists lacked the conventional military strength to seize and hold major towns. According to the allies' political assessment (which turned out to be correct), the Communists could count on little help from urban citizens who, while often hostile or apathetic toward the Saigon regime, were far from ready to rise on behalf of the National Liberation Front." Thus, Westmoreland and his intelligence officials thought that information of an attack on the cities was, in fact, a ruse.

The MACV commander also thought that the offensive would come before or after TET. The most likely time would be after TET because he felt the enemy would use the holiday period to move and prepare for its offensive. As Westmoreland recounts, he did not believe that the North would violate a holiday so valuable to the people they were trying to convince to come to their side.

The MACV intelligence officer, General Davidson, reinforced this thinking. He later said, "Neither of us saw a high probability of an attack on the day of TET, so harsh and disaffecting it would be the psychological impact on the very people the enemy was trying to rally to his side."

Westmoreland did act, however, upon some of this intelligence. In the III ARVN Corps region, upon request of the I Field Force Commander, General Frederick Weyand, who had intelligence about some enemy action against Saigon, he postponed a planned operation against enemy positions near the Cambodian border. Many of these US combat forces took up new positions near Saigon. They would be critical to the fight for the city later.

As mentioned, Westmoreland had also decided to reroute some new deployments, such as elements of the rest of the 101st Airborne Division and some of the 1st Cavalry, northward. He further alerted his commanders of the intelligence of some significant enemy attack just before, during or after the TET holiday. Finally, he tried to get the RVN to cancel the TET truce, and, not doing that, convince the ARVN leadership to limit the leaves of their forces for the holiday.

The MACV commander further alerted his superiors to what the intelligence was, and his views on what it meant. On 20 December, he sent a message to Admiral Sharp and General Wheeler alerting them to his views. Westmoreland said, "The enemy has already made a crucial decision concerning the conduct of the war.... The enemy decided that prolongation of his past policies for conducting the war would lead to his defeat, and that he would have to make a major effort to reverse the downward trend.... His decision, therefore, was to undertake an intensified countrywide effort, perhaps a maximum effort, over a relatively short period."

The General continued to describe what he thought may be some of the outcomes of this offensive. He wrote, "If the enemy is successful in winning a significant military victory somewhere in [South Vietnam], or gaining even an apparent position of strength, he may seek to initiate negotiations. If, on the other hand, he fails badly, we do not believe that he will negotiate from weakness, but will continue the war at a reduced intensity." He clarified that although he thought there might be some country-wide attacks, the main effort would be in the I Corps region to cut it off from the rest of the country and seek to organize an alternative communist government there.

Admiral Sharp did not believe that the enemy would conduct an all-out attack. He disagreed with Westmoreland that such an assault was likely because the enemy thought he was losing. He did believe that the communists may try to launch "some sharp blows," but the "likelihood of a final effort… remains remote." Wheeler, meanwhile, focused on the enemy activity at Khe Sanh – primarily because the President was asking several times a day whether it could be defended.

However, the Chairman agreed with the MACV commander about a major offensive, and that it would be primarily directed in northern I Corps. Indeed, there was ample reason to focus on the plight of the base. Now there were some two divisions of more than 20,000 PAVN soldiers massed in the mountainous terrain surrounding it. Westmoreland, by the end of January, had positioned almost 50,000 troops in and near the base.

On 21 January the NVA launched a ground assault on one of the Marine outposts surrounding Khe Sanh. It was an unsuccessful and costly attack. They also began a continuous and fierce artillery and rocket bombardment of the base. This led to a spectacular explosion of one of its ammunition dumps and damage to some aircraft supplying the Marines. These actions fit well into the news reporting on the fight at the base. Correspondents could obtain shots of the action and, like that of the rest of the war, they rushed the dramatic film footage to American TV news stations for viewing to the public.

With the North Vietnamese now constructing trenches that appeared as a preparation for a ground assault on Khe Sanh itself – as Giap had done at Dien Bien Phu – Westmoreland began to get more than a little concerned. Though the President had authorized the use of B52 strikes, and they had already been occurring, the MACV commander directed his staff to start planning for the use of tactical nuclear weapon strikes should the NVA launch a major ground attack that threatened the loss of the base. To his staff, he remarked, "We are not, repeat not, going to be defeated at Khe Sanh."

Attack and Counterattack: The First Attacks and Battles in Saigon

As already explained in Chapter 7, confusion over the actual start of the TET new year resulted in a premature communist attack on 30 January in some areas of southern I Corps and northern II Corps. Just after midnight, PLAF forces attacked eight towns and cities – the major ones being at Da Nang, Ban Me Thuot and Nha Trang. These attacks lacked coordination, and some units got lost in trying to attack their specific objectives. At Da Nang during a fierce VC assault on ARVN I Corps headquarters, South Vietnamese soldiers fought well. The attack quickly ended.

In the central region town of Ban Me Thuot, the ARVN division commander, who had captured an attack plan and had canceled all leaves for TET, battled two thousand PLAF soldiers at the center of the city. It lasted for nine hours before the VC withdrew after losing half of its force. At Nha Trang on the coast, five sapper companies attacked the South Vietnamese Naval Training facilities there and critical targets in the downtown area. US Special Forces and an ARVN Ranger Battalion quickly killed or captured most of the VC sappers.

These premature attacks alerted most American and South Vietnamese officials. President Thieu canceled the TET cease-fire and ordered all armed forces back to their units. He further placed all local security units on alert. However, it would take days for many South Vietnamese soldiers to return to their organizations. In some cases, many did not show up until weeks after the communist offensive began.

MACV had sent out similar alerts. While most commanders knew something was afoot, few still expected the breadth of the attack to follow. Westmoreland still focused on the Khe Sanh area. This continued attention was despite his intelligence officer's warning, "this is going to happen in the rest of the country tonight and tomorrow morning."

Sure enough, it happened – in much more fury than expected. Shortly before 3:00 AM on January 31, more than 85,000 communist troops, primarily PLAF main and VC local units, conducted attacks against more than three-quarters of the provincial capitals, most of the major cities, and many of the ARVN and American military facilities and bases.

As historian James Willbanks describes the situation, "Although the attacks varied in size and scope, they generally followed the same pattern. They began with a barrage of mortar and rocket fire, followed closely thereafter by a ground assault spearheaded by sappers, who penetrated the defensive perimeter. Once inside the cities, the commandos linked up with troops who had previously infiltrated and with local sympathizers, who often acted as guides. Main force units, which quickly seized predetermined targets, followed. They were usually accompanied by propaganda teams that tried to convince the local populace to revolt against the Saigon government. The attackers were both skillful and determined and had rehearsed their attacks beforehand."

While these assaults were stunning in scope and caused much confusion and even shock, as mentioned in Chapter 3, the ultimate result turned out to be a military disaster for the communists. What Westmoreland predicted - that if they attacked the cities, they would not be able to hold them and would suffer catastrophic casualties - is precisely what happened. Of the three principal targets of their planned campaign – Saigon, Da Nang, and Hue - only in the latter city would the communists even be able to hold on for some extent of time.

In Saigon, the communists committed thirty-five battalions to attack six primary targets. Eleven VC battalions directly attacked targets within Saigon. Another nine assaulted the American bases at Long Binh and Bien Hoa. Three went to overrun Tan Son Nhut airbase. The remaining VC battalions positioned themselves to ambush reinforcements from the outlying areas.

General Weyand, the American commander in the area, remembered that his situation map reminded him of "a pinball machine, one light after another going on as it was hit." However, he had been ready for this assault. His movement of forces closer to the city a month prior paid off.

The General quickly ordered US reinforcements to land by helicopter to reinforce the garrison at Long Binh and counterattack the enemy forces assaulting Bien Hoa. He also sent an armored ground force from its base toward Bien Hoa. It fought through the VC roadblocks and ambushes before getting there after a series of fierce fights.

At Long Binh, General Bruce Palmer, now the Commander of US Army, Vietnam, recalls being "very proud of the performance of HQ USARV and the many support-type units which manned the huge perimeter protecting the base. Battalion-size VC attacks struck hard at our clerks and mechanics at several points, but their defenses were never penetrated."

Meanwhile, in the downtown Saigon area ARVN forces, aided by South Vietnamese police and other security elements, thwarted the attacks against the Joint General Staff headquarters, the RVN government Independence Palace, and the state radio station. ARVN units quickly reinforced them either in the city or adjacent to it. In the case of the Joint Staff headquarters, some VC overran surprised guards and gained entry to the compound. ARVN airborne and marine units came to the rescue. After a series of brief firefights, they killed the intruders.

South Vietnamese police forces went after any VC that escaped. They captured many enemy soldiers; some executed on the spot. Such was the case of the head of police, Brigadier General Nguyen Ngoc Loan's killing of a VC local force leader, Bay Lop. Hardly an innocent captured enemy soldier, Bay Lop had been charged with rounding up key Saigon leaders for assassination. His unit had already killed scores of innocent Saigon civilians.

As outlined in some detail in Chapter 4, the most famous Saigon attack was at the US Embassy. It was also the smallest and least damaging regarding destruction and death of the entire TET offensive. At 2:45 AM a squad of VC sappers, thirteen strong, blew a hole through the embassy's outer wall. MP guards at once engaged them and killed their leader and several others. Some of these MPs were themselves killed by return fire of the remaining VC.

Other MPs rushed to the Embassy and joined in a six-hour firefight with the remaining VC, who had not been able to penetrate the Embassy building. After a platoon of the 101st Airborne Division had landed on the roof of the Embassy, American forces killed the remaining Communist soldiers. Five Americans died in the brief fight.

As also described in Chapter 4, because of its symbolism and his proximity, General Westmoreland showed up at the Embassy soon after US forces secured it. Before he had arrived, an AP reporter had already sent a bulletin that the VC had overrun and captured the Embassy. Some of the news reporters that had gathered before the General had gotten there had already taken dramatic pictures of the fight; one of which was two of the American dead.

This reporting was the first instance that the American public would see the overall American Commander in Vietnam during the TET offensive. Westmoreland at once gave an impromptu interview to a CBS news team on the scene. The General tried to assure the reporters at the Embassy. He said, "the enemy's well-laid plans went afoul." He then, unfortunately, stated that he thought the attack against Saigon was a diversion and that the main attacks would be in the North where they were ready for it. According to Willbanks, "The reporters were stunned…They could hardly believe their ears. Westmoreland was standing in the ruins and saying everything was great."

Although the TET offensive had just begun, the MACV commander stood by his earlier belief that it would turn out to be a disaster for the communists. As he relates in his memoirs, "My efforts at perspective went for naught…. What would they have had me say, that the walls were tumbling down when I knew they were not? That the enemy was winning when I knew he was on the verge of a disastrous military defeat?... Was the word of a professional military man who bore overall military responsibility for the war in South Vietnam and who personally gone through the Embassy building to have no precedence over rumor? Had the level of credibility and the art of reporting sunk to such a low?"

Attack and Counterattack: The Battles in Hue and its Vicinity

At the time, of course, the results of the communist offensive were not yet clear to the reporters, or to the US military in Vietnam or Washington, or to the American public. In Saigon, the fight would last for several more weeks before the ARVN uprooted the last VC holdouts. In Hue, the most prolonged battle of the offensive had just begun. It would last several months. It would also be the bloodiest.

With a population of some 140,000 people, Hue was the third largest city in the South. It had been the old capital of Vietnam – Ho, Giap, Le Duan, and Diem had at some stage of their lives lived and gone to school there. It was now the capital of the South Vietnamese province of Thua Thien. Although there had been some mortar or rocket attacks in and around the city, it had escaped the major fighting of the war – until January 1968 that is.

The city consisted of two parts, each divided by the Perfume River. In the north was the Old City or Citadel. It was a place of gardens, pagodas, and some old stone buildings. An outer wall some thirty feet high and forty feet thick surrounded it. It had been the residence of the ancient emperors of central Vietnam.

The headquarters of the 1st ARVN Infantry Division – considered by many Americans to be the best of the South Vietnam divisions – was in the central part of the old city. The headquarters had a small staff and a 36-man reconnaissance platoon in the actual citadel. There were several ARVN training camps around the city with a mixture of support and small combat units.

The only Americans in the city were one-hundred advisors and a few marine guards who lived in a compound south of the Perfume River. There were other US units near Hue, however. To the south of the city was the US Marine base at Phu Bai, some twenty miles away. To the north were a series of brigade size firebases of elements of the American 1st Cavalry and 101st Airborne Divisions – fifteen to twenty miles distance. These are units that Westmoreland had recently moved north from the ARVN II Corps area.

Army Historian Erik Villard's account, *The 1968 Tet Offensive Battles of Quang Tri City and Hue*, explains that the communists had spent the last two months preparing for its assault on Hue. "Communist agents used patient and discrete observation, as well as human informants, to obtain up-to-date tactical intelligence about the military facilities in Hue. From those reports, the Communists concluded that a quick capture of the city was possible because Hue was 'nearly unprotected' and the soldiers defending it had a weak morale and a poor combat capability."

Villard continues to explain that "guerrillas made regular night excursions through the villages around Hue to make the local dogs bark, thus desensitizing the inhabitants to their canine alarms. Enemy scouts drew detailed maps of the routes the attacking units were to take and spent many hours observing the routines of South Vietnamese soldiers. North Vietnamese logisticians stockpiled supplies in mountain camps to the west and south of Hue, and the enemy established aid stations and hospitals staffed by both military and civilian personnel."

For the assault, the communists assembled a total of thirteen battalions, including eight PAVN. In the first wave would be five thousand soldiers attacking almost a hundred designated targets. As in other attacks, PLAF leaders prepared a list of key officials to capture and dispatch to special camps for punishment after the battle. They had planned to assassinate some as well.

The premature attacks on 30 January had alerted General Ngo Quang Troung, the ARVN 1st Division commander. As Mark Bowden describes him, the General was not the typical looking or acting ARVN senior officer. He was a soldier's leader who led from the front and gave little care to looking like a general. Most American officers who knew him thought he was the best senior officer the ARVN had. A US infantry officer at the time by the name of Norman Schwarzkopf, who would command US troops in the early Gulf War in 1989-90, was an advisor in his division. He had told others then and after the war that this officer was "the most brilliant tactical commander I'd ever known."

General Troung dispatched elements of his force around Hue to key positions, primarily in the outskirts. Moving into these positions, these ARVN forces noticed that shops in the city had closed early; streets were unusually deserted, and almost no one was celebrating TET. One American advisor to them noted that the city's local bordello had closed, which never had happened before.

Early morning of the 31st, an element of Troung's reconnaissance unit reported a column of PAVN soldiers moving along the Perfume River toward Hue. Shortly after, a regional force unit to the north of the city fired upon a group of other NVA soldiers moving southward toward the city. About 0330 that morning, two PAVN and one PLAF battalions began their primary attacks.

These attacks overwhelmed much of the initial ARVN opposition. A PAVN battalion had broken through the gates to the Citadel and attacked the ARVN division headquarters. General Troung, his staff, and soldiers from his recon outfit, held them off. Another PAVN battalion had attacked the MACV compound in the southern part of the city. The American advisors and their staff repeatedly repelled the assaults. By daylight, however, the communists controlled most of the center of Hue.

As in Saigon, and other cities and hamlets they had attacked, VC political cadres rounded up South Vietnamese whom they had identified as political officials or other influential individuals. Most of these were never seen alive again. Later, after the battle was over, South Vietnamese soldiers found a hastily constructed mass grave site containing several thousand bodies.

Both General Troung and the American advisors were frantically reacting to the attacks and calling for help. The 1st ARVN Division commander got in touch with one of his regiments to counterattack from its position northwest of the city toward the citadel. Troung's superior, General Hoang Xuan Lam, who now commanded the ARVN I Corps region, was trying to find out what was going on throughout his area.

Soon the ARVN Corps commander realized that Hue was one of the more important communist goals. He ordered several of his reserve airborne battalions and an armored cavalry troop to join Truong's regiment in the counterattack. On the way to the citadel, the ARVN reinforcements met stiff resistance but fought valiantly to reach the 1st Division headquarters at the northeast corner of the Citadel.

Meanwhile, the US III MAF commander, General Robert Cushman, ordered a Marine Task Force to counterattack from Phu Bai along Route 1 toward Hue and reinforce the besieged MACV compound. Unlike his South Vietnamese counterpart, Cushman and his subordinate American commander were less aware of the massive NVA assault that was taking place. With little intelligence on the size of the force that attacked Hue, the Task Force Commander dispatched only two Marine companies for the mission.

Picking up a few tanks on the way, the Marines succeeded with heavy losses in reaching the MACV compound. Still unaware of the size of the overall enemy force, the Task Force Commander further ordered an attack to relieve the ARVN headquarters element across the river. That attack failed. Some 300 Marines did not know they were now up against over 10,000 hard-core NVA and VC soldiers determined to liberate not only the city but all South Vietnam. Neither did Cushman or General Westmoreland in Saigon realize that this was not only a significant attack but would turn out to be the fiercest of the entire TET offensive.

Hours after the initial Marine attack, both General Cushman and General Lam became aware of what they were up against. They decided to dispatch significant forces to counterattack. The ARVN commander agreed to clear the part of the city north of the Perfume River, to include the Citadel. The American commander agreed to clear the south part. He also ordered US units from their base at Camp Evans north of Hue to cut off any further NVA reinforcements and seal off any escape routes north and west of the city. The commanders then decided on how to employ their overall forces throughout the I Corps region against other PAVN and PLAF forces attacking other cities and hamlets.

As the combined US/ARVN counterattack continued for the next several days in Hue City, American and ARVN senior commanders committed more forces. In touch with General Westmoreland, who had been slow to realize the severity of the communist attack against Hue, had finally set up a MACV forward headquarters to aid General Cushman. The III MAF commander eventually had to employ a brigade of Marines and a brigade of the 1st Cavalry Division to complete the initial clearing of their part of the city and its western environs. It took twelve days for the Marines, who lost 38 dead and 320 wounded during this phase of the fight.

The fight to the west of Hue by the Camp Evans US units was also difficult. It further shows how much the US command underestimated the strength and determination of the NVA assault on the city. As described in detail in his *Hue 1968*, Mark Bowen captures the confusion, intensity, and courage of both American and North Vietnamese and PLAF soldiers.

Eventually, it would take an entire brigade of the 1st Cavalry Division to dislodge the NVA units that had entrenched to the west of Hue. One reason is that the PAVN Front command headquarters had set up its command post in a small village there called La Chu to oversee its operations to capture Hue. A reinforced PAVN battalion protected it and was to stop any reinforcements trying to recapture HUE. Other NVA forces were moving to reinforce those who had already seized the citadel. All these NVA forces were well armed and ready for a fight.

Much like what happened to the Marines who initially counterattacked out of Phu Bai, those Army units moving from the 1st Cavalry's base at Camp Evans had underestimated the communist strength on their way to Hue. Thus, there was only one battalion that moved toward Hue. When it ran into the PAVN forces, the latter surrounded the Americans. Another infantry battalion later joined in the fight, supported by massive artillery and air. It took almost a week for the US forces to prevail. The American infantrymen in the two infantry battalions lost over sixty killed and nearly five hundred wounded. Somewhere near one-thousand enemy died in the fighting as well.

The ARVN fighting in the northern part of Hue also lost heavily. However, they could not retake the Citadel. An entire PAVN battalion had dug in there. It was determined to hold on until reinforcements arrived. The ARVN command requested that the Americans, who had more firepower, take up the attack.

On 17 February, the US Marines began their main attack on the Citadel. The attacking battalion lost 47 killed and 240 wounded in five days. The commander regrouped, and with reinforcements continued the attack again. The American force then penetrated the Citadel fortress, killing most of the defenders. At that juncture, MACV decided that the ARVN would conduct the final assault to clear the northern part of the city. On 24 February, the remaining PAVN soldiers gave up the fight and withdrew to the west. In another week, on 2 March, the battle for Hue was over.

According to Willbanks in his book on TET, "In the twenty-six days of combat, the ARVN lost 384 killed and more than 1,800 wounded, plus 30 missing in action. The U.S. Marines suffered 147 dead and 857 wounded. The U.S. Army sustained 74 dead and 507 wounded in the battles that raged in the area surrounding the city.

The allies claimed over 5,000 communists killed in the city and an estimated 3,000 killed in the fighting in the surrounding area. Actual figures of VC and PAVN casualties are not known, but it is clear that the Communists forces had paid dearly in the bitter fighting." The cost for the people of Hue was also catastrophic. 40% of the city was destroyed. 110,000 of its inhabitants were homeless. Some 5,800 civilians had perished.

As depicted in Chapter 4, the Press captured on film much of the fighting, killing, and destruction there. The News Media showed it to Americans at home, who already were either bewildered about what was happening or convinced that the VC were winning. The battle for Hue became the symbol of American failure in the war. It was in Hue that Walter Cronkite had observed what was happening during the TET offensive. What he saw and heard influenced him to go back and report on the war as one that "was mired in stalemate" and that it "seems now more certain than ever that the bloody experience of Vietnam is to end in a stalemate."

Alternative Strategy Revisited: Westmoreland and the 206K Call for Reinforcements

As the fighting in Hue had continued, Westmoreland began focusing on counterattacking the vulnerable main forces of the enemy throughout Vietnam participating in the TET assault. For him, the opportunity was ripe to achieve his original objective of destroying them and removing them as a threat to pacification. He issued orders for a sustained counteroffensive. American commanders complied.

However, the countryside was in turmoil. Pacification efforts had been severely set back. The communist offensive had devastated the South Vietnamese regional and local security forces. Most importantly, the enemy remained as elusive as ever. With such turmoil, some of the regional and local VC forces still put up a fight for the hamlets they controlled. The main PAVN and PLAF units which had participated in the offensive had begun to withdraw from the cities to their mountain and jungle bases to wait for further orders.

While much of the PLAF main and local forces, along with the political cadres, had suffered severe damage, the mainstay of the North's aggression, the PAVN units, were able to regroup and eventually recover. Most of them - except for those around Khe Sanh and in the Hue battle - the COSVN high command had not significantly committed to the offensive.

Moreover, the lifeline for their existence to fight another day, the Ho Chi Minh Trail, was still operational. The North still had enough manpower to rebuild its main forces for that other day. They had not given up the fight. Indeed, by the end of April, North Vietnam would send another 90,000 PAVN soldiers south to replace losses from the TET offensive initial attacks.

During the fierce fighting in Hue, and while US and ARVN forces were engaged in other cities, Khe Sanh remained a fixture in Westmoreland's mind. He still expected a significant attack to come from that area and across the DMZ with the uncommitted PAVN forces. So was the Administration in Washington. On February 3, Chairman General Earle Wheeler sent a message to Westmoreland asking if he needed any additional reinforcements for the defense of Khe Sanh. According to Wheeler, he sent upon request and concern of the President.

Because Wheeler's cable focused on Khe Sanh, Westmoreland's response was limited to what he thought would be an added capability that he did not have enough of if the communists finally launched an all-out assault on the base. Thus, his response was for some more munitions and airlift capability that was needed to keep the base supplied.

As explained in Chapter 3, Wheeler had more in mind. The Chairman had become acutely aware of the weaknesses in the ability of the US military to respond to circumstances should there be a significant crisis outside of Vietnam. Indeed, such circumstances were brewing and happening in the Middle East, Europe, and Northeast Asia.

Just before TET, North Korea had seized an intelligence ship in international waters 16 miles from its shores. Also, the Chairman was further worried by the clashes between US and South Korean troops near the DMZ with North Korea. As the TET offensive continued, Wheeler had his staff study the problem with the strategic reserve. The results were as bleak as he had feared.

General Wheeler now felt that the entire TET offensive presented an opportunity to revisit the troop reinforcement and mobilization issue. In fact, in several meetings with the President, LBJ had indicated that he would support more reinforcements "should they be needed." As mentioned in Chapter 3, in a meeting on 6 February, Wheeler heard the President reiterate his pledge to give Westmoreland "everything he wants."

On the 7th of February, the Chairman sent another backchannel message encouraging the MACV commander to ask for reinforcements, stating that the US Government "is not prepared to accept defeat in South Vietnam." He told him that right now he could get the 82d Airborne Division and half of a marine division if needed. Wheeler further suggested that the MACV commander could use these in a counteroffensive against any communist attack coming out of the DMZ. He strongly encouraged Westmoreland to "not be bound by earlier [troop] agreements" and ended, "if you need more troops, ask for them."

About the same time, Admiral Sharp, Westy's Pacific Command superior, chimed in. He said that he thought this was an "opportune moment to ask for additional men and equipment." As he recalls in his memoirs, the Admiral also told both Westmoreland and Wheeler that he was further in favor of revisiting the issue of increased bombings in North Vietnam, the mining of Haiphong, and the use of an amphibious landing against North Vietnam.

Responding to Wheeler's 7 February cable, Westmoreland sent another message to Wheeler and Sharp on 9 February. His summary of the situation in South Vietnam was quite confident. In the II and III Corps areas, he felt that his "posture was adequate," and he could "cope with the situation." He told Wheeler that, while he felt he could hold Khe Sanh, he "welcomed reinforcements at any time they can be made available. These would permit him to carry out my campaign plans [for 1968]." Westy further explained that if the North invaded the northern provinces, he could thwart that attack as well, using the additional marines and airborne troops [he and Wheeler had discussed] in an amphibious operation in the rear of any thrust out of the North.

As explained in Chapter 3, Wheeler shared this memo with the President and Secretary McNamara, who was on the way out as Secretary of Defense. The President called a meeting of the JCS at the White House on 11 February, with McNamara, his designated replacement Clark Clifford, and others to discuss the MACV commander's 9 February cable. The minutes of this meeting are in the *Foreign Relations of the US*. It is a remarkable document. While Chapter 3 mentions this meeting, it is worth a more detailed examination here.

Westmoreland's 9 February message had confused the President and others about the situation in South Vietnam and his need for reinforcements. At the meeting, LBJ asked "Is it true that General Westmoreland is not recommending or requesting additional troops now?" Wheeler said yes. McNamara and Clifford agreed that there did not seem to be an urgency in the need for more forces.

General Maxwell Taylor, whom the President had asked to attend, said that he read Westmoreland's message differently. While it did not explicitly ask for reinforcements, Taylor noted that it seemed that his "forces were tied down" and he had "no reserves." Thus, it would greatly benefit Westmoreland, he thought, if the President send more reinforcements to enhance the field commander's ability to react to the aftermath of the enemy offensive.

Secretary of State Dean Rusk said best what all were thinking. He caustically remarked, "I must say if General Westmoreland is requesting troops in this cable he has a poor Colonel doing the drafting for him." At the end of the meeting, LBJ remarked that if Westmoreland was not asking for more troops, "I don't feel worried." However, he remarked, "I think we should tell Westmoreland that if he really isn't asking for more troops and find out if that interpretation is correct. In my mind I think he really wants more troops."

Wheeler must have been dumbfounded and embarrassed. At first, the Chairman sent another message urging the MACV commander send a formal request specifying what he needed in more explicit terms to get Washington to lift the troop deployment restrictions. The Chairman said, "Please understand that I am not trying to sell you on the deployment of additional forces which in any event I cannot guarantee. However, my sensing is that the critical phase of the war is upon us, and I do not believe that you should refrain from asking for what you believe is required under the circumstances."

General Wheeler, perhaps having misgivings about the clarity and forcefulness of the MACV commander's previous messages, followed this up with yet another message the same day in which he related the results of the White House meeting. Now, in more forceful words, he told Westmoreland that those at this meeting had concluded, "you can use more troop units, but you are not expressing a firm demand for them; in sum, you do not fear defeat if you are not reinforced."

Now Westmoreland got the gist of what Wheeler was telling him. He sent another message on 12 February. It was, of course, decidedly different in tone from his 9 February one. He emphasized that the enemy had changed his strategy from one of "protracted war" to one that he hoped to win a "quick military/political victory during the American election year." In response, he thought the US "must change" his strategy.

To underscore the shift in the war brought about by the enemy's change in strategy, the MACV commander stated, "This has been a limited war with limited objectives, fought with limited means and programmed for the utilization of limited resources. This was a feasible proposition on the assumption that the enemy was to fight a protracted war. We are now in a new ball game where we face a determined, highly disciplined enemy, fully mobilized to achieve a quick victory. He is in the process of throwing in all his military chips to go for broke."

Westmoreland's tone now turned much more forceful than his earlier messages. He continued, "we must seize the opportunity to crush him." To do so, the MACV commander emphatically said that he "desperately" needed reinforcements. He stated that he had not yet received all the reinforcements promised – about 25,000 troops. He further said that he wanted those forces "now."

These were the brigades from the 82d and the Marines that he and Wheeler had talked about. Then he said he needed the "remaining elements of those two divisions at a later time."

Hinting that his request was to change the strategy in response to the enemy offensive, General Westmoreland stated, "we face a situation of great opportunity as well as heightened risk. However, time is of the essence here, too. I do not see how the enemy can long sustain the heavy losses which his new strategy is enabling us to inflict on him. Therefore, adequate reinforcements should permit me not only to contain his I Corps offensive but also to capitalize on his losses by seizing the initiative in other areas. Exploiting this opportunity could materially shorten the war."

Most curiously, and most confusing at this time for those civilian leaders and advisors who would see this message in Washington, he did not elaborate on what 'seizing the initiative' meant. Nor did he explain how it would 'materially shorten the war.'

When this message hit Washington, Wheeler at once sent it to McNamara. That night, the outgoing Defense Secretary called the President. He knew what the two military men were trying to do – raise the threshold of reinforcements and obtain the mobilization that the JCS had been arguing for in the last several years. He urged the President to exercise caution to the request and its implied troop changes. He stated, "I think it'd be a mistake to call up the reserves and plan on permanent augmentation of our forces out there above the planned 525 [thousand]."

LBJ replied in his usual fashion, "A—I don't have a position of deserting my commander in time of war. B—I don't have a position of deserting my home folks and acting imprudently or getting involved where I can't pull out." He then called for a meeting to address his "commander in time of war" request, and, as implied, a way to avoid a situation from which he "can't pull out."

Apparently, in this time of crisis, the President was more concerned about the appearance of not supporting his commander in the field, than what needed to be done to defeat the enemy. As usual, he was looking for a way out of a difficult decision.

Again, as summarized in Chapter 3, the next day the President met with his senior foreign policy advisors. Everyone agreed that the President should order the sending of the immediate reinforcements – a brigade from the 82d Airborne and a Marine brigade. However, Wheeler and McNamara disagreed on the question of calling up reserves and raising the ceiling of any follow-on forces. LBJ deferred on this issue. He told the Secretary and Chairman to reach some consensus.

Following the meeting, the JCS dispatched an order for the sending of the two brigades. They would begin arriving in two weeks. The Joint Staff and Office of the Secretary of Defense, meanwhile, prepared the usual papers on the pros and cons of mobilization and additional forces. To seek clarity on what was on the mind of his commander in Vietnam, LBJ dispatched Wheeler to Saigon to discuss the future with Westmoreland and report back to him the results.

Wheeler arrived in Vietnam on 23 February. The meeting was low key and informal – meaning the Chairman's party was small and no reporters involved. In his memoirs, Westmoreland remembered, Wheeler appeared to be "a tired man, seemingly near the point of exhaustion" and "mirrored the gloom that pervaded official circles in Washington, a reflection of the doomsday reporting by press and television."

According to Westmoreland, his discussions with Wheeler surrounded future operations that could take advantage of the vulnerability of the communist forces resulting from their attacks. They both expected a reappraisal by Washington of the current policies. They both saw this reconsideration as an opportunity to alter the restrictions on troop strength and the reluctance to conduct ground operations outside of South Vietnam.

Although previously he had not pushed hard for mobilization and their emergency procedures, Westmoreland now agreed with Wheeler that these must be lifted; not only to provide forces necessary for a counteroffensive but to reconstitute the national reserve. He and Wheeler further thought that the possibilities of a reassessment and the lifting of the troop and mobilization restrictions were high because of the change over from McNamara to Clifford. They both surmised that there was bound to be a change because the latter was known as a 'hawk' when it came to the war.

General Westmoreland further recounts that "with additional strength and removal of the old restrictive policy, we could deal telling blows – physically and psychologically – well within the time-frame of the reservists one-year term." His discussions with Wheeler then turned to possible operations against the enemy. Many of these he had already developed as contingency plans, such as FULL CRY, that he had prepared and had hoped to execute as part of his Optimum Force package he asked for in the Spring of 1967. As he further tells it in his memoirs, "If I could execute those moves fairly rapidly following the heavy losses the enemy had incurred in the TET offensive, I saw the possibility of destroying the enemy's will to continue the war."

Wheeler, in an oral interview years later, confirmed the subject of these talks. He further stated that while he discussed future operations, such as an attack into Laos and an amphibious assault against the North, he told Westmoreland that the forces for these would not be available until perhaps the fall of 1968. However, he felt that at least the immediate reinforcements that they had already discussed in Washington could be in South Vietnam by the end of the month and perhaps a division more in April.

Westmoreland further explains that he and Wheeler agreed that the total forces needed to carry out the future operations, such as an offensive into Laos, entailed the same numbers from his 'Optimum Force' option he had sent to Washington and discussed in Manila. That force was approximately 206,000 soldiers and marines.

According to the Army's official history *Staying the Course* the Generals decided that the request would consist of three deployment increments, based on what Wheeler thought their availability would be. "The first increment of 108,000 troops consisted of the 5th Infantry Division (Mechanized), the 6th Armored Cavalry, the remainder of the 5th Marine Division, five Air Force tactical fighter squadrons and various support units. It was to arrive in Vietnam no later than 1 May 1968."

"The second package of 42,000 men was to be ready by 1 September, and the third increment of 56,000 was to be available by 1 December. The second and third groups would go to Vietnam only if the president decided to pursue a more aggressive strategy, such as allowing MACV to invade Laos or Cambodia, or if the Communists launched another major offensive. Otherwise, those 98,000 troops would be used to reconstitute the strategic reserves in the continental United States."

Since Washington already was familiar with the overall 206K figures, Wheeler argued that would be a suitable number to offer as those forces needed should the President agree to lift the troop ceiling and agree to mobilization. As Westmoreland recalls, the Chairman would focus on the numbers first; rather than a lengthy presentation of what they would be used for. Numbers, after all, is something that the Pentagon and Washington were interested in.

The MACV commander agreed with Wheeler's focus on numbers of troops in his attempt to sell the Administration on this new strategy. He facetiously states in his memoirs, "I can hardly fault General Wheeler's approach…Who among the civilians would appreciate a policy of exploiting the enemy's defeat, of reinforcing success? Having read the newspapers, who among them would even believe there was success? Better to exploit their belief in crisis to get the troops, then argue new strategy later. One thing at a time."

As recounted in detail in Chapter 3, when General Wheeler returned to Washington, DC he failed in his attempt to get the forces for the new strategy that he and Westmoreland envisioned. Ironically, he failed because those to whom he presented the numbers did not understand how they would make any difference. For General Wheeler, his approach to use numbers backfired. The effect he produced was further confusion. To most, it created a sense that the war in Vietnam was out of control.

Neither the Chairman of the Joint Chiefs nor the Commander of forces in the war presented a clear, new approach that would have isolated South Vietnam from the North's ability to reinforce the South. No responsible military man presented an approach that could have critically changed any COSVN ability to gain the initiative after its defeat during TET.

Arguably, the alternative strategy Westmoreland envisioned, could have denied the North the ability to send PAVN forces to the South. Along with improvements to an emboldened ARVN following its successes in TET, and a reconstituted and reinvigorated pacification program, this approach could have created new conditions in South Vietnam. This new situation then may have led to a favorable negotiated conclusion to the war. More on this later.

TET Ends; Westmoreland Leaves

As explained in Chapter 7, the communists followed up the January attacks with two more – one in the late spring and another at the end of the summer that lasted until the end of September. None were successful.

In mid-March, it became apparent that they would not be a major assault on Khe Sanh. The PAVN and PLAF had suffered anywhere between 10,000 to 15,000 soldiers to divert attention from the lowland and city attacks. In April MACV launched OPERATION PEGASUS to relieve the base. Later, MACV abandoned and then reoccupied the area when the South Vietnamese began LAM SON 719.

Just after Wheeler's battle to obtain reinforcements, when it appeared that nowhere close to the 206,000 figures would prevail, Westmoreland decided to back off his alternative strategy. He reinforced the civilian perceptions of nothing new by once again indicating that he could still win the war with fewer than the optimum force. He dispatched yet another confusing message to Washington that with the fewer forces he did not need to adjust his strategic aims. He could still ultimately prevail with whatever they provided, given the time of course.

Again, he would not 'pull a MacArthur.' At a time that demanded bold, effective military advice and action, he chose not to confront his commanders. He chose not to argue for and pursue a possible military solution that had a reasonable chance at forcing his opponent to abandon his goals. Unlike MacArthur, he did not have to disobey orders. He just needed to convince his civilian leaders that he had a way to end the war favorably without provoking a Chinese intervention; had they provided the means to do so.

Why did he not choose to argue for a reasonable course that may have also saved thousands of lives of the soldiers of America's mothers and fathers? Perhaps the reason lies in the way Westmoreland got to be a four-star general. He got there by not challenging his superiors…by being someone who would just obey and not upset those who held sway over his future.

Or perhaps, he just figured that his civilian leaders just would not approve of his alternative strategy because of the uproar of the TET offensive and it was not worth any effort to convince them to the contrary. Or perhaps, the General was just frustrated over the fact that his civilian superiors would not understand how his alternative strategy could work? Or perhaps, the MACV commander just thought his present course would eventually work and that it would just take more time.

Time, according to Napoleon, is a very fleeting commodity that can never be recovered if lost in war. With nowhere to go but more of the same, America's leaders may have lost the time in mid-1968 to wage a protracted war – or any war that would take more casualties without results. The American public would no longer accept the numbers that their government had contrived and given to show the US could win the war.

Two months after the communist TET offensives ended, there was a new leader. This new President vowed to end the war with honor – whatever that meant at the time he said it.

There would also be a new MACV commander sooner than a new President. On 10 June Westmoreland relinquished command to his deputy – General Creighton Abrams. As he left, as Lewis Sorely recounts, he gave a press conference at which he adamantly continued to say that the current strategy of attrition would "make continued fighting intolerable to the enemy."

Meanwhile, Le Duan and his supporters in the Politburo were still intent on a military victory – whatever the costs. All they needed was time and the Ho Chi Minh Trail. That time would be gained through yet another US peace initiative that sought an end to the conflict through goodwill, rather than the prudent and practical use of military force.

Chapter 10: A Better War?

This chapter examines the changing nature of the war following the TET 1968 offensives. It focuses on General Abrams' attempts to support President Nixon's Vietnamization policy described in Chapter 5, and the efforts to extricate the American military from direct ground combat in Vietnam. Some have argued that Abrams pursued a decidedly 'better war' than his predecessor that could have, if he had more time or if he could have executed sooner, won the war.

As we examine Abrams mission change, strategy, and operations, the chapter discusses in detail his 'one war' approach and whether it could have made a difference had the US gained more time to conduct it. It further explores the relationship between General Abrams and his civilian superiors, their failure to end the war favorably for the US, and the US role in the fall of South Vietnam in 1975.

Section 10.1 – The Changing Nature of the War, Abrams' Theater Military Strategy and Vietnamization

As mentioned in the last chapter, the US, ARVN, and other allied forces defeated the main TET offensive that began at the end of January, and the two other communist offensives afterward in May and August. By the fall of 1968, it had become clear to the US military that the North Vietnamese general offensives of 1968 had significantly altered, for the time being, the military balance in South Vietnam in favor of the free-world forces.

Allied forces had regained significant control in the countryside. They had severely bloodied the enemy's main forces and much of his local forces and political cadres. The ARVN had fought well. It had gained confidence that it had never felt before in its capability to fight and win against the communists' forces.

Moreover, the South Vietnamese government saw that its citizens had reacted negatively toward the communist destruction and terror. Most people had refused to join them in their offensive to overthrow the South Vietnam government. By not joining, they voted for the South's government – regardless of how inept or corrupt it may have been.

President Thieu, bolstered by the reaction, called for a general mobilization of the people into the Armed Forces. He reasoned that the time would soon be right for some reforms and legitimate elections. To the US State Department officials in Saigon, these were all very positive signs that a quasi-democratic RVN may be possible.

However, as depicted in Chapters 3 and 4, the American political leaders and the Public drew different conclusions than the US military and the South Vietnamese government. Influenced by the adverse American Press reporting, for the most part the US government and a large segment of its populace believed that TET had been a defeat for US policy in Vietnam. LBJ's announcement on 31 March 1968 to seek a negotiated conclusion to the war and that he would not accept another term as President gave impetus to these perceptions. It also decisively altered the international and domestic politics behind the war.

By the end of the year, both sides had agreed to meet in Paris and begin negotiations on ending the war. Meanwhile Richard Nixon in his run for the Presidency promised if elected, he would bring the troops home and end the war honorably. American cries to bring home the troops grew louder and even more militant.

These circumstances, in turn, would come to alter the military ends, ways, and means significantly to seek a favorable conclusion to the further conduct of the war. As explained in Chapter 5, the Nixon Administration would cleverly but significantly change the original objective of preventing the imposition of communist' rule in South Vietnam. It would now be a matter for the Vietnamese people to choose. The question remained, however, how free would that choice be.

Meanwhile, as historian Lien-Hang Nguyen reveals, the PAVN and PLAF high command proclaimed the TET offensive a "'resounding success with 630,000 enemy troops killed. Le Duan and the militants in his Politburo, however, knew that their roll of the dice had failed, just as it had in 1964."

Still resolved to find a way to defeat the Southern Vietnamese militarily and end American involvement, Le Duan had 'grudgingly agreed' to direct discussions with the Americans so that he could create the semblance of wanting a peaceful solution. This move would, he felt, further undermine the American civilian leaders' efforts to gain a favorable negotiating position at the talks, while offering time to reconstitute his military power for continuance of his military solution to the war.

Taking Charge

Amidst these changes, Westmoreland's Deputy, General Creighton Abrams, in June 1968 had taken charge of the war in South Vietnam. The General had been in country since May of 1967. Westmoreland had used him primarily to track the progress of the ARVN forces in their role in protecting the populated areas and, in some instances, their ability to conduct operations with US forces. When US Army forces reinforced the I Corps region just before TET, Abrams had aided in commanding and controlling them as the head of MACV Forward placed there. In that role, the Deputy MACV got along much better with the Marine Corps commanders than his chief had.

A reason for that rapport may have been the contrast of personalities between the two Army leaders. Per Westmoreland's and Abrams' biographer, Lewis Sorley, that contrast was significant. Indeed, the two seemed to be complete opposites. Whereas Westmoreland always appeared 'spit and polish' with his emblems of rank visible and his uniforms neat; Abrams - much of the time - looked like he had just jumped out of bed wearing his fatigues as pajamas, making it difficult to see the four stars on his collars. Westmoreland always appeared the consummate patrician leader and often projected a high degree of 'formalism;' reflecting his South Carolinian background and demeanor. Abrams was gruff, cigar-smoking, and swore often; reflecting the combat aura he had gotten in World War Two.

Moreover, Westmoreland seemed out of touch with the ordinary soldier, but impressed the foreign leaders and American politicians he met. Abrams rather be with soldiers than experience the high trappings of command around prominent politicians. Withdrawing to their quarters at Tan Son Nhut airbase after an arduous day, Westmoreland would go to bed early and read himself to sleep. Abrams stayed up late and took solace in drinking scotch and listening to Wagnerian operas.

The differences between the two were also evident in the way that Westmoreland left and Abrams took command. As described by Sorley in *Thunderbolt*, the former left in much fanfare with a final press conference proclaiming a decisive victory during TET. To the contrary, the latter did not have the customary 'change of command' ceremony formally decreeing his authority. Rather, he ordered the fine furniture and carpets removed from the MACV commander's office and gathered his staff for the latest update on the military situation then unfolding at Khe Sanh.

Right after his assumption of command and before the 1968 elections, the Johnson Administration was giving directions to Abrams that would eventually lead to a new approach in the theater. For example, under increasing public pressure, Secretary of Defense Clifford directed the Joint Chiefs to come up with a proposal to shift the burden of combat to the ARVN. As premature as this was with the ongoing communist offensives during the summer and fall, the JCS further directed MACV to draft a concept.

As the Deputy MACV, Abrams had already been involved in planning for improvement to the ARVN and in envisioning ways it could take a more active role in the war. He approved and signed off on a resultant "RVNAF Improvement and Modernization Plan" before he took over command. Absent any higher detailed guidance; the plan included Abrams thinking on how to do that transfer. It also made certain assumptions about future negotiations regarding a mutual withdrawal of US and NVA forces given the Johnson Administration's renewed efforts to seek a negotiated end to the war.

As described in the MACV history, the plan "assumed that after any mutual withdrawal of North Vietnamese and US combat forces, five years would be needed to develop an RVNAF able to hold its own against the Viet Cong, who were expected to continue receiving North Vietnamese manpower and logistical support. In the interim, an American 'residual force' would remain to aid the South Vietnamese."

The history further explains that "The plan called for a force buildup along the lines proposed in March, with the South Vietnamese reaching their peak combat strength in 1970. Thereafter, gradual reductions in regular and territorial infantry would release manpower for new fixed-wing and helicopter air units and an enlarged seagoing and riverine navy."

To support the plan, "MACV prepared delivery schedules for significant quantities of equipment ranging from M16 [rifles] to M48 tanks. Assuming negotiated withdrawals began on 1 July 1968, the plan's US residual force would decline from 61,500 men in June 1969 to 20,000 by June 1973 and still be at a level of about 16,600 indefinitely thereafter to perform tasks still beyond RVNAF capabilities."

As the history further explains, "In late June, the Defense Department approved the plan. To complement this concept, Abrams further worked with his South Vietnamese counterparts to expand the ARVN and the South Vietnamese security forces." The General also began to work with the South Vietnamese on a revitalized pacification plan.

Abrams put this plan on the back burner at the beginning of the fall to await the results of the US Presidential elections. Meanwhile, he turned his attention to continuing the military operations to further damage or destroy the NVA and VC forces that had exposed themselves during their 1968 offensives. Thus, as the MACV history relates, "during his first months as COMUSMACV, General Abrams urged his U.S. commanders to seek out and destroy the enemy units exposed by the Communist offensives."

The history also explains that Abrams "strongly rejected administration suggestions, transmitted through Wheeler, that MACV cut back on offensive operations to reduce casualties. The best way to keep American losses down, he argued, was to interpose a formidable array of combat power where the enemy is planning to fight."

Abrams stated at his first commanders' conference that the "critical problem" was to "determine a practical way to inflict significant attrition on [the enemy], to grab hold of him and to destroy him. This is the payoff—to kill the enemy," he declared. Expecting the enemy's August offensive in 1968, Abrams directed his commanders to preempt the communists by launching attacks of their own.

At his commander's meeting during his first year in charge, Abe's confidence and aggressive attitude showed. He declared: "I intend to accommodate the enemy in seeking battle and in fact to anticipate him wherever possible... We must anticipate him, fix his major forces as far away as possible from our vital areas, and defeat him decisively... We must concentrate every last element of available combat power on the enemy when he is located... We must defeat his forces, then pursue them and destroy them."

Thus, despite his differences in appearances and demeanor with Westmoreland, early in his command he shared with his predecessor the desire to conduct offensive operations against the enemy's main forces. This is because he recognized that the enemy TET offensives presented an opportunity to damage the enemy and their infrastructure significantly.

Abrams also experienced much of the same frustration with the Press and the civilian advisors in the Defense Department of his predecessor. An examination of Lewis Sorley's transcripts of Abrams staff meetings found in *Vietnam Chronicles: The Abrams Tapes, 1968 to 1972* shows this exasperation. For example, in several meetings after the NVA offensive in the early fall of 1968 had ended, he remarks that "the conventional wisdom in Washington is that we are losing….." In another meeting, he comments on the effectiveness of the communist propaganda over their 1968 offensives and their claims that they are winning. He facetiously comments that "75 or 80 percent of the people believe [the enemy is winning]" … and "100 percent of the press."

As Abrams continued to press for offensive action going into 1969, the numbers began to show how much of a military defeat the communists had suffered in 1968 as a result of their offensive. According to the US Army official history, "MACV estimated that the Communists had committed 124,000 troops to the Tet offensive—84,000 in the initial battles of 30–31 January, plus another 40,000 over the next several weeks. These had suffered mightily. During February 1968, the allies had killed about 50,000 enemy personnel. Of this number, 40,000 had been soldiers and 10,000 had been individuals not carried on MACV's roster of enemy military units. MACV arbitrarily evenly divided the latter category into two groups—members of the infrastructure and civilians who, either willingly or not, had served the enemy as guides, auxiliaries, or laborers."

In addition, "To the dead were added thousands more who either had surrendered, been captured, or who had been detained as suspects. The number of enemy wounded was unknown, but MACV postulated that 14,000 enemy personnel had been hurt seriously enough to have either died or been permanently incapacitated. In contrast, the command reported 7,277 allied military dead—5,025 Vietnamese, 2,105 Americans, and 147 from the other Free World forces."

Despite the remarkable successes of the Allied counteroffensives throughout the rest of 1968, the home front continued to exhibit not only war weariness, but a growing call for retreat from Vietnam. For someone who had fought as an armor commander in the battles in the European Theater of World War Two, the aura of defeat in Washington and the rest of America must have been incredibly exasperating.

One War Strategy: A New Approach to a Better War?

In the fall of 1968, after the last of the enemy offensives, Abrams had ben to change his emphasis on operations. One reason, the MACV history asserts, is that captured enemy documents and defectors showed that COSVN and Hanoi had come to realize that their three 1968 offensives were failures and had severely damaged their forces. While the considerable damage was to the local and main VC forces, the PAVN engagements at Khe Sanh and Hue, and their other efforts to lure American forces away from the cities had bloodied them as well.

Abrams sensed that now was the time to make up some ground in the fight for the lowland regions and their populated areas. He reasoned that he needed to counter what he perceived as an enemy strategy to establish as much political and military control as possible over these areas to give them leverage in the Paris peace talks.

Another reason for Abrams change of emphasis was that the Saigon government had embarked upon an effort to enlarge and improve their local forces. Many of these had performed well during TET. Some had not. However, what was now sure is that when they did perform well much of what they did turned the tide and enabled the ARVN forces to counterattack effectively. In conjunction with this build up, and because of the Allied counteroffensive against the TET attacks, the Thieu government, encouraged by MACV, launched what they called an 'accelerated pacification plan.'

At several of his command and staff meetings in September, October, and November, Abrams verbalized his thinking on the way ahead. In mid-September, he told his staff to change the focus of their command and staff meetings. He said they needed to look at "an assessment of all elements, not just military…so we can try to produce…a reasonably comprehensive picture of the whole game Hanoi is playing in South Vietnam…" He added, "we need to work against the system" that the communist forces use to employ their forces to include his supply caches, the local forces he depends upon, and the population that he is trying to subvert.

At an October meeting, he explained that he wanted efforts simultaneously launched at this 'system.' He expounded," where they have withdrawn to their base areas somebody should be getting at the base areas…keeping the pressure on. Somebody should be out here trying to intercept the supplies and getting after the guerrillas and the guys that are carrying this stuff, the guys that are leading them, and so on."

In November, he argued that the cross-border base areas were also part of the system, and they had to attack them as well. In fact, he declared that those bases were "decisive in the outcome of this war" and that he thought the policies, particularly toward Cambodia, "have got to be changed."

Recognizing the importance of these bases to the enemy's strategy, Abrams emphasized: "I think it's criminal to let these enemy outfits park over here, fatten up, reindoctrinate, get their supplies, and so on." Later, specifically to his superiors at Pacific Command and in the Pentagon, he referred to this concept of attacking the enemy's system as his "one war" approach.

The new MACV commander began to publish this 'one war' approach in the allied Combined Campaign Plan for 1969. While the plan repeated some of the same objectives of Westmoreland's plans, it assumed no increase in American forces. It did, however, mention the increase in and the need for improvement and modernization of the ARVN. The plan specifically reemphasized pacification, reflecting the already set up accelerated pacification efforts of the RVN.

The most significant departure from the Westmoreland campaign plans, however, was the elimination of the "division of functions under which the Americans had fought the enemy's big units while the South Vietnamese Army concentrated on pacification support. Henceforward, all allied units were to take part equally in the four primary military missions - attacking enemy main forces and base areas, guarding the borders and the Demilitarized Zone, defending the cities, and supporting pacification."

Abrams guidance and orders also directed, "Under the new dispensation, South Vietnamese infantry divisions were to be relieved from territorial security tasks by the Regional and Popular Forces as rapidly as the improvement of the territorial forces allowed. The South Vietnamese regulars were to direct their 'primary efforts' to the destruction of the North Vietnamese and Viet Cong main forces, alongside the Americans and eventually replacing them."

Abrams, unlike his predecessor, also saw the need for a published longer-range plan. While Westmoreland had directed tasks and priorities in his yearly directives, the new MACV commander saw the need to pull everything together – operations against the enemy, improvements to the Southern armed forces, and pacification programs in a document that would show what the US and South Vietnamese needed to accomplish beyond the one-year view. To make this happen and knowing of their previous work, the General asked for and received some officers from the Army staff that had worked on the PROVN concept during 1965.

The resultant MACV Strategic Objectives Plan, finished after the 1969 campaign plan, did just that and more. Under Abrams' close supervision, the plan tied the accelerated pacification plan and the ARVN improvement plan to a MACV schedule of redeployment of US forces. The American redeployment in this plan, in turn, was to include an assessment of progress in pacification and improvement of ARVN capabilities. All of this was without interference from Washington at the time.

As this plan took effect in 1969, the communists, as mentioned in Chapter 7, were significantly changing the nature of the war. While they continued many of their attacks during TET of 1969, the degree and sustainment of them were much diminished. Indeed, by the summer of 1969, the Politburo issued a resolution calling for continued attacks, but these were to be mainly small unit assaults. The spirit of the resolution was heavily worded regarding a more protracted war than the more bellicose words of a general offensive.

At the same time, the Politburo directed its negotiators in Paris to adhere to a hard line that it knew the Americans would not settle on. The object was to gain time and 'talk while fighting.' The opportunity, Le Duan thought, would eventually come 'while talking' for yet another offensive that would result in a settlement favorable to the North.

Meanwhile, the communists continued their infiltration of forces and supplies in the South. These were to replace the TET losses, especially in the PLAF main and local force units. By mid-1969, indeed, these units were PLAF in name only. In some cases, these organizations consisted of entirely North Vietnamese soldiers.

The MACV intelligence apparatus noticed the increased infiltration. That apparatus had been continuously improving, and by 1969 US intelligence personnel had acquired the capability to intercept communist communications. These intercepts frequently and accurately reported the status of units in the infiltration pipeline.

For the first time in the war, MACV had a reliable source on the movement of forces southward, the bases they were using on the way, the rate of their movement, and the amount of material moving along with them. Abrams tracked this information daily and considered it the most crucial factor in the enemy system he wanted to attack.

American intelligence had improved in other areas as well. Intelligence organizations focused more efficiently on finding the VC political infrastructure. This improvement paid dividends to the

Phoenix program's systematic efforts to disrupt or eliminate that infrastructure. Taking advantage of its intelligence, to include extensive use of informants, the program's operatives targeted the VC political cadres at the hamlet level for arrest or assassination. The program also gathered critical information on COSVN plans and directives for the South.

Under the CORDS new director, William Colby, who had replaced Komer after TET, the controversial program over the next three years would account for, according to John Prados in his *The Hidden History of the Vietnam War*, almost 29,000 captured and over 20,000 killed VC infrastructure cadre. Moreover, in his Vietnam account *Lost Victory* and public talks, Colby made much of the fact that "he was able to drive through Quang Tin Province on the back of a motorbike at night in 1970." What made the program so controversial was the backlash Phoenix later received because of press reports of the use of assassination and other supposed atrocities program personnel used to target suspects.

Because of this new and improved intelligence and the Phoenix activities, Abrams became aware of the shift to a more protracted small unit war the enemy was trying to wage in South Vietnam. He shifted as well. By the beginning of 1969, he directed his commanders to break down into smaller units to find, fix and engage the enemy as the situation allowed. He also began to increase the cooperation and combined operations of US units with South Vietnamese regional forces in the lowland areas, much like the Marine Corps Combined Action Program instituted by General Walt in 1965-66.

He did not restrict his subordinate commanders, however, from launching large-scale operations. Indeed, the armor officer in Abrams instinctively told him to press the fight against an enemy hurt in the 1968 campaigns. Thus, he encouraged his commanders in the beginning of 1969 to keep the pressure on when the opportunity arises to corner and engage the enemy's main forces. Indeed, the statistics – as reported to and tracked by the Defense Department and found in Guenter Lewy's *America in Vietnam* – show that ground operations of battalion size or higher increased at first under Abrams' command from 71 in July 1968 to 89 the next year.

One of those battalion or larger operations in May of 1969 became infamous in the history of the war when senior US commanders in I Corps decided that there was a significant build up again in the A Shau Valley area and sent a brigade-size force to engage it. The resultant battle of Hamburger Hill produced yet another massive body count of enemy forces and their withdrawal back into Laos to recoup. However, the public reaction, as described in Chapter 4, brought Washington pressure once again for Abrams to limit such engagements and reduce American casualties.

Soon after Hamburger Hill, Abrams over the next year, under continual pressure from Nixon's Defense Secretary Laird and others in Washington and against his better judgment, limited large operations from 89 in July 1969 to 58 in January 1970. This decrease, in turn, reduced combat fatalities from 638 to 343 - a considerable drop that obviously must have pleased Washington.

While these battalion and more extensive operations decreased, the nature of these operations changed significantly. Though operations along the borders against enemy base areas still had some focus, US actions began to concentrate more on the populated areas. One reason is that Abrams wanted more American combat activities combined with the South Vietnamese regular and self-defense forces directed at protecting the populated areas.

The MACV commander mentioned that these operations would eventually have a two-fold effect. First, they would continue to enlarge the hold of the South Vietnamese government over those areas seized during the TET offensive. Second, it would also improve both the ARVN and self-defense forces combat readiness.

The irony about this shift, Guenter Lewy notes, is that while it resulted in reduced American casualties – because US forces were not facing the enemy's main forces on his terrain and near his border sanctuaries - it caused more civilian casualties and an increase in refugees. The damages to the civilians, moreover, often were a result of the habit of using firepower assets in any engagement; a standard operating procedure developed over the last four years in combating the enemy's main forces in remote areas.

By the summer of 1969, the Secretary of Defense through the Chairman of the JCS issued new orders to Abrams that stymied the MACV commander's intent to continue the use of large formations in offensive operations. This Washington pressure to reduce both offensive operations and casualties disturbed the MACV commander. His remarks recorded in *The Abrams Tapes*, demonstrate on numerous occasions his frustrations on such restrictions.

For example, on the fighting in the A Shau Valley, he remarked, "Why are you out in the A Shau? Well, it's better than fighting in Hue." Abrams on another occasion chided about a press conference at which Laird used the phrase 'protective reaction' as his new instructions to the commander in Vietnam. At another staff meeting the MACV commander ranted on about "all this crap about the way to save casualties is to stay in your base camp" …and "just sit back there and give the son of a bitch a free ride" …while they "clobber the hell out of you."

Perhaps best demonstrating his frustration, the seasoned World War Two combat veteran went on to further say his soldiers were better off to go home. For example, at a February 1970 staff briefing he remarked, "If you're going to have American infantry sitting around in base camps over here, I don't want to do it. I think they're better off home, because all they're doing [here] is preparing themselves to be killed." Moreover, in an attempt to bring humor to what he saw as a ridiculous situation in a war zone, he remarked that if he followed Washington's instructions, his aide would be required to take his firearm away from him.

Despite these frustrated remarks about sitting around in base camps and firebases, and reducing offensive operations, Abrams had to give in to the pressure from Washington. To new reporters and visiting member of Congress, however, the General continued to give optimistic appraisals of actions against the enemy in South Vietnam and the improvements in the South Vietnamese Armed Forces. For the next two years, while the NVA and PLAF were still recovering from their TET offensive defeat this optimism seemed valid.

Meanwhile, the resultant reduction in large-scale offensive operations led to US combat units relying on and staying at these fixed locations more and more from the end of 1969 and into 1970. Furthermore, as the withdrawal of US forces kicked in at a high rate at the end of 1970 and into 1971, large bases became important as staging areas for units moving out of country.

The use of and reliance upon firebases and other fixed locations was particularly true in the I Corps area from late 1969 through 1970. During that time PAVN infiltration and staging were more prevalent there than in the other Corps areas. For example, NVA forays from the north through the

DMZ increased, and Marine units more than ever continued to watch and interdict them from their camps along the southern edge of that border.

In the 101st Airborne Division area to the west and south, the command used an array of firebases along the eastern edge of the A Shau Valley to monitor NVA use of the valley trails. Often commanders used artillery and air strikes or spoiling attacks with swift but limited ground assaults to interdict any attempts to move against the coastal cities.

One such firebase was Ripcord. As described by Shelby Stanton in his *The Rise and Fall of an American Army*, "Fire Support Base Ripcord was built in April 1970 by the 101st Airborne Division (Airmobile) about twenty-five miles west of Hue in Thua Thien Province. It was a key forward artillery base in the division's summer offensive plans against the A Shau Valley. Like most firebases, Ripcord was built as part of a network of individually isolated posts which garnered mutual protection because they were within artillery range of each other."

Unmolested for three months, in July the NVA began operations against the firebase because of the effectiveness of its use of ground ambushes and firepower against its infiltration and base areas in the region. They started with their first of what would become daily mortar attacks. From then on small but fierce firefights took place around the base. NVA units regularly attacked the patrols that the US commander dispatched from Ripcord.

Attesting to the effectiveness of the position almost two divisions of PAVN forces surrounded Ripcord. They brought in anti-aircraft weapons that shot down numerous US helicopters. American forces struck back, mainly with massive air and artillery attacks. These actions killed many enemy soldiers but did not stop their attempts to overrun the base.

Finally, US commanders decided to vacate the base. Overall, the operations around it had resulted in 75 American dead. Enemy casualties were unknown. The NVA also attacked other 101st Airborne Division Fire Support Bases (FSBs) in the area. They harassed many with rockets and mortars. PAVN sappers attacked others with various success. As US commanders abandoned these as well, B52s carpet bombed the area.

As US troop withdrawals were about to start, General Abrams' observations on the danger of relying on these fixed positions and to "just sit back there" …while they "clobber the hell out of you" were coming true. The use of these static bases to monitor and disrupt NVA traffic was not only dangerous but also becoming futile. In the end, the US had to "give the son of a bitch a free ride" in the enemy's steady buildup in the South. Such was the result of the change in mission to reduce offensive operations to ensure fewer casualties.

Finding a Way to Support Vietnamization

The pressure from Washington to alter Abrams' offensive tactics and his new theater strategic approach had begun well before the setup of Ripcord and other firebases around the A Shau Valley. That pressure had begun in March 1969 when the new Secretary of Defense Melvin Laird visited MACV. He brought with him his and the new President's ideas on how to bring peace with honor to South Vietnam. This meeting, and subsequent actions, would significantly alter Abrams' plans for improving the ARVN that he had already launched.

As summarized in Chapter 5, Laird's ideas pointedly differed from Abrams on what both thought was inevitable - the withdrawal of US forces from South Vietnam. For example, as explained above, Abrams' planning included a 'residual' American force. The MACV commander felt that no amount of improvement or modernization would enable the ARVN forces to combat the PAVN main forces on their own successfully. His planning had assumed that some American forces would be necessary for the near term – four to five years after the withdrawal of most American units at least – to enable the ARVN to combat any main PAVN invasion or general offensive in the South.

Like Korea and even Europe, Abrams believed that for a long-term defense plan to be useful for South Vietnam, some continuing US ground force commitment would be necessary. Abrams had shared these views with Laird and the President in his response to the questions in Kissinger's NSSM-1 explained in Chapter 5.

In his first meeting with Abrams in March 1969, however, Laird explained his belief that the American public and the Congress would never agree to such an arrangement. The war had become too controversial. TET had convinced much of the American public and its representatives that the South Vietnamese government and armed forces needed to now defend itself without more American bloodshed.

Recalling further from Chapter 5, during this meeting, Abrams expressed the need for a residual force, much like what the US had in Korea. He said that he had sent his thoughts on the withdrawal and ARVN improvements to Washington as part of his inputs to the Administration's call for inputs on a new approach to the war. At the end of their meeting, Laird emphasized that Abrams needed to plan for withdrawals that would consider ARVN capabilities and communist threats, but would not result in any American residual forces.

Meanwhile, the Secretary alerted Abrams that he should accelerate his planning for American withdrawals and make recommendations on some for 1969. Abrams did not object to or further counter the Secretary's guidance on a residual force. Though a much more aggressive officer than Westmoreland, like his predecessor, he deferred from arguing with his civilian superior on the matter.

In mid-May President Nixon called Abrams to Washington to discuss the turnover of the war to the South Vietnamese. Nixon emphasized that he wanted a 'systematic and orderly' turnover and withdrawal. Abrams indicated that he wanted redeployments tied to enemy activity and got the assurances from the President that he would support the General's recommendations. The MACV commander, who had his staff working on a withdrawal of US forces during 1969 based on his conversations with Laird, told Nixon that he could start withdrawals this year.

Abrams' first plans for the extraction of US forces had been well thought-out. He desired to start the withdrawal of the Marine forces in the northern I Corps area. There were two excellent reasons for that despite the obvious threat from PAVN forces across the DMZ. One was that the best ARVN unit, the 1st Infantry Division, was in I Corps. The second was that the Marines would withdraw to Okinawa, where they could readily redeploy to South Vietnam should the situation warrant.

Once MACV completed this phase of the withdrawal, Abrams would order other forces from the II Corps to start based on the enemy situation there. The General wanted to withdraw the American units around Saigon last, where the enemy threat remained the highest. In both cases, the MACV commander would also track the progress of the ARVN in taking over from their American counterparts. He would schedule the order of US forces within the ARVN Corps regions to the ability of the South Vietnamese armed force in their area to take over operations. All of this made imminently good military sense.

However, good military sense was not to be the predominant factor for Vietnamization and the US troop withdrawal. A significant problem that Abrams faced was that the President and his National Security advisor differed from the Secretary of Defense in their approach to both. As Lewis Sorley explains in his Abrams biography, *Thunderbolt*, "there were continual contests within the administration as to emphasis and timing, if not the basic elements of Vietnamization and withdrawal, with Nixon and Kissinger and Haig pushing for forceful prosecution of the war, usually with Wheeler's agreement, while Laird was pushing for disengagement as quickly as possible."

In the end, again as related in Chapter 5, Laird would be more successful in pursuit of his approach. He knew how to manipulate the budget, and deal with a Congress that was more than willing to pull all the troops out as quickly as possible. Thus, like Westmoreland, Abrams had to deal with Presidential assurances of support for his strategy, and the realities of the lack of fulfillment of those promises.

While Laird was pushing Abrams down this path that was militarily inadvisable, as previously mentioned, the Defense Secretary turned out to be the most astute observer of American public mood and its support for the war. While in 1969 it seems that US public opinion was willing to give Nixon's policies a chance, Americans were impatient and wanted to get on with getting out of Vietnam. The domestic reactions to continued high US casualties was a case in point. As related previously, the Hamburger Hill battle reaction was a good example.

Responding to public pressures to 'bring the forces home' as he had promised, in June 1969, President Nixon announced the withdrawal of 25,000 US forces by the end of August. From then on withdrawal schedules became more a factor of public calls for the troops to come home and Congressional funding impacts than the capability of the ARVN forces or the enemy threat.

The MACV history best summarizes the situation that Abrams and the US military faced: "General Abrams, along with Admiral McCain [his commander in Hawaii] and the Joint Chiefs of Staff, exercised at the best limited influence on the development of President Nixon's overall Vietnamization policy. Domestic political considerations, congressional pressures, budgetary limitations, and intra-administration maneuvering, more than military advice, determined Nixon's course."

Indeed, budget projections and Congressional appropriations in 1970 began to affect military operations directly. While South Vietnam military aid increased over the next few years, much of the operating funds for American forces were cut. Particularly affected were the air sorties in support of ground operations. In fact, Abrams' directives for operations reflected both the Administration's Vietnamization and withdrawal guidelines and the realities of reduction in funds. In his directive for operations in 1970, Abrams warned, "The realities of the American political situation indicate a need to consider time limitations in developing a strategy to win…[and] time is running out."

Thus, as early as the beginning of 1970 it had become clear to Abrams that he may never be able to get the time he needed to effect Vietnamization fully. As the Army official history notes, "Abrams and his superiors harbored and expressed, deep doubt that Laird's goal of South Vietnamese military self-sufficiency could be achieved. Nevertheless, when pressed, they produced the necessary plans along with explanations of why they would work and periodic reports of progress. As did Westmoreland before him, Abrams loyally supported and carried out administration strategy, never publicly or privately challenging its basic assumptions."

As the MACV history further explains, "as a military adviser, General Abrams played an ambivalent role. Especially during the first two years of redeployment, he warned of risks, advocated deliberation, and cut-and-try, and sought to postpone the loss of his American combat power. Yet privately, one of his chief withdrawal planners recalled, Abrams realized from the start that 'we were going to get out completely' and that all he could do was try to see that the United States disengaged in an orderly fashion and did not 'completely bug out' on the Vietnamese and leave them flat and unable to defend themselves."

Thus, despite his attempts to set up a modified strategy that still focused on the attrition of the enemy's capabilities, Abrams faced fighting a rear-guard war. He understood early that he would need to coordinate operations with the ARVN and find a way to bring American power to bear to effectively aid in the turnover to the South Vietnamese Armed Forces. He also hoped that the American withdrawal would not turn out to be a precipitous retreat.

In short, by early 1970 General Abrams and his senior subordinates had to come to grips with how the unilateral American withdrawal would affect the combat efforts in the field. During the last months of 1969 and throughout 1970 and afterward, Abrams consistently talked to his commanders about the need to keep their forces combat ready as best they could as the withdrawal began and then precipitously continued.

The US Withdrawal and its Impact: How Do You Ask a Soldier to be the Last to Die in Vietnam?

Though Nixon had announced his first troop withdrawals in the summer of 1969, and by the end of that year some US forces began to come home, it was not until 1970 that troop units began to leave Vietnam in large numbers. It was also in 1970 that some of the adverse effects of Abrams' change of mission and its implied defense posture began to manifest themselves on the forces. Increasingly in his command and staff meetings, the MACV commander voiced concern over the increasing signs of drug abuse, racial tensions and incidents, combat refusals, and the alarming reports of atrocities.

Statistics, observations, and conclusions on these problems have historically had enormous disparities; depending on one's viewpoint on the war, and the sources and how one uses them. For example, if someone takes at face value the remarks of some ex-servicemen against the war, one might adopt the view that these problems were widespread in Vietnam because that person was there and said it was pervasive.

For instance, John Kerry - in his testimonies before the Senate in 1971 on his service in Vietnam - said that there were all kinds of atrocities in Vietnam and that it was command driven. Also, in the years after the war, some film producers, who fought in the war have taken poetic license and created works such as the immensely popular movie, *Platoon*, that have led to a particular "belief" that these events not only occurred but were endemic to American fighting units.

Additionally, one can gain access to an overwhelming amount of testimony - some true - to draw conclusions and make claims that seem accurate on atrocities, but ignore other evidence and make general judgments based on the most outrageous claims. As an example, just recently a researcher by the name of Nick Turse wrote a book based on his review of civilian killing investigations and courts-martial in the National Archives.

In that work, called *Kill Anything that Moves*, Turse argues that US soldiers caused all sorts of atrocities, fueled in many cases by drug use, lack of discipline, and inept leadership. He confirms Kerry's view that they were command driven by the need for body counts and the use of free fire zones, as well as by a break down in overall discipline and leadership.

Turse further makes an overall claim that atrocities were 'ubiquitous' throughout the war and not just a symptom of troop withdrawals and discipline problems. He argues that American system of war caused "cold-blooded slaughter" on the Vietnamese civilians. The US "killing machine," he claims, unleashed unfathomable misery upon the civilian population. Turse further announces that "every infantry, cavalry, and airborne division" that served Vietnam committed these atrocities.

To be sure, we know that American unit and individual civilian killings and atrocities occurred. Many are aware of the My Lai massacre that took place in 1968 and was made public in late 1969. Here the story of a US infantry platoon's execution of nearly 200 Vietnamese civilians further fueled the antiwar movement and affected the American public's perception of the war – and rightly so. It was repugnant to many soldiers who had served honorably and suffered wounds in the war, as well. We also know that there were other My Lai-like events, especially toward the end of the war, in which innocent civilians were killed without cause, or, deliberately.

In many instances of US units killing civilians, however, it was a result of the kind of war that both sides waged in Vietnam. Because the VC chose to blend in with the civilian population, it became essential to try to weed them out. That caused civilians casualties when leaders and soldiers made mistakes in judgment as who was the enemy and who was not.

Moreover, operations in the populated areas, as in all wars, caused inadvertent civilian casualties; especially in Vietnam as the enemy often took refuge among the civilian population to fight or to escape or to use them as a shield. Furthermore, by design, the communist VC, especially at the local level, took part in a wanton assassination of civilians to undermine any government control of the population. To be fair, certainly US bombing of North Vietnam also caused significant civilian casualties and suffering.

Thus, regarding measuring atrocities, one is remiss indeed, and even duplicitous to some extent, if he or she ignores these instances from both sides of the war. One is also remiss if they focus solely on the Vietnam War as one in which soldiers on both sides did anything different or in more murderous ways than other wars. The battlefields of Vietnam, while as described above different in some respects, were strikingly similar to the battlefields of other wars to an infantryman engaged in close combat.

Those who have not experienced war and combat have no idea what it is like – the disparagement of human life, the terror of someone trying to kill you, the necessity to murder another human being, the utter horror of the sights, sounds, and smells of the battlefield. For an infantryman, combat is devoid of the norms of human values. As it is happening, whether it be for a few minutes, hours, or days, the grunt must step over the fine line of sanity to survive, and step back afterward. Some never step back. More than that, the experience of killing becomes the grunt's norm for a time; and resides inside them forever afterward. That is the nature of, and the lasting effect, of war from a grunt's experience.

Criticisms of Turse's research and judgments rightly point this out. In fact, Rudolph Rummel, a professor of political science at the University of Hawaii, has spent his career studying data on violence in war and has accomplished much in his analysis of the Second Indochina War. His results show the extent of civilian deaths in the Vietnam War from both sides and show that it was extensive but not solely the purview of American units. In fact, his data shows that the communists caused more deliberate killing of civilians than either the US or the South Vietnamese military.

Of course, this does not justify any illegal killing of civilians by either side. These are usually the result of a breakdown in military discipline, and in the absence of leader motivation and sense of duty. However, war is an atrocity, and it involves as its fundamental purpose, killing. Accidental killing is a natural phenomenon. Bullets, shells, mines, and bombs do not discern between friend and foe; soldier and civilian; mother, child, or adult once they are launched against what one thinks is an enemy.

Wanton killing can also happen if not checked by the soldier's leader. But checking it is difficult. It is near impossible to stop a soldier in close combat from killing an enemy who has been trying to kill them by just shouting cease-fire or even through an attempt to restrain. The adrenaline just propels one forward to harm or kill. The killing will go on for a while; just as in a football game when the referee blows a whistle and contact continues to occur for a period after.

Students, historians, lawyers, news reporters, the person reading a book or sitting in a movie theater – or any person who has never seen war – cannot understand this. It is hard enough for one who has experienced it to live with or understand for the rest of one's life.

As far as the problem of the erosion of discipline as the war for American forces spiraled down, there are statistics available that can lead to a reasonable conclusion of the actual extent of the discipline problem and its effect on the conduct of the war. Some professional historians, who do not seem to have a point to prove, have analyzed these. For example, historian Guenter Lewy does a credible job of explaining what the problem was, the apparent extent of it, and how it affected the US military in Vietnam.

In his *America in Vietnam*, Lewy explains the extent and presents causes of this "erosion of discipline" among US organizations during the withdrawal period. As for the causes, he offers several credible ones. He believes that the growing antiwar movement, both at home and in the military, was one. As one indicator to support this assertion, he explains the growth of underground newspapers in the military of which there were a total of around 245 by 1972. Many of these were popular and circulated amongst soldiers as they awaited rotation back to the States. Some of these were actually influenced by North Vietnam's propaganda campaign. Moreover, American soldiers had access to some of the broadcasts from Hanoi calling for desertion and refusal of orders. Jane Fonda – or Hanoi Jane as known to many soldiers then and now – was one such broadcaster.

Lewy also argues that many soldiers interviewed after the war, some of whom were actively involved in this underground, admitted that the antiwar demonstrations that they heard about from the news and letters from family and loved ones had a growing influence on them, especially after the announcement that the US was pulling out of Vietnam. This was particularly true among those military members who had returned to Vietnam late in LBJ's Administration and during the Nixon's and had witnessed the antiwar sentiment in the States while there and then returned for a second tour of duty.

The Professor further claims that the most critical cause of indiscipline in many of its forms was from the idleness and disillusionment toward the war as the troop withdrawals proceeded. Shelby Stanton, a staunch admirer of US troop performance in the war, agrees. Stanton writes, "lowered troop morale and discipline were manifested in increased crime, racial clashes, mutinous disregard of orders, anti-war protests, and monetary corruption in black market currency exchanges, as well as drug use." Stanton argues that these incidents further led to serious degradations "in unit cohesion and operational slippages."

So, what was the extent of this problem that General Abrams had to contend with? Lewy offers a view on the scope based on defense department records and statistics examined by various Congressional committees. These seem to be the most pertinent and reliable records. As far as drug abuse, his data shows that in the year 1971, the height of the troop withdrawals, "50.9 percent of Army personnel in Vietnam smoked marijuana, 28.5 percent had used narcotics such as heroin and opium, and 30.8 percent had used other psychedelic drugs."

What Lewy also shows is that this data was not much higher than other military theaters outside of Vietnam, and more importantly, most of those who were drug abuses had used drugs before they had entered the military. Unfortunately, there is no breakdown between those who took drugs in combat units and those who did in non-combat organizations. This latter statistic would have been more an indicator of how widespread drug use and a breakdown in discipline was in those units who had to carry the fight to the enemy.

However, anecdotal evidence from interviews of Vietnam Veterans indicates that drug use was much more prevalent in the rear areas. Combat unit norms seem to be that the use of drugs would so impair a soldier that it would put all at risk in a firefight. Thus, any drug use that did occur would wait until the unit returned to a firebase or larger unit camp. The author's experience verifies this observation.

Three of the most written about statistics, and the most controversial and misrepresented in accounts of the war, concern refusals to go on operations, insubordination, and fraggings. The latter incident involved the use of grenades against leaders, primarily those who continue to be aggressive in their tactics and operations and placed soldiers at risk of being killed. Critics of the war, especially those who argue that it was immoral and illegal, claim anywhere between over a thousand to multiple thousands of these incidents from 1969 to 1972. Lewy's data show that these were more likely a number close to a total of a little over 700, with nearly 200 of these reported as possible incidents but not confirmed.

More recently, George Lepre, in his book *Fragging: Why US Soldiers Assaulted Their Officers in Vietnam* says the numbers may never be known since many incidents were not reported. However, his exhaustive research, which includes extensive interviews, shows that the numbers ranged between 600-850 – far below the thousands that some argue occurred. While these were serious incidents resulting in deaths, they were not as widespread as many had reported and much more believed. Nevertheless, as George Lepre's research shows, the US Army - both in Vietnam and elsewhere - took these incidents seriously, investigated all reported incidents, and prosecuted them vigorously.

As for refusals to go on operations and insubordination, they are even more difficult to measure. Again, Lewy's figures seem the most reliable of those recorded. He shows that in 1969 there were a total of 128 trial cases of all those charged with a 'willful refusal to obey orders.' That increased to 152 in 1970. Of the 152, moreover, military courts convicted 131. Though these 1970 convictions represented a rate of .44 per 1000 soldiers, it is reasonable to assume there may have been more than reported. However, it is also reasonable to assume that they were no way near claims in the news or made by some on TV, such as one this author viewed and described later, that most soldiers in Vietnam were disobeying orders to go on operations or fight.

Last of the indicators of soldier problems during the withdrawal was the number of racial incidents, especially the number of black on white or vice versa hostile acts. Though there were some racially motivated incidents, the numbers reported are apparently, according to many who have attempted to do so, difficult to determine how pervasive it was. Some statistics, however, show a higher percentage of incidents of court-martials for disobedience or drug use among more Blacks than Whites. For example, during 1970 Black servicemen accounted for 43 percent of aggravated assaults and 71 percent of the robberies in Vietnam, while the percentage of Blacks serving in country was only 9.1 percent.

Guenter Lewy makes an interesting observation as to why the Black percentages were so high in the above instances. He surmises that the rhetoric of Black leaders in the civil-rights movement was a significant factor. Without the real numbers to show otherwise, Black soldiers tended to believe Martin Luther King's claim that the Government was using them as 'cannon fodder.' The fact is, however, that the number of Black soldiers killed in action was in proportion to the numbers of Blacks serving in Vietnam.

Whatever the real numbers are, or even if the numbers were skewed based on bias, the fact is that from the end of 1969 to the end of US troop service in Vietnam, discipline indicators rose steadily; showing that the drawdown had a significant effect upon the US Army in Vietnam during that period. However, as a demonstration of combat breakdown these figures are incomplete, anecdotal, or for some, suspect because they were government owned.

Despite the analysis above, to be honest the authors view is that the degree of American soldier and unit participation in unlawful and immoral activities was and still is in the eyes of the beholder. Consequently, anyone trying to conclude those activities, or the overall degree of the US military's disintegration should keep in mind Mark Twain's warning, "Figures can lie; and liars can figure."

Section 10.2 – Buying Time, 1970 - 1972

Despite the difficulties that would have to be addressed in both Vietnamization and the troop withdrawals, the situation for the US in Vietnam as Abrams' One War strategy kicked in was bright. As William Turley summarizes in his *The Second Indochina War*, "Under the combined pressure of US troops, a growing ARVN, and accelerated pacification, the Communists had been unable to recover from losses suffered in the Tet Offensive." The picture was bleak indeed from Hanoi's perspective. Their forces in the South had declined by more than 50,000 from 1968 to 1971. They had lost many of their party cadres and political leaders.

Meanwhile, the ARVN forces had fought well since 1968. Their forces were growing and would number over a million in arms into the seventies. Hanoi leaders were also aware that the South Vietnamese military was now becoming better equipped with the latest US armaments. They were further aware that the South Vietnam government had grown stronger, and was in 1970, though still politicized, over the turmoil of the post-Diem assassination.

Considering the gains described above and others, Lewis Sorley, in his history of the war during Abrams' command, *A Better War*, writes, "There came a time when the war was won. The fighting wasn't over, but the war was won." With what had already occurred in the planning and execution of Vietnamization explained in Section I – to include the political pressure to increase the withdrawal and the guidance to not leave any American forces behind – it is difficult to understand how Sorley's claim could be valid.

Contrary to his view, the historical record, as it now stands, is clear on what the situation was during the first years of Abrams' tenure. The US, ARVN, and third world militaries had won a significant victory in 1968. The Communist North Vietnamese leadership recognized this. They were posturing to recover. They had the means to do so; especially with the Ho Chi Minh Trail intact and now even expanding. They were also aware of the clamor in the US to withdraw its troops; and President Nixon's pledge to do so.

The US leaders, moreover, had not taken advantage of that 1968 military victory. America was now going to withdraw from the war. The terms of any negotiation were not yet clear. What was clear, was that the communist forces were building up and, as early as the beginning of 1970, lurking on the border sanctuaries for another major offensive.

General Abrams and his subordinate commanders, as well as their ARVN counterparts, recognized this situation. They all knew that they had to buy some time for the development and transition of an ARVN and South Vietnamese security force race to withstand another assault that they all knew would come. Yet, as he had told his commanders and staff, the MACV commander sensed that "time was running out."

Cambodian Incursion

Buying time was the main reason for the Cambodian incursion in May 1970. The opportunity came, as described in Chapter 5, with the Lon Nol coup against Prince Sihanouk. When the query came from the White House as to the feasibility of launching an ARVN offensive against the Cambodian bases, Abrams was quick to respond favorably. He argued for not just an ARVN incursion, but a combined US and ARVN assault.

Abrams thought that the key to the defense of South Vietnam was to go after the cross-border bases. They were part of the communist war-making system that he wanted to dismantle in his one war concept. He had welcomed the earlier B52 bombing of these sanctuaries. However, he knew that the bombing alone could not critically damage the communist forces in them.

Before the Nixon go ahead, during his staff and commander discussions about Cambodia, many had argued that they should 'inadvertently' conduct ground assaults despite the US policy to not do so. Both Abrams and his deputy, General Goodpaster, would not condone that. They did, however, keep ground operations plans should an opportunity arise that would call for an attack.

Both Ambassador Bunker, and the new leader of CORDS, Ambassador Colby, supported Abrams views on the criticality of the Cambodian bases to the enemy and had been saying in their cables back to the State Department. In several of his discussions with his commanders, Abrams hoped that he would get the approval for the use of US forces in such an operation.

Since 1969, there had already been some ground actions against the Cambodia bases. MACV conducted limited, small unit covert actions under the control of its Studies and Observations Group or SOG. More recently, the ARVN had conducted several larger unit cross-border attacks, without their American advisors, in support of the Lon Nol forces now embattling the Cambodian Communist Khmer Rouge. Abrams, however, felt frustrated with the small results. He would welcome any opportunity to turn these limited attacks into something much more substantial.

Abrams had gotten more precise intelligence on the location of these bases and had reliable estimates on the number of supplies and forces that were in them. Communications intercepts had also found the site of the COSVN headquarters. He had been passing this intelligence on to his superiors and hoped that General Wheeler would gain support from the new Administration to launch an attack against them.

As the Lon Nol faction struggled against the Cambodian Communists and their North Vietnamese supporters, the Nixon Administration had tried at first to help it with the use of a CIA-sponsored program of supplying arms and munitions. This action, however, did not give the anti-communist forces with the means to counter a combined North Vietnamese and Cambodian Communist offensive. By early April it appeared that the communists would defeat the Lon Nol forces. Again, as related in Chapter 5, Nixon then ordered the combined ARVN and US assault into Cambodia. However, the President wanted to minimize public reaction. So, he insisted that they limit the attack in distance and duration to 30 km in depth and that all American forces withdraw from Cambodia by 30 June.

Between 28 April and 1 May 1970, 32,000 US and 48,000 ARVN forces attacked along two major avenues and several minor ones against fourteen known major base areas along the border and deeper into Cambodia. A combined ARVN and US force made the main attack from the III ARVN Corps region against two areas called the 'Fishhook' and the 'Parrot's Beak.' The former jutted out from Cambodia toward War Zone C north of Saigon. It was the area where US intelligence had found the location of COSVN. The latter area pointed toward northwest Saigon and had bases some 20 miles from the Capital.

To the north, in the II Corps area, a mostly American force attacked west to seize base areas threatening Pleiku and Ban Me Thuot. While these attacks followed the rough outline of previously drawn contingency operations, some of them occurred with as little as a week's notice. Moreover, the US I Field Force commander had to reverse his plans for the movement of forces for a planned out of country withdrawal and reposition them for the offensive.

Over the next sixty days, there were no large-scale battles, but many small but fierce encounters. The COSVN headquarters, warned by Saigon agents, made its escape deeper into Cambodia well before the beginning of the offensive. The incursion was a success in many ways. Allied forces claimed 11,000 PAVN and PLAF soldiers killed and 2,300 prisoners. Allied forces also seized or destroyed more than 25,000 weapons, 1,700 tons of ammunition, and 6,800 tons of rice. Most notably, there was a treasure trove of intelligence – millions of pages of enemy documents as well as the information from the interrogation of POWs.

Within thirty days of its launch, Abrams declared that the attacks had "disrupted enemy operations, preempted enemy planned activities, and removed pressure from the pacification program in the COSVN area." To his staff and commanders, he said "the performance of the South Vietnamese forces has really been extraordinary. After all, they had not engaged in this kind of operation, in this magnitude, with this much movement, and the requirement of this much coordination in the whole history of their armed forces." Indeed, all of this was good news. MACV had gained some added time for Vietnamization.

However, Abrams knew that this operation was not decisive by any stretch of the imagination. He had told his staff, as the time limit for US forces in Cambodia approached, "What we need right now is another division—go in deep. We need to go west from where we are, we need to go north and east from where we are. And we need to do it now... Christ—it's so clear. Don't let them pick up the pieces. Don't let them pick up the pieces. Just like the Germans—you give them thirty-six hours and, goddamn it, you've got to start the war all over again."

Apparently, he must have been thinking of the days when commanders in the field could use their initiative to exploit military success to reach a decisive gain. Those days were absent in this war; they belonged in the past now.

While no American ground forces stayed in Cambodia, South Vietnam continued, on a regular but limited basis, other cross-border operations. These were mostly in support of Lon Nol's armed forces, which struggled against the superior communist onslaught. Moreover, the Nixon Administration continued to offer funds and materials from the foreign aid budget to Lon Nol's forces. In addition, MACV training assistance in South Vietnam now included Cambodian forces at South Vietnamese training centers. American air attacks also continued.

Abrams also used his Mobile Riverine Force to try to seal the border between Cambodia and the southwest delta region of South Vietnam. This force, formed in the summer of 1967 and fully operational in 1968, consisted of a fleet of US Navy armored troop carriers and gunboats teamed with a brigade of the US 9th Infantry Division. This combined Navy-Army team, commanded by a US Navy Admiral, was a force much like one that the Federal government used in the American Civil War to operate in the Mississippi Delta region against the Confederate States. This unique combined Navy-Army joint force by 1970 had become quite useful in the IV Corps area of South Vietnam. Their use in sealing the border, while not entirely successful, was compelling enough to further reduce infiltration into South Vietnam's delta area in 1970.

By the end of that year, Lon Nol's forces were in a campaign of attrition with the North Vietnam and Khmer Rouge Communist forces. Moreover, North Vietnam had suffered a severe blow to their ability to launch offensive operations into South Vietnam. This was particularly the case in the III Corps region for the latter part of 1970 and all of 1971.

Allied actions had also severed the North's sea supply lines through Sihanoukville. This action would make their lines of supply via the Ho Chi Minh Trail much more critical. Throughout 1970 and into the first months of 1971, the PAVN further improved the routes along the Ho Chi Minh Trail and their defenses.

Laos and Lam Son 719: The Test of Vietnamization

The Nixon Administration had also decided to step up its attacks on the trail in Laos. Throughout the latter part of 1969 and all of 1970, air attacks, to now include the use of B52s, had increased in Laos. Abrams had a role in the choice of attacks, but the President insisted on controlling most from Washington. The MACV commander also had a role in the allocation of sorties. Frequently, however, his views on where the air strikes would go and their allocation, particularly over the use of B52s, came into conflict with those of the President and Kissinger. Conflict over their use will continue until the end of the war.

Both Abrams and his Commander-in-Chief, however, shared views on a ground attack against the trail in Laos. They both realized that any significant disruption of the use of this critical infiltration route could set back significantly the North's plans for an offensive in the South. Thus, such an attack could also give much needed time to make Vietnamization work.

By 1971, as James Willbanks describes in his *A Raid Too Far: Operation Lam Son 719 and Vietnamization in Laos*, the much-improved Ho Chi Minh Trail "was a system of roads, command centers, transshipment points, base areas, and way stations, which were called binh trams. The binh trams were located about a day's march from each other, and each operated as a complete logistical center with an assigned area of responsibility and its own medical, engineering, storage, transportation, and maintenance support as well as infantry and anti-aircraft troops to provide security."

As mentioned in Chapter 7, this elaborate support system now consisted of about thirteen thousand kilometers of trails and roads. At this point in the war some were only a meter wide; just enough for foot and bicycle transport. Some were hard bed roads that could handle trucks, and in some cases, armored vehicles.

Since TET and after the Cambodian incursion the North had increased its infiltration dramatically along the trail. By 1971, US intelligence had estimated that a total 630,000 PAVN soldiers had moved to the South using this transportation route; along with some one hundred thousand tons of foodstuff, another four hundred thousand weapons, and fifty tons of ammunition. This estimate is very close to what the PAVN official history claims.

There were three major base areas in Laos – numbered 604, 611, and 612 – at which PAVN forces staged before entering South Vietnam. Upon assembling in them, PAVN forces would then move via an east-west highway called Route 9 into the A Shau Valley at the northwest corner of Thua Thien Province in South Vietnam. From there they would set up forward bases in that valley and could threaten the major cities, especially the provincial and district cities, such as Quang Tri and Hue.

At the end of 1970, MACV intelligence was reporting that movement to these areas had picked up to six thousand PAVN troops a month. The same intelligence reported a dramatic buildup of weapons, ammunition, and equipment in Base Area 604. All indications were for yet another major offensive into the northern two provinces of the ARVN I Corps region during 1971 or during the 1972 election year at the latest. Abrams sent much of this intelligence, and his and Ambassador Bunker's concerns, to Washington.

As the MACV history recounts, on 6 December 1970, Admiral Moorer, the Chairman of the Joint Chiefs succeeding Wheeler, informed Admiral McCain, the current Pacific Command leader, that the President wanted concepts for offensives into either Cambodia again, or Laos early in the new year. The Cambodian offensive would support, once again, Lon Nol's struggle against the communists and attack the sanctuaries reestablished by the NVA. The Laos offensive aim was to counter the PAVN buildup for an expected attack in the ARVN I Corps area.

It is not entirely clear from the current historical evidence who favored and pushed for the Laos invasion. This is probably because of its poor results. Several participants have pointed the finger at others to exonerate themselves from the ultimate failure. The evidence does show that both those in the MACV command and the policy-makers in Washington did discuss at length and shared the risks associated with a Laotian offensive.

Those risks were significant. Given the damage to the Cambodian sanctuaries, strong PAVN forces using the mature base areas in Laos could and would react aggressively to any attack. The PAVN high command could reinforce those forces quickly from reserves out of North Vietnam. Thus, the risks of a significant ARVN defeat and significant losses were high.

As previously mentioned, the ARVN forces would for the first time be operating without their American advisors in any venture outside of South Vietnam due to Congressional restrictions. The advisors were the ones who called for air and artillery support that was critical for such an offensive. Laos, moreover, was not Cambodia. The terrain, weather, and enemy in the former were much more formidable than the latter. Finally, this would be the first time that the ARVN would employ sizeable forces over some significant distances away from their bases without American ground forces.

However, the gains from such an attack could be significant. If successful, this would be the first time that ground forces would cut the trail. Destruction of the North's forces and bases in Laos could set back any communist offensive operation in the South for many months, if not over a year or even more. Moreover, an ARVN victory over the PAVN there would prove their ability to cope with a force that many thought they could not handle.

Consequently, American leaders could find out the answer to the most crucial question about Vietnamization – the viability of the ARVN against the PAVN without significant American support. Moreover, some, to include General Abrams, thought that the operation could lead to the most decisive campaign of the entire war.

Another contributing factor for conducting the offensive was that 1971 was the last time a significant offensive into Laos was possible. That was because such an attack would depend on

American air and artillery support from bases in the South for any chance of success. As James Willbanks writes, "with US troops being steadily drawn down, early 1971 would be the last opportunity for the South Vietnamese to go on such an offensive while substantial US combat forces would still be in South Vietnam to provide support."

Though the Administration favored at first another attack upon Cambodia, the advantages of a Laotian attack intrigued President Nixon. One major factor in his mind was that a victory there could offer an advantage at the Paris Peace Talks, which remained deadlocked. In mid-December, the President sent General Haig to Saigon to hear what General Abrams thoughts were on and his concept for a Laotian offensive.

Immediately after the initial tasking in early December, Abrams set about to explore, with Admiral McCain's enthusiastic support, plans for an ARVN attack. He consulted with his deputy, General Fred Weyand, and the American commanders in I Corps and II Corps, Generals James Sutherland, and Michael Davison, respectively. Abrams tasked them to develop concepts for attacks from each of their regions.

After reviewing each of his subordinates' ideas, the MACV commander accepted Sutherland's concept as the best. It incorporated a main offensive by an ARVN Corps size (several divisions) element along the central east to the west highway, Route 9 to seize several main base areas in Laos. He discussed this concept with Ambassador Bunker, President Thieu, and the Chief of the South Vietnamese General Staff, General Vien. The three of them endorsed the concept.

Abrams, with Bunker present, presented this more detailed outline to Haig on 13 December. Haig had with him a concept of his own, which he had developed with his small Security Council Staff in Washington and had already briefed his immediate boss, Kissinger. The Laos offensive he had in mind was an attack into the Laotian panhandle to the south of the thrust that Abrams envisioned. It was not as bold in that it was further away from the main base areas and the majority of the PAVN forces.

Following that meeting, they all met with Thieu and Vien, who reiterated their support for Abrams's concept. Before leaving, Haig cabled the White House. He endorsed Abrams' bold plan. The concept, he explained later when back in Washington, envisioned using several ARVN divisions supported by American helicopters and air support in Laos, and artillery from positions along the Laotian and South Vietnamese border.

As Haig relates in his memoirs, the Abrams plan appeared to meet the President's guidance "to carry the battle to the enemy to the greatest extent possible." Haig further related to Nixon when he returned that General Abrams had told him that the operation was "potentially the most decisive operation of the war." Therefore, after conferring with his key advisors and with the support of Admiral Moorer, the President gave his approval for further planning.

Once Nixon gave his blessing all seemed to be on board for this offensive. This agreement included Kissinger, though he had reservations. These misgivings were significant, especially after some discussion with the Army Chief of Staff, General Westmoreland. As related in Chapter 5, the former MACV commander did not think the ARVN could be successful without accompanying American advisors and units.

As described in the MACV history, "During January, [the US] XXIV Corps and [ARVN] I Corps, and their subordinate commands drafted detailed plans and orders for the offensive, which Abrams and Vien reviewed and approved. The final plan for the operation, labeled DEWEY CANYON II in its American first phase and LAM SON 719 in its remaining three South Vietnamese phases, closely followed Abrams' original concept. The forward operating base in South Vietnam was to be at Khe Sanh, site of the 1968 siege, which XXIV Corps would secure and reopen during Phase I."

"Besides the armored brigade, a Ranger group, and two regiments of the 1st Infantry Division from I Corps, President Thieu committed the airborne and marine divisions of his national reserve to the offensive under General Lam's operational control. Generals Sutherland and Lam were to direct the battle through cooperation with and coordination from forward command posts.... Under the legislative ban on American ground troops in Laos, the American advisers to South Vietnamese units would still be in South Vietnam. However, the operation depended entirely on massive American air support in all its forms, from B-52 strikes to helicopter lift of troops, artillery, and supplies; and US ground forces would be engaged on the South Vietnamese side of the border."

As James Willbanks explains, while the offensive was bold and risky, the South Vietnamese high command envisioned it as a spoiling attack. That meant that the ARVN forces would not stay in Laos, as Westmoreland had previously planned for US forces. Moreover, the expectations of the South Vietnamese and the Americans were significantly different for the length of the campaign. The South Vietnamese were anxious to end their time in Laos after attacking the main base areas. On the other hand, Abrams and Nixon expected a more prolonged period; thereby producing a decisive cutting of the Trail and the destruction of the main PAVN forces that would mass to protect it.

The Allies took special precautions to prevent communist intelligence of the operation. Both the Americans and South Vietnamese restricted the numbers of staff members involved in the planning. They limited the time that lower-level commanders, brigade and below, were aware of the beginning of the offensive. MACV banned the news media from reporting on any preparations or even that there was a significant operation intended.

The restriction backfired. MACV did not usually set up a ban on reporting daily operations or even future ones. Thus, the Press became enraged; some reporters even indignant. They were incited to find out on their own what was going on. As the MACV history states, the "embargo proved quite porous, both in Vietnam and Washington. During the first days of February, reports and speculation on the coming invasion of Laos were widespread, as was an editorial denunciation of the military's attempt to muzzle the news media. "

Shortly before the launching of the first phase of the assault, both American and South Vietnamese commanders feared enemy intelligence operatives had gained information on some details of the operation. Some postwar stories collaborate that communist spies in the ARVN I Corps headquarters had gained specific times and places for the attacks. Other communist accounts relate that though they knew of the general timeframe and the aims of the attack, the details were unknown.

For sure, PAVN commanders knew that something was about to happen when they garnered information about the preparations, notably the reopening of Khe Shan. They also knew that if the ARVN launched an offensive, it would rely heavily on helicopter support. Accordingly, they planned for the ambushes of likely landing zones and moved in more air defense formations.

Thus, the PAVN command in Laos was ready for the offensive. At the end of January, they had massed a total of 23,000 troops near the expected main objective, Tchepone. Another 40,000 were in position to move and thwart an ARVN attack into Laos against the main base areas. Overall, the ARVN forces during the campaign would be outnumbered more than two to one.

On 29 January, American forces from the 1st Brigade of the 5th Mechanized Infantry Division began a movement from its main base camp west along Route 9 to set up a firebase near a place called Ca Lu. This firebase was to offer fire support for the reopening of Khe Sanh. Other American units positioned themselves to protect the route for the forces that would deploy to Khe Sanh by road.

An air assault into the former marine base soon followed. There American infantry, engineer, artillery, aviation, and support units began setting up positions to support the follow-on ARVN forces that would stage there for further air assaults into Laos. The aviation group of the 101st Airborne Division would conduct most of the air movements. Over 500 helicopters would take part.

Meanwhile, ARVN units began employing near the Laotian border. US forces gave security to their assembly areas for the offensive. The American Press, now privy to most of these moves, began reporting these preparations. The North Vietnamese, already prepared to meet the offensive, now knew from the news reports that it was imminent.

On 8 February, the assault into Laos began. After a B52 preparatory strike, ARVN engineer units moved out to repair the narrow Route 9 running toward the primary objective. ARVN armored forces followed with American air cavalry elements offering aerial observation as they moved west. As each element crossed the border, they waved at members of the Press gathered there to watch. If they knew how these news people were about to treat the entire operation, they would not have been so hospitable.

As the American air cavalry scouted ahead of the ground forces, seven ARVN airborne and ranger battalions air assaulted into pre-designated landing zones north and south of the route of advance. PAVN forces, which had set up ambushes at many of the sites, heavily engaged the disembarking soldiers. Enemy air defense units also engaged American helicopters, shooting several down as they approached the LZs.

Meanwhile, the ARVN armored forces found that despite the engineer efforts, Route 9 was too narrow and run down to afford rapid advances. It became clear to the ARVN high command, and their co-located American advisors in South Vietnam, that most of the offensive would have to rely on helicopter movement for major advances and resupply. The mild weather that had characterized the operation during its preparatory phase now turned bad. This critically hampered air movement and support, on which all now depended.

Despite the harsh weather and poor roads, in two days ARVN forces had penetrated about twenty kilometers into Laos. Despite some initial ambushes, units had set up secure locales and had fanned out to conduct operations to find the enemy and destroy their base areas. As the main attack along Route 9 slogged forward, ARVN elements positioned a series of fire support bases to support their offensive into Laos. The units selected for this operation were the best in the ARVN. Therefore, despite the difficulties in terrain, weather, and continued enemy resistance they moved forward.

The PAVN high command had not yet moved reinforcements in reaction to the initial attack. They wanted to ensure that the attack along Route 9 was not a feint. Now, less than a week into the offensive, they became emboldened. The forty thousand PAVN soldiers in reserve began to rapidly move toward the ARVN locations along the flanks of the route of advance. These PAVN units included heavy artillery, heavy air defense guns, and the latest Soviet tanks and other armored vehicles.

Just as this force started to bear down on the ARVN flanks, the ARVN high command began to lose control. The officer in charge of the operation, General Lam, did not issue orders for later moves. ARVN division and brigade officers did not take any initiative to continue the momentum toward Tchepone.

Compounding the delay and confusion in the field, President Thieu became cautious. He wanted to avoid significant casualties. The President ordered Lam to ensure that his forces were not spread out and that the flanks of the main advance were secure. It seems that as his forces became more engaged, the RVN President became increasingly worried that he may lose his best and most loyal forces.

General Abrams knew that this lack of aggressiveness could be fatal to the operation. He and General Sutherland went to Lam's forward command post where they expressed these concerns. This consultation seemed to work. Lam issued orders to continue the attack. However, now the NVA was about to launch a coordinated counterattack.

As Willbanks explains, "When the speed and momentum of the attack, which gave the ARVN their only chance for success, evaporated, the would-be attackers soon found themselves under attack by a much stronger enemy than they had anticipated and were coming under heavy rocket and long-range artillery fire. Additionally, the increased number of enemy antiaircraft weapons on the mountain slopes to the south, as well as north of Route 9, made airmobile operations and aerial resupply more and more dangerous as Lam Son continued."

Sensing the vulnerability of the ARVN forces, the NVA now directed an all-out effort to destroy them. Elements of four PAVN divisions relentlessly attacked. They aimed to isolate various ARVN positions along the main ground avenue of advance and defeat them one at a time. The resultant fighting over the next several weeks would be amongst the heaviest of the war.

With the main ground advance stalled, the ARVN high command decided to conduct a series of airmobile advances toward Tchepone. American aviation units supported these, with the final one into the immediate vicinity of the small outpost town near the final objective being the most extensive air assault of the war. While this attack attained some success in destroying bases and supplies near the town, the ARVN forces came under a massive PAVN counterattack consisting of tanks and supporting infantry.

Shortly after other ARVN forces seized Tchepone. Feeling that his troops had succeeded in the overall operation, Thieu told Abrams that he would curtail the entire campaign. He would withdraw his troops from Laos by the first week of April. The senior ARVN commander had lost any stomach for any further offensive action.

Overall, The ARVN junior leaders and their companies and battalions had fought bravely throughout the operation. They stood their ground repeatedly; often outnumbered and faced with a force they had never faced before – tanks and other armored vehicles.

They had depended heavily, however, on the American military support. Though they were without their usual American advisors, US Army aviation kept them supplied with ammunition and shifted forces about the battlefield. Moreover, US Air Forces and Army gunships gave critical close air support. The Air Force launched B52 attacks against NVA forces more vulnerable than ever because their conventional formations were now dependent on roads and sustainment of fuel.

Furthermore, the ARVN forces had faced two formidable circumstances outside of their control - other than the PAVN relentless counterattacks – that would inhibit or appear to prevent their overall success. These were the adverse press reporting, and their inexperience in this new form of combat. Both were primarily an American doing.

The American Press had already played a role in tipping off the PAVN in the launching of the offensive. Now their reporting would, much like it had done in TET 68, affect the perceptions of the American public on the nature of the fighting and its confidence in an ally that the US had been supporting for more than a decade.

The first significant example of the impact of the Press occurred two weeks into the offensive. It involved one of the ARVN positions set up north of the main route of advance at a place called Ranger Base North. There, a battalion of ARVN Rangers, some 430 strong, fought and held off an NVA regiment three times their numbers. The ARVN Rangers lost 326 men, killed, wounded, or missing while killing 639 PAVN soldiers. After the battle ended, US helicopters flew in the extract the remaining rangers.

An American press team photographed some unwounded ARVN Rangers trying to get out of their LZ by frantically holding on to the skids of the medical evacuation helicopters. The resulting news stories with those pictures in the *New York Times* and *Washington Post* painted a picture of cowardly South Vietnamese soldiers running away from the battle. These stories and pictures "set the tone for the lasting public perception of Lam Song 719 amongst the American people."

Abrams Losses Favor with Washington

Nixon and Kissinger, like LBJ and McNamara three years before, became susceptible to this constant adverse reporting. They plummeted Abrams with requests for updates. They also began to directly order the MACV commander to move troops and resources as the battles ensued.

When they found out about Thieu's order to cease the campaign by the first part of April, both the President and his National Security Advisor became angry at and lost faith in General Abrams. They insisted that he order the South Vietnamese to continue the operation until the end of April. They felt that keeping them there for another month would prevent the semblance of a hasty retreat in the face of the strong PAVN counterattacks.

Abrams relayed Nixon's desires to Thieu. However, the RVN President did not want to risk further damage or a major catastrophe. He felt that the seizure of Tchepone was proof enough that the ARVN had fought hard and accomplished their primary objective. Thieu continued his orders to withdraw.

In response to both Nixon's and Kissinger's frequent inquiries, General Abrams continued to express confidence in the ARVN capabilities to inflict damage on the NVA network in Laos. He also tried to get the South Vietnamese High Command to commit more forces to the operation.

They would only do so, they argued, if the US would commit ground forces to the Laos fighting. Abrams knew that this was not possible. Instead, he told them that they could count on increasing B52 support.

The MACV commander was becoming increasingly aware that the South Vietnamese forces were dependent on American firepower and air support for survival. Therefore, by the middle of March, he gave up on the thought that the ARVN could win a decisive major battle against Northern forces.

Instead of opposing Thieu's desires for a curtailed operation, he now began to support the South Vietnam President's call for a departure in early April. In response, Nixon and Kissinger, as explained in Chapter 5, dispatched their senior military advisor, General Alexander Haig, to Saigon to obtain his views on what was going on in Operation Lam Son 719 and assess Abrams' performance.

After Haig arrived in country on 17 March, he went to visit General Sutherland's headquarters in I Corps. There he related to Abrams and his officers the President's desires for the ARVN to stay in Laos through April. Abrams told him that the withdrawal was already underway and remaining longer in Laos was not possible.

At once, Haig cabled back to Washington that "ARVN enthusiasm for continuation of the operation in Laos is completely lacking... The extended period of intense combat has convinced the ARVN commanders that the operation should be called off as quickly as possible." The next day Haig followed up with another message stating, "the ARVN have lost their stomach for Laos, and the problem isn't to keep them in but rather to influence them to pull out in an orderly fashion."

In later cables, Haig criticized the American leadership role in the operation. He wrote, "it was clear that the operation was not receiving the kind of leadership and management from the American force structure that it should have." Haig reinforced all this criticism personally with Nixon and Kissinger when he returned home several days later.

These events all led to the 23 March discussion, also related in Chapter 5, of the firing of Abrams and his replacement with Haig. It is unknown how much Abrams' knew of Haig's backstabbing. He never wrote any memoirs, did not give interviews to the Press, and did not say much to his subordinates and staff about his relationship with his superiors or Haig.

Withdrawing under enemy pressure is one of the most challenging military operations to execute. The ARVN executed one, but only through the extraordinary brave efforts of American helicopter pilots and their crews. The PAVN shot down several of these more than once executing their missions. Many of these 'shoot downs' were inflicted on US helicopters trying to extract isolated and exposed ARVN units from pick up zones under enemy fire. Some of these pilots and crews were never found. They remain today among the list of American MIAs in Indochina.

Besides the role of the Press in the perception of failure in Lam Son 719, the other circumstance that influenced the ARVN performance was the American effort to train and turn over operations under the Vietnamization program. The weaknesses that the ARVN showed in Laos were, in large part, an American failure.

As discussed in detail in Chapter 8, the US had never intended until after TET 1968 to adequately organize, equip, and train the South Vietnamese Armed Forces for many capabilities that they lacked. Close air support, artillery support, intelligence operations, logistics for sustained combat operations were just a few that MACV had assumed would be supplied mostly by American forces and advisors. Now they were not present.

Moreover, the ARVN high command was not ready to command and control large formations in a Corps size operation, which Lam Son 719 was. They just did not know how and had not exercised properly to do so. Senior commanders at the division and brigade level, likewise, had not trained or operated in division-size operations, which the Lam Son 719 operations concept demanded. Neither did they have the wherewithal to do so; given the fact that American advisors were absent.

This was not just an American training failure. Haig was partially correct that it was also an American command problem. General Abrams should have known that such an operation was outside of the capability of an Army that he had had the responsibility for organizing, equipping, and training for nearly four years – one year as Westmoreland's Deputy and three as the MACV commander.

Instead, the General had succumbed to the desire, as others had done, to demonstrate the result of American efforts to build an Army that could win. He merely, but erroneously, wanted the ARVN to win the decisive campaign of the war that an American Army should have conducted. Thus, while the ARVN high command and its subordinate senior leaders made serious errors in judgment and showed a lack of military professionalism endemic to its political orientation, the American press and military contributed to the perception of and the realities of failure in Laos.

By 25 March ARVN forces were out of Laos. Two weeks later MACV ordered the American base at Khe Sanh once again abandoned. Per their official history, the operation resulted in 13,000 North Vietnamese dead, and the loss of 88 tanks and some 2,000 other vehicles. As with other such offensives, ARVN forces destroyed significant ammunition and food supplies, as well.

General Abrams and Ambassador Bunker told Washington that they thought Lam Son 719 set back the enemy for any major offensive into South Vietnam for the rest of 1971. Publicly, Nixon and his advisors tried to sell these arguments to the American Press and Public. They would not believe any of it. They just continued to call for an end to the war.

In June, the Senate passed the Mansfield Amendment calling for the withdrawal of all American forces from Vietnam. By the beginning of 1972, most American major combat forces had left. The Paris peace talks continued with one significant development. The Americans agreed that PAVN forces would not have to withdraw from the South. The fate of the ARVN and its government was sealed.

Post Lam Son 719 Improvements, Changes, and Lingering Scars

While General Abrams continued to paint Lam Son 719 in a positive light, to his credit he acted to improve the ARVN deficiencies that were prominent during the campaign. Most notably, he formed several American 'joint support groups' to advise the ARVN Corps and Division commanders and their staffs in higher unit operations – particularly in logistics, combat support operations, and coordination of units larger than battalion size.

The group staff training also acted to improve on ARVN use of fire support and use of aviation assets. Abrams further asked for, received, and aided the ARVN in forming some new armored units. These had improved American battle tanks to counter the PAVN armored formations encountered during the Laos campaign.

During some heavy fighting on the Cambodian border at the end of 1971, ARVN Corps and divisions used some of these improvements in tactics and techniques successfully. By the end of the year, the US replenished materials lost during Lam Son 719. Of course, they could not replace many of the brave junior leaders lost.

There were also unseen scars that the withdrawal from Laos had caused among several of the elite ARVN units. There was also much resentment on how the American press had reported the operation and a realization that they were still heavily dependent on American advisors and air support.

The months after Lam Son 719 was eerily silent in South Vietnam. MACV reported steady improvement in Vietnamization and Pacification. The RVN was now relatively stable. At the beginning of 1972, American troop strength was down to 139,000, with only about 6,000 of those combat forces. The latter was standing down and preparing for the final withdrawal at the end of the year.

MACV had altered the US advisory organization. It reduced the number of American advisors at the division level and below. For example, at the height of the advisory effort, there were on average seventy-five Americans in each regiment. Advisory teams went down to the company level. Now there were only two Americans at the regiment level and none below. The command also consolidated other advisors at the Corps level. They further organized them into new 'regional assistance teams.' The total drawdown and reorganization resulted in many ARVN units being without American teams that could quickly call for US artillery and air support.

Despite this drawdown of American advisory support, the ARVN at the end of 1971 was a formidable force. As Andrew West in *Forgotten Army* describes, "Within the impressive catalog of military might, the ARVN had expanded to more than 400,000 troops, while the Territorial Forces had risen in strength to more than 500,000 men. Both the ARVN and the Territorial Forces also received new weaponry, eventually including 175mm artillery pieces, M-48A3 tanks, and TOW wire-guided antitank missiles."

"The South Vietnamese Navy and Air Force also saw similar expansions and upgrades in equipment, with the staple of the South Vietnamese Air Force, the outdated A-1 Skyraider, gradually replaced by the A-37 and F-5A jet fighter-bombers. Training of the expanded military forces of South Vietnam also improved and centered on the strengthening of areas of weaknesses exhibited during the Laotian incursion, including coordination of fire support, airmobile operations, and logistical support."

Despite these improvements, the inherent weaknesses of corruption and political intrigue among the ARVN senior commanders remained prevalent. Abrams tried to cure these flaws. He often made recommendations to President Thieu for alterations in the senior command structure. Thieu agreed to some but kept those who were the most politically loyal and influential in their fiefdoms in office.

Many middle-level leaders were aware of this 'business as usual' at the top and had begun to get disillusioned about any eventual reform for the future. At the troop level, desertions continued, especially because the South Vietnamese economy wilted as the Americans withdrew and their spending no longer fueled local economies.

Supporting the 1972 Easter Invasion: A Crisis in Command

Meanwhile, the North Vietnamese had been reviewing their lessons and conclusions from Lam Son 719, which they also planned to act upon. As explained in Chapter 7, both the Politburo and the PAVN high command felt that they had faced the best that the ARVN could field in a major operation and had defeated them. They felt that the PAVN had dealt a devastating blow to American Vietnamization.

Communist agents in the South reinforced this view. They reported serious morale problems among those ARVN forces that had taken part in the Lam Son 719 campaign. They also reported that desertions in the ARVN were growing higher than ever before.

With the Americans now devoted to a withdrawal from South Vietnam, Le Duan believed that the ARVN was now vulnerable to an all-out attack. While their losses had been significant, the North Vietnamese had the rest of 1971 to reconstitute and prepare for another offensive in 1972. Because of the high anti-war sentiment in the US, most in the Politburo did not think that Nixon would risk US military intervention against an offensive in an election year.

As early as March 1971, Le Duan had begun arguing before the Politburo his case for a 1972 all-out invasion of South Vietnam. He was successful. Immediately after, Le Duan visited Moscow and Beijing to obtain state of the art military assistance to further build the PAVN into a powerful conventional force. As military hardware and supplies for the offensive flowed into the North during the rest of the year, General Giap, reinstated after some vindication from the costly TET offensive, devised a campaign plan. It consisted of an invasion of the South using a four-prong attack.

As detailed in Chapter 7, the plan called for an advance of three divisions directly across the DMZ toward Quang Tri. A secondary attack from Laos consisting of another three divisions would support that DMZ thrust. The ultimate goal was Hue. The second advance of two divisions came from Laos toward Kontum. Its final objective was Qui Nhon on the coast. A third attack came from Cambodia toward An Loc directed at Saigon. It consisted of three divisions as well. The final advance was a two-division attack out of southern Cambodia into the ARVN IV Corps delta area.

Recall from previous descriptions that nearly the entire PAVN would take part in the offensive – involving a total of 200,000 North Vietnamese soldiers. Giap labeled this campaign the Nguyen Hue Offensive, named after an emperor who had launched a successful surprise attack against the Chinese in 1789. It would be almost entirely a conventional type offensive. North Vietnam would finally reveal the real nature of its conquest of the South. Gone for the time being were any pretenses that its attack would be in support of an uprising prompted by southern insurgents.

North Vietnamese preparations and build up for this offensive, like that for TET 68, did not go unnoticed by MACV or the South Vietnamese High Command. Reconnaissance flights, long-range patrols, radio intercepts gave ample signs that a major offensive was imminent by the end of 1971. As Westmoreland had done before TET 68, Abrams cabled Washington to warn them of a significant communist assault. Everyone thought the timing of the coming attack would be a repeat of the 1968 offensive. So, both Abrams and the South Vietnamese Joint Staff thought it would come during the TET holiday in 1972. It did not.

On March 30, 1972, spearheaded by Soviet tanks, PAVN units finally attacked simultaneously on all four fronts. Once again, the offensive surprised both MACV and the South Vietnamese. The largest surprise was the conventional nature of the NVA offensive. Though American military leaders had long worried about an invasion from the North across the DMZ, there was no ARVN effective defense there. The string of outposts south of the DMZ, taken over from the US Marines during 1971, was no real defense against PAVN armor and heavy artillery. They fell quickly, leaving the route open for the seizure of Quang Tri.

General Truong, who would soon take over the fight in the I Corps areas, later wrote, "The unexpected assault across the DMZ caught the forward elements of the 3rd Division in movement, only partially settled into defensive positions they had not been in for some time, locally outnumbered three-to-one, and outgunned by the enemy artillery. The ARVN defenses in the DMZ area were designed to counter infiltration and local attacks. There were no positions prepared to give the depth to the battlefield that would be required to contain an attack of the size and momentum of the one that had now fallen upon them."

As Willbanks claims, many of the ARVN soldiers' morale dropped immediately because they felt abandoned by their American advisors. There seemed no other recourse than retreat. It was just a matter of how far and in what condition to resist further.

In the II Corps region, PAVN forces quickly overran ARVN elements on the border. Like the I Corps area, ARVN commanders had employed their forces in firebases and other large unit bases taken over from the Americans the previous year. Unlike the northern region, PLAF units, with mostly NVA fillers, aided their PAVN brethren by attacks in the lowland areas as well. This was particularly true in the coastal province of Binh Dinh, which had been a communist stronghold resisting many of the clear and hold operations over the years.

As the offensive continued, ARVN forces increasingly put up a fierce fight. They slowed the PAVN advance, using American B52 strikes out of it Thailand bases. By early May, however, two PAVN divisions closed in on Kontum, the headquarters of the ARVN Corps and its remaining American advisors.

The PAVN offensive in the III Corps region came out of the bases that the ARVN and American forces had attacked in their Cambodia incursion in 1970. The infamous 9th PLAF Division, which the Americans had 'destroyed' several times in their large sweeps of War Zones C and D and the Iron Triangle, led the assault out of the 'Parrots Beak' area toward Saigon. That division was now made up of mostly North Vietnamese soldiers. Two PAVN divisions also attacked out of the 'Fishhook' bases toward Saigon. Their intermediate aim was An Loc, where the ARVN Corps headquarters and its American advisor team were.

ARVN resistance along the border had been more effective than that in the two other Corps areas. However, by 13 April the PAVN reached An Loc. There the ARVN, expecting that the NVA would attack Saigon along an axis going through An Loc, had assembled a formidable force to defend the city. The PAVN could not overrun it and settled in for a siege to capture it.

The road going through An Loc was essential for the communist attack against the South Vietnamese capital. Thus, the Northern forces were determined to seize it. Meanwhile, MACV monitored the battle in Saigon. Regional advisors often sent Abrams reports. The General also visited the ARVN Corps headquarters when he could. He also sent his deputy, General Weyand, to ARVN units to assess the situation.

Nixon and Kissinger once again daily asked Abrams for updates. Distrusting their field commander, Nixon and Kissinger again sent Haig on periodic visits to Saigon. As mentioned in Chapter 5, they now depended on their military aide for an assessment of the situation. They habitually relied more on a junior military officer than the JCS or MACV for military advice. Haig was a willing agent. His ambition far surpassed his loyalty and courtesy to any sense of service to the profession of arms that he should have followed.

As also related in Chapter 5, the President and his National Security Assistant had become so infuriated with Abrams that they had ever since Lam Son considered his replacement. At first, they wanted it to be Haig; now they were considering General DePuy, who had served under Westmoreland in Vietnam and now was his Deputy Chief of Staff or the Army.

One reason for their continued dismay with the MACV commander was that Abrams reports were again characteristically optimistic. Abe naturally wanted the ARVN, which had undergone significant improvements in materials, to show the fruits of his efforts. He eventually began to believe, however, that the ARVN just could not hold their own against the NVA onslaught.

On 1 May Abrams' reports took a dramatic negative shift. He reported to Secretary Laird: "As the pressure has mounted and the battle has become brutal the senior military leadership has begun to bend and in some cases, break. In adversity, it is losing its will and cannot be depended upon to take the measures necessary to stand and fight." He concluded, there was "no apparent basis for confidence Hue could be held."

Besides monitoring and reporting on the offensive, Abrams only other recourse to affect the battle was to coordinate the only support he now had available - airpower. There were only two US combat brigades left in country, and they were preparing for withdrawal to the States. Consequently, they were of no use. However, he could still call upon much air support from forces in country, on carriers in the South China Sea, and some strategic air forces in adjacent bases primarily in Thailand and Guam.

As the communist onslaught continued, because of their payload and the terror they produced on enemy units, B52s were becoming the 'weapon of choice.' Periodically, as mentioned, the use of the strategic bombers in South Vietnam competed with the bombing the North. This issue created further friction between Abrams and Nixon.

Again, as related in Chapter 5, Nixon was increasingly taking over operations in Southeast Asia. Now he was passing orders on B52 strikes directly to the Pacific Commander, Admiral McCain - the father of then POW and future Senator John McCain.
These orders demanded a shift in B52 assets from Abrams.

Admiral McCain did so, but without informing Abrams. McCain was technically the superior to the MACV commander, so he was well within his authority. However, in wartime, it is of tantamount importance that one commander, whatever his relationship with another, keep another commander informed of the use of assets that the latter is dependent upon. In this instance, McCain had violated that basic professional courtesy and necessity.

According to Lewis Sorley in his biography, Abrams became infuriated. Already under much stress, he penned a message to McCain that was, in essence, a letter of resignation informing the Admiral that without the B52 assets he had counted on, he "would be unable to discharge the responsibilities assigned to me." In response, McCain reallocated a portion of the B52s that Abrams said he needed immediately.

By the end of May, the NVA offensive started to slow down and then stop in all four regions. There were three reasons for this. First, the PAVN high command had their problems of coordinating their movements. This massive unit offensive was new to them. Though they had done some training for it, their preparations had not given them the wherewithal needed for the coordinated division and corps size operations over vast distances. They experienced the same difficulties that the ARVN high command had in Lam Son 719.

Second, PAVN movements were now depended upon the major road networks. That made them highly vulnerable to American air interdiction. These attacks had become intense – hundreds of sorties each day. Senior American Advisors, now available at the Corps headquarters and some sent to ARVN divisions, effectively coordinated them. As described in the MACV history, "Airpower was the Military Assistance Command's decisive weapon in the 1972 battles. During the crisis, MACV's single management system, tried and perfected since 1968, enabled General Abrams to mass his airplanes where and when they were needed."

Finally, the ARVN units, competently led by some division commanders and many junior leaders, began to hold. In the I Corps region, the first defeat had resulted in the relief of the ARVN Corps commander. His replacement was one of the finest officers and leaders of the South Vietnamese Army – General Ngo Quang Truong. Truong had been the 1st ARVN Division head during TET 68. In that position, he was mostly responsible for the ARVN successful counterattack at Hue. Now Thieu ordered him to defend Hue again.

The new ARVN I Corps commander asked for and received much-needed reinforcements. Rather than preparing a static defense, Truong launched a series of small counterattacks to stall the NVA offensive. It worked. PAVN troops never made it to Hue. Aided by the fortune of clear weather and massive American air attacks, he then ordered a major counteroffensive.

That assault began at the end of June. It was successful in recapturing much of the lost ground and firebases in the western portions of the I Corps provinces; however, the key avenue of the A Shau Valley remained in communist hands. The recapture of Quang Tri – the capital city of the South's northern most province - was much more problematic. After a month-long battle in house-to-house fighting, the ARVN finally retook the city on 16 September. Afterward, ARVN forces were exhausted. They were unable to retake the area between the city and the DMZ. There PAVN forces reassembled and prepared for future operations.

In the II Corps area, the ARVN reinforced their units around Kontum. The ARVN commander, bolstered by his American Advisor John Paul Vann and American airpower, successfully held off the first attacks. Soon, however, the ARVN commander lost control, and Vann took over.

This civilian advisor was the same American who, as a military officer and advisor, had been present at the infamous battle of Ap Bac in 1963. He had returned to South Vietnam as a civilian in charge of American CORDS efforts in the II Corps region. Now he took over the battle for this central region city. If Kontum fell, then the principal west to east road to the coast would be open for the PAVN armored forces. Communist forces would have cut South Vietnam in half.

Vann convinced President Thieu to replace the ARVN Corps commander. Thieu did so. The President also sent more reinforcements. With Vann calling for and directing an immense amount of American air power, the ARVN defenses held against several PAVN assaults. Some of these had penetrated the defenses. However, some Southern units quickly countered and forced the NVA to withdraw. Later, John Paul Vann died when his helicopter crashed as he was reviewing the battlefield. His body was recovered and brought back for burial at Arlington Cemetery. He died believing South Vietnam would finally be able to survive communist aggression.

By June the PAVN gave up the fight and withdrew to the western areas of the II Corps area. There they would set up bases and establish control of large areas of the westernmost provinces. For the time being, they were militarily neutralized. They had lost over 4,000 dead and around 20,000 wounded during the campaign – much of that in the battle for Kontum.

The PAVN main thrust toward Saigon, like that in the II Corps region, stalled and bogged down outside a major city – An Loc. As the communist offensive had moved toward Saigon, it, like others, became dependent on the main road, Route 13, to move its armored formations. Route 13 ran through An Loc. That provincial capital city became the ARVN's 'battle of Bastogne.' Initially defended by the ARVN 5th Division, the South Vietnamese Corps commander reinforced the defenses with another division before the PAVN attack took place.

From 13 April to 18 June, elements of three PAVN divisions besieged the city. Wave after wave of NVA infantry and armor launched head-on attacks against a solid ARVN defense helped by American advisors. The advisors directed American airpower to thwart those assaults. Finally, the PAVN had to break off their attack and withdraw to the northwest areas next to the border region. There, they settled in to gain control of the local populace and set up bases for future operations.

The battle and siege of An Loc, recounted in historical narratives like Andrew Wiest's *Forgotten Army* and Lam Quang Thi's *Hell in An Loc*, are stories of heroism and determination of both the ARVN soldier and their American Advisors. Thi, an ARVN officer who took part in the battle and later escaped to America, best summarizes the battle's success. He wrote, "The South Vietnamese army had indeed won a decisive victory against overwhelming odds." Thi notes, "according to Maj. Gen. James F. Hollingsworth, Senior Advisor to ARVN III Corps, 'The real credit goes to the little ARVN soldier. He is just tremendous, just magnificent. He stood in there, took all that fire and gave it back."

The experiences and later fate of those 'little ARVN' soldiers are worthy of reading. A recent book *South Vietnamese Soldiers: Memories of the Vietnam War and After*, by a daughter of a former South Vietnam diplomat named Nathalie Huynh Chau Nguyen, is full of oral testimonies of these men, what motivated them, and how they survived. It is heartbreaking.

Despite all that heroism without their American advisors it is doubtful that the ARVN would have been successful. As Lam Quang Thi's narrative further explains the ARVN success, "Special credit should also be given to the American advisors who fought valiantly alongside their counterparts and, more importantly, gave effective air support and coordinated resupply and medevac operations for the beleaguered garrison. Their mere presence constituted a tremendous boost to the morale of ARVN troops because it embodied the U.S. commitment to support South Vietnam in these darkest hours of its history."

As the battles raged in South Vietnam, the Nixon Administration, as described in Chapter 5, launched the most extensive and sustained bombing of the North. The US Navy also mined Haiphong harbor and other Northern ports. These operations, along with the successful defense and counteroffensive of the ARVN against the PAVN forces, brought an end to the Easter Offensive.

As in Lam Son 719, both sides claimed victory. President Nixon once again argued that it was a validation of the entire Vietnamization policy. General Abrams publicly praised the bravery and tenacity of the ARVN forces. Privately he knew that it had been a near disaster. He realized that there were still problems to overcome. One that was especially clear was the continued incompetence of several of the politically corrupt senior leaders. Another was the persistent inability of Thieu to set up a competent senior command structure.

Abrams also knew that without American airpower and advisory teams, the ARVN would not have been able to hold its own. He also realized that it was all out of his hands now. He, like the South Vietnamese leaders, understood what the concessions at Paris meant to the South's ability to defend itself. On top of that, there would soon be no US residual force, a severe reduction of Congressional aid, and no American airpower to help.

Beyond the victory claims, the reality was that the PAVN had severely bloodied the ARVN. The South Vietnamese Army lost over 100,000 casualties. There had been more than 25,000 civilians killed and almost a million refugees.

The North also paid the price. The PAVN lost nearly 100,000 casualties. American airpower had virtually destroyed its armored forces. The defeat resulted in the discrediting of both General Giap and the PAVN high command. The Politburo purged the General Staff.

Giap, whom many have seen as a brilliant strategist responsible for the military victories over the American Army, was never to plan or command future operations again in the war. He would remain as Minister of Defense, primarily in the role of overseeing the continued raising and training of PAVN forces, and titular head of the Peoples' Army of North Vietnam.

As detailed in Chapters 5 and 7, the failure of the Easter Offensive and the Nixon directed extensive bombing convinced the North to negotiate an end to the fighting. This was primarily to finalize American military involvement and reconstitute its losses. Thus, Le Duan directed Le Duc To to sign the Paris Peace Accords in January 1973. Though he had not achieved the military victory he had sought, Le Duan knew that he could eventually defeat the South, who could not hold out without American military support. It was now, he thought, just a matter of time.

Section 10.3 - The Final Collapse

As mentioned several times, the Paris accords allowed the North Vietnamese forces that were in the South after the Easter Offensive to remain there. The North would reinforce them, reconstitute its conventional capabilities, and, over the next two years, consolidate and expand its hold over some of the territorial gains from its Nguyen Hue Offensive.

In July 1973, the US Congress passed legislation that prohibited the use of American combat forces in Indochina. By his involvement in the Watergate affair and Congress's later investigations, Nixon eventually resigned in August 1974. This resignation nullified any hope for Thieu that President Nixon might intervene as he had promised he would if the North again launched a major offensive. Congress, reflecting the American publics' call for an ending of US military involvement in the war, steadily and critically reduced funding for South Vietnam and its armed forces.

US Command Changes

Immediately after the Paris Peace Accords, American force strength in South Vietnam stood at a little over 23,000 personnel, who were mostly administrative and support elements. The US also made significant changes to its command structure. General Weyand, replacing Abrams, who took over as Army Chief of Staff from Westmoreland, disbanded MACV and reorganized it into several entities.

The first was an American contingent to the "Four - Party Joint Military Commission." This Commission, called for under the accords, would plan for and oversee the return of the American POWs and supervise the cease-fire. The second was the headquarters, US Support Activities Group and 7th Air Force. This headquarters, about 600 personnel, would be stationed in Thailand. Its primary function was to command and control American Air Force support for continued operations in South Vietnam, Laos, and Cambodia (until Congress prohibited it later).

The Support Group in Thailand would also oversee the Defense Attaché Office in Saigon. The DAO - consisting of some 55 military personnel and supported by over thousand indigenous Vietnamese and American contractors - would continue to oversee US aid to South Vietnam. Meanwhile, the American mission in Saigon, now headed by Ambassador Graham Martin, continued to work with the RVN. While Thieu and his government continued to hold elections, their rule remained autocratic. True reform stayed elusive.

On 29 March 1973, the last US troops left South Vietnam. That evening, President Nixon announced that the US had "prevented the imposition of a Communist government by force on South Vietnam." The same day General Weyand held a ceremony terminating MACV.

As described by James Willbanks in his *Abandoning Vietnam*, Weyand's last report to Washington applauded the accomplishments of the ARVN in the Easter Offensive and its aftermath. But, he also warned that without continued US air power, the ARVN would find it more difficult to oppose an outright invasion from the North. Prophetically, he pointed out that the ARVN lacked enough mobile reserves to counter any North Vietnamese major attack. The main reason, he emphasized, was that the shifting of ARVN forces would be problematic because their family connections tied them to the regions in which they were garrisoned.

The Aftermath of the Paris Accords and the 'War of the Flags'

After the signing of The Paris Peace Accord, there was a total of about 219,000 PAVN forces in South Vietnam. PAVN General Tran Van Tra, the B2 Front commander, recalls that they "were fatigued, had not had time to make up for their losses [from the 1972 offensive], and all units were in disarray."

However, they occupied sizeable chunks of territory. Much of the DMZ from the 17th Parallel to the Thach Han River, where US Marines had survived the heavy rocket and artillery attacks against their outposts guarding the northernmost province, was now a PAVN enclave. To the West, NVA forces also controlled the A Shau Valley, where the US Army had fought many battles to include the one at Hamburger Hill in May 1969.

PAVN units further occupied other tracts of territory in the II and III Corps regions where American forces had fought to destroy PAVN and PLAF main forces, in areas such as Dak To, and War Zones C and D. Meanwhile, significant NVA forces also stayed in the borderland bases. For example, by the end of January 1973, as William Le Gro in his *Vietnam from Cease-Fire to Capitulation* states, there were 70,000 NVA soldiers in Laos and 30,000 in Cambodia.

Just before the RVN and DRV had signed the accords, both sides tried to seize and control as much of South Vietnam as possible. Each side tried to mark a hamlet or village complex under their political control by planting their national flag. The North continued its ruse that disgruntled Southern VC represented the NLF. Therefore, communist forces planted the NLF flag. All of this activity became known as the 'war of the flags.'

William Turley summarizes that "From January 1973 to mid-1974, Saigon claimed to have placed a thousand added hamlets under its control; three hundred were retaken from the Communists, who had seized them just before the ceasefire. Ninety had been under Communist control for a long time. The Communists had a slightly different assessment. They retook nearly all of the 394 hamlets we had liberated prior to the signing of the Agreement." The only thing sure about this 'war of the flags' was that many of these flag planting episodes involved fighting - much of it heavy – and killing.

After the signing of the accords, Le Duan and the North Vietnam Politburo had wanted a period of relative peace in the South. They wanted to use this time to enable the replenishment of their combat power and the reestablishment of the communist political cells, particularly in the areas they claimed in the 'war of the flags.' They were unable to do so.

The main reason was the determination of the Thieu government not to honor the agreements. The RVN President recognized that the Paris accords, which the Americans had forced them to sign, had heavily favored the North. Therefore, he wanted to obtain as much territory as possible to gain some advantages before the inevitable North offensive.

A close second reason was that the southern fraction of the communists, what little of it was left, did not want the RVN to be able to gain such a strong foothold that it would be impossible to regain any political control. For them, the Northern Communist call for more emphasis on political action was reminiscent of the situation after the 1954 Geneva Accords.

Thus, the Southern Communists put a lot of pressure on their Northern comrades to change their approach. Until that was done, they just "ignored orders and pushed the ARVN out of their positions." Soon, after some debate in the meeting of its 21st Plenum, the North's Politburo passed a resolution to wage a "fierce revolutionary war to defeat the enemy and win complete victory." Fighting during the first year of 'peace' took the lives of 80,000 Vietnamese, including some 14,000 civilians.

As mentioned in Chapter 7, during the year after the combatants signed the treaty, somewhere between 100,000 to 120,000 PAVN troops infiltrated into the South. This brought the number of regular communist forces there to approximately 330,000. This reinforcement included new tanks and heavy artillery to replace losses as well as troops.

To support the movement of troops and material, the North further improved the Ho Chi Minh Trail. 10,000 trucks now moved unhindered along newly built and improved roads to bring supplies for a future offensive. Because much of the traffic included copious amounts of armored and wheeled vehicles, PAVN engineers also built a new 5000-kilometer pipeline to transport fuel to forward bases along and just inside the borders of South Vietnam.

Free from US bombing, the traffic soon became so high that the North built a supplemental, new route that paralleled the Ho Chi Minh complex. This one was in South Vietnam. It stretched from the DMZ to Loc Ninh, just one-hundred kilometers' northwest of Saigon. This new route, called the Truong Son Corridor, would play a significant role in the later capture of Saigon.

Meanwhile, in the first year following the signing of the treaty, US aid, though diminished, continued to flow to the South. Much like the North, the South had to replenish its Easter Offensive losses. US aid helped its Armed Forces to grow to a strength of over a million personnel. The ARVN grew by 320,000 soldiers, which included more armored forces and improved artillery in some new organizations. Further enhancing their material buildup was the equipment left behind by Allied forces. The result was that during the increased fighting in 1974, ARVN forces could hold their own and even win some important battles.

During 1974, however, Congress began to cut US aid drastically. As Le Gro notes, "on 23 and 24 September, the House and Senate appropriated only $700 million for Vietnam in the Defense Appropriations Bill for FY 75. The $700 million appropriations, furthermore, covered all shipping expenses, certain undelivered FY 73-74 items, as well as the operational costs or the DAO itself, leaving less than $500 million to be applied to the operational requirements of the [Republic of Vietnam Armed Forces]."

Thus, as the Chief of the South Vietnam Armed Forces, General Vien, explains in his postwar monograph, *The Final Collapse,* the South Vietnamese Armed Forces had to: "inactivate, return, or destroy almost 300 air force fighters and bombers; cut flying hours in half on the rest; reduce helicopter lift capability by 70 %; reduce airlift by 50%; cut replacement parts but 33%; and lower fuel consumption by 50%." Even these draconian reductions did not show the full impact of the Congressional cuts. Ammunition stocks were down to ten days in critical regions.

The overall impact on the ARVN was catastrophic. In General Vien's words, "the South Vietnamese soldier of 1974-75 marched into combat with the deep concern that his ammunition might not be replenished as fast as it was consumed and that, if wounded, he might have to wait much longer for evacuation to a hospital. The time of abundant supplies and fast helo lifts had gone.

It was now the turn of the soldier's family to become concerned about his safety in the face of growing shortages. The most tragic result of the shortage was increased casualties. A price in blood was paid by the soldier for every round of ammunition he was not issued."

Vien further asserts that "The debates and votes in the US Congress and the exact amount of military aid finally appropriated were too widely known for our comfort. Both we and the enemy knew and could anticipate all the difficulties and weaknesses of our armed forces. To our side, it was a matter for anxiety; to the enemy, it offered an excellent opportunity."

Despite these drastic reductions and their impact on the South Vietnamese Armed Forces, Thieu and his senior advisors, as Willbanks recounts, still thought that the US would not abandon them. Reminiscent of the arguments of LBJ's advisors in 1964-1965, many South Vietnamese government officials thought that such an action would most surely damage America's reputation as a 'guarantor of freedom from communism.' However, to the contrary, in 1974 the American Public and Congress wanted nothing to do with guaranteeing South Vietnamese freedom. They just wanted the entire episode of US involvement in Southeast Asia to go away.

The Third Indochina War

The North Vietnamese had been planning for the opportunity General Vien mentioned in earnest since mid-1974. The planning, William Turley claims, was contentious. The PAVN Chief of Staff, General Van Tien Dung, oversaw drafting them. The initial concept envisioned a two-phase campaign, with an initial attack to test what the American response would be. If there were no response, then significant attacks would take place in all three ARVN Corps regions simultaneously.

As Willbanks further explains in *Abandoning Vietnam*, a forward PAVN headquarters in the ARVN II Corps region would coordinate the three attacks. To synchronize forces, something the PAVN high command had failed to do in 1972, the PAVN further grouped their divisions into Corps. Each Corps commander was answerable to their Front commander, who would oversee the offensive in his region.

General Tran Van Tra disagreed with Dung's concept of operations. He believed that the Easter Offensive had shown how difficult it was to coordinate three separate and geographically distant advances. He argued that each Front commander in the three regions conduct their operations without regard initially to the other attacks.

General Tra further argued that his attack should not wait on the other three, as General Dung's preliminary plan called for. His primary concern was the difficulty of synchronizing the assaults. Specifically, he argued that the attacks could bog down, allowing the ARVN to shift forces between regions and fall back onto enclaves that they could defend indefinitely.

Tra's argument prevailed. The High Command changed the plan. It would begin in the central region with a primary target at first being the seizure of Ban Me Thuot. From there PAVN forces would drive to the coast and split South Vietnam in half. During that attack, if there were no US response, Tra would attack Saigon using a series of short assaults gradually defeating the ARVN defenses with a final push when the opportunity arose. PAVN forces would attack the ARVN I Corps region coincidentally, but not synchronized, with the other two advances.

In January 1975, there was an unexpected PAVN victory in the ARVN III Corps region, resulting in the seizure of an entire province northwest of Saigon. This operation had not been part of the overall offensive plan. There was no military reaction from the Americans. As a result, the PAVN High Command thought the time was right to launch the planned offensive against Ban Me Thuot in March 1975. Therefore, on 5 February, General Dung left Hanoi to go to the South Vietnam highland headquarters to assume supreme command of the campaign.

After some diversionary moves, on 9 March General Dung ordered an attack against Ban Me Thuot. Outnumbering the ARVN force there by five to one, the attack quickly succeeded. PAVN forces overcame a hasty counterattack. ARVN forces began a withdrawal toward the coast that turned into a rout. The ARVN II Corps commander lost all control of his forces to obey President Thieu's orders to move them toward Na Trang to set up an enclave of resistance that the ARVN command could continue to support from the sea.

Faced with a catastrophe in the II Corps region, President Thieu on 11 March called for a meeting of his principal military advisors in Saigon. Per General Vien, Thieu decided that defending all South Vietnam was not possible. Pointing to a map the South Vietnamese President proposed that forces be 'redeployed' to "hold and defend only those populous and flourishing areas which were really the most important."

The map Thieu showed and marked on during the meeting denoted the southeast part of II Corps, the III Corps areas minus the border regions, and almost all of IV Corps as the 'most important areas.' The map also showed a series of phase lines running from northern I Corps south to the southeast area of the Central Highland region. The intent was for the ARVN forces in the north to conduct a fighting withdrawal to these phase lines.

General Vien told Thieu that he agreed with the need for the redeployment of forces. What he did not convey was that he believed that it would cause a sense of defeat and panic and would present some significant problems with most of the ARVN divisions that were to withdraw from the I and II Corps regions. In his words, "experience had proved that most South Vietnamese population fled the Communists if they could. And 'population' also meant military dependents who were the source of comfort and support for the combat troops. It was unthinkable to try to separate them for any length of time because they always tended to get together."

As Vien further explains, "This was especially true, as previously mentioned, considering the traditional Vietnamese family attachment and the marginal living conditions of the troops and their dependents in general. All this had to be carefully considered whenever an attempt was made to separate troops from their families for any lengthy period." Vien's musings, of course, were after the fact. Whether he felt that way in his meeting with Thieu, or made these observations after the ARVN defeat, is unknowable.

Regardless, the South Vietnamese head of the General Staff's misgivings were soon vindicated. When the ARVN II Corps commander tried to withdraw to enclaves along the coastal areas, fleeing civilians clogged the roads. Many were dependents of the ARVN forces trying to hold back the attacking NVA elements. Seeing their loved ones trying to get away and unable to get to safety, they left their units to aid them. Now the ARVN military was disintegrating attempting to help their loved ones. Any cohesive military operation became impossible.

As the II Corps regional defense began to break down, PAVN forces along the DMZ attacked the ARVN I Corps forces. The able ARVN commander in the north, General Ngo Quang Truong - the one who defended Hue during the 1968 TET and the 1972 Easter Offensives - tried an orderly withdrawal of his forces to Da Nang. There he intended to set up and defend an enclave, which the ARVN could support from the sea.

However, as had occurred in the Central Region, the civilians fleeing the communist attack disrupted any orderly movement. What happened in the II Corps area repeated itself. The famous 1st ARVN Division, with a deserved reputation of the best in the Army, dissolved when its soldiers tried to help their dependents trying to escape the communist onslaught.

The Ho Chi Minh Campaign

As the attacks in the I and II Corps regions continued, PAVN General Dung began to reevaluate his planned offensive. The rapid success had surprised him. The preliminary attacks in the III Corps region, planned as preparations for the final assault on Saigon, were going well. On April 7, as Dung was assessing what to do next, Le Duc Tho – the one who had won the Pulitzer Prize for the Paris Treaty and refused it because he knew it did not end the war – arrived at Dung's headquarters.

Though the North Vietnamese had considered the setup of some interim government resulting from a hard-fought campaign in the South, the rapid collapse that they were now seeing precluded that. The Northern Communists would now settle for nothing less than total victory. As the representative of the Politburo, Le Duc Tho approved General Dung for the decisive final drive on Saigon.

Attacking Saigon, with a population at the time of two and a half million, would be no easy task – even for an Army experienced in urban combat. The 1975 PAVN had no such experience. Except for its senior leaders, most of its unit commanders were new. Like the American Army, the long war had killed off many of its experienced small unit leaders.

General Dung, and the able and experienced COSVN military commander General Tra, came up with a plan of attack. Most of all, the communist military commanders wanted to avoid a long drawn out campaign around Saigon and its outskirts. They also wanted to capture the city intact, with as little damage as possible.

To do so, they envisioned a maneuver against the outer defenses that would cut off the ARVN defenders and prevent them from withdrawing into the built-up areas of Saigon. Meanwhile, PAVN mechanized units would bypass the outer defenses as much as possible, penetrate the center of the city, and seize the 'nerve centers' of the South's government and its military. They dubbed this final assault, 'The Ho Chi Minh Campaign.'

On 29 April 1975, the communists launched the main attack. It consisted of fifteen main force divisions supported by an assortment of local units, a force of 50,000 soldiers. Political cadres also infiltrated amongst fleeing civilians to contact operatives in Saigon to aid in setting up quickly a new communist government. Where they met stiff resistance, they bypassed it, as planned. Some ARVN soldiers continued to fight bravely and to the finish. More shed their uniforms and tried to melt into the civilian populace.

Many South Vietnamese fled or tried to flee the country. Among them were leaders in the government and ARVN command, to include Thieu, Air Marshal Ky, General Vien, General Troung, and the former Saigon Chief of Police, General Loan. Some 140,000 followed that year. More than two million others would leave - many of them by shabby, overcrowded boats – over the next decades.

On April 30, at 1045, a Soviet-made T-54 tank, bearing the flag of the PLAF/VC but manned by PAVN soldiers, crashed through the gates of the Independence Palace – the center of the Government of the Republic of South Vietnam. A North Vietnamese crew member ran into the palace and made it up to the roof. There he raised the flag.

Right to the end, the PAVN High Command had assured that the tremendous successful ruse that the VC had fought a revolutionary war against an oppressive regime supported by a foreign power would still make the American newscasts. The ruse had worked masterfully for almost thirty years. They had won. The wars for the unification of Vietnam were now over.

The American Reaction and Evacuation

As James Willbanks relates, The DAO in Saigon, as well as the US Mission, kept the American government thoroughly informed of the situation during the fighting in March and April. They also asked for emergency aid for the South Vietnamese Armed Forces to resist the communist offensive.

In reaction to these reports, President Ford sent several cables to Thieu assuring him that the US was "determined to stand firmly behind the Republic of Vietnam at this crucial hour." Ford also dispatched General Weyand to Saigon. The General met with President Thieu and assured him of the President's "steadfast support." Upon leaving, he told Thieu, "We will get you the assistance you need and will explain your needs to Congress."

President Ford earnestly tried to gain some last minute Congressional support. None was forthcoming. In reaction to the requests, Congressional leaders voiced outrage over Nixon's secret commitments, which the former President had not consulted with them about. Besides, the American people wanted the entire experience of the Vietnam War to go away. Congress inaction reflected this view. The American Press was bombarding the public with news of a rapid, ignominious retreat involving little ARVN resistance that would ensure the South's defeat. The message was, why should America stand by people who would not fight for themselves?

Of concern to most in America, however, was the evacuation of some three thousand Americans still in South Vietnam. President Ford and his key advisors – notably Henry Kissinger, who had become his Secretary of State – were directly in touch with Ambassador Martin to obtain his views on an evacuation. The Ambassador was cautious in ordering a full evacuation.

Graham felt that the specter of Americans leaving the country would add to the sense of panic that was growing stronger as the communist offensive gained more momentum. Besides, he still clung to the belief that the South could hold on to significant portions of the III Corps area. Adding to this belief was the ARVN defense at Xuan Loc, a city northeast of Saigon that, if held, could thwart a significant approach to the capital. There an ARVN division fought bravely; holding for over a week against a PAVN assault of three divisions.

As Graham hesitated, the US Mission and the DAO were reviewing their plans for the evacuation.

Dubbed FREQUENT WIND, these plans included details on numbers and names of evacuees, assembly and pick up points in Saigon for their ground transport to departure areas, and air routes to further areas outside of South Vietnam where they would await transport to the US or other sites. As the Defense Attaché, General Homer Smith relates in his paper, *The Final Forty-Five Days in Vietnam*, the plan review revealed several flaws as the situation on the ground unfolded.

The primary one was that the plan assumed South Vietnamese forces would provide security for the evacuation. Now, this assumption was unreliable. So, the DAO increased the use of a small Marine contingent from the embassy and asked for reinforcements from the US naval forces afloat in the South China Sea.

Also noteworthy was the necessity to keep most of the evacuation orders secret and low key to avoid tipping off local VC cadres. The review further prompted DAO to ask for permission from Graham to begin a drawdown of some in the DAO and their dependents before he ordered the larger evacuation. This the Ambassador allowed, but he ordered the discrete execution of its movements.

The drawdown began on 1 April – April fools' day, the same day thirty years earlier LBJ had ordered American Marines in Da Nang to go on the offensive in South Vietnam.

The plans called for the air movement of most out of Tan Son Nhut airport at the northern outskirts of Saigon. So, as the aircraft landed there, many bringing in some material and supplies from the US Support Activities Group in Thailand, officials and dependents loaded on them and left. Among them were some South Vietnamese who were not on the list of dependents or employees for evacuation. American officials, many of them having served with these South Vietnamese, had smuggled them onto the aircraft.

As documented in General Smith's account and depicted in a PBS documentary called, *Last Days in Vietnam*, the identification of the South Vietnamese considered for evacuation was extraordinarily problematic. The ones authorized and identified were those who worked in an official capacity for the US and subject to communist reprisals. There were also some American citizens' married dependents.

However, there were many Vietnamese who did not have the official documentation. They either had not yet bothered to obtain them or were not in the official category. Many of the latter were Vietnamese women who were American girlfriends or wives without proper visas.

The DAO and the Embassy devised a system and created paperwork to authorize many previously not considered for evacuation. There were many others – mainly family members of those Vietnamese who eventually gained the authorization – that needed to go as well. There were also other Vietnamese who had ties to the Americans in the DAO and the Embassy that their American counterparts wanted to help. Compounding all of this was that Ambassador Martin, in the eyes of some, was dragging his feet and just waiting too long to execute the full evacuation.

On 20 April Graham finally ordered the full evacuation. By that time, the gathering of South Vietnamese in and around the Embassy and DAO was growing. Numerous Vietnamese just wanted to get out; many of them having associations with Americans in Saigon and elsewhere that made them, in their view, targets to the communists.

Further compounding the removal of people was that several days after the evacuation order, Tan Son Nhut airport came under attack and was unusable. The DAO and Embassy had to revert to helicopter withdrawal from their compounds and several other sites in Saigon.

The resultant rotary wing movement turned out to be a remarkable feat; and the largest in aviation history to that point. Marine Corps helicopters moved some 400 US and over 4,000 Vietnamese from the DAO compound, and another 978 and about 1,000 from the Embassy. These made their way to US ships awaiting them off the coast.

Thousands of Vietnamese had already crowded these ships by sailing or flying out to them in makeshift boats or American helicopters provided through the US assistance program. To make further room, American sailors shoved helicopters into the sea. Incoming ARVN rotary wing pilots ditched the aircraft after discharging their passengers. Estimates are that some 120,000 Vietnamese may have escaped to these ships or on ships they sailed to other places.

Meanwhile, thousands of other Vietnamese still gathered around the Embassy and DAO Compound – still hoping for escape. They would not get to go. Countless thousands would languish in communist 're-education camps' for years. Some committed suicide.

A contingent of Marines stayed on the roof of the Embassy. They seemed forgotten. The Marines saw PAVN forces entering the center of Saigon. Then, a day after the evacuation, a single CH-53 Marine helicopter took them away. The Marines had barricaded the stairway to the roof. Right after they left, a crowd of Vietnamese men, women, and children overcame the barricade and moved onto the roof. They waited for American aircraft to take them away. They never came.

The American War to ensure a South Vietnam free from communism ended. For many American civilians watching the evacuation of terrified Vietnamese people scrambling to get away on TV, the havoc and confusion symbolized the futility of it all.

For American servicemen who fought in Vietnam, the end is perhaps best described by Michael Kerr in his book, *Dispatches* – "The war ended, and then it really ended, the cities fell, I watched the choppers I'd loved dropping into the South China Sea as their Vietnamese pilots jumped clear, and one last chopper revved it up, lifted up, and flew out of my chest."

Chapter 11: The Failure of US Policies and Strategies for Vietnam, 1950-1975

The last three chapters have focused on the military strategies and operations that the major American military commanders developed to achieve their Commander-in-Chiefs' policies during the Vietnam War. This chapter summarizes and relates these military strategies and operations back to the Presidential policies and decisions presented in Chapters 1 (for Truman and Eisenhower), 2 (for JFK), 3 (for LBJ) and 5 (for Nixon). In so doing, the narrative concludes this story of the Vietnam War, and makes a series of observations and conclusions on the effectiveness of the overall US strategic formulation for the war, and why America's leaders lost and the North Vietnamese won.

The interrelationship between what the policymakers wanted and how that translated into effective military actions in Vietnam are critical to understanding the outcomes of the war. The military commanders in Southeast Asia did not develop their plans and execute them in a vacuum. They tried - to the best of their abilities, knowledge, and experiences - to carry out their Commander-in-Chiefs' guidance as they understood it.

What the chapters mentioned above and the last three have shown is that overall American civilian leaders were confused or uncertain about how to apply military force to solve the political-military dilemma they faced in Indochina. For the most part, they also imposed decisive restrictions or ordered unwise actions without a full understanding of the consequences or the viability of the assumptions driving them, and their impact on the successful outcomes they were seeking.

Because of the above, US civilian leaders' war policies were gravely flawed. They lacked a broad understanding of the situation in Indochina, did not properly consider their enemy, and did not address the problems they faced with a clear understanding of the costs involved or the restrictions or orders they imposed. Consequently, they failed to develop the clarity of purpose that could translate into effective military action. In the end, their lack of determination, courage, or moral compass gravely inhibited a military solution and severely shook the social, political, and moral fabric of the nation they swore to serve and preserve.

Moreover, US military commanders and senior advisors equally failed their civilian leaders. They did not clearly and forcibly present a unified air-sea-land military strategy that could have achieved the political-military problem they faced. They blindly followed, without serious objection or argument, directions that they eventually realized were flawed. In so doing they foolishly pursued a military course that they could only hope would eventually convince rather than force their enemy to surrender. In the end, that folly cost tens of thousands of American and millions of Vietnamese lives.

The reasons for the above are complicated. But it is essential to understand why this happened so that we can avoid any future outcome and turmoil like that experienced in the Vietnam War. Accordingly, this chapter ends with a presentation of six deductions on the US failures and their enemy's successes. These conclusions will serve as the basis for the discussions and arguments on the lessons learned from the Vietnam War in the last two chapters, and why they matter today.

Section 11.1 - The Truman and Eisenhower Years: The Evolution of Vietnam as a Vital US Interest and the Quest for a Political-Military Solution for its Defense, 1950 to 1961

As we saw in Chapter 1, when the US first got involved in Vietnam, primarily after the Korean War, the US effort focused on aiding the French in their struggle against a communist-dominated movement to gain Vietnamese independence from the yoke of colonialism. Moreover, the importance of France to the containment of Soviet power in Europe was a significant incentive for the US in supporting France in Indochina. From the onset, US executive direction for Vietnam was to prevent communist control, not only of Vietnam but the Southeast Asia region.

As described and explained at the end of Chapter 1, the circumstances following the end of World War Two and the US-led victory over the Nazis and Japanese set the stage for what later happened in Vietnam. First, the primary lesson drawn from the war and later applied by all US Presidents in Southeast Asia was, in the words of Jeffrey Record in *Making War, Thinking History*, "appeasement of aggression only invites more aggression, and its therefore imperative that early and effective force be used to stop it."

This conclusion is what was, and still is, called the 'Lesson of Munich' or the 'Munich Syndrome' – Munich being a city in Germany where in 1938 British Prime Minister Neville Chamberlain gave in to Adolph Hitler's demands over the territorial acquisition of lands in Czechoslovakia. Afterwards, as historians and political scientists studied the war's causes, they determined that this 'giving in to demands' encouraged Hitler's later aggression, leading to the world war.

As Record further explains "implicit in this lesson is the notion that the twentieth-century phenomenon of totalitarianism, be it fascism or communism, [only] understands the language of force." Thus, as described in Chapter 1, the Cold War had its roots in the need to stop Communist Soviet leader Joseph Stalin from expanding the Soviet Union's boundaries into Europe and eventually elsewhere in the world.

With the US emerging as a global superpower after the war, it was natural for it to take on the mantle and challenge of containing that expansion. When communism spread to Asia via China and later Indochina, it became axiomatic that the US policy of containment, which was so successful in Europe, now be applied in Asia.

Vietnam and Containment
By the mid-fifties, then, US involvement in Southeast Asia was entirely in consonance with the existing national security policy of containment. That policy, by its promulgation in NSC 68, sought to contain communist expansion wherever it may surface in the world. Now - with the 'loss of China,' its resultant Chinese communist state recognition of and support for the Viet-Minh, and the blatant attack on Korea – containment had become an Asian problem along with a continued defense issue in Europe. Moreover, Southeast Asia became the resultant battleground for the future of containment of communism in Asia.

Some historians, such as George Herring, have criticized the American involvement in South Vietnam from its beginning as ill-advised and without consideration of the local factors involved. This story has tried to show, while in retrospect that historical view may be logical, the US commitment to defend that country was entirely reasonable given the perceived threats to Southeast

Asia, its geopolitical importance, the domestic temperament at the time, and the lessons of the causes of World War Two.

These influences were together so strong that Truman and Eisenhower declared Southeast Asia and Vietnam vital to the containment of communism. These factors would later affect the choices and decisions of JFK, LBJ, and Nixon. In the opinion of this work, to ignore the importance of these determinants at the time is to judge too harshly and errantly the motives and judgments of US leaders during the entire American experience in South Vietnam. While in retrospect, they seem wrong because of the outcomes, at the time they were perfectly logical and even necessary.

The problem the American decision makers faced was how to employ US power to attain the goal of containment in the region. At first, Truman and Eisenhower, despite their misgivings, thought that supporting the French could do so. They were aware, of course, that such a choice involved portraying the US as a supporter of imperialism and colonialism. To counter that they encouraged, even pushed, the French to create a new state of Vietnam under the banner of the French Union.

Supporting the French
The French would not do so. Their efforts focused on the creation of a pseudo-nationalist proxy government to give the illusion of giving the Vietnamese people a choice, and an indigenous Vietnamese Army to make up for their inability to field a strong French citizen Army. Their need to restore their national prestige in the aftermath of the Second World War was their primary motivation to reestablish control over Indochina. Though French leaders ironically relied on foreign fighters to restore that prestige through the force of arms, they thought that French command and direction of a victory there would fulfill the restoration of national pride.

Consequently, there never really was any genuine French effort to build a workable Vietnamese nationalist state that could serve as an alternative to the communist one created in the aftermath of World War Two. Moreover, the US primary instrument in supporting the French effort was military aid to thwart what was at the time primarily a political and economic problem. Thus, from the very beginning, American involvement in South Vietnam oriented on a military solution, rather than one focused on economic and political factors to build a working government to rule its populace as an alternative to communism.

The French not only did not create a sufficient political entity to rule Vietnam, but they also neglected the effective building of an indigenous army to support their efforts to defeat the Viet-Minh led revolution. As described in some detail in Chapter 8, this had an everlasting effect on the efficacy of ARVN leadership and competency. Thus, the French sowed the seeds of ineffectiveness in both their attempts to create a political entity and a corresponding armed force to protect it.

That failure would impede and haunt future US actions in their attempts from 1954 to 1973 to build a viable independent South Vietnam and an effective ARVN. Thus, in many ways, as Bernard Fall argued in his *Street Without Joy*, the US ignorance or disregard of the French experience in Vietnam in many ways contributed to America's woes in their attempts to produce a workable South Vietnamese alternative to the communist political movement and military aggression there.

Of course, the masterful leadership and strategy of Ho Chi Minh and Giap had something to do with it. Ho ensured that the Viet-Minh struggle stood for the idea of nationalism and unification for all Vietnamese. Though he was a genuine communist, he was primarily a nationalist and pragmatist. He failed in the aftermath of the war to convince America of his cause, though it is not certain if his wooing of US leaders was to gain favor or support toward power.

Ignored, he gained critical support from the Chinese and Soviets, which throughout the wars with the French and the Americans offered the means for both independence and unification. As a genuine nationalist figure, Ho could get many Vietnamese to identify with and admire him. His political prowess and fatherly image were crucial to the founding of a nation in the North; albeit a nation that suffered from the imposition of a Vietnamese communist brand of totalitarianism that bred suffering and want.

Giap gave the leadership and organizational skills to form and employ a capable and motivated Viet-Minh military force. Though he sometimes overreached in his schemes against the French, his brilliant handling of his PAVN under a unique Vietnamese application of Mao's Peoples War resulted in a resounding military victory. It also eventually led to the fielding of a competent, motivated Army that would fight courageously against the Americans.

Yet, like the French failure to build a political entity that could challenge the communist nationalistic attraction and an army to serve it, the Americans would fail to examine the reasons for the Viet-Minh's military success and learn from them.

After the First Indochina War: Finding a New Way to Contain Communism

After France lost this First Indochina War, the US decided to try to accomplish what the French could not do - build an effective political governing body that could eventually stand up to communist aggression. There was some increase in economic aid to do so. Economic aid had worked under the Truman doctrine in Southeast Europe. That approach had been immensely successful in restoring democratic states throughout all postwar torn Europe. It had held back communist expansion to Western Europe. Thus, it appeared to be the right solution in Vietnam as well.

However, Southeast Asia was nothing like Southeast or Western Europe. There was no tradition of democracy or individualism. There were few inherent incentives for individual enterprise under a capitalistic society. US goals to set up a nation built solely on American ideals and attitudes could never take hold. US Administrations never came to realize that nations build nations, not other nations. Instead of building a viable polity based on Vietnamese cultural and historical roots of its mandarin past, it chose to force the new state and its leader, Ngo Dinh Diem, to forge a US vision of a western democracy.

As for the employment of US military force to contain communism, though President Eisenhower had proclaimed that Vietnam and other Indochina states were vital to US interests, he did not commit to using significant US combat ground forces to intervene to protect that interest. IKE did explore intervention to help at Dien Bien Phu. But, he was unsure whether to do so. He had met with and had to contend with three key opposition groups.

The first was the military itself. Though his CJCS and Chief of Staff Air Force recommended the use of airpower and even tactical nuclear weapons, the more astute Army Chief, General Matthew Ridgeway, vehemently opposed the use of American military power in an Asian war that could eventually involve over a half of a million soldiers. A second group was the Congress. Ironically a Senator by the name of Johnson from Texas led the resistance. The Congressmen that IKE consulted would not give their support without strong backing and even help of European allies. This third opposition group, led by Great Britain, would have nothing to do with Vietnam; especially as Europe was still recovering from the war.

Eisenhower chose to support the creation of a new regime – the Republic of South Vietnam – and its American backed leader, Diem. To do so, however, the IKE Administration increased its aid primarily to organize, train and advise a new Republic of Vietnamese Armed Forces (RVNAF). With this force in place to confront any North Vietnam invasion, IKE oversaw the development of military plans that would rely on the use of tactical nuclear weapons to ensure defense of the area. This was consistent with IKE's New Look or Massive Retaliation Policy.

Consistent with IKE's view on international security, he also chose to set up a new international organization to provide a defense mechanism to deter any further communist aggression in Southeast Asia – the Southeast Asia Treaty Organization (SEATO). Like NATO, the Eisenhower Administration hoped that a future SEATO would provide the political and military will and forces to prevent China from encouraging any further North Vietnamese moves to subjugate the South. Once again, however, what worked in Europe did not in Asia.

As recounted in Chapter 8, this US national security policy and structure for Southeast Asia at first entailed a military strategy and plans to confront a conventional threat, and the military forces to resist it. Thus, the JCS in Washington began to develop a military strategy for the region that entailed the use of US and SEATO troops for the defense of Laos and the rest of Indochina. For the US command in South Vietnam that meant to develop plans and actions to defend against a Peoples' Army of North Vietnam or PAVN threat to South Vietnam. Meanwhile, the indigenous movement in the South had not yet surfaced as a significant security problem.

Previous actions and experience in Asia reinforced this initial US military strategy for South Vietnam. The US Army had just fought Chinese Communist forces to a standstill. US leaders had committed to a long-term military commitment to the defense of South Korea, and still had significant military forces in South Korea and the region. As a result, the US had contained communism there. In 1954, it was natural for the American military leadership to plan for an eventuality that they had just experienced, that is, a conventional defense of a country from the threat of a communist state with an army that they thought, with military support from Red China and the Soviet Union, could launch an attack at any time and overrun it.

Thus, the first US military strategy and plans for the defense of South Vietnam and the organization and training of its armed forces in many ways made sense. Besides, there were limited funds available. Building an Army takes much time and effort. So, it was natural to build and organize the ARVN along the lines of an infantry division baseline. The thought was that such an organization would be easy to build, inexpensive, and basic to train. The initial design also took into consideration that a light infantry division could be useful for internal missions. Thus, though the intent was to organize them for a primary external threat, the US military argued that the ARVN could also quickly adapt to deal with internal threats. Moreover, it did so.

In preparing for the defense of South Vietnam in the late fifties, American contingency planners also relied on augmenting the South with American combat forces. Thus, they planned for the deployment of such forces into South Vietnam in the eventuality of a PAVN invasion. This planning further affected the design of the ARVN. With the augmentation of US combat forces, the ARVN would not need much of the traditional support and more expensive combat support forces, such as heavy artillery and aviation units. This would not only lessen the cost of forming a new ARVN but would alleviate the difficulty of training the South Vietnam Armed Forces in general.

Thus, the dependence upon American forces to supplement ARVN capabilities was an instrumental part of the design and organization of the South Vietnamese Armed Forces from its very beginning. Moreover, throughout its existence that army would rely on American military support. Later when that US military support was no longer available, there would be neither time or other resources to create it.

Another factor during this period that would affect the ARVN throughout its existence is that, from its birth in 1954, its primary purpose, focus, and experiences were in defending an autocratic regime from internal political groups and individuals that threatened its existence. The result was that the Army's senior leaders developed a sense of personal loyalty to the regime's leaders, more than to their service to their nation. Later US actions, such as the removal of Diem, would further this focus on political regime survival, rather than on national service and preservation.

As the nature of the war changed in South Vietnam - primarily when the North decided to send PAVN regroupees south to reinforce the struggling insurgency - the South Vietnamese forces tried to adapt. Under the advice and with the help of the Americans, the ARVN formed lighter and more mobile forces. The latter were its ranger, airborne and marine units that were not bound to a province. They could move throughout the country to counter the insurgency and its Northern elements supporting it.

American commanders and the small number of advisors then also began to teach and train South Vietnamese forces on counter-guerrilla doctrine and the use of helicopters. This adaptation, along with a more offensive use of some of the ARVN regular divisions against the insurgency, in the late fifties and the first two years of the sixties was mostly successful against the insurgent movement.

We now know that the Communist Northern leadership, which directed the revolutionary elements in the South, had emphasized mostly political action after the 1954 Geneva Convention and until the late fifties. Thus, there was no significant North Communist conventional or even Southern Communist insurgent threat during the fifties.

In fact, it was the Southern success in the late fifties, under the direction of Republic of Vietnam's President Diem, that changed the situation in all Southeast Asia. With that success, the new Northern leader - Le Duan - decided that the southern conflict could not be won without significant PAVN forces, leadership, and direction. Therefore, in the early sixties he embarked upon a military build-up, and the creation of a primary lifeline to the south – the Ho Chi Minh Trail – to enable the infiltration of major PAVN forces to the South. As a new US President was about to take over, this Northern decision to defeat the ARVN, topple its government, and defeat the American support effort, was about to turn the tide against the South Vietnamese and their US benefactors.

To sum the observations and conclusions of these early years, Vietnam became a vital interest to the US as an area to contain the spread of communism in Asia as America had done in Europe. This was logical, even necessary, in the minds of the major American civilian leaders and their advisors during the Truman and Eisenhower Administrations, especially considering the lessons of the recent world war and the aggression in Korea. Both Presidents chose military aid and advice as the primary means to do stop communist expansion.

Furthermore, both Truman and Eisenhower believed that the US demonstration of commitment to South Vietnam independence, coupled later with the building of an international alliance structure – like they had in Europe – could deter any Soviet and Communist China expansion. After the French left Indochina, they saw North Vietnam as an immediate regional military threat, but as the lackey of China and the Soviet Union. Thus, at first, any further military threat would be like what happened in Korea – a conventional attack by the North, supported by China and the Soviet Union.

The US military leaders and advisors labored to find a solution to support this national policy. At first, they relied on military aid and advice to the French military to defeat a communist-led and supported Army fighting a war for independence. The French failed. Yet, the American military ignored the lessons of this failure. This ignorance would plague its efforts to build a South Vietnamese Armed force in the years ahead, as well as its commitment of its own Armed Forces in direct combat a decade later.

In the last years of the fifties it became evident to the Eisenhower Administration and his military advisors in Vietnam that an insurgency seemed to replace the North's conventional threat. US military leaders in the South then believed and relied on ARVN light infantry forces to triumph over the ill-equipped and poorly trained guerrillas. At first, under Diem's ruthless counterattacks against the VC, this seemed to be working.

The challenge ahead was whether the US could ever overcome the already discernable deficiencies in the South's political and military capabilities, and whether they could prevail in an atmosphere of increasing support from the North. In 1961, a new President came into office thinking that he had an innovative approach that, with the determination to pay any price and bear any burden, would turn the tide and lead to success.

Section 11.2 – The Kennedy Years: McNamara, The JCS, Harkins, and the US Counterinsurgency Strategy, 1961 - 1963

While the Kennedy Administration continued to support South Vietnam by enhancing the capabilities of the South Vietnam Armed Forces, it instituted a change in both policy and the military means to do so. JFK directed that his national security policy, from the onset, overcome the weaknesses and liabilities of Eisenhower's 'New Look.' Central to that change was the adoption of Maxwell Taylor's flexible response ideas. For Kennedy that meant a focus on adopting a new approach to counter Soviet Premier Khrushchev's announced support for wars of national liberation.

Counterinsurgency as a Test Case

As described in Chapter 2, Kennedy's counterinsurgency policy in South Vietnam was to be a test case to thwart communist exploitation of the breakdown of the old colonial systems following the Second World War. Vietnam was a place that typified that breakdown. Like Eisenhower, however, this new policy still depended on the establishment of a western oriented government under Diem. Unlike the IKE years, however, now the Communist Democratic Republic of Vietnam in the north had decided to reverse the Diem gains against the VC in the south and use military force to unify Vietnam.

General Paul Harkins, as the first MACV commander, tried to institute JFK's policy of counterinsurgency from January 1962 to June 1964. Harkins was a protégé of General Maxwell Taylor. He, like most of the senior American commanders at the beginning of the war, was a veteran of World War Two. Besides his relationship with Taylor, his other qualifications to institute a counterinsurgency policy in Vietnam was that he had experience in military assistance operations – namely in Turkey – and was familiar with SEATO defense plans for Southeast Asia.

Harkins had no education or experience in strategic formulation in general. Neither was he a military man who dwelled upon high ideas of military strategic theory. But, he was a good soldier who could obey orders, developed a good relationship with both US Ambassador Nolting and Diem, and was confident that he could be successful.

Like many officers in the American armed forces at the time, he was also determined to carry out his mission. After all, the US military had succeeded in forcing unconditional surrender of two of history's most militant regimes. From the war, Harkins had learned that in the face of difficulty, show faith in overcoming adversity. As he took over the reins of command, *Time* magazine quoted him as saying, "I am an optimist; and I am not going to allow my staff to be a pessimist."

Under Kennedy, resources for his counterinsurgency policy increased dramatically. As detailed in both Chapters 2 and 8, much of this emphasis was toward military aid and advice. With General Harkins' oversight this enhancement did, initially, improve ARVN battlefield performance. At one point in late 1962, McNamara's measures of effectiveness showed that the South Vietnamese could counter the indigenous insurgency successfully. He told his President and the Press that the US was winning the war.

A good measure of how successful Diem was in suppressing the VC insurgency is how his enemy reacted to his actions. As we have seen and noted in Chapters 6 and 7, by the early sixties, the Northern leaders, because of Diem's successes with the help of Harkins and his command, knew that they could not obtain success in the South and obtain their goal of unification without its critical contribution in leadership, strategic direction, and forces. North Vietnam was to be the strategic base of operations for the achievement of that goal. The umbilical cord between the fight in the South and the resources and direction from the North was the Ho Chi Minh Trail.

At first, under Le Duan, the DRV sent small detachments of PAVN 'regroupees.' These were mainly former Viet-Minh soldiers who had fought in the South but had moved north after the Geneva accords. Their return was to be a precursor for larger, more capable PAVN regulars. Initially, they advised existing small Southern VC elements and began the setup of base areas and assembly areas for follow-on forces. By 1962, they were ready to receive additional forces along the Ho Chi Minh trail.

By 1963 these communist forces were beginning to make a significant impact on the fighting. PAVN support for engagements with South Vietnamese units increased. Some large battles, such as Ap Bac in January 1963, ended with considerable damage to the ARVN forces. Diem had foreseen that the use of these infiltration routes would make a decisive difference. As early as 1961 he had lamented to the US that this was a critical threat to his country. But Kennedy, who was not interested in dealing with any matters that may embroil his Administration in a regional conflict, ignored this warning.

Strategic Void

Thus, while some on his staff – to include General Maxwell Taylor and his deputy National Security Advisor Walt Rostow – also pointed out the importance of the trail to the war in the South and the role that the North was playing in the insurgency, Kennedy refused to take any significant military action to address it. His approach was primarily diplomatic – to neutralize Laos.

This action did nothing to solve the problem of the North's presence of its troops there, or, more importantly, the passage of its soldiers and supplies to the South. As explained in Chapter 2, a reason for this is that JFK had little confidence in his military advisors' or commanders' abilities to plan for or execute sizeable military ground operations anywhere in Southeast Asia.

Indeed, a fundamental failure in JFK's approach to Vietnam was that he and his advisors never developed a strategy to implement his counterinsurgency policy. The Kennedy Administration did not have a coherent, established approach for any application of, or concept for, the use of military forces in Indochina. Moreover, there was no assessment of how much force was necessary or where it should be employed for what purpose to counter both the enemy operations in the South and the supporting infiltration from the North.

The closest the Kennedy Administration came to develop one was the study and report that Taylor and Rostow submitted in the Fall of 1961 after their several weeks visit to South Vietnam. However, Kennedy refused to consider any major direct military action against the unfolding insurgency or to punish the North. Instead, he chose to increase advisors and a contingent of US military forces, such as helicopter and special force units, that could add to the military capabilities to thwart the insurgency, but, most importantly, would not significantly add to the footprint of US military action in South Vietnam.

Thus, JFK and his advisors – especially McNamara - saw the application of their counterinsurgency 'strategy' in terms of the development of forces specialized in unconventional warfare, and military assistance to the South Vietnamese government to increase the size of its armed forces. In lieu of a strategy, his Secretary of Defense instituted and assessed measures for the war – numbers of secure hamlets, amount of operations, etc. McNamara's systems analysts were more than eager to assign and evaluate them. However, as Greg Daddis reminds us in his study, *No Sure Victory*, "systems analyst techniques" were not enough in filling the void in national security strategic thinking for Indochina and Vietnam.

Without a concentrated effort to come up with a regional perspective and strategy, most of JFK's decisions were reactionary, and focused on McNamara's budget programs to show progress. The object of many of Kennedy's decisions on Vietnam was just to keep our commitment and 'wait and see' what would happen next. The result was that JFK and his main advisors focused on reports, statistics and assessments based on individual opinions and measures that were easy to assess. No one designed an achievable end state that would assist them in knowing whether their efforts were having any bearing on the conflict.

McNamara devoted himself to having enough statistics that he could use to manage the war. He seemed more than confident that such an approach would eventually lead to some solution. He and his Whiz Kids did what they knew best – analyze and manage. They had no idea of what war was all about, or any sense of what kind of national security strategy was necessary to meet the challenges in Southeast Asia. Nevertheless, when queried on how the US was doing in South Vietnam, the Defense Secretary reported that "all indicators say we are winning."

Moreover, Kennedy and McNamara's military commanders and advisors were dormant in pushing for such a strategy. The JCS struggled against the President's and McNamara's complete lack of confidence in them and could not obtain a voice in the JFK Administration on Vietnam and other matters. Their focus was on the resources that Kennedy was willing to support for his counterinsurgency policies in the budget and programming process. The result was that the Chiefs of the Services embroiled themselves in a constant fight for those resources instead of what was the proper military strategic advice for the conflict that was unfolding in Vietnam. JFK further ignored their advice on Vietnam in part because of their internal bickering over roles and missions, and the budget.

Another result of all this was that General Harkins simply did not have any strategic guidance from Washington to plan or coordinate a theater strategy. One seemed to exist on paper – the National Level Operation Plan for Counterinsurgency adapted from the earlier MAAG plan. Later, MACV planners further developed a National Campaign Plan in coordination with the new South Vietnamese General Staff. However, these were more blueprints for operations rather than a coordinated plan for the achievement of concrete objectives and the use of resources and concepts to achieve them on a regional scale.

Besides, the MACV commander mostly ignored these 'blueprints' of operations and focused on measures of effectiveness. Why should he pay that much attention to any 'blueprint' or military strategy for Vietnam? His Commander-in-Chief was not interested in such formal plans. His Secretary of Defense did not care to discuss any or push for one. As McNamara would later say, military strategies no longer mattered, only efficient management policies.

In short, General Harkins' focus was on the politics of his relationship with Diem, his struggle with showing success in his counterinsurgency plan (mostly the strategic hamlet program), countering the unfavorable American Press reports, and pleasing his superiors. He paid attention only to those things that his bosses, primarily McNamara, focused on – and that was numbers and how they showed progress.

All of this left any strategic approach in South Vietnam to Diem, who was intent on defeating the communists, but who was most worried about keeping power. At the end, when Diem left, any semblance of an approach to the war against the growing communist threat left with him. There was no South Vietnamese leader that could replace him.

The Kennedy Vietnam Legacy

In sum, without a coherent national strategy for Vietnam, President Kennedy confused the initial symptoms of the conflict with the actual causes. He was too narrow-minded to see the bigger strategic picture of who and what was causing the war, and how to address the struggle that was growing in the South. In so doing, JFK left a legacy consisting of two lasting views on the conflict that would affect both the future conduct of, and American public reaction to, the war that would follow.

The first is that in trying to execute a new approach in Vietnam – counterinsurgency - JFK, and his civilian and military advisors, tried to make the conflict in the South something it was not. They portrayed it as primarily an insurgency caused by dissatisfaction and disenchantment with the Southern Government's rule. They also portrayed it as a grassroots uprising of the Southern Vietnamese – fought by peasants in black pajamas armed with old flintlocks and pitchforks. Indeed, news reports, interviews, and film clips about Vietnam during this time - influenced by JFK and his senior advisors' statements and policies - became the one that dominated much of the American public's image of the war. This lasted, for many Americans, particularly in the antiwar movement, until the very end of US involvement.

Indeed, JFK's Administration bears the burden of the creation of the greatest myth about the Vietnam War – that it was a grass roots insurgency. Ironically, in doing so Kennedy and his advisors furthered the North's approach to winning the war – creating the aura of an insurgency mostly fought by people who wanted to rid themselves of an illegal government that did not represent them. The North was merely trying to help their Vietnamese brethren in that endeavor.

As this story argues, it was not as JFK and others thought and portrayed it. From the beginning of his Presidency, the conflict in Vietnam was primarily a military offensive to overthrow the South Vietnamese government by force and reunify Vietnam under Communist Northern Vietnamese rule.

Once again Clausewitz's statements on war seem pertinent here. "The first, the supreme, the most far-reaching act of judgment that the statesman and commander have to make is to establish the kind of war on which they are embarking; neither mistaking it for, nor trying to turn it into, something that is alien to its nature. This is the first of all strategic questions and the most comprehensive."

Kennedy's second strategic legacy of the Vietnam War is related to the former. Because they did not understand the nature of the conflict, JFK and his advisors in Washington continually laid the blame for its policy failures on the South Vietnam government – namely on Diem's shoulders. Thus, all that had to be done, they concluded, was to fix this situation with the removal of Diem. When it occurred, Kennedy at once saw the mistake. He was shaken. He realized that it had been an error that could lead to an unstable Government in South Vietnam that it could never recover from.

Not only did Diem's assassination lead to instability, but Diem's removal encouraged the North to increase its military action once again – a major military offensive to defeat the South before the US could do anything about it. With a commitment to overthrowing the South by force and defeating what they called the US Special War, the North outwardly turned a limited conflict to one that ultimately had international repercussions. For the fledging South and its military, it also led to an assault and greater conflict with the PAVN from which it was unable to defend itself.

The Diem assassination would have long-lasting effects on the ability of the South's military forces to defend against what became a cleverly disguised Northern invasion consisting of a well-trained, motivated, regular force – its PAVN. Faced with that, and the aftermath of Diem's death that caused the turnover of military commanders trying to survive the various juntas and leaders' purges, the situation in 1964 and the first six months of 1965 created a near fatal death blow to the ARVN. Only an American combat force intervention in 1965 would save them.

Section 11.3 – The LBJ – McNamara Years: Limited War, Graduated Response, and Westmoreland's Strategy of Attrition

As noted in previous chapters the assassination of Diem and later Kennedy convinced Le Duan and the Politburo to conduct a major offensive to defeat the South Vietnamese armed forces and overthrow its government in the latter part of 1964. His main means to accomplish these aims was through the infiltration of his main regular forces over the Ho Chi Minh Trail to reinforce the Peoples' Liberation Army forces there.

In Washington throughout most of 1964 LBJ's primary attention was getting elected as 'a legitimate President in his own right.' While days after JFK's death he had reaffirmed the US commitment to Vietnam in NSAM 273, upon recommendations of his advisors, he decided to address the unfolding crisis in South Vietnam by relying mostly on covert operations under OPLAN 34.

Per guidance from Washington, Admiral Sharp and General Westmoreland executed the operations under this plan primarily with South Vietnamese military conducting most of the operations, but with increasing US support and direction. The intent was to convince the North to give up its support for the insurgency. Inadvertently, these covert actions resulted in a direct military confrontation between the DRV and the US in the Tonkin Gulf.

The Application of Limited War and Graduated Response

Following the Gulf of Tonkin crisis, its resultant Congressional resolution, and his reelection, the new President focused on his Washington civilian advisors' advocacy of a limited war, graduated response policy. Its premise was to use carefully calculated airpower strikes along with gestures like bombing pauses to prompt a negotiated end to the conflict.

As detailed in Chapter 3, LBJ's choice to pursue a Limited War and Graduated Response policy, whose chief proponent was Robert McNamara, was a way for the President to ensure that Vietnam would not become a wider war with the Chinese. As his contemporary comments and later memoirs and interviews show, war with China is something he worried a great deal about, mainly because of their past intervention in Korea. This approach also afforded him an acceptable way to control the costs of a military intervention in Vietnam. This control would allow him to pursue his domestic agenda – Johnson's main priority and what he had hoped would be his legacy as a President.

President Johnson's graduated response had its origins in the Kennedy Administration. As George Herring noted in an address at the Air Force Academy in 1990, "The Kennedy administration's successful handling of the Cuban Missile Crisis seems to have reinforced in the minds of US officials the value of such an approach. 'There is no longer any such thing as strategy, only crisis management,' McNamara exclaimed in the aftermath of Kennedy's victory."

Armed with that belief, with now a new crisis in Vietnam on the horizon in late 1964 and early 1965, McNamara sought to manage his way toward a resolution using gradual signals carefully controlled. The consequence was that the Johnson Administration began a war without a discussion of how to fight it; without Congressional consultation (other than the Tonkin Gulf Resolution) and debate; and without the nation fully understanding the worth or the reasons.

The principal instrument of the Limited War and Graduated Response policy was the ROLLING THUNDER air campaign. As described in Chapters 3 and 8, LBJ and McNamara picked the nature of the targets, their location and ordered when to execute each strike. The primary aim of the bombing - to convince the North Vietnamese leaders to give up their efforts in the South and bring them to the negotiating table - shows how much the Johnson Administration misunderstood their opponents and their overall goals, as demonstrated in Chapters 6 and 7.

LBJ and his national security civilian advisors further thought the bombing would fulfill their desires for a 'low key' cheap method to employ military force. They undertook this approach despite several government agency disagreements. The CIA and other intelligence organizations offered several estimates on how and why the bombings would not work. JCS war games showed the futility of reliance on gradual aerial attacks, and even predicted that instead of bringing North Vietnam to negotiate it would have just the opposite effect. Finally, the JCS continually but fruitlessly argued against this piecemeal approach and called for a more forceful bombing campaign to convince the communist to stop its aggression.

Soon after the bombing began, LBJ began to doubt that bombing alone would work. He then bought into McNamara's argument that the employment of some ground combat forces to enclaves along the coast of Vietnam would send an even more effective signal that would pressure the North to cease its aggression.

Contrary to what their chief military advisors and commanders on the ground wanted, Johnson, Bundy, and McNamara did not intend, either with the use of air or ground operations, to impose the US will upon the North using force. It would be too risky to a widening of the war. They only wanted to show US resolve to convince the communist leaders to give up their aggression. Despite signs indicating that their enemy was determined in his actions, the reasoning continued to be that the demonstration of US determination to defend South Vietnam from military conquest would persuade the North to come to its senses and seek a negotiated end to hostilities.

For Johnson's principal civilian advisors this logic transcended the Vietnam conflict problem. The threat and limited use of force was further intended for the international community - allies and enemies alike. Now that the US had crossed the use of major combat force threshold, LBJ's primary civilian advisors thought the world would see that the US willingness to employ military force in Southeast Asia would prove to other international powers that it had the resolve to do so in other areas of the globe. Hence the linking of US prestige became more important, even critical to the outcome of their commitments of force.

Most startling, as the signaling continued to show it did not have the effect intended, LBJ's primary advisors – namely Bundy, McNamara, and McNaughton – then began to argue that even if this demonstration of US military power did not work - the world would see America as having tried and just could not salvage a broken, corrupt South Vietnamese government. The expression these security advisors used was that any US failure in Vietnam would be like 'a doctor who had tried to save a patient who just couldn't be saved.'

There was nothing intrinsically wrong with LBJ's decision for limited war. In the age of nuclear weapons, it made not only sense but was a necessity. However, the objectives and assumptions behind the use of military force and their prescribed limits, especially on how to use or not use force and where, are essential elements of whether the ends, ways, and means to pursue success are productive, and the probabilities of the war resulting in victory and with acceptable cost. In this case, as the US moved dangerously closer to the use of increased force, neither the President or his closest advisors understood this.

As it turned out, the President's civilian advisors' reasoning did not work. It could not work. First, it did not account for the fact that such judgment was alien to the nature of war. The use of force in war does not follow such logic. Even limited war needs to consider what level of force is necessary, given the restraints demanded, to force a decision upon the enemy. If such does not exist under those limits, as Clausewitz argues, then one must look to other uses of power, or change the constraints imposed and take a different approach, or accept the fact that the use of constrained military force cannot obtain the object desired.

The gradual signaling approach, moreover, did not account for 'knowing your enemy' or the fact that the enemy 'has a vote.' As shown in Chapter 7, that 'vote' was much different than what American leaders' thought they could change. Le Duan and his supporters were not interested in meaningful negotiations to end the war with concessions short of unification on their terms. To them, negotiations were only useful if they had a decisive bargaining chip on the battlefield – and decisive meant that they could eventually be assured of their goal for the unification of Vietnam.

Thus, Le Duan wanted nothing to do with and ignored any US action that was intended to bend his will to the Americans because they had shown they are powerful, but peace-seeking. Moreover, the North's Politburo was not like LBJ's Congress, where every person had a price and could be convinced to compromise. Or like academic gamers who, as Bundy and McNamara thought, would respond to actions that they were supposed to, based on rational human beings of similar thought patterns. US policy makers just did not know or understand their enemy.

By June 1965, only a couple of months after it began, LBJ and his advisors finally recognized that ROLLING THUNDER and the small ground force commitment to South Vietnam would not keep Communist North Vietnam from defeating the ARVN and taking over South Vietnam. Johnson had already been looking for a solution on 'how to kill more VC' with more ground forces. Unsure himself on how to wage war, now, as it appeared that the South was breaking apart, he turned to his advisors and asked for guarantees on what it would take to 'win' should he commit major ground cmbat forces to the fight. His primary civilian advisor, McNamara, queried his Whiz kids to define what winning meant. In response, his assistant secretary of defense McNaughton wrote his famous memo defining winning as preserving US prestige and demonstrating its willingness to commit military power to stop communism.

When McNamara discussed this memo with Bundy, they both yet again agreed, not knowing their enemy, that all that they needed to do was to show further resolve of a great power and North Vietnam – only a small state for a little over ten years - would give up. In their views, it would be unreasonable and illogical to think otherwise. After all, game theory and limited war strategies, concepts that the National Security Advisor had studied in academia, presumed this outcome. Faced already with results that showed otherwise, not knowing anything about war, the 'Best and Brightest' still thought they could apply their brain power, as JFK had hired them to do, and solve the problem with a little more analysis and a little more assessment of numbers.

Thus, all that had to be done was for the US to commit a larger, but still limited number of ground forces to show even greater resolve and the North would come to its senses. Moreover, even if the war still went on, and for some unknown reason North Vietnam did not seek a negotiated peace, the

US could just withdraw, and the world could still see the US as a great power who tried to do its best, but its patient just died.

The US military in Washington, Honolulu, and Saigon was either unaware of, or passively resisted this thinking at the time. They continued to believe that the President wanted to achieve the political objectives declared in the National Security documents. LBJ reinforced this notion by continuing to tell them on several occasions "to kill more VC."

Therefore, when Secretary McNamara referred the President's question of how to guarantee a win in Vietnam to the JCS in the summer of 1965, the resultant study used the official, declared objectives and the President's urgings to describe what was necessary to win. Thus, it focused on how to kill more VC to force the North to cease its aggression, rather than convincing its leaders to quit or preserving US prestige. Its author, General Andrew Goodpaster concluded, "there appears to be no reason we cannot win if such is our will—and if that will is manifested in strategy and tactical operations."

The Goodpaster Study's 'strategy and tactical operations,' as explained in Chapter 3, spelled out the need to conduct a large-scale ground attack against the North's principal lines of communication - the Ho Chi Minh Trail. The object was to isolate the battlefield in the South by stopping the North's infiltration of forces there. By severing the trail, the study reasoned the North would have to fight to keep it open, and that would lead to the destruction of its main regular forces that were key to forcing the DRV to stop the war. If that could be done, then the combined US and ARVN military could defeat the enemy in South Vietnam, cut off from its base and lifeline, and preserve the Republic of South Vietnam's freedom.

In devising this military strategy to win, Goodpaster and his planners did not neglect the critical political-military concerns over a widening war with China. They assumed, based on a CIA reasonable assessment of the internal situation in China at the time, that the Communist Chinese would not intervene unless the US invaded North Vietnam or forced the North to surrender through massive bombing. Thus, the study's planners considered an attack into Laos to sever the trail as a moderate risk for Chinese military intervention.

Furthermore, Goodpaster and his planners also felt that 'if such is our will' to win than the US would also have to provide the means to execute its operational maneuver in Laos. That meant mobilizing or calling up enough reserves to generate the combat and support forces necessary to conduct the concepts of operation for the strategy. The study assumed that it would be reasonable to do so and would not prompt any significant Chinese or Soviet action to intervene in Southeast Asia.

Goodpaster, under orders of the Chairman, shared the study's concepts and results with the JCS. He also shared it with Sharp and Westmoreland in a July 1965 visit to Saigon. Both the Service Chiefs and field commanders said it was in concert with their thinking on a military strategy for achieving victory in Vietnam.

As emphasized in Chapter 3, LBJ's civilian policymakers never seriously considered this study. There is no evidence that it was ever passed to the President. Neither were previous estimates that General Westmoreland had sent in March or in June. Later in August a JCS paper, with similar ideas and conclusions of the Goodpaster study, was again submitted to the Secretary. It too was shelved.

Rather, with McNamara in the lead, the principal civilian advisors continued to march toward the commitment of US ground forces to South Vietnam and a continuance of air attacks against the North without due care to the possible consequences they were already alerted to. They were also headed forward with several key assumptions about that commitment that would later affect the execution of the military strategy against their principal opponent – Communist North Vietnam - to the latter's advantage.

The Key Assumptions Driving Actions on South Vietnam

As discussions and planning continued into July for the commitment of US ground forces, LBJ, Bundy, and McNamara and his principal defense assistants held on to some critical assumptions that would drive that commitment. They believed, some more stronger than others, that any military ground operation directed outside of South Vietnam would cause Chinese intervention.

Moreover, the President strongly felt that any reserve call-up or mobilization would incite the Chinese or Soviets to go to a war footing in Asia or Europe. These assumptions and resultant restrictions were the key factors in not only limiting the US military's use of force in South Vietnam and the Southeast Asia region, but in directing a faulty application of Westmoreland's US military strategy during the LBJ Administration.

Here, it is interesting to explain the reasons why and how LBJ's and his civilian advisors adopted these assumptions, and why they in turn drove the restrictions on military operations. The work of Yuen Foong Khong in his *Analogies of War* is quite instructive. In this book, Professor Khong examines the use of analogies for decision making during the Vietnam War. His findings are a valuable contribution to understanding some of those decisions.

One of Dr. Khong's principal arguments is that "The historical analogy that played the most influential role in the decision making of the 1960s was that of Korea." He contends that the use of this analogy "can help explain why the Johnson Administration decided to intervene in Vietnam, as well as why the American intervention took the form it did."

According to Khong's research and analysis of discussions at the time, the form of intervention in Vietnam was based upon the American principal decision and policy makers' lessons from the Chinese intervention in Korea. Here Khong shows how the 'China Factor' influenced and drove the limitations on the breadth and scope of both the bombing campaign against the North, and combat actions against the North Vietnam's lines of communication.

The professor offers some interesting observations on the reasons for the limitation. He says that "the ghost of the Yalu debacle of 1950" haunted LBJ and many of his advisors on what to do in Vietnam. That is, they were concerned about any action that China may see as threatening their survival, such as what MacArthur did in crossing the 38th parallel and advancing to the Yalu River border with China.

Khong's analysis of the evidence further demonstrates that, in part, the President's decision not to call up the reserves, to limit the bombing in North Vietnam, and to restrict ground operations against the North and in Laos were based on the assumption that China would intervene if the US took any of those actions.

In short, in selecting these critical limiting assumptions, the President and his principal advisors did not consult their intelligence or military experts or advisors. Rather they chose to apply a false historical precedent that had influenced actions in an environment and time completely different from the one they faced.

All of this begs the question, why did no one seriously challenge these assumptions and the resultant restrictions they imposed on the application of military force? As we have seen, there certainly existed proposed estimates and strategies that not only questioned the rationale for the limiting assumptions, but also proposed alternative ones.

For example, as mentioned, there existed CIA and other estimates that pointed to the unlikelihood of Chinese intervention happening unless there was an invasion of the North that threatened China's borders, an all-out bombing campaign that would obliterate the North and destroy it as a state, or the use of tactical nuclear weapons in Southeast Asia. As described, the Goodpaster study drew upon those estimates in making alternative assumptions about Chinese intervention. In so doing, it did not think that operations into Laos, or mobilization would reasonably incite China to confront directly another war with the US. In addition, in November 1965, as also described in Chapter 3, there was a JCS proposed military strategy that rejected the Korean War analogies and resultant restricting assumptions imposed on military actions.

Later, Westmoreland presented an alternative strategy in early 1967 and after TET in 1968 based on the same assumptions as the Goodpaster Study and the CJCS November 65 strategy. However, the MACV commander, as explained in Chapter 9, did not make a case for these alternatives or challenge directly the imposed restrictions for operations in Laos.

So if there were alternative military strategies, studies and views that brought into question the LBJ and McNamara assumptions limiting military action, why did the alternative assumptions that they used not brought to the attention and explained to the President and other principals who believed otherwise? Alternatively, as some were brought to the attention of several key policy makers, such as McNamara and Bundy, why were they ignored?

Strategic Void Again: The Failure to Produce a Long-Term National Military Strategy for the War

The answers to the above inquiries reside in the circumstance that at the critical stage in going to war in Vietnam, from April to July 1965, LBJ, Bundy, and McNamara never called for or had a systematic and complete discussion at the highest levels of the Johnson Administration on what their long-term strategy would be for Vietnam. Neither did the Chairman of the Joint Chiefs, General Wheeler, insist upon one.

For sure, as described in Chapter 3, the President, his chief civilian and military advisors, and some other participants such as the 'Wise Men' had many meetings. At these meetings there were discussions on options and how to guarantee winning in Vietnam. There was some discussion on convincing the North to stop its aggression. There was also some Presidential guidance, such as 'kill more VC.'

But throughout the spring to mid-summer 1965 there was never a thorough review or discussion of a national military strategy that tied the purposes, means and ways for the conflict unfolding in

Vietnam. There was no high-level consideration of what may have been North Vietnam's strategy entailing the same, or what may have been the enemy's weaknesses and strengths.

There was the appearance of consideration, as well as the appearance of argument. There were questions asked. In fact, at some of the meetings in July, particularly the ones on 21 July, some very important inquiries came from LBJ on such things such as how will the enemy react to our sending in the forces; how will US troops be able to perform in the weather and terrain in Vietnam? The President encouraged full airing of views in answering these questions.

But the answers were usually short and never fully discussed. Those forwarded to the State, Defense, Joint Chiefs, and Intelligence staffs were not really examined in detail at later meetings. There was the semblance of what should be done to win – but what winning meant was never thoroughly defined or discussed amongst both the principal senior civilian and military advisors present at the same time at meetings.

By the admission of many present at these meetings, most discussions and any decisions reached were done behind the doors of other closed gatherings or over private discussions. Though McNamara was always willing and able to recite numbers "without pause or hesitation," according to Jack Valenti, these discussions were without the benefit of detailed military analyses or strategic considerations. For the most part these were devoid of any real debate, and only in an atmosphere of reaching a consensus of doing what the President wanted or what some thought he wanted, not what he should be told or what should be done.

This lack of thoughtful consideration of ends, ways and means to conduct the war in Vietnam was irresponsible. Clausewitz's dictum that "No one starts a war - or rather, no one in his senses ought to do so - without first being clear in his mind what he intends to achieve by that war and how he intends to conduct it" is most pertinent here.

Not only did this neglect fail to give adequate and detailed guidance for the field commanders, but it prevented a thorough examination of evidence that may have refuted the critical assumptions on the restrictions imposed as described above. This lack of 'how [the President] intends to conduct [the war in Vietnam]' also resulted, as mentioned frequently in the preceding chapters, in the absence of consideration of North Vietnam's actions to the success or failure of US actions, and the costs of involvement in a potential long war in Vietnam and Indochina for America.

So, who in the LBJ Administration was responsible for the conduct of a systematic review resulting in a comprehensive strategy before the starting of a war in Vietnam, and even after; and why did they not do so?

As outlined in Chapter 1, by the National Security Act of 1947, modified under IKE, and more importantly as the position evolved under JFK, the National Security Advisor McGeorge Bundy was most responsible for coordinating issues of national security, and preparing papers and studies for deliberation before the President. Hence, he was certainly a person responsible for ensuring a thorough and thoughtful combined civilian and military consideration and review of issues leading to some detailed national military strategic guidance for Vietnam.

Yet, as described in Chapter 3, mentioned in Chapter 8, and outlined again above, he not only did not produce a national long-term look and guidance for the employment of force in Vietnam, but ignored or rejected the military strategy produced by General Goodpaster and his group. The irony is that this study, having been undertaken as a result of the inquiries of the President and directed by the Secretary of Defense, may have been that it was just the kind of examination that could have prompted a thorough review resulting in the formulation of a national military strategy.

But it is unfair to blame just McGeorge Bundy on this matter. Robert McNamara, as Secretary of Defense under the National Security Acts, was responsible to the President for the management of the Defense Department, defense affairs and matters, and was second in command of US military forces. As such, he should have ensured that the President was "clear in his mind what he [intended] to achieve [in a war in Vietnam] and how he [intended] to conduct it."

Yet, as mentioned in Chapters 3 and 8, the second in command to the Commander-in-Chief never made sure that such a discussion took place. Indeed, he prevented one from happening by not verifying that Bundy forwarded the July Goodpaster Study or any of the Westmoreland estimates of March or June to the President. Or that they received a full hearing before him for approval. Rather the Secretary settled for a series of discussions, many of which were devoid of any military advisors, in which options were deliberated without basic military strategic considerations, and selected based upon system analysis techniques and formulas.

But it is still unfair to blame just Bundy or McNamara. General Wheeler, as the Chairman of the Joint Chiefs, was responsible for military guidance from the Chiefs of Staff of the Services on the war to the Secretary of Defense and the President. In that capacity he should have established a draft national military strategy for the war in Vietnam before the President's commitment of forces in July 1965, if not before, and ensured that it received full examination by the President.

Thus, as the Goodpaster Study was such a draft, Wheeler should have checked and confirmed that one was delivered for discussion and approval of the President and his chief civilian advisors. As far as the evidence now shows, the CJCS did not do that and the strategy never went anywhere. Moreover, even after the first American troops were in combat and dying, the Chairman still did not ensure that a national military strategy went to the President for consideration - even though another was developed in November 1965 and forwarded to the Secretary of Defense. Like the Goodpaster Study it too went nowhere.

Thus, there were three principal advisors for the President – two civilians and one military - who failed to see to the formulation of a national military strategy for the war. But there is one person who bears the overall responsibility for being "clear in his mind what he [intended] to achieve by that war and how he [intended] to conduct it." That is the individual where, in the words of Harry Truman, the 'buck stops' - the President of the US and Commander-in-Chief. Above all it is he who is responsible for the formulation of national strategies to give guidance and to explain to his Administration and, for those unclassified parts that can be released, to the Public how he intended to win the war he chose to embark on.

However, Johnson - though he pondered continuously the Vietnam issue, sought sympathy for his dilemma on how to solve it, and asked how we are going to win - gave very little guidance, beyond kill more VC, to his subordinates on how to win or conduct the war. What he did was delegate the responsibility for determining what he wanted to achieve and how to run the war in Vietnam to his Secretary of Defense. In doing so, he failed to ensure that he had the best advice he could get from his military advisors for sound decisions, and failed to provide clear guidance and direction to his commanders.

What about the question why did the above people responsible for strategic direction in the form of a well-thought out and clear directive not do so? From the evidence and narrations of the earlier chapters, there appear to be three basic and interrelated reasons that are common to those individuals discussed above.

First, all believed that the actions of the US to convince North Vietnam to cease its aggression would work and work fairly quickly. Though LBJ voiced discomfort to his Senate colleagues whether the graduated responses would be effective, he was willing to believe his National Security Advisor and Defense Secretary in July 1965 that the policy would be successful.

As mentioned several times, Bundy and McNamara were students or supporters of game theory and conflict management thought. These methods, for them, were reinforced by the success of settling the Cuban Missile Crisis successfully. Thus, they thought it would also work in Southeast Asia. As for Wheeler, at first, he went along with the policy because he also believed that ROLLING THUNDER would eventually work as well.

Why would it not? They all knew that the US was the most powerful nation on earth; had held communism at bay in Europe and in Northeast Asia; and had rebuilt Europe and Japan. Moreover, North Vietnam had been a mere colony before the end of the war. Yes, it had won a war against the French, but the French had lost easily to Germany in the World War. Besides the Expeditionary Force it deployed against the Viet-Minh was mostly made up of mercenaries – Foreign Legionnaires – and colonial troops. That French led Army was thus not motivated, weak, and its leaders inept.

Related to the above, a second reason for the absence of a comprehensive long term national strategy for the war was that those mentioned above ignored, or misunderstood, or were contemptible of their enemy. As demonstrated and explained in the previous chapters, all of the US senior decision makers above made little effort to learn about the enemy they would face, did not care to understand their motives, and ignored those in the Administration who did.

Hence, they mirror imaged how North Vietnam would respond to their actions, ignored the lessons from the war with the French, and did not believe the Northern leaders' words that they would wage a long war despite the damages the US could inflict. As a consequence, the US launched a war with no idea of who their opponents were, were shortsighted on what it would take to force them to capitulate, and did not know how to respond to the long war that followed.

The third reason for no comprehensive national military strategy was that the above policy and decision makers just did not see or understand the necessity for one. Neither Bundy nor McNamara knew anything about military strategies. They were students of economic theories and systems analysis. Moreover, as already mentioned, McNamara had declared that strategies were no longer needed, in their stead crisis management now was the only direction process required. As we also have seen, the Defense Secretary focused on systems analysis as the primary method to find the answers to the use of military force.

So why did not the Chairman or any of the Chiefs make demands for a national strategy for the direction of the war and its combat operations. The evidence seems to indicate that General Wheeler, though a competent officer, was not a strategist and had no combat experience. Thus, he was not aware of the importance of melding military operations with clear and meaningful military objectives that reflected political aims. He was, as a schooled mathematician, mostly focused on numbers. Indeed, it seems that Wheeler later recognized this failure. As related in Chapter 3, he later recanted that is lack of support for and inaction on making sure a sound military strategy went before the President was one of the worst mistakes he made as Chairman.

As for the military Chiefs, they were, for the most part, focused on their particular Services and how they were employed by the field commander, as well as the impact of deployments to the readiness of their Service forces worldwide. Besides, Service roles and missions, and budget share continued to embroil them in bickering between themselves.

A Commander Struggles to Derive a Wartime Theater Military Strategy without a National Strategy as a Guide

The one person who saw the need for a military strategy for the war at its very beginning was the MACV Commander. Thus, General Westmoreland really drove the development of how to conduct the war in 1965 from his point of view. Before the July 1965 decisions, however, this strategy was very conceptual, not detailed in how he would accomplish his war of attrition, did not challenge his civilian leader assumptions, narrowly focused on his area of responsibility, and though fixated on his needs for the resources to execute it ignored the necessity for the reserves to support it.

As early as the spring of 1965, as the communist offensive was taking a toll on the South Vietnamese armed forces and it appeared that the South might succumb to the North's attacks, the MACV commander sensed the timing was right to send to Washington his first ideas on how to use US forces to keep the ARVN from defeat and the Republic of Vietnam from falling. This first proposed military strategic concept sent in his 26 March cable was, as detailed in Chapter 8, "a classic Leavenworth style analysis." It outlined his force requirements and ideas on how they were to be employed. It stated that it would save the South from immediate defeat. It argued for the necessity of more effort and forces, warned of the distinct prospect of a more protracted war, and the need to prepare for such a war.

LBJ and his primary security advisors never read, studied, or debated the objective or concepts in that cable or other military analyses – such as those produced by the Sigma War Games, or like the later Goodpaster report, or the JCS strategy produced in the fall of 1965. It was not until thirty years later that McNamara lamented in his memoirs that he should have questioned the MACV commander's strategy that he did not even care to see.

In June, a little over a month before the July decision to go to war, General Westmoreland forwarded the 'bombshell' message to Washington that propelled the Administration toward the President's decision. Once again, led by McNamara, no one seemed interested in the more detailed concepts for the US force employment to stem the tide. The principal civilian advisors did question the troop levels, however. They sensed that they were on the verge of having to use large numbers of troops to halt the disaster confronting them.

Despite concerns and questions on how to win the war, troop deployment numbers remained the focus of the President's civilian advisors, as well as many in the JCS, and thus were the main issues brought forth to the President for consideration and decisions. That is because numbers for them, especially McNamara, showed budget and political costs, which they understood.

Besides, they did not understand what offensive or defensive operations were all about. They did not know what an attrition or exhaustion or destruction strategy entailed other than the need to 'kill more VC.' How could they; no one from the JCS bothered to explain, and MACV was embroiled in trying deal with and stop a disaster from happening while Washington deliberated. Besides, had the Chairman done so, it would have been an uphill battle – given Wheeler's lack of military strategy and McNamara's belief it was an irrelevant subject.

After the July decision, with the apparent failure of the calculated and graduated bombing of North Vietnam and with no national military strategy for the war, as the first American combat troops arrived in theater, Westmoreland was left on his own to develop a more thorough theater strategy to deal with the increasingly dire situation in the South. He was, in his mind, up to the challenge and not hesitant to do so. Contrary to the images of a dull-minded, military martinet portrayed in works such as Lewis Sorley's *Westmoreland* and *Better War*, General Westmoreland had a detailed and solid, if not brilliant or bold, grasp of military doctrine and strategy.

Westmoreland's Strategy of Attrition: A Strategy for an Unwinnable War?

As explained in Chapter 8, Westmoreland's military strategy - as now detailed not only to Washington but also through directives to his subordinates – was to carry out what he thought was his chief political objective as he knew it. That was explicitly stated in the November 1963 NSAM 273 - "It remains the central object of the United States in South Vietnam to assist the people and Government of that country to win their contest against the externally directed and supported Communist conspiracy. The test of all U. S. decisions and actions in this area should be the effectiveness of their contribution to this purpose."

For Westmoreland, as he explains in his memoirs and as is consistent with his wartime directives, the focus of his campaigns was to defeat the North's main forces in the South to achieve the political object explained above. Without their defeat, he reasoned, South Vietnam could never be defended and pacified. Without their destruction, South Vietnam would never be able to be free from communist subjugation from the North.

Moreover, the most capable forces to achieve this military objective, the MACV commander decided, were the American combat forces. The ARVN - and South Vietnamese territorial forces – were the most appropriate to provide security for the South Vietnam populace and build support for its government. This was a reasonable division of labor at the time - especially in light of the turmoil and the defeats that the ARVN experienced in the years after Diem's assassination.

Encouraged by the Secretary of Defense, the MACV commander's primary military objective, consistent with LBJ's policy and guidance to convince the North to desist support for the war, was to destroy enough forces to convince the Northern leadership that they could not win militarily in the South. This had to be the solution to the central strategic problem of the war as he saw it, as his first major combat units arrived in theater and he was preparing to employ them against the enemy. It was a matter of how to achieve this military aim with the forces and restrictions Washington was giving and directing him.

Despite later criticisms and post-war recantations, both LBJ and McNamara not only bought into this approach but later finally set specific operational objectives for it. At the 1966 Honolulu meeting, they provided their field force commander a key measure of effectiveness to kill or disable more enemy than the communists could replace. This so-called 'cross-over point,' became the focus of the LBJ Administration in the first two and a half years of the conflict for determining the success of their limited war in South Vietnam. Contrary to some histories, this was an LBJ and McNamara goal and not one that Westmoreland contrived to fit his ideas of how to win in Vietnam, or one that he derived to fashion his strategy of attrition.

Westmoreland's operational approach - his search and destroy operations - was consistent with this guidance. In the field, US commanders set body counts as the critical measure of success in each engagement, major battle, and campaign. This too was consistent with the LBJ Administration's focus and guidance, which, in the absence of any previous or current military strategy from Washington, civilian leaders and advisors were making up as the war progressed.

As the historical evidence shows, moreover, Westmoreland - contrary to the view of some historians - recognized the importance of pacification and the necessity to gain support for the RVN. His directives and plans consistently stated the importance of this task. However, he firmly believed that pacification would never be able to take root unless his forces could defeat the enemy's main combat units. Absent any other guidance from his commanders in Washington, this made sense to him at the time.

Again, the central issue for his military strategy as mentioned above and described in Chapter 9, was whether he could confront and bloody the main forces enough to allow for pacification to proceed; or whether he could have executed pacification while just keeping the enemy's main forces at bay. Contrary to most critiques of Westmoreland's strategy, it was not really whether he should have focused more on the main forces 'war,' or more on the local guerrilla forces' security threat 'war.'

Dale Andrade's article of June 2008 in *The Small Wars Journal* on this point is right on and worthy of mention in this chapter's overview. He observes, "It remains difficult to see why [Westmoreland's attrition strategy] has come to be regarded as controversial. Those who argue that there was a choice between two approaches—one that first sought to neutralize the enemy main forces, and one that would have instead emphasized counterinsurgency—ignore the stark realities on the ground." The stark realities on the ground were that Westmoreland needed to do both. This problem was his primary dilemma and one that he could not solve given his chosen theater military strategy and the restrictions that influenced it.

Interestingly, as we have seen in Chapter 7, it was also a dilemma that the North Vietnamese High Command was counting on; that is, that the Americans would be unable to do so because they would be spread too thin to do both, and their forces would be able to circumvent American operations to fix and destroy their main units. In short, the enemy was counting on an American military strategy that would be handicapped by employing too little forces, to accomplish too much, over large expanses of area.

To summarize from other explanations, there were three primary reasons the General could not solve this dilemma. The first reason was the geographic and force limitations that his superiors imposed upon him. These restrictions unduly hampered his ability to find, fix and destroy the enemy's main forces. The second was that when he was unable to convince his commanders in Washington to change those restrictions, Westmoreland just gave in and, despite evidence to the contrary, persisted that his attrition strategy could eventually work and that it just would take more time.

The third reason, related to the second, was that in complying with of his civilian superiors' decisions to continue the limitations, the General seriously miscalculated his ability to execute his attrition strategy without relief from those imposed limits. The paragraphs ahead address the impact of these restrictions in more detail, as well as Westmoreland's acquiescence and miscalculations when he failed to obtain relief from them.

As mentioned, the force limitations that Westmoreland contended with throughout late 1965 and through 1968 severely inhibited his ability to engage the enemy and find, fix, and destroy his main forces. As explained in Chapters 3 and 7, LBJ's decision not to mobilize and put the nation on a war footing was a major reason that the MACV commander could not get the forces in the numbers and at the times he required them.

Moreover, though initially promised that he would get all that he needed over time, as early as the beginning of 1966 and thereafter, Secretary McNamara convinced the President, without consulting with his field commanders, to limit deployments to control inflation and sustain US forces at a constant level. Furthermore, when Westmoreland attempted to change his strategy and attack the enemy's key lines of communication in the Spring of 1967, the President, based on McNamara's recommendation, refused to provide the reinforcements necessary to execute it.

Despite these force restrictions, however, in all instances when Westmoreland did not get his reinforcements, he gave in to the troop reductions and delays without any significant disagreement or forceful counterargument. According to Westmoreland in his remarks at the time and later in his memoirs, the General thought that he could live with any delays and modifications in force levels because he thought that he could still succeed, but that the war would just take a little longer.

It is important to note here once again that the enemy still had 'an important vote' on the outcome of Westmoreland's ultimate plans for offensive operations to destroy its main forces – something that the General may have ignored. Indeed, even with all his requested forces in the timeframe he suggested, it would have been still problematic for the US field commander to engage the enemy successfully and defeat them within the confines of South Vietnam. This was because the communists, most of the time, chose when and where to engage the Americans. They also had the safe havens of the cross-border base areas to withdraw for reconstitution as necessary.

In fact, in the General's attrition strategy, which he thought would eventually defeat the enemy in South Vietnam, Westmoreland miscalculated his ability to destroy their main forces and thereby allow for the pacification of the countryside. Most importantly, Westmoreland errored seriously and foolishly thinking that in going after the PAVN and PLAF base camps in South Vietnam he could either engage the enemy main forces and destroy them or drive them out of South Vietnam.

Indeed, Westmoreland's major military objective of his attrition strategy – to force the enemy's main forces to fight in his base areas and defeat them - was a "fool's errand." To obtain his stated 'end state' for victory, Westmoreland would have had to achieve one of three conditions. One, he would have had to convince the North Vietnamese to abandon its efforts at infiltration into the South and have destroyed or neutralized the enemy's main forces in the South. Neutralizing in this case means render any of the enemy's main forces incapable of interfering effectively with pacification.

Two, the General would have had to seal the borders of South Vietnam to prevent such infiltration if the North persisted, while defeating or neutralizing its remaining main forces in South Vietnam. Three, the MACV commander would have had to deny any enemy main forces from interfering with pacification by destroying them or neutralizing them, and interdicting and halting any further reinforcements with air forces.

None of these conditions was possible. We have seen that the North was intent on continuing its infiltration because it was the 'sine qua non' for any success in forceful reunification. Aerial interdiction could slow or make costly this continued infiltration but could not stop it. Sealing over a thousand miles of mountains, densely vegetated borders from the DMZ to the Mekong Delta was impossible. The US could not even seal the seventy-mile DMZ from infiltration during the war. Finally, the ability to corner and destroy the enemy main forces within the South was also impossible. The terrain, the mobility and the nature of the enemy forces, and the presence of safe havens across the borders prevented that from happening.

Moreover, as argued throughout this story, the chief enabler of the North's ability to wage war was its main infiltration route for its forces and supplies into South Vietnam. As we have seen in Chapter 7 and elsewhere, the Ho Chi Minh Trail throughout the war was the key to the North's ability to fight in the South. Without it, North Vietnam could never have been able to reverse the situation in South Vietnam in the early sixties, could not have launched the 1968 TET attack, and could not have conducted its 1972 and 1975 offensives.

In short, without this Ho Chi Minh Trail complex, the North could not have won the war. The trail complex was for them, in Clausewitz's terms a "center of gravity," or "the hub of all power and movement, on which everything depends." Thus, it is entirely possible that if Westmoreland could have had permission to attack into Laos and permanently sever the trail with ground forces he could have had a reasonable chance of military success in Vietnam.

To conclude this summary of the 'Strategy of Attrition' there are four primary observations. First, absent a well thought-out and coordinated national military strategy, Westmoreland devised the best theater military strategy he could, given the restrictions imposed by Washington. Second, even if LBJ had provided the forces Westmoreland requested for his attrition strategy, it is doubtful, even impossible without one of the three conditions mentioned above, that the object of destroying or neutralizing the North's PAVN forces could have been achieved.

Three, the attrition strategy did stop the initial communist onslaught, and achieved a stalemate by the end of 1967, but the US public and Congress would not continue to support such an end state given the cost to achieve it in terms of casualties and time. Finally, the choice to follow a strategy of attrition, given the restrictions imposed from 1965 to 1968 and the pressures after TET to get out of Vietnam, was not only a fool's choice, but ultimately led to an unwinnable war.

However, the above observations do not mean that General Westmoreland was stupid and solely responsible for the US failure in Vietnam, as Lewis Sorley implies in his subtitle of his book on Westmoreland – "The General Who Lost Vietnam." There were many to blame and to account for the end result; not the least the North Vietnamese and the policies and actions that followed in the Nixon Administration. Moreover, the General, to his credit at the time, recognized that his attrition strategy was in trouble in 1967 and tried, in his way, to seek an alternative solution. Having failed in 1967, he again tried to resurrect the alternative in 1968, and again failed.

As explained in Chapters 3 and 9, this alternative theater military strategy had merit, and may have succeeded in ending the war by achieving the NSAM aims. Why this alternate course never occurred, and how it may have been a lost opportunity is worthy of further review here.

Westmoreland's Alternative Strategy: A Lost Opportunity to Attack the Enemy Center of Gravity?

General Westmoreland had recognized the trail's importance to the war in the south early on. Thus, in March 1965 he included in his estimate and concept for the employment of US forces their possible use against the trail. In his memoirs, he explains that he did not consider such an employment in the evolution of his later attrition strategy because of LBJ and McNamara's concerns on limiting the war for fear of Chinese intervention.

Besides, at the time, he thought that the use of air interdiction of the North's forces and supplies moving along the trail would have a decided effect. Whether this was wishful thinking, a genuine belief in airpower, or most likely, just following Administration policy we may never know. But we do know that by June 1965 he saw that this aerial interdiction could not halt enemy infiltration, and that without a massive infusion of US ground forces the Republic of South Vietnam would fall.

The General cites reasons other than LBJ's restrictions why he did not pursue such an attack against the Trail in 1965 and for a while thereafter. Westmoreland explains that he did not consider operations outside of South Vietnam in 1965 through 1966 because to launch such an offensive would have taken more troops than he had available; especially considering the need for a sizeable logistic force to support it. In addition, South Vietnam just did not have the infrastructure to support a build-up on its borders for such an offensive in that time frame.

By late 1966 and into early 1967, as mentioned above and explained in Chapter 9, it appeared to Westmoreland that it may not be possible to kill more VC than North Vietnam could replace in the South. His intelligence about the enemy's interdiction demonstrated that despite his large-scale operations, enemy strength in South Vietnam had actually increased. Thus, he questioned whether the elusive cross over point that was set as his key objective at Honolulu early that year may not have been achievable given his current approach.

Moreover, Westmoreland may have also realized that he may not have the time he thought he would need to execute his strategy of attrition as he had envisioned. At the Honolulu Conference in early 1966 and later in early 1967 to the Congress he stated to his audience that a critical factor for his conduct of the war was whether the American public would continue to support it over time. He further voiced his concern that the enemy thought that the US people would grow weary of the war, as the French had done in their defeat in Indochina.

As also explained in Chapter 9, there were two opportunities that Westmoreland seized to challenge the geographic restriction and asked for the wherewithal to execute his contingency plans for cutting the Ho Chi Minh Trail in Laos. One was in March in 1967 with his inputs for force reinforcements for 1968 as part of his Optimum Force Package. The other was in his 206K reinforcement request a year later as the TET 1968 offensive was occurring. On both occasions, however, Westmoreland fell off his requests and did not forcibly argue for them to launch offensive operations outside of his geographic restrictions.

On both occasions, moreover, Westmoreland continued to argue - despite indications that his attrition strategy was not working given its geographic restrictions and the difficulty in finding and destroying the enemy's main units - that he could win the war, but it would just take more time. He continued, despite evidence to the contrary, to rely on his calculation that he would eventually be successful. Of course, we now know he would never get that time. LBJ would resign and give up trying to kill more VC.

It is interesting to speculate further at this point in the story on why Westmoreland did not press more strongly for his requests for the necessary forces and lifting of the geographic restrictions for an offensive into Laos. The most obvious reason, as mentioned several times, was that he foolishly thought that he still would be able to be successful given more time to carry out his attrition strategy.

But, there appears that there may have been other reasons as well. As we saw in Chapter 9, he was not stupid. He most likely knew in early 1967 that more forces more quickly and their use against the Trail had a better chance at success than relying on his attrition strategy within the confines of South Vietnam.

So why else, besides his continued reliance and belief in his original strategy, may he have given in so easily? Why did he not argue more forcibly for his alternative strategy? What would have been the obstacles and counterarguments? Furthermore, would his alternative strategy to attack the Ho Chi Minh Trail have offered more decisive results, and could Westmoreland have had a reasonable chance to achieve them given the situation at the time?

First, as to the alternative's chances and viability as a strategy, in military terms this alternative could have been an acceptable, feasible, and an adequate concept to decisively alter the stalemate that had developed in 1967 in the favor of the US. That is, it is entirely possible that the operation could have been launched and executed at reasonable costs to the attacking forces (i.e., it was acceptable). Moreover, by the time he first envisioned this attack could happen, late 1967, Westmoreland's logistics and sustainment bases and lines in South Vietnam could have supported such an offensive (i.e., it was feasible). And, as already explained in Chapter 9, it was entirely possible that such an operation could have led to a situation that would have forced the North into submission had it resulted in the closing of the Ho Chi Minh Trail (i.e., it was an adequate concept).

Of course, this is a retrospective judgment, and we will never know for sure whether it would have worked. But the above brief assessment is reasonable, based on the evidence that the trail complex had become critical to the North Vietnamese war effort. Indeed, by 1967 it is highly probable Le Duan and his PAVN high command would have had to react to such an offensive, much as they had to in 1971.

Moreover, the campaign would most probably have been a fiercely contested one – but also would have presented an opportunity to gain the initiative over the enemy and force him to do battle with his main forces. Having forced the enemy to fight to defend and preserve the Trail, Westmoreland would have favorable circumstances to bring the full power of the American military to bear upon and destroy the PAVN/PLAF main forces committed to battle. Once the Trail severed, the North would not have the wherewithal to reinforce the South. The communist war in the South may very well have faltered and disintegrated.

How about the obstacles and counterarguments Westmoreland may have faced? Chapters 3 and 9 explain the reasons that neither LBJ or McNamara in 1967 and then the President and Clifford in 1968, did not decide to execute Westmoreland's alternative. But then, Westmoreland had not forcibly made an argument. What if he had? What if he had insisted that such an operation could have stopped the North's infiltration, finally brought its main forces to fight in a decisive campaign, and conceivably led to victory or a favorable settlement? What kind of resistance may he have faced then?

First, besides the reasons explained in the above chapters, it is also probable McNamara and his analysts may have argued vigorously against this alternative because military strategies and operations, by nature, are fraught with risks, unknowns, contradictions, and difficulties. As Clausewitz reminds his students, "No other human activity is so continuously or universally bound up with chance. And through the element of chance, guesswork, and luck come to play a great part in war…. Absolute, so-called mathematical factors never find a firm basis for military calculations."

Westmoreland's alternative strategy of a strike against the trail in Laos was full of these imponderables and unknowns. Explaining these unknowns or other issues do not lend themselves to mathematical models or statistical analysis. They require assumptions. While you can test some assumptions, using probability calculations for instance, they often demand risks that can only be calculated by how one feels about that assumption. For calculating military risks, those feelings can mainly be measured by how confident one may be of accomplishing something based on previous experiences or even intuition. Can you imagine trying to explain the rationale of the assumptions based on intuition and experience to number crunching analysts who are naturally suspicious, even contemptuous, of the military?

We have already examined what the civilian and military members of the Johnson Administration have said of one another, and what a divide there was between the military and civilians in the Department of Defense. Therefore, it is reasonable to say that it would have been an uphill battle to convince them of the acceptability, feasibility, and adequacy of such an alternative strategy. What added to this improbability was, as already mentioned, the lack of respect and confidence between the civilian analysts and the military planners.

Given the evidence of the propensity of the civilian defense analysts and McNamara to reject arguments that were not quantifiable, it would have been on the shoulders of both Wheeler and Westmoreland to make a convincing argument in favor of such a strategy to LBJ or even Clark Clifford who were more open to less quantifiable methods of analysis than McNamara. Why did they not do that?

For Westmoreland, the answer, in part, relates to his way of dealing with his superiors – both civilian and military. Throughout the war, it appears that he chose not to directly involve himself in the issues affecting his theater strategy in the high circles of government. For example, throughout his tenure, he either left the issues involving his troop requests to the Chiefs of Staff and the Chairman, or acquiesced to the President's or Secretary of Defense's points of view or decisions.

Westmoreland also saw himself as a dutiful soldier who, after presenting his ideas, did not choose to argue them or seek support for them at the higher command level. Yes, he had gone to Congress and the American people to explain his strategy and give a progress report in 1967, but it was because the President had ordered him to do so. Moreover, though he had served in the Pentagon, he did not see himself, like most of the military officers in the Vietnam timeframe, as a 'political general.'

Therefore, Westmoreland did not see his place to debate what he saw as political factors with his civilian leaders, even though they affected military operations. He had been, as some observed, stoic, even unconcerned when the President and his advisors did not act on his alternative strategy. In a passage in his memoirs on his relationship with the President, he revealed, he "had no intention of crossing the President in any way." Indeed, LBJ, the reluctant commander, had chosen just the right field general for his limited war.

Westmoreland also relied on his immediate superior, the Commander of the Pacific Command, or the Chairman of the Joint Chiefs to argue his case for his strategic approach to Washington bureaucrats. Apparently, as indicated in his memoirs, he loathed doing so himself; and either did not feel comfortable in his position to do so, or felt that it was above his role as a theater commander, or both.

Besides, the reinforcement issue was, at least during the TET period, Wheeler's notion. Though it certainly would give him forces he could use for his contingency, it was not his idea at the time. As for Admiral US Sharp, in his memoirs he admits that he did not see it as within his purview to interfere with ground war matters in South Vietnam. He saw his primary task as overseeing air operations against North Vietnam.

Thus, Lewis Sorley, who has done a disservice in his overall portrayal of the General, may have been partly right in his views on Westmoreland – especially during the time of the 1968 TET offensive. He just was not a risk taker, nor did he see himself as a bold strategic thinker. He had chosen a strategy that had not worked, and he must have realized that he was running out of time to continue it. However, he was unwilling to change the course he now stubbornly stuck to. Thus, as Sorley observes, "Westmoreland's strengths eventually propelled him to a level beyond his understanding and abilities."

Answering the question of why for Wheeler during this timeframe is more difficult. This is because Wheeler did not leave a memoir, and as of this time, there has not been an acclaimed, thorough biography on him. However, one can speculate on why based on the transcripts in the FRUS, several oral histories, some contemporary memoirs, and the Presidential tapes.

As already mentioned above and explained in Chapter 3, Wheeler was more a staff officer than a combat soldier. President Johnson had chosen Wheeler because he knew him to be a consummate team man. Johnson was right about him. Wheeler was an excellent team participant and chose to obtain a consensus from the Chiefs before presenting a JCS position on an issue in the Johnson White House. He had settled on his position as a messenger to the Chiefs on Presidential decisions. Because the Chiefs were not in unison on strategic alternatives – except more rigorous bombing – Wheeler chose not to bring up alternative strategies at any time unless the President asked for one or would be acceptable to one.

General Wheeler had also become an excellent bureaucrat. He had served in the Pentagon for eight straight years. He knew how his civilian superiors thought. His boss for five of those years had been McNamara. Thus, Wheeler knew that if anything sold, he would have to concentrate on the numbers. So, as mentioned in Chapter 3 and detailed in Chapter 9, he convinced Westmoreland that the CJCS would take the lead in convincing Washington's civilians to the opportunities ahead and for the increases in troop levels and a decision on reserve call-up. Wheeler had it all figured out.

But somewhere along the road, Wheeler may have panicked or just become frustrated on how to obtain the force increases. His presentation to the National Security Council on the situation in South Vietnam in late February bordered upon depicting TET as a near disaster. Afterward, he let Clifford and his team make up their minds about what to do next. He had presented the numbers and explained where they all fit – but not in a way that anyone knew whether the numbers mattered. As we know, absent any military alternative to doing more of the same, Clifford recommended the reduction of the US commitment and negotiating an end of the war. Like his predecessor, he felt the war was unwinnable.

As for the other Joint Chiefs regarding the question of why they did not push for an alternative strategy, the situation at the time relegated them to the bench or backseat of decision making. Wheeler had become their spokesman. They had seldom met with the President. Most of their focus now was not on strategic issues, but on preserving the readiness of their forces. The evidence, and the scholarly stories resulting from it, show that Interservice rivalries over the operational use of the service forces dominated their consideration of issues toward Vietnam.

Besides, McNamara had already demonstrated that he did not take the Service Chiefs' advice seriously at Congressional hearings. Moreover, as explained in Chapter 8, the Chief with the most to say on the risks and viability of the concept, General Harold Johnson, just did not want to challenge LBJ's directions. Much like Westmoreland, Johnson was content to obey orders apparently without regard to the consequences to the soldiers putting their lives at risk.

In short, though the alternative strategy had merit and offered a way to change the conflict around for the US, no military man was willing or able to offer it in understandable military terms, other than in numbers of troops, that had a chance to alter their civilian leaders' views to change their imposed restrictions and take the risks involved. Westmoreland did not see it as his role. Wheeler did not have the strategic view necessary and believed that arguing numbers would work. The JCS was too focused elsewhere.

Despite all the above speculation, there is no way of knowing whether LBJ would have chosen this new offensive strategy, especially given his state in March 1968. Smart historians remind us that 'what ifs' in history are conjectures that are often filled with assumptions about unknowns. They do not recognize, being in retrospect, that other forces, reactions, motives – unknown to the speculator - may not support the proposed supposition. Thus, as George Herring has noted, what-ifs can be a 'dubious methodology' to determine whether a result of the past could have been different.

Thus, even if LBJ had decided to choose this strategy, it is impossible to know if it would have worked and changed the course of the war and its final result. So, the question whether this 'what if' in the Vietnam War would have worked – resulting in a winnable war - at least during Westmoreland's tenure as commander – is a mute issue.

More important, at least to this author, is that the relationships between LBJ, his civilian advisors, and his military commander and advisors, precluded an in-depth discussion of this alternative; and thus, any possibility that it would be seriously considered, much less whether it would have worked. These relationships will be explored in more detail in the next chapter. They are key to understanding why America lost the war.

Section 11.4 – The Nixon and Kissinger Years: Abrams, Vietnamization, and 'The Better War'

Unlike LBJ, Richard Nixon had – even before he took over the Presidency - some ideas on how he wanted to approach the Vietnam problem he would face in 1969. Also unlike LBJ, he would not be reluctant to apply these ideas to force the North to do his bidding.

As explained in Chapter 5, Nixon thought he had to bring pressure on the North's two major supporters, Red China and the Soviet Union, to get their ally to negotiate a compromise peace to end the conflict. He also felt that more military pressure needed to be better applied to further convince the North that it was not in their interest to continue their aggression against the South. Hence, he favored some limited attacks against their sanctuaries and bases outside of Vietnam to gain some leverage at the peace tables, as well as to further apply military power to punish the North and gain time to turn over the ground war to South Vietnam.

These diplomatic and military actions were the main components of Nixon's grand strategy to end the war. There was nothing new to this combination of diplomacy and military action in grand strategies. Indeed, they were the basic parts of what Henry Kissinger knew as 'balance of power international politics." Hence, who better to pursue this approach, Nixon thought, then Henry Kissinger, whom he chose as the basic architect and executioner of this strategy.

Nixon and Kissinger early on decided to make a complete review of the Vietnam situation to further develop their 'grand strategy' for their approach to finding peace with honor in Vietnam. Hence, they sent out a survey, NSSM-1, to gather views from the field, the cabinet offices, and other agencies. Nixon and Kissinger took the results of this survey and further promulgated some of its ideas in NSSD-9, which outlined the basic tenets of the Nixon strategy specifically directed toward Vietnam and the Indochina region.

The NSSD's basic components were to continue operations against the communist forces in the South to regain and expand security there, to expand and accelerate improvements in the Armed Forces of South Vietnam, and to begin withdrawal of US forces matched to the South Vietnamese military and security improvements. The overall 'buzzword' for these parts of Nixon's grand strategy was "Vietnamization."

As discussed in Chapter 10, turning over the fighting to the South Vietnamese had already been an ongoing task from Clifford for General Abrams when the latter took over from Westmoreland in June of 1968. Moreover, Abrams had already drafted plans when Laird came to visit in March of 1969 to discuss with him the ongoing deliberations in Washington on what Nixon was thinking about in his new strategy.

Thus, for Abrams and his MACV staff, it seemed that all that needed to be done to carry out Nixon's aims in Vietnamization would be some minor alterations to their already well thought out plans. However, Laird, as we have seen, had other ideas that would clash with these early MACV plans.

Vietnamization: Another Opportunity Lost?

As detailed in Chapter 10, Abrams' plans, based on his years of experience overseeing ARVN operations and his political-military sense of what would work, were based on three major premises. The first was that any transfer of the war's operations to the ARVN would have to be based on a program to improve their capabilities. What was needed, in addition to time and opportunity, was greater US aid to modernize and improve the ARVN to make up for its lack of capabilities that US forces had, up to this point in the war, provided. These capabilities and improvements were in individual armaments - such as the American M-16 rifle - artillery, aviation, and some engineers; and certainly, the training to use them. These would also require the organization of additional units and staffs that needed further field training for operations against their enemy.

The second premise was that Abrams knew that the US had to keep the pressure on the enemy main forces primarily with American combat forces to keep them at bay for Vietnamization to continue effectively. He realized that in 1969 he finally had the strategic initiative against the PAVN and what was left of the PLAF. Thus, he wanted to continue the offensive against them to keep them off balance, while he renewed and improved the security and pacification in the countryside. Recognizing that this would take time, resources, and a continued American combat presence, any withdrawal of American forces would, Abrams knew, have to be tied to both the enemy's actions and the ARVN's progress.

The third premise of Abrams' view on a US withdrawal and ARVN take over was that there would have to be some continued US military residual presence in South Vietnam if the ARVN was ever to prevail against the North. Thus, at a minimum, the South Vietnamese military would need US advisors; maybe not of the level at its height, but at some level. Also, there would be a requirement for the US military to intervene on behalf of the South Vietnamese armed forces against any significant PAVN offensive. Those forces did not have to be ground forces, but certainly supporting air power would be necessary.

As it turned out Abrams' plans, which would give the South Vietnamese a chance to survive without major US ground combat forces, had to change dramatically. From the onset, Laird's guidance during his visit in March and later invalidated most of Abrams' premises. Indeed, one of the reasons that the US failed in Vietnam is the collective changes that altered Abrams' original concept for Vietnamization and the principles behind it.

Part of the responsibility for this lies with General Abrams. He recognized that these changes would seriously affect Vietnamization, at least in the beginning. Yet, he did not steadfastly object, at least by the current historical record, to the changes imposed upon him by Washington.

His folly was believing that despite these changes he could still succeed. He even clung to the belief that Vietnamization was working during the Cambodian incursions, and argued that because of its progress, the ARVN could succeed in Laos. Just as Westmoreland had foolishly insisted that his attrition strategy could succeed over time, Abrams insisted Vietnamization could work, despite the fact that his civilian leaders rejected his original arguments for success.

Therefore, despite their differences in demeanor and experiences, Westmoreland and Abrams were more alike in their actions in Vietnam than some historians claim. Like Westmoreland, Abrams was the obeying soldier who did not see his place as seriously challenging his superior civilian directions. Like Westmoreland, despite his military judgment to the contrary at times, Abrams continued to execute military actions with a foolish belief that he could be successful despite the evidence that he would fail.

Though the President was initially supportive of Abrams views on Vietnamization, he also soon gave in to the realization that Public and Congressional pressures clamored for more rapid withdrawal of US forces. To accommodate the more rapid withdrawal, offset the potential impact especially at the negotiating table, and to protect and reassure his South Vietnamese allies, Nixon chose to conduct military operations against the North's bases in Cambodia and Laos to prevent or delay communist military actions that could upset or derail Vietnamization. He also employed massive doses of airpower against North Vietnam and its forces.

These all failed ultimately as well. There were four major reasons. First, the Cambodian operations, because of their territorial and time limitations, did not prevent subsequent communist offensives that disrupted Vietnamization. Second, the Laotian offensive, because of lack of support from the Congress and its denial of the necessary US advisor support, was a massive failure. The result was that it prompted confidence and plans for the North's ultimate decision to launch offensives in 1972 and later in 1975 that defeated South Vietnam.

Third, Nixon and Kissinger agreed to allow North Vietnamese forces to remain in South Vietnam as part of their effort to gain a negotiated peace. They further indicated that they would not intervene militarily if there was a 'decent interval' between the final peace accords and a major North Vietnamese effort to overrun South Vietnam. Finally, the Watergate Affair led to the departure of Nixon and thus negated his promise to defend South Vietnam with massive airpower strikes in the event of a major Northern offensive.

A Better War?

The above interpretation of the failure of Abrams in his approach to Vietnamization and role in the war is counter to Lewis Sorley's accounts of the Vietnam War and his biography of Abrams. Sorley's opinions and suppositions are first that General Abrams' theater strategic approach and leadership led to a near victory in Vietnam. He claims in *A Better War* that the war was won in 1970, because of Abrams' one war concept.

In Sorley's version Westmoreland's replacement focused more on pacification and destruction of the guerrilla forces, which enabled more control over the South Vietnamese countryside. Sorley further argues that Abrams revitalized the ARVN and South Vietnamese Territorial Forces in ways that Westmoreland neglected during his command, thus enabling it to better perform against the North's regular forces, and preventing it from disrupting pacification.

Thus, in Sorley's telling, Abrams rescued the war effort by focusing operations more at the local level in which the rooting out of the VC threats and gaining support from the populace was decisive, and by revitalizing the South Vietnam armed forces. As for the failures in Vietnamization, he seems to blame that on Westmoreland, who the author claims, did not offer the necessary equipment or the tactical opportunity that would have made a difference by the seventies in their capabilities to defend against the enemy's main offensives.

Critics of Sorley and a more careful reading (and listening) of the historical record during Abrams command, support more closely the narrative presented in this story and its summary. While certainly Abrams was a leader and soldier to be admired, he was no magician. Moreover, he suffered from and made decisions based upon political restrictions and policy decisions as did Westmoreland. Like his predecessor, he did not forcibly challenge them.

Thus, the war was far from won in the late 1969 and 1970 timeframe. As pointed out in Chapter 7, Le Duan and his PAVN were merely recovering and reconstituting from the TET 68 debacle to enable the North Vietnam leader to end the war militarily through an all-out offensive at some later time.

Where Sorley seems right is that in the timeframe in which Abrams took over, there was a chance to impose further setbacks on the enemy's ability to control large areas in the South that he had seized during TET. That occasion, of course, was a result of the military defeat of the PLAF forces from TET. Taking advantage of that opportunity, Abrams' combined allied counteroffensive in the latter part of 1968, coupled with several aggressive attacks on supporting PAVN forces in the lowland areas in early 1969, made great strides in recapturing and reinstating RVN control in the countryside. As a result, the PAVN main forces were mostly, but not entirely, driven into their mountain and border sanctuaries.

In fact, Abrams, far from just focusing on pacification - as historians such as Greg Daddis and Andrew Birtle have shown - continued to push for search and destroy operations, now called 'reconnaissance in force.' However, then in mid-1969, Washington pulled the rug out from under him. Laird, with Nixon's later support, changed his mission. They ordered him, through the JCS, to cut back on offensive operations. This was, like his Vietnamization plans, against his better judgment. However, like his orders on Vietnamization, Abrams obeyed without much resistance.

Moreover, in attacking and decisively disrupting the Ho Chi Minh Trail, which was a critical part of his one war concept, Abrams faced the same problem that Westmoreland had. He too recognized that the trail was the linchpin of the North's war effort in the South. Despite the dramatic improvement in the ability to track the movements on the trail, Abrams was extraordinarily frustrated on ways to affect the infiltration of forces to the South.

Thus, when Nixon ordered the Cambodian incursions, the MACV commander was elated. But the President's orders restricted the effectiveness of this interdiction. Eventually, the enemy would reinstate its bases, forces, and their supplies in the same areas that Abrams had attacked in 1970. Like the changes to his Vietnamization plans, Abrams did not seriously object to the restrictions imposed on the Cambodian incursion. He, like Westmoreland, was an obedient soldier who would be silent on matters that ultimately cost American and Vietnamese lives and lost the war.

Because he recognized the importance the trail complex, especially so at this juncture of the war, General Abrams was an ardent supporter of the Laotian offensive. While he may have had misgivings about the ability of the ARVN to conduct such a risky operation, he favored it because of the high payoff that such an attack could have. When it failed, he lost whatever confidence and support he had with the President. He must have winced and gagged over Haig's imperial visits to Saigon. His retreats to his quarters to enjoy his scotch and classical music were undoubtedly deserved.

Once again, Dale Andrade has some interesting observations about the failure of Abrams' one war approach and comparing it to Westmoreland's attrition strategy that are most noteworthy. He writes, "Both Westmoreland and Abrams found themselves in a quandary: unless a significant part of their forces sought out the enemy main forces, there could be no security in South Vietnam. Therefore, the key to either general's plan had to be the ability to keep the main forces away from the population; whether the operational method was called 'search and destroy' or 'one war' made little difference. Judged by that standard, both generals failed. Despite the progress made by pacification in the years 1967 through 1972, it made no significant difference in the end."

Andrade further argues, "Indeed, both MACV commanders were caught on the horns of the same dilemma. While Westmoreland concentrated on the main forces and failed to prevent a guerrilla offensive in 1968, Abrams placed great emphasis on pacification and failed to prevent a conventional buildup in 1972. In the end neither commander had the resources or the opportunity to handle both threats simultaneously."

Moreover, like Westmoreland's failure to obtain approval of his alternative strategy, one should question why Abrams was not more forceful in objecting to the changes to his original Vietnamization plan and his supporting scheme of offensive operations against the enemy main forces. Unlike Westmoreland, Abrams left no memoir or statement or interview that sheds any light. The transcripts of his command meetings in the Abrams' Tapes reveal only his frustrations and further emphasize his beliefs in what should have been done, rather than any explanation why he did not try to change the imposed alterations from Washington.

As explained in Chapters 5 and 10, the most likely reason was that Abrams' relationship with Nixon, Kissinger, and Haig had deteriorated so that he felt he had no chance to contest them. His relationship with Laird was much better, but he did not challenge the Secretary, who remained adamant that they had lost US public support for the war and for leaving any military force in South Vietnam. The only conclusion that is plausible at this time is that, like Westmoreland and other senior officers of the period, he did not see it as his place to confront his civilian superiors though the consequences to American soldiers was profound.

Personal Experience and Observations, 1969 to 1970

As mentioned in Chapter 5, it was during Abrams' command that I was in South Vietnam. As an infantry platoon leader and company commander I participated in operations at the village/hamlet level, and in the base areas of the main NVA/VC forces. My first experience was with South Vietnamese regional forces. The US command referred to these as the RFs. We called them the 'rough-puffs.' Our mission was to conduct operations near the villages of a district along the coast of Binh Thuan Province, while training the RF forces in small unit tactics – mostly patrolling and ambushing techniques.

As we teamed and trained with the 'rough-puffs,' the district US advisors worked with the South Vietnamese revolutionary development teams in the villages to establish government programs. During this time, I saw that South Vietnam government officials had set up control in the larger population areas, like the district town and the province capital at Phan Thiet. However, in the villages and hamlets I operated in, the RVN government was present during daylight but retreated to the larger cities at night. That left our forces to deal with the population and any enemy at nightfall and daybreak that intruded and threatened the village population.

During the time we worked with the RFs in the villages we had no translators. American soldier contact with the population was limited. We concentrated on improving the RFs, who appeared to be interested, but only acted when American forces did. We also, on two occasions, became engaged with NVA/VC forces that attempted to infiltrate into the village and attack our positions. They wanted to show that the villages were never entirely safe from their forces.

Thus, for me, pacification was only in the eyes of the beholder. There never was complete security as long as there were enemy forces that could come from their bases and threaten the populace. There was never complete government control unless government officials permanently stayed in the villages to administer effective government programs. These two circumstances depended, furthermore, on the permanent stationing of competent forces that could defend the numerous villages and allow the above to happen on a sustained basis.

Therefore, these security and pacification operations, like the Marine CAPs described in Chapter 8, worked if you had enough forces to do the job. But our battalion was the only one in this part of the province - 600 American soldiers assigned, but only 350 in the field. There were over fifty large hamlets in the province, and hundreds of villages. It took almost an entire infantry company to patrol and defend one. So, at any one time, we could only protect three.

There were also two suspected enemy main force base areas in the mountain and forested areas near the hamlets. When we were no longer tied to the RFs and separate from the defensively oriented ARVN forces in the area, we conducted reconnaissance in force operations to find them. When we did find them often the PAVN and PLAF forces, warned of our approach, had abandoned them. We tried to destroy as much of the base as we could. Invariably, either the enemy would return to the damaged base after we had left, or found another place to create another.

On several occasions, the enemy decided to fight it out. Often that was when we had managed to move and find them, and they had no ample warning. The ensuing firefights were intense but short. Our area of operations in the province was on the coast of the South China Sea, far from the more dangerous border bases and areas. Therefore, our enemy did not have much ammunition for a prolonged battle.

Operations to find the enemy bases were in the densely jungled mountainous areas – in terrain that the French mobile forces had operated in the fifties, and earlier American units had operated from 1966 to 1968. While the terrain was the same, the enemy was different. There were no truly VC units. The enemy soldiers we fought against were all from the North. They wore VC clothing but carried NVA weapons, ammunition, and other accruements - such as a red star belt buckle or canteen. They fought bravely, but as mentioned, briefly for lack of ammunition.

After seven months, higher headquarters assigned me to the division base. This was the 101st Airborne Division (Airmobile) at Camp Eagle. As large a size as the town I grew up in, and two others nearby, Camp Eagle was like any other stateside US Army base. If I did not hear the distant artillery fire and experience an occasional rocket attack, I would have thought I was at Fort Campbell, Kentucky – the home base of the division in the States.

As mentioned in Chapter 5, there I got to meet General officers who were talking about the war. Most of their talk was about the restrictions on offensive operations to avoid casualties. The last division large operation had been MASSACHUSETTS STRIKER and had resulted in the battle of Hamburger Hill.

Their conversations were also about the inevitable. The NVA units that now lingered along the Laotian border and gathered in the A Shau Valley would eventually overrun this country. All the sweat, blood and tears would be over nothing. In 1975, it became true.

I met General Abrams while at Camp Eagle. He looked like an old soldier who was frustrated and worn down. I overheard his comments about being forced on the defensive and his anger over the Press and the 'bureaucrats' in Washington.

As previously recounted, he and his fellow general officers' greatest dismay and anger was the rapid and irresponsible withdrawal of American forces, and what they were sure would eventually follow. PAVN units were then on the western edges of the A Shau Valley, lurking and waiting for the final coup de grace.

I wondered then why Abrams, his fellow general officer subordinates, and those in Washington had not, as Westmoreland should have, pressed for bold military action to wrest the initiative from the enemy and prevent him from winning. I understand now from what I have researched.

Since then, after South Vietnam was no longer, after so many of my friends and soldiers died there, after growing old, I still wonder why our Generals did not at least try to change the directions from their civilian leaders first by trying to convince them to do otherwise – and, if failing, resigning in protest.

Section 11.5 - Conclusions

So, what can we conclude from the summary and observations in this chapter about the American policies and strategies for the conduct of the Vietnam War, and the decisions made or not made that resulted in the failure of the US to reach its aims?

The first conclusion - related to all the others that follow - is that the JFK, LBJ and Nixon Administrations never developed a comprehensive and coordinated strategy for their military activities in Vietnam and Indochina. The one President who came closest was Richard Nixon. However, though Nixon had a preconceived strategy for what he wanted to do about ending the war, he never fully coordinated it and later deviated from its basic tenets – primarily in matching US withdrawals to the security situation in South Vietnam. Overall then, George Herring's conclusion that "American strategy in Vietnam was improvised rather than carefully designed" seems correct.

The lack of a well thought out comprehensive national military strategy, and, in its absence an improvised one, was a primary reason for the US failure. Once again – it bears repetition - Clausewitz seems pertinent in reminding strategists that, "No one starts a war—or rather, no one in his senses ought to do so—without first being clear in his mind what he intends to achieve by that war and how he intends to conduct it….This is the governing principle which will set its course, prescribe the scale of means and effort which is required, and make its influence felt throughout down to the smallest operational detail."

Why was this so? First, as explained in many of the preceding chapters, JFK, LBJ, and Nixon, to various degrees, chose to not use the formal structure for setting up national security policies and strategies. They felt more at ease and believed it would be more effective, to use smaller either ad hoc or created group meetings to discuss policies and reach decisions. Of course, as President they had every right to do so. There is nothing sacrosanct about the National Security Acts that prevent them from modifying the procedures and organizations to fit a President's needs. But in making changes to their designs and intent for use, the Executive Branch of the US government needs to be aware of the drawbacks.

While using a formalized structure and process may not have resulted in or guaranteed an effective and comprehensive national strategy, it most certainly would have exposed the Presidents and their principal civilian advisors to more and broader expertise than they had access to or had ignored. This is especially pertinent to the use of the Joint Chiefs and their military staffs. However, for the structures and procedures to work there must be a relationship between civilian and military leaders and advisors that are respectful, trusted, open, and willing to accept differences and compromises. There must be a sense of shared responsibility for the derivation of policies and plans and their execution. This was completely missing throughout the Vietnam period of US military engagement from 1960 to 1975.

Another reason for not developing a comprehensive, coordinated strategy is that the Presidents did not understand the need for one; or care to spend the energy and time to develop or thoroughly coordinate one. In part this is because the Presidents, whom themselves lacked an in-depth understanding of military affairs and strategy, chose to neglect, or disregard collective military advice from the American military establishment.

There are understandable reasons for this neglect. As explained in several chapters, senior military men's attitudes over the use of nuclear weapons, disregard for political factors, and debates over Service roles and missions contributed to this disregard. However, by not being more inclusive or paying attention to a broader spectrum of advice – especially its military, all three Presidents missed some very thorough and more thoughtful insights on the problem and issues they faced in Vietnam.

For example, JFK ignored the experts in the CIA and State Department who were warning that the conflict in Vietnam was a regional issue, sustained more by Northern support and direction of the conflict in the South more than a people's dissatisfaction and insurgency. LBJ never got to see or consider the results of the Sigma War Games, the Goodpaster Study, and the JCS strategy that would have provided some alternative thinking to McNamara's and his assistants' flawed gradualism argument. Nixon never considered Abrams' plans for Vietnamization, his arguments to not change his mission statement, or CIA estimates that indicated that Northern leadership for the war was intent on a military solution to the conflict.

Moreover, Presidents sometimes sought information and recommendations from a select, even biased number of advisors who were not able to offer the full range subject area expertise. For example, for military advice, JFK relied primarily on General Maxwell Taylor who not only was biased in his views toward the flexible response concept, but became a personal friend of the family. Despite his credentials as a combat leader and soldier-scholar and his experience and language abilities in parts of Asia, he was largely ignorant of Southeast Asia; as well as many facets of joint and combined operational doctrine.

LBJ relied on General 'Bus' Wheeler. He was a competent bureaucrat and staff officer but lacked both the military experience and knowledge to recommend on matters of military policy and strategy. Besides, he acquiesced to the President's lack of attention to the JCS, and did not insist on a national military strategy that Westmoreland could have benefited from.

Finally, Nixon turned to Colonel and later General Alexander Haig, who provided him with information and recommendations that the President was predisposed to rather than what he needed to know. Haig became a substitute not only for the CJCS but, dangerously and foolishly, a substitute for the field commander in Vietnam, General Abrams.

A second conclusion on American policies and strategies is that once the LBJ Administration committed to the use of force, its senior civilian leaders gave mixed signals to their military commanders and advisors as to their political purpose. For example, the President, from time to time, said that he wanted the US military to 'kill more VC.' Yet, his restrictions seemed to contradict that aim. Besides, killing more VC was not, in of itself, a political aim.

Johnson's primary 'minister of war,' Secretary of Defense Robert McNamara, gave other directions to his commanders in the field that were from time to time different or took the President's remarks literally without due consideration for their military effect. At first, the Defense Secretary told them that he wanted US force directed at convincing the North it could not win. His intent was not just to kill more VC, but kill just enough to convince the North it could not win – a precision or abstraction that is beyond reason in war. That translated explicitly at the Honolulu Conference in early 1966 to "inflicting casualties on their forces at a rate as high as their capability to put men into the field."

McNamara's obsession with statistics drove this aim toward the absurd as the war continued. In Washington, the Secretary's statisticians toiled all hours into the night figuring out kill ratios. These became the sole calculation and factor that drove recommendations on troop deployments, resulting in 1967 with a Presidential decision not to give the forces necessary to make a change in military strategy in Vietnam. In Saigon and throughout Vietnam MACV staff officers, and commanders in the field, fixated on body counts to measure progress in the field, resulting in come cases in inflated assessments and, at times, dictating the tempo and place of military operations.

Further muddying the field of political guidance and objectives, McNamara's primary assistant, John McNaughton, sent to the Secretary a set of political purposes, which in themselves added more confusion to what the specific political intent was in South Vietnam and Indochina. For example, McNaughton's number one aim was "To avoid a humiliating US defeat (to our reputation as guarantor)." In fact, during most of the civilian-only discussions in the summer of 1965 over sending major combat forces to South Vietnam, McGeorge Bundy and Robert McNamara used 'preserve US prestige' as the chief political aim. No wonder no one knew what to do about the unfolding crisis in South Vietnam.

If all of this was not confusing enough, National Security documents had yet another statement of goals. For example, days after taking over President Johnson signed National Security Action Memorandum (NSAM) – 273. This document declared that "it remains the central object of the United States in South Vietnam to assist the people and government of that country to win their contest against the externally directed and supported communist conspiracy. The test of all US decisions and actions in this area should be the effectiveness of their contribution to this purpose."

Neither the President nor the NSC ever rescinded this political aim. In fact, in further discussions and reports in March 1964 LBJ and his senior advisors reconfirmed the political goal of preventing Southeast Asia from falling to communist aggression. Later, Westmoreland, Goodpaster, and the JCS in general used this political goal in devising the military strategies they either proposed or used, and their civilian leaders ignored or dispelled.

Further confusing the US military about what the civilian leaders wanted, were the restrictions they placed on military operations to convince the North to stop their aggression, or to preserve US prestige as a guarantor, or to assist or defend South Vietnam from a communist takeover. These restrictions affected all aspects of the operations against the Northern homeland, its lines of operations to the South, and the ground operations in South Vietnam.

Most of these, moreover, came to benefit the enemy rather than to convince him to negotiate an end to the war. Thus, they were in fact counterproductive to any 'contribution to assisting the people and government of South Vietnam to win their contest against the externally directed and supported communist conspiracy.'

For example, the restrictions dictated the nature of and the intensity of the bombing of the North's ability to conduct the war. Along with the bombing halts, US limited air operations encouraged the Communist DRV leaders to continue pursuit of their war rather than desist. Moreover, US limitations to operations in South Vietnam gave both the strategic and tactical initiative to the NVA and VC. Most critical of all, restrictions allowed the lifeline of the Ho Chi Minh Trail to continue to give sustenance to sustained operations at will against the US and ARVN forces.

From a military perspective, moreover, these limitations were contradictory to the varying political aims. How could Westmoreland kill more VC when they could withdraw at will to sanctuaries? How could MACV kill more VC than the North could infiltrate replacements as and when needed when he could not stop them? How could the commanding general in the field employ the necessary force to execute his campaign plans without timely reinforcements and mobilization?

Thus, both the confusing nature of the political aims and the imposed restrictions prohibited a sound application of military force against the North and its military throughout Indochina. The observations of Bernard Brodie in his *War and Politics* seem most appropriate here. "War takes place within a political milieu from which it derives all of its purposes." The "influence of the purposes" on the military application of force is "continuing and pervasive." Thus, in the application of force in the Vietnam War, confusion and lack of clarity of political purpose most certainly resulted in misunderstanding and lack of precision in and effectiveness of military operations.

The civilian leaders were not solely at fault for this confusion and its impacts on the application of force. LBJ's military commanders and senior advisors should have asked for more clarification and understanding of the political aims. They also should have more forcibly challenged the restrictions. In doing so, they should have shown how the logical lifting of some restrictions could have been more effective in defeating enemy forces, without raising the risk of Chinese or Soviet intervention. Similarly, they should have argued how military force may not have been appropriate or their operations effective in achieving the proposed or stated political aims.

Though this second conclusion thus far has focused on the Johnson years, a comparable situation existed in the Nixon Administration. During this time, mainly as Vietnamization and the US withdrawal were in full swing, again the US military's lack of challenge of decisions affecting the use of its forces and concepts for Vietnamization continued. In this case, Neither Abrams nor the JCS objected to the restrictions and changes to MACV's well thought out, prudent plans for Vietnamization – to include the need to tie the US military withdrawal and the ARVN improvement program to North Vietnamese military actions, and the necessity of some residual force presence after US major force withdrawals.

Furthermore, the aim to create time for Vietnamization by attacking the enemy sanctuaries failed. This was due to Nixon's imposed restrictions on the time and space allocated for the Cambodian offensive that was to create more time by crippling communist capabilities to launch any offensives toward the III Corps region. Though one can find in the Abrams tapes the MACV commander's concerns over these political impositions, the General did not effectively object to them.

A third conclusion on US national policies and strategies, directly related to the previous two, is that American involvement in Southeast Asia was based on a set of policy assumptions that drove US leaders to commit US forces to war without careful consideration of the consequences and costs. This was because, for the most part, decision-makers did not make an earnest, detailed assessment of the long-term effects of their commitment toward containment in South Vietnam or Indochina in general.

Truman began to aid the French initially because of their importance to bolstering the defense of western Europe and containment of the Soviet Union. Later he increased it because of the perceived need to contain Chinese Communist expansion in Asia due to the Korean War. In so doing he directed American policy of containment not just to Asia but committed US deterrent capability specifically to a failed effort to stem the rise of nationalism in Southeast Asia. Yet, there was no assessment of what a French failure would do to longer-term American continued involvement in the area.

While he decided not to commit direct combat forces to save the French from defeat, IKE did pledge the US to a continued and longer-term commitment to defense of Indochina and Southeast Asia. He increased American military aid and set up a NATO-like security structure to defend South Vietnam and the region around it. In doing so, US prestige as a defender of freedom from communist subjugation was now at stake. Yet, there was no detailed assessment of the long-term costs of such US assurances or the possibility of success in that commitment.

JFK not only continued that US commitment but again raised the stakes. His determination that the situation in Southeast Asia was a result of a monolithic communist offensive through supporting wars of national liberation increased America's military involvement. Kennedy, though not admitting it, further committed American troops to battle by employing significant numbers of special forces, advisors, and capable combat units such as helicopter and close air support organizations. This decision further raised the importance of and reputation of the US military to resist such aggression. US prestige was now fully committed.

From what JFK had begun, LBJ fully committed the US to armed conflict in Southeast Asia. During Johnson's tenure, the situation there seemed to confirm the need for a military ground combat commitment to the defense of South Vietnam, which was now the bulwark of US defenses against communism in Southeast Asia. LBJ increased the use of direct US military action in a confrontation that if lost, could mean defeat not only in Asia but a setback for US prestige throughout the world.

With all that was at stake, however, LBJ sought to wage a graduated approach that guaranteed for him a limited war, which would enable him, he thought, to control the costs. Yet, without a thorough assessment of the consequences of his actions from the beginning, and with no consideration of their enemy, Johnson and his civilian advisors underestimated the price in military, economic and political terms.

Nixon chose a more aggressive military approach than Johnson to gain time for his Vietnamization policy. However, he too underestimated the time, force, and political support he would need for such an enterprise. Meanwhile, his emphasis on a more aggressive and complementary diplomatic action did not account for the tenacity of his enemy, and their unwillingness to bend to his military and diplomatic pressures. In the end, his quest for a negotiated, honorable, and meaningful settlement turned out to be ruinous as well as devious. The costs in terms of US and Vietnamese lives, hardships to countless numbers of other Vietnamese and US wounded servicemen, and to the reputation and confidence in the US and its institutions were immense.

In short, the JFK, LBJ and Nixon Administrations went to war without considering the achievability of their aims and the long-term costs to the nation and its people. Here, once again, it is worthy to note Clausewitz's enduring wisdom on the need to not only consider your enemy and how you conduct a war against them, but to consider the worth of any endeavor that seeks to use military force. He states, "Since war is not an act of senseless passion but is controlled by its political object, the value of this object must determine the sacrifices to be made for it in magnitude and also in duration. Once the expenditure of effort exceeds the value of the political object, the object must be renounced and peace must follow."

While these words are more easily quoted than followed, the basic wisdom of them is profound. There must be an effort made, assessed and, most of all, considered of the human, material, and moral costs of waging a war before and while doing so. Otherwise a leader will find, as both LBJ and Nixon did, that the circumstances will force a decision that is not only unforeseen but less than desirable.

A fourth conclusion on US policies and strategies is that US military senior leaders and advisors, except for a few, acquiesced to the involvement in South Vietnam without thoughtful assessment of or argument against the utility of the American military instrument to achieve policy goals. The most noted exception and objection came from the Army's Chief of Staff, Matthew Ridgeway, during the Eisenhower Administration. Another was General Andrew Goodpaster, whose study group thoroughly evaluated what it would take "to win," and argued that to do so restrictions on force levels, mobilization, and operations in Laos had to be changed. To a lesser degree, CJCS Wheeler did approve and forward JCS war game results and proposed military strategies either warning of or against certain uses of US military force. In the cases of the Goodpaster study and the JCS November 65 strategy, however, the CJCS did not ensure that the Secretary of Defense acted upon them, or that the President had an opportunity to consider them.

During the summer of 1965 and sometimes thereafter, there was some argument over the degree of the use of force and the restrictions imposed. There was also disagreement over the lack of call-up of reserves and mobilization. But no military person, though several – notably General Harold Johnson - recognized the consequences, pushed or demanded that these crucial factors on the use of force be reconsidered or the consequences realized. Indeed, the Presidential decision to not involve the reserves was one of the most critical of the war. It drove the ability to provide the adequate and prompt deployment of the forces necessary to carry the fight to the enemy whatever the theater military strategy MACV adopted.

Moreover, when LBJ and McNamara reduced US deployments beginning as early as spring 1966, no one objected persuasively enough to contest the decision. In fact, the Service chiefs by voicing their concerns over the strain on their services, actually encouraged the reductions. Furthermore, the field commander, General Westmoreland, acquiesced to his boss over the issue of meeting his force requests, putting his faith – and folly – in the hope that the war would go on and he would eventually prevail.

The two major attempts to modify the original purpose for the employment of force during LBJ's presidency and change direction were Westmoreland's alternative strategy attempts in 1967 and after TET. However, as described, neither the President's field commander or senior military advisor presented any challenge or convincing argument to even make such an alternative possible.

During the Nixon Administration, General Abrams, similarly, did not bother to vehemently challenge the Administration over several issues that were critical to the MACV one war strategy and the execution of Vietnamization. While Abrams objected to his mission change, there is yet no evidence that he forcibly laid out the consequences of the reduction to offensive operations to his continued ability to affect pacification or improve the South Vietnamese Armed Forces. While he knew and recognized that the agreement to leave PAVN forces in South Vietnam could critically diminish the ARVN's ability to defend itself, he did not provide forceful criticism of the decision.

A fifth major conclusion is that American leaders, both civilian and military, did not know their enemy and properly take them into consideration in their policies and strategies. As we discovered, particularly in Chapters 6 and 7, there was little effort amongst the main US decision makers to gain some sense of the motives or objectives of the Communist Vietnamese leaders. After the First

Indochina War, US Presidents and their senior advisors did not even know who the DRV Communist decision makers were.

Truman and Eisenhower had dismissed the Viet-Minh leadership. They thought that Ho and Giap were taking their cues from the Soviets and the Chinese. Similarly, JFK thought that the conflict in South Vietnam was an effort of a monolithic communist policy to take advantage of wars of national liberation, and that the main directors were in Moscow and Beijing. LBJ and Nixon thought that the disposed Ho Chi Minh and Giap were still calling the shots. Thus, from the onset, US leaders did not take the North Vietnamese leaders as independent actors, seeking their own nationalistic goals, or just did not pay close attention to who was really running the North Vietnamese conduct of the war.

Moreover, LBJ and Nixon, and their principal advisors viewed their opponents' reactions to their policies and actions through their personal prisms. They did not pay serious attention to what the main North Vietnamese leaders had experienced, or that they would pay any price and bear any burden to succeed. Due to their personal beliefs and experiences, American Presidents thought, in the case of LBJ, that the communist leaders could be convinced, as rational men, to accept 'an offer that they could not refuse.' In the case of Nixon, he just arrogantly thought he was smarter than others and could force the North to desist its aggression or make them think that he would even resort to the use of nuclear weapons to win.

Again, Clausewitz' remarks seem valid, "To discover how much of our resources must be mobilized for war, we must first examine our own political aim and that of the enemy. We must gauge the strength and situation of the opposing state. We must gauge the character and abilities of its government and people and do the same regarding our own."

Without regard to the factors that Clausewitz' mentions, it is difficult to understand how American decision-makers could have expected their policies and plans to produce results. This is a particularly pertinent issue for LBJ's reliance on his gradual response policy to convince the North to give up its support for the war in the South.

Specifically, how could gradualism have convinced North Vietnam leaders to give up their war aims, if US policymakers did not understand their enemy's motives for the war, or even who was waging it? How could Westmoreland have been convinced that killing enemy soldiers in the South would persuade the enemy to give up its military aggression if he did not understand North Vietnamese reasons for their sacrifice on the battlefield, or their willingness to lose so many soldiers?

Disregard for Vietnamese custom, culture, and history also led American leaders to not understand their South Vietnamese ally. JFK and LBJ wanted the Vietnamese to build a government that was democratic and inclusive of the people in the South. They did not realize that inclusiveness was not possible of all groups that lived there – they were either too diverse, or too focused on the family unit to engage in larger community structures.

Kennedy and Johnson and their advisors, civilian and military, were further ignorant and dismissive of the Confucian heritage, and its effect on views of the Vietnamese. They did not understand the aversion to individual rights and advocacy of family and village ties. American frustration with Diem did not allow them to understand what Diem knew. That he could not, and would not even if he could build an American system in Vietnam.

The sixth and final conclusion on US policies and strategies is that civil-military relationships throughout the JFK, LBJ, and Nixon Administrations were characterized by a lack of understanding of political and military cultures and experiences. This resulted in mistrust and even disdain that led to a divisive, dysfunctional, and ineffective strategic formulation atmosphere. This atmosphere, in many ways, accounts for the lack of a coherent military strategy mentioned above, as well as the inability to judge the nature of the war and its potential costs correctly.

Indeed, the most critical reason for the US failure in the Vietnam War was that there was a huge breakdown in the interactions between civilian and military leaders and advisors. This breakdown is the central factor that resulted in all the above-summarized deficiencies and conclusions. In all three war Presidencies – Kennedy, Johnson, and Nixon - when it was the most critical time for formulating effective policies and strategies for Vietnam, there was no cohesive working relationship to ensure a thorough, candid exchange of views, and workable solutions to the difficult strategic issues confronting US leaders.

Consequently, civilian policymakers disregarded key and important military information and analyses that should have been considered and acted upon. Military advisors and commanders often became frustrated or confused on both the overall political direction of the war, and how to effectively offer and convince their civilian leaders of courses of action that may have remedied critical strategic issues and problems. With such poor relationships, and similar problems in strategic formulation, no wonder US leaders underestimated and cast aside their enemy.

Therefore, the most crucial finding of this story is that in a quest to find out what went wrong and how the US lost the Vietnam War, personal relationships, interactions, and shared responsibilities are more important factors than missed opportunities, misplaced actions, or fixing blame for mistakes. Moreover, as a corollary to this finding of the US failure in Vietnam, we need to ask what we can learn from it? Are these the most pertinent and useful lessons from Vietnam and do they still have meaning for us today? The next two chapters try to answer these questions and find lessons that we can apply in the future.

Chapter 12: The Heavy Shadow of Vietnam

Henry Kissinger wrote of America's involvement in Vietnam, "No war since the Civil War has seared the national consciousness like Vietnam. The controversies surrounding it tore the country apart while the war was raging, and its legacies shaped the national approach to foreign policy for a generation." H.R. McMaster, the author of a Vietnam history and a soldier who fought in the wars to follow, adds: "the war's legacies proved to be as profound as the war was traumatic. It led Americans to question the integrity of their government as never before. Thirty years later, after the end of the Cold War, the shadow of the American experience in Vietnam still hangs heavy over American foreign and military policy, and over American society."

This chapter examines, from this author's perspective, "the heavy shadow" the war cast on US national security policy and strategy, and its armed forces in the first two decades after its end in 1975. It first looks at the immediate aftermath of the war during which the US Armed Forces had to recover and rebuild from the agony and defeat of Vietnam. Then it surveys the results of that recovery and reconstitution up to the end of the First Gulf War, and its impact on US national security affairs.

In the Chapter's conclusion, the narrative offers insights on the lessons learned from the US defeat in Vietnam. It further explains, demonstrates, and concludes how the appropriate use of these lessons from the Vietnam War can guide US leaders, both civilian and military, in the effective formulation and execution of strategies in wartime.

Section 12.1 – Immediate Post-Vietnam Years, 1975 to 1988: America's Struggle to Find Meaning

As George Herring notes in his *America's Longest War,* "In the immediate aftermath of the [Vietnam] war, the nation experienced a self-conscious, collective amnesia." It was if President Ford's remarks on the fall of South Vietnam had at once taken hold: "Today, Americans can regain the sense of the pride that existed before Vietnam. But it cannot be achieved by re-fighting the war." Indeed, to regain that 'pride' most of America chose not to indulge in any immediate self-searching to figure out why it had lost. Instead, the seventies turned out to be a period of self-indulgence; and forgetting the war and its travails.

Of course, there was a group of Americans that could not forget. They were some of the 2.7 million men and women who had served in the war. For those who saw combat in Vietnam, the war's experience haunted them. Furthermore, unlike those who came home from World War Two, there were no jubilant or welcome home parades. Just the opposite occurred.

The soldiers who had served in Vietnam and then stayed in service endured most of the blame for the war. It seemed that the public expressed its feelings of Nixon's Watergate disgrace and the overall disillusionment with American institutions in its aftermath on those who fought the war - some spit at soldiers, called them baby killers, and ostracized their families from the communities they returned to. A 1970s' public survey rated the profession of arms just above garbage collectors.

Some scholars claim that Veteran stories of the spitting on soldiers and calling them names was a 'myth.' These are, in many cases, the same college professors who had escaped the draft and led the anti-war campaigns on their campuses. It was no myth to me when I returned home through San Francisco in 1970. It was no fable on how some Americans treated my wife, while I was serving in Vietnam. It was not some delusion on how some treated us as we drove across the country for our new assignments in the early seventies.

The treatment of America's soldiers - and their families - would eventually change for the better. The attempts to forget Vietnam would soon give way to a deep soul-searching about what had happened and why we had failed there. By the early eighties film producers, historians, political scientists, politicos, and pundits began flooding the bookshops, newspapers, magazines, journals, and movie screens with propositions about what, why, and how the war had happened and who was to blame.

For those American segments of society and institutions most affected by the war and its aftermath, the agony of defeat gave way to a rebirth of confidence, reconstitution, and reform. My journey to find out what had happened, in retrospect, was a microcosm of that larger quest for answers. Because of all of this, a plethora of lessons learned sprouted – some ridiculous; some sublime; some in between.

This section examines and summarizes the aftermath of the Vietnam War, its perceived early lessons, and its impact upon the US Armed Forces and the national security making apparatus from the fall of South Vietnam in 1975 through the Reagan Administration in 1988.

The 'All-Volunteer' Force

In 1972, the Nixon Administration actions to end the draft, begun years prior and as promised in his 1968 campaign, resulted in the end of the service induction authority. At the time, of course, this came as a relief to many who had been on the mandatory conscription rolls. For Nixon, it was a way of ameliorating the impact of the anti-war movement on his actions to end the war and to fulfill his commitments after that. The end of the draft represented one of the first major impacts of the Vietnam War on America. This action would have a lasting effect on American social, political, and military life for decades afterward and even to the present day.

The immediate effect was in America's armed forces. The end of conscripted service heralded in the all-volunteer force that we know today. For the Army, it began an era fraught with unknowns and challenges. One of the most undetermined and difficult issues was how to obtain volunteers to fill its ranks - especially considering the anti-war and anti-military climate that existed in the early seventies.

Ironically, General Westmoreland, who was the Army Chief of Staff when conscription ended, would oversee the beginning of this experiment. At first, the Army labeled this effort as VOLAR or Volunteer Army. To begin with, Westmoreland brokered with the Administration and Congress the strength and structure of the force. This was set at a lower level, at about 780,000 active soldiers, than the Vietnam Army, which had numbered around one and a half million. Then he set up a headquarters group and several stateside Army posts as experimental organizations to start the concept. Finally, he went about changing Army regulations and policies to furnish guidance in its recruiting, training, and quality of life programs that would induce volunteers into service.

Later, when General Abrams took over from Westmoreland, the new Chief reorganized and restructured the Army. Most significantly, Abrams decided to organize the active divisions, the mainstay organization of the Army (at about 15,000 soldiers each), with one of its three brigades – its main subordinate elements – as a reserve unit. Abrams also moved some key support organizations from the active force to the reserve. That way, as Abrams explained, the Army could never go to war again without some call-up of the reserves. This decision reflected yet another primary lesson from the Vietnam War – do not go to war without the involvement of the people whom the reserves stood for.

I was intimately involved in this VOLAR experiment as an infantry captain at Fort Lewis, Washington from 1972 through 1975. There I commanded the first infantry company formed of the newly reactivated 9th Infantry Division. I experienced the problems that the Army first had in this all-volunteer experiment.

My unit received the first soldiers in the division recruited under a concept known as 'unit of choice recruiting.' That concept was the Army's first step in trying the find soldiers for its main organizations. It called for each division to recruit its soldiers in the region that it had its home base, send them to regional basic training centers for their initial training, and then incorporate them into each new unit for further indoctrination.

Finding enough and the 'right kind' of volunteers was the most challenging task. In the overall Army during this first year, there were 14,000 soldiers less recruited than the organization needed to fill its active divisions. For the 9th Infantry Division in the northwest region of the US, we initially recruited enough to fill only one-third of the soldiers needed. Of the nine infantry battalions in the division in its first year, only three could be fully manned.

My infantry company, being the first to form, filled its one-hundred enlisted soldiers. However, they were not all the 'right kind.' Some could hardly read or write and became a difficult or even intractable training problem. Some, about 10%, were hardened criminals whom judges had told, "go into the Army or go to jail." We had to get rid of this cancerous criminal group as quickly as possible.

Moreover, about half of the initial entry soldiers were married, some with a child or two. This was a unique issue for the new volunteer armed forces. Previously the Army, on average, had less than 10% of its enlisted lower rank soldiers married. The problems I faced were typical of the rest of the Army. There was no on Post housing available for enlisted soldiers and their families. Finding adequate and affordable living arrangements were extremely difficult and time-consuming.

During the first several years, the signs at the Army level were that the experiment was faltering. It was painful and a slow process to get rid of the criminal element. There were barracks larcenies and drug sales to deal with. Racial tensions in American society continued to spill over to the military. There was an inordinate amount of minority blacks recruited, especially from the lower income and education segment of American youth. Black soldiers hung around together, to the resentment of some of the white recruits. Racially sparked fights broke out. Many of these incidents, and the criminality and drug use, was in the public light.

The reputation of the Army - and to a lesser degree the other services - suffered. News publicity of these actions further adversely affected the recruiting of quality first-term soldiers. The pressures on recruiters resulted in scandals where they misrepresented quotas, and, in some cases, misappropriated recruitment bonuses. Moreover, the Army did not have the budget resources to enhance recruiting efforts. Nor did it have the necessary money to improve quality of life programs for those recruited. These shortages were due, in part, to the afflictions of the mid-seventies economic crisis resulting from the Vietnam War.

In my own microcosmic experience, the one benefit that made our 'experiment' get through these problems and issues was the caliber and commitment of the Vietnam War veterans who stayed in the Service. These men had survived the war, usually had been wounded, and had undergone much public malice. Yet, they decided to still be in the Army - despite the low pay, hardships to their families, and atmosphere in America against its Armed Forces.

My sergeants - the same ones who had mostly been the young soldiers in the waning years of the war - stuck it out, dealt with the uneducated, helped get rid of the derelicts, aided the soldiers with families, and served as examples of dedicated professional soldiers to the newly recruited volunteers. They did that and got through the personnel problems to create challenging, meaningful, and rewarding training to induce the first entries worthy of retention to stay in the Army. This commitment and professionalism of the noncommissioned leaders in my outfit were prevalent throughout the other divisions in the Army by similar professional soldiers with the same dedication and grit.

By the late 70s, the Army as an institution began to find its way out of the early years of this all-volunteer force. To solve the recruiting problem, the Department of the Army formed a new Recruiting Command. The Army assigned highly qualified soldiers to lead it, supervise the recruiting, and motivate young Americans to join. The pool of recruits grew – to include more women who wanted to join and serve. Many veterans, who had tried to rejoin society and found that very difficult to do, rejoined the Army. The Department of Defense set higher education and quality standards for recruits. With the help of Congress, the Army offered more incentives.

The Army shred - to the chagrin of its 'old soldiers' to include me – some of its traditions in appearance and living conditions. Post engineers built new 'VOLAR' structures that looked more like college dorms than traditional barracks. Army post commanders oversaw the hiring of civilian contractors to perform the menial kitchen police and other soldierly duties of the past. There was a vast improvement in off-duty theaters, shops, and athletic facilities on the posts that served as home to the major divisional organizations. Soon, raises in pay levels began to kick in. Enlisted soldiers and their families began to slowly emerge out of the 'poverty level' of living as a soldier in America in the seventies.

Further driving the post-war Army on to a newly formed volunteer force was a revolution in its thinking about its future role and its training. Army doctrine - the codification of its purpose for, role in, and methods of performing the nation's common defense - began to change and focus its reason for being.

Under the leadership of such Vietnam veterans as General DePuy, who had served as Westmoreland's deputy for operations and later as a division commander in Vietnam, that doctrine, with its supporting training manuals, refocused the Army's future on fighting a war in Europe against its most important foe – the Soviet Union. In support of that doctrine and its implementing training directives, the Army built new training centers that revolutionized how its organizations trained to fight its future wars. Many future Army leaders and Vietnam veterans took part in this revolution. It would serve them well in the two decades after the Vietnam War.

By the early eighties, the volunteer force experiment began to take hold. While there were still some units that could not be fully manned or equipped, America's armed forces had survived some very trying years. The worst years seemed behind. For those at the Army institutional level, to include the senior officers, and those at the field level from senior Colonels to the sergeants that made it materialize, much of what happened to make this all-volunteer concept work was in memory of those who had fallen on the battlefields of Vietnam. Indeed, the lost cause of the Vietnam War became the motivation for a new Army that would emerge at the end of the eighties.

Vietnam Syndrome

In addition to affecting its military, the war, in George Herring's words, "shattered the Cold War consensus that had existed since the late 1940s" in America. Immediately after the war ended for the US, support for Government actions abroad that could lead the US into another conflict came to an abrupt halt. Reflecting the public mood, the Congressional 'War Powers Act,' passed in the fall of 1973, required the President to notify Congress within 48 hours of committing armed forces to military action. It forbade the US Armed Forces from remaining for more than 60 days after any commitment without a Congressional authorization for the use of military force or a declaration of war by the United States.

This loss of support for the use of military force in foreign policy and international action was not just because the American people had become disenchanted with military conflicts. It was also due to the loss of faith of the public in its leaders and institutions, especially the President of the US and the Executive Branch. This was not just because of the Vietnam War, but was also due to the entire Watergate Affair and Nixon's resultant resignation.

Adding to the humiliating twin events of the lost war in South Vietnam and a President's resignation, were the economic woes that besieged the country. LBJ's decision to fund both a war and a flurry of social programs during the sixties, without a corresponding rise in taxes, brought upon a severe period of inflation in the seventies. This double-digit inflation, as well as a crisis in the middle east that brought on an oil embargo that seriously affected American dependence on the automobile, 'shattered' more than the Cold War consensus. It severely affected American family pocketbooks. Besides the rise in the cost of gasoline, there was also a significant increase in the cost of a home mortgage.

The great boom of the post-Second World War, described in Chapters 1 and 4, came to a screeching halt. Along with it, the grand expectations of the decades following the Second World War also deflated; replaced by a sense that America's greatest days were behind her - cloaked in the gloom and despair caused by its failure in Vietnam.

The Vietnam wartime concerns of all three Administrations – that US prestige was at stake and its loss of the war could undermine it – seemed confirmed as the seventies unfolded. Allies in Europe and Asia became concerned over the American public mood. A drastic reduction in US defense spending further showed a lack of interest in international security commitments and issues.

Concern turned to alarm when the Soviet Union became more adventuresome in the Middle East – supporting Egypt in its war against Israel. Meanwhile, the Soviets also significantly increased its military power in eastern Europe. It further reasserted itself in the western hemisphere, with Cuba and Nicaragua; and expanded its influence in Africa in such places as Angola. Then, in 1979, it invaded Afghanistan. To many in America of the political right, the loss of prestige from the Vietnam War defeat contributed to this alarming spread of communist influence and power in the world.

The most celebrated symbol of the apparent American paralysis in foreign affairs and its neglect of the military in the post-Vietnam War years of the seventies was the seizure of American embassy personnel in Tehran in November 1979. Resulting from Iranian militant reaction to US medical treatment of the exiled Shah of Iran, Iranians stormed the US embassy and seized 52 American hostages. They stayed hostages for over a year, with the US President, Jimmy Carter, unable to do anything to gain their release. An American military operation to free the hostages was unsuccessful. That result was proof not only the helplessness of US foreign policy, but the inadequacies of American military power.

The Iranian Hostage crisis became the embodiment of a term that emerged from this period in American history – the 'Vietnam Syndrome.' It is not exactly clear how the term came to mean 'a paralysis in the use of force to seek foreign policy objectives resulting from the Vietnam War experience.'

According to Christian Appy in his *American Reckoning*, the term evolved from an early 1970s medical diagnosis referring to the psychological distress of post-Vietnam War veterans. Physicians began to label that condition as 'post-Vietnam syndrome.' That term equated to then what today people know as Post Traumatic Stress Disorder or PTSD. As Appy explains, this terminology later morphed into a shorter and different meaning phrase simply called, the 'Vietnam Syndrome.' In its first known public use in an article in *Business Week* magazine published in March 1979 that phrase became synonymous to "The Decline of US Power."

The phrase caught on. As Professor Appy notes, the term's most famous application was in Ronald Reagan's speech to the Veterans of Foreign Wars after the Iranian hostage crisis in 1980. Reagan equated the "Vietnam syndrome" not only with a reluctance on the part of the American public to support US military interventions, but also with feelings of guilt and doubt over the morality of America's intentions and actions during the Vietnam War. He argued that America had fought for "a noble cause," blaming the war in Vietnam exclusively on North Vietnam's aggression.

The future President further said: "For too long, we have lived with the 'Vietnam Syndrome.' Much of that syndrome has been created by the North Vietnamese aggressors who now threaten the peaceful people of Thailand. Over and over they told us for nearly 10 years that we were the aggressors bent on imperialistic conquests. They had a plan. It was to win in the field of propaganda here in America what they could not win on the field of battle in Vietnam. As the years dragged on, we were told that peace would come if we would simply stop interfering and go home."

Reagan continued to elaborate that "It is time we recognized that ours was, in truth, a noble cause. A small country newly free from colonial rule sought our help in establishing self-rule and the means of self-defense against a totalitarian neighbor bent on conquest. We dishonor the memory of 50,000 young Americans who died in that cause when we give way to feelings of guilt as if we were doing something shameful, and we have been shabby in our treatment of those who returned. They fought as well and as bravely as any Americans have ever fought in any war. They deserve our gratitude, our respect, and our continuing concern."

He then expounded on a lesson of that war that was contrary to all that had been said in the aftermath of US defeat. Reagan said, "There is a lesson for all of us in Vietnam. If we are forced to fight, we must have the means and the determination to prevail or we will not have what it takes to secure the peace. And while we are at it, let us tell those who fought in that war that we will never again ask young men to fight and possibly die in a war our government is afraid to let them win."

The Nightingale's Song

A young journalist and Vietnam Veteran Marine by the name of Robert Timberg, who had been severely wounded and burned by a landmine during the war, first noticed Reagan's speech while he was covering Jimmy Carter's campaign headquarters in the 1980 presidential election. As Timberg recalls, he was talking to some of Carter's young campaign aides when they started to ridicule an article they had posted on a wall in their headquarters that demonstrated the "looniness of the GOP standard bearer" at the time. The article's headline was "Reagan Calls Vietnam Noble Cause."

Timberg, whose first reaction to the article had been how could Vietnam have been a noble cause, saw "red" when "Reagan's remark was met with ridicule not just by the Carter aides but by press colleagues who dismissed it with superior grins and smug putdowns, the newsroom equivalent of boos and hisses."

A few years later, after Reagan became President, Timberg further recalled that emotional reaction to the 'Noble Cause' article at Carter's campaign headquarters. He also thought about the new President's remarks afterward about Vietnam, and how they touched many Vietnam veterans. He decided to write a book about his Naval Academy classmates who also had fought in the war, and how they had not only reacted to Reagan's words of praise but also had decided to rejoin the cause by serving in the Reagan Administration. He called it, *The Nightingale's Song*.

As Timberg explains in that book, his choice of the title reflects the scientific fact that a "Nightingale has a template in its brain that contains all the notes for the music [it knows and can sing], but that the bird cannot sing unless its song is triggered by another nightingale." Thus, like the nightingale who does not know the song until it hears it from another, Vietnam Veterans remained silent until their 'nightingale,' Ronald Reagan, sang their song that the war was a noble cause.

As Timberg further explains - to him, his academy brethren he writes about, and many Vietnam Vets – "the Nightingale's Song, as rendered by Ronald Reagan, did more than recast the Vietnam War as a noble cause. Throughout that 1980 campaign and well into his presidency, Reagan regularly portrayed servicemen not as persons to be feared and reviled – ticking time bombs, baby-killers, and the like – but as men to whom the nation should be grateful, worthy of respect and admiration. To the men of the armed forces, he had a single, unvarying theme: I appreciate what you have done. The whole nation does. Wear your uniforms with pride."

The Reagan Presidency began a new era for Vietnam Vets. It rejuvenated them, made them feel proud of their service in Vietnam, and to show their pride in their continued service once again. Those who had stuck it out in the military during the bleak seventies began to feel that the soldier was no longer the scapegoat of the American seventies' doubts and despairs.

For me, one of the most significant symbols of the recovery of pride, was when the Army uniform regulations changed in the early eighties. Previously, just after the Vietnam War ended, service regulations prohibited soldiers from wearing their uniform in public places – primarily to escape either embarrassment of a civilian's adverse reaction, or to avoid provoking such a response. In the early eighties, authorities revoked that order.

Reagan did more than rejuvenate the military's spirit and sense of pride. He significantly raised the defense budget. Increases in military pay doubled in some cases. Enlisted married soldiers, who had lived well below the poverty line, now could support their families. Senior noncommissioned officers and mid to higher grade officers could afford decent off-post housing.

The Army and other Services began to modernize their old Vietnam War equipment and major systems. This was the time that the Abrams tanks, Bradley fighting vehicles, and Apache and Blackhawk helicopters – made so famous later – came into the inventory. These personnel and equipment improvements, along with a revolution in training, would dramatically change the Armed Services by the end of the eighties.

Meanwhile, the Army and other branches of the US Armed Forces had a new mission. Before he had left office, Carter confronted the Soviet threat in the Middle East by proclaiming that area as vital to the interests of the US. Accordingly, he charged the American military with the defense of countries in the middle east should the Soviets decide to spread their control further than Afghanistan.

This new mission called for an influx and enhancement of the ability to project military power into areas, unlike Europe, which did not have the infrastructure to sustain military forces. The Defense Department began to fund significant programs for new airlift, sealift and prepositioning of equipment outside of the NATO area. These programs would have a dramatic effect on future operations into the last decade of the nineties and this century.

Beirut, Grenada, and the Goldwater-Nichols Act

While willing to use the American military to engage in operations in support of foreign policy goals, the Reagan Administration's application of military force would be fraught with difficulties. Some of this resulted from the extended period of languish and neglect in the military following the aftermath of Vietnam. Some of this was a lack of understanding in defining clear objectives and missions that should have been learned from the Vietnam experience.

The first of these was the Beirut peacekeeping mission in Lebanon. In the early fall of 1983, because of a conflict between the Israeli military and Iranian and Syrian-backed forces in Lebanon, President Reagan ordered US Marines to take part in an international peacekeeping force to separate these warring factions.

Reagan's cabinet was divided in their advice for this military deployment. His Secretary of State George Schultz, a proponent of getting the US more involved in international affairs, supported the participation. His Secretary of Defense Casper Weinberger opposed the mission. The latter, rightly so in retrospect, argued that US support for Israel in its attack on Lebanon would put US troops in a dangerous position. This was because the Muslim factions in Lebanon would see the US as a supporting force for Israel. In that case, they may use force against them.

Reagan chose to support Schultz. He approved the dispatch of a Marine Battalion Landing Team to take part in the peacekeeping mission with French and Italian forces.
After the Marines landed the situation soon worsened. Rather than just offering separation of the factions that could lead to some UN settlement, the various groups in Lebanon, primarily minority Christian and several Muslim majority factions, came into conflict. The Marines and other UN forces found themselves inserted in a violent Civil War.

Making the situation worse was the presence of some Iranian-sponsored outside Muslim militant organizations. Instead of withdrawing the Marines, the Reagan Administration continued to think that the persistent presence of American forces would eventually lead to some resolution in the fighting. The Marines higher command transmitted new orders to the Marines there to provide 'presence.' No one understood what that meant; especially difficult was for the Marines to understand what security measures they were authorized to institute for such a mission.

That presence did not assure anyone to keep the peace. Soon the exact opposite occurred. Against the advice of the Marine Commander present, US warships off the coast of Lebanon fired against targets that the overall US commander in the region perceived as threatening the Marines in Beirut. Muslim militias and militant groups saw this American use of force as further evidence of overall US support of the Christian Lebanese forces. American forces now became a prime target for Muslim militants.

On 23 October 1983, a truck drove into to the Beirut International Airport, where the US Marines had their base. Once onto the airport the driver, who turned out to be an Iranian national and suspected member of the Iranian guard, further maneuvered his truck - loaded with about 21,000 TONS of explosives - toward the Marine barracks. The truck passed between two sentry posts. It then drove through an open gate in the perimeter fence and crashed through a guard shack in front of the building. The vehicle finally smashed into the lobby of the building serving as the barracks for the 1st Battalion, 8th Marines and exploded.

The sentries at the gate had been operating under strict rules of engagement. They could not fire upon anyone unless fired upon. This situation had made it very difficult to respond quickly to the moving vehicle. They did not have their weapons loaded. Thus, they were not able to stop what they had initially thought was supposed to be a routine water truck supplying the barracks.

The force of the explosion collapsed the four-story building into rubble, crushing many inside. 241 Marines perished. Afterward, in retaliation for the bombing, the USS New Jersey battleship fired 300, 16-inch shells at Syrian militants thought to be responsible for the bombing. In February of 1984, President Reagan, recognizing the futility of their presence, finally withdrew the Marines.

In this incident, unlike the Iranian hostage rescue attempt, the failure of the American force mission was not due to unit readiness flaws. Despite President Reagan's investment in rebuilding the US Armed Forces, the Beirut employment of US Marines and the later terrorist bombing of their barracks showed how little experience the Reagan Administration had in giving clear, meaningful missions to its military. For many Vietnam War veterans, the episode proved what can happen when there is a lack of clarity in purpose for military operations. Many invoked the perceived lessons of what happened in Vietnam, where many veterans believed that there was no clear mission and it had led to defeat.

The lesson to several Vietnam military veterans now in senior positions, was the tragedy in Beirut showed that need for clear and specific missions and objectives was still an issue. They - particularly those who were now occupying key uniformed senior positions - were intent on avoiding this lesson in the future.

The Beirut bombing of the Marine barracks and its aftermath coincided with the first employment of US forces in a large operation since the Vietnam War. This was the Grenada invasion, or as the military labeled it, OPERATION URGENT FURY. This operation would involve elements of an Army division, several battalions of special forces, a Marine amphibious group, over seven ships of a Navy carrier battle group, and several Air Force wings. The total troop commitment consisted of over 7,600 soldiers, sailors, marines, and airmen.

Grenada is a small island just one hundred miles off the northern coast of Venezuela. It had gained its independence from the British in the seventies. Throughout the latter part of that decade, the new state struggled to gain some stability in governance. A leftist organization had gained power in 1979. Subsequently, it set up ties to a new Cuban adventurous movement in the Caribbean and Central America area supported by the Soviets.

In the early eighties, an internal power struggle again developed between that leftist faction and a new revolutionary group seeking reform. The latter had gained power briefly, but leftist reactionaries in 1983, supported by the Cuban military, seized control after killing the revolutionary group leader.

President Reagan, after he had taken over, began speaking out on the Soviet-supported Cuban threat in the Caribbean and Central America. He specifically noted the development of new military capable airfields in Grenada and Nicaragua, which could handle Soviet heavy transports and bomber aircraft. When the Grenadian leftists seized power in October 1983, Reagan ordered a US military force to attack Grenada to restore a democratic government. The mission was also to rescue several hundred American students attending a medical school there who seemed threatened.

That mission fell to the US Commander of the Atlantic Command; a four-star Admiral based in Norfolk, Virginia. He formed a task force under his Second Fleet Commander to conduct the operation. The Army, Air Force and Marine forces under the Fleet Commander came from the newly formed Rapid Deployment Joint Task Force stationed primarily along the east coast. The

American military had formed this RDJTF in the late seventies in response to the need to develop forces that could deploy to defend against Soviet and other threats primarily to the Middle East.

The plan for the invasion was to conduct a simultaneous attack on the principal airfields and the military unit locations that had threatened American students and the deposed Grenadian government officials. Army Rangers and airborne forces would attack the large Point Salines International Airport on the southern end of the island. They would then attack suspected locations of Cuban paramilitary forces nearby.

Marines would conduct an amphibious assault to seize a small airfield, called Pearls airport, on the eastern end. They would then attack the nearby location of Grenadian military forces. Meanwhile, Special Forces units would helicopter assault to free and secure the students and government officials at two separate locations. Finally, Naval forces would cordon off the island to ensure that no Cuban reinforcements could counter the invasion.

The invasion started in the early hours of 25 October 1983. From the onset, things went wrong. Heavy seas caused the Navy seals sent to scout the Salines airfield to drown. Significant anti-aircraft and ground fire met the Army Rangers parachuting on to Salines airfield. Special operations helicopters also ran into intense anti-aircraft fire and could not land where they believed the students were. The only success on the first day was where the Marines landed near Pearls' airport and had not met any resistance.

In the attempts to change his plans the Task Force commander ran into significant difficulties. The makeshift joint staff formed for the task force had problems in understanding each other's operating and planning methods. Army, Marine and Air Force units could not always talk to one another. They used different communications equipment that was incompatible. At one point, there was a need to use Marine helicopters to move Army forces. That move became difficult and delayed because of different Service command and control procedures.

Though they did not execute their plans as envisioned, senior commanders with combat experience succeeded in getting forces to their objectives. US rangers finally rescued the students. They also freed and reinstated the Grenadian officials. Friendly losses were light with 19 Americans killed in action and 116 wounded. Cuban forces lost 25 killed, 59 wounded, and 638 captured. Grenadian force casualties amounted to 45 killed and 358 wounded.

The one major event of the invasion that seemed to capture the attention of the American public was the freeing of the US students. Several had rejoiced when the Army Rangers arrived. Media reporters captured this and later displayed the students' warm greetings on American TV. It seemed that for a moment at least, the American public attitude toward their military may have taken a turn for the better from the latter days of the Vietnam War.

The American military and Congress scrutinized the failures in the Iranian hostage and Grenadian operations. Both operations had shown a severe lack of interoperability between Service units and a cumbersome military high command structure. Both were, in large part, due to Service rivalries and lack of cooperation in building systems and command structures that could provide wartime operational effectiveness between the Services. Many of these failures seemed to be the same experience during the Vietnam War. Service parochialism and differences were very much alive and well in the US military culture.

To address these failures and operational lessons, as well as some difficulties and waste in defense procurement as the defense budget expanded, Congress formed a task force to study the overall Defense Department structure and the National Security Act responsibilities and powers. This work resulted in the Goldwater-Nichols Act of 1986.

This legislation was the most significant effort to reform the national security organization since the National Security Acts of the forties and early fifties.

To correct the lack of effectiveness in strategic advice and planning, the Act made the Chairman of the Joint Chiefs the principal military strategic advisor to the President. The JCS would still collaborate and make recommendations on strategic issues, but the Chairman was now solely responsible to the President and his Secretary of Defense for the resultant recommendations. The Commander-in-Chief was now to focus on one uniformed military advisor for military strategic development and planning and not a council of military advisors who had a stake in their own service's future.

The Act also sought to decrease the JCS focus on Service programs dominated by their Chiefs of Staff. Such a focus had often resulted in parochial bickering, arguments over the primacy of specific programs and budgets, and decisions that resulted in less than optimal compromises. These, as we have seen, were some of the same problems experienced in the Vietnam War.

While the Service Chiefs still had primacy over what was best for their specific Service in organizing, training, and providing their forces, the Chairman would now make the final recommendations to the President and Secretary of Defense, in consultation with the military field commanders, on their employment. The intent was for the Chairman to offer a recommendation that was not on what would satisfy all the Services, but what would be operationally effective for the multi-service joint force to execute a mission to achieve national strategic objectives.

To enhance this new role of the Chairman, the new law stipulated that the Joint Staff was now to be the Chairman's staff; and not a staff for all the Chiefs. Now the Joint Staff would take its direction from the CJCS as the President's principal advisor. It was to produce products and recommendations for the Chairman, and not for the entire JCS as a council of equals.

The Act further created a Vice Chairman who was to aid the Chairman in offering assessments, priorities, and advice on budget and programming issues. The intent here was to offer a joint perspective across Service programs on what would best improve effectiveness when the Service Branches operated together as a joint force – such as being able to talk on their radios together. To further enhance this joint outlook, the Commanders of the major geographic regions, who were responsible for the employment of the armed forces in their area, had new roles in the programming and budgeting process.

The impetus of Goldwater-Nichols was the recent operational lessons learned and a dire need to reform the defense budget and acquisition systems. However, the problems the Act addressed were significant strategic and command and control issues also experienced during and since the Vietnam War. These problems were service parochialism, unclear lines of command, and lack of field commanders' involvement in resource issues affecting their abilities to carry out their missions.

Section 12.2 – Vietnam War Lessons Learned Applied: Panama, 1989

It was during the time of rejuvenation in the early to mid-Eighties – in this period of the 'Nightingale's Song' – that my West Point classmates and I became field grade officers commanding battalions and brigades instead of leading platoons and companies as we had in Vietnam. It was during this period that field grade officers of the Vietnam War – like Norman Schwarzkopf and Colin Powell - became general officers.

Indeed, the senior command structure – Colonels through Generals - of the American military in the last decade of the 20th and the first decade of the 21st Century would now consist of those who had fought in Vietnam and experienced the aftermath and recovery from that war. They brought into those senior positions their views on why America had failed in Vietnam and vowed not to repeat them.

Lessons Learned Emerge

During the seventies, despite the public attitude to forget the war, there had been some works written on Vietnam. These were primarily early reactions to the US involvement and resultant failure in the war. In general, they were written by journalists who had served in Vietnam; several biographies and memoirs from those who had served in the three Administrations; and some Cold War historians who tried to place Vietnam in the perspective of communist containment.

The most notable ones were David Halberstam's, *The Making of a Quagmire: America and Vietnam during the Kennedy Era (1965)* and *The Best and the Brightest (1972)*; Arthur Schlesinger's *Thousand Days: JFK in the White House (1965)*; LBJ's *Vantage Point (1971)*; Henry Kissinger's *The White House Years (1979)*; and George Herring's first edition *America's Longest War: The United States and Vietnam, 1950-1975 (1979)*.

These early views had dominated attitudes about how and why we got involved in Vietnam, and the lessons we should have derived from the decisions that led to that involvement and defeat. Not surprisingly, because of the mindsets of the American journalists and intellectuals who wrote such works, the general conclusions were that Vietnam was a needless and unwinnable war.

Furthermore, these authors had further concluded that the US could not have won due to two reasons. The first was because of the ineptness and corruption of the South Vietnamese. The second was a result of the arrogant, gradual, and ill-advised policies and strategies of the various US Presidents and their advisors. These works also generally argued that we wrongfully got involved because we misread the nature of the war (i.e., it was primarily a revolutionary war fought by nationalists against a puppet regime) and because it was never in the US national interest to do so.

These views and attitudes, referred to by historians as the orthodox view of the war, continued into the early eighties in such works as Stanley Karnow's *Vietnam: A History (1983)*; Neil Sheehan's *A Bright and Shining Lie: John Paul Vann and American in Vietnam (1988)*; and John Lewis Gaddis' *Strategies of Containment: A Critical Appraisal of Postwar American National Security Policy (1982)*.

However, several books in the eighties soon began to question the validity of the view that the war was wrong and unwinnable. Two specific works addressed this issue: Harry Summers' *On Strategy: A Critical Analysis of the Vietnam War (1982)*, and Andrew Krepinevich's *The Army and Vietnam (1986)*. Interesting enough, both authors were or had been Army officers. Colonel (Retired) Summers had also fought in South Vietnam and had taken part in the American delegation to oversee the Paris Peace Accords. Their service was the one thing they had in common. Their views on how the war was fought and lost, however, differed significantly.

Krepinevich argued that the US did not conduct the war properly because the American armed forces fought it conventionally, rather than focusing on waging a counterinsurgency conflict. He contended that Westmoreland's military strategy sought to engage the enemy's main forces rather than focusing on winning the war against the guerrillas and pacifying the countryside. The implication here was that if the military command had devised a different military strategy and the American forces employed differently, then the US may have won the war.

Summers also thought that the war could have been won; if it had been fought differently. Using Clausewitz's analytical framework, he argued that the civilian leaders made some significant strategic policy mistakes that could have altered the outcome. One was the failure to mobilize the nation in support of the war. Another was that they misjudged the nature of the war. In Summers' view, the war was conventional. Thus, if the US civilian leaders had focused more on the conventional threat of the Northern aggressor by decisively bombing its infrastructure from the beginning and cutting the Ho Chi Minh Trail, the US could have won the war. The author's main suggestion was that civilian leaders and their military advisors failed to follow Clausewitz' principles of the use of military force to win.

Thus, by the latter part of the eighties, arguments over whether the US should have gotten involved in Vietnam, could have won the war, why it did not, and who was at fault for the US failure there had fallen into two major camps. Such is the case today. However, what is important to what follows is that several senior military men who had fought in Vietnam were able to draw upon their own ideas and lessons learned in their service there to incorporate into military doctrine and apply to future conflicts.

The Weinberger and Powell Doctrines

The senior officer who brought his own Vietnam War lessons to bear upon the events of the mid-eighties to mid-nineties was General Colin Powell. Powell was born in New York City just before the Second World War into a Jamaican immigrant family. In his autobiography, *My American Journey*, he recalls memories of that war, in which his uncle fought with an armored division in Europe.

His fascination with his uncle's accounts of the war motivated him to be a soldier. Consequently, the young Powell joined the ROTC program at the City College of New York. After his graduation, he went into the Army and chose the infantry.

The future Chairman of the Joint Chiefs first assignments were typical to a young infantry lieutenant at the time – serving a tour in Europe early on, and an assignment in the states preparing to go to deploy to Europe should the Soviet Union attack NATO. Many stateside assignments at the time were at Army posts in the South. The black officer Powell experienced prejudice that was then prevalent in such cities as Columbus, Georgia near Fort Benning, where all infantry officers went to branch schooling and airborne school. Nevertheless, he enjoyed serving in the Army where he had his opportunity to serve just like those of all races and creeds.

As a Captain in 1962, he deployed to South Vietnam, where he served as an advisor in the ARVN 1st Infantry Division. When he returned to Vietnam in 1968, he served as a division staff officer as a Major after the main TET offensive had ended. Like most company and junior field grade officers who served in Vietnam, his war and post-war experiences would leave an indelible mark on his remaining service.

Powell, because of his dedication and competency, rose through the ranks rapidly. After Vietnam, he served in several positions under influential Army leaders who were involved in the post-war recovery. His first significant command was under the legendary General "Gunfighter' Emerson, who was one of the most notable and decorated Army leaders from the Vietnam War. Emerson groomed him for further responsibilities and service in the Army of the late seventies and early eighties.

Powell also attended graduate school at Georgetown University, where he received an MBA and, in his words, "a large dose of anti-war feelings on campus." His service and reputation gave him an opportunity to get into the prestigious White House Fellow Program.

It was as a member of that program that now Colonel Powell began a series of assignments, while still on active duty, which involved influential political figures. For example, during the Fellow Program, he went to the Office of Management and Budget (or OMB), a government agency that oversaw the vast federal budget. There he served with the agency's head and its deputy – Casper Weinberger and Frank Carlucci. These two men would later hold important defense department positions in the Reagan Administration. They would call on Powell to help them with military matters.

While at the OMB, as he recounts in his memoir, Powell learned much about government service and bureaucracies. One of the lessons he took with him was: "Organization doesn't really accomplish anything. Plans do not accomplish anything, either. Theories of management do not much matter. Endeavors succeed or fail because of the people involved." He also visited such places as the Soviet Union and China – experiences that enlightened him on these cultures and histories.

Powell's career rotated between high-level assignments in the Pentagon, the Executive building next to the White House, and the US military. His Army field assignments gave him the perspective he needed to keep in touch with his first love – soldiers and command. He had his battalion duty in Korea, and a brigade at Fort Campbell, Kentucky.

He also attended the Service Schools that kept him abreast of military doctrine and strategic concepts and theory. While at the Command and General Staff College at Fort Leavenworth, Kansas he got to know Colonel Harry Summers. At the National War College, he studied and later used the ideas of Carl Clausewitz, the grandfather of all military theorists.

Powell was a dedicated and serious student and graduate of his professional military schools. Unlike many military students, who saw their schooling as a respite between arduous assignments, he took his studies seriously and recognized their utility in his later service. Furthermore, he retained what he learned. Again, unlike many officers attending their military schooling, he did not look at what he learned as merely theoretical and something to be discarded in the 'real world' of soldiering.

In 1978 Colonel Powell had been serving as a military assistant to one of the Assistant Defense Secretaries in the Carter Administration. He then went with one of his bosses to the Department of Energy. While there the Army promoted him to Brigadier General. When the Reagan Administration came in, he hoped to get back to troops, but the new President had decided to make Casper Weinberger his Defense Secretary, who in turn appointed Frank Carlucci as his Deputy.

Because the new Deputy knew him, and he was still in Washington, Powell became Carlucci's senior military assistant. After a brief tour as an assistant Division commander followed by an assignment at Fort Leavenworth from 1980 to 1983, he once again returned to the Pentagon. This time he was Secretary of Defense Weinberger's senior military aide.

During these Washington tours, now General Powell could watch the country's civilian leaders perform during some of the crises previously mentioned. He observed and learned how senior government officials tended to act. When he was with the Carter administration, he could see some of the decision making and reactions to the Iranian hostage rescue fiasco. As Carlucci's and then Weinberger's military assistant, he saw how the Beirut and Grenada operations unfolded, and the effects of the aftermath.

In his memoirs, Powell recalls of the Iranian hostage rescue, "You have to plan thoroughly, train as a team, match the military punch to the political objective, go in with everything you need—and then some—and not count on wishful thinking." On the Beirut situation, he remembered, "I was developing a strong distaste for the antiseptic phrases coined by State Department officials for foreign interventions which usually had bloody consequences for the military, words like 'presence,' 'symbol,' 'signal,' 'option on the table,' 'establishment of credibility.' Their use was fine if beneath them lay a solid mission. But too often these words were used to give the appearance of clarity to mud."

He also describes his reaction to URGENT FURY. He writes, "Relations between the services were marred by poor communications, fractured command and control, Interservice parochialism, and micromanagement from Washington. The operation showed how far cooperation among the services still had to go. The invasion of Grenada succeeded, but it was a sloppy success."

Powell observed that of all the crises the one that affected Secretary Weinberger most was the Beirut disaster. As mentioned, the Defense Secretary had recommended against it because he did not see the insertion of the Marines as a practical military option. As his assistant, Powell saw firsthand the Secretary's reaction.

He recalls in his memoirs, "I knew that Weinberger, for all his outward self-possession, had been deeply troubled by the tragic bombing of the Marine barracks in Beirut. I did not realize how deeply until a singular draft document came out of his office. He asked me to take a look at it and circulate it to the administration's national security team."

The General further remembered that "Weinberger had applied his formidable lawyerly intellect to an analysis of when and when not to commit the United States military forces abroad. He was put off by fancy phrases like 'interpositional forces' and 'presence' that turned out to mean putting U.S. troops in harm's way without a clear mission. He objected to our troops being 'used' in the worst sense of that word. He had come up with six tests for determining when to commit American forces."

These tests, as Powell refers to them, were a list of considerations that Weinberger thought any decision maker should consider before committing American forces to a crisis. Reagan's Defense Secretary announced them in an address to the National Press Club on November 28, 1983.

As Powell recalls, "I went with him to hear him describe the tests he recommended when we are weighing the use of U.S. combat forces abroad. (1) Commit only if our or our allies' vital interests are at stake. (2) If we commit, do so with all the resources necessary to win. (3) Go in only with clear political and military aims. (4) Be ready to change the commitment if the objectives change, since wars rarely stand still. (5) Only take on commitments that can gain the support of the American people and the Congress. (6) Commit U.S. forces only as a last resort."

Powell's comments on these tests are revealing. In his *American Journey,* he says, "Clausewitz would have applauded. And in the future, when it became my responsibility to advise Presidents on committing our forces to combat, Weinberger's rules turned out to be a practical guide. However, at the time of the speech, I was concerned that the Weinberger tests, publicly proclaimed, were too explicit and would lead potential enemies to look for loopholes." Later, when asked about the Weinberger tests and his thoughts, he again invoked Clausewitz and reiterated his thoughts on using doctrine as a sound basis for the employment of force.

These comments are revealing because Powell was not thinking about these tests as a laundry list of things that had to be checked off before committing forces. Instead, he thought that several of Weinberger's thoughts reflected what he had learned from Clausewitz's teachings. The most important revelation here is that Powell was not going to be someone who relied on sacrosanct tests; instead, he reflected on his own gained wisdom on Clausewitz's ideas on the use of force based on his military education.

In short, the future Chairman knew that theory, doctrine, and guidelines had utility, but only if one does not follow them blindly. That is, as Clausewitz emphasizes to his readers, "Theory cannot equip the mind with formulas for solving problems, nor can it mark the narrow path on which the sole solution is supposed to lie by planting a hedge of principles on either side. But it can give the mind insight into the great mass of phenomena and of their relationships, then leave it free to rise into the higher realms of action."

Later, when he became Chairman of the Joint Chiefs, the Press would often criticize Powell's approach to the commitment of forces in the First Gulf War and other crises, and how he rigidly followed his former boss's rules. However, as stated above, the General never really established a hard set of rules. He did believe in the use of long-established doctrine, as he had learned it through the professional military education he had received first at the Army's Command and Staff College, and later at the National War College.

After leaving the position as Weinberger's military assistant, a position that usually results in some senior general assignment afterward, Powell would go on to command a Corps in Europe, one of the most prestigious assignments in the Army. He then led the Army's Forces Command – the stateside organization that oversaw all the Army forces in the US. Both commands gave him a ringside seat on the status of the Army in the mid-eighties.

In between important and demanding Army assignments, which offered him a unique view of the status of the Army's recovery from the post-Vietnam era, at the end of 1986 he returned to Washington as President Reagan's National Security Advisor. That position, as in the Vietnam War, was still responsible to the President for the integration of domestic, foreign, and military policies relating to national security.

Powell, as he explains in his autobiography, interpreted his new assignment as follows: "a lot of different agencies and people compete for the President's ear where war and peace are concerned, and consequently he needed a "referee," a body with no ax to grind that would present to him, balanced and unbiased, the views of each contender, along with the National Security Advisor's own position. A good advisor was an honest broker."

While he served in this position from 1986 to 1988, Powell had to ensure that the President had ample information on issues surrounding arms control and the changing nature of the Soviet Union under Gorbachev. There were also dangers of escalation and interruption of oil from the Middle East due to a war between Iraq and Iran.

Finally, he also had to deal with the revelations over what became known as the Iran-Contra Affair. This latter situation, which had embroiled the National Security Council before Powell arrived, involved the release of the American hostages in Iran through the prohibited sale of arms to them and the resultant money transferred illegally to fund the Contra group (an anti-Government rebel organization) in Nicaragua.

None of these issues would be entirely settled during Powell's tenure as National Security Advisor. However, the experience he gained into the workings (or lack) of the National Security apparatus with top senior officials in government was invaluable to his future. That future arrived quickly after his brief three-month command in Georgia of the US Army Forces Command. In the summer of 1989, President Bush chose him to be the 12th Chairman of the Joint Chiefs of Staff. He was the first African-American to serve in that position and the youngest at the age of 52.

The new Chairman was fully aware of the authorities that the Goldwater-Nichols Act had given to the position he now occupied. However, his experience in the Government and the Army at the pinnacle of both organizations taught him that the effective use of power and authority would depend upon his working relationship with others. He recognized that it was through personal relationships that power worked or failed.

Seeing that the adage that power corrupts and can offer an inflated view of oneself, he also sought to keep his perspective on his rank and authority. On his first day in his office in the Pentagon that overlooked the Potomac and Washington, DC, he hung a framed letter that Lincoln had signed and said, "it was easier to make new generals than to replace lost horses." With that perspective, the new Chairman vowed to listen to the advice of knowledgeable officers and officials he would work with to gain the expertise on matters he would face. On the other hand, he would not accept at face value the opinions of experts who only knew a narrow slice of the bigger picture.

Chairman Powell also brought to this new office his thoughts on lessons learned from the Vietnam War. Before taking over, he recalled of the Vietnam era Generals, "Our senior officers knew the war was going badly. Yet they bowed to groupthink pressure and kept up pretenses, the phony measure of body counts, the comforting illusion of secure hamlets, the inflated progress reports. As a corporate entity, the military did not talk straight to its political superiors or to itself. The top leadership never went to the Secretary of Defense or the President and said, this war is unwinnable the way we are fighting it."

He further reflected, "Many of my generation, the career captains, majors, and lieutenant colonels seasoned in that war, vowed that when our turn came to call the shots, we would not quietly acquiesce in halfhearted warfare for half-baked reasons that the American people could not understand or support. If we could make good on that promise to ourselves, to the civilian leadership, and to the country, then the sacrifices of Vietnam would not have been in vain."

The Panama Crisis: First Application of Vietnam War Lessons Learned

Immediately after he took over as Chairman, General Powell faced a significant issue involving US relations with Panama. Panama had been a vital strategic location for the US since President Teddy Roosevelt had pushed for and the US had built a canal there in 1914. By treaty, the US had controlled and stationed forces in a zone extending five miles on both sides of the canal.

In 1979, the Carter Administration agreed to relinquish American control of the zone to the Panamanians. By this treaty, the US would withdraw its military forces stationed there when the Panamanians took over complete control in the year 2000. Until then, there were over 10,000 US military and over 25,000 American dependents living within the US zone of the canal.

By the mid-eighties, a military dictator named Manuel Noriega controlled Panama. He did this through his use and the loyalty of the Panamanian Defense Force (PDF) of approximately 12,000 paramilitary soldiers. Noriega had sided with the US, particularly during the Reagan Administration, in the latter's actions to rid central America of its leftist, communist movements – particularly in Nicaragua – and in its anti-drug operations. In doing so, the CIA had paid him handsomely for his services.

A few years later Noriega became bellicose toward US officials and forces in the area. He also had become more entrenched and dependent on loyal PDF units, which he used to thwart several coups attempts and harass any democratic Panamanian hopefuls. Beginning in October 1989, Noriega's PDF began to harass US members of the armed forces and their dependents.

All of this came to a head when on 16 December PDF soldiers fired upon, wounded, and killed several American military personnel. They also detained another naval officer and his spouse. Reports were that PDF members beat the officer and sexually threatened his wife.

Because of these rising tensions with Noriega and his PDF 'thugs,' the US commander in Panama, Army General Max Thurman, had been working and refining contingency plans to take actions against the Panamanian dictator and his forces. The main plan, labeled BLUE SPOON, called for several options. They ranged from using Special Forces to 'snatch' Noriega, to a full-scale US invasion to topple his government and restore known Panamanian democratic leaders. In anticipation of executing all or some of these options, Thurman, and his supporting and subordinate commanders, trained their troops extensively in the execution of the plan.

With the 16 December killing of American servicemen and the kidnapping of another officer and his wife, President H.W. Bush reviewed the tense situation in Panama with his senior civilian and military advisors. Before the meeting with President, however, General Powell wanted to pave the way to ensure a meeting that would enable him to offer the best military advice he could give on the situation.

The first thing he did was to contact General Thurman to get his recommendations on what to do. Thurman recommended the full execution of their contingency plan, which called for not only the removal of Noriega, but the defeat of his PDF and the restoration of a democratic government. After asking several questions about that plan, Powell asked whether Thurman's forces were ready to execute. The latter assured him that they could begin preparations immediately, and gave a specific timetable for the accomplishment of the mission.

To ensure that the man who would be supporting him in Washington knew about his intent for the execution of his plan, Thurman further told Powell that the plan should be executed at night, preferably an hour after midnight. He explained to the Chairman that launching the operation in those circumstances would give enough time to get the forces in place for a simultaneous assault on the many targets, and enough nighttime to make most of the operation under darkened conditions.

Generals Thurman and Powell further agreed to prepare for the restoration of government by getting in touch with the democratic elements of the Panamanian populace. The Chairman was now confident that he knew enough to explain the commander on the ground's concept of operations. This would be crucial to the Chairman's explanation of the plan to his civilian bosses and getting their approval.

Powell then turned to obtain the views of the Service Chiefs. As he relates, the Senior Military Advisor to the President recognized at the time that this crisis would be the "first serious test of the chairman's new role under Goldwater-Nichols. The chiefs had great skill and experience. They were the ones who provided the trained and ready forces to the [Commanders in Chiefs – like Thurman]. I was not likely to ignore their wisdom. But now, as Chairman, I was no longer limited to a messenger role." However, he still wanted to present a consensus at best, or at least be able to inform the Secretary of Defense, now Richard Cheney, and the President of any dissenting views and why.

Powell's meeting with the Chiefs before consulting with the President shows how things had changed since the Vietnam era. Unlike what had happened during most of that war, he did not try to hide anything from the Chiefs or get their consensus for the field commander's plan. He also did not feel that he needed to get their approval for what he and General Thurman were about to do. Instead, he informed them about the commander's plan was, that he had discussed it with General Thurman, and offered his views on its viability.

Prudently, he further asked the Chiefs whether there was anything in that plan that disregarded or needed further consideration in the use of their Service's forces. In short, the Chairman was not only keeping those members of the JCS who would have to oversee the provision of forces in the crisis informed, as he should have, but wanted to discover whether there was anything that the field commander may have forgotten or needed that he overlooked.

With the Chairman allowing for open discussion, the Chiefs, in turn, gave their views and recommendations. On one occasion a Service Chief brokered to have more of his Service forces involved. It appeared for a moment that the parochialism that had infected unity of purpose in the Vietnam War may still be alive. However, Powell tactfully declined this by saying that the Commander on the ground has a "solid plan, ready to go, and we're not going to delay it or add anything unnecessary." As the meeting ended, he obtained the unanimous support he wanted but did not need.

The meeting with the President on what to do also went according to what Powell wanted, and what the field commander about to launch American troops into harm's way needed. One reason is that the Chairman had already set up a rapport with and the confidence of his civilian boss, Secretary Richard Cheney, whom he had met and got to know when he had worked for Reagan.

He had also answered most of Cheney's questions about the military aspects of the plan and made him at ease by educating him on those military features the Secretary did not understand. Moreover, unlike many such meetings during the Vietnam War, the President and his senior advisors were open to and listened to the Chairman, whom they knew and respected for his previous high government and military experience.

As Powell recounts the meeting: "Except for Cheney, the others were hearing an expanded BLUE SPOON plan for the first time. I started off with our prime objective: we were going to eliminate Noriega and the PDF. If that succeeded, we would be running the country until we could set up a civilian government and a new security force. Since this plan went well beyond 'getting Noriega,' I paused to make sure that this point had sunk in, with all its implications. No one objected."

As Chairman Powell further recalls, those present asked many questions. These were the normal ones that political leaders and advisors would want to know in anticipation of Congressional and Press inquiries and concerns. The General, because his political savvy, had anticipated them. Some of the typical questions were: was there enough provocation to intervene; how many casualties would there be; what collateral damage would there be; are we confident we can capture Noriega?

The Chairman answered these in simple, straightforward, and understandable terms, but would not offer guesses or optimistic estimates. He did not try to get bogged down in figures or answers on the unknowns. However, as the military expert present, he set out to educate his civilian bosses and their advisors on military operations. He reassured them that the military had taken into consideration casualties and damages; they would be minimized, but could not be avoided. He emphasized that in any military operation things would go wrong; soldiers would die; civilian property and persons would be destroyed and hurt. At the end of the two-hour meeting, he recalled, "Bush, after everyone had had his say, gripped the arms of his chair and rose. Okay, let us do it."

OPERATION JUST CAUSE was one of the most successful military operations of the Post-Vietnam era. The simultaneous air, sea and ground assaults overwhelmed the opposition with minimum casualties. Eventually, American forces deposed Noriega. They defeated and dissolved the PDF. Soon after, they helped the Panamanians appoint a temporary leader and ensured the protection for freely elected democratic government and its restoration. Of the nearly 28,000 US troops involved, 23 were killed and 325 wounded. The PDF lost about 205 killed and an unknown number of wounded. About 300 civilians perished.

General Powell spent most of his time during the crisis and operation as a political-military intermediary between the commanders on the ground and the civilian leaders in Washington. He also served as a screen between those in the Bush Administration who wanted to query the US military in Panama on ongoing operations and, in some instances, give unwanted and unhelpful guidance. He further found himself playing a pivotal role in dealing with the Press: mainly because it had become a twenty-four hour, seven days a week media influx to the public and Congress on what was going on.

The new Chairman recalls in his memoirs that he was pleased that the operation had restored public pride and confidence in their military. He also observed, "The lessons I absorbed from Panama confirmed all my convictions over the preceding twenty years, since the days of doubt over

Vietnam. Have a clear political objective and stick to it. Use all the force necessary, and do not apologize for going in big if that is what it takes. Decisive force ends wars quickly and eventually saves lives. Whatever threats we faced in the future, I intended to make these rules the bedrock of my military counsel."

Section 12.3 - Vietnam War Lessons Learned and Applied: DESERT SHIELD and DESERT STORM, 1990-1991

After the Panama crisis, General Powell turned his attention to what he believed was the most essential military strategic issue the nation confronted – the demise of the Soviet Union and what that would mean to US national security and the future of its military. Working with the Joint Staff, he convinced both Cheney and the President to support his vision of a post-Cold War national security strategy, military strategy, and force structure. The force structure levels he called the 'Base Force.' That name indicated the minimum force levels needed to support the President's national security strategy and its military component.

The day that President Bush announced his new national strategy for the post-Cold War world, Saddam Hussein invaded Kuwait. This middle east crisis was one of those expected in Powell's 'Base Force' strategy. In reacting to the Iraq invasion, President Bush established the crisis as in the national interest of the US, and ordered, with the consent of the Saudi government, US forces to Saudi Arabia to defend against any further military threat that may emerge from Saddam Hussein against that nation.

On 7 August 1990 US forces began deploying to the region to defend Saudi Arabia. The military labeled the operation DESERT SHIELD. The US commander of the region, General Norman Schwarzkopf, began execution of a draft contingency plan for movement to the peninsula. As the Commander of Central Command recalls in his autobiography, *It Doesn't Take A Hero*, the execution "would mean a seven-thousand-mile shift of five and one-third divisions, or 120,000 troops, in four months" …to the Saudi peninsula.

Similar to the movement of about the same number of forces to South Vietnam in the first six months of that war, the deployment would be no small feat – especially because these forces would also have to move everything needed to feed, move, and fight the force. Unlike the Vietnam War, however, the American field commander would eventually obtain from the President and his advisors precisely what he needed – to include a mobilization of the resources and personnel to move and support his command to execute his eventual campaign.

Like General Powell, Schwarzkopf was a veteran of the Vietnam War. He had also served two tours – one as an advisor and one as a commander of a US infantry battalion. Like most Vietnam Veterans he was bitter about the defeat and his treatment during his homecoming. He recalls the day that Saigon fell… "I sat motionless in front of the TV listening to reports that the only South Vietnamese forces still putting up any resistance were remnants of the airborne at Tan Son Nhut air base. I knew that the Airborne's cause was lost and that men who were my friends, like Hop, Hao, and Hung, were probably fighting to the death, at that moment."

Like many soldiers who had fought there and wondered about the cost of the futile effort of Vietnam, he "took out a bottle of scotch and got drunk... Never mind that the communists won—geopolitical pros and cons were irrelevant to me—the war never should have been allowed to end that way. I conjured up the countless thousands of lost lives and mutilated bodies and ruined marriages and wondered what we had accomplished." Now, as the commander of over a hundred thousand American troops, he wanted to get this war right.

While their personalities were dramatically different, the President's primary military advisor and his field commander were determined to work together to ensure success. Powell, with his knowledge and experience in Washington circles and his intent to use his Goldwater-Nichols powers, would manage the political-military affairs in the US and the capital. Schwarzkopf would then be able, particularly with his background and knowledge of the Middle East and his extensive troop experience, develop his campaign plan and execute it with Powell as a screen between himself and the American politicos and the Press. Moreover, the Chairman, in close coordination with the field commander and the supporting Service Chiefs, would see to it that the combat commander executing his campaign would get everything he needed to be successful.

The credentials these two men had, plus the great relationship they forged between themselves, enabled an effective merging of national aims to a theater strategic campaign with clear and achievable military objectives. In addition, there would be no brakes on the means to achieve those aims. This would be in stark contrast to what had happened in Vietnam.

This is not to say that there were no problems and issues between the military and its senior civilian superiors. From the onset of DESERT SHIELD, there was an issue with what the President was saying publicly, what the initial objectives were, and what the senior military officers could infer from what was being said to the Press.

As Schwarzkopf relates in his autobiography, "I couldn't see where the operation was supposed to lead. I told Powell that the longer Saddam waited to launch his invasion, the more certain we were of being able to defend Saudi Arabia. But suppose the invasion never came? I couldn't imagine the United States simply pulling out while Iraq still occupied Kuwait."

Meanwhile, General Powell had also been carefully following President Bush's remarks to the Press. The Chairman noted that he saw the President's reaction to a question that if Saddam continued to refuse to withdraw from Kuwait what would he do? Bush emphatically said, "This will not stand." Powell astutely recognized that those words differed significantly from Bush's early stance that the US was "drawing a line in the sand."

To the politically perceptive Chairman, 'drawing a line in the sand,' meant the continued, and long-term, defense of Saudi Arabia. 'This will not stand,' on the other hand, meant that if Saddam did not withdraw from Kuwait, an offensive military theater strategy would be necessary to force him out. This seeming contradiction had to be resolved if military planning, strategies, and operations could continue effectively to achieve meaningfully and understood political direction.

Unlike General Wheeler in the Vietnam War, as Chairman General Powell was not waiting for guidance or seeking just to see what the Commander-in-Chief wanted to do. The Chairman had to resolve any confusion to obtain what he knew the Field Commander needed - a clear and meaningful political objective that could guide a military strategy. He also wanted to get ahead of his political seniors and resolve Presidential statements or clear up whatever confusion existed that would either contradict the current directions for or redirect the use of force. In doing so, he also wanted to influence any changes in direction before politics in Washington and the Press unduly influenced his senior leaders elsewhere.

General Powell used his new powers under the Goldwater-Nichols Act to do just that. He first went to Cheney to make sure his immediate superior, who was the one who would issue orders to the Commander in the field, was aware of the existing plans and what they could carry out. He also wanted to alert the Defense Secretary as to what the President was saying and what that may mean for any change to military missions and operations.

His relationship and dealings with the Secretary went far beyond just informing him of the military's plans and future possibilities. Using his staff, he went about to answer any questions that the inquisitive Cheney might have and to educate him on military matters. Sometimes this education occurred in the meeting place of the JCS, called 'the tank.' On occasion, he asked Schwarzkopf to take time out from his busy schedule and come to Washington to brief the Secretary on his plans, and give updates on the military situation. Often Powell held 'classroom' on military matters for the Secretary in his office.

In his memoirs, Powell mentions that as the Gulf crisis unfolded he "considered Dick's education complete. My Joint Staff operations officer, Tom Kelly, organized a ceremony, and we presented Dick with a certificate stating that Richard Bruce Cheney was now an honorary graduate of all the war colleges." The above description explains what senior military advisors must do to educate their civilian leaders on military action to obtain sound political guidance for the use of force.

As the principal military advisor to the President, moreover, Powell was not hesitant to ask for an audience with Bush. Often, of course, he informed Cheney of his need to see the Commander-in-Chief and the Secretary would go with him. There were several times that Powell saw the President alone as well. He would then inform his boss of what happened between them.

There were other times in which the Chairman met with the President in a small group, what Powell called the 'gang of eight,' which consisted of a select number of the President's advisors. The General realized that sometimes too large a meeting could get unruly, or at other times they just resulted in nothing. At small meetings, with the principals' present, there was a better discussion of the options, and a better opportunity to explain the pros and cons of them.

Encouraged by General Powell, Bush also chose to use the National Security Council for more formal meetings and more comprehensive discussions. These more extensive meetings ensured that more experts had an opportunity to present their considerations, views, and recommendations. In sum, unlike the relationships between military advisors and commanders and the civilian leaders and advisors during the Vietnam War, the Bush Administration maintained an operative chain of communication and cooperation that eventually led to effective policies and strategies for the First Gulf War.

Personal Experiences and Observations

I was on General Powell's Joint Staff at the time and gained some first-hand knowledge of what happened during this time. As one of his senior military planners, it fell on me and the officers I worked with to respond to the needs of the Chairman for information and analysis. Some of this work was to prepare papers for his use in his deliberations with his civilian superiors or meetings with the Chiefs. Sometimes the papers consisted of military considerations and courses of action based on General Powell's guidance or questions.

We also prepared information or gave briefings to the Chairman's representatives who took part in the National Security Council meetings. At times, we went with these representatives or the Chairman to these gatherings. On occasion, we also attended the Chairman's consultations with the Secretary of Defense or his Deputy.

Along with other officers from all parts of the Joint Staff, we worked several of the critical issues for General Powell. It was instructive to obtain his views and 'musings' on several them. The first issue of importance was to develop some papers and a few briefing charts for the Chairman's use of political and military objectives for the war. These were not just for the war itself, but what we thought US objectives should be for after the conflict. As we struggled with these based on what the President had announced (e.g., A line in the sand; this will not stand) and what the Chairman and his principal assistants to the National Security Council meetings had discussed, we often met with General Powell to discuss and obtain his views.

Frequently in these meetings, the General reminded us of his perspective on the lack of clarity in the political and military objectives in Vietnam. He also encouraged us not to be shy about developing our thoughts on what the political considerations and aims should be, though it was outside of our direct responsibility. What he wanted was something that we could propose at NSC meetings that could offer some ideas to the President's NSC staff, who were working on a National Security Directive for the war. The overall aim was to assist in melding whatever the possible political goals might be to any valid military objectives and actions they may require.

The General also told us to look beyond the immediate crisis. From what I recall he said, "Propose objectives for what we want after the shooting ends. Do not just focus solely on what the military objective could be or should be. Step outside of your military hats, and determine what our civilian masters need to be instructed on regarding what political objectives might be necessary to bring a favorable conclusion to the war and the peace to follow."

During discussions with the Chairman and some of his other general officer assistants, we did just that. For example, we developed a political objective to "ensure that the US is better postured in the Gulf region to respond to other post-war crises." Its corresponding military objective was to "obtain basing rights and a forward military headquarters in the Gulf region." The former would be an aim for the President to consider in any National Security Guidance he may issue; while the latter would be something the Secretary of Defense or the Chairman would provide in their orders to the field commander to achieve as part of his campaign plan.

In discussions with some of the State Department and CIA experts, General Powell became concerned about any long-term military commitment to the region should there develop any tendency for regime change and occupation of Iraq during or after the war. In these discussions, he became aware of the tremendous divide that existed in Iraq between the Sunni and Shia population. The General did not think it wise, from a political-military perspective to get involved in any civil war that may develop.

His feelings and concerns about the political, social, cultural, and religious background in the Middle East and Iraq, in particular, led to further meetings between his staff and experts from the CIA and State Department. During these meetings as a member of the Chairman's staff in attendance, we gained a thorough understanding of this region's history and background and obtained a vast amount of knowledge about the problems in the region that any American occupying force would have to face. We brought this information back to the Chairman and gave him an earful of the issues, problems, and difficulties that US commanders would face.

Thus, the Chairman eventually decided that it would be in the interest of our worldwide military commitments to avoid such a predicament. Accordingly, the General thought it wise to limit the war to the Saudi Arabia – Kuwait – Southern Iraq area. In his mind, a more protracted war and a prolonged military occupation would have long-term repercussions to defending vital interests in other areas in Europe and Asia with the military capabilities the US then had.

Besides, he warned, such an objective would not coincide with UN resolutions and may result in an unraveling of the coalition of Arab forces that were supporting our efforts. As he explains in his autobiography, he further thought it was in the US interest at the time to continue to have an Iraq that could counterbalance the Iranian ambitions in the Gulf Region.

As a result, he had us prepare papers for his use on arguments for a possible discussion of the issue should anyone trying to make a case for regime change and occupation of Iraq. He wanted it available to offer his best military advice on why he thought it a disastrous idea. In short, General Powell was prepared to discuss the pros and cons of limiting the war and avoiding a post-war situation of the occupation of a broken state which could lead to unacceptable long-term costs.

Another problem that we spent much time on was the nature and size of the US forces for the offensive phase to force Iraq out of Kuwait. In this issue, General Powell wanted to take the lead for the ground commander. He would, of course, consult with General Schwarzkopf, but he wanted to persuade the President to not piecemeal the necessary forces that would be decisive to evict the Iraqis from Kuwait. With an eye toward the post-war outlook in the Gulf region, he also wanted to make sure the US had enough and the right force to destroy the elite and offensive forces of the Iraqi Army – the so-called Republican Guard.

The resultant First Gulf War – the defensive DESERT SHIELD and offensive phase DESERT STORM – was a resounding victory for the US. Though some have criticized it in retrospect (that we should have removed Saddam, for example), all the ultimate political and military objectives were achieved. General Powell's role in that was extraordinary and decisive. So was the role, work, and leadership of the military commanders in the theater of war who developed a sound military theater strategy and executed it superbly.

Making this all possible was the civilian leadership from the President down to his primary advisors and the Secretary of Defense. They created a collaborative atmosphere that made full use of a national security structure that ensured sound military advice, the development of effective political war policies and objectives, and the generation of decisive forces for that victory.

I witnessed this collaborative and shared-responsibility atmosphere and working relationship. It was in stark contrast to what I would learn afterward about civil-military workings in the Vietnam War.

Several weeks after the so-called "100-hour ground war" ended, President Bush declared "we've kicked the Vietnam syndrome once and for all." Considering what happened after the terrorist attacks on 9/11 and the continuing war on terror since, this seems premature. However, it certainly reflected the feelings of many Americans at the time. To the war's Generals and other senior commanders who led the divisions and brigades in Saudi Arabia, Kuwait, and southern Iraq, it also was a welcomed catharsis for the aftermath of the Vietnam War.

As General Powell recounts in his memoirs, "The celebrations were no doubt out of proportion to the achievement. We had not fought another World War II. Yet, after the stalemate of Korea and the long agony in Southeast Asia, the country was hungry for victory. We had given America a clear win at low casualties in a noble cause, and the American people fell in love again with their armed forces. The way I looked at it, if we got too much adulation for this one, it made up for the neglect the troops had experienced coming home from those other wars."

For me, then and now, the First Gulf War serves as a counterpoint for how senior civilian and military leaders conceived and waged the Vietnam War. The former is a model for effective civil-military cooperation in the development of a sound national and military strategy for a conflict. The latter was not. If one ponders the questions how and why the US failed in the Vietnam War, the comparison between it and the First Gulf War offers a useful analytical approach to understand why one was so successful and the other such a tragic loss.

The Powell Model of Effective Military Advice for Decision Making and Strategic Formulation

Over the years, as I pondered the reasons for the Vietnam War and why it was lost, I kept going back to my experiences, not only in the war itself but most of all to my years serving under General Colin Powell. It was not his 'Powell doctrine' or his list of rules that he kept on his desk that I kept going back to. It was his personal and candid remarks on his relationships with the civilian leaders he served with or for, his role in strategic decision making, and how he offered his military advice.

What I remember most - and what is most pertinent to me in my journey to find answers about the loss of Vietnam - were the General's genuine and insightful observations, forged by his experiences and education, on how useful advice and consent are provided, discussed, and decided upon on national security strategic matters.

Often, he reflected that senior civilian leaders knew little about military strategy and the military itself. He cautioned, therefore, that military advisors had to be leery of how to approach military matters with them. Usually, straightforward advice coupled with the risks and costs of military actions needed to be offered in terms leaders who are uneducated and inexperienced in military affairs can understand.

Moreover, he always reminded us that military jargon and war college solutions with military graphics and phrases could easily confuse senior leaders. The adage 'keep it simple stupid' is part of the solution; but putting military advice in understandable terms of how to produce the decisive effects, results, and costs without confusing details are even better. This approach, moreover, also works best in describing military matters to the Press and the Public.

I saw this approach several times during the First Gulf War. For example, in several meetings, we discussed how to present to Secretary Cheney and President Bush the transition from DESERT SHIELD to DESERT STORM and what was necessary to carry out the mission to eject the Iraqi forces from Kuwait. At the last of these meetings, General Powell directed that we come up with a straightforward graphic that he would use to explain this transition and what is necessary to defeat the Iraqi military. It turned out to be a simple chart with two axes. One showed time, and the other showed the deployment of US forces in theater over that time.

General Powell explains how he used this chart and how he described it to both Cheney and Bush in his autobiography. His use of the chart of numbers went well beyond the figures. He described in simple language what the numbers meant regarding decisions that the Chairman and the military commander in the field would need from the President to do the tasks that the numbers were intended to carry out. That approach, along with several straightforward answers to their questions, worked effectively and convinced the President to support the military strategy resulting in the war's success.

Another example was the General's Press conference in January 1991 just after air operations were underway against Iraqi forces. At a meeting with him several days prior, he considered how to explain the elaborate military campaign that General Schwarzkopf had developed to defeat the Iraqi forces in Kuwait. He charged us with developing several simple charts, one of which showed in general terms the Iraqi Army positions in Kuwait. That was it.

At a Press conference later that month, he showed the chart with the Iraqi forces in Kuwait. Pointing to the unclassified broad array of Iraq Army units, he said: "Our strategy in going after this army is very simple. First, we are going to cut it off, and then we are going to kill it." The effect was electrifying.

In recalling these two examples, I now think of the ineptness of both Westmoreland and Wheeler in their attempts to explain an alternative approach to the attrition strategy in Vietnam. I also ponder what could have been had they had the personal and professional skills to show how numbers translate into the means to execute a successful military course of action.

General Powell also pondered on occasion with us his role as the Chairman of the Joint Chiefs. He believed that the Chairman had to be more than just an advisor on military strategy and operations. As the military officer responsible for that advice, he thought that to be effective he also had to be a teacher and moderator on military affairs and strategic concepts for the President and his Secretary of Defense. In that role, in close coordination with the field commander, the Chairman's significant contribution to the employment of military force is to ensure that he could both educate and advise the civilian leaders on the best way to employ military force, as often and convincingly as necessary.

He further reflected on what if these leaders do not take that advice. His thoughts focused on the consequences to the soldiers, sailors, marines, and airmen that would bear the costs of whatever the alternatives were or of taking no action. If the risks and costs are high, he believed, then it is the duty of the military advisor or the commander to forcefully object to the decision; stating the costs and risks involved in no uncertain terms.

If then the civilian superior still insists on some alternative or to do nothing, then one is faced with the most difficult decision in one's life. There can be no cookie cutter solution. It is up to one's conscience as much as any oath that an officer takes to the constitution. Perhaps the main factor is to weigh the consequences. Even that, however, will be full of speculation and unknowns. If one resigns, that act may unravel any support for the application of force that may be underway and cause more casualties than any protest could prevent.

Soon after this discussion I recall a session that I had with some of my military peers at the time over this issue. Many felt that one's oath to the constitution demands resignation. This is because, while in our system of government the military man owes his allegiance to those elected civilian leaders he serves, an officer's oath of allegiance is to the Constitution, not any individual. Thus, in assessing the expected results of the civilian leader's decision, if the costs and risks of the loss of the lives of the soldiers, sailors, marines, and airmen are unacceptable, and the civilian leader persists, an officer must resign.

In the end, I had a new appreciation for the dilemma senior officers must have in facing the possibility of having to resign over their advice to a civilian superior. While I have been harsh in my criticisms of such men as General Harold K. Johnson, he must have faced a heart-wrenching decision. He chose to not resign. In retrospect it is easy to judge. But resignation is the last definitive statement one can make as a senior military officer in a high position that can still have an effect on a bad decision that may cost thousands of lives.

Another fundamental lesson I drew from my experiences as a senior military planner and advisor to the Chairman of the Joint Chiefs in prominent levels of the US government is that it is not the organization or process or the bureaucracy that makes for good or bad decision-making. While stated and established policies, organizational processes, theories and doctrines, and their resultant belief systems and ideas all have a vital role, it is the personal dealings and the way people interact that are the main factors and influences in decision making.

If these relationships are weak, then so will be the decisions and their corresponding outcomes. Moreover, because most civilian leaders have no real education or practice in military affairs, senior military officers need to mentor the senior civilian officials they serve. This in no way alters the relationship of civilian control over the military. Instead, it enhances it by ensuring the relationship can work through mutual respect, understanding, and shared responsibility.

Section 12.4 – Lessons Learned for the Future: Relationships Matter

The importance of interpersonal relationships that I learned from General Powell offers for me an essential perspective on a primary reason for how and why we lost the Vietnam War. We lost, in large part, because America's highest leaders – both civilian and military - did not listen to, trust, respect, and learn from one another.

Because of this, American senior decision makers were unable to develop and execute an effective military strategy that stipulated the right ends, ways, and means to fight the Vietnam War effectively. Nor did they have an in-depth discussion, from the beginning, on the potential long-term costs to the US military and public support.

These observations and conclusions do not mean that the war was solely lost because of US mistakes. As this story has tried to show, the Vietnamese enemy and their allies had a lot to do with the American loss in Vietnam. As explained in Chapters 6 and 7, North Vietnamese leaders were intent on winning the war primarily through military means. They were persistent in their methods and goals for their purpose.

Ho Chi Minh and then Le Duan were masterful in their obtainment of Soviet and Chinese aid and support for the war – without which they would never have been able to confront the military power of the United States. They prevailed mostly because of the resolute pursuit of their goal of unification. Moreover, and most ironically, American leaders inadvertently aided the pursuit of their aims. That is because American desires to seek a negotiated settlement coupled with 'gradual military use of force' encouraged the Northern Communists in their quest for victory.

The North Vietnamese leaders were also effective in mobilizing their nation, and building and providing the necessary military force to attain their long-sought objective of unification. In fact, as all the evidence confirms, without North Vietnamese direction, military force capabilities, and ability to give both over uninterrupted lines of communication via the Ho Chi Minh Trail, the war could not have been won in South Vietnam.

Moreover, US decision-makers responses to their enemy's actions and what they thought of them mattered a great deal in the conduct of the war. As explained in Chapters 6 and 7 and concluded in the last chapter, American leaders misunderstood and misjudged the North Vietnam motives and actions, not just because they did not know them or ignored them, but because they did not listen to or disregarded those who did.

Robert McNamara's claim that "our government lacked experts for us to consult to compensate for our ignorance," is just false. While there is some truth that the US lost some ability in Asian affairs after the McCarthy 'purge,' there was still sufficient expertise in the State Department and in the CIA to offer information on the skills and motives of the North Vietnamese leaders. And they did; only to be dismissed.

As Rufus Phillips, himself a veteran of the State Department who served in South Vietnam, states so emphatically in his *Why Vietnam Matters*, "McNamara simply rejected advice that did not conform to his preconceptions. No set of 'experts' could have overcome that obstacle…." Moreover, it was not just McNamara. Many of his colleagues, hand-picked because their views matched his own, also chose not to pay attention to the experts – those who they derisively referred to as unthinking bureaucrats.

The inability to open the minds of American decision makers to points of view about their enemy is a complicated issue. Some have argued that it was due to some 'can do spirit' of the decision makers and their primary advisors. According to this argument, much of this spirit was because America had just won the greatest war of the modern age. There is some evidence that this was a factor.

As explained in Chapter 1, this victory was a monumental feat. That total victory imbued civilian and military leaders alike to believe in America's immense power and infallibility. Coupled the fact that America emerged as the greatest power on earth after the war, it was entirely natural for those in the post-war environment as America's "new generation" of leaders to feel that they could do whatever it takes to further America's destiny. That attitude was the theme and thrust of JFK's inaugural address.

Others argue that the inability to understand the enemy was due to the intellectual arrogance of the best and brightest. This arrogance created a sense that they knew the answers to the unique and complex strategic issues they confronted because of their successes and mindsets forged in the civilian political, business, or academic backgrounds. While they had no or little meaningful military education or experience, their views on such things as 'limited' war, game theory, systems analyses, and crises management drove their thinking on how to approach the Vietnam situation.

Again, Rufus Phillips' remarks seem right on the mark – "Top policy makers in Washington, with egos inflated by meritorious careers, had a low tolerance for different views based on firsthand experience. The standardized flow of information up through the bureaucracy, telling details strained out, was too often distorted by an optimistic patina of progress."

Given the lessons learned and applied as outlined above, and remembering the words of General Powell about how effective decision making is about human relationships, it seems like the best conclusion is that the failures to not know the enemy, as well as the inability to formulate sound strategies, are shared responsibilities between both American senior civilian and military leaders and advisors in the Vietnam War.

For me, however, just affixing blame is just not enough. Why was that relationship flawed? How could it have been more effective?

In my quest for answers on the how and why of the American Vietnam War failures, and the corollary inquiries of how and why the civilian-military relationships were flawed, there was one main phrase that at first haunted me, and then enlightened me. It is a saying often attributed to the Greek general and historian I have mentioned – Thucydides.

"A nation that makes a great distinction between its scholars and warriors will have its thinking done by cowards and its fighting done by fools." Whoever is the right author of this phrase, and whether quoted correctly, this expression in my view is extraordinarily pertinent to the understanding of American decision-making in the Vietnam War.

For any chance of a successful American outcome in that war, or any war for that matter, it was of paramount importance for the scholars or thinking men - in this case, the civilian best and brightest – and for the warriors – the military commanders and advisors serving them – to understand one another and work together in mutual respect.

To create these conditions of understanding and mutual respect, moreover, there must have been some degree of knowledge and appreciation of the two cultures that they lived in. There also must have been some common point of view on the nexus of politics and military affairs, and how they must work together to produce this connection. Through common points of view and understanding, and the resultant mutual respect and trust, they may have developed a more effective military strategy and conducted a more thorough assessment of the costs for the war.

That need for shared responsibility and understanding in war is not new. It should have been self-evident if they had studied together past examples of success and failures in war. Noteworthy political and military commentators and theorists of the past have written about it. Plato, Machiavelli, and Clausewitz paid tribute to the necessity.

Not available then, but for any statesmen and military men interested now, there are many histories on this subject and examples to examine. A few are: Eliot Cohen's *Supreme Command: Soldiers, Statesmen, and Leadership in Wartime*; Murray, Sinnreich, and Lacey's *The Shaping of Grand Strategy: Policy, Diplomacy, and War*; Joseph Glatthaar's *Partners in Command: The Relationships Between Leaders in the Civil War*; James McPherson's *Tried By War: Abraham Lincoln as Commander in Chief*; Nigel Hamilton's *The Mantle of Command: FDR at War, 1941-1942*; Joseph Persico's *Roosevelts Centurions: FDR and the Commanders He Led to Victory in World War Two*; and Matthew Moten's *Presidents and Their Generals: An American History of Command in War*.

Yet, the difficulty is not just to recognize this need but to discuss how to foster, maintain, or in its absence, create it. Thus, drawing upon the explanations, descriptions, and observations from the earlier eleven chapters, the rest of this section summarizes the nature of the breakdown in political-military relations in decision-making during the Kennedy, Johnson, and Nixon Administrations. It also explains why this may have happened, and how it affected the war.

The narrative that follows does not focus on the full gamut of what political scientists, such as Samuel Huntington, would call civil-military relations. But it narrows on the nature of the relationships of the military and civilian policy makers and their impact on the decisions and formulation of policies and strategies for the war. The intent is to find some further understanding of that breakdown and offer Vietnam War lessons learned on this subject that, if applied, may offer antidotes for the future.

JFK Administration Civil-Military Relations

As we have seen in Chapter 2, JFK came to the Presidency with a preconceived notion of senior military officers. From his experience in World War Two - somehow and at some time - he had developed a distaste for the military 'brass,' whom he saw as uninspiring and having shown poor judgment. Moreover, just as Richard Neustadt's *Presidential Power* influenced his view of the Presidency, in general, Barbara Tuchman's *Guns of August* molded his views of military thinking, advice, and planning.

President Kennedy often mentioned Tuchman's portrayal of military generals in the first crisis weeks of August 1914 as unthinking leaders bent on blindly executing their plans without regard to political factors. This had resulted in military escalation actions that led to a horrific world war. He cited the book during his deliberations over the Cuban missile crisis. He also asked his only military advisor whom he respected, General Maxwell Taylor, if he had ever read Tuchman's account. This was during a discussion with the General, as Taylor's biographer relates, on Kennedy's belief that there exists a military mindset that often produces unthinking prescribed solutions, which are unimaginative and without flexibility.

Kennedy's dealings with the Joint Chiefs of Staff during the three crises that were the 'crucibles' of his presidency – the Bay of Pigs, Laos, and Cuban Missile Crisis – reinforced this learned, preconceived notion. His biographers' accounts of these interactions are full of descriptions on how JFK sat, "biting his lip…tapping his front teeth…running his hand through his hair" and becoming increasingly "irritated" and "frustrated" with their briefings and comments. Robert Dallek further describes "how tense the president was listening to Lemnitzer [his first Chairman of the Joint Chiefs], who used thirty-eight flip charts sitting on easels" to describe military options for intervention in Laos.

Moreover, when the President asked questions about how the enemy may react or about the military planners' questionable assumptions, he got puzzled looks and irrational answers. One such answer during the Laos crisis set him off. He asked what if the Chinese were to intervene. Lemnitzer answered, "You start using atomic weapons! If we are given the right to use nuclear weapons, we can guarantee victory." Furious after that meeting, Schlesinger recalls, Kennedy said to his civilian advisors, "And we call ourselves the human race."

JFK's meetings with the JCS during the Cuban missile crisis best illustrate this gulf between himself and his military advisors. Recall from Chapter 2 that it was in one of these that General LeMay said that the President was in a 'fix' – indicating that the crisis was the President's problem and not the Joint Chiefs.' LeMay made other outrageous remarks. In response to the President's consideration of a blockade over a massive air attack against the missiles, the Air Force Chief responded, "This blockade and political action, I see leading into war. I do not see any other solution. It will lead right into war. This is almost as bad as the appeasement at Munich."

General LeMay, who had a favorable following in Congress and the Media, also indirectly threatened Kennedy with making his dissent public. He said, "I think that a blockade, and political talk, would be considered by a lot of our friends and neutrals as being a pretty weak response to this. And I'm sure a lot of our own citizens would feel that way, too."

LeMay epitomized JFK's notion of how senior military advisors were inept at giving sound advice in the age of potential nuclear holocaust. After one such meeting, Kennedy summed up his thoughts on his views on the efficacy of military advice: "These brass hats have one great advantage in their favor. If we listen to them and do what they want us to do, none of us will be alive later to tell them that they were wrong."

As Mark Perry explains in his *Four Stars*, most of the Chiefs early in Kennedy's tenure were highly decorated World War Two combat leaders. For example, LeMay had led the US Army Air Force attacks against the Japanese homeland. General Tom White, Le May's predecessor, had ably led Army Air Forces in the large Pacific battles around the Philippines and Okinawa. Arleigh Burke, the Chief of Naval Operations, had fought in the Pacific as a naval officer in charge of destroyer task forces and had earned the Navy Cross during the battles in the Solomon Islands. General George Decker had led Army forces under MacArthur in the Pacific and won the Silver Star in combat. General David Shoup, the Commandant of the Marine Corps, had won the Medal of Honor in the brutal fighting at the Tarawa Atoll in the Pacific.

These experiences naturally influenced their attitudes toward and advice on the use of force. For most, if not all, General MacArthur's famous saying, 'There is no substitute for victory' held sway over their advice on the use of force. Moreover, this experience, and the resultant prestige of the victory in the war, certainly made them more than able to advise on the use of force in combat situations.

However, that war experience did not give them an understanding of the potential changes occurring with the advent of nuclear weapons on the future of armed conflict. Nor did it provide an understanding of the necessity more than ever to consider political factors in recommending the use of force in an era of potential nuclear war.

Indeed, the atomic bomb had made their experience somewhat of an anachronism. It certainly made the use of force more dangerous, in that any escalation or confrontation between powers having those weapons could result in a disastrous nuclear exchange. These combat veterans, and national heroic figures, just did not adapt and understand that this bomb was not just another weapon.

Their experience, moreover, did not take into consideration political factors that their actions had resulted from or caused. Now, in the nuclear age, in which, according to Bernard Brodie, the "basic utility of war is in question," their combat experiences of World War Two seemed irrelevant at first. At the very least one could conclude that warfare had changed, and they were caught in the trap of their past experiences.

Exasperating this change in warfare due to the nuclear age, the Kennedy Joint Chiefs had taken part in the Eisenhower Administration's dependence on the nuclear arsenal. Thus, they were tainted and overly influenced, by their service in IKE's government. Since the central national policy and strategy was massive retaliation, these senior officers had served in positions that planned for and promoted the development of nuclear forces in each of their Services.

The plans that they developed and fit with the Eisenhower's policies called for the use of nuclear weapons as the necessary and deciding means for victory. This policy and the corresponding responsibility for planning for their use reinforced their view that nuclear weapons were interchangeable with any other weapon at their disposal.

Furthermore, they had not thought about and had ignored the evolving deterrence theory and limited war policies that the academic community was then proposing and arguing over. These combat-experienced military men, unfamiliar with and unsure of thinking about new, revolutionary concepts, relegated this evolving strategic theory on the use of force in a nuclear age to university professors and other highly educated civilians who were developing new ideas on controlled escalation, deterrence ladders, and game theories.

Besides as the new Kennedy group took over in Washington in 1961 the military brass anticipated that things would be different for them. As Richard Betts explains in his article in *American Civil-Military Relations: The Soldier and the State in a New Era*, "It was a harsh jolt for the leaders of the military's World War II generation to move overnight from answering to five-star General Eisenhower to taking orders from Lieutenant Kennedy."

In short, the military top brass simply just did not fit into the same mind frame as the new Kennedy Administration's younger civilian leaders. What seemed to the new President and his civilian advisors as insane and ridiculous in the military's recommendations was previously the norm for his senior military advisors. These men were now being asked to give advice that demanded a new mindset that they just did not have. The result, according to Richard Betts, was that the Chiefs advice "inhibited the civilians' interest in using force or frustrated the military when intervention proceeded with less force than they recommended."

To remedy the military advice 'problem' as the new President saw it after the Bay of Pigs fiasco, JFK chose to recall General Maxwell Taylor to active duty. As explained before, there were several reasons for this. First, Kennedy had read Taylor's *The Uncertain Trumpet*, which described and promoted a call for a more flexible military capability than the massive retaliation policy of the Eisenhower Administration had produced. The new President, therefore, thought it fitting to recall him to aid in developing his new national security policy of flexible response.

Secondly, in Taylor JFK thought he could have a military man with whom he could interact and listen to. This General was unlike any that Kennedy had known. He was an intellectual as well as an experienced and respected combat military man. The Kennedys liked him and socialized with him.

The former commander of the renowned 101st Airborne Division during the Normandy campaign could entertain them with war stories over dinners at RFK's home in a Washington suburb. Meanwhile, he also conversed with Jackie Kennedy in fluent French. Indeed, this general was fluent in several languages. He also had experience in the Orient, which, the Kennedy's thought, would undoubtedly help the Administration in executing any military actions in Asia.

However, as mentioned in Chapter 2, this appointment and personal connection soured the relationship with the JCS. As Kennedy's special military assistant, the Chiefs saw Taylor, rightly so as it turned out, as a means for the President to obtain military advice without consulting them. Even when Taylor became the new Chairman, the other Chiefs felt that he continued to serve as personal representative and go-between for Kennedy and his Secretary of Defense.

Thus, collectively the JCS senior military advisors believed this situation continued to keep them from offering their face to face and more frequent personal military advice to the President. Of course, that is just what JFK wanted. The result was that no matter how well Taylor tried to keep the President informed, the Commander-in-Chief would be unable to receive some of the more pertinent military details of the armed services capabilities that would have enabled him to receive better military advice.

Further exasperating the relationship between the President and the Chiefs was the appointment of Robert McNamara to the position of Secretary of Defense. Indeed, Dale Herspring, a scholar of civil-military relations during the Vietnam War, has written that, "Of all the decisions that Kennedy took in office, none would impact civil-military relations more negatively than his appointment of Robert McNamara…. [The Defense Secretary] had no interest in creating shared responsibility, and he had little respect for the military or its culture."

As also mentioned in Chapter 2, JFK bought the former President of Ford Motor Company on board with a significant action to reform the Defense Department. This task was no small chore. In so doing, McNamara rigidly held to his belief that tried and true business management techniques were translatable to military affairs. His brief military experience, which entailed number crunching on bombing statistics, did not provide him with any insights on military operations or strategic matters. Moreover, knowledge of military affairs did not matter to McNamara. In managing the Department most of his interface with the Service Chiefs and their staffs would entail parochial service interests in the budget. He saw this programming and budget role, not strategic advice, or formulation, as the primary one for the Service Chiefs.

In reforming the business aspects of the Defense Department, McNamara was in his element. As Larry Freedman notes, "his capacity to digest information, zoom in on discrepancies, compute costs, and assess alternatives astonished and alarmed subordinates. The military appeared as amateurs in his presence, fumbling for answers to questions that had never been asked before, expected to explain their programs without recourse to the normal slogans or a sense of what the political marketplace would bear."

McNamara's utter faith in numbers and quantifiable systems analysis significantly influenced civil-military relationships. On the Secretary's part, according to Freedman, he announced, "I am certain that no significant military problem will be wholly susceptible to purely quantitative analysis." However, he further emphasized, the more 'quantitative analysis,' the better; for it removes "uncertainty from our process of making a choice."

As he became more successful in his reform of the Pentagon's program and budgeting problems, the Defense Secretary became emboldened over his systems analysis successes. He became convinced that it would be the new method for determining military strategies for solving complex political-military problems. As previously mentioned, he announced that there is no longer any use for the term 'military strategy.' Like the President, he also became convinced that military thinking was too dull, unoriginal, and outmoded to the new frontier that the Kennedy Administration confronted.

The "Whiz Kids" he brought in with him to reform the Department had similar analytical backgrounds and attitudes toward the military. Mostly business analysts and men with pronounced academic backgrounds, McNamara positioned these men in key positions throughout his staff. The two individuals who best represented the attitudes, views, and methods of the Whiz Kids were Alain Enthoven and John McNaughton.

Enthoven had worked at the Rand Corporation, applying his economics and systems analysis educational background from Stanford, Oxford, and MIT. McNamara thought that his knowledge and applications of his analytical methods, and his knowledge of the thoughts behind strategic weapons theory, would be ideal for his reform plans. H. R. McMaster, in his book on the relationship between the military and civilians in the Pentagon, observes that he "became McNamara's point man in establishing firm civilian control over the Defense Department. His flair for quantitative analysis was exceeded only by his arrogance."

Enthoven, like McNamara, held military experience in low regard and considered military men intellectually inferior. He likened leaving the military decision making to the professional military to allowing welfare workers to develop national welfare programs. Enthoven suggested that military experience can even be a disadvantage because it discourages seeing the larger picture. He and many of his colleagues believed that most people in the Department of Defense just tried to advance their particular project or their service or their department. He was convinced that "there was little in the typical officer's early career that qualifies him to be a better strategic planner than… a graduate of the Harvard Business School."

Enthoven would derive most of the performance measures that McNamara would rely on for progress in Administration's Vietnam policies. His main statistic, as demonstrated in several memos in *The Pentagon Papers*, was the kill ratio. As mentioned in earlier chapters, his arguments against Westmoreland's call for reinforcements would focus on how more forces would not increase these kill ratios appreciably; thus, it would not be worth the cost in the budget. McNamara based his resistance to MACV troop increases mainly on Enthoven's recommendations.

John McNaughton, who was not one of the former Whiz Kids at Ford as Enthoven was, would become the Assistant Secretary of Defense for International Security Affairs. He was McNamara's right-hand man for his gradualism approach to crises. Like Enthoven, his memos to McNamara would dominate much of the analyses, as exhibited in *The Pentagon Papers*.

He had been a Harvard Law School professor; but his real interests were in strategic weapons, nuclear arms control, and limited war theory. At Harvard, he had taught with and maintained contacts with the prominent strategic weapons and limited war scholars of the time. One such man was Thomas Schelling, who had written a pioneering study of conflict behavior just before Kennedy became President called *The Strategy of Conflict*.

The dominant theme of Schelling's 1960 book was conflict management. Mostly unschooled in military theory or history, the Harvard educated economist primarily relied on the economic theories of bargaining and gaming. From these theories, he coined in this book his philosophy and theory of conflict behavior. In several of his chapters, he introduced the ideas of the importance of credibility, gradual escalation techniques, and incentives for inducing enemy responses to alter their behavior.

McNaughton thought that in applying Schelling's theories and techniques, a solution could be found to any problem "by simply dissecting it into all its elements and then piecing together the resultant formula." Like McGeorge Bundy, he was a proponent of game theory and would apply it in his recommendations for the ROLLING THUNDER operations. During JFK's Administration, he advised McNamara on his belief in control of military arms to prevent escalation and signal an opponent to affect his choices and decisions. In the Cuban Missile Crisis McNamara relied upon him in his recommendations to the President on how to control military force.

Military members of the Defense Department almost immediately responded to these two men and others in the 'Whiz Kid' gang with a lack of trust and understanding in kind. For example, many military staff officers in the Pentagon saw "McNamara's staff as adversaries. Differences arose between the JCS and McNamara's office over new management techniques, the military budget, and weapons procurement. The officers resented the lack of respect for military experience among those whom they nicknamed derisively McNamara's happy little hotdogs."

Furthermore, as "General Thomas D. White wrote bitterly in 1963: In common with many other military men, active and retired, I am profoundly apprehensive of the pipe-smoking, tree-full-of-owls type of so-called professional defense intellectuals who have been brought into this Nation's Capital. I don't believe a lot of these often over-confident, sometimes arrogant young professors, mathematicians, and other theorists have sufficient worldliness or motivation to stand up to the kind of enemy we face."

In summary of civil-military relations during the Kennedy years, given the nature of his views and those of his civilian advisors, it is reasonable to deduce that JFK's disdain for and lack of trust in his military advisors decisively influenced his decisions on the use of military actions in Southeast Asia. As a result, Presidential decisions lacked full consideration to critical military factors, overreliance on academic models and treatises on crisis management and game theory, and the lack of an overall national military strategy for Indochina and Vietnam.

Though Kennedy would not live to see the results of his decisions on the war, his advisors would. These advisors would continue to make recommendations on Vietnam during the most critical early years of the Johnson Administration. They would also have a critical effect on LBJ's views on the military and the war. Thus, JFK's adoption of the gradual response approach to international crises would survive his death. His distrust of the military, and those best and brightest scholars he brought into government would also influence his successor and his relationships with the military.

LBJ Administration Civil-Military Relations

As mentioned in Chapter 3, LBJ sought continuity between his Presidency and that of Kennedy. While keeping the bulk of JFK's advisors, he almost immediately endorsed the assassinated President's pledge to keep South Vietnam from communist domination. Indeed, Johnson publicly said that he would not become known as the one who had lost Vietnam to the communists. These two acts, retaining JFK's advisors and his policies, would set the stage for the relations between himself, his senior civilian advisors, and the American military for the rest of his term.

Moreover, despite this apparent pledge not to lose Vietnam, LBJ indicated early on in his Presidency to a few close associates, and some biographers afterward, that he did not want to be known as a war president. As emphasized in Chapter 3 and elsewhere, he was leery that that 'bitch' of a war would detract from what he wanted to carry out in his Presidency – his domestic programs. This ambivalence of not wanting to be a war president, and yet not wanting to lose the war, would have two further significant effects on the war and civil-military relations.

First, as detailed before, LBJ felt that he had to walk a fine line between waging a war to stop communism, and controlling it so that it would not get out of hand and ruin his domestic agenda. Thus, he chose, upon the recommendation of Robert McNamara, to follow a cautious, limited, and gradual approach to the conduct of the war to personally control it so that he could wage his war on poverty. This approach, given the published, stated purpose of defending South Vietnam against aggression, set him at odds with the JCS, who thought that they needed to apply force in an all-out effort against the North to stop communist belligerence in Southeast Asia.

Second, LBJ had shared his predecessor's distrust of the military. To his Senate colleagues in 1964 he said that he suspected that the JCS were trying to pull him further into the war in Vietnam, and even another World War, to satisfy their lust for glory. In 1966, he told General Westmoreland not to pull another MacArthur. Moreover, his continued insistence on applying force in a limited, piecemeal fashion, yet telling his advisors to kill more VC, further confused the relationship between himself and his military advisors and commanders.

The Presidential tapes illustrate how confused and uncertain of the military and its advice LBJ thought he was getting about the conflict in Vietnam. To his friend Senator Russell, he complained about the seeming recklessness of the JCS, sometimes exaggerating and saying, "They're ready to put a million men in there real quick and all that... Now, none of us want to do what the Joint Chiefs of Staff say you ought to do to win—and that's 'go in and bomb the hell out of [North Vietnam].' And I'm refusing to do that...They're awfully irresponsible... They just scare you."

As the war unfolded, the President consistently demanded from his military that they be loyal and not rock the boat. In his rare meetings with the JCS, he demanded that they give him ways to guarantee how to win the war. When the military situation seemed glum, such as during Khe Sanh, he asked for further guarantees and even pledges that the enemy would not win.

In essence, LBJ's treatment of his principal military advisors prevented him from getting the advice he needed. It also stifled any disagreement and, in effect, silenced the Joint Chiefs from voicing any disagreement. As Richard Betts argues, "professional military opposition to the Johnson administration's planned strategy for Vietnam was unknown to the public [for the first two years of the war]. This in turn reduced the constraints on Johnson, made it easier for him to avoid the choice between the extremes of withdrawal and overwhelming force, and facilitated the descent into disaster that did not end until a decade later, at a price far higher than a choice of either of the extremes in 1965 would have cost."

Furthermore, when Johnson confronted a significant decision on the war - such as the mobilization issue or lifting the restrictions on the bombing, or attacking the Ho Chi Minh Trail with major American ground forces - he always sought a compromise solution. Compromise is what he had done in the Congress. It had made him a highly successful politician. But compromise and one-way pledges are hardly the ways for a leader in wartime to garner confidence, or certainly to gain mutual trust and understanding.

George Herring, in his study of Johnson as a war leader *LBJ and Vietnam*, summarizes best Johnson's legacy as Commander-in-Chief of one of the most complex and controversial wars in US history. He writes, "Although he took quite seriously his role as commander in chief, he preferred to deal with other matters, the Great Society and the legislative process he understood best and so loved. In contrast to Lincoln, Roosevelt, and even Harry Truman, he had little interest in military affairs and no illusion of military expertise. He had read virtually nothing of such things and had done only brief and token service in World War II."

As Herring further notes, "Lyndon Johnson's entirely political manner of running the war, his consensus-oriented modus operandi, had the effect of stifling debate. Throughout his political career, on the most controversial of issues he had always positioned himself comfortably in the middle, and on Vietnam, he did the same. On such issues as bombing targets and bombing pauses, troop levels and troop use, by making concessions to each side without giving any what it wanted, he managed to keep dissent and controversy under control. From the beginning of the war to the end, as Clark Clifford has observed, Johnson acted more as a legislative leader maintaining consensus among his divided colleagues than a commander in chief running a war."

Under pressure to increase reinforcements, with the war having no end in sight, and continuously self-pressured by news reports and television images of anti-war demonstrations, LBJ, from time to time, let into the Chiefs and other military senior officers. As early as 1965 he showed his frustration and lack of respect for his senior military advisors in an outburst over the bombing. As related by McMaster in his study, a frustrated Johnson said to his Joint Chiefs, "Bomb, bomb, bomb. That's all you know...You generals have all been educated at the taxpayer's expense, and you're not giving me any ideas and any solutions for this little pissant country. Now I don't need ten generals to come in here ten times to tell me to bomb."

Months later, at a JCS meeting on the war and in an account by a Marine Corps officer present, the President "screamed obscenities, he cursed them personally, he ridiculed them for coming to his office with their 'military advice.' Noting that it was he who was carrying the weight of the free world on his shoulders, he called them filthy names-shitheads, dumb shits, pompous assholes-and used 'the F-word' as an adjective more freely than a Marine in boot camp would use it. He then accused them of trying to pass the buck for World War III to him. It was unnerving, degrading."

Under enormous pressure and unsure of himself as a wartime leader, LBJ had Robert McNamara as his right-hand man to depend upon to get things right on Vietnam. The Commander-in-Chief was confident that his Secretary of Defense could handle the war that the President did not want. By this time, McNamara had completed his management reform of the unwieldy defense department. He had also replaced several of the Chiefs. He had 'handpicked' General Earle Wheeler, a military man comfortable with numbers, but ignorant on most military strategic matters.

As George Herring again notes, these latest military men were a 'new breed.' They lacked the prestige of combat. They were at home behind the desk. They were "planners and thinkers, not heroes." The Secretary made it clear to them that he wanted "team men, not gladiators."

Despite McNamara's 'mea culpa' in his *In Retrospect*, the evidence, especially the presidential tapes, shows that the defense secretary was confident in 1965 that he could keep Vietnam limited and apply his beloved gradualism approach to convince the North Vietnamese to cease their aggression. When he saw Westmoreland's June 1965 request for more troops, he knew that the nature of the US commitment to South Vietnam had reached a crossroads.

He told the President so. The challenge for McNamara, as he saw it then, was how to manage the flow of troops and the corresponding budget to ensure that the war did not get out of hand. As in the JFK years, his business acumen, belief in statistics, and faith in his intellect convinced him that he could manage the war. War was no different from running a business, he thought. There was be no need for a military strategy. In his mind, such a necessity was outdated. As a result, in the words of George Herring, "he was out of his element when compelled to go beyond the managerial aspects of military policy."

The very first thing that the Defense Secretary sought to do in mid-1965 was to bring Westmoreland under control. As the situation in Vietnam was getting out of hand, he had been upset with the way the MACV commander had somehow wrestled the reins of 'managing' the conflict and escalating it through a series of requests for increasingly more reinforcements.

Into the following year, his statistics had not shown any decisive results. He and his principal assistants – namely McNaughton and Enthoven – were intent on bringing the war back under their direction. "Under control," to these business-oriented academicians meant a cost-efficient level of commitment until the forces of economic diminishing returns convinced the enemy to give up.

With the unwitting help of Westmoreland himself, who did not care to get involved with these civilians and left such matters up to those in Washington, McNamara slowed or reduced force deployments. The Secretary began to not only marginalize the theater commander regarding what was needed to wage war but continued to minimize and bypass the Joint Chiefs on what they thought it would take to conduct the war more successfully. The goal for McNamara in 1967 was to wait out the enemy until he would just agree to negotiate.

As the evidence shows, and as George Herring explains, McNamara, frustrated that his cost-effective management and systems analysis techniques had failed, had given up on a military solution that would convince the enemy to stop its aggression. In mid-1967, without any consultation with the military and after thousands of American and Vietnamese dead, the Secretary went as far as to tell LBJ that he must find a negotiated solution. That solution was to offer the North a significant concession on allowing the southern communists to take part in elections to decide the South's fate – a concession that all had believed since the early sixties would lead to a communist victory. That is when LBJ decided to get rid of his trusted war manager.

As the Defense Secretary lost faith in any favorable outcome, the relationship between McNamara and the JCS continued to grow worse. Indeed, several accounts - mainly Lewis Sorley's biography of Harold Johnson, *Honorable Warrior*; and Mark Perry's *Four Stars* - state that the Chiefs considered resigning in protest over the Administration's, meaning McNamara's, Vietnam policies.

According to Sorley, whose account primarily cites Army staff officers serving for Johnson, the Army Chief of Staff was a strong proponent of calling up the reserves. As mentioned in previous chapters, he argued the criticality of the reserve call-up to McNamara. He said that without them, Army forces would be hard pressed to deploy in the numbers that Westmoreland needed. He also stated that the Army might not be able to meet its commitments in Europe and elsewhere.

General Johnson, a Bataan death march survivor, and Korean War veteran, said that he thought this was the most crucial decision of the entire war. To staff officers, and during a question and answer session in a visit to the Army War College after the war, he said that he thought of resigning in protest over this failure to call up the reserves.

The General decided against this act, saying, "But if I resign, they'll just put in somebody in who will vote the way they want him to." He also told some students at the War College, that resignation "would be disruptive, deciding instead to serve on and do the best he could under the circumstances."

The Army Chief of Staff's rationale, which seems self-serving given the consequences, is hard to accept. One could certainly question the title of Sorley's book, given the thousands of American soldiers, sons, and fathers, who died in the war and whose fate may have been different if the reserve mobilization had occurred.

Mark Perry's account narrates an instance in which all of Chiefs contemplated resigning. It occurred over testimony before the Stennis' hearings in August 1967 narrated in Chapter 4. Though there is no hard proof that this incident occurred, what may have happened reflects that nature of the civil-military relationship in the Johnson Administration and the deterioration of the personal relationships between the Joint Chiefs and Robert McNamara in 1967.

According to the story, the JCS were upset over McNamara's testimony before the committee over the bombing campaign against North Vietnam. Before that same committee, the JCS had previously testified that the campaign, which the Administration was thinking of cutting back on, should be expanded. Days afterward the Secretary refuted this claim. He confidently, and some thought arrogantly, said that the Chiefs were wrong.

Using his usual mastery of statistics, McNamara then vehemently said that the employment of airpower had already severely crippled the North's ability to support the war in the South. Any more bombing, he added, would be useless and could lead to the loss of innocent civilians. To the JCS, in Perry's telling of this incident, it seemed that McNamara was not only denying their arguments over the ineffectiveness of the US interdiction efforts against the North, but selectively, erroneously, and deceptively distorting the war's progress to the Congress.

Perry claims, using remarks from officers on the JCS staff, that Wheeler and the other Chiefs met in the Chairman's office after McNamara's testimony and discussed resigning. The Chairman led the discussion. He swore everyone to secrecy over the meeting. He proposed that they all resign at a press conference that he would call for the next morning. The meeting lasted from noon well into the evening. At its end, they had all decided to go along with Wheeler's suggestion.

Afterward, Wheeler had second thoughts. He again got the Chiefs together in his office the next morning. The General suggested that if they did resign, with a war going on, it would be a 'mutiny.' They had taken an oath to obey orders. Besides, the Chairman further reasoned, it would not matter. The Administration would find someone in their place. The resignation would all be for naught because it would quickly be forgotten. The best they could do was to continue to present their views to the President and the Congress when called upon to do so.

Whether this story is true or not – Wheeler and the other Chiefs denied it happened and there is nothing of this episode in the official JCS histories - this anecdote symbolizes what much of the evidence indicates was the actual civil-military atmosphere of the time. By late 1967, all the military advisors in Washington knew that the Administration's policy of gradualism and limited war was prohibiting the American military from taking the initiative and affecting the North's ability to pursue the war.

As we have seen in the earlier chapters, the indecisive course of the war was not entirely due to the civilians' faulty and faint-hearted policies. The two US military men most responsible for the war up until mid-1968 contributed to this indecision and poor direction in their own ways. Both had not been able to understand entirely their follies in agreeing, at first, to their civilian leaders' choices and direction for the war. They were also reluctant or unable to argue a course that could have gained the initiative and effectively imposed a solution upon the North. These two military men, of course, were General Earle Wheeler and General William Westmoreland.

As explained in earlier chapters, Wheeler was trying to improve a problematic situation between his military colleagues in the Pentagon, the commanders in the field at US Pacific Command and MACV, and his civilian bosses, McNamara, and Johnson. At the same time, he had a heart disease which further added to or was a symptom of the discord. His attempts to show respect and loyalty to LBJ and the Secretary, while voicing the concerns of the JCS and military commanders, resulted in divided military advice in Washington.

While Wheeler left no detailed memoir or autobiography, his oral testimonies on the war, found in the LBJ library, show that he had an intense friendship for LBJ. The President often called him 'Bus,' and through the typical Johnson methods, it appears that Wheeler was touched by the personal affection LBJ demonstrated. The President also tried to bond with his chief military advisor over their mutual cardiac problems.

Eventually, after the President noticed McNamara's negativity toward and resulting strain from the war, Johnson even began to rely more on Wheeler for advice. LBJ made him a member of the Tuesday luncheon group. After that, the Chairman became increasingly sympathetic to the pressures brought on the President, mainly by the animosity of the anti-war movement. In short, it seems that the General fell under the spell that LBJ cast upon others at times – making his chief military advisor sympathetic to the Commander-in-Chief's woes and worries.

It is what Wheeler did not do, however, that is most noteworthy. As the President's senior advisor, he did not try to educate LBJ on military affairs or strategy. He continued to let the President give meaningless advice, such as kill more VC, or seek guarantees of victory rather than discussions and assessments of critical strategic issues. Though Johnson sought none of this and was uninterested in such matters, Wheeler had the responsibility to ensure that his Commander-in-Chief address such in wartime. Of course, the General would have had to be knowledgeable in military strategy and operations to do so; and that knowledge was profoundly lacking.

As the war progressed and Westmoreland continuously asked for more reinforcements, Wheeler, as noted previously, fell into the trap of the 'numbers game.' Instead of insisting that he and the Joint Staff and Chiefs argue the merits of the force requests regarding military factors, concepts of operations, enemy capabilities, and possible outcomes, the Chairman relinquished the initiative to the civilian analysts.

Consequently, McNamara and his team of 'Whiz Kids,' packaged each of the MACV requests into force cases, or levels, or options – the language of management enthusiasts arguing cost-effective solutions. These Defense program management specialists assessed each one of these cases. In doing so, they examined pros and cons regarding measured and assessed budget costs, inflationary impacts, kill ratio effects, and whether they could be supported without mobilization.

As a result, Wheeler and the JCS and its staff found themselves in a continuous game of defending numbers rather than how each request could affect the military strategy or operations. It is no wonder then, that when Wheeler tried to obtain forces that could take advantage of the NVA/VC TET defeat, he got himself involved in yet again another argument on numbers. McNamara's choice to recommend him as Chairman because he was not a 'Gladiator' but a good team staff manager paid off. LBJ got precisely what he wanted when he selected him because he would be loyal and ardent personal supporter of his decisions.

Meanwhile, as he admits in his memoirs and as already mentioned, General Westmoreland was content to let Wheeler manage the numbers game in Washington. While he offered an operational concept for his reinforcement requests, he let Wheeler justify them. The irony is that, other than a few officers in the joint and service staffs, no civilian leaders paid any attention to those operational concepts. As mentioned and as best we can now determine, the President never saw them.

As related and emphasized several times previously, one startling fact about the MACV commander is that while he gave his reasoning behind the force levels, he did not forcibly argue for the reinforcements he needed when McNamara and LBJ rejected them. Moreover, by his own accounts - and supported by much of the documentation since – Westmoreland did not argue the risks associated with fewer forces. While offering some thoughts, such as the war would just be more prolonged, he seemed to accept the adjustments without vigorously pointing out the downside.

This story has already offered some speculation on why he did not argue strenuously for the reinforcements and his alternative strategy. Recall that it may have been, at least in the beginning, that he realized that his logistics and support system in South Vietnam could not entirely give the throughput that was necessary for these forces. At other times, as mentioned, he seemed to assume that he could do what he wanted even with fewer forces, it would just take more time. We have also reasoned that Westmoreland did not persist because he left these decisions to his superior commander in Hawaii and the senior advisor in Washington. Another was that it was not in his nature to argue with his superiors.

Here – to gain a different perspective on this critical issue - we need to examine his acquiescence and lack of strong counterargument regarding the personalities involved and the relationships of the military commanders, advisors, and their senior civilian leaders.

As explained in Chapter 9 and further concluded in the last chapter, one year into the war Westmoreland finally realized that his original object might not be obtainable – at least, in his assessment - not as quickly as would be needed given the faltering support on the Homefront. That is when he began to have his staff develop contingency plans for an offensive into Laos to sever the Ho Chi Minh Trail. He discussed this concept, furthermore, with his superior in Hawaii.

The MACV commander and Admiral Sharp both agreed that such a concept could force the North Vietnam Army into a campaign that would result in a decisive contest that the US could win. At the very least, the trail would be permanently severed. At best, the PAVN would be dealt a decisive blow that would end or severely delay its ability to threaten the South. In preparing for such a contingency, should the President authorize it, Westmoreland eventually set up the US base at Khe Sanh.

Once again, from the perspective now of personal and professional relationships - why did Westmoreland not forcefully push the execution of this new offensive military strategy? As the narratives in the earlier chapters have shown, there were at least two documented times that he broached the concept with the President. The first was in March-April of 1967. The second, right after the TET offensive began. At neither of these times was he forceful enough or did he make a convincing case for this change in military strategy.

Going beyond previous speculations, as summarized above, one can further deduce from some of the historical evidence that Westmoreland's relationship with his civilian leaders had become so strained that he just gave up on dealing with them. Thus, he was so frustrated with McNamara and especially the Secretary's assistants and others in Washington that he thought it would merely be futile for him to try.

Much of the evidence of this frustration is limited mostly to his memoirs. That is primarily because the General was very guarded in his reactions to and criticisms of his chain of command. There are no prominent tapes or written records of meetings that reveal this frustration. However, a close reading of his recollections and a statement that the General later made in an oral history shows this frustration on civilians in Washington with whom he had to deal or those who seemed to him to 'second guess' his decisions.

For example, in his recall of McGeorge Bundy's visit and experience during the VC attacks on American facilities in February 1965, the General notes that Bundy was "distressed that what he and other civilian officials in Washington had been hopefully predicting …[that is, an end to Northern aggression in the south due to US bombing] would not happen, had happened." ...Moreover, as he continued to speculate, he notes that it seems that like other "civilians in positions of some government authority, once he smelled a little gunpowder he developed a field marshal psychosis."

In another part of his memoirs in the discussion of the bombing pauses against North Vietnam, Westmoreland states, many in LBJ's Administration did not "have any real understanding of the application of power." He then goes on to name such officials as John McNaughton and Alain Enthoven. The General says of McNaughton that his "views, in particular, were incredible."

Later the MACV commander recalls, "over the months to come lesser civilian officials in the offices of the Assistant Secretaries of Defense for Systems Analysis and International Security Affairs constantly sought to alter strategy and tactics with naïve, gratuitous advice. So, too, the Department of State from time to time tried to impose views differing from the agreed strategy...Although the cables went out over the name of Secretary Rusk, I suspect some of the self-appointed field marshals in the Vietnam Task Force were responsible."

In his most protracted and most revealing explanation of his view of the role of LBJ's civilian interference and his apparent frustration with it, Westmoreland notes further McNaughton's and other civilian meddling. He states, "Those officials and some White House and State Department advisors appeared to scorn professional military thinkers in a seeming belief that presumably superior Ivy League intellects could devise some political hocus pocus or legerdemain to bring the enemy to terms without using force to destroy his war making capability."

The General then continues, "However desirable the American system of civilian control of the military, it was a mistake to permit appointive civilian officers who lack military experience and knowledge of military history and who are oblivious to the lessons of Communist machinations to wield undue influence in the decision-making process." In a later 1986 oral interview for the LBJ library, an aging Westmoreland further relates that "over control by the civilians of the conduct of the war was a major problem for him and," the source of detailed control [was the Secretary of Defense] whose views on the war – including how it was to be fought and the sources to be provided – were paramount."

In sum of this discussion of civil-military relations during the Johnson years, there are three major conclusions. First, LBJ brought to his administration the same senior civilian advisors that JFK had in his. Consequently, he inherited the poor atmosphere that had already existed in the Kennedy years in civil-military relations. Compounding this appalling state of personal relationships between civilians and military, LBJ had no experience in military affairs, and because of what he had observed under Kennedy, had developed a distrust toward the military and was suspicious of and lacked confidence in their military advice.

Second, in part due to this inherited state of relations and continued lack of rapport, the civilians and the military advisors in Washington failed to formulate, coordinate, assess, and understand political aims and military objectives and strategies. At first, military advisors became defensive and reluctant to challenge this civilian takeover of military affairs by a group of business systems analysts that challenged their military judgment and experience with numbers. As the relationships further deteriorated, the senior military advisors rejected forceful action to challenge the policies imposed upon them with little consultation and much circumvention in the decision-making process.

Third, a reason that the field commander, General William Westmoreland, did not press strongly for his sound alternative military strategy and its prerequisite forces in 1966 and 1968 is that he had become frustrated with the civilian defense officials he had been dealing with in Washington, and thought it would be futile to do so. Thus, he was more than willing for others, namely the Chairman of the Joint Chiefs General Bus Wheeler to do so for him. Unfortunately, the latter was not up to the task and failed to do so.

To complete then this part of the discussion of civil-military relations during the Vietnam War, the distrust and lack of respect between the Johnson civilian and military advisors and leaders led to a serious void in shared responsibility for the Vietnam War. All of that was a significant contributor to the flawed national policies and strategies of LBJ's Administration toward Vietnam, as well as an inability to develop effective theater strategies to direct operations there that had a possibility of defeating the enemy.

Nixon Administration Civil-Military Relations

There is an aphorism that says, "Just when you don't think things can get worse, they do." Such seems accurate when one views the state of civil-military relations during the Nixon Administration contrasted to that of Kennedy and Johnson. While JFK shunned the advice of the JCS and LBJ manipulated them, Nixon just bypassed them. Indeed, he built his substitute national security mechanism for the legal one promulgated by the National Security Acts of the forties and fifties. He created it, as described in Chapter 5, by relying on Kissinger and his expanded personal office for national security affairs.

As Robert Dallek portrays in his book *Nixon and Kissinger* both men shared the same views and desires for decision making – one in which they personally directed policies, and avoided interference from both within the executive branch and from any other outside agency or organization; most notably the Press and Congress. To do this, they bypassed their secretaries of defense and state, built their private military council, and controlled information between themselves and others.

Dale Herspring notes in his *Civil-Military Relations and Shared Responsibility*, that the Nixon-Kissinger informal organization "put the White House in the center of the decision-making process. The White House staff grew from 292 under Johnson to 583 by the end of Nixon's first term. Chaired by the president's national security assistant, these committees comprised the Vietnam Special Studies Group, the Washington Special Actions Group (to deal with international crisis), the Defense Programs Review Committee, the Verification Panel (to deal with strategic arms talks), the 40 Committee (to deal with covert actions), and the Senior Review Group (to deal with all other policy issues)."

These special White House groups seldom coordinated their activities with other agencies or offices in the Nixon government, unless the President or Kissinger specifically told them to do so. Again, as Herspring explains, "Often, key officials had no idea what was going on. For example, no one from the White House informed Secretary of State William Rogers in advance of the administration's most innovative foreign policy initiative—the opening to China, which Nixon visited in February 1972." Moreover, the Nixon Presidential tapes are full of the President's remarks, more like orders, to key staffers in these groups to avoid and not share their papers or insights into national security matters with others in the Administration.

The JCS official history during the Nixon years describes the office of the Joint Chiefs as bypassed entirely on major military issues. Indeed, the history quotes several of the Chiefs as referring to themselves as total 'bystanders' to the war during these years. Hence, more than the JFK and LBJ years, the JCS as a body played no significant role in the Vietnam War during Nixon's reign.

One of the primary reasons was that the JCS Chairman, Admiral Moorer, whom Nixon and Kissinger personally chose, obeyed the President's orders not to involve the other Chiefs in decisions on the Vietnam War. Herspring argues that CJCS Moorer was "just the kind of officer the Nixon White House preferred; he made little effort to inform his fellow chiefs of what was happening at the White House. He was fully aware of the existence of the back-channel communications system in the Pentagon's basement that was under twenty-four-hour guard and reported directly to Kissinger, thereby bypassing Laird."

From time to time even Moorer was left in the dark on several critical issues. This was for fear that he might confide them to the Secretary of Defense Melvin Laird. Thus, the Admiral set up his own White House JCS liaison office, whose function was to send any secret or any other relevant document that it could get its hands on to the Chairman. When Nixon found out about this, he dismantled the office but decided to keep on the indispensable Moorer, who was still willing to do the President's bidding.

This breakdown of formal civil-military communications also characterized the relationship between Washington and the military headquarters overseeing the war - the Pacific Command and MACV. Nixon circumvented that chain of command and used Moorer to transmit orders directly to operational commanders on several occasions. After a while, both the Pacific Commander, Admiral John McCain, and the MACV commander, General Abrams, had to ensure that their subordinates were aware that they had been bypassed, and needed to be kept informed should the President or his National Security advisor approach them directly.

As an example of the above, at one point during LINEBACKER - according to several accounts - Nixon told Moorer that, as Commander-in-Chief, he was now directly in charge of the bombing operations. While he did not take formal direct command, he did try to completely redo the command structure for the war to his liking. While this would have placed the region under one commander – what Commanders-in-Chief should have done from the beginning – it would at that juncture in the war have disrupted ongoing operations. Thus, Moorer convinced Nixon that working with him would get the orders passed to the President's liking, and would guarantee more effective operations.

It is during this time, in May 1972, that the Presidential Tapes relate one extraordinary incident that characterizes the worse of civil-military relations during the Nixon Administration, and perhaps the worst of all of the Vietnam War experience. On 19 May, Nixon was meeting with his Vice President Spiro Agnew in the oval office. Agnew had just returned from a trip to Southeast Asia and some US airbases there. He told the President that "there's some remorse" in the US military over limits placed on the bombing of North Vietnam. The President became ballistic and asked to see Admiral Moorer at once.

While waiting for the Chairman, Nixon turned to Kissinger, who also was present, and said, "I've given them the latitude and the Air Force dropped the ball in a miserable way. They aren't worth a goddamn. They aren't worth a goddam. I want the head of that son of a bitch of the Air Force – Ryan [the Chief of Staff] today. He's out. Out. Out. Out." The President then turns his tirade to the actual pilots flying the missions over North Vietnam, saying, "They're scared. They're scared to go in under the ceiling."

When the Chairman comes to his office, Nixon tells him, "Ryan has got to get off his goddamn ass or he's out. I'm tired of him anyway. He's a soft man. I mean, of course, he should be; I mean, his son killed and all that sort of thing. But let me say, you know and I know, I have ordered that goddamn Air Force time and time again to do anything, and they can't bomb, because they say … they need a 4,000-foot ceiling. You know and I know that they do not have restrictions. The only restriction they've got is the one within ten miles of Hanoi *at the present time*, which they didn't have before and the Air Force didn't do a *goddamn thing* for the last three days, as you know… I want the military to shape up or there's going to be a new chief of staff all up and down the line. Now, you go take care of it right now. Is that clear?"

Moorer responded in an unemotional voice, "Yes sir." This episode was not the first time that the Admiral underwent a tongue lashing from Nixon. The tapes during this time, as the Easter Offensive was ongoing, show Nixon at his lowest in how he treated people. He had come under much pressure realizing that if the North had been successful in its invasion all would be lost in settling his 'Peace with Honor.' Moreover, he had become just as furious with Abrams as Moorer, and the rest of the JCS.

At this time, Moorer had come as disillusioned about Abrams as Nixon had. The Chairman had become concerned that Abrams' assessments of the South Vietnamese Armed Forces were much too confident. Even the entire JCS thought that they were tainted too much by his wishful thinking. Instead of discussing this directly with General Abrams, Admiral Moorer assigned his Director of the Joint Staff, Air Force General John Vogt, to Abrams staff. His role was primarily to keep the Chairman advised of any information on how the MACV commander was making decisions.

This officer became a de facto spy for Moorer. As the JCS history points out, "The Chairman now had his trusted man on the scene and, increasingly, would rely on him for appraisals and advice. Very soon, at Moorer's direction, Vogt began cabling a daily personal assessment marked 'For the Chairman's Eyes Only,' through special channels bypassing General Abrams and Admiral McCain. The Assistant Chief of Staff for Intelligence, USAF, delivered these messages to Admiral Moorer who passed copies to Dr. Kissinger."

Thus, as a result of Nixon's bombastic tirades and threats, and Admiral Moorer's system of spy rings and informants, by mid-1972 the entire US chain of command for the war had become unraveled. With senior military officers so afraid of Nixon's threats, and the JCS leader finding the need to spy on the US field commander, there was not even a semblance of capable direction of the war.

Nixon and Kissinger further soured relationships and added to the breakdown in military command by relying upon personal military assistant Alexander Haig. As previously explained, Colonel, and in 1972 Brigadier General Haig was the head of Kissinger's informal council for military assessments and advice. Indeed, it was this informal council that drafted some of the strategic plans that Nixon asked his National Security Advisor to draft. The most notable was the DUCK HOOK plan explained in Chapter 5.

However, Haig's principal role was to travel between the White House and Saigon to assess first-hand the situation there. He would then personally report back to both Kissinger and the President his views on the efficiency and effectiveness of the MACV commander and his actions. This task the military officer undertook with enthusiasm, and without loyalty or remorse. At every opportunity, he seemed to relish reporting on his senior's drinking habits and mistakes.

Consequently, as we have seen in Chapter 5, as Nixon grew more dissatisfied with Abrams performance, he thought of having Haig take command. This was a prime sign that Nixon knew little about military culture, and could care less. Blinded by ambition, evidently Haig did not care to inform the President that the move would have been not only unprecedented but further ruinous to military discipline and order in a war zone.

While both Nixon and Kissinger claim respect for and confidence in their military advisors in their memoirs, the tapes of their conversations, such as the one above, show dramatically otherwise. This is particularly clear during the period after the Laos offensive. Moreover, in many of the taped conversations during and after the Easter Offensive in 1972 Nixon continually ridicules the military; often implying not only incompetence but cowardice in their operations. These comments are particularly offensive because under Nixon's presidency the US military lost over twenty thousand troops to achieve his 'Peace with Honor.'

These tapes also show that both the President and his National Security Advisor thought they were experts in military history and operations, and, therefore, did not need military advice. For example, in one conversation on April 4, 1972, Nixon and Kissinger discuss the inability of the military to move and mass air and naval forces adequately and in a prompt fashion to counter the North's offensive operations against the South. They regularly refer to how Napoleon could attack and defeat his enemies with "lightning strikes;" and imply that the US military was missing opportunities to "really clobber" the North Vietnamese that, if they were in the field in direct command, they could remedy.

Nixon's rants about how Abrams drinking is particularly ironic. As mentioned in Chapter 5, some evidence suggests that the President had an alcohol problem. It even seems that the two may have had much in common in this regard. Abrams supposedly drank and often listened to classical music for comfort. Nixon drank and repeatedly watched the movie, *Patton,* to regain his composure and confidence.

In sum, the views and behavior that got Richard Nixon impeached characterized his relationships and dealings with his senior military commanders and advisors, as well. His suspicion and distrust toward the Press and his political opponents were only slightly greater than that of his attitude toward the military. He thought that his actions would be more effective if he relegated his commanders and senior advisors to 'bystanders' in his grand scheme of how to end the war. In so doing, he completely shattered the 'sine qua non' for success in war – the military chain of command and its ability to translate political direction into sound military operations.

Conclusion: How Scholars and Warriors Can Become Cowards and Fools

To conclude this chapter, the key lessons of the Vietnam War for the future are not the 'what ifs' or 'could have beens' regarding changing the course of the past, and seeking recipes for the future. Instead, practical choices for and decisions in the national security arena, mainly when they call for the use of military force, are dependent in a democracy on constructive and productive relationships between the civilian decision makers and their military advisors and commanders.

As Bob Woodward has discovered in his attempts to capture the policy-making in more recent times, "Decision making at the highest levels of national government is a complex human interaction. The inside story of government involves conversations, arguments, meetings, phone calls, personal attitudes, backgrounds, and relationships. This human story is the core of understanding decisions at the highest level of government."

Indeed, the 'human story' of the Vietnam War is one of a great tragedy. In the American system of government, the conduct of foreign affairs and wars is a shared responsibility. However, it is on the shoulders of the Chief Executive, the President of the United States, the Commander-in-Chief of the Armed Forces, that the successes or failures in war rest. Truman's standard remains applicable – "The Buck Stops Here!"

Each of the Presidents involved in the Vietnam saga had their tragic flaws. The most common flaw, regarding the Chief Executive's responsibilities as Commander-in-Chief of the US Armed Forces, was that they either ignored or rejected the advice of their senior military commanders and advisors. Yet, they did not have a sound background or understanding of the use of military force. Even if they had, it was incumbent upon the President to find and choose military commanders and advisors whom he could have confidence in and trust. That is what made Lincoln and Franklin Roosevelt such great Commanders-in-Chiefs, and successful war leaders.

Lincoln and FDR not only eventually chose great military war leaders, but they listened and learned from them. Through this on the job instruction, supplemented by their self-education on military affairs, they gained a sense of the difficulty of waging war, exhibited great determination and courage to choose the right strategic course and stick to it, and provided the appropriate guidance to their military commanders for victory on the battlefield. On the other hand, the three major Vietnam War Commanders, JFK, LBJ, and Nixon, floundered and folded in both purpose and determination to build and nurture a relationship with their military that may have altered their flawed policies and created a more effective war strategy. Thus, each in their way, contributed to the failed outcome of America's most complex and controversial conflict.

Throughout his presidency, JFK adhered to a belief that military men are inherently inflexible, and will always argue for the use of force on the road to war that may, like in the *Guns of August*, lead to the destruction of that which we want to preserve. Thus, he hesitated in finding a decisive military solution to the Vietnam dilemma. His hesitation over the Diem removal and assassination also led to a decisive turn in the South's long-term struggle to set up a workable government to counter the insurgency and outside aggression.

LBJ shared JFK's distrust of the military. He also inherited, by choice, Kennedy's civilian advisors who thought they knew better than the American military on how to wage war. Johnson sought to limit the war so that he could engage in and gain what he wanted as the measure of his legacy as President – his Great Society programs. All his decisions were gauged toward limiting a war and convincing his opponents to cease their aggression. Those decisions turned out to be wrong because the North could not be convinced using limited force when it was fighting an unlimited war.

LBJ also deceived his military commanders into believing that they would have his support in pursuing a military strategy of their choosing. As he wished for an easily negotiated settlement, the war just would not go away. His opponents had a vote in this matter, and the great 'vote getter' could not understand why his powers of persuasion could not work as they had before on the campaign trail and in the Congress.

In the end, his chief war manager, Robert McNamara – the best and brightest of the best and brightest – succumbed to failure and also broke down under pressure. He had waged a war he thought could be won by measuring it to success. Meanwhile, his Commander-in-Chief, as distraught as the man he had turned the war over to, surrendered to the media's portrayal of defeat in Vietnam. His senior military advisor and commander aided in that surrender by not providing the determination, advice, and support needed in the face of adversity. In short, they all quit at a critical moment. In so doing, they were as cowardly in their actions, or lack of, as a soldier on the battlefield who runs away from the enemy.

In the aftermath of this surrender, the most flawed of American Presidents – Richard Nixon - thought he could still win the war single-handedly. Amid public dismay toward the war, Nixon gave birth to the Imperial Presidency and ruled as a Shogun warrior. His desire to prove that he could convince the North to desist his aggression using force led to his approval of the US military to attack the enemy's safe havens and the unleashing of American airpower against the North's homeland.

However, these assaults, long advocated by the military, proved indecisive because they were temporary, ill-designed, and not supported. His delusion of military greatness and his illusion of power created distrust, even loathing, in his administration and most importantly in the Congress. While he publicly praised his warriors and paid homage to them, he privately disrespected and degraded them. This Commander-in-Chief wasted the lives of over twenty thousand troops in his personal invective cause while negotiating what he knew to be a flawed peace with honor. Eventually, these tragic flaws led to his resignation and a disgraceful end to the Vietnam War.

In this 'human story' of the great tragedy of the Vietnam War, the American military share in this defeat through their follies. In an era that demanded a new way to view warfare, those in Washington close to the seat of power clung to the old ideas of 'no substitute for victory' even though it could lead to the extinction of humanity. They divorced themselves from their obligation to explore new theories and doctrines on the use of force in the atomic age. Instead, they focused on justifying their parochial service views on obtaining a fair share of the budget and promoted the use of their service forces to gain more prominence in the programming games of the Pentagon.

In fact, while there were a few who tried to grapple with new concepts for dealing with unconventional wars and there was military doctrine on the subject, the concept of counterinsurgency for the most senior military in Washington meant obtaining more money from restricted budgets. Consequently, they did not know how to employ military force in an era in which limited war was becoming a necessity. They did not understand how political constraints had to be considered, and advice rendered on the effect of those constraints on the effective use of force and its consequences on the political and military objects of war.

Furthermore, during the JFK, LBJ, and Nixon Administrations, the Chairmen and Service Chiefs knew that they were being circumvented from their prescribed duties, yet were derelict to object and forcibly argue their views and attempt to correct their superiors flawed strategic concepts. Some just decided to adhere to their civilian bosses' ways. Some took solace in the view that if they resigned the Administration would just find substitutes. It was better - all convinced themselves - to carry on, obey orders, and to do the best they could under the circumstances.

They saw their duty to obey their superior civilian leaders. They neglected or ignored their obligation to the soldiers, sailors, marines, and airmen, and their American fathers and mothers who had entrusted their sons to them for their service to their country.

In Vietnam, the first American commander, General Paul D. Harkins, sought to do his duty as he knew it. Convinced that half the battle was to show enthusiasm for his mission, he showed an uninhibited fervor to carry out that mission. In a 'fool's errand,' he reported progress, believing that the mission would be accomplished if one sustained a 'can do' spirit. Of course, he was only doing what his civilian bosses wanted and checked on.

The one soldier whom most blame for the military defeat in Vietnam is General William Westmoreland. Unfairly chastised for his military strategy, he did what he was supposed to do – develop a military strategy in the absence of one from Washington. He focused, rightly so, on the most capable military force that the enemy had committed to winning the war. He disseminated and within reason supervised the execution of his concept of operation.

Westy did so despite the opposition from some disgruntled Washington military officers seeking more emphasis on their Service. Above all, he tried to employ force as he had experienced in World War Two, but had modified to the environment of Vietnam – that is to find, fix, and destroy the enemy. This was despite the interference from Administration civilian systems analysts who thought they had better ideas on how to kill more enemy soldiers to win the war. Yet, Westmoreland had been straightforward, and essentially correct, in warning from the onset that this was to be a long war dependent on American public support. He was ignored in the beginning and blamed eventually for its happening in the end.

General Westmoreland was also a loyal commander who tried to do his best with what he had; even though his civilian leaders did not deliver what they promised for his operations. Yet he foolishly believed that he could make his plans work within the constraints the President assigned. Despite the admission that the enemy usually had the initiative and enjoyed sanctuaries outside of South Vietnam where they could recoup losses and reconstitute units, Westmoreland believed he could inflict grave losses, drive them from South Vietnam, and prevent their return over thousands of miles of borders. He did so without due regard to the combat 'grunts' who bore the brunt of battle and to their families who still grieve for them.

Westmoreland - and the military man in Washington responsible during most of the war for advising the President, General Earle Wheeler - let their Commander-in-Chief down at a very critical time and juncture in the war. Wheeler, the consummate staff officer who had become mesmerized by the McNamara numbers game, sought to foolishly play that game during a moment that demanded sound military advice beyond just numbers. In the aftermath of TET, when both the President and his new Defense Secretary were looking for some decisive action plan, both Wheeler and Westmoreland failed to provide one.

General Westmoreland had a potential military course that may have been decisive. It was to take the initiative and conduct offensive operations against the one area that the enemy had to commit to defending – the Ho Chi Minh Trail. They should have done so. Any sound military analysis, albeit in retrospect, shows that such an offensive had a high probability of forcing the enemy to fight with his most capable forces, the same ones that he depended on for victory in the South, and creating a situation in which the power of the American military could be brought to bear and defeat the enemy's prime forces in a 'coup de main.'

It would then have been up to the President to decide whether an effort is undertaken to gain the public and Congressional support needed. In not arguing persuasively for this alternative practical military strategy, Westmoreland and Wheeler added, decisively, to the President's dismay and defeatist attitude.

Finally, some historians have fostered a myth that a soldier on a white horse came along who could have salvaged all of this – General Creighton Abrams. As mentioned in Chapter 10, this argument does not stand up to scrutiny. In fact, the success that occurred in South Vietnam during the first two years of Abrams command was a direct result of the PAVN/VC defeat during the 1968 TET offensive and later counterattacks.

A careful examination of the historical evidence shows that the claim by the end of 1969 that the war was won is absurd. Without a decisive denial of the Ho Chi Minh Trail, and attacks against the border sanctuaries, US leaders allowed the North to recover from its TET military debacle. When the North accomplished that recovery and the US military hastily withdrawn, it was inevitable that the South Vietnamese would be defeated. Abrams could do nothing to reverse these outcomes. The further deterioration of civil-military relations during the Nixon years was a fundamental reason.

General Abrams had fallen into the same pattern as most American military leaders and advisors in the Vietnam War. He accepted the Washington restrictions placed upon operations, loyally tried to execute what he knew as a flawed concept for Vietnamization, and battled with the Administration over allocations and employment of military assets for the war and lost.

Though he threatened to resign at one point over the air allocation issue, he dutifully followed through on orders he knew to be ruinous to the South Vietnamese military and showed wishful thinking on his programs to enhance the capabilities of the ARVN to thwart PAVN and VC main force offensives. In short, Abrams was just as willing to keep on serving without any forceful objections to the actions of his civilian leaders as any of the other military senior officers who served during the war.

To conclude, there is ample blame to go around for someone who seeks answers as to how, why and who lost the Vietnam War. American civilian and military leaders and their advisors all share that in that blame. The credit for the American defeat also needs to be shared with the North Vietnamese leaders and their PAVN and VC forces. They were determined and competent in their pursuit of a war of unification, as well as persistent and brave on the battlefield.

However, seeking blame is not the real value for or lesson of the American failure in the Vietnam War. If we Americans are to learn anything from that experience, we need to study and absorb the personal relationships and their impact on decisions of the civilian and military leaders waging war in Indochina from 1960 to 1973. It is through that study of personal relationships, and the need to develop what Dale Herspring calls 'shared responsibility' for national security decision making in our Government, wherein lay the true lessons of the Vietnam war and their relevance and utilization for today and beyond.

This lesson and its importance to today's national security environment is the subject of the next and concluding chapter of this story. In the further telling of what has been occurring in the US national security arena from 1991 through 2016, and the applicability of the lessons of the Vietnam War experience to that, the reader will see how those lessons are not only pertinent but why they still matter.

Chapter 13: Have We Learned Anything?

The preceding chapters have tried to find answers on why the US lost the Vietnam War. The resultant story has concluded that what was most important to the American experience in that war is that the primary cause for failure was a breakdown in relations between senior civilian and military policymakers. That breakdown, in no small measure, led to erroneous and egregious decision making in the conduct of the war.

There is still, however, one last question. So what? Is that central lesson of the American experience in the Vietnam War pertinent to today's national security environment and decision making? If it is, then can that lesson help solve any of the problems we face today? The purpose of this chapter is to explore these questions.

The following narrative briefly examines the evolution of the US national security environment since the end of the Cold War to today's war on terror. That survey outlines how we got to today's national security decision making atmosphere in which the US is beset with an ongoing, open-ended, and seemingly unsolvable conflict that drains our national treasure of human capital and financial wealth.

The conclusion is that we have many of the same conditions and problems today in the formulation of a national security strategy that we experienced in the Vietnam War. Moreover, we have not learned from that experience and applied its pertinent and applicable lessons. Thus, our senior leaders, both civilian and military, need to find a way to collectively study and apply these lessons, as appropriate, to improve today's national security formulation to address and solve our national security problems. Toward the end of the chapter, the author proposes a way.

Section 13.1 - The 21st Century American National Security Environment: From 'The End of History' to the 'Long War'

With the end of the Soviet Union the decades-old US containment policy, which led to our involvement in Indochina, was obsolete. The specter of communism that prompted the 'Domino Theory' ended. Some political scientists, such as Francis Fukuyama, proclaimed *The End of History*. He declared that democracy had won its struggle against totalitarian regimes. With that triumph, he added, the likelihood of conflict in the future would diminish.

Others, such as Fareed Zakaria in *The Post American World*, pronounced that the new world that would emerge would have a more multi-faceted political orientation. The great power politics of the last four centuries would fade away; replaced by a globalized world more equal and prosperous.

Still others, like Joseph Nye, argued that America would be the only super-power, and was *Bound to Lead* in this new world order. For the most part, these authors' crystal balls were full of optimism about the future.

Certainly, as General Colin Powell had expected, there would be as at the end of other American Wars a peace dividend. The question was how much; and what effect it would have on the nation's armed forces and its security. Indeed, when the William Jefferson Clinton Administration swept into power in 1993, defense budgets dropped. The initial impact was dramatic. The US Army, flushing with its victory in DESERT STORM, went from an active duty strength of some 728,000 soldiers to 529,000. Despite the First Gulf War, peace seemed at hand.

We now know this was but a brief illusion of peace. Before Clinton's first term was over, the US was involved in military deployments and conflicts in Haiti, Somalia, and the Balkans. Clinton also continued Bush's no-fly zone prohibitions over Iraq. He further employed special operations units and other forces in attempts to kill the head of an international terrorist organization called al-Qaeda.

Then, there was September 11, 2001. The unprecedented al-Qaeda planned and executed attacks against the US homeland affected Americans much like the Japanese attack on Pearl Harbor. President George W. Bush, who had followed Clinton, declared a "Global War on Terror."

US forces invaded Afghanistan and toppled, but did not defeat, the Taliban ruling power. Several years later, Bush waged a preventative war against Iraq – forcibly removing Saddam Hussein and occupying that country. As of this writing, we are still involved militarily in both countries, as well as other parts of the globe in constant military conflicts, mostly as part of a war on terror extremists.

The optimism of only twenty-five years ago has turned sour. Some of this sourness is a result of the open-ended commitment to a no end in sight war on terror. Moreover, the US military is the force of choice to counter terrorism in continuous operations in what some now call 'The Long War.'

No End to War in Sight - A National Security Environment in Disarray

One of the more frequent, vociferous, and articulate critics of this no 'light at the end of the tunnel' situation that is characterized by the constant use of American military force is Professor Andrew

Bacevich. A former military officer, a veteran of the Vietnam War, a teacher at West Point, and now a professor at Boston University, Bacevich has written a plethora of books on the effects of this constant conflict.

Bacevich worries that this has or is resulting in *The New American Militarism*. His central theme reflects on James Madison's warnings about standing militaries and warfare. In 1795, Madison warned, "War is the parent of Armies. From these proceed debts and taxes. And armies, debts, and taxes are the known instruments for bringing the many under the domination of the few.... No nation could preserve its freedom in the midst of continual warfare." This Army officer turned Professor warns that this condition may very well be happening in America today.

Professor Bacevich includes several examples of the decisions of America's leaders that have led to this condition. With a soldier-scholars eye, he unveils several interesting and disturbing trends in this decision making that are reminiscent of the Vietnam War experience. For example, regarding Bush's decision to launch Operation Iraqi Freedom in 2003, he argues that "The folly and hubris of the policy makers who heedlessly thrust the nation into an ill-defined and open-ended 'global war on terror' without the foggiest notion of what victory would look like, how it would be won, and what it might cost...." has resulted in a series of conflicts without end. As is described in this story, this situation is eerily reminiscent of the LBJ and McNamara decision to employ ground forces in the summer of 1965 to South Vietnam without a military strategy and no idea of the long-term costs.

Bacevich also faults current American civilian leaders for following an ideology that, like the Vietnam War, does not take into consideration how the world is diverse, and, therefore, such dogma simply may not apply. That creed to him is reflected in each Presidents' and their advisors' constant pronunciations' that American power must be employed throughout the world to keep the peace, promote stability, and build democratic institutions. In that sense, he supports the argument of many that the US now pursues a "Pax Americana" in the 21st Century much like Great Britain sought a "Pax Britannica" in the 19th Century.

To Bacevich, and other like-minded scholars and soldiers, the American military is being employed continuously as an imperial force to 'Americanize' regions that have their local traditions and culture that defy US aims. A corollary to this warning is that, in areas of so-called 'failed states,' only a nation can build a nation; no outside force can do so. Yet, as in both Iraq and Afghanistan, we have tried to build a nation that appears beyond reach. Again, this is disconcertingly like what we tried to do in South Vietnam.

Bacevich joins some other scholars and former warriors who further argue that the now decades old volunteer force is an enabler to the US civilian leaders in their pursuit of an American-dominated world. This is because the US citizenry does not take part in the military. Few Americans fight and die, in these continual conflicts. As James Fallows writes in *The Atlantic Magazine*, "Now the American military is exotic territory to most of the American public.... As a country, America has been at war nonstop for the past 13 years. As a public, it has not. A Total of about 2.5 million Americans, roughly three-quarters of 1 percent, served in Iraq and Afghanistan at any point in the post-9/11 years, many of them more than once."

Critics like Bacevich and Fallows remind us that fewer still politicians and their civilian experts, moreover, have served in the military, much less in the wars they are propagating. One consequence is that there is no accountability for the policies that promote a militaristic approach to national security and foreign policy. The danger of this condition is that our leaders can, and have already, committed our Armed Forces to war without the attention of its citizenry or even the authority of the Constitution.

Critics of the present-day decision-makers and their proclivity for regular employment of force include some in the military. These military detractors are quick to point out that what characterizes American wars since 9/11 is that we have not won any. One reason they argue is that there is the trend of senior military leaders to be managers and yes men. In being so, they have abandoned the precepts of solid military theory and doctrine, focused on tactics rather than strategy, and have served merely by obeying orders and getting ahead. This reproach is reminiscent of the arguments about the military's senior leaders in the last stages and the aftermath of the Vietnam War.

Thomas Ricks, a journalist who specializes in defense topics and has reported for *the Wall Street Journal* and *Washington Post* is one such critic. In his recent book *The Generals,* Ricks traces the development and the effectiveness of Army general officers from World War Two to the present. His main thrust is that there has been a deterioration of accountability in the senior ranks since World War Two. While there are exceptions, he faults them, and their education and training, for being too tactically and not strategically oriented. In their interface with civilian leaders, moreover, he finds that senior generals have become too familiar with their counterparts and lack the wherewithal to engage them in a frank professional dialogue about military affairs.

Most disturbing, Mr. Ricks recounts a mid-nineties survey of professional officers at Fort Leavenworth that is reminiscent of one that followed the Vietnam War. The more recent survey reveals that many mid-career officers felt that Army senior officers are too "over controlling" and that they micromanage to keep from getting poor efficiency reports. These officers felt that the Army has become too bureaucratic and businesslike. There was also an overall lack of trust between those senior officers and their subordinates.

There are similar critics amongst some senior officers who have taken part in the conflicts in Iraq and Afghanistan. One of the most outspoken is a General Daniel Bolger. Bolger has shown up in the media - such as National Public Radio and some TV talk shows – and written a book called *Why We Lost: A General's Inside Account of the Iraq and Afghanistan Wars.*

This former Army division commander in Iraq and the general officer who had overseen advisors in Afghanistan, begins his book, "I am a United States Army general, and I lost the Global War on Terrorism. It's like Alcoholics Anonymous; step one is admitting you have a problem. Well, I have a problem. So do my peers. And thanks to our problem, now all of America has a problem, to wit: two lost campaigns and a war gone awry."

Bolger then candidly states, "What went right involved the men and women who fought…. What went wrong squandered the bravery, sweat, and blood of these fine Americans. Our primary failing in the war involved generalship. If you prefer the war-college lexicon, we—guys like me— demonstrated poor strategic and operational leadership." His book then tells a story of the military high command following a flawed strategic view and operational concept that adhered to a belief in the success of a counterinsurgency doctrine that was ill-suited to the enemy we fought against, and its imposed limitations.

Refrains similar to Ricks' and Bolger's are in other historians' works who have served as active duty commanders during the current long war period. For example, Colonels Gia Gentile and Greg Daddis, in their books *Wrong Turn: America's Deadly Embrace of Counterinsurgency* and

Withdrawal: Reassessing America's Final Years in Vietnam strike comparable themes on America's military follies in pursuing the wars in Iraq and Afghanistan. All of this sounds strikingly familiar to the Vietnam War years as recounted in the story of the earlier chapters.

At first glance then it appears that the US national security apparatus may now have a problem much as we had experienced in the Vietnam War; even worst in some respects. The rest of this section seeks to examine briefly what the current nature of civil-military relations may be, and whether the lessons of Vietnam are pertinent to them. Moreover, if there is a problem, and there seems to be, the section concludes with some speculation on how lessons from the Vietnam War may be the basis for some solution.

To enable this survey, there is an assortment of accounts and commentaries since the First Gulf War that relates many of the problems in waging satisfactory conclusions to the fighting in the current conflicts to US civil-military relations. There are interesting comparisons, furthermore, to the lessons of Vietnam. Here the works of Dale Herspring, *Civil-Military Relations and Shared Responsibility* and Suzanne Nielsen's and Don Snider's *American Civil-Military Relations: The Soldier and the State in a New Era* are helpful. So are some of the memoirs of Presidents Clinton (*My Life*) and George W. Bush (*Decision Points*); Defense Secretaries Rumsfeld (*Known and Unknown*) and Gates (*Duty*); and military leaders Generals Tommy Franks (*American Soldier*) and Hugh Shelton (*Without Hesitation*).

In addition, Bob Woodward's detailed accounts of the Bush Administration - such as *Plan of Attack*, and *Bush at War* - focus on the policy-making process of this presidency. They provide, with some caution, insights on some of the recent state of government decision making. Woodward has also published a similar book of some of Obama's Presidency called *Obama's Wars*. These works, in the author's words, "recount the strategies, meetings, phone calls, planning sessions, motivations, dilemmas, conflicts, doubts and raw emotions" in the debates and decision points of the Bush and Obama Administrations. As such, they can enlighten one on the civil-military relationships during the first decade of the 21st century.

While much in these is hearsay, circumstantial, conjecture or in the case of some memoirs self-serving, there is enough evidence to convince one that during this period of prolonged conflict decision making and civil-military relations was and still is in a dismal stage in US history. What follows is not only a brief survey of these but a more detailed sketch of some of the issues and how we may address and correct them using the lessons of the Vietnam War.

US Civil-Military Relations and Decision-Making in the Clinton Administration

Clinton was the first president since World War Two who had not served in the military. He had avoided the draft during the Vietnam War and had said publicly that he "loathed the military." Herspring claims that "Clinton's method of operating was much like that of LBJ. He avoided tough decisions, primarily deferred to his defense secretary, and though he and Powell got along, did not follow the latter's advice on the President's campaign pledge to avoid the 'gays in the military' issue."

As an example and symbol of the Clinton Administration's overall view of the military and its relations, early in that Presidency the Press wrote a story of a White House staff member who snubbed General Barry McCaffrey, a decorated Vietnam veteran and joint staff officer for Powell, in a hallway of the White House in 1993. When the general said hello to the staffer, she replied, "I don't talk to the military."

Clinton's cabinet selections further indicated what the relationships between his civilian leaders and advisors and the military might be during his tenure as well. For instance, his defense secretary, Les Aspin, who had been a member of Congress and opponent of General Powell's concept for a base force military in the aftermath of the Cold War, fostered a shift away from the preeminence in defense policy that the military seemed to have gained during the first Bush Administration. Other than defense budget issues, Aspin had no experience or real interests in military affairs. His rumbled looks and awkward salutes often portrayed him as an out of place Defense Secretary. Moreover, Aspin became somewhat of a lightning rod in many of Clinton's ostensible anti-military policies, such as allowing open gays in the military, which sought to change the military culture through social policy-making.

Soon after President Clinton took over in discussions with the President, Secretary Aspin, and other civilian advisors about the use of military force in peacekeeping missions in Africa and the Balkans, General Powell warned against making hasty decisions without defined objectives to employ the military. With leaks on these talks from some of Clinton's inner circle, the Press found out about the General's cautionary remarks and began criticizing him for his reluctance to use force.

William Safire, writing for *The New York Times*, was one such critic. He compared Powell to General George McClellan, a Union commander during the Civil War who refused to take risks under the orders of President Lincoln. Powell responded with his editorial that not only countered Safire's criticism but sought to remind the public that "we have learned the proper lessons of history, even if some journalists have not."

Criticism for General Powell's advice was not only from the Press. Madeline Albright, who was one of Clinton's Secretaries of State, criticized the General over his reticence to recommend the use of the US military to the President in several other crises. Albright reportedly said to the Chairman, "What's the use of having this superb military that you're always talking about if we can't use it?" Per Herspring's version, Powell became livid over Albright's cavalier attitude. He admonished the Secretary for viewing the military as a set of 'toys' to be used haphazardly.

Other instances involving the use of US forces and relationships with senior commanders further illustrate a strain in civil-military relations during the Clinton Administration. For example, in Somalia Secretary Aspin denied a request for reinforcements from the commander of US special operation forces employed there to capture a warlord who seemed responsible for much of the interference in the humanitarian aid effort. The Secretary reportedly denied the reinforcements because they may have sent the 'wrong message' on US intents to harm the Somalian populace.

Those supports, an armored force for protection in urban conflicts, were later needed during a firefight that ensued when Army Rangers engaged Somali paramilitary forces and civilians in downtown Mogadishu. The Rangers lost 18 killed. Afterward, without asking for military advice, Clinton summarily withdrew these special forces without allowing them to carry out their mission. Aspin's denial of reinforcements and Clinton's withdrawal order infuriated many in the military, who thought such a retreat would bode ill for the US ahead.

Later, in Eastern Europe, Clinton launched an operation against Bosnian Serbs. They had attacked innocent civilians in their war against other Bosnian factions and Albanians in Kosovo. The operation, dubbed ALLIED FORCE, primarily involved the use of airpower under the leadership of the US overall commander in Europe, General Wes Clark – a wounded and decorated veteran of Vietnam.

Aspin's successor as Secretary of Defense, William Cohen, had appointed Clark to the position, but afterward had grown concerned that the General had used his position as Supreme Commander of NATO forces to vary from the Clinton Administration's policy toward actions in East Europe. To Cohen, Clark had exceeded his authorities as the US commander and showed an extraordinary ambitious attitude that contradicted the Secretary's orders.

The poor relationship between the two came to a head when Cohen ordered the then CJCS, General Hugh Shelton, a special forces officer who seemed out of his league when dealing with political matters and did not like Clark, to tell the US commander in Europe to stay off the television and away from other media. As related in Herspring's account, Shelton called and said, "The Secretary of Defense asked me to give you some verbatim guidance, so here it is: 'Get your fucking face off the TV. No more briefings, period. That's it.' I just wanted to give it to you like he said. Do you have any questions?"

Though the Serbs finally gave up their actions to subjugate areas next to their country, the US remained divided on how to settle the peace. There was much debate in Washington on US force contributions to a peacekeeping force. Clinton stayed aloof and difficult to obtain any definitive guidance. The rumors became rampant about his affair with a White House intern. They turned out to be true, and the impeachment proceedings that followed interfered with any White House decisions for resolution of military affairs.

Clinton's actions, both personal and public, created a schism between what had been a previously proper relationship between the security apparatus civilians and the military. Meanwhile, the departure of General Powell, a political savvy Chairman, and his replacement with less politically knowledgeable officers, created a vacuum in the US military's ability to work with a new group of senior civilians who were less willing to cooperate and understand military affairs.

US Civil-Military Relations and Decision-Making in the Bush Administration

In 2001, George W. Bush came into power. In many circles in Washington, and amongst the military in general, the return of a Bush and the conservatives to power was a blessing. The younger Bush seemed to regenerate his father's administration regarding people he chose to serve in key positions. His Vice President became Dick Cheney, who had been his father's Defense Secretary. Now retired General Colin Powell returned as the Secretary of State. Donald Rumsfeld, whom Cheney had had a long association and who had been a Secretary of Defense during the Ford Administration, returned for an unprecedented second term as a Defense Secretary. To some these appointments indicated a return to a closer relationship between the civilian leaders and their military commanders and advisors.

These men, and several others in central defense department and national security positions such as Paul Wolfowitz, Elliot Abrams, and Richard Perle, became known as the neo-conservatives. They were outwardly committed to the spread of American democracy abroad, and, especially after 9/11, the use of American force to counter terrorist attacks. They were all also more than willing to dominate views toward the use of force, however, without close coordination with their senior military advisors and commanders.

This group profoundly influenced Bush's policies. After the attacks on the Twin Towers and the Pentagon, the President announced a new policy of preemptive attacks. This policy said that the US would preemptively attack any state that harbored terrorists who might threaten America. The most famous of his preventative attacks was against Iraq in 2003.

The primary person who seemed to personify that war - and the state of civil-military affairs during the Bush Administration - was Donald Rumsfeld. As a former businessman, like McNamara, he was intent on reforming the defense establishment and recreating it as he saw fit. In Herspring's words, "Rumsfeld was convinced that the U.S. military and especially the U.S. Army was living in the last century. It was time to modernize it by making greater use of technology, thereby decreasing the need for reliance on large numbers of troops. As he put it on February 1, 2002, transformation was, the military buzzword for a change from heavy, slow-moving forces to lighter, more agile units, employing the latest information technology, to wage computerized warfare."

For Rumsfeld, this primarily meant modernizing the Army into a lighter, more lethal force. He became a major critic of the Service's inability to do so. This was even though the Army, under its then Chief of Staff, General Eric Shinseki - a wounded Vietnam War veteran who was highly respected – was trying to move in that direction. By Rumsfeld's way of dealing with things, he thought that the movement was much too slow. He publicly criticized Shinseki and the Secretary of the Army Tom White – another decorated Vietnam veteran - for dragging their feet.

Rumsfeld also had some significant problems with the JCS. As Herspring recounts, "Rumsfeld's style in dealing with the Joint Chiefs quickly became apparent. General Hugh Shelton, the chairman of the Joint Chiefs of Staff at the time, discovered that Rumsfeld expected to play a leading role in all significant military decisions. He even went to the point of suggesting to Shelton that—in violation of the Goldwater-Nichols Act—he go through him before speaking to the president. Shelton refused. In short, while the Joint Chiefs appreciated Bush, they had little respect for his secretary of defense, a man who relegated Shelton and his staff to the status of 'second-rate citizens.' As another senior officer put it, the fact is, [Rumsfeld] is disenfranchising people."

Rumsfeld's principal motive for his actions, some have speculated, was that he felt that the JCS had gained too much power over defense matters. He therefore, sought not just to reestablish some balance but wanted to wrestle most of the power for defense matters and military strategy in his own hands. Moreover, as McNamara wanted to do, he also felt that the Department was in much need for reform. He wanted to bring the Defense Department and its military branches "into the twenty-first century."

Secretary Rumsfeld had many opportunities to show off how much he was in charge shortly after 9/11. He dominated both the planning for and the execution of the US invasion of Afghanistan. The resultant overthrow of the Taliban was quick and carried out with mostly special forces. The American commander, General Tommy Franks, taking continuous direction from the Defense Secretary, had limited the number of regular and special troops employed without regard to a well thought out end result to his hastily created campaign plan. Thus, after the first successes, military operations suffered some serious deficiencies and setbacks.

For example, at a place called Tora Bora along the Afghan-Pakistan border, it appeared that the US had the al-Qaeda leader, Osama Bin Laden, cornered in a mountainous area. A request came into Franks for the employment of more troops to complete the encirclement. With no reserve for such contingencies, the General declined; saying that it would take too much time, and the intelligence was not specific enough.

Consequently, Osama escaped into Pakistan. Afterward, several military subordinates revealed that with some reinforcements they could have not only captured the Al Qaeda leader but destroyed the remainder terrorist force before it escaped to Afghanistan.

The foremost example, however, of Rumsfeld's domination of the military and military strategy was the Iraq War. As most of the contemporary sources tell it, Rumsfeld determined not only the strategic goals but the level of forces employed. General Tommy Franks, by some accounts, gave in to every issue without argument or advice.

For Rumsfeld, Iraq was a test of his overall desire to show that technological breakthroughs and new methods could replace the old thinking and ways of the Pentagon brass. To him, the Iraq War would 'Shock and Awe' everyone into realizing that he had single-handedly brought the American military into a revolution in military affairs.

As Andrew Bacevich writes in *Breach of Trust*, "Whether Franks personally devised the plan for invading Iraq or whether Rumsfeld coached, cajoled, and bullied his field commander into accepting an approach incorporating his own predilections one thing is certain. Conceptually, the operation dubbed Iraqi Freedom reflected both the ideas of those intent on refashioning the armed forces into something never seen and the vision of a high-tech power-projection army that Sullivan [a former Army Chief] and his colleagues had laid out a decade before. The media termed the result—put on vivid display as U.S. forces dashed toward Baghdad in March 2003—shock and awe."

During the Iraq War Rumsfeld dominated the senior officers in Washington, such as the Chairman of the JCS, General Myer, who became silent on advice to the President or the field commander. Without a Chairman or any other higher General officer in Washington to rely on for perspective, General Franks concentrated solely on the war at hand and how Rumsfeld wanted to execute its operations. He and Rumsfeld paid little attention to the aftermath.

Woodward's account in *Plan of Attack* relates how much the Secretary was involved in the minute details of the planning of the Iraq War and its execution. "For Rumsfeld, each day had been like a month, even a year. The excuses were broken helicopters, fouled-up communications, and weather delays. He had pounded on Franks very hard with increasing fury. I don't understand, Rumsfeld had said. Why can't we do this? Soon the secretary was trickling down into lower-level operational decisions, demanding details and explanations."

These accounts are strangely reminiscent of McNamara's handling of the Vietnam War; LBJ's daily inquiries into operational and tactical matters on Khe Sanh; and Nixon's orders for the employment of B-52s during the 1972 Easter Invasion. Like these civilian leaders, Rumsfeld had no idea of what Clausewitz refers to as the 'fog and friction' of war – the many happenings in armed conflict that prevent plans from going right and add to the confusion and uncertainty so characteristic of wartime operations.

As a result of Rumsfeld's constant meddling, the entire national security process broke down - as it had in the Nixon years during the Vietnam War. The National Security Advisor, Condoleezza Rice - an intellectual who had been a political science professor at Stanford and had worked at the Rand Corporation - was unable to coordinate any efforts between the State and Defense Departments.

Part of the problem was that Secretary of Defense Rumsfeld and Secretary of State Colin Powell did not get along or agree on most issues. Consequently, as the *Washington Post* reported, Rice got nowhere on making plans for postwar stability or to advance an agenda in the Mideast after the war. Powell - upset that hardly any attention was being paid to the aftermath of the war - had warned Bush and other cabinet members that a regime change in Iraq would break it apart, and the US would have the responsibility to fix it. The warning went unheeded.

The role of the Chairman of the Joint Chiefs and the Chiefs in the planning for and execution of OPERATION IRAQI FREEDOM was ambiguous at best. As Herspring and some media reports claim, Rumsfeld's chosen Chairman, General Richard Myers, quietly acquiesced to the Cheney-Franks plans and strategy for the invasion and its aftermath. It seems that Myers' role, like Wheeler's in the Vietnam War, was to work to achieve consensus among the Chiefs for the operation for Secretary Cheney. In doing so, the Chairman played no role as an Advisor to the President.

Not all senior military in the Government agreed with Rumsfeld. General Shinseki, in testimony before Congress, veered from Rumsfeld's push to limit the size of the overall forces involved and estimated that the force, especially for operations afterward, was too small. For that Rumsfeld's deputy, Paul Wolfowitz chastised and ostracized him from the Bush Administration. Shinseki resigned shortly after.

Later, the Director of Operations for the Joint Staff, General Greg Newbold, went public and said that he wished he had resigned in protest over the entire planning and execution for Iraq. Throughout all of this, Marine Corps General Peter Pace, who replaced Myers as Chairman, remained a silent and loyal advisor to Rumsfeld. He was careful to not contradict his boss before the press or even in private. All of this, again, is too reminiscent of Vietnam.

As we now know not only were the forces too small, especially for the post-invasion stability operations, but they were unable to find and destroy any weapons of mass destruction - ostensibly the purpose of the war. Yet, Rumsfeld continued to display tremendous shortsightedness, even stubbornness, over the unfolding nature of the war. He dismissed reports of the effectiveness of the unconventional Iraqi tactics during the invasion. He then further rejected the insurgency that developed afterward.

The entire botched occupation and initial counterinsurgency ineffectiveness fell on his shoulders. However, he was unable to come to grips with it. After the dissatisfaction between Rumsfeld and his military advisors finally became known, and the media continued to press him on what was going on in Iraq, the Secretary finally resigned in November 2006.

For Bush, Rumsfeld's resignation did not end the frustrations and the poor relationships with his military commanders and senior advisors. Paul Bremmer, a former foreign service officer who had taken charge of much of the post-war Iraq situation from the military under Rumsfeld, had dismissed former Iraqi Baathist Party governing officials. There were no others to replace them. Without regard to the consequences, he also decided to disband the rest of the Iraqi Army. This decision led to a lack of security, rioting, and dissatisfaction with the American presence.

The instability and lawlessness eventually resulted in a Sunni insurrection against the new Iraqi Shiite government and its American protectors. The religious divide between the traditional Islamic factions added to the bloodshed. A civil war ensued. Throughout all of this, no senior military officer had cautioned Bremmer on his decisions.

Faced with this turmoil, General Franks quickly retired. He wanted nothing to do with a situation that may detract from, what he perceived as, one of the most brilliant campaigns in military history. Before leaving, reporters had asked him about what he had planned to do about the postwar Iraq before the invasion. He answered, "I had a war to fight," and that was his priority.

Further revealing his lack of strategic insight at lectures he gave afterward at the war colleges, he answered a fundamental question on what kind of war was Afghanistan by saying, "That's a great question for historians." Clearly, by these remarks, the American military commander did not have a clue about how to end a war, and, consequently, had a significant role in the failures that were evident in both Afghanistan and Iraq.

General John Abizaid replaced Franks at CENTCOM, the name of the US combatant command for that area. General Ricardo Sanchez took over military operations in Iraq. Powell sent his right-hand man from State, Richard Armitage, a Marine Corps Vietnam War veteran, to size up the situation under Sanchez. He reported back to the Secretary, "I came away from my first meeting with him saying this guy doesn't get it."

Absent any guidance from Washington, Sanchez and Bremmer needed to work together to coordinate resources and operations. Relations between them became strained. They soon refused to even talk to one another. Meanwhile, the General issued little direction to his subordinates. Various American units developed their own concepts of operations to deal with the insurrection, and a growing al-Qaeda presence. In the spring of 2004, a story broke out about American abuse of prisoners at a prison at Abu Ghraib. The situation proved to be too much for Sanchez, whose incompetence was evident to Rumsfeld's replacement, Robert Gates.

In the aftermath of the failures of American commanders in Iraq, there was little 'soul-searching' that characterized the post-Vietnam War military. That would be left to the critics. One such one was Thomas Ricks. He writes in the *Generals*, "Under both Franks and Sanchez, the failures of the American military in Iraq were not those of frontline soldiers. American troops deployed to Iraq fit and well trained. However, training tends to prepare one for known problems, while education better prepares one for the unknown, the unpredictable, and the unexpected."

Ricks further relates that "Like their civilian overseers, the generals leading the Army in Iraq had a major gap in their educations. They were not mentally prepared for the war they encountered in Iraq." Ironically, while the First Gulf War Vietnam veterans remembered the political-military lessons of Vietnam and sought to apply them, senior generals - most a generation removed - had forgotten many of the operational and tactical lessons by the time of IRAQI FREEDOM.

General George Casey – the son of a general officer killed in Vietnam - took over from Sanchez and tried to restore order. He quickly developed plans and issued orders that coordinated most actions of American military units. His main guidance was to focus on training a new Iraqi Army and police force to replace US units in their security missions – all reminiscent of the Vietnamization efforts during the Nixon Presidency in Vietnam.

The new commander insisted that the only way out of the Iraqi dilemma was to get the Iraqi government and forces to work together and offer security. Indeed, as the Iraqi resistance caused more American casualties, the media began to harken back to the Vietnam War experience, calling the Iraq War another stalemate and quagmire. American failures in Vietnam were now nearly continuously compared to what was happening in Iraq and Afghanistan.

An impatient President Bush soon lost confidence in Casey. He became frustrated by the General's consistent assessment that the Iraqis could only overcome the insurrection and it would take time. Time was something that the President was no longer willing to provide. This was because of the constant bad press on the war. He searched for the proverbial "man on horseback," who could ride in and make everything work.

Through the advice of some outside of his Administration, Bush selected General David Petraeus. Petraeus had commanded a division in the Iraqi War. Afterward, he oversaw the training of Iraqi forces for its newly forming Army and police forces. Now, in the Spring of 2007, he would command US and allied forces in Iraq. His first primary task was to direct a new surge of forces – an added 30,000 troops - that the President ordered to reverse the situation there.

Using ideas from a new counterinsurgency doctrine that he had developed for the Army, which he based on lessons learned from Vietnam, Petraeus seemingly turned the situation around in Iraq within a year. He also had arranged for several hand-picked officers to go with him in this endeavor. He groomed others on his ideas toward protecting the population as the key to accomplishing the defeat of the insurrection.

By 2008, the American Press and his superiors hailed Petraeus as the victor of the Iraq War surge. At the end of that year, he turned over his command to one of his protégés, General Raymond Odierno. At the ceremony, Secretary of Defense Gates declared, "history will regard you as one of our nation's greatest battle captains." The highly-exaggerated comment aside, Petraeus did oversee a turnaround without much real support from what had become a dysfunctional national security team under Bush.

Meanwhile, the situation in Afghanistan, which had taken 'second fiddle' to the Iraq War for several years, had deteriorated significantly. The Bush Administration had even contemplated withdrawing forces from there; leaving it to the NATO community to decide what to do. However, a Taliban resurgence and most importantly the presence of al-Qaeda in the western Pakistan region, kept US forces there. From 2004 to 2009 the number of Taliban contact incidents increased nine times. As 2009 approached, and as violence continued to grow, a corrupt Afghan government became increasingly intransigent to US advice.

US Civil-Military Relations and Decision-Making in The Obama Administration

The Afghanistan neglect was about to change with a new US Administration. Barack Obama had run on a foreign policy plank that Iraq had been the wrong war, and the US should withdraw from there. On the other hand, Afghanistan was where the US should rejuvenate its efforts. Because of his admitted lack of experience in military matters, Obama appointed an ex-military man to be his National Security Advisor.

Retired General James Jones was a forty-year Marine Corps veteran. He was a veteran of the Vietnam War who had served as the Commandant of the Marines and the NATO Allied commander in Europe. When on active duty he had told, according to Bob Woodward, his fellow Marine General Peter Pace, "You should not be the parrot on the secretary's shoulder." After accepting Obama's offer, Jones was determined to revamp his position and that of the Chairman of the JCS.

He further wanted to re-energize the entire NSC process.

To shift toward a renewed emphasis on Afghanistan while drawing down in Iraq, the new President kept Robert Gates on as his Secretary of Defense. Gates, in turn, selected Admiral Mike Mullen as his new Chairman. Gates told Mullen that he thought that the Chairman position had been dormant and overlooked. He wanted to revitalize it. Mullen, who had been the Chief of Naval Operations, was also intent on reestablishing the Chairman as the principal military advisor to the President.

While having all good intentions, and choosing people who seemed extremely qualified, Obama's selections and their determinations would eventually run into severe bureaucratic roadblocks. Like what happened in the Nixon Administration during Vietnam, the White House would begin to both block and ignore the primary national security actors and the process. Like Kissinger and Haig, the White House staff - run by its Chief, Rahm Emanuel, and consisting of some of the President's closest political associates - began to control everything that went to and from the President.

It seems that, as Woodward reported, the White House civilian political team never shrugged off the spirit and determination to look at things purely from the viewpoint of the next election. They, consequently, were protective of the public affairs message that the President should continuously develop and portray. In doing so, they often blocked or manipulated access to the President of both Retired General Jones and Admiral Mullen, and sought to convey to Obama their views of what his military advisors were trying to say and do. They did so with little regard to and without any experience on the assessments and recommendations of the military.

Early on, however, Obama demanded that all be involved in an initial assessment of the situation in Afghanistan and what to do there. From his national security team that included Secretary Gates, Admiral Mullen, General Petraeus- now the CENTCOM commander - and the then commander in Afghanistan, General David McKiernan, there began a thorough review of the situation in Afghanistan. The means for that assessment consisted of several meetings, both formal NSC, and other informal gatherings, and focused on an old request McKiernan had made for added troops – some 30,000 more.

At first, as related by Woodward in *Obama's Wars*, these discussions were quite extensive and went beyond just the numbers of troops. To Obama's credit, he asked some very pointed, often insightful questions. He pointed out to all that any action would have to take into consideration the recession that the country faced because of the financial crisis. The President also emphasized, "The ultimate strategy must explain the logic for adding more troops and show how the fight would be carried out going forward." The discussions eventually focused on two courses of action in Afghanistan. Simply said and described, these two courses were whether to pursue a theater strategy of counterinsurgency or one labeled counterterrorism.

Obama decided on the counterinsurgency course. The argument and reputation of General Petraeus, supported by Secretary Gates, carried the day. Later, the President also decided to change the commander in Afghanistan. He agreed to appoint General Stanley McChrystal, a former leader of the special operations conducted in Iraq. McChrystal also had the confidence of Secretary Gates, Admiral Mullen and was a protégé of Petraeus.

While the President chose the course, there was still some debate on how to execute it and with what resources – namely how many troops. McChrystal's first task as the new commander was to assess the situation there and come back with some answers to those questions.

The new commander did so. When Washington received it, the Administration made a public release statement that gave few details but hinted at the need for more troops. Gates, Mullen, and Petraeus were all called upon to testify on their views of the release. They were careful in their comments, but all hinted at the need for more troops in Afghanistan.

As the Obama Administration considered it, an unknown official leaked the assessment to the Press. The 66-page document was a startling evaluation. It argued for substantial reinforcements, over 40,000, and included details on how those forces would be employed. McChrystal's assessment further argued that the US would fail in Afghanistan if the full complement of forces did not go there.

As Woodward relates, others in the media sensationalized the leak. One reporter wrote, "The domestic political-military stakes have been ramped up considerably with this leak. It is not quite a 3-A.M.-phone-call crisis, but it is probably the most serious national security test the Obama team has confronted thus far." The incident was reminiscent of the 206k reinforcement leak during the TET 68 offensive.

The debates and discussions on the McChrystal Report continued. Some of the issues that Obama wanted answers for were again quite insightful and meaningful. They included how could the Taliban or al-Qaeda be defeated when they had Pakistani sanctuaries and support? Can a counterinsurgency strategy work with a corrupt and inept Afghan government? However, eventually, the numbers are what mattered to the White House staff because of the political and possible economic repercussions.

Obama's politicos in the White House thought that the military brass was trying to influence the President through their testimonies. More alarming, they believed that McChrystal leaked his report to put pressure on the President for his troop request. As time went on, relations between the White House and the Commander in Afghanistan deteriorated. Eventually, as he sought to execute his counterinsurgency strategy, McChrystal would resign over an article that claimed he and his staff had made disparaging remarks about civilian officials in the Obama Administration.

Section 13.2 – Observations, Insights, and Conclusions on Civil-Military Relations Pertinent for Today

This section extracts observations from Section 1's review of the 21st Century security environment and its survey of three presidencies' civil-military relationships. It seeks to conclude how lessons from Vietnam can potentially improve future national security policies and strategies.

Four Trends

The Section 1 summary of civil-military relations and national security issues from the first Bush to the Obama Administrations show four major disturbing trends and problems for today's US national security environment. Many of these are reminiscent of the Vietnam War.

First, the close and cooperative relationships between and among the civilian and military advisors and commanders that marked the decision making during George H. W. Bush's presidency seems to have critically eroded. This may explain why there was a failure to derive and achieve an effective strategy to end both 2001 Afghanistan and 2003 Iraqi invasions.

For example, in the First Gulf War President Bush, through the close cooperation and workings of the national security apparatus' people and its processes, set up clear and obtainable political aims of restoring the Kuwaiti Government to power and deterring any further Iraqi offensives or interventions in the Gulf region. Through that same process, and in close coordination with the President and his primary civilian advisors, the US military clearly established achievable, feasible and acceptable military objectives to defeat the Iraqi Army in Kuwait, destroy their offensive military capability, and set up forward bases to deter and deny Iraqi military from further incursions of its neighbors.

Though there were discussions on removing Sadam Hussein from power, both civilian and military leaders determined that the resultant necessity of some military occupation and restoration of a viable government would not be worth the costs and was too risky. Those costs and risks resulted from a thorough and wide-ranging review by national security policy experts, both civilian and military, who knew the history, culture, and geopolitical factors of the area in general, and Iraq and the Middle East in particular.

Yet, from the brief survey of the evidence, it appears that in neither the invasion of Afghanistan in 2001 nor Iraq in 2003 were there clear, open, and thorough discussions or assessments of civilian leaders' aims on how to end these wars favorable for the US. Consequently, there were also no considerations on the use of force for a long-term favorable ending of the war and an enduring peace to follow. Neither was there an assessment of the overall costs in the long term. Much the same seems to have occurred in the Obama Administration's pursuit of a favorable conclusion in Afghanistan.

The reasons for this were primarily relationship-driven. In both 2001 and 2003, it appears that Rumsfeld felt he knew more about what the proper military objectives and courses were to follow, rather than his military advisors or commanders. The latter mostly acquiesced to and did not challenge the Secretary's course. As in the Vietnam War, there was a clear dereliction of duty on the part of the JCS to ensure a comprehensive national military strategy for the war, how to end it, what to do in the postwar vacuum that was sure to follow, and an assessment of the long-term costs and risks.

The President, meanwhile, did not facilitate a discussion or debate of his Defense Secretary's strategy. He accepted it without complete knowledge of the difficulties, risks, or consequences. It appears that George W. Bush succumbed to the fancy of the 'Shock and Awe' vision that Rumsfeld used to convince him of his concept for victory. Like LBJ in the Vietnam War, Bush put his blind faith in someone who knew little about war. Rumsfeld, like McNamara, thought that the application of sound business and system analysis techniques would work in managing the conflict.

The second trend in today's national security environment is that the balance between the ability and responsibility to coordinate, assess and make recommendations on national security policies and their related military strategies have shifted away from the intent of the Goldwater-Nichols Act. The ability of the Chairman to be the primary military advisor to the President has diminished dramatically.

The Secretary of Defense and his office now dominate strategic issues and how they are presented to the President. The White House staff has also helped in this alteration by having the ability to limit or control the subject and manner of access to the military advisors and commanders to the President. Making matters worse, many of the Presidential selectees and appointees to these offices are soulfully lacking in national security and military affairs knowledge.

The one who seems to have been responsible most for this shift in balance is Donald Rumsfeld. Like Robert McNamara in the sixties, Rumsfeld was intent on reforming the Department of Defense. Like McNamara, Rumsfeld's personality and views so dominated Defense matters that he was able to smother the views of his subordinates who may have had different ones. A consequence is that the ability and the power of the JCS and the Combatant Commanders has diminished since the early nineties dramatically.

As Andrew Bacevich notes in his *Washington Rules*, "The institutional influence of the Joint Chiefs of Staff [has] remained at an all-time low: Through the 'Long War's first decade, there was no major issue on which the Chiefs collectively can be said to have had a major impact…. The JCS chairman, nominally occupying the uppermost rung of the military profession, wielded about as much influence as a moderately prominent assistant secretary of defense. As for the service chiefs, charged with building and maintaining the various uniformed services, they had long since been banished from the inner circle of power."

This sidelining of the US military's advisors has resulted in a deterioration of the relationship in government between the military and civilian national security players. Aiding in this diminution have been the various Chairmen of the JCS, who either have not wanted to challenge the obstructers or have acquiesced to it, either through lack of desire or ability to do so.

Both above trends can also be attributed to the US Commander-in-Chiefs. Since H.W. Bush, we have not had a President knowledgeable about military affairs. Clinton loathed it and delegated as much as possible national security matters to his inept and inexperienced advisors. George W. Bush, an absent for duty reservist during the Vietnam War, had little knowledge in military matters and did not care to learn. Like Clinton, he chose to delegate and defer these matters to his civilian advisors.

He did have an unshakable faith in the use of military force to further American values and virtues in the world. However, he often said that he saw his role as the President to give guidance and then let the military carry out their mission without further interference from him. In other words, he wanted to divest himself from matters dealing with military operations once they were underway.

At least President Obama was aware of his shortcomings in military affairs when he took office. There is evidence that he had tried to make up for his lack of experience and knowledge by reading about military affairs. He also initially selected experienced ex-military advisors who could help him. However, Obama primarily relied on his closest associates and political friends, who have little experience, for national security matters. Moreover, as mentioned, his White House staff steadily worked to control both the President's agenda and visitors, which enabled them also to govern how much contact he would have with his military commanders and advisors.

A third trend, which is most troubling for today's national security environment, has been a drift of senior military officers away from the knowledge of, experience in, and an interest in military strategy and national security matters. This is a significant theme in Tom Ricks' and Andrew Bacevich's works, as well as several other recent commentators on foreign and military affairs.

General Barry McCaffrey, a retired military officer with experience in the Pentagon and as a civilian in the White House also notices this trend and makes a case to change it. In his foreword to *American Civil-Military Relations: The Soldier and the State in a New Era* he states, "many of our senior flag officers who encountered the arrogance, disingenuous behavior, and misjudgments of Secretary of Defense Donald Rumsfeld during the initial years of Operation Iraqi Freedom were ill-prepared to respond effectively."

"Although these uniformed leaders came to senior military positions with enormous accumulated experience, technical skills, and integrity, some lacked the confidence that could have been derived from an earlier and broader set of experiences, such as graduate education and other assignments outside their services, to give them an essential sense of history, the law, languages, and other cultures, and how our constitutional form of government really works. They simply were not prepared to take the initiative to shape the political-military dialogue responsibly."

He adds, "It is not enough to say that a senior military leader has only the options of obedience to the Republic or principled resignation. The nation needs senior military flag officers who are respectful of civilian authority, principled in their behavior, deeply experienced in their understanding of strategy and the international environment, and masters of the history of U.S. national security and governance."

This trend has also been noted in several surveys and professional articles of officers serving at the Service colleges. For example, in a recent military journal article from a graduate of the Army's School of Advanced Military Studies or SAMS noted, "America's generals have failed to prepare our armed forces for war and advise civilian authorities on the application of force to achieve the aims of policy... If the policymaker desires ends for which the means he provides are insufficient, the general is responsible for advising the statesman of this incongruence."

This young Army officer then wrote of his experiences in Iraq. He criticized several general officers for not challenging Secretary Rumsfeld when the latter denied that there was a significant insurgency erupting after the IRAQI FREEDOM operation. He concluded his article with a charge that "the generals of 2006 were repeating the mistakes of Vietnam, having failed to prepare their forces for the war they fought or to provide Congress and the American people with "an accurate assessment" of the Iraq war."

My own experiences reinforce this sentiment and criticism. I saw a similar attitude amongst upcoming senior officers and general officers as a professor at the National War College in the mid-nineties, and later as a consultant to a senior defense official in the Pentagon in the first decade of the 2000s. On those occasions, I saw senior officers who did not have a rudimentary grasp of military strategic theory. They treated the subject of military doctrine, the basic concepts derived from that theory that is supposed to guide military strategy and operations, as too academic and irrelevant.

I also saw events in which Generals or Admirals did not seek to give their advice on military matters to senior civilian defense officials. It appeared that they did not want the controversy that such a confrontation may result in. In fact, in the Pentagon, the general atmosphere among Flag Officers was to survive and get back to their service organizations, where they felt more at ease with less strategic and political matters. In much of the senior officer student body at the war college, their education on strategic matters seems to take a back seat to getting back to units where their promotions hang in the balance.

This attitude and atmosphere was and still is partly a result of the regular deployment of forces and leaders in the conflicts in Iraq and Afghanistan and other areas abroad. As Andrew Bacevich writes, "The generation of officers represented by Petraeus… came to view war as commonplace, a quasi-permanent aspect of everyday reality. Moreover, their experiences in Iraq and Afghanistan persuaded them to see armed conflict as an open-ended enterprise. To be a soldier was either to be serving in a war zone or to be recently returned—in which case preparations for the next combat deployment were already under way or soon would be. Wars no longer ended. At best, they subsided, a semblance of order replacing disorder and a semblance of stability displacing instability—with even this limited achievement requiring many years of struggle."

Thus, the most common refrain of this generation of senior military officers seems to be 'we don't have time to think about such lofty strategic matters and ideas, we have to fight a real war.' The result is that the continual conflict generated by the Global War on Terror or The Long War has produced a group of senior officers who are "eager to get into the fight," do not want to be labeled as academics, and do not want to waste their time at educational institutions or assignments. Consequently, they are now education adverse and strategically shortsighted.

A fourth and final disturbing trend has been the continued growth of intellectual, academic, and business experienced experts in Washington, DC waiting for government positions. This new breed of experts perennially serve in government, persistently advise on national security affairs, and, yet, have little experience and proper education in military matters. Many of these 'experts' reside in what has become known as 'think tanks' – research and marketing organizations that generate policy-oriented research, ideas, and advice. Many of these people are graduates of distinguished institutions of higher learning, who continue to hold teaching positions there, and who take part in these think tanks at one time or another. They also have associations with large corporations, particularly those that have significant monetary defense contracts.

The typical modus operandi of these 'experts' perpetuates their service in Washington as part of an established national security policy click. When a party comes into office, these 'professionals' serve in government as Presidential appointees or senior official selectees. They are strikingly similar in backgrounds to the "Best and Brightest" of the JFK and LBJ Administrations, having comparable educational backgrounds and intellectual reputations.

When a party vacates the government, these authorities then go back to the 'think tank' from which they came, or academia or business or a combination of each to await the next Presidential election. Depending on the results of that next election, they return to government if there is a Presidential or Government official who wants to sponsor them. This cycle then repeats itself as long as the expert desires, and is in favor with their political sponsor, and is alive.

The existence of such 'think tanks' and experts is not a recent phenomenon. FDR, for example, appointed and depended upon certain economic specialists with similar educational backgrounds for advice during the creation of his New Deal program. As we have seen, JFK appointed many of his advisors from academia and the business world. McNamara had been a professor at Harvard, a President of Ford Corporation and appointed many of the Rand Corporation – a "Think Tank" of its day - as his Whiz Kids.

What is also like the Vietnam War era is that many of these modern 'Whiz Kids' have similar attitudes about the military, and are more than willing to exert themselves in defense policy and military affairs even though they do not have professional military backgrounds, experiences, or know how.

What has changed since the Vietnam War is the remarkable growth in these organizations, and the continual association they have with political parties and senior national security officials. Today there is a total of 1835 think tanks in the US [not all in national security field]. This growth is tenfold from the end of the Vietnam War. Some of these a federally funded, most are non-profits. Many depend on funds from their government work, or from affiliated business corporations, or from political parties and other political fundraising organizations, or a combination of all. The most prominent and largest organizations are in Washington, DC, or its close environs.

A review of the backgrounds of some who have served in critical national security positions in the Clinton, Bush and Obama Administrations illustrates the prominence and influence of think tanks (and other experts' havens) to government policymaking. For example, of the National Security Advisors during the Clinton years - Anthony Lake and Richard Berger - had relationships or worked for the Partnership for Secure America and the Brookings Institute. Berger was also on the board of directors of a major oil corporation. Both individuals had already worked in some capacity in the Carter Administration.

Likewise, in the George W. Bush Administration, National Security Advisor Condoleezza Rice had been a fellow at Stanford, where she also taught, and a member of the Hoover Institute and the Council on Foreign Relations. Obama's advisor, Susan Rice, who had also served in earlier democratic cabinets, was a member of the Board of the Atlantic Council and has served as a fellow from time to time at the Brookings Institute and on the Council of Foreign Relations. None of these advisors have any direct experience or formal education in military affairs.

A survey of Secretaries of Defense shows similar backgrounds. William Perry, who served at the beginning of the Clinton Presidency, gained his experience in business - founding and owning his own tech company. He was later a director of an investment firm. He spent much of his time out of government as a professor at Stanford University and as an advisor to the Roosevelt Institute, a liberal think tank in New York City.

Robert Gates had extensive experience in government before serving as Bush's and then Obama's Secretary. When out of government, he has been a lecturer at Harvard, Dean of Texas A&M and Professor at William and Mary. He has also been a member of the board of a dominant defense contracting firm, and a member of the prestigious Council on Foreign Relations.

Obama's last Defense Secretary, Ashton Carter, had extensive academic credentials, being a Yale graduate and Rhodes Scholar. He has spent much of his time when not in government teaching at MIT. He also had high-level experience in industry and finances, having been a consultant at Goldman Sachs and a member of the board of MITRE – a defense contractor. Like so many, he has also served as a fellow at the Council on Foreign Relations.

As one can see from this brief survey, there is indeed a similar pattern of education, experience, and service for members of the national security policy elite in government, whether they are affiliated with a particular party or both. Andrew Bacevich refers to this elite a group of "policy wonks: or "eggheads." He warns that this group - following in the footsteps of their forerunners during the Vietnam era - "infest present-day Washington, where their presence strangles common sense and has brought to the verge of extinction the simple ability to perceive reality. A benign appearance — well-dressed types testifying before Congress, pontificating in print and on TV, or even filling key positions in the executive branch — belies a malign impact. They are like Asian carp let loose in the Great Lakes."

Most importantly, as mentioned, these people have little formal education in strategic or military affairs. Their analyses, arguments, and views usually rehash security issues that are highly politicized and, thus, the same old issues repeated over and over, with much hype sometimes to make them more palatable for election purposes or their selection in the next government.

In sum, the four above described developments – the erosion of civil-military relationship and cooperation; the balance of the responsibility and authority for military strategic advice shifting to the civilian defense officials; the disinterest in, distaste for and ignorance of strategic matters among the current senior officer generation; and the growth of a national security self-serving elite whose intellectual, academic, business and defense policy involvement do not match to experience, education, and skills in military affairs – are disturbing trends.

These current tendencies hauntingly remind one of some of the reasons for the American failure in the Vietnam War. The central question then, and application of why Vietnam matters, is whether we can learn from the past and avoid the same mistakes of the Vietnam War?

Why the Vietnam War Still Matters, What We Can Learn from its Lessons, and How Can We Apply Them?

In the 2008 National Defense Authorization Act, Congress empowered the Secretary of Defense to conduct a program on behalf of the nation to commemorate the 50th Anniversary of the Vietnam War. On Memorial Day 2012, President Obama began this commemoration to honor the veterans of the war, which was to last from that day until Veterans Day 2025.

Some would think that this is an ironic act. This is because, in their minds, the Congress did not provide adequate funds to South Vietnam to defend themselves. Consequently, South Vietnam fell to the North Vietnamese Communists. Now the Congress was enacting the remembrance of a war that America lost in large part due to the Congress' past acts.

Others have argued that the commemoration is nothing more than a propaganda campaign, commemorating American soldiers who had served but ignoring the horrors and killings for which they were responsible. Thus, this official government commemoration has, in part, reopened the controversies and old wounds of the Vietnam experience to those of the sixties that lived through it.

In many respects, the commemoration further highlights a Déjà Vu examination of the conflicts today with our Vietnam experience. There has been a plethora of articles, documentaries, and books on the Vietnam War – much of it surrounding why we lost and comparing past actions and decisions to those involving our actions and decisions over Iraq, Afghanistan, Syria, and other places.

For example, the National Review published an article on Obama's decisions for the calls for troops needed in current conflicts and how they relate to LBJ's actions in July 1965. That same periodical had an article on the fall of Saigon, whose central premise was that US restraint during the Vietnam War showed how such inaction could cause "stalemate and defeat" in war.

There has been a flood recently of articles and 'op-eds' in major newspapers remembering the lessons of Vietnam, especially considering President Obama's recent visit there, as well as criticisms of the Obama decisions over Afghanistan, Iraq, and Syria. Andrew Bacevich, in his offensive with books and articles on *America's War for the Greater Middle East*, has gone as far as to compare US involvement there as "creating a twenty-first century slow-motion Vietnam."

With some exception - most notably books such as McMaster's *Dereliction of Duty*, Herspring's *The Pentagon and the Presidency*, Orrin Schwab's *A Clash of Cultures*, and Matthew Moten's *Presidents and Their Generals* - much of this opening of old wounds has also reopened many of the old lessons. These repeat the often written, old refrain and arguments of 'if we did this or did not do that we could have won;' or 'we should never have been there;' or the 'responsibility for failure fell upon the military or the politicians, or the press or the antiwar movement.' It goes on and on about we 'shoulda,' 'coulda,' 'woulda,' and repeats the 'blame game' irrelevant arguments over the years since the Vietnam War ended.

Warriors and Fools argues that the most responsible use of the Vietnam War lessons learned, and their best application on the use of military power in today's environment, is through improving the civil-military relationships of our civilian and military leaders who hold steward over policies and strategies dealing with the employment of our armed forces for the nations common defense and security.

But how do we do that?

The best way of improving that relationship, as in any relationship, is to build an understanding of the roles, responsibilities, processes, mechanisms, organizations, risks and rewards, norms, motives, experiences, attitudes, between two diverse, often conflicting cultures.

An approach to doing that is to set up and execute a mutually participatory educational experience for senior political and military decision-makers before they are thrust into their positions of power and responsibility. This can be a workable method to build the understanding, trust and shared view of each culture that can lead to effective action or inaction if such is the best case, which their positions will demand.

There are some existing mechanisms, processes, and institutions that can be changed, expanded, or used as examples for such an educational approach. The professional military education programs, with its senior war colleges, can serve as one way to further the spirit and methodology of this education. For example, the war colleges can expand its attendance of civilian students, to include those members of think tanks who consistently serve in government. The National War College executes a unique education program for general officer selectees, referred to as 'charm school.' Some modification or expansion of this program could also be a useful mechanism.

The Presidential transition process can be changed or expanded to incorporate some program to bring together senior military and new administration personnel to discuss relations and case studies. Here the key would be to bring in outside, reputable veterans (civilian and military) of the national security apparatus who do not have a current stake in government to discuss and lead debates on effective organizations, processes, and interactions for strategic formulation and execution. Some combination of these programs and mechanisms might work as well.

Continued meetings and seminars at a place such as Camp David is another mechanism. Taking some long weekends, or other periods, during an Administration can further improve and maintain relationships, knowledge, and lessons learned. These off-site meetings - just like what businesses, educational institutions, and others do - can continue to foster and build up efforts that have been already established.

In whatever way that can be done, the main lessons of the Vietnam War - described in this work as effective civil-military relationships that help the understanding of cultures, the building of trust, and developing a shared view of strategic policy decision making – can serve the national security elite well. Specific examples of case studies that may be appropriate from the Vietnam War are: JFK's relationship with military in forging a counterinsurgency strategy for Vietnam; the failure to know the North Vietnamese leaders and their strategy in the derivation of the gradual response strategy; LBJ's decision to employ combat forces in 1965; the American military's failure to produce and offer a viable strategic alternative in 1967 or during the TET offensive.

This educational experience and its venue should not be an experience to build policy consensus or to develop a cookie-cutter approach to national security policies or issues. Instead, the object is to allow an opportunity for senior national security decision-makers to realize that whatever their education and experience – however great, prestigious, enlightening, fulfilling, rewarding it may have already been for them – there is a need for more education and understanding of national security issues, and ways to address them using past lessons of history – especially those of the Vietnam War.

The method for this education can refer to Richard Neustadt's and Ernest May's, *Thinking in Time: The Uses of History for Decision Makers.* They have based this book on the courses and educational methods they have tried at Harvard to incorporate historical cases and lessons learned. They have shared what can be the value of studying specific historical decision-making cases and the pitfalls.

As Neustadt and May write in their book, "We hope that with a modicum of care as well as luck, care of the sort suggested by this book, future decision-makers will be spared the Kennedy complaint to Theodore Sorenson at the moment of the disaster in the Bay of Pigs: 'How could I have been so stupid." Of course, the key would be to convince potential leaders and office holders to use history not to justify actions but to gain an appreciation from the past and insights into future actions. Such an experience may well cure what JFK also complained about to Robert McNamara in 1961 – "there is no school for Presidents and Defense Secretaries."

As Historian Mark Moyar, in his latest work on Obama's foreign policy, writes, "A nation must study its own history with care and sobriety, and shield historical inquiry from the pressures of politicians and academics [and military officers] who would use it to their own ends. A nation's government must empower strategists who can discern what should and should not be learned from history and put the advice of the strategists ahead of partisan politics."

In this author's view, the empowerment for our nation's senior civilian and military leaders through education is not only needed, but it must also be an obligation of those who take the oath to serve the nation for its common defense and welfare. It can be achieved only if senior civilian decision makers in national security positions of our government recognize that it is their solemn duty to do so. After all, education on war is too important a subject to be left to the Generals.

Section 13.3 - Conclusion: Our Story's Main Characters... The Final Role They Played and What Happened to Them?

This section's narrative reviews the roles that the principal characters played in this book and recounts what happened to them afterward. It concludes the story presented herein by reminding the reader that the waging of war is, above all, a human affair, wherein civilian leaders and their warriors seek to impose their wills on others who oppose them. As such, it is the most complex and challenging endeavor that national leaders can undertake because of the uncertainties, risks, sufferings, destruction, and death that characterizes warfare.

The Americans

The assassination of **John Fitzgerald Kennedy** on 22 November 1963 is one of those events, like the Pearl Harbor or 9/11 attacks, that Americans at the time say they will always remember. His sudden death, coupled with his relative youth and his promises of things that could have been, have engrained JFK even into the memory of many Americans who were not living at the time. Today, most Americans rank him as one of the most popular Presidents. His gravesite with its eternal flame at Arlington Cemetery is one of the most often visited sites in Washington.

JFK's death represents two main turning points in this Vietnam War story. The first is that his passing marked a dramatic change of eras for America in general and the war in particular. It seems that after the assassination America began to lose faith in its leaders, in its institutions, and in its future. His death also marked the end of the post-war boom era unbridled confidence and the beginning of our Vietnam nightmare era with unremitting self-doubt.

The second turning point was that, through JFK's own doing, his Administration's last act led to the removal of South Vietnamese leader Ngo Dinh Diem. After that, South Vietnam began its dramatic slide toward defeat from which it could not save itself. It was also no accident that the North Vietnamese leadership themselves saw these two events as significant opportunities, and decided to increase its infiltration and step up its attacks shortly after. Both these turning points would come to haunt Kennedy's successor when he finally had to turn his attention to waging a war that he did not want and wished would just go away.

Five years after Kennedy's death, **Lyndon Baines Johnson** would leave office a broken man. For years afterward, unlike the man he succeeded, Americans would see him as one of the least popular Presidents. After he saw Richard Nixon sworn in on January 20, 1969, LBJ got on a plane to fly back to his beloved ranch in Texas. As the plane's front door closed, he pulled out a cigarette – his first since his 1955 heart attack. One of his daughters admonished him for so doing. Johnson shot back, "I'm no longer President now I'm going to enjoy myself." He would have only a few years to do so.

When Johnson got to his ranch, he grew his hair down to shoulder length, looking like an older 'hippy' who had once chanted obscenities outside his White House. He also gained over twenty-five pounds and set to work on his memoirs, which was published in 1971. Ignoring his daughters and doctors continued warnings about his weight and smoking, he would have two heart attacks between 1970 and 1971. A third on January 22, 1973, killed him. He was buried near his ranch and birthplace. General Westmoreland, forever his obedient general, laid a wreath at the foot of his coffin.

LBJ is an excellent example of Aristotle's *Poetics* Greek tragic figure in this story. What had gotten him at the head of his chosen and beloved political life - his ability to bargain with and convince others to do his bidding - did not work in his approach to waging war in Vietnam. His political judgments on the campaign trail and in the Senate had no place in the logic of war. His experience in cajoling and flattery got him nowhere with a determined foe, whose years of prosecution in French prisons had hardened them to flattery and had steeled them on accomplishing what Johnson wanted to stop.

Johnson told everyone that he did not want to be a wartime President. Yet, he chose to wage a war he did not want. He had pledged not to be a President to lose a war. He did so by his own doing. He depended on those who could not help. He ignored or sidelined those who might have helped, but did not.

Thus, his character led to his downfall. In many ways, he personified America's undoing in the Vietnam saga. I have always thought it was ironic that my West Point Class, which lost the most of any Academy class fighting in this war, had marched in his inaugural parade.

Johnson's replacement **Richard Mulhouse Nixon** was another tragic figure in this story. He turned out to be the epitome of what Aristotle had in mind for tragically flawed characters. His legacy as 'Tricky Dick' seems to say it all. What he saw as honor and peace were unlike what most honorable, and peace-loving people understand as such. His policy of 'Peace with Honor' turned into a thoroughly dishonorable one of selling out the South Vietnamese people and leaving them to the mercy of their enemies. Ultimately, he recognized it to be a 'sell-out.' However, in his postwar memoirs, he blamed Congress for it.

Nixon was no doubt a brilliant man. Yet, he was entirely beset with suspicions that others were out to destroy him. He trusted no one. He ordered the wiretapping of his closest advisors – even Henry Kissinger, whom he often referred to as that 'Jew Boy.' He formed his secret investigative group to spy on and to gather intelligence on individuals and groups. It led to Watergate and his downfall.

When he left the White House in disgrace on August 9, 1974, he and his wife flew to their San Clemente, California home where he worked to regain his stature as an international statesman. In retirement, he wrote ten books, several of which received critical acclaim. These, along with a famous interview with David Frost and meetings with several heads of state, seemed to have regained his standing in the public eye as a respectable ex-President.

When he died of a stroke in April 1994, all five then living Presidents attended. The line to view his casket was three miles long with an estimated 42,000 people. Today thousands more than those at his funeral can listen to *YouTube* renditions of his Presidential Tape recordings that include his expletive-filled tirades of his belittling everyone from his cabinet members, aides, and military advisors to heads of state and ethnic and religious groups. Thus, the tapes not only show his role in Watergate but reveal his true character and demeanor as a crude wartime leader responsible for thousands of American and tens of thousands of Vietnamese lives lost.

After leaving office in April 1968, **Robert Strange McNamara** spent over thirteen years as head of the World Bank. He reveled in that role, using his considerable managerial skills – especially his systems analysts' cost-effectiveness measures - to reform and improve the bank's functions. During these years, he stayed out of the public light – refusing to join the speaking circuit on the lessons of the Vietnam War. However, he could not escape entirely from public scrutiny. Even before the war ended, in 1972, a passenger on a ferry to Martha's Vineyard tried to throw him overboard because "he just wanted to confront him on Vietnam."

Staying silent for many years, in 1995 McNamara finally published his account of the war. Most famously, the memoir admitted that he and others were "wrong, terribly wrong." *In Retrospect* was met with much notoriety and some ridicule – mainly because he revealed that he thought the war was lost well before he recommended against it, and after the loss of thousands of lives.

Today one can listen to his defense on numerous *YouTube* videos and documentaries that have played on public television stations. His persona in these reminds one of what he did during the war. He stands confidently, almost defiantly, expounding on his thoughts and reasons on 'what went wrong.' He does this in the same manner as when he explained to the Public what was going right as he advised two Presidents on his measures that showed the US was winning in Vietnam.

McNamara died in his sleep at his home in Washington, DC on July 6, 2009. He is buried at Arlington Cemetery on the same grounds as the President who hired him to reform the Department of Defense, and amongst the thousands of young men who died for his measures of effectiveness.

During the Watergate Affair, **Henry Alfred Kissinger** was untouched by the scandals that shook Washington. Most of his duties had kept him out of town and out of the attempts by Nixon to sweep the entire affair under the rug. As it further embroiled the President and began to tarnish US foreign policy, Kissinger recommended that the President resign. The night before Nixon left office, he and the President shared several shots of brandy and some tears together in the White House. Nixon even asked his "Jew Boy" to kneel in prayer with him over his ordeal. Upon Nixon's departure, Kissinger continued to serve as both National Security Advisor and Secretary of State for the new President Gerald Ford.

After Carter defeated Ford for the Presidency in 1976, Kissinger would not again hold an official position in the US Government. He, however, remained the acknowledged American expert in foreign affairs writ large in the eyes of many. He gradually became one of the most famous personages in American public and private life. He wrote books, founded his consultancy, made public appearances, appeared on television news programs, was a sought-after public speaker, and was one of the most wanted single men in America before his marriage. This all made him a very wealthy man. He is still famous and well-off today at the age of 94 – the only living principal cast member of this story.

Despite all his fame and wealth, he does not escape untarnished from the Vietnam War tragedy. Before Watergate forced his resignation, Nixon had decided to bring Haig in to serve as his Chief of Staff, insulting Kissinger in the process. After Haig had taken over, he told Kissinger about the secret White House taping system. As a biographer recounts, "Kissinger, with a reverence for history's judgment and a self-awareness of how bad his groveling might sound when played publicly, was horrified. He knew that he had been caught on tape assenting to, even encouraging, Nixon's darker musings and paranoid prejudices."

So it remains for posterity. All one has to do is to listen to one of the Nixon-Kissinger tapes to see how this American statesman icon flattered, stimulated, reaffirmed, and bent to Nixon's views. He shamelessly reassured Nixon at every step to do whatever the President said he wanted to do. After hearing how complicit Kissinger was in the Nixon decisions on the Vietnam War, one knows how much he shares in the outcome and disgrace of the 'Peace with Honor' approach in ending it.

General **Maxwell Davenport Taylor** continued to play a role in the Vietnam War after he departed as Ambassador to Vietnam. He served as Special Consultant to Presidents Johnson and Nixon from 1965 to 1969. As such he continued to advise on the war, usually agreeing with the field commanders and sometimes giving public speeches explaining why the US was involved. Johnson sometimes sent him to Congressional hearings to explain Westmoreland's military strategy, which the President never understood. He also spoke up in favor of Westmoreland's alternative strategy to strike the Ho Chi Minh Trail after TET 1968 but kept quiet when his man failed to press the issue.

Taylor's retired life was much as he had served - a soldier-scholar known and often revered for his wartime exploits, but also admired for his scholarly pursuits. He continued to defend his views on Vietnam in his memoirs, *Swords, and Plowshares*, published in 1972, while, of course, it seemed that the US might still end the war favorably. As the US withdrew and after South Vietnam's fall, Taylor continued to write articles for such journals as *Foreign Affairs* supporting the use of force as an instrument of policy during times in which it never seemed the US would engage in conflict again. In the eighties, he also continued to write about the need for reform in the office of the Chairman of the Joint Chiefs.

A vigorous golfer and sailor, his activities rapidly declined when he contracted Lou Gehrig's disease. The ailment caused several serious falling accidents. After one such grave incident, paramedics rushed him to Walter Reed Hospital, where he died on April 19, 1987. He was interned at Arlington; joining some of his 'Screaming Eagle' comrades from World War Two, and his two friends, John, and Robert Kennedy.

Taylor's role in this war saga has often been ambiguous. He oscillated in his recommendations for the use of US ground forces. He was an ardent supporter of gradualism in the beginning and then for the employment of combat forces as quickly as possible. When US forces began operations in earnest in 1966, he became a fervent advocate of Westmoreland's attrition strategy, but also argued for their use in the protection of the populated areas and pacification. Recently, Army General and historian H. R. MacMaster contended that he was complicit in keeping the views of the Joint Chiefs from the President. Yet, he had always been an advocate of effective JCS advice to the Commander-in-Chief. Above all - like all the military senior commanders and advisors in this story - he was willing to bend to the will of his civilian leaders without convincing counter arguments or adamant dissension.

General Taylor had many protégés that fought in the Vietnam War. His most famous was General **William Childs Westmoreland**. As this story shows 'Westy' tried to do the best he could to find a way to win the war. Having little help from his civilian leaders and military advisors in Washington, the MACV commander developed a flawed military strategy. It was flawed because he assumed that he could force the enemy main forces into battle by attacking their base camps and destroying them within the borders of South Vietnam. He did not have the forces, or the time, or the cooperation of the enemy to do so.

When he saw that it could not work, to his credit, he developed an alternative approach that may have achieved a positive outcome. His attempts to sell this approach, however, lacked the forcefulness, clarity, and reasoning needed to convince the President and others that it could decisively turn the tide in the war. His most significant flaw was that he did not think it his duty to challenge his civilian leaders when he recognized that their guidance and direction could not lead to success. When bold, imaginative leadership was necessary, he let his superiors and most importantly his soldiers down.

When Westmoreland retired as the Army Chief of Staff in 1972, he returned to his home in Charleston, South Carolina. Two years later he ran for the Republican Party nomination for Governor. He lost. When Saigon fell to the North Vietnamese, he took the brunt of the criticism for the loss of Vietnam. In 1976, he published his memoirs explaining his actions and thoughts on the strategy he created for the war. Despite his explanations, some historians continue to blame him for the loss; sometimes unfairly criticizing him for neglecting critical aspects of the war.

Regardless of this criticism, the General continued to make public appearances and give interviews. One such interview with CBS led to that network's airing of a documentary charging him for deliberately suppressing intelligence to deceive his civilian leaders and the public. Unknown to the public in this documentary the issue was over the disparity in estimates of the guerrilla forces, which were always suspect even to the communist leaders.

Westmoreland sued for libel. After a long and costly battle, he settled for some rewording of the findings and withdrew the suit. Afterward, the General suffered from Alzheimer's disease and lived in a retirement home. His fading memory may have finally given him some respite from the blame and anguish of the criticism he had to endure for Vietnam. 'Westy' died on July 18, 2005, at the age of 91. He is buried at West Point, NY, where, as Superintendent of the United States Military Academy, he was once revered as one of the most distinguished generals in the US Army.

General **Creighton Williams Abrams** - thanks to the praise and adulation of one recent historian - did not suffer the criticism and humiliation that the war brought upon his West Point classmate. Indeed, after he left MACV command and took over as Army Chief of Staff, many contemporaries and historians credit him with saving the Army after its Vietnam disaster. Always a heavy cigar smoker, before he could complete his tenure as Army Chief, he died at Walter Reed Hospital on 4 September 1974. Like many of the soldiers he commanded in two wars, Abrams rests in Arlington Cemetery in Virginia.

A history of the Vietnam War gives Abrams acclaim for almost winning in 1969 - 1970. Yet, as this story relates, these latter triumphs benefited from the communist military defeat during TET that actually occurred during Westmoreland's command. Moreover, like his classmate, the civilian direction and guidance provided to Abrams was equally flawed in that it derailed his sound plans for US troop withdrawals and turning the war over to the Vietnamese Armed Forces. Also like Westmoreland, he was unable to convince his superiors to change that direction. Furthermore, as the released Presidential tapes reveal, he received much ridicule from the President and his National Security Advisor, whom both indicated a lack of confidence in him and a desire to relieve him of command from time to time.

Thus, this work tells a different story from that of Lewis Sorley's of General Abrams role in the Vietnam War and its defeat. While 'Abe' recognized what needed to be done and had the opportunity to follow up on the TET communist defeat, he was unable to do so. That failure was as much his responsibility and fault as that of his superiors. He, like Westmoreland, failed his soldiers in not forcefully bringing his views to his superiors and getting their attention to the consequences of withdrawing US forces unilaterally before its counterpart ARVN was ready. In the end, Abrams was as much responsible for the American abandoning of South Vietnam to communist aggression and defeat as anyone.

The Vietnamese

The major Vietnamese figure that dominated the war was, of course, **Ho Chi Minh**. William Duiker's portrait of Ho's role and description of his significant contributions to the independence and unification of Vietnam is mostly accepted in this story. He was a charismatic and unifying figure in the conflict. Many Vietnamese, both in the South and North, rallied around him in that struggle. He was instrumental in the founding of the modern-day Vietnam independence and unification movement and became its leader and mentor for many other participants. His determination and inspiration were fundamental factors in their success.

Duiker's argument that he was both a nationalist and a communist makes sense. His devotion to communist ideology was equally as motivating as his nationalist fervor. For him, the two notions were intertwined. An integral part of communist ideology explained colonial subjugation. The fact that he was a communist as much as a nationalist is essential to this story. In the late forties and into the fifties, Americans and their leaders saw all communists as the same. Thus, with a communist as their leader, the Viet-Minh were all communists, and their nationalist struggle was naturally a communist-driven desire to enlarge its hold on the world.

There is much irony in the American view of Ho. He so dominated their overall sense of the struggle that they did not realize that Ho was not the one calling the shots on the war in North Vietnam. While he still performed an important function as a diplomat and a ceremonial role to the people as 'Uncle Ho,' he was no longer a decision maker. However, Ho played another role in the war as a distractor and deceiver. As an apparently reasonable man who delved in western political ideas and a world traveler, American leaders thought they could reason with him and convince him of the futility of the irrational pursuit of war against the world's greatest power.

By 1969 'Uncle Ho' was in rapidly failing health. He could no longer perform his role of rallying the people for the war while enduring hardship, destruction, and harm. On the day of recognizing their independence, September 2, 1969, his heart stopped. 100,000 people attended his funeral four days later. Always rejecting pomp and circumstance, his comrades, however, decided that it was too important to their cause, and their enduring power, to erect a tomb and later a museum in his name. In April 1975, his name also supplanted Saigon as the main city in the southern part of a unified Socialist Republic of Vietnam (SRV). Today, he rightly remains the founder of the SRV and is portrayed as the main reason for its success in wars against two powerful western oppressors of Vietnamese independence and unification. Yet, in the overall portrait of Ho we cannot forget that as a communist he also brought a system to his people that resulted in much hardship, death, and destitution. Vietnam today is still trying to recover from his belief in communism as a way of life for the Vietnamese.

While Ho was America's most well-known North Vietnamese leader, **Vo Nguyen Giap** was a close second. While the architect and founder of the People's Army of North Vietnam (PAVN) and the victory at Dien Bien Phu, he played a secondary role in the war against the Americans. As this story shows, communist leaders during the American war sidelined him for most of the time. This move was primarily because his reputation and closeness to Ho Chi Minh made him a threat to the authority of the Politburo leaders who had seized power.

Giap was also an opponent to, or at least not in favor of, the Party leaders' aggressive general offensive strategy. Thus, the Politburo's more militant leaders needed to minimize his views on the conduct of the war. Yet, they did not entirely remove him from the Party and kept him as Minister of Defense. This is because, like Ho, Giap served a useful role in the North's deceptions against the Americans. It appears that letting the American leaders believe that the hero of Dien Bien Phu was in charge, played into their overall ruse of confusing the Americans on who was really in control of military affairs. It also fit in well with the design to lure US forces away from the cities in preparation for TET. Thus, they made it appear that Giap was personally in charge at Khe Sanh and about to launch another Dien Bien Phu assault. It worked.

After TET, Giap did have a role in the Easter and Ho Chi Minh offensives. It may have been to use him as a scapegoat should those offensives fail. Indeed, after the Easter Offensive, the Politburo did place some blame on him. After the war ended, however, the Party leaders stripped him of power, and he lost any real position in the Party or Government. Yet, because of his renown, they found it useful for him to play a ceremonial role in some official affairs. He also wrote several books glorifying his part in the wars against the French and Americans. In the end, Giap survived his opponents. He lived to the ripe old age of 102. The Government gave him a state funeral. Today, he is buried in his hometown in the Province of Quang Binh.

Unknown to American leaders and most experts on North Vietnam, we now know that the real person calling the shots in Hanoi was **Le Duan**. He kept up the ruse that Ho and Giap oversaw the war to confuse the Americans on who was making the decisions. It worked. While the primary American policy was to use limited force to reach a negotiated peace, he was intent on pursuing a military victory at all costs. He had constructed a police state that devoted all its resources to the war and suppressed any opposition. Meanwhile, often Le Duan gained a respite from American bombing in his enemy's pursuit of a negotiated ending. This lack of 'knowing who your enemies are' turned out to be the colossal US intelligence failure in the war, and one of the most effective ruses in modern warfare.

Following the 'liberation' of Saigon in April 1975, the taciturn Le Duan, and his right-hand subordinates Le Duc Tho and General Van Tien Dung, celebrated the end of their fifteen-year struggle for unification. A year later, the victorious General Secretary renamed the unified Vietnam state the Socialist Republic of Vietnam. In that year, he oversaw the continued suppression of all opposition, the imprisonment, and re-education of thousands of former South Vietnamese, and the continued Soviet-style socialization of the new Republic.

These domestic policies would result in a downward spiral for all Vietnamese economically, and nearly ruin all aspects of their lives in both the former northern and southern portions for decades. Moreover, by the end of the decade, Vietnam went to war with their former Khmer Rouge allies in Cambodia, as well as with the Chinese once again on their northern frontier. Victorious on both counts, the wars further plummeted the country into economic stagnation and super inflation. These conflicts also led to their isolation from a growing, prosperous Southeast Asian economic block that may have rescued them from their plight.

Throughout the first five years of the next decade, Le Duan continued to rule with an iron hand. Vietnam also continued its economic stagnation and its militaristic ventures. In the latter case, its reputation gained from its defeat of American arms led to other states' requests of PAVN advisors and their dispatch to aid the Sandinistas in Nicaragua and the Soviets in Afghanistan. By 1986, however, Le Duan succumbed to the trials and tribulations of years in French jails and contracted lung problems. Though he had hoped one day to return to the South, he died July 10, 1986. He is buried in a national cemetery in Hanoi. Two years later his loyal subordinates, Le Duc Tho and Van Tien Dung, followed. With these deaths came an end of the hard-line communist rule in Vietnam, a return to normalcy with other Southeast Asian countries, and normalization of relations with the United States.

Ngo Dinh Diem, the first President of the Republic of South Vietnam, was in many ways the personification of the many complexities, contradictions, ironies, and tragedies of the Vietnam War story in this work. He was a devout Catholic in a country that consisted of mostly Buddhists. He was a staunch anti-communist, whom the Vietnamese Communists wanted to join their cause. He was a devoted nationalist but did not have the personality or the ability to govern a nation. The communists and others called him a lackey of the Americans, yet he resisted American pressures to reform. Some historians view him as a bumbling idiot, a despot and an out of touch elitist; others as a far-sighted leader, the last of the Mandarin type patriot who wanted much for his people and could have delivered, just not in the American way. Like many of his American counterparts, his character traits that initially led to his astounding successes from 1954 to 1960, led to his downfall and death in 1963.

While his personality and his abilities as a leader were multifaceted and remain controversial, this story argues that his assassination was a significant turning point in the war. His removal did nothing to solve or relieve the perceived or real faults that led to his elimination. To the contrary, it led to a worsened situation in the South that eventually enabled Northern Communist success and American combat force intervention.

Diem's actual assassination is a micro example within the broader panorama of misfits, misfires, incompetencies, deceits, disloyalties, and dishonors among and between the South Vietnamese and American officers and diplomats during the war. As related in Chapter 2, several members of the Kennedy Administration, mainly Ambassador Lodge, were complicit in encouraging a coup against Diem. When it happened on 1 November 1963, Diem called Lodge to see what he could arrange through the Americans for transportation to leave the country. Lodge purposely did not take the call. Meanwhile, the Coup leaders had differing views about what to do with Diem. Some wanted him safely transported somewhere outside of South Vietnam. Others wanted him killed. When finally caught, his captors placed Diem and his brother in an Armored Personnel Carrier to be transported back to the South Vietnamese Armed Forces headquarters. Before arriving there, they brutally killed them.

Afterward, there was another debate on what to do with the bodies. The South Vietnamese generals ultimately decided to hide the location of his burial. To this day, the actual site is still unknown. It was a sad and shameful ending for a man whom LBJ had once labeled 'The Winston Churchill' of Southeast Asia, and whom the US had spent millions of dollars and dozens of lives to support as the head of a state which was to contain the spread of communism in Asia.

The End: De Quoi S'Agit-il? (What is it all About?)

In his classic work *War and Politics* Bernard Brodie begins by recounting the French General Ferdinand Foch's reflection on the violence and chaos of the First World War – "De Quoi S-Agit-iL." Foch, who had led the French armies in several futile offensives resulting in massive casualties, was looking back over what had occurred in the war and questioning himself and others in the Allied High Command on the rationale for and worth of all those casualties.

This reflection of what is it all about, in Brodie's theme for *War and Politics*, is what more senior officers and their political overseers must ask before they embark on such an important venture as going to war. To not do so is to invite disaster. As this story has tried to show, such was the case for the American political and military leaders for the Vietnam War.

What resulted was one of the greatest tragedies in US history. That tragedy transcended the politicians and soldiers directly involved. As shown in this chapter and the one before, the Vietnam War - whether recognized or not, whether directly or indirectly – has left a permanent mark on our lives and is destined to continue affecting thoughtful citizens of this republic as long as it exists.

As the great theorist, Carl von Clausewitz reminds us, "War is an act of human intercourse...It is part of man's social existence...Thus, it is fitting that we finish this tragic story with the above summary of what happened to its principal characters. For this has been a human story of what occurred in the Vietnam War decades ago. What happened in that war and its results were primarily due to the interactions of leaders and policymakers in a world that was different from today. Though the times have changed, the types of personal interactions described in this story - with all their human strengths, qualities, determinations, frailties, weaknesses, and misunderstandings – live on.

Epilogue

As I neared the completion of this story of the Vietnam War, every day I saw or heard or read something about that war. Its heavy shadow continues to fall on us from film, television, books, magazines, news stories, and the ubiquitous internet. Why does this remain so?

There are some obvious reasons. First, now that the war is more than fifty years past its 1965 or whatever start point historians assign it, there has been an increase in the availability of sources on the war – from American, Vietnamese, and other participants' archives and holdings – that have prompted a dramatic increase in histories on the event. Also prompting the upsurge in these accounts has been the availability of oral histories of its veterans. For example, the Department of History at the United States Military Academy has launched a program of capturing the thoughts and memories from the war's participants and posting them online for all to hear and witness. There are other oral history sites on the war, as well. Most recently, Ken Burns, the master storyteller using the oral history genre, has just finished his rendition of the Vietnam War on the Public Broadcasting System television. Reactions to that work are about as controversial as the war was.

Second, as World War Two and Korean veterans reach the limits of their life expectancies and fade away in large numbers, Vietnam War veterans have come to replace them on the stage of remembrances of American past foreign wars. As a result, tens of thousands of communities have commemorated their citizens' service in the war with monuments and ceremonies. My West Point classmate, Al Nahas, has produced a fascinating book called, *Warriors Remembered*, which describes over one thousand memorials to those who fought there and tells the intensely human story of those who created them.

Third, Vietnam Veterans themselves have reached some reconciliation with the war. There are thousands of web pages on the internet on which these veterans share their lives after the war and their current thoughts and memories of it. My old outfit, the 3rd Battalion, 506th Infantry has one labeled the "Stand Alone Battalion." Moreover, one continually reads or hears about Vietnam reunions well attended, and well infused with beverages that prompt or encourage the telling of the proverbial 'war stories.' My West Point Class of 1967 just had our 50th Reunion celebration at which we honored the 29 classmates who perished in Vietnam.

As mentioned in the closing chapter, a not so apparent reason, but most profound, is that the war was a defining moment in American history that has touched every facet of American life. In Ken Burns' work on the war, the filmmaker claims that Vietnam stands alongside the US Civil War in its impact on Americans and their history. This book has tried to capture this importance in several chapters, as I saw it years back when I began its story. Indeed, the memory of Vietnam will continue to live on in our lives and history books well beyond the lifespans of its veterans. After the present generations are gone, people will continue to try to understand the Vietnam War and its meaning alongside the times in which it happened.

I am sure that the meaning for America and its populace to come will continue to be full of controversy, misinterpretations, and dramatic conclusions. The Vietnam experience as history is full of complex meanings and lessons for the future. The continued study and use of the war's lessons can benefit our leaders, as I have argued in the last chapters of this book.

My feelings about what lessons Americans have learned and applied remain mixed. Presently, most books and articles on the war continue to fall into the orthodox and revisionist camps. These, as mentioned in this book and its appendices, mostly focus on what should have or not have been; what we should have done or not; and whether we could have won the war or not. These arguments and their conclusions tend, in my view, to seek some definitive answer or solution to any issue at hand, and further use it as a defense for a point of view that someone wants to get across. I am sure that some statesman or woman will use one or two lessons from the war as an analogy, as Professor Yuen Foong Khong demonstrates in his book on *Analogies at War*, to justify their argument or decision for going or not going to war in the future.

In my view, there will continue to be a misuse of the history of the war. Decision makers of the future will try to replicate answers or solutions to present problems based on misinterpreted or misused lessons of the past. This has already occurred. For example, as Retired Colonels Daddis and Gentile have argued, some government officials have tried to wrongly apply the Lewis Sorley interpretation of the Vietnam War to both Iraq and Afghanistan to justify troop surges and military courses of action there.

As I have tried to show in this book, for me at least, the real value of history is to illustrate how humans interact, and how we may find a better way of discourse that will enable more information and points of view considered in the solving of any problem in the national security arena. This improved discourse, and the attempts to produce it, can create a sense of shared responsibility that seems essential to effective decision making. As mentioned in the last chapter, this has been the theme of my story of the Vietnam War.

My experience in Government and the military - in war and preparing for war, and my education in military affairs and strategic formulation - reinforce my point of view about history in general, and about this story in particular. Like theory and doctrine, history should be a guide, a litmus test, an example of human interaction and understanding, or misunderstanding, of issues and problems. Such is its real contribution to understanding the use of force and the conduct of war.
Present day problems in governing and in the employment of force in conflicts beg not only this use of history but demand the application of the lessons learned from Vietnam that I have found in my research and presented in this story.

Currently, there are many lessons of Vietnam that journalists, historians, and officials are now writing about or arguing over for their application of or use in the current conflicts America is involved in – Afghanistan, Iraq, and Syria, for example. Too many of these proposed lessons surround such issues as whether these conflicts are winnable or not; whether they are in the national interest or not; whether politicians are too restrictive or not in the application of military force. Sound familiar? These were issues in the Vietnam War, and now so-called 'experts,' many from the prolific 'think tanks,' are arguing for some solution based on what happened or not in the American experience in Vietnam.

It seems that what is important here is whether the US has the right people in government and its national security apparatus to wrestle with the current day issues requiring sound strategic formulation and the effective employment of force, whatever and wherever that may be. It is also profoundly important, based on the lessons of Vietnam explored in this work, whether these people are effectively working together to give the President the necessary and pertinent information and analyses to enhance his judgment on these issues of war and peace. It is further critical that the government's national security advisors and responsible military commanders inform the

Commander-in-Chief of the US Armed Forces of the issues and make reasonable recommendations that ensure he is knowledgeable enough to make sound decisions on issues that will result in the loss of American lives.

We need advisors, particularly those who wear the uniform, to educate their civilian leaders on the many aspects of war; how difficult it is to wage and how things will always go wrong or different from expected. To do so, we not only need military commanders and advisors who have combat experience, but who are educated on military history in a way that they can confront issues of war and peace armed with the perspective of the past.

We need military advisors and commanders who can explain that war results in death and destruction – purposefully produced and accidentally created. War is not some game. Theories of conflict do not prescribe exact solutions to war. It is a human endeavor that at its very core is waged to impose one's will on another through force. Though perhaps currently it may seem crude or politically incorrect, one should recall what Sherman said of war – "War means fighting and fighting means killing." Despite the age of computers and robots, this means we need soldiers, sailors, marines, and airmen who can kill others.

Lastly, we need Commanders-in-Chief who are knowledgeable of the basics of strategic formulation and the employment of military force so that they can make informed, reasonable decisions on the use of military force – especially its difficulties and uncertainties. Whether they acquire that knowledge through a program like that proposed in this work, or through an education provided by their primary military advisors, or from self-study, or a combination of all, is irrelevant. What is relevant is that the President must know something about the employment of military force, and it must be more than some half-baked article, or book, or political-savvy civilian advisor, or prep school. The fact is that the most important decisions in the US Government on national security matters are the purview of the President whether he desires it or not. The buck stops with the Commander-in-Chief.

With the new Trump Administration coming into office the application of the lessons of the past, and, in particular Vietnam, seems especially relevant to the current situation in the US government. Though I am not in a position to expound on the goings on in the current government, there are ample, convincing reports, which do not seem to be 'fake news,' that should be alarming in this regard.

The situation in the Trump Administration is in many ways similar and analogous to those who had confronted the issue of war in the Vietnam era. First, despite Trump's stated belief that his military prep school experience is comparable to military service, the new President brings no military or national security experience to his office. In fact, like Clinton, he was mainly a draft dodger who got one of the menial deferments for a 'bone spur.' Second, most of his civilian advisors that he has appointed to his White House staff, the State Department, and in the intelligence arena lack any military experience or education.

Moreover, most of the background of the new Commander-in-Chief and his civilian advisors are in business. As we have seen in this story, the application of business techniques may be of use in managing the vast government bureaucracy and even the Department of Defense but does not translate well to the use of force or waging of war. Thus, there is and will continue to be a need for some education and acquired knowledge for these civilians, to include the President. Unfortunately, it appears that this will have to consist of an 'on the job' effort, as most new US governments do in learning about national security.

Trump has included several retired and active duty military personnel in his Administration. For example, as of this writing he has appointed retired Generals Mattis and Kelly as his Secretary of Defense and Chief of Staff, respectively, and Lieutenant General H.R. McMaster as his National Security Advisor. This action seems to make up for his and his other civilian appointees' lack of military experience. However, as we have seen in the story in this book, this act onto itself will not solve the lack of knowledge amongst the Trump Administration civilians of military affairs and the use of force. It does not absolve the President from gaining sufficient knowledge, whatever that may be, about the use of military force in national security issues.

The recent appointment of McMaster is particularly interesting and hopeful in ensuring the new President and his chief civilian advisors will obtain comprehensive and useful knowledge and advice on national security matters. After all, the General has written a book on the Vietnam War, *Dereliction of Duty*, which I have used extensively in my research for this work. McMaster's conclusions in his book are very much similar as in this work. Perhaps his knowledge gained from history and his extensive military experience will make a difference.

As mentioned in the last several chapters of this story, the most complex and pressing issue is the continued, seemingly never-ending use and employment of the US Armed Forces to counter and defeat extreme terrorist groups – namely ISIS and al-Qaeda. Whether one can agree with Andrew Bacevich's arguments about the overuse of force in American international politics, he makes one major point that the current and any future American governments will have to address – the poor existing state of civil-military relations and its impact on policies for the continual use of force. In his book *The Long War* Bacevich supports the argument in this work that "among the many explanations for the debacle of Vietnam, the atmosphere of civil-military dishonesty and mistrust prevailing throughout the war deserves a place of honor." Moreover, Bacevich further claims, as does this work, that civil-military relationships have, with few exceptions, since that war been "less than admirable and effective."

Rather, the dialogue between our civilian and military leaders and advisors has been fraught with "mutual manipulation informed by suspicion and mistrust," instead of a healthy "give and take, candid and at times even contentious" discussion of the issues and views. The result is that we have not had a detailed, honest assessment and reevaluation of the current trends and effectiveness of overall US national security policies or the long war on terrorism.

Thus, I agree with Bacevich's assertions on the present state of US civil-military relations in our national security making. That must change for any useful, necessary reassessment of where the future of the US lays in the national security arena. Moreover, using the lessons of the Vietnam War's example can serve well in fixing that quality if policymakers are willing to do so.

Indeed, it seems that the current number of ex or current military experienced advisors and leaders can help. Retired Generals Mattis and Kelly have had excellent service records and have demonstrated skills in their craft. General McMaster seems the ideal National Security Advisor for bringing about change. He has the credentials of being a soldier-scholar with a unique historical perspective on policymaking, who can bring an "open and honest dialogue that is consistent with civilian supremacy."

Just having military or retired military advisors in high government positions, however, does not in itself guarantee that sound political-military dialogues will occur, or effective decisions will be made. Current reports are not favorable for such a dialogue to happen. McMaster has no experience in the machinations of the Washington world of dealing with politicians and policy wonks. The President and many of the civilians in his White House team and cabinet posts know little about the employment of military force and other instruments of power. They are not well-versed in history. As mentioned, their primary background is in business. We saw in Vietnam how business practices are not in consonance with the employment of military force.

At this juncture, the most that can be said, from this author's perspective is that the road ahead will be a tough one. There have not been any apparent breakthroughs in our current operations in Syria, Afghanistan, Iraq or anywhere else in the Middle East. Moreover, there are situations in the Pacific – North Korean belligerence and Chinese adventurism – that could break out in a conflict involving US interests and forces. Finally, there is also the Russian question. Will Russia continue its aggressive policies toward its neighbors, and where will their past efforts to disrupt the election process in the US go? The world remains a dangerous place. The need for sound decision-making in national security affairs has never been more necessary. The need to gain perspective from the past has never been greater.

Source Notes

This appendix lists and outlines the sources that I consulted and have heavily relied on for each chapter and the epilogue of *Warriors and Fools*. In the Bibliography that follows, there is another set cited that I have also consulted for the story in this book. It is inclusive of the sources in this appendix.

Many of these sources are electronic books – either in Amazon Kindle or Barnes and Noble Nook or Apple iBook formats. Some others are electronic documents found on various web pages or downloaded in PDF layout. One reason there are no footnotes in the narrative is that these eBooks and other electronic source formats have no paginations, or the pages vary depending on how they display.

I have used electronic sources as much as possible. Electronic displays ease the usage of these sources while researching (allows for automatic note-taking and storage) and writing and citing (enables direct cut and paste of quotes, the inclusion of actual documents, and notations) in the book's narrative. Direct copy and paste from electronic sources also enable more exact citation and use.

General Sources

I met three major problems in finding and using general sources that cover the entire Vietnam War for this book. The first was that most general histories or accounts cover various aspects of the war during varying periods. For example, some general narratives only cover the period of direct US major combat commitment of forces. Others only involve events during specific US administrations. Still others focus on only US activities. Finally, some of the more popular general histories now lack information from sources that have become available since published.

My choices for general sources, to include primary and secondary, entailed several parameters. I wanted those that most authors of the American Vietnam War experience used and cited in their accounts. Secondly, I sought those that were more inclusive of US involvement in Indochina and Vietnam near the end of World War Two – circa early 1945 - to the fall of Saigon in 1975. Thirdly, I wanted the most recent general histories. Fourth, I wanted works that also focused on the Vietnamese perspectives. Fifth, I sought to use primary source materials available online. Finally, I set a timeframe for the publication that, of course, limited my ability to find or research all general sources. This was the result.

The *National Archives* online is a vast collection of materials available for general research and educational use. I used this site primarily to access the complete collection of *The Pentagon Papers*. One can download these as PDF files, which are useful for documents that were pertinent to in-depth research on various issues. I also consulted *The National Archive YouTube Channel* for Vietnam War videos. A select number of these are embedded in the iBook version of this book. I was also able to use its military reports and records to find specific daily situation reports on the service of my battalion during the summer and fall of 1969. Also available at the Archives online site are links to *The Presidential Libraries*.

An essential primary source is the *Foreign Relations of the United States* (FRUS) series of historical documents. This is also available online. They are organized into Presidential Administration collections. Researchers can download specific volumes or documents for in-depth use. Documents include specific decision memoranda, transcripts of meetings and telephone conversations, and memoranda of record. In many cases, there are notations to other source materials that a document or meeting transcript refers to such as other files found in the national archives or private paper collections at various sites.

The University of Virginia's *The Miller Center* online web page is another indispensable site. It advertises itself as a "nonpartisan institute for the understanding of the presidency, policy, and political history, providing critical insights for the national's governance challenges." The site consolidates and provides the Presidential Recordings of the Truman, Eisenhower, Kennedy, Johnson, and Nixon Administrations for the Vietnam War as well as other events. Particularly useful given the sometimes inferior quality of the tapes, are several slide shows and transcripts of select tapes. For example, there are valuable transcripts of the JFK recordings in the *Great Crises* work edited by Timothy Naftali and Philip Zelikow. Moreover, for all three Vietnam War Presidents there are many transcripts of tales in the "Presidential Recordings Digital Edition." As in the national archive site, there are links to *The Presidential Libraries* and online versions of very useful oral histories.

Presidential Libraries offer a host of documents and tapes, as does the Miller Center. However, they also offer, in most instances, more than *The Miller Center*. For example, at the JFK library, there are transcripts of the tapes that allow a better understanding of the conversations because they include some editorial comment in the context of the meetings and telephone conversations. In the Nixon library, as in the other libraries to varying degrees, one can find original memos and correspondence for use and download. One will have to alternate between online sites between the archives, *The Miller Center*, and Libraries to find the most valuable online materials for their research and publication.

The *CIA's Freedom of Information Act Electronic Reading Room* is an important primary source for National Intelligence Estimates, Presidential Daily Intelligence Briefs, investigations, and other CIA reports. This site can be valuable to find intelligence materials that are not found in other sources or places, such as those not in the *FRUS* or other official sources.

Texas Tech University's *The Vietnam Center and Archive* "collects and preserves the documentary record of the Vietnam War." The Center advertises its material as "more personal in nature – personal photographs, letters home, etc." Many of these sources, especially those collected and donated by Douglas Pike, offer insights on the war from the North Vietnamese and the southern Communist side. Available sources are in a searchable, virtual archive of over 4 million pages of scanned materials, including photos, maps, oral histories, and interviews. There are also materials for teachers at all levels, such as proposed course syllabi and lesson plans.

Another valued general source is *The U.S. Government and the Vietnam War: Executive and Legislative Roles and Relationships* by William Conrad Gibbons. This work, written by a historian and former congressional staffer, is in four parts covering the events and US policy making from 1945 to January 1968. Like the *Pentagon Papers,* it includes both commentary and primary source materials. Unlike the *Papers,* it also includes comments on several interviews or references that are not readily available elsewhere - such as oral testimonies, letters between noted officials and

Westmoreland papers on file at the US Army Center of Military History. Extracts and summaries of Gibbons' work can be found on the website in his name.

The Chairman of the Joint Chiefs of Staff's Office of Joint History has published on the Joint Electronic Library web page *The Joint Chiefs of Staff and National Policy series, the Joint Chiefs of Staff and Vietnam series, and Institutional History series*. These histories of the JCS are essential to an understanding of its role and the issues it faced in the timeframe of this book. All three series have a total of twenty-four downloadable PDF files for use. Reputable historians have written these electronic books, which are mainly based on JCS files in the National Archives. In addition, journalist Mark Perry has written a general history of the Joint Chiefs called *Four Stars*. It is useful in that it is primarily based on interviews of senior – even some former Chiefs - and some junior officers who had served at various times in the OJCS.

The Branches of the US Armed Forces have also published their general histories of the war. Like the JCS series, historians have written these based on official records, participant papers, and interviews. The most noteworthy are *The US Army Official Histories and Studies*, the US Marine Corps, *US Marines in Vietnam series*, and *The United States Air Force in Southeast Asia, 1961-1973*. These can be found online. The Army's history is at the *US Army's Center of Military History site*; The Marine Corps is at *USMC History and Museum Division site*; and the Air Force's is found at the *Defense Technical Information site*. They all can be downloaded as PDF files for use.

A major online encyclopedia, *Wikipedia.org*, has vast amounts of information on the war as well as any other historical subject. The site can help in any venture to find materials online. While varied in authoritative sources and quality, for the Vietnam War it is a wonderful place to start to search for more detailed information or to collect general information on Vietnam and related materials. The service gives the capability to create a *Wikipedia book* (see print/export/create a book functionality) that compiles pages anywhere from its site on any subject. A researcher can download the resultant mini-encyclopedia or book compilation and use it as a reference for further researching and writing.

The availability and abundance of online source material on the Vietnam War, in my view, is a revolution in historical research, as well as a challenge to any researcher. The latter can easily feel overwhelmed. Anyone trying to 'follow in my footsteps' can receive help from Richard Werking and Brian Etheridge's article, "Teaching the Vietnam War in the Internet Age: Libraries, Websites, and Information Literacy" in *Understanding and Teaching the Vietnam War* from editors John Tully, Matthew Masur and Brad Austin.

In the over fifty years since LBJ decided to commit major US forces to combat in South Vietnam, there have been a plethora of general books written on the war. I have read and included much of the following historical general accounts of the war in my story. Some of these are electronic books from Kindle and Apple Bookstores.

The histories of David Halberstam (*The Best and the Brightest*), Neil Sheehan (*The Bright Shining Lie*) and Stanley Karnow (*Vietnam: A History*) are the earliest written general accounts that I used. I had used Karnow's book in my course on the war at the National War College at the beginning of the 1990s, supplemented with excerpts from the others, along with the *Pentagon Papers*. I remain awed by his story telling abilities. All three of these journalists' works are great reads and offer contemporary commentary. They are also heavily prejudiced against the war and lack recent knowledge from both the Vietnamese side and the US. Another early general history that I consulted was Guenter Lewy's *America and Vietnam*. It challenged several early antiwar accounts' views, to include these journalists, on the morality of the war.

Two other general histories that challenge the views of these earlier works are Harry Summers' *On Strategy* and Andrew Krepinevich's *The Army and Vietnam*. These books were also included in my course at the National War College. While they focus more on the military aspects of the war, they offer different views on what may have gone wrong in the US military strategic formulation and execution. Like other histories written during their timeframe, they lack valuable perspectives from key decision makers on both sides.

More recent and relatively inclusive general accounts I used are: Mark Atwood Lawrence's *The Vietnam War: A Concise International History*; William Turley's *The Second Indochina War: A Short Political and Military History, 1954-1975*; John Prado's *The Hidden History of the Vietnam War*; Robert Schulzinger's *A Time For War: The United States and Vietnam, 1941-1975*; and Mark Moyar's *Triumph Forsaken: The Vietnam War, 1954-1965*. All are more contemporary than the accounts mentioned in the previous two paragraphs. Consequently, they offer sources and views not only from the American side but the Vietnamese as well. Moyar's book is the first of a two-volume history to be published. The second volume is to cover the period up to the fall of Saigon. Because Moyar's first volume challenged much of the orthodox view of the war, Andrew Wiest and Michael Doidge have edited and compiled a series of essays and notes on his work that is useful in *Triumph Revisited: Historians Battle for the Vietnam War*.

George Herring's *America's Longest War: The United States and Vietnam, 1950-1975* in my view stands above all general sources on the war. While Professor Herring first wrote this account in 1986, he has updated it in several editions, the latest being a Kindle Book in 2014. While in the traditional or orthodox camp of historical views on the war, his most recent rendition is inclusive of the main historical views and tries to embrace recent studies on the Vietnamese side and the revisionist historians. Professor Herring's article, "Teaching the Vietnam War: Recollections and Reflections from More Than Thirty Years," in *Understanding and Teaching the Vietnam War* is also well worth a read along with his updated general account.

Of course, I had to include the most recent work of Ken Burns and Geoffrey Ward, *The Vietnam War: An Intimate History* because of its most recent notoriety. I mostly used it to compare it to both the orthodox and revisionist historian treatments. Perhaps, the best use I got out of it was some of the more recent pictures, film and narrative on Le Duan and other North Vietnamese oral histories. I found the oral history series, upon which the book is based, as a useful addition to the more current works I had consulted. However, in my view, many of the veteran stories that were presented seem to have been done because they could be considered more interesting for television viewing, rather than balanced first person witness accounts. Nevertheless, as a combat veteran they confirmed what I already knew: one's memory of the war is intensely personal, varies greatly between where and when one was in Vietnam, and suffers from the shock of the unnatural experience of killing, death, mutilation, and destruction that war is all about.

There are also a number of dictionaries and encyclopedias available on the war. Several that I used were: William Duiker and Bruce Lockhart, *Historical Dictionary of Vietnam*; James Willbanks, *Vietnam War: The Essential Reference Guide* and *Vietnam War Almanac*; and Spencer Tucker, Paul Pierpaoli, Jr., and Merle Pribbenow, *The Encyclopedia of the Vietnam War: A Political, Social and Military History*. Overall, the works in this paragraph can be invaluable in providing summaries of key events, persons, dates, and organizations for use in perspectives or checking on names and facts for the war.

Within time and my capabilities, I have tried to include the Vietnamese Communist side of the war as much as possible. The general accounts that I used are: William Duiker's *The Communist Road to Power* and *Sacred War: Nationalism and Revolution in a Divided Vietnam*; L-H Nguyen's *Hanoi's War: An International History of the War for Peace in Vietnam*; Mark Bradley's *Vietnam at War*; and Ang Cheng Guan's *The Vietnam War from the Other Side: The Vietnamese Communists' Perspective* and *Southeast Asia and the Vietnam War*. The first of Guan studies covers the Vietnamese Communists views and decision-making from 1954 to 1969. The second broadens the opinion of the conflict to include all Southeast Asia. Michael Hunt's *A Vietnam War Reader* gives a selection of Vietnamese printed sources. These are mostly published accounts and writings with some interview transcripts. Noted below in the appropriate chapters are other Vietnamese views in less general accounts.

Of course, the South Vietnamese view is also essential. Up until recently, it has also been neglected. I tried to incorporate some material from their side. The two overall general accounts I used were Robert Bringham, *ARVN: Life and Death in the South Vietnamese Army* and Andrew Wiest's *Vietnam's Forgotten Army*. Several parts of the book, as noted below, discuss, or note monographs and memoirs of ARVN officers and a few works on Diem. A most recent book from Australian Research Council researcher by the name of Nathalie Huynh Chau Ngyuen called *South Vietnamese Soldiers: Memories of he Vietnam War and After* is a fascinating compilation of South Vietnamese military recollections on the war and their experiences afterward recovering primarily as exiles and emigrants to other countries. One only needs to read many of these, translated from the Vietnamese and painstakingly collated by the daughter of a South Vietnamese senior soldier to get a feeling for the pride that many South Vietnamese soldiers had in their service, as well as the suffering that many occurred.

To obtain an overview of the general, but differing views and interpretations of the war I relied on *The Columbia History of the Vietnam War*. This is a series of articles and essays, compiled by Columbia historian David Anderson, on the war from many perspectives. Professor Anderson explains that this work, which is available in electronic formats, "strives to be an authoritative narration and explanation of this still controversial event." The breadth and depth of views in this anthology of essays are a must-read for anyone seeking an understanding of the many diverse and controversial views of the Vietnam War from so many different perspectives.

Equally as informative and useful is Gary Hess' *Vietnam: Explaining America's Lost War*. While Hess admits that his views on the war are in line with the "dovish-orthodox tradition," the essays that he includes are representative of the many views, both contemporary and historical, on the American involvement. Besides being a compilation of essays on the historiography of the war, it includes a list of books that researchers can use as a useful initial bibliography. For the teacher, Hess gives a series of questions that could be assigned to students for debate in the classroom.

Finally, to provide both a geopolitical and military map understanding of the war, I used several atlases. The *Philip's Atlas of World History*, edited by Patrick O'Brien was an excellent source, especially as it is a general atlas that was electronic and download capable. Harry Summers' *Historical Atlas of the Vietnam War* was also valuable for a military understanding. So was the United States Military Academy History Department's *Maps of the Vietnam War*, available on their website. Each official history of the US Armed Services of the war include many maps that are very useful, even critical, to understanding the military operations conducted in Vietnam and its environs.

The following includes the particular sources, in more detail, that I consulted and used in the research and writing of each chapter of the book. In an appendix that follows, I have included some essays that comment on and critique many of the sources mentioned.

Chapter 1: The Best of Times; The Worst of Times

The works that I consulted and used for Section I and its description of American domestic affairs and the impact of the war on them varied. I started with Eric Goldman's classic but dated, *The Crucial Decade and After, America, 1945 – 1960*. Goldman's history of that period had been considered a classic because the author – a distinguished scholar at Princeton University – had challenged the popular notion of the time that the era of the fifties was an era of prosperity but little meaning. Goldman's main thesis was that the decade and a half following the Second World War saw the success and institutionalization of liberal political and social reforms of the FDR years at home and abroad. I began using Goldman's history because I had read and used it in my Graduate School studies in the seventies. Thus, it was originally a baseline for my knowledge of America in the postwar period.

However, the main secondary source that I relied upon for my narrative in this Chapter, and in part in Chapter 4, was James Patterson's *Grand Expectations*. Published in 1997, Paterson's work is much more contemporary than Goldman's. Moreover, as an Oxford History of the US series book and winner of the Bancroft Prize for history, it is considered one of the best histories of the attitudes and moods of the American postwar period.

I have adopted Paterson's theme and argument that the postwar years were full of grand expectations resulting in an optimistic mood that engulfed American affairs and produced an almost fatalistic belief in the future promise of continued wealth and good times. This mood not only affected the general public but our public leaders from Truman through Kennedy and into the LBJ Presidency.

To supplement both Goldman and Paterson I also consulted Peter Jennings, *The Century* – a chronicle of the accomplishments in America during the twentieth century that offered some interesting observations of the attitudes of post-World War Two American. I also extracted some observations from the scholarly essays in Mark Carnes' *Columbia History of Post World War II America* to provide further insights and analyses on the postwar attitudes and their consequent impacts on US social, political, religious issues and events.

Truman's Volume Two of his memoirs, *Years of Trial and Hope, 1946-1952*, David McCullough's *Truman* and Stephen Ambrose's *Eisenhower* were the primary sources that provided me with Truman's and later Eisenhower's views on and actions upon both domestic and international affairs. McCullough and Ambrose also offer their takes on domestic impacts on US containment policies and what was going on in Vietnam during this period. For my rendition of the MacArthur relief, I used Truman's memoirs, McCullough's account, and supplemented them with William Manchester's *American Caesar*.

For Section II and the events and impacts of the end of the war and the origins of the Cold War and containment policy and strategies I relied upon Gerhard Weinberg, *A World at Arms*, and John

Gaddis' *The United States and the Origins of the Cold War, 1941-1947*, and *Strategies of Containment* and *The Cold War: A New History*. Many scholars consider both these historians as the most authoritative in their fields.

I read both Gaddis' and Weinberg's works while in graduate school, where Weinberg was also one of my Professors in my graduate studies. I later attended, as a faculty member at the National War College several of Gaddis' lectures on his themes and arguments in his works on containment and their pertinence to the Vietnam War and other international events – to include the end of the Cold War in 1989. I also read and extracted some files, particularly those covering the development of NSC 68, from the *FRUS 1950, Volume 1*, and related some events from Dean Acheson's *Present at the Creation*.

For my views and narratives on American military affairs, policies, strategies, plans and actions during these years of the post-war period and the early part of the Cold War, I used Steven Rearden's *Council of War: A History of the Joint Chiefs of Staff, 1942-1991*; James Schnabel's *History of the Joint Chiefs of Staff: Volume I, The Joint Chiefs of Staff and National Policy 1945-1947*; Ronald Cole, et. al., *History of the Unified Command Plan, 1946-2012*; Carter, *The US Army Before Vietnam, 1953-1965*; and Maxwell Taylor's memoir *The Uncertain Trumpet*.
Finally, in my views and narrative on US-French relations, particularly US support of their actions in Indochina and Vietnam, I relied on my Graduate Dissertation, *The Politics of Common Defense: France and the Cold War, 1945-1949*. It is an unpublished source at the University of North Carolina. I researched much of the material for this in the National Archives in Washington, DC, and used primary French leader sources as well.

Though written in the mid-seventies, I still think the thesis is right on in countering the then prevalent revisionist historian's view that American political and economic ambitions were a cause of the Cold War. The thesis demonstrated how much American leaders were taken in by their French counterparts who were intent on using the Soviet and the internal communist threat as a means to gain favor and assistance from the US. The key role of the French, as depicted in this section of the Chapter and later, in the reconstruction economically and militarily of Europe in the late forties and early fifties was a major reason for American support in Vietnam.

In reconstructing and explaining the US role and American attitudes toward the First Indochina War in Section II, I further relied on William Conrad Gibbons' *The US Government and the Vietnam War: Executive and Legislative Roles and Relationships, Part I: 1945-1960*; Matthew Moten, *Presidents and the Generals: An American History of Command in War*; David Armstrong, *The Joint Chiefs of Staff and the First Indochina War*; Bernard Fall, *Street Without Joy* and *Hell in a Very Small Place*; Fredrik Logevall's Pulitzer Prize-winning *Embers of War* and his later *Origins of the Vietnam War*; and Mark Lawrence's *Assuming the Burden: Europe and the American Commitment to War in Vietnam*.

Chapter 2: The Best and the Brightest

The general accounts that I relied on for this chapter are George Herring's *America's Longest War: The United States and Vietnam, 1950-1975*; David Halberstam's *The Best and Brightest*; Neil Sheehan's *Bright and Shining Lie*; Stanley Karnow's *Vietnam: A History*. Of these, as mentioned previously, the Halberstam, Sheehan and Karnow works are the most dated. I used them primarily because of their contemporary views and descriptions of both the personalities of the Kennedy Administration and what they observed as journalists.

I have offset some of these works with some equally as valid - and perhaps more in tune with some of the recent revelations of the North Vietnamese - with arguments from Mark Moyar's, *Triumph Forsaken*. I also relied heavily on Larry Freedman *Kennedy's Wars* for his in-depth and insightful analysis of JFK as a commander-in-chief and his views of the military; as well as Daalder and Destler's *In the Shadow of the Oval Office* for the way Kennedy and George McBundy's organized and used the NSC apparatus.

The three main biographies of JFK that I relied on were Dallek's *Unfinished Life*, Ted Sorenson's *Kennedy*, and Arthur Schlesinger's *A Thousand Days*. While Dallek's is certainly less engrossed with the JFK legacy and legend and more recent, Schlesinger and Sorenson offer some interesting observations on JFK's attitude toward his military advisors during his time in office.

My first use of the Presidential tapes comes into play in this chapter. For that I relied on John F. Kennedy Library, Presidential Recordings (meetings and telephone calls), and The Miller Center's, *Presidential Recordings* (Kennedy Tapes, Norton Transcripts, Exhibits, *Presidential Recordings Project*, Ernest May, and **Philip Zelikow**, editors). The written transcripts in the Miller Center were downloadable and of particularly useful in understanding the conversations in the sometimes very poorly taped and hard to hear sessions. I also used several of the tape transcripts as presented in John Prados' *The White House Tapes: Eavesdropping on the President*.

Other biographies, memoirs and secondary sources on various members of the JFK Administration that I used were: David Milne's *America's Rasputin: Walt Rostow and the Vietnam War;* Maxwell Taylor's *Swords and Plowshares*; his son's biography Robert Taylor's *The American Soldier;* Gordon Goldstein's , *Lessons in Disaster: McGeorge Bundy and the Path to War in Vietnam*, which purportedly is based on notes and conversations the author had with Bundy before his death; Kai Bird's The *Color of Truth: McGeorge Bundy and William Bundy: Brothers in Arms;* and Thomas Zeiler's *Dean Rusk*. I was particularly pleased to get Max Boot's recent biography of Edward Lansdale called, *The Road Not Taken* to use in portraying how he differed with Robert McNamara in the initial stages of the development of the counterinsurgency strategy, and how McNamara dominated the development of JFK's policy in Vietnam.

I also used some of the oral testimonies found in the John F. Kennedy Library *Oral History Collection*. Particularly useful were those of Nolting, Harkins, Taylor, and Rostow.
In a league of its own is Robert McNamara's memoirs, *In Retrospect*. It became, honestly, more increasingly repulsive to me as I read more of the primary source materials in the Presidential libraries, the FRUS series, the *Pentagon Papers* and as I contrasted what he said in his memoirs with his actions and views at the time. This is particularly true when one listens to his reports and conversations on the tapes and reads the transcripts. I tried to balance my feelings with video tapes that McNamara made explaining his memoirs and his actions that are readily accessible on *You Tube*, as well as his testimony in the Errol Morris production " The Fog of War," which I used primarily by extracting pieces from the published version by James Blight and Janet Lang. This effort did nothing to alleviate my disgust with his attitudes in the beginning of the war and his later cowardly acts to cover them up and retreat from what he had created.

Besides the recordings and memoirs most of the other primary sources I used for this chapter were from William Gibbons, US Government and the Vietnam War, Part II: 1961-1964; John Glennon, ed, Foreign Relations of the United States, 1961-1963, Volume I: Vietnam, 1961; Kaplan, L. (2013) *History of the Office of the Secretary of Defense: The McNamara Ascendancy, 1961-1965*, National Archives, *Pentagon Papers, Part IVB, The Kennedy Commitments 1961-1963.*

As for a focus on JFK Administration's civil-military affairs and interrelationships, besides Larry Freedman, I consulted Matthew Moten's, *Presidents and the Generals: An American History of Command in War*; Jack Shulimson's (editor) *History of the Joint Chiefs of Staff: The Joint Chiefs of Staff and The War in Vietnam, Part 1, 1960-1968*; H. R. McMaster's *Dereliction of Duty*; and Robert Buzzanco's *Masters of War: Military Dissent and Politics in the Vietnam Era*. Though not focused solely on the military, a very useful secondary source on those who were involved in the National Security Council and its proceeding was David Rothkopf's *Running the World: The Inside Story of the National Security Council and the Architects of American Power*.

For the transition narration at the end of Section II, I used Robert Caro's *The Years of Lyndon Johnson: The Passage of Power* and Doris Kearns Goodwin's, *Lyndon Johnson and the American Dream*.

Chapter 3: The Reluctant Commander-in-Chief

Because LBJ decided to keep on many of JFK's advisors, I continued to use some of the memoirs, biographies, and oral histories of Bundy, Rostow, Rusk, McNamara, and Taylor mentioned above. Unfortunately, General Wheeler left no memoir, and there is yet no biography. His oral histories in the LBJ library are useful but limited, as are any of the taped conversations. Joseph Califano's memoir, *The Triumph and Tragedy of Lyndon Johnson* provide some very useful insights on the personality and pressures on LBJ by one of his closest civilian advisors in the White House, as does Jack Valenti's *My Life*.

Here I also began relying on George Ball's *The Past Has Another Pattern* for his recollections on his role as a devil's advocate in the road to war in late 1964 to mid-1965.
I also relied heavily on LBJ's two main commanders' memoirs for the war: William Westmoreland's *A Soldier Reports* and U.S. Grant Sharp's *Strategy for Defeat*. I supplemented Westmoreland's account with some help from Dr. Erik Villard's postings on his Vietnam War History website, which included several of Westmoreland's directives and memos from the latter's papers at the Army's Center of Military History.

To these, I added for this period: Lewis Sorley's *Honorable Warrior: General Harold K. Johnson and the Ethics of Command* and *Westmoreland: The General Who Lost Vietnam*; and Robert Jordan's *An Unsung Soldier: The Life of Gen. Andrew J. Goodpaster*. I have already given my views on Sorley's works on the war in the body of much of the narrative of the story.

I continued to use some of the general sources, which covered the Johnson years. I found the following added general sources very useful. George Herring's *LBJ and Vietnam: A Different Kind of War* and his US Air Force Academy Harmon Memorial Lecture entitled LBJ's *Conduct of Limited War in Vietnam*. Both offered some great insights on LBJ as a war president. Herring's contrast to LBJ's experiences in the Congress and his lack of adapting his leadership style to one that was needed as Commander-in-Chief were particularly noteworthy. He also gave some examples and explanations of LBJ's distrust of the military.

Most interesting was Herring's analysis of the use of limited war theory in Vietnam and its misapplication to the situation that the US faced at the time. Other sources for this chapter were Larry Bergman's *Planning a Tragedy* and his *Lyndon Johnson's War*. Bergman's main contribution was his argument that LBJ's advisors were hardly the 'yes' men portrayed in some histories. Also consulted was Michael Hunt's *Lyndon Johnson's War* and Randall Woods' *LBJ: Architect of American Ambition*.

I also used the following memoirs and biographies on LBJ: Lyndon Johnson's *Vantage Point*; Robert Caro *The Years of Lyndon Johnson: The Master of the Senate, Volume 3* (for LBJ's personality traits and experiences in the Senate) and *The Passage of Power, Volume 4*; Doris Kearns Goodwin, *Lyndon Johnson and the American Dream*; and Robert Dallek's *Lyndon B. Johnson: Portrait of a President*.

The Presidential tapes remain a prime source for this chapter. These are particularly pertinent because LBJ used the telephone so extensively in his consultations with his former colleagues in the Senate, and with others he relied upon either for advice or solace – particularly President Eisenhower, whom he used as a personal military advisor at times. At other times, LBJ used his conversations with IKE to show to the Republicans that he was interested in obtaining the wisdom of their leader.

In addition, these other accounts were useful in that they integrated the tapes into their historical analysis or served as edited transcripts with historical context that were extraordinarily insightful: George Herring's *The War Bells Have Rung: The LBJ Tapes & The Americanization of the War;* Mark Updegrove's *Indomitable Will: LBJ in the Presidency*; Mark Beschloss, *Taking Charge: The Johnson White House Tapes, 1963-1964* and *Reaching for Glory: Lyndon Johnson's Secret White House Tapes, 1964-1965*; The Miller Center's *Educational Resources: Exhibits* on LBJ and Vietnam; Lyndon Baines Johnson Library's *Oral History Collection* (Wheeler, McNamara, Clifford, Dirksen, George Ball).

One unique and valuable source for the decisions in 1965 to send US ground combat forces to Vietnam is Yuen Foong Khong's recent study *Analogies at War: Korea, Munich, Dien Bien Phu, and the Vietnam Decisions of 1965*. Professor Young, a professor at Oxford University, has provided a seminal source on the use of historical analogies in the decision-making process for national security affairs and the government in general, as well as the Johnson Administration's rationale for sending in combat forces in 1965.

I also continued to use the following sources pertinent to this chapter: William Gibbons' *The US government and the Vietnam War, Parts III and IV* covering the period February 1965 to January 1968; the Central Intelligence Agency's *Library of Reports*; John Glennon, editor, *The Foreign Relations of the United States, 1964-1968 Volumes I- VI*; The National Archives' *Pentagon Papers: Evolution of Commitment, The Johnson Commitments, 1964-1968*.

For LBJ's relationships with his military advisors and the views and actions of the JCS, I utilized Graham Cosmas' *History of the Joint Chiefs of Staff: The Joint Chiefs of Staff and the War in Vietnam, 1960-1968, Parts 2 and 3*; Walter Poole's *History of the Joint Chiefs of Staff: The Joint Chiefs of Staff and the War in Vietnam, 1965-1968*; H. R. McMaster's *Dereliction of Duty*; Matthew Moten, *Presidents and the Generals: An American History of Command in War*; Mark Perry's, *Four Stars*; Orrin Schwab's *A Clash of Cultures: Civil-Military Relations During the Vietnam War*; and James Robbins' *This Time We Win: Revisiting the TET Offensive*.

Chapter 4: America in Crisis

For this chapter, I relied heavily on the following general works of the period and topic: John Andrew's *Lyndon Johnson and the Great Society*; Mark Carns' *Columbia History of Post World War II America*; Terry Anderson's, *The Movement and the Sixties*; Tom Brokaw's *Boom! Voices of the Sixties*; James Patterson's *Great Expectations*; Fredrik Logevall's *Origins of the Vietnam War*; and David Farber and Beth Bailey's *The Columbia Guide to America in the Sixties*.

To capture LBJ's reactions and feeling toward the domestic events and actions in this chapter I continued to use: Lyndon Johnson's *Vantage Point*; Doris Kearns Goodwin, *Lyndon Johnson and the American Dream*; Dallek's *Lyndon B. Johnson: Portrait of a President*; and Mark Updegrove's *Indomitable Will: LBJ in the Presidency*.

For the civil rights movement, I consulted: The Charles River Editors; *The Civil Rights Movement*; Lawson and Payne's *Debating the Civil Rights Movement, 1945-1968*; Academy of Achievement's online course and eBook entitled, *The Road to Civil Rights*; David Farber and Beth Bailey's, editors' *The Columbia Guide to America in the 60*; and Christian Appy's *Patriots: The Vietnam War Remembered From All Sides* and *American Reckoning: The Vietnam War and Our National Identity*.

For the anti-war movement narrative, I primarily used: Simon Hall's, *Rethinking the American Anti-War Movement*; Paul Joseph's "Direct and Indirect Effects of the Movement Against the Vietnam War" in Werner and Huyck's *The Vietnam War: Vietnamese and American Perspectives*; and David Steigerwald's, "Teaching the Anti-War Movement" in *Understanding and Teaching the Vietnam War*.

In addressing the Press's role in the war I used: William Hammond's *United States Army in Vietnam: Public Affairs: The Military and the Media, 1962-1968*, and *Public Affairs: The Military and the Media, 1968-1973*; John Cooke, editor, *Reporting the War: Freedom of the Press From the American Revolution to the War on Terror*; Donald Ritchie, *Reporting From Washington: The History of the Washington Press Corps*; Peter Braestrup's *Big Story* and *Oral History* in the LBJ Library; David Culbert's article "Television's Visual Impact on Decision-Making in the USA, 1968", *Journal of Contemporary History*, July 1998; and Daniel Hallin, *The Uncensored War: The Media and Vietnam*.

My views on the role and impact of public opinion in this chapter are based on Adam Berinsky's *In Time of War: Understanding American Public Opinion from World War II to Iraq*; William Darley's "War Policy, Public Support, and the Media in *Parameters*, Summer 2005; David Steigerwald's "Teaching the Antiwar Movement: Confronting Popular Myths", in *Understanding and Teaching the Vietnam War*; William Lunch and Peter Sperlich's "American Public Opinion and the War in Vietnam" in *The Western Political Quarterly*, March 1979.

Finally, for Congress's role in the war I relied on: Gibbons, *The U.S. Government and the Vietnam War*, all volumes; Joseph Fry, *Debating Vietnam: Fulbright, Stennis and their Senate Hearings*; Andrew Johns, *Vietnam's Second Front: Domestic Politics, the Republican Party, and the War*; and Mark Perry's, *Four Stars*.

Chapter 5: Peace with Honor

The general sources that I used to cover the Nixon years are primarily: George Herrings' *America's Longest War*; Major-General ® Ira Hunt's *Losing Vietnam*; Jeffrey Kimball's *Nixon's Vietnam War*; David Schmitz's *Richard Nixon and the Vietnam War*; James Willbanks' *Abandoning Vietnam*; Larry Berman's *No Peace, No Honor*; Burr and Kimball, *Nixon's Nuclear Spector*; Robert Schulzinger, *A Time For War*; and Daadler and Destler, *In the Shadow of the Oval Office*.

To obtain Nixon's and his biographers views on his personality and policies I used Richard Nixon's *Memoirs*; Robert Dallek's *Nixon and Kissinger*; Evan Thomas' *Being Nixon*; Tim Weiner's *One Man Against the World*; Stephen Ambrose's *Nixon: The Triumph of a Politician*; Anthony Summers' *The Arrogance of Power*; and Rick Perlstein's *Nixonland*.

The memoirs and biographies of Nixon's key advisors and members of his Administration I relied upon for this chapter were: Henry Kissinger's *The White House Years* and *Ending the Vietnam War*; Walter Isaacson's *Kissinger: A Biography*; Robert Halderman's *The Halderman Diaries*; Dale Van Atta's *With Honor: Melvin Laird in War, Peace and Politics*; Alexander Haig's, *Inner Circle*; Lewis Sorley's *Thunderbolt: General Creighton Abrams and the Army of His Times* and *Vietnam Chronicles: The Abrams Tapes*.

For continued revelations of Nixon's and Kissinger's policy making in the Nixon tapes, I used Ken Hughes' *Fatal Politics* and *Chasing Shadows*. These are fascinating and extremely useful volumes that links Hughes' interpretations about the Nixon – Kissinger Administration's foreign policy. To support his views, Hughes, a former CIA official who now works at the Miller Center, provides hyperlinks to the transcripts and taped conversations in the Miller Center. Some of these tapes with the narrative are also available on a YouTube channel named "Fatal Politics".

For other revelations from the Presidential Tapes I used, Brinkly and Nichter's two volumes of *The Nixon Tapes*; the Nixon Presidential Library's Nixon's White House Tapes and Documents; and the Miller Center's *Educational Resources: The Nixon Exhibits*. The latter source was particularly useful in offering presentations on such issues as Nixon's reactions and views toward the antiwar movement, obtaining South Vietnam support for the peace talks, his and Kissinger's views on the viability of South Vietnam's continued ability to win the war without US assistance (the 'decent interval' issue).

In addition, there are scores of YouTube videos available online that also present some of the taped conversations between Nixon and his advisors, particularly Kissinger. While many focus on the sensational aspects of Nixon's prejudices, his alcohol use, and Watergate some also present ongoing views on the war.

I continued to use the primary sources pertinent to the Nixon years from Keefer, *FRUS, 1969-1976, Volumes VI and VII* for Nixon's NSC meetings and policy papers. I supplemented these from the JCS' view with Walter Pooles, *The Joint Chiefs of Staff and National Policy 1969-1972*; Willard Webb's, *The Joint Chiefs of Staff and The War in Vietnam, 1969-1970*; and William Webb's and Walter Poole's, *The Joint Chiefs of Staff and The War in Vietnam 1971-1973*.

Chapter 6: Know Your Enemy and Chapter 7: The Enemy Gets a Vote

For Section I's geopolitical overview of Indochina in general and Vietnam in particular, I relied upon: Bruce Lockhart and William Duiker's *Historical Dictionary of Vietnam*; The *Philip's Atlas of World History*; the United States Military Academy History Department's *Maps of the Vietnam War*; Colin Gray and Geoffrey Sloan, editors, *Geopolitics, Geography and Strategy*; Saul Cohen's, *Geopolitics: The Geography of International Politics*; W. Gordon East's *The Geography Behind History*; Margaret Scott and Westenley Alcenat's "Revisiting the Pivot: The Influence of Heartland Theory in Great Power Politics," *Comparative Strategy*, Vol. 22; and John Gaddis, *Strategies of Containment*.

The general sources on the Communist Vietnamese and North Vietnam's actions and policies in both Chapters 6 and 7 that I used were: William Duiker's *The Communist Road to Power* and *Sacred War: Nationalism and Revolution in a Divided Vietnam*; L-H Nguyen's *Hanoi's War: An International History of the War for Peace in Vietnam*; Pierre Asselin, *Hanoi's Road to War, 1954-1965*; Mark Bradley's *Vietnam at War*; Eric Logevall, *Embers of War* and *Origins of the Vietnam War*; Francis Fitzgerald's *The Fire in the Lake*; Ang Cheng Guan's *The Vietnam War from the Other Side*; and David Elliot, *The Vietnamese War: Revolution and Social Change in the Mekong Delta, 1930-1975, Vol. 1*.

For biographies and memoirs of some key leaders and participants from the Vietnamese Communist view, I relied on: William Duiker, *Ho Chi Minh: A Life*; Pierre Brocheux's *Ho Chi Minh: A Biography*; Cecil Currey, *The Genius of Vietnam's General Vo Nguyen Giap*; James Warren's *Giap: The General Who Defeated America in Vietnam*; Truong Nhu Tang's *A Vietcong Memoir*; Tran Van Tra's *Vietnam: History of the Bulwark B2 Theater*; Bui Tin's *Following Ho Chi Minh: The Memoirs of a North Vietnamese Colonel*; Larry Berman's *Perfect Spy: The Incredible Life of Pham Xuan An*; and Le Ly Hayslip, *When Heaven and Earth Changed Places*.

There are other communist documents and personal views that I used in these two chapters found in Michael Hunt, ed. *A Vietnam War Reader*; Christian Appy's *Patriots: The Vietnam War Remembered From All Sides*; Jayne Werner and Luu Doan Huynh, editors, *The Vietnam War: Vietnamese and American Perspectives*; and selections from Ken Burns and Geoffrey Ward's *The Vietnam War: An Intimate History*.

For the DRV and PAVN high command perspective and its actions and roles in the war I used: The Military History Institute of Vietnam's, translated by Merle Pribbenow, *Victory in Vietnam: The Official History of the People's Army of Vietnam, 1954-1975*; Bernard Fall's *Street Without Joy* and *Hell in a Very Small Place*; Douglas Pike's *PAVN: The People's Army of Vietnam*; Lanning and Cragg's *Inside the VC and NVA*; Gordon Rottman's *North Vietnamese Army Soldier, 1958-1975*; and Warren Wilkins's *Grab Their Belts to Fight Them: The Viet Cong's Big Unit War Against the US, 1965-1966*.

For the period in Chapters 6 and 7 on Diem and his actions, and observations of some Vietnamese other than communists I used: Bui Diem's, *In the Jaws of History*; Seth Jacobs' *Cold War Mandarin: Ngo Dinh Diem and the Origins of America's War in Vietnam, 1950-1963*; Jessica Chapman's *Cauldron of Resistance: Ngo Dinh Diem, The United States and 1950s South Vietnam*.

Chapter 8: The Unwinnable War; Chapter 9: The Agony of Defeat; Chapter 10: A Better War; and Chapter 11: US Policies and Strategies for the Vietnam War, 1950-1975

As general sources for these chapters I continued to use, as appropriate to the topic under discussion, the histories of David Halberstam (*The Best and the Brightest*), Neil Sheehan (*The Bright Shining Lie*) and Stanley Karnow (*Vietnam: A History*). Once again, I primarily used these three to present their perspectives on operations in country which they observed or reported on.

To balance these accounts, I also consulted and used Mark Moyar's *Triumph Forsaken: The Vietnam War, 1954-1965*, George Herring's *America's Longest War: The United States and Vietnam, 1950-1975*; William Turley's *The Second Indochina War: A Short Political and Military History, 1954-1975*; John Prado's *The Hidden History of the Vietnam War*; and Robert Schulzinger's *A Time For War: The United States and Vietnam, 1941-1975*.

General sources that focused more on the military strategic and operational views presented that I used were: Harry Summers' *On Strategy*; Andrew Krepinevich's *US Army in Vietnam*; Lewis Sorley's *A Better War: The Unexamined Victories and Final Tragedy of American's Last Years in Vietnam* , Gregg Daddis' *Westmoreland's War: Reassessing American Strategy I Vietnam, No Sure Victory: Measuring US Army Effectiveness and Progress in the Vietnam War* and *Withdrawal: Reassessing America's Final Years in Vietnam*; Thomas Thayer's, *War Without Front: The American Experience in Vietnam*; Douglas Kinnard's *The War Managers*; Michael Hennessy, *Strategy in Vietnam: The Marines and Revolutionary Warfare in I Corp, 1965-1972*; Andrew Birtle's *US Army Counterinsurgency and Contingency Operations Doctrine, 1942-1976*; Gian Gentile's *Wrong Turn: America's Deadly Embrace of Counterinsurgency*; and Robert Gillespie's, *Black Ops, Vietnam*.

The memoirs and biographies that I consulted for these chapters were: McNamara's *In Retrospect*; Haig's *Inner Circles*; Maxwell Taylor's *Swords and Plowshares*; Westmoreland's *A Soldier Reports*; U.S Grant Sharp's *Strategy for Defeat*; Lewis Walt's *Strange War Strange Defeat*; Palmer's *The 25-Year War*; Ira Hunt's *Losing Vietnam*; and Lewis Sorley's *Westmoreland: The General Who Lost Vietnam, Thunderbolt: General Creighton Abrams and the Army of His Times,* and *Vietnam Chronicles: The Abrams Tapes, 1968-1972.*

One major note on several of the above sources. Lewis Sorley's flurry of books published at the end of 1999 and into the next decade – his biographies of Westmoreland, Abrams, and Johnson, plus his *Abrams Tapes* and book on the war during Abrams' years, *A Better War* – have an overriding theme that has caught on in some circles of the historiography of the war. That theme is that Westmoreland's strategy for the war was seriously flawed from the start in that it ignored the pacification aspects of counterinsurgency that were critical to denying the enemy access to the population.

Sorley further argues that Westmoreland also did not focus the priority on building government control in the countryside and neglected the establishment of effective security forces and an ARVN that could defeat the Communist forces. In so doing, Sorley has, in effect, made General Westmoreland the main villain in the American defeat. He further elevated General Abrams to one who had tried to rectify his former commander's mistakes but did not have enough time.

As Andrew Birtle, Gregg Daddis, and Gian Gentile have shown, however, Sorley's research and writing are shortsighted. He misinterpreted some historical evidence and ignored key parts of the historical record. While contributing to the narrative of the war - especially in the Abrams, Nixon years - his criticisms of Westmoreland have seriously distorted that General's attempts to find a suitable military strategy to fulfill the guidance and aims of his superiors.

Sorley further ignored the realities of the battlefield and the enemy's capabilities and intent. So, though I have used Sorley's works, I have tried – using the works of Birtle, Gaddis, and Gentile - to bring balance to my presentation of Westmoreland, the strategic dilemmas he faced, and the attempts he made to find a suitable military solution to a very complex strategic and operational problem.

As in Chapter 5, in focusing on the development of Westmoreland's theater military strategy and his attempts to find an alternative in 1967 and after TET, I continued to use the National Archives', *Pentagon Papers, The Johnson Commitments, US Ground Strategy and Force Deployments, 1965-1967*, Glennen, the *FRUS, V. 2*, and The Miller Center's, *Presidential Recordings, Nixon, Exhibits.*

Once again, as in the narratives in Chapters 2, 3 and 5, I found the Presidential Tapes extremely important in understanding the relationship and views of Westmoreland and Abrams military advice to the Presidents and his advisors. As I have mentioned in the text of this book, what the civilians say in their memoirs about that relationship and advice is very different from what they portray on the tapes.

In describing the military campaigns and operations, and their relationship to the theater military strategy, I relied heavily on The United States Army in Vietnam series. This included: Graham Cosmas' *MACV: The Joint Command in the Years of Escalation, 1962-1967 and MACV: The Joint Command in the Years of Withdrawal* , Ronald Spector's, *Advice and Support: The Early Years, 1941-1960*, Alexander Cochran, "American Planning for Ground Combat in Vietnam, 1952-1965", *Parameters Journal* , Jeffrey Clarke, *Advice and Support: The Final Years, 1965-1973*, John Carland, *Combat Operations: Stemming the Tide, May 1965 to October 1966*, George MacGarrigle, *Combat Operations: Taking the Offensive, October 1966 to October 1967*, and Eric Villard's *Combat Operations: Staying the Course, October 1967 to September 1968*.

I further used the US Army's Vietnam Studies series to include: George Eckhardt, *Command and Control, 1950-1969*, Joseph McChristian, *The Role of Military Intelligence, 1965-1967*, Joseph Heiser, *Logistics Support*, Carroll Dunn, *Base Development, 1965-1970*, John Tolson, *Airmobility, 1961-1971*, Bernard Rogers, *Cedar Falls and Junction City, A Turning Point*, and William Le Gro, *Vietnam from Cease-Fire to Capitulation*.

I am once again indebted to Erik Villard of the US Army Center of Military History at Carlisle Barracks, PA. for materials in these chapters. He put together a Facebook site called "Vietnam War History Org: History Forum." The site has attracted many Vietnam War veterans, historians and other scholars who have offered innumerable first-hand accounts of their experiences in or works on Vietnam. Villard has also provided from time to time materials from the Centers' archives on the war – to include items from the Westmoreland Papers at the Center. I extracted from the site directives and correspondence that helped in gaining an appreciation for Westmoreland's periodic guidance to his field commanders.

One such set of correspondence, of note, was between Westmoreland and General Lewis Walt. It showed that Walt struggled between his concepts of protection and pacification of the countryside and his realization that he had to conduct major operations against the NVA and PLAF main forces to be able in the long run secure the population. As I tried to show in the narrative, this was the major strategic dilemma that Westmoreland tried to solve but was unsuccessful at doing so for several reasons. As also noted, Westmoreland finally realized that he could not solve this conundrum, and thus sought an alternative strategy.

Regarding Westmoreland's attempt to develop an alternative strategy I am also indebted to the excellent work of Colonel Casey Brower. His "Strategic Assessment in Vietnam: The Westmoreland 'Alternative Strategy of 1967-1968", *A Naval War College Advanced Research Program Paper*, written in 1990, is a thorough investigation of Westmoreland's guidance and planning on attacking the Ho Chi Minh Trail complex and decisively imposing a military condition in which the North would be compelled to cease its critical support for military operations in the South. Brower's analysis of the feasibility of this approach was very valuable and central to my argument on the viability of such an alternative strategy.

To revisit the Wheeler – Westmoreland 206K troop request during TET, Brower was again helpful. In addition, an article in Foreign Policy in Fall 1971 written by John B. Henry was also very valuable. Tipped off by George Herring's use of this source I found Henry's interviews of Wheeler and Westmoreland very useful in expanding what both were thinking in February 1968 about their attempts to get these reinforcements and change the overall theater strategy.

To supplement the US Army series and studies on operational and tactical actions, I also relied upon the remarkable work of Shelby Stanton's *The Rise and Fall of an American Army*. Stanton not only describes the battles and campaigns in clear and understandable prose but dispels the myth of an American Army that relied on firepower at the expense of maneuver and other more effective ways of defeating an enemy.

As he attempts to rightly explain to the reader, the American Army usually fought small, intense engagements, often heavily outnumbered and disadvantaged by the enemy's knowledge of the terrain. The firepower at an infantry unit's disposal – artillery, aerial rockets and gunships, and naval and air force close air support, offset these disadvantages and often proved the difference between life and death of the American infantryman. As he ends his tribute to the American soldier, Stanton accurately describes the result of the Vietnam experience for the US Army...." An entire American army was sacrificed on the battlefield of Vietnam. When the war was finally over, the United States Military had to build a new volunteer army form the smallest shreds of its tattered remains."

The US Marines in Vietnam series was also extremely useful in telling the Marines Corps role in combat operations. The primary works I used were: Jack Shulimson and Charles Johnson, *The Landing and the Build Up, 1965*, Jack Shulimson, *An Expanding War, 1966*, Gary Telfer, Lane Rogers and V. Keith Fleming, *Fighting the North Vietnamese*. For the Air Force view of operations, I consulted Jacob Staaveren, *The United States Air Force in Southeast Asia, 1961-1973* and Mark Clodfelter's classic study of bombing operations against the North in his *The Limits of Airpower: The American Bombing of North Vietnam*.

To gain an appreciation for and present the argument for a decisive military defeat of the Communist TET 68 offensives I used Erik Villard, *The 1968 TET Offensive Battles of Quang Tri City and Hue*; James Willbanks, *The TET Offensive*; and the most recent accounts by James Robbins', *This Time We Win;* and Mark Bowen's *TET 68*.

For further analysis of the tactical situation that US forces faced in Vietnam, I read and extracted descriptions and explanations from Harold Moore and Joseph Galloway, *We Were Soldiers Once...moreover, Young*; S.L.A. Marshall, *Battles in the Monsoon*; Samuel Zaffiri, *Hamburger Hill*; Michael Herr, *Dispatches*; F.J. West, *The Village*; and Stuart Herrington, *Silence Was A Weapon*. In addressing the highly critical views of the US Army's performance in Vietnam, I have consulted the works of Richard A. Gabriel and Richard Savage in their *Crisis in Command: Mismanagement in the Army* and more recently the work of Nick Turse entitled, *Kill Anything that Moves: The Real American War in Vietnam*.

While the Gabriel and Savage work I had read in the seventies and felt then that it had some truth to it, I remained convinced that their arguments, and their statistics that have been since put into perspective by others, were overstated and generalized to the point where they have not done the Army any service then or now. As for Turse's arguments, they have not only been overstated but, unfortunately, have resurfaced the anti-war movements exaggerations and myths of the atrocities and war crimes that American soldiers committed in Vietnam.

Finally for these chapters in presenting some of the South Vietnamese side of the story I relied on Jessica Chapman, *Cauldron of Resistance, Ngo Dinh Diem, the United States, and 1950s Southern Vietnam;* Seth Jacobs, *Cold War Mandarin: Ngo Dinh Diem and the Origins of America's War in Vietnam, 1950-1963*; Bui Diem's *In the Jaws of History*; Robert Bringham, *ARVN: Life and Death in the South Vietnamese Army*; Andrew Wiest, *Vietnam's Forgotten Army*; Nathalie Huynh Chau Nguyen, *South Vietnamese Soldiers: Memories of the Vietnam War and After*; James Lawton Collins, *The Development and Training of the South Vietnamese Army, 1950-1972*; Ngo Quang Truong, *The Easter Offensive of 1972*; Cao Van Vien, *The Final Collapse*; Lam Quang Thi, *The Twenty-Five Year Century* and *Hell in An Loc*; James Willbanks, *A Raid Too Far: Lam Son 719 and Vietnamization in Laos*; and Gordon Rottman, *Army of the Republic of Vietnam, 1955-75*.

Chapter 12: The Heavy Shadow of Vietnam

For the importance of the impact of the war on the US, see Henry Kissinger, *The White House Years*, H.R. McMaster, *Dereliction of Duty*. The effect of the war on the US initially and then into the Reagan years is related in George Herring, *America's Longest War*; Christian Appy, *American Reckoning*; David Anderson and John Ernst, *The War that Never Ends*; Rufus Phillips, *Why Vietnam Matters*; and Robert Timberg, *The Nightingale's Song*.

Besides my recollections of the Grenada, Panama and First Gulf War I used Bob Woodward, *The Commanders*; Colin Powell, *My American Journey*; H. Norman Schwartzkopf, *It Doesn't Take a Hero*; Jeffrey Clarke, *Operation Urgent Fury*; Ronald Cole, *Operation Just Cause: The Planning and Execution of Joint Operations in Panama*; and Mark Perry, *Four Stars*.

My comments on civil-military relationships is supplemented by Dale Herspring's, *Civil-Military Relations and Shared Responsibilities* and *The Pentagon and the Presidency*; Orin Schwab's *A Class of Cultures;* and Suzanne Nielson and Don Snider's anthology *American Civil-Military Relations: The Soldier and the State in a New Era*.

Chapter 13: Have We Learned Anything?

For interpretations of what the end of the Cold War meant at the time see Francis Fukuyama, *End of History*; Fareed Zakaria, *The Post American World*; Joseph Nye, *Bound to Lead*; and Paul Kennedy's *The Rise and Fall of the Great Powers*.

On changes brought about by the shift to an all-volunteer force and the employment of the US military in the Long War see, Andrew Bacevich's, *Washington Rules, The New American Militarism, Breach of Trust*, and The *Long War*; Rachel Maddow, *Drift;* and Christian Appy, *American Reckoning: The Vietnam War and Our National Identity*. While I do not agree with all that is said and argued in these works, I have found many of the views compatible. I have also found them in line with my post active service experiences as an advisor to several officials in the Department of Defense.

Criticisms of the US military noted are from Thomas Ricks,' *The Generals*; Gian Gentile, *Wrong Turn*; and Daniel Bolger, *Why We Lost*.

For policies, plans and actions in support of military actions since the First Gulf War I relied on Bob Woodward's *Plan of Attack, Bush at War,* and *Obama's Wars*; Bill Clinton's *My Life*; George Bush's, *Decision Points*, Rumsfeld's, *Known and Unknown*; Gates' *Duty*, Franks, *American Soldier*; and Hugh Shelton's, *Without Hesitation*.

My observations on civil-military relations and effective policy making also relied upon the views of Dale Herspring in his *Civil-Military Relations and Shared Responsibility*, and *The Pentagon and the Presidency*; Orrin Schwab's *A Clash of Cultures*; Matthew Moten, *Presidents and their Generals*; Eliot Cohen's *Supreme Command* and Suzanne Nielson and Don Snider's anthology *American Civil-Military Relations: The Soldier and the State in a New Era*. This last work, which includes a series of papers resulting from a conference at West Point on the subject, was of particular use in gaining some insights on others' views of the current state of civil-military relations.

For the use of history in policymaking see Richard Neustadt and Earnest May, *Thinking in Time*, and Ernest May's *Lessons in History*. As already mentioned Yuen Foong Khong's recent study *Analogies at War: Korea, Munich, Dien Bien Phu, and the Vietnam Decisions of 1965* is also a very useful work to use as part of the program outlined in this chapter.

Bibliography

Academy of Achievement. 2012. *The Road to Civil Rights*. Washington, DC: Academy of Achievement.

Acheson, Dean. 1987. *Present at the Creation: My Years in the State Department*. New York: New York: WW Norton and Co.

Ambrose, Stephen. 1988. *Nixon: The Triumph of a Politician 1962-1972*. eBook edition ed. New York: Simon & Schuster.

Ambrose, Stephen. 2003. *Eisenhower: Soldier and President*. Condensed e–Book edition of Paperback ed. New York: Simon and Schuster.

Anderson, David, ed. 2011. *Columbia History of the Vietnam War*. e–Book edition ed. New York: Columbia University Press.

Anderson, Terry. 1995. *The Movement and the Sixties*. New York: New York: Oxford University Press.

Andrew, John A. III. 1998. *Lyndon Johnson and the Great Society*. eBook edition ed. Chicago, Ill.: Dee Inc.

Appy, Christian. 2015. *American Reckoning: The Vietnam War and Our National Identity*. Penguin Edition ed. New York: Viking.

Appy, Christian. 2003. *Patriots: The Vietnam War Remembered From All Sides*. eBook edition ed. New York: New York: Penguin Group.

Asselin, Pierre. 2013. *Hanoi's Road to the Vietnam War: 1954-1965*. eBook edition ed. Berkley, CA: University of California Press.

Associated Press. 1983. *The Eyewitness History of the Vietnam War, 1961-1975*. Ballantine Books Inc.

Atta, Dale Van. 2008. *With Honor: Melvin Laird in War, Peace, and Politics*. Kindle eBook ed. Madison, WS: University of Wisconsin Press.

Bacevich, Andrew. 2010. *Washington Rules: America's Path to Permanent War*. eBook version ed. New York: New York: Metropolitan Books.

Bachevich, Andrew. 2010. *The New American Militarism*. eBook ed. New York: New York: Metropolitan Books.

Bachevich, Andrew. 2007. *The Long War: A New History of US National Security Strategy Since World War II*. eBook ed. New York: New York: Columbia University Press.

Berger, Carl, ed. 2015. *The US Air Force in Southeast Asia, 1961-1973*. Smashwords edition ed. Washington, DC: Office of Air Force History.

Berinsky, Adam. 2001. *In Time of War: Understanding American Public Opinion from World War II to Iraq*. eBook ed. Chicago, ILL: University of Chicago Press.

Berman, Larry. 1982. *Planning a Tragedy: The Americanization of the War in Vietnam*. eBook edition 2010 ed. WW Norton and Co.: New York: New York.

Berman, Larry. 2007. *A Perfect Spy: The Incredible Double Life of Pham Xuan An*. eBook ed. Toronto, Canada: Harper Gilians.

Berman, Larry. 2001. *No Peace, No Honor: Nixon, Kissinger, and Betrayal in Vietnam*. Kindle eBook Touchstone Books ed. New York: New York: Simon and Schuster.

Berman, Larry. 1989. *Lyndon Johnson's War: The Road to Stalemate*. WW Norton and Co. New York: New York

Beschloss, Michael. 1997. *Taking Charge: The Johnson White House Tapes, 1963-1964*. New York, NY: Simon & Schuster.

Beschloss, Michael. 2001. *Reaching for Glory: Lyndon Johnson's Secret White House tapes, 1964-1965*. United States: New York: Simon & Schuster, c2001.

Bird, Kai. 1999. *The Color of Truth*. New York: Simon & Schuster.

Birtle, Andrew. 2006. *US Army Counterinsurgency and Contingency Operations Doctrine, 1942-1976*. PDF edition ed. Carlisle Barracks, PA: Center of Military History.

Blight, James G. and Lang, Janet, M. 2005. *The Fog of War: Lessons from the Life of Robert McNamara*. Lanham: Maryland. Rowan and Littlefield, Publishers.

Bolger, Daniel. 2010. *Why We Lost: A General's Inside Account of the Iraq and Afghanistan Wars*. eBook ed. New York: New York: First Mariner Books.

Boot, Max. 2018. *The Road Not Taken: Edward Lansdale and the American Tragedy in Vietnam*. iBook edition. New York: New York. Liveright Publishing Corporation

Bowden, Mark. 2017. *Hue 1968: A Turning Point of the American War in Vietnam*. eBook ed. New York: NY: Atlantic Monthly Press.

Bradley, Mark. 2009. *Vietnam at War*. iBook edition ed. New York: Oxford University Press.

Braestrup, Peter. 1994. *Big Story: How the Press and Television Reported the Crisis of TET in Vietnam and Washington*. Presidio, CA: Presidio Press.

Bringham, Robert. 2007. *ARVN: Life and Death in the South Vietnamese Army*. Lawrence, KS: University of Kansas Press.

Brinkley, Douglas, and Luke Nichter, eds. 2014. *The Nixon Tapes, 1971-1972*. Boston, MA: Houghton, Mifflin, Harcourt.

Brinkly, Douglas, and Luke Nichter, eds. 2015. *The Nixon Tapes: 1973*. First Mariner Books edition, 2016th ed. New York: New York: Houghton Mifflin Harcourt.

Brocheux, Pierre. 2007. *Ho Chi Minh: A Biography*. Cambridge, MA: Cambridge University Press.

Brodie, Bernard. 1973. *War and Politics*. New York: New York. The MacMillan Company

Brokaw, Tom. 1998. *The Greatest Generation*. New York: Random House USA Inc.

Brokaw, Tom. 2007. *Boom! Voices of the Sixties*. eBook edition 2012 ed. New York: New York: Random House.

Burns, Ken and Geoffrey Ward. 2017. *The Vietnam War: An Intimate History*. eBook ed. New York: Alfred Knopf

Burr, William, and Jeffrey Kimball. 2015. *Nixon's Nuclear Specter: The Secret Alert of 1969, Madman Diplomacy and the Vietnam War*. Kansas City: KA: Kansas University Press.

Bush, George W. 2010. *Decision Points*. New York: Enfield: Publishers Group UK [distributor].

Buzzanco, Robert. 1997. *Masters of War: Military Dissent and Politics in the Vietnam era*. 1st ed. Cambridge: Cambridge University Press.

Califano, Joseph A., Jr. 2000. *The Triumph and Tragedy of Lyndon Johnson*. iBook Touchstone ed. New York: Simon and Schuster, Inc.

Carland, John. 2000a. *The United States Army in Vietnam: Stemming the Tide, May 1965- October 1966*. Washington, DC: US Army Center of Military History.

Carland, John. 2000b. *The United States Army in Vietnam: Taking the Offensive, October 1966 - October 1967*. Washington, DC: US Army Center of Military History.

Carns, Mark, ed. 2007. *Columbia History of Post World War II America*. eBook edition ed. New York: New York: Columbia University Press.

Caro, Robert. 2013. *The Years of Lyndon Johnson: The Passage of Power, Volume 4*. Knopf Doubleday Publishing Group.

Caro, Robert. 1982. *The Years of Lyndon Johnson: The Path to Power*. Vintage Books Edition, 1990th ed. New York: Random House.

Caro, Robert. 1990. *The Years of Lyndon Johnson: Means of Ascent*. Vintage Books Edition, 1991st ed. New York: Random House.

Center, The Vietnam, Archive, and Michael Dutill. 2013. "The Vietnam center and archive Homepage." October 23. https://www.vietnam.ttu.edu/ (December 30, 2016).

Chapman, Jessica. 2013. *Cauldron of Resistance: Ngo Dinh Diem, the United States, and 1950s Southern Vietnam*. Ithaca, NY: Cornell University Press

Clinton, William. 2004. *My Life*. eBook ed. New York: New York: Alfred Knopf.

Clodfelter, Mark. 1989. *The Limits of Airpower: The American Bombing of North Vietnam*. iBook edition. New York: New York. The Free Press.

Cloud, David, and Greg Jaffe. 2012. *The Fourth Star: Four Generals and the Epic Struggle for the Future of the United States Army*. eBook ed. New York: New York: Crown.

Cohen, Eliot. 2003. *Supreme Command: Soldiers, Statesmen, and Leadership in Wartime*. Knopf Doubleday Publishing Group.

Cohen, Saul. 2014. *Geopolitics: The Geography of International Relations*. eBook ed. New York: New York: Rowman and Littlefield.

Cole, Ronald. 1995. *Operation Just Cause: The Planning and Execution of Joint Operations in Panama, February 1988 - January 1990*. PDF ed. Washington, DC: Joint History Office.

Cole, Ronald. 1997. *Operation Urgent Fury: The Planning and Execution of Joint Operations in Grenada, 12 October - 2 November 1983*. PDF ed. Washington, DC: Joint History Office.

Collins, Lawton. 1975. *The Development and Training of the South Vietnamese Army*. Vietnam Studies eBook Edition by Pickle Publishers ed. Carlisle Barracks, PA: USA Center of Military History.

Cooke, John. 2007. *Reporting the War: Freedom of the Press from the American Revolution to the War on Terrorism*. eBook edition ed. New York: New York: Pelgrave McMillian.

Cosmas, Graham. 2006a. *The United States Army in Vietnam: MACV The Joint Command in the Years of Escalation, 1962–1967*. Washington, DC: Center of Military History United States Army.

Cosmas, Graham. 2006b. *The United States Army in Vietnam: MACV The Joint Command in the Years of Withdrawal, 1968–1973*. Washington, DC: US Army Center of Military History.

Cosmas, Graham. 2012. *The Joint Chiefs of Staff and the War in Vietnam, 1960-1968, Part 2*. PDF in Joint Electronic Library ed. Washington, DC: The Joint History Office.

Cosmas, Graham. 2009. *The Joint Chiefs of Staff and the War in Vietnam, 1960-1968, Part 3*. PDF in Joint Electronic Library ed. Washington, DC: The Joint History Office.

C. Richard Nelson. 2016. *The Life and Work of General Andrew J. Goodpaster: Best Practices in National Security Affairs*. Kindle Book edition. Lanham, MD: Rowman and Littlefield.

Currey, Cecil Barr. 1996. *Victory at Any Cost: The Genius of Viet Nam's Gen. Vo Nguyen Giap*. Washington [DC]: Brassey's Inc.

Daalder, Ivo, and I. M. Destler. 2009. *In the Shadow of the Oval Office: Profiles of the National Security Advisors and the Presidents They Served - From JFK to George W. Bush*. eBook ed. New York: New York: Simon and Schuster.

Daddis, Gregory. 2017. *Withdrawal: Reassessing American's Final Years in Vietnam*. New York: Oxford University Press.

Daddis, Gregory. 2014. *Westmoreland's War: Reassessing American Strategy in Vietnam*. New York: Oxford University Press Inc.

Daddis, Gregory. 2011. *No Sure Victory: Measuring U.S. Army Effectiveness and Progress in the Vietnam War.* New York: Oxford University Press.

Dallek, Robert. 2004. *Lyndon B. Johnson: Portrait of a President.* USA: Oxford University Press.

Dallek, Robert. 2003. *An Unfinished Life: John F. Kennedy, 1917-1963.* Boston, MA: Little, Brown and Company.

Dallek, Robert. 2007. *Nixon and Kissinger.* New York: HarperCollins eBooks.

Diem, Bui and Chanoff, David. 1987. *In The Jaws of History.* Indianapolis Indiana: Indiana University Press.

Drea, Edward. 2013. *History of the Unified Command Plan, 1946-2012.* PDF in the Joint Electronic Library ed. Washington, DC: The Joint History Office.

Duiker, William. 2000. *Ho Chi Minh: A Life.* iBook version. Hyperion.

Duiker, William. 1981. *The Communist Road to Power.* Paperback Edition ed. Boulder, Colorado: Westview Press.

Duiker, William J. 1994. *Sacred war: Nationalism and Revolution in a Divided Vietnam.* New York: McGraw Hill Higher Education.

Duiker, William, and Bruce Lockhart. 2006. *Historical Dictionary of the Vietnam War.* eBook by Scarecrow Press ed. Lanham, MD: Rowman and Littlefield.

Dunn, Caroll. 1972. *Base Development, 1965-1970.* Vietnam Studies eBook ed. Carlisle, PA: USA Center of Military History.

East, W. Gordon. 1965. *The Geography Behind History.* New York: New York: W.W. Norton Co.

Eckhardt, George. 1974. *Command and Control, 1950-1969.* Vietnam Studies eBook by Pickle Publishing ed. Carlisle Barracks, PA: USA Center of Military History.

Elliot, David. 2003. *The Vietnamese War: Revolution and Change in the Mekong Delta, 1930-1975.* Armonk, NY: ME Sharpe, Inc.

Fairchild, Byron, and Walter Poole. 1986. *The Joint Chiefs of Staff and National Policy, Vol. VII, 1957 - 1960.* PDF in JCS Electronic Library ed. Washington, DC: Joint History Office.

Fall, Bernard. 1994. *Street Without Joy.* eBook edition of paperback edition ed. New York: Stackpole Books.

Fall, Bernard. 1968a. *Hell in a Very Small Place: The Siege of Dien Bien Phu.* Vintage Books edition ed. New York: New York: Random House Inc.

Fall, Bernard. 1968b. *Hell in a Very Small Place: The Siege of Dien Bien Phu.* Vintage Books ed. New York: New York: Random House Inc.

Farber, David, and Beth Bailey, eds. 2001. *The Columbia Guide to America in the Sixties*. eBook ed. New York: New York: Columbia University Press.

Fisher, David. 1970. *Historians' Fallacies: Toward a Logic of Historical Thought*. Harper Torchbooks. New York: New York

Fitzgerald, Francis. 1972. *Fire and the Lake: The Vietnamese and Americans in Vietnam*. 2009 eBook ed. New York: New York: Little, Brown and Co.

Franks, Tommy. 2010. *American Soldier*. eBook ed. New York: New York: Harper Collins.

Freedman, Lawrence. 2000. *Kennedy's Wars: Berlin, Cuba, Laos and Vietnam*. eBook ed. New York: New York: Oxford University Press.

Fry, Joseph. 2006. *Debating Vietnam: Fulbright, Stennis and their Senate Hearings*. Kindle eBook ed. Lanham, MD: Roman and Littlefield.

Fukuyama, Francis. 1992. *The End of History and the Last Man*. New York: New York: Avon Books.

Gabriel, Richard A. and Paul L. Savage. 1978. *Crisis in Command: Mismanagement in the Army*. New York: New York. Hill and Hang

Gaddis, John. 2005. *Strategies of Containment: A Critical Appraisal of American National Security Policy During the Cold War*. expanded and revised eBook ed. New York: New York: Oxford University Press.

Gaddis, John Lewis. 2006. *The Cold War: A New History*. New York: Penguin Press HC, The.

Gates, Robert M. 2015. *Duty: Memoirs of a Secretary at War*. United States: Vintage.

Gentile, Colonel Gian. 2013. *Wrong Turn: America's Deadly Embrace of Counterinsurgency*. United States: The New Press.

Gibbons, William Conrad. 1986a. *The US Government and the Vietnam War: Executive and Legislative Roles and Relationships, Part I, 1945 - 1960*. Princeton, NJ: Princeton University Press.

Gibbons, William Conrad. 2014. *The U.S. Government and the Vietnam War: Executive and legislative roles and relationships: Part III, January - July 1965*. Princeton, NJ, United States: Princeton University Press, [1986]-.

Gibbons, William Conrad. 1986b. *The US Government and the Vietnam War: Executive and Legislative Roles and Relationships, Part II, 1961- 1964*. Princeton, NJ: Princeton University Press.

Gibbons, William Conrad. 1995. *The U.S. Government and the Vietnam War: Executive and legislative roles and relationships, Part IV, July 1965 - January 1968*. Princeton, NJ: Princeton University Press.

Gillespie, Robert. 1988. *Black Ops, Vietnam: The Operational History of MACVSOG*. eBook ed. Annapolis, MD: Naval Institute Press.

Glennon, John, ed. 1998. *Foreign Relations of the United States, 1950: Vol. I, National Security Affairs; Foreign Economic Policy*. eBook version Feb 26, 2015th ed. Washington, DC: Government Printing Office.

Glennon, John, ed. 1988. *Foreign Relations of the United States, 1961-1963, Vol. I: Vietnam, 1961*. eBook version 21 May 2013 ed. Washington, DC: Government Printing Office.

Glennon, John, ed. 1992. *Foreign Relations of the United States, 1964-1968, Vol. I: Vietnam, 1964*. eBook version 21 May 2013 ed. Washington, DC: Government Printing Office.

Goldman, Eric. 1960. *The Crucial Decade and After, America, 1945 - 1960*. Vintage Books ed. New York: New York: Random House, Inc.

Goldstein, Golden. 2008. *Lessons in Disaster: McGeorge Bundy and the Path to War in Vietnam*. Holt Paperback and eBook Edition ed. New York: Henry Holt and Company.

Goodwin, Doris Kearns. 2015. *Lyndon Johnson and the American Dream*. eBook ed. New York: New York: Open Road Media.

Gravel, Mike, ed. 1971. *The Pentagon Papers: The Defense Department History of the United States Decision Making in Vietnam*. The Gravel Edition ed. Boston, MA: Beacon Press.

Gray, Colin, and Geoffrey Sloan, eds. 2013. *Geopolitics, Geography and Strategy*. eBook ed. New York: New York: Rutledge Press.

Greenstein, Fred I., John P Burke, Larry Berman, and Richard Immerman. 1991. *How Presidents Test Reality: Decisions on Vietnam, 1954 and 1965*. New York: Russell Sage Foundation Publications.

Gro, William. 1985. *Vietnam: From Ceasefire to Capitulation*. PDF edition in Vietnam Studies Series ed. Washington, DC: Center of Military History.

Guan, Ang Cheng. 2002. *The Vietnam War From the Other Side*. eBook ed. New York: New York: Routledge Curzon.

Gustavson, Carl G. 1955. *A Preface to History*. New York: New York. MacGraw Hill.

Haig, Alexander, and Charles McCarry. 1998. *Inner Circles: How America Changed the World*. United States: Grand Central Publishing.

Halberstam, David. 2001. *The Best and the Brightest*. eBook Modern Library edition ed. New York: New York: Random House, Inc.

Haldeman, H. 1994. *Haldeman Diaries: Inside the Nixon White House*. United Kingdom: New York: G.P. Putnam's, c1994.

Hall, Simon. 2012. *Rethinking the American Anti-War Movement*. eBook ed. New York: New York: Rutledge.

Hallin, Daniel. 1986. *The Uncensored War: The Media and Vietnam*. eBook ed. Berkeley, CA: University of California Press.

Hayslip, Le Ly. 1989. *When Heaven and Earth Changed Places: A Vietnamese Woman's Journey from War to Peace*. eBook ed. New York: New York: Doubleday Co.

Heiser, Joseph. 1972. *Logistic Support*. USA Center of Military History PDF ed. Washington, DC: HQ Department of Army.

Herr, Michael. 1968. *Dispatches*. Avon Paperback ed. New York: New York: Alfred Knopf.

Herring, George. 2014. *America's Longest War: The United States and Vietnam,1950-1975*. 5th Edition ed. New York, NY: McGraw Hill.

Herring, George. 1994. *LBJ and Vietnam: A Different Kind of War*. eBook edition ed. Austin, Texas: University of Texas Press.

Herring, George. 2015. *The War Bells Have Rung: The LBJ Tapes and the Americanization of the Vietnam War*. e–book edition ed. University of Virginia: University of Virginia Press.

Herrington, Stuart. 1982. *Silence Was a Weapon: The Vietnam War in the Villages*. Balantine Paperback ed. Presidio, CA: Presidio Press.

Herspring, Dale. 2005. *The Pentagon and the Presidency: Civil Military Relations from FDR to George W. Bush*. Lawrence, KS: University of Kansas Press.

Herspring, Dale. 2013. *Civil Military Relations and Shared Responsibility*. eBook ed. Baltimore, MD: Johns Hopkins Press.

Hess, Gary. 2008. *Vietnam: Explaining America's Lost War*. Malden, MA: Wiley Blackhold.

Hughes, Ken. 2015a. *Fatal Politics: The Nixon Tapes, The Vietnam War, and the Casualties of Reflection*. eBook edition by Miller Center ed. Charlottesville, VA: University of Virginia Press.

Hughes, Ken. 2015b. *Chasing Shadows: The Nixon Tapes, the Chennault Affair, and the Origins of Watergate*. Kindle eBook Miller Center ed. Charlottesville, VA: University of Virginia Press.

Hunt, Ira. 2013. *Losing Vietnam: How America Abandoned Southeast Asia*. University Press of Kentucky.

Hunt, Michael. 1996. *Lyndon Johnson's War: America's Cold War Crusade in Vietnam, 1945-1965*. New York: Hill and Wang

Hunt, Michael, ed. 2010. *A Vietnam War Reader: A Documentary History From the American and Vietnamese Perspective*. eBook ed. Chapel Hill, NC: University of North Carolina Press.

Isaacs, Arnold. 1997. *Vietnam Shadows: The War, Its Ghosts, and Its Legacy*. Baltimore: The Johns Hopkins University Press.

Isaacson, Walter. 2005. *Kissinger: A Biography*. eBook ed. New York: New York: Simon and Schuster.

Jacobs, Seth. 2006. *Cold War Mandarin: Ngo Dinh Diem and the origins of American's War in Vietnam, 1950-1963*. Kindle Book Edition. Lanham: MD. Rowman and Littlefield Publishers.

Johns, Andrew. 2010. *Vietnam's Second Front: Domestic Politics, The Republican Party, and the War*. eBook ed. Lexington, KY: University of Kentucky Press.

Johnson, Lyndon B. 1971. *The Vantage Point: Perspectives of the Presidency, 1963-1969*. New York: Holt Rinehart Winston.

Jordan, Robert. 2013. *An Unsung Soldier: The Life of Gen. Andrew J. Goodpaster*. Annapolis, MD: Naval Institute Press.

Kagan, Donald. 2009. *Thucydides: The Reinvention of History*. United States: Penguin Group (USA).

Kaplan, Lawrence. 2013. *History of the Office of the Secretary of Defense: The McNamara Ascendancy, 1961-1965, Vol. V*. Smashwords Edition ed. Washington, DC: US Government.

Karnow, Stanley. 1983. *Vietnam: A History*. New York: Viking Press.

Keefer, Edward, ed. 2006. *Foreign Relations of the United States, 1969- 1976, Vol, VI: Vietnam, January 1969- July 1970*. eBook version 21 May 2013 ed. Washington, DC: Government Printing Office.

Keefer, Edward, ed. 2010. *Foreign Relations of the United States, 1969-1976, Vol. VII: Vietnam, July 1970- January 1972*. eBook version 21 May 2013 ed. Washington, DC: Government Printing Office.

Kennedy, Paul. 1987. *The Rise and Fall of the Great Powers*. 1989 Vintage book eBook ed. New York: New York: Random House.

Khong, Yuen Foong. 1992. *Analogies at War: Korea, Munich, Dien Bien Phu, and the Vietnam Decisions of 1965*. Princeton, NJ. Princeton University Press.

Kimball, Jeffrey. 1998. *Nixon's Vietnam War*. Lawrence, Kan.: University Press of Kansas.

Kinnard, Douglas. 1977. *The War Managers*. Hanover, NH: University Press of New England.

Kissinger, Henry. 2003. *Ending the Vietnam War*. New York, NY: Simon & Schuster.

Kissinger, Henry. 1979. *The White House Years*. Boston, MA: Little and Brown.

Kolko, Gabriel. 1986. *Vietnam: Anatomy of a War*. 1997 Kindle Book edition ed. New York: New York: Routledge.

Krepinevich, Andrew. 1986. *The Army and Vietnam*. Baltimore: Johns Hopkins Press.

LaFantasie, Glenn, ed. 1996. *Foreign Relations of the United States, 1964-1968, Vol. II: Vietnam, January - June 1965*. eBook version 21 May 2013 ed. Washington, DC: Government Printing Office.

LaFantasie, Glenn, ed. 1998. *Foreign Relations of the United States, 1964-1968, Vol. III: Vietnam, June - December 1965*. eBook version 21 May 2013 ed. Washington, DC: Government Printing Office.

Lanning, Michael, and Dan Cragg. 1992. *Inside the VC and NVA*. Kindle e Book ed. College Station, TX: Texas A&M Press.

Lawrence, Mark. 2005. *Assuming the Burden: Europe and the American Commitment to War in Vietnam*. Berkley, CA: University of California Press.

Lawrence, Mark. 2008. *The Vietnam War: A Concise International History*. Oxford University Press. New York: New York

Leshikar, Chuck. 1998. *Delta Raiders*. Petersburg, FL: Southern Heritage Press.

Lewy, Guenter. 1978. *America in Vietnam*. New York: Oxford University Press.

Logevall, Fredrik. 2013. *The Origins of the Vietnam War*. New York, NY: Routledge.

Logevall, Fredrik. 2012. *Embers of War*. eBook edition ed. New York: Random House.

Maddox, Rachel. 2012. *Drift: The Unmooring of American Military Power*. eBook edition ed. New York: New York: Broadway Books.

Manchester, William. 1998. *American Caesar: Douglas MacArthur, 1880-1964*. eBook edition 2008 ed. New York: New York: Little Brown, Inc.

Manchester, William. 2013. *The Glory and the Dream*. eBook ed. New York: New York: Rosetta Books.

Marshall, S. L. A. 1967. *Battles in the Monsoon: Campaigning in the Central Highlands, South Vietnam, Summer 1966*. New York: New York: William Morrow and Com.

May, Ernest. 1973. *Lessons of the Past: The Use and Misuse of History in American Foreign Policy*. New York: New York: Oxford University Press.

McChristian, Joseph. 1994. *The Role of Military Intelligence*. PDF Vietnam Studies series ed. Washington, DC: Center of Military History.

McCullough, David. 1992. *Truman*. New York: Simon & Schuster Adult Publishing Group.

McMaster, H.R. 1997. *Dereliction of Duty: Lyndon Johnson, Robert McNamara, the Joint Chiefs of Staff, and the Lies that Led to Vietnam*. New York: Harper Collins Publishers.

McNamara, Robert, and Brian Vandemark. 1995. *In Retrospect: The Tragedy and Lessons of Vietnam*. New York: Times Books.

Milne, David. 2008. *America's Rasputin: Walt Rostow and the Vietnam War*. eBook by Hill and Wang ed. New York: New York: Farrar, Straus and Giroux.

Moody, Walter. 2004. *The Joint Chiefs of Staff and the First Indochina War, 1947-1954*. PDF in Joint Electronic Library ed. Washington, DC: The Joint History Office.

Moore, Harold, and Joseph Galloway. 1992. *We Were Soldiers Once...And Young: Ia Drang - the Battle that Changed the War in Vietnam.* eBook by Open Roads ed. New York: New York: Random House.

Moten, Matthew. 2014. *Presidents and Their Generals: An American History of Command in War.* eBook kindle edition ed. Cambridge, MA: Harvard University Press.

Moyar, Mark. 2006. *Triumph Forsaken: The Vietnam War, 1954-1965, V. 1.* eBook Kindle ed. New York: Cambridge University Press.

Moïse, Edwin. 1996. *Tonkin Gulf and the escalation of the Vietnam War.* United States: The University of North Carolina Press.

Murray, Williamson, Richard Sinnreich, and James Lacey. 2011. *The Shaping of Grand Strategy: Policy, Diplomacy, and War.* United Kingdom: Cambridge University Press.

Neustadt, Richard, and Ernest May. 1986. *Thinking in Time: The Uses of History for Decision Makers.* New York: New York: The Free Press.

Nguyen, Lien-Hang. 2012. *Hanoi's War: An International History of the War for Peace in Vietnam.* Chapel Hill: University of North Carolina Press.

Nguyen, Nathalie Huynh Chau. 2016. *South Vietnamese Soldiers: Memories of the Vietnam War and After.* iBook. Santa Barbara, CA: ABC-CIO LLC

Nielson, Suzanne C. and Snider, Don M. 2009. *American Civil-Military Relations: The Soldier and the State in a New Era.* Baltimore: Md. The Johns Hopkins Press.

Nixon, Richard. 1978. *The Memoirs of Richard Nixon.* eBook ed. New York: Simon & Schuster.

Nixon, Richard. 1984. *No More Vietnams.* eBook edition by Nixon Foundation 2012 ed. New York: New York: Simon and Schuster.

Nye, Joseph S. 1990. *Bound to lead: The changing nature of American power.* New York: Basic Books.

O'Brien, Patrick, ed. 2005. *The Philips Atlas of World History.* eBook ed. London, England: Octopus Publishing Group.

O'Brien, Tim. 1990. *The Things They Carried.* eBook ed. New York: First Mariner Books.

Palmer, Bruce. 1984. *25-Year War: American Military Role in Vietnam.* eBook ed. Lexington, KY: University of Kentucky Press.

Paterson, David, ed. 1998. *Foreign Relations of the United States, 1964-1968, Vol. IV: Vietnam, 1966.* eBook version 21 May 2013 ed. Washington, DC: Government Printing Office.

Paterson, David, ed. 2002a. *Foreign Relations of the United States, 1964- 1968 Vol. IV: Vietnam, 1966.* eBook version 21 May 2013 ed. Washington, DC: Government Printing Office.

Paterson, David, ed. 2002b. *Foreign Relations of the United States, 1964- 1968, Vol. VI: Vietnam, 1967*. eBook version 21 May 2013 ed. Washington, DC: Government Printing Office.

Patterson, James. 1996. *Grand Expectations: The United States, 1945-1974*. New York: Oxford University Press Inc, USA.

Perlstein, Rick. 2009. *Nixonland: America's Second Civil War and the Divisive Legacy of Richard Nixon, 1965-1972*. London: Simon & Schuster Adult Publishing Group.

Perry, Mark. 1989. *Four Stars*. Boston, MA: Houghton Mifflin Co.

Phillips, Rufus. 2008. *Why Vietnam Matters: An Eyewitness Account of Lessons not Learned*. Annapolis, MD: Naval Institute Press.

Pike, Douglas. 1986. *PAVN: People's Army of Vietnam*. Novato, California: Presidio Press.

Poole, Joseph. 1998. *The Joint Chiefs of Staff and National Policy, Vol. IV, 1950-1952*. PDF in JCS Electronic Library ed. Washington, DC: Joint History Office.

Poole, Joseph. 1986a. *The Joint Chiefs of Staff and National Policy, Vol. VIII, 1961-1964*. PDF in Joint Electronic Library ed. Washington, DC: Joint History Office.

Poole, Joseph. 1986b. *The Joint Chiefs of Staff and National Policy, 1965-1968*. PDF in Joint Electronic Library ed. Washington, DC: Joint History Office.

Poole, Joseph. 1986c. *The Joint Chiefs of Staff and National Policy, 1969-1972*. PDF in Joint Electronic Library ed. Washington, DC: Joint History Office.

Poole, Walter. 2007. *The Joint Chiefs of Staff and the War in Vietnam, 1971-1973*. PDF in the Joint Electronic Library ed. Washington, DC: The Joint History Office.

Powell, Colin, and Joseph Persico. 1995. *My American Journey*. New York: Random House Publishing Group.

Prados, John. 1995. *The Hidden History of the Vietnam War*. eBook ed. Chicago, IL: Elephant Paperback.

Preston, Andrew. 2010. *The War Council: McGeorge Bundy, the NSC, and Vietnam*. United States: Harvard University Press.

R, Herspring, Dale. 2005. *The Pentagon and the Presidency: Civil-military Relations from FDR to George W. Bush*. United States: Lawrence: University Press of Kansas, c2005.

Rather, Dan. 1996. *The War in Vietnam*. CD-ROM. New York: New York. Macmillan Digital

Rafalko, Frank. 2011. *MH/Chaos: The CIA's Campaign Against the Radical New Left and the Black Panthers*. Kindle eBook ed. Annapolis, MD: Naval Institute Press.

Rearden, Steven. 2013. "History of the Office of the Secretary of Defense, Volume One - The Formative Years: 1947-1950. Smashwords Edition ed. U.S. Government, Department of Defense Smashwords.

Rearden, Steven. 2012. *Council of War: A History of the Joint Chiefs of Staff, 1942-1991*. eBook ed. Washington, DC: NDU Press.

Record, Jeffrey. 2002. *Making War, Thinking History*. eBook. Annapolis, MD: Naval Institute Press.

Ricks, Thomas. 2012. *The Generals: American Military Command from World War II to Today*. New York: Penguin Group (USA) Incorporated.

Ritchie, Donald. 2005. *Reporting From Washington: The History of the Washington Press Corps*. eBook ed. New York: New York: Oxford University Press.

Robbins, James. 2012. *This Time We Win: Revisiting the TET Offensive*. eBook ed. New York: Encounter Books

Rogers, Bernard. 1973. *Cedar Falls and Junction City: A Turning Point*. PDF Vietnam Studies edition ed. Washington, DC: Center of Military History.

Rothkopf, David. 2005. *Running the World: The Inside Story of the National Security Council and the Architects of American Power*. eBook Edition. Perseus Books Group. Cambridge: MA

Rothmann, Harry. 1976. "The Politics of Common Defense: France and the Cold War, 1945-1949." Dissertation University of North Carolina.

Rothmann, Harry. 2014. *None Will Surpass: A Story of the Four Decade Service and Sacrifice of the West Point Class of 1967*. Amazon Paperback edition ed. Orlando, FL: RCI Publications.

Rottman, Gordon. 2009. *North Vietnamese Soldier, 1958-1975*. eBook ed. New York: New York: Osprey Press.

Rumsfeld, Donald. 2011. *Known and unknown: A memoir*. New York: Penguin Group (USA).

Schlesinger, Arthur. 1965. *A Thousand Days: John F. Kennedy in the White House*. First Mariner Books Edition, 2002nd ed. Boston, MA: Houghton, Mifflin Company.

Schmitz, David. 2014. *Richard Nixon and the Vietnam War: the end of the American century*. United States: Rowman & Littlefield Publishers.

Schnabel, James, and Robert Watson. 1998. *The Joint Chiefs of Staff and National Policy, Vol. III, The Korean War, Part I*. PDF in Joint Electronic library ed. Washington, DC: The Joint History Office.

Schnabell, James. 1996. *History of the Joint Chiefs of Staff and National Policy, Vol. I, 1945-1947*. PDF in Joint Electronic Library ed. Washington, DC: Joint History Office.

Schulzinger, Robert. 1997. *A Time for War: The United States and Vietnam, 1941-1975*. New York: Oxford University Press.

Schwab, Orrin. 2006. *A Clash of Cultures: Civil-Military Relations during the Vietnam War (In War and in Peace: U.S. Civil-Military Relations)*. United States: Praeger Security International General Interest-Cloth.

Schwarzkopf, Norman, and Peter Petre. 1992. *It Doesn't Take a Hero: The Autobiography of General H. Norman Schwarzkopf.* New York: Bantam Dell Pub Group.

Sharp, U.S. Grant. 1978. *Strategy for Defeat: Vietnam in Retrospect.* San Rafael, California: Presidio Press.

Sheehan, Neil. 1989. *A Bright Shining Lie: John Paul Vann and America in Vietnam.* New York: Knopf Doubleday Publishing Group.

Shelton, Hugh. 2010. *Without Hesitation: The Odyssey of an American Warrior.* eBook ed. New York: New York: ST. Martin Press.

Shulimson, Jack. 2011. *The Joint Chiefs of Staff and the War in Vietnam, 1960-1968, Part 1.* PDF in Joint Electronic Library ed. Washington, DC: The Joint History Office.

Shulimson, Jack. 1982. *US Marines in Vietnam: An Expanding War, 1966.* Washington, DC: History and Museum Directorate, USMC HQ.

Shulimson, Jack, and Charles Johnson. 1978. *US Marines in Vietnam: The Landing and the Buildup, 1965.* eBook ed. Washington, DC: History and Museum Directorate, USMC HQ.

Shulimson, Jack, Charles Smith, and David Dawson. 1997. *US Marines in Vietnam: The Defining Year, 1968.* Pickle Partners Publishing edition, 2015th ed. Washington, DC: History and Museum Directorate, USMC HQ.

Snepp, Frank. 2002. *Decent Interval: An Insiders Account of Saigon's Indecent End.* eBook edition ed. Lawrence, KS: University of Kansas.

Sorenson, Ted. 1965. *Kennedy.* 2009 Edition ed. New York: Harper Collins.

Sorley, Lewis, ed. 2004. *Vietnam Chronicles: The Abrams Tapes, 1968-1972 (Modern Southeast Asia Series).* Texas Tech University Press.

Sorley, Lewis. 2011. *Westmoreland: The General Who Lost Vietnam.* e–Book edition ed. New York: Houghton Mifflin Harcourt.

Sorley, Lewis. 2008. *Thunderbolt: General Creighton Abrams and the Army of His Times.* 2nd ed. United States: Indiana University Press.

Sorley, Lewis. 1999. *Honorable Warrior: General Harold K. Johnson and the Ethics of Command.* United States: University Press of Kansas.

Stanton, Shelby. 1985. *The Rise and Fall of an American Army: US Ground Forces in Vietnam, 1965-1973.* Ballantine eBook iBookstore edition ed. New York: New York: Random House.

Summers, Anthony. 2000. *The Arrogance of Power: The Secret World of Richard Nixon.* eBook ed. New York: New York: Penguin Books.

Summers, Harry. 1982. *On Strategy: A Critical Analysis of the Vietnam War.* Presidio, CA: Presidio Press.

Summers, Harry, and Stanley Karnow. 1995. *Historical Atlas of the Vietnam War*. Boston: Houghton Mifflin (Trade).

Taylor, John M., and Lewis F. Powell. 2002. *An American Soldier: The Wars of General Maxwell Taylor*. United States: Random House Publishing Group.

Taylor, Maxwell. 1960. *The Uncertain Trumpet*. New York: New York: Harper Brothers.

Taylor, Maxwell D. 1990. *Swords and Plowshares*. New York, NY: Da Capo Press.

Telfor, Jack, Lane Rogers, and Keith Fleming. 1984. *US Marines in Vietnam: Fighting the North Vietnamese, 1967*. Washington, DC: History and Museum Directorate, USMC HQ.

Thayer, Thomas. 1985. *War Without Fronts: The American Experience in Vietnam*. eBook ed. Annapolis, MD: Naval Institute Press.

Thomas, Evan. 2015. *Being Nixon: A Man Divided*. Colophon e-Book edition ed. New York: New York: Random House.

Timberg, Robert. 1995. *The Nightingale's Song*. New York: Simon & Schuster.

Tra, Tran Van. 1983. *Vietnam: History of the Bulwark B2 Theater, Vol.5 - Concluding the 30-Years War*. PDF in Vietnam Monographs ed. Leavenworth, KS: Combat Studies Institute.

Truman, Harry. 1956. *Memoirs, Vol II: Years of Trial and Hope, 1946-1952*. Garden City. NJ: Doubleday.

Truong, Nhu Tang, David Chanoff, and Van Toai Do an. 1986. *A Viet Cong Memoir: An Inside Account of the Vietnam War and Its Aftermath*. First Vintage Books Edition ed. New York: Random House.

Tucker, Spencer C and Pierpaoli, Paul, editors. 2011. *The Encyclopedia of The Vietnam War: A Political, Social, and Military History*. 2nd Edition. E-Book. Santa Barbara, CA: ABC CLIO Publishers

Tully, John, Matthew Masur, and Brad Austin, eds. 2013. *Understanding and Teaching the Vietnam War*. eBook Kindle ed. Madison, WS: University of Wisconsin Press.

Turley, William. 2009. *The Second Indochina War: A Concise Political and Military History*. 2d Edition ed. New York: Roman and Littlefield Press.

Updegrove, Mark. 2012. *Indomitable Will: LBJ in the Presidency*. eBook ed. New York: New York: Random House.

Valenti, Jack. 2007. *This Time, This Place: My Life in War, the White House, and Hollywood*. iBook edition. New York: New York. Harmony Books, Crown Publishers

Vietnam, Staff of The Military History Institute of, Merle Pribbenow, and William Duiker. 2002. *Victory in Vietnam: The Official History of the People's Army of Vietnam, 1954--1975: The Military History Institute of Vietnam*. University Press of Kansas.

Villard, Eric. 2008. *The 1968 TET Offensive Battles of Quang Tri City and Hue.* eBook Pickle Publishers edition ed. Washington, DC: HQ Department of the Army.

Villard, Eric. 2017. *Combat Operations: Staying the Course, October 1967 to September 1968.* Washington, DC: US Army, Center of Military History.

Walt, Lewis. 1970. *Strange War, Strange Strategy: A General's Report on Vietnam.* New York: New York: Funk and Wagnall's.

Warren, James. 2013. *Giap: The General Who Defeated America in Vietnam.* eBook by Palgrave ed. New York: New York: MacMillan.

Webb, Williard. 2008. *The Joint Chiefs of Staff and the Prelude to the War in Vietnam, 1954-1959.* PDF in Joint Electronic Library ed. Washington, DC: The Joint History Office.

Webb, Williard. 2002. *The Joint Chiefs of Staff and the War in Vietnam, 1969-1970.* PDF in the Joint Electronic Library ed. Washington, DC: The Joint History Office.

Weinberg, Gerhard. 1994. *A World At Arms: A Global History of World War II.* New York: New York: Cambridge University Press.

Weiner, Tom. 2015. *One Man Against the World.* Henry Holt e–Book edition ed. New York: New York: MacMillan.

Werner, Jayne and Huynh, Luu Doan, ed. 1993. *The Vietnam War: Vietnamese and American Perspectives.* iBook, 2015 edition. New York: New York. Routledge.

West, F. J. 1985. *The Village.* Madison, WS: University of Wisconsin Press.

Westmoreland, William. 1976. *A Soldier Reports.* Garden City, New York: Doubleday and Company.

Wiest, Andrew. 2008. *Vietnam's Forgotten Army: Heroism and Betrayal in the ARVN.* eBook ed. New York: New York: NYU Press.

Wiest, Andrew, and Michael Doidge, eds. 2010. *Triumph Revisited: Historians Battle for the Vietnam War.* eBook edition by Taylor & Francis ed. New York: Routledge.

Wilkins, Warren. 2011. *Grab Their Belts to Fight Them: The Viet Cong's Big-Unit War Against the U.S., 1965-1966.* United States: Naval Institute Press.

Willbanks, James. 2014. *A Raid Too Far: Operation Lam Son 719 and Vietnamization in Laos.* eBook ed. College Station, TX: Texas A&M University Press.

Willbanks, James. 2007. *The TET Offensive: A Concise History.* eBook ed. New York: New York: Columbia University Press.

Willbanks, James H. 2008. *Abandoning Vietnam: How America Left and South Vietnam Lost its War.* Lawrence, KS: University Press of Kansas.

Willbanks, James H. 2013. *Vietnam War: The Essential Reference Guide*. iBook Edition. Santa Barbara, CA: ABC-CLIO, LLC

Willbanks, James H. 2013. *Vietnam War Almanac*. iBook Edition. New York: New York. Skyhorse Publishing,

Woods, Randall B. 2006. *LBJ: Architect of American Ambition*. iBook Edition. New York: New York. Free Press.

Woodward, Bob. 1991a. *The Commanders*. New York: Simon & Schuster.

Woodward, Bob. 2003. *Bush at War*. United States: Simon & Schuster Adult Publishing Group.

Woodward, Bob. 2006. *State of Denial: [Bush at war, part III]*. United States: New York: Simon & Schuster, c2006.

Woodward, Bob. 2008. *The War Within: A Secret White House History, 2006-2008*. United States: Simon Spotlight Entertainment.

Woodward, Bob. 2010. *Obama's Wars*. United States: Simon & Schuster Adult Publishing Group.

Woodward, Bob. 1991b. *The Commanders*. New York: Simon & Schuster.

Woodward, Bob, and Alice Mayhew. 2004b. *Plan of attack*. New York: Simon & Schuster Adult Publishing Group.

Zaffiri, Samuel. 1988. *Hamburger Hill, May 11-20, 1969*. Presidio, CA: Presidio Press.

Zakaria, Fareed. 2008. *The Post-American World*. New York: Norton, W. W. & Company.

Zeiler, Thomas. 2000. *Dean Rusk: Defending the American Mission Abroad*. Wilmington, DE: Scholarly Resources, Inc.

"LBJ Presidential Library." http://www.lbjlibrary.org/ (January 23, 2015a).

"US Department of State." http://history.state.gov/historicaldocuments.

"CIA Library." http://www.foia.cia.gov/collection/vietnam-collection?page=13.

"US National Archives." http://www.archives.gov/research/pentagon-papers/.

"Nixon Presidential Library." http://www.nixonlibrary.gov/virtuallibrary/documents/index.php.

"Vietnam War 50th Commemoration Site. http://www.vietnamwar50th.com/"

"The Vietnam Center and Archive: Virtual Vietnam Archive." http://www.vietnam.ttu.edu/virtualarchive/ (May 2, 2015h).

"The Vietnam war: 1954-1975." http://www.mcu.usmc.mil/historydivision/Pages/Publications/The_Vietnam_War_1954_1975.aspx (December 10, 2015i).

http://www.cc.gatech.edu/fac/Thomas.Pilsch/Vietnam.html (March 31, 2016j).

"RVNHS: The republic of Vietnam historical society Homepage - Việt Nam Cộng Hòa." http://rvnhs.com/ (September 7, 2016k).

"Department of history - Vietnam War." http://www.westpoint.edu/history/SitePages/Vietnam%20War.aspx (December 21, 2016).

"Archives.gov." https://www.archives.gov/ (December 30, 2016l).

"Miller center." http://millercenter.org/ (December 30, 2016).

"Historical documents - office of the historian." https://history.state.gov/historicaldocuments (December 30, 2016m).

"Joint electronic library, doctrine." http://www.dtic.mil/doctrine/mobile/app.htm (January 2, 2017n).

"John F. Kennedy presidential library & museum." https://www.jfklibrary.org/ (January 3, 2017o).

"U.S. Army in Vietnam - U.S. Army center of military history." http://www.history.army.mil/html/bookshelves/collect/usavn.html (January 7, 2017p).

Center, The Vietnam, Archive, and Justin Saffell. 2013. "The Vietnam Center and Archive Homepage." October 23. http://www.vietnam.ttu.edu/index.php (March 30, 2016).

Made in the USA
Monee, IL
26 March 2022